International Marketing

THE IRWIN/MCGRAW-HILL SERIES IN MARKETING

International Marketing

TENTH EDITION

Philip R. Cateora
Fellow, Academy of International Business
University of Colorado

John L. Graham
University of California, Irvine

Irwin
McGraw-Hill

Boston   Burr Ridge, IL   Dubuque, IA   Madison, WI   New York   San Francisco   St. Louis
Bangkok   Bogotá   Caracas   Lisbon   London   Madrid
Mexico City   Milan   New Delhi   Seoul   Singapore   Sydney   Taipei   Toronto

Irwin/McGraw-Hill

A Division of The **McGraw·Hill** Companies

INTERNATIONAL MARKETING

Copyright ©1999 by The McGraw-Hill Companies, Inc. All rights reserved. Previous editions © 1966, 1971, 1975, 1979, 1983, 1987, 1990, 1993, and 1996 by Richard D. Irwin, a Times Mirror Higher Education Group, Inc. company. Printed in the United States of America. Except as permitted under the United States Copyright Act of 1976, no part of this publication may be reproduced or distributed in any form or by any means, or stored in a data base or retrieval system, without the prior written permission of the publisher.

This book is printed on acid-free paper.

international   1 2 3 4 5 6 7 8 9 0 VNH/VNH 9 3 2 1 0 9 8
domestic   1 2 3 4 5 6 7 8 9 0 VNH/VNH 9 3 2 1 0 9 8

ISBN 0-256-25982-8
ISBN 0-07-366132-5 (*Business Week* edition)

Vice president and editorial director: *Michael W. Junior*
Publisher: *Gary Burke*
Sponsoring editor: *Karen Westover*
Senior developmental editor: *Diane E. Beausoleil*
Senior marketing manager: *Colleen J. Suljic*
Senior project manager: *Gladys True*
Senior photo research coordinator: *Keri Johnson*
Photo research: *Charlotte Goldman*
Production supervisor: *Heather D. Burbridge*
Art director: *Francis Owens*
Cover designer: *Gary Palmatier/Ideas to Images*
Cover images: *Courtesy of Microsoft, Inc.; Courtesy of Shops.net;*
   © Steve Brown/Leo de Wys, Inc.; Courtesy of Digital Stock, a division of Corbis
Supplement coordinator: *Marc Mattson*
Compositor: *ElectraGraphics, Inc.*
Typeface: *10/12 Times Roman*
Printer: *Von Hoffmann Press, Inc.*

Library of Congress Cataloging-in-Publication Data

Cateora, Philip R.
   International marketing / Philip R. Cateora, John L. Graham. —
  10th ed.
     p.   cm.
   Includes index.
   ISBN 0-256-25982-8
   1. Export marketing.   2. International business enterprises.
  I. Graham, John L.   II. Title.
  HF1009.5.C35   1999
  658.8´48—dc21   98-21048

INTERNATIONAL EDITION
Copyright © 1999. Exclusive rights by The McGraw-Hill Companies, Inc. for manufacture and export. This book cannot be re-exported from the country to which it is consigned by McGraw-Hill. The International Edition is not available in North America.

When ordering the title, use ISBN 0-07-115673-9

http://www.mhhe.com

To Nancy and Thomas, Maggie, and Angela
To Steven A. Graham

PREFACE

There has never been a time in modern economic history when more change has occurred in so short a period than that which has occurred in the last decade of the 20th century. New markets are springing forth in emerging economies from Eastern Europe, the Commonwealth of Independent States, China, Indonesia, Korea, India, Mexico, Chile, Brazil, Argentina—in short, globally. These emerging economies hold the promise of huge markets in the future. In the more mature markets of the industrialized world, opportunity and challenge also abound as consumers' tastes become more sophisticated and complex and as increases in purchasing power provide them with the means of satisfying new demands.

Opportunities in today's global markets are on a par with the global economic expansion that existed after World War II. Today, however, the competitive environment within which these opportunities exist is vastly different from that earlier period when United States multinationals dominated world markets. From the late 1940s through the 1960s, multinational corporations (MNCs) from the United States had little competition; today, companies from almost all the world's nations vie for global markets.

There is no better illustration of the changes that have occurred in the competition for global markets in the last quarter century than that experienced by General Electric Lighting (GEL). GEL, begun in 1887, dominated the U.S. lighting market until traditional rival Westinghouse sold its lamp operations to Philips Electronics of Holland in 1983. "Suddenly," reflected GEL's chief, "we have bigger, stronger competition. They're coming to our market, but we're not in theirs. So we're on the defensive." Not long after, GEL acquired Tungsram, a Hungarian lighting company, and Thorn EMI in Britain, and then moved into Asia via a joint venture with Hitachi. As recently as 1988, GE Lighting got less than 20 percent of its sales from outside the U.S; in 1997, more than half came from abroad. What

happened at GE Lighting has occurred over and over again to MNCs in the United States, Europe, and Asia. The companies that succeed in the 21st century will be those capable of adapting to constant change and adjusting to new challenges.

The economic, political, and social changes that have occurred over the last decade have dramatically altered the landscape of global business. Consider the present and future impact of:

- Emerging markets in Eastern Europe, Asia, and Latin America, where more than 75 percent of the growth in world trade over the next 20 years is expected to occur.

- The reunification of Hong Kong, Macau, and China, which finally puts all of Asia under the control of Asians for the first time in over a century.

- The European Monetary Union and the switch from local country currencies to one monetary unit for Europe.

- The rapid move away from traditional distribution structures in Japan, Europe, and many emerging markets.

- The growth of middle-income households the world over.

- The continued strengthening and creation of regional market groups such as the European Union (EU), the North American Free Trade Area (NAFTA), ASEAN Free Trade Area (AFTA), the Free Trade Area of the Americas (FTAA), the Southern Cone Free Trade Area (Mercosur), and the Asian-Pacific Economic Cooperation (APEC).

- The successful completion of the Uruguay Round of the General Agreement on Tariffs and Trade (GATT) and the creation of the World Trade Organization (WTO).

- The continuing privatization and deregulation of telecommunications throughout the world.
- The restructuring, reorganizing, and refocusing of companies such as IBM, Eastman Kodak, General Motors, Levi Strauss, and Nike as they respond to the changing competitive milieu of the global marketplace.
- The transformation of the Internet from a toy for "cybernerds" to a major international business tool for research, advertising, communications, exporting, and marketing.

These are not simply news reports. These are changes that affect the practice of business worldwide, and they mean that companies will have to constantly examine the way they do business and remain flexible enough to react rapidly to changing global trends to be competitive.

As global economic growth occurs, understanding marketing in all cultures is increasingly important. *International Marketing* addresses global issues and describes concepts relevant to all international marketers, regardless of the extent of their international involvement.

Not all firms engaged in overseas marketing have a global perspective, nor do they need to. Some companies' foreign marketing is limited to one country; others market in a number of countries, treating each as a separate market; and still others, the global enterprises, look for market segments with common needs and wants across political and economic boundaries. All, however, are affected by competitive activity in the global marketplace. It is with this future that the tenth edition of *International Marketing* is concerned.

Emphasis is on the strategic implications of competition in different country markets. An environmental/cultural approach to international marketing permits a truly global orientation. The reader's horizons are not limited to any specific nation or to the particular ways of doing business in a single nation. Instead, the book provides an approach and framework for identifying and analyzing the important cultural and environmental uniqueness of any nation or global region. Thus, when surveying the tasks of marketing in a foreign milieu, the reader will not overlook the impact of crucial cultural issues.

The text is designed to stimulate curiosity about management practices of companies, large and small, seeking market opportunities outside the home country and to raise the reader's consciousness about the importance of viewing international marketing management strategies from a global perspective.

Although this revised edition is infused throughout with a global orientation, export marketing and the operations of smaller companies are not overlooked. Issues specific to exporting are discussed where strategies applicable to exporting arise and examples of marketing practices of smaller companies are examined.

New and Expanded Topics in This Edition

The new and expanded topics in this tenth edition reflect issues in competition, changing marketing structures, ethics and social responsibility, negotiations, and the development of the manager for the 21st century. Competition is raising the global standards for quality, increasing the demand for advanced technology and innovation, and increasing the value of customer satisfaction. The global market is swiftly changing from a seller's market to a buyer's market. This is a period of profound social, economic, and political change. To remain competitive globally, companies must be aware of all aspects of the emerging global economic order.

Additionally, the evolution of global communications and its known and unknown impact on how international business is conducted cannot be minimized. In the third millennium people in the "global village" will grow closer than ever, and will hear and see each other as a matter of course. An executive in Germany will be able to routinely pick up his/her videophone to hear and see his/her counterpart in an Australian company or anywhere else in the world. In many respects, distance is becoming irrelevant. Telecommunications, videophones, facsimile machines, the Internet, and satellites are helping companies optimize their planning, production, and procurement processes. Information—and, in its wake, the flow of goods—is moving around the globe at lightning speed. Increasingly powerful global networks spanning the globe enable the delivery of services that reach far beyond national and continental boundaries, fueling and fostering international trade. The connections of global communications bring people all around the world together in new and better forms of dialogue and understanding.

This dynamic nature of the international marketplace is reflected in the number of new and expanded topics in this tenth edition, including:

- The Internet and its expanding role in international marketing.
- Negotiations with customers, partners, and regulators.
- Big Emerging Markets (BEMS).
- Evolving global middle-income households.
- The Uruguay Round of GATT.
- World Trade Organization (WTO).
- North American Free Trade Area (NAFTA).
- ASEAN Free Trade Area (AFTA).
- Asia-Pacific Economic Cooperation (APEC).
- Multicultural research.
- Qualitative and quantitative research.
- Country-of-origin effect and global brands.
- Industrial trade shows.

- ISO 9000.
- Trends in channel structures in Europe, Japan, and developing countries.
- Ethics and socially responsible decisions.
- Green marketing.
- Changing profiles of global managers.

Structure of the Text

The text is divided into six parts. The first two chapters, Part I, introduce the reader to the environmental/cultural approach to international marketing and to three international marketing management concepts: Domestic Market Expansion Concept, Multidomestic Market Concept, and Global Marketing Concept. As companies restructure for the global competitive rigors of the 21st century, so too must tomorrow's managers. The successful manager must be globally aware and have a frame of reference that goes beyond a country, or even a region, and encompasses the world. What global awareness means and how it is acquired is discussed early in the text; it is at the foundation of global marketing.

Chapter 2 focuses on the dynamic environment of international trade and the competitive challenges and opportunities confronting today's international marketer. The importance of the Uruguay Round of the General Agreement on Tariffs and Trade (GATT) and the creation of the World Trade Organization (WTO), the successor to GATT, are fully explored. The growing importance of the Internet in conducting international business is explored in depth, creating a foundation on which specific applications in subsequent chapters are presented.

The five chapters in Part II deal with the cultural environment of global marketing. A global orientation requires the recognition of cultural differences and the critical decision of whether or not it is necessary to accommodate them.

Geography and history (Chapter 3) are included as important dimensions in understanding cultural and market differences among countries. Not to be overlooked is concern for the deterioration of the global ecological environment and the multinational company's critical responsibility to protect it.

Chapter 4 presents a broad review of culture and its impact on human behavior as it relates to international marketing. Specific attention is paid to Geert Hofstede's study of cultural values and behavior. The elements of culture reviewed in Chapter 4 set the stage for the in-depth analysis in Chapters 5, 6, and 7, business customs and the political and legal environments. Ethics and social responsibility are presented in the context of the dilemma that often confronts the international manager; that is, balancing corporate profits against the social and ethical consequences of their decisions.

The three chapters in Part III are concerned with assessing global market opportunities. As markets expand, segments grow within markets, and as market segments across country markets evolve, marketers are forced to understand market behavior within and across different cultural contexts. Multicultural research and qualitative and quantitative research and a discussion of the Internet as a tool in the research task are explored in Chapter 8.

Chapters 9 and 10 in Part III explore the impact of the three important trends in global marketing: (1) the growth and expansion of the world's big emerging markets; (2) the rapid growth of middle-income market segments; and (3) the steady creation of regional market groups that include the North American Free Trade Area (NAFTA), the European Union (EU), ASEAN Free Trade Area (AFTA), Asian-Pacific Economic Cooperation (APEC), and the evolving Free Trade Area of the Americas (FTAA). The sagging leadership role of the United States in influencing the development of the FTAA and the accelerating influence of Brazil are explored. Also discussed is the disturbing number of trade agreements that have been executed by the European Union and Japan with the FTAA and some Latin American countries.

The strategic implications of the dissolution of the USSR, the emergence of new independent republics, the shift from socialist-based to market-based economies in Eastern Europe, and the return of South Africa and Vietnam to international commerce are examined. Attention is also given to the efforts of the governments of India and many Latin-American countries to reduce or eliminate barriers to trade, open their countries to foreign investment, and privatize state-owned enterprises.

These political, social, and economic changes that are sweeping the world are creating new markets and opportunities, making some markets more accessible while creating the potential for greater protectionism in others.

In Part IV, Developing Global Marketing Strategies, planning and organizing for global marketing is the subject of Chapter 11. The discussion of Collaborative relationships, including strategic alliances, recognizes the importance of relational collaborations among firms, suppliers, and customers in the success of the global marketer. Many multinational companies realize that to fully capitalize on opportunities offered by global markets, they must have strengths that often exceed their capabilities. Collaborative relationships can provide technology, innovations, productivity, capital, and market access that strengthen a company's competitive position.

Chapters 12 and 13 focus on product management, reflecting the differences in strategies between consumer and industrial products and the growing importance in world markets for business services. Additionally, the discussion on the development of global products stresses the importance of approaching the adaptation issue from the viewpoint of building a standardized product platform that can be adapted to reflect cultural differences. The competitive importance in today's global market for quality, innovation, and technology as the keys to marketing success is explored.

Chapter 14 takes the reader through the distribution process, from home country to the consumer, in the target-country market. The structural impediments to market entry imposed by a country's distribution system are examined in the framework of a detailed presentation of the Japanese distribution system. Additionally, the rapid changes in channel structure that are occurring in Japan, as well as in other countries, and the emergence of the World Wide Web as a distribution channel are presented.

In Chapter 15, the special issues involved in moving a product from one country market to another, and the accompanying mechanics of exporting, are addressed. In addition, the importance of the Internet in assisting the exporter to wade through the details of exporting is discussed in the context of the revised export regulations.

Chapter 16 covers advertising and addresses the promotional element of the international marketing mix. Included in the discussion of global market segmentation are recognition of the rapid growth of market segments across country markets and the importance of market segmentation as a strategic competitive tool in creating an effective promotional message. Chapter 17 discusses personal selling and sales management and the critical nature of training, evaluating, and controlling sales representatives.

Price escalation and ways it can be lessened, countertrade practices, and price strategies to employ when the dollar is strong or weak relative to foreign currencies are concepts presented in Chapter 18.

In Part V, Chapter 19 is a thorough presentation of negotiating with customers, partners, and regulators. The discussion stresses the varying negotiation styles found among cultures and the importance of recognizing these differences at the negotiation table.

Pedagogical Features of the Text

The text portion of the book provides a thorough coverage of its subject, with specific emphasis on the planning and strategic problems confronting companies that market across cultural boundaries.

The use of the Internet as a tool of international marketing is stressed throughout the text. In all occasions where data used in the text originated from an Internet source, the Web address is given. Problems that require the student to access the Internet are included with end-of-chapter questions. Internet-related problems are designed to familiarize the student with the power of the Internet in his/her

research, to illustrate data available on the Internet, and to challenge the reader to solve problems using the Internet. Many of the examples, illustrations, and exhibits found in the text can be explored in more detail by accessing the Web addresses that are included.

Current, pithy, sometimes humorous, and always relevant examples are used to stimulate interest and increase understanding of the ideas, concepts, and strategies presented in emphasizing the importance of understanding cultural uniqueness and relevant business practices and strategies.

Each chapter is introduced with a Global Perspective, a real-life example of company experiences that illustrate salient issues discussed in the chapter. Companies featured in the Global Perspectives range from exporters to global enterprises.

The boxed "Crossing Borders," an innovation of the first edition of *International Marketing,* have always been popular with students. This tenth edition includes more than 30 new incidents that provide insightful examples of cultural differences while illustrating concepts presented in the text. They reflect contemporary issues in international marketing and can be used to illustrate real-life situations and as the basis for class discussion. They are selected to be unique, humorous, and of general interest to the reader.

Besides the special section of color maps found in Chapter 3, there are numerous maps that reflect changes important to the chapter and that help the reader observe features of countries and regions discussed in the text.

New photographs of current and relevant international marketing events are found throughout the text, as well as three special photo essays. One on advertising around the world, one on Microsoft as a global marketer of services, and the third on Solar, a global marketer of industrial goods.

"The Country Notebook—A Guide for Developing a Marketing Plan," found in Part VI, Supplementary Material, is a detailed outline that provides both a format for a complete cultural and economic analysis of a country, and guidelines for developing a marketing plan.

Cases

In addition to "The Country Notebook," Part VI comprises a selection of short and long cases. The short cases focus on a single problem, serving as the basis for discussion of a specific concept or issue. The longer, more integrated cases are broader in scope and focus on more than one marketing management problem.

More than half of the cases are new or revised. New cases focus on healthcare marketing, negotiations, using the Internet, services and industrial marketing, and marketing research. The cases can be analyzed by using the information provided. They also lend themselves to more in-depth analysis, requiring the student to engage in additional research and data collection.

Supplements

We have taken great care to offer new features and improvements to every part of the teaching aid package. Below is a list of specific features:

Instructor's Manual and Test Bank: The Instructor's Manual, prepared by the authors, contains lecture notes and/or teaching suggestions for each chapter. A section called "Changes to This Edition" is included to help instructors adapt their teaching notes to the tenth edition. A case correlation grid at the beginning of the case notes offers alternative uses for the cases.

The Test Bank, prepared by Ron Weir of East Tennessee State University, is bound with the Instructor's Manual for ease of use. The Test Bank contains over 2,000 questions, including true/false, critical thinking, and essay formats. Computest, computerized testing software with an on-line testing feature is also available in Windows and Macintosh formats.

Videos: The video program has been revised for the tenth edition and contains new footage of companies, topics videos, and unique footage of global marketing operations. An accompanying booklet offers teaching notes and questions relevant to each chapter in the text.

Powerpoint Slides: The PowerPoint presentation that accompanies *International Marketing,* tenth edition, contains approximately 150 exhibits from the text and other sources. Fourteen maps from the text are included as well.

World Wide Web Home Page: The home page for *International Marketing,* tenth edition, can be found at **www.mhhe[DB2]need**. Included on the site will be instructor resources, such as key supplements to be downloaded. There will also be a resource for students that includes updates on information given in the text.

Business Week Edition: A special version of *International Marketing,* the *Business Week* Edition provides students with a value-priced, 16-week subscription to *Business Week* magazine, a respected source of business information and trends, and one that is cited throughout this text.

Acknowledgments

The success of a text depends on the contributions of many people, especially those who take the time to share their thoughtful criticisms and suggestions to improve the text.

We would especially like to thank the following reviewers who gave us valuable insights into this revision:

Robert Allerheiligen
Colorado State University

Shirley Anderson
California State University—Northridge

Susan Cremins
Westchester Community College

Samuel M. Gillespie
Texas A & M University

Bonnie S. Guy
Appalachian State

David Jamison
University of Florida

Nancy Miller
University of North Texas

Mark Mitchell
School of Business
USC—Spartanburg

Chiesl Newell
Indiana State University

Juanita Roxas
California State Polytechnic University

Farid Sadrieh
Temple University

Miriam B. Stamps
University of South Florida

Charles R. Taylor
Villanova University

Hope K. Torkornoo
Kennesaw State University

Sushila Umashankar
University of Arizona

Frank E. Vaughn
Kent State University

Steven White
Bridgewater State College

Terrence H. Witkowski
California State University

In addition, over 200 instructors, unfortunately too many to list here, responded to surveys that helped shape the content and structure of this edition, as well as provided impetus for some very positive changes in the supplement package.

We appreciate the help of all the many students and professors who have shared their opinions of past editions, and we welcome their comments and suggestions on this and future editions of *International Marketing.*

A very special thanks to Karen Westover, Sponsoring Editor; Diane Beausoleil, Senior Developmental Editor; Colleen Suljic, Senior Marketing Manager; Gladys True, Senior Project Manager; Francis Owens, Art Director; and Charlotte Goldman, Photo Researcher, at Irwin/McGraw-Hill, whose enthusiasm, creativity, constructive criticisms, and commitment to excellence has made this edition possible.

Philip R. Cateora
John L. Graham

BRIEF CONTENTS

Contents

PART III

ASSESSING GLOBAL MARKET OPPORTUNITIES

LIST OF "CROSSING BORDERS" BOXES

GLOBAL PERSPECTIVE

International Marketing Is for Small Companies Too

It's not news that Coca-Cola is a global company or that 25 percent of all of General Motors' profits for the past five years came from General Motors do Brazil. After all that's what international marketing and the global economy are all about, companies like IBM, Intel, Nike, and McDonald's doing business around the world. But you might be surprised to learn that the global economy now reaches every corner of the United States and that internationalization now involves not just the giant corporations but also many small companies that have only recently ventured outside of the United States seeking new markets. In fact, export growth of small businesses selling everything from window screens to abrasives has been one of the major engines of the United States' long economic expansion. According to a study by the Institute for International Economics, the 50 largest exporters account for 30 percent of the nation's merchandise exports; the rest comes from "middle and lightweights." Facing stiff competition and saturated markets at home, many small and medium-size companies are discovering the opportunity of foreign markets. Consider the following examples:

- Red Spot Paint & Varnish Co.'s international sales used to be so rare that the president handled them on Saturday mornings. Today, a staff of four full-timers covers exports that account for 20 percent of the company's $90 million annual sales. Red Spot sells paints and other coatings to auto makers on six continents and competes with the likes of Du Pont Co. When they started, people asked, "How in the world can you sell Red Spot Paint outside the tri-state area?"

- Hanover Wire Cloth made its first attempts to sell screens abroad nine years ago by visiting foreign trade shows. Today the company's factory runs round-the-clock, six days a week. Its international department, now seven strong, sells products in 35 countries. Foreign sales reached $9.4 million, 16 percent of the company's total revenues. Over the last five years the company has made two major equipment upgrades to accommodate the special needs of the new markets. Hanover Wire Cloth now turns out wire screening in metric widths as

well as inch widths, and in nontraditional colors to suit market tastes—green for Europe, gold for the Philippines, and black for Australia and Canada.

- In the mid-1980s, only about 10 percent of Bromide Engineered Abrasives' sales were outside the U.S.—and those were to Big Three automakers' factories across the river in Canada. By 1997, 60 percent of the business was overseas. The company employs 35 people to manufacture, sell, and ship "little sticks," 6-inch-long sticks used like a file or whetstone to polish and fine-tune the metal molds for plastic parts. To obtain a glossy-smooth finish on a telephone, for example, the steel or aluminum plastic-injection molds must be carefully maintained. Overseas customers in 27 different countries buy these "little sticks" despite tariffs and duties imposed to keep foreign products out. Customers in India, for example, who are not allowed to write checks for more than $5,000 to non-Indian companies, get around the restriction by splitting orders into less than $5,000 each.

- Not to be overlooked is Hawg Heaven Bait Co., whose exports account for 20 percent of its sales. "Japan is really becoming a country that likes to bass fish," says Hawg's owner, pulling out a $9,600 Japanese order for his Twin Screws Super Craw fishing lures.

It wasn't too long ago that international marketing was left to the big boys while the rest dabbled in exporting only once in a while. Today, however, international marketing is a contributor to the revenue streams of more and more companies. If all the global trends we discuss in this chapter and throughout the text continue, the world will experience an economic boom of unparalleled proportions in the 21st century. To participate, you and your companies must become aware of global challenges and opportunities; we present this text as a step in that direction.

Sources: Laurent Belsie, "Small Items from Small Towns Are Now Big Part of U.S. Exports," *Christian Science Monitor,* November 13, 1996, p. 1; "Brazil Plan Is Bitter Pill for U.S. Multinationals," *The Wall Street Journal,* November 13, 1997, p. A17; Robert L. Rose and Carl Quintanilla, "Tiptoeing? Abroad: More Small U.S. Firms Take Up Exporting, with Much Success," *The Wall Street Journal,* December 20, 1996, p. A1; and Peter Grier, "Exports: Rocket Fuel of U.S. Economy Selling Sandpaper's 'Sticks' to India," *Christian Science Monitor,* October 1, 1997, p. 1.

Never before in American history have U.S. businesses, large and small, been so deeply involved in and affected by international global business. A global economic boom, unprecedented in modern economic history, is under way as the drive for efficiency, productivity, and open, unregulated markets sweeps the world. Powerful economic, technological, industrial, political, and demographic forces are converging to build the foundation of a new global economic order on which the structure of a one-world economic and market system will be built.

Whether or not a U.S. company wants to participate directly in international business, it cannot escape the effect of the ever-increasing number of North American firms exporting, importing, and/or manufacturing abroad, nor can it ignore the number of foreign-based firms operating in U.S. markets, the growth of regional trade areas, the rapid growth of world markets, and the increasing number of competitors for global markets.

Of all the trends affecting global business today, three stand out as the most dynamic, the ones that will influence the shape of international business in the future: (1) the rapid growth of regional free trade areas such as NAFTA, EC, and AFTA;[1] (2) the trend toward the acceptance of the free market system among developing countries in Latin America, Asia, and Eastern Europe; and (3) as a result of these two, the evolution of large emerging markets such as Brazil, China, South Korea, and Poland.

Today most business activities are global in scope. Technology, research, capital, investment, production, and marketing, distribution, and communications networks all have global dimensions. Every business must be prepared to compete in an increasingly interdependent global economic environment, and all businesspeople must be aware of the effects of these trends when managing a domestic company that exports or a multinational conglomerate. As one international expert noted, every American company is international, at least to the extent that its business performance is conditioned in part by events that occur abroad. Even companies that do not operate in the international arena are affected to some degree by the success of the European Community, the export-led growth in South Korea, the revitalized Mexican economy, and the economic changes taking place in China.

It is less and less possible for business to avoid the influence of the internationalization of the United States economy, the globalization of the world's markets, and the growth of new emerging markets. As competition for world markets intensifies, the number of companies operating solely in domestic markets will decrease. Or, to put it another way, it is increasingly true that *the business of American business is international business.* The challenge of international marketing is to develop strategic plans that are competitive in the intensifying global markets. For a growing number of companies, being international is no longer a luxury but a necessity for economic survival. These and other issues affecting the world economy, trade, markets, and competition will be discussed throughout this text.

The Internationalization of U.S. Business

Current interest in international marketing can be explained by changing competitive structures coupled with shifts in demand characteristics in markets throughout the world. With the increasing globalization of markets, companies find they are unavoidably enmeshed with foreign customers, competitors, and suppliers, even within their own borders. They face competition on all fronts—from domestic firms and from foreign firms. A significant portion of all tape players, VCRs, apparel, and dinnerware sold in the United States is foreign made. Sony, Laura Ashley, Norelco, Samsung, Toyota,

---

[1] NAFTA is the North American Free Trade Area, EC is the European Community, and AFTA is the Asian Free Trade Area.

CROSSING BORDERS 1–1

One World, One Ford: Yesterday—Today

Yesterday

Henry Ford built a 100 percent American-made automobile. Ford's Rouge plant in Dearborn, Michigan, was built in 1919 to turn out the country's first Model Ts. The plant had its own steel mill, glass factory, and 32 other separate manufacturing plants under one roof. The only foreign element in a Model T was rubber from Malaysia, and Henry Ford made a valiant but vain effort to grow rubber trees. Not until the advent of synthetic rubber in the 1940s did the Ford become 100 percent American. It was manufactured entirely in the Rouge plant, then the world's largest single industrial complex.

In the early 1960s things began to change. A Ford memorandum stated, "In order to further the growth of our worldwide operations, each purchasing activity should consider the selection of sources of supply anywhere in the world," or to paraphrase: If it's cheaper abroad, get it abroad. Ford's memorandum was a harbinger of American business to come.

Today

World cars—developed, manufactured, and assembled all over the world and sold all over the world—are a fact. Ford's Festiva was designed in the U.S., engineered by Mazda in Japan, and is being built by Kia in Korea. Mercury Tracer has a Ford design, built on a Mazda platform in Hermosillo, Mexico, with a Ford engine manufactured in Mexico and other components from Taiwan.

As emerging countries come into the market for automobiles, Ford is developing two low-cost "value vehicles"—one a small passenger car, the other a compact utility vehicle—that can be sold for about $8,000 to $9,000 in markets such as India, China, Brazil, and Russia beginning in 2001–02. Smaller than the Escort, these value vehicles will share some components with the next-generation Fiesta minicar that's currently being developed in Europe.

Under the Ford 2000 plan, Ford's U.S. and European operations will be formally merged into one super organization; Latin American and Asian operations will follow later. The idea is to create and use the same systems and processes around the world to design products that can be built and sold in different places with only modest local variations.

Since Europe is chiefly a smaller-car market, Ford's European operations will be responsible for creating front-wheel-drive cars. The same platform and the same manufacturing and design processes will be used to build small cars for the U.S. market. Four U.S. vehicle project centers will be responsible for designing bigger cars and trucks which will be marketed worldwide, and may even be built worldwide with common manufacturing systems and almost identical basic platforms. The company envisions huge savings from engineering a product only once.

Ford 2000 is not a one-car-fits-all idea. It looks like centralization but really involves decentralizing. Although it will produce fewer basic car platforms, it will result in very different vehicles from the same platform. A small world car designed by Ford Europe will have the same engine, transmission, and other major components around the world, but will have styling tailored to local tastes. One World, One Ford Today!

Sources: Adapted from Nancy W. Hatton, "Born and Bred in the USA," *Detroit News*, March 12, 1983; Jerry Flint, "One World, One Ford," *Forbes*, June 20, 1994, pp. 40–41; Paul Lienert, "Ford Plans World Car under $10,000," *Detroit News*, October 20, 1997, p. C1; and Katherine Yung, "Coming to Grips with Ford 2000: How Ambitious Overhaul Affects the Mind-set, Lives of 3 Middle Managers," *Detroit News*, March 2, 1997, p. C1. Visit the Ford homepage for an interesting view of how many countries Ford has operations. **http://www.ford.com/global/**.

EXHIBIT 1–1   **Foreign Acquisitions of U.S. Companies**

U.S. Company	Foreign Owner
J. Walter Thompson (advertising)	Britain
Spiegel (catalog retailing)	Germany
Mack Trucks (automotive)	France
Giant Food Stores (supermarkets)	Netherlands
Pillsbury, Hueblein	Britain
CBS Records (music and entertainment)	Japan
Magnavox (televisions)	Netherlands
Carnation (Coffee-Mate, Friskies pet food)	Switzerland
Chesebrough-Pond's (Vaseline)	Netherlands
Vermont American (garden tools)	Germany
Northwest Airlines	Netherlands

Source: Adapted from "Soon to Be Extinct: American TV Brands," *U.S. News & World Report,* July 31, 1995, p. 13; and Gustavo Lombo, "Creating American Jobs," *Forbes,* July 28, 1997, p. 222.

and Nescafé are familiar brands in the United States, and for U.S. industry they are formidable opponents in a competitive struggle for U.S. and world markets.

Many familiar U.S. companies are now foreign controlled. When you drop in at a 7-Eleven convenience store or buy Firestone tires, you are buying directly from a Japanese company. Some well-known brands no longer owned by U.S. companies are Carnation (Swiss), Burger King (British), and the all-American Smith and Wesson handgun that won the U.S. West, which is owned by a British firm. The last U.S.-owned company to manufacture TV sets was Zenith, but it was recently acquired by South Korea's LG Electronics, Inc., which manufactures Goldstar TVs and other products. Pearle Vision, Universal Studios, and many more are currently owned or controlled by foreign multinational businesses (see Exhibit 1–1). Foreign investment in the United States is in excess of $1.5 trillion. Companies from the United Kingdom lead the group of investors, with companies from the Netherlands, Japan, Germany, and Switzerland following in that order.[2]

Other foreign companies that entered the U.S. market through exporting their products into the U.S. realized sufficient market share to justify building manufacturing plants in the U.S. Fuji Photo Film invested more than $1 billion in a plant to service its 12 percent share of the U.S. film market.[3] Honda, BMW, and Mercedes are all manufacturing in the U.S. Investments go the other way as well. Ford bought Jaguar; Pacificorp acquired Energy Group, the U.K.'s largest electricity supplier and second largest gas distributor; and Wisconsin Central Transportation, a medium-sized U.S. railroad, controls all U.K. rail freight business and runs the queen's private train, via its English, Welsh & Scottish Railway unit. It has also acquired the company that runs rail shuttles through the Channel Tunnel.[4] Investments by U.S. multinationals abroad are nothing new. They have been roaming the world in mass since the end of World War II, buying companies and investing in manufacturing plants. What is relatively new for U.S. companies is having their global competitors competing with them in "their" market, the United States.

Once the private domain of domestic businesses, the vast U.S. market that provided an opportunity for continued growth must now be shared with a variety of foreign companies and products. Companies with only domestic markets have found it increasingly difficult to sustain customary rates of growth and many are seeking foreign markets in which to expand. Companies with foreign operations find foreign earnings are making an important overall contribution to total corporate profits. A four-year Conference

---

[2] Gustavo Lombo, "Creating American Jobs," *Forbes,* July 28, 1997, p. 222.
[3] Philip Siekman, "A Surge in Foreign-Owned Factories," *Fortune,* July 21, 1997, p. 95.
[4] "Investing in Each Other," *Europe,* September 1997, p. 12.

Barnyard Babies, Inc. is a good example of entrepreneurs that are finding opportunities through exporting. Barnyard Babies export stuffed toy figures that can be colored and washed and colored again. (© Ken Touchton)

Board study of 1,250 U.S. manufacturing companies found that multinationals of all sizes and in all industries outperformed their strictly domestic U.S. counterparts. They grew twice as fast in sales and earned significantly higher returns on equity and assets. Further, the U.S. multinationals reduced their manufacturing employment, both at home and abroad, more than domestic companies.

Exhibit 1–2 illustrates how important profit generated on investments abroad is to U.S. companies. In many cases, foreign sales are more profitable than U.S. sales and foreign return on assets are better than in the United States—all important reasons for going international.[5]

Companies that never ventured abroad until recently are now seeking foreign markets.[6] Companies with existing foreign operations realize they must be more competi-

---

[5] Lawrence Chimerine, "The New Economic Realities in Business," *Management Review,* January 1997, p. 47.

[6] "Wal-Mart Spoken Here," *Business Week,* June 23, 1997, p. 138.

EXHIBIT 1–2   Some Big U.S. Players in the Global Game*

Company	Foreign Revenues (Percent of Total)	Foreign Profits (Percent of Total)	Foreign Assets (Percent of Total)
E.I. du Pont de Nemours	43.1%	28.9%	40.6%
Procter & Gamble	50.1	36.9	40.5
Coca-Cola	67.1	67.8	37.7
Motorola	45.0	92.4	35.7
Johnson & Johnson	49.6	46.1	45.3
Sara Lee	39.7	53.8	51.3
Colgate-Palmolive	71.6	83.6	60.4
Gillette	63.1	41.1	62.6
Compaq Computer	46.5	51.7	31.4
McDonald's	57.0	49.6	55.0
Avon Products	65.3	58.9	59.0
Intel	58.4	38.4	20.2
RJR Nabisco	36.2	53.8	20.2

* 1996 data.

Source: Adapted from Brian Zajac, "Buying American," *Forbes* July 28, 1997, p. 218. Visit some of the home pages of these companies and see how extensive their international holdings are: **http://www.Nestle.com/**, **http://www.pg.com**, and **http://www.colgate.com**.

tive to succeed against foreign multinationals. They have found it necessary to spend more money and time improving their marketing positions abroad because competition for these growing markets is intensifying. For the firm venturing into international marketing for the first time and for those already experienced, the requirement is generally the same: a thorough and complete commitment to foreign markets and, for many, new ways of operating.

International Marketing Defined

International marketing is the performance of business activities designed to plan, price, promote, and direct the flow of a company's goods and services to consumers or users in more than one nation for a profit. The only difference in the definitions of domestic marketing and international marketing is that marketing activities take place in more than one country. This apparently minor difference ". . . *in more than one nation* . . ." accounts for the complexity and diversity found in international marketing operations. Marketing concepts, processes, and principles are universally applicable, and the marketer's task is the same whether doing business in Dimebox, Texas, or Dar es Salaam, Tanzania. Businesses' goal is to make a profit by promoting, pricing, and distributing products for which there is a market. If this is the case, what is the difference between domestic and international marketing?

The answer lies not with different concepts of marketing but with the environment within which marketing plans must be implemented. The uniqueness of foreign marketing comes from the range of unfamiliar problems and the variety of strategies necessary to cope with different levels of uncertainty encountered in foreign markets.

Competition, legal restraints, government controls, weather, fickle consumers, and any number of other uncontrollable elements can, and frequently do, affect the profitable outcome of good, sound marketing plans. Generally speaking, the marketer cannot control or influence these uncontrollable elements, but instead must adjust or adapt to them in a manner consistent with a successful outcome. What makes marketing interesting is the challenge of molding the *controllable elements* of marketing decisions (product, price, promotion, and distribution) within the framework of the *uncontrollable*

Representing the biggest-ever Campbell product launch in Asia, the line of four corn soups offered in Hong Kong, Singapore, and Taiwan reflects the company's strategy to offer products that have been consumer-tested and tailored to meet local tastes. (Courtesy of Campbell Soup Company)

elements of the marketplace (competition, politics, laws, consumer behavior, level of technology, and so forth) in such a way that marketing objectives are achieved. Even though marketing principles and concepts are universally applicable, the environment within which the marketer must implement marketing plans can change dramatically from country to country or region to region. The difficulties created by different environments are the international marketer's primary concern.

The International Marketing Task

The international marketer's task is more complicated than that of the domestic marketer because the international marketer must deal with at least two levels of uncontrollable uncertainty instead of one. Uncertainty is created by the uncontrollable elements of all business environments, but each foreign country in which a company operates adds its own unique set of uncontrollables. Exhibit 1–3 illustrates the total environment

Exhibit 1–3   The International Marketing Task

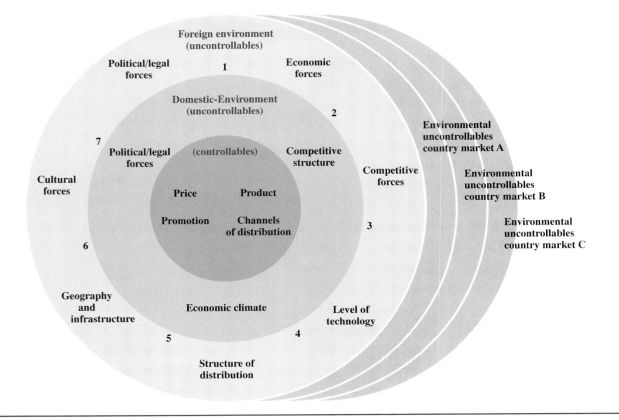

of an international marketer. The inner circle depicts the controllable elements that constitute a marketer's decision area, the second circle encompasses those environmental elements at home that have some effect on foreign-operation decisions, and the outer circles represent the elements of the foreign environment for each foreign market within which the marketer operates. As the outer circles illustrate, each foreign market in which the company does business can (and usually does) present separate problems involving some or all of the uncontrollable elements. Thus, the more foreign markets in which a company operates, the greater the possible variety of foreign environmental uncontrollables with which to contend. Frequently, a solution to a problem in country market A is not applicable to a problem in country market B.

Marketing Controllables

The successful manager constructs a marketing program designed for optimal adjustment to the uncertainty of the business climate. The inner circle in Exhibit 1–3 represents the area under control of the marketing manager. Assuming the necessary overall corporate resources, the marketing manager blends price, product, promotion, and channels-of-distribution activities to capitalize on anticipated demand. The controllable elements can be altered in the long run and, usually, in the short run, to adjust to changing market conditions, consumer tastes, or corporate objectives.

The outer circles surrounding the market controllables represent the levels of uncertainty that are created by the domestic and foreign environments. Although the marketer can blend a marketing mix from the controllable elements, the uncontrollables are precisely that and there must be active evaluation and, if needed, adaptation. That effort, the adaptation of the marketing mix to the uncontrollables, determines the ultimate outcome of the marketing enterprise.

Domestic Uncontrollables

The second circle in Exhibit 1–3, representing the *domestic uncontrollables,* includes home-country elements that can have a direct effect on the success of a foreign venture and are out of the immediate control of the marketer: political and legal forces, economic climate, and competition.

A political decision involving domestic foreign policy can have a direct effect on a firm's international marketing success. For example, the U.S. government placed a total ban on trade with Libya to condemn Libyan support for terrorist attacks, imposed restrictions on trade with South Africa to protest apartheid, and placed a total ban on trade with Iraq, whose actions constituted a threat to the national security of the United States and its allies. In each case, the international marketing programs of United States' companies, whether it was IBM, Exxon, or Hawg Heaven Bait Company, were restricted by these political decisions, all domestic uncontrollables. The U.S. government has the constitutional right to restrict foreign trade when such trade adversely affects the security or economy of the country, or when such trade is in conflict with U.S. foreign policy. Conversely, positive effects occur when there are changes in foreign policy and countries are given favored treatment. Such were the cases when South Africa abolished apartheid and the embargo was lifted, and when the U.S. government decided to uncouple human rights issues from foreign trade policy and grant most favored nation status (MFN) to China. In both cases, opportunities were created for U.S. companies.

The domestic economic climate is another important home-based uncontrollable variable with far-reaching effects on a company's competitive position in foreign markets. The capacity to invest in plants and facilities, either in domestic or foreign markets, is to a large extent a function of domestic economic vitality. It is generally true that capital tends to flow toward optimum use; however, capital must be generated before it can have mobility. Furthermore, if internal economic conditions deteriorate, restrictions against foreign investment and purchasing may be imposed to strengthen the domestic economy.

For a variety of economic reasons, the most pressing condition affecting U.S. international marketers during the mid-1980s was the relative strength of the dollar in world markets. Because the U.S. dollar's value was high compared to most foreign currencies, U.S. goods were expensive for foreign buyers. This gave a price advantage to foreign competitors by making American products relatively expensive, and thus caused a downturn in export sales. By the 1990s, the U.S. dollar had weakened compared to world currencies, and export sales increased as U.S. products became bargains for foreign customers. For example, an English citizen planning to buy a $15 American-made product in 1984, when the exchange rate was £1 = $1.15, had to exchange £13 to get $15 U.S. By 1997, when the British pound equaled $1.66, that same $15 item would cost him or her £9.03, £3.97 less than in 1984. From the American's perspective, the situation in 1997 was more favorable for the sale of U.S. products than was the case in 1984. Currency value, then, is another influence the home environment's economy has on the marketer's task.

Competition within the home country can also have a profound effect upon the international marketer's task. Until recently, Eastman Kodak dominated the U.S. film market and could depend on achieving profit goals that provided capital to invest in foreign markets. Without having to worry about the company's lucrative base, management had the time and resources to devise aggressive international marketing programs. However, the competitive structure changed when Fuji Photo Film became a formidable competitor by lowering film prices in the United States, opening a $300 million plant, and gaining 12 percent of the U.S. market. As a result, Kodak had to direct energy and resources back to

CROSSING BORDERS 1–2

Is a Cheeto a Cheeto If It Doesn't Taste Like Cheese?

PepsiCo, the maker of Cheetos, announced a $1 million joint venture to produce the little crispy-tasting cheese puffs in Guangdong province, China. The estimated market for Western snack foods in Guangdong province is $40 million to $70 million. The province, with 70 million consumers, represents a market that is one-third the size of the United States. Between-meal snacking is rising rapidly along with disposable income as the Chinese economy gains momentum and work hours increase.

This is the first time a major snack-food brand will be produced in China for Chinese tastes. In adapting Cheetos to the Chinese market, a new flavor had to be found. Cheese is not a mainstay in the Chinese diet and in focus groups the cheese taste of American Cheetos did not test well. More than 600 flavors, ranging from Roasted Cuttlefish to Sweet Caramel, were tested before settling on Savory American Cream (a buttered popcorn flavor) and Zesty Japanese Steak (a teriyaki-type taste).

But, is it a Cheeto if it doesn't taste like cheese? "It's still crispy, it has a Cheeto shape, and it's fun to eat, so it's a Cheeto," says the general manager of PepsiCo Foods International.

The introduction of Cheetos will be backed by television, print advertising, and promotions based on Chester Cheetah, the brand's feline symbol, riding a Harley-Davidson motorcycle. The packages will carry the Cheeto logo in English along with the Chinese characters *qi duo,* which translates to *new surprise.*

Source: Adapted from Glenn Collins, "Chinese to Get a Taste of Cheese-less Cheetos," *The New York Times,* September 2, 1994, p. C4; and Glenn Collins, "Going Global Involves More Than Many U.S. Companies Think," *The New York Times,* January 2, 1997, p. C1.

the United States.[7] Competition within their home country affects a company's domestic as well as international plans. Inextricably entwined with the effects of the domestic environment are the constraints imposed by the environment of each foreign country.

Foreign Uncontrollables

In addition to uncontrollable domestic elements, a significant source of uncertainty is the number of foreign *uncontrollables* (depicted in Exhibit 1–3 by the outer circles). A business operating in its home country undoubtedly feels comfortable in forecasting the business climate and adjusting business decisions to these elements. The process of evaluating the uncontrollable elements in an international marketing program, however, often involves substantial doses of cultural, political, and economic shock.

A business operating in a number of foreign countries might find polar extremes in political stability, class structure, and economic climate—critical elements in business decisions. The dynamic upheavals in some countries further illustrate the problems of dramatic change in cultural, political, and economic climates over relatively short periods of time. A case in point is China, which has moved from a communist legal system in which all business was done with the state to a transitional period while a commercial legal system is developing.[8] In this transitional phase, new laws are passed but are left to

---

[7] For a report on Kodak's home problems see Mark Maremont and William M. Bulkeley, "Kodak's 10,000 Job Cuts May Amount to Just 8,000," *The Wall Street Journal,* November 13, 1997, p. A1.

[8] Richard Tomlinson, "A Much Criticized Legal System Takes Tentative Steps toward Reform," *International Herald Tribune,* November 25, 1996, p. IV.

be interpreted by local authorities, where confusion prevails as to what rules are still in force and what rules are no longer applicable. For example, commercial contracts can be entered into with a Chinese company or individual only if they are considered a "legal person." To be a legal person in China, the company or person must have registered as such with the Chinese government. To complicate matters further, negotiations may only take place with "legal representatives" of the "legal person" to have the power to bind the company. So if your company enters into negotiations with a Chinese company or person, you must ask for signed, legal documents establishing the right to do business. The formalities of the signature must also be considered. Will a signature on a contract be binding or is it necessary to place a traditional Chinese seal on the document? Even when all is done properly, the government still might change its mind. Coca-Cola had won approval for its plan to build a new facility to produce product for its increasing Chinese market share but before construction began the Chinese parliament raised the issue that Coca-Cola appeared to be too successful in China,[9] so negotiations continue. Such are the uncertainties of the uncontrollable political and legal factors of international business.

The more significant elements in the uncontrollable international environment, shown in the outer circles of Exhibit 1–3, include (1) political/legal forces, (2) economic forces, (3) competitive forces, (4) level of technology, (5) structure of distribution, (6) geography and infrastructure, and (7) cultural forces. They constitute the principal elements of uncertainty an international marketer must cope with in designing a marketing program. Although each will be discussed in depth in subsequent chapters, consider the level of technology and political/legal forces as illustrations of the nature of foreign uncontrollables.

The level of technology is an uncontrollable element that can often be misread because of the vast differences that may exist between developed and undeveloped countries. A marketer cannot assume that the understanding of the concept of preventive maintenance for machinery and equipment or the level of technical support are the same in other countries as in the United States. Technical expertise may not be available at a level necessary for product support and the general population may not have an adequate level of technical knowledge to properly maintain equipment. In those situations, a marketer will have to take extra steps to make sure that the importance of routine maintenance is understood and carried out. Further, if technical support is not readily available, locals will have to be specially trained or the company will have to provide the support.

Political and legal issues face a business whether operating at home or in a foreign country. However, the issues abroad are often amplified by the "alien status" of the company, which increases the difficulty of properly assessing and forecasting the dynamic international business climate. There are two dimensions to the alien status of a foreign business: alien in that foreigners control the business, and alien in that the culture of the host country is alien to management. The alien status of a business means that, when viewed as an outsider, it can be seen as an exploiter and receive prejudiced or unfair treatment at the hands of politicians and/or legal authorities. Political activists can rally support by advocating the expulsion of the "foreign exploiters," often with open or tacit approval of authorities. The Indian government, for example, gave Coca-Cola the choice of either revealing its secret formula or closing up shop and leaving the country. Coke chose to leave. When it was welcomed back several years later, it faced harassment and constant interference with its operations from political activists, inspired by competing soft drink companies.

Furthermore, in a domestic situation political details and the ramifications of political and/or legal events are often more transparent than they are in some foreign countries. For instance, while in the United States there are established legal procedures and due process to which each party in a dispute has access, legal systems in other countries may be evolving. In Russia and China, corruption may prevail, foreigners may receive unfair treatment, or the laws are so different from those in the home country that they

---

[9] Byron J. Lawler, "China: A Legal Check-list for Doing Business," *Trade Culture,* January 1996, p. 45.

CROSSING BORDERS 1–3

So, Jose Antonio Martinez de Garcia, Are You Señor Martinez or Señor Garcia?

In the United States, we try to get on a first-name basis quickly. In some countries, however, to do so makes you appear brash, if not rude. The best policy is to use the last name with a proper and respectful title until specifically invited to do otherwise. But the problem doesn't end there because the "proper" last name can vary among cultures.

In Brazil and Portugal, people are addressed by their Christian names, along with the proper title or simply Mr., so that Manuel Santos is Señor Manuel. In Spain and Spanish-heritage South America, it is not unusual to use a double surname—from the paternal and maternal family names. The paternal family name is the one to use. It is generally the second from last while the maternal name is the last, so that Jose Antonio Martinez de Garcia is Señor Martinez. In written communications, both last names may be used, but in verbal communication, only the paternal name.

In China, the order of names is just the reverse of the United States: last name, middle name, and first name. Hence, in the name Chang Wu Jiang, Chang is the family surname, Wu is a middle name, and Jiang is the first name. This person would be addressed with a title plus the surname, that is, Mr. Chang. To address him as Mr. Jiang would be calling him by his first name, which might appear as being too informal. The problem in China is further complicated by the fact that few surnames exist. There are only 438 Chinese surnames, the most common being Wang, Zhang, and Li; 10 percent of the total population (over 100 million) are named Zhang; 60 percent have only 19 surnames; 90 percent have only 100 surnames. The Chinese themselves generally address each other by the family name and an appropriate title or by both the family name and full given name together, with the family name first. The obvious reason for this custom is that it helps distinguish all the Wangs, Zhangs, and Lis from one another.

Sources: Adapted from Lennie Copeland and Lewis Griggs, *Going International* (New York: Random House, 1985), p. 158; and Wayne A. Conaway and Terri Morrison, "What's in a Name?" *Industry Week,* September 23, 1997, p. 31.

are misinterpreted. The point is that a foreign company is foreign and thus always subject to the political whims of the government to a greater degree than a domestic firm.

Political/legal forces and the level of technology are only two of the foreign uncontrollables that will be discussed in subsequent chapters. The uncertainty of different foreign business environments creates the need for a close study of the uncontrollable elements within each new country. Different solutions to fundamentally identical marketing tasks are often in order and are generally the result of changes in the environment of the market. Thus, a strategy successful in one country can be rendered ineffective in another by differences in political climate, stages of economic development, level of technology, or other cultural variation.

Environmental Adjustment Needed

To adjust and adapt a marketing program to foreign markets, marketers must be able to interpret effectively the influence and impact of each of the uncontrollable environmental elements on the marketing plan for each foreign market in which they hope to do business. In a broad sense, the uncontrollable elements constitute the culture; the difficulty facing the marketer in adjusting to the culture (i.e., uncontrollable elements of the marketplace) lies in recognizing their impact. In a domestic market the reaction to much of the uncontrollables' (cultural) impact on the marketer's activities is automatic; the various cultural influences that fill our lives are simply a part of our history, and we react in a manner acceptable to our society without thinking about it because we are culturally responsive to our environment. The experiences we have gained throughout life have become second nature and serve as the basis for our behavior.

The task of cultural adjustment, however, is the most challenging and important one confronting international marketers; they must adjust their marketing efforts to cultures to which they are not attuned. In dealing with unfamiliar markets, marketers must be aware of the frames of reference they are using in making their decisions or evaluating the potential of a market because judgments are derived from experience that is the result of the enculturative process. Once a frame of reference is established, it becomes an important factor in determining or modifying a marketer's reaction to situations—social and even nonsocial—especially if experience or knowledge of accustomed behavior is lacking.

When a marketer operates in other cultures, marketing attempts may fail because of unconscious responses based on frames of reference acceptable in one's own culture but unacceptable in different surroundings. Unless special efforts are made to determine local cultural meanings for every market, the marketer is likely to overlook the significance of certain behaviors or activities and proceed with plans that result in a negative or unwanted response.

For example, a Westerner must learn that white is a symbol of mourning in parts of Asia, quite different from Western culture's white for bridal gowns. Also, time-conscious Americans are not culturally prepared to understand the meaning of time to Latin Americans. These differences must be learned to avoid misunderstandings that can lead to marketing failures. Such a failure actually occurred in the one situation when ignorance led to ineffective advertising on the part of an American firm; and a second misunderstanding resulted in lost sales when a "long waiting period" in the outer office of a Latin American customer was misinterpreted by an American sales executive. Cross-cultural misunderstandings can also occur when a simple hand gesture has a number of different meanings in different parts of the world. When wanting to signify something is OK, most people in the United States raise a hand and make a circle with the thumb and forefinger. However, this same hand gesture means "zero" or "worthless" to the French, "money" to the Japanese, and a general sexual insult in Sardinia and Greece. A U.S. president sent an unintentional message to some Australian protesters when he held up the first two fingers with the back of his hand to the protesters. Meaning to give the "victory" sign, he was unaware that in Australia the same hand gesture is equivalent to holding up the middle finger in the United States.

To avoid such errors, the foreign marketer should be aware of the principle of *marketing relativism;* that is, marketing strategies and judgments are based on experience, and experience is interpreted by each marketer in terms of his or her own culture. We take into the marketplace, at home or in a foreign country, frames of reference developed from past experiences that determine or modify our reactions to the situations we face.

Cultural conditioning is like an iceberg—we are not aware of nine-tenths of it. In any study of the market systems of different peoples, their political and economic structures, religions, and other elements of culture, foreign marketers must constantly guard against measuring and assessing the markets against the fixed values and assumptions of their own cultures. They must take specific steps to make themselves aware of the home-cultural reference in their analyses and decision making.

Self-Reference Criterion: An Obstacle

The key to successful international marketing is adaptation to the environmental differences from one market to another. Adaptation is a conscious effort on the part of the international marketer to anticipate the influences of both the foreign and domestic uncontrollable environments on a marketing mix and then to adjust the marketing mix to mini-mize the effects.

The primary obstacle to success in international marketing is a person's *self-reference criterion (SRC)* in making decisions, that is, an unconscious reference to one's own cultural values, experiences, and knowledge as a basis for decisions. The SRC impedes the ability to assess a foreign market in its true light.

When confronted with a set of facts, we react spontaneously on the basis of knowledge assimilated over a lifetime—knowledge that is a product of the history of our culture. We seldom stop to think about a reaction; we simply react. Thus, when faced with a problem in another culture, the tendency is to react instinctively and refer to our SRC for a solution. Our reaction, however, is based on meanings, values, symbols, and behavior relevant to our own culture and usually different from those of the foreign culture. Such decisions are often not valid.

To illustrate the impact of the SRC, consider misunderstandings that can occur about personal space between people of different cultures. In the United States, unrelated individuals keep a certain physical distance between themselves and others when talking or in groups. We do not consciously think about that distance; we just know what feels right without thinking. When someone is too close or too far away, we feel uncomfortable and either move farther away or get closer to correct the distance. In doing so, we are relying on our SRC. In some cultures the acceptable distance between individuals is substantially less than that which is comfortable to Americans. When someone from another culture approaches an American too closely, unaware of another culture's acceptable distance the American unconsciously reacts by backing away to restore the proper distance (i.e., proper by American standards), and confusion results for both parties. Americans assume foreigners are pushy, while foreigners assume Americans are unfriendly and standoffish. Both react to the values of their own SRCs, making them all victims of a cultural misunderstanding.

Your self-reference criterion can prevent you from being aware that there are cultural differences or from recognizing the importance of those differences. Thus, you either fail to recognize the need to take action, you discount the cultural differences that exist among countries, or you react to a situation in a way offensive to your hosts. A common mistake made by Americans is to refuse food or drink when offered. In the United States, a polite refusal is certainly acceptable, but in Asia or the Middle East, a host is offended if you refuse hospitality. While you do not have to eat or drink much, you do have to accept the offering of hospitality. Understanding and dealing with the self-reference criterion are two of the more important facets in international marketing.

The SRC can influence an evaluation of the appropriateness of a domestically designed marketing mix for a foreign market. If U.S. marketers are not aware, they may evaluate a marketing mix on U.S. experiences (i.e., their SRC) without fully appreciating the cultural differences requiring adaptation. Esso, the brand name of a gasoline, was a successful name in the United States and would seem harmless enough for foreign countries; however, in Japan, the name phonetically means "stalled car," an undesirable image for gasoline. Another example is "Pet" in Pet Milk. The name has been used for decades, yet in France the word *pet* means, among other things, flatulence—again, not the desired image for canned milk. Both of these examples of real mistakes made by major companies stem from relying on SRC in making a decision. In U.S. culture, a person's SRC would not reveal a problem with either Esso or Pet, but in international marketing relying on one's SRC could produce an inadequately adapted marketing program that ends in failure.

When marketers take the time to look beyond their own SRCs, the results are more positive. A British manufacturer of chocolate biscuits (cookies in American English), ignoring its SRC, knows that it must package its biscuits differently to accommodate the Japanese market. Thus, in Japan McVitie's chocolate biscuits are wrapped individually, packed in presentation cardboard boxes, and priced about three times higher than in the U.K.—the cookies are used as gifts and thus must look and be perceived as special.[10] Unilever, appreciating the uniqueness of its markets, repackaged and reformulated its detergent for Brazil. For one, the lack of washing machines among poorer Brazilians made a simpler soap formula necessary. Next, since people wash their clothes in rivers, the powder was packaged in plastic rather than paper so it would not get soggy. Finally, because the Brazilian poor are price conscious and buy in small quantities, the soap was packaged in small, low-priced packages.[11] Even McDonald's modifies its traditional Big Mac in India where it is known as the "Maharaja Mac." This burger features two mutton patties, since most Indians consider cows sacred and don't eat beef.[12] In each of these examples, had the marketers' own SRCs been the basis for decisions, none of the changes would have been readily apparent based on home-market experience.

The most effective way to control the influence of the SRC is to recognize its existence in our behavior. Although it is almost impossible for someone to learn every culture in depth and to be aware of every important difference, an awareness of the need to be sensitive to differences and to ask questions when doing business in another culture can avoid many of the mistakes possible in international marketing. Asking the appropriate question helped the Vicks Company avoid making a mistake in Germany. It discovered that in German "Vicks" sounds like the crudest slang equivalent of intercourse, so they changed the name to "Wicks" before introducing the product.[13]

Be aware, also, that not every activity within a marketing program is different from one country to another; indeed, there probably are more similarities than differences. For example, the McVitie's chocolate biscuits mentioned earlier are sold in the United States in the same package as in the U.K. Such similarities, however, may lull the marketer into a false sense of apparent sameness. This apparent sameness, coupled with our self-reference criterion, is often the cause of international marketing problems. Undetected similarities do not cause problems; however, the one difference that goes undetected can create a marketing failure.

To avoid errors in business decisions, it is necessary to make a cross-cultural analysis isolating the SRC influences. The following steps are suggested as a framework for such an analysis.

Step 1: Define the business problem or goal in *home-country* cultural traits, habits, or norms.

Step 2: Define the business problem or goal in *foreign-country* cultural traits, habits, or norms. Make no value judgments.

Step 3: Isolate the SRC influence in the problem and examine it carefully to see how it complicates the problem.

Step 4: Redefine the problem without the SRC influence and solve for the optimum business goal situation.[14]

This approach requires an understanding of the culture of each foreign market as well as one's own culture. Surprisingly, understanding one's own culture may require additional study because much of the cultural influence on market behavior remains at a subconscious level and is not clearly defined.

Developing a Global Awareness

Opportunities in global business abound for those who are prepared to confront myriad obstacles with optimism and a willingness to continue learning new ways. The successful

---

10 Alison Maitland, "Across the Frontiers," *Financial Times,* October 24, 1996, p. 14.

11 Bill Britt, "Unilever Tests Small Sizes," *Advertising Age International,* March 1997, p. I-3.

12 "Globalization," *Across the Board,* February 1997, p. 5.

13 David A. Ricks, *Blunders in International Business* (Cambridge, Mass.: Blackwell Publishers, 1993), p. 43.

14 James A. Lee, "Cultural Analysis in Overseas Operations," *Harvard Business Review,* March–April 1966, pp. 106–11.

businessperson in the 21st century will have *global awareness* and have a frame of reference that goes beyond a region or even a country and encompasses the world. To be globally aware is to have:

- Objectivity.
- Tolerance[15] of cultural differences.
- Knowledge of cultures, history, world market potential, and global economic, social, and political trends.

To be globally aware is to be objective. Objectivity is important in assessing opportunities, evaluating potential, and responding to problems. Millions of dollars have been lost by companies that blindly entered the Chinese market on the belief that there were untold opportunities when, in reality, opportunities were only in very select areas and generally for those with the resources to sustain a long-term commitment. Many were caught up in the euphoria of envisioning one billion consumers, not seeing the realities of low income and purchasing power, poor distribution and logistics, inadequate media infrastructure, and differences in tastes and preferences between Chinese and Western consumers. Thus, uninformed and not very objective decisions were made.

To be globally aware is to have tolerance toward cultural differences. Tolerance is understanding cultural differences and accepting and working with others whose behaviors may be different from yours. You do not have to accept, as your own, the cultural ways of another but you must allow others to be different and equal. The fact that punctuality is less important in some cultures does not make them less productive, only different. The tolerant person understands the differences that may exist between cultures and uses that knowledge to relate effectively.

A globally aware person is knowledgeable about cultures and history. Knowledge of cultures is important in understanding behavior in the marketplace or in the board room. Knowledge of history is important because the way people think and act is influenced by their history. Some Latin Americans' reluctance about foreign investment, Chinese reluctance to open completely to outsiders, or British persons' hesitance about the tunnel between France and England can all be understood better if you have a historical perspective.

Global awareness also involves knowledge of world market potentials and global economic, social, and political trends. Over the next few decades there will be enormous changes in market potentials in almost every region of the world, all of which a globally aware person must continuously monitor. Finally, a globally aware person will keep abreast of the global economic, social, and political trends because a country's prospects can change as these trends shift direction or accelerate. The former republics of the USSR, along with Russia, Eastern Europe, China, India, Africa, and Latin America are undergoing economic, social, and political changes that have already altered the course of trade and defined new economic powers. The knowledgeable marketer will identify opportunity long before it becomes evident to others.[16] It is the authors' goal in this text to guide the reader toward acquiring a global awareness.

Being International

Once a company has decided to be international, it has to decide the degree of marketing involvement and commitment it is prepared to make. These decisions should reflect

---

[15] The Webster unabridged dictionary defines tolerance as a fair and objective attitude toward those whose opinions, practices, race, religion, nationality, etc., differ from one's own: freedom from bigotry. It is with this meaning that the authors are using tolerance.

[16] For an insightful study of the characteristics of successful international business managers see Brendan J. Gray, "Profiling Managers to Improve Export Promotion Targeting," *Journal of International Business Studies,* Second Quarter 1997, p. 387.

NAFTA has multiplied opportunities in Mexico, where phasing out of tariffs is giving consumers a broader range of supermarket choices of a greater value while providing sharper competition in the Mexican economy. (Courtesy of Campbell Soup Company)

considerable study and analysis of market potential and company capabilities—a process not always followed. Many companies begin tentatively in international marketing, growing as they gain experience and gradually changing strategy and tactics as they become more committed. Others enter international marketing after much research and with fully developed long-range plans, prepared to make investments to acquire a market position.[17]

Stages of International Marketing Involvement

Regardless of the means employed to gain entry into a foreign market, a company may, from a marketing viewpoint, make no market investment—that is, its marketing involvement may be limited to selling a product with little or no thought given to development of market control. Or a company may become totally involved and invest large sums of money and effort to capture and maintain a permanent, specific share of the market. In general, one of five but overlapping stages can describe the international marketing involvement of a company. Although the stages of international marketing involvement are presented here in a linear order, the reader should not infer that a firm progresses from one stage to another; quite to the contrary, a firm may begin its international involvement at any one stage or be in more than one stage simultaneously. For example,

---

[17] The importance of experiential knowledge in the internationalization process is detailed in Kent Eriksson, Jan Johanson, Anders Majkgard, and D. Deo Sharma, "Experiential Knowledge and Cost in the Internationalization Process," *Journal of International Business Studies,* Second Quarter, 1997, p. 337.

because of a short product life cycle and a thin but widespread market for many technology products, many high-tech companies large and small see the entire world, including their home market, as a single market and strive to reach all possible customers as rapidly as possible.

No Direct Foreign Marketing.   A company in this stage does not actively cultivate customers outside national boundaries; however, this company's products may reach foreign markets. Sales may be made to trading companies as well as other foreign customers who come directly to the firm. Or products reach foreign markets via domestic wholesalers or distributors who sell abroad on their own without explicit encouragement or even knowledge of the producer. As companies develop web pages on the Internet, many receive orders from international "web surfers." Often an unsolicited order from a foreign buyer is what piques the interest of a company to seek additional international sales.

Infrequent Foreign Marketing.   Temporary surpluses caused by variations in production levels or demand may result in infrequent marketing overseas. The surpluses are characterized by their temporary nature; therefore, sales to foreign markets are made, as goods are available, with little or no intention of maintaining continuous market representation. As domestic demand increases and absorbs surpluses, foreign sales activity is withdrawn. In this stage, there is little or no change in company organization or product lines. Few companies today fit this model as customers seek long-term commitments and there are companies that offer this option.

Regular Foreign Marketing.   At this level, the firm has permanent productive capacity devoted to the production of goods to be marketed on a continuing basis in foreign markets. A firm may employ foreign or domestic overseas middlemen or it may have its own sales force or sales subsidiaries in important foreign markets. The primary focus of operations and production is to service domestic market needs. However, as overseas demand grows, production is allocated for foreign markets and products may be adapted to meet the needs of individual foreign markets. Profit expectations move from being seen as a bonus to regular domestic profits to the position where the company becomes dependent on foreign sales and profits to meet its goals.

Meter-Man, Inc., a small company (25 employees) in southern Minnesota that manufactures agricultural measuring devices, is a good example of a company at this stage. In 1989, the 35-year-old company began exploring the idea of exporting; by 1992 the company was shipping product to Europe. Today, a third of Meter-Man's sales are in 35 countries and by the end of this decade, the company expects international sales to account for about half of its business. "When you start exporting, you say to yourself, this will be icing on the cake," says the director of sales and marketing. "But now I say going international has become critical to our existence."[18]

International Marketing.   Companies at this stage are fully committed and involved in international marketing activities. Such companies seek markets all over the world and sell products that are a result of planned production for markets in various countries. This generally entails not only the marketing but also the production of goods outside the home market. At this point a company becomes an international or multinational marketing firm.

The experience of Fedders, a manufacturer of room air-conditioners, typifies a company that begins its international business at this stage. Even though it is the largest manufacturer of air-conditioners in the United States, the firm faced constraints in its

---

[18] Christopher Farrell and Edith Updike, "Selling Overseas: So You Think the World Is Your Oyster," *Business Week,* June 9, 1997, p. 4.

domestic market. Its sales were growing steadily but air-conditioner sales (the company's only product) are seasonal and thus there are times when domestic sales do not even cover fixed costs. Furthermore, the U.S. market is mature, with most customers buying only replacement units. Any growth would have to come from a rival's market share and the rivals, Whirlpool and Matsushita, are formidable. Fedders decided that the only way to grow was to venture abroad.

Fedders decided that Asia, with its steamy climate and expanding middle class, offered the best opportunity. China, India, and Indonesia were seen as the best prospects. China was selected because sales of room air-conditioners had grown from 500,000 units to over 4 million in five years, which still accounted for only 12 percent of the homes in cities like Beijing, Shanghai, and Guangzhou. The company saw China as a market with terrific growth potential. After careful study, Fedders entered a joint venture with a small Chinese air-conditioner company that was also looking for a partner and a new company, Fedders Xinle, was formed. They immediately found that they needed to redesign their product for this market. In China air-conditioners are a major purchase seen as a status symbol, not as a box to keep a room cool as in the U.S. The Chinese also prefer a split-type-air-conditioner, the unit containing the fan inside the room and the heat exchanger mounted on a wall outside. Since Fedders did not manufacture split models, it designed a new product that is lightweight, energy-efficient, and packed with features such as a remote control and an automatic air-sweeping mechanism. The joint venture appears to be successful, and the company is exploring the possibility of marketing to other Asian markets and Japan and maybe even back to the United States with a new product that it developed for the China market.[19] As Fedders expands into other markets and makes other commitments internationally, it continues to evolve as an international or multinational company. The company may remain at this stage, as most companies do, or go through a change in orientation and become a global company.

Global Marketing.   At the global marketing level, the most profound change is the orientation of the company toward markets and its planning. At this stage, companies treat the world, including their home market, as one market. In contrast to the multinational or international company that views the world as a series of country markets (including their home market) with unique sets of market characteristics for which marketing strategies must be developed, a global company develops a strategy to reflect the existing commonalties of market needs among many countries to maximize returns through global standardization of its business activities—whenever it is cost effective and culturally possible. The entire operations, its organization structure, sources of finance, production, marketing, and so forth, take on a global perspective.

Perhaps the former president of Coca-Cola, Roberto Goizueta, put it most simply and succinctly when he said, "The culture of The Coca-Cola Co. has moved from being an American company doing business internationally to an international company that happens to be headquartered in Atlanta. This change is pervasive throughout our organization. . . . If you go back to our 1981 annual report, you will see references to 'foreign' sales or 'foreign' earnings. Today, the word foreign is 'foreign' to our corporate language."[20] He went on to say that Coke had been global before global was fashionable.

Mr. Goizueta was referring to organizational changes that better reflected the global nature of the company. Coca-Cola had been a global company for years and the organizational change was the last step in recognizing the changes that had already occurred. Initially, all international divisions reported to an executive vice president in charge of international operations who, along with the vice president of United States operations, reported to the president. The new organization consists of six international

---

[19] "China Investment: U.S. Air-conditioning Firm's Success," *The Economist,* April 6, 1996, p. 35.

[20] As quoted in "Roberto Goizueta in His Own Words," *The Wall Street Journal,* October 20, 1997, p. B-1.

divisions—five Coca-Cola divisions and one Coca-Cola Foods division. The United States business unit accounts for about 20 percent of profits and has been downgraded to just part of one of the six international business units in the company's global geographic regions. The new structure does not reduce the importance of the company's North American business; it just puts other areas on an equal footing. It is recognition, however, that future growth is going to come from emerging markets outside the United States.[21]

International operations of businesses in global marketing reflect the heightened competitiveness brought about by the globalization of markets, interdependence of the world's economies, and the growing number of competing firms from developed and developing countries vying for the world's markets. Global companies and global marketing are terms frequently used to describe the scope of operations and marketing management orientation of companies at this stage.

Changes in International Orientation

As mentioned earlier, companies rarely fit neatly into any one of these five stages of international marketing involvement; the definitions are more to give the reader a sense of varying degrees of involvement and commitment. Companies may begin in one stage and move to another or stay at the same stage. Companies at different stages have different attitudes toward their foreign operations and, as they evolve from one stage to another, their orientation or attitudes toward international operations also change.

Experience shows that a significant change in the international orientation of a firm occurs when the company relies on foreign markets to absorb permanent production surpluses and depends on foreign profits. The complexity and sophistication of international marketing activity is greater and the degree of internationalization to which management is philosophically committed is more intense between the first and last stages of international involvement. Such commitment affects the specific international strategies and decisions of the firm.

International Marketing Concepts

Although not articulated as such in current literature, it appears that the differences in the international orientation and approach to international markets that guide the international business activities of companies can be described by one of three orientations to international marketing management:

1. Domestic market extension concept.
2. Multidomestic market concept.
3. Global marketing concept.

It is to be expected that differences in the complexity and sophistication of a company's marketing activity depend on which orientation guides its operations. The ideas expressed in each concept reflect the philosophical orientation that also can be associated with successive stages in the evolution of the international operations in a company.

Among the approaches describing the different orientations that evolve in a company in different stages of international marketing—from casual exporting to global marketing—is the often-quoted EPRG schema.[22] The authors of this schema suggest

---

[21] "Coca-Cola's 6 Global Units to Report to Its President," *The Wall Street Journal,* January 15, 1996, p. B-3.

[22] Yoram Wind, Susan P. Douglas, and Howard V. Perlmutter, "Guidelines for Developing International Marketing Strategy," *Journal of Marketing,* April 1973, pp. 14–23.

that firms can be classified as having an *e*thnocentric, *p*olycentric, *r*egiocentric, or *geo*-centric orientation (EPRG), depending on the international commitment of the firm. Further, the authors state that "a key assumption underlying the EPRG framework is that the degree of internationalization to which management is committed or willing to move towards affects the specific international strategies and decision rules of the firm." The EPRG schema is incorporated into the discussion of the three concepts that follows in that the philosophical orientations described by the EPRG schema help explain management's view when guided by one of the concepts.

Domestic Market Extension Concept

The domestic company seeking sales extension of its domestic products into foreign markets illustrates this orientation to international marketing. It views its international operations as secondary to and an extension of its domestic operations; the primary motive is to market excess domestic production. Domestic business is its priority and foreign sales are seen as a profitable extension of domestic operations. Even though foreign markets may be vigorously pursued, the firm's orientation remains basically domestic. Its attitude toward international sales is typified by the belief that if it sells in Peoria it will sell anywhere else in the world. Minimal, if any, efforts are made to adapt the marketing mix to foreign markets; the firm's orientation is to market to foreign customers in the same manner the company markets to domestic customers. It seeks markets where demand is similar to the home market and its domestic product will be acceptable. This domestic market extension strategy can be very profitable; large and small exporting companies approach international marketing from this perspective. Firms with this marketing approach are classified as *ethnocentric* in the EPRG schema. Meter-Man, Inc., discussed earlier, could be said to follow this orientation.

Multidomestic Market Concept

Once a company recognizes the importance of differences in overseas markets and the importance of offshore business to the organization, its orientation toward international business may shift to a multidomestic market strategy. A company guided by this concept has a strong sense that country markets are vastly different (and they may be, depending on the product) and that market success requires an almost independent program for each country. Firms with this orientation market on a country-by-country basis, with separate marketing strategies for each country.

Subsidiaries operate independently of one another in establishing marketing objectives and plans, and the domestic market and each of the country markets have separate marketing mixes with little interaction among them. Products are adapted for each market without coordination with other country markets; advertising campaigns are localized, as are the pricing and distribution decisions. A company with this concept does not look for similarity among elements of the marketing mix that might respond to standardization; rather, it aims for adaptation to local country markets. Control is typically decentralized to reflect the belief that the uniqueness of each market requires local marketing input and control. Firms with this orientation would be classified in the EPRG schema as *polycentric*. Fedders, as it progresses in its plans, fits this orientation.

Global Marketing Concept

A company guided by this orientation or philosophy is generally referred to as a global company, its marketing activity is global marketing, and its market coverage is the world. A company employing a global marketing strategy strives for efficiencies of scale by developing a standardized product, of dependable quality, to be sold at a reasonable price to a global market, that is, the same country market set throughout the world. Important to the global marketing concept is the premise that world markets are being "driven toward a converging commonalty"[23] seeking in much the same ways to satisfy their needs and desires. Thus, they constitute significant market segments with similar demands for the same product the world over. With this orientation a company attempts to standardize as much of the company effort as is practical on a worldwide basis. Some decisions are viewed as applicable worldwide, while others require consideration of local influences. The world as a whole is viewed as the market and the firm develops a global marketing strategy. The global marketing company would fit the *regiocentric* or *geocentric* classifications of the EPRG schema. Coca-Cola Company, Ford Motor Company (see Exhibit 1–1), General Motors, and several other companies can be described as global companies.

The global marketing concept views an entire set of country markets (whether the home market and only one other, or the home market and 100 other countries) as a unit, identifying groups of prospective buyers with similar needs as a global market segment and developing a marketing plan that strives for standardization wherever it is cost and culturally effective. This might mean a company's global marketing plan has a standardized product but country-specific advertising, or has a standardized theme in all countries with country- or cultural-specific appeals to a unique market characteristic, a standardized brand or image but adapted products to meet specific country needs, and so on. In other words, the marketing planning and marketing mix are approached from a global perspective, and where feasible in the marketing mix, efficiencies of standardization are sought. Wherever cultural uniqueness dictates the need for adaptation of the product, its image, and so on, it is accommodated. The company standardizes its processes, logo, most of its advertising, store decor and layouts, and so forth when and wherever possible. However, you will find wine on the menu in France and beer in Germany, a Filipino-style spicy burger in Manila, pork burgers in Thailand, and Vegetable McNuggets and Vegetable McBurgers in New Delhi—all to accommodate local tastes and customs.[24] The point is, to be global is a mindset, a way of looking at the market for commonalties that can be standardized across regions or country market sets.

What is suggested as a global orientation is analogous to the normal operations of a U.S. domestic company in the U.S. market. The entire United States is viewed as a single market—or if a company's objectives exclude some of the 50 states, then the states where they intend to market are viewed as a market unit. There are fewer uncontrollables to relate to among the 50 states but nevertheless the approach is to view the entire group of states as one market. The marketing mix is standardized for the entire market except where there are differences requiring adaptation for acceptance in the market. For example, automobiles have to be adapted to stricter emission controls in California than in the other 49 states, and fabric is heavier in men's winter suits destined for the northern and northeastern markets than for milder southern or western markets.

As the competitive environment facing U.S. businesses becomes more internationalized—and it surely will—the most effective orientation for many firms involved in marketing into another country will be a *global orientation*. This means operating as if all the country markets in a company's scope of operations (including the domestic market) are approachable as a single global market and standardizing the marketing mix where culturally feasible and cost effective. This does not, however, mean a slavish adherence to one orientation. Depending on the product and market, other orientations may make more marketing sense. For example, Procter & Gamble may pursue a global strategy for disposable diapers, but a multidomestic one in Asian markets for detergents.[25] As these ideas are tested and debated it is becoming more evident that

[23] Theodore Levitt, "The Globalization of Markets," *Harvard Business Review,* May–June 1983, p. 92.

[24] Ban Biers and Miriam Jordan, "McDonald's in India Decides the Big Mac Is Not a Sacred Cow," *The Wall Street Journal,* October 14, 1996, p. A13.

[25] Susan Segal-Horn, "The Limits of Global Strategy," *Strategy & Leadership,* November 21, 1996, p. 12.

companies actually use a composite of the various orientations. The global market is too complex to deal in absolutes.[26]

We must acknowledge at least two dimensions to the question of global business: one side focuses on orientation of firms as just discussed; the other questions whether a global market exists as defined by Levitt. In other words, do segments exist across several countries with similar needs and wants that can be satisfied with a single standardized product?

Although the world has not become a homogeneous market, there is strong evidence of identifiable groups of consumers (segments) across country borders with similar values, needs, and behavior patterns. Regardless of the degree to which global markets exist, a company can benefit from a global orientation. The issues of whether marketing programs should be standardized or why they are localized are not as critical as the recognition that marketing planning processes need to be standardized.[27]

Global Markets

Theodore Levitt's article, "The Globalization of Markets," has spawned a host of new references to marketing activities: global marketing, global business, global advertising, and global brands, as well as serious discussions of the processes of international marketing. Professor Levitt's premise is that world markets are being driven "toward a converging commonalty."[28] Almost everyone everywhere wants all the things they have heard about, seen, or experienced, via the new technologies. He sees substantial market segments with common needs, that is, a high quality, reasonably priced, standardized product. The "global corporation sells the same thing in the same way everywhere."

Professor Levitt argues that segmenting international markets on political boundaries and customizing products and marketing strategies for country markets or on national or regional preferences are not cost effective. The company of the future, according to Levitt, will be a global company that views the world as one market to which it sells a global product. Competition in the future will require global marketing rather than international or multinational marketing.

As with all new ideas, interpretations abound and discussions and debates flow. Professor Levitt's article has provoked many companies and marketing scholars to reexamine a fundamental idea that has prevailed for decades; that is, products and strategies must be adapted to the cultural needs of each country when marketing internationally. This approach is contrasted with a global orientation suggesting a commonalty in marketing needs and thus a standardized product for the entire world. While the need for cultural adaptation exists in many markets and for many products, the influence of mass communications in the world today and its influence on consumer wants and needs cannot be denied. Satellite and cable television transmit to hundreds of millions of potential consumers everywhere in the world via MTV, Cable News Network (CNN), and television programs that include everything from "LA Law" to "Lifestyles of the Rich and Famous."

Certainly the homogenizing effect of mass communications in the United States has eliminated many of the regional differences that once existed. It is difficult to deny the influences of mass media and communications on American tastes and consumer behavior. Based on American experiences, it seems reasonable to believe that people in other

---

[26] William L. Shanklin and David A. Griffith, "Crafting Strategies for Global Marketing in the New Millennium," *Business Horizons,* September 1996, p. 11.

[27] An excellent discussion on standardizing channels of distribution is presented in Bert Rosenbloom, Trina Larsen, and Rajiv Mehta, "Global Marketing Channels and the Standardization Controversy," *Journal of Global Marketing,* Vol. 11, No. 1, 1997, p. 64.

[28] Levitt, "Globalization," p. 92.

cultures exposed to the same influences will react similarly and that there is indeed a converging commonalty of the world's needs and desires.

Does this mean markets are now global? The answer is yes; there are market segments in most countries with similar demands for the same product. Levi Strauss, Revlon, Toyota, Ford, McDonald's, and Coca-Cola are companies that sell relatively standardized products throughout the world to market segments seeking the same products to satisfy their needs and desires. Does this mean there is no need to be concerned with cultural differences when marketing in different countries? The answer is "it depends"; for some products adaptation is not necessary, but for other products more sensitive to cultural values, adaptation is still necessary. The issue of modification versus standardization of marketing effort cannot be answered as easily as yes or no. The astute marketer always strives to present products that fulfill the perceived needs and wants of the consumer. Some products successful in one culture are equally acceptable in another; Pepsi-Cola is a good example. Other products demonstrate the vast differences in what is acceptable from one market to another. Turkey testicles, wings, and necks (considered gourmet fare in Taiwan and preferred to white meat, which they consider disgusting) would probably need some creative adaptation to sell for Thanksgiving dinner in Peoria, Illinois.

Marketing internationally should entail looking for market segments with similar demands that can be satisfied with the same product, standardizing the components of the marketing mix that can be standardized, and, where there are significant cultural differences that require parts of the marketing mix to be culturally adapted, adapting.[29] Throughout the text, the question of adaptation versus standardization of products and marketing effort—that is, global marketing—will be discussed.

Orientation of *International Marketing*

Most problems encountered by the foreign marketer result from the strangeness of the environment within which marketing programs must be implemented. Success hinges, in part, on the ability to assess and adjust properly to the impact of a strange environment. The successful international marketer possesses the best qualities of the sociologist, psychologist, diplomat, lawyer, prophet, and businessperson.

In light of all the variables involved, with what should a text in foreign marketing be concerned? It is the opinion of the authors that a study of foreign-marketing environments and cultures and their influences on the total marketing process is of primary concern and is the most effective approach to a meaningful presentation.

Consequently, the orientation of this text can best be described as an environmental/cultural approach to international strategic marketing. By no means is it intended to present principles of marketing; rather it is intended to demonstrate the unique problems of international marketing. It attempts to relate the foreign environment to the marketing process and to illustrate the many ways in which culture can influence the marketing task. Although marketing principles are universally applicable, the cultural environment within which the marketer must implement marketing plans can change dramatically from country to country. It is with the difficulties created by different environments that this text is primarily concerned.

The text is concerned with any company marketing in or into any other country or groups of countries, however slight the involvement or the method of involvement. Hence, this discussion of international marketing ranges from the marketing and busi-

---

[29] An excellent essay on the issue of standardization is provided by Jeryl Whitelock and Carole Pimblett, "The Standardisation Debate in International Marketing," *Journal of Global Marketing,* Vol. 10, No. 3, 1997, p. 45.

ness practices of small exporters such as a Colorado-based company that generates more than 50 percent of its $40,000 annual sales of fish-egg sorters in Canada, Germany, and Australia to the practices of global companies such as Motorola, Avon, and Johnson and Johnson, all of which generate more than 50 percent of their annual profits from the sales of multiple products to multiple country-market segments all over the world.

The first section of *International Marketing* offers an overview of international marketing, including a brief discussion of the global business environment confronting the marketer. The next section deals exclusively with the uncontrollable elements of the environment and their assessment, followed by chapters on assessing global market opportunities. Then, management issues in developing global marketing strategies are discussed. In each chapter, the impact of the environment on the marketing process is illustrated.

The importance of the Internet as a marketing tool and its impact on the marketing mix will be presented in the appropriate chapters. World Wide Web (WWW) addresses for unique information sources will be included both in the body of the text and in footnotes. These WWW sites will lead you to a vast assortment of company and government information in addition to many of the original sources for the topics being discussed in the chapter.

Space prohibits an encyclopedic approach to all the issues of international marketing; nevertheless, the authors have tried to present sufficient detail so readers appreciate the real need to make a thorough analysis whenever the challenge arises. The text provides a framework for this task.

Questions

1. Define:

   international marketing   foreign uncontrollables
   controllable elements   marketing relativism
   uncontrollable elements   self-reference criterion (SRC)
   domestic uncontrollables   global awareness

2. "The marketer's task is the same whether applied in Dimebox, Texas, or Dar es Salaam, Tanzania." Discuss.

3. How can the increased interest in international marketing on the part of U.S. firms be explained?

4. Discuss the four phases of international marketing involvement.

5. Discuss the conditions that have led to the development of global markets.

6. Differentiate between a global company and a multinational company.

7. Differentiate among the three international marketing concepts.

8. Relate the three international marketing concepts to the EPRG schema.

9. Prepare your lifelong plan to be globally aware.

10. Discuss the three factors necessary to achieve global awareness.

11. Define and discuss the idea of global orientation.

12. Visit the Bureau of Economic Analysis homepage (www.bea.doc.gov). Select the section, International articles, and find the most recent information on Foreign Direct Investments in the United States. Which country has the highest dollar amount of investment in the United States? Second highest?

CHAPTER

2

THE DYNAMIC ENVIRONMENT OF INTERNATIONAL TRADE

Chapter Learning Objectives

What you should learn from Chapter 2
- The basis for the reestablishment of world trade following World War II.
- The importance of balance-of-payment figures to a country's economy.
- The effects of protectionism on world trade.
- The seven types of trade barriers.
- The provisions of the Omnibus Trade and Competitiveness Act.
- The importance of GATT and the World Trade Organization.
- The emergence of the International Monetary Fund and World Bank Group.
- The keiretsu system.
- The importance of the Internet to global business.

Does NAFTA Really Eliminate Trade Barriers?

We know the story about our trade disputes with Japan. Japan has so many trade barriers and high tariffs that U.S. manufacturers are unable to sell in Japan as much as Japanese companies sell in the United States. The Japanese claim that "unique" Japanese snow requires skis made in Japan, and U.S. baseballs are not good enough for Japanese baseball. Even when Japan opened their rice market, the popular California rice had to be mixed and sold with inferior grades of Japanese rice.

The Japanese are not alone; it seems every country takes advantage of the open U.S. market while putting barriers in the way of U.S. exports. The French, for example, protect their film and broadcast industry from foreign competition by limiting the number of American shows that can appear on television, the percentage of American songs broadcast on radio, and the proportion of U.S. movies that can be shown in French theaters. Not only do these barriers and high tariffs limit how much U.S. companies can sell; they also raise prices for imported products much higher than they sell for in the United States.

But wait. Is that the whole story? Congress permits only 1.7 million pounds of imported peanuts (that is less than one-tenth of 1 percent of the U.S. crop) into the country. As a consequence, U.S. consumers pay more for peanuts than they would if there were no quotas. Quotas on sugar mean that consumers pay about twice as much as the price outside the United States—about $1.4 billion each year. Not only are many products taxed as they come into the United States, but it is often the lower priced items that receive the highest tariffs. An imported plastic school satchel has a 20 percent duty imposed but one of reptile leather has only a 4.7 percent duty. Mink furs are free of tariffs but affordable polyester sweaters for a baby carry a 34.6 percent tariff.

You would think with the NAFTA agreement, that there would be very low or no tariffs between the United States and Mexico. That is basically true, but not completely. It all started over some brooms. The NAFTA accord did lower tariffs and other trade barriers among Canada, the United States, and Mexico but the accord contains a provision that allows member nations to protect domestic industries threatened by cheaper foreign imports.

U.S. broom manufacturers complained that a flood of low-cost Mexican brooms eliminated 200 jobs and, if left unchecked, would sweep their industry away. The U.S. International Trade Commission agreed and tariffs were raised on corn-straw brooms to their pre-NAFTA level— 33 percent import tax on all imports that exceed an annual quota of brooms allowed duty free.

Two weeks later Mexico raised import taxes on U.S. wine from 14 percent to 20 percent, on brandy from 12.2 percent to 20 percent, and on previously duty-free sparkling wine. Wine shipments fell 61 percent, and Mexico went from the fifth largest export market for U.S. wineries to 13th. U.S. wineries are worried because Mexico also has negotiated a separate agreement with Chile that will begin scaling back tariffs for Chilean wine to duty-free access in four years.

Now you know the rest of the story: all countries do it. Barriers to trade, both tariff and nontariff, are one of the major issues confronting international trade. On average, tariffs have been reduced to a record low and substantial progress has been made on eliminating nontariff barriers. However, nations continue to use trade barriers for a variety of reasons, some rational some not so rational. As you read this chapter, you will see the benefits and losses generated by trade policy. Ask yourselves whether the examples discussed are justifiable.

Sources: Adapted from Todd G. Buchholz, "Free Trade Keeps Prices Down," *The Consumers' Research Magazine,* October 1995, p. 22; and Ted Appel, "Wine Held Hostage, State's Vintners Are Caught in a Trade Battle with Mexico," *The Press Democrat,* January 12, 1997, p. E1.

Yesterday's competitive market battles were fought in Western Europe, Japan, and the United States; tomorrow's competitive battles will extend to Latin America, Eastern Europe, Russia, India, Asia, and Africa as these emerging markets open to trade. More of the world's people, from the richest to the poorest, will participate in the world's wealth through global trade. The emerging global economy in which we live brings us into worldwide competition with significant advantages for both marketers and consumers.

Exhibit 2–1   **Top Ten 1996 U.S. Trading Partners ($ billions)**

Country	U.S. Exports	U.S. Imports	Total	Surplus Deficit
Canada	$132.6	$155.8	$288.4	–$23.2
Japan	67.5	115.2	182.7	–47.7
Mexico	56.8	74.3	131.1	–17.5
U.K.	30.9	29.0	59.9	+1.9
Germany	23.4	33.9	57.3	–15.5
China	12.0	51.5	63.5	–39.5
South Korea	26.6	22.7	49.3	+3.9
Taiwan	18.4	29.9	48.3	–11.5
Singapore	16.7	20.3	37.0	–3.6
Hong Kong	14.0	9.9	23.9	+4.1

Source: Compiled from **http://www.stat-usa.gov/BEN/databases.html** (select Imports/Exports by Country).

Marketers benefit from new markets opening and smaller markets growing large enough to become viable business opportunities. Consumers benefit by being able to select from the widest range of goods produced anywhere in the world at the lowest prices.

Bound together by satellite communications and global companies, consumers in every corner of the world are demanding an ever-expanding variety of goods. As Exhibit 2–1 illustrates, world trade is an important economic activity. Because of this importance, the inclination is for countries to control international trade to their own advantage. As competition intensifies, the tendency toward protectionism gains momentum. If the benefits of the social, political, and economic changes now taking place are to be fully realized, free trade must prevail throughout the global marketplace. The creation of the World Trade Organization (WTO) is one of the biggest victories for free trade in decades.

This chapter includes a brief survey of the United States' past and present role in global trade and some concepts important in understanding the relationship between international trade and national economic policy. A discussion of the logic and illogic of protectionism, the major impediment to trade, is followed by a review of the General Agreement on Tariffs and Trade (GATT) and its successor, the World Trade Organization (WTO), two multinational agreements designed to advance free trade. A brief look at the Japanese keiretsu, a strategic component of the international trade environment, is followed by a review of the Internet and its potential impact on global business.

The Twentieth to the Twenty-first Century

At no time in modern economic history have countries been more economically interdependent, have greater opportunities for international trade existed, or has the potential for increased demand existed than now, during the last decade of the 20th century. In the preceding 90 years, world economic development has been erratic.

The first half of the century was marred by a major worldwide economic depression that occurred between two world wars and that all but destroyed most of the industrialized world. The last half of the century, while free of a world war, was marred by struggles between countries espousing the socialist Marxist approach and those following a democratic capitalist approach to economic development. As a result of this ideological split, traditional trade patterns were disrupted.

After World War II, as a means to dampen the spread of communism, the United States set out to infuse the ideal of capitalism throughout as much of the world as possi-

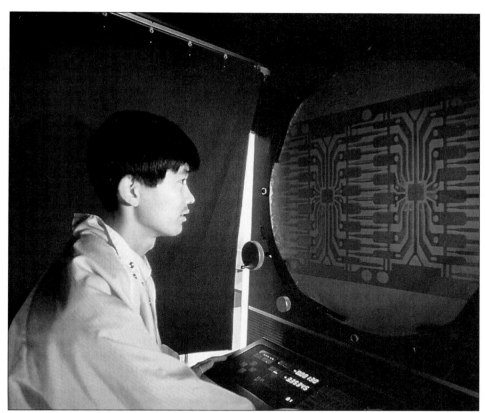

Investments like Motorola's semiconductor assembly plant near Tianjin, China, where workers quickly become high achievers, help to fuel the emerging markets of Asia. (Forest Anderson/Liaison International)

ble. The Marshall Plan[1] to assist in rebuilding Europe, financial and industrial development assistance to rebuild Japan, and funds channeled through the Agency for International Development and other groups designed to foster economic growth in the underdeveloped world were used to help create a strong world economy. The dissolution of colonial powers created scores of new countries in Asia and Africa. With the striving of these countries to gain economic independence and the financial assistance offered by the United States, most of the noncommunist world's economies grew and new markets were created.

The benefits from the foreign economic assistance given by the United States flowed both ways. For every dollar the United States invested in the economic development and rebuilding of other countries after World War II, hundreds of dollars more returned in the form of purchases of U.S. agricultural products, manufactured goods, and services. This overseas demand created by the Marshall Plan and other programs was important to the United States economy since the vast manufacturing base built to supply World War II and the swelling labor supply of returning military created a production capacity well beyond domestic needs. The major economic boom and increased standard of living the United States experienced after World War II was fueled by fulfilling pent-up demand in the United States and demand created by the rebuilding of war-

---

[1] To read more about the Marshall Plan see Martin Walker, "George Marshall: His Plan Helped Save Europe," *Europe*, April 1997, p. 22. The table of contents for issues of *Europe* magazine can be found at web site **http://www.eurunion.org/magazine/index.htm**.

torn countries of Europe and Asia. In short, the United States helped to make the world's economies stronger, which enabled them to buy more from us.

In addition to U.S. economic assistance, a move toward international cooperation among trading nations was manifest in the negotiation of the General Agreement on Tariffs and Trade (GATT). International trade had ground to a halt following World War I when nations followed the example set by the U.S. enactment of the Smoot-Hawley Law (1930), which raised average U.S. tariffs on more than 20,000 imported goods to levels in excess of 60 percent. In retaliation, 60 countries erected high tariff walls and international trade was stalled, along with most economies. A major worldwide recession catapulted the world's economies into the Great Depression when trade all but dried up after tariffs and other trade barriers were raised to an intolerable height.

Determined not to repeat the economic disaster following World War I, world leaders created GATT, a forum for member countries to negotiate a reduction of tariffs and other barriers to trade. The forum proved successful in reaching those objectives. With the ratification of the Uruguay Round agreements, the GATT became part of the World Trade Organization (WTO) and its 117 original members moved into a new era of free trade.

World Trade and U.S. Multinationals

The rapid growth of war-torn economies and previously underdeveloped countries, coupled with large-scale economic cooperation and assistance, led to new global marketing opportunities. Rising standards of living and broad-based consumer and industrial markets abroad created opportunities for American companies to expand exports and investment worldwide. During the 1950s, many U.S. companies that had never before marketed outside the United States began to export, and others made significant investments in marketing and production facilities overseas.

At the close of the 1960s, U.S. multinational corporations (MNCs) were facing major challenges on two fronts: direct investment and export markets. Large investments by U.S. businesses in Europe and Latin America heightened the concern of these countries about the growing domination of U.S. multinationals. The reaction in Latin American countries was to expropriate direct U.S. investments or to force companies to sell controlling interests to nationals. In Europe, apprehension manifested itself in strong public demand to limit foreign investment. Concern that "Britain might become a satellite where there could be manufacturing but no determination of policy" led to specific guidelines for joint ventures between British and U.S. companies. In the European Community, U.S. multinationals were rebuffed in ways ranging from tight control over proposed joint ventures and regulations covering U.S. acquisitions of European firms to strong protectionism laws.

The threat felt by Europeans was best expressed in the popular book, *The American Challenge,* published in 1968, in which the French author, J. J. Servan-Schreiber, wrote:

> Fifteen years from now it is quite possible that the world's third greatest industrial power, just after the United States and Russia, will not be Europe but *American Industry in Europe.* Already, in the ninth year of the Common Market, this European market is basically American in organization.[2]

Servan-Schreiber's prediction did not come true for many reasons, but one of the more important was that U.S. MNCs were confronted by a resurgence of competition from all over the world. The worldwide economic growth and rebuilding after World War II was beginning to surface in competition that challenged the supremacy of American industry. Competition arose on all fronts; Japan, Germany, most of the industrialized world, and many developing countries were competing for demand in their own countries and were looking for world markets as well. Countries once classified as less

---

[2] J. J. Servan-Schreiber, *The American Challenge* (New York: Atheneum Publishers, 1968), p. 3.

EXHIBIT 2-2   **The Nationality of the World's 100 Largest Industrial Corporations (by country of origin)**

	1963	1979	1984	1990	1993	1995	1996
United States	67	47	47	33	32	24	24
Germany	13	13	8	12	14	14	13
Britain	7	7	5	6	4	1	2
France	4	11	5	10	6	12	13
Japan	3	7	12	18	23	37	29
Italy	2	3	3	4	4	3	4
Netherlands–United Kingdom	2	2	2	2	2	2	2
Netherlands	1	3	1	1	1	2	2
Switzerland	1	1	2	3	3	3	5
Argentina	—	—	1	—	—	—	—
Belgium	—	1	1	1	—	—	—
Brazil	—	1	—	1	1	—	—
Canada	—	2	3	—	—	—	—
India	—	—	1	—	—	—	—
Kuwait	—	—	1	—	—	—	—
Mexico	—	1	1	1	1	—	1
Venezuela	—	1	1	1	1	—	1
South Korea	—	—	4	2	4	2	4
Sweden	—	—	1	2	1	—	—
South Africa	—	—	1	1	—	—	—
Spain	—	—	—	2	2	—	—
Turkey	—	—	—	—	1	—	—

developed were reclassified as newly industrialized countries (NICs). NICs such as Brazil, Mexico, South Korea, Taiwan, Singapore, and Hong Kong experienced rapid industrialization in selected industries and became aggressive world competitors in steel, shipbuilding, consumer electronics, automobiles, light aircraft, shoes, textiles, apparel, and so forth. In addition to the NICs, developing countries such as Venezuela, Chile, and Bangladesh established state-owned enterprises (SOEs) that operated in other countries. One state-owned Venezuelan company has a subsidiary in Puerto Rico that produces canvas, cosmetics, chairs, and zippers; there are also Chilean and Colombian companies in Puerto Rico; in the U.S. state of Georgia, there is a Venezuelan company in agribusiness; and Bangladesh, the sixth largest exporter of garments to the United States, also owns a mattress company in Georgia.

In short, economic power and potential became more evenly distributed among countries than was the case when Servan-Schreiber warned Europe about U.S. multinational domination. Instead, the U.S. position in world trade is now shared with other countries. For example, in 1950 the United States represented 39 percent of world Gross National Product (GNP) but by 1995, it represented 26 percent. In 1953, the United States accounted for 45 percent of the world's manufacturing output but by 1990, it accounted for 22 percent.[3] In the meantime, however, the global GNP was much larger, as was the world's manufacturing output—all countries shared in a much larger economic pie. This change was reflected in the growth of MNCs from other countries as well. Exhibit 2–2 shows the dramatic change between 1963 and 1996. In 1963, the United States had 67 of the world's largest industrial corporations; by 1996, that number had dropped to 24 while Japan moved from having three of the largest to 29 and South Korea from none to four.

---

[3] Peter Beinart, "The False Promise of Globalization, *The New Republic*, October 20, 1997, p. 21.

EXHIBIT 2-3   U.S. Current Account by Major Components, 1983–96 ($ billions)

	1987	1988	1989	1990	1991	1992	1993	1994	1995	1996
1. Merchandise trade										
a. Exports	$249.6	$319.9	$362.1	$389.3	$416.9	$440.4	$456.9	$502.5	$575.9	$612.1
b. Imports	409.9	446.4	477.4	498.3	491.0	536.5	589.4	668.6	749.4	803.2
c. Balance	−160.3	−126.5	−115.2	−109.0	−74.1	−96.1	−132.5	−166.1	−173.5	−191.2
2. Business services										
a. Exports	59.4	69.1	116.5	136.6	153.7	164.4	174.5	193.8	205.1	231.2
b. Imports	58.0	63.2	86.9	98.7	101.6	104.4	112.7	125.9	129.6	143.1
c. Balance	+1.4	+5.9	+29.6	+37.9	+52.1	+60.0	+61.8	+67.9	+75.5	+88.1
3. Other goods and services										
a. Exports	12.0	10.6	10.3	10.6	9.5	12.2	10.3	5.0	5.5	5.5
b. Imports	15.8	16.2	15.0	18.3	16.0	16.5	15.3	13.0	12.6	13.5
c. Balance	−3.8	−5.6	−4.7	−7.7	−6.5	−4.3	−5.0	−8.0	−7.1	−8.0
4. International investment income										
a. Receipts	103.8	108.2	152.5	160.3	136.9	114.4	113.9	137.6	182.6	206.4
b. Payments	83.4	105.6	138.9	139.6	122.1	109.9	109.9	147.0	190.7	203.6
c. Balance	+20.4	+2.6	+13.6	+20.7	+14.8	+4.5	+4.0	−9.4	−8.1	+2.8
5. Total goods and services										
a. Exports	424.8	507.8	641.4	696.8	717.0	731.4	755.6	838.9	980.1	1,055.2
b. Imports	565.3	629.6	718.2	754.9	730.7	767.3	827.3	954.5	1,107.5	1,163.5
c. Balance	−140.5	−121.8	−76.7	−58.1	−13.7	−35.9	−71.7	−115.6	−113.2	−108.2
6. Net unilateral transfers	−13.4	−13.6	−26.1	−33.7	+6.7	−31.9	−32.0	−35.8	−35.1	−40.0
7. Current account balance	−153.9	−135.4	−102.8	−91.8	−7.0	−67.8	−103.7	−151.4	−148.2	−148.2

Sources: Survey of Current Business, U.S. Department of Commerce, Bureau of Economic Analysis, **http://www.stat-usa.gov/BEN/bea1/sch.html**, February 1998.

Another dimension of world economic power, the balance of merchandise trade, reflected the changing role of the United States in world trade. Between 1888 and 1971, the United States sold more to other countries than it bought from them; that is, the United States had a favorable balance of trade. By 1971, however, the United States had a trade deficit of $2 billion that grew steadily until it peaked at $160.3 billion in 1987. After that, the deficit in merchandise trade declined to $74.1 billion in 1991 but began increasing again and by 1996 had reached $148.2 billion. (See Exhibit 2–3.)

Imports of oil and other petroleum products account for a substantial chunk of the deficit, but demand for automobiles, consumer electronics, apparel, microwave ovens, and other consumer products continues to add to the deficit. Between 1971 and 1991, American companies' share of the U.S. market for color TVs dropped from 90 percent to 10 percent, machine tools from 100 percent to just about 35 percent, and VCRs from 10 percent to 1 percent. It is ironic that the economic problems facing the United States at the close of the 20th century are, in part, proof of the success of U.S. economic assistance programs. The countries that benefited most are the competitors that U.S. businesses now face in markets the world over, including in the United States.

This heightened competition for U.S. businesses raised questions similar to those heard in Europe two decades earlier: how to maintain the competitive strength of American business, to avoid the domination of U.S. markets by foreign multinationals, and to forestall the buying of America. In the 1980s, the U.S. saw its competitive position in capital goods such as computers and machinery erode sharply. From 1983 to 1987, almost 70 percent of the growth of the merchandise trade deficit was in capital goods and automobiles. At the time, those were America's high-wage, high-skill industries. U.S.

industry got a wake-up call and responded by restructuring its industries, in essence, "getting lean and mean." By the middle of the 1990s, the U.S. was holding its own in capital goods. Moreover, it began exporting advanced technology products such as aircraft and high-tech equipment that produced a $26 billion surplus in such goods in 1996.

Among the more important questions raised were those concerning the ability of U.S. firms to compete in foreign markets and the fairness of international trade policies of some countries. Trade friction revolved around Japan's sales of autos and electronics in the U.S. and Japan's restrictive trade practices.[4] The United States, a strong advocate of free trade, was confronted with the dilemma of how to encourage trading partners to reciprocate with open access to their markets without provoking increased protectionism.[5] Besides successfully pressuring Japan to open its markets for some types of trade and investment,[6] the U.S. was a driving force behind the establishment of the WTO. It is too early to tell how successful this organization will be, although early indications are that it is making progress in causing countries to lower trade restraints and thus helping to equalize trade imbalances.

By the last decade of the 20th century profound changes in the way the world will trade in the decades ahead were already under way. The final integration of the countries of the European Union, the creation of NAFTA, and the rapid evolution of APEC are the beginnings of global trading blocks that many experts expect to dominate trade patterns in the future. With the return of Hong Kong in 1997 and Macao in 2000 to China, all of Asia will be controlled and managed by Asians for the first time in 400 years.[7] During the decades since World War II, the West set the patterns for trade, but increasingly Asia will be a major force, if not the leading force.[8]

The First Decade of the 21st Century and Beyond

Trends already under way in the last decade of the 20th century are destined to change the patterns of trade for years to come. The economies of the industrialized world have begun to mature and the rates of growth will be more modest in the future than they have been for the past 20 years. The Organization for Economic Cooperation and Development (OECD) estimates that the economies of OECD member countries will expand about 3 percent annually for the next 25 years, the same rate as in the past 25 years. Conversely, the economies of the developing world will grow at unprecedented rates—from an annual rate of 4.5 percent in the past quarter century to a rate of 6.7 percent for the next 25 years.[9] Their share of world output will rise from about one-sixth to nearly one-third over the same period. The World Bank estimates that five countries—Brazil, China, India, Indonesia, and Russia—whose share of world trade is barely a third of that of the European Union, will by 2020 be 50 percent higher than that of the EU.[10] As a consequence, there will be a definite shift in economic power and influence away from industrialized countries—Japan, the United States, and the European Union—to countries in Latin America, Eastern Europe, Asia, and Africa.

---

[4] Michael J. Mandel, "Why This Trade Gap Isn't So Terrifying," *Business Week*, June 2, 1997, p. 38.

[5] Arthur J. Alexander, "U.S. Direct Investment in Japan; Another Dimension of Economic Ties," *JEI Report*, May 2, 1997, p. 46.

[6] Japan rose from ninth as a target for U.S. direct investment in 1980 to fourth in 1995.

[7] John Naisbitt, "At Last—Asia for the Asians," *Across the Board*, April 1997, p. 13.

[8] For a provocative book on the United States as a world power see Donald W. White, *The American Century* (New Haven, Conn.: Yale University Press, 1997).

[9] Olivier Bouin and David O'Connor, "The World Economy in 2020," *OECD Observer*, August 18, 1997, p. 9. Information about the OECD and selected articles from the *OECD Observer* can be found at **http://www.oecd.org/**.

[10] "World Bank Says 'Big Five' Could Re-draw Global Economic Map over Next 25 Years," *The World Bank Group*, September 1997, News Release No. 98/1454, **www.worldbank.org/**.

CROSSING BORDERS 2–1

The Globalization of the American Economy

America's involvement in the global economy has passed through two distinct periods: a development era during which the United States sought industrial self-sufficiency in the 18th and 19th centuries, and a free-trade era in the early and middle 20th century during which open trade was linked with prosperity. Now America has entered a third, more dangerous era—an age of global economic interdependence.

With surprising swiftness, the United States has shifted from relative economic self-sufficiency to global interdependence. In 1960, trade accounted for only 10 percent of the country's gross national product; by the mid-1980s, that figure had more than doubled. American farmers now sell 30 percent of their grain production overseas; 40 percent of U.S. farmland is devoted to crops for export. In fact, more acres of U.S. farmland are used to feed the Japanese than there are acres of farmland in Japan. American industry exports more than 20 percent of its manufacturing output, and the Department of Commerce estimates that, on average, 19,100 jobs result for every $1 billion of merchandise exports. More than 70 percent of American industry now faces stiff foreign competition within the U.S. market.

Sources: Adapted from Pat Choate and Juyne Linger, "Tailored Trade: Dealing with the World as It Is," *Harvard Business Review,* January–February 1988, pp. 87–88; and "U.S. Trade Facts," *Business America,* April 6, 1992, p. 34.

Exports and investments are on a steadily accelerating growth curve in emerging markets where the greatest opportunities for growth will be. China, for example, is projected by the World Bank to have the world's largest economy by 2010 and, if it continues the reform program started in the 1990s, it should eliminate absolute poverty by 2020.[11] As much as 50 percent of the expected increase in global exports, from approximately $4 trillion in 1993 to $7 trillion in 2005, will come from developing countries. It is estimated that between 1995 and 2000, the number of households with annual incomes approaching $18,000 in Pacific Rim countries will increase from 32.5 million to over 73 million. Demand in Asia for automobiles is expected to more than triple, from 16 to 58 million in less than a decade. Such increases in consumer demand are not limited to automobiles; the shopping lists of the hundreds of millions of households that will enter or approach the middle class over the next decade will include washing machines, televisions, and all the other trappings of affluence. Similar changes are expected to occur in Latin America and Eastern Europe as well.

This does not mean that markets in Europe, Japan, and the United States will cease to be important; those economies will continue to produce large, lucrative markets and the companies established in those markets will benefit. It does mean that if a company is to be a major player in the next century, now is the time to begin laying the groundwork. How will these changes that are taking place in the global marketplace impact on international business? For one thing, the level and intensity of competition will change as companies focus on gaining entry into or maintaining their position in emerging markets, regional trade areas, and the established markets in Europe, Japan, and the United States.

[11] "China in the Year 2020: World Bank Charts Path to Sustained Growth," World Bank News Release, September 18, 1997, **http://www.worldbank.org/html/extdr/extme/1490.htm/**.

Companies are looking for ways to become more efficient, improve productivity, and expand their global reach while maintaining an ability to respond quickly to deliver a product that the market demands. For example, large multinational companies such as Matsushita of Japan continue to expand their global reach. Nestlé is consolidating its dominance in global consumer markets by acquiring and vigorously marketing local-country major brands. Samsung of South Korea has invested $500 million in Mexico to secure access to markets in the North American Free Trade Area. Whirlpool, the U.S. appliance manufacturer which secured first place in the global appliance business by acquiring the European division of the appliance maker, N. V. Philip's, immediately began restructuring itself into its version of a global company. These are a few examples of changes that are sweeping multinational companies as they gear up for the next century.

Global companies are not the only ones aggressively seeking new market opportunities. Smaller companies are using novel approaches to marketing and seeking ways to apply their technological expertise to exporting goods and services not previously sold abroad. A small Midwestern company that manufactures and freezes bagel dough for supermarkets to bake and sell as their own saw opportunities abroad and began to export to Japan. International sales, though small now, showed such potential that the company sold its U.S. business in order to concentrate on international operations. Other examples of smaller companies include Nochar Inc., which makes a fire retardant it developed a decade ago for the Indianapolis 500. The company now gets 32 percent of its sales overseas, in 29 countries. The owner of Buztronics Inc., a maker of promotional lapel buttons, heard from a friend that his buttons, with their red blinking lights, would do great in Japan. He made his first entry in exporting to Japan and after only a year, 10 percent of Buztronics sales come from overseas. While 50 of the largest exporters account for 30 percent of U.S. merchandise exports, the rest come from middle and small firms like those mentioned above.[12] There is a flurry of activity in the business world as companies large and small adjust to the internationalization of the marketplace at home and abroad.

As is always true in business, the best-laid plans can fail or be slowed by dramatic changes in the economy. When the U.S. economy was less involved in international trade, economic upheavals abroad often went unnoticed except by the very largest companies. Today, when the stock market in Hong Kong drops precipitously as it did in 1997 and South Korea and several Southeast Asia economies faltered shortly thereafter, the U.S. stock market reacted with its largest daily drop in several years. The fear was the potential negative impact on U.S. technology industries if the economies of Asian customers slowed. Two years later most of the world's emerging markets were on a somewhat slower but nevertheless positive growth path than before the financial crisis of 1997.

Balance of Payments

When countries trade, financial transactions among businesses or consumers of different nations occur. Products and services are exported and imported, monetary gifts are exchanged, investments are made, cash payments are made and cash receipts received, and vacation and foreign travel occurs. In short, over a period of time, there is a constant flow of money into and out of a country. The system of accounts that records a nation's international financial transactions is called its *balance of payments.*

A nation's balance-of-payments statement records all financial transactions between its residents and those of the rest of the world during a given period of time—usually

---

[12] Robert L. Rose and Carl Quintanilla, "Tiptoeing Abroad: More Small Firms Take Up Exporting, with Much Success," *The Wall Street Journal,* December 20, 1996, p. A1.

one year. Because the balance-of-payments record is maintained on a double-entry bookkeeping system, it must always be in balance. As on an individual's financial statement, the assets and liabilities or the credits and debits must offset each other. And like an individual's statement, the fact that they balance does not mean a nation is in particularly good or poor financial condition. A balance of payments is a record of condition, not a determinant of condition. Each of the nation's financial transactions with other countries is reflected in its balance of payments.

A nation's balance of payments presents an overall view of its international economic position and is an important economic measure used by treasuries, central banks, and other government agencies whose responsibility is to maintain external and internal economic stability. A balance of payments represents the difference between receipts from foreign countries on one side and payments to them on the other. On the plus side of the U.S. balance of payments are export sales, money spent by foreign tourists, payments to the United States for insurance, transportation, and similar services, payments of dividends and interest on investments abroad, return on capital invested abroad, new foreign investments in the United States, and foreign government payments to the United States.

On the minus side are costs of goods imported, spending by tourists overseas, new overseas investments, and the cost of foreign military and economic aid. A deficit results when international payments are greater than receipts. It can be reduced or eliminated by increasing a country's international receipts (i.e., gain more exports to other countries or more tourists from other countries) and/or reducing expenditures in other countries. A balance-of-payments statement includes three accounts: the current account—a record of all merchandise exports, imports, and services plus unilateral transfers of funds; the capital account—a record of direct investment, portfolio investment, and short-term capital movements to and from countries; and the official reserves account—a record of exports and imports of gold, increases or decreases in foreign exchange, and increases or decreases in liabilities to foreign central banks. Of the three, the current account is of primary interest to international business.

Current Account

The *current account* is important because it includes all international merchandise trade and service accounts, that is, accounts for the value of all merchandise and services imported and exported and all receipts and payments from investments. Exhibit 2–3 gives the current account for the United States since 1987. Clearly, services trade and receipts from foreign investments (lines 2c and 4c) are important because they are positive and help reduce the overall deficit in the current account (item 7).

It is important to note that in Exhibit 2–3 both merchandise and services trade figures may be underrepresented substantially due to the way in which trade transactions are recorded. In one year imports reported by all countries exceeded their counted exports by $98 billion, but because one country's exports are another's imports the two reported figures should be in balance. Import figures are considered to be the more accurate figure between export and import tallies since tariffs are collected on imports. Since the United States is the world's largest exporter, it only seems reasonable that a large share of U.S. exports have gone unreported. There are data that support this notion that exports from the U.S. are underreported. For instance, services are very difficult to record because there are many ways exports of services miss being recorded. A few are the fees paid a consultant who travels to a German firm and whose fees are often not recorded as exports; the sales of software by firms via the Internet—the buyer from France gives a credit card number and the software is downloaded over the telephone; or the revenue of U.S. catalog companies to foreign customers, which often escapes being listed as an export in the United States but is recorded as an import in the buyer's country. Inadequate procedures also account for much underreporting. A former Customs official comments that he had no idea how to determine the value of containers of computer software being shipped abroad from the port where he worked. The solution was to weigh the CD-ROMs on which the software was recorded and price them as plastic at $1^1/_2$ cents per pound.[13] Just a few small oversights can result in a lower deficit or even a surplus. For instance, if 10 percent of U.S. exports were missed in 1996, the trade deficit would drop from the reported $114 billion to only $31 billion. A 15 percent undercount would mean an actual surplus of $11 billion. U.S. Customs was scheduled to implement an Automated Export System in 1998 that should correct some of the underreporting.

Balance of Trade

The relationship between merchandise imports and exports (lines 1a and 1b in Exhibit 2–3) is referred to as the *balance of merchandise trade* or trade balance. If a country exports more goods than it imports, it has a favorable balance of trade; if it imports more goods than it exports, as did the United States in 1993, it has an unfavorable balance of trade, as shown on line 1c. Usually a country that has a negative balance of trade also has a negative balance of payments. Both the balance of trade and the balance of payments do not have to be negative—at times a country may have a favorable balance of trade and a negative balance of payments or vice versa. This was the case for the United States during the Korean and Vietnam wars. The imbalance was caused by heavy foreign aid assistance by the United States to other countries and the high cost of conducting the Korean and Vietnam wars.

Since 1970 the United States has had a favorable balance of trade in only three years. This means that for each year there was an unfavorable balance the United States imported goods with a higher dollar value than the goods it exported. These imbalances resulted primarily from U.S. demand for oil, petroleum products, cars, consumer durables, and other merchandise. Such imbalances have drastic effects on balance of trade, balance of payments, and, therefore, the value of U.S. currency in the world marketplace. Factors such as these eventually require an adjustment in the balance of payments through change in exchange rate, prices, and/or incomes. In short, once the wealth of a country whose expenditures exceed its income has been exhausted that country, like an individual, must reduce its standard of living. If its residents do not do so voluntarily, the rate of exchange of its money for foreign monies declines; and through the medium of the foreign exchange market, the purchasing power of foreign goods is transferred from that country to another. As can be seen in Exhibit 2–4, the U.S. dollar fell steadily against most of the other major currencies for a number of years until 1988. As U.S. deficits began to decline after 1987, the exchange rate relative to currencies of other industrialized countries stabilized somewhat, except against the Japanese yen, where the dollar continued its downward slope until 1994.

EXHIBIT 2–4   What Would One U.S. Dollar Buy? (Selected Years)

	1985	*1987*	*1988*	*1992*	*1993*	*1994*	*1995*	*1996*	*1997*
British pound	.86	.67	.54	.56	.66	.68	.63	.64	.59
French franc	9.60	7.55	5.40	5.29	5.67	5.55	4.95	5.12	5.94
Japanese yen	250.23	123.32	123.70	126.70	111.08	102.18	93.96	108.78	129.15
Swiss franc	2.25	2.07	1.29	1.41	1.48	1.37	1.18	1.24	1.43

Source: For information on exchange rates see *The Wall Street Journal.*

---

[13] A. Gary Shilling, "The Buck Will Get Stronger," *Forbes,* May 19, 1997, p. 64.

When foreign currencies can buy more dollars, U.S. products are less expensive for the foreign customer and exports increase, and foreign products are more expensive for the U.S. customer and the demand for imported goods is dampened.

Protectionism

International business must face the reality that this is a world of tariffs, quotas, and nontariff barriers designed to protect a country's markets from intrusion by foreign companies. Although the General Agreement on Tariffs and Trade (GATT) has been effective in reducing tariffs, countries still resort to measures of *protectionism*. Nations utilize legal barriers, exchange barriers, and psychological barriers to restrain entry of unwanted goods. Businesses work together to establish private market barriers while the market structure itself may provide formidable barriers to imported goods. The complex distribution system in Japan is a good example of a market structure creating a barrier to trade. However, as effective as it is in keeping some products out of the market, in a legal sense it cannot be viewed as a trade barrier.

Protection Logic and Illogic

Countless reasons to maintain government restrictions on trade are espoused by protectionists,[14] but essentially all arguments can be classified as follows: (1) protection of an infant industry, (2) protection of the home market, (3) need to keep money at home, (4) encouragement of capital accumulation, (5) maintenance of the standard of living and real wages, (6) conservation of natural resources, (7) industrialization of a low-wage nation, (8) maintenance of employment and reduction of unemployment, (9) national defense, (10) increase of business size, and (11) retaliation and bargaining. Economists in general recognize as valid only the arguments for infant industry, national defense, and industrialization of underdeveloped countries.[15] The resource conservation argument becomes increasingly valid in an era of environmental consciousness and worldwide shortages of raw materials and agricultural commodities. There might be a case for temporary protection of markets with excess productive capacity or excess labor when such protection could facilitate an orderly transition. Unfortunately such protection becomes long term and contributes to industrial inefficiency while detracting from a nation's realistic adjustment to its world situation.

Most protectionists argue the need for tariffs on one of the three premises recognized by economists—whether or not they are relevant to their products. Proponents are likely also to call on the maintenance-of-employment argument because it has substantial political appeal. When arguing for protection, the basic economic advantages of international trade are ignored. The fact that the consumer ultimately bears the cost of tariffs and other protective measures is conveniently overlooked. Sugar and textiles are good examples of protected industries in the United States that cannot be justified by any of the three arguments. U.S. sugar prices are artificially held higher than world prices for no sound economic reason.

To give you some idea of the cost to the consumer, consider the results of a recent study of 21 protected industries. The research showed that U.S. consumers paid about $70 billion in higher prices in 1990 because of tariffs and other protective restrictions. On average, the cost to consumers for saving one job in these protected industries was $170,000 per year, or six times the average pay (wages and benefits) for manufacturing

[14] Lorraine Woellert, "Why Do Nations Tariff?" *The World & I,* July 1997, p. 64.
[15] Steven Suranovic, "Why Economists Should Study Fairness," *Challenge,* September 19, 1997, p. 109.

CROSSING BORDERS 2-2

Trade Barriers, Hypocrisy, and the United States

The United States thinks of itself as the leader in free trade and frequently brings actions against nations as unfair trade partners. Section 301* of the Omnibus Trade and Competitiveness Act authorizes the U.S. government to investigate and retaliate against specific foreign trade barriers judged to be unfair and to impose up to 100 percent tariffs on exports to the U.S. from guilty nations unless they satisfy U.S. domestic demands. But critics say the United States is somewhat hypocritical in some of the stands taken since the U.S. is just as guilty of protecting its markets with trade barriers. A Japanese government study alleges that the U.S. engages in unfair trade practices in 10 of 12 policy areas reviewed in the study. Notably, the U.S. imposes quotas on imports, has high tariffs, and abuses antidumping measures. Are the critics correct? Is the U.S. being hypocritical when it comes to free trade? You be the judge.

The U.S. launched a Section 301 investigation of Japanese citrus quotas. "The removal of Japan's unfair barriers could cut the price of oranges for Japanese consumers by one third," said the U.S. trade representative. Coincidentally, the U.S. had a 40 percent tariff on Brazilian orange juice imports when the investigation was initiated.

The U.S. brought a 301 case against Korea for its beef import quotas even though the U.S. has beef import quotas that are estimated to cost U.S. consumers $873 million annually in higher prices. Another 301 case was brought against Brazil, Korea, and Taiwan for trade barriers on footwear even though the U.S. maintains tariffs as high as 67 percent on footwear imports.

Can you believe that we have two phone-book-size volumes of the U.S. customs code that includes restrictions on such innocuous items as scissors, sweaters, leather, costume jewelry, tampons, pizzas, cotton swabs, ice cream from Jamaica, and even products we do not produce such as vitamin B12. We also have restrictions on more sensitive products as cars, supercomputers, lumber, and every type of clothing imaginable. Would-be Latin American exporters find hundreds of their most promising export products such as grapes, tomatoes, onions, steel, cement, asparagus, and shoes on the customs list. Visit **http://www.usitc.gov/taffairs.htm** and select the Interactive Tariff Database to see some other examples.

So, is the U.S. as guilty as the rest or not?

---

* Section 301, a provision of U.S. trade law, enables the U.S. government to take action against countries deemed to have engaged in "unreasonable, unjustifiable, or discriminatory" practices that restrict U.S. commerce.

Sources: Abstracted from James Bovard, "A U.S. History of Trade Hypocrisy," *The Wall Street Journal,* March 8, 1994, p. A10; "The Great Trade Violator?" *World Press Review,* August 1994, p. 41; and Jeb Blount, "Protectionism, Made in USA," *Latin Trade,* November 1996, p. 62.

workers. Those figures represent the average of 21 protected industries, but the cost is much higher in selected industries. In the steel industry, for example, countervailing duties and antidumping penalties on foreign suppliers of steel since 1992 have saved the jobs of 1,239 steelworkers at a cost of $835,351 each. Anyone who buys a car can assume that at least $3,000 to $5,000 of the price they pay represents the effect of voluntary quotas on Japanese cars that allow both U.S. and Japanese companies to boost prices in the U.S. Unfortunately, protectionism is politically popular, but it rarely leads to renewed growth in a declining industry. And the jobs that are saved are saved at a

The French won the right to protect their citizens from the pernicious effects of U.S. films. (Jean-Pierre Amet/SYGMA)

EXHIBIT 2–5   The Price of Protectionism

Industry	Total Costs to Consumers (in $ millions)	Number of Jobs Saved	Cost per Job Saved
Textiles and apparel	$27,000	640,000	$ 42,000
Carbon steel	6,800	9,000	750,000
Autos	5,800	55,000	105,000
Dairy products	5,500	25,000	220,000
Shipping	3,000	11,000	270,000
Meat	1,800	11,000	160,000

Source: Michael McFadden, "Protectionism Can't Protect Jobs," *Fortune,* May 11, 1987, p. 125. © 1987 Time, Inc. All rights reserved.

very high cost, which constitutes a hidden tax that consumers unknowingly pay.[16] (See Exhibit 2–5.)

Trade Barriers

To encourage development of domestic industry and protect existing industry, governments may establish such barriers to trade as tariffs, quotas, boycotts, monetary barriers, nontariff barriers, and market barriers. Barriers are imposed against imports and against foreign businesses. While the inspiration for such barriers may be economic or political, they are encouraged by local industry. Whether or not the barriers are economically logical, the fact is they exist.

---

[16] For a complete report on the study, see Gary Clyde Hufbauer and Kimberly Ann Elliott, *Measuring the Costs of Protection in the United States* (Washington, D.C.: Institute for International Economics, 1994), p. 125.

Tariffs.   A *tariff,* simply defined, is a tax imposed by a government on goods entering at its borders. Tariffs may be used as a revenue-generating tax or to discourage the importation of goods, or for both reasons. In general, tariffs:

Increase	Inflationary pressures.
	Special interests' privileges.
	Government control and political considerations in economic matters.
	The number of tariffs (they beget other tariffs).
Weaken	Balance-of-payments positions.
	Supply-and-demand patterns.
	International understanding (they can start trade wars).
Restrict	Manufacturers' supply sources.
	Choices available to consumers.
	Competition.

In addition, tariffs are arbitrary, discriminatory, and require constant administration and supervision. They often are used as reprisals against protectionist moves of trading partners. In a dispute with the European Community over pasta export subsidies, the United States ordered a 40 percent increase in tariffs on European spaghetti and fancy pasta. The EC retaliated against U.S. walnuts and lemons. The pasta war raged on as Europe increased tariffs on U.S. fertilizer, paper products, and beef tallow, and the United States responded in kind. The war ended when the Europeans finally dropped pasta export subsidies.

Imports are restricted in a variety of ways other than tariffs. These *nontariff barriers* include quality standards on imported products, sanitary and health standards, quotas, embargoes, and boycotts. Exhibit 2–6 gives a complete list of nontariff barriers.[17]

Quotas.   A quota is a specific unit or dollar limit applied to a particular type of good. There is a limit on imported television sets in Great Britain, and there are German quotas on Japanese ball bearings, Italian restrictions on Japanese motorcycles, and U.S. quotas on sugar, textiles, and, of all things, peanuts. Quotas put an absolute restriction on the quantity of a specific item that can be imported. Like tariffs, quotas tend to increase prices. U.S. quotas on textiles are estimated to add 50 percent to the wholesale price of clothing.

Voluntary Export Restraints.   Similar to quotas are the voluntary export restraints (VER) or orderly market agreements (OMA). Common in textiles, clothing, steel, agriculture, and automobiles, the VER is an agreement between the importing country and the exporting country for a restriction on the volume of exports. Japan has a VER on automobiles to the United States; that is, Japan has agreed to export a fixed number of automobiles annually. When televisions were still manufactured in the United States, Japan signed an OMA limiting Japanese color television exports to the United States to 1.56 million units per year. However, as a result of the OMA, Japanese companies began investing in television manufacturing in the U.S. and as a result they regained the entire market share that had been lost through the OMA, eventually dominating the entire market.[18] A VER is called voluntary because the exporting country sets the limits; however, it is generally imposed under the threat of stiffer quotas and tariffs being set by the importing country if a VER is not established.

---

[17] Anjuli Bhargaza, "Non-tariff Barriers in 16 Markets Hinder Exports," *Business Standard,* April 29, 1997, p. 10.

[18] John B. Goodman, Debora Spar and David B. Yoffie, "Foreign Direct Investment and the Demand for Protection in the United States," *International Organization,* September 1996, p. 565.

EXHIBIT 2–6   Types of Nontariff Barriers

Specific Limitations on Trade:
  Quotas
  Import licensing requirements
  Proportion restrictions of foreign to domestic goods (local content requirements)
  Minimum import price limits
  Embargoes

Customs and Administrative Entry Procedures:
  Valuation systems
  Antidumping practices
  Tariff classifications
  Documentation requirements
  Fees

Standards:
  Standards disparities
  Intergovernmental acceptances of testing methods and standards
  Packaging, labeling, marking standards

Governmental Participation in Trade:
  Government procurement policies
  Export subsidies
  Countervailing duties
  Domestic assistance programs

Charges on Imports:
  Prior import deposit requirements
  Administrative fees
  Special supplementary duties
  Import credit discriminations
  Variable levies
  Border taxes

Others:
  Voluntary export restraints
  Orderly marketing agreements

Source: A. D. Cao, "NonTariff Barriers to U.S. Manufactured Exports," *The Columbia Journal of World Business,* Summer 1980, p. 94.

Boycotts.   A government boycott is an absolute restriction against the purchase and importation of certain goods from other countries. A public boycott can be either formal or informal and may be government sponsored or sponsored by an industry. The United States uses boycotts and other sanctions against countries with which there is a dispute. For example, Cuba, Iran, and Iraq had or still have sanctions imposed by the United States. There is rising concern, however, that government-sponsored sanctions cause unnecessary harm for both the United States and the country being boycotted without reaching desired results.[19] It is not unusual for the citizens of a country to boycott goods of other countries at the urging of their government or civic groups.[20] Nestlé products were boycotted by a citizens group that considered the way Nestlé promoted baby milk formula misleading to Third World mothers and harmful to their babies.[21]

---

[19] Dick Kirschten, "Economic Sanctions: Speaking Loudly but Carrying Only a Small Stick?" *National Journal,* January 4, 1997, p. 43.

[20] *Corporations and the Impact of Public Advocacy on Corporate Strategy: Nestlé and the Infant Formula Controversy* (Boston: Kluwer Academic Press, 1994), p. 4113.

[21] For a comprehensive review, see Thomas V. Greer, "International Infant Formula Marketing: The Debate Continues," *Advances in International Marketing* 4, 1990, pp. 207–225.

CROSSING BORDERS 2-3

A Word for Open Markets

Bastiat's century-old farcical letter to the French Chamber of Deputies points up the ultimate folly of tariffs and the advantages of utilizing the superior production advantage of others.

To the Chamber of Deputies:

We are subjected to the intolerable competition of a foreign rival, who enjoys such superior facilities for the production of light that he can inundate our national market at reduced price. This rival is no other than the sun. Our petition is to pass a law shutting up all windows, openings, and fissures through which the light of the sun is used to penetrate our dwellings, to the prejudice of the profitable manufacture we have been enabled to bestow on the country.

Signed: Candlestick Makers,
F. Bastiat

Monetary Barriers. A government can effectively regulate its international trade position by various forms of exchange-control restrictions. A government may enact such restrictions to preserve its balance-of-payments position or specifically for the advantage or encouragement of particular industries. There are three barriers to consider: blocked currency, differential exchange rates, and government approval requirements for securing foreign exchange.

Blocked currency is used as a political weapon or as a response to difficult balance-of-payments situations. In effect, blockage cuts off all importing or all importing above a certain level. Blockage is accomplished by refusing to allow importers to exchange national currency for the sellers' currency.

The *differential exchange rate* is a particularly ingenious method of controlling imports. It encourages the importation of goods the government deems desirable and discourages importation of goods the government does not want. The essential mechanism requires the importer to pay varying amounts of domestic currency for foreign exchange with which to purchase products in different categories. For example, the exchange rate for a desirable category of goods might be one unit of domestic money for one unit of a specific foreign currency. For a less-desirable product, the rate might be two domestic currency units for one foreign unit. For an undesirable product, the rate might be three domestic units for one foreign unit. An importer of an undesirable product has to pay three times as much for the foreign exchange as the importer of a desired product.

Government approval to secure foreign exchange is often used by countries experiencing severe shortages of foreign exchange. At one time or another, most Latin American and East European countries have required all foreign exchange transactions to be approved by a central minister. Thus, importers who want to buy a foreign good must apply for an exchange permit, that is, permission to exchange an amount of local currency for foreign currency.

The exchange permit may also stipulate the rate of exchange, which can be an unfavorable rate depending on the desires of the government. In addition, the exchange permit may stipulate that the amount to be exchanged must be deposited in a local bank for a set period prior to the transfer of goods. For example, Brazil has at times required funds to be deposited 360 days prior to the import date. This is extremely restrictive because funds are out of circulation and subject to the ravages of inflation. Such policies cause major cash flow problems for the importer and greatly increase the price of imports. Needless to say, these currency-exchange barriers constitute a major deterrent to trade.

Standards.   Nontariff barriers of this category include standards to protect health, safety, and product quality. The standards are sometimes used in an unduly stringent or discriminating way to restrict trade, but the sheer volume of regulations in this category is a problem in itself. A fruit content regulation for jam varies so much from country to country that one agricultural specialist says, "A jam exporter needs a computer to avoid one or another country's regulations." Different standards are one of the major disagreements between the United States and Japan. The size of knotholes in plywood shipped to Japan can determine whether or not the shipment is accepted; if a knothole is too large, the shipment is rejected because quality standards are not met.

The United States and other countries require some products (automobiles in particular) to contain a percentage of "local content" to gain admission to their markets. The North American Free Trade Agreement (NAFTA) stipulates that all automobiles coming from member countries must have at least 62.5 percent North American content to deter foreign car makers from using one member nation as the back door to another.

Trade restrictions abound, and the United States is among the governments applying them. According to one source, approximately 45 percent of U.S. manufactured imports are subject to some form of nontariff barrier. For more than a decade, U.S. government officials have arranged "voluntary" agreements with the Japanese steel and automobile industries to limit sales to the United States. Similar negotiations with the governments of major textile producers have limited textile imports into the United States. While countries create barriers to trade, they appreciate the growing interdependence of the world's economies and thus strive to lower barriers in a controlled and equitable manner. The General Agreement on Tariffs and Trade (GATT) and the World Trade Organization (WTO) both have as their goal the elimination of trade barriers.[22]

Easing Trade Restrictions

Lowering the trade deficit has been a priority of the U.S. government for a number of years. Of the many proposals brought forward, most deal with fairness of trade with some of our trading partners instead of reducing imports or adjusting other trade policies. Many believe that too many countries are allowed to trade freely in the United States without granting equal access to U.S. products in their countries. Japan is the trading partner with which we have the largest deficit and with which there is the most concern about fairness. The Omnibus Trade and Competitiveness Act of 1988 addressed the trade fairness issue and focused on ways to improve U.S. competitiveness.

The Omnibus Trade and Competitiveness Act

The *Omnibus Trade and Competitiveness Act of 1988* is many faceted, focusing on assisting businesses to be more competitive in world markets as well as on correcting perceived injustice in trade practices. The trade act was designed to deal with trade deficits, protectionism, and the overall fairness of our trading partners. Congressional concern centered on the issue that U.S. markets were open to most of the world but markets in Japan, Western Europe, and many Asian countries were relatively closed. The act re-

---

22 Charles Oliver, "National Issue: For Trade, Now the Hard Part," *Investor's Business Daily,* January 20 , 1997, p. A6.

The explosion of Western products in Moscow, advertised on buildings, buses, and sidewalks, has triggered a backlash among many Russians that has been partly responsible for a resurgence of nationalism. (Robert Wallis/SABA)

flected the realization that we must deal with our trading partners based on how they actually operate, not on how we want them to behave. Some see the act as a protectionist measure, but the government sees it as a means of providing stronger tools to open foreign markets and to help U.S. exporters be more competitive. The bill covers three areas considered critical in improving U.S. trade: market access, export expansion, and import relief.

The issue of the openness of markets for U.S. goods is addressed as *market access.* There are many barriers that restrict or prohibit goods from entering a foreign market. Unnecessarily restrictive technical standards, compulsory distribution systems, customs barriers, tariffs, quotas, and restrictive licensing requirements are just a few. The act gives the U.S. president authority to restrict a country's products in the U.S. market if that country imposes unfair restrictions on U.S. products. Further, if a foreign government's procurement rules discriminate against U.S. firms, the U.S. president has the authority to impose a similar ban on U.S. government procurement of goods and services from the offending nation.

Besides emphasizing market access, the act also recognizes that some problems with U.S. export competitiveness stem from impediments on trade imposed by U.S. regulations and export disincentives. Export controls, the Foreign Corrupt Practices Act (FCPA), and export promotion were specifically addressed in the *export expansion* section of the act. Export licenses could be obtained more easily and more quickly for products on the export control list. In addition, the act reaffirmed the government's role in being more responsive to the needs of the exporter. Two major contributions facilitating export trade were computer-based procedures to file for and track export license requests, and the creation of the National Trade Data Bank (NTDB) to improve access to trade data.[23]

Export trade is a two-way street: We must be prepared to compete with imports in the home market if we force foreign markets to open to U.S. trade. Recognizing that foreign penetration of U.S. markets can cause serious competitive pressure, loss of market share, and, occasionally, severe injury, the *import relief* section of the Omnibus Trade and Competitiveness Act provides a menu of remedies for U.S. businesses adversely affected by imports. Companies seriously injured by fairly traded imports can petition the government for temporary relief while they adjust to import competition and regain their competitive edge.

The act has resulted in a much more flexible process for obtaining export licenses, in fewer products on the export control list, and in greater access to information, and has established a basis for negotiations with India, Japan, and other countries to remove or lower barriers to trade.

As the global marketplace evolves, trading countries have focused attention on ways of eliminating tariffs, quotas, and other barriers to trade. Three ongoing activities to support the growth of international trade are GATT, the International Monetary Fund (IMF), and The World Bank Group.

General Agreement on Tariffs and Trade[24]

Historically, trade treaties were negotiated on a bilateral (between two nations) basis, with little attention given to relationships with other countries. Further, there was a tendency to raise barriers rather than extend markets and restore world trade. The United States and 22 other countries signed the *General Agreement on Tariffs and Trade (GATT)* shortly after World War II. Although not all countries participated, this agreement paved the way for the first effective worldwide tariff agreement. The original agreement provided a process to reduce tariffs and created an agency to serve as watchdog over world trade. GATT's agency director and staff offer nations a forum for negotiating trade and related issues. Member nations seek to resolve their trade disputes bilaterally; if that fails, special GATT panels are set up to recommend action. The panels are only advisory and have no enforcement powers.

The GATT treaty and subsequent meetings have produced agreements significantly reducing tariffs on a wide range of goods. Periodically, member nations meet to reevaluate trade barriers and establish international codes designed to foster trade among members. In general, the agreement covers these basic elements: (1) trade shall be conducted on a nondiscriminatory basis; (2) protection shall be afforded domestic industries through customs tariffs, not through such commercial measures as import quotas; and (3) consultation shall be the primary method used to solve global trade problems.

Since GATT's inception there have been eight "rounds" of intergovernmental tariff negotiations. The most recently completed was the Uruguay Round (1994), which built on the successes of the Tokyo Round (1974)—the most comprehensive and far-reaching round undertaken by GATT up to that time. The Tokyo Round resulted in tariff cuts and set out new international rules for subsidies and countervailing measures, antidumping, government procurement, technical barriers to trade (standards), customs valuation, and import licensing. While the Tokyo Round addressed nontariff barriers, there were some areas not covered which continued to impede free trade.

In addition to market access, there were issues of trade in services, agriculture, and textiles; intellectual property rights; and investment and capital flows. The United States was especially interested in addressing services trade and intellectual property rights

---

[23] See the Appendix to Chapter 8 for a discussion of the NTBD.
[24] For a complete description and history of GATT visit **http://www.wto.org/wto/about/about.htm**.

since neither had been well protected. Based on these concerns, the eighth set of negotiations (Uruguay Round) was begun in 1986 at a GATT Trade Minister's meeting in Punta del Este, Uruguay, and finally concluded in 1994. By 1995, 80 GATT members including the United States, the European Union (and its member states), Japan, and Canada had accepted the agreement.

The market access segment (tariff and nontariff measures) was initially considered to be of secondary importance in the negotiations, but the final outcome went well beyond the initial Uruguay Round goal of a one-third reduction in tariffs. Instead, virtually all tariffs in 10 vital industrial sectors with key trading partners were eliminated. This resulted in deep cuts (ranging from 50 to 100 percent) on electronic items and scientific equipment, and the harmonization of tariffs in the chemical sector at very low rates (5.5 to 0 percent).

U.S. exporters of paper products serve as a good example of the opportunities that will be opened as a result of these changes. Currently, U.S. companies competing for a share of the paper products market in the European Community have to pay tariffs as high as 9 percent while European competitors enjoy duty-free access within the EU. Once the results of the Uruguay Round market-access package are implemented, these high tariffs will be eliminated. Another example is Korean tariffs as high as 20 percent on scientific equipment, which will be reduced to an average of 7 percent, permitting U.S. exporters to be more competitive in that market.

An important objective of the United States in the Uruguay Round was to reduce or eliminate barriers to international trade in services. While there is still much progress to be made before free trade in services will exist throughout the world, the *General Agreement on Trade in Services (GATS)* is the first multilateral, legally enforceable agreement covering trade and investment in the services sector. It provides a legal basis for future negotiations aimed at eliminating barriers that discriminate against foreign services and deny them market access. For the first time, comprehensive multilateral disciplines and procedures covering trade and investment in services have been established. Specific market-opening concessions from a wide range of individual countries were achieved, and provision was made for continued negotiations to further liberalize telecommunications and financial services.

Equally significant were the results of negotiations in the investment sector. *Trade-Related Investment Measures (TRIMs)* established the basic principle that investment restrictions can be major trade barriers and therefore are included, for the first time, under GATT procedures. An initial set of prohibited practices included local content requirements specifying that some amount of the value of the investor's production must be purchased from local sources or produced locally; trade balancing requirements specifying that an investor must export an amount equivalent to some proportion of imports or condition the amount of imports permitted on export levels; and foreign exchange balancing requirements limiting the importation of products used in local production by restricting its access to foreign exchange to an amount related to its exchange inflow. As a result of TRIMs, restrictions in Indonesia which prohibit foreign firms from opening their own wholesale or retail distribution channels can be challenged. And so can investment restrictions in Brazil that require foreign-owned manufacturers to buy most of their components from high-cost local suppliers and that require affiliates of foreign multinationals to maintain a trade surplus in Brazil's favor by exporting more than they sell within.

Another objective of the United States for the Uruguay Round was achieved by an agreement on *Trade Related Aspects of Intellectual Property Rights (TRIPs)*. The TRIPs agreement establishes substantially higher standards of protection for a full range of intellectual property rights (patents, copyrights, trademarks, trade secrets, industrial designs, and semiconductor chip mask works) than are embodied in current international agreements, and it provides for the effective enforcement of those standards both internally and at the border. The Uruguay Round also provides for a better integration of the agricultural and textiles areas into the overall trading system. The reductions of export subsidies, internal supports, and actual import barriers for agricultural products are in-cluded in the agreement. The Uruguay Round also includes another set of improvements in rules covering antidumping, standards, safeguards, customs valuation, rules of origin, and import licensing. In each case, rules and procedures were made more open, equi-table, and predictable, thus leading to a more-level playing field for trade. Perhaps the most notable achievement of the Uruguay Round was the creation of a new institution as a successor to the GATT—the World Trade Organization.

World Trade Organization[25]

At the signing of the Uruguay Round trade agreement in Marrakech, Morocco, in April 1994, U.S. representatives pushed for an enormous expansion of the definition of trade issues. The result was the creation of the *World Trade Organization (WTO),* which will encompass the current GATT structure and extend it to new areas not adequately cov-ered in the past. The WTO is an institution, not an agreement as was GATT. It will set the rules governing trade between its 132 members, provide a panel of experts to hear and rule on trade disputes between members, and, unlike GATT, issue binding deci-sions. It will require, for the first time, the full participation of all members in all aspects of the current GATT and the Uruguay Round agreements, and, through its enhanced stature and scope, provide a permanent, comprehensive forum to address the trade is-sues of the 21st century global market.

All member countries will have equal representation in the WTO's ministerial con-ference, which will meet at least every two years to vote for a director general who will appoint other officials. Trade disputes will be heard by a panel of experts selected by the WTO from a list of trade experts provided by member countries. The panel will hear both sides and issue a decision; the winning side will be authorized to retaliate with trade sanctions if the losing country does not change its practices. While the WTO has no actual means of enforcement, international pressure to comply with WTO decisions from other member countries is expected to force compliance. The WTO ensures that member countries agree to the obligations of all the agreements, not just those they like. For the first time, member countries, including developing countries (the fastest-grow-ing markets of the world), will undertake obligations to open their markets and to be bound by the rules of the multilateral trading system.

There was some resistance to the World Trade Organization provision of the Uruguay Round before it was finally ratified by the three super powers, Japan, European Union (EU), and the United States. A legal wrangle between European Union countries centered on whether the EU's founding treaty gives the European Commission the sole right to negotiate for its members in all areas covered by the WTO.

In the United States, ratification was challenged because of concern for the possible loss of sovereignty over its trade laws to WTO, the lack of veto power (the U.S. could have a decision imposed on it by a majority of the WTO's members), and the role the United States would assume when a conflict arises over an individual state's laws that might be challenged by a WTO member. The GATT agreement was ratified by the U.S. Congress and soon after, the EC, Japan, and more than 60 other countries followed. All 117 members of the former GATT supported the Uruguay agreement. Since almost im-mediately after its inception on January 1, 1995, WTO's agenda has been full with is-sues ranging from threats of boycotts and sanctions and the membership of China. In-stead of waiting for various "rounds" to iron out problems, the WTO offers a framework for a continuous discussion and resolution of issues that retard trade.

WTO has its detractors but from most indications it is gaining acceptance by the trading community.[26] The number of countries that have joined and those that want to

---

[25] Visit the WTO homepage for complete details on the WTO. **http://wto.org/**

[26] Daniel B. Moskowitz, "Lukewarm Success," *International Business,* January 1997, p. 45.

become members is a good measure of its importance. Another one is the accomplishments since its inception: It has been the forum for successful negotiations to opening markets in telecommunications and in information technology equipment, something the United States had sought for the last two rounds of GATT. It also has been active in settling trade disputes and it continues to oversee the implementation of the agreements reached in the Uruguay Round.[27] But, with its successes come other problems, namely, how to counter those countries that want all the benefits of belonging to WTO but also want to protect their markets.

Skirting the Spirit of GATT and WTO

Unfortunately, as is probably true of every law or agreement, since its inception there have been those who look for loopholes and ways to get around the provisions of the WTO. For example, China has asked to become a member of the WTO but to be accepted it has to show good faith in reducing tariffs and other restrictions on trade.[28] To fulfill the requirements to join the WTO, China has reduced tariffs on 5,000 product lines and has eliminated a range of traditional nontariff barriers to trade, including quotas, licenses, and foreign exchange controls. At the same time, U.S. companies have begun to notice an increase in the number and scope of technical standards and inspection requirements. As a case in point, China recently has applied safety and quality inspection requirements on such seemingly benign imported goods as jigsaw puzzles. It also has been insisting that a long list of electrical and mechanical imports undergo an expensive certification process that requires foreign companies but not domestic companies to pay for on-site visits by Chinese inspection officials. Under WTO rules, China will have to justify the decision to impose certain standards and provide a rationale for the inspection criteria. However, the foreign companies will have to request a review before the WTO will investigate. The WTO recognizes the need for standards (safety, health, and so on) although it advocates worldwide harmonization of product standards.[29]

Antidumping duties are becoming another favorite way for nations to impose duties, under the justification that a foreign company is selling at unfair prices. Most nations have dumping laws which ostensibly are designed to keep foreign companies from "dumping" product, that is, selling below cost in order to unfairly gain a share of market and lessen competition. This law always has been difficult to interpret because "selling below cost" is difficult to measure; most countries have defined it whatever way necessary to serve their purpose. When companies are found to be dumping, the country places an extra tax on the product to offset the advantage of the lower price. If the government has subsidized the company that is found guilty of dumping, an additional countervailing duty is collected to offset the subsidy.

In an attempt to standardize the definition, the WTO defines dumping as selling at a lower price in the foreign market than in other markets or selling at below average total costs. The interpretation and calculation of average total costs creates the most difficulty in evaluating cases. Antidumping actions do not require evidence of predatory behavior, or intentions to monopolize, or of any other efforts to drive competitors out of business.

Under U.S. antidumping law, the burden of proof falls upon the industry or firm that is accused. Foreign firms are presumed guilty until proven innocent. Under current U.S. law, any industry can approach the Department of Commerce and International Trade Commission (ITC) and claim foreigners are pricing exports lower in the U.S. than

---

[27] "What Is It, and What Use Is It . . . ?" November 18, 1997. **http://www.wto.org/wto/faqs/faq.htm/**

[28] "Slow Dance with the Dragon," *Business Week,* April 7, 1997, p. 52.

[29] Richard Brecher and Catherine Gelb, "As China Inches Closer to the WTO, U.S. Companies Need to Rethink Their China Strategies," *China Business Review,* May 1997, p. 26.

CROSSING BORDERS 2–4

Antidumping: The New Trade Barrier?

Historically tariffs and nontariff trade barriers have impeded free trade, but over the years they have been eliminated or lowered through the efforts of GATT and WTO. Now there is a new nontariff barrier: antidumping laws that have emerged as a way of keeping foreign goods out of a market. Antidumping laws were designed to prevent foreign producers from "predatory pricing," a practice whereby a foreign producer would intentionally sell their products in the U.S. for less than the cost of production in order to undermine the competition and take control of the market. It was intended as a kind of antitrust law for international trade. Violators are assessed "antidumping" duties for selling below cost and/or assessed "countervailing duties" to prevent the use of foreign government subsidies to undermine American industry. Many countries have similar laws, and they are allowed under WTO rules.

Recent years have seen a staggering increase in antidumping cases in the U.S. In one year, 12 U.S. steel manufacturers launched antidumping cases against 82 foreign steel-makers in 30 countries. Many economists felt that there was no need for these antidumping charges because of the number of companies and countries involved; supply and demand could have been left to sort out the best producers and prices. Nevertheless, antidumping cases are becoming de facto trade barriers. The investigations are very costly, they take a long time to resolve, and until they are resolved they effectively limit trade. Further, the threat of being hit by an antidumping charge is enough to keep some companies out of the market.

A Brazil-based firm targeted in a dumping case found it was saddled with costs of more than $1 million just to comply with U.S. antidumping laws. The company had to fill out a four-part questionnaire, each part of which was about 40 pages long. Five investigators spent 45 staff days going over the company's books. The investigation was one of the worst experiences the company has had—"It was like being invaded by little green men. It is so difficult to comply with the law that at one point we almost had to stop production at the company." Despite their efforts, the company was assessed countervailing duties of 5.88 percent and antidumping duties of 42.08 percent on its exports, effectively pricing the company out of the market.

Even companies that win their cases do not win in the end. Colombian flower producers have been investigated nine times in the last 10 years without ever being assessed an antidumping duty of more than 3.2 percent. The cost to members is between $3 million and $5 million annually to comply. The law has been called the "32 cent petition," because all it takes to trigger an investigation is a letter from an American producer and a 32-cent stamp. Under U.S. law, once charged, the "dumping" company must prove its innocence and that takes time and money.

The burden is not all on the backs of the companies that are taxed, however. According to a recent study, 119 of 192 nonsteel dumping cases led to $4.8 billion in additional cost to U.S. consumers. The 19 steel cases added $3.3 billion increase in the cost of steel products.

The United States is not the only country misusing antidumping laws. China has been the target of 69 charges that cover almost 20 percent of its exports to the European Union. At last count the EU had 159 antidumping actions in force against foreign exporters. In NAFTA, the charges go in all directions, Canadians against Mexico, Mexico against the United States, and on and on. Certainly many of the antidumping or subsidy complaints are valid. Countries do subsidize their industries and companies do sell below market prices in order to unfairly gain footholds in other markets. In fact, an Organization for Economic Cooperation and Development (OECD) study showed that the vast majority of the world's antidumping cases had no economic rationale. There are enough incidents where charges of antidumping are less than compelling that make it plausible to say that antidumping laws are the new nontariff barriers.

Sources: Adapted from Jeb Blount, "Protectionism, Made in U.S.A.," *Latin Trade,* November 1996, p. 62; Shada Islam, "Invisible Barriers: Asians Say Politics Is Behind EU Anti-dumping Action," *Far Eastern Review,* June 12, 1997, p. 68; and Nancy E. Kelly, "Nafta Battles Continue among Participants," *American Metal Market,* May 29, 1997, p. 11A.

at home.[30] The Department investigates and the ITC determines whether material injury has occurred. Antidumping duties are imposed when foreign merchandise is sold in the United States for less than "fair" value. A duty is assessed equal to the amount by which the estimated foreign market value exceeds U.S. price.

Although the definition of fair value leaves room for interpretation, the most egregious tactic is the requirement for the "offending" firm to complete a detailed questionnaire of information on costs. Just the volume of data required in such cases is a deterrent to trade. The Department of Commerce presents an accused foreign firm with a questionnaire as long as 100 pages that requests specific accounting data on individual sales in the home market, data on sales in the U.S., and detailed data needed to adjust for tariffs, shipping, selling, and distribution costs. Information has to be recorded and transmitted to the Department of Commerce in English and in a computer-readable format within a short deadline.[31] (See Crossing Borders 2–4.)

Following the example of the United States (the region's most prolific user of antidumping cases) Mexico and other Latin American countries have increased their use of antidumping and countervailing duties as protectionist measures. As one Mexican official involved in antidumping cases noted, "We have learned our trade in the United States and learned it well."[32] Despite the "clever" tactics used by some countries to skirt its provisions, the WTO is considered to have a positive effect on international trade.

The International Monetary Fund and World Bank Group

The International Monetary Fund and the World Bank group are two global institutions created to assist nations in becoming and remaining economically viable. Each plays an important role in the environment of international trade by helping to maintain stability in the financial markets and by assisting countries that are seeking economic development and restructuring.

Inadequate monetary reserves and unstable currencies are particularly vexing problems in global trade. So long as these conditions exist, world markets cannot develop and function as effectively as they should. To overcome these particular market barriers which plagued international trading before World War II, the *International Monetary Fund (IMF)* was formed. Originally 29 countries signed the agreement; now there are 181 countries as members. Among the objectives of the IMF are the stabilization of foreign exchange rates and the establishment of freely convertible currencies to facilitate the expansion and balanced growth of international trade. Member countries have voluntarily joined to consult with one another in order to maintain a stable system of buying and selling their currencies so that payments in foreign money can take place between countries smoothly and without delay. The IMF also lends money to members having trouble meeting financial obligations to other members.

To cope with universally floating exchange rates, the IMF developed *special drawing rights (SDRs),* one of its more useful inventions. Because both gold and the U.S. dollar have lost their utility as the basic medium of financial exchange, most monetary statistics relate to SDRs rather than dollars. The SDR is in effect "paper gold," and represents an average base of value derived from the value of a group of major currencies. Rather than being denominated in the currency of any given country, trade contracts are frequently written in SDRs because they are much less susceptible to exchange-rate

---

[30] Paul Magnusson, "Uncle Sam Isn't Playing Fair with the WTO," *Business Week,* March 10, 1997, p. 38.

[31] David M. Gould and William C. Gruben, "Will Fair Trade Diminish Free Trade?" *Business Economics,* April 1997, p. 7.

[32] Jeb Blount, "Protectionism, Latin Style," *Latin Trade,* March 1997, p. 59.

fluctuations. Even floating rates do not necessarily accurately reflect exchange relationships. Some countries permit their currencies to float cleanly without manipulation (clean float) while other nations systematically manipulate the value of their currency (dirty float), thus modifying the accuracy of the monetary marketplace. Although much has changed in the world's monetary system since the IMF was first established, it still plays an important role in providing short-term financing to governments struggling to pay current-account debts, as well.

While the International Monetary Fund has some severe critics, most agree that it has performed a valuable service and at least partially achieved many of its objectives.[33] To be sure, the IMF proved its value in the financial crisis among some Asian countries in 1997. The impact of the crisis was lessened substantially as a result of actions taken by the IMF. During the financial crisis, the IMF provided loans to several countries including Thailand, Indonesia, and South Korea.[34] Had these countries not received aid ($60 billion to Korea alone), the economic reverberations may have led to a global recession.[35] As it was, all the major equity markets reflected substantial reductions in market prices and the rate of economic growth in some countries was slowed.

Sometimes confused with the IMF, the *World Bank Group* is a separate institution that has as its goal the reduction of poverty and the improvement of living standards by promoting sustainable growth and investment in people. The Bank provides loans, technical assistance, and policy guidance to developing-country members to achieve its objectives. There are five institutions in the World Bank Group, each of which has a specific function. The IBRD[36] lends money to the governments of developing countries to finance development projects in education, health, and infrastructure. The IDA provides assistance to governments for developmental projects to the poorest developing countries (per capita incomes of $925 or less). The IFC lends directly to the private sector. Its goal is to help strengthen the private sector in developing countries with long-term loans, equity investments, and other financial assistance. The MIGA provides investors with investment guarantees against "noncommercial risk," such as expropriation and war. The purpose is to create an environment in developing countries that will attract foreign investment. Finally, the ICSID was founded to promote increased flows of international investment by providing facilities for the conciliation and arbitration of disputes between governments and foreign investors. It also provides advice, carries out research, and produces publications in the area of foreign investment law.[37] Since their inception, these institutions have played a pivotal role in the economic development of countries throughout the world and thus contributed to the expansion of international trade since World War II.

Keiretsu: A Formidable Competitor?

Although today fewer barriers to trade exist than at any time in the recent past, the efforts of GATT, the U.S. government, and other countries to improve global trade relations and lower tariffs have not yet provided a level playing field for international trade. Some companies are deriving a substantial competitive advantage not only from protec-

---

[33] Visit the IMF homepage for detailed information. **http://www.imf.org/**

[34] Namju Cho, "South Korea Seeks IMF Aid, but Strings Will Be Attached," *The Wall Street Journal,* November 24, 1997, p. A2.

[35] Jackie Calmes, "IMF Bailout of Asian Economy Gets Financial Backing of APEC," *The Wall Street Journal,* November 26, 1997, p. A5.

[36] The International Bank for Reconstruction and Development (IBRD); The International Development Association (IDA); The International Finance Corporation (IFC); The Multilateral Investment Guarantee Agency (MIGA); and the International Center for the Settlement of Investment Disputes (ICSID).

[37] For more information on the World Bank Group and links to databases see **http://www.worldbank.org/**.

EXHIBIT 2–7   **The Core Members in Mitsubishi Keiretsu***

The Flagship Members

Mitsubishi Corporation (32%)
Mitsubishi Bank (26%)
Mitsubishi Industries (20%)

Twenty-Five Core Members

Mitsubishi Paper Mills (32%)
Mitsubishi Kasei (23%)
Mitsubishi Plastics Industries (57%)
Mitsubishi Petrochemical (37%)
Mitsubishi Gas Chemical (24%)
Kirin Brewery (19%)
Mitsubishi Oil (41%)
Mitsubishi Steel Manufacturing (38%)
Mitsubishi Cable Industries (48%)
Mitsubishi Estate (25%)
Mitsubishi Warehousing and Transportation (40%)
Mitsubishi Metal (21%)
Mitsubishi Construction (100%)
Asahi Glass (28%)
Mitsubishi Rayon (25%)
Mitsubishi Electric (17%)
Mitsubishi Kakoki (37%)
Mitsubishi Aluminum (100%)
Mitsubishi Mining & Cement (37%)
Tokio Marine & Fire Insurance (24%)
Meiji Mutual Life Insurance (0%)
Mitsubishi Trust & Banking (28%)
Nippon Yusen (25%)
Mitsubishi Motors (55%)
Nikon Corp. (27%)
and
Hundreds of other Mitsubishi-related companies.

* Percentages represent shares of each company held by others in the group.

Sources: Adapted from "Mighty Mitsubishi Is on the Move," *Business Week,* September 24, 1990, p. 99; and "Why Japan Keeps on Winning," *Fortune,* July 15, 1991, pp. 76 and 81.

tive tariffs but also from the way they are organized and their relationship to other companies. The *keiretsu,* which means "order" or "system," is a unique form of business organization that links companies together in industrial groups that provide Japanese business with a substantial competitive edge over non-keiretsu organizations.

Keiretsus are collections of dozens of major companies spanning several industries and held together by cross-shareholding, old-boy networks, interlocking directorates, long-term business relationships, and social and historical links. There are six major Japanese industrial keiretsu groups and 11 lesser ones. Together, the sales in these groups are responsible for about 25 percent of the activities of all Japanese companies, and keiretsus account for 78 percent of the value of all shares on the Tokyo Stock Exchange. Exhibit 2–7 illustrates the range and complexity of the relationships among the members of the Mitsubishi Group, a vertical keiretsu led by Mitsubishi Bank and Mitsubishi Heavy Industries, the country's largest machinery manufacturer, with interests ranging from aircraft to air-conditioning equipment. Altogether the Mitsubishi Group, with annual sales of $175 billion, involves 160 companies, of which 124 are listed on the Tokyo Stock Exchange. Each is entirely independent with its own board of directors.

There are three types of keiretsus: (1) financial, (2) production, and (3) sales-distribution. The financial keiretsus are loose federations of powerful, independent firms clustered around a core bank that provides funds to a general trading company and other member firms. The production, or vertical, keiretsu is a web of interlocking, long-term relationships between a big manufacturer and its main suppliers. Vertical keiretsu are pyramids of companies that serve a single master—a manufacturer that dictates virtually everything, including prices it will pay, to hundreds of suppliers who are often prohibited from doing business outside the keiretsu. Production keiretsus are typically found in the automotive industry and consist of vertically integrated systems—from the manufacturer to suppliers. A large manufacturing firm will have a group of primary subcontractors, which in turn farm out work to thousands of little firms.

The third category, sales-distribution keiretsus, consists of fully integrated manufacturing and distribution companies. The trading company,[38] the center of a distribution keiretsu, coordinates a complex manufacturing entity that involves thousands of small companies which sell through the keiretsus' distribution network. The keiretsu controls its own retail system, enabling it to dictate prices, profit margins, and exclusive representation through the system. Matsushita, a distribution keiretsu of consumer electronics, controls 60 wholesalers who sell to 25,000 keiretsu stores.

Keiretsus have their critics in Japan[39] and in the United States. It is evident that Japan's keiretsus, vertical and horizontal, restrict the flow of imports into Japan and many Japanese feel that the power of the keiretsu and its control of distribution results in higher prices, inefficiencies that lead to higher prices, and less variety for consumers. Outside Japan, keiretsus favor trade among member companies and they will almost always support their own suppliers at home or abroad before buying from an outsider. Japan is building relationships in other Asian countries that tie the non-Japanese members to keiretsus and, in effect, create the same "loyalty" to keiretsu members as found in Japan. A survey in Taiwan found that half of the Japanese subsidiaries indicated they had to follow Japan's strict lead on marketing matters.[40] First choice is a keiretsu company, second is a Japanese supplier, and third, a local company.

In the past six years, hundreds of U.S. companies—from IBM to smaller companies in industries as diverse as computers, semiconductors, autos, farm implements, and motorcycles—have sought alliances and links vertically with suppliers and horizontally with university research labs, and with their peers. What is emerging is an enterprise model that borrows from Japan's keiretsus to improve competitiveness. Motorola has reorganized its supplier network in the United States based on its Japanese experience in dealing with keiretsus. This move is designed to build stronger ties with suppliers and to boost quality and productivity. Ford, General Motors, and Chrysler are cooperating in "pre-competitive research" on new materials and electric-car batteries to avoid the "waste of money on duplicate research."[41] Strategic International Alliances (SIAs), discussed in Chapter 11, illustrate one way companies are adapting characteristics of the keiretsu system to U.S. business.[42]

The Internet and Global Business

The Internet (the Net) is changing so rapidly that it is hard to keep up with its progress. While it is still full of opinions, chat forums, games, and such, it is also becoming a gold mine for the small business interested in international marketing. Each day it seems that more companies, nations, and global organizations post pages on the World Wide Web

---

[38] The trading company will be discussed in some detail in Chapter 13.

[39] Takatoshi Ito, "Japan's Economy Needs Structural Change," *Finance & Development,* June 1997, p. 16.

[40] Kozo Yamamura, "Japan Keeping U.S. Products out of Asia; Intricate Network Known as 'Keiretsu' Excludes 'Outsiders,'" *The Baltimore Sun,* November 9, 1997, p. 6F.

[41] Jordan D. Lewis, "Business World: Western Companies Improve Upon Japanese 'Keiretsu,'" *The Wall Street Journal Europe,* January 2, 1996, p. 7.

[42] Hiroyuki Tezuka, "Success as the Source of Failure? Competition and Cooperation in the Japanese Economy," *Sloan Management Review,* January 1997, p. 83.

(WWW). Originally many of these Web sites were just statements about the companies or tourist information for countries. While that type of information is still available, sources of information and data that was once only available in reference books and government documents are made available over the Internet free or for a relatively low price.

As one media consultant noted, new technology goes through three stages: hype, rejection, and finally the realization that there is something valuable to be developed. The Net is moving past phase two and rapidly into phase three. Federal Express conducted a survey among 751 export managers of businesses with fewer than 100 employees in 1997. More than 75 percent expect to use the Internet to conduct commerce in the next five years, especially to pursue international markets more aggressively. Nearly 30 percent of small businesses surveyed use e-mail to keep in touch with customers, distributors, and suppliers.[43] Another study found that almost 75 percent of Canadian businesses expect to buy and sell on the Net by 2000. Some analysts estimate the business-to-business market at $8 billion and predict it will swell to $327 billion by 2002.

The number of commercial Web sites has grown from 23,000 in 1995 to over 220,000 in 1996. Firms are now beginning to explore ways to increase productivity and efficiency through the use of the Internet. Firms are using the Net to advertise, conduct customer research, locate partners and distributors, provide product information, communicate with customers, provide service information, and collect data for market analysis.[44] In the future, companies operating internationally will realize a much broader range of benefits from this medium's potential as both a communication and a transaction vehicle.

The use of the Internet for telephone communications and facsimile transmissions, for example, is growing at such a rate that large telecommunications companies such as AT&T-Jens, an AT&T Corporation venture in Japan, have begun to provide services for Internet telephony. The savings over regular telephone charges are substantial. A three-minute call from Japan to Britain is 135 yen ($1.10) with the AT&T venture compared with 770 yen ($6.27) with a traditional Japanese carrier. A similar call to the U.K. is 99 yen, instead of 450 yen. WorldCom Inc., of the U.S., is planning to offer an Internet-based fax service that is 35 to 55 percent cheaper than traditional faxing. One U.S. research firm estimates that by the end of 1999, Internet telephone services worldwide will grow from virtually nothing to a $560 million business. Another company estimates that it could reach $1.8 billion by 2001.[45]

Small businesses have traditionally lacked a fast and efficient way to find partners and distributors in other countries. Electronic messaging gives those small companies a way to find one another and set up working relationships without as much trouble and expense as a series of face-to-face meetings would require. This can be achieved by visiting the home sites of potential partners or distributors or by using the various services provided by the Department of Commerce and other foreign or domestic organizations that offer such services for a fee.

Companies like World Merchandise Exchange Online (Womex Online), a private "members-only" electronic information service, are designed for the worldwide general merchandise trading community. Womex maintains a database carrying tens of thousands of products from thousands of manufacturers, provides members with free electronic mail and online discussion forums, and offers links to industry publications, trade associations, and other resources.

Encore Sale Ltd., a distributor of private-label merchandise to drugstores, department stores, and discount stores throughout Canada, provides a good example of how

---

[43] "EC Enables Small Business to Compete Internationally," *Electronic Commerce News,* November 3, 1997, p. 26.

[44] Using the Internet in marketing research, distribution, advertising/communications, and exporting will be discussed in detail in the respective chapters (Chapters 8, 14, 15, and 16).

[45] Gautam Naik, "Internet Phones Are Catching On as Global Experiment," *The Wall Street Journal,* November 24, 1997, p. B5.

companies like Womex Online can save money and make a small company's efforts more efficient. Encore used to source the more than 5,000 products distributed by its firm the old-fashioned way; that is, the company subscribed to dozens of industry magazines, paged tirelessly through piles of specialty catalogs, and traveled to endless trade shows to find cheap and reliable manufacturers of everything from stationery to baby care products. Because 90 percent of the goods Encore distributed came from the Pacific Rim, the company ran up enormous fax and telephone expenses communicating with potential suppliers.

As a member of Womex Online, Encore now logs on to the network, searches the database, and finds detailed specifications, including photographs, packaging data, case markings, weight measurements, and pricing estimates of potential products to distribute. It is able to investigate the financial history of the manufacturers, send e-mail inquiries to interesting leads, and begin the sensitive negotiation process with in-depth online discussions. No more placing midnight telephone calls to non-English-speaking switchboards. No more faxing page after page of questions or requests for additional material to China, Korea, or Taiwan hoping that timely and intelligible replies would be forthcoming. Best of all, Encore's base of suppliers has increased because many smaller manufacturers that don't advertise in international publications are on the Womex list. This has given the company a much richer pool of potential suppliers with which to work.

In addition to commercial sites like Womex Online, individual companies like Sony of Japan are posting their procurement needs and product information on the Web. Sony accepts electronic inquiries from any interested party. A small compact disc maker in Alabama, for example, visited Sony's procurement page[46] and initiated an e-mail exchange with Sony buyers,[47] which was followed by negotiations for a sale.

The Internet has some rough spots involving security and privacy, as well as differing international rules on consumer protection, product liability, and the collection of import duties and national taxes. These issues are being addressed and will be solved. The technology industry is working with businesses to establish standards for encryption, authentication, password controls, and firewalls that are supported worldwide by trustworthy security management infrastructures.[48] The Organization for Economic Cooperation and Development (OECD) conference on "Dismantling the Barriers to Global Electronic Commerce" laid out preliminary groundwork for a major conference in 1998. The OECD has published a series of policy briefs to keep the public informed of their work in this area. The first brief, Electronic Commerce, is available at **http://www. oecd.org/publications/Pol_brief/9701_Pol.htm**.[49]

Although helpful, the World Wide Web does not offer complete soup-to-nuts solutions for transacting global business. You would never cut a final deal through e-mail, so there will always be a need to travel and establish business relationships in more traditional ways. And although the Net will ease some of the difficulties of global commerce, it will never eliminate the need for good business practices.[50] Many businesspeople make the mistake of viewing the Internet as a replacement for their existing business when they should view it as an alternative channel or extension and a means to make practices more efficient and effective.

You will notice that Web sites are provided throughout the text. Visit these sites; they will provide you with additional information on the subject being discussed or links to other relevant information. The Internet is an important innovation in the dynamic environment of international trade and is rapidly becoming an indispensable

---

[46] Browse the Sony Japan home page at **http://www.sony.co.jp/** and search for procurement.

[47] "Japan and the Internet: Surf's Up! Part 2 of 2" *JEI Report*, June 13, 1997, p. 22.

[48] Shahla Aly, "Surfing for Dollars" *The Financial Post Weekly*, October 11, 1997, p. 8.

[49] If this specific site is not available, then go to **http://www.oecd.org**, the home page of OECD, and search the archives for OECD Policy Brief No.1, Electronic Commerce.

[50] "The Framework for Global Electronic Commerce," *Business America*, January 1998, p. 5.

tool—it will have a profound effect on how international business is conducted in the 21st century.[51]

Summary

Regardless of the theoretical approach used in defense of international trade, it is clear that the benefits from absolute or comparative advantage can accrue to any nation. Heightened competitors from around the world have created increased pressure for protectionism from every region of the globe at a time when open markets are needed if world resources are to be developed and utilized in the most beneficial manner. It is true there are circumstances when market protection may be needed and may be beneficial to national defense or the encouragement of infant industries in developing nations, but the consumer seldom benefits from such protection.

Free international markets help underdeveloped countries become self-sufficient, and because open markets provide new customers, most industrialized nations have, since World War II, cooperated in working toward freer trade. Such trade will always be partially threatened by various governmental and market barriers that exist or are created for the protection of local businesses. However, the trend has been toward freer trade. The changing economic and political realities are producing unique business structures that continue to protect certain major industries. The future of open global markets lies with the controlled and equitable reduction of trade barriers.

Questions

1. Define:

GATT	IMF
balance of payments	nontariff barriers
balance of trade	voluntary export restraint (VER)
current account	keiretsu
tariff	WTO
protectionism	

2. Discuss the globalization of the U.S. economy.

3. Differentiate among the current account, balance of trade, and balance of payments.

4. Explain the role of price as a free market regulator.

5. "Theoretically, the market is an automatic, competitive, self-regulating mechanism which provides for the maximum consumer welfare and which best regulates the use of the factors of production." Explain.

6. Interview several local businesspeople to determine their attitudes toward world trade. Further, learn if they buy or sell goods produced in foreign countries. Correlate the attitudes and report on your findings.

7. What is the role of profit in international trade? Does profit replace or complement the regulatory function of pricing? Discuss.

8. Why does the balance of payments always balance even though the balance of trade does not?

9. Enumerate the ways in which a nation can overcome an unfavorable balance of trade.

10. Support or refute each of the various arguments commonly used in support of tariffs.

11. France exports about 18 percent of its gross domestic product, while neighboring Belgium exports 46 percent. What areas of economic policy are likely to be affected by such variations in exports?

12. Does widespread unemployment change the economic logic of protectionism?

13. Review the economic effects of major trade imbalances such as those caused by petroleum imports.

14. Discuss the main provisions of the Omnibus Trade and Competitiveness Act of 1988.

15. The Tokyo Round of GATT emphasized the reduction of nontariff barriers. How does the Uruguay Round differ?

16. Discuss the impact of GATS, TRIMs, and TRIPs on global trade.

17. Discuss the evolution of world trade that has led to the formation of the WTO.

18. Discuss the impact of the keiretsu system on trade competition.

19. Visit **http://www.usitc.gov/taffairs.htm** (U.S. Customs tariff schedule) and look up the import duties on leather footwear. You will find a difference in the duties on shoes of different value, material composition, and quantity. Using what you have learned in this chapter, explain the reasoning behind these differences. Do the same for frozen and/or concentrated orange juice.

20. The GATT has had a long and eventful history. Visit **http://www.wto.org/wto/about/about.htm** and write a short report on the various Rounds of GATT. What were the key issues addressed in each round?

---

[51] Arielle Emmett, "Beyond 2001: A Telecommunications Odyssey?" *America's Network*, January 15, 1997, p. 27

GEOGRAPHY AND HISTORY: THE FOUNDATIONS OF CULTURAL UNDERSTANDING

Chapter Learning Objectives

What you should learn from Chapter 3

- The importance of geography and history in the understanding of international markets.

- The effects of topography and climate on products, population centers, transportation, and economic growth.

- The growing problem and importance of environmental damage to world trade.

- The social and moral responsibility each citizen has to protect the environment.

- The importance of nonrenewable resources.

- The effects on the world economy of population increases and shifts, and of the level of employment.

- The importance of the history of each culture in understanding its response to international marketing.

GLOBAL PERSPECTIVE

Birth of a Nation—Panama in 67 Hours

The Stage Is Set

June 1902
U.S. offers to buy Panama Canal Zone from Colombia for $10 million.

August 1903
The Colombian Senate refuses the offer. Theodore Roosevelt, angry on hearing of the refusal, is alleged to have referred to the Colombian Senate as "those contemptible little creatures in Bogota." Roosevelt agrees to a plot, led by Dr. Manuel Amador, a secessionist, to assist a group to secede from Colombia.

October 17
Panamanian dissidents travel to Washington and agree to stage a U.S.-backed revolution. Date of revolution set for November 3 at 6 P.M.

October 18
Flag, constitution, and declaration of independence created over the weekend. Panama's first flag was designed and sewn by hand in Highland Falls, New York, using fabric bought at Macy's.
Bunau-Varilla, a French engineer associated with the bankrupt French-Panama canal construction company and who had no permanent residence in Panama, was named Panama's ambassador to the United States.

A Country Is Born

Tuesday, November 3
Precisely at 6 P.M. bribes are paid to the Colombian garrison to lay down their arms. The revolution begins, the U.S.S. Nashville steams into Colon harbor, and the junta proclaims Panama's independence.

Friday, November 6
By 1:00 P.M. the United States recognizes the sovereign state of Panama.

Saturday, November 7
The new government sends an official delegation from Panama to the United States to instruct the Panamanian ambassador to the United States on provisions of the Panama Canal Treaty.

Wednesday, November 18
6:40 P.M. The Panamanian ambassador signs the Panama Canal Treaty. At 11:30 P.M., the official Panamanian delegation arrives at Washington, D.C., railroad station and is met by their ambassador, who informs them that the treaty was signed just hours earlier.

The Present

1977
United States agrees to relinquish control of Panama Canal Zone on December 31, 1999.

September 1997
Law creating Autoridad del Canal de Panama, the canal authority that will assume control from the Panama Canal Commission (U.S. federal agency).

2000
Panama Canal Zone reverts to Panama ????

The past has a direct influence on current events. If you were a citizen of Panama, what would your attitude be toward a foreign power that controls the most profitable part of your country, the Panama Canal? If you were from China, how would you feel about foreigners who forced you to relinquish territory (Hong Kong and Macau) to them for almost a century? Consider what your feelings and attitude will be when Macau reverts to your control and you know that all of Asia is, for the first time in over a century, finally under control of Asians?

Sources: Bernard A. Weisberger, "Panama: Made in U.S.A.," *American Heritage*, November 1989, pp. 24–25; and "Canal Control," *Latin Trade*, September 1997, p. 20.

If a marketer is to interpret a society's behavior and basic attitudes, it is essential to have some idea of a country's geography and history. Marketers can observe the nuances of a culture, but without an appreciation for the role geography and history play in molding that culture, they cannot expect to understand fully why it responds as it does. Culture can be defined as a society's program for survival, the accepted basis for responding to external and internal events. Without an awareness of the geographical characteristics to which a culture has had to adapt and to which it must continuously respond or an appreciation of the historical events that have shaped its cultural evolution, the fundamental attitudes or behavior of a society cannot be fully understood.

The goal of this chapter is to introduce the reader to the impact of geography and history on the marketing process. The influence of geography on markets, trade, and environmental issues as well as the influence of history on behavior and attitudes toward foreign marketers will be examined.

Geography and Global Markets

Geography, the study of the earth's surface, climate, continents, countries, peoples, industries, and resources, is an element of the uncontrollable environment that confronts every marketer but which receives scant attention. The tendency is to study the aspects of geography as isolated entities rather than as important causal agents of the marketing environment. A significant determinant in shaping the culture of a society and its economy is the ongoing struggle to supply its needs within the limits imposed by a nation's physical makeup.[1] Thus, the study of geography is important in the evaluation of markets and their environment.

This section discusses the important geographic characteristics the marketer needs to consider when assessing the environmental aspects of marketing. Examining the world as a whole provides the reader with a broad view of world markets and an awareness of the effects of geographic diversity on the economic profiles of various nations. Climate and topography are examined as facets of the broader and more important elements of geography. A brief look at the earth's resources and population—the building blocks of world markets—completes the presentation on geography and global markets.

Climate and Topography

As elements of geography, the climate and physical terrain of a country are important environmental considerations when appraising a market. The effect of these geographical features on marketing ranges from the obvious influences on product adaptation to more profound influences on the development of marketing systems.[2]

Altitude, humidity, and temperature extremes are climatic features that affect the uses and functions of products and equipment. Products that perform well in temperate zones may deteriorate rapidly or require special cooling or lubrication to function adequately in tropical zones. For example, manufacturers have found that construction equipment used in the United States requires extensive modifications to cope with the intense heat and dust of the Sahara Desert.

Within even a single national market, climate can be sufficiently diverse to require major adjustments. In Ghana, a product adaptable to the entire market must operate effectively in extreme desert heat and low humidity and in tropical rain forests with consistently high humidity. And the climate differences of Europe caused Bosch-Siemens to alter its washing machines: Because the sun does not shine regularly in Germany or in Scandinavia, washing machines must feature a minimum spin cycle of 1,000 rpm with the maximum approaching 1,600 rpm. The clothes must be dryer coming out of the washer because users don't have the luxury of hanging them out to dry. In Italy and Spain, on the other hand, it's quite sufficient to have a spin cycle speed of 500 rpm because of the abundant sunshine.[3]

South America represents an extreme but well-defined example of the importance of geography in marketing considerations. The economic and social systems there can

---

[1] For an interesting history of the spread of societies and the influence of geography, see Robert P. Clark, *The Global Imperative: An Interpretive History of the Spread of Humankind* (Boulder, Colo.: Westview Press, 1997)

[2] The impact of physical geography on the economic growth of a country is discussed in some detail in Jeffery Sachs, "Nature, Nurture and Growth," *The Economist,* June 14, 1997, p. 46.

[3] Scot Stevens and Dan Davis, "Battle of the Brands," *Appliance,* February 1997, p. B21.

CROSSING BORDERS 3–1

Fog, Fog Everywhere and Water to Drink

When you live in Chungungo, Chile, one of the country's most arid regions with no nearby source of water, you drink fog! Of course!! Due to legend and resourceful Canadian and Chilean scientists, Chungungo now has its own supply of drinkable water after a 20-year drought. Before this new source of water, Chungungo depended on water trucks that came twice a week.

Chungungo has always been an arid area, and legend has it that the region's original inhabitants used to worship trees. They considered them sacred because a permanent flow of water sprang from the treetops producing a constant interior rain. The legend was right—the trees produced rain! Thick fog forms along the coast and, as it moves inland and is forced to rise against the hills, it changes into tiny raindrops, which are in turn retained by the tree leaves producing the constant source of rain. Scientists set out to take advantage of this natural phenomenon.

The nearby ancient eucalyptus forest of El Tofo hill provided the clue that scientists needed to create an ingenious water-supply system. To duplicate the water-bearing effect of the trees, they installed 50 "fog catchers" on the top of the hill—huge nets supported by 12-foot eucalyptus pillars, with water containers at their base. About 1,900 gallons of water are collected each day and then piped into town. This small-scale system is cheap, clean, and provides the local people with a steady supply of drinking water.

Sources: Adapted from "Drinking Fog," *World Press Review;* and "The Harvest from the Fog-Bank," *The Economist,* January 7, 1995, p. 32.

be explained, in part, in terms of the geographical characteristics of the area. It is a continent 4,500 miles long and 3,000 miles wide at its broadest point. Two-thirds of it is comparable to Africa in its climate, 48 percent of its total area is made up of forest and jungle, and only 5 percent is arable. Mountain ranges cover South America's west coast for 4,500 miles, with an average height of 13,000 feet and a width of 300 to 400 miles. This is a natural, formidable barrier that has precluded the establishment of commercial routes between the Pacific and Atlantic coasts. Building railroads and highways across the United States was a monumental task, but cannot be compared to the requirements for building a railroad from northeast Brazil to the Peruvian West through jungles and mountains. Once the Andes are surmounted, the Amazon basin of 2 million square miles lies ahead. It is the world's greatest rain forest, almost uninhabitable and impenetrable. Through it runs the Amazon, the world's second largest river, which with its tributaries has almost 40,000 miles of navigable water. On the east coast is another mountain range covering almost the entire coast of Brazil, with an average height of 4,000 feet.

South America's natural barriers inhibit national growth, trade, and communication. It is a vast land area with population concentrations on the outer periphery and an isolated and almost uninhabited interior. National unity and an equal degree of economic development are nearly impossible when inadequate roads and poor communication often separate major cities from each other. Many citizens of South America are so isolated they do not recognize themselves as part of the nation that claims their citizenship. Geography has always separated South America into secluded communities.

Characteristic of Latin American countries is the population concentration in major cities. In almost every case, a high percentage of the total population of each country lives in a few isolated metropolitan centers with most of the wealth, education, and power. The surrounding rural areas remain almost unchanged from one generation to the next, with most of the people existing at subsistence levels. In many areas, even the language of the rural people is not the same as that of metropolitan residents.[4] Such circumstances generally preclude homogeneous markets. As a case in point, Colombia has four major population centers separated from one another by high mountains. Even today these mountain ranges are a major barrier to travel. The airtime from Bogota to Medellin, the second-largest city in Colombia, is 30 minutes; by highway, the same trip takes 10 to 12 hours. Because of the physical isolation, each center has a different style of living and population characteristics; even the climates are different. From a marketing view, the four centers constitute four different markets.[5]

Other regions of the world that have extreme topographic and climatic variations are China, Russia, India, and Canada, each of which has formidable physical and/or climatic conditions within its borders. In Canada, one observer notes that vast distances and extreme winter weather have a major influence on distribution. Reorder points and safety stock levels must be higher than normally expected for given inventories because large cities such as Montreal can be isolated suddenly and completely by heavy snowfalls.[6] At such times, delivery delays of three to four days are common. Additionally, shipment delays can result from a shortage of insulated railcars and trucks, and the high cost of heating railcars on long hauls in extreme weather can add 10 percent or more to a company's freight bill. Imagine the formidable problems of appraising market potential or devising a marketing mix that would successfully reconcile the diversities in such situations.

The effect of natural barriers on market development is also important. Because of the ease of distribution, coastal cities or cities situated on navigable waterways are more likely to be trading centers than are landlocked cities; cities not near natural physical transportation routes generally are isolated from one another. Consequently, natural barriers rather than actual miles may dictate distribution points. For example, in discussing distribution in Africa, one marketer pointed out that a shipment from Mombasa on the Kenya east coast to Freetown on the bulge of West Africa could require more time than a shipment from New York or London to Kenya over established freight routes.

Contrast that to more economically advanced countries where formidable mountain barriers have been overcome. A case in point is the 7.2-mile tunnel that cuts through the base of Mont Blanc in the Alps. This highway tunnel brings Rome and Paris 125 miles closer and provides a year-round route of only 170 miles between Geneva and Turin. Before the tunnel opened, it was a trip of nearly 500 miles when snow closed the highway over the Alps.

In some cases countries have preserved physical barriers as protection from potential enemies; in other cases, governments have been reluctant to eliminate barriers in order to preserve economic isolation. Such attitudes are yielding to the desire many countries have to participate in economic opportunities and challenges of the global marketplace. Three major projects completed or under way illustrate how globalization has caused old attitudes to be reexamined: the Eurotunnel and Oresund Link in Europe and the Colonia Bridge in South America.

After more than 200 years of speculation, a tunnel under the English Channel between Britain and France was officially opened in 1994. Historically, the British had resisted a tunnel; they did not trust the French or any other European country and saw the English Channel as protection. When they became members of the European Community, however, economic reality meant that a tunnel had to be built. The Eurotunnel or

---

   [4] This discussion is based in part on a monograph of Herbert V. Prochnow, "Economic, Political, and Social Trends in Latin America" (Chicago: First National Bank of Chicago, n.d.).

   [5] For more information on Latin America and its countries visit **http://www.latinsynergy.org**, the Latin American Alliance home page.

   [6] Peter M. Banting, et al., "Canadian Distribution Is Different," *International Journal of Physical Distribution*, February 1972, p. 76.

Chunnel, as it is sometimes called, has had its financial problems but it carries over 50 percent of London to Paris passenger traffic[7] and freight shipments have increased substantially since its opening.[8]

An agreement between Sweden and Denmark to build a bridge and tunnel across the Baltic Strait to Continental Europe also reflects a change away from isolation to closer economic ties. The 10-mile-long Oresund Link, to be completed in 2000, will accommodate freight and high-speed passenger trains and a four-lane motorway. When completed, a five-hour trip between Copenhagen and Aarhus, Denmark, will be reduced to two and one half-hours. Ultimately, it will be possible to drive from Lapland in northernmost Scandinavia to Calabria in southern Italy. Politically the agreement is seen as a powerful, tangible symbol that these nations are ending their political isolation from the rest of Europe and are linking themselves economically to the Continent's future and membership in the European Community.[9]

After 50 years of discussion, commitment to Mercosur[10] has resulted in an agreement to build the Colonia Bridge between Argentina and Uruguay. When completed in 1999 it will be the longest bridge in the world (a span of 41 km) and decrease the overall driving distance between Buenos Aires and Montevideo from 342 miles to 154 miles. Shipping costs for all member countries are expected to drop substantially.[11]

Geographic hurdles have a direct effect on a country's economy, markets, and the related activities of communication and distribution. Furthermore, there are indirect effects on its society and culture that are ultimately reflected in market behavior. Europe and North America have been blessed with stronger economies and relatively favorable geographical makeup compared to countries in parts of Asia, Latin America, or Africa. Consequently it has been easier for industrialized nations to overcome geographic obstacles than for other, less fortunate areas.

Geography, Nature, and Economic Growth

Always on the slim margin between subsistence and disaster, less-privileged countries suffer disproportionately from natural and human-assisted catastrophes. Climate and topography coupled with civil wars, poor environmental policies, and natural disasters push these countries further into economic stagnation. Without irrigation and water management, they are afflicted by droughts, floods, soil erosion, and creeping deserts, which reduce the long-term fertility of the land. Population increases, deforestation, and overgrazing intensify the impact of drought and lead to malnutrition and ill health, further undermining their ability to solve their problems.[12] Cyclones cannot be prevented, nor inadequate rainfall, but there are means to control their effects. Unfortunately, each disaster seems to push these countries further away from effective solutions. Countries that suffer the most from major calamities are among the poorest in the world. Many have neither the capital nor the technical ability to minimize the effects of natural phenomena; they are at the mercy of nature.

As countries prosper and expand their economies, natural barriers are overcome. Tunnels are dug, bridges and dams built, all in an effort to control or to adapt to climate,

---

[7] Charles Batchelor, "Eurostar: London & Continental Moves towards Breakeven," *Financial Times,* July 9, 1997, p. 3.

[8] "Letter from the Channel Tunnel, The Disorient Express," *The Economist,* March 15, 1997, p. 37.

[9] Martha Andersson, "Ancient Nordic Rivals Link Up in Bridge Project," *The Christian Science Monitor,* April 10, 1997, p. 7.

[10] Mercosur (Southern Cone Common Market) is the common market agreement among Argentina, Brazil, Paraguay, and Uruguay.

[11] "Mercosur's Big Bridge," *Business Latin America,* April 7, 1997, p. 6.

[12] For insights into geography and economic development, see Paul Krugman, *Development, Geography & Economic Theory (Ohlin Series)* (Philadelphia: MIT Press, 1997).

CROSSING BORDERS 3–2

Climate and Success

A major food processing company had production problems after it built a pineapple cannery at the delta of a river in Mexico. It built the pineapple plantation upstream and planned to barge the ripe fruit downstream for canning, load them directly on ocean liners, and ship them to the company's various markets. When the pineapples were ripe, however, the company found itself in trouble: crop maturity coincided with the flood stage of the river. The current in the river during this period was far too strong to permit the backhauling of barges upstream; the plan for transporting the fruit on barges could not be implemented. With no alternative means of transport, the company was forced to close the operation. The new equipment was sold for 5 percent of original cost to a Mexican group that immediately relocated the cannery. A seemingly simple, harmless oversight of weather and navigation conditions was the primary cause for major losses to the company.

Source: David A. Ricks, *Blunders in International Business* (Cambridge, Mass.: Blackwell Publishers, 1993), p. 16.

topography, and the recurring extremes of nature. Humankind has been reasonably successful in overcoming or minimizing the effects of geographical barriers and natural disasters, but as they do they must contend with problems of their own making. The construction of dams is a good example of how an attempt to harness nature for good has its bad side. To a developing country, dams are considered a cost-effective solution to a host of problems. Dams create electricity, help control floods, provide water for irrigation during dry periods, and can be a rich source of fish. However, there are side effects; dams displace people—the Three Gorges dam in China will displace 1.3 million people[13]—and silt that ultimately clogs the reservoir is no longer carried downstream to replenish the soil and add nutrients.[14] In short, the costs of these projects often outweigh the benefits.

As the global rush toward industrialization and economic growth accelerates, environmental issues become more apparent. Disrupting ecosystems, relocation of people, inadequate hazardous waste management, and industrial pollution are all problems that must be addressed by the industrialized world and those seeking economic development.[15] The problems are mostly by-products of processes that have contributed significantly to economic development and improved life-styles. During the decade of the 1990s, there has been considerable effort on the part of governments and industry to develop better ways to control nature and to allow industry to grow while protecting the environment.[16]

Social Responsibility and Environmental Management

The 1990s have been called the "Decade of the Environment," in that nations, companies, and people reached a consensus: Environmental protection is not an optional extra—it is

---

[13] "The Human Debris of China's Mega-Dams," *World Press Review,* August 1997, p. 7.

[14] "Dambuilders and Dambusters," *The Economist,* April 19, 1997, p. 6.

[15] See "Is Economic Growth Good for the Environment?" *London Business School Economic Outlook,* January 2, 1997, p. 18, for an interesting discussion on the effects of economic growth on the environment—is it good or bad?

[16] Visit **http://www.gemi.org** for information on *Global Environmental Management Initiative,* an organization of 22 U.S. multinational companies dedicated to environmental protection.

One of the side effects of rapid industrial growth that has brought prosperity to Asia is pollution. With every uptick in industrial production comes a surge in smoke and hazardous waste and with every point in GDP growth comes an almost precisely predictable increase in garbage. (Adrian Bradshaw/SABA)

an essential part of the complex process of doing business.[17] Many view the problem as a global issue rather than a national issue and one that poses common threats to humankind and thus cannot be addressed by nations in isolation.[18] Of special concern to governments and businesses are ways to stem the tide of pollution and to clean up decades of neglect.

Companies looking to build manufacturing plants in countries with more liberal pollution regulations than they have at home are finding that regulations everywhere have gotten stricter. Many Asian governments are drafting new regulations and enforcing existing ones.[19] A strong motivator for Asia and the rest of the world is the realization that pollution is on the verge of getting completely out of control. According to one report, Asia has the most heavily polluted cities, and its rivers and lakes are among the world's most contaminated. An examination of rivers, lakes, and reservoirs in China revealed that toxic substances polluted 21 percent and that 16 percent of the rivers were seriously polluted with excrement.[20]

One of the revelations after Eastern Europe became independent was the seriousness of pollution in those countries. Described as the world's greatest polluter, the countries of Eastern Europe have a long, hard road to bring their environment under control. Most factories are antiquated, use the cheapest and most polluting fuels, and have few laws to control pollution. The list of environmental problems is overwhelming: nitrates contaminate Bulgaria's drinking water; and sewage, oil, and industrial waste pollutes the Black Sea.[21] In Hungary, the Danube River runs black with industrial and municipal wastes, and drinking water in the south is seriously contaminated with arsenic. Neither Europe nor the rest of the industrialized world is free of environmental damage. Rivers are polluted and the atmosphere in many major urban areas is far from clean (e.g., Los Angeles, Denver, and Mexico City to mention a few).

---

[17] Bill L. Long, "Environmental Regulation: The Third Generation," *The OECD Observer,* June 1, 1997, pp. 14–18.

[18] Visit **http://www.webdirectory.com** for "Amazing Environmental Organization Web Directory," a search engine for environmental subjects.

[19] "Asia's Environmental Quality Deteriorates: ADB," *Xinhua News Agency,* May 11, 1997.

[20] Susan Moffat, "Asia Stinks," *Fortune,* December 9, 1996, p. 64.

[21] "Russia Black Sea Faces Pollution Disaster," *ITAR-TASS* news agency, January 27, 1997.

CROSSING BORDERS 3–3

Listen Up Los Angeles: Don't Like the Smog? Move the Mountain

One of the characteristics that distinguishes humankind from the rest of the animal kingdom is the ability to devise ways to overcome the harshness of the environment. But what about that which it creates? Smog is a well-known human-created problem the world over. Mention Los Angeles or Mexico City and the first thing that comes to mind is smog. One of the unfortunate "rewards" of economic growth is pollution. Lanzhou, China, is no exception. Surrounded by mountains, Lanzhou has become one of the world's worst smog traps after four decades of unplanned industrialization.

When Mr. Zhu Qihua left 15 years ago to seek his fortune, Lanzhou was a pristine village. After earning his fortune ($12 million), Mr. Zhu wants his legacy to be that he cleaned up the smog. His method? Level Big Green Mountain and let fresh air sweep the valley clean. There are skeptics but that doesn't stop the determined Mr. Zhu.

Mr. Zhu's project is underway and the mountain is shrinking. Ten thousand gallons of water a day flows up and down the mountain. First, the water is pumped up the mountain to a reservoir and then the water is released in a small stream about a yard wide that zigzags down the mountain. Workers hack at the crumbling soil allowing it to be carried away by the water. By Mr. Zhu's calculations, a quart of water can carry 1.3 cubic yards of dirt down the slope at a cost of 20 cents, a fraction of the cost of moving 3.9 million cubic yards of mountain by truck. "As long as we keep the water full of soil, we will be on schedule and have the mountain moved in two years," says Mr. Zhu.

So Los Angeles, there is a solution—Oh! but then you also have a water problem. Maybe you should consider a giant fan on top of the mountain or a fan hung from a helium balloon—two of the other proposals suggested by visionaries in Lanzhou before Mr. Zhu's project got under way.

Reprinted by permission from *The Wall Street Journal,* © 1997 Dow Jones & Company, Inc. All Rights Reserved Worldwide.

The very process of controlling industrial wastes leads to another and, perhaps equally critical issue: the disposal of hazardous waste, a by-product of pollution controls. Estimates of hazardous wastes collected annually exceed 300 million tons; the critical issue is disposal that does not move the problem elsewhere.[22]

The export of hazardous wastes by developed countries to lesser-developed nations has ethical implications and environmental consequences. Countries finding it more difficult to dispose of wastes at home are seeking countries willing to assume the burden of disposal. Waste disposal is legal in some developing countries as governments seek the revenues that are generated by offering sites for waste disposal. In other cases, illegal dumping is done clandestinely, often without proper protection for those who unknowingly come in contact with the poisons. Countries are beginning to close their borders to legal dumping and imposing penalties for illegal dumping. China became a target dumping ground after many countries in Latin America and Asia closed their borders to dumping. But now China also has taken steps to control the "invasion of foreign garbage."[23] A 1992 treaty among members of the Basel Convention that required prior approval before dumping could occur was

---

[22] Dian Turnheim, "Containing Toxic Waste," *The OECD Observer,* June 1997, p. 46.

[23] "China-Environment: No More Dumping in Our Backyard Says Beijing," *Inter Press Service English News Wire,* March 21, 1997.

revised in 1995 to a total ban on the export of hazardous wastes by developed nations starting in 1998.[24] The influence and leadership provided by this treaty are reflected in a broad awareness of pollution problems by businesses and people in general.[25]

Governments, organizations, and businesses are becoming increasingly concerned with the social responsibility and ethical issues surrounding the problem of maintaining economic growth and the protection of the environment for future generations.[26] The Organization for Economic Cooperation and Development (OECD), the United Nations, the European Community, and international activist groups are undertaking programs to strengthen environmental policies. The issue that concerns all is, can economic development and protection for the environment co-exist? *Sustainable development,* a joint approach among those (governments, businesses, environmentalists, and others) who seek economic growth with "wise resource management, equitable distribution of benefits and reduction of negative efforts on people and the environment from the process of economic growth," is the concept that guides many governments and multinational companies today. The United Nations' conference on Environment and Development in 1992 (also known as the Rio Summit or Earth Summit) resulted in a set of propositions that encompass the concept of sustainable development and serve as a foundation for practice. The key propositions are:[27]

- There is a crucial and potentially positive link between economic development and the environment.
- The costs of inappropriate economic policies on the environment are very high.
- Addressing environmental problems requires that poverty be reduced.
- Economic growth must be guided by prices that incorporate environmental values.
- Since environmental problems pay no respect to borders, global and regional collaboration is sometimes needed to complement national and regional actions.

Although these principles serve as a solid base, companies faulted them for not being more specific about taking into account the interests of shareholders. Thus, the various interpretations by multinationals incorporate specific reference to the importance of shareholders to the long-term survival of the company. Typical of these interpretations is a multinational company whose statement includes the phrase, "The realization of competitive advantage by serving the needs of our shareholders, employees, customers, and the residents of local communities, while simultaneously maintaining the integrity of the environment for future generations."[28] More and more companies are embracing the idea of sustainable development as a "win-win" opportunity.[29] Responsibility for protecting the environment does not rest solely with governments, businesses, or activist groups, however; each citizen has a social and moral responsibility to include environmental protection among his or her highest goals.[30]

---

[24] Asahi Shimbun, "Special: Major Global Environmental Issues," *Asahi Evening News,* June 23,1997.

[25] See Geoffrey Dobilas and Alan MacPherson, "Environmental Regulation and International Sourcing Policies of Multinational Firms," *Growth and Change (Special Issue: Industry and the Environment),* Winter 1997, pp. 7–24, for a study on how MNC selection of suppliers is affected by environmental standards.

[26] Ismail Serageldin, "Sustainable Development: From Theory to Practice," *Finance & Development,* December 1996, p. 3.

[27] Andrew Steer, "Ten Principles of the New Environmentalism," *Finance & Development,* December 1996, pp. 4–6.

[28] Blair W. Feltmate, "Making Sustainable Development a Corporate Reality," *CMA—the Management Accounting Magazine,* March 1, 1997, p. 9.

[29] Kent Gilges, "Sustainable Development: Beyond the Greenwash," *Chemical Engineering,* April 1, 1997, pp. 681–801.

[30] For a discussion of environmental strategies by Volvo, Polaroid, and Procter & Gamble see James Maxwell, Sandra Rothenberg, Forrest Briscoe, and Alfred Marcus, "Green Schemes: Corporate Environmental Strategies and Their Implementation," *California Management Review,* March 22, 1997, p. 118.

Resources

The availability of minerals and the ability to generate energy are the foundations of modern technology. The location of the earth's resources, as well as the available sources of energy, are geographic accidents, and the world's nations are not equally endowed, nor does a nation's demand for a particular mineral or energy source necessarily coincide with domestic supply.

Energy is necessary to power the machinery of modern production and to extract and process the resources necessary to produce the goods of economic prosperity. In much of the underdeveloped world, human labor provides the preponderance of energy. The principal supplements to human energy are animals, wood, fossil fuel, nuclear power, and to a lesser and more experimental extent, the ocean's tides, geothermal power, and the sun. Of all the energy sources, petroleum usage is increasing most rapidly because of its versatility and the ease with which it is stored and transported.

Many countries that were self-sufficient during much of their early economic growth have become net importers of petroleum during the past 25 years and continue to become increasingly dependent on foreign sources. A spectacular example is the United States, which was almost completely self-sufficient until 1942, became a major importer by 1950, and between 1973 and 1995 increased its dependency from 36 percent to over 50 percent of its annual requirements.[31] Exhibit 3–1 compares U.S. domestic energy consumption and production. The area between the curves reflects the growth of imports, particularly petroleum, to meet increasing energy needs—the all-time high was reached by the mid-1990s. If present rates of consumption continue, predictions are that the United States will be importing over 70 percent of its needs by the early 2000s.[32]

Since World War II, concern for the limitless availability of seemingly inexhaustible supplies has become a prominent factor. The dramatic increase in economic growth in the industrialized world and the push for industrialization in the remaining world has put tremendous pressure on the earth's energy resources. This rapid change to market-driven economies and increasing reliance on petroleum supplies from areas of political instability in two major petroleum exporting regions—the Middle East and the former Soviet Union—creates a global interdependence of energy resources. This means that political upheavals and/or price changes will have a profound impact on the economies of the industrialized and industrializing countries. Exhibit 3–2 shows the world dependence on OPEC oil between 1973 and 2010. The higher the index values the greater the probability of experiencing large price increases and the greater the impact on the economy.

As an environmental consideration in world marketing, the location, quality, and availability of resources will affect the pattern of world economic development and trade for at least the remainder of the century. This factor must be weighed carefully by astute international marketers in making worldwide international investment decisions. In addition to the raw materials of industrialization, there must be an available and economically feasible energy supply to successfully transform resources into usable products.

Because of the great disparity in the location of the earth's resources, there is world trade between those who do not have all they need and those who have more than they need and are willing to sell. Importers of most of the resources are industrial nations with insufficient domestic supplies. Aluminum is a good example; Australia, Guinea, and Brazil account for over 65 percent of the world's reserves, and one country, the United States, consumes 35 percent of all aluminum produced. As the global demand

---

[31] Matthew L. Wald, "U.S. Dependence on Imported Oil Grows," *The New York Times,* August 11, 1997, p. B-12.

[32] "The USGS World Energy Program," *USGS Fact Sheet FS-007-97.*

Exhibit 3–1   United States Consumption and Production of Energy—1950–1995

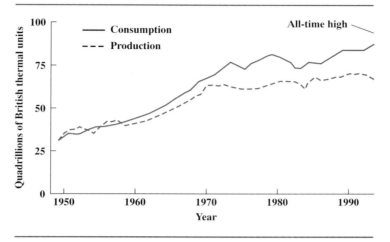

Exhibit 3–2   World Dependence on OPEC Oil between 1973 and 2010*

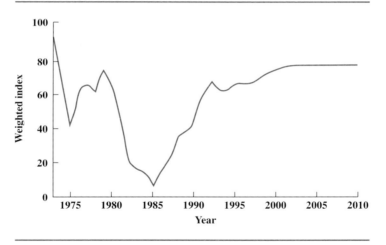

* The higher the index value, the greater the probability of experiencing large price increases and the greater the impact on the economy.

"The USGS World Energy Program," *USGS Fact Sheet FS-007-97.*

for resources intensifies and prices rise, resources will continue to increase in importance among the uncontrollable elements of the international marketer's decisions.

World Population Trends

Current population, rural/urban population distribution, rates of growth, age levels, and population growth controls help determine today's demand for various categories of goods. While not the only determinant, the existence of sheer numbers of people is significant in appraising potential consumer demand. Changes in the composition and distribution of population among the world's countries will profoundly affect future demand.

CROSSING BORDERS 3-4

How Many Energy Robots Work for You?

A healthy, hard-working person can produce just enough energy to keep a 100-watt bulb burning. This may seem unimportant, but it is a humbling reminder that muscle power is really very puny. Supplementary energy now exceeds muscle energy in every part of our lives, from food production to recreation. It is like a gang of silent "energy robots" who labor continually and uncomplainingly to feed, clothe, and maintain us. The energy comes, of course, from mineral resources such as coal, oil, and uranium, not from real robots, but everyone on the earth now has energy robots. . . . In India the total supplementary energy produced is equivalent to the work of 15 energy robots, each working an eight-hour day, for every man, woman, and child. In South America everyone has approximately 30 energy robots; in Japan, 75; Russia, 120; Europe, 150; and in the United States and Canada, a huge 300. The concept of energy robots demonstrates how utterly dependent the world has become on mineral resources. If the energy robots were to strike (which means if the supplies ran out), the world's peoples could not keep themselves alive and healthy. Reverting to muscle power alone would bring starvation, famine, and pestilence. Nature would quickly reduce the population.

Source: Brian J. Skinner, *Earth Resources,* 2d ed. 1976, pp. 3–4. Reprinted by permission of Prentice Hall, Inc., Englewood Cliffs, NJ.

Recent estimates indicate there are over 5.7 billion people in the world, of whom 80 percent are in less-developed regions. Further, Exhibit 3–3 shows that 83 percent of the population will be concentrated in less-developed regions by 2015 and, if growth rates continue, 88 percent by 2050. Barring some unforeseen change in growth rates, these estimates in the numbers of people who will live in less-developed regions in the future should be reasonably accurate.

Rapid population increases without commensurate economic development creates a number of problems. Among the most pressing are the numbers of new jobs needed to accommodate the flood of people entering the labor pool. In the 1970s, 200 million people entered the labor market in the Third World. The International Labor Organization (ILO) estimates that 1.2 billion jobs must be created worldwide by 2025 to accommodate new entrants. Further, most of the new jobs will need to be created in urban areas where most of the population will reside.[33]

The mismatch between population growth and economic growth is a major problem to be faced in the next century. Most of the population increases are occurring in the developing world while most of the jobs are being created in the developed world. The vast majority of new workers—500 to 700 million—will be found in developing countries while the majority of jobs will be found in the industrialized world. Even though it is true that cheap labor costs, brought on in part by vast labor pools in less-developed countries, attract labor-intensive manufacturers from higher-cost industrialized countries, the number of new jobs created will not be sufficient to absorb the projected population growth.

Rural/Urban Shifts. A relatively recent phenomenon is a pronounced shift of the world's population from rural to urban areas. In the early 1800s, less than 3.5 percent of

---

[33] "Employment and Economic Reform in Developing Countries" *World Employment 1996/97* (Geneva: International Labour Office,1996). For other sources of information from the International Labour Office, visit **http://www.ilo.org**.

EXHIBIT 3–3   **World Population by Region 1996–2050**
Life Expectancy at Birth 1990–1995 (millions)

Regions	1996	2015	2050	Life Expectancy at Birth 1990–1995
World	5,768	7,286	9,367	64
More-developed regions*	1,175	1,214	1,162	74
Less-developed regions†	4,593	6,072	8,205	62
Least-developed countries‡	595	945	1,632	50
Africa	739	1,181	2,046	52
Asia	3,488	4,381	5,443	65
Europe	729	717	638	73
Latin America	484	625	810	68
Northern America	299	345	384	76
Oceania	29	37	46	73

* More-developed regions comprise all regions of Europe and Northern America, Australia–New Zealand, and Japan.

† Less-developed countries comprise all regions of Africa, Asia (excluding Japan) and Latin America, and the regions of Melanesia, Micronesia, and Polynesia.

‡ Least-developed countries as defined by the United Nations General Assembly include 48 countries of which 33 are in Africa, 9 in Asia, 1 in Latin America, and 5 in Oceania. They are included in less-developed regions.

Source: Compiled from "World Population—1996," United Nations Population Division, Department of Economic and Social Information and Policy Analysis, 1997 (**http://www.undp.org/popin/** select World Population 1996).

the world's people were living in cities of 20,000 or more and less than 2 percent in cities of 100,000 or more; today, more than 40 percent of the world's people are urbanites and the trend is accelerating.

By 2025, it is estimated that more than 60 percent of the world's population will live in urban areas (see Exhibit 3–4), and at least 27 cities will have populations of 10 million or more, 23 of which will be in the less-developed regions.[34] Tokyo has already overtaken Mexico City as the largest city on Earth with a population of 26 million, a jump of almost 8 million since 1990.

Migration from rural to urban areas is largely a result of a desire for greater access to sources of education, health care, and improved job opportunities. Once in the city, perhaps three out of four migrants make economic gains. Family income of a manual worker in urban Brazil is almost five times that of a farm laborer in a rural area.

Although migrants experience some relative improvement in their living standards, intense urban growth without investment in services eventually leads to profound problems. Slums populated with unskilled workers living hand to mouth put excessive pressure on sanitation systems, water supplies, and other social services. At some point, the disadvantages of unregulated urban growth begin to outweigh the advantages for all concerned.[35]

Consider conditions that exist in Mexico City today. Over 14,000 tons of garbage are produced every day but only 8,000 tons are processed; the rest is dumped in landfills or left to rot in the open. More than 2 million families have no running water or sewage facilities in their homes. Sewage facilities are so overtaxed that tons of wastes are left in gutters or vacant lots where it dries and is blown into the atmosphere. The problem is so severe that one Mexico City newspaper reported, "If fecal matter were fluorescent, the city wouldn't need lights."[36]

Smog, garbage, and pollution are not the only major problems facing Mexico City; local water supplies are nearly exhausted as well. Water consumption from all sources is

[34] Gerard Piel, "The Urbanization of Poverty Worldwide," *Challenge,* January 11, 1997, p. 7.
[35] Eugene Linden, "The Exploding Cities of the Developing World," *Foreign Affairs,* January 1996, p. 52.
[36] "Mexico: Running on Empty," *Business Latin America,* March 31, 1997, p. 3.

Exhibit 3-4   **Urban–Rural Population and Percentage Urban 1994–2025 (Population—millions)**

Regions	Urban		Rural		Percent urban	
	1994	*2025*	*1994*	*2025*	*1994*	*2025*
World	2,520	5,065	3,109	3,229	44.8	61.1
More-developed regions*	868	1,040	295	198	74.7	84.0
Less-developed regions†	1,653	4,025	2,814	3,031	37.0	57.0
Least-developed countries‡	122	506	437	657	21.9	43.5
Africa	240	804	469	692	33.8	53.8
Asia	1,159	2,718	2,244	2,242	34.1	54.8
Europe	532	598	194	120	73.3	83.2
Latin America	349	601	125	109	73.7	84.7
Northern America	221	313	69	56	76.1	84.8
Oceania	20	31	8	10	70.3	74.9

* More-developed regions comprise all regions of Europe and Northern America, Australia–NewZealand, and Japan.

† Less-developed countries comprise all regions of Africa, Asia (excluding Japan) and Latin America, and the regions of Melanesia, Micronesia, and Polynesia.

‡ Least-developed countries as defined by the United Nations General Assembly include 48 countries of which 33 are in Africa, 9 in Asia, 1 in Latin America, and 5 in Oceania. They are included in the less-developed regions.

Source: Compiled from "World Urbanization Prospects: The 1994 Revisions," United Nations Population Division, Department of Economic and Social Information and Policy Analysis, 1997 (**http://www.undp.org/popin/** select World Population 1996).

about 16,000 gallons per second while the underground aquifers are producing only 2,640 gallons per second. Water has to be imported from hundreds of miles away and pumped from an elevation of 3,600 feet to Mexico City's elevation of 7,440 feet.[37] This is a grim picture of a city that is at the same time one of the most beautiful and sophisticated in Latin America. Such problems are not unique to Mexico; throughout the developing world, poor sanitation and inadequate water supplies are consequences of runaway population growth.

Many political scientists fear that as we approach the next century the bulging cities will become fertile fields for social unrest unless conditions in urban areas are improved. Prospects for improvement are not encouraging because most of the growth will take place in developing countries already economically strained. Further, there is insufficient progress in controlling birthrates in the fastest-growing countries.[38]

Controlling Population Growth.   Faced with the ominous consequences of the population explosion, it would seem logical for countries to take appropriate steps to reduce growth to manageable rates, but procreation is one of the most culturally sensitive uncontrollables. Economics, self-esteem, religion, politics, and education all play a critical role in attitudes about family size.

The prerequisites to population control are adequate incomes, higher literacy levels, education for women, universal access to health care, family planning, improved nutrition, and, perhaps most important, a change in basic cultural beliefs toward the importance of large families. Unfortunately, progress in providing improved conditions and changing beliefs is hampered by the increasingly heavy demand placed on institutions responsible for change and improvement. India's population will exceed that of China by 2050 unless its fertility rate can be reduced. India's population was once fairly stable but with improved health conditions resulting in lower infant mortality, population has soared. The government's attempts to institute change has been hampered by a variety

[37] "Mexico City's Watery Grave," *Business Latin America,* March 24, 1997, p. 1.
[38] "The Human Flood That Could Swamp India," *Business Week,* June 16, 1997, p. 58.

of factors, including slow change in cultural norms and political ineptitude. In those states with the highest birth rates, local administrators provide little or no leadership in providing for primary education and access to family planning.[39]

In many cultures, the prestige of a man, whether alive or dead, depends on the number of his progeny, and a family's only wealth is its children. Such feelings are strong. When she was Prime Minister of India Mrs. Indira Gandhi found out how strong when she attempted mass forced sterilization of males: She was defeated in a subsequent election.[40]

Many religions discourage or ban family planning and thus serve as a deterrent to control. Nigeria has a strong Muslim tradition in the north and a strong Roman Catholic tradition in the east, and both faiths favor large families. Most traditional religions in Africa encourage large families; in fact, the principal deity for many is the goddess of land and fertility.

Population control is often a political issue as well. Overpopulation and the resulting problems have been labeled by some as an imperialist myth to support a devious plot by rich countries to keep Third World population down and maintain the developed world's dominance of the globe. Instead of seeking ways to reduce population growth, some politicians encourage growth as the most vital asset of poor countries. As long as such attitudes prevail, it will be extremely difficult, if not impossible, to control population.

Governments try to control explosive birthrates by encouraging birth control. China has the strictest policy: only one child is allowed per couple except in rural areas where, if the first child is female, a second child is permitted. The program has been moderately successful except in rural areas, where the desire for more than one child is still strong.[41] Experience tells us that real change in population control comes with economic growth. A decline in the fertility rate is a function of economic prosperity. A recent shift in population growth has occurred in Spain, where families have gone from having six or more children to one of the lowest birth rates in Europe, an average of 1.24 per woman. Several factors are behind this change, including the opportunity for more women to have meaningful careers and society's distancing from the Roman Catholic Church and its ban on contraception.[42] Growing industrialization, urbanization, universal literacy, and improved social status for women and a decline in infant mortality all contributed to the lowering of birth rates in Europe and the United States.[43]

Developed-World Population Decline.   While the developing world faces a rapidly growing population, it is estimated that the industrialized world's population will decline. Birthrates in Western Europe and Japan have been decreasing since the early or mid-1960s; more women are choosing careers instead of children, and many working couples are electing to remain childless. As a result of these and other contemporary factors, population growth in many countries has dropped below the rate necessary to maintain present levels. The populations of France, Sweden, Switzerland, and Belgium are all expected to drop within a few years. Austria, Denmark, Germany, Japan, and several other nations are now at about zero population growth and probably will slip to the minus side in another decade. Recent reports by the Japanese government indicate that Japan's birthrate has dropped to 1.46 births per female, which is below the 2.08 presumed necessary to maintain a nation's population. Japan's rural areas have steadily lost young people to the cities and, to counteract the trend, governments in rural prefectures are giving mothers "Congratulatory Birth Money"—up to 3 million yen ($30,400)—to

---

[39] "India's Growing Pains," *The Economist,* February 27, 1997, p. 53.

[40] Martin Wold, "Progress: Democracy for the Few," *Financial Times,* August 1, 1997, p. 6.

[41] Renee Schoof, "China Tries to Ease Tensions over Policy Limiting Family Size," *Associated Press,* July 5, 1997.

[42] "Spaniards Having Fewest Kids," *Associated Press,* July 5, 1997.

[43] Daniel J. Ncayiyana, "Population Control? Bah, Humbug!" *The Lancet,* May 24, 1997, p. 1540.

EXHIBIT 3-5   Percentage of World Population—by Age Group

Regions	Under Age 15	65 or Older	Density (% pop per sq. km)
World	32	7	43
More-developed regions*	19	14	22
Less-developed regions†	35	5	55
Least-developed countries‡	45	3	29
Africa	46	3	24
Asia	32	5	110
Europe	19	14	32
Latin America	33	5	24
Northern America	22	13	14
Oceania	26	10	3

* More-developed regions comprise all regions of Europe and Northern America, Australia–New Zealand, and Japan.

† Less-developed countries comprise all regions of Africa, Asia (excluding Japan) and Latin America, and the regions of Melanesia, Micronesia, and Polynesia.

‡ Least-developed countries as defined by the United Nations General Assembly include 48 countries of which 33 are in Africa, 9 in Asia, 1 in Latin America, and 5 in Oceania. They are included in less-developed regions.

Source: Compiled from "World Population—1996," United Nations Population Division, Department of Economic and Social Information and Policy Analysis, 1997 (**http://www.undp.org/popin/** select World Population 1996).

have a seventh child. The national government gives a $5,000 award for the third and fourth child.[44]

Europe, Japan, and the United States have special problems because of the increasing percentage of elderly people who must be supported by shrinking numbers of active workers.[45] The elderly require higher government outlays for health care and hospitals, special housing and nursing homes, and pension and welfare assistance, but the workforce that supports these costs is dwindling. In addition, a shortage of skilled workers is anticipated in these countries because of the decreasing population. The part of the world with the largest portion of people over 65 is also the part of the world with the fewest number of people under age 15 (Exhibit 3–5).

The trends of increasing population in the developing world with substantial shifts from rural to urban areas, and declining birthrates in the industrialized world will have profound effects on the state of world business and world economic conditions well into the next century.

World Trade Routes

Trade routes bind the world together, minimizing distance, natural barriers, lack of resources, and the fundamental differences between peoples and economies. As long as one group of people in the world wants something another group somewhere else has and there is a means of travel between the two, there is trade. Early trade routes were overland; later came sea routes and, finally, air routes to connect countries. One of the better known ancient overland trade routes between east Asia and Europe, known as the "Silk Road," is regaining its importance as a major trade route now that the Soviet Union is no longer a block between the West and Central Asia.[46] The mariners of Carthage, a Phoenician colony on the North African coast, roamed the Mediterranean

---

[44] "The Baby Shortage," *World Press Review,* August 1997, p. 35.

[45] "The Aging of Japan," *World Press Review,* August 1997, pp. 34–35.

[46] William Spain, "Turkey Carving a New Silk Road: Tenacity Tested in Region That Bridges Markets in Asia, Europe" *Advertising Age International,* March 1, 1997.

CROSSING BORDERS 3–5

Where Have All the Women Gone?

Three converging issues in China have the potential of causing a serious gender imbalance by the year 2000: Issue 1—China, the world's most populous country, has a strict one-child policy to curb population growth; Issue 2—Traditional values dictate male superiority and a definite parental preference for boys; and Issue 3—Prenatal scanning allows women to discover the sex of their fetuses and thereby abort unwanted female fetuses.

As a consequence, Chinese statisticians have begun to forecast a big marriage gap for the generation born in the late 1980s and early 1990s. In 1990, China recorded 113.8 male births for every 100 female births, far higher than the natural ratio of 106 to 100. In rural areas where parental preference for boys is especially strong, newborn boys outnumber girls by an average of 144.6 to 100. In one rural township the ratio was reported to be 163.8 to 100.

Not only will there be a gender mismatch after the year 2000, but there may also be a social mismatch since most of the men will be peasants with little education, while most of the women will live in cities and more likely have high school or college degrees. In China, men who do physical labor are least attractive as mates, while women who labor with their minds are least popular.

One solution has been to put female babies up for adoption. China has become the top provider of babies for international adoption by Americans. Over 1,000 reside in the New York area alone. They are almost all girls, the casualties of China's one-child policy.

Sources: Adapted from "Sex Determination before Birth," Reuters News Service, May 3, 1994; "Seven Times as Many Men," AP News Service, March 31, 1994; and "Adopted Chinese Girls in New York: Noticing and Being Noticed," *The New York Times,* August 18, 1997.

---

trading wine, dried fish, fabrics, and other goods as far as Spain, Britain, and perhaps even to the Americas.[47] Whether the Phoenicians' trade routes actually extended to the Americas is speculative but in 1571 a trade route was established between Spain, South America, and China. The Spanish empire founded the city of Manila in the Philippines to receive its silver-laden galleons bound for China. On the return trip the ship's cargo of silk and other Chinese goods would be off-loaded in Mexico, carried overland to the Atlantic, and put on Spanish ships to Spain. By 1571, this trade route linked Asia with the Americas, Europe, and Africa—and each with the other.[48]

Trade routes represent the attempts of countries to overcome economic and social imbalances created in part by the influence of geography. Today the major world trade routes, as Exhibit 3–6 illustrates, are among the most industrialized countries of the world: Europe, North America, and Japan.

A careful comparison among world population figures in Exhibit 3–6, Triad trade figures in Exhibit 3–6, and world trade figures in Exhibit 3–7 illustrates how small a percentage of the world's land mass and population account for the majority of trade. It is no surprise that the major sea-lanes and the most developed highway and rail systems link these major trade areas. The more economically developed a country is, the better developed the surface transportation infrastructure is to support trade.

---

[47] Charles Leroux, "Caribbean Cruise Carthaginians; Trade Routes May Have Included the Americas," *Chicago Tribune,* December 26, 1996.

[48] Marcus W. Brauchli, "Echoes of the Past," *The Wall Street Journal,* September 26, 1996, p. R24.

EXHIBIT 3–6   The Triad: Trade between the United States and Canada, the European Community, and Japan, 1995 ($ billions)

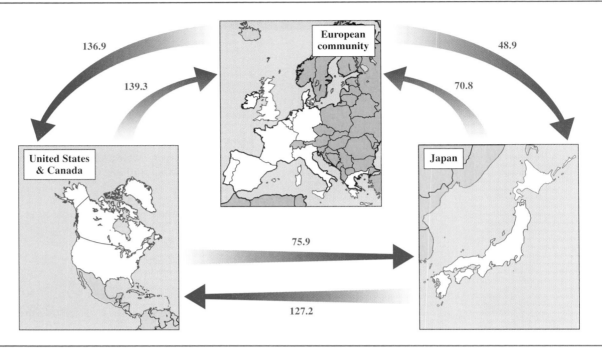

For additional trade figures see "Indicators of Market Size for 115 Countries, Part I," *Crossborder Monitor,* August 27, 1997, pp. 4–8.

EXHIBIT 3–7   Leading World Trading Countries, 1995 ($ millions)

Country*	Exports	Imports	Total
U.S.A.	582.5	770.9	1,353.4
Germany	509.3	443.8	953.1
Japan	443.0	335.9	778.9
United Kingdom	239.4	262.5	501.9
Italy	231.7	204.3	436.0
Netherlands	58.6	138.5	197.1
Canada	190.2	167.4	357.6
Belgium/Luxembourg	128.3	166.3	294.6
Hong Kong	173.5	192.8	366.3
China	148.8	132.0	280.8
Spain	91.6	114.8	206.4
South Korea	125.4	135.2	260.6
Taiwan	111.8	103.7	215.5
Switzerland	81.4	80.1	161.5
Singapore	118.2	124.4	242.6

* Order determined by total dollar value of exports and imports.

For additional trade data, see "Indicators of Market Size for 115 Countries, Part 1," *Crossborder Monitor,* August 27, 1997, pp. 4–8.

Although airfreight is not extremely important as a percentage of total international freight transportation, an interesting comparison between surface routes and air routes is air service to the world's less-industrialized countries. Although air routes are the heaviest between points in the major industrial centers, they are also heavy to points in less-developed countries. The obvious reason is that for areas not located on navigable waters or where the investment in railroads and effective highways is not yet feasible, air service is often the best answer. Air communications have made otherwise isolated parts of the world reasonably accessible.

Geographic hurdles must be recognized as having a direct effect on marketing and the related activities of communications and distribution. Furthermore, there may be indirect effects from the geographical ramifications on society and culture that are ultimately reflected in marketing activities. Many of the peculiarities of a country (i.e., peculiar to the foreigner) would be better understood and anticipated if its geography were studied more closely.

Historical Perspective in Global Business

History helps define a nation's "mission," how it perceives its neighbors, how it sees its place in the world, and how it sees itself. Insights into the history of a country are particularly effective for understanding attitudes about the role of government and business, the relations between managers and the managed, the sources of management authority, and attitudes toward foreign multinational corporations (MNCs).

To understand, explain, and appreciate a people's image of itself and the attitudes and unconscious fears that are often reflected in its view of foreign cultures, it is necessary to study the culture as it is now as well as to understand the culture as it was, that is, a country's history.

History and Contemporary Behavior

Unless you have a historical sense of the many changes that have buffeted Japan—seven centuries under the shogun feudal system, the isolation before the coming of Admiral Perry in 1853, the threat of domination by colonial powers,[49] the rise of new social classes, Western influences, the humiliation of World War II, and involvement in the international community—it is difficult to fully understand its contemporary behavior. Why do the Japanese have such strong loyalty toward their companies? Why is the loyalty found among participants in the Japanese distribution systems so difficult for an outsider to develop? Why are decisions made by consensus? Answers to such questions can be explained in part by Japanese history.

Loyalty to family, to country, to company, and to social groups and the strong drive to cooperate, to work together for a common cause, permeate many facets of Japanese behavior and have historical roots that date back for thousands of years. Loyalty and service, a sense of responsibility, and respect for discipline, training, and artistry have been stressed since ancient times as necessary for stability and order. Confucian philosophy, taught throughout Japan's history, emphasizes the basic virtue of loyalty "of friend to friend, of wife to husband, of child to parent, of brother to brother, but, above

---

[49] Several years after Perry arrived and Japan was opened to the West, the shogunate signed treaties with the United States, Britain, Holland, Russia, and France that extended their jurisdiction onto Japanese soil and limited the country's right to impose taxes on imports. According to one account, these unequal and humiliating treaties had much to do with shaping Japan's goal to make itself the West's industrial and military equal. For an excellent insight into Japanese history and contemporary issues see Patrick Smith, *Japan: A Reinterpretation* (New York: Alfred A. Knopf, 1997).

Theodore "Teddy" Roosevelt in Cuba. As the leader of the "Rough Riders," Teddy was beginning a lifetime of involvement in Latin America. (UPI/Corbis-Bettmann)

Port-au-Prince residents cheer a group of U.S. soldiers in a tank patrolling the city as troops arrive in Haiti—the most recent intrusion of U.S. military into Latin America. (REUTERS/Lee Celano/ARCHIVE PHOTOS)

all, of subject to lord," that is, to country. A fundamental premise of Japanese ideology reflects the importance of cooperation for the collective good. Japanese achieve consensus by agreeing that all will unite against outside pressures that threaten the collective good. A historical perspective gives the foreigner in Japan a basis on which to begin developing cultural sensitivity and a better understanding of contemporary Japanese behavior.

History Is Subjective

History is important in understanding why a country behaves as it does, but history from whose viewpoint? Historical events always are viewed from one's own biases and SRC, and thus what is recorded by one historian may not be what another records, especially if the historians are from different cultures. Historians traditionally try to be objective, but few can help filtering events through their own cultural biases. Not only is history sometimes subjective, but there are other subtle influences to our perspective. Maps of the world sold in the United States generally show the United States as the center, as maps in Britain show Britain at the center, and so on.[50]

A crucial element in understanding any nation's business and political culture is the subjective perception of its history. Why do Mexicans have a love–hate relationship toward the United States? Why were Mexicans required to have majority ownership in

---

[50] Professor Lyn S. Amine of St. Louis University brought this observation to our attention.

most foreign investments until recently? Why did dictator General Porfíario Diáz lament, "Poor Mexico, so far from God, so near the United States"? Because Mexicans see the United States as a threat to their political, economic, and cultural independence. Most citizens of the United States are mystified by such feelings.

After all, the United States has always been Mexico's good neighbor. Most would agree with President John F. Kennedy's proclamation during a visit to Mexico, "Geography has made us neighbors, tradition has made us friends." North Americans may be surprised to learn that most Mexicans "felt it more accurate to say 'Geography has made us closer, tradition has made us far apart.' "

Citizens of the United States feel they have been good neighbors. They see the Monroe Doctrine as protection for Latin America from European colonization and the intervention of Europe in the governments of the Western Hemisphere. Latin Americans, on the other hand, tend to see the Monroe Doctrine as an offensive expression of U.S. influence in Latin America. Or to put it another way, "Europe keep your hands off, Latin America is only for the United States," an attitude perhaps typified by former U.S. president Ulysses S. Grant, who, in a speech in Mexico in 1880, described Mexico as a "magnificent mine" that lay waiting south of the border for North American interests.[51]

United States Marines sing with pride of their exploits "from the halls of Montezuma to the shores of Tripoli." To the Mexican, the "halls of Montezuma" is remembered as U.S. troops marching all the way to the center of Mexico City and extracting as tribute 890,000 square miles that included Arizona, California, New Mexico, and Texas. Los Niños Heroes (the boy heroes), who resisted U.S. troops, wrapped themselves in Mexican flags, and jumped to their deaths rather than surrender, are remembered by a prominent monument at the entrance of Chapultepec Park. Mexicans can recount the heroism of Los Niños Heroes and the loss of Mexican territory to the United States. Every September 13, the President of Mexico, his Cabinet, and the diplomatic corps assemble at the Mexico City fortress to recall the defeat[52] that led to the "despojo territorial" (territorial plunder).[53]

The Mexican Revolution, which overthrew dictator Diáz and launched the modern Mexican State, is particularly remembered for the expulsion of foreigners, especially North American businessmen who were the most visible of the wealthy and influential entrepreneurs in Mexico.[54]

Manifest Destiny and the Monroe Doctrine were accepted as the basis for U.S. foreign policy during much of the 19th and 20th centuries. *Manifest Destiny,* in its broadest interpretation, meant that Americans were a chosen people ordained by God to create a model society. More specifically, it referred to the desires of American expansionists in the 1840s to extend the U.S. boundaries from the Atlantic to the Pacific. The idea of Manifest Destiny was used to justify U.S. annexation of Texas, Oregon, New Mexico, and California and later, U.S. involvement in Cuba, Alaska, Hawaii, and the Philippines.

The *Monroe Doctrine,* a cornerstone of U.S. foreign policy, was enunciated by President James Monroe in a public statement proclaiming three basic dicta: no further European colonization in the New World, abstention of the United States from European political affairs, and nonintervention of European governments in the governments of the Western Hemisphere.

---

[51] Enrique Krauze, *Mexico: Biography of Power—A History of Modern Mexico, 1810–1996* (New York: Harper Collins, 1997) p. 6.

[52] Mark Stevenson, "Mexicans Recall U.S. Invasion," *Associated Press,* September 13, 1997.

[53] Margot Hornblower, "Northern Exposures Amid the Current Crisis, Mexicans Reflect on Their Neighbor: America the Bully, America the Bountiful," *Time,* March 6, 1995. p. 40.

[54] Those who are interested in knowing more about Mexico's history and the role politics, religion, Spanish colonialism, and United States interventions have on contemporary Mexico are strongly urged to read Enrique Krauze, *Mexico: Biography of Power—A History of Modern Mexico, 1810–1996* (New York: Harper Collins, 1997).

CROSSING BORDERS 3-6

What Do the Mexican–American War, Ireland, and Gringo All Have in Common?

Revered in Mexico, honored in Ireland, and all but forgotten in the United States are the San Patricios (the St. Patrick's Battalion). During the Mexican–American War the San Patricios were approximately 250 mostly Irish men who made up a battalion of defectors from the U. S. Army and fought for Mexico.

The San Patricios fought well but when they ended up back in American hands, 50 of them died by hanging and many others were branded on the right cheek with a two-inch letter D for deserter.

The Mexican–American conflict that lasted from 1846–1848 may be dismissed as irrelevant "history" north of the border, but not south of it. Every year the San Patricios are remembered with a ceremony in Mexico City and County Galway, Ireland, home of the brigade's commanding officer.

These immigrant Irish soldiers deserted from the U.S. Army. A year later, just as Mexico City's Chapultepec Castle fell to the Americans, U.S. Colonel William S. Harney gave the sign to hang 30 of the rebel prisoners of St. Patrick's Battalion. The war was over and Mexico was forced to cede half its territory to the United States. During the two-year conflict, the immigrant deserters forged a strong alliance with the Mexicans. Most were executed for their pains, but they became a symbol of Mexican independence and defense against imperialism.

O.K., now we know what Ireland and the Mexican–American War have in common, but what about *gringo?* According to some sources, at day's end the San Patricios would sit around their campfires singing a song called, "Green Grow the Lilacs." The story goes that the Mexican soldiers began to refer to their comrades as "los greengros."[60] To be fair, we should share the other explanation for gringo: Some historians say the word was used in Spain prior to the discovery of America and was an alteration of *griego (Greek)* for gibberish or "it's Greek to me."

Source: James Callaghan, "The San Patricios," *American Heritage,* November 1995, p. 58; and James O. Clifford, "Historians Keep the Saga of the 'San Patricios' Green," *Los Angeles Times,* March 16, 1997, p. C-4.

After 1870, interpretation of the Monroe Doctrine became increasingly broad. In 1881, its principles were evoked in discussing the development of an interoceanic canal across the Isthmus of Panama. Theodore Roosevelt further applied the Monroe Doctrine with what became known as the *Roosevelt Corollary* to the Monroe Doctrine. The corollary stated that not only would the United States prohibit non-American intervention in Latin American affairs but it would also police the area and guarantee that Latin American nations met their international obligations. The corollary sanctioning American intervention was applied in 1905 when Roosevelt forced the Dominican Republic to accept the appointment of an American economic adviser who quickly became the financial director of the small state. It was used also in the acquisition of the Panama Canal Zone from Colombia in 1903 and the formation of a provisional government in Cuba in 1906.[55]

The manner in which the United States acquired the land for the Panama Canal Zone typifies the Roosevelt Corollary—whatever is good for the United States is justifi-

---

[55] For more about the return of the Panama Canal to Panama, see John Otis, "Panama Countdown," *Latin Trade,* February 1997, pp. 46–50.

CROSSING BORDERS 3–7

Exporting Ice to India

A mainstay of New England's 19th-century commerce was the ice trade between New England and the world. In 1806, before the invention of mechanical ice making, a demand for ice in the tropics led a New England resident, Frederic Tudor, to pioneer the transportation of ice to the tropics. His first shipment to Martinique, 130 tons, was harvested from a family pond in New England. The venture was not at first a financial success. Tudor had to solve problems with inefficiency in harvesting, keeping the ice from melting, and developing a market. He demonstrated how ice could be used to make ice cream; he promoted the use of iceboxes for keeping food fresh; he fostered the medical application of ice in reducing fever; and he sold his ice cheaply to encourage customers and to build his market. The ice was stored in insulated icehouses where preservation was improved by the simple innovation of packing sawdust between the ice blocks.

By 1833 his ice-exporting business was a financial success. It was at this time that he began exporting ice to Calcutta. His ice exporting was such a success in India that three icehouses were built to store the ice once it arrived by ship. An icehouse at Madras still stands today. And so went one of the first global marketing ventures.

Source: Reprinted By Permission of *American Heritage* magazine, a division of Forbes, Inc., © 1991 Forbes, Inc.

able. As the Global Perspective at the beginning of this chapter illustrates, the creation of the country of Panama was a total fabrication of the United States. Today such adventures hardly would be condoned by the United States or its allies, yet it is also true that the United States sent troops to Panama in 1990 to bring Panama's President Noriega to justice and, in 1994, the United States sent more than 20,000 troops to occupy Haiti and return "democracy" there.[56]

According to U.S. history, these Latin American adventures were a justifiable part of our foreign policy; to Latin Americans, they were unwelcome intrusions in Latin American affairs. The way historical events are recorded and interpreted in one culture can differ substantially from the way those same events are recorded and interpreted in another. A comparison of histories goes a long way in explaining the differences in outlooks and behavior of people on both sides of the border. Many Mexicans believe that their "good neighbor" to the north is not reluctant to throw its weight around when it wants something. There are suspicions that self-interest is the primary motivation in good relations with Mexico today, whether it is fear of Fidel Castro or eagerness for Mexican oil.

By seeing history from a Latin American's perspective, it is understandable how a national leader, under adverse economic conditions, can point a finger at the United States or a U.S. multinational corporation and evoke a special emotional, popular reaction that would divert attention away from the government in power. As a case in point, after the U.S. House of Representatives voted to censure Mexico for drug corruption, President Zedillo was under pressure to take a hard stand with Washington. He used the anniversary of Mexico's 1938 expropriation of the oil industry from foreign companies to launch a strong nationalist attack. He praised the state oil monopoly Pemex as a

---

[56] As this is written in 1998, U.S. troops remain in Haiti. See Ray Suarez, "Haiti: United States Military Will Remain in Haiti," *Talk of the Nation,* National Public Radio (Washington, D.C.: Federal Document Clearing House, January 1998).

"symbol of our historical struggles for sovereignty." Union members cheered him on, waving a huge banner that read: "In 1938 Mexico was "decertified" because it expropriated its oil and it won . . . today we were decertified for defending our dignity and sovereignty."[57]

The leader might be cheered for expropriation or confiscation of a foreign investment, even though the investment was making an important contribution to the economy. To understand a country's attitudes, prejudices, and fears, it is necessary to look beyond the surface of current events to the inner subtleties of the country's entire past for clues. Comments by two Mexicans best summarize this section:[58]

> History is taught one way in Mexico and another way in the United States . . . the U.S. robbed us but we are portrayed in U.S. textbooks as bandits who invaded Texas.

and

> We may not like gringos for historical reasons, but today the world is dividing into commercial blocks, and we are handcuffed to each other for better or worse.

Summary

One British authority admonishes foreign marketers to study the world until "the mere mention of a town, country, or river enables it to be picked out immediately on the map." Although it may not be necessary for the student of foreign marketing to memorize the world map to that extent, a prospective international marketer should be reasonably familiar with the world, its climate, and topographic differences. Otherwise, the important marketing characteristics of geography could be completely overlooked when marketing in another country. The need for geographical and historical knowledge goes deeper than being able to locate continents and their countries. For someone who has never been in a tropical rain forest with an annual rainfall of at least 60 inches (and sometimes more than 200 inches), it is difficult to anticipate the need for protection against high humidity

or to understand the difficult problems caused by dehydration in constant 100-degrees-plus heat in the Sahara region. Further, without an historical understanding of a culture, the attitudes within the marketplace may not be fully understood.

Aside from the simpler and more obvious ramifications of climate and topography, there are complex geographical and historical influences on the development of the general economy and society of a country. In this case, the need for studying geography and history is to provide the marketer with an understanding of why a country has developed as it has rather than as a guide for adapting marketing plans. Geography and history are two of the environments of foreign marketing that should be understood and that must be included in foreign marketing plans to a degree commensurate with their influence on marketing effort.

Questions

1. Define:
   Manifest Destiny   Sustainable development
   Roosevelt Corollary   Monroe Doctrine

2. Visit the United Nations home page (**http://www.un.org**), select topic, Economic and Social Development, then select topic, Population, then select topic, Population and Urbanization. Answer the following questions: How does education help control population growth? What are major problems of rapid urbanization growth?

3. Why study geography in international marketing? Discuss.

4. Pick a country and show how employment and topography affect marketing within the country.

5. Discuss the bases of world trade. Give examples illustrating the different bases.

6. The marketer "should also examine the more complex effect of geography on general market characteristics, distribution systems, and the state of the economy." Comment.

7. The world population pattern trend is shifting from rural to urban areas. Discuss the marketing ramifications.

8. Select a country with a stable population and one with a rapidly growing population. Contrast the marketing implications of these two situations.

9. "The basis of world trade can be simply stated as the result of equalizing an imbalance in the needs and wants of society on one hand and its supply of goods on the other." Explain.

---

[57] Debora Montesinos, "Mexico's Zedillo Attacks Foreign Meddling," *Reuters,* March 18, 1997.

[58] Margot Hornblower, "Northern Exposures Amid the Current Crisis, Mexicans Reflect on Their Neighbor: America the Bully, America the Bountiful," *Time,* February 1996, p. 43.

10. How do differences in people constitute a basis for trade?

11. "World trade routes bind the world together." Discuss.

12. Why were the 1990s called the "Decade of the Environment"? Explain.

13. Some say the global environment is a global issue rather than a national one. What does this mean? Discuss.

14. How does an understanding of history help an international marketer?

15. Why is there a love–hate relationship between Mexico and the United States? Discuss.

16. Discuss how your interpretation of Manifest Destiny and the Monroe Doctrine might differ from a Latin American's.

CULTURAL DYNAMICS IN ASSESSING GLOBAL MARKETS

Chapter Learning Objectives

What you should learn from Chapter 4

- The importance of culture to an international marketer.
- The effects of the self-reference criterion (SRC) on marketing objectives.
- The elements of culture.
- The impact of cultural borrowing.
- The strategy of planned change and its consequences.

GLOBAL PERSPECTIVE

Culture and Consumer Behavior: How Markets Differ

When multinational companies develop strategies for their global markets, they need to be flexible and alert to local culture. Although there are many stories of mistakes, flubs, and failures, there are far more successes than failures. And all the success stories have one thing in common: When the market demands it, successful marketing strategies reflect local custom. Here are a few examples of the cultural issues multinational companies confront.

In the U.S., Domino's Pizza stresses its delivery system as a way to differentiate itself from other pizza companies, but abroad it is not so easy. In Britain, customers don't like the idea of the deliveryman knocking on their doors—they think it's rude. In Japan, houses aren't numbered sequentially so finding an address means searching among rows of houses numbered willy-nilly. In Kuwait, pizza is more likely to be delivered to a waiting limousine than to someone's front door. And in Iceland, where much of the population doesn't have telephone service, Domino's has teamed with a drive-in movie theater chain to gain access to consumers. Customers craving a reindeer-sausage pizza—one of the most popular flavors—flash their turn signals, and a theater employee brings them a cellular phone to order a pizza that is delivered to the car.

When Pillsbury Company decided to market its Green Giant brand vegetables abroad, it started with canned sweet corn because the company felt that corn was unlikely to require any flavor changes across international markets. But to Pillsbury's surprise adjustments had to be made—not to flavor, but to how it was marketed. The French add corn to salad and eat it cold instead of as a hot side dish. In Britain, corn is used as a sandwich filler and pasta topping. In Japan, school children snack on canned corn as after-school treats. And in Korea, sweet corn is sprinkled over ice cream. Needless to say, the advertising created for the U.S. market wouldn't do, so Pillsbury created different spots for each market showing corn kernels falling off a cob into salads or pasta, or topping an ice cream sundae. It's still canned corn, but it is used differently in other parts of the world.

A $10 million Chicago company makes automotive cleaners, waxes, and other car-care products that it ships to markets as diverse as Russia, Thailand, Japan, and Mexico. Thirty percent of its sales come from abroad. Its success is explained by the owner's comment, "If it needs customization we'll do it. The only thing we won't compromise on is quality." So, what has to be changed in car wax? In Japan, the distributor told the company that the premium car wax would do better if it were pink and smelled like roses. It was done. In Saudi Arabia, fruity smells are preferred so the tire protectant was given an orange scent.

Marketing in the European Common Market is no piece of cake, either. Clothing manufacturers have found that children's clothes aren't well received in France, where children are dressed as small adults. In southern Europe, form-fitting clothes sell well but are sure losers in the Netherlands in northern Europe. Dutch women wear loose-fitting clothing, many because they bicycle to work.

What these examples illustrate is that people express their needs and wants differently from culture to culture. They all eat canned corn, polish and wax their cars, and wear clothes but each culture has a way of doing it a bit differently. The marketer's challenge is to understand cultural similarities and differences and mold marketing strategies to fit the particular needs of a market. In short, a marketer must develop a sensitivity to cultural dynamics.

Sources: Adapted from Tara Parker-Pope, "The Most Successful Companies Have to Realize a Simple Truth: All Consumers Aren't Alike," *The Wall Street Journal,* September 26, 1996, p. R22; "Study Analyzes Cultural Impact on Retailing," *Industry Week,* September 27, 1997 (also available on the Web at **http://www.industryweek.com/**); and Lawrence R. Quinn, "Global Warning," *Sales & Marketing Management,* April 1997, p. 54.

Culture deals with a group's design for living. It is pertinent to the study of marketing, especially international marketing. If you consider the scope of the marketing concept—the satisfaction of consumer needs and wants at a profit—it is apparent that the successful marketer must be a student of culture. What a marketer is constantly dealing with is the culture of the people (the market). When a promotional message is written, symbols recognizable and meaningful to the market (the culture) must be used. When designing a product, the style, uses, and other related marketing activities must be made culturally acceptable (i.e., acceptable to the present society) if they are to be operative and meaningful. In fact, culture is pervasive in all marketing activities—in pricing, promotion, channels of distribution, product, packaging, and styling—and the marketer's efforts actually become a part of the fabric of culture. The marketer's efforts are judged in a cultural context for acceptance, resistance, or rejection. How such efforts interact with a culture determines the degree of success or failure of the marketing effort.

Humans are born creatures of need; as they mature, want is added to need. Economic needs are spontaneous and, in their crudest sense, limited. Humans, like all living things, need a minimum of nourishment, and like a few other living things, they need shelter. Unlike any other being, they also need essential clothing. Economic wants, however, are for nonessentials and, hence, are limitless. Unlike basic needs, wants are not spontaneous and not characteristic of the lower animals. They arise not from an inner desire for preservation of self or species but from a desire for satisfaction above absolute necessity. To satisfy their material needs and wants, humans consume.[1]

The manner in which people consume, the priority of needs and the wants they attempt to satisfy, and the manner in which they satisfy them are functions of their culture that temper, mold, and dictate their style of living. *Culture* is the human-made part of human environment—the sum total of knowledge, beliefs, art, morals, laws, customs, and any other capabilities and habits acquired by humans as members of society. Culture is "everything that people have, think, and do as members of their society."[2]

The marketer's frame of reference must be that markets are not (static), they become (change); they are not static but change, expand, and contract in response to marketing effort, economic conditions, and other cultural influences. Markets and market behavior are part of a country's culture. One cannot truly understand how markets evolve or how they react to a marketer's effort without appreciating that markets are a result of culture. Markets are dynamic living phenomena, expanding and contracting not only in response to economic change but also in response to changes in other aspects of the culture. Markets are the result of the three-way interaction of a marketer's efforts, economic conditions, and all other elements of the culture. Marketers are constantly adjusting their efforts to cultural demands of the market, but they also are acting as agents of change whenever the product or idea being marketed is innovative. Whatever the degree of acceptance in whatever level of culture, the use of something new is the beginning of cultural change and the marketer becomes a change agent.

This is the first of four chapters that focus on culture and international marketing. A discussion of the broad concept of culture as the foundation for international marketing is presented below. The next chapter, "Business Customs in Global Marketing," discusses culture and how it influences business practices. The third and fourth chapters examine elements of culture essential to the study of international marketing, the political environment, and the legal environment.

This chapter's purpose is to heighten the reader's sensitivity to the dynamics of culture. It is not a treatise on cultural information about a particular country; rather, it is designed to emphasize the need for study of each country's culture and all its elements, and to point up some relevant aspects on which to focus.

Culture and Its Elements

The student of foreign marketing should approach an understanding of culture from the viewpoint of the anthropologist. Every group of people or society has a culture because culture is the entire social heritage of the human race—"the totality of the knowledge

---

[1] An interesting Web site that has information on various cultural traits, gestures, holidays, languages, religion, and so forth and a "question corner" where you can ask about the cultural nuances of a particular nation or ethnic group can be found at **http://www.worldculture.com/**.

[2] Gary P. Ferraro, *The Cultural Dimension of International Business,* 3rd ed. (Englewood, Cliffs, NJ: Prentice Hall, 1997), p. 16.

CROSSING BORDERS 4–1

"Teeth Are Extracted by the Latest Methodists"

So reads a sign by a Hong Kong dentist. Translating a message and getting the right meaning is a problem for all cultures. The following examples illustrate:

A Polish menu: "Beef rashers beaten up in the country people's fashion."

An Acapulco hotel gives new meaning to quality control: "The manager has personally passed all the water served here."

In an Austrian hotel catering to skiers: "Not to perambulate the corridors in the hours of repose in the boots of ascension."

In an attempt to add prestige to the labels of products for sale in China, a Japanese firm included English translations on its labels. A few examples: "Liver Putty" (Japanese equivalent of Spam); "My Fanny" (brand of toilet paper); "Strawberry Crap Dessert" (ready-to-eat pancakes); "Hot Piss" (name of an antifreeze spray); and "Specialist in Deceased Children" (slogan for a pediatrician).

A Bangkok dry cleaner: "Drop your trousers here for best results."

Sign in a Rome doctor's office: "Specialist in Women and Other Diseases."

A Zurich hotel: "Because of the impropriety of entertaining guests of the opposite sex in the bedroom, it is suggested that the lobby be used for this purpose."

A sign posted in Germany's Black Forest: "It is strictly forbidden on our Black Forest camping site that people of different sex, for instance, men and women, to live together in one tent unless they are married with each other for that purpose."

A Swiss restaurant menu: "Our wines leave you nothing to hope for."

A Tokyo car-rental firm's driving manual: "When passengers of foot heave in sight, tootle the horn, trumpet him melodiously at first, if he still obstacles your passings, then tootle him with vigor."

A detour sign in Japan: "Stop: Drive Sideways"

And finally, truth in advertising in a Copenhagen airline ticket office: "We take your bags and send them in all directions."

Sources: From the authors; Charles Goldsmith, "Look See! Anyone Do Read This and It Will Make You Laughable," *The Wall Street Journal,* November 19, 1992, p. B-1; "Cook's Travelers' Tales," *World Press Review,* June 1994, p. 26; and "Some Strawberry Crap Dessert, Dear?" *South China Morning Post,* December 9, 1996, p. 12.

and practices, both intellectual and material of society . . . [it] embraces everything from food to dress, from household techniques to industrial techniques, from forms of politeness to mass media, from work rhythms to the learning of familiar rules."[3] Culture exists in New York, London, and Moscow just as it does among the Navajos, the South Sea islanders, or the aborigines of Australia.

It is imperative for foreign marketers to learn to appreciate the intricacies of cultures different from their own if they are to be effective in a foreign market. A place to begin is to make a careful study of the elements of culture.

Elements of Culture

The anthropologist studying culture as a science must investigate every aspect of a culture if an accurate, total picture is to emerge. To implement this goal, there has evolved

---

[3] Colette Guillaumin, "Culture and Cultures," *Cultures* 6, No. 1 (1979), p. 1.

CROSSING BORDERS 4–2

Cultures Just Different, Not Right or Wrong, Better or Worse

We must not make value judgments as to whether or not cultural behavior is good or bad, better or worse. There is no cultural right or wrong, just difference.

People around the world feel as strongly about their cultures as we do about ours. Every country thinks its culture is the best and for every foreign peculiarity that amuses us, there is an American peculiarity that amuses others. The Chinese tell American dog jokes, reflecting their amazement that we could feel the way we do about an animal that the Chinese consider better for eating than petting. And we're surprised that the French take their dogs to the finest restaurants, where the dogs might be served at the table.

Source: Adapted from Lennie Copeland and Lewis Griggs, *Going International* (New York: Plume, 1997), p. 7.

a cultural scheme that defines the parts of culture. For the marketer, the same thoroughness is necessary if the marketing consequences of cultural differences within a foreign market are to be accurately assessed.

Culture includes every part of life. The scope of the term *culture* to the anthropologist is illustrated by the elements included within the meaning of the term. They are:[4]

1. Material culture
   Technology
   Economics
2. Social institutions
   Social organization
   Education
   Political structures
3. Humans and the universe
   Belief systems
4. Aesthetics
   Graphic and plastic arts
   Folklore
   Music, drama, and dance
5. Language

In the study of humanity's way of life, the anthropologist finds these five dimensions useful because they encompass all the activities of social heritage that constitute culture. Foreign marketers may find such a cultural scheme a useful framework for evaluating a marketing plan or studying the potential of foreign markets. All the elements are instrumental to some extent in the success or failure of a marketing effort because they constitute the environment within which the marketer operates. Furthermore, because we automatically react to many of these factors in our native culture, we must purposely learn them in another. Finally, these are the elements with which marketing efforts interact and so are critical to understanding the character of the marketing system of any society. It is necessary to study the various implications of the differences of each of these factors in any analysis of a specific foreign market.

---

[4] Melvin Herskovits, *Man and His Works* (New York: Alfred A. Knopf, 1952), p. 634. See also Chapter 3, Culture, in Raymond Scupin, *Cultural Anthropology: A Global Perspective,* 3rd ed. (Englewood Cliffs, NJ: Prentice Hall, 1998).

Material Culture.   *Material culture* is divided into two parts, technology and economics. Technology includes the techniques used in the creation of material goods; it is the technical know-how possessed by the people of a society. For example, the vast majority of U.S. citizens understand the simple concepts involved in reading gauges, but in many countries of the world this seemingly simple concept is not part of their common culture and is, therefore, a major technical limitation.

A culture's level of technology is manifest in many ways. Such concepts as preventive maintenance are foreign in many low-technology cultures. In the United States, Japan, Germany, or other countries with high levels of technology, the general population has a broad level of technical understanding that allows them to adapt and learn new technology more easily than populations with lower levels of technology. Simple repairs, preventive maintenance, and a general understanding of how things work all constitute a high level of technology. One of the burdens of China's economic growth is providing the general working population with a modest level of mechanical skills, that is, a level of technology.

Economics is the manner in which people employ their capabilities and the resulting benefits. Included in the subject of economics is the production of goods and services, their distribution, consumption, means of exchange, and the income derived from the creation of utilities.

Material culture affects the level of demand, the quality and types of products demanded, and their functional features, as well as the means of production of these goods and their distribution.[5] The marketing implications of the material culture of a country are many. For example, electrical appliances sell in England and France but have few buyers in countries where less than 1 percent of the homes have electricity. Even with electrification, economic characteristics represented by the level and distribution of income may limit the desirability of products. Electric can openers and electric juicers are acceptable in the United States, but in less-affluent countries not only are they unattainable and probably unwanted, they would be a spectacular waste because disposable income could be spent more meaningfully on better houses, clothing, or food.

Social Institutions.   *Social institutions* include social organization, education, and political structures that are concerned with the ways in which people relate to one another, organize their activities to live in harmony with one another, teach acceptable behavior to succeeding generations, and govern themselves. The positions of men and women in society, the family, social classes, group behavior, age groups, and how societies define decency and civility are interpreted differently within every culture.[6] In cultures where the social organizations result in close-knit family units, for example, it is more effective to aim a promotion campaign at the family unit than at individual family members. Travel advertising in culturally divided Canada pictures a wife alone for the English audience but a man and wife together for the French segments of the population because the French are traditionally more closely bound by family ties.

The roles and status positions found within a society are influenced by the dictates of social organizations. In India the election of a low-caste person—once called an "untouchable"—as president made international news because it was such a departure from traditional Indian culture. Decades ago, brushing against an untouchable or even glancing at one was considered enough to defile a Hindu of status. Even though the caste system had been outlawed, it remained as part of the culture; perhaps the election of a member of Hinduism's lowest class signals a meaningful change in social class in India.[7]

---

5 See, for example, Jose Luis Nueno and Harvey Bennett, "The Changing Spanish Consumer," *International Journal of Research in Marketing,* Vol. 14, 1997, p. 19.

6 Amelie Oksenberg Rorty, "From Decency to Civility by Way of Economics: First Let's Eat and Then Talk of Right and Wrong," *Social Research,* March 22, 1997, p. 112.

7 "India Gets 1st Low-Caste President," *Associated Press,* July 17, 1997.

Education, one of the most important social institutions, affects all aspects of the culture from economic development to consumer behavior. The literacy rate of a country is a potent force in economic development. Numerous studies indicate a direct link between the literacy rate of a country and its ability for rapid economic growth. According to the World Bank no country has been successful economically with less than 50 percent literacy, but when countries have invested in education the economic rewards have been substantial.[8] Literacy has a profound affect on marketing. It is much easier to communicate with a literate market than to one where the marketer has to depend on symbols and pictures to communicate. Each of the social institutions has an effect on marketing because each influences behavior, values, and the overall patterns of life.

Humans and the Universe.   Within this category are religion (belief systems), superstitions, and their related power structures. The impact of religion on the value systems of a society and the effect of value systems on marketing must not be underestimated. Religion impacts people's habits, their outlook on life, the products they buy, the way they buy them, even the newspapers they read.

Acceptance of certain types of food, clothing, and behavior are frequently affected by religion, and such influence can extend to the acceptance or rejection of promotional messages as well. In some countries, focusing too much attention on bodily functions in advertisements would be judged immoral or improper and the products would be rejected. What might seem innocent and acceptable in one culture could be considered too personal or vulgar in another. Such was the case when Saudi Arabian customs officials impounded a shipment of French perfume because the bottle stopper was in the shape of a nude female.

Religion is one of the most sensitive elements of a culture. When the marketer has little or no understanding of a religion, it is easy to offend, albeit unintentionally. Like all cultural elements, one's own religion is often not a reliable guide of another's beliefs. Many do not understand religions other than their own, and what is "known" about other religions is often incorrect. The Islamic religion is a good example of the need for a basic understanding of all major religions.[9] There are between 800 million and 1.2 billion people in the world who embrace Islam, yet major multinational companies often offend Muslims. The French fashion house of Chanel unwittingly desecrated the Koran by embroidering verses from the sacred book of Islam on several dresses shown in its summer collections. The designer said he had taken the design, which was aesthetically pleasing to him, from a book on India's Taj Mahal palace and that he was unaware of its meaning. To placate a Muslim group that felt the use of the verses desecrated the Koran, Chanel had to destroy the dresses with the offending designs along with negatives of the photos taken of the garments.[10] Chanel certainly had no intention of offending Muslims since some of its most important customers embrace Islam. This example shows how easy it is to offend if the marketer, in this case the designer, has not familiarized himself with other religions.

Superstition plays a much larger role in a society's belief system in some parts of the world than it does in the United States. What an American might consider as mere superstition can be a critical aspect of a belief system in another culture. For example, in parts of Asia, ghosts, fortune telling, palmistry, head-bump reading, phases of the moon, demons, and soothsayers are all integral parts of certain cultures. Astrologers are rou-

---

[8] Patrisha Joan F. de Leon, "Focus: State of Philippine Literacy: Interest in Reading," *Business World Manila,* July 21, 1997, p. 7.

[9] For an interesting article on the Islamic world, see the report on a speech by Prime Minister Datuk Seri Dr Mahathir Mohamad, "The Islamic World and Global Co-operation: Preparing for the 21st Century in Petaling Jaya," *The New Straits Times,* April 26, 1997.

[10] Advertising and research also are affected by religion. For an insightful study on attitudes toward advertising in Islam see Safran S. Al-Makaty, G. Norman Van Tubergen, S. Scott Whitlow, and Douglas A. Boyd, "Attitudes toward Advertising in Islam," *Journal of Advertising Research,* May 15, 1996.

CROSSING BORDERS 4-3

Gaining Cultural Awareness in 17th and 18th-Century England—The Grand Tour

Gaining cultural awareness has been a centuries-old need for anyone involved in international relations. The term *Grand Tour,* first applied over three hundred years ago in England, was, by 1706, firmly established as the ideal preparation for soldiers, diplomats, and civil servants. It was seen as the best means of imparting to young men of fortune a modicum of taste and knowledge of other countries. By the summer of 1785, there were an estimated 40,000 English on the Continent.

The Grand Tourist was expected to conduct a systematic survey of each country's language, history, geography, clothes, food, customs, politics, and laws. In particular, he was to study its most important buildings and their valuable contents, and he was encouraged to collect prints, paintings, drawings, and sculpture. All this could not be achieved in a few weeks, and several years were to lapse before some tourists saw England's shores again. Vast sums of money were spent. At times, touring was not the relatively secure affair of today. If the Grand Tourist managed to avoid the pirates of Dunkirk, he then had to run a gauntlet of highwaymen on Dutch roads, thieves in Italy and France, marauding packs of disbanded soldiery everywhere, and the Inquisition in Spain, to say nothing of ravenous wolves and dogs.

He had to be self-contained; he carried with him not only the obligatory sword and pistols but also a box of medicines and other spices and condiments, a means of securing hotel rooms at night and an overall to protect his clothes while in bed. At the end of these Grand Tours, many returned with as many as eight or nine hundred pieces of baggage. These collections of art, sculpture, and writings can be seen today in many of the mansions throughout the British Isles.

Source: Nigel Sale, *Historic Houses and Gardens of East Anglia* (Norwich, England: Jerrold Colour Publications, 1976), p. 1.

tinely called on in Thailand to determine the best location for a structure. The Thais insist that all wood in a new building must come from the same forest to prevent the boards from quarreling with each other. Houses should have an odd number of rooms for luck, and they should be one story because it is unlucky to have another's foot over your head.

It's called art, science, philosophy, or superstition, depending on who is talking but the Chinese practice of "feng shui" is an important ancient belief held by Chinese, among others. Feng shui is the process that links humans and the universe to ch'i, the energy that sustains life and flows through our bodies and surroundings, in and around our homes and workplaces. The idea is to harness this ch'i to enhance good luck, prosperity, good health, and honor for the owner of a premise and to minimize the negative force, "sha ch'i," and its effect. Feng shui requires engaging the services of a feng shui master to determine the positive orientation of a building in relation to either the owner's horoscope, the date of establishment of the business, or the shape of the land and building.[11] It is not a look or a style, and it is more than aesthetics: Feng shui is a strong belief in establishing a harmonious environment through the design and placement of furnishings and the avoidance of buildings facing northwest, the "devil's entrance," and southwest, the "devil's backdoor."

---

[11] "Corporate Feng Shui with Dr. R. Yong," *Business Times,* October 15, 1997, p. 6.

These Nike shows were withdrawn from the market after complaints that Muslims could interpret the logo on the shoes as resembling the Arabic for "Allah." (Greg Gibson/APA Wide World Photos)

Too often, one person's beliefs are another person's funny story. It is a mistake to discount the importance of myths, beliefs, superstitions, or other cultural beliefs, however strange they may appear, because they are an important part of the cultural fabric of a society and influence all manner of behavior. For the marketer, it can be an expensive mistake to make light of superstitions in other cultures when doing business there. To make a fuss about being born in the right year under the right phase of the moon and to rely heavily on handwriting and palm-reading experts, as in Japan, can be worrisome to a Westerner who seldom sees a 13th floor in a building, refuses to walk under a ladder, or worries about the next seven years after breaking a mirror.

Aesthetics.   Closely interwoven with the effect of people and the universe on a culture are its *aesthetics,* that is, its arts, folklore, music, drama, and dance. Aesthetics are of particular interest to the marketer because of their role in interpreting the symbolic meanings of various methods of artistic expression, color, and standards of beauty in each culture. Customers everywhere respond to images, myths, and metaphors that help them define their personal and national identities and relationships within a context of culture and product benefits.[12] The uniqueness of a culture can be spotted quickly in symbols having distinct meanings. A long-standing rivalry between the Scottish Clan Lindsay and Clan Donald caused McDonald's Corporation some consternation when they chose the Lindsay tartan design for new uniforms for its restaurant hosts and hostesses. Godfrey Lord Macdonald, Chief of Clan Donald, was outraged and complained that McDonald's had a "complete lack of understanding of the name."[13] While Lord Macdonald's "outrage" may have been in part tongue in cheek, such was not the case with a symbolic misstep by Nike Inc. over a logo used on athletic shoes. The logo was intended to represent flames or heat rising off a blacktop for a line of shoes to be sold with the names *Air Bakin', Air Melt, Air Grill,* and *Air B-Que.* Unfortunately, the logo

12 Jeanne Binstock van Rij, "Trends, Symbols, and Brand Power in Global Market: The Business Anthropology Approach," *Strategy & Leadership,* November 21, 1996, p. 18.
13 "McDonald's Tartan Choice Upsets Scottish Clan," *Advertising Age,* May 12, 1997, p. 78.

inadvertently resembled the Arabic script for the word "Allah," the Arabic word for God. After receiving complaints from Muslim leaders, Nike recalled the offending shoes.

Myths also seem to trip up athletic shoemakers. Reebok had to remove "Incubus," the designation of its women's running shoe, from all shoeboxes and labels because Incubus is the name of a mythical demon who preys on (that is, "has his way with") sleeping women.[14]

Without a culturally correct interpretation of a country's aesthetic values, a whole host of marketing problems can arise. Product styling must be aesthetically pleasing to be successful, as must advertisements and package designs. Insensitivity to aesthetic values can offend, create a negative impression, and, in general, render marketing efforts ineffective. Strong symbolic meanings may be overlooked if one is not familiar with a culture's aesthetic values. The Japanese, for example, revere the crane as being very lucky for it is said to live a thousand years; however, the use of the number four should be avoided completely because the word for four, *shi,* is also the Japanese word for death.

Language.   The importance of understanding the language of a country cannot be overestimated. The successful marketer must achieve expert communication, and this requires a thorough understanding of the language as well as the ability to speak it. Advertising copywriters should be concerned less with obvious differences between languages and more with the idiomatic meanings expressed. It is not sufficient to say you want to translate into Spanish, for instance, because, in Spanish-speaking Latin America the language vocabulary varies widely. *Tambo,* for example, means a roadside inn in Bolivia, Colombia, Ecuador, and Peru; in Argentina and Uruguay, it means a dairy farm; and in Chile, a tambo is a brothel. If that gives you a problem, consider communicating with the people of Papua, New Guinea. Some 750 languages, each distinct and mutually unintelligible, are spoken there.[15]

A dictionary translation is not the same as an idiomatic interpretation, and seldom will the dictionary translation suffice. A national food processor's familiar "Jolly Green Giant" translated into Arabic as "Intimidating Green Ogre." One airline's advertising campaign designed to promote its plush leather seats urged customers to "fly on leather"; when translated for its Hispanic and Latin American customers, it told passengers to "fly naked." The U.S. chicken entrepreneur Frank Perdue's translation of one of his very successful U.S. advertising slogans, "It takes a tough man to make a tender chicken," came out in Spanish as, "It takes a virile man to make a chicken affectionate." Schweppes was not pleased with its tonic water translation into Italian: "Il Water" idiomatically means the bathroom.

Carelessly translated advertising statements not only lose their intended meaning but can suggest something very different, obscene, offensive, or just plain ridiculous. For example, in French-speaking countries the trademark toothpaste brand name, "Cue," was a crude slang expression for derriere. The intent of a fountain pen company advertising in Latin America suffered in translation when the new ink was promoted to "help prevent unwanted pregnancies." The intent was also lost in translation when "hydraulic rams" came out as "wet sheep."[16] The poster of an engineering company at a Russian trade show did not mean to promise that its oil well completion equipment was dandy for "improving a person's sex life."[17] Oh, don't forget the accent marks found in many

---

[14] "Nike Recalls Shoes Bearing Logo That Muslims Found Offensive," *Associated Press,* June 25, 1997.

[15] Bernard Kong, "Papua New Guinea: A Land of Extreme Contrasts," *Trade & Culture,* May/July 1997, p. 40.

[16] Gary P. Ferraro, "The Need for Linguistic Proficiency in Global Business," *Business Horizons,* May/June 1996, p. 39.

[17] For other examples of language translation mistakes, see David A. Ricks, *Blunders in International Business* (Cambridge, Mass.: Blackwell Publishers, 1994).

languages; left out or incorrectly placed, they can change the whole meaning of a word. For example, the "~" over a word in Spanish can change the entire meaning of a word— *años,* with the ~ accent means *years,* but omit the ~ and it becomes *anuses!*

Language may be one of the most difficult cultural elements to master, but it is the most important to study in an effort to acquire some degree of empathy. Many believe that to appreciate the true meaning of a language it is necessary to live with the language for years. Whether or not this is the case, foreign marketers should never take it for granted that they are communicating effectively in another language. Until a marketer can master the vernacular, the aid of a national within the foreign country should be enlisted; even then, the problem of effective communications may still exist. One authority suggests that we look for a *cultural translator,* that is, a person who translates not only among languages but also among different ways of thinking and among different cultures.

Analysis of Elements

Each cultural element must be evaluated in light of how it could affect a proposed marketing program; some may have only indirect impact, while others may be totally involved. Generally, it could be said that the more complete the marketing involvement or the more unique the product, the more need for thorough study of each cultural element. If a company is simply marketing an existing product in an already developed market, studying the total culture is certainly less crucial than for the marketer involved in total marketing—from product development, through promotion, to the final selling.

A food court reflects the diverse multicultural society found in Singapore. Chinese, Indian, and Malay food are served. (© Munshi Amed)

CROSSING BORDERS 4–4

It's Not the Gift That Counts, but How You Present It

Giving a gift in another country requires careful attention if it is to be done properly. Here are a few suggestions:

Japan

Do not open a gift in front of a Japanese counterpart unless asked and do not expect the Japanese to open your gift.

Avoid ribbons and bows as part of gift-wrapping. Bows as we know them are considered unattractive and ribbon colors can have different meanings.

Do not offer a gift depicting a fox or badger. The fox is the symbol of fertility; the badger, cunning.

Europe

Avoid red roses and white flowers, even numbers, and the number 13. Do not wrap flowers in paper.

Do not risk the impression of bribery by spending too much on a gift.

Arab World

Do not give a gift when you first meet someone. It may be interpreted as a bribe.

Do not let it appear that you contrived to present the gift when the recipient is alone. It looks bad unless you know the person well. Give the gift in front of others in less personal relationships.

Latin America

Do not give a gift until after a somewhat personal relationship has developed unless it is given to express appreciation for hospitality.

Gifts should be given during social encounters, not in the course of business.

Avoid the colors black and purple; both are associated with the Catholic Lenten season.

China

Never make an issue of a gift presentation—publicly or privately.

Gifts should be presented privately, with the exception of collective ceremonial gifts at banquets.

Source: Adapted from "International Business Gift-Giving Customs," available from The Parker Pen Company, n.d.

While analysis of each cultural element vis-a-vis a marketing program could ensure that each facet of a culture is included, it should not be forgotten that culture is a total picture, not a group of unrelated elements. Culture cannot be separated into parts and be fully understood. Every facet of culture is intricately intertwined and cannot be viewed singly; each must be considered for its synergistic effects. The ultimate personal motives and interests of people are determined by all the interwoven facets of the culture rather than by the individual parts. While some specific cultural elements have a direct influence on individual marketing efforts and must be viewed individually in terms of their potential or real effect on marketing strategy, the whole of cultural elements is manifested in a broader sense on the basic cultural patterns. In a market, basic consumption patterns—that is, who buys, what they buy, frequency of purchases, sizes purchased, and so on—are established by cultural values of right and wrong, acceptable and unacceptable. The basic motives for consumption that help define fundamental needs and different forms of decision making have strong cultural underpinnings that are critical knowledge for the marketer. Gaining cultural knowledge is a beginning.

Cultural Knowledge

There are two kinds of knowledge about cultures. One is *factual knowledge* about a culture; it is usually obvious and must be learned. Different meanings of color, different tastes, and other traits indigenous to a culture are facts that a marketer can anticipate, study, and absorb. The other is *interpretive knowledge*—an ability to understand and to appreciate fully the nuances of different cultural traits and patterns. For example, the meaning of time, attitudes toward other people and certain objects, the understanding of one's role in society, and the meanings of life can differ considerably from one culture to another and may require more than factual knowledge to be fully appreciated. In this case, interpretive knowledge is also necessary.

Factual versus Interpretive Knowledge

Frequently, factual knowledge has meaning as a straightforward fact about a culture but assumes additional significance when interpreted within the context of the culture. For example, that Mexico is 98 percent Roman Catholic is an important bit of factual knowledge. But equally important is what it means to be a Catholic within Mexican culture versus being Catholic in Spain or Italy. Each culture practices Catholicism in a slightly different way. For example, All Soul's Day is an important celebration among some Catholic countries; in Mexico; however, the celebration receives special emphasis. The Mexican observance is a unique combination of pagan (mostly Indian) influence and Catholic tradition. On the Day of the Dead, as All Soul's Day is called by many in Mexico, it is believed that the dead return to feast. Hence, many Mexicans visit the graves of their departed, taking the dead's favorite foods to place on the graves for them to enjoy. Prior to All Soul's Day, bakeries pile their shelves with bread shaped like bones and coffins, and candy stores sell sugar skulls and other special treats to commemorate the day. As the souls feast on the food, so do the living celebrants. Although the prayers, candles, and the idea of the soul are Catholic, the idea of the dead feasting is very pre-Christian Mexican. Thus, a Catholic in Mexico observes All Soul's Day quite differently from a Catholic in Spain. The interpretive, as well as factual, knowledge about religion in Mexico is necessary to fully understand this part of Mexican culture.

Another conflict that can arise if one possesses factual knowledge but little interpretive knowledge occurs in interpersonal relations. One of the facts about Taiwanese cultures is that the Taiwanese emphasize the collective while Westerners emphasize the individual. Emphasis on the collective results in close-knit, highly supportive teams among Taiwanese staff that create a mindset which does not always work in meeting with Western clients. The problem is that when local staffs act humble and cautious, in deference to the group, a Westerner's lack of interpretive knowledge results in perceiving their humility as ignorance or lack of interest.[18]

---

[18] Laurie Underwood, "One Office Two Cultures," *Topics—American Chamber of Commerce in Taipei,* April 1997. *Topics* can be viewed on the Web at **http://www.amcham.com.tw/**.

CROSSING BORDERS 4–5

Green: A Double Whammy

The trend in many U.S. communities is to visit a foreign country in a search for foreign trade. These trips can prove that sometimes the simplest thing can cause problems. As a case in point, a county commissioner and 20 business representatives seeking business connections arrived in Taiwan bearing gifts of green baseball caps.

The trip was scheduled a month before elections. No one knew that green was the color of the political opposition party. In addition, the visitors learned too late that according to Taiwan culture a man wears green to signify that his wife has been unfaithful. "I don't know whatever happened to those green hats but the trip gave us an understanding of the extreme differences in our culture," said the county commissioner. While a green hat may spell trouble in Taiwan, the color green symbolizes exuberance and youth in other Asian countries.

Sources: From a public address and Roger Axtell, *The Do's and Taboos of International Trade: A Small Business Primer* (New York: John Wiley and Sons, 1994), p. 227.

Interpretive knowledge requires a degree of insight that may best be described as a feeling. It is the kind of knowledge most dependent on past experience for interpretation and most frequently prone to misinterpretation if one's home-country frame of reference (SRC) is used. Ideally, the foreign marketer should possess both kinds of knowledge about a market. Most facts about a particular culture can be learned by researching published material about that culture. This effort can also transmit a small degree of empathy, but to appreciate the culture fully it is necessary to live with the people for some time. Because this ideal solution is not practical for a marketer, other solutions are sought. Consultation and cooperation with bilingual nationals with marketing backgrounds is the most effective answer to the problem. This has the further advantage of helping the marketer acquire an increasing degree of empathy through association with people who understand the culture best—locals.

Cultural Sensitivity and Tolerance

Successful foreign marketing begins with *cultural sensitivity*—being attuned to the nuances of culture so that a new culture can be viewed objectively, evaluated, and appreciated. Cultural sensitivity, or cultural empathy, must be carefully cultivated. Perhaps the most important step is the recognition that cultures are not right or wrong, better or worse; they are simply different. For every amusing, annoying, peculiar, or repulsive cultural trait we find in a country, there is a similarly amusing, annoying, or repulsive trait others see in our culture. We bathe, perfume, and deodorize our bodies in a daily ritual which is seen in many cultures as compulsive, while we often become annoyed with those cultures less concerned with natural body odor.

Just because a culture is different does not make it wrong. Marketers must understand how their own cultures influence their assumptions about another culture. The more exotic the situation, the more sensitive, tolerant, and flexible one needs to be. Being culturally sensitive will reduce conflict, improve communications, and thereby increase success in collaborative relationships.

It is necessary for a marketer to investigate the assumptions on which judgments are based, especially when the frames of reference are strictly from his or her own culture. As products of our own culture we instinctively evaluate foreign cultural patterns from a personal perspective. One major U.S. firm could have avoided a multimillion dollar mistake in Japan had it not relied on an American frame of reference by assuming all Japanese homes had ovens in which to bake cakes made from the company's mixes. From the U.S. firm's perspective, it was unnecessary to ask if Japanese had home ovens; in fact, they had few ovens, so attempts to market the product failed. As one expert warns, the success or failure of operations abroad depends on an awareness of the fundamental differences in cultures and the willingness to discard as excess baggage cultural elements of one's own culture. Some understanding of cultural values helps the marketer to understand differences and similarities in cultures.

Cultural Values

Underlying the cultural diversity that exists among countries are fundamental differences in *cultural values*. The most useful information on how cultural values influence various types of business and market behavior comes from a seminal work by Geert Hofstede.[19] Studying over 90,000 people in 66 countries, he found that the cultures of the nations studied differed along four primary dimensions and that various business and consumer behavior patterns can be closely linked to these four primary dimensions. Hofstede's approach has been widely and successfully applied to international marketing[20] and research by others has reaffirmed these linkages.[21] Research evidence indicates that the four cultural dimensions can be used to classify countries into groups that will respond in a similar way in business and market contexts. The four dimensions are: (1) the Individualism/Collective Index (IDV),[22] which focuses on self-orientation; (2) the Power Distance Index (PDI), which focuses on authority orientation; (3) the Uncertainty Avoidance Index (UAI), which focuses on risk orientation; and (4) the Masculinity/Femininity Index (MAS), which focuses on achievement orientation.[23]

Individualism/Collective Index (IDV)

The *Individualism/Collective Index* refers to the preference of behavior that promotes one's self-interest. Cultures that are high in IDV reflect an "I" mentality and tend to reward and accept individual initiative, while those low in individualism reflect a "we" mentality and generally subjugate the individual to the group. This does not mean that individuals fail to identify with groups when a culture scores high on IDV, but rather that personal initiative is accepted and endorsed. Individualism pertains to societies in which the ties between individuals are loose; everyone is expected to look after himself or herself and his or her immediate family. Collectivism as its opposite pertains to societies in which people from birth onward are integrated into strong, cohesive groups, which throughout people's lifetime continue to protect them in exchange for unquestioning loyalty.

Power Distance Index (PDI)

The *Power Distance Index* measures the tolerance of social inequality, that is, power inequality between superiors and subordinates within a social system. Cultures with high PDI scores tend to be hierarchical, with members citing force, manipulation and inheritance as sources of power. Those with low scores, on the other hand, tend to value

[19] Geert Hofstede, *Culture's Consequences: International Differences in Work Related Values* (Beverly Hills, CA: Sage Publications, 1980).

[20] Joel West and John L. Graham, "Measuring Culture in International Marketing Research: A Comparison of Values-Based and Linguistic Indicators," *Working Paper: University of California, Irvine,* 1998.

[21] See, for example, Scott Shane, "Uncertainty Avoidance and the Preference for Innovation Championing Roles," *Journal of International Business Studies,* March 1995, p. 47.

[22] Sometimes referenced as (IND).

[23] In a subsequent study a fifth dimension, Long-Term Orientation (LTO), was identified as focusing on a temporal orientation.

equality and cite knowledge and respect as sources of power. Thus, cultures with high PDI scores are more apt to have a general distrust of others since power is seen to rest with individuals and is coercive rather than legitimate. High power scores tend to indicate a perception of differences between superior and subordinate and a belief that those who hold power are entitled to privileges. A low score reflects the opposite attitude.

Uncertainty Avoidance Index (UAI)

The Uncertainty Avoidance Index explains the intolerance of ambiguity and uncertainty among members of a society. Cultures with high UAI scores are highly intolerant of ambiguity, and as a result tend to be distrustful of new ideas or behaviors.[24] They tend to have a high level of anxiety and stress and a concern with security and rule following. Accordingly, they dogmatically stick to historically tested patterns of behavior, which in the extreme become inviolable rules. Those with very high levels of UAI thus accord a high level of authority to rules as a means of avoiding risk. Cultures scoring low in uncertainty avoidance are associated with a low level of anxiety and stress, a tolerance of deviance and dissent, and a willingness to take risks. Thus, those cultures low in UAI take a more empirical approach to understanding and knowledge while those high in UAI seek a more "absolute truth."

As can be seen in Exhibit 4–1, the United States has a UAI score of 46 while France has a much higher score of 86. This difference in uncertainty avoidance in the two countries can often lead to cultural conflict between managers and their superiors. For example, one American manager working in France was frustrated with his boss's insistence that he constantly submit reports. The manager complained of the accountability trail, which meant that he had to write down everything, even summarize phone calls. The boss complained that the American had difficulty in following a rigid framework, a procedure that is typically French.[25] Germans also rank high on the UAI score and they display attitudes toward rules and instructions similar to the French. Job descriptions, clear-cut procedures, and specific instructions are all hallmarks of German management style.[26]

Masculinity/Femininity Index (MAS)

The Masculinity/Femininity Index refers to one's desire for achievement and entrepreneurial tendencies, and the extent to which the dominant values in society are "masculine." Assertiveness, the acquisition of money and not caring for others, and the quality of life or people are all cultural traits in countries with high MAS scores. Low-scoring cultures are associated with fluid sex roles, equality between the sexes, and an emphasis on service, interdependence, and people. Some cultures allow men and women to take on many different roles, while others make sharp divisions between what men should do and what women should do. In societies that make a sharp division, men are supposed to have dominant, assertive roles and women more service-oriented, caring roles.[27] An interesting study showed that tipping appeared to be less prevalent in countries with feminine values (low MAS scores) that emphasized social relationships compared with countries with masculine values (high MAS scores) that emphasized achievement and economic relationships.[28]

---

[24] Niraj Dawar, Philip M. Parker, and Lydia J. Price, "A Cross-Cultural Study of Interpersonal Information Exchange," *Journal of International Business Studies,* September 1996, p. 497.

[25] Claire Gouttefarde, "American Values in the French Workplace," *Business Horizons,* March–April 1996, p. 60.

[26] Ursula Glunk, Celeste Wilderom, and Robert Ogilvie, "Finding the Key to German-Style Management," *International Studies of Management and Organization,* Fall 1996, p. 93.

[27] Robert W. Armstrong, "The Relationship between Culture and Perception of Ethical Problems in International Marketing," *Journal of Business Ethics,* Vol. 15, 1996, p. 1199.

[28] Michael Lynn, George M. Zinkhan, and Judy Harris, "Consumer Tipping: A Cross-Country Study," *Journal of Consumer Research,* December 1993, p. 478.

EXHIBIT 4-1   Hofstede's Cultural Values and Scores Selected Countries

Country or Region	IDV Score†	Rank*	PDI Score‡	Rank	UAI Score§	Rank	MAI Score‖	Rank
Arab Countries	38	26/27	80	7	68	27	53	23
Australia	90	2	36	41	51	37	61	16
Brazil	38	26/27	69	14	76	21/22	49	27
Canada	80	4/5	39	39	48	41/42	52	24
Colombia	13	49	67	17	80	20	64	11/12
Finland	63	17	33	46	59	31/32	26	41
France	71	10/11	68	15/16	86	10/15	43	35/36
Germany	67	15	35	42/44	65	29	66	9/10
Great Britain	89	3	35	42/44	35	47/48	66	9/10
Greece	35	30	60	27/28	112	1	57	18/19
Guatemala	6	53	95	2/3	101	3	37	43
India	48	21	77	10/11	40	45	56	20/21
Indonesia	14	47/48	78	8/9	48	41/42	46	30/31
Iran	41	24	58	29/30	59	31/32	43	35/36
Japan	46	22	54	33	92	7	95	1
Mexico	30	32	81	5/6	82	18	69	6
Netherlands	80	4/5	38	40	53	35	14	51
New Zealand	79	6	22	50	49	39/40	58	17
Pakistan	14	47/48	55	32	70	24/25	50	25/26
South Korea	18	43	60	27/28	85	16/17	39	41
Taiwan	17	44	58	29/30	69	26	45	32/33
Turkey	37	28	66	18/19	85	16/17	45	32/33
United States	91	1	40	38	46	43	62	15
Uruguay	36	29	61	26	100	4	38	42
Venezuela	12	50	81	5/6	76	21/22	73	3

* Rank is based on 53 countries.

† IDV Range of scores: US 91—Guatemala 6.

‡ PDI Range of scores: Malaysia 100—Austria 11.

§ UAI Range of scores: Greece 112—Singapore 8.

‖ MAI Range of scores: Japan 95—Sweden 5.

There is a relationship between specific cultural values as defined by Hofstede and certain aspects of behavior: Those societies that have relatively similar scores on the value dimensions tend to respond in a similar fashion. Power distance, for example, can be directly related to the use of social or symbolic brand image. The greater the culture's power distance (PDI), the greater the appeal of images that project social class status and affiliation. In managing personnel from other cultures, differences in cultural values between the countries involved can be the bases for cultural misunderstanding if cultural values are not carefully evaluated. Mexico is high on power distance, low on individualism, high on uncertainty avoidance, and high on masculinity. Just the opposite, the U.S. is low on power distance, high on individualism, low on uncertainty avoidance, and high on masculinity (see Exhibit 4–1). As a consequence, management practices that are typical in the United States can cause difficulty in Mexico. For example, an American manager of a steel mill in Mexico launched a complaint and grievance system similar to one in the U.S. Because no grievances were brought up, he assumed all was well—until the entire plant walked out. In countries with high PDI scores like Mexico, workers respect authority and would not directly confront a supervisor, thus no grievances were filed. However, strong unions (low IDV equals strong group/union affiliation) made it acceptable to walk out with the group.[29] Since Turkey, like Mexico, is high

---

[29] Randall S. Schuler, Susan E. Jackson, Ellen Jackofsky, and John W. Slocum, Jr., "Managing Human Resources in Mexico: A Cultural Understanding," *Business Horizons,* May–June 1996, p. 55.

on PDI and low on IDV, it would be no surprise that behavior patterns similar to those in Mexico would exist there.[30] Hofstede's cultural values, which will be discussed further in subsequent chapters, are one more tool available to the international marketer to evaluate the cultural environment.

Besides knowledge of cultural values, a marketer also should have appreciation of how cultures change and accept or reject new ideas. Because the marketer usually is trying to introduce something completely new or to improve what is already in use, how cultures change and the manner in which resistance to change occurs should be thoroughly understood.

Cultural Change

Culture is dynamic in nature; it is not static, but a living process. But that change is consta _____ because another important attribute of culture is that it is conserva _____ mic character of culture is significant in assessing ne _____ ace resistance. There are a variety of ways society c _____ on them by war (for example, the changes in Japan a _____ ster. More commonly, change is a result of a society s _____ created by its existence. One view is that culture is t _____ est solutions to problems faced in common by mem _____ rds, culture is the means used in adjusting to the bio _____ al, and historical components of human existence. _____ s to some problems; invention has solved many other _____ ies have found answers by looking to other cultures _____ Cultural borrowing is common to all cultures. Although _____ situations facing it, most problems confronting all soci _____ rations for each particular environment and culture.

_____ ple effort to borrow those cultural ways seen as helpful _____ o a society's particular problems. If what it does adopt _____ he adaptation becomes commonplace, it is passed on as _____ unique in their own right are the result, in part, of bor _____ for example, American culture (United States) and the

_____ ge from the eastern Mediterranean, a cantaloupe from Persia, or _____ atermelon. After his fruit and first coffee he goes on to waffles, _____ n technique from wheat domesticated in Asia Minor. Over these _____ ed by the Indians of the Eastern U.S. woodlands. As a side dish _____ pecies of bird domesticated in Indo-China, or thin strips of the _____ ated in Eastern Asia which have been salted and smoked by a _____ n Europe.

_____ s the news of the day, imprinted in characters invented by the an _____ al invented in China by a process invented in Germany. As he ab _____ gn troubles he will, if he is a good conservative citizen, thank a _____ ropean language that he is 100 percent American.[32]

_____ correct to assume that he or she is 100 percent American be _____ l cultural facets has been adapted to fit his or her needs, _____ ican habits, foods, and customs. Americans behave as they

_____ : A Dualistic Business Culture," *Trade & Culture,* May/July 1997, p. 44.
_____ ocative article on how Protestant evangelicals are having a profound cultural
_____ e Jeb Blount, "A Question of Faith," *Latin Trade,* July 1997, p. 32.
_____ n (New York: Appleton-Century-Crofts, 1936), p. 327.

New ideas, new needs and new wants arise when societies are introduced to products from other cultures. These Malaysian shoppers represent profound cultural changes that are occurring as multinational companies carry the products of diverse cultures throughout the world. (© Munshi Ahmed)

do because of the dictates of their culture. Regardless of how or where solutions are found, once a particular pattern of action is judged acceptable by society, it becomes the approved way and is passed on and taught as part of the group's cultural heritage. Cultural heritage is one of the fundamental differences between humans and other animals. Culture is learned; societies pass on to succeeding generations solutions to problems, constantly building on and expanding the culture so that a wide range of behavior is possible. The point is, of course, that although many behaviors are borrowed from other cultures, they are combined in a unique manner that becomes typical for a particular society. To the foreign marketer, this similar-but-different feature of cultures has important meaning in gaining cultural empathy.

Similarities: An Illusion

For the inexperienced marketer, the similar-but-different aspect of culture creates illusions of similarity that usually do not exist. Several nationalities can speak the same lan-

CROSSING BORDERS 4–6

Spit Three Times over Your Left Shoulder . . .

. . . is the response to a compliment or positive comment to ward off bad luck. This is one of the many superstitions found in Russia. Innocent words or actions can be considered a threat that must be remedied by performing specific rituals. Superstitions are found in all societies but in some they may be taken more seriously than others may. For the international marketer it is not just idle curiosity to know a culture's superstitions. If you are not aware of the superstitions, you run the risk of making terrible mistakes. For example, the Principal Financial Group has as its logo a triangle, a rather innocuous symbol in the United States. But in Hong Kong or Korea a triangle is considered a negative shape.

As you read some of the following superstitions think how a company could unintentionally create a negative advertisement, packaging, or product by not being aware. Or, how you might give the wrong impression.

Red is popular in Denmark, but represents witchcraft and death in many African countries.

Don't stick chopsticks vertically in a bowl of rice in Japan because that is done at Japanese funeral dinners to mark the dish that belonged to the dead person. It is considered a terrible gesture and is believed to bring bad luck.

Give only odd numbers of flowers to people in Russia; even numbers are for funerals and the dead.

In Russia, never shake hands or kiss over a threshold. Step inside first, or risk offending your host and also Damovoi, a house spirit that lives on the threshold, and can bring bad luck.

In India, witchcraft, or "baanaamathi" as it is called, is real among some simple villagers. A baanaamathi can manifest itself in several ways. A buffalo may suddenly stop yielding milk or a woman may suddenly go into fits of rage or a crop may abruptly wither. When this happens, villagers try to find whoever performed the baanaamathi and expel them from the village.

Before you leave this Crossing Borders feeling smug, consider the urban myth that continues to circulate in the United States: A businessman meets an attractive woman in a bar. She buys him a drink. The next thing he remembers is waking up in an ice-filled bathtub. "Call 911 or you will die," reads a note on the wall. He examines himself for injuries and discovers a row of clumsy stitches on his back or a plastic tube or duct tape. One of his kidneys has been stolen, presumably for sale on the black market. This organ-napping rumor has been circulating for several years. New Orleans and Las Vegas often are named as the cities where the fictional crime takes place. Do people believe it? Deluged with inquiries, the police in both cities have had to issue statements assuring nervous tourists that the rumors lack even a kernel of truth.

Sources: Adapted from Dave Carpenter, "Old Superstitions Retain Hold on Citizens of the New Russia," *Associated Press,* June 12, 1997; R. J. Rajendra Prasad, "India: Blame It on the Sorcerer," *The Hindu,* March 19, 1997, p. 16; and "The Kidney Heist," *U.S. News & World Report,* October 27, 1997.

guage or have similar race and heritage, but it does not follow that similarities exist in other respects—that a product acceptable to one culture will be readily acceptable to the other, or that a promotional message that succeeds in one country will succeed in the other. Even though a people start with a common idea or approach, as is the case among English-speaking Americans and the British, cultural borrowing and assimilation to meet individual needs translate over time into quite distinct cultures. A common language does not guarantee a similar interpretation of even a word or phrase. Both the British and the American speak English, but their cultures are sufficiently different so that a single phrase has different meanings to each and can even be completely mis-understood. In England, one asks for a lift instead of an elevator, and an American, when speaking of a bathroom, generally refers to a toilet, while in England a bathroom is a place to take a tub bath. Also, the English "hoover"[33] a carpet whereas Americans vacuum.

Differences run much deeper than language differences, however. The approach to life, values, and concepts of acceptable and unacceptable behavior may all have a com-mon heritage and may appear superficially to be the same, yet in reality profound differ-ences do exist. Among the Spanish-speaking Latin American countries, the problem be-comes even more difficult because the idiom is unique to each country, and national pride tends to cause a mute rejection of any "foreign-Spanish" language. In some cases, an acceptable phrase or word in one country is not only unacceptable in another; it can very well be indecent or vulgar. Mitsubishi first sold its jeep-type vehicle in Europe un-der the model name Pajero (quite close to the Spanish term for bird). It took them some exasperating months to learn its baser meaning in Madrid. They quickly relabeled the mode the *Montero* in Spain. Similarly, in Spanish, coger is the verb "to catch," but in some countries it is used as a euphemism with a baser meaning. Across Latin American countries, and even within, there can be important variations in behavior. For instance, Argentina's Buenos Aires is very European whereas Venezuela's Caracas has a Carib-bean atmosphere. Barranquilla, Colombia, also shares a Caribbean flavor, in contrast to the colder interior city of Bogota, which is more European.

Just as Latin Americans are often thought of as one cultural group, Asians are fre-quently grouped together as if there were no cultural distinctions among Japanese, Ko-reans, and Chinese, to name but a few of the many ethnic groups in the Pacific region. Asia cannot be viewed as a homogeneous entity, and the marketer must understand the subtle and not-so-subtle differences among Asian cultures. Each country (culture) has its own unique national character.

There is also the tendency to speak of the "European consumer" as a result of grow-ing economic unification of Europe. Many of the obstacles to doing business in Europe have been or will be eliminated as the EC takes shape, but marketers, anxious to enter the market, must not jump to the conclusion than an economically unified Europe means a common set of consumer wants and needs. Cultural differences among the members of the EC are the product of centuries of history that will take centuries to erase.

Even the United States has many subcultures that today, with mass communications and rapid travel, defy complete homogenization. It would be folly to suggest that the South is in all respects culturally the same as the Northeastern or Midwestern parts of the United States, just as it would be folly to assume that the unification of Germany has erased cultural differences that have arisen from 30 years of political and social separation.

A single geopolitical boundary does not necessarily mean a single culture. For ex-ample, Canada is divided culturally between its French and English heritages although it is politically one country, and successful marketing strategy among the French Canadi-ans may be a certain failure among remaining Canadians.[34] Within most cultures there are many subcultures that can have marketing significance. The possible existence of more than one culture in a country, as well as subcultures, should be explored before a marketing plan is final. In fact, subcultures in some country markets may be meaningful

---

[33] This is also a good example of a brand name becoming generic, e.g., asking someone to Xerox a letter instead of asking it to be photocopied. The Hoover brand vacuum cleaner was among the first popular brands in England, ergo, "hoover" the carpet.

[34] Wilson Baker, "O Canada," *American Demographics/Marketing Tools*, June 1997. Available on the Web at **http://www.demographics.com//**.

target market segments just as subcultures (Hispanics, Blacks, teenagers, and Generation Xers, to name a few) are important market segments in the U.S.

Marketers must assess each country thoroughly in terms of the proposed products or services and never rely on an often-used axiom that if it sells in one country, it will surely sell in another. As worldwide mass communications and increased economic and social interdependence of countries grow, similarities among countries will increase and common market behavior, wants, and needs will continue to develop. As the process occurs, the tendency will be to rely more on apparent similarities when they may not exist. A marketer is wise to remember that a culture borrows and then adapts and customizes to its own needs and idiosyncrasies and thus, what may appear to be the same on the surface may be different in its cultural meaning. As one research cautions, "Assumptions of similarity can prevent executives from learning about critical differences."[35]

The scope of culture is broad. It covers every aspect of behavior within a society. The task of foreign marketers is to adjust marketing strategies and plans to the needs of the culture in which they plan to operate. Whether innovations develop internally through invention, experimentation, or by accident, or are introduced from outside through a process of borrowing or immigration, cultural dynamics always seem to take on a positive and, at the same time, negative aspect.

Resistance to Change

A characteristic of human culture is that change occurs. That people's habits, tastes, styles, behavior, and values are not constant but are continually changing can be verified by reading 20-year-old magazines. However, this gradual cultural growth does not occur without some resistance; new methods, ideas, and products are held to be suspect before they are accepted, if ever, as right.

The degree of resistance to new patterns varies. In some situations new elements are accepted completely and rapidly, and in others, resistance is so strong that acceptance is never forthcoming. Studies show the most important factor in determining what kind and how much of an innovation will be accepted is the degree of interest in the particular subject, as well as how drastically the new will change the old—that is, how disruptive the innovation will be to presently acceptable values and behavior patterns. Observations indicate that those innovations most readily accepted are those holding the greatest interest within the society and those least disruptive. For example, rapid industrialization in parts of Europe has changed many long-honored attitudes involving time and working women. Today, there is an interest in ways to save time and make life more productive; the leisurely continental life is rapidly disappearing. With this time-consciousness has come the very rapid acceptance of many innovations which might have been resisted by most just a few years ago. Instant foods, laborsaving devices, fast-food establishments, all supportive of a changing attitude toward work and time, are rapidly gaining acceptance.

Although a variety of innovations are completely and quickly accepted, others meet with firm resistance. India has been engaged in intensive population-control programs for over 20 years, but the process has not worked well and India's population remains among the highest in the world; it is forecasted to exceed 1.1 billion by the year 2000. Why has birth control not been accepted? Most attribute the failure to the nature of Indian culture. Among the influences that help to sustain the high birthrate are early marriage, the Hindu religion's emphasis on bearing sons, dependence on children for security in old age, and a low level of education among the rural masses. All are important cultural patterns at variance with the concept of birth control. Acceptance of birth con-

---

[35] Shawna O'Grady and Henry W. Lane, "The Psychic Distance Paradox," *Journal of International Business Studies,* 2nd Quarter 1996, p. 309.

trol would mean rejection of too many fundamental cultural concepts. For the Indian people, it is easier and more familiar to reject the new idea.

The process of change and the reactions to it are relevant to the marketer, whether operating at home or in a foreign culture, for marketing efforts are more often than not cultural innovations. As one anthropologist points out, "The market survey is but one attempt to study this problem of acceptance or rejection of an internal change . . . [and] in every attempt to introduce, in a foreign society, a new idea, a new technique, a new kind of goods, the question [of acceptance or rejection] must be faced."

Most cultures tend to be *ethnocentric;* that is, they have intense identification with the known and the familiar of their culture and tend to devalue the foreign and unknown of other cultures. Ethnocentrism complicates the process of cultural assimilation by producing feelings of superiority about one's own culture and, in varying degrees, generates attitudes that other cultures are inferior, barbaric, or at least peculiar. Ethnocentric feelings generally give way if a new idea is considered necessary or particularly appealing.

There are many reasons cultures resist new ideas, techniques, or products. Even when an innovation is needed from the viewpoint of an objective observer, a culture may resist that innovation if the people lack an awareness of the need for it. If there is no perceived need within the culture, then there is no demand. Frozen foods, for example, were first developed and introduced to the U.S. market by Birdseye in 1924 but did not even begin to be accepted until convenience became important in the mid-1950s and stores and households had freezers.

Ideas may be rejected because local environmental conditions preclude functional use and thus useful acceptance, or they may be of such complex nature that they exceed the ability of the culture either to effectively use them or to understand them. Other innovations may be resisted because acceptance would require modification of important values, customs, or beliefs. All facets of a culture are interrelated, and when the acceptance of a new idea necessitates the displacement of some other custom, threatens its sanctity, or conflicts with tradition, the probability of rejection is greater.

Although cultures meet most newness with some resistance or rejection, that resistance can be overcome. Cultures are dynamic and change occurs when resistance slowly yields to acceptance so the basis for resistance becomes unimportant or forgotten. Gradually there comes an awareness of the need for change, ideas once too complex become less so because of cultural gains in understanding, or an idea is restructured in a less complex way, and so on. Once a need is recognized, even the establishment may be unable to prevent the acceptance of a new idea. For some ideas, solutions to problems, or new products, resistance can be overcome in months; for others approval may come only after decades or centuries.

An understanding of the process of acceptance of innovations is of crucial importance to the marketer. The marketer cannot wait centuries or even decades for acceptance but must gain acceptance within the limits of financial resources and projected profitability periods. Possible methods and insights are offered by social scientists that are concerned with the concepts of planned social change. Historically, most cultural borrowing and the resulting change has occurred without a deliberate plan, but increasingly changes are occurring in societies as a result of purposeful attempts by some acceptable institution to bring about change, that is, planned change.

Planned and Unplanned Cultural Change

The first step in bringing about planned change in a society is to determine which cultural factors conflict with an innovation, thus creating resistance to its acceptance. The next step is an effort to change those factors from obstacles to acceptance into stimulants for change. The same deliberate approaches used by the social planner to gain ac-

CROSSING BORDERS 4–7

California Rice—Who Can Tell the Difference? Ethnocentrism at Its Best

An example of the resistance to change because of customs, values, and beliefs is *o-kome*—honorable rice—in Japan. In the Shinto religion, sake, rice cakes, and other rice products are the most sacred of offerings. To politicians, rice is a symbol of independence to a nation that must import much of its food. Stores called *kome-ya* sell only rice. Like wine shops, they offer many varieties, identified by strains and home regions; Japanese rice is felt to be superior to all others.

Motoori Norinaga, an 18th-century historian, proclaimed that the superiority of Japan over other countries could be simply demonstrated by the quality of its rice, which surpassed that grown elsewhere. Rice is sacred and represents the soul of the nation, an idea supported by the government, the powerful agriculture community, and many Japanese consumers. Stiff import controls protect the market from inferior rice.

So what happened when poor weather resulted in a 10 percent shortfall of the annual need? The word went out: Ease controls on imported rice and ban all sales of pure domestic rice. All domestic rice would be blended with imported rice and the Japanese would have to eat foreign rice. Dire consequences were predicted— there would be riots, hoarding of domestic rice, even thefts. TV watchers and magazine readers were bombarded with all kinds of taste tests and contests about whether Japanese rice really is better than the much cheaper California variety. This was, after all, the country that tried to bar the import of French skis, claiming that Japanese snow was different than inferior European snow, and where an agriculture minister opposed beef imports on the grounds that Japanese stomachs were different from those of foreigners.

The emperor was enlisted to ease the expected crisis. The Imperial Household Agency said he had consented "to eat foreign rice mixed with Japanese rice," and he had survived. Sumo wrestlers were persuaded to give foreign rice their weighty endorsement. These were touching gestures, but the emperor and the wrestlers need not have bothered. The great rice crisis did not happen. It seems that most cannot tell the difference between Japanese and California or Chinese rice. The prime minister was quoted as saying, "If I hadn't been told it was blended rice, I wouldn't have known." His statement mimicked the results of taste tests. They found out what Japanese executives who had worked in the United States knew all along: They often imported bags of California rice when transferred back home.

One explanation offered for the similarity of Japanese rice with California rice is that Japanese immigrants carried the seeds to California some 100 years ago. Nevertheless, rice served at school lunches must continue to be pure Japanese. In that way, the government explains, children will better understand the place of rice in Japanese tradition.

Sources: Adapted from Brenton R. Schlender, "What Rice Means to the Japanese," *Fortune,* November 1, 1993, pp. 150–156; "Going Against the Grain in Japan," *The Economist,* April 23, 1994, p. 34; Jack Russell, "California Soft Sells Its Rice in Japan," *Advertising Age International,* May 16, 1994, p. I-18.5; and Hirai Michiko, "An Appetite for Homegrown Food," *Look Japan,* June 1997, p. 132.

ceptance for hybrid grains, better sanitation methods, improved farming techniques, or protein-rich diets among the peoples of underdeveloped societies can be adopted by marketers to achieve marketing goals.[36]

Marketers have two options when introducing an innovation to a culture: they can wait, or they can cause change. The former requires hopeful waiting for eventual cultural changes that prove their innovations of value to the culture; the latter involves introducing an idea or product and deliberately setting about to overcome resistance and to cause change that accelerates the rate of acceptance.

Obviously not all marketing efforts require change to be accepted. In fact, much successful and highly competitive marketing is accomplished by a *strategy of cultural congruence.* Essentially this involves marketing products similar to ones already on the market in a manner as congruent as possible with existing cultural norms, thereby minimizing resistance. However, when marketing programs depend on cultural change to be successful, a company may decide to leave acceptance to a *strategy of unplanned change*—that is, introduce a product and hope for the best. Or, a company may employ a *strategy of planned change*—that is, deliberately set out to change those aspects of the culture offering resistance to predetermined marketing goals.

As an example of unplanned cultural change, consider how the Japanese diet has changed since the introduction of milk and bread soon after World War II. Most Japanese, who are predominantly fish eaters, have increased their intake of animal fat and protein to the point that fat and protein now exceed vegetable intake. As many McDonald's hamburgers are apt to be eaten in Japan as the traditional rice ball wrapped in edible seaweed, and American hamburgers are replacing many traditional Japanese foods. Burger King recently purchased Japan's homegrown Morinaga Love restaurant chain, home of the salmon burger—a patty of salmon meat, a slice of cheese, and a layer of dried seaweed, spread with mayonnaise and stuck between two cakes of sticky Japanese rice pressed into the shape of a bun—an eggplant burger and other treats.[37] The chain will be converted and will sell Whoppers instead of the salmon-rice burger.

The Westernized diet has caused many Japanese to become overweight. To counter this, the Japanese are buying low-calorie, low-fat foods to help shed excess weight and are flocking to health studios. All this began when U.S. occupation forces introduced bread, milk, and steak to Japanese culture. The effect on the Japanese was unintentional but, nevertheless, change occurred.[38] Had the intent been to introduce a new diet—that is, a strategy of planned change—specific steps could have been taken to identify resistance to dietary change and then to overcome these resistances, thus accelerating the process of change.

As an example of planned change, consider Pillsbury's strategy when it introduced its Green Giant brand of frozen vegetables to the Asian diet. Although vegetables are a significant part of the Asian diet, the time it took to prepare the family meal was a source of pride for Japanese mothers. Using frozen vegetables was considered an unwelcome shortcut that caused some guilt—a shortcut that was in conflict with the mother's perception of a "good" mother's role. The solution was to change the cultural perception. Pillsbury's strategy of planned change was to convince moms that using frozen vegetables gave them the opportunity to prepare their families' favorite foods more often. Green Giant focused on a frozen mixture of julienne carrots and burdock

---

[36] For an interesting text on change agents, see Gerald Zaltman and Robert Duncan, *Strategies for Planned Change* (New York: John Wiley & Sons, 1979).

[37] Steven Butler, "The Whopper Killed the Salmon Burger: Burger King's Plans for Meat-Loving Japanese," *U.S. News & World Report,* January 20, 1997, p. 57.

[38] Initially unintentional when meat and milk products were first introduced after WW II, there was, however, nothing unintentional about McDonald's or Burger King's plans to continue to accelerate the cultural change.

CROSSING BORDERS 4–8

Ici on Parle Francais

Frequently there is a conflict between a desire to borrow from another culture and the natural inclination not to pollute one's own culture by borrowing from others. France offers a good example of this conflict. On the one hand, the French accept such U.S. culture as the "Oprah Winfrey" show on television, award Sylvester "Rambo" Stallone the Order of Arts and Letters, listen to Bruce Springsteen, and dine on all-American gastronomic delights such as the Big Mac and Kentucky Fried Chicken. At the same time, there is an uneasy feeling that accepting so much from America will somehow dilute the true French culture. Thus, in an attempt to somehow control cultural pollution, France is embarking on a campaign to expunge examples of "franglais" from all walks of life, including television, billboards, and business contracts. If the culture ministry has its way, violators will be fined. Lists of correct translations include *heures de grande ecoute* for "prime time," *coussin gonflable de protection* for "airbag," sable americain for "cookie," and some 3,500 other less-offensive expressions. While the demand for hamburgers and U.S. TV shows cannot be stemmed, perhaps the language can be saved.

With a tongue-in-cheek response, an English lawmaker said he would introduce a bill in Parliament to ban the use of French words in public. Order an aperitif in a British bar or demand an encore at the end of an opera and you might be in trouble—and so goes the "language wars."

Perhaps the French should be concerned. After years of "Law and Order"-type TV dramas seen in France, it is reported that French prisoners address a judge in a courtroom as "Your Honor," rather than the traditionally acceptable "Mr. President." They also ask to have their "Miranda rights read to them" and routinely demand to see a warrant when police want to search their homes. Neither is part of the French legal code.

Postscript. The use of foreign words in media and advertising got a last-minute reprieve when France's highest constitutional authority struck down the most controversial parts of the law, saying it only applies to public services and not to private citizens.

Sources: Adapted from Maarten Huygen, "The Invasion of the American Way," *World Press Review*, November 1992, pp. 28–29; "La Guerre Franglaise," *Fortune*, June 13, 1994, p. 14; "Briton Escalates French Word-War," *Reuters*, June 21, 1994; and Jeanne Binstock van Rij, "Trends, Symbols, and Brand Power in Global Market: The Business Anthropology Approach," *Strategy & Leadership*, November 21, 1996, p. 18.

root, a traditional Asian root vegetable that requires several hours of tedious preparation. Additionally, the company introduced individual seasoned vegetable servings for school lunch boxes. Although fresh vegetables still dominate the market, the strategy of planned change is working, and frozen varieties account for half the company's vegetable sales in Japan.[39]

Just introducing a product whose acceptance requires change begins the process of cultural change even if the company does nothing consciously to change behavior. An innovation that has advantages but requires a culture to learn new ways to benefit from these advantages establishes the basis for eventual cultural change. Both a strategy of unplanned change and a strategy of planned change as in the Green Giant example produce cultural change. The fundamental difference is that unplanned change proceeds at its own pace whereas in planned change, the process of change is accelerated by the

---

[39] Tara Parker-Pope, "The Most Successful Companies Have to Realize a Simple Truth: All Consumers Aren't Alike," *The Wall Street Journal,* September 26, 1996, p. R22.

change agent. While culturally congruent strategy, strategy of unplanned change, and strategy of planned change are not clearly articulated in international business literature, the three situations occur. The marketer's efforts become part of the fabric of culture—planned or unplanned.

Marketing strategy is judged culturally in terms of acceptance, resistance, or rejection. How marketing efforts interact with a culture determines the degree of success or failure, but even failures leave their imprint on a culture. All too often marketers are not aware of the scope of their impact on a host culture.

The foreign marketer can function as a change agent and design a strategy to change certain aspects of a culture to overcome resistance to an innovative product. If a strategy of planned change is implemented, the marketer has some responsibility to determine the consequences of such action.

Consequences of an Innovation

When product diffusion (acceptance) occurs, a process of social change may also occur. One issue frequently addressed concerns the consequences of the changes that happen within a social system as a result of acceptance of an innovation. The marketer seeking product diffusion and adoption may inadvertently bring about change that affects the very fabric of a social system. Consequences of diffusion of an innovation may be functional or dysfunctional, depending on whether the effects on the social system are desirable or undesirable. In most instances, the marketer's concern is with perceived functional consequences—the positive benefits of product use. Indeed, in most situations innovative products for which the marketer purposely sets out to gain cultural acceptance have minimal, if any, dysfunctional consequences, but that cannot be taken for granted.

On the surface, it would appear that the introduction of a processed feeding formula into the diet of babies in underdeveloped countries where protein deficiency is a health problem would have all the functional consequences of better nutrition and health, stronger and faster growth, and so forth. There is evidence, however, that in at least one situation the dysfunctional consequences far exceeded the benefits. In Nicaragua, as the result of the introduction of the formula, a significant number of babies annually were changed from breast-feeding to bottle-feeding before the age of six months. In the United States, with appropriate refrigeration and sanitation standards, a similar pattern exists with no apparent negative consequences. In Nicaragua, however, where sanitation methods are inadequate, a substantial increase in dysentery and diarrhea and a higher infant mortality rate have resulted.

A change from breast-feeding to bottle-feeding at an early age without the users' complete understanding of purification has caused dysfunctional consequences. This was the result of two factors: the impurity of the water used with the milk and the loss of the natural immunity to childhood disease that a mother's milk provides. This was a case of planned change that resulted in devastating consequences. The infant formula company set out to purposely change traditional breast-feeding to bottle-feeding. Advertising, promotions of infant formula using testimonials from nurses and midwives, and abundant free samples were used to encourage a change in behavior. It was a very successful marketing program but the consequences were unintentionally dysfunctional. An international boycott of its products by several groups resulted in the company agreeing to alter its marketing programs to encourage breast-feeding. This problem first occurred over 20 years ago and is still causing trouble for the company.[40] The consequences of

---

[40] "UNICEF Criticizes Firms Promoting Breastmilk Substitutes," *Agence France-Presse,* July 22, 1997; and Jacqui Wise, "Baby Milk Companies Accused of Breaching Marketing Code," *British Medical Journal,* January 18, 1997, p. 167

the introduction of an innovation can be serious for society and the company responsible, whether the act was intentional or not.[41]

Some marketers may question their responsibility beyond product safety as far as the consequences of being change agents are concerned. The authors' position is that the marketer has responsibility for the dysfunctional results of marketing efforts whether intentional or not. Foreign marketers may cause cultural changes that can create dysfunctional consequences. If proper analysis indicates negative results can be anticipated from the acceptance of an innovation, it is the responsibility of the marketer to design programs not only to gain acceptance for a product but also to eliminate any negative cultural effects.

Summary

A complete and thorough appreciation of the dimensions of culture may well be the single most important gain to a foreign marketer in the preparation of marketing plans and strategies. Marketers can control the product offered to a market—its promotion, price, and eventual distribution methods—but they have only limited control over the cultural environment within which these plans must be implemented. Because they cannot control all the influences on their marketing plans, they must attempt to anticipate the eventual effect of the uncontrollable elements and plan in such a way that these elements do not preclude the achievement of marketing objectives. They can also set about to effect changes that lead to quicker acceptance of their products or marketing programs. Planning marketing strategy in terms of

the uncontrollable elements of a market is necessary in a domestic market as well, but when a company is operating internationally each new environment influenced by elements unfamiliar and sometimes unrecognizable to the marketer complicates the task. For these reasons, special effort and study are needed to absorb enough understanding of the foreign culture to cope with the uncontrollable features. Perhaps it is safe to generalize that of all the tools the foreign marketer must have, those that help generate empathy for another culture are the most valuable. Each of the cultural elements is explored in depth in subsequent chapters. Specific attention is given to business customs, political culture, and legal culture in the following chapters.

Questions

1. Define:

cultural sensitivity	social institutions
culture	factual knowledge
ethnocentrism	interpretive knowledge
strategy of cultural congruence	cultural values
	cultural borrowing
cultural translator	material culture
strategy of unplanned change	aesthetics
	strategy of planned change

2. Which role does the marketer play as a change agent?

3. Discuss the three cultural change strategies a foreign marketer can pursue.

4. "Culture is pervasive in all marketing activities." Discuss.

5. What is the importance of cultural empathy to foreign marketers? How do they acquire cultural empathy?

6. Why should a foreign marketer be concerned with the study of culture?

7. What is the popular definition of culture? What is the viewpoint of cultural anthropologists? What is the importance of the difference?

8. It is stated that members of a society borrow from other cultures to solve problems that they face in common. What does this mean? What is the significance to marketing?

9. "For the inexperienced marketer, the 'similar-but-different' aspect of culture creates an illusion of similarity that usually does not exist." Discuss and give examples.

10. Outline the elements of culture as seen by an anthropologist. How can a marketer use this "cultural scheme"?

11. What is material culture? What are its implications for marketing? Give examples.

12. Social institutions affect marketing in a variety of ways. Discuss, giving examples.

13. Discuss the implications and meaning of the statement, "Markets are not, they become."

14. "Markets are the result of the three-way interaction of a marketer's efforts, economic conditions, and all other elements of the culture." Comment.

15. What are some particularly troublesome problems caused by language in foreign marketing? Discuss.

---

[41] See Case 1–3, Nestlé—The Infant Formula Incident, for a complete discussion of this example,

16. Suppose you were requested to prepare a cultural analysis for a potential market. What would you do? Outline the steps and comment briefly on each.

17. Cultures are dynamic. How do they change? Are there cases where changes are not resisted but actually preferred? Explain. What is the relevance to marketing?

18. How can resistance to cultural change influence product introduction? Are there any similarities in domestic marketing? Explain, giving examples.

19. Visit Channel A homepage (**http://www.channela. com/?eu**) and select, People and Culture. Read the information at the people and culture location and compare aspects of the Asian culture with your culture.

20. Innovations are described as being either functional or dysfunctional. Explain and give examples of each.

21. Defend the proposition that a multinational corporation has no responsibility for the consequences of an innovation beyond the direct effects of the innovation such as the product's safety, performance, and so forth.

22. Find a product whose introduction into a foreign culture may cause dysfunctional consequences and describe how the consequences might be eliminated and the product still profitably introduced.

BUSINESS CUSTOMS IN GLOBAL MARKETING

Chapter Learning Objectives

What you should learn from Chapter 5

- The obstacles to business transactions in international marketing.
- The influences of a culture on the modes of doing business.
- The effect of high-context, low-context cultures on business practices.
- The effects of disparate business ethics on international marketing.
- A guide to help make ethical and socially responsible decisions.

GLOBAL PERSPECTIVE

Different Cultures, Different Business Customs

Cultural misunderstandings can raise havoc on even the best business plans. Such was the case with an American businessman who flew to Tokyo to sign a contract with a Japanese company. His detailed itinerary allowed him a week to "get the contract in hand" and be back home.

On Monday, his first day in Tokyo, his Japanese counterpart invited him to play golf. They played, and the American won the game by a couple of strokes. The next day, the American expected to have a business meeting, but his counterpart wanted to play golf again. They did, and the American won again. When his host suggested another game the next day, the American blurted out in frustration, "But when are we going to start doing business?" His host, taken aback, responded, "But we have been doing business!"

Because the American did not realize what was going on, he probably didn't make the best business use of those golf outings. At the very least, he could have tried to lose on the second day (although his host, not wanting a guest to lose face, might have made it difficult for him to do so). As it turned out, they started meetings on the third day and a contract was signed on Saturday, but the American was in such a hurry to conclude the contract within the week that he conceded a number of points as his self-imposed deadline approached.

Conflicting culture-based business customs can jeopardize a deal before it even gets started. In this example, where were the conflicts and what are the possible consequences? First, each of the businessmen had different objectives. The Japanese executive was not focused on signing a contract. His culture is strongly collective, where life in general depends on close relationships, beginning with one's immediate family. In business, a contract is merely a guideline pertaining to one small transaction of a larger relationship between the parties. What he wanted was to get to know the American, to determine whether this was someone on whom he could depend in the future, and to build a relationship that would lead to not just one contract but many.

The American's primary objective, on the other hand, was to get a signature on that contract. His culture is strongly individualistic, one that emphasizes self-reliance and individual accomplishment. He had promised to return home with a signed contract for this transaction, not with some vague understanding for unknown deals that might or might not ever come to pass. The consequence was a missed opportunity to establish a strong relationship with the Japanese executive.

Second, each had different concepts of time. For the Japanese executive, time is important but it takes a back seat to getting things right. For him, the relationship needed to get off to a good start, and this could take as much time as needed. Then, in discussing the terms of the contract, everything had to be fully understood. This too could take as much time as needed. Conversely, for the American time is a precious commodity, not to be wasted on golf or nit-picking the terms of a standard contract that was comprehensible only to lawyers. The bottom line for him was that the contract needed to be signed by the end of the week.

The consequence, again, was a missed opportunity to build a strong relationship and a better understanding by both parties of the contractual obligations. A better understanding of the contract could prove helpful in avoiding disputes and, should a dispute occur, resolutions more easily mediated.

Third, the American displayed frustration. The American's focus was a completed deal and any activity perceived as delaying the final outcome was difficult to tolerate. Japanese society places a strong emphasis on maintaining harmony and avoiding surface confrontation. The consequence was a loss of stature that could make the American less effective in future business relations. When the American blurted out his frustration about not getting down to business he probably lost stature in his host's mind. For Japanese to show anger or frustration in a business relationship is to lose face. It also may have made it easier, in the eyes of the Japanese, to negotiate for concessions.

Fourth, the American was culturally naïve. By not understanding Japanese business customs, the American inadvertently was putting himself in a position for possible manipulation by the host. There is the possibility that the Japanese executive knew that the American businessman was culturally naïve and would become frustrated as each day slipped by with no direct discussion of the business deal. The consequence is the possibility that a host may take advantage of the cultural naïveté of their counterparts and create situations that force compromises and hasty decisions.

Source: "Different Cultures, Different Business Customs," Adapted from David James, "Cultural Flubs Can Kill International Business Deals," *Asian Business*, April 21, 1997. Also available at **http://www.channela.com/business/doingbiz/Djames/**

Business customs are as much a cultural element of a society as is the language. Culture not only establishes the criteria for day-to-day business behavior but also forms general patterns of attitude and motivation. Executives are to some extent captives of their cultural heritages and cannot totally escape language, heritage, political and family ties, or religious backgrounds. One report notes that Japanese culture, permeated by Shinto precepts, is not something apart from business but determines its very essence. Although international business managers may take on the trappings and appearances of the business behavior of another country, their basic frame of references is most likely to be that of their own people.

In the United States, for example, the historical perspective of individualism and "winning the West" seems to be manifest in individual wealth or corporate profit being dominant measures of success. Japan's lack of frontiers and natural resources and its dependence on trade have focused individual and corporate success criteria on uniformity, subordination to the group, and society's ability to maintain high levels of employment. The feudal background of southern Europe tends to emphasize maintenance of both individual and corporate power and authority while blending those feudal traits with paternalistic concern for minimal welfare for workers and other members of society. Various studies identify North Americans as individualists, Japanese as consensus-oriented and committed to the group, and central and southern Europeans as elitists and rank conscious. While these descriptions are stereotypical, they illustrate cultural differences that are often manifest in business behavior and practices.[1]

A lack of empathy for and knowledge of foreign business practices can create insurmountable barriers to successful business relations. Some businesses plot their strategies with the idea that counterparts of other business cultures are similar to their own and are moved by similar interests, motivations, and goals—that they are "just like us." Even though they may be just like us in some respects, enough differences exist to cause frustration, miscommunication, and, ultimately, failed business opportunities if they are not understood and responded to properly.[2]

Knowledge of the business culture, management attitudes, and business methods existing in a country and a willingness to accommodate the differences are important to success in an international market. Unless marketers remain flexible in their own attitudes by accepting differences in basic patterns of thinking, local business tempo, religious practices, political structure, and family loyalty, they are hampered, if not prevented, from reaching satisfactory conclusions to business transactions. In such situations, obstacles take many forms, but it is not unusual to have one negotiator's business proposition accepted over another's simply because "that one understands us."

This chapter focuses on matters specifically related to the business environment. Besides an analysis of the need for adaptation, it will review the structural elements, attitudes, and behavior of international business processes, concluding with a discussion of ethics and socially responsible decisions.

Required Adaptation

Adaptation is a key concept in international marketing and willingness to adapt is a crucial attitude. Adaptation, or at least accommodation, is required on small matters as well as large ones. In fact, the small, seemingly insignificant situations are often the most

---

[1] Edward T. Hall and Mildred Reed Hall, *Understanding Cultural Differences* (Yarmouth, Maine: Intercultural Press, 1990), p. 196. Also see Edward T. Hall, *The Dance of Life: The Other Dimension of Time* (New York: Peter Smith Publications, 1996).

[2] Haruyasu Ohsumi, "Cultural Differences and Japan–U.S. Economic Frictions," *Tokyo Business Today,* February 1995, pp. 49–52.

Securities market in Oman. Respect for cultural
differences is imperative for successful business
relations. (Dod Miller/Network/SABA)

crucial. More than tolerance of an alien culture is required. There is a need for affirmative acceptance, that is, open tolerance of the concept "different but equal." Through
such affirmative acceptance, adaptation becomes easier because empathy for another's
point of view naturally leads to ideas for meeting cultural differences.

As a guide to adaptation, there are ten basic criteria that all who wish to deal
with individuals, firms, or authorities in foreign countries should be able to meet. They
are: (1) open tolerance, (2) flexibility, (3) humility, (4) justice/fairness, (5) ability to
adjust to varying tempos, (6) curiosity/interest, (7) knowledge of the country, (8) liking
for others, (9) ability to command respect, and (10) ability to integrate oneself into
the environment. In short, add the quality of adaptability to the qualities of a good executive for a composite of the perfect international marketer. It is difficult to argue with
these ten items. As one critic commented, "They border on the 12 Boy Scout laws."
However, as we complete this chapter we see that it is the obvious that we sometimes
overlook.

Degree of Adaptation

Adaptation does not require business executives to forsake their ways and change to
conform to local customs; rather, executives must be aware of local customs and be
willing to accommodate those differences that can cause misunderstanding. Essential to
effective adaptation is awareness of one's own culture and the recognition that differences in others can cause anxiety, frustration, and misunderstanding of the host's intentions. The self-reference criterion (SRC) is especially operative in business customs. If
we do not understand our foreign counterpart's customs, we are more likely to evaluate
that person's behavior in terms of what is acceptable to us.

The key to adaptation is to remain American but to develop an understanding and willingness to accommodate differences that exist. A successful marketer knows that in China it is important to make points without winning arguments; criticism, even if asked for, can cause a host to "lose face." In Germany, it is considered discourteous to use first names unless specifically invited to do so; always address a person as *Herr, Frau,* or *Fraulein* with the last name. In Brazil, do not be offended by the Brazilian inclination to touch during conversation. Such a custom is not a violation of your personal space but rather the Brazilian way of greeting, emphasizing a point or as a gesture of goodwill and friendship.

A Chinese, German, or Brazilian does not expect you to act like one of them. After all, you are not Chinese, German, or Brazilian, but American, and it would be foolish for an American to give up the ways that have contributed so notably to American success. It would be equally foolish for others to give up their ways. When different cultures meet, open tolerance and a willingness to accommodate each other's differences are necessary. Once a marketer is aware of the possibility of cultural differences and the probable consequences of failure to adapt or accommodate, the seemingly endless variety of customs must be assessed. Where does one begin? Which customs should be absolutely adhered to? Which others can be ignored? Fortunately, among the many obvious differences that exist between cultures, only a few are troubling.

Imperatives, Adiaphora, and Exclusives

Business customs can be grouped into *imperatives,* customs that must be recognized and accommodated; *adiaphora,* customs to which adaptation is optional; and *exclusives,* customs in which an outsider must not participate. An international marketer must appreciate the nuances of cultural imperatives, cultural adiaphora, and cultural exclusives.

Cultural Imperatives.   *Cultural imperatives* refer to the business customs and expectations that must be met and conformed to or avoided if relationships are to be successful. Successful businesspeople know the Chinese word *guan-xi,* the Japanese *ningen kankei,* or the Latin American *compadre.* All refer to friendship, human relations, or attaining a level of trust. They also know there is no substitute for establishing friendship in some cultures before effective business negotiations can begin.

Informal discussions, entertaining, mutual friends, contacts, and just spending time with others are ways *guan-xi, ningen kankei, compadre,* and other trusting relationships are developed. In those cultures where friendships are a key to success, the businessperson should not slight the time required for their development. Friendship motivates local agents to make more sales and friendship helps establish the right relationship with end users, leading to more sales over a longer period. Naturally, after-sales service, price, and the product must be competitive, but the marketer who has established *guan-xi, ningen kankei,* or *compadre* has the edge. Establishing friendship is an imperative in many cultures.[3] If friendship is not established, the marketer risks not earning trust and acceptance, the basic cultural prerequisites for developing and retaining effective business relationships.

In some cultures a person's demeanor is more critical than in other cultures. For example, it is probably never acceptable to lose your patience, raise your voice, or correct someone in public however frustrating the situation. In some cultures such behavior would only cast you as boorish, but in others it could end a business deal. In China, Japan, and other Asian cultures it is imperative to avoid causing your counterpart to "lose face." In China to raise your voice, to shout at a Chinese person in public, or to correct them in front of their peers will cause them to lose face.[4]

---

³ "Business in Egypt Is Personal," *Business America,* December 1996, p. 8.
⁴ "Tips on Business Etiquette—Taiwan," *Asia Pulse,* May 27, 1997.

A complicating factor in cultural awareness is that what may be an imperative to avoid in one culture is an imperative to do in another. For example, in Japan prolonged eye contact is considered offensive and it is imperative that it be avoid. However, with Arab and Latin American executives it is important to make strong eye contact or you run the risk of being seen as evasive and untrustworthy.[5]

Cultural Adiaphora.[6]   *Cultural adiaphora* relates to areas of behavior or to customs that cultural aliens may wish to conform to or participate in but that are not required; in other words, it is not particularly important but permissible to follow the custom in question. The majority of customs fit into this category. One need not greet another man with a kiss (a custom in some countries), eat foods that disagree with the digestive system (so long as the refusal is gracious), or drink alcoholic beverages (if for health, personal, or religious reasons). On the other hand, a symbolic attempt to participate in adiaphora is not only acceptable but also may help to establish rapport. It demonstrates that the marketer has studied the culture. Japanese do not expect a Westerner to bow and to understand the ritual of bowing among Japanese, yet a symbolic bow indicates interest and some sensitivity to their culture that is acknowledged as a gesture of goodwill. It may help pave the way to a strong, trusting relationship.

For the most part adiaphora are customs that are optional, although adiaphora in one culture may be perceived as imperative in another. In some cultures one can accept or tactfully and politely reject an offer of a beverage, while in other cases the offer of a beverage is a ritual and not to accept is to insult. In the Czech Republic an aperitif or other liqueur offered at the beginning of a business meeting, even in the morning, is a way to establish good will and trust. It is a sign that you are being welcomed as a friend. It is imperative that you accept unless you make it clear to your Czech counterpart that the refusal is because of health or religion.[7] Chinese business negotiations often include banquets at which large quantities of alcohol are consumed in an endless series of toasts. It is imperative that you participate in the toasts with a raised glass of the offered beverage but to drink is optional. Your Arab business associates will offer coffee as part of the important ritual of establishing a level of friendship and trust; you should accept even if you only take a ceremonial sip.[8] Cultural adiaphora are the most visibly different customs and thus more obvious. Often, it is compliance with the less obvious imperatives and exclusives that is more critical.[9]

Cultural Exclusives.   *Cultural exclusives* are those customs or behavior patterns reserved exclusively for the locals and from which the foreigner is excluded. For example, a Christian attempting to act like a Muslim would be repugnant to a follower of Mohammed. Equally offensive is a foreigner criticizing a country's politics, mores, and peculiarities (that is, peculiar to the foreigner) even though locals may, among themselves, criticize such issues. There is truth in the old adage, "I'll curse my brother but, if you curse him, you'll have a fight." There are few cultural traits reserved exclusively for locals, but a foreigner must carefully refrain from participating in those that are reserved.

Foreign managers need to be perceptive enough to know when they are dealing with an imperative, an adiaphora, or an exclusive and have the adaptability to respond to each. There are not many imperatives or exclusives, but most offensive behavior results

---

[5] Erika Rasmusson, "Beyond Miss Manners: The Importance of International Business Etiquette," *Sales & Marketing Management,* April 1, 1997, p. 84.

[6] Adiaphora can be considered to mean cultural options.

[7] Lou Vargo, "Avoiding Cross-Cultural Blunders," *Trade & Culture,* February/March 1997, p. 47.

[8] "Minding Your Manners in the Middle East," *International Business,* November 1997, p. 25.

[9] See, for example, Edward Peck, "Doing Business without Condescension," *Trade & Culture,* October/November 1996, p. 47.

CROSSING BORDERS 5-1

Jokes Don't Travel Well

Cross-cultural humor has its pitfalls. What is funny to you may not be funny to others. Humor is culturally specific and thus rooted in people's shared experiences. Here are examples:

President Jimmy Carter was in Mexico to build bridges and mend fences. On live television President Carter and President Jose Lopez Portillo were giving speeches. In response to a comment by President Portillo, Carter said, "We both have beautiful and interesting wives, and we both run several kilometers every day. In fact, I first acquired my habit of running here in Mexico City. My first running course was from the Palace of Fine Arts to the Majestic Hotel where my family and I were staying. In the midst of the Folklorico performance, I discovered that I was afflicted with Montezuma's Revenge." Among Americans this may have been an amusing comment but it was not funny to the Mexican. Editorials in Mexico and U.S. newspapers commented on the inappropriateness of the remark.

Most jokes, even though well intended, don't translate well. Sometimes a translator can help you out. One speaker, in describing his experience, said, "I began my speech with a joke that took me about two minutes to tell. Then my interpreter translated my story. About thirty seconds later the Japanese audience laughed loudly. I continued with my talk which seemed well received," he said, "but at the end, just to make sure, I asked the interpreter, 'How did you translate my joke so quickly?' The interpreter replied, 'Oh I didn't translate your story at all. I didn't understand it. I simply said our foreign speaker has just told a joke so would you all please laugh.'"

Who can say with certainty that anything is funny? Laughter, more often than not, symbolizes embarrassment, nervousness, or even scorn. Hold your humor until you are comfortable with the culture.

Sources: Robert T. Moran, "What's Funny to You May Not Be Funny to Other Cultures," *International Management,* July–August 1987, p. 74; Richard Hill, "No Laughing Matter," *Trade & Culture,* November–December 1994, pp. 68–69; and Richard D. Lewis, *When Cultures Collide* (London: Nicholas Brealey Publishing, 1997), pp. 20–24.

from not recognizing them. It is not necessary to obsess over committing a faux pas. Most sensible businesspeople will make allowances for the occasional misstep. But the fewer you make the smoother the relationship will be. When in doubt, rely on good manners and respect for those with whom you are associating.

Methods of Doing Business

Because of the diverse structures, management attitudes, and behaviors encountered in international business, there is considerable latitude in ways business is conducted. No matter how thoroughly prepared a marketer may be when approaching a foreign market, a certain amount of cultural shock occurs when differences in contact level, communications emphasis, tempo, and formality of foreign businesses are encountered. Ethical standards are likely to differ, as will the negotiation emphasis. In most countries, the foreign trader is also likely to encounter a fairly high degree of government involvement. Among the four dimensions of Hofstede's cultural values discussed in Chapter 4,

In many emerging markets, timely telephone calls were often impossible before the advent of cell phones like the one being used in front of the Forbidden City (Beijing). (Forrest Anderson/Liaison International)

Individualism/Collectivism (IDV) and Power Distance (PDI) are especially relevant in examining methods of doing business among countries.

Sources and Level of Authority

Business size, ownership, public accountability, and cultural values that determine the prominence of status and position (PDI) combine to influence the authority structure of business. In high PDI countries like Mexico and Malaysia, understanding the rank and status of clients and business partners is much more important than in more egalitarian (low PDI) societies like Denmark and Israel. In high PDI countries subordinates are not likely to contradict bosses, but in low PDI countries they often do. Although the international businessperson is confronted with a variety of authority patterns, most are a variation of three typical patterns: top-level management decisions; decentralized decisions; and committee or group decisions.

Top-level management decision making is generally found in those situations where family or close ownership gives absolute control to owners and where businesses are small enough to make such centralized decision making possible. In many European businesses, such as in France, decision-making authority is guarded jealously by a few at the top who exercise tight control. In other countries, such as Mexico[10] and

---

[10] Gregory K. Stephens and Charles R. Greer, "Doing Business in Mexico: Understanding Cultural Differences," *Organizational Dynamics*, June 1995, p. 39.

CROSSING BORDERS 5–2

Meishi—Presenting a Business Card in Japan

In Japan the business card, or *Meishi,* is the executive's trademark. It is both a mini résumé and a friendly deity that draws people together. No matter how many times you have talked with a businessperson by phone before you actually meet, business cannot really begin until you formally exchange cards.

The value of a *Meishi* cannot be overemphasized; up to 12 million are exchanged daily and a staggering 4.4 billion annually. For a businessperson to make a call or receive a visitor without a card is like a Samurai going off to battle without his sword. There are a variety of ways to present a card, depending on the giver's personality and style:

> *Crab style*—held out between the index and middle fingers.
>
> *Pincer*—clamped between the thumb and index finger.
>
> *Pointer*—offered with the index finger pressed along the edge.
>
> *Upside down*—the name is facing away from the recipient.
>
> *Platter fashion*—served in the palm of the hand.

The card should be presented during the earliest stages of introduction, so the Japanese recipient will be able to determine your position and rank and know how to respond to you. The normal procedure is for the Japanese to hand you their name card and accept yours at the same time. They read your card and then formally greet you either by bowing or shaking hands or both.

Not only is there a way to present a card, there is also a way of receiving a card. It makes a good impression to receive a card in both hands, especially when the other party is senior in age or status. Do not put the card away before reading or you will insult the other person, and never write on a person's card in their presence as this may cause offense.

Sources: Adapted from "Meishi," *Sumitomo Quarterly,* Autumn 1986, p. 3; Boye Lafayette DeMente, *Japanese Etiquette and Ethics in Business.* 6th ed. (Lincolnwood, IL: NTC Business Books, 1994), p. 24; and "Tips on Business Etiquette—Japan, *Asia Pulse,* April 4, 1997.

Venezuela, where a semi-feudal, land-equals-power heritage exists, management styles are characterized as autocratic and paternalistic. Decision-making participation by middle management tends to be deemphasized; dominant family members make decisions that tend to please the family members more than to increase productivity. This is also true for government-owned companies where professional managers have to follow decisions made by politicians, who generally lack any working knowledge about management.[11] In Middle Eastern countries, the top man makes all decisions and prefers to deal only with other executives with decision-making powers. There, one always does business with an individual per se rather than an office or title.

As businesses grow and professional management develops, there is a shift toward decentralized management decision making. Decentralized decision making allows executives at different levels of management authority over their own functions. This is typical of large-scale businesses with highly developed management systems such as those found in the United States. A trader in the United States is likely to be dealing

---

[11] Mike Johnson, "Untapped Latin America: Challenges of Doing Business In Latin America," *Management Review,* July 1996, p. 31.

CROSSING BORDERS 5–3

The Eagle: An Exclusive in Mexico

According to legend, the site of the Aztec City of Tenochtitlán, now Mexico City, was revealed to its founders by an eagle bearing a snake in its claws and alighting on a cactus. That image is now the official seal of the country and appears on its flag. Thus, Mexican authorities were furious to discover their beloved eagle splattered with catsup by an interloper from north of the border: McDonald's.

To commemorate Mexico's Flag Day, two Golden Arches outlets in Mexico City papered their trays with placemats embossed with a representation of the national emblem. Eagle-eyed government agents swooped down and confiscated the disrespectful placemats. A senior partner in McDonald's of Mexico explained, "Our intention was never to give offense. It was to help Mexicans learn about their culture."

It is not always clear what symbols or what behavior patterns in a country are reserved exclusively for locals. In McDonald's case there is no question that the use of the eagle was considered among Mexicans as an exclusive for Mexicans only.

Source: Matt Moffett, "For U.S. Firms, Franchising in Mexico Gets More Appetizing, Thanks to Reform," *The Wall Street Journal,* January 3, 1991, p. A8. Read more about the legend of the eagle and snake in Enrique Krauze, *Mexico: Biography of Power* (New York: Harper Collins, 1997), p. 11.

with middle management, and title or position generally takes precedence over the individual holding the job.

Committee decision making is by group or consensus. Committees may operate on a centralized or decentralized basis, but the concept of committee management implies something quite different from the individualized functioning of the top management and decentralized decision-making arrangements just discussed. Because Asian cultures and religions tend to emphasize harmony and collectivism, it is not surprising that group decision making predominates there. Despite the emphasis on rank and hierarchy in Japanese social structure, business emphasizes group participation, group harmony, and group decision making—but at top management level.

The demands of these three types of authority systems on a marketer's ingenuity and adaptability are evident. In the case of the authoritative and delegated societies, the chief problem would be to identify the individual with authority. In the committee decision setup, it is necessary that every committee member be convinced of the merits of the proposition or product in question. The marketing approach to each of these situations differs.

Management Objectives and Aspirations

The training and background (i.e., cultural environment) of managers significantly affect their personal and business outlooks. Society as a whole establishes the social rank or status of management, and cultural background dictates patterns of aspirations and objectives among businesspeople. These cultural influences affect the attitude of managers toward innovation, new products, and conducting business with foreigners. To fully understand another's management style, one must appreciate an individual's objectives and aspirations that are usually reflected in the goals of the business organization and in the practices that prevail within the company. In dealing with foreign business, a marketer must be particularly aware of the varying objectives and aspirations of management.

CROSSING BORDERS 5-4

Business Protocol in a Unified Europe

Now that 1992 has come and gone and the European Community is now a single market, does it mean that all differences have been wiped away? For some of the legal differences, yes! For cultural differences, no!

There is always the issue of language and meaning even when you both speak English. English and American English are often miles apart. If you tell someone his presentation was "quite good," an American will beam with pleasure. A Brit will ask you what was wrong with it; you have just told him politely that he barely scraped by. Then there is the matter of humor. The anecdote you open a meeting with may fly well with your American audience; however, the French will smile, the Belgians will laugh, the Dutch will be puzzled, and the Germans will take you literally. Humor doesn't travel well.

And then there are the French, who are very attentive to hierarchy and ceremony. When first meeting with a French-speaking businessperson, stick with *monsieur, Madame,* or *mademoiselle;* the use of first names is disrespectful to the French. If you don't speak French fluently, apologize. Such apology shows general respect for the language and dismisses any stigma of American arrogance.

The formality of dress can vary with each country also. The Brit and the Dutchman will take off their jackets and literally roll up their sleeves; they mean to get down to business. The Spaniard will loosen his tie, while the German disapproves—he thinks they look sloppy and unbusinesslike, and he keeps his coat on throughout the meeting. So does the Italian, but that was because he dressed especially for the look of the meeting.

With all that, did the meeting decide anything? It was, after all, a first meeting. The Brits were just exploring the terrain, checking out the broad perimeters and all that. The French were assessing the other players' strengths and weaknesses and deciding what position to take at the next meeting. The Italians also won't have taken it too seriously. For them it was a meeting to arrange the meeting agenda for the real meeting. Only the Germans will have assumed it was what it seemed and be surprised when the next meeting starts open-ended.

Sources: Adapted from Barry Day, "The Art of Conducting International Business," *Advertising Age,* October 8, 1990, p. 46; and Brad Ketchum Jr., "Faux Pas Go with the Territory," *Inc.,* May 1994, pp. 4–5.

Personal Goals.   In the United States, we emphasize profit or high wages while in other countries security, good personal life, acceptance, status, advancement, or power may be emphasized. Individual goals are highly personal in any country, so it is hard to generalize to the extent of saying that managers in any one country always have a specific orientation. For example, studies have shown that Kuwaiti managers are more likely than American managers to make business decisions consistent with their own personal goals. Swedish managers were found to express little reluctance in bypassing the hierarchical line, while Italian managers believed that bypassing the hierarchical line was a serious offense.[12]

Security and Mobility.   Personal security and job mobility relate directly to basic human motivation and therefore have widespread economic and social implications. The

---

[12] William J. Bigoness and Gerald L. Blakely, "A Cross-National Study of Managerial Values," *Journal of International Business Studies,* Winter 1996, p. 739.

word *security* is somewhat ambiguous and this very ambiguity provides some clues to managerial variation. To some, security means good wages and the training and ability required for moving from company to company within the business hierarchy; for others, it means the security of lifetime positions with their companies; to still others, it means adequate retirement plans and other welfare benefits. In European companies, particularly in the countries late in industrializing such as France and Italy, there is a strong paternalistic orientation, and it is assumed that individuals will work for one company for the majority of their lives. For example, in Britain managers place great importance on individual achievement and autonomy, whereas French managers place great importance on competent supervision, sound company policies, fringe benefits, security, and comfortable working conditions. There is much less mobility among French managers than British.[13]

Personal Life.   For many individuals, a good personal life takes priority over profit, security, or any other goal. In his worldwide study of individual aspirations, David McClelland discovered that the culture of some countries stressed the virtue of a good personal life as being far more important than profit or achievement. The hedonistic outlook of ancient Greece explicitly included work as an undesirable factor that got in the way of the search for pleasure or a good personal life. Perhaps at least part of the standard of living that we enjoy in the United States today can be attributed to the hardworking Protestant ethic from which we derive much of our business heritage.

To the Japanese, personal life is company life. Many Japanese workers regard their work as the most important part of their overall lives. Metaphorically speaking, such workers may even find themselves "working in a dream." The Japanese work ethic—maintenance of a sense of purpose—derives from company loyalty and frequently results in the Japanese employee maintaining identity with the corporation.

Social Acceptance.   In some countries, acceptance by neighbors and fellow workers appears to be a predominant goal within business. The Asian outlook is reflected in the group decision making so important in Japan, and the Japanese place high importance on fitting in with their group. Group identification is so strong in Japan that when a worker is asked what he does for a living, he generally answers by telling you he works for Sumitomo or Mitsubishi or Matsushita, rather than that he is a chauffeur, an engineer, or a chemist.

Power.   Although there is some power-seeking by business managers throughout the world, power seems to be a more important motivating force in South American countries. In these countries, many business leaders are not only profit-oriented but also use their business positions to become social and political leaders.

Communications Emphasis

Probably no language readily translates into another because the meanings of words differ widely among languages. Even though it is the basic communication tool of marketers trading in foreign lands, managers, particularly from the United States, often fail to develop even a basic understanding of a foreign language, much less master the linguistic nuances that reveal unspoken attitudes and information. One writer comments that "even a good interpreter doesn't solve the language problem." Seemingly similar business terms in English and Japanese often have different meanings. In fact, the Japanese language is so inherently vague that even the well educated have difficulty communicating clearly among themselves. A communications authority on the Japanese language estimates that the Japanese are able to fully understand each other only about

---

[13] Ibid., p. 740.

CROSSING BORDERS 5–5

You Don't Have to Be a Hollywood Star to Wear Dark Glasses

Arabs may watch the pupils of your eyes to judge your responses to different topics.

A psychologist at the University of Chicago discovered that the pupil is a very sensitive indicator of how people respond to a situation. When you are interested in something, your pupils dilate; if you hear something you don't like, your eyes tend to contract. The Arabs have known about the pupil response for hundreds if not thousands of years. And because people can't control the response of their eyes, many Arabs wear dark glasses, even indoors.

These are people reading the personal interaction on a second-to-second basis. By watching the pupils, they can respond rapidly to mood changes. That's one of the reasons why they use a closer conversational distance than Americans do. At about five feet, the normal distance between two Americans who are talking, we have a hard time following eye movement. But if you use an Arab distance, about two feet, you can watch the pupil of the eye.

Direct eye contact for an American is difficult to achieve because we are taught in the United States not to stare, not to look at the eyes that carefully. If you stare at someone, it is too intense, too sexy, or too hostile. It also may mean that we are not totally tuned in to the situation. Maybe we should all wear dark glasses.

Source: Authors.

85 percent of the time. The Japanese often prefer English-language contracts where words have specific meanings.

The translation and interpretation of clearly worded statements and common usage is difficult enough, but when slang is added the task is almost impossible. In an exchange between an American and a Chinese official, the American answered affirmatively to a Chinese proposal with, "It's a great idea, Mr. Li, but who's going to put wheels on it?" The interpreter, not wanting to lose face but not understanding, turned to the Chinese official and said, "And now the American has made a proposal regarding the automobile industry"; the entire conversation was disrupted by a misunderstanding of a slang expression.

The best policy when dealing in other languages, even with a skilled interpreter, is to stick to formal language patterns. The use of slang phrases puts the interpreter in the uncomfortable position of guessing at meanings. Foreign language skills are critical in all negotiations, so it is imperative to seek the best possible personnel. Even then, especially in translations involving Asian languages, misunderstandings occur.

Linguistic communication, no matter how imprecise, is explicit, but much business communication depends on implicit messages that are not verbalized. E. T. Hall, professor of anthropology and, for decades, consultant to business and government on intercultural relations, says, "In some cultures, messages are explicit; the words carry most of the information. In other cultures . . . less information is contained in the verbal part of the message since more is in the context."[14]

---

[14] E. T. Hall, "Learning the Arabs' Silent Language," *Psychology Today,* August 1979, pp. 45–53. Hall has several books that should be read by everyone involved in international business: *Beyond Culture* (New York: Anchor Press-Doubleday, 1976); *The Hidden Dimension* (New York: Doubleday, 1966); and *The Silent Language* (New York: Doubleday, 1959).

EXHIBIT 5-1 Contextual Background of Various Countries

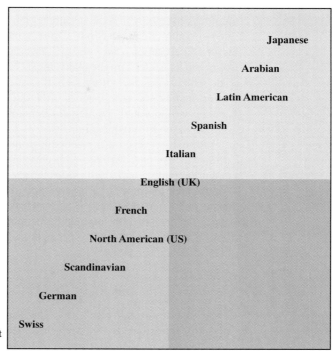

Note: Patterned after E. T. Hall.

Hall divides cultures into high-context and low-context cultures. Communication in a high-context culture depends heavily on the context or nonverbal aspects of communication, whereas the low-context culture depends more on explicit, verbally expressed communications (see Exhibit 5–1).

Recent studies have identified a strong relationship between Hall's high/low context and Hofstede's individualism/collectivism (IDV) and power distance (PDI) indices. For example, low-context American culture scores relatively low on power distance and high on individualism, while high-context Arab cultures score high on power distance and low on individualism.[15] Managers in general probably function best at a low-context level because they are accustomed to reports, contracts, and other written communications.

In a low-context culture, one gets down to business quickly. In a high-context culture it takes considerably longer to conduct business because of the need to know more about a businessperson before a relationship develops. High-context businesspeople simply do not know how to handle a low-context relationship with other people. Hall suggests that, "in the Middle East, if you aren't willing to take the time to sit down and have coffee with people, you have a problem. You must learn to wait and not be too eager to talk business. You can ask about the family or ask, 'How are you feeling?' but avoid too many personal questions about wives because people are apt to get suspicious. Learn to make what we call chitchat. If you don't, you can't go to the next step. It's a little bit like a courtship." Even in low-context cultures, our communication is heavily dependent on our cultural context. Most of us are not aware of how dependent we are on

---

[15] H. Rika Houston and John L. Graham, "Some Antecedents and Consequences of Corruption in Foreign Markets," *Working Paper, University of California, Irvine,* 1988.

the context, and, as Hall suggests, "Since much of our culture operates outside our awareness, *frequently we don't even know what we know.*"[16]

As an example of this phenomenon, one study discusses hinting, a common trait among Chinese, which the researcher describes as "somewhere between verbal and nonverbal communications."[17] In China, comments such as, "I agree," might mean "I agree with 15 percent of what you say"; "we might be able to" could mean "not a chance"; or "we will consider" might really mean "we will, but the real decision maker will not." The Chinese speaker often feels that such statements are very blunt with a clear hint; unfortunately, the U.S. listener often does not get the point at all. Prior experience, the context within which a statement is made, and who is making the comment are all important in modifying meaning.

Probably every businessperson from America or other relatively low-context countries who has had dealings with counterparts in high-context countries can tell stories about the confusion on both sides because of the different perceptual frameworks of the communication process. It is not enough to master the basic language of a country; the astute marketer must have a mastery over the language of business and the silent languages of nuance and implication. Communication mastery, then, is not only the mastery of a language but also a mastery of customs and culture. Such mastery develops only through long association.

Formality and Tempo

The breezy informality and haste that seem to characterize the American business relationship appear to be American exclusives that businesspeople from other countries not only fail to share but also fail to appreciate. This apparent informality, however, does not indicate a lack of commitment to the job. Comparing British and American business managers, an English executive commented about the American manager's compelling involvement in business, "At a cocktail party or a dinner, the American is still on duty."

Even though Northern Europeans seem to have picked up some American attitudes in recent years, do not count on them being "Americanized." As one writer says, "While using first names in business encounters is regarded as an American vice in many countries, nowhere is it found more offensive than in France," where formality still reigns. Those who work side by side for years still address one another with formal pronouns. France ranks fairly high on the power distance value orientation (PDI) scale while the United States ranks much lower, and such differences can lead to cultural misunderstandings. For example, the formalities of French business practices as opposed to Americans' casual manners are symbols of the French need to show rank and Americans' tendency to downplay it. Thus, the French are dubbed snobbish by Americans, while the French consider Americans Philistines.[18]

Haste and impatience are probably the most common mistakes of North Americans attempting to trade in the Middle East. Most Arabs do not like to embark on serious business discussions until after two or three opportunities to meet the individual they are dealing with; negotiations are likely to be prolonged. Arabs may make rapid decisions once they are prepared to do so, but they do not like to be rushed and they do not like deadlines. The managing partner of the Kuwait office of KMPG Peat Marwick LLP says

---

[16] For a detailed presentation of the differences in high- and low-context cultures, see Edward T. Hall and Mildred Reed Hall, *Hidden Differences: Doing Business with the Japanese* (New York: Doubleday Anchor Books, 1990), p. 172.

[17] Jeanette W. Gilsdorf, "Metacommunication Effects on International Business Negotiating In China," *Business Communication Quarterly,* June 1997, p. 20.

[18] Claire Gouttefarde, "American Values in the French Workplace," *Business Horizons,* March–April 1996, p. 60.

CROSSING BORDERS 5–6

You Say You Speak English?

The English speak English and North Americans speak English, but can the two communicate? It is difficult unless you understand that in England:

Newspapers are sold at *bookstalls.*

The *ground floor* is the main floor, while the *first floor* is what we call the second, and so on up the building.

An apartment house is a *block of flats.*

You will be putting your clothes not in a closet, but in a *cupboard.*

A closet usually refers to the W.C. or *water closet,* which is the toilet.

When one of your British friends says she is going to "spend a penny," she is going to the ladies' room.

A *bathing dress* or *bathing costume* is what the British call a bathing suit, and for those who want to go shopping, it is essential to know that a *tunic* is a blouse; a *stud* is a collar button, nothing more; and *garters* are suspenders.

Suspenders are *braces.*

If you want to buy a sweater, you should ask for a *jumper* or a *jersey* as the recognizable item will be marked in British clothing stores.

A *ladder* is not used for climbing but refers to a run in a stocking.

If you *called up* someone, it means to your British friend that you have drafted the person—probably for military service. To *ring someone up* is to telephone them.

You put your packages in the *boot* of your car, not the trunk.

When you *table* something, you mean you want to discuss it, not postpone it as in the United States.

Any reference by you to an *M.D.* will probably not bring a doctor. The term means mental deficient in Britain.

When the desk clerk asks what time you want to be *knocked up* in the morning, he is only referring to your wake-up call.

A *billion* means a million million (1,000,000,000,000) and not a thousand million as in the United States.

Sources: Adapted from Margaret Zellers, "How to Speak English," *Denver Post,* date unknown; and Copeland and Griggs, *Going International,* pp. 101–102.

---

of the "flying-visit" approach of many American businesspeople, "What in the West might be regarded as dynamic activity—the 'I've only got a day here' approach—may well be regarded here as merely rude."

Marketers who expect maximum success have to deal with foreign executives in ways that are acceptable to the foreigner. Latin Americans depend greatly on friendships but establish these friendships only in the South American way: slowly, over a considerable period of time. A typical Latin American is highly formal until a genuine relationship of respect and friendship is established. Even then the Latin American is slow to get down to business and will not be pushed. In keeping with the culture, *mañana* (tomorrow) is good enough. How people perceive time helps to explain some of the differences between U.S. managers and those from other cultures.

P-Time versus M-Time

North Americans are a more time-bound culture than Middle Eastern and Latin cultures. Our stereotype of those cultures is "they are always late," and their view of us is "you are always prompt." Neither statement is completely true though both contain some truth. What is true, however, is that we are a very time-oriented society—time is money to us—whereas in other cultures time is to be savored, not spent.

Edward Hall defines two time systems in the world: monochronic and polychronic time. *M-time,* or monochronic time, typifies most North Americans, Swiss, Germans, and Scandinavians. These Western cultures tend to concentrate on one thing at a time. They divide time into small units and are concerned with promptness. M-time is used in a linear way and it is experienced as being almost tangible in that we save time, waste time, bide time, spend time, and lose time. Most low-context cultures operate on M-time. *P-time,* or polychronic time, is more dominant in high-context cultures where the completion of a human transaction is emphasized more than holding to schedules. P-time is characterized by the simultaneous occurrence of many things and by "a great involvement with people." P-time allows for relationships to build and context to be absorbed as parts of high-context cultures.

One study comparing perceptions of punctuality in the United States and Brazil found that Brazilian timepieces were less reliable and public clocks less available than in the United States. Researchers also found that Brazilians more often described themselves as late arrivers, allowed greater flexibility in defining early and late, were less concerned about being late, and were more likely to blame external factors for their lateness than were Americans.

The American desire to get straight to the point, to get down to business, and other indications of directness are all manifestations of M-time cultures. The P-time system gives rise to looser time schedules, deeper involvement with individuals, and a wait-and-see-what-develops attitude. For example, two Latins conversing would likely opt to be late for their next appointments rather than abruptly terminate the conversation before it came to a natural conclusion. P-time is characterized by a much looser notion of on time or late. Interruptions are routine; delays to be expected. It is not so much putting things off until *mañana* but the concept that human activity is not expected to proceed like clockwork.[19]

Most cultures offer a mix of P-time and M-time behavior, but have a tendency to be either more P-time or M-time in regard to the role time plays. Some are similar to Japan, where appointments are adhered to with the greatest M-time precision but P-time is followed once a meeting begins. The Japanese see U.S. businesspeople as too time-bound and driven by schedules and deadlines which thwart the easy development of friendships. The differences between M-time and P-time are reflected in a variety of ways throughout a culture.

When businesspeople from M-time and P-time meet, adjustments need to be made for a harmonious relationship. Often clarity can be gained by specifying tactfully, for example, whether a meeting is to be on Mexican time or American time. An American who has been working successfully with the Saudis for many years says he has learned to take plenty of things to do when he travels. Others schedule appointments in their offices so they can work until their P-time friend arrives. The important thing for the U.S. manager to learn is adjustment to P-time in order to avoid the anxiety and frustration that comes from being out of synchronization with local time. As global markets expand, however, more businesspeople from P-time cultures are adapting to M-time.

---

[19] For an entertaining book on time around the world see Robert Levine, *A Geography of Time: The Temporal Misadventures of a Social Psychologist, or How Every Culture Keeps Time Just a Little Bit Differently* (New York: Basic Books, 1997).

CROSSING BORDERS 5-7

When Yes Means No, or Maybe, or I Don't Know, or ?

Once my youngest child asked if we could go to the circus and my reply was, "Maybe." My older child asked the younger sibling, "What did he say?" The prompt reply, "He said NO!"

All cultures have ways to avoid saying no when they really mean no. After all, arguments can be avoided, hurt feelings postponed, and so on. In some cultures, saying "no" is to be avoided at all costs—to say no is rude, offensive, and disrupts harmony. When the maintenance of long-lasting, stable personal relationships is of utmost importance, as in Japan, to say no is to be avoided because of the possible damage to a relationship. As a result, the Japanese have developed numerous euphemisms and paralinguistic behavior to express negation. To the unknowing American, who has been taught not to take no for an answer, the unwillingness to say no is often misinterpreted to mean that there is hope—the right argument or more forceful persuasion is all that is needed to get a yes. But don't be misled—the Japanese listen politely and, when the American is finished, respond with *hai*. Literally it means yes, but usually it only means, "I hear you." When a Japanese avoids saying yes or no clearly, it most likely means that he or she wishes to say no. One example at the highest levels of government occurred in negotiations between the Prime Minister of Japan and the President of the United States. The prime minister responded with, "We'll deal with it," to a request by the president. It was only later that the U.S. side discovered that such a response generally means no—to the frustration of all concerned. Other euphemistic, decorative no's sometimes used by Japanese: "It's very difficult." "We will think about it." "I'm not sure." "We'll give this some more thought." Or they leave the room with an apology.

Americans generally respond directly with a yes or no and then give their reasons why. The Japanese tend to embark on long explanations first, and then leave the conclusion extremely ambiguous. Etiquette dictates that Japanese may tell you what you want to hear, may not respond at all, or are evasive. This ambiguity often leads to misunderstanding and cultural friction.

Sources: Adapted from Mark Zimmerman, *How to Do Business with the Japanese* (New York: Random House, 1985), pp. 105–110; and Laurie Underwood, "Topics—American Chamber of Commerce in Taipei," *American Chamber of Commerce in Taipei*, April 1997, p. 12.

Negotiations Emphasis

All the just-discussed differences in business customs and culture come into play more frequently and are more obvious in the negotiating process than any other aspect of business. The basic elements of business negotiations are the same in any country; they relate to the product, its price and terms, services associated with the product, and finally, friendship between vendors and customers. But it is important to remember that the negotiating process is complicated and the risk of misunderstanding increases when negotiating with someone from another culture. This is especially true if the cultures score differently on Hofstede's PDI and IDV value dimensions.

Attitudes brought to the negotiating table by each individual are affected by many cultural factors and customs often unknown to the other individuals and perhaps unrecognized by the individuals themselves. Each negotiator's understanding and interpretation of what transpires in negotiating sessions is conditioned by his or her cultural background. The possibility of offending one another or misinterpreting each other's motives is especially high when one's SRC is the basis for assessing a situation. One standard rule in negotiating is "know thyself" first, and second, "know your opponent." The SRCs of both parties can come into play here if care is not taken. How business customs and culture influence negotiations is discussed in Chapter 19.

Gender Bias in International Business

The gender bias toward women managers that exists in many countries creates hesitancy among U.S. multinational companies to offer women international assignments. Questions such as, Are there opportunities for women in international business? and Should women represent U.S. firms abroad? frequently arise as U.S. companies become more international. As women move up in domestic management ranks and seek career-related international assignments, companies need to examine their positions on women managers in international business.[20]

In many cultures—Asian, Arab, Latin American, and even some European—women are not typically found in upper levels of management.[21] Traditional roles in male-dominated societies often are translated into minimal business opportunities for women. This cultural bias raises questions about the effectiveness of women in establishing successful relationships with host country associates. An often-asked question is whether it is appropriate to send women to conduct business with foreign customers. To some it appears logical that if women are not accepted in managerial roles within their own cultures, a foreign woman will not be any more acceptable. This is but one of the myths used to support decisions to exclude women from foreign assignments.[22]

It is a fact that men and women are treated very differently in some cultures. In Saudi Arabia, for example, women are segregated, expected to wear veils, and forbidden even to drive. Evidence suggests, however, that prejudice toward foreign women executives may be exaggerated and that the treatment local women receive in their own cultures is not necessarily an indicator of how a foreign businesswoman is treated.[23]

When a company gives management responsibility and authority to someone, a large measure of the respect initially shown that person is the result of respect for the firm. When a woman manager receives training and the strong backing of her firm, she usually receives the respect commensurate with the position she holds and the firm she represents.[24] Thus, resistance to her as a female either does not materialize or is less severe than anticipated. Even in those cultures where a female would not ordinarily be a manager, foreign female executives benefit, at least initially, from the status, respect, and importance attributed to the firms they represent. In Japan, where Japanese women rarely achieve even lower-level management positions, representatives of U.S. firms are seen first as Americans, second as representatives of firms, and then as males or females.

Similarly, women in China are seen as foreigners first and women second. Being foreign is such a major difference that being a woman is relatively minor. As one researcher notes, in China "businesswomen from the West are almost like 'honorary men' "[25] Once

---

[20] Nancy J. Adler, "Women Managers in a Global Economy," *Training and Development,* April 1994, pp. 31–36.

[21] See Calvin Reynolds, "Strategic Employment of Third Country Nationals: Keys to Sustaining the Transformation of HR Functions," *Human Resource Planning,* March 3, 1997, p. 33.

[22] Nancy J. Adler, "Going Global: Women Managers in a Global Economy," *HRMagazine,* September 1993, p. 52.

[23] Sully Taylor and Nancy Napier, "Working in Japan: Lessons from Women Expatriates," *Sloan Management Review,* Spring 1996, p. 76.

[24] Michelle Martinez, "Prepared for the Future: Training Women for Corporate Leadership," *HRMagazine,* April 1997, p. 80.

[25] Jeanette W. Gilsdorf, "Metacommunication Effects on International Business Negotiating in China," *Business Communication Quarterly,* June 1997, p. 24.

World Maps

1 The Americas

EXHIBIT 5–2   **Transparency International 1997 Corruption Perception Index***
(Selected Countries 1997 & 1996)

Country†	CPI 1997	CPI 1996	Country	CPI 1997	CPI 1996
Denmark (1)	9.94‡	9.33	Italy (30)	5.03	3.42
Finland (2)	9.48	9.05	S Korea (34)	4.29	2.96
Norway (7)	8.92	8.87	Brazil (36)	3.56	2.96
Singapore (9)	8.66	8.80	China (41)	2.88	2.43
Switzerland (11)	8.61	8.76	India (45)	2.75	2.63
U.S.A. (16)	7.61	7.66	Mexico (47)	2.66	5.50
France (20)	6.66	6.96	Russia (49)	2.27	2.58
Czech Rep. (27)	5.20	5.37	Nigeria (52)	1.76	0.69

* The ranking is based on the 52 countries studied.

† ( ) number is rank in 1997 study.

‡ The maximum score is 10.00; the minimum score is 0. A perfect score of 10.00 would be a totally corrupt free country.

Source: "Transparency International Publishes 1997 Corruption Perception Index," *TI Press Release,* July 31, 1997. Available at **http://www.uni-goettingen.de/~uwvw** or alternatively **http://www.uni-goettingen.de/%7Euwvw**.

nalized. Leaders of the region realize that democracy depends on the confidence the people have in the integrity of their government, and that corruption undermines economic liberalization. The actions of the OAS coupled with those of the OECD will obligate a majority of the world's trading nations to maintain a higher standard of ethical behavior than has existed before. Unfortunately, India, China, and other Asian and African countries are not members of either organization.

The actions of the OECD and OAS also reflect the growing concern among most trading countries of the need to bring corruption under control. International businesspeople often justify their actions in paying bribes and corrupting officials as necessary because "corruption is part of their culture," failing to appreciate that it takes "two to tango"—a bribe giver and a bribe taker.

Since 1993 an international organization called Transparency International (TI) has been dedicated to "curb[ing] corruption through international and national coalition encouraging governments to establish and implement effective laws, policies and anti-corruption programmes." Among its various activities, TI conducts an international survey of businesspeople, political analysts, and the general public to determine their perception of corruption in various countries. In the 1997 Corruption Perception Index (CPI), shown in Exhibit 5–2, Denmark, with a score of 9.94 out of a maximum of 10, was perceived to be the least corrupt and Nigeria, with a score of 1.76, as the most corrupt. TI is very emphatic that its intent is not to expose villains and cast blame, but to raise public awareness that will lead to constructive action. As one would expect, those countries receiving low scores are not pleased; however, the effect has been to raise public ire and debates in parliaments around the world—exactly the goal of TI.[36]

Bribery: Variations on a Theme

While bribery is a legal issue, it is also important to see bribery in a cultural context in order to understand different attitudes toward bribery. Culturally, attitudes are significantly different among different peoples. Some cultures seem to be more open about taking bribes, while others, like the United States, are publicly contemptuous of such practices but are far from virtuous. Regardless of where the line of acceptable conduct is

---

[36] Transparency International homepage is **http://www.transparency.de//**. The 1997 CPI report is available at the TI Web address.

CROSSING BORDERS 5-8

The Loser Wins When Mah-jongg and Bribery Meet

A fashionable way of disguising bribes, payoffs, or gifts in both business and political circles in Japan is to purposely lose when playing Mah-jongg or golf. If you can lose skillfully, your services may be in demand. Losing at Mah-jongg and golf are classic examples of indirect but preferred ways the Japanese use when it comes to greasing palms.

Mah-jongg is a Chinese table game played with ivory tiles, having rules similar to gin rummy. Gambling is a minor crime in Japan whereas bribery is a major one. To skirt the law, Japanese businesspeople invite officials or others to a discreet, high-class restaurant or club that provides a salon for private Mah-jongg games. Executives of the host company bring along young employees noted for their abilities to deftly lead their opponent to a successful win at a substantial loss for themselves. If your guests prefer golf to Mah-jongg, no problem. They can have a golf game with the company's "reverse pro," that is, a duffer who specializes in hooking and slicing his way to sure defeat.

Source: Adapted from "Those Who Lose Really Win in Japan: The Fine Art of Mah-jongg as Bribery," *The Wall Street Journal,* January 20, 1984, p. 28. Reprinted with permission from *The Wall Street Journal.* © 1984 Dow Jones & Company, Inc. All Rights Reserved Worldwide.

drawn, there is no country where the people consider it proper for those in position of political power to enrich themselves through illicit agreements at the expense of the best interests of the nation. A first step in understanding the culture of bribery is to appreciate the limitless variations that are often grouped under the word *bribery.* The activities under this umbrella term range from extortion through subornation to lubrication.

Bribery and Extortion. The distinction between bribery and extortion depends on whether the activity resulted from an offer or from a demand for payment. Voluntarily offered payments by someone seeking unlawful advantage is *bribery.* For example, it is bribery if an executive of a company offers a government official payment if the official will incorrectly classify imported goods so the shipment will be taxed at a lower rate than correct classification would require. On the other hand, it is *extortion* if payments are extracted under duress by someone in authority from a person seeking only what they are lawfully entitled to. An example of extortion would be a finance minister of a country demanding heavy payments under the threat that a contract for millions of dollars would be voided.

On the surface, extortion may seem to be less morally wrong because the excuse can be made that "if we don't pay we don't get the contract" or "the official (devil) made me do it." But even if it is not legally wrong, it is morally wrong—and in the United States it is legally *and* morally wrong.

Subornation and Lubrication. Another variation of bribery is the difference between lubrication and subornation.[37] *Lubrication* involves a relatively small sum of cash, a gift, or a service given to a low-ranking official in a country where such offerings are

---

[37] Hans Schollhammer, "Ethics in an International Business Context," *MSU Business Topics,* Spring 1977, pp. 53–63.

CROSSING BORDERS 5–9

Time: A Many Cultured Thing

Time is cultural, subjective, and variable. One of the most serious causes of frustration and friction in cross-cultural business dealings occurs when counterparts are out of sync with each other. Differences often appear with respect to the pace of time, its perceived nature, and its function. Insights into a culture's view of time may be found in its sayings and proverbs. For example:

"Time is money." *United States*

"Those who rush arrive first at the grave." *Spain*

"The clock did not invent man." *Nigeria*

"If you wait long enough, even an egg will walk." *Ethiopia*

"Before the time, it is not yet the time; after the time, it's too late." *France*

The precision of clocks also tells a lot about a culture. In a study on how cultures keep time, the researcher found:

Clocks are slow or fast by an average of just 19 seconds in Switzerland.

When a man in Brazil was queried about the time, he was more than three hours off when he said it was "exactly 2:14."

When the researcher ask the time in Jakarta, he was told by a postal employee in the central post office that he didn't know the time but to go outside and ask a street vendor.

Sources: Adapted from Edward T. Hall and Mildred Reed Hall, *Understanding Cultural Differences* (Yarmouth, Maine: Intercultural Press, 1990), p. 196; Gart M. Wederspahn, "On Trade and Cultures," *Trade and Culture,* Winter 1993–1994, pp. 4–6; and Alan Zarembo, "What If There Weren't Any Clocks to Watch?" *Newsweek,* June 30, 1997.

not prohibited by law. The purpose of such a gift is to facilitate or expedite the normal, lawful performance of a duty by that official. This is a practice common in many countries of the world. A small payment made to dock workers to speed up their pace so unloading a truck takes a few hours rather than all day is an example of lubrication.

Subornation, on the other hand, generally involves giving large sums of money, frequently not properly accounted for, designed to entice an official to commit an illegal act on behalf of the one offering the bribe. Lubrication payments accompany requests for a person to do a job more rapidly or more efficiently; subornation is a request for officials to turn their heads, to do their jobs more quickly, to not do their jobs, or to break the law.

A third type of payment that can appear to be a bribe but may not be is an agent's fee. When a businessperson is uncertain of a country's rules and regulations, an agent may be hired to represent the company in that country. For example, an attorney may be hired to file an appeal for a variance in a building code on the basis that the attorney will do a more efficient and thorough job than someone unfamiliar with such procedures. While this is often a legal and useful procedure, if a part of that agent's fees is used to pay bribes, the intermediary's fees are being used unlawfully. Under U.S. law, an official who knows of an agent's intention to bribe may risk penalties of up to five years in jail. The Foreign Corrupt Practices Act (FCPA) prohibits U.S. businesses from paying bribes openly or using middlemen as conduits for a bribe when the U.S. official knows that part of the middleman's payment will be used as a bribe. There are many middlemen (attorneys, agents, distributors, and so forth) who function simply as conduits for illegal payments. The process is further complicated by legal codes that vary from country to country; what is illegal in one country may be winked at in another and legal in a third.[38]

The answer to the question of bribery is not an unqualified one. It is easy to generalize about the ethics of political payoffs and other types of payments; it is much more difficult to make the decision to withhold payment of money when the consequences of not making the payment may affect the company's ability to do business profitably or at all. With the variety of ethical standards and levels of morality that exist in different cultures, the dilemma of ethics and pragmatism that faces international business cannot be resolved until the anticorruption accords among the OECD and OAS members are fully implemented and multinational businesses refuse to pay extortion or offer bribes.

The Foreign Corrupt Practices Act has had a positive effect. The Secretary of Commerce has stated that bribery and corruption cost U.S. firms $64 billion in lost business in just one year, the implication being that had there been no FCPA there would have been no lost business.[39] Even though there are numerous reports indicating a definite reduction in U.S. firms paying bribes,[40] however, the lure of contracts is too strong for some companies. Lockheed Corporation made $22 million in questionable foreign payments during the 1970s. For example, the company pled guilty in 1995 to paying $1.8 million in bribes to Dr. Leila Takla, a member of the Egyptian national parliament,[41] in exchange for Dr. Takla to lobby successfully for three air cargo planes worth $79 million to be sold to the military. Lockheed was caught, fined $25 million, and cargo plane exports by the company were banned for three years. Lockheed's actions during the 1970s were a major influence on the passing of the FCPA. The company now maintains one of the most comprehensive ethics and legal training programs of any major corporation in the United States.[42]

It would be naïve to assume that laws and the resulting penalties alone will put an end to corruption. Change will come only from more ethically and socially responsible decisions by both buyers and sellers and governments willing to take a stand.[43]

Ethical and Socially Responsible Decisions

To behave in an ethically and socially responsible way should be the hallmark of every businessperson's behavior, domestic or international. It requires little thought for most of us to know the socially responsible or ethically correct response to questions about knowingly breaking the law, harming the environment, denying someone his or her rights, taking unfair advantage, or behaving in a manner that would bring bodily harm or damage. Unfortunately, the difficult issues are not the obvious and simple right or wrong ones. In many countries the international marketer faces the dilemma of responding to sundry situations where there is no local law, where local practices appear to condone a certain behavior, or where the company willing to "do what is necessary" is favored over the company that refuses to engage in certain practices.[44] In short, being socially responsible and ethically correct is not a simple task for the international marketer operating in countries whose cultural and social values, and/or economic needs are different from those of the marketer.

In normal business operations there are five broad areas where difficulties arise in making decisions, establishing policies, and engaging in business operations: (1) em-

[38] For example, see Sheila M. Puffer and Daniel J. McCarthy, "Finding the Common Ground in Russian and American Business Ethics," *California Management Review,* Winter 1995, pp. 29–46.

[39] Patricia Digh, "Shades of Gray in the Global Marketplace," *HRMagazine,* April 1997, p. 90.

[40] Greg Steinmetz, "U.S. Firms Are among Least Likely to Pay Bribes Abroad, Survey Finds," *The Wall Street Journal,* August 25, 1997, p. B5a.

[41] Gregory L. Miles, "Crime, Corruption and Multinational Business," *International Business,* July 1995, p. 34.

[42] Consequently, and perhaps somewhat ironically, when you access **www.ethics.org** on the Web you get the homepage of Lockheed.

[43] Sally Washington, "Managing Government Ethics," *The OECD Observer,* February/March 1997, p. 15.

[44] "Corruption: Stopping the Rot," *Business Asia,* January 13, 1997, p. 2.

ployment practices and policies; (2) consumer protection; (3) environmental protection; (4) political payments and involvement in political affairs of the country; and (5) basic human rights and fundamental freedoms. In many countries, the law may help define the borders of minimum ethical or social responsibility, but the law is only the floor above which one's social and personal morality is tested. The statement that "there is no controlling legal authority"[45] may mean that the behavior is not illegal but it does not mean that the behavior is morally correct or ethical. "Ethical business conduct should normally exist at a level well above the minimum required by law"[46] or "controlling legal authority."[47] In fact, laws are the markers of past behavior that society has deemed unethical or socially irresponsible.

There are three ethical principles that provide a framework to help the marketer distinguish between right and wrong, determine what ought to be done, and properly justify his or her actions. Simply stated they are:

Principle	Question
Utilitarian ethics	Does the action optimize the "common good" or benefits of all constituencies?
Rights of the parties	Does the action respect the rights of the individuals involved?
Justice or fairness	Does the action respect the canons of justice or fairness to all parties involved?

Answers to these questions can help the marketer ascertain the degree to which decisions are beneficial or harmful, right or wrong, or whether the consequences of actions are ethical or socially responsible. Perhaps the best framework to work within is defined by asking: Is it legal? Is it right? Can it withstand disclosure to stockholders, to company officials, to the public?[48]

One researcher suggests that regardless how corrupt a society might be there are core human values that serve as the underpinning of life, no matter where a person lives. Participants in 43 countries and more than 50 faiths were given 17 values and asked to rate each as a core value. Five values—*compassion, fairness, honesty, responsibility, and respect for others*—were the most often selected regardless of culture.[49] The researcher suggests that an action should only be taken if the answer is no to the question, "Is the action a violation of a core human value?"[50] When people are clear about their own values and can identify the principles and core values that make up ethical behavior, they have the tools for looking at potential decisions and deciding whether or not a decision is ethical.[51]

[45] "There is no controlling legal authority that says this was in violation of the law," Vice President Albert Gore. Charles Krauthammer, "No Controlling Legal Authority," *The San Diego Union-Tribune,* March 10, 1997, p. B6.

[46] "A Code of Worldwide Business Conduct and Operating Principles," published by Caterpillar Inc., n.d., p. 4.

[47] "The Law Is a Flawed Tool for Judging Immorality," *The Sunday Patriot-News Harrisburg,* March 16, 1997, p. F1.

[48] For a discussion of other guiding principles of ethical and socially responsible behavior, see Joel Makower and Business for Social Responsibility, *Beyond the Bottom Line: Putting Social Responsibility to Work for Your Business and the World* (New York: Simon and Schuster, 1994).

[49] Patricia Digh, "Shades of Gray in the Global Marketplace," *HRMagazine,* April 1997, p. 90.

[50] Charlene Marmer Solomon, " Prepare to Walk a Tightrope: Put Your Ethics to a Global Test," *Personnel Journal,* January 1996, p. 66.

[51] For "ethical and social responsibility" issues facing U.S. multinationals, see Case 4–15 "Making Socially Responsible and Ethical Marketing Decisions: Selling Tobacco to Third World Countries," in this text. See William Beaver, "Levi's Is Leaving China," *Business Horizons,* March–April 1995, pp. 35–40.

Summary

Business customs and practices in different world markets vary so much that it is difficult to make valid generalizations about them; it is even difficult to classify the different kinds of business behavior that are encountered from nation to nation. The only safe generalizations are that businesspersons working in another country must be sensitive to the business environment and must be willing to adapt when necessary. Unfortunately, it is not always easy to know when such adaptation is necessary; in some instances adaptation is optional while in others it is actually undesirable. Understanding the culture you are entering is the only sound basis for planning.

Business behavior is derived in large part from the basic cultural environment in which the business operates and, as such, is subject to the extreme diversity encountered among various cultures and subcultures.[52] Environmental considerations significantly affect the attitudes, behavior, and outlook of foreign businesspeople. Motivational patterns of such businesspeople depend in part on their personal backgrounds, their business positions, their sources of authority, and their own personalities.

Varying motivational patterns inevitably affect methods of doing business in different countries. Marketers in some countries thrive on competition, while in others they do all possible to eliminate it. The authoritarian, centralized decision-making orientation in some nations contrasts sharply with democratic decentralization in others. International variation characterizes contact level, ethical orientation, negotiation outlook, and nearly every part of doing business. The foreign marketer can take no phase of business behavior for granted.

The new breed of international businessperson that has emerged in recent years appears to have a heightened sensitivity to cultural variations.[53] Sensitivity, however, is not enough; the international trader must be constantly alert and prepared to adapt when necessary. One must always realize that, no matter how long in a country, the outsider is not a local; in many countries that person may always be treated as an outsider. Finally, one must avoid the critical mistake of assuming that knowledge of one culture will provide acceptability in another.

Questions

1. Define:

   cultural imperative   M-time
   cultural adiaphora   subornation
   cultural exclusive   principle of utilitarian ethics
   FCPA   principle of justice or fairness
   P-time   silent language

2. "More than tolerance of an alien culture is required; there is a need for affirmative acceptance of the concept 'different but equal.'" Elaborate.

3. "We should also bear in mind that in today's business-oriented world economy, the cultures themselves are being significantly affected by business activities and business practices." Comment.

4. "In dealing with foreign businesses, the marketer must be particularly aware of the varying objectives and aspirations of management." Explain.

5. Suggest ways in which persons might prepare themselves to handle unique business customs that may be encountered in a trip abroad.

6. Business customs and national customs are closely interrelated. In which ways would one expect the two areas to coincide and in which ways would they show differences? How could such areas of similarity and difference be identified?

7. Identify both local and foreign examples of cultural imperatives, adiaphora, and exclusives. Be prepared to explain why each example fits into the category you have selected.

8. Contrast the authority roles of top management in different societies. How do the different views of authority affect marketing activities?

9. Do the same for aspirational patterns.

10. What effects on business customs might be anticipated from the recent rapid increases in the level of international business activity?

11. Interview some foreign students to determine the types of cultural shock they encountered when they first came to your country.

12. Differentiate between:
    Private ownership and family ownership
    Decentralized and committee decision making

13. In which ways does the size of a customer's business affect business behavior?

14. Identify and explain five main patterns of business ownership.

15. Compare three decision-making authority patterns in international business.

16. Explore the various ways in which business customs can affect the structure of competition.

17. Why is it important that the business executive be alert to the significance of business customs?

---

[52] See for example, "India's Spreading Blight," *Business Asia,* January 27, 1997, p. 1.

[53] Daniel B. Turban and Daniel W. Greening, "Corporate Social Performance and Organizational Attractiveness to Prospective Employees," *Academy of Management Journal,* June 1997, p. 658.

18. Suggest some cautions that an individual from a high-context culture should bear in mind when dealing with someone from a low-context culture. Do the same for facing low- to high-context situations.

19. Political payoffs are a problem. How would you react if you faced the prospect of paying a bribe? If you knew that by not paying you would not be able to complete a $10 million contract?

20. Differentiate among the following:
    subornation   lubrication
    extortion   bribery

21. Distinguish between P-time and M-time.

22. Discuss how a P-time person reacts differently from an M-time person in keeping an appointment.

23. What is meant by "laws are the markers of past behavior that society has deemed unethical or socially irresponsible"?

24. What are the three ethical principles that provide a framework to help distinguish between right and wrong? Explain.

25. Visit Transparency International's Web page and check to see how the CPI Index for countries listed in Exhibit 5–2 has changed. Searching TI's databank, explain why the changes have occurred. The site is found at **http://www. transparency.de/**.

THE POLITICAL ENVIRONMENT:

A Critical Concern

Chapter Learning Objectives

What you should learn from Chapter 6

- The political environment for foreign investment and the factors that affect stability.

- The importance of the political system to international marketing and its effect on foreign investors.

- The risks and controls associated with investments in foreign markets.

- The means of protecting an investment in foreign market.

- Alternatives to loss of markets through political instability.

GLOBAL PERSPECTIVE

The Pajama Caper

Four headlines illustrate the entanglements that can result when national sovereignty and international business collide:

"Wal-Mart Ignites Row by Pulling Cuban Pajamas off Shelves in Canada"

"Cuban Quandary: Wal-Mart in Hot Water for Yanking Pajamas"

"Canada, U.S. Wager Diplomatic Capital in a High-Stakes Pajama Game"

"Wal-Mart Puts Cuban Goods Back on Sale"

The controversy arose over a U.S. embargo forbidding U.S. businesses to trade with Cuba, and whether or not the embargo could be enforced in Canada. Wal-Mart was selling Cuban-made pajamas in Canada. When Wal-Mart officials in the U.S. became aware of the origin of manufacture, they issued an order to remove all the offending pajamas because it is against U.S. law (Helms-Burton Act)* for a U.S. company or any of its foreign subsidiaries to trade with Cuba. Canada was incensed at the intrusion of U.S. law on Canadian citizens. The Canadians felt that they should have the right to buy Cuban-made pajamas if they so chose. Wal-Mart was caught in the middle of a Canada–U.S. foreign policy feud. Wal-Mart Canada was breaking U.S. law if it continued to sell the pajamas, and was subject to a million-dollar fine and possible imprisonment. However, if the company pulled the pajamas out of Canadian stores as the home office ordered, it was subject to $1.2 million fine under Canadian law.†

Sources: *Boston Globe,* March 3, 1997, *St. Louis Post-Dispatch,* March 9, 1997, *Washington Post,* March 14, 1997, p. A6; and *The Wall Street Journal,* March 14, 1997, p. B4.

* Officially known as the Cuban Liberty and Democratic Solidarity Act of 1996, the Act strengthens the ongoing U.S. embargo of trade with Cuba. Earlier embargoes against Cuba were the result of presidential executive order and could be changed at the discretion of the president. Under the Helms-Burton Act, no president can lift or even relax the embargo until Fidel Castro and the existing Cuban regime fall from power. Trade with Cuba by American citizens is illegal, including foreign subsidiaries of U.S. corporations. In addition to other provisions, it bars foreign companies operating in the U.S. from investing in U.S. property seized by the Castro regime and prohibits foreign companies operating in the U.S. from investing in U.S. products with Cuban content. For more information about this Act and the politics behind its passage see William M. Leogrande, "Enemies Evermore: U.S. Policy towards Cuba after Helms-Burton," *Journal of Latin American Studies,* February 1997, pp. 211–222.

† After discussion with Canadian authorities Wal-Mart resumed selling the pajamas. As of this printing, U.S. authorities had the case under study—which means they probably will not bring any charges.

No company, domestic or international, large or small, can conduct business without considering the influence of the political environment within which it will operate. One of the most undeniable and crucial realities of international business is that both host and home governments are integral partners. A government reacts to its environment by initiating and pursuing policies deemed necessary to solve the problems created by its particular circumstances. Reflected in its policies and attitudes toward business are a government's ideas of how best to promote the national interest, considering its own resources and political philosophy. A government controls and restricts a company's activities by encouraging and offering support or by discouraging and banning or restricting its activities—depending on the pleasure of the government.

International law recognizes the sovereign right of nations to grant or withhold permission to do business within its political boundaries and to control where its citizens conduct business. Thus, the political environment of countries is a critical concern for the international marketer. This chapter examines some of the more salient political considerations in assessing global markets.

The Sovereignty of Nations

In the context of international law, a *sovereign state* is independent and free from all external control; enjoys full legal equality with other states; governs its own territory; selects its own political, economic, and social systems; and has the power to enter into agreements with other nations. *Sovereignty* refers to both the powers exercised by a state in relation to other countries and the supreme powers exercised over its own members. It sets requirements for citizenship, defines geographical boundaries, and controls trade and the movement of people and goods across its borders. Additionally, a citizen is subject to the state's laws even when beyond national borders. It is with the extension of national laws beyond a country's borders that much of the conflict in international business arises. This is especially true when another country considers its own sovereignty to be compromised.[1]

Nations can and do abridge specific aspects of their sovereign rights in order to coexist with other nations. The European Union (E.U.),[2] North American Free Trade Agreement (NAFTA), and North Atlantic Treaty Organization (NATO) are examples of nations voluntarily agreeing to give up some of their sovereign rights in order to participate with member nations for a common, mutually beneficial goal. Even though a state often relinquishes certain of its sovereign rights in order to coexist with others, any breach of a sovereign right to which it has not consented is considered an unfriendly act. The sovereignty of nations is a fundamental principle governing relations among nations and a significant component of the political environment within which multinational companies operate.

The "pajama game" discussed in the global perspective above is not unusual for multinational corporations (MNCs). The laws of multiple nation-states, the laws of the host countries, and the laws of its home country affect an MNC. And, as was the case with Wal-Mart, an MNC must also be concerned with the relationships between its home country, the host countries, and countries of product origin because foreign policy issues between countries can impact the multinational's ability to operate. Often MNCs are subject to extra scrutiny since they may be larger than many of their host countries and, rightly or wrongly, may be perceived as having more power than the host country. What all this means is that the international firm is subject to the laws of multiple countries and the political, legal, and foreign policy issues revolving around host and home countries are of paramount importance in assessing the environment in which the firm must operate.

The ideal political climate for a multinational firm is a stable, friendly government. Unfortunately, governments are not always friendly and stable, nor do friendly, stable governments remain so; changes in attitudes and goals can cause a stable and friendly situation to become risky. Changes are brought about by any number of events: a radical shift in the government when a political party with a philosophy different from the one it replaces ascends to power, government response to pressure from nationalist and self-interest groups, weakened economic conditions that cause a government to recant trade commitments, or increasing bias against foreign investment. Since foreign businesses are judged by standards as variable as there are nations, the friendliness and stability of the government in each country must be assessed as an ongoing business practice.

Stability of Government Policies

At the top of the list of political conditions that concern foreign businesses is the stability or instability of prevailing government policies. Governments might change or new

---

[1] Miguel de la Madrid, "National Sovereignty and Globalization," *Houston Journal of International Law,* Spring 1997, p. 553.

[2] James G. Dickinson, "Must Global Marketing Cost US Sovereignty?" *Medical Marketing & Media,* June 1997, p. 10.

political parties might be elected, but the concern of the multinational corporation is the continuity of the set of rules or code of behavior—regardless of which government is in power. A change in government, whether by election or coup, does not always mean a change in the level of political risk. In Italy, for example, there have been more than 50 different governments formed since the end of World War II. While the political turmoil in Italy continues, business goes on as usual. In contrast, India has had 51 different governments since 1945 with several in the past few years favorable to foreign investment and open markets;[3] however, much government policy remains hostile to foreign investment. This is a result of senior civil servants not directly accountable to the electorate but remaining in place despite the change of the elected government. Even after elections of parties favoring economic reform, the bureaucracy continues to be staffed by old-style central planners.[4]

Conversely, radical changes in policies toward foreign business can occur in the most stable governments. Until 1997, the same political party, the Institutional Revolutionary Party (PRI), had controlled Mexico for over 60 years. But during that period, the political risk for foreign investors ranged from expropriation of foreign investments through Mexico's membership in the North American Free Trade Agreement (NAFTA) and an open door for foreign investment and trade. Now that the PRI party no longer controls both houses of Congress, how will Mexico's policies change? The PRI controls the Senate while the opposition party, National Action Party (PAN), controls the Chamber of Deputies (lower house), the mayoralty of Mexico City,[5] and six governorships. This change could result in gridlock between the two houses of Congress, or worse, radical change in current policy. Sensing the potential for chaos, the President of Mexico is urging a "mature, constructive" embrace of the country's new political pluralism.[6] Of importance to the foreign investor and Mexico's trading partners is whether Mexico will continue on the road of open markets and free trade as epitomized by NAFTA or revert to a less stable political environment.

Some African countries are among the unstable with seemingly unending civil wars, boundary disputes, and oppressive military regimes. Sierra Leone has had three changes in government in five years, and the most recent (1997) coup d'etat ended the country's brief experiment with democracy.[7]

The one region with the greatest number of questions concerning long-term stability, trade policy, and a host of other issues is Hong Kong. Since China gained control in 1997, the "official" message is that nothing will change and thus far all seems to be going smoothly.[8] However, most political analysts suggest that it is too early to determine how the business climate will change, if at all.

If there is potential for profit and if permitted to operate within a country, multinational companies can function under any type of government as long as there is some long-run predictability and stability. PepsiCo, for example, operated profitably in the Soviet Union when it had one of the world's most extreme political systems.[9] Years

---

[3] Marijeet Kripalani, "Commentary: As the Politicians Squabble India Stagnates," *Business Week,* May 5, 1997, p. 27.

[4] "India: Living Barriers to Reform," *Country Forecast,* The Economist Intelligence Unit Unlimited, August 8, 1997.

[5] "Mexico. Fox Hunting," *The Economist,* July 19, 1997, p. 14.

[6] Dianne Solis, "Mexico's Congress Is Urged to Accept Political Pluralism," *The Wall Street Journal,* September 2, 1997, p. A1.

[7] "Sierra Leone: Political Instability, Isolation and Economic Gloom," *Country Report,* Intelligence Unit, August 21, 1997 (**http://www.eiu.com/**). Visit this site for abstracts of EIU's country reports of current political and economic data.

[8] For a detailed profile of Hong Kong, visit the PRS Group's Web online site (**http://www.prsgroup.com/**). See the feature of the month for August 18–September 22, 1997, "Hong Kong Profile," or a more recent feature.

[9] Visit the Pepsi Web site in Russia for a history of Pepsi in Russia, Pepsi advertising in Russia, and other information: **http//www.pepsi.ru/**.

before the disintegration of the Communist Party, PepsiCo established a very profitable business with the USSR by exchanging Pepsi syrup for Russian vodka.

Socioeconomic and political environments invariably change as they have in the USSR and Mexico, both within home and host countries. These changes are often brought about or reflected in changes in political philosophy and/or a surge in feelings of nationalistic pride.

Political Parties

Particularly important to the marketer is knowledge of the philosophies of all major political parties within a country, since any one of them might become dominant and alter prevailing attitudes. In those countries where there are two strong political parties that typically succeed one another in control of the government, it is important to know the direction each party is likely to take. In Great Britain, for example, the Labour Party traditionally has tended to be more restrictive on foreign trade than the Conservative Party. The Labour Party, when in control, has limited imports, while the Conservative Party has tended to liberalize foreign trade when it is in power. A foreign firm in Britain can expect to seesaw between the liberal trade policies of the Conservatives and the restrictive ones of the Liberals.

Even in Mexico, where a dominant party (PRI) maintained absolute control until 1997, knowledge of the philosophies of all political parties is important. Over the years, the doctrines of opposing parties have had an influence on the direction of Mexican policy. With the recent wins of the PAN party it is even more essential to know the philosophy and direction of that group as their influence mounts. The Mexican President's call for harmony between parties is a strong signal of the influence PAN philosophy will have in the future.

In Russia, now that President Boris Yeltsin has indicated he will not seek re-election in 2000,[10] those seeking the presidency will be surfacing and the guessing game begins. Will Yeltsin's successor continue the political and economic reforms begun several years ago?[11] It depends on who is elected. If it happens to be Russian ultra-nationalist Vladimir Zhirinovsky, whose party is the third largest in the Lower House of Parliament, there could be a radical change in attitudes toward foreign investment. In a recently reported incident, Zhirinovsky tore apart and trampled, in front of parliament, a McDonald's Big Mac in order to drive home his point that imports of "poisonous beef" for Western fast-food restaurants be banned.

Changes in direction a country may take toward trade and related issues are caused not only by political parties with differing philosophies but also by politically strong interest groups and factions within different political parties that cooperate to affect trade policy. In the United States, for example, strong, vocal groups in both political parties in Congress oppose the expansion of NAFTA to countries beyond Canada and Mexico.[12]

Similarly, it will be interesting to watch the PRI party in Mexico, as there are indications that many within the party have pro-PAN sentiments.[13] Further, some are defecting to opposing parties. One outgoing federal congressman for the PRI joined the left of center PRD (Democratic Revolutionary Party) saying it was a place where he could express his convictions.[14]

---

[10] For current election news from around the world including the United States and links to the world's newspapers visit **http//www.klipsan.com/elecnews.htm/**.

[11] Betsy McKay, "Yeltsin Won't Run in 2000, Launching Race for Successor," *The Wall Street Journal*, September 2, 1997, A1.

[12] Ann Devroy, "Battle Lines Forming over Clinton's Bid 'Fast-Track' Trade Powers," *Washington Post*, August 31, 1997, p. A15.

[13] Geri Smith, "Mexico: Now the Ruling Party Will Crumble Even Faster," *Business Week*, July 21, 1997, p. 42.

[14] Dianne Solis, "Powerful Opposition Chief in Mexico Mixes Bombast with Political Craft," *The Wall Street Journal*, August 29, 1997, p. A8.

The point is that an astute international marketer must understand all aspects of the political landscape to be properly informed about the political environment. Unpredictable and drastic shifts in government policies deter investments, whatever the cause of the shift. In short, an assessment of political philosophy and attitudes within a country is important in gauging the stability and attractiveness of a government in terms of market potential.[15]

Nationalism

Economic nationalism, which exists to some degree within all countries, is another factor important in assessing business climate. *Nationalism* can best be described as an intense feeling of national pride and unity, an awakening of a nation's people to pride in their country. This pride can take an anti-foreign business bias, and minor harassment and controls of foreign investment are supported, if not applauded. Economic nationalism has, as one of its central aims, the preservation of national economic autonomy in that residents identify their interests with the preservation of the sovereignty of the state in which they reside. In other words, national interest and security are more important than international consideration.

These feelings of nationalism are manifested in a variety of ways including a call to "buy our country's products only" (e.g., "Buy American"),[16] restrictions on imports, restrictive tariffs, and other barriers to trade. They may also lead to control over foreign investment, often regarded with suspicion, which then becomes the object of intensive scrutiny and control. Generally speaking, the more a country feels threatened by some outside force, the more nationalistic it becomes in protecting itself against the intrusion. For example, as China has increasingly opened its market to foreign competition it has also become more nationalistic toward foreign products. Sony, Samsung, and Sharp products sold in China have been criticized as being of poor quality compared with Chinese-made electronic equipment.[17]

Nationalism can also be the banner under which politicians campaign. In the 1996 United States presidential primaries, rhetoric against NAFTA, the World Trade Organization, and foreign imports was heard from candidates of major and minor political parties alike.

During the period after World War II when many new countries were founded and many others were seeking economic independence, manifestations of militant nationalism were rampant. Expropriation of foreign companies, restrictive investment policies, and nationalization of industries were common practices in some parts of the world. This was the period when India imposed such restrictive practices on foreign investments that companies like Coca-Cola, IBM, and many others chose to leave rather than face the uncertainty of a hostile economic climate. In many Latin American countries, similar attitudes prevailed and led to expropriations and even confiscation[18] of foreign investment.

The World Bank Group has reported that between 1960 and 1980 a total of 1,535 firms from 22 different capital-exporting countries had been expropriated in 511 separate actions by 76 nations. By the late 1980s, that level of militant nationalism had sub-

---

[15] For political information from countries over the world including elections, political sites, governments, media, and political parties, visit **http://www.agora.stm.it/politic/**. For links to other sites visit the home page: **http://www.agora.stm.it/**.

[16] It is interesting that when consumers in the United States were initially encouraged to "buy American" in the 1940s it had little to do with saving U.S. jobs from foreign competitors; the goal was to protect consumers from inferior imports. Laura M. Litvan, "National Issue Is 'Made in USA' Label Obsolete," *Investor's Business Daily,* June 4, 1997, p. A1.

[17] "Blazing Away at Foreign Brands," *Business Week,* May 12, 1997, p. 58.

[18] Confiscation occurs when a government takes property without payment to the owners, and expropriation exists when a country takes property and reimburses the owners. Both involve unwilling transfer of ownership of property to the government. These concepts and others are discussed in detail in the next section of this chapter.

sided and today the foreign investor, once feared as a dominant tyrant that threatened economic development, is often sought after as a source of needed capital investment. Nevertheless, strong nationalistic feelings prevail among many Asian countries, especially those that were colonies of Western countries. The Prime Minister of Malaysia, who said, "It is time that Asia too is accorded the regard and the respect it is due,"[19] best expresses the attitudes. Nationalism comes and goes as conditions and attitudes change, and foreign companies welcome today may be harassed tomorrow and vice versa.

While militant economic nationalism has subsided, nationalistic feelings can be found even in the most economically prosperous countries. When Japanese investors purchased Rockefeller Center, Pebble Beach golf course, Columbia Records, and other high-profile properties in the U.S., politicians, labor unions, the press, and others raised questions about the need to restrict the Japanese from "buying America." Similarly, the Japanese have nationalistic feelings about U.S. products marketed in Japan. When U.S. negotiators pushed Japan to import more rice to help balance the trade deficit between the two countries, nationalistic feelings rose to a new high. Deeply rooted Japanese notions of self-sufficiency, self-respect, and the welfare of Japanese farmers resisted any change for several years. It was only after a shortfall in the Japanese rice harvest in 1993 and 1994 that restrictions on rice imports were temporarily eased. Even then, all imported foreign rice had to be mixed with Japanese rice before it could be sold. When normal harvests returned, so did calls for rice self-sufficiency.[20]

It is important to appreciate that no nation–state, however secure, will tolerate penetration by a foreign company into its market and economy if it perceives a social, cultural, or economic threat to its well-being.

Political Risks of Global Business

Issues of sovereignty, differing political philosophies, and nationalism are manifest in a host of governmental actions that enhance the risks of global business. Risks can range from confiscation to many lesser but still significant government rules and regulations such as exchange controls, import restrictions, and price controls that directly impact the performance of business activities. Although not always officially blessed initially, social or political activist groups can provoke governments into action that proves harmful to a business. Of all the political risks, the most severe are those actions that result in a transfer of equity from the company to the government with or without adequate compensation.

Confiscation, Expropriation, and Domestication

The most severe political risk is *confiscation,* that is, the seizing of a company's assets without payment. The two most notable recent confiscations of United States property occurred when Fidel Castro became the leader in Cuba and later when the Shah of Iran was overthrown. The Helms-Burton Act, discussed earlier, is part of a continuing embargo against Cuba as retaliation for the confiscation of U.S. assets in Cuba.[21] The United States also has imposed an embargo against trade with Iran.

Less drastic, but still severe, is *expropriation,* which requires some reimbursement for the government-seized investment. A third type of risk is *domestication,* which

[19] Richard Halloran, "Nationalism Driving Asians: Their Policies Rooted in Customs, Anti-Colonialism," *Chicago Tribune,* August 17, 1997, p. 7.

[20] Hirai Michiko, "An Appetite for Homegrown Food," *Look Japan,* June 1997, p. 14.

[21] Guy de Jonquieres, "Trade Talks: Keeping the Lid on Helms Burton," *Financial Times,* July 31, 1997.

The Great Wall in China was an early political statement. (Philip R. Cateora)

occurs when host countries take steps to transfer foreign investments to national control and ownership through a series of government decrees. Governments seek to domesticate foreign-held assets by mandating:

- A transfer of ownership in part or totally to nationals.
- The promotion of a large number of nationals to higher levels of management.
- Greater decision-making powers resting with nationals.
- A greater number of component products locally produced.
- Specific export regulations designed to dictate participation in world markets.

A combination or all of these mandates are issued over a period of time and eventually control is shifted to nationals. The ultimate goal of domestication is to force foreign investors to share more of the ownership and management with nationals than was the case before domestication.

A change in government attitudes, policies, economic plans, and/or philosophy toward the role of foreign investment in national economic and social goals is behind the decision to confiscate, expropriate, or domesticate existing foreign assets. Risks of confiscation and expropriation have lessened over the last decade because experience has shown that few of the desired benefits materialized after government takeover.[22] Rather than a quick answer to economic development, expropriation and nationalization often led to nationalized businesses that were inefficient, technologically weak, and noncompetitive in world markets.[23] Today, countries which are concerned that foreign invest-

---

[22] Even though confiscation and expropriation have lessened, they still occur. In 1992 the government of Zaire (now Congo) seized the assets of Chevron, Mobil, and three other oil companies, and turned the assets over to state-owned Petro-Zaire. See Kenneth B. Noble, "Zaire Seizes Chevron Assets," *The New York Times,* June 8, 1992, p. C2.

[23] For a look at expropriation activity over the last three decades see Michael S. Minor, "The Demise of Expropriation as an Instrument of LDC Policy, 1980–," *Journal of International Business,* Spring 1994, pp. 177–189.

ments may not be in harmony with social and economic goals often require prospective investors to agree to share ownership, local content, labor and management agreements, and participation in export sales as a condition of entry.

As the world has become more economically interdependent and it has become obvious that much of the economic success of countries such as South Korea, Singapore, and Taiwan is tied to foreign investments, countries are viewing foreign investment as a means of economic growth. Countries throughout the world that only a few years ago restricted or forbade foreign investments are now courting foreign investors as a much-needed source of capital and technology. Additionally, they have begun to privatize telecommunications, broadcasting, airlines, banks, and other nationally owned companies.

The benefits of privatizing are many. In Mexico, for example, privatization of the national telephone company resulted in almost immediate benefits when the government received hundreds of millions of dollars of much-needed capital from the sale. In addition, Mexico's antiquated telephone system is being replaced by the latest technology, and service to many who have not had access to telephones is planned—something the financially strapped government could not do. A similar scenario is being played out in Brazil, Argentina, India, and many Eastern European countries. Ironically, many of the businesses that were expropriated and nationalized earlier are now being privatized.

Political risk is still an important issue, despite a more positive attitude toward MNCs and foreign investment. The transformation of China, the Commonwealth of Independent States (CIS), and Eastern Europe from Marxist–socialist economies to free-market economies will take years to achieve. Even if there is an ideological shift back toward Marxist–socialist economies in some of these countries, it is doubtful that leaders will revert to expropriation and harm their countries' links with the international economic system. Instead, companies will face political and economic uncertainty, currency conversion restrictions, unresponsive bureaucrats, and other kinds of political risks.

Economic Risks

Even though expropriation and confiscation are waning in importance as a risk of doing business abroad, international companies are still confronted with a variety of economic risks often decreed with little warning. Restraints on business activity may be imposed under the banner of national security to protect an infant industry, to conserve scarce foreign exchange, to raise revenue, or to retaliate against unfair trade practices, self-sufficiency, and a score of other real or imagined reasons. These economic risks are an important and recurring part of the political environment that few international companies can avoid.

Exchange Controls. *Exchange controls* stem from shortages of foreign exchange held by a country. When a nation faces shortages of foreign exchange, controls may be levied over all movements of capital or selectively against the most politically vulnerable companies to conserve the supply of foreign exchange for the most essential uses. A recurrent problem for the foreign investor is getting profits and investments into the currency of the home country.

Exchange controls also are extended to products by applying a system of multiple exchange rates to regulate trade in specific commodities classified as necessities or luxuries. Necessary products are placed in the most favorable (low) exchange categories, while luxuries are heavily penalized with high foreign exchange rates. Myanmar,[24] for example, has three exchange rates: the official rate (Kt6:U.S. $1); the market rate (Kt100–125:U.S. $1); and an import duty rate (Kt100:U.S. $1). Since the kyat (Kt) is not convertible—that is, not officially exchangeable for currencies that can be spent out-

---

[24] Formerly known as Burma.

side the country—investors are severely impacted by tax liability and their ability to send profits outside the country.[25] Under such exchange rates, tax liability can be very high. For instance, a profit of Kt 135,000 is worth U.S. $22,500 at the official exchange rate of Kt6:U.S. $1, but at the market rate, the investor has earned only U.S. $1,000. The exchange rate difference means the investor has to pay tax on U.S. $21,500 of nonexistent, unearned income.[26]

Currency convertibility can be a problem because many countries maintain regulations for control of currency, and, in the event an economy should suffer an economic setback or foreign exchange reserves suffer severely, the controls on convertibility are imposed quickly.

Local-Content Laws.   In addition to restricting imports of essential supplies to force local purchase, countries often require a portion of any product sold within the country to have local content, that is, to contain locally made parts. This restriction often is imposed on foreign companies that assemble products from foreign-made components. Contrary to popular belief, local-content requirements are not restricted to Third World countries. The European Community has had a local-content requirement as high as 45 percent for "screwdriver operations," a name often given to foreign-owned assemblers, and the North American Free Trade Agreement (NAFTA) requires 62 percent local content for all cars coming from member countries.

Import Restrictions.   Selective restrictions on the import of raw materials, machines, and spare parts are fairly common strategies to force foreign industry to purchase more supplies within the host country and thereby create markets for local industry. Although this is done in an attempt to support the development of domestic industry, the result is often to hamstring and sometimes interrupt the operations of established industries. The problem then becomes critical when there are no adequately developed sources of supply within the country.

Tax Controls.   Taxes must be classified as a political risk when used as a means of controlling foreign investments. In such cases, they are raised without warning and in violation of formal agreements. A squeeze on profit results from taxes being raised significantly as a business becomes established. In those underdeveloped countries where the economy is constantly threatened with a shortage of funds, unreasonable taxation of successful foreign investments appeals to some governments as the handiest and quickest means of finding operating funds.

Price Controls.   Essential products that command considerable public interest, such as pharmaceuticals, food, gasoline, and cars, are often subjected to price controls. Such controls applied during inflationary periods can be used to control the cost of living. They also may be used to force foreign companies to sell equity to local interests. A side effect to the local economy can be to slow or even stop capital investment.

Labor Problems.   In many countries, labor unions have strong government support that they use effectively in obtaining special concessions from business. Layoffs may be forbidden, profits may have to be shared, and an extraordinary number of services may have to be provided. In fact, in many countries foreign firms are considered fair game for the demands of the domestic labor supply. In France, the belief in full employment is almost religious in fervor; layoffs of any size, especially by foreign-owned companies, are regarded as national crises.

---

[25] As will be discussed in Chapter 17, companies faced with this kind of problem will have to engage in some type of barter or countertrade to be able to realize any profits outside the country.

[26] "Myanmar's Three Exchange Rates: Changing Kyat," *Business Asia,* July 1, 1996, p. 12.

Political Sanctions[27]

In addition to economic risks, one or a group of nations may boycott another nation, thereby stopping all trade between the countries, or issue sanctions against the trade of specific products. The United States has long-term boycotts of trade with Cuba, Iran, and Libya. Less severe and more often imposed are sanctions against the trade in specific products. For example, the United States joined the United Nations' sanction of trade with Libya in hydrocarbon equipment.[28]

Social issues may also be a basis for restricting trade to a country, as was the case in South Africa when several countries boycotted that nation to force elimination of apartheid. Once apartheid was renounced, boycotts were lifted and business resumed, but during the several years the boycott was in force multinational corporations were denied operations in that market.

Companies caught in the crossfire of such political disputes between countries or between political factions within a country can become unwitting victims of political reprisals. Such was the case with an auto dealer in California which entered an agreement with the government of Cameroon to provide 500 vehicles and a service center for $24 million. The company got EximBank (the Export Import Bank) financing and the State Department's blessing for the transaction. To complete the financing, the auto dealer used his personal savings, mortgaged buildings he owned, and refinanced his home. He sent engineers to Cameroon to begin preliminary work and ordered the special cars from General Motors. Just as the cars were to be delivered, the State Department reversed itself and imposed sanctions against trade in these "special vehicles," as they would be used by abusive police. The auto dealer was forced to sell two of his four dealerships to help repay the $750,000 he had already spent.[29]

Political and Social Activists

Although not usually officially sanctioned by the government, the impact of political and social activists (PSAs) can also interrupt the normal flow of trade. PSAs can range from those who seek to bring about peaceful change to those who resort to violence and terrorism to affect change. When well organized, the actions of PSAs can be effective.

One of the most effective and best-known PSA actions was against Nestlé and the sale of baby formula in Third World markets. The worldwide boycott of Nestlé products resulted in substantial change in the company's marketing.[30] More recently, activists of the Free Burma Campaign (FBC) have applied enough pressure to cause several U.S. garment companies to stop importing textiles from Burma (now known as Myanmar).[31] Furthermore, activists on several U.S. college campuses have boycotted Pepsi-Cola drinks and Pepsi-Cola-owned Pizza Hut and Taco Bell stores saying that the company contributes to abysmal human rights in Myanmar. The results of the boycott were serious enough that Pepsi-Cola sold its stake in its joint venture in Myanmar and withdrew from that market. The concern was that potential losses in the United States outweighed potential profits in Myanmar.[32] Holland's Heineken and Denmark's Carlsberg beer companies withdrew from Myanmar for similar reasons.

---

[27] For a detailed discussion of sanctions see Robert P. O'Quinn, "A User's Guide to Economic Sanctions," *The Heritage Foundation,* Re Backgrounder No. 1126, June 25, 1997, available from **http://www. heritage.org/heritage/library/library** (select "economics" under Economic and Political Theory).

[28] "Libya: Sanctions Bite," *The Economist Intelligence Unit,* August 18, 1997.

[29] Christopher Farrel and Edith Updike, "So You Think the World is Your Oyster," *Business Week,* June 9, 1997.

[30] See Case 1–3, "Nestlé—The Infant Formula Incident," for details of this incident.

[31] See "Outlook 97," *Control Risks Group* **http://www.crg.com/ControlRisks/report/**. Depending when you access this site, Outlook 97 may be found in archives. If not available, similar more current reports will be available.

[32] "Pepsi May Rethink Burma Deal," *Associated Press,* April 17, 1997.

The Free Burma Campaign also has pressured U.S. state and city administrations to pass "selective purchasing" agreements that impose bans on doing business with any company operating in Myanmar. Consequently, Mitsubishi Heavy Industries failed to win a lucrative contract with the city of San Francisco because of its operations in Myanmar.

Although not usually government-initiated, violence is another related risk for multinational companies to consider in assessing the political vulnerability of their activities. The State Department reported 296 terrorist incidents worldwide in 1996, down from 665 in 1987. Of those, 227 were directed at U.S. businesses resulting in 50 personnel being killed or wounded.[33] While the incidence of international terrorism has dropped sharply, the overall threat remains very serious. The death toll from acts of international terrorism rose from 163 in 1995 to 311 in 1996. Violence can be directed so that it embarrasses a government and its relationship with multinational firms by forcing the government to take action against the multinationals to placate those who have instigated the violence. In other cases, kidnapping and robbery are used to generate funds to finance the goals of terrorists. In many of these cases, the multinational company is a source of ready cash and is caught in the middle of political or social disputes not specifically directed at it.[34]

Assessing Political Vulnerability

There are at least as many reasons for a product's political vulnerability as there are political philosophies, economic variations, and cultural differences. Some products appear to be more politically vulnerable than others, in that they receive special government attention. Depending on the desirability of the product, this special attention may result in positive actions toward the company or in negative attention.

Unfortunately, there are no absolute guidelines a marketer can follow to determine whether or not a product will be subject to political attention. It is not unusual for countries seeking investments in high-priority industries to excuse companies from taxes, customs duties, quotas, exchange controls, and other impediments to investment.

Conversely, firms marketing products not considered high priority or that fall from favor often face unpredictable government restrictions.

As a case in point, Continental Can Company's joint venture to manufacture cans for the Chinese market faced a barrage of restrictions when the Chinese economy weakened. China decreed that canned beverages were wasteful and must be banned from all state functions and banquets. Tariffs on aluminum and other materials imported for producing cans were doubled and a new tax was imposed on canned-drink consumption. For Continental Can, an investment that had the potential for profit after a few years was rendered profitless by a change in the attitude of the Chinese government.

Politically Sensitive Products

While there are no specific guidelines to determine a product's vulnerability at any point, there are some generalizations that help to identify the tendency for products to be politically sensitive. Products that have an effect upon or are perceived to have an effect upon the environment, exchange rates, national and economic security, and the wel-

---

[33] For detailed information see "1996 Patterns of Global Terrorism Report," U.S. State Department, 1997, at **http://www.state.gov/www/global/terrorism/1996Report/**.

[34] For a report on how companies attempt to manage terrorism, see Michael G. Harvey, "A Study of Corporate Programs for Managing Terrorist Threats," *Journal of International Business Studies,* Third Quarter 1993, pp. 465–478.

CROSSING BORDERS 6–1

Coke's Back and It Still Has the Secret

For ninety-one years, the formula for making Coca-Cola had been a closely guarded secret. Then the government of India ordered Coca-Cola to disclose it or cease operations in that country. A secret ingredient called 7-X supposedly gives Coke its distinctive flavor. The government's minister for industry told the Indian parliament that Coca-Cola's Indian branch would have to transfer 60 percent of its equity shares to Indians and hand over its know-how by April 1978, or shut down.

Indian sales accounted for less than 1 percent of Coca-Cola's worldwide sales, but the potential market in India, a country of 800 million, is tremendous. The government refused to let the branch import the necessary ingredients and Coke—once as abundant as bottled drinking water sold in almost every Indian town of more than 50,000—packed up its bags and left the country. The minister for industry said that Coca-Cola activities in India "furnish a classic example of how multinational corporations operating in a low-priority, high-profit area in a developing country attain run-away growth and . . . trifle with the weaker indigenous industry." Coke said it wouldn't give up the formula and India said it had to leave.

Sixteen years later, India's attitudes toward foreign investment changed and Coke reentered the market without having to divulge its formula. During Coke's 16-year exile, however, Pepsi-Cola came to India and captured a 26 percent market share. Not to worry; there is plenty of growth potential for both considering India's per capita consumption is just three eight-ounce bottles a year, versus about 12 for Pakistan and 731 in the United States.

Sources: "Indian Government Rejects Coke's Bid to Sell Soft Drinks," *The Wall Street Journal*, March 16, 1990, p. B5; and "Coke Adds Fizz to India," *Fortune*, January 10, 1994, pp. 14–15.

fare of people, and are publicly visible or subject to public debate, are more apt to be politically sensitive.

Fast-food restaurants, obviously visible, have often been lightning rods for groups opposed to foreign companies. For example, Kentucky Fried Chicken (KFC) has faced continued problems since opening stores in India. Health authorities closed KFC's first restaurant for health reasons (two flies were seen in the kitchen) and a second store was closed because "chicken contained excessive levels of monosodium glutamate," a flavor enhancer, although the amount used was below international and India's acceptable standards. These closings followed months of protesters arguing that foreign investment should be limited to high technology. "India does not need foreign investment in junk-food," said the leader of the protesting farmers' group. Both stores were later opened by court order.[35] KFC faired better in India than Enron Corporation, which had a $2.8 billion contract to build a power plant cancelled. The company had spent $300 million on the project when the contract was repudiated.[36]

Health is often the subject of public debate, and products that effect or are affected by health issues can be sensitive to political concern. Hormone-treated beef has been banned by the European Union (EU) for more than a decade. There is a question about

---

[35] Miriam Jordan, "Farmers Protesting Foreign Investment in India Storm a KFC Fast-Food Outlet," *The Wall Street Journal*, January 31, 1996, p. A12.

[36] Shiraz Sidhua, "Alive and Well: Against the Odds, Enron Makes a Go of It in India," *Far Eastern Economic Review*, December 11, 1997, p. 62.

India's xenophobia, rooted in its
colonial past, has led to demonstrations
aimed at Pepsi. Politicians rail against
the "foreign devil" and call for
demonstrations against Pepsi in which
bottles of the beverage are smashed.
(Sharad Saxena/India Today)

whether the ban is a valid health issue or just protection for the European beef industry. Even though the World Trade Organization (WTO) concluded in 1989 that the ban had no scientific basis, the United States had to appeal again in 1997 to the WTO for a ruling to force the EU to lift the ban. The WTO ruled in favor of the United States and the last word was that the EU had appealed WTO's ruling.[37]

Depending on the philosophy of those in power, a company might expect to receive favorable political attention if it contributes to the achievement of national goals or, conversely, unfavorable attention if it is nonessential in view of current national needs. For products judged nonessential, the risk would be great, but for those that were thought to be making an important contribution, encouragement and special considerations could be available.

Forecasting Political Risk

In addition to qualitative measures of political vulnerability, a number of firms are employing systematic methods of measuring political risk. *Political risk assessment* is an attempt to forecast political instability to help management identify and evaluate political events and their potential influence on current and future international business decisions. Political risk assessment can:

- Help managers decide if risk insurance is necessary.
- Devise an intelligence network and an early warning system.
- Help managers develop contingency plans for unfavorable future political events.
- Build a database of past political events for use by corporate management.
- Interpret the data gathered by its intelligence network to advise and forewarn corporate decision makers about political and economic situations.

Risk assessment is used not only to determine whether or not to make an investment in a country but also to determine the amount of risk a company is prepared to accept. In

---

[37] "EU to Appeal WTO's Ruling on Hormone-Treated Beef Ban," *The Wall Street Journal,* September 10, 1997, p. B6.

the Commonwealth of Independent States (CIS) and China the risk may be too high for some companies, but stronger and better-financed companies can make long-term investments in those countries that will be profitable in the future. Early risk is accepted in exchange for being in the country when the economy begins to grow and risk subsides.

During the chaos that arose in 1991 after the political and economic changes in the USSR, the newly formed republics were anxious to make deals with foreign investors, yet the problems and uncertainty made many investors take a wait-and-see attitude. However, one executive warned, "If U.S. companies wait until all the problems are solved, somebody else will get the business." Certainly the many companies that are investing in the CIS or China do not expect big returns immediately; they are betting on the future. The unfortunate situation is with the companies that do not assess the risk properly. After making a sizable initial investment they realize they are not financially able to bear all the future risks and costs while waiting for more prosperous times, so they lose their capital. Better political risk analysis might have helped them make the decision not to go into a risky market but to make an investment in a country with more predictability and less risk instead.

There are a variety of methods used to measure political risk. They range from in-house political analysts to external sources that specialize in analyzing political risk. Although none of the methods are perfect, the very fact that a company attempts to systematically examine the problem is significant.

For a marketer doing business in a foreign country, a necessary part of any market analysis is an assessment of the probable political consequences of a marketing plan since some marketing activities are more susceptible to political considerations than others. Basically, it boils down to evaluating the essential nature of the immediate activity. The following section explores additional ways businesses can reduce political vulnerability.

Reducing Political Vulnerability

Even though a company cannot directly control or alter the political environment of the country within which it operates, there are measures that can lessen the degree of susceptibility of a specific business venture to politically induced risks.

Foreign investors frequently are accused of exploiting a country's wealth at the expense of the national population and for the sole benefit of the foreign investor. This attitude is best summed up in a statement made by a recent president of Peru: "We have had massive foreign investment for decades but Peru has not achieved development. Foreign capital will now have to meet government social goals."

These charges are not wholly unsupported by past experiences, but today's enlightened investor is seeking a return on investment commensurate with the risk involved. To achieve such a return, hostile and generally unfounded fears must be overcome. Some countries, especially the less developed, fear foreign investment for many reasons. They fear the multinationals' interest is only to exploit their labor, markets, or raw materials and to leave nothing behind except the wealthy that become wealthier.

Good Corporate Citizenship

As long as such fears persist, the political climate for foreign investors will continue to be hostile. Are there ways of allaying these fears? A list of suggestions made years ago is still appropriate for a company that intends to be a good corporate citizen and thereby minimize its political vulnerability. A company is advised to remember:

1. It is a guest in the country and should act accordingly.
2. The profits of an enterprise are not solely any company's; the local national employees and the economy of the country should also benefit.

Political unrest within a country can have a far-reaching effect on world trade.
The student uprising at Tiananmen Square (Beijing) continues to be an issue in
U.S.–Chinese relations. (Baldev/SYGMA)

3. It is not wise to try to win over new customers by completely Americanizing them.
4. Although English is an accepted language overseas, a fluency in the local language goes far in making sales and cementing good public relations.
5. The company should try to contribute to the country's economy and culture with worthwhile public projects.
6. It should train its executives and their families to act appropriately in the foreign environment.
7. It is best not to conduct business from the United States but to staff foreign offices with competent nationals and supervise the operation from the U.S.

By changing the way they operate, companies can minimize their political vulnerability and often survive the most hostile environments. Companies that establish deep local roots and show, by example rather than meaningless talk, that their strategies are aligned with the long-term goals of the host country stand the best chance of prospering. Companies often have an opportunity to assist countries in their pursuit for progress. Most all the emerging market countries need sophisticated technical assistance. Merrill Lynch is helping India devise regulatory policy for stock markets. In China, Procter & Gamble is helping local schools and universities to train and educate leaders. And in Malaysia, Motorola and Intel have instituted training programs to enhance the skills of local workers.[38] Such activities might render a marketer's activities and products less politically vulnerable, and although the risks of the political environment might not be eliminated completely, the likelihood and frequency of some politically motivated risks might be reduced.

Managing External Affairs

Companies manage external affairs in foreign markets to ensure that the host government and the public are aware of their contributions to the economic, social, or human development of the country.

---

[38] Jeffrey E. Garten, "Troubles Ahead in Emerging Markets," *Harvard Business Review,* May–June 1997, pp. 38–49.

Government–MNC relations are generally positive if the investment (1) improves the balance of payments by increasing exports or reducing imports through import substitution; (2) uses locally produced resources; (3) transfers capital, technology, and/or skills; (4) creates jobs; and/or (5) makes tax contributions.

An external affairs program, however well designed and executed, is never better than the behavior of the company. Regardless of how well multinational companies lessen political vulnerability through investment and business decisions, a task they all face is maintaining a positive public image where they do business. The public recognition Coca-Cola Company received when they were awarded the Corporate Council on Africa Award for good corporate citizenship for "continued help to drive long-term sustainable economic growth across the [African] continent" is what all companies seek.[39]

Faced with growing anti-Japanese sentiment, Japanese companies with U.S. subsidiaries have mounted an extensive advertising campaign to promote an all-American image for their U.S. operations. Additionally, they have developed an extensive program of corporate philanthropy worldwide.[40]

Most companies today strive to become good corporate citizens in their host countries, but because of overheated feelings of nationalism, or political parties seeking publicity or scapegoats for their own failures, the negative aspects of MNCs, whether true or false, are the ones which frequently reach the public.[41] The only effective defense for the multinational company is to actively tell its own story. As one authority states, "Passivity is passé. It is high time for a high profile."

Strategies to Lessen Political Risk

In addition to corporate activities focused on the social and economic goals of the host country and good corporate citizenship, MNCs can use other strategies to minimize political vulnerability and risk.

Joint Ventures.   Typically less susceptible to political harassment, joint ventures can be with either locals or other third-country multinational companies; in both cases, a company's financial exposure is limited. A joint venture with locals helps minimize anti-MNC feelings, and a joint venture with another MNC adds the additional bargaining power of a third country.

Expanding the Investment Base.   Including several investors and banks in financing an investment in the host country is another strategy. This has the advantage of engaging the power of the banks whenever any kind of government takeover or harassment is threatened. This strategy becomes especially powerful if the banks have made loans to the host country; if the government threatens expropriation or other types of takeover, the financing bank has substantial power with the government.

Marketing and Distribution.   Controlling distribution in markets outside the country can be used effectively if an investment should be expropriated; the expropriating country would lose access to world markets. This has proved especially useful for MNCs in the extractive industries where world markets for iron ore, copper, and so forth, are crucial to the success of the investment. Peru found that when Marcona Mining Company was expropriated, the country lost access to markets around the world and ultimately had to deal with Marcona on a much more unfavorable basis than first thought possible.

---

[39] "Africa-Coca-Cola Gets Prestigious African Award," *Africa News Service,* April 23, 1997.

[40] Barbara Wanner, "Japanese Corporate Citizenship: Beyond the Growing Pains," *JEI Report,* January 10, 1997.

[41] "For Business, No More 'Mr. Bad Guy' Thinking Ahead," *International Herald Tribune,* May 2, 1997.

Licensing. A strategy some firms find that eliminates almost all risks is to license technology for a fee. Licensing can be effective in situations where the technology is unique and the risk is high. Of course, there is some risk assumed because the licensee can refuse to pay the required fees while continuing to use the technology.

Planned Domestication. The strategies just discussed can be effective in forestalling or minimizing the effect of a total takeover. However, in those cases where an investment is being domesticated by the host country, the most effective long-range solution is planned phasing out, that is, *planned domestication.* This is not the preferred business practice, but the alternative of government-initiated domestication can be as disastrous as confiscation. As a reasonable response to the potential of domestication, planned domestication can be profitable and operationally expedient for the foreign investor. Planned domestication is, in essence, a gradual process of participating with nationals in all phases of company operations.

Initial investment planning provides for eventual sale of a significant interest (perhaps even controlling interest) to nationals and incorporation of national economic needs and national managerial talent into the business as quickly as possible. Such a policy is more likely to result in reasonable control remaining with the parent company even though nationals would hold important positions in management and ownership. Company-trained nationals would be more likely to have a strong corporate point of view than a national perspective.

Local suppliers developed over a period of time could ultimately handle a significant portion of total needs, thus meeting government demands for local content. Further, a sound, sensible plan to sell ownership over a number of years would ensure a fair and equitable return on investment, in addition to encouraging ownership throughout the populace. Finally, if government concessions and incentives essential in early stages of investment were rendered economically unnecessary, the company's political vulnerability would be lessened considerably.

Today, the climate for foreign investment is more positive than a decade ago, so planned domestication may not be necessary. However, planned domestication is a meaningful strategy to help avoid hostility toward an investment. Better to plan to blend into a foreign market on your own terms than have the host country force domestication or, worse, employ expropriation.

Political Payoffs

One approach to dealing with political vulnerability is the *political payoff*—an attempt to lessen political risks by paying those in power to intervene on behalf of the multinational company. Political payoffs, or bribery, have been used to lessen the negative effects of a variety of problems. Paying heads of state to avoid confiscatory taxes or expulsion, paying fees to agents to ensure the acceptance of sales contracts, and providing monetary encouragement to an assortment of people whose actions can affect the effectiveness of a company's programs are decisions that frequently confront multinational managers and raise ethical questions.

Bribery poses problems for the marketer at home and abroad since it is illegal for U.S. citizens to pay a bribe even if it is a common practice in the host country. There may be short-run benefits to political payoffs, but in the long run the risks are high and bribery should be avoided.

Government Encouragement of Global Business

Governments, both foreign and U.S., also encourage foreign investment. In fact, within the same country some foreign businesses fall prey to politically induced harassment while others may be placed under a government umbrella of protection and preferential treatment. The difference lies in the evaluation of a company's contribution to the nation's interest.

Foreign Government Encouragement

The most important reason to encourage foreign investment is to accelerate the development of an economy. An increasing number of countries are encouraging foreign investment with specific guidelines aimed toward economic goals. Multinational corporations may be expected to create local employment, transfer technology, generate export sales, stimulate growth and development of local industry, and/or conserve foreign exchange as a requirement for market concessions. Recent investments in China, India, and the former republics of the USSR include provisions stipulating specific contributions to economic goals of the country that must be made by foreign investors.

Many countries open to foreign investment impose requirements similar to those discussed in planned domestication as a precondition for entry or continued expansion. This practice is especially evident in China, where companies are more and more expected to pay with some economic contribution for access to their market or be left out. For example, as a condition for its continued presence in the rapidly growing Chinese telecommunications market, Japan's NEC corporation was "encouraged" to build a semiconductor manufacturing and assembly plant. Although NEC did not need the plant in China, it complied with the request. On the other hand, as part of a billion-dollar minivan deal, Chrysler Corporation refused to give up patent rights to technology used in making vans and lost the deal to Mercedes.[42]

The most recent trend in India has been toward dropping preconditions for entry and liberalizing requirements in order to encourage further investment. In just the few years between the time Pepsi-Cola was given permission to enter the Indian market and the Coca-Cola Company reentered, requirements were eased considerably. Pepsi was restricted to a minority position (40 percent) in a joint venture. In addition, Pepsi was required to develop an agricultural research center to produce high-yielding seed varieties, construct and operate a snack food processing plant and a vegetable processing plant, and, among other foreign exchange requirements, guarantee that export revenues would be five times greater than money spent on imports. Pepsi agreed to these conditions and by 1994 had captured 26 percent of the Indian soft-drink market. In contrast, when Coke reentered the Indian market a few years later, requirements for entry were minimal. Unlike Pepsi, Coca-Cola was able to have 100 percent ownership of its subsidiary.

Along with direct encouragement from a host country, an American company may receive assistance from the U.S. government. The intent is to encourage investment by helping to minimize and shift some of the risks encountered in some foreign markets.

U.S. Government Encouragement

The U.S. government is motivated for economic as well as political reasons to encourage American firms to seek business opportunities in countries worldwide, including those that are politically risky. It seeks to create a favorable climate for overseas business by providing the assistance that helps minimize some of the more troublesome politically motivated financial risks of doing business abroad. The Department of Commerce (DOC) is the principal department that supports U.S. business. The International Trade Administration (ITA), a bureau in the DOC, is dedicated to helping U.S. business compete in the global marketplace.[43]

---

[42] "Price of Entry Into China Rises Sharply: U.S. Firms Face Growing Pressure to Transfer Technology," *The Wall Street Journal,* December 19, 1996, p. A12.

[43] Visit **http://www.ita.doc.gov/** for the home page of the International Trade Administration.

Other agencies that provide assistance to U.S. companies include the ExportImport Bank (Eximbank), a U.S. government agency that underwrites international trade and investment activities of American firms. Through the Foreign Credit Insurance Association (FCIA), an agency of the Eximbank, an exporter can insure against nonpayment of a buyer's obligation when it is due to political reasons.

The Eximbank also provides guarantees against political risks. For a cost of 0.5 percent per year of the guarantee coverage, an investor can get coverage in selected countries of up to 95 percent of loss because of political risks. Those insurable risks include inconvertibility, war, confiscation, civil disturbances, and the cancellation or restriction of export or import licenses.[44]

The Agency for International Development (AID), in conjunction with its aid to underdeveloped countries, has provisions for limited protection in support of "essential" projects in approved countries and for approved products. The costs of coverage are similar to those of the Eximbank, and coverage extends to the basic political risks of convertibility, confiscation or expropriation, and war.

The Overseas Private Investment Corporation (OPIC) provides political-risk insurance for companies investing in less-developed countries.[45] In addition to governments sponsoring political risk insurance, private sources such as Lloyd's of London will issue insurance against political risk but at a substantially higher cost.

Summary

Vital to every marketer's assessment of a foreign market is an appreciation for the political environment of the country within which he or she plans to operate. Government involvement in business activities abroad, especially foreign-controlled business, is generally much greater than business is accustomed to in the United States. The foreign firm must strive to make its activities politically acceptable or it may be subjected to a variety of politically condoned harassment. In addition to the harassment that can be imposed by a government, the foreign marketer frequently faces the problem of uncertainty of continuity in government policy. As governments change political philosophies, a marketing firm accepted under one administration might find its activities completely undesirable under another. An unfamiliar or hostile political environment does not necessarily preclude success for a foreign marketer if the marketer's plans are such that the company becomes a local economic asset. The U.S. government may aid American business in its foreign operations, and if a company is considered vital to achieving national economic goals, the host country often provides an umbrella of protection not extended to others.

Questions

1. Define:

sovereign state	political risk assessment
sovereignty	confiscation
nationalism	domestication
expropriation	planned domestication

2. Why would a country rather domesticate than expropriate?

3. How can government-initiated domestication be the same as confiscation?

4. Discuss planned domestication as an alternative investment plan.

5. "A crucial fact when doing business in a foreign country is that permission to conduct business is controlled by the government of the host country." Comment.

6. What are the main factors to consider in assessing the dominant political climate within a country?

7. Why is a working knowledge of political party philosophy so important in a political assessment of a market? Discuss.

8. What are the most common causes of instability in governments? Discuss.

9. Discuss how governmental instability can affect marketing.

10. What are the most frequently encountered political risks in foreign business? Discuss.

11. Expropriation is considered a major risk of foreign business. Discuss ways in which this particular type of risk has been minimized somewhat as a result of company activities.

---

[44] Visit **http://www.exim.gov/**, the Eximbank home page, for an in-depth coverage of Eximbank's activities.

[45] Visit **http://www.opic.gov/**, the OPIC home page, for an in-depth coverage of OPIC's activities.

Explain how these risks have been minimized by the activities of the U.S. government.

12. How do exchange controls impede foreign business? Discuss.

13. How do foreign governments encourage foreign investment? Discuss.

14. How does the U.S. government encourage foreign investment? Spell out the implications in foreign marketing.

15. Discuss measures a company might take to lessen its political vulnerability.

16. Select a country and analyze it politically from a marketing viewpoint.

17. The text suggests that violence is a politically motivated risk of international business. Comment.

18. There is evidence that expropriation and confiscation are less frequently encountered today than just a few years ago. Why? What other types of political risks have replaced expropriation and confiscation in importance?

19. Visit the homepage of Control Risks Group (**http://www.crg.com**), select resource base, select reports. Read the report, Outlook 1998 or later and write a brief summary of political problems facing MNCs in various countries.

THE INTERNATIONAL LEGAL ENVIRONMENT:

Playing by the Rules

Chapter Outline

Chapter Learning Objectives

What you should learn from Chapter 7

- The four heritages of today's legal systems.
- The important factors in jurisdiction of international legal disputes.
- The problems of protecting intellectual property rights.
- The legal differences between countries that affect international marketing plans.
- The importance of green marketing.
- The complications for U.S. marketers in adhering to U.S. laws while marketing internationally.

GLOBAL PERSPECTIVE

Protecting Brand Names, Trademarks, and Logos: The Law Differs Internationally

Caffè Latte is a hit in Japan. But it's not the mix of hot espresso and frothy steamed milk made famous in the Pacific Northwest by Seattle-based Starbucks Corporation. Japan's "Caffè Latte" is a registered trademark for a cold espresso coffee drink sold by Morinaga Milk Industry Co. That could force Starbucks, which is considering expansion in Japan, to rename its product there.

Trade-law experts in Japan say the dispute serves as a reminder that U.S. companies must protect popular products from admirers in Japan. U.S. companies don't think about this, but they moan when it's too late. If they are interested in doing business in Japan, they need to be aggressively registering trademarks in Japan. The law is different there.

Morinaga says it registered "Caffè Latte" in Japanese and English over two years ago. It sells cold espresso coffee and milk in sealed cups in 20,000 convenience stores and supermarkets. On billboards, Jodie Foster smiles over a cup of "Caffè Latte" with a familiar-looking green logo.

Starbucks says it's all too familiar: "It looks like our cup [and] it looks like our logo. We don't think Morinaga's trademark will stand up. Morally, you have to ask if it's right for one company to take another company's ideas. I don't think so," said the head of international sales for Starbucks.

Legal authorities say Starbucks may be right but an appeal could be expensive. It took McDonald's 10 years to win its appeal of a trademark granted to a Japanese company to sell "Macburgers." Japan has historically granted trademarks for product names that were believed to be rare in Japan.

Another Seattle-based coffee company, Java Trading Co., operates three outlets in Tokyo and is trying to avoid trademark problems with Morinaga. "What [Morinaga] sells is nothing like real caffe latte. We make real caffe latte, but we can't use the name. We advertise 'caffè late' spelled with one 't' instead of two."

Morinaga says its coffee drink was "born in trendy Seattle," although its product tastes little like the Seattle product. Advertisements feature dome-topped cups—ringers for the cups used by Starbucks—superimposed over a picture of Seattle's famed Space Needle and nearby Mount Rainier. Mount Rainier also is featured on Morinaga's logo for the product.

"Our product was not modeled on theirs. It was based on market research," said a Morinaga spokesman. "We have people traveling around the world all the time, looking for ideas," he said. "In developing this particular product, people were looking in many places, mainly in the U.S. Most likely Seattle was looked at."

Starbucks has entered the Japanese market and is also moving into other parts of Asia. Since entering Japan, there have been several copycats. The most blatant is Megabucks Enterprise, a Nagoya-based company with two coffee bars that are so obviously a Starbucks replica that Starbucks says it may sue. In fact, the president of Megabucks says he did model his stores after Starbucks and uses a logo that's almost identical to Starbucks.

This example illustrates but one of the myriad legal entanglements that a company doing business abroad can encounter. Both Morinaga and Starbucks have the legal right to the "Caffè Latte" trademarks in their respective countries. And if Starbucks wants to challenge Morinaga's rights to the trademark it must do so in Japan, where the laws and traditions are different than in the United States. There is no international court for commercial law to which Starbucks can appeal. How could Starbucks have avoided this problem? Read on and see.

Sources: Adapted from Alan K. Ota, "Late Da!" *The Oregonian*, July 21, 1995, p. B1; and Nancy J. Kim, "Starbucks' Strategy: Full Steam into Asia," *American City Business Journals*, October 17, 1997, p. 1.

How would you like to play a game where the stakes were high; there was no standard set of rules to play by; whenever a new player entered the game the rules changed; and when a dispute arose, the referee used the other players' rules to interpret who is right? That fairly well describes the international legal environment. Since no single, uniform international commercial law governing foreign business transactions exists, the international marketer must pay particular attention to the laws of each country within which it operates. An American company doing business with a French customer has to contend

Morinaga's registered "Caffè Latte" trademark, a Starbuck's knockoff? (Alan K. Ota/The Oregonian)

with two jurisdictions (U.S. and France), two tax systems, two legal systems, and a third supranational set of European Community laws and regulations that may override French commercial law. The situation would be similar when doing business in Japan, Germany, or any other country. Laws governing business activities within and between countries are an integral part of the legal environment of international business.

Legal systems of different countries are so disparate and complex that it is beyond the scope of this text to explore the laws of each country individually. There are, however, issues common to most international marketing transactions that need special attention when operating abroad. Jurisdiction, dispute resolution, intellectual property, extraterritoriality of United States laws, and associated problems will be discussed in this chapter to provide a broad view of the international legal environment. While space and focus limits an in-depth presentation, it should be sufficient for the reader to conclude that securing expert legal advice is a wise decision when doing business in another country.[1] The foundation of a legal system profoundly affects how the law is written, interpreted, and adjudicated. The place to begin is with a discussion of the different legal systems.

Bases for Legal Systems

Three heritages form the bases for the majority of the legal systems of the world: (1) common law, derived from English law and found in England, the United States, Canada,[2] and other countries once under English influence; (2) civil or code law,

---

[1] For a variety of reports, treaties, laws, and other information on legal issues in international trade see **http://www.ljextra.com/** (select *practice areas* and then *international trade*).

[2] All of the provinces of Canada have a common law system with the exception of Quebec, which is a code-law province. All states in the United States are common law with the exception of Louisiana, which is a code-law state.

derived from Roman law and found in Germany, Japan, France, and in non-Islamic and non-Marxist countries; and (3) Islamic law, derived from the interpretation of the Koran and found in Pakistan, Iran, Saudi Arabia, and other Islamic states. A fourth heritage for a commercial legal system is the Marxist–socialist economies of Russia and the republics of the former Soviet Union, Eastern Europe, China, and other Marxist–socialist states. The legal system that existed in the Marxist–socialist states centered on the economic, political, and social policies of the state. As each country moves toward its own version of a free market system and enters the global market, a commercial legal system is also evolving from those Marxist–socialist tenets.[3]

The differences among these four systems are of more than theoretical importance because due process of law may vary considerably among and within these legal systems. Even though a country's laws may be based on the doctrine of one of the four legal systems, its individual interpretation may vary significantly—from a fundamentalist interpretation of Islamic law as found in Pakistan to a combination of several legal systems found in the United States, where both common and code law are reflected in the laws.

Common and Code Law

The basis for *common law* is tradition, past practices, and legal precedents set by the courts through interpretations of statutes, legal legislation, and past rulings. Common law seeks "interpretation through the past decisions of higher courts which interpret the same statutes or apply established and customary principles of law to a similar set of facts." *Code law,*[4] on the other hand, is based on an all-inclusive system of written rules (codes) of law. Under code law, the legal system is generally divided into three separate codes: commercial, civil, and criminal.

Common law is recognized as not being all-inclusive, while code law is considered complete as a result of catchall provisions found in most code-law systems. For example, under the commercial code in a code-law country, the law governing contracts is made inclusive with the statement that "a person performing a contract shall do so in conformity with good faith as determined by custom and good morals." Although code law is considered all-inclusive, it is apparent from the foregoing statement that some broad interpretations are possible in order to include everything under the existing code.

Steps are being taken in common-law countries to codify commercial law even though the primary basis of commercial law is common law, that is, precedents set by court decisions. An example of the new uniformity and a measure of codification are the acceptance of the Uniform Commercial Code by most states in the United States. Even though U.S. commercial law has been codified to some extent under the Uniform Commercial Code, the philosophy of interpretation is anchored in common law.

As we discuss later in the section on protection of intellectual property rights,[5] laws governing intellectual property offer the most striking differences between common-law and code-law systems. Under common law, ownership is established by use; under code law, ownership is determined by registration. In some code-law countries, certain agreements may not be enforceable unless properly notarized or registered; in a common-law country, the same agreement may be binding so long as proof of the agreement can be established. Although every country has elements of both common and code law, the differences in interpretation between common- and code-law systems regarding contracts, sales agreements, and other legal issues are significant enough that an interna-

---

[3] For a detailed report on the magnitude of the challenge to develop a legal framework in a Marxist–Socialist economy see Pham van Thuyet, "Legal Framework and Private Sector Development in Transitional Economies: The Case of Vietnam," *Law and Policy in International Business,* March 1996, p. 48.

[4] Also known as the Napoleonic Code.

[5] Industrial property rights and intellectual property rights are used interchangeably. The more common term used today is *intellectual property rights* to refer to patents, copyrights, trademarks, and so forth.

When conducting business in the United Arab Emirates, Islamic law and customs must be respected. (© 1993 Ed Kashi)

tional marketer familiar with only one system must enlist the aid of legal counsel for the most basic legal questions.

Another illustration of where fundamental differences in the two systems can cause difficulty is in the performance of a contract. Under common law in the United States, it is fairly clear that impossibility of performance does not necessarily excuse compliance with the provisions of a contract unless it is impossible to comply for reasons of an act of God, such as some extraordinary happening of nature not reasonably anticipated by either party of a contract. Hence, floods, lightning, earthquakes, and similar occurrences are generally considered acts of God. Under code law, acts of God are not limited solely to acts of nature but are extended to include "unavoidable interference with performance, whether resulting from forces of nature or unforeseeable human acts," including such things as labor strikes and riots.

Consider the following situations: A contract was entered into to deliver a specific quantity of cloth. In one case, before the seller could make delivery an earthquake caused the destruction of the cloth and compliance was then impossible. In the second case, pipes in the sprinkler system where the material was stored froze and broke, spilling water on the cloth and destroying it. In each case, loss of the merchandise was sustained and delivery could not be made. Were the parties in these cases absolved of their obligations under the contract because of the impossibility of delivery? The answer depends on the system of law invoked.

In the first situation, the earthquake would be considered an act of God under both common and code law and impossibility of performance would excuse compliance under the contract. In the second situation, courts in common-law countries would probably rule that the bursting of the water pipes did not constitute an act of God if it hap-

CROSSING BORDERS 7–1

Ceské Budějovic, Privatization, Trademarks— What Do They Have in Common with Anheuser-Busch?

Budweiser, that's what!

Anheuser-Busch has launched a massive public relations program in the small Czech town of Ceské Budějovic, where a local brewery produces Budweiser Budvar—no relation to Anheuser-Busch. Anheuser-Busch's goal is to win support for a minority stake in the Czech state-owned brewery, Budějovice Budvar N.P., when the government privatizes it. Thanks to Anheuser-Busch, trees are being planted along main avenues, a new cultural center was recently opened offering free English courses to citizens and management advice to budding entrepreneurs, and newspaper ads tout the possibilities of future cooperation.

So why the interest in a brewery whose annual production of 500,000 barrels is the equivalent of two days' output for Anheuser-Busch? Part-ownership is critically important to Anheuser-Busch for two reasons. They are in search of new markets and Europe is their target, and they want to be able to market the Budweiser brand in Europe to achieve a presence there. So what's the connection? They don't have the rights to use the Budweiser brand in Europe because it is owned by Budějovice Budvar N.P.

Anheuser-Busch established the name Budweiser in the U.S. when German immigrants founded the St. Louis family brewery in the latter part of the eighteenth century. The Czechs claim they have been using the name since before Columbus discovered the New World, even though they did not legally register it until the 1920s. The Anheuser-Busch Company markets Budweiser brand beer in North America, but in Europe it markets Busch brand beer since the Czechs have the rights to the use of the name Budweiser. The Czech government has given Anheuser-Busch the right to negotiate for a minority stake in Budvar as part of the privatization of the brewery, which claims to have its roots when beer-making was licensed by Bohemian King Otakar II in 1256. If all goes well and Anheuser-Busch is allowed to buy a one-third interest in Budvar, it will be able to settle the trademark battle over the Czech Budweiser brand.

Visit the Budvar homepage for history of Budvar and a tour of the plant at **http://www.centraleurope.com/sponsor/budvar/budvar.html/**.

Sources: Adapted from "Anheuser-Busch Says Skoal, Salud, Prosit," *Business Week,* September 20, 1993, pp. 76–77; and "This Bud's for Whom?" *Reuters News Service,* July 1, 1994.

pened in a climate where freezing could be expected. Therefore, impossibility of delivery would not necessarily excuse compliance with the provisions of the contract. In code-law countries, where the scope of impossibility of performance is extended considerably, the destruction might very well be ruled an act of God, and thus release from compliance with the contract could be obtained.

Islamic Law

The basis for the Shari'ah (Islamic law) is interpretation of the Koran.[6] It encompasses religious duties and obligations as well as the secular aspect of law regulating human acts. Broadly speaking, Islamic law defines a complete system that prescribes specific

---

[6] Abdulaziz Sachedina, "What Is Islam?" *The World & I,* September 1997, p. 26.

patterns of social and economic behavior for all individuals. It includes issues such as property rights, economic decision making, and types of economic freedom. The overriding objective of the Islamic system is social justice.[7]

Among the most unique aspects of Islamic law is the prohibition against the payment of interest. The Islamic law of contracts states that any given transaction should be devoid of *riba,* defined as unlawful advantage by way of excess of deferment, that is, interest or usury. Prohibiting the receipt and payment of interest is the nucleus of the Islamic system. However, other principles of Islamic doctrine advocate risk sharing, individuals' rights and duties, property rights, and the sanctity of contracts. The Islamic system places emphasis on the ethical, moral, social, and religious dimensions to enhance equality and fairness for the good of society. Another principle of the Islamic legal system is the prohibition against the investment in those activities that violate the Shari'ah. For example, any investment in a business dealing with alcohol, gambling, and casinos would be prohibited.

Prohibition against the payment of interest impacts banking and business practices severely. However, there are acceptable practices that adhere to Islamic law and permit the transaction of business. These practices meet the requirements of Shari'ah by enabling borrowers and lenders to share in the rewards as well as losses in an equitable fashion. They also ensure that the process of wealth accumulation and distribution in the economy is fair and representative of true productivity. Of the several ways to comply with Islamic law in financial transactions, trade with markup or cost-plus sale (*murabaha*) and leasing (*ijara*)[8] are the most frequently used. In both *murabaha* and *ijara,* a mutually negotiated margin is included in the sale price or leasing payment. Such an arrangement is frowned on by strict fundamentalists but it is practiced and is an example of the way the strictness of Islamic law can be reconciled with the laws of non-Islamic legal systems.

Because the laws are based on interpretation of Islamic law, the international marketer must have knowledge of the law and understand the way the law may be interpreted in each region. Regional courts can interpret Islamic law from the viewpoint of fundamentalists (those that adhere to a literal interpretation of the Koran) or they may use a more liberal translation. A company can find local authorities in one region willing to allow payment of interest on deferred obligations as stipulated in a contract, while in another region all interest charges may be deleted and replaced with comparable "consulting fees." In yet another, authorities may void a contract and declare any payment of interest illegal. Marketers conducting business in Islamic-law countries must be knowledgeable about this important legal system.

Marxist–Socialist Tenets

As socialist countries become more directly involved in trade with non-Marxist countries, it has been necessary to develop a commercial legal system that permits them to engage in active international commerce. The pattern for development varies among the countries because each has a different background and each is at a different stage in its development of a market-driven economy. For example, Central European countries such as the Czech Republic and Poland had comprehensive codified legal systems before communism took over, and their pre-World War II commercial legal codes have been revised and re-instituted. Consequently, they have moved toward a legal model with greater ease than some others have.[9] Russia and most of the Republics of the for-

7 Zamir Iqbal, "Islamic Financial Systems," *Finance & Development,* June 1997, p. 42.

8 David Wohabe, "Islamic Leasing as a Form of Financing," *Trade & Culture,* February–March 1997, p. 43.

9 Loukas A. Mistelis, "A Look at . . . the Law after Communism; For Law or Money in Warsaw," *The Washington Post,* June 22, 1997, p. C-3.

CROSSING BORDERS 7–2

Counterfeit, Pirated, or the Original— Take Your Choice

Intellectual properties—trademarks, brand names, designs, manufacturing processes, formulas—are valuable company assets that U.S. officials estimate are knocked off to the tune of $200 billion a year due to counterfeiting and/or pirating. Some examples from China:

- Design Rip-Offs. Beijing Jeep Corporation, a Chrysler Corporation joint venture, found more than 2,000 four-wheel-drive vehicles designed to look nearly identical to its popular Cherokee model.
- Product Rip-Offs. Exact copies of products made by Procter & Gamble, Colgate-Palmolive, Reebok, and Nike are common throughout Southern China. Exact copies of any Madonna album are available for as little as $1, as are CDs and movies. One executive says, "They'll actually hire workers away from the real factories." In addition, fake "3M" floppy disks are manufactured by a Chinese firm.
- Brand Name Rip-Offs. Bausch & Lomb's Ray Ban sunglasses become Ran Bans. Colgate in the familiar bright red tube becomes Cologate. The familiar Red Rooster on Kellogg's Corn Flakes appears on Kongalu Corn Strips packages that state "the trustworthy sign of quality that is famous around the world."
- Book Rip-Offs. Even the rich and powerful fall prey to pirating. Soon after "My Father, Deng Xiaoping," a biography written by Deng Rong, daughter of Deng Xiaoping, was published, thousands of illegal copies flooded the market. The true owners also sell original versions of the products mentioned above in China.

Sources: Adapted from Marcus W. Brauchli, "Chinese Flagrantly Copy Trademarks of Foreigners," *The Wall Street Journal,* June 26, 1994, p. B-1; "How Heinz and Procter & Gamble Fight Counterfeiting," *Business China,* November 25, 1996, p. 6; and "Chinese Businessmen Convicted for Counterfeiting 3M Trademark," *Xinhua News Agency,* December 16, 1997.

Because patents, processes, trademarks, and copyrights are valuable in all countries, some companies have found their assets appropriated and profitably exploited in foreign countries without license or reimbursement. Further, they often learn not only that other firms are producing and selling their products or using their trademarks, but that the foreign companies are the rightful owners in the countries where they operate.

There have been many cases where companies have legally lost the rights to trademarks and have had to buy back these rights or pay royalties for their use. The problems of inadequate protective measures taken by the owners of valuable assets stem from a variety of causes. One of the more frequent errors is assuming that because the company has established rights in the United States, they will be protected around the world, or that rightful ownership can be established should the need arise. Such was the case with McDonald's in Japan, where enterprising Japanese registered its "Golden Arches" trademark as their own. Only after a lengthy and costly legal action with a trip to the Japanese Supreme Court was McDonald's able to regain the exclusive right to use the trademark in Japan. After having to "buy" its trademark for an undisclosed amount, McDonald's maintains a very active program to protect its trademarks.

Similarly, a South Korean company legally uses the Coach brand on handbags and leather goods. The company registered the Coach trademark first and has the legal right to use that mark in Korea. The result is that a Coach-branded briefcase that is virtually

CROSSING BORDERS 7–3

Aspirin in Russia, Bayer in the United States— It's Enough to Give You a Headache

Russia's patent office awarded the German chemical company, Bayer AG, the registered trademark to the word "aspirin." If the trademark award holds, Bayer will have the exclusive right to market pain relievers under the brand name Aspirin in Russia. The word and labeling "aspirin" fell out of use in Russia in the 1970s, when the chemical name acetylsalicylic acid, aspirin's main ingredient, came into use. Bayer AG believes its trademark rights will be upheld and they will be the only company able to sell acetylsalicylic acid as Aspirin; the Russian patent office agrees. There are several reasons for granting Bayer the trademark: aspirin has fallen out of popular use in Russia; Bayer was the world's first manufacturer of aspirin and marketed acetylsalicylic acid under the brand name Aspirin nearly a century ago; Bayer holds trademark rights to Aspirin in many countries; and they registered the name first.

In the United States it's a different story. Bayer AG lost the exclusive right to Aspirin when U.S. courts declared aspirin as the generic term for acetylsalicylic acid. Later, Bayer AG lost the right to the name Bayer as well. Bayer AG does not sell the famous Bayer aspirin in the United States, where Sterling Winthrop, Inc., owns the Bayer trademark. The U.S. government confiscated the domestic assets of Bayer AG after World War I, and in 1919 sold them along with the rights to the Bayer name. While Sterling Winthrop has the exclusive use of the name Bayer, it does not have the exclusive use of the term aspirin since U.S. courts ruled aspirin to be a generic term.

Ownership changes rapidly in international business. Bayer of Germany bought Sterling Winthrop, the U.S. owner of the Bayer brand, from the Kodak Company in 1994, and now Bayer of Germany once again owns the brand Bayer worldwide. The change in ownership in the United States, however, does not affect the trademark dispute over the brand name Aspirin discussed above.

The moral to the story? Patent and trademark protection is a complicated issue for international companies.

Sources: Adapted from Marya Fogel, "Bayer Trademarks the Word 'Aspirin' in Russia, Leaving Rivals Apoplectic," *The Wall Street Journal,* October 29, 1993, p. A-9; and Andrew Wood, "Companies: Bayer Corp.; New Recognition for an Old Name," *Chemical Week,* September 10, 1997, p. 051.

---

indistinguishable from the U.S. product can be purchased for $135 in South Korea versus $320 in the United States.[24] A United States attorney who practices with a South Korean firm noted that he has seen several cases where a foreign company will come to Korea, naively start negotiating with a Korean company for distribution or licensing agreements, and the Korean company will register that trademark in its own name. Later, they will use that leverage in negotiations or, if the negotiations fall apart, sell the trademark back to the company. Many businesses fail to take proper steps to legally protect their intellectual property because they are under the misconception that if it is protected in the U.S., it is protected elsewhere. They fail to understand that some countries do not follow the common-law principle that ownership is established by prior use or that registration and legal ownership in one country does not necessarily mean ownership in another.

---

[24] David Holley, "S. Korea's Counterfeiters Make It Hard to Knock Off Knockoffs," *Los Angeles Times,* January 1, 1996, p. 1.

Prior Use versus Registration

In the United States, a common-law country, ownership of intellectual property rights is established by prior use—whoever can establish first use is typically considered the rightful owner. In many code-law countries, however, ownership is established by registration rather than by prior use—the first to register a trademark or other property right is considered the rightful owner. For example, a trademark in Jordan belongs to whoever registers it first in Jordan. Thus, you can find "McDonald's" restaurant, "Microsoft" software, and "Safeway" groceries all legally belonging to a Jordanian. A company that believes it can always establish ownership in another country by proving it used the trademark or brand name first is wrong and risks the loss of these assets.

Besides the first to register issue, companies may encounter other problems with registering. China has improved intellectual property rights protection substantially and generally recognizes "first to invent." However, a Chinese company can capture the patent for a product invented elsewhere; it needs only to "reverse engineer" or reproduce the product from published specifications and register it in China before the original inventor. Latvia and Lithuania permit duplicate registration of trademarks and brand names. A cosmetics maker registered Nivea and Niveja cosmetics brands in the former Soviet Union in 1986 and again in Latvia in 1992, but a Latvian firm had registered and had been selling a skin cream called Niveja since 1964. Neither the Soviet nor the Latvian authorities notified either firm. It is up to applicants to inform themselves about similar trademarks already registered. The case is being taken to the Supreme Court of Latvia.[25] It is best to protect intellectual property rights through registration. Several international conventions provide for simultaneous registration in member countries.

International Conventions

Many countries participate in international conventions designed for mutual recognition and protection of intellectual property rights. There are three major international conventions.

1. The Paris Convention for the Protection of Industrial Property, commonly referred to as the Paris Convention, includes the United States and 100 other countries.
2. The Inter-American Convention. It includes most of the Latin American nations and the United States.
3. The Madrid Arrangement, which established the Bureau for International Registration of Trademarks. It includes 26 European countries.

In addition, the World Intellectual Property Organization (WIPO) of the United Nations is responsible for the promotion of the protection of intellectual property and administration of the various multilateral treaties through cooperation among its member States.[26] Furthermore, two multicountry patent arrangements have streamlined patent procedures in Europe. The first, the Patent Cooperation Treaty (PCT), facilitates the application of patents among its member countries. It provides comprehensive coverage in that a single application filed in the United States supplies the interested party with an international search report on other patents to help evaluate whether or not to seek protection in each of the countries cooperating under the PCT.[27] The second, the European

---

[25] "Baltic States: The Name Game," *Business Eastern Europe,* May 19, 1997, p. 5.

[26] Visit the homepage of the WIPO for detailed information of the various conventions and the activities of WIPO: **http://www.wipo.org/**.

[27] For several articles on patent conventions, the PCT, EPC, and other means of protecting intellectual property see the home page of Ladas & Parry, a law firm specializing in international law: **http://www.ladas.com/**.

CROSSING BORDERS 7-4

Patent Law: The United States versus Japan— Differences in Culture Do Matter

The goal of Western patent systems is to protect and reward individual entrepreneurs and innovative businesses, to encourage invention, and to advance practical knowledge. The intent of the Japanese patent system is to share technology, not to protect it. In fact, it serves a larger, national goal: the rapid spread of technological know-how among competitors in a manner that avoids litigation, encourages broad-scale cooperation, and promotes Japanese industry as a whole.

This approach is entirely consistent with the broader characteristics of Japanese culture, which emphasizes harmony, cooperation, and hierarchy. It favors large companies over small ones, discourages Japanese entrepreneurship, and puts foreign companies that don't appreciate the true nature of the system at a substantial disadvantage. Below is a comparison of patent laws in the United States and Japan.

United States	*Japan*
Protects individual inventors.	Promotes technology sharing.
Patent applications are secret.	Patent applications are public.
Patents granted in up to 24 months.	Patents granted in 4 to 6 years.
Patents valid for 17 years from date issued.	Patents valid 20 years from application.

Sources: Adapted from Donald M. Spero, "Patent Protection or Piracy—A CEO Views Japan," *Harvard Business Review,* September–October 1990, p. 58; "Clay Jacobson Calls It Patently Unfair," *Business Week,* August 19, 1991, p. 48; and "Differences in National Patent Laws Breed Discord and Confusion," *Jane's Defense Contracts,* September 1997, p. 9.

Patent Convention (EPC), established a regional patent system allowing any nationality to file a single international application for a European patent. Once the patent is approved, the patent has the same effect as a national patent in each individual country designated on the application.

In addition, the European Union (EU) has approved its Trademark Regulation, which will provide intellectual property protection throughout all member states. Companies have a choice between relying on national systems when they want to protect a trademark in just a few member countries, or the European system, when protection is sought throughout the European Union. Trademark protection is valid for 10 years and is renewable; however, if the mark is not used for five years, protection is forfeited.

Once a trademark, patent, or other intellectual property right is registered, most countries require that these rights be worked and properly policed. The United States is one of the few countries where a patent can be held by an individual throughout the duration of the patent period without it being manufactured and sold. Other countries feel that in exchange for the monopoly provided by a patent, the holder must share the product with the citizens of the country. Hence, if patents are not produced within a specified period, usually from one to five years (the average is three years), the patent reverts to public domain.

This is also true for trademarks; products bearing the registered mark must be sold within the country or the company may forfeit its right to a particular trademark. McDonald's faced that problem in Venezuela. Even though the McDonald's trademark was properly registered in that code-law country, the company did not use it for more than two years. Under Venezuelan law, a trademark must be used within two years or it is lost. Thus, a Venezuelan-owned "Mr. McDonald's," with accompanying golden arches, is operating in Venezuela. The U.S. McDonald's Corporation faces a potentially costly legal battle if it decides to challenge the Venezuelan company.

Individual countries expect companies to actively police their intellectual property by bringing violators to court. Policing can be a difficult task, with success depending in large measure on the cooperation of the country within which the infringement or piracy takes place. A lack of cooperation in some countries may stem from cultural differences of how intellectual property is viewed. In the United States, the goal of protection of intellectual property is to encourage invention and to protect and reward innovative businesses. In Korea, the attitude is that the thoughts of one person should benefit all. In Japan, the intent is to share technology rather than protect it; an invention should serve a larger, national goal with the rapid spread of technology among competitors in a manner that promotes cooperation. In light of such attitudes, the lack of enthusiasm toward protecting intellectual property is better understood. The United States is a strong advocate of protection, and at U.S. insistence many countries are becoming more cooperative about policing cases of infringement and piracy.[28]

Commercial Law within Countries

When doing business in more than one country, a marketer must remain alert to the different legal systems. This problem is especially troublesome for the marketer who formulates a common marketing plan to be implemented in several countries. Although differences in languages and customs may be negated, legal differences between countries may still prevent a standardized marketing program.

Marketing Laws

All countries have laws regulating marketing activities in promotion, product development, labeling, pricing, and channels of distribution. In some, there may be only a few laws with lax enforcement; in others, there may be detailed, complicated rules to follow that are stringently enforced. There often are vast differences in enforcement and interpretation among countries having laws covering the same activities. Laws governing sales promotions in the European Community offer good examples of such diversity.

In Austria, premium offers to consumers come under the discount law, which prohibits any cash reductions that give preferential treatment to different groups of customers. Because most premium offers would result in discriminatory treatment of buyers, they normally are not allowed. Premium offers in Finland are allowed with considerable scope as long as the word *free* is not used and consumers are not coerced into buying products. France also regulates premium offers which are, for all practical purposes, illegal because it is illegal to sell for less than cost price or to offer a customer a gift or premium conditional on the purchase of another product. Furthermore, a manufacturer or retailer cannot offer products different from the kind regularly offered (i.e., a detergent manufacturer cannot offer clothing or kitchen utensils). German law covering promotion in general is about as stringent as can be found. Building on an 80-year-old statute against "unfair competition," the German courts currently prevent businesses from offering all sorts of incentives to lure customers. Most incentives that target particular groups of customers are illegal, as are most offers of gifts. Similarly, enterprises may not offer price cuts of more than 3 percent of a product's value.

[28] Jon Choy, "Tokyo Updates Protections for Intellectual Property," *JEI Report,* January 1, 1997, p. 26.

The various laws concerning product comparison, a natural and effective means of expression, are another major stumbling block. In Germany, comparisons in advertisements are always subject to the competitor's right to go to the courts and ask for proof of any implied or stated superiority. In Canada, the rulings are even more stringent: All claims and statements must be examined to ensure that any representation to the public is not false or misleading. Such representation cannot be made verbally in selling or contained in or on anything that comes to the attention of the public (such as product labels, inserts in products, or any other form of advertising including what may be expressed in a sales letter). Courts have been directed by Canadian law to take into account in determining whether a representation is false or misleading the "general impression" conveyed by the representation as well as its literal meaning. The courts are expected to apply the "credulous person standard," which means that if any reasonable person could possibly misunderstand the representation, the representation is misleading. In essence, puffery, an acceptable practice in the United States, could be interpreted in Canada as false and misleading advertising. Thus, a statement such as "the strongest drive shaft in Canada" would be judged misleading unless the advertiser had absolute evidence that the drive shaft was stronger than any other drive shaft for sale in Canada.

In Puerto Rico and the Virgin Islands, the law requires that the rules for any promotion must be printed in Spanish and English. And during the entire time of the promotion both versions must be printed in at least one general circulation newspaper once a week. If the promotion includes a drawing, Puerto Rico requires that a notary be present when the drawing takes place.[29] Such diversity of laws among countries extends to advertising, pricing, sales agreements, and other commercial activities.

There is some hope that the European Community will soon have a common commercial code. While the EC is a beautiful picture of economic cooperation, there is still the reality of dealing with 15 different countries, cultures, and languages, as well as 15 different legal systems. Cultural norms are difficult to change, although Germany's complicated trade laws are changing but with resistance. Helping to maintain the status quo is an industry–finance organization called the Center for Combating Unfair Competition. Its 20 lawyers file a thousand lawsuits a year, going after, for example, a grocery store that offers discount coupons or a deli that gives a free cup of coffee to a customer who has already bought 10. Both practices are illegal in Germany.[30]

The goal of full integration and a common commercial code has not been totally achieved in the EC; however, decisions by the European Court continue to strike down individual country laws that impede competition across borders. In a recent decision, the European Court ruled that a French cosmetics company could sell its wares by mail in Germany by advertising them at a markdown from their original prices, a direct violation of German law. One German lawyer commented, "The decision marks the beginning of the end of German advertising law." Slowly but surely, the provisions of the Single European Market Act will be attained, but until then many of the legal and trade differences that have existed for decades will remain.

Green Marketing Legislation

Multinational corporations also face a growing variety of legislation designed to address environmental issues. Global concern for the environment extends beyond industrial pollution, hazardous waste disposal, and rampant deforestation to include issues that focus directly on consumer products. Green marketing laws focus on product packaging and its effect on solid waste management and environmentally friendly products.[31]

---

[29] Maxine Lans Retsky, "Global Promotions Are Subject to Local Laws," *Marketing News,* May 12, 1997, p. 8.

[30] Greg Steinmetz, "Mark Down: German Consumers Are Seeing Prices Cut in Deregulation Push," *The Wall Street Journal,* August 15, 1997, p. A1.

[31] For an interesting discussion of taxation as a motivator in the "green movement" see Jean-Philippe, " 'Green' Taxation," *The OECD Observer,* June 1997, p. 8.

Germany has passed the most stringent green marketing laws that regulate the management and recycling of packaging waste. The new packaging law was introduced in three phases. The first phase required all transport packaging such as crates, drums, pallets, and Styrofoam containers to be accepted back by the manufacturers and distributors for recycling. The second phase requires manufacturers, distributors, and retailers to accept all returned secondary packaging, including corrugated boxes, blister packs, packaging designed to prevent theft, packaging for vending machine applications, and packaging for promotional purposes. The third phase requires all retailers, distributors, and manufacturers to accept returned sales packaging including cans, plastic containers for dairy products, foil wrapping, Styrofoam packages, and folding cartons such as cereal boxes. The requirement for retailers to take back sales packaging has been suspended as long as the voluntary green dot program remains a viable substitute.

Many European countries also have devised schemes to identify products that comply with certain criteria that make them more environmentally friendly than similar products. Products that meet these criteria will be awarded an "eco-label" that the manufacturer can display on packaging as a signal to customers of an environmentally friendly product. Alarmed at the diversity of green laws and eco-labeling that were evolving and the difficulty of harmonizing them across the EC, the EC Commission has issued similar laws. The strategic marketing implications of eco-labeling and the German and EC packaging laws will be discussed in more detail in the chapter on consumer products (Chapter 11).

Antitrust: An Evolving Issue

With the exception of the United States, antitrust laws have been either nonexistent or not enforced in most of the world's countries for the better part of the 20th century. However, the European Community, Japan, and many other countries have begun to actively enforce their antitrust laws patterned after those in the United States. Antimonopoly, price discrimination, supply restrictions, and full-line forcing are areas in which the European Court of Justice has dealt severe penalties. For example, before Procter & Gamble Company was allowed to buy VP-Schickedanz AG, a German hygiene products company, it had to agree to sell off one of the German company's divisions that produced Camelia, a brand of sanitary napkins. P&G already marketed a brand of sanitary napkins in Europe, and the Commission was concerned that allowing them to keep Camelia would give them a controlling 60 percent of the German sanitary products market and 81 percent of Spain's. In another instance, Coca-Cola was fined $1.8 million for anticompetitive practices by France's antitrust authority; two months later Coca-Cola paid a $2 million fine in Venezuela for violating laws that prohibit market concentrations restrictive to free competition.[32]

As is frequently the case with antitrust decisions, decisions that are logical from a strategic sense can be seen as potentially damaging to competition. Such was the case with a proposed joint venture by Coca-Cola and Carlsberg A/S to bottle and distribute Coca-Cola. European Union antitrust regulators were concerned that the proposed venture would create a stranglehold on the Scandinavian market.[33] Of similar concern was the Boeing-McDonnell merger. After a year-long investigation, U.S. antitrust regulators approved the merger, but initially EU regulators did not. Permission came only after Boeing made several important concessions. Among the concessions was that Boeing had to discontinue a 20-year exclusive contract to supply parts with three major U.S. airlines.[34]

---

[32] Charles Fleming and Nikhil Deogun, "French Unit Fines Coke $1.8 Million for Sales Practices," *The Wall Street Journal,* January 30, 1997, p. B12.

[33] "EU Is Said to Prepare Full Probe of Coca-Cola, Carlsberg Venture," *The Wall Street Journal,* May 2, 1997, p. B3.

[34] "Commission Clears Merger between Boeing and McDonnell Douglas with Conditions and Obligations," *The European Union Press Releases,* No. 53/97, July 30, 1997 (**http://www.eurunion.org/ news/press/1997-3/**).

Developing nations see intracorporate limitations imposed by a parent company on its subsidiary within their country as the major violation of free trade. Thus, restraint of trade reflects concern with a parent multinational firm restraining the competitive activities of its subsidiary within the country. In all these situations, the MNC is confronted with various interpretations of antitrust. To confuse the marketer further, its activities in one country may inadvertently lead to antitrust violations in another. Active antitrust enforcement worldwide is just one more important law that each multinational firm must consider in its strategic decision making.

U.S. Laws Apply in Host Countries

All governments are concerned with protecting their political and economic interests domestically and internationally; any activity or action, wherever it occurs, that adversely threatens national interests is subject to government control. As such, leaving the political boundaries of a home country does not exempt a business from home-country laws. Regardless of the nation where business is done, a U.S. citizen is subject to certain laws of the United States. What is illegal for an American business at home can also be illegal by U.S. laws in foreign jurisdictions for the firm, its subsidiaries, and licensees of U.S. technology.

Laws that prohibit taking a bribe, trading with the enemy, participating in a commercial venture that negatively affects the U.S. economy, participating in an unauthorized boycott such as the Arab boycott, or any other activity deemed to be against the best interests of the United States, apply to U.S. businesses and their subsidiaries and licensees, regardless of where they operate. Thus, at any given time a U.S. citizen in a foreign country must look not only at the laws of the host country, but at home law as well.

The question of jurisdiction of U.S. law over acts committed outside the territorial limits of the country has been settled by the courts through application of a long-established principle of international law, "objective theory of jurisdiction." This concept holds that, even if an act is committed outside the territorial jurisdiction of U.S. courts, those courts can nevertheless have jurisdiction if the act produces effects within the home country. The only possible exception may be when the violation is the result of enforced compliance with local law.[35]

Foreign Corrupt Practices Act

Recall from Chapter 5 that the Foreign Corrupt Practices Act (FCPA) makes it illegal for companies to pay bribes to foreign officials, candidates, or political parties. Stiff penalties can be assessed against company officials, directors, employees, or agents found guilty of paying a bribe or of knowingly participating in or authorizing the payment of a bribe. However, also recall that bribery, which can range from lubrication to extortion, is a common business custom in many countries.

The original FCPA lacked clarity, and early interpretations were extremely narrow and confusing. Even simple payments to expedite activities (grease) were considered illegal. Another troubling part of the law for U.S. executives was the provision that executives could be held liable for bribes paid by anyone in their organizations, including agents in the foreign country, if they had any "reason to know." Many U.S. firms restricted their agents from business as usual for fear the agents were paying bribes. The Omnibus Trade and Competitiveness Act of 1988 amended the FCPA and reduced the potential liability of corporate offices from "have reason to know" to "know of or autho-

---

[35] Andre Simons, "Foreign Trade and Antitrust Laws," *Business Topics,* Summer 1962, p. 27.

rize" illegal payments. In addition, if it is customary in the culture, the law permits small (grease or lubrication) payments made to encourage officials to complete routine government actions such as processing papers, stamping visas, and scheduling inspections.[36]

The debate continues as to whether or not the law puts U.S. business at a disadvantage. Some argue that U.S. businesses are at a disadvantage in international business transactions in those cases where bribery payments are customary, while others contend that it has little effect, indeed, that it helps companies to "just say no." The truth probably lies somewhere in between. A study by the Commerce Department stated that foreign firms using bribery to undercut U.S. firms' efforts have won contracts worth about $45 billion.[37] How many of these contracts would have been won by U.S. firms if bribes were not paid is anyone's guess. Clearly, many U.S. businesses are living within the law; the consensus is that most comply in good faith.

National Security Laws

U.S. firms, their foreign subsidiaries, or foreign firms that are licensees of U.S. technology cannot sell a product to a country where the sale is considered by the U.S. government to affect national security. Further, responsibility extends to the final destination of the product regardless of the number of intermediaries that may be involved in the transfer of goods. Thus, a U.S. company cannot legally sell a controlled product to someone if the U.S. company could reasonably know that the product's final destination would be in a country where the sale would be illegal.

The control of the sale of goods for national security reasons has abated somewhat with the improved trade relations among nations that have come with the end of the Cold War. When the former USSR, China, and other communist countries were viewed as major threats to U.S. security, the control of the sale of goods considered to have a strategic and military value was extremely strict, although considered by some to be of doubtful importance. In one case, the Fruehauf Corporation was caught in the middle when its French subsidiary signed a $20 million contract to sell Fruehauf trailers to a French truck manufacturer. The French truck company planned to sell the truck and trailer as a unit to China, thus the U.S. trailers would go to China.[38] At the time, the United States was not trading with China, and in order not to be in violation of the Trading with the Enemy Act, Fruehauf (U.S.) canceled the contract. The French government was outraged and intervened by legally seizing the French subsidiary and completing the sale of the trailers to the truck company, which then sold them to China.

Since the Fruehauf case, U.S. relations with China have changed dramatically and there is extensive trade between the two countries. The difference between today and the height of the Cold War is that there are now fewer controlled products and the position of the U.S. government has been to liberalize export controls. Nevertheless, a U.S. company, its subsidiaries, joint ventures, or licensees still cannot sell controlled products without special permission from the U.S. government.

The consequences of violation of the Trading with the Enemy Act can be severe: fines, prison sentences, and in the case of foreign companies, economic sanctions. Toshiba Machine Tool Company of Japan sold the Soviet Union milling machines to make ultraquiet submarine propellers. A U.S. company licensed the technology for the milling machines to the Japanese company, and sale to Russia was forbidden. Besides sanctions taken against Toshiba in Japan for violation of Japanese law, the U.S. Trade Bill of 1988 specifically banned all government purchases from Toshiba Corporation, parent of Toshiba Machine Company, for three years. The estimated losses annually

---

[36] Skip Kaltenheuser, "The Real Cost of Doing Business; Ignorance Is No Protection," *World Trade,* June 1997, p. 80.

[37] "Foreign Practices," *Across the Board,* October 1996, p. 11.

[38] See Chapter 14 for a complete discussion of export controls.

CROSSING BORDERS 7-5

Whatever You Call It—It's Still a Bribe

U.S. expressions such as bribe or payoff all sound a little stiff and cold. In some countries, the terms for the same activities have a little more character.*

Country	Term	Translation
Japan	Kuroi kiri	Black mist
Germany	Schmiergeld	Grease money
Latin America	El soborno	Payoff
Mexico	La mordida	The bite
Middle East	Baksheesh	Tip, gratuity
France	Pot-de-vin	Jug of wine
East Africa	Chai	Tea
Italy	Bustarella	Little envelope

*Other terms are *wairo* (Japan), *dash* (Nigeria), and *backhander* (India).

were about 3 percent of the company's total exports to the United States. Protection of U.S. technology that has either national security or economic implications is an ongoing activity of the U.S. government.[39]

In addition to the reasons discussed above, exports are controlled also for the protection and promotion of human rights, as a means of enforcing foreign policy, because of national shortages, to control technology, and a host of other reasons the U.S. government deems necessary to protect its best interests. In years past, the government has restricted trade with South Africa (human rights) and restricted the sale of wheat to Russia in retaliation for Russia's invasion of Afghanistan (foreign policy). Currently, the government restricts the sale of leading-edge electronics (control of technology) and prohibits the export of pesticides that have not been approved for use in the U.S. (to avoid the return of residue of unauthorized pesticides in imported food and protect U.S. consumers from the so-called "circle of poison"). In each of these cases, U.S. law binds U.S. businesses regardless of where they operate.[40]

Antitrust Laws

Antitrust enforcement has two purposes in international commerce. The first is to protect American consumers by ensuring that they benefit from products and ideas produced by foreign competitors as well as by domestic competitors. Competition from foreign producers is important when imports are, or could be, a major source of a product or when a single firm dominates a domestic industry. This becomes relevant in many joint ventures, particularly if the joint venture creates a situation where a U.S. firm entering a joint venture with a foreign competitor restricts competition for the U.S. parent in the U.S. market.

---

[39] E. J. Prior, "The Future of, and in, Export Controls: It's Not Futile, If You Play Your Cards Right," *The Export Practitioner,* January 15, 1997, p. 16.

[40] For an insightful discussion of export controls see James B. Burnham, "The Heavy Hand of Export Controls," *Society,* January 11, 1997, p. 39.

The second purpose of antitrust legislation is to protect American export and investment opportunities against any privately imposed restrictions. The concern is that all U.S.-based firms engaged in the export of goods, services, or capital should be allowed to compete on merit and not be shut out by restrictions imposed by bigger or less-principled competitors.

The questions of jurisdiction and how U.S. antitrust laws apply are frequently asked but only vaguely answered. The basis for determination ultimately rests with the interpretation of Sections I and II of the Sherman Act: Section I states that "every contract, combination . . . or conspiracy in restraint of trade or commerce among the several states or with foreign nations is hereby declared to be illegal"; Section II makes it a violation to "monopolize, or attempt to monopolize, or combine or conspire with any other person or persons, to monopolize any part of the trade or commerce among the several states, or with foreign nations."

The Justice Department recognizes that application of U.S. antitrust laws to overseas activities raises some difficult questions of jurisdiction. It recognizes that U.S. antitrust-law enforcement should not interfere unnecessarily with the sovereign interest of a foreign nation. At the same time, however, the Antitrust Division is committed to control foreign transactions at home or abroad that have a substantial and foreseeable effect on U.S. commerce. When such business practices occur, there is no question in the Antitrust Division of the Department of Justice that U.S. laws apply.

Antiboycott Law

Under the antiboycott law enacted in 1977, U.S. companies are forbidden to participate in any unauthorized foreign boycott; further, they are required to report any request to cooperate with a boycott. The antiboycott law was a response to the Arab League boycott of Israeli businesses.[41] The Arab League boycott of Israel has three levels: (1) a primary boycott bans direct trade between Arab states and Israel; (2) a secondary boycott bars Arab governments from doing business with companies that do business with Israel; and (3) a tertiary boycott bans Arab governments from doing business with companies that do business with companies doing business with Israel.

When companies do not comply with the Arab League's[42] boycott directives, their names are placed on a blacklist and they are excluded from trade with members of the Arab League.[43] U.S. companies are caught in the middle: If they trade with Israel, the Arab League will not do business with them, and if they refuse to do business with Israel in order to trade with an Arab League member, they will be in violation of U.S. law. One hospital supply company that had been trading with Israel was charged with closing a plant in Israel in order to have the company taken off the Arab blacklist. After an investigation, the company pleaded guilty, was fined $6.6 million, and was prohibited from doing business in Syria and Saudi Arabia for two years.[44] The Gulf Cooperation

---

[41] For a complete description of the antiboycott regulations see "Antiboycott Compliance Requirements," *Bureau of Export Administration:* **http://www.bxa.doc.gov/oacprogr.htm/**.

[42] The antiboycott law only applies to those boycotts not sanctioned by the U.S. government. Sanctioned boycotts, such as the boycotts against trade with Cuba and Iraq, are sanctioned by the United States and must be honored by U.S. firms.

[43] For those non-U.S. companies trading with the Arab League and complying with the boycott, each was required to include a statement on the shipping invoices. On an invoice for 10 buses to be shipped from Brazil to Kuwait the following statement appeared: "We certify that we are the producer and supplier of the shipped goods; we are neither blacklisted by the Arab Boycott of Israel nor are we the head office branch or subsidiary of a boycotted company. No Israeli capital is invested in this firm, no company capital or capital of its owners is invested in any Israeli company; our products are not of Israeli origin and do not contain Israeli raw material or labor."

[44] Thomas M. Burton, "How Baxter Got Off the Arab Blacklist, and How It Got Nailed," *The Wall Street Journal,* March 26, 1993, p. A1.

Council[45] lifted the secondary and tertiary boycotts in 1995 but they remained in effect for the other Arab states until the Arab–Israeli Accord was reached in 1996. However, that accord soon fell apart, and as conditions worsened, the Arab League passed a resolution to restore an economic boycott against Israel.[46]

Extraterritoriality of U.S. Laws

The issue of the extraterritoriality of U.S. laws is especially important to U.S. multinational firms because the long arm of the United States legal jurisdiction causes anxiety for heads of state. Foreign governments fear the influence of American government policy on their economies through U.S. multinationals.[47]

Especially troublesome are those instances when U.S. law is in conflict with host countries' economic or political goals. Conflict arises when the host government requires joint ventures to do business within the country and the U.S. Justice Department restricts or forbids such ventures because of their U.S. anticompetitive effects. Host countries see this influence as evidence of U.S. interference. When U.S. MNCs' subsidiaries are prohibited from making a sale in violation of the U.S. Trading with the Enemy Act, host governments react with hostility toward the extraterritorial application of U.S. foreign policy.

When the intent of any kind of overseas activity is to restrain trade, there is no question about the appropriateness of applying U.S. laws. There is a question, however, when the intent is to conclude a reasonable business transaction. If the U.S. government encourages U.S. firms to become multinational, then the government needs to make provisions for resolution of differences when conflict arises between U.S. law and host government laws.

Summary

Business faces a multitude of problems in its efforts to develop a successful marketing program. Not the least of these problems is the varying legal systems of the world and their effect on business transactions. Just as political climate, cultural differences, local geography, different business customs, and the stage of economic development must be taken into account, so must such legal questions as jurisdictional and legal recourse in disputes, protection of industrial property rights, extended U.S. law enforcement, and enforcement of antitrust legislation by U.S. and foreign governments. A primary marketing task is to develop a plan that will be enhanced, or at least not adversely affected, by these and other environmental elements. The myriad questions created by different laws and different legal systems indicate that the prudent path to follow at all stages of foreign marketing operations is one leading to competent counsel well versed in the intricacies of the international legal environment.

Questions

1. Define:

common law	code law
Islamic law	Marxist–socialist tenets
prior use versus registration	conciliation
arbitration	litigation

2. How does the international marketer determine which legal system will have jurisdiction when legal disputes arise?

3. Discuss the state of international commercial law.

4. Discuss the limitations of jurisdictional clauses in contracts.

5. What is the "objective theory of jurisdiction"? How does it apply to a firm doing business within a foreign country?

6. Discuss some of the reasons why it is probably best to seek an out-of-court settlement in international commercial legal disputes rather than to sue.

---

[45] Of the 21 member Arab League, six (Saudi Arabia, Bahrain, Kuwait, Oman, Qatar, and United Arab Emirates) are members of the Gulf Cooperation Council.

[46] "Arab League Approves Resolution to Freeze Ties with Israel," *Compass Middle East News Service,* March 31, 1997. It should be noted that the secondary boycott against third parties trading with Israel was not called for in the resolution.

[47] See also Chapter 6.

7. Illustrate the procedure generally followed in international commercial disputes when settled under the auspices of a formal arbitration tribunal.

8. What are intellectual property rights? Why should a company in international marketing take special steps to protect them?

9. In many code-law countries, registration rather than prior use establishes ownership of intellectual property rights. Comment.

10. Discuss the advantages to the international marketer arising from the existence of the various international conventions on trademarks, patents, and copyrights.

11. "The legal environment of the foreign marketer takes on an added dimension of importance since there is no single uniform international commercial law which governs foreign business transactions." Comment.

12. What is the "credulous person standard" in advertising and what is its importance in international marketing?

13. Differentiate between the European Patent Convention (EPC) and the Patent Cooperation Treaty (PCT) in their effectiveness in protecting industrial property rights.

14. Discuss the recent changes in the Foreign Corrupt Practices Act made in the Omnibus Trade and Competitiveness Act of 1988.

15. Why is conciliation a better way to resolve a commercial dispute than arbitration?

16. Differentiate between conciliation and arbitration.

DEVELOPING A GLOBAL VISION THROUGH MARKETING RESEARCH

Chapter Learning Objectives

What you should learn from Chapter 8

- Additional marketing factors involved in international market research.

- The problems of availability and use of secondary data.

- Quantitative and qualitative research methods.

- Multiculture sampling and its problems in less-developed countries.

- How to analyze and use research information.

- The function of multinational marketing information systems.

- Sources of available secondary data.

GLOBAL PERSPECTIVE

Selling Apples in Japan Can Be a Bruising Business

Selling apples in Japan—whether they are of the edible or computer variety—can be a bruising business. In both cases, designing effective and competitive marketing strategies requires a deep knowledge of buyer behavior that may be distinctly different from that which marketers encounter in the United States.

It took Washington State apple growers 24 years to get their fruit past customs inspectors in Japan. The door finally opened to Red and Golden Delicious apples in 1995, and Japanese consumers immediately gobbled up nearly 8,500 tons. But in 1996, sales dropped precipitously to only 800 tons. The slide in sales can be attributed in part to the fact that U.S. apple growers did not anticipate the strength of Japanese consumers' seasonal preferences; Americans buy and eat apples year round, but Japanese consumers do not. The growers also did not anticipate the lasting effects of nationalism among many Japanese. As one older Japanese woman wrote to her sister in the United States, "Younger Japanese people simply do not have any respect. They just buy those American apples with no shame. They do not have any loyalty to the Japanese farmers. All they care about is the lower price." And it's not just consumer behaviors that are giving the Washington apple growers fits; competitors are beginning to nibble on the Japanese apple market, too. New Zealand fruit is already on the shelves in Tokyo and, after years of complaining about European fruit flies and fungi, the Japanese authorities now are allowing in apples from France as well.

As for apples of the computer variety, Apple Computers traditionally have been a huge success in Japan, where it is the number-two computer vendor behind domestic producer NEC. Its 14 percent market share there is nearly double its penetration in the United States, and it hopes to maintain its industry-leading growth rate (44 percent in 1995) through the end of the century. But it won't be easy to continue taking a big bite out of the $30 billion Japanese personal computer (PC) market. Apple is having big problems at home, and the losses in market share and reputation in the United States will certainly have an effect on buyers' perceptions in Japan. Moreover, the Japanese PC market works differently than that in the United States. For one, Japanese businesses have been relatively slow to use PCs to boost productivity and managers prefer to network in face-to-face settings rather than via electronic hookups. Additionally, there are few informational professionals in Japan compared to the United States. Such circumstances suggest that the rate of adoption of PCs in the Japanese workplace will not parallel that in the United States, meaning Apple will have a smaller market in which to operate.

Yes, selling either kind of apple in Japan will require the best marketing research efforts of U.S. firms. The basis of a marketing budget is the all-important forecast of demand, which requires statistical analyses and macroeconomic data from Japan. But before those data are collected, consumer focus groups and surveys must be conducted. U.S. marketers must also travel across the Pacific for visits to grocery stores or office buildings to see firsthand these evolving markets at their cores.

Sources: "U.S. Apple Growers Go After Japanese Consumers," *Chicago Tribune*, July 29, 1996, p. 4; "Japan 'Unfair to U.S. Apples,'" *Financial Times*, October 1, 1996, p. 5; personal correspondence given to authors; David Owens and Emiko Terazano, "French Apples May Yet Appeal to Japan," *Financial Times*, August 14, 1997, p. 5; and "Wiring Corporate Japan, Doing It Differently," *The Economist*, April 19, 1997, pp. 62–64. For the latest information on its current performance and growth plans for the Japanese market, see Apple's Web site at **http://www.apple.com**.

Information is the key component in developing successful marketing strategies and avoiding major marketing blunders. Information needs range from the general data required to assess market opportunities to specific market information for decisions about product, promotion, distribution, and price. Sometimes the information can be bought from trusted research vendors or supplied by internal marketing research staff. But sometimes even the highest level executives have to "get their shoes dirty" by putting in the miles and talking to key customers and/or directly observing the marketplace in action.[1] As an enterprise broadens its scope of operations to include international markets,

---

[1] Peter Drucker's wisdom improves with age. In his *Wall Street Journal* article (May 11, 1990, p. A15) he most eloquently makes the case for direct observation of the marketplace by even the most senior executives. For the most substantive argument in that same vein see Gerald Zaltman's description of the emotional

the need for current, accurate information is magnified. Indeed, some researchers maintain that entry into a fast-developing, new-to-the-firm foreign market is one of the most daunting and ambiguous strategic decisions an executive can face.[2] A marketer must find the most accurate and reliable data possible within the limits imposed by time, cost, and the present state of the art. The measure of a competent researcher is twofold: (1) the ability to utilize the most sophisticated and adequate techniques and methods available within these limits; and (2) the effective communication of insights to the decision makers in the firm. The latter often requires involving senior executives directly in the research process itself.

Marketing research is traditionally defined as the systematic gathering, recording, and analyzing of data to provide information useful in marketing decision making. While the research processes and methods are basically the same whether applied in Columbus, Ohio, or Colombo, Sri Lanka, *international marketing research* involves two additional complications. First, information must be communicated across cultural boundaries. That is, executives in Chicago must be able to "translate" their research questions into terms that consumers in Guangzhou, China, can understand. Then the Chinese answers must be put into terms (i.e., reports and data summaries) that American managers can comprehend. Fortunately, there are often internal staff and research agencies that are quite experienced in these kinds of cross-cultural communication tasks.

Second, the environments within which the research tools are applied are often different in foreign markets. Rather than acquire new and exotic methods of research, the international marketing researcher must develop the ability for imaginative and deft application of tried and tested techniques in sometimes totally strange milieus. The mechanical problems of implementing foreign marketing research often vary from country to country. Within a foreign environment, the frequently differing emphases on the kinds of information needed, the often limited variety of appropriate tools and techniques available, and the difficulty of implementing the research process constitute the challenges facing most international marketing researchers.

This chapter deals with the operational problems encountered in gathering information in foreign countries for use by international marketers. Emphasis is on those elements of data generation that usually prove especially troublesome in conducting research in an environment other than the United States.

Breadth and Scope of International Marketing Research

The basic difference between domestic and foreign market research is the broader scope needed for foreign research.[3] Research can be divided into three types based on information needs: (1) general information about the country, area, and/or market; (2) information necessary to forecast future marketing requirements by anticipating social, economic, consumer, and industry trends within specific markets or countries; and (3) specific market information used to make product, promotion, distribution, and price decisions and to develop marketing plans. In domestic operations, most emphasis is placed on the third type, gathering specific market information, because the other data are often available from secondary sources.

---

aspects of managerial decision making in "Rethinking Market Research: Putting People Back In," *Journal of Marketing Research,* XXXIV, November 1997, pp. 424–437.

2 Hugh Courtney, Jane Kirkland, and Patrick Viguerie, "Strategy under Uncertainty," *Harvard Business Review,* 75(6), November–December 1997, pp. 66–79.

3 Still the best reference on the topic is Susan P. Douglas' and C. Samuel Craig's *International Marketing Research* (Englewood Cliffs, NJ: Prentice Hall, 1983).

Microsoft's Bill Gates takes his company's advertising slogan, "Where do you want to go today?" very seriously. While he and his ads espouse the advantages of virtual travel, his own actual international travel schedule is also quite heavy. He finds face-to-face meetings with foreign vendors, partners, customers, and regulators a crucial part of his trying to understand international markets. Here he talks with reporters and France's President Jacques Chirac while attending the IT Forum Computer Show in Paris. (© William Stevens/Liaison International)

A country's political stability, cultural attributes, and geographical characteristics are some of the kinds of information not ordinarily gathered by domestic company marketing research departments but which are required for a sound assessment of a foreign market. This broader scope of international marketing research is reflected in Unisys Corporation's planning steps, which call for collecting and assessing the following types of information:

1. *Economic:* General data on growth of the economy, inflation, business cycle trends, and the like; profitability analysis for the division's products; specific industry economic studies; analysis of overseas economies; and key economic indicators for the United States and major foreign countries.

2. *Sociological and political climate:* A general noneconomic review of conditions affecting the division's business. In addition to the more obvious subjects, it also covers ecology, safety, leisure time, and their potential impact on the division's business.

3. *Overview of market conditions:* A detailed analysis of market conditions the division faces, by market segment, including international.

4. *Summary of the technological environment:* A summary of the "state of the art" technology as it relates to the division's business, carefully broken down by product segments.

5. *Competitive situation:* A review of competitors' sales revenues, methods of market segmentation, products, and apparent strategies on an international scope.

Such in-depth information is necessary for sound marketing decisions. For the domestic marketer, most such information has been acquired after years of experience with a single market, but in foreign markets this information must be gathered for each new market.

There is a basic difference between information ideally needed and that which is collectible and/or used. Many firms engaged in foreign marketing do not make decisions with the benefit of the information listed. Cost, time, and the human elements are critical variables. Some firms have neither the appreciation for information nor adequate time or money for implementation of research. As a firm becomes more committed to foreign marketing and the cost of possible failure increases, however, greater emphasis is placed on research. Consequently, a global firm is or should be engaged in the most sophisticated and exhaustive kinds of research activities.

The Research Process

A marketing research study is always a compromise dictated by limits of time, cost, and the present state of the art. The researcher must strive for the most accurate and reliable information within existing constraints. A key to successful research is a systematic and orderly approach to the collection and analysis of data. Whether a research program is conducted in New York or New Delhi, the *research process* should follow these steps:

1. Define the research problem and establish research objectives.
2. Determine the sources of information to fulfill the research objectives.
3. Consider the costs and benefits of the research effort.
4. Gather the relevant data from secondary and/or primary sources.
5. Analyze, interpret, and summarize the results.
6. Effectively communicate the results to decision makers.

Although the steps in a research program are similar for all countries, variations and problems in implementation occur because of differences in cultural and economic development. While the problems of research in England or Canada may be similar to those in the United States, research in Germany, South Africa, or Mexico may offer a multitude of different and difficult distinctions. These distinctions become apparent with the first step in the research process—formulation of the problem. Subsequent text sections illustrate some frequently encountered difficulties facing the international marketing researcher.

Defining the Problem and Establishing Research Objectives

The research process should begin with a definition of the research problem and the establishment of specific research objectives. The major difficulty here is converting a series of often ambiguous business problems into tightly drawn and achievable research objectives. In this initial stage, researchers often embark on the research process with only a vague grasp of the total problem.

This first, most crucial step in research is more critical in foreign markets because an unfamiliar environment tends to cloud problem definition. Researchers either fail to anticipate the influence of the local culture on the problem or fail to identify the self-reference criterion (SRC) and so treat the problem definition as if it were in the researcher's home environment. In assessing some foreign business failures it is apparent that research was conducted, but the questions asked were more appropriate for the U.S. market than for the foreign one. For example, all of Disney's years of research and ex-

CROSSING BORDERS 8-1

Headache? Take Two Aspirin and Lie Down

Such advice goes pretty far in countries like Germany, where Bayer invented aspirin more than 100 years ago, and in the United States. But people in many places around the world don't share such "Western" views about medicine and the causes of disease. Many Asians, including Chinese, Filipinos, Koreans, Japanese, and Southeast Asians, believe illnesses such as headaches are the result of the imbalance between the *yin* and *yang*. *Yin* is the feminine, passive principle that is typified by darkness, cold, or wetness. Alternatively, *yang* is the masculine, active principle associated with light, heat, or dryness. All things result from their combination, and bad things like headaches result from too much of one or the other. Acupuncture and/or moxibustion (heating crushed wormwood or other herbs on the skin) are common cures for *yin* outweighing *yang,* or vice versa. Many Laotians believe pain can be caused by one of the body's 32 souls being lost or by sorcerers' spells. The exact cause is often determined by examining the yolk of a freshly broken egg. In other parts of the world such as Mexico and Puerto Rico, illness is believed to be caused by an imbalance of one of the four body humors: "blood—hot and wet; yellow bile—hot and dry; phlegm—cold and wet; and black bile—cold and dry." Even in the high-tech U.S., many people believe that pain is often a "reminder from God" to behave properly.

For companies such as Bayer a key question to be addressed in marketing research is how and to what extent can aspirin be marketed as a supplement to the traditional remedies. That is, will little white pills mix well with phlegm and black bile?

Source: Adapted from Larry A. Samovar, Richard E. Porter, and Lisa A. Stefani, *Communication between Cultures.* 3rd edition. (Belmont, CA: Wadsworth Publishing Co., 1998), pp. 224–225; the direct quote is from N. Dresser, *Multicultural Manners: New Rules for Etiquette for a Changing Society* (New York, NY: John Wiley & Sons, 1996), p. 236.

perience in keeping people happy standing in long lines could not help them anticipate the scope of the problems they would run into at EuroDisney. The firm's experience had been that the relatively homogeneous clientele at both the American parks and Tokyo Disneyland were cooperative and orderly when it came to queuing up. Actually, so are most British and Germans. But the rules about queuing in other countries such as Spain and Italy are apparently quite different, creating the potential for a new kind of intra-European "warfare" in the lines. Understanding and managing this multinational customer service problem has required new ways of thinking. Isolating the SRC and asking the right questions are crucial steps in the problem formulation stage.

Other difficulties in foreign research stem from failure to establish problem limits broad enough to include all relevant variables. Information on a far greater range of factors is necessary to offset the unfamiliar cultural background of the foreign market. Consider proposed research about consumption patterns and attitudes toward hot milk-based drinks. In the United Kingdom, hot milk-based drinks are considered to have sleep-inducing, restful, and relaxing properties and are traditionally consumed prior to bedtime. People in Thailand, however, drink the same hot milk-based drinks in the morning on the way to work and see them as being invigorating, energy-giving, and stimulating. If one's only experience is the United States, the picture is further clouded since hot milk-based drinks are frequently associated with cold weather, either in the morning or the evening, and for different reasons each time of day. The market researcher must be certain the problem definition is sufficiently broad to cover the whole range of response possibilities and not be clouded by his or her self-reference criterion.

Once the problem is adequately defined and research objectives established, the researcher must determine the availability of the information needed. If the data are available—that is, if they have been collected already by some other agency—the researcher should then consult these *secondary data* sources.

Problems of Availability and Use of Secondary Data

The breadth of many foreign marketing research studies and the marketer's lack of familiarity with a country's basic socioeconomic and cultural patterns result in considerable demand for information like that generally available from secondary sources in the United States. The U.S. government provides comprehensive statistics for the United States; periodic censuses of U.S. population, housing, business, and agriculture are conducted and, in some cases, have been taken for over 100 years. Commercial sources, trade associations, management groups, and state and local governments also provide the researcher with additional sources of detailed U.S. market information.

Unfortunately, the quantity and quality of marketing-related data available on the United States is unmatched in other countries. The data available on and in Japan is a close second, and several European countries do a good job of data collection and reporting them. Indeed, on some dimensions the quality of data collected in these latter countries can actually exceed that in the U.S. However, in many countries substantial data collection has been initiated only recently. Through the continuing efforts of organizations such as the United Nations and the Organization for Economic Cooperation and Development (OECD) improvements are being made worldwide.

In addition, with the emergence of Eastern European countries as potentially viable markets, a number of private and public groups are funding the collection of information to offset a lack of comprehensive market data. Several Japanese consumer goods manufacturers are coordinating market research on a corporate level and have funded 47 research centers throughout Eastern Europe. As market activity continues in Eastern Europe and elsewhere, market information will improve in quantity and quality. To build a data base on Russian consumers, one Denver, Colorado, firm used a novel approach to conduct a survey: it ran a questionnaire in Moscow's *Komsomolskaya Pravda* newspaper asking for replies to be sent to the company. The 350,000 replies received (3,000 by registered mail) attested to the willingness of Russian consumers to respond to marketing inquiries. The problems of availability, reliability, comparability of data, and validating secondary data are described below.

Availability of Data

Much of the secondary data an American marketer is accustomed to having about United States markets is just not available for many countries. Detailed data on the numbers of wholesalers, retailers, manufacturers, and facilitating services, for example, are unavailable for many parts of the world, as are data on population and income. Most countries simply do not have governmental agencies that collect on a regular basis the kinds of secondary data readily available in the United States. If such information is important, the marketer must initiate the research or rely on private sources of data.

Reliability of Data

Available data may not have the level of reliability necessary for confident decision making for many reasons. Official statistics are sometimes too optimistic, reflecting national pride rather than practical reality, while tax structures and fear of the tax collector often adversely affect data.

Although not unique to them, less-developed countries are particularly prone to being both overly optimistic and unreliable in reporting relevant economic data about their countries. China's National Statistics Enforcement Office recently acknowledged that it had uncovered about 60,000 instances of false statistical reports since beginning a crackdown on false data reporting several months earlier. Seeking advantages or hiding failures, local officials, factory managers, rural enterprises, and others filed fake numbers on everything from production levels to birthrates. For example, a petrochemical plant reported one year's output to be $20 million, 50 percent higher than its actual output of $13.4 million. Finally, if you believe the statistics, Chinese in Hong Kong are the world-champion consumers of fresh oranges—64 pounds per year per person, twice as much as Americans. However, apparently about half of all the oranges imported into Hong Kong, some $30 million worth, actually find their way into Greater China, where U.S. oranges are (wink, wink) illegal.[4]

Willful errors in the reporting of marketing data are not uncommon in the most industrialized countries, either. Often print media circulation figures are purposely overestimated even in OECD countries.[5] The European Community (EC) tax policies can affect the accuracy of reported data also. Production statistics are frequently inaccurate because these countries collect taxes on domestic sales. Thus, some companies shave their production statistics a bit to match the sales reported to tax authorities. Conversely, foreign trade statistics may be blown up slightly because each country in the EU grants some form of export subsidy. Knowledge of such "adjusted reporting" is critical for a marketer who relies on secondary data for forecasting or estimating market demand.

Comparability of Data

Comparability of available data is the third shortcoming faced by foreign marketers. In the United States, current sources of reliable and valid estimates of socioeconomic factors and business indicators are readily available. In other countries, especially those less developed, data can be many years out of date as well as having been collected on an infrequent and unpredictable schedule. Naturally, the rapid change in socioeconomic features being experienced in many of these countries makes the problem of currency a vital one. Further, even though many countries are now gathering reliable data, there are generally no historical series with which to compare the current information.

A related problem is the manner in which data are collected and reported. Too frequently, data are reported in different categories or in categories much too broad to be of specific value. The term *supermarket,* for example, has a variety of meanings around the world. In Japan a supermarket is quite different from its American counterpart. Japanese supermarkets usually occupy two-or three-story structures; they sell foodstuffs, daily necessities, and clothing on respective floors. Some even sell furniture, electric home appliances, stationery, and sporting goods, and have a restaurant. General merchandise stores, shopping centers, and department stores are different from stores of the same name in the United States. Furthermore, data from different countries are often not comparable. One report on the problems of comparing European cross-border retail store audit data states, "Some define the market one way, others another; some define price categories one way, and others another. Even within the same research agency, auditing peri-

---

[4] Evelyn Iritani, "China Orange Trade Sour, Sweet," *Los Angeles Times,* August 12, 1997, pp. A1 and A6; "China's Faked Numbers Pile Up," *The Wall Street Journal,* August 26, 1994, p. A6; and "Chinese Call for an End to Misreported Statistics," *The New York Times,* August 18, 1994, p. C17.

[5] Patrick M. Reilly and Ernest Beck, "Publishers Often Pad Circulation Figures," *The Wall Street Journal,* September 30, 1997, p. B12.

ods are defined differently in different countries."[6] As a result, audit data are largely not comparable.

Validating Secondary Data

The shortcomings discussed here should be considered when using any source of information. Many countries have similarly high standards of collection and preparation of data generally found in the United States, but secondary data from any source, including the United States, must be checked and interpreted carefully. As a practical matter, the following questions should be asked to effectively judge the reliability of secondary data sources:

1. Who collected the data? Would there be any reason for purposely misrepresenting the facts?
2. For what purposes were the data collected?
3. How were the data collected? (methodology)
4. Are the data internally consistent and logical in light of known data sources or market factors?

Checking the consistency of one set of secondary data with other data of known validity is an effective and often-used way of judging validity. For example, a researcher might check the sale of baby products with the number of women of childbearing age and with birthrates, or the number of patient beds in hospitals with the sale of related hospital equipment. Such correlations can also be useful in estimating demand and forecasting sales.

In general, the availability and accuracy of recorded secondary data increase as the level of economic development increases. There are exceptions; India is at a lower level of economic development than many countries but has accurate and relatively complete government-collected data.

Fortunately, interest in collecting quality statistical data rises as countries realize the value of extensive and accurate national statistics for orderly economic growth. This interest to improve the quality of national statistics has resulted in remarkable improvement in the availability of data over the last 20 years. However, where no data are available, or the secondary data sources are inadequate, it is necessary to begin the collection of primary data.

The Appendix to this chapter includes a comprehensive listing of secondary data sources, including World Wide Web sites on a variety of international marketing topics. Indeed, almost all secondary data available on international markets can now be discovered or acquired via the Internet. For example, the most comprehensive statistics regarding international financial, demographic, consumption, exports, and imports are accessible through a single source, the U.S. Department of Commerce at **www.stat-usa.gov**. Many other government, institutional, and commercial sources of data can be tapped into on the Internet as well.

Gathering Primary Data: Quantitative and Qualitative Research

If, after seeking all reasonable secondary data sources, research questions are still not adequately answered, the market researcher must collect *primary data*—that is, data

---

[6] "Cross-Border Market Research: Braun Battles National Diversity," *Business Europe,* February 21–27, 1994, pp. 7–8.

CROSSING BORDERS 8–2

International Data: Caveat Emptor

The statistics that are usually attached to economic data are subject to more than the usual number of caveats and qualifications concerning comparability. Statistics on income and consumption were drawn from national-accounts data published regularly by the United Nations and the Organization for Economic Cooperation and Development. These data, designed to provide a "comprehensive statistical statement about the economic activity of a country," are compiled from surveys sent to each of the participating countries (118 nations were surveyed by the UN). However, despite efforts by the UN and the OECD to present the data on a comparable basis, differences among countries concerning definitions, accounting practices, and recording methods persist. In Germany, for instance, consumer expenditures are estimated largely on the basis of the turnover tax, while in the United Kingdom tax-receipt data are frequently supplemented by household surveys and production data.

Even if data-gathering techniques in each country were standardized, definitional differences would still remain. These differences are relatively minor except in a few cases. For example, Germany classifies the purchase of a television set as an expenditure for "recreation and entertainment," while the same expenditure falls into the "furniture, furnishings, and household equipment" classification in the United States.

Expenditures, as defined by both the UN and the OECD, include consumption outlays by households (including individuals living alone) and private nonprofit organizations. The latter include churches, schools, hospitals, foundations, fraternal organizations, trade unions, and other groups which furnish services to households free of charge or at prices that do not cover costs.

Source: David Bauer, "The Dimensions of Consumer Markets Abroad," *The Conference Board Record*, reprinted with permission.

---

collected specifically for the particular research project at hand. The researcher may question the firm's sales force, distributors, middlemen, and/or customers to get appropriate market information. In most primary data collection, the researcher questions respondents to determine what they think about some topic or how they might behave under certain conditions. Marketing research methods can be grouped into two basic types: quantitative and qualitative research. In both methods, the marketer is interested in gaining knowledge about the market.

In *quantitative research,* usually a large number of respondents are asked to reply either verbally or in writing to structured questions using a specific response format (such as yes/no) or to select a response from a set of choices. Questions are designed to get specific responses to aspects of the respondents' behavior, intentions, attitudes, motives, and demographic characteristics. Quantitative research provides the marketer with responses that can be presented with precise estimations. The structured responses received in a survey can be summarized in percentages, averages, or other statistics. For example, 76 percent of the respondents prefer product A over product B, and so on. Survey research is generally associated with quantitative research, and the typical instrument used is the questionnaire administered by personal interview, mail, telephone, and most recently over the Internet.

Scientific studies often are conducted by engineers and chemists in product-testing laboratories around the world. There, product designs and formulas are developed and

As the saying goes, "There's no accounting for taste." But that's exactly what Campbell's tries to do in its consumer research in international markets. Here Mexican consumers taste new products and view packaging ideas in a focus group setting. (Courtesy of Campbell Soup Company)

tested in consumer usage situations. Often those results are integrated with consumer opinions gathered in concurrent survey studies. One of the best examples of this kind of marketing research comes from Tokyo. You may not know it, but the Japanese are the world champions of bathroom and toilet technology. Their biggest company in that industry, Toto, has spent millions of dollars in developing and testing consumer products. "Thousands of people have collected data [using survey techniques] on the best features of a toilet, and at the company's 'human engineering laboratory,' volunteers sit in a Toto bathtub with electrodes strapped to their skulls, to measure brain waves and 'the effects of bathing on the human body.'"[7] Toto is now introducing one of its high-tech (actually low-tech compared to what they offer in Japan) toilets in the U.S. market. It's a $600 seat, lid, and control panel that attaches to the regular American bowl. It features a heated seat and deodorizing fan.

In *qualitative research*, if questions are asked they are almost always open-ended and/or in-depth, and unstructured responses that reflect the person's thoughts and feelings on the subject are sought after. Direct observation of consumers in choice or product usage situations is another important qualitative approach to marketing research. One researcher spent two months observing birthing practices in American and Japanese hospitals to gain insights into the export of health care services.[8] Nissan Motors Corp. has sent a researcher to live with an American family (renting a room in their house for six weeks) to directly observe how Americans use their cars.[9] Qualitative research seeks to interpret what the "people in the sample are like, their outlooks, their feelings, the dynamic interplay of their feelings and ideas, their attitudes and opinions, and their re-

---

[7] Mary Jordon and Kevin Sullivan, "But Do They Flush?" *The Washington Post,* May 15, 1997, pp. A1 and A31. For a tour of their toilets, see Toto's Web site at **http://www.totousa.com**.

[8] H. Rika Houston, *Medicine, Magic and Maternity: An Ethnographic Study of Ritual Consumption in Contemporary Urban Japan,* an unpublished doctoral dissertation, the Graduate School of Management, University of California, 1997.

[9] Eric Bailey, "Nissan Says Corporate Snoop Suit Is 'Absurd,'" *Los Angeles Times,* December 9, 1989, p. C1.

sulting actions."[10] The most often-used form of qualitative questioning is the focus group interview. However, oftentimes in-depth interviewing of individuals can be just as effective while consuming fewer resources.

Qualitative research is used in international marketing research to formulate and define a problem more clearly and to determine relevant questions to be examined in subsequent research. It is also used where interest is centered on gaining an understanding of a market, rather than quantifying relevant aspects. For example, a small group of key executives at Solar Turbines International, a division of Caterpillar Tractor Co., called on key customers at their offices around the world. They discussed in great depth with both financial managers and production engineers potential applications and the demand for a new size of gas-turbine engine the company was considering developing. The data and insights gained during the interviews to a large degree confirmed the validity of the positive demand forecasts produced internally through macroeconomic modeling. The multi-million-dollar project was then implemented. Additionally, during the discussions new product features were suggested by the customer personnel that proved most useful in the development efforts.

Qualitative research is also helpful in revealing the impact of sociocultural factors on behavior patterns and in developing research hypotheses that can be tested in subsequent studies designed to quantify the concepts and relevant relationships uncovered in qualitative data collection. Procter & Gamble has been one of the pioneers of this type of research—the company has systematically gathered consumer feedback for some 70 years.[11] It was the first company to conduct in-depth consumer research in China. In 1994 P&G began working with the Chinese Ministry of Health to develop dental hygiene programs and has now reached over one million children in 28 cities. The company will soon offer Crest toothpaste in two flavors and toothbrushes in four colors to Chinese consumers.[12] Procter & Gamble also conducts research with washing-machine manufacturers to develop the best products given the evolving technology in the home-appliance industry.[13] The details of Procter & Gamble's integration of qualitative and quantitative marketing research efforts in Egypt provide a good case in point:

For years Procter & Gamble had marketed Ariel Low Suds brand laundry detergent to the 5 percent of homes in the Egyptian market that had automatic washing machines. P&G planned to expand its presence in the Egyptian market, and commissioned a study to: (1) identify the most lucrative opportunities in the Egyptian laundry market; and (2) develop the right concept, product, price, brand name, package, and advertising copy once the decision was made to pursue a segment of the laundry market.

The "Habits and Practices" study, P&G's name for this phase, consisted of home visits and discussion groups (qualitative research) to understand how the Egyptian housewife did her laundry. The company wanted to know her likes, dislikes, and habits (the company's knowledge of laundry practices in Egypt had been limited to automatic washing machines). From this study, it was determined that the Egyptian consumer goes through a very laborious washing process to achieve the desired results. Among the 95 percent of homes that washed in a nonautomatic washing machine or by hand, the process consisted of soaking, boiling, bleaching, and washing each load several times. Several products were used in the process; bar soaps or flakes were added to the main wash, along with liquid bleach and bluing to enhance the cleaning performance of the poor quality of locally produced powders. These findings highlighted the potential for a

---

[10] Sidney J. Levy has been a long-term advocate of qualitative methods. See his "What Is Qualitative Research?" *The Dartnell Marketing Manager's Handbook* (Chicago: The Dartnell Corporation, 1994), p 275. For the most recent insights see Gerald Zaltman, "Rethinking Marketing Research: Putting People Back In," *Journal of Marketing Research,* XXXIV, November 1997, pp. 424–437; and Craig J. Thompson, "Interpreting Consumers: A Hermeneutical Framework of Deriving Marketing Insights from the Texts of Consumers' Consumption Stories," *Journal of Marketing Research*, XXXIV, November 1997, pp. 438–455.

[11] See **www.pg.com**.

[12] See the October 21, 1996, news release on P&G's Web site: **http://www.pg.com**.

[13] "Procter & Gamble Unveils New 'High Efficiency' Tide Detergent," *Dow Jones News Service,* March 20, 1997.

At Procter & Gamble's international research center, P&G laundry detergents are tested using water and washing machines from different countries. (Louis Psihoyos/Matrix International)

high-performing detergent that would accomplish everything that currently required several products. The decision was made to proceed with the development and introduction of a superior-performing high-suds granular detergent.

Once the basic product concept (i.e., one product instead of several to do laundry) was decided on, the company needed to determine the best components for a marketing mix to introduce the new product. The company went back to focus groups to assess reactions to different brand names (the choices were Ariel, already in the market as a low-suds detergent for automatic washers, and Tide, which had been marketed in Egypt in the 1960s and 1970s), to get ideas about the appeal and relevant wording for promotions, and to test various price ranges, package design, and size. Information derived from focus group encounters helped the company eliminate ideas with low consumer appeal and to focus on those that triggered the most interest. Further, the groups helped refine advertising and promotion wording to ensure clarity of communication through the use of everyday consumer language.

At the end of this stage, the company had well-defined ideas garnered from several focus groups, but did not have a "feel" for the rest of the people in the target market. Would they respond the same way the focus groups had? To answer this question, the company proceeded to the next step, a research program to validate the relative appeal of the concepts generated from focus groups with a survey (quantitative research) of a large sample from the target market. Additionally, brand name, price, size, and the product's intended benefits were tested in large sample surveys. Information gathered in the final surveys provided the company with the specific information used to develop a marketing program that led to a successful product introduction and brand recognition for Ariel throughout Egypt.[14]

---

[14] This material was adapted from Mahmoud Aboul-Fath and Loula Zaklama, "Ariel High Suds Detergent in Egypt—A Case Study," *Marketing Research Today,* May 1992, pp.130–134.

Oftentimes the combination of qualitative and quantitative research proves quite useful, as in the example of P&G's research on Ariel or as demonstrated in other industrial and business-to-business marketing settings. In one study the number of personal referrals used in buying legal, banking, and insurance services in Japan was found to be much greater than in the United States.[15] The various comments made by the executives during the personal interviews in both countries proved invaluable in interpreting the quantitative results, suggesting implications for managers and providing ideas for further research. Likewise, the comments of sales managers in Tokyo during in-depth interviews helped researchers understand why individual financial incentives were found not to work with Japanese sales representatives.[16]

As we shall see later in this chapter, using either research method in international marketing research is subject to a number of difficulties brought about by the diversity of cultures and languages encountered.

Problems of Gathering Primary Data

The problems of collecting primary data in foreign countries are different only in degree from those encountered in the United States. Assuming the research problem is well defined and the objectives are properly formulated, the success of primary research hinges on the ability of the researcher to get correct and truthful information that addresses the research objectives. Most problems in collecting primary data in international marketing research stem from cultural differences among countries, and range from the inability of respondents to communicate their opinions to inadequacies in questionnaire translation.

Ability to Communicate Opinions

The ability to express attitudes and opinions about a product or concept depends on the respondent's ability to recognize the usefulness and value of such a product or concept. It is difficult for a person to formulate needs, attitudes, and opinions about goods whose use may not be understood, that are not in common use within the community, or that have never been available. For example, it may be impossible for someone who has never had the benefits of an office computer to express accurate feelings or provide any reasonable information about purchase intentions, likes, or dislikes concerning a new computer software package. The more complex the concept, the more difficult it is to design research that will help the respondent communicate meaningful opinions and reactions. Under these circumstances, the creative capabilities of the international marketing researcher are challenged.

No company has had more experience in trying to understand consumers with communication limitations than Gerber. Babies may be their business, but babies often can't talk, much less fill out a questionnaire. Over the years Gerber has found that talking to and observing both infants and their mothers are important in marketing research. In one study Gerber found that breast-fed babies adapted to solid food more quickly than bottle-fed babies because breast milk changes flavor depending on what the mother has eaten. For example, infants were found to suck longer and harder if their mother had recently eaten garlic. In another study, weaning practices were studied around the world. Indian babies were offered lentils served on a finger. Some Nigerian children got fermented sorghum, fed by the grandmother through the funnel of her hand. In some parts

15 R. Bruce Money, Mary C. Gilly, and John L. Graham, "National Culture and Word-of-Mouth Referral Behavior in the Purchase of Industrial Services in the U.S. and Japan," *Journal of Marketing,* October 1998.

16 R. Bruce Money and John L. Graham, "Sales Performance, Pay, and Satisfaction: Tests of a Model Using Data Collected in the U.S. and Japan," *Journal of International Business Studies,* forthcoming 1998.

of tropical Asia mothers "food-kissed" prechewed vegetables into their babies' mouths. All this research helps the company decide which products are appropriate for which markets. For example, the Vegetable and Rabbit Meat and the Freeze-Dried Sardines and Rice flavors popular in Poland and Japan, respectively, most likely won't make it to American store shelves.[17]

Willingness to Respond

Cultural differences offer the best explanation for the unwillingness or the inability of many to respond to research surveys. The role of the male, the suitability of personal gender-based inquiries, and other gender-related issues can affect willingness to respond. In some countries, the husband not only earns the money but also dictates exactly how it is to be spent. Because the husband controls the spending, it is he, not the wife, who should be questioned to determine preferences and demand for many consumer goods.

In some countries, women would never consent to be interviewed by a male or a stranger. A French Canadian woman does not like to be questioned and is likely to be reticent in her responses. In some societies, a man would certainly consider it beneath his dignity to discuss shaving habits or brand preference in personal clothing with anyone—most emphatically not a female interviewer.

Anyone asking questions about any topic from which tax assessment could be inferred is immediately suspected of being a tax agent. Citizens of many countries do not feel the same legal and moral obligations to pay their taxes as do U.S. citizens. So, tax evasion is an accepted practice for many and a source of pride for the more adept. Where such an attitude exists, taxes are often seemingly arbitrarily assessed by the government, which results in much incomplete or misleading information being reported. One of the problems revealed by the government of India in a recent population census was the underreporting of tenants by landlords trying to hide the actual number of people living in houses and flats. The landlords had been subletting accommodations illegally and were concealing their activities from the tax department.

In the United States, publicly held corporations are compelled by the Securities and Exchange Commission (SEC) to disclose certain operating figures on a periodic basis. In many European countries, however, such information is seldom if ever released and then most reluctantly. Attempts to enlist the cooperation of merchants in setting up an in-store study of shelf inventory and sales information ran into strong resistance because of suspicions and a tradition of competitive secrecy. The resistance was overcome by the researcher's willingness to approach the problem step-by-step. As the retailer gained confidence in the researcher and realized the value of the data gathered, more and more requested information was provided. Besides the reluctance of businesses to respond to surveys, local politicians in underdeveloped countries may interfere with studies in the belief that they could be subversive and must be stopped or hindered. A few moments with local politicians can prevent days of delay.

Although such cultural differences may make survey research more difficult to conduct, it is possible. In some communities, locally prominent people could open otherwise closed doors; in other situations, professional people and local students have been used as interviewers because of their knowledge of the market. Less direct measurement techniques and nontraditional data analysis methods may also be more appropriate.[18] In one study, Japanese supermarket buyers rated the nationality of brands (foreign or domestic) as relatively unimportant in making stocking decisions when asked directly;

---

[17] Adapted from Geraldine Brooks, "It's Goo, Goo, Goo, Goo Vibrations at the Gerber Lab," *The Wall Street Journal*, December 4, 1996, pp. A1 and A10. See the Gerber Web site for more information: **http://www.gerber.com**.

[18] See Chapter 15 in Mary Jo Bitner and Valeri Zeithaml, *Services Marketing* (New York: McGraw-Hill, 1996).

however, when an indirect, paired-comparison questioning technique was used, brand nationality proved to be the most important factor.[19]

Sampling in Field Surveys

The greatest problem of sampling stems from the lack of adequate demographic data and available lists from which to draw meaningful samples. If current, reliable lists are not available, sampling becomes more complex and generally less reliable. In many countries, telephone directories, cross-index street directories, census tract and block data, and detailed social and economic characteristics of the population being studied are not available on a current basis, if at all. The researcher has to estimate characteristics and population parameters, sometimes with little basic data on which to build an accurate estimate.

To add to the confusion, in some South American, Mexican, and Asian cities, street maps are unavailable, and in some Asian metropolitan areas, streets are not identified nor are houses numbered. In contrast, one of the positive aspects of research in Japan and Taiwan is the availability and accuracy of census data on individuals. In these countries, when a household moves it is required to submit up-to-date information to a centralized government agency before it can use communal services such as water, gas, electricity, and education.

The effectiveness of various methods of communication (mail, telephone, and personal interview) in surveys is limited. In many countries, telephone ownership is extremely low, making telephone surveys virtually worthless unless the survey is intended to cover only the wealthy. In Sri Lanka, fewer than 10 percent of the residents—only the wealthy—have telephones. Even if the respondent has a telephone, the researcher may still not be able to complete a call.

The adequacy of sampling techniques is also affected by a lack of detailed social and economic information. Without an age breakdown, for example, the researcher can never be certain of a representative sample requiring an age criterion because there is no basis of comparison with the age distribution in the sample. A lack of detailed information, however, does not prevent the use of sampling; it simply makes it more difficult. In place of probability techniques, many researchers in such situations rely on convenience samples taken in marketplaces and other public gathering places.

McDonald's recently got into trouble over sampling issues. The company was involved in a dispute in South Africa over the rights to its brand name in that fast-emerging market. Part of the company's claim revolved around the recall of the McDonald's name among South Africans. In the two surveys the company conducted and provided as proof in the proceedings, the majority of those sampled had heard the company name and could recognize the logo. However, the Supreme Court judge hearing the case took a dim view of the evidence because the surveys were conducted in "posh, white" suburbs when 76 percent of the South African population is black. Based in part on these sampling errors, the judge threw out McDonald's case.[20]

Inadequate mailing lists and poor postal service can also be problems for the market researcher using mail to conduct research. In Nicaragua, delays of weeks in delivery are not unusual, and expected returns are lowered considerably because a letter can be mailed only at a post office. In addition to the potentially poor mail service within countries, the extended length of time required for delivery and return when a mail survey is conducted from another country further hampers the use of mail surveys. Although airmail reduces this time drastically, it also increases costs considerably.

---

[19] Frank Alpert, Michael Kamins, Tomoaki Sakano, Naoto Onzo, and John L. Graham, "Retail Buyer Decision-Making in Japan: What US Sellers Need to Know," *International Business Review,* 6(2), 1997, pp. 91–112.

[20] "Management Brief—Johannesburgers and Fries," *The Economist,* September 27, 1997, pp. 75–76.

The kinds of problems encountered in drawing a random sample include:

- No officially recognized census of population.
- No other listings that can serve as sampling frames.
- Incomplete and out-of-date telephone directories.
- No accurate maps of population centers. Thus, no cluster (area) samples can be made.

While all the conditions described do not exist in all countries, they illustrate why the collection of primary data requires creative applications of research techniques when firms expand into many foreign markets.

Language and Comprehension

The most universal survey research problem in foreign countries is the language barrier. Differences in idiom and the difficulty of exact translation create problems in eliciting the specific information desired and in interpreting the respondents' answers. Equivalent concepts may not exist in all languages. Family, for example, has different connotations in different countries. In the United States, it generally means only the parents and children. In Italy and many Latin countries it could mean the parents, children, grandparents, uncles, aunts, cousins, and so forth. The meaning of names for family members can have different meanings depending on the context within which they are used. In the Italian culture, aunt and uncle are different for the maternal and paternal sides of the family. The concept of affection is a universal idea but the manner in which it is manifest in each culture may differ. Kissing, an expression of affection in the West, is alien to many Eastern cultures and even taboo in some.

Literacy poses yet another problem. In some less-developed countries with low literacy rates, written questionnaires are completely useless. Within countries, too, the problem of dialects and different languages can make a national questionnaire survey impractical. In India, there are 14 official languages and considerably more unofficial ones. One researcher has used pictures of products as stimuli and pictures of faces as response criterion in a study of eastern German brand preferences to avoid some of the difficulties associated with language differences and literacy in international research.[21]

Furthermore a researcher cannot assume that a translation into one language will suffice in all areas where that language is spoken. Such was the case when one of the authors was in Mexico and requested a translation of the word *outlet,* as in *retail outlet,* to be used in Venezuela. It was read by Venezuelans to mean an electrical outlet, an outlet of a river into an ocean, and the passageway into a patio. Needless to say, the responses were useless—although interesting. Thus, it will always be necessary for a native speaker of the target country's language to take the "final cut" in any translated material.

All marketing communications, including research questionnaires, must be written perfectly. If not, consumers and customers will not respond with accuracy, or even at all. The obvious solution of having questionnaires prepared or reviewed by a native speaker of the language of the country is frequently overlooked. Even excellent companies like American Airlines bring errors into their measurement of customer satisfaction by using the exact same questionnaire in Spanish for their surveys of passengers on routes to Spain and Mexico. To a Spaniard orange juice is *"zumo de naranja";* a Mexican would order *"jugo de naranja."* These apparently subtle differences are no such things to Spanish speakers. In another case, a German respondent was asked the number of wash-

---

[21] Christina Roemer, *Perceived Domination and Brand Preference: Understanding Eastern German Rejection of Western German Products,* unpublished doctoral dissertation, Graduate School of Management, University of California, Irvine (1996). See also Gerald Zaltman's "Rethinking Marketing Research: Putting People Back In," *Journal of Marketing Research,* XXXIV, November 1997, pp. 424–437.

CROSSING BORDERS 8–3

Oops! Even the Best Companies Can Make Mistakes

Mexican users of the Spanish-language version of Microsoft Word 6.0 are angry. One might also say they are mad, burning, violent, bothered, steaming, raging, stormy, furious, irate, livid, frothy, piqued, annoyed, seething, resentful, infuriated, irked, vexed, roiled, enraged, ireful, ruffled, churlish, wrathful, and irritated.

The problem is the thesaurus, or synonym dictionary, that Microsoft included with the popular word processing program. When asked to provide alternatives for the word *Indian,* the thesaurus generates suggestions that include *cannibal* and *savage.* In Mexico, where most people can claim indigenous ancestry, that just isn't right. It's not kosher or politically correct for that matter, either.

Similar problems arise with the words *lesbian*—suggested alternatives are *pervert* and *depraved person*—and *western*—suggested alternatives *Aryan, white,* and *civilized.*

Critics minced no words. "I see this as profoundly dangerous because it is a lack of respect for our dignity as Mexicans and for our indigenous roots," said Adriana Luna, a Mexican congresswoman. Another deputy called the dictionary "fascist" and "conservative."

For Microsoft that translates into "public relations disaster." Its response, however, was swift. The company said the thesaurus was created by an outside contractor, but accepted full responsibility all the same. Calling the word suggestions "offensive" and "mistaken," it "asked for forgiveness of customers who have been offended." Microsoft also promised a revised dictionary, will attempt to make its Spanish-language products more sensitive to different countries' usage, and promised to provide the new version to current users free of charge.

Microsoft seems suitably embarrassed . . . as well as ashamed, humbled, distressed, disgraced, and chastened. But under the circumstances, we suggest that all avoid using another synonym for their situation: red-faced.

Source: *Latin Trade,* September 1996, p. 16.

---

ers (washing machines) produced in Germany for a particular year; the reply reflected the production of the flat metal disk. Marketers use three different techniques, back translation, parallel translation, and decentering, to help ferret out translation errors ahead of time.

• **Back Translation.** In *back translation* the questionnaire is translated from one language to another, then a second party translates it back into the original. This process pinpoints misinterpretations and misunderstandings before they reach the public. A soft-drink company wanted to use a very successful Australian advertising theme, "Baby, it's cold inside," in Hong Kong. They had the theme translated from English into Cantonese by one translator and then retranslated by another from Cantonese into English, where the statement came out, "Small Mosquito, on the inside it is very cold." Although "small mosquito" is the colloquial expression for small child in Hong Kong, the intended meaning was lost in translation.

• **Parallel Translation.** Back translations may not always ensure an accurate translation because of commonly used idioms in both languages. *Parallel translation* is used to overcome this problem. In this process, more than two translators are used for the back translation; the results are compared, differences discussed, and the most appropriate translation selected.

• **Decentering.** A third alternative, known as *decentering,* is a hybrid of back translation. It is a successive iteration process of translation and retranslations of a questionnaire, each time by a different translator. For example, an English version is translated into French and then translated back to English by a different translator. The two English versions are compared and where there are differences, the original English version is modified and the process is repeated. If there are still differences between the two English versions, the original English version of the second iteration is modified and the process of translation and back translation is repeated. The process continues to be repeated until an English version can be translated into French and back translated, by a different translator, into the same English. In this process, wording of the original instrument undergoes a change, and the version that is finally used and its translation have equally comprehensive and equivalent terminologies in both languages.

Regardless of the procedure used, proper translation and perfect use of the local language in a questionnaire are of critical importance to successful research design.

Because of cultural and national differences, confusion can just as well be the problem of the researcher as of the respondent. The question itself may not be properly worded in the English version, or English slang or abbreviated words are often translated with a different or ambiguous meaning. Such was the case mentioned above with the word *outlet* for *retail outlet.* The problem was not with the translation as much as it was of the term used in the question to be translated. In writing questions for translation, it is important that precise terms, not colloquialisms or slang, are used in the original to be translated. One classic misunderstanding which occurred in a *Reader's Digest* study of consumer behavior in Western Europe resulted in a report that France and Germany consumed more spaghetti than did Italy. This rather curious and erroneous finding resulted from questions that asked about purchases of "packaged and branded spaghetti." Italians buy their spaghetti in bulk; the French and Germans buy branded and packaged spaghetti. Since the Italians buy little branded or packaged spaghetti, the results underreported spaghetti purchases by Italians. Had the goal of the research been to determine how much branded and packaged spaghetti was purchased, the results would have been correct. However, because the goal was to know about total spaghetti consumption, the data were incorrect. Researchers must always verify that they are asking the right question.

Finally, some of the problems of cross-cultural marketing research can be addressed after data have been collected. For example, we know that consumers in some countries such as Japan tend to respond to rating scales more conservatively than Americans. That is, on a 1 to 7 scale anchored by "extremely satisfied" and "extremely dissatisfied," Japanese may tend to answer more toward the middle (more 3s and 5s), while Americans' responses may tend toward the extremes (more 1s and 7s). Such a response bias can be managed through statistical standardization procedures to maximize comparability. Some translation problems can also be detected and mitigated post hoc through other statistical approaches as well.[22]

Multicultural Research: A Special Problem

As companies become global marketers and seek to standardize various parts of the marketing mix across several countries, multicultural studies become more important. A

---

[22] Mahesh Rajan and John L. Graham, "Methodological Considerations in Cross-Cultural Research: A Discussion of the Translation Issue," a paper delivered at the Academy of International Business Meetings, Monterrey, Mexico, October 8–12, 1997. See also John L. Graham and Alma Mintu-Wimsat, "Culture's Influence on Business Negotiations in Four Countries," *Group Decision Making and Negotiation,* 6, 1997, pp. 483–502.

company needs to determine to what extent adaptation of the marketing mix is appropriate. Thus, market characteristics across diverse cultures must be compared for similarities and differences before a company proceeds with standardization on any aspect of marketing strategy. The research difficulties discussed thus far have addressed problems of conducting research within a culture. When engaging in multicultural studies, many of these same problems further complicate the difficulty of cross-cultural comparisons.

Multicultural research involves dealing with countries that have different languages, economies, social structures, behavior, and attitude patterns. When designing multicultural studies, it is essential that these differences be taken into account. An important point to keep in mind when designing research to be applied across cultures is to ensure comparability and equivalency of results. Different methods may have varying reliabilities in different countries. It is essential that these differences be taken into account in the design of a multicultural survey. Such differences may mean that different research methods should be applied in individual countries.

In some cases the entire research design may have to be different between countries to maximize the comparability of the results. For example, Japanese, compared to American businesspeople, tend not to respond to mail surveys. This problem was handled in two recent studies by using alternative methods of questionnaire distribution and collection in Japan. In one study, attitudes of retail buyers regarding pioneer brands were sought. In the U.S. setting a sample was drawn from a national list of supermarket buyers and questionnaires were distributed and collected by mail. Alternatively, in Japan questionnaires were distributed through contact people at 16 major supermarket chains and then returned by mail directly to the Japanese researchers.[23] The second study sought to compare the job satisfaction of American and Japanese sales representatives. The questionnaires were delivered and collected via the company mail system for the U.S. firm. For the Japanese firm, participants in a sales training program were asked to complete the questionnaires during the program.[24] While the authors of both studies suggest that the use of different methods of data collection in comparative studies does threaten the quality of the results, the approaches taken were the best (only) practical methods of conducting the research.

The adaptations necessary to complete these cross-national studies serve as examples of the need for resourcefulness in international marketing research. However, they also raise serious questions about the reliability of data gathered in cross-national research. There is evidence that often insufficient attention is given not only to nonsampling errors and other problems that can exist in improperly conducted multicultural studies, but also to the appropriateness of research measures that have not been tested in multicultural contexts.

Research on the Internet: A New Opportunity

It is literally impossible to keep up with the worldwide growth in Internet usage. We know that at this writing there are more than 20 million users in more than 194 countries.[25] While about 58 percent of the hosts are in the United States, international Internet usage is growing almost twice as fast as American usage. Growth in countries such as Costa Rica has been spurred by the local government's early (1989) decision to reclassify computers as "educational tools," thus eliminating all import tariffs on the hard-

23 Frank Alpert et al., "Retail Buyer Decision-Making in Japan: What U.S. Sellers Need to Know," *International Business Review,* 6(2), 1997, pp. 91–112.

24 R. Bruce Money and John L. Graham, "Salesperson Performance, Pay, and Job Satisfaction: Tests of a Model Using Data Collected in the U.S. and Japan," *Journal of International Business Studies,* forthcoming 1998.

25 "By the Numbers," *Scientific American,* July 1997, p. 26.

ware.[26] The demographics of users worldwide are: 60%–40% male-female; average age about 32; about 60% college educated; median income of about $60,000; usage time about 2.5 hours/week; and main activities are e-mail and finding information.[27] The percentage of home pages by language is English—82.3%, German—4.0%, Japanese—1.6%, French—1.5%, Spanish—1.1%, and all others less than 1%.[28]

For many companies the Internet provides a new and increasingly important medium for conducting a variety of international marketing research. New product concepts and advertising copy can be tested over the Internet for immediate feedback. Worldwide consumer panels might be created to help test marketing programs across international samples. Indeed, it has been suggested that there are six different uses for the Internet in international research:[29]

(1) *On-line surveys*—these can include incentives for participation, and they have better "branching" capabilities (asking different questions based on previous answers) than more expensive mail and phone surveys.

(2) *On-line focus groups*—bulletin boards can be used for this purpose.

(3) *Web visitor tracking*—servers automatically track and time visitors' travel through Web sites.

(4) *Advertising measurement*—servers track links to other sites and their usefulness can therefore be assessed.

(5) *Customer identification systems*—many companies are installing registration procedures that allow them to track visits and purchases over time, creating a "virtual panel."

(6) *E-mail marketing lists*—customers can be asked to sign up on e-mailing lists for future direct marketing efforts via the Internet.

It is quite clear that as the Internet continues to grow, even more kinds of research will become feasible, and it will be quite interesting to see the extent to which new translation software has an impact on marketing communications and research over the Internet.[30] Finally, as is the case in so many international marketing contexts, privacy is and will continue to be a matter of personal and legal consideration. A vexing challenge facing international marketers will be the cross-cultural concerns about privacy and the enlistment of cooperative consumer and customer groups.

The ability to conduct primary research is one of the exciting aspects about the Internet. However, there are some severe limitations because of the potential bias of a universe composed solely of Internet respondents. Nevertheless, as more of the general population in countries gain access to the Internet, this tool will be all the more powerful and accurate for conducting primary research.

Today the real power of the Internet for international marketing research is the ability to easily access volumes of secondary data. These data have been available in print form for years but now they are much easier to access and, in many cases, more current. Instead of leafing through reference books to find two- or three-year-old data, as is the case with most printed sources, you can often find up-to-date data on the Internet. Such Internet sites as **http://stat-usa.gov** provide almost all data that are published by the U.S. government. If you want to know the quantity of a specific product being shipped to a country, the import duties on a product, and whether or not an export license is required, it's all there via your computer.

In addition to government sources, there are many private Web sites that provide

[26] Sue Mullin, "CyberCentral (America)," *Latin Trade,* November 1997, pp. 67–70.

[27] Bruce H. Clark, "Welcome to My Parlor . . .," *Marketing Management,* Winter 1997, pp. 11–25.

[28] Alis Technologies and the Internet Society 1997 (**http://www.babel.alis.com:8080/palmares.html**).

[29] Much of this material is adapted from an excellent article: John A. Quelch and Lisa R. Klein, "The Internet and International Marketing," *Sloan Management Review,* Spring 1996, pp. 60–75.

[30] Marie-Claude Lotrie, "Parlez-Vous Internet?" *Los Angeles Times,* October 20, 1997, pp. D1 and D10.

information free or for a nominal price. Visit **http://www.exporthotline.com/guide 2.htm** and find market research for 80 countries, directories of business listings, import/exports by product and country—just to name a few of the sources. For people interested in doing business in Japan, JETRO (**http://jetro.go.jp**), a Japanese trade organization, provides information from how to do business in Japan to specific product studies. Likewise, many universities offer sites that have links to sources all over the world. One of the best is **http://www.ciber.bus.msu.edu/busres.htm**.

The point is that there are volumes of good secondary data that can be accessed from your computer that will make international marketing research much easier and more efficient than it has ever been. Keep in mind, however, that this information must be validated, just as any secondary information should.

Problems in Analyzing and Interpreting Research Information

Once data have been collected, the final steps in the research process are the analysis and interpretation of findings in light of the stated marketing problem. Both secondary and primary data collected by the market researcher are subject to the many limitations just discussed. In any final analysis, the researcher must take into consideration these factors and, despite their limitations, produce meaningful guides for management decisions.

Accepting information at face value in foreign markets is imprudent. The meanings of words, the consumer's attitude toward a product, the interviewer's attitude, or the interview situation can distort research findings. Just as culture and tradition influence the willingness to give information, they also influence the information given. Newspaper circulation figures, readership and listenership studies, retail outlet figures, and sales volume can all be distorted through local business practice. To cope with such disparities, the foreign market researcher must possess three talents to generate meaningful marketing information.

First, the researcher must possess a high degree of cultural understanding of the market in which research is being conducted. In order to analyze research findings, the social customs, semantics, current attitudes, and business customs of a society or a subsegment of a society must be clearly understood. Indeed, at some level it will be absolutely necessary to have a native of the target country involved in the interpretation of the results of any research conducted in a foreign market.

Second, a creative talent for adapting research findings is necessary. A researcher in foreign markets often is called on to produce results under the most difficult circumstances and short deadlines. Ingenuity and resourcefulness, willingness to use "catch as catch can" methods to get facts, patience, a sense of humor, and a willingness to be guided by original research findings even when they conflict with popular opinion or prior assumptions are all considered prime assets in foreign marketing research.

Third, a skeptical attitude in handling both primary and secondary data is helpful. For example, it might be necessary to check a newspaper press run over a period of time to get accurate circulation figures, or deflate or inflate reported consumer income in some areas by 25 to 50 percent on the basis of observable socioeconomic characteristics. Indeed, where data are suspect, such "triangulation" through the use of multiple research methods will be crucial.

These essential traits suggest that a foreign marketing researcher should be a foreign national or should be advised by a foreign national who can accurately appraise the data collected in light of the local environment, thus validating secondary as well as primary data. Moreover, regardless of the sophistication of a research technique or analysis, there is no substitute for decision makers themselves getting into the field for personal observation.

Responsibility for Conducting Marketing Research

Depending on the size and degree of involvement in foreign marketing, a company in need of foreign market research can rely on an outside foreign-based agency or on a domestic company with a branch within the country in question. It can conduct research using its own facilities or employ a combination of its own research force with the assistance of an outside agency.

Many companies have an executive specifically assigned to the research function in foreign operations; he or she selects the research method and works closely with foreign management, staff specialists, and outside research agencies. Other companies maintain separate research departments for foreign operations or assign a full-time research analyst to this activity. For many companies, a separate department is too costly; the diversity of markets would require a large department to provide a skilled analyst for each area or region of international business operations.

A trend toward decentralization of the research function is apparent. In terms of efficiency, it appears that local analysts are able to provide information more rapidly and accurately than a staff research department. The obvious advantage to decentralization of the research function is that control rests in hands closer to the market. Field personnel, resident managers, and customers generally have a more intimate knowledge of the subtleties of the market and an appreciation of the diversity that characterizes most foreign markets. One disadvantage of decentralized research management is possible ineffective communications with home-office executives. Another is the potential unwarranted dominance of large-market studies in decisions about global standardization. That is to say, the larger markets, particularly the United States, justify more sophisticated research procedures and larger sample sizes, and results derived via simpler approaches that are appropriate in smaller countries are often unnecessarily discounted.

A comprehensive review of the different approaches to multicountry research suggests that the ideal approach is to have local researchers in each country, with close coordination between the client company and the local research companies. This cooperation is important at all stages of the research project from research design to data collection to final analysis. Further, two stages of analysis are necessary. At the individual country level, all issues involved in each country must be identified, and at the multicountry level, the information must be distilled into a format that addresses the client's objectives. Such recommendations are supported on the grounds that two heads are better than one and that multicultural input is essential to any understanding of multicultural data. With just one interpreter of multicultural data, there is the danger of one's self-reference criterion (SRC) resulting in data being interpreted in terms of one's own cultural biases. Self-reference bias can affect the research design, questionnaire design, and interpretation of the data.

If a company wants to use a professional marketing research firm, many are available. Most major advertising agencies and many research firms have established branch offices worldwide. There also has been a healthy growth in foreign-based research and consulting firms. Of the 10 largest (based on revenues) marketing research firms in the world, four are based in the U.S. including the biggest, two are in France, two are in Germany, one is in the U.K., and one is in Japan.[31] In Japan, where it is essential to understand the unique culture, the quality of professional market research firms is among the best. A recent study reports that research methods applied by Japanese firms and American firms are generally quite similar, but with notable differences in the greater emphasis of the Japanese on forecasting, distribution channels, and sales research.[32] A

---

[31] Jack Honomichl, "Global 25 Marketing Research Firms," *Marketing News*, September 23, 1996, pp. H1, H20.

[32] Earl Naumann, Donald W. Jackson, Jr., and William G. Wolfe, "Examining the Practices of United States and Japanese Marketing Research Firms," *California Management Review*, Summer 1994, pp. 49–69.

listing of international marketing research firms is printed every July as an advertising supplement in the *Marketing News.*[33]

Estimating Market Demand

In assessing current product demand and forecasting future demand, reliable historical data are required.[34] As previously noted, the quality and availability of secondary data frequently are inadequate; nevertheless, estimates of market size must be attempted to plan effectively. Despite limitations, there are approaches to demand estimation usable with minimum information. The success of these approaches relies on the ability of the researcher to find meaningful substitutes or approximations for the needed economic and demographic relationships. Some of the necessary but frequently unavailable statistics for assessing market opportunity and estimating demand for a product are current trends in market demand.

When the desired statistics are not available, a close approximation can be made using local production figures plus imports, with adjustments for exports and current inventory levels. These data are more readily available because they are commonly reported by the United Nations and other international agencies. Once approximations for sales trends are established, historical series can be used as the basis for projections of growth. In any straight extrapolation, however, the estimator assumes that the trends of the immediate past will continue into the future. In a rapidly developing economy, extrapolated figures may not reflect rapid growth and must be adjusted accordingly. For this reason, three other methods are recommended: expert opinion, analogy, and income elasticity.

Expert Opinion

For many market estimation problems, particularly in new foreign countries, *expert opinion* is advisable. In this method, experts are polled for their opinions about market size and growth rates. Such experts may be companies' own sales managers or outside consultants and government officials. The key in using expert opinion to help in forecasting demand is triangulation, that is, comparing estimates produced by different sources. One of the tricky parts is how best to combine the different opinions. Developing scenarios is useful in the most ambiguous situations, such as predicting demand for accounting services in emerging markets like China and Russia.

Analogy

Another technique is to estimate by *analogy*. This assumes that demand for a product develops in much the same way in all countries as comparable economic development occurs in each country. First, a relationship must be established between the item to be estimated and a measurable variable in a country that is to serve as the basis for the analogy. Once a known relationship is established, the estimator then attempts to draw an analogy between the known situation and the country in question. For example, suppose a company wanted to estimate the market growth potential for a beverage in country X, for which it had inadequate sales figures, but the company had excellent beverage

---

[33] See, for example, *Marketing News,* July 21, 1997, pp. 13–32. CLT Research, which is based in the U.S. and has affiliates in 54 countries, is located at **http://www.cltresearch.com**; Marketing Intelligence Corporation (MIC) in Japan is also worth the visit at **http://www.mictokyo.co.jp/mic/**. In addition, the 1998 *Marketing News* Directory may be on-line. Check the American Marketing Association at **http://www.ama.org**.

[34] Although more than a decade old, still the best summary of forecasting methods and their advantages, disadvantages, and appropriate applications is David M. Georgoff and Robert G. Murdick, "Manager's Guide to Forecasting," *Harvard Business Review,* January–February 1986, pp. 110–120.

CROSSING BORDERS 8-4

Forecasting the Global Health Care Market

In 1996 Johns Hopkins Hospital in Baltimore treated 6,000 patients from foreign countries. That's up from just 600 in 1994. And there were no hassles with insurance companies and HMOs. In fact, many of these patients paid cash—even for $30,000 surgical procedures! The Mayo Clinic in Rochester, MN, has been serving foreigners for decades. The number there has jumped by about 15 percent in five years. Similar growth is happening in places like Mount Sinai Hospital in Miami, the University of Texas Cancer Center, and the UCLA Medical Center. The Mayo Clinic has even set up a Muslim prayer room to make patients and their families feel more comfortable. Fast growth, yes (some say exponential), but will it continue? Forecasting this demand so decisions can be made about staffing and numbers of beds is a daunting project indeed.

Demand in Mexico and Latin America seems to be coming primarily for treatment of infectious and digestive diseases and cancer. Demand from the Middle East stems more from genetic diseases, heart diseases, cancer, and asthma. From Asia, wealthy patients are coming mainly to California for treatment of cancer and coronary diseases. Europeans travel to the U.S. for mental illness services, cancer and heart disease, and AIDS treatments.

But perhaps the strangest market to forecast is global war wounded. Last year Johns Hopkins contracted to replace limbs for soldiers involved in the recent border clash between Ecuador and Peru at $35,000 per patient. Perhaps the descriptions in *The Wall Street Journal* article are a bit overzealous? "There are wars all over the world, bombs all over the world. Casualty patients are a new and enriching market niche."

Sources: "U.S. Hospitals Attracting Patients from Abroad," *USA Today*, July 22, 1997, p. 1A; and Lucette Lagnado, "Hospitals Court Foreign Patients to Fill Beds," *The Wall Street Journal*, October 7, 1996, pp. B1 and B6.

data for neighboring country Y. In country Y it is known that per capita consumption increases at a predictable ratio as per capita gross domestic product (GDP) increases. If per capita GDP is known for country X, per capita consumption for the beverage can be estimated using the relationships established in country Y. Caution must be used with analogy because the method assumes that factors other than the variable used (in this example GDP) are similar in both countries, such as the same tastes, taxes, prices, selling methods, availability of products, consumption patterns, and so forth. Despite the apparent drawbacks to analogy, it is useful where data are limited.

Income Elasticity

Measuring the changes in the relationship between personal or family income and demand for a product also can be used in forecasting market demand. In *income elasticity* ratios, the sensitivity of demand for a product to income changes is measured. The elasticity coefficient is determined by dividing the percentage change in the quantity of a product demanded by the percentage change in income. With a result of less than one, it is said that the income–demand relationship is relatively inelastic; conversely, if the result is greater than one the relationship is elastic. As income increases, the demand for a product increases at a rate proportionately higher than income increases. For example, if the income coefficient elasticity for recreation is 1.20, it implies that for each 1 percent change in income, the demand for recreation could be expected to increase by 1.2 percent; if the coefficient is 0.8, then for each 1 percent change in income, demand for recreation could be expected to increase only 0.8 percent. The relationship also occurs when income decreases, although the rate of decrease might be greater than when income increases. Income elasticity can be very useful, too, in predicting growth in demand for a particular product or product group.

The major problem of this method is that the data necessary to establish elasticities may not be available. However, in many countries income elasticities for products have been determined and it is possible to use the analogy method described (with all the caveats mentioned) to make estimates for those countries. Income elasticity measurements only give an indication of change in demand as income changes and do not provide the researcher with any estimate of total demand for the product.

As is the case in all market demand estimation methods described in this section, income elasticity measurements are no substitute for original market research when it is economically feasible and time permits. Indeed, the best approach to forecasting is almost always a combination of such macroeconomic data base approaches and interviews with potential and current customers. As more adequate data sources become available, as would be the situation in most of the economically developed countries, more technically advanced techniques such as multiple regression analysis or input–output analysis can be used.

Communicating with Decision Makers

Most of the discussion in this chapter has regarded *getting* information from or about consumers, customers, and competitors. It should be clearly recognized, however, that getting the information is only half the job. That information must also be *given* to decision makers in a timely manner. High-quality international information systems design will be an increasingly important competitive tool as commerce continues to globalize, and resources must be invested accordingly.

Decision makers, often top executives, should be directly involved not only in problem definition and question formulation, but when the occasion warrants it (as in new foreign markets), they should also be involved in the field work of seeing the market and hearing the voice of the customers in the most direct ways. Top managers should have a "feel" for their markets which even the best marketing reports cannot provide.

Summary

The basic objective of the market research function is providing management with information for more accurate decision making. This objective is the same for domestic and international marketing. In foreign marketing research, however, achieving that objective presents some problems not encountered on the domestic front.

Customer attitudes about providing information to a researcher are culturally conditioned. Foreign market information surveys must be carefully designed to elicit the desired data and at the same time not offend the respondent's sense of privacy.

Besides the cultural and managerial constraints involved in gathering information for primary data, many foreign markets have inadequate and/or unreliable bases of secondary information. Such challenges suggest three keys to successful international marketing research: (1) the inclusion of natives of the foreign culture on research teams; (2) the use of multiple methods and triangulation; and (3) decision makers, even top executives, who must on occasion talk directly to and/or directly observe customers in foreign markets.

Questions

1. Define:

marketing research	international marketing
research process	research
secondary data	primary data
back translation	multicultural research
expert opinion	parallel translation

   analogy   decentering
   income elasticity

2. Discuss how the shift from making "market entry" decisions to "continuous operations" decisions creates a need for different types of information and data.

3. Discuss the breadth and scope of international marketing research. Why is international marketing research generally broader in scope than domestic marketing research?

4. The measure of a competent researcher is the ability to utilize the most sophisticated and adequate techniques and methods available within the limits of time, cost, and the present state of the art. Comment.

5. What is the task of the international market researcher? How is it complicated by the foreign environment?

6. Discuss the stages of the research process in relation to the problems encountered. Give examples.

7. Why is the formulation of the research problem difficult in foreign market research?

8. Discuss the problems of gathering secondary data in foreign markets.

9. "In many cultures, personal information is inviolably private and absolutely not to be discussed with strangers." Discuss.

10. What are some problems created by language and the ability to comprehend in collecting primary data? How can a foreign market researcher overcome these difficulties?

11. Discuss how decentering is used to get an accurate translation of a questionnaire.

12. Discuss when qualitative research may be more effective than quantitative research.

13. Sampling offers some major problems in market research. Discuss.

14. Select a country. From secondary sources found on the Internet compile the following information for at least a 5-year period prior to the present:

principal imports	principal exports
gross national product	chief of state
major cities and population	principal agricultural crop

15. "The foreign market researcher must possess three essential capabilities to generate meaningful marketing information." Discuss.

Appendix: Sources of Secondary Data

For almost any marketing research project, an analysis of available secondary information is a useful and inexpensive first step. Although there are information gaps, particularly for detailed market information, the situation on data availability and reliability is improving. The principal agencies that collect and publish information useful in international business are presented here, with some notations of selected publications.

A. U.S. Government

The U.S. government actively promotes the expansion of U.S. business into international trade. In the process of keeping U.S. businesses informed of foreign opportunities, the U.S. government generates a considerable amount of general and specific market data for use by international market analysts. The principal source of information from the U.S. government is the Department of Commerce, which makes its services available to U.S. businesses in a variety of ways. First, information and assistance are available either through personal consultation in Washington, D.C., or through any of the U.S. & FCS (Foreign Commercial Service) district offices of the International Trade Administration (ITA) of the Department of Commerce located in key cities in the United States. Second, the Department of Commerce works closely with trade associations, chambers of commerce, and other interested associations in providing information, consultation, and assistance in developing international commerce. Third, the department publishes a wide range of information available to interested persons at nominal cost.

1. Foreign Trade Report, FT 410. U.S. exports—commodity by country. The FT 410 provides a statistical record of all merchandise shipped from the United States to foreign countries, including both quantity and dollar value of these exports to each country during the month covered by the report. Additionally, it contains cumulative export statistics from the first of the calendar year. You can learn which of more than 150 countries have bought any of more than 3,000 U.S. products. By checking the FT 410 over a period of three or four years, you can determine which countries have the largest and most consistent markets for specific products.

2. International Economic Indicators. Quarterly reports providing basic data on the economy of the United States and seven other principal industrial countries. Statistics included are gross national product, industrial production, trade, prices, finance, and labor. This report measures changes in key competitive indicators and highlights economic prospects and recent trends in the eight countries.

3. Market Share Reports. An annual publication prepared from special computer runs shows U.S. participation in foreign markets for manufactured products during the last five-year period. The 88 reports in a country's series represent import values for the U.S. and eight other leading suppliers, and the U.S. percentage share for about 900 manufactured products.

4. International Marketing Information Series. Publications that focus on foreign market opportunities for U.S. suppliers. This series is designed to assemble, under a common format, a diverse group of publications and reports available to the U.S. business community. The following publications are made available on a continuing basis under this program:

　　a. Global market surveys. Extensive foreign market research is conducted on
　　　　target industries and target business opportunities identified by the Commerce
　　　　Department. Findings are developed into global market surveys. Each survey
　　　　condenses foreign market research conducted in 15 or more nations into
　　　　individual country market summaries.
　　b. Country market sectoral surveys. These in-depth reports cover the most
　　　　promising U.S. export opportunities in a single foreign country. About 15
　　　　leading industrial sectors usually are included. Surveys currently available deal
　　　　with Brazil, Nigeria, Venezuela, Indonesia, and Japan.
　　c. Overseas Business Reports (OBR). These reports provide basic background
　　　　data for businesspeople who are evaluating various export markets or
　　　　are considering entering new areas. They include both developing and
　　　　industrialized countries.
　　d. Foreign economic trends and their implications in the United States. This series
　　　　gives in-depth reviews of current business conditions, current and near-term
　　　　prospects, and the latest available data on the gross national product, foreign
　　　　trade, wage and price indexes, unemployment rates, and construction starts.
　　e. Business America. The Department of Commerce's principal periodical, a
　　　　monthly news magazine, provides an up-to-date source of worldwide business
　　　　activity covering topics of general interest and new developments in world and
　　　　domestic commerce.

5. Trade Opportunities Program (TOP). Overseas trade opportunities, private and government, are transmitted to the TOP computers through various American embassies and councils. U.S. business firms can indicate the product or products they wish to export and the types of opportunities desired (direct sales and representation) in countries of interest. The TOP computer matches the foreign buyer's agent's or distributor's product interest with the U.S. subscriber's interest. When a match occurs, a trade opportunity notice is mailed to the U.S. business subscriber.

6. Commercial Information Management System (CIMS). CIMS is a computer system linking the Department of Commerce to worldwide resources. It enhances the ability of Commerce officers to assist exporters in overseas markets by providing detailed information on a more timely basis than the hard copy of past years that frequently was a year or more out of date before it became available. CIMS, an interactive system, dramatically shortens the time it takes to move information from foreign markets to international trade specialists at the department's district offices. Interested exporters contact a trade specialist who queries the CIMS data base about specific criteria such as country, product, industry, and marketing information. CIMS then constructs a package of information drawing from all parts of the system's data base. The system's information base is continually refined because new data are added to the data base as they are collected.

7. Single Internal Market Information Service (SIMIS).   Operated by the Commerce Department's International Trade Administration, SIMIS serves as the major contact point within the U.S. government for U.S. business questions on commercial and trade implications of the European Community's Single Market program. SIMIS maintains a comprehensive data base of EC directives and regulations, as well as specialized documentation published by the EC Commission, the U.S. government, and the private sector.

8. Business Information Service for the Newly Independent States (BISNIS).   This is a one-stop source for U.S. firms interested in obtaining assistance on selling in the markets of the Newly Independent States of the former Soviet Union. BISNIS provides information on trade regulations and legislation, defense conversion opportunities, commercial opportunities, market data, sources of financing, government and industry contacts, and U.S. government programs supporting trade and investment in the region.

9. National Trade Data Bank (NTDB).   The Commerce Department provides a number of the data sources mentioned above and others in their computerized information system in the National Trade Data Bank (NTDB). The NTDB is a "one-step" source for export promotion and international trade data collected by 17 U.S. government agencies. Updated each month and released on the Internet, the NTDB enables the reader to access more than 100,000 trade-related documents. The NTDB contains: (1) the latest Census data on U.S. imports and exports by commodity and country; (2) the complete CIA (Central Intelligence Agency) World Factbook; (3) current market research reports compiled by the U.S. & Foreign Commercial Service; (4) the complete Foreign Traders Index, which contains over 55,000 names and addresses of individuals and firms abroad that are interested in importing U.S. products; (5) State Department country reports on economic policy and trade practices; (6) the publications Export Yellow Pages, A Basic Guide to Exporting, and the National Trade Estimates Report on Foreign Trade Barriers; (7) the Export Promotion Calendar; and many other data series. The NTDB is also available at over 900 federal depository libraries nationwide.

In addition, the Department of Commerce provides a host of other information services. Besides the material available through the Department of Commerce, consultation and information are available from a variety of other U.S. agencies. For example, the Department of State, Bureau of the Census, and Department of Agriculture can provide valuable assistance in the form of services and information for an American business interested in international operations.

B. Other Sources[35]

1. Bibliographies

    a. International Directory of Business Information Sources and Services. 2d ed. London: Europa, 1996. Provides directory information on over 5,000 organization, including details of libraries and publications.

    b. Weekly, James K., *Information for International Marketing: An Annotated Guide to Sources* (Bibliographies and Indexes in Economics and Economic History, No. 3), Westport, CT: Greenwood, 1986. Lists and briefly annotates more than 190

---

[35] This section is adapted from *An International Marketing Research Bibliography,* prepared by Dr. Judith A. Truelson, Director, Doheny Electronic Resources Center at the University of Southern California for Taylor W. Meloan and John L. Graham's *International & Global Marketing: Concepts and Cases* (Chicago: Irwin/McGraw-Hill, 1998).

government publications, databases, periodicals, and basic reference sources. Appendixes present brief directory listings for publishers, state trade contacts, U.S. foreign service offices in foreign countries, foreign embassies in the U.S., the U.S. International Trade Administration, and international marketing journals.

c. *World Directory of Marketing Information Sources*. London: Euromonitor, 1996. [also on CD-ROM]. Provides 6,000 entries, including libraries, market research companies, trade associations, trade journals, online sources, and international business contacts.

2. Directories

a. *American Export Register*. New York: Thomas Publishing Co., International Division. Annual. Includes an alphabetical product list with over 220,000 product/service listings in more than 4,200 separate categories as well as lists of U.S. and foreign embassies and consulates, chambers of commerce, world trade center clubs, U.S. and world ports, and banks.

b. Arpan, Jeffrey S., and David A. Ricks. *Directory of Foreign Manufacturers in the United States*. 5th enl. ed. Atlanta: Publishing Services Division, College of Business Administration, Georgia State University, 1993. Lists nearly 6,000 foreign-owned manufacturing firms in the U.S.

c. *D. & B. Principal International Businesses Directory*. Wilton, CT: Dun's Marketing Services. Annual. [also on CD-ROM]. Covers approximately 55,000 companies in 140 countries, listing businesses by product classification and alphabetically.

d. *Directory of American Firms Operating in Foreign Countries*. 14th ed. New York: World Trade Academy Press, 1996. Alphabetically lists U.S. firms with foreign subsidiaries and affiliates operating in over 125 countries; also lists the foreign operations grouped by countries.

e. *Directory of United States Importers and Directory of U.S. Exporters*. New York: Journal of Commerce. Annual. [also on CD-ROM]. Contains verified business profiles on a total of 60,000 active trading companies. These annual guides also include a product index with the Harmonized Commodity Code numbers, customs information, foreign consulates, embassies, and international banks.

f. *Encyclopedia of Global Industries*. Detroit: Gale, 1995. Alphabetically covers 125 vital international industries, providing in-depth information including statistics, graphs, tables, charts, and market share.

g. *Export Yellow Pages*. Washington, D.C.: Venture Publishing North-America; produced in cooperation with the Office of Export Trading Company Affairs and International Trade Administration. Annual. Provides detailed information on over 12,000 export service providers and trading companies, agents, distributors, and companies outside the U.S.; also includes a product/service index and an alphabetical index.

h. *FINDEX: The Worldwide Directory of Market Research Reports*. London: Euromonitor. Annual. [also on CD-ROM]. Abstracts and indexes more than 9,000 market research and company reports, spanning 12 broad product sectors.

i. *International Brands and Their Companies*. Detroit: Gale, 1990-. Annual. Lists nearly 65,000 international consumer brand names attributed to 15,000 manufacturers, importers, and distributors, giving for each brand a description of the product, company name, and a code for the source from which the information was taken.

j. *International Companies and Their Brands*. 4th ed. Detroit: Gale, 1994. Lists 25,000 manufacturers, importers, and distributors and the nearly 80,000 brand names attributed to them, giving for each company the firm's address and telephone number and an alphabetical listing of its trade names.

   k. International Directory of Corporate Affiliations. New Providence, NJ: National
   Register Publishing Co. Semiannual. Contains critical information on over 2,300
   corporate parents with revenues of more than $50 million annually, 42,000
   subsidiaries worldwide, and 54,000 key executives.

   l. International Tradeshow. Frankfurt: m+a Publishers for Fairs, Exhibitions
   and Conventions Ltd. Semiannual. Contains detailed information on
   global trade fairs and exhibitions that are of national and international
   significance.

   m. Trade Directories of the World. San Diego, CA: Croner Publications. Looseleaf.
   Includes more than 3,000 trade, industrial, and professional directories in 1,000
   categories in 175 countries.

   n. World Directory of Consumer Brands and Their Owners. London: Euromonitor,
   1996. Provides information on 17 market sectors including consumer electronics,
   consumer healthcare, and leisure and entertainment.

   o. World Directory of Trade and Business Associations. London: Euromonitor,
   1995. [also on CD-ROM]. Contains entries from a broad range of sectors, giving
   details of publications produced, aims and objectives of the association, and
   whether they provide assistance in further research.

   p. World Retail Directory and Sourcebook. 2d ed. London: Euromonitor,
   1995. [also on CD-ROM]. Identifies over 2,000 retailers, breaking them
   down by country and classifying them by organization and type of product
   sold.

   q. Worldwide Franchise Directory. Detroit: Gale. Irregular. Provides information
   concerning some 1,574 franchising companies in 16 countries, arranged by type
   of business in more than 80 categories.

3. Marketing Guides

   a. Export Market Locator. Wilton, CT: Dun & Bradstreet. Annual. [also on
   CD-ROM]. Identifies the five largest and five fastest growing global markets for
   a product; software version provides statistical information on more than 5,000
   product lines, allowing searching by SIC code, harmonized code, or keyword
   commodity description. Report available for single products.

   b. Exporters Encyclopaedia. Wilton, CT: Dun & Bradstreet. Annual.
   Comprehensive world marketing guide, in five sections; section two, "Export
   Markets," gives important market information on 220 countries (import and
   exchange regulations, shipping services, communications data, postal
   information, currency, banks, and embassies); other sections contain general
   export information. Also available are regional guides for Asia-Pacific, Europe,
   and Latin America, and Export Guides for a single country.

   c. International Business Handbook. Binghamton, NY: Haworth Press, 1990.
   Includes a global overview as well as separate chapters on 15 countries or
   regions, covering such topics as consumer cultures, business customs, methods
   of entry, and global strategies.

   d. Reference Book for World Traders: A Guide for Exporters and Importers. San
   Diego, CA: Croner Publications. Looseleaf. Provides information required for
   market research and for planning and executing exports and imports to and from
   all foreign countries; under each country provides listing of services to exporters
   and importers including marketing research organizations, marketing
   publications, and custom brokers.

   e. U.S. Custom House Guide. Hightstown, NJ: K-III Directory Co. Annual.
   Provides a comprehensive guide to importing including seven main sections:
   import how-to, ports sections, directory of services, tariff schedules (Harmonized
   Tariff Schedules of the U.S.), special and administrative provisions, custom
   regulations, and samples of import documents.

4. Demographic Data

a. *Consumer Europe.* London: Euromonitor, 1976- . Annual. Provides demographic data on consumer products for the major countries of Europe, Eastern Europe, totals for the European Community, and comparison between the European Community, Japan, and the U.S.

b. *European Marketing Data and Statistics.* London: Euromonitor, 1965-Annual. [also on CD-ROM]. Presents data from 32 European countries on everything from economic indicators to transport infrastructure in spreadsheet form, including a 10-year trend data for each country and a full list of useful information sources.

c. *International Marketing Data and Statistics.* London: Euromonitor, 1976- . Annual. [also on CD-ROM]. Presents extensive marketing data for all countries outside Europe, including 10-year trend data for most series.

d. *World Consumer Markets, 1996/7.* London: Euromonitor, 1996. [also on CD-ROM]. Provides volume and value market size data for over 230 consumer products across 55 countries for 1990–1995, with expert forecasts to 2000.

e. *World Market Share Reporter.* 2d ed. Detroit: Gale, 1996. Provides market share data for hundreds of products, services, and commodities in countries of regions other than North America and Mexico.

f. *World Marketing Forecasts, 1997.* London: Euromonitor, 1996. [CD-ROM file]. Provides detailed forecast data for the period 1995 to 2010 in 54 countries, mapping out global changes for the next 15 years, illustrated by a large number of social, demographic, and economic forecasts.

5. Periodical Indexes

a. *ABI/INFORM.* Charlotte, NC: UMI/Data Courier. Weekly. [computer file and CD-ROM]. Indexes and abstracts articles from some 1,000 business and management periodicals published worldwide. More than half the journals are indexed cover-to-cover, the others selectively. Abstracts are about 200 words long; available online on Data-Star, European Space Agency, Lexis-Nexis, Orbit Search Service, STN International, University Microfilm International, Ovid Technologies, and Knight-Ridder Information; and on CD-ROM as *ABI/INFORM Global Edition.*

b. *Predicasts F & S Index Europe.* Foster City, CA: Information Access Co. Monthly. [print file, computer file, and CD-ROM]. Covers company, product, and industry information for the European Community (Common Market), Scandinavia, other regions in Western Europe, the former USSR, and East European countries in financial publications, business-oriented newspapers, trade magazines, and special reports; available online through Ovid Technologies, Data-Star, and Knight-Ridder Information and on CD-ROM as *Predicasts F & S Index Plus Text.* Abstracts in the computer file and on CD-ROM vary in length from 400 to 600 words and contain full text for many shorter articles.

c. *Predicasts F & S Index International.* Foster City, CA: Information Access Co. Monthly. [print file, computer file, and CD-ROM]. Covers company, product, and industry information for Canada, Latin America, Africa, the MidEast, Asia, and Oceania in financial publications, business-oriented newspapers, trade magazines, and special reports; available online through Ovid Technologies, Data-Star, and Knight-Ridder Information and on CD-ROM as *Predicasts F & S Index Plus Text.* Abstracts in the computer file and on CD-ROM vary in length from 400 to 600 words and contain full text for many shorter articles.

6. Periodicals

a. Business Briefings. *Business Africa, Business Asia, Business China, Business Eastern Europe, Business Europe, Business Latin America, Business Middle*

East, Russia, India Business Intelligence, Crossborder Monitor, Ostwirtschafts-report. New York: Business International. Biweekly or monthly. [also on CD-ROM]. Reports issued for each title provide current news about companies, products, markets, and recent developments in laws and practices.

b. Business Operations Report. *Eastern Europe, Middle East & Africa, Latin America, Asia.* [also on CD-ROM]. Provides hands-on operating information for setting up or operating a business, including information and commentary on new marketing and sales challenges and import and export policies.

c. *China Hand.* New York: Business International. Monthly. [also on CD-ROM]. Provides comparative information on provinces and sites for setting up new operations and keeping up-to-date with regulatory changes and business developments.

d. *East Asian Business Intelligence.* Washington, D.C.: International Executive Reports. Biweekly. Provides sales and contracting opportunities for East Asian countries, including a brief description of the business opportunity, the person to contact, address, plus phone and fax numbers.

e. *Investing Licensing and Trading Abroad.* New York: Business International. Semiannual. [also on CD-ROM]. Directed toward companies that export directly or that have established subsidiaries, joint ventures, or licensing arrangements abroad, outlining business requirements for overcoming restrictions and other legal hurdles in 60 countries.

f. *Marketing in Europe.* New York: Economists Intelligence Unit. Monthly. Contains detailed studies of markets for consumer products in France, Germany, Italy, Belgium, and the Netherlands, including food, drink, tobacco, clothing, furniture, leisure goods, chemists' goods, household goods, and domestic appliances.

g. *Market Research International.* London: Euromonitor. Monthly. Each issue features diverse products and markets focusing on international market review, global market trends and developments, U.S.A. market report, Japan market report, emerging market report, and market focus.

h. *World Commodity Forecasts: Industrial Raw Materials; and Food, Feedstuffs and Beverages.* New York: Business International. Annual, with updates. Provides analysis of market trends, with specific price forecasts up to two years ahead for 28 commodities.

7. **Web Sites for Multinational Marketing**

a. *STAT-USA/Internet:* **http://www.stat-usa.gov/**. Clearly the single most important source of data on the Internet. STAT-USA, a part of the U.S. Department of Commerce's Economics and Statistics Administration, produces and distributes at a nominal subscription fee the most extensive government-sponsored business, economic, and trade information data bases in the world today, including National Trade Data Bank (see above), Economic Bulletin Board, and Global Business Procurement Opportunities.

b. *BEMS (Big Emerging Markets):* **http://www.stat-usa.gov/itabems.html**. BEMS is a service of the International Trade Administration of the U.S. Department of Commerce, targeting markets of the 21st century such as China, Indonesia, Mexico, and Brazil.

c. *GEMS (Global Export Market Information System):* **http://www.itaiep. doc.gov/**. GEMS is a service of the Market Access and Compliance Group of the International Trade Administration of the U.S. Department of Commerce, providing the latest in country and regional information for American exporters.

d. U.S. Census: **http://www.census.gov/ftp/pub/foreign-trade/www/**. Provides a variety of international trade statistics.

  e. U.S. Customs Service: **http://www.customs.ustreas.gov**. Provides information regarding customs procedures and regulations.

  f. Overseas Private Investment Corporation (OPIC): **http://www.opic.gov**. Provides information regarding services of OPIC.

  g. Export-Import Bank of the United States (EX-IM Bank): **http://www.exim.gov**. Provides information related to trade financing services provided by the U.S. government.

  h. International Monetary Fund (IMF): **http://www.imf.org**. Provides information about the IMF and international banking and finance.

  i. World Trade Organization (WTO): **http://www.wto.org**. Provides information regarding the operations of the WTO.

  j. Organization of Economic Cooperation and Development (OECD): **http://www.oecd.org**. Provides information regarding OECD policies and associated data for 29 member countries.

  k. Japan External Trade Organization (JETRO): **http://www.jetro.go.jp**. The best source for data on the Japanese market.

  l. Euromonitor: **http://www.euromonitor.com**. A company providing a variety of data and reports on international trade and marketing.

  m. The Web of Culture: **http://www.worldculture.com**. Provides a variety of data on cultural dimensions such as language, gestures, and religion for a large number of countries.

  n. *Doing Business around the World:* **http://www.eyi.com/tdbaw.htm**. Ernst & Young's *Doing Business around the World* series has been converted to a Folio Infobase format for Internet viewing. The series provides country profiles that overview the investment climate, forms of business organization, and business and accounting practices in more than 40 countries.

  o. University-based Web sites, all connected to several data sources include: Michigan State University Center for International Business Education and Research: **http://ciber.bus.msu.edu/busres.htm**. U. C. Berkeley: **http://berkeley.edu.busi/bbbg8.html**. University of Kansas: **http://bschool.ukans.edu.intbuslib/trade.htm**.

  p. *VIBES (Virtual International Business and Economic Sources):* **http://www.uncc.edu/lis/library/reference/intbus/vibehome.htm**. VIBES provides links to sources of international business information. These include links to full-text files (in English), statistical tables, and graphs on topics related to international business available on Gopher sites and Web sites. VIBES does not include Telnet sites, fee-based services, or business directories.

  q. World Network of Chambers of Commerce and Industry: **http://www.worldchambers.com**. Provides data and addresses regarding chambers of commerce around the world.

  r. The Internet Public Library: **http://www.ipl.org/ref/RR/static/bus4700.html**. Provides Internet addresses for dozens of sources of trade data worldwide.

  s. World Trade Center Association: **http://www.wtca.org**. Provides information about services provided by the World Trade Centers in the U.S. including export assistance, trade leads, training programs, and trade missions.

  t. World Trade Magazine: **http://www.worldtrademag.com**. Provides on-line its annual *Resource Guide* to products, goods, and services for international trade.

EMERGING MARKETS

Chapter Learning Objectives

What you should learn from Chapter 9

- The political and economic changes affecting global marketing.

- The connection between the economic level of a country and the marketing task.

- Marketing's contribution to the growth and development of a country's economy.

- The growth of developing markets and their importance to regional trade.

- The political and economic factors that affect the stability of regional market groups.

- The NIC growth factors and their role in economic development.

GLOBAL PERSPECTIVE

Wal-Mart, Tide, and Three-Snake Wine

Developing markets all over the world are experiencing rapid industrialization, creating growing industrial and consumer markets, economic growth, and new opportunities for foreign investment. Consider the following illustration:

In China, it is just a few shopping days before the advent of the Year of the Ox and the aisles at the local Wal-Mart supercenter are jammed with bargain hunters pushing carts loaded high with food, kitchen appliances, and clothing. It could be the pre-holiday shopping rush in any Wal-Mart in Middle America, but the shoppers here are China's nouveau riche. Alongside Campbell's soup and Bounty paper towels are racks of dried fish and preserved plums. One shelf is stacked high with multiple brands of *congee,* a popular southern Chinese breakfast dish, and another has *nam yue* peanuts and packets of bamboo shoots. In the liquor section in the back of the store is the three-snake rice wine, complete with the dead serpents' bodies coiled together in the potent liquid.

Megastores such as this Wal-Mart have opened in a number of Chinese cities as U.S. retail giants rush into the world's largest potential market. As one executive commented, "It boggles the mind to think if everybody washed their hair every day, how much shampoo you would sell."

The China market can be difficult to tap and may not be profitable for years to come. Most foreign retailers are in a learning mode about the ways and tastes of the East that are so different from those on Main Street U.S.A. Pricesmart designed its Beijing store with two huge loading docks to accommodate full-sized diesel trucks in anticipation of the big deliveries needed to keep shelves well-packed. What the company found was Chinese dis-

tributors arriving with goods in car trunks, on three-wheel pedicabs, or strapped to the backs of bicycles.

Procter & Gamble offered Powdered Tide detergent in large quantities but China's oppressive summer humidity turned it into unwieldy clumps. Stocking large quantities of paper towels and disposable diapers didn't work well either—most customers didn't know what a paper towel was and diapers were too expensive a luxury for most. Package sizes also posed a problem—small Chinese apartments couldn't handle the large American-sized packages.

On top of all that, foreign retailers have had to learn to deal with the uncertainty of China's complex and rapidly changing business climate, where personal connections matter more than business plans, and rules and regulations often are a matter of interpretation. "It doesn't matter what the law says," notes one retailer. "What matters is what the guy behind the desk interprets the law to say."

How do you sell $75 jeans or $150 wireless phones in a country where the per capita gross domestic product is only a couple thousand dollars a year? One answer marketing researchers have found is that extended families are showering their money on the kids, a common form of conspicuous consumption in the developing world. Even in China the spending power of youth is nothing to discount. Studies have shown that the average 7–12-year-old in a large city has $182 a year in spending money—admittedly less than the $377 in France or $493 in the U.S. but still a significant amount considering the huge population.

Sources: Adapted from Keith B. Richburg, "Attention Shenzen Shoppers!; U.S. Retail Giants Are Moving into China, and Finding the Learning Curve Formidable," *Washington Post,* February 12, 1997.

China and other emerging markets throughout the world will account for 75 percent of the world's total growth in the next decade and beyond, according to Department of Commerce estimates. The transition from socialist to market-driven economies, the liberalization of trade and investment policies in developing countries, the transfer of public-sector enterprises to the private sector, and the rapid development of regional market alliances are changing the way countries will trade and prosper in the next century.

No more than a decade ago, large parts of the developing world were hostile toward foreign investment and imposed severe regulatory barriers to foreign trade. Today, the view is different. With the collapse of the Marxist–socialist, centrally planned economic model and the spectacular economic success of Taiwan, South Korea, Singapore, and other Asian economies, it became apparent to many that the path to prosperity was open trade and direct investment. As a result, many developing countries are experiencing some degree of industrialization, urbanization, rising productivity, higher personal incomes, and technological progress, although not all at the same level or rate of development. Few nations are content with the economic status quo; now, more than ever, they seek economic growth, improved standards of living, and an opportunity for the good life most people want as part of the global consumer world.

China, Taiwan, Hong Kong, Singapore, South Korea, Poland, Argentina, Brazil, Mexico, and India are some of the countries undergoing impressive changes in their economies and emerging as vast markets. In these and other countries there is an ever-expanding and changing demand for goods and services. Markets are dynamic, developing entities reflecting the changing life-styles of a culture. As economies grow, markets become different, larger, and more demanding.

When economies grow and markets evolve beyond subsistence levels, the range of tastes, preferences, and variations of products sought by the consumer increases; they demand more, better, and/or different products. As countries prosper and their people are exposed to new ideas and behavior patterns via global communications networks, old stereotypes, traditions, and habits are cast aside or tempered, and new patterns of consumer behavior emerge. Twenty-nine-inch Sony televisions in China, Avon cosmetics in Singapore, Wal-Mart discount stores in Argentina, Brazil, Mexico, China, and Thailand, McDonald's beefless Big Macs in India, Whirlpool washers and refrigerators in Eastern Europe, Sara Lee food products in Indonesia, and Amway products in the Czech Republic represent the opportunities that are arising in emerging markets.

A pattern of economic growth and global trade that will extend well into the 21st century appears to be emerging. It consists of three multinational market regions that comprise major trading blocks: Europe, Asia, and the Americas. Within each trading block are fully industrialized countries as typified by Germany, Japan, and the United States; rapidly industrializing countries such as Mexico, Singapore, and South Korea that are close on the heals of the fully industrialized; and other countries that are achieving economic development but at more modest rates. Outside the triad of Europe, Asia, and the Americas are others at different levels of development striving to emulate their more prosperous neighbors. Indonesia, Malaysia, Thailand, and the Philippines are beginning to chase the leaders' tails though from much lower levels of income. All four groups are creating enormous global markets. This chapter and the next explore the emerging markets and the multinational market regions and market groups that comprise the global trading blocks of the future.

Marketing and Economic Development

The economic level of a country is the single most important environmental element to which the foreign marketer must adjust the marketing task. The stage of economic growth within a country affects the attitudes toward foreign business activity, the demand for goods, distribution systems found within a country, and the entire marketing process. In static economies, consumption patterns become rigid, and marketing is typically nothing more than a supply effort. In a dynamic economy, consumption patterns change rapidly. Marketing is constantly faced with the challenge of detecting and providing for new levels of consumption, and marketing efforts must be matched with ever-changing market needs and wants.

Economic development presents a two-sided challenge. First, a study of the general aspects of economic development is necessary to gain empathy for the economic climate within developing countries. Second, the state of economic development must be studied with respect to market potential, including the present economic level and the economy's growth potential. The current level of economic development dictates the kind and degree of market potential that exists, while knowledge of the dynamism of the economy allows the marketer to prepare for economic shifts and emerging markets.

Economic development is generally understood to mean an increase in national production that results in an increase in the average per capita gross domestic product (GDP).[1] Besides an increase in average per capita GDP, most interpretations of the concept also imply a widespread distribution of the increased income. Economic development, as commonly defined today, tends to mean rapid economic growth-improvements achieved "in decades rather than centuries"—and increases in consumer demand.

Stages of Economic Development

The best-known model for classifying countries by stage of economic development is the five-stage model presented by Walt Rostow. Each stage is a function of the cost of labor, technical capability of the buyers, scale of operations, interest rates, and level of product sophistication. Growth is the movement from one stage to another, and countries in the first three stages are considered to be economically underdeveloped.

Briefly, the stages are:[2]

Stage 1: *The traditional society.* Countries in this stage lack the capability of significantly increasing the level of productivity. There is a marked absence of systematic application of the methods of modern science and technology. Literacy is low, as are other types of social overhead.

Stage 2: *The preconditions for take-off.* This second stage includes those societies in the process of transition to the take-off stage. During this period, the advances of modern science are beginning to be applied in agriculture and production. The development of transportation, communications, power, education, health, and other public undertakings are begun in a small but important way.

Stage 3: *The take-off.* At this stage, countries achieve a growth pattern which becomes a normal condition. Human resources and social overhead has been developed to sustain steady development. Agricultural and industrial modernization lead to rapid expansion in these areas.

Stage 4: *The drive to maturity.* After take-off, sustained progress is maintained and the economy seeks to extend modern technology to all fronts of economic activity. The economy takes on international involvement. In this stage, an economy demonstrates that it has the technological and entrepreneurial skills to produce not everything, but anything it chooses to produce.

Stage 5: *The age of high mass consumption.* The age of high mass consumption leads to shifts in the leading economic sectors toward durable consumers' goods and services. Real income per capita rises to the point where a very large number of people have significant amounts of discretionary income.

---

[1] Gross domestic product (GDP) and gross national product (GNP) are two measures of a country's economic activity. GDP is a measure of the market value of all goods and services produced within the boundaries of a nation, regardless of asset ownership. Unlike gross national product (GNP), GDP excludes receipts from that nation's business operations in foreign countries, as well as the share of reinvested earnings in foreign affiliates of domestic corporations.

[2] Walt W. Rostow, *The Stages of Economic Growth.* 2d ed. (London: Cambridge University Press, 1971), p. 10. See also W.W. Rostow, *The Stages of Economic Growth: A Non-Communist Manifesto* (London: Cambridge University Press, 1991).

EXHIBIT 9–1   Economic and Social Data for Selected Countries

	Consumer Spending				Hospital		
Country	Food ($millions)**	Percent of Total*	Clothing ($millions)	Percent of Total*	Beds per (000s) Population	Number of Beds	Literacy (percent)
U.S.A.	$833,159	17.0%	$221,800	5.2%	5.1	560,300	99.5%
Argentina	76,557	29.2	31,618	12.0	5.3	96,000	93.9
Brazil	95,331	35.1	14,202	5.2	3.5	169,488	77.8
Colombia	18,364	33.0	5,898	10.6	1.5	29,353	85.2
Mexico	43,758	34.1	11,584	9.0	0.7	130,000	87.6
Venezuela	20,246	36.7	5,239	9.5	2.6	28,400	84.7

* Percent of all consumer spending.

** In U.S. dollars, basis 1985.

Sources: For additional information, see *International Trade Statistics Yearbook* (New York: United Nations, 1997); *Demographic Yearbook 1997* (New York: United Nations, 1997); and *International Marketing Data and Statistics, 1997* (London: Euromonitor Publications, 1997).

While Rostow's classification has met with some criticism because of the difficulty of distinguishing among the five stages, it provides the marketer with some indication of the relationship between economic development and the types of products a country needs, and the sophistication of its industrial infrastructure.

The United Nations uses a system to classify a country's stage of economic development based on its level of industrialization. It groups countries into three categories: MDCs (more-developed countries)—industrialized countries with high per capita incomes such as Canada, England, France, Germany, Japan, and the United States; LDCs (less-developed countries)—industrially developing countries just entering world trade, many of which are in Asia and Latin America, with relatively low per capita incomes; and LLDCs (least-developed countries)—industrially underdeveloped, agrarian, subsistence societies with rural populations, extremely low per capita income levels, and little world trade involvement. LLDCs are found in Central Africa and parts of Asia. The UN classification has been criticized because it no longer seems relevant in the rapidly industrializing world today. In addition, many countries that are classified as LDCs are industrializing at a very rapid rate while others are advancing at more traditional rates of economic development. It is interesting to note in Exhibit 9–1 the differences in consumer spending among the Latin American countries and the United States.

Newly Industrialized Countries

Countries that are experiencing rapid economic expansion and industrialization and do not exactly fit as LDCs or MDCs are more typically referred to as *newly industrialized countries (NICs)*. These countries have shown rapid industrialization of targeted industries and have per capita incomes that exceed other developing countries. They have moved away from restrictive trade practices and instituted significant free-market reforms; as a result, they attract both trade and foreign direct investment. Chile, Brazil, Mexico, South Korea, Singapore, and Taiwan are some of the countries that fit this description. NICs have become formidable exporters of many products including steel, automobiles, machine tools, clothing, and electronics, as well as vast markets for imported products.

Brazil[3] provides an example of the growing importance of NICs in world trade, exporting everything from alcohol to carbon steel. Brazilian orange juice, poultry, soy-

---

[3] "Brazil. Is It for Real?" *The Economist*, May 17, 1997, p. 24.

beans, and weapons (Brazil is the world's sixth largest weapons exporter) compete with the United States for foreign markets. Embraer, a Brazilian aircraft manufacturer, has sold planes to over 60 countries and provides a substantial portion of the commuter aircraft used in the United States and elsewhere.[4] Even in automobile production, Brazil is a world player; it ships more than 200,000 cars, trucks, and buses to Third World countries annually. Volkswagen has produced more than 3 million VW Beetles in Brazil and is now investing more than $500 million in a project to produce the Golf and Passat automobiles, and General Motors is investing $600 million in its production facilities. All in all, auto and parts makers are investing more than $2.8 billion aimed at the 200 million people in the Mercosur market, the free-trade group formed by Argentina, Brazil, Paraguay, and Uruguay.[5]

Among the NICs, South Korea, Taiwan, Hong Kong, and Singapore have had such rapid growth and export performance that they are discussed as the "Four Tigers" of Southeast Asia. The Four Tigers have almost joined the ranks of developed economies in terms of GDP per head. In addition, personal incomes in these countries have increased from just one-sixth of U.S. levels in the early 1960s to over two-thirds today,[6] making them major markets for industrial and consumer goods.

These four countries began their industrialization as assemblers of products for U.S. and Japanese companies, but are now major world competitors in their own right.[7] Korea, for example, exports such high-tech goods as petrochemicals, electronics, machinery, and steel, all of which are in direct competition with Japanese and U.S.-made products. In consumer products, Hyundai, Kia, Samsung, and Lucky-Goldstar are among the familiar Korean-made brand names in automobiles, microwaves, and televisions sold in the United States. Korea is also making sizable investments outside its borders. A Korean company recently purchased 58 percent of Zenith, the last remaining TV manufacturer in the U.S.[8] At the same time, Korea is dependent on Japan and the United States for much of the capital equipment and components needed to run its factories.

NIC Growth Factors

Both Rostow's and the UN's designations for stages of economic development reflect a static model in that they do not account for the dynamic changes in economic, political, and social conditions in many developing countries, especially among NICs. Why have some countries grown so rapidly and successfully while others with similar resources or more plentiful resources languished or had modest rates of growth is a question to which many have sought answers. Is it cultural values,[9] better climate, more energetic population, or just an "Asian Miracle"? There is ample debate as to why the NICs have grown while other underdeveloped nations have not. Some attribute their growth to cultural values, others to cheap labor, and still others to an educated and literate population. Certainly all of these factors have contributed to growth but there are other important factors that are present in all the rapidly growing economies, many of which seem to be absent in those nations that have not enjoyed comparable economic growth.

One of the paradoxes of Africa is that its people are for the most part desperately poor while its land is extraordinarily rich.[10] East Asia is the opposite: It is a region

---

[4] Jack Epstein, "David and Goliath: Brazil's Embraer Takes Up the Battle for the Lucrative Regional Jet Market," *Latin Trade*, October 1997, p. 26.

[5] "Building a Detroit in Latin America," *Business Week*, September 15, 1997, p. 58.

[6] Jeffrey D. Sachs and Steven C. Radelet, "Emerging Asia's Bright Prospects," *The Asian Wall Street Journal*, May 19, 1997, p. 8.

[7] "The Asian Miracle: Is It Over?" *The Economist*, March 1, 1997, p. 28.

[8] Kim Suk-hi, "In My View: LG's Acquisition of Zenith," *The Korea Herald*, August 1, 1997.

[9] William Pfaff, "Inherited Social Values May Be Stalling India," *International Herald Tribune*, August 8, 1997, p. 5.

[10] Digby Larner, "Into Africa? New Investing Views Despite Economic Growth, Some Doubt Continent's Viability," *International Herald Tribune*, July 19, 1997, p. 19.

mostly poor in resources that over the last few decades has enjoyed an enormous economic boom. When several African countries in the 1950s (for example Congo, the former Zaire) were at the same income level as many East Asian countries (for example South Korea) and were blessed with far more natural resources, it might have seemed reasonable for the African countries to have prospered more than their Asian counterparts. While there is no doubt that East Asia[11] enjoyed some significant cultural and historical advantages, its economic boom relied on other factors that have been replicated elsewhere but were absent in Africa. The formula for success in East Asia was an outward-oriented, market-based economic policy coupled with an emphasis on education and health care. This is a model that most newly industrialized countries have followed in one form or another.[12]

The factors that existed to some extent during the economic growth of NICs were:

- Political stability in policies affecting their development.
- Economic, political, and legal reforms.
- Entrepreneurship. In all of these nations, free enterprise in the hands of the self-employed was the seed of the new economic growth.
- Planning—a central plan with observable and measurable development goals linked to specific policies.
- Outward orientation—production for the domestic market and export markets with increases in efficiencies and continually differentiating exports from competition.
- Factors of production. If deficient in the factors of production—land (raw materials), labor, capital, management, and technology—an environment existed where these factors could easily come from outside the country and be directed to development objectives.[13]
- Industries targeted for growth. Strategically directed industrial and international trade policy was created to identify those sectors where opportunity existed. Key industries were encouraged to achieve better positions in world markets by directing resources into promising target sectors.
- Incentives to force a high domestic rate of savings and to direct capital to update the infrastructure, transportation, housing, education, and training.[14]
- Privatized state-owned enterprises (SOEs) that placed a drain on national budgets. Privatization released immediate capital to invest in strategic areas and gave relief from a continuing drain on future national resources. Often when industries are privatized, new investors modernize thus creating new economic growth.[15]

The final factors that have been present are large, accessible markets with low tariffs. During the early growth of many of the NICs, the first large open market was the United States, later joined by Europe and now, as the fundamental principles of the World Trade Organization (WTO) are put into place, much of the rest of the world.

While it is customary to think of the NIC growth factors applying only to industrial growth, Chile is an example of economic growth that can occur with agricultural development as its economic engine. Chile's economy has expanded at an average rate of 7.2 percent since 1987. But since 1976, when Chile opened up trade, the relative size of its manufacturing sector has declined from 27 percent of GDP in 1973 to 16.8 percent in 1995. Agriculture, on the other hand, has not declined. Exports of agricultural products

---

[11] "Beyond Myths," *The Economist*, January 4, 1997, p. 36.

[12] Nicholas D. Kristof, "From Asia's Tigers, a Lesson for Impoverished Africa," *The New York Times*, May 27, 1997, p. 1.

[13] Robert Isaak, "Making 'Economic Miracles': Explaining Extraordinary National Economic Achievement," *American Economist*, Spring 1997, p. 59.

[14] See Carl Nelson, "Economic Development and Political Reality," *The World & I*, April 1997, p. 330.

[15] Jay Solomon, "Privatization," *Far Eastern Economic Review*, January 30, 1997, p. 54.

For example, after nearly a decade of frustration in trying to effectively market and service its products in China, IBM took a bold step and entered a venture with the Railways Ministry that allowed IBM to set up IBM service centers dubbed the "Blue Express." The agreement created a national network of service centers in railway stations that enable IBM to ship computer parts via the railroad around the country within 24 hours whereas competitors must book cargo space weeks in advance. Plus, the ministry's staff of more than 300 computer engineers helps out in providing customer services on IBM products.

As the process of modernization continues in developing nations, distribution and the entire process of widening the market will lead the way. Marketing is an economy's arbitrator between productive capacity and consumer demand. The marketing process is the critical element in effectively utilizing production resulting from economic growth; it can create a balance between higher production and higher consumption.

Although marketing may be considered a passive function, it is instrumental in laying the groundwork for effective distribution. An efficient distribution system matches production capacity and resources with consumer needs, wants, and purchasing power. To eliminate some of the inefficiencies that sap the economies of underdeveloped and less-developed countries, a fully developed distribution system with adequate financing of the distribution of goods must evolve. Marketing helps make that happen.

Marketing in a Developing Country

A marketer cannot superimpose a sophisticated marketing program on an underdeveloped economy. Marketing efforts must be keyed to each situation, custom tailored for each set of circumstances. A promotional program for a population that is 90 percent illiterate is vastly different from a program for a population that is 90 percent literate. Pricing in a subsistence market poses different problems than pricing in an affluent society. The distribution structure should provide an efficient method of matching productive capacity with existing demand. An efficient marketing program is one that provides for optimum utility at a single point in time, given a specific set of circumstances. In evaluating the potential in a developing country, the marketer must make an assessment of the existing level of marketing development within the country.

Level of Marketing Development

The level of the marketing function roughly parallels the stages of economic development. Exhibit 9–3 illustrates various stages of the marketing process as they evolve in a growing economy. The table is a static model representing an idealized evolutionary process. As discussed earlier, economic cooperation and assistance, technological change, and political, social, and cultural factors can and do cause significant deviations in this evolutionary process. However, the table focuses on the logic and interdependence of marketing and economic development. The more developed an economy, the greater the variety of marketing functions demanded, and the more sophisticated and specialized the institutions become to perform marketing functions. The evolution of the channel structure illustrates the relationship between marketing development and the stage of economic development of a country.

As countries develop, the distribution system also develops. In the retail sector, specialty stores, supermarkets, and hypermarkets emerge and "mom and pop" stores give way to larger establishments. In short, the number of retail stores declines and the volume of sales per store increases. Additionally, a defined distribution structure from manufacturer to wholesaler to retailer develops and replaces the import agent that traditionally assumed all the functions between importing and retailing.

Advertising agencies, facilities for marketing research, repair services, specialized consumer financing agencies, and storage and warehousing facilities are supportive

CROSSING BORDERS 9–2

Got Distribution Problems? Call Grandma!

One of the problems facing any marketer of consumer products in emerging markets is physically getting the product to the consumer. Poor roads, an inadequate or nonexistent middleman network, or too few retailers are some of the problems plaguing the marketer. Of all the emerging markets, China may be among the most difficult in which to attain effective distribution.

Shanghai is large, crowded, and growing. Its small narrow streets were barely adequate when bicycles were the main mode of personal transportation and now with the onslaught of new automobiles and trucks there is massive congestion. In an attempt to manage this congestion, local authorities are constantly changing traffic rules and regulations. Coke, whose success depends on getting its product to the consumer when the consumer wants it, was having problems with Shanghai's two main shopping streets, Nanjing Lu and Huaihai Lu. The area was becoming too expensive for the small stores that offered Coke. Further, traffic regulations were constantly changing, downtown deliveries required a special pass, and street vendors were banned. So how did Coke get its product to market? Enter one of the lingering remnants of the old Communist regime, that bastion of the geriatric busybody, the Chinese street committee.

Initially the Chinese street committee consisted of older people whose job was to make sure all within their territory were being "good Chinese citizens." If not, they scolded scofflaws and if that didn't work, the committee reported them to higher authorities. To carry out their jobs committee members had privileged status. Anyone wearing the *zhi qin* (on duty) armband could pretty much go where they liked and do whatever they wanted.

With the beginning of civil society and a rudimentary legal system—not to mention an increasing unwillingness of the people to be spied on and bossed around by self-important old people—the traditional role of the street committee was becoming redundant. The members, however, retained their privileged status which, as Coke managers noted, meant they could push sales carts laden with ice-cold Coke around traffic and through street vendor-restricted areas of downtown Shanghai. Their access is such that Coke has signed up enough of them to warrant a fleet of 150 push carts and 300 specially designed tricycles.

The street committees keep their Coke vehicles in the local street committee lock-up (where they usually also have room for a large ice-making machine). Each committee is contracted on an exclusive basis to store, chill, and sell ice-cold Coke on its turf.

The moral to the story? You have to be creative for success in emerging markets.

Sources: "Coke Pours into Asia," *Business Week,* October 28, 1996, p. 72; and "Those Ever-Resourceful Coke Boys: Distribution Is It," *Business China,* April 28, 1997, p. 12.

facilitating agencies created to serve the particular needs of expanded markets and economies. It is important to remember that these institutions do not come about automatically, nor does the necessary marketing institution simply appear. Part of the marketer's task when studying an economy is to determine what in the foreign environment will be useful and how much adjustment will be necessary to carry out stated objectives. In some developing countries it may be up to the marketer to institute the foundations of a modern marketing system.

The limitation of Exhibit 9–3 in evaluating the market system of a particular country stems from the fact that the marketing system is in a constant state of flux. To expect neat, precise progression through each successive growth stage, as in the geological sciences, is to oversimplify the dynamic nature of marketing development.

EXHIBIT 9–3 Evolution of the Marketing Process

Stage	Substage	Example	Marketing Functions	Marketing Institutions	Channel Control	Primary Orientation	Resources Employed	Comments
Agricultural and raw materials (Mk.(f) = prod.)*	Self-sufficient	Nomadic or hunting tribes	None	None	Traditional authority	Subsistence	Labor Land	Labor intensive No organized markets
	Surplus commodity product	Agricultural economy—such as coffee, bananas	Exchange	Small-scale merchants, traders, fairs export-import	Traditional authority	Entrepreneurial Commercial	Labor Land	Labor and land intensive Product specialization Local markets Import oriented
Manufacturing (Mk.(f) = prod.)	Small scale	Cottage industry	Exchange Physical distribution	Merchants, wholesalers, export-import	Middlemen	Entrepreneurial Financial	Labor Land Technology Transportation	Labor intensive Product standardization and grading Regional and export markets Import oriented
	Mass production	U.S. economy 1885–1914	Demand creation Physical distribution	Merchants, wholesalers, traders, and specialized institutions	Producer	Production and finance	Labor Land Technology Transportation Capital	Capital intensive Product differentiation National, regional, and export markets
Marketing (Prod.(f) = mk.)	Commercial—transition	U.S. economy 1915–1929	Demand creation Physical distribution Market information	Large-scale and chain retailers	Producer	Entrepreneurial Commercial	Labor Land Technology Transportation Capital Communication	Capital intensive Changes in structure of distribution National, regional, and export markets
	Mass distribution	U.S. economy 1950 to present	Demand creation Physical distribution Market information Market and product planning, development	Integrated channels of distribution Increase in specialized middlemen	Producer Retailer	Marketing	Labor Land Technology Transportation Capital Communication	Capital and land intensive Rapid product innovation National, regional, and export markets

* Mk.(f) = prod.: Marketing is a function of production.

237

Exhibit 9-4   Market Indicators in Selected Countries

	Population (millions)	GDP per Capita	Cars in Use (000)	TVs in Use (000)	Telephones in Use (000)	Trucks and Buses
United States	263	$27,540	147,172	215,000	164,624	48,298
Argentina	34.6	8,089	4,186	7,165	5,532	1,427
Australia	18.1	19,260	7,734	8,000	9,200	1,915
Brazil	156.8	4,603	12,128	30,000	12,083	2,379
Canada	19.6	19,103	13,470	17,400	17,457	3,773
China	1205.0	578	1,765	126,000	40,706	4,927
France	58.0	26,501	24,500	29,300	32,400	5,140
Germany	81.6	26,044	39,918	30,500	40,400	4,154
India	935.7	351	1,491	20,000	11,970	2,177
Indonesia	193.8	1,022	610	11,000	3,291	2,620
Italy	57.9	18,482	29,600	17,000	24,845	2,745
Japan	125.6	40,689	44,940	100,000	61,106	24,784
Mexico	94.8	2,637	8,175	56,000	8,801	3,679
Poland	38.6	2,957	3,506	10,000	5,729	430
South Africa	41.2	3,240	3,815	3,485	3,919	1,579
South Korea	44.9	10,144	6,500	9,101	18,600	2,898
Spain	39.2	14,268	13,790	17,000	15,098	2,959
U.K.	58.6	18,880	23,832	20,000	29,408	3,605

Sources: For additional information see "Indicators of Market Size for 115 Countries," *Crossborder Monitor,* August 27, 1997; and *International Trade Statistics Yearbook* (New York: United Nations, 1997).

A significant factor in evaluating a developing market is the influence of borrowed technology on the acceleration of market development. Countries or areas of countries have been propelled from the 18th to the 21st century in the span of two decades by the influence of borrowed technology. And in fact, marketing structures of many developing countries are simultaneously at many stages. It would not be unusual to find traditional marketing retail outlets functioning side-by-side with advanced, modern markets. This is true especially in food retailing, where a large segment of the population buys food from small produce stalls while the same economy supports modern supermarkets equal to any found in the United States.

Demand in a Developing Country

Estimating market potential in less-developed countries involves myriad challenges. Most of the difficulty arises from *economic dualism,* that is, the coexistence of modern and traditional sectors within the economy. The modern sector is centered in the capital city and has jet airports, international hotels, new factories, and a small Westernized middle class. Alongside this modern sector is a traditional sector containing the remainder of the country's population. Although the two sectors may be very close geographically, they are centuries apart in production and consumption. This dual economy affects the size of the market and, in many countries, creates two distinct economic and marketing levels. India is a good example. The eleventh largest industrial economy in the world, India has a population of over 900 million, of which 250 million are an affluent middle class. The modern sector demands products and services similar to those available in any industrialized country; the remaining 650 million in the traditional sector, however, demand items more indigenous and basic to subsistence. As one authority on India's market observed, "A rural Indian can live a sound life without many products. Toothpaste, sugar, coffee, washing soap, bathing soap, kerosene are all bare necessities of life to those who live in semi-urban and urban areas."

In countries with dual sectors, there are at least two different market segments. Each can prove profitable but each requires its own marketing program and products appropriate for its market characteristics. Many companies market successfully to both

Displays, like this one in Shanghai, are important in Gillette's marketing strategy in emerging markets.
(Adrian Bradshaw/SABA)

the traditional and the modern market segments in countries with mixed economies. The traditional sector may offer the greatest potential initially, but as the transition from the traditional to the modern takes place (i.e., as the middle-income class grows), an established marketer is better able to capitalize on the growing market.

Tomorrow's markets will include expansion in industrialized countries and the development of the traditional side of less-developed nations, as well as continued expansion of the modern sectors of such countries. The greatest long-range growth potential is to be found in the traditional sector, where the realization of profit may require a change in orientation and willingness to invest time and effort for longer periods. The development of demand in a traditional market sector means higher initial marketing costs, compromises in marketing methods, and sometimes redesigning products. But market investment today is necessary to produce profits tomorrow.

New markets often also mean that the marketer has to help educate the consumer. Procter & Gamble, Colgate, and Unilever all are aggressively pursuing dental health education programs—from school visits to scholarships at dental universities to sponsorship of oral care research. While creating new markets for their products they are also helping to spread more healthful practices. In China, for instance, only about 20 percent of the population in rural areas brush daily. Most view brushing as purely cosmetic, rather than medicinal. P&G's efforts may change that attitude as school children frolic with Crest's giant inflatable Tooth Mascot that comes out when the mobile dental van makes a stop in the countryside.[20]

---

[20] Laurel Wentz and Rebecca A. Fannin, "Crest, Colgate Bare Teeth in Competition for China," *Advertising Age International,* November 1996, p. 13.

CROSSING BORDERS 9–3

Third World Faces Up to Progress

Much of the marketing challenge in the developing world, which is not accustomed to consumer products, is to get consumers to use the product and to offer it in the right sizes. For example, because many Latin-American consumers can't afford a 7-ounce bottle of shampoo, Gillette sells it in half-ounce plastic bubbles. And in Brazil, the company sells Right Guard in plastic squeeze bottles instead of metal cans.

But the toughest task for Gillette is convincing Third World men to shave. The company recently began dispatching portable theaters to remote villages—Gillette calls them mobile propaganda units—to show movies and commercials that tout daily shaving. In South African and Indonesian versions, a bewildered bearded man enters a locker room where clean-shaven friends show him how to shave. In the Mexican film, a handsome sheriff is tracking bandits who have kidnapped a woman. He pauses on the trail to shave every morning. The camera lingers as he snaps a double-edged blade into his razor, lathers his face, and strokes it carefully. In the end, of course, the smooth-faced sheriff gets the woman. In other places, Gillette agents with an oversized shaving brush and a mug of shaving cream lather up and shave a villager while others watch. Plastic razors are then distributed free and blades—which must be bought—are left with the local storekeeper.

Once the men get used to the idea of shaving, Gillette introduces them to shaving cream. Gillette discovered a while back that only 8 percent of Mexican men who shave use shaving cream. The rest soften their beards with soapy water or just plain water. Since Gillette sells neither, it introduced plastic tubs of shaving cream that sell for half the price of aerosol.

After five years of selling shaving products in Thailand, Gillette introduced a new product to the market: dental floss. Most Thais don't floss so Gillette is marketing the floss through local government health programs that encourage dental hygiene. The average usage is about 0.92 yard per person, well below the U.S. standard.

From packaging blades so that they can be sold one at a time to educating the unshaven about the joys of a smooth face and extolling the virtues of flossing, Gillette is pursuing a growth strategy in the developing world.

Source: Adapted from David Wessel, "Gillette Keys Sales to Third World Taste," *The Wall Street Journal,* January 23, 1986, p. 30; and G. Pascal Zachary, "Major U.S. Companies Expand Efforts to Sell to Consumers Abroad," *The Wall Street Journal,* June 13, 1996, p. A1.

The companies that will benefit in the future from emerging markets in Eastern Europe, China, Latin America, and elsewhere are the ones that invest when it is difficult and initially unprofitable. In some of the less-developed countries, it may be up to the marketer to institute the very foundations of a modern marketing system, thereby gaining a foothold in an economy that will someday be highly profitable. The price paid for entering in the early stages of development may be lower initial returns on investment, but the price paid for waiting until the market becomes profitable may be a blocked market with no opportunity for entry. The political price a company must be willing to pay for entry into a less-developed country market is that the host country will at first enjoy most of the benefits of the company's activities. When financial markets in Southeast Asia took a tumble in early 1997 and many currencies were devalued, foreign companies had the choice of raising prices to keep their margins intact or cutting prices and assuming the majority of the risk. The attitude of many was like that of Microsoft: "[We gave] up some of our profit margins. We're in those countries for the long term. These markets have grown like a weed for us. We still see them as having huge poten-

CROSSING BORDERS 9–4

In Developing Countries, Opportunity Means Creating It

There are vast rewards in emerging markets for those with patience that will offer incentives for progress and go the extra mile. For example, after 13 years of talks (patience), Nestlé was finally invited to help boost milk production in China. When Nestlé opened a powdered milk and baby cereal plant, it faced an inadequate source of milk and an overburdened infrastructure. Local trains and roads made it almost impossible to collect milk and deliver the finished product efficiently. Nestlé's solution was to develop its own infrastructure by weaving a distribution network known as the "milk roads" between 27 villages and the factory collection points (the extra mile). Farmers pushing wheelbarrows, pedaling bicycles, or walking on foot delivered their milk and received payment on the spot, another innovation for China. Suddenly the farmers had an incentive to produce milk and the district herds grew from 6,000 to 9,000 cows in a matter of months. To train the farmers in rudimentary animal health and hygiene, Nestlé hired retired teachers who were paid commissions on all sales to Nestlé (incentive). The result? Business took off. In three years, Nestlé factory production rose from 316 tons of powdered milk and infant formula to 10,000 tons. Capacity has tripled with the addition of two factories.

Seventeen years after talks began, Nestlé's $200 million sales were just barely profitable. However, a year later they had risen to $250 million (patience). Nestlé has exclusive rights to sell the output of its factories throughout China for 15 years (reward) and predictions are that sales will hit $700 million by 2000.

Sources: Abstracted from Carla Rapoport, "Nestlé's Brand Building Machine," *Fortune,* September 19, 1994, pp. 147–56; and Mark L. Clifford, Dexter Roberts, and Pete Engardio, "How You Can Win in China," *Business Week (International Edition),* May 26, 1997, p. 38.

tial."[21] Once profitability is assured, many companies will want to get into the market, but generally those there first will have the advantage.

Developing Countries and Emerging Markets

The Department of Commerce estimates that over 75 percent of the expected growth in world trade over the next two decades will come from the more than 130 developing and newly industrialized countries (NICs); a small core of these countries will account for more than half of that growth. Commerce researchers also predict that imports to the countries identified as Big Emerging Markets (BEMs),[22] with half the world's population and accounting for 25 percent of the industrialized world's GDP today, will by 2010 be 50 percent of that of the industrialized world. With a combined GDP of over $2 trillion, the BEMs already account for as large a share of world output as Germany and the United Kingdom combined, and exports to the BEMs exceed exports to Europe and Japan combined.[23]

---

[21] Ronald Henkoff, "Asia: Why Business Is Still Bullish," *Fortune,* October 27, 1997, p. 139.

[22] "Big Emerging Markets: 1996 Outlook and Sourcebook," Department of Commerce, 1997.

[23] For a comprehensive report on BEMs and their affect on the global economy see Jeffrey E. Garten, *The Big Ten: The Big Emerging Markets and How They Will Change Our Lives* (New York: Basic Books, 1997).

Big Emerging Markets share a number of important traits.[24] They:

- Are all physically large.
- Have significant populations.
- Represent considerable markets for a wide range of products.
- Have strong rates of growth or the potential for significant growth.
- Have undertaken significant programs of economic reform.
- Are of major political importance within their regions.
- Are "regional economic drivers."
- Will engender further expansion in neighboring markets as they grow.

While these criteria are general in nature and each country does not meet all the criteria, the Department of Commerce has identified those listed in Exhibit 9–5 as BEMs. Other countries such as Venezuela and Colombia may warrant inclusion in the near future. The list is fluid in that some countries will drop off while others will be added as economic conditions change. The message is clear: the Department of Commerce is focusing on countries that demonstrate the greatest potential for growth. Inducements for those doing business in BEMs include Export–Import Bank loans and political-risk insurance that will be channeled into these areas.

The BEMs differ from other developing countries because they import more than smaller markets and more than economies of similar size. As they embark on economic development, demand for capital goods to build their manufacturing base and develop infrastructure increases. Increased economic activity means more jobs and more income to spend on products not yet produced locally. Thus, as their economies expand, there is an accelerated growth in demand for goods and services, much of which must be imported. BEM merchandise imports are expected to be nearly one trillion dollars ($1,000,000,000,000) higher than they were in 1990; if services are added, the amount jumps beyond the trillion dollar mark.

Because many of these countries lack modern infrastructure, much of the expected growth will be in industrial sectors such as information technology, environmental technology, transportation, energy technology, health care technology, and financial services. India, for example, has less than 10 million telephone lines to serve a population of 900 million and Turkey's plans for improving health services will increase the demand for private hospital services and investments in new equipment.

What is occurring in the BEMs is analogous to the situation after World War II when tremendous demand was created during the reconstruction of Europe. As Europe rebuilt its infrastructure and industrial base, demand for capital goods exploded and, as more money was infused into its economies, consumer demand also increased rapidly. For more than a decade, Europe could not supply its increasing demand for industrial and consumer goods. During that period, the U.S. was the principal supplier since most of the rest of the world was rebuilding or had underdeveloped economies.[25] Meeting this demand produced one of the largest economic booms the United States had ever experienced. As we shall see later in the chapter, consumer markets and market segments are already booming. Unlike the situation after WWII, the competition will be fierce as Japan, Europe, the NICs, and the United States vie for these big emerging markets.[26]

The Americas[27]

A silent political and economic revolution has been taking place in the Americas (see Map 9–1) over the last decade. Most of the countries have moved from military

---

[24] For up-to-date information on BEMs visit **http://www.stat-usa.gov/itabems.html/**.

[25] For an interesting warning of possible problems ahead for some emerging markets see Jeffrey E. Garten, "Troubles Ahead in Emerging Markets," *Harvard Business Review,* May–June 1997, p. 38.

[26] "Troubles Ahead in Emerging Markets," *Harvard Business Review,* May–June 1997, p. 38.

[27] There are several Web sites for information on countries in the Americas. Visit these sites: **http:// www.enterweb.org/latin.htm/**, **//info.lanic.utexas.edul/**, and **http://www.sice.oas.org/datae.stm/**.

EXHIBIT 9-6   Eastern European Markets

	Population (millions)	GDP ($billions)	GDP ($per capita)	Exports ($millions)	Imports ($millions)
Albania	3.28	$ 2.7	$ 820	$ 80	$ 147
Bosnia/Herzegovina*	2.66	0.8	300	NA	NA
Bulgaria	9.00	11.3	1,336	4,273	5,596
Croatia*	4.78	26.3	5,600	4,633	7,582
Czech†	10.30	45.7	4,421	17,338	23,255
Hungary	10.30	35.4	3,435	12,540	15,073
Macedonia*	2.05	4.8	2,400	1,244	1,420
Poland	38.40	83.6	2,178	22,892	29,052
Romania	22.80	40.7	1,794	7,516	9,256
Slovakia†	5.27	9.3	1,763	8,585	9,070
Slovenia*	1.96	21.0	10,700	8,268	9,452

* Former republics of Yugoslavia.

† Former republics of Czechoslovakia.

Sources: For additional data, see "Indicators of Market Size for 115 Countries," *Crossborder Monitor,* August 27,1997; and *International Trade Statistics Yearbook* (New York: United Nations, 1997).

low living standards are enormous.[37] The chosen five are much richer today than just a few years ago although their per capita income is still barely a third of the EU average.[38]

While capitalism is taking root in most East European countries, incomes are increasing and a viable middle class earns enough to buy sophisticated goods. Poland, for example, has seen per capita GDP grow annually from 3–7 percent, rising by more than $2,000 in six years to about $3,500. All has not been smooth, however. Rapid economic growth and poor fiscal policy have caused a financial crisis that threatens the devaluation of their currencies. A similar problem in recent years in Mexico and Asia caused those countries to slow their rate of growth. While serious, many believe that with rapid growth, such problems are inevitable[39] and with budget cutting and monetary tightening a currency crisis can be avoided. For the long run, the outlook is bullish.[40]

Besides an increase in foreign investment from Europe, the United States, and Asia,[41] Eastern Europe has another engine for growth: the entrepreneur. Freedom from communism has provided the opportunity for the risk-taker to blossom. Nowhere is this more evident than in Hungary. A Hungarian entrepreneur, Imre Somody, hit upon an idea to catch the health craze blooming in Hungary. He came up with a vitamin-C tablet that dissolves in water to become a fizzy drink. The state-owned drugmaker where Somody worked rejected the idea, so in 1988 he quit and founded Pharmavit. In less than a year Hungary's best-known brand, Plusssz, was created—vitamins packaged in bright plastic tubes. An Olympic swimming gold medalist was signed up to lead the marketing blitz. The company expanded into generic drug manufacturing and by 1995 sales had soared to about $42 million. Bristol-Myers recently paid $110 million for Pharmavit and put Somody in charge of all products in Hungary, from cancer drugs to Clairol hair care.[42]

[37] "Eastward Ho!" *Europe,* September 1997, p. 4.

[38] Lionel Barber, "Growth Pains May Need to Be Soothed," *Financial Times,* January 5, 1998, p. 4.

[39] "Something Horrible Out There," *The Economist,* October 16, 1997, p. 38.

[40] Karen Lowry Miller, "Hungary: After Painful Austerity, a Solid Recovery," *Business Week,* October 27, 1997, p. 23.

[41] Christopher Elliott, "All Business on the Eastern Front," *Journal of Business Strategy,* March–April 1997, p. 34.

[42] "Piling into Central Europe," *Business Week,* July 1, 1996, p. 45.

Map 9-2   Eastern Europe and the Baltic States

The Baltic States.[43]   The States of the Baltic Republic—Estonia, Latvia, and Lithuania—are three of the top performing postcommunist countries. Estonia became the first Baltic Republic to create its own national currency and was among the first to attract foreign investments. Like their East European neighbors, however, the Baltic States also underwent a banking crisis that had short-term negative effects on their economies.[44] They seemed to have weathered the banking "crisis" and there has been a

---

[43]   Visit **//www.msen.com/~okno/linkfsu.html/** for links to various Web sites of countries of former Soviet Union.

[44]   Colin Jones, "Go to the Top of the Class," *The Banker,* April 1997, p. 57.

Economic growth is creating a voracious appetite for energy in emerging markets. Enron, a U.S. energy multinational, is completing construction of a gas-fired 150 megawatt electrical generating plant in China. (Greg Girard/CONTACT Press Images)

steady improvement in living standards, solidifying middle classes. Lithuania and Latvia each posted nearly 2 percent economic growth in 1996, and both expect to double that rate in 1997. Estonia experienced a 3 percent expansion in its economy in 1996 and expects a 4 percent rise for 1997. Unemployment is a fraction of that suffered by Russia, and salaries are the highest in the 15 newly independent states. These three Baltic states like to compare themselves favorably with the "tiger" economies of Southeast Asia. While they have a way to go to achieve that goal, they have experienced the most encouraging economic growth of those countries in the former Soviet Union. The Baltic States are positioned to be a bridge for trade between the West and the former USSR. With their past experience as exporters to the USSR of manufactured goods made from Russian raw materials, the Baltics see themselves as a logical location for Western investors seeking markets in the former Soviet Union.

Like their Eastern European neighbors, the Baltic States are in the sphere of influence of the European Community. There is a natural tendency for them to look to the

EC for assistance and, eventually, membership. Of these countries, Estonia is furthest along in gaining membership in the EU.[45] Agenda 2000 of the EU recommends that negotiations with Estonia begin in 1998, with possible admission by 2000. In addition, Latvia and Lithuania have been invited into partnerships with the EU to help speed up their preparations for membership.[46]

Asia[47]

Asia (see Map 9–3) has been the fastest growing area in the world for the past three decades and the prospects for continued economic growth over the long run are excellent.[48] Beginning in 1996, the leading economies of Asia (Japan, Hong Kong, South Korea, Singapore, and Taiwan) experienced a serious financial crisis, which culminated in the meltdown of the Asian stock market. A tight monetary policy, an appreciating dollar, and a deceleration of exports all contributed to the downturn.[49] Despite this economic adjustment, the 1993 International Monetary Fund (IMF) estimates that Asian economies will have 29 percent of the global output by the year 2000 is still on target.[50] Both as sources of new products and technology and as vast consumer markets, the countries of Asia—particularly those along the Pacific Rim—are just beginning to gain their stride (see Exhibit 9–7).

Asian Pacific Rim.   The most rapidly growing economies in this region, other than Japan, are the group of countries sometimes referred to as the Four Tigers (or Four Dragons): Hong Kong, South Korea, Singapore, and Taiwan. Often described as the "East Asian miracle," they were the first countries in Asia, besides Japan, to move from a status of developing countries to newly industrialized countries (NICs).[51] They have grown from suppliers of component parts and assemblers of Western products to become major global competitors—in electronics, shipbuilding, heavy machinery, and a multitude of other products. In addition, each has become a major influence in trade and development in the economies of the other countries within their spheres of influence. The rapid economic growth and regional influence of the member countries of the Association of Southeast Nations (ASEAN)[52] over the last decade has prompted the Department of Commerce to include ASEAN as one of its big emerging markets.[53] They are vast markets for industrial goods and, as will be discussed later, important emerging consumer markets.

The Four Tigers are rapidly industrializing and extending their trading activity to other parts of Asia. Japan was once the dominant investment leader in the area and was a key player in the economic development of China, Taiwan, Hong Kong, Korea, and other countries of the region, but as the economies of other Asian countries have strengthened and industrialized, they are becoming more important as economic

---

[45] Amy Serrill, "Estonia: A Shining Example of Economic Transformation," *Business America,* August 1997, p. 7.

[46] "Agenda 2000: For a Stronger and Wider Union," *The European Union,* available from **http://www.europa.eu.int/comm/agenda2000/overview/en/agenda.htm/**. Visit the Europa homepage for additional information on the EU at **http://www.europa.org/**.

[47] For a list of Web sites on Asia, see **http://www.netlink.co.uk/users/euromktg/gbc/en/busasia.html/**; also see **http://www.feer.com/Restricted/bestweb_hk.html/** for a very comprehensive list of Asian Web sites.

[48] "Developments in Selected Non-OECD Countries," *OECD Economic Outlook,* June 1997, p. 117.

[49] "The Asian Tigers Lose Their Grip," *The Economist,* July 19, 1997, p. 45.

[50] R. M. Torre, "Tigers and Slugs," *International Business,* July/August 1997, p. 19.

[51] Reuven Glick and Ramon Moreno, "The East Asian Miracle: Growth Because of Government Intervention and Protectionism or in Spite of It?" *Business Economics,* April 1997, p. 20.

[52] ASEAN will be discussed in detail in Chapter 10.

[53] "What You Need to Know about the ASEAN Four," *Asiaweek,* October 31, 1997. This article can also be found in the Asiaweek archives at **http://www.asiaweek.com/**.

Map 9–3   Asia

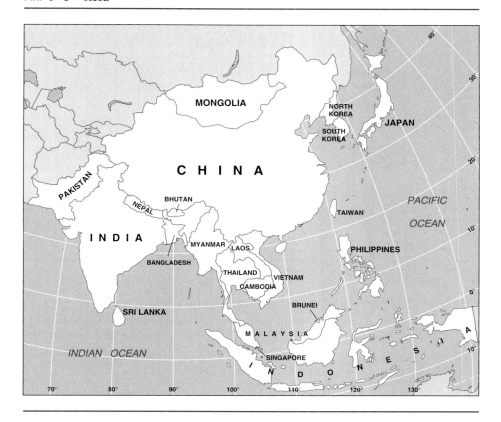

Exhibit 9–7   Asian Markets—Selected Countries

	Population (millions)	GDP ($billions)	GDP (per capita)	Exports ($ millions)	Imports ($ millions)
Australia	18.1	$ 290.7	$ 347.6	$ 52,966	$ 61,347
China	1,205	697	578	148,755	132,007
Hong Kong	6.2	140.2	22,613	173,546	192,764
India	935.4	328.4	351	30,537	34,456
Indonesia	193.8	198.1	1,022	43,285	39,456
Japan	125.6	5,110.5	40,689	443,000	335,871
South Korea	44.9	455.5	10,144	125,365	135,153
Taiwan	21.1	260.2	12,274	111,837	103,652

Sources: For additional information, see "Indicators of Market Size for 115 Countries," *Crossborder Monitor,* August 27,1997; and *International Marketing Data and Statistics, 1997* (London: Euromonitor Publications, 1997).

leaders.[54] For example, South Korea[55] is the center of trade links with north China and the Asian republics of the former Soviet Union. South Korea's sphere of influence and trade extends to Guangdong and Fujian, two of the most productive Chinese Special Economic Zones, and is becoming more pronounced in intraregional investment as well. In fact, intraregional direct investment from South Korea, Taiwan, and Singapore totaled $356 billion in 1994, about three times as much as the $117 billion from Japan, the United States, and Europe combined.[56] Japan's leadership is still dominant but now it shares the area with other Asian nations.[57]

China.[58]   The economic and social changes occurring in China since it began actively seeking economic ties with the industrialized world have been dramatic. China's dual economic system, embracing socialism along with many tenets of capitalism, produced an economic boom with expanded opportunity for foreign investment that has resulted in annual GNP growth averaging nearly 10 percent since 1970. Most analysts predict that an 8–10 percent average for the next 10 to 15 years is possible.[59] At that rate China's GNP should equal that of the U.S. by 2015. All of this is dependent on China's ability to deregulate industry, import modern technology, privatize overstaffed, inefficient SOEs (state-owned enterprises), and continue to attract foreign investment. The prospects look good.

A new era in China's internal development took place when Premier Deng Xiaoping died in 1997 and Jiang Zemin rose to the top to head the government. Proclamations during the early days of Jiang's tenure make it appear that Jiang will move further away from the socialist model to one that can be described as "capitalism with Chinese characters," rather than Deng's "socialism with Chinese characters."[60] Jiang's reform agenda included six major proposals:

1. Restructure state enterprises. SOEs account for about two-fifths of industrial output but soak up four-fifths of investment.
2. Strengthen financial markets. Expand and ensure the integrity of capital markets.
3. Sell state assets. Sell off all but 1,000 of China's 305,000 state enterprises and allow some to go bankrupt.
4. Build social services. Create housing, pension programs, and other services to relieve burdens on SOEs and to care for millions who may lose jobs.
5. Slash tariffs. Reduce average tariffs to 17 percent in 1997 and to 15 percent by 2000 as part of China's bid to join the World Trade Organization.

These reforms will answer many of the problems facing China in the near future.

The most difficult reform for Jiang to achieve will be the restructuring and privatization of state-owned enterprises.[61] SOEs are a burden on the economy but dismantling

---

[54] Purnendra C. Jain, "Japan's Relations with South Asia," *Asian Survey* (The Regents of the University of California), April 1997, p. 340.

[55] For current information on South Korea and other countries, visit **http://www.stat-use.gov/** (select Export and International Trade, then select International Marketing Insights).

[56] Suvendrini Kakuchi, "Asia-Trade: South Koreans Challenge Japanese on Region's Roads," *Global Information Network,* June 7, 1997.

[57] "Japanese Industrial Strategy—Government and Business," *The Hindu,* February 2, 1997, p. 34.

[58] China is divided into 23 provinces (including Taiwan) and 5 autonomous border regions. The provinces and autonomous regions are usually grouped into six large administrative regions: Northeastern Region, Northern Region (includes Beijing), Eastern Region (includes Shanghai), South Central Region, Southwestern Region, and Northwestern Region.

[59] Andrew Tanzer, "Stepping-Stones to a New China?" *Forbes,* January 27, 1997.

[60] "China: Future Tense—Out of Deng's Shadow," *World Press Review,* November 1997, p. 6.

[61] "Can China Reform Its Economy?" *Business Week,* September 29, 1997, p. 116.

CROSSING BORDERS 9–5

Two Faces of Chinese Industry

Since China has been on the road to open markets its industrial base has gradually evolved into two distinct types of companies—one representing the slowly declining past, the other representing the future.

Inside the gritty state-owned Wuxi Qingfeng Group Ltd. building, women work in choking dust and an ear-shattering racket as looms spin cotton and silk into yarn for everything from pillowcase covers to uniforms for the People's Liberation Army, its main customer. Despite laying off 1,700 workers, Qingfeng is still unprofitable. And like most state industries, it must pay for cradle-to-grave welfare benefits for a staff of 10,000, half of whom are retired. There are tens of thousands of factories around China like Wuxi Qingfeng.

Just across town sits Wuxi Little Swan Company in a three-story whitewashed head-quarters that hums with blue-smocked workers assembling the latest in washing machines. With its efficient work, Little Swan has sales of $163 million and 18 percent of China's market for clothes washers. It also exports to Southeast Asia, South America, and the Middle East. Fortunately there are thousands of companies like Little Swan that have learned to thrive in a market economy.

Source: Adapted from "Can China Reform Its Economy?" *Business Week,* September 29, 1997, p. 120. Reprinted from the September 29, 1997, issue of *Business Week* by special permission. © 1997 The McGraw-Hll Companies, Inc.

them could create extraordinary social unrest because they provide salaries and social services for over 100 million workers and their families.[62] If the government is not prepared to support the idled workers, there could be serious social and political consequences. Jiang's tenure could be affected since not all in the Chinese government agree with the reforms. In fact, Jiang has been careful not to call the process of reform of SOEs "privatization," and assures his comrades that "advancing socialism" is the ultimate aim. Nevertheless, the reform plans outline a program of merging state companies in key sectors (e.g., telecommunications, petrochemicals, and high-tech electronics) to form 1,000 huge corporations modeled on Japanese and Korean conglomerates. Eventually these corporations will be open to foreign and domestic share ownership. Hundreds of thousands of other companies will have to fend for themselves, go bankrupt, be sold to workers, or be peddled to foreign investors.[63] China has followed a path of "gradualism" with excellent results, but now the test will be in the next big step: privatization. Some predict the outcome could be a $2 trillion economy by 2010.[64]

In addition to the reforms articulated by Jiang Zemin, China has two other important steps to take if the road to economic growth is to be smooth: improve human rights and reform the legal system. Both of these issues were raised during Jiang Zemin's official state visit to the United States. The human rights issue has been a sticking point with the U.S. since the Tiananmen Square massacre and the jailing of dissidents as well as in light of China's treatment of Tibet. The Clinton administration continues to be under pressure from Congress and various groups to restrict trade with China until human rights changes are made; however, in 1994 the U.S. government made a major change in

---

[62] "China: Country Commercial Guide 1996-97," available on the internet at **http://www.ita.doc.gov/ uscs/ccgochin.html/** and on the National Trade Data Bank on CD-ROM.

[63] "China's New Revolutionary?" *The Economist,* September 13, 1997, p. 32.

[64] "Time for a Fresh Start," *Business Week,* November 3, 1997, p. 54.

U.S. foreign-trade policy, uncoupling China's trade status from its human-rights record and renewing China's Most Favored Nation (now Normal Trade Relations—NTR)[65] status.

The U.S. government's decision reflected, in part, the growing importance of China in the global marketplace and the perception that trade with China was too valuable to be jeopardized over a single issue. However, the issue remains delicate both within the U.S. and between the U.S. and China. During Jiang's visit, the President and Jiang had an exchange over human rights and the responses of the two are indicative of the distance that exists between the two nations on this issue. When asked about this issue by reporters, Jiang responded "It goes without saying that China observes the general rules of human rights universally abided by in the world." Then he assured reporters that he had no regrets about the suppression of dissidents at Beijing's Tiananmen Square. To the contrary, Jiang said the crackdown helped assure the "political stability" that allowed the "reform and opening-up we have today." Jiang went on to say that China and the United States have different "historic and cultural traditions and the concepts on democracy, on human rights, and on freedoms are relative."[66] The President responded that, "On so many issues, China is on the right side of history, and we welcome it. But on this issue, we believe the policy of the government is on the wrong side of history." Jiang did promise peaceful cooperation with the U.S. and stated that China would move toward democracy and greater openness.[67]

Jiang has also stated on several occasions that China would continue to institute legal reforms to provide legal protection and legal recourse for foreign companies. Nonetheless, the American Embassy in China has seen a big jump in complaints from disgruntled U.S. companies fed up with their lack of protection under China's legal system. Outside the major urban areas of Beijing, Shanghai, and Guangzhou, companies are discovering that local protectionism and cronyism make business tough even when they have local partners. Many are finding that a Chinese partner with local political clout can rip off its foreign partner and, when complaints are taken to court, influence courts to rule in their favor.[68]

An American manager, a 10-year veteran in China, says that shakedowns by officials have steadily increased, and rampant and blatantly open corruption is now prevalent at all levels. The government office that issues licenses for cars and drivers expects "donations" of gasoline and cash in exchange for prompt service. The Chinese press has to be paid off with lavish meals and cash to attend corporate press conferences. A Mercedes-Benz and $10,000 deposited in a Hong Kong bank is not an unusual payment for connections made or agreements reached in a major contractual deal. Indeed, it is estimated that such "gifts" to Chinese officials account for up to 5 percent of operating costs for large Hong Kong companies. Such practices are difficult to deal with, but they are part of the current business culture confronting companies that want to participate in the growth of the largest of all the Big Emerging Markets (BEMs). Despite the problems, China is working to build a commercial legal system and to reform current practices.

Because of China's size, diversity, and political organization, it is better to think of it as a group of six regions rather than a single country—a grouping of regional markets

---

[65] Most Favored Nation (MFN) has been replaced by the term Normal Trade Relations (NTR). The feeling in Congress was that MFN is a term that has led to public misunderstanding. Since MFN tariff rates are the same as the U.S. extended to all but eight countries, NTR is a more accurate description of the relationship. See Harry Dunphy, "Sen's Agree to Dump Old Trade Term," *Washington Post*, September 11, 1997.

[66] John F. Harris, "U.S.-China Pacts Reached in Shadow of Discord on Rights," *Washington Post*, October 30, 1997, p. A1.

[67] Helen Dewar and John Yang, "Jiang Vows Cooperation, but on China's Terms," *Washington Post*, October 31, 1997, p. A1.

[68] "Cheated in China?" *Business Week*, October 6, 1997, p. 142.

CROSSING BORDERS 9–6

The Planting Season—Plant Now, Sow Later

The NEC executive turned the radio on to hear that China was considering a new tax on exports. Just what it needed, another tax. NEC's $200 million joint venture was already riddled with unstable power supplies, export quotas, duties on imported equipment, and meddlesome politicians. To get the agreement to build a joint-venture chip plant it had invested $200 million at 29 percent interest. Along with the money, NEC will hand over state-of-the-art 0.5-to-0.35-micron process technology. That will enable China to turn out its first 8-inch logic and memory chips in 1999.

Why do people put up with all this just to get into China? Because they are afraid not to. Industrializing at incredible speed, China (including Hong Kong) has passed Taiwan to become Asia's top semiconductor market after Japan. A market research firm figures the chip market in China is worth $5.6 billion and is growing at over 30 percent per year.

"Long term China will become a huge market and you can't wait until it is too late to get involved." As the NEC executive speaks, he jots down the three characters that form the Chinese phrase "old friends." The point is clear: The Chinese will remember those who helped them industrialize in the early days. Doing business in China can be a headache, but no pain, no gain.

Sources: Adapted from Neil Weinberg, "Planting Season," *Forbes*, October 20, 1997, p.112.

rather than a single market. There is no one-growth strategy for China. Each region is at a different stage economically and has its own link to other regions as well as links to other parts of the world. Each has its own investment patterns, is taxed differently, and has substantial autonomy in how it is governed. But while each region is separate enough to be considered individually, each is linked at the top to the central government in Beijing.

In many respects, the transition from socialism to capitalism has lurched out of the central government's control, creating a free-for-all atmosphere among the regions. As a result, fierce competition among political regions often interferes with the free flow of trade and creates inefficiencies in the system. China is neither an economic paradise nor an economic wasteland, but a relatively poor nation going through a painfully awkward transformation from a socialist market system to a hybrid socialist/free-market system, not yet complete and with the rules of the game still being written.

Actually there are two Chinas, one a maddening, bureaucratic, bottomless money pit, the other an enormous emerging market. There is the old China, where holdovers of the Communist Party's planning apparatus heap demands on multinational corporations, especially in politically important sectors such as autos, chemicals, and telecom equipment. Companies are shaken down by local officials, whipsawed by policy swings, railroaded into bad partnerships, and squeezed for technology. McDonnell Douglas, Peugeot, and BellSouth all have been burned on big investments. But there is also a new, market-driven China that is emerging fast. Consumer areas, from fast-food to shampoo, are now wide open. Even in tightly guarded sectors, the barriers to entry are eroding as provincial authorities, rival ministries, and even the military challenge the power of Beijing's technocrats.[69]

---

[69] "Investing in China: Between the Extremes," *Business Asia,* October 6, 1997, p. 6.

No industry better illustrates the changing rules than information technology. Chinese planners once limited imports of PCs and software to promote home-grown industries but the Chinese preferred smuggled imports to the local manufacturers. Beijing eventually loosened the restraints, and Microsoft is now the dominant PC operating system and the PC market is a stronghold of U.S. brands.[70] A market whose modernization plan calls for imports of equipment and technology of over $100 billion per year, with infrastructure expenditures amounting to $250 billion through the remainder of the decade, is worth the effort.[71]

Hong Kong.   After 155 years of British rule, Hong Kong reverted to China in 1997. Many thought the territory's laissez-faire ways, exuberant capitalism, and gung-ho spirit would prove unbearable for Beijing's heavy-handed Communist leaders but early evidence suggests that except for changes in tone and emphasis, even opponents of communist rule concede that Beijing is honoring the "one country, two systems" policy (see Exhibit 9–8). The first test came when the Hong Kong financial markets had a meltdown in 1997 that reverberated around the financial world and directly threatened the mainland's interests. Beijing's officials kept silent and when they said anything, they expressed confidence in the ability of Hong Kong authorities to solve their own problems.[72]

The decision to let Hong Kong handle the crisis on its own is considered strong evidence that the relationship is working for the best for both sides, considering that China has so much riding on Hong Kong. Among other things, Hong Kong is the largest investor in the mainland, investing more than $100 billion over the last few years for factories and infrastructure. Further, the Hong Kong stock market is the primary source of capital for some of China's largest state-owned enterprises. China Telcom, for example, recently raised $4 billion in an initial public offering. There are, however, some problems coming mostly from new investors from China, including allegations of insider-trading tips and rumors of takeovers by company directors who benefit from rising stock prices. All of this is complicated by the difficulty in getting accurate information from mainland companies. Most of the problems stem from fundamental concepts such as clear rules and transparent dealings that are not understood the same way on the mainland as they are in Hong Kong.[73] China's ascension to the ranks of a global economic power will have been realized if the integration of Hong Kong with the mainland continues to be successful.

India.[74]   The wave of change that has been washing away restricted trade, controlled economies, closed markets, and hostility to foreign investment in most developing countries has finally reached India. Since its independence in 1950, the world's largest democracy had set a poor example as a model for economic growth for other developing countries and was among the last of the economically important developing nations to throw off traditional insular policies. India's growth had been constrained and shaped by policies of import substitution and an aversion to free markets. Real competition in internal markets was practically eliminated through import bans and prohibitive tariffs on foreign competition. Industry was so completely regulated that those with the proper license could count on a specific share of market. While other Asian countries were wooing foreign capital, India was doing its best to keep it out. Multinationals, seen as

---

[70] "How You Can Win in China," *Business Week,* May 26, 1997, p. 66.

[71] For a detailed report on China's market in five major sectors see "China—Big Emerging Sectors" available from **//www.stat-usa.gov/bems/bemschi/chibes.html**.

[72] For a current report see "Hong Kong Economic Indicators: Still on Track but It May Be Uphill for a While," *International Market Insight Reports,* November 5, 1997. This article is also available at **//www.stat-use.gov/** (select Export and International Trade, then select International Marketing Insights).

[73] "The Wild West of the East," *The Economist,* July 12, 1997, p. 17.

[74] For information on India and links to other sites, see **//www.indiantl.com/**.

EXHIBIT 9–8   Framework for the Hong Kong Special Administrative Region (HKSAR)

The framework for the transition of sovereignty on July 1, 1997, from British to Chinese control stipulates the HKSAR's capitalist system and way of life shall remain unchanged for 50 years after July 1. During the period, the HKSAR is to remain autonomous in all but two areas: foreign affairs and defense. Other key provisions with respect to the economic and legal system are:

- The rights of private ownership of property and investment shall be protected by the law.
- The HKSAR will have its own tax system and its own tax laws, and will enjoy freedom from taxation by the central government of China.
- The monetary relationship between China and Hong Kong is defined under the concept of "one country, two systems" as one country with two monetary systems, and two monetary authorities which are mutually independent.
- The Hong Kong dollar will remain the legal tender and a freely convertible currency fully backed by foreign exchange.
- The HKSAR shall maintain autonomy in its external economic relations, including the status of a free port and a tariff-free zone, separate customs territory, and participation in international organizations.

Source: Aasim M. Husain, "Hong Kong, China in Transition," *Finance & Development,* September 1997, p. 6.

vanguards of a new colonialism, were shunned. As a result, India lost its technological connection with the rest of the world. Technological change in many manufactured products was frozen in time. Automobiles were protected by a complete ban on importation. The Ambassador, India's mass-produced automobile, has been unchanged since it was introduced 40 years ago—40 years of technological progress bypassed the Indian auto industry. Aside from textiles, Indian industrial products found few markets abroad other than in the former Soviet Union and Eastern Europe.

Now, however, times have changed and India has embarked on the most profound transformation since it won political independence from Britain. The new direction promises to adjust the philosophy of self-sufficiency that had been taken to extremes and to open India to world markets.

India now has the look and feel of the next China or Latin America. But it continues to have problems. While it has overthrown the restrictions of earlier governments, it is not moving toward reforms and open markets with the same degree of vigor found in other emerging markets. In the first five years of the free-market reforms, India's economy grew dramatically. But reforms began to grind to a halt because of arguments among the centrist and leftist parties that make up the Prime Minister's coalition government. Resistance to change comes from bureaucrats, union members, and farmers, as well as from some industrialists who have lived comfortably behind protective tariff walls that excluded competition. Socialism is not dead in the minds of many in India, and religious, ethnic, and other political passions flare easily. Nationalism, whipped up by local politicians, helped block a Cargill, Inc., unit from building a salt plant; yet one recent survey found that roughly half of the nation wants foreign investment. India's present problems are not solely economic but a mix of political, psychological, and cultural attitudes.

Despite these uncertainties, being included among the BEMs reflects the potential of India's market. With a population expected to reach one billion by the year 2000, India is second in size only to China, and both contain enormous low-cost labor pools. India has a middle class numbering some 250 million, about the population of the United States.[75] Among its middle class are large numbers of college graduates, 40 percent of

---

[75] "Why Is India a Big Emerging Market?" found at **http://www.stat-usa.gov/bems/bemsind/ bemsind.htm/**.

whom have degrees in science and engineering. India has a diverse industrial base and is developing as a center for computer software. These advantages give India's reform program enormous potential.

Even India's weak infrastructure, which makes many aspects of doing business there difficult and costly, creates potential since the Indian government plans to address these deficiencies. Recent policy changes now permit private-sector entry into power generation, oil and gas exploration, telecommunications, and civil aviation. India's telecommunications industry is also open to foreign investors, a market projected to be over $50 billion. Approval for private investment in cellular telephones alone is expected to total $5 billion. The power industry will require billions of dollars a year, as will roads and ports.

The consumer-goods sector is another important draw for the foreign investor. An estimated 100 to 300 million Indians possess sufficient disposable income to form an expanding consumer class. Imported consumer items are still banned, but foreign investment in 22 consumer sectors is now welcome. One of the negotiating points for India to join the World Trade Organization is to allow imports of some consumer goods and to permit imports of agricultural commodities.[76]

General Electric, Ford, McDonald's, Coca-Cola, and Kentucky Fried Chicken (KFC) recently have made direct investments with spotty success. India is not a large market for branded consumer goods. Coca-Cola sells more bottles in South Korea than in India, where the bulk of the consumer market is still for cheap, unbranded goods. Further, the size of and purchasing power of the middle class might be substantially overstated. Ford, for example, entered a joint venture with a local company in southern India to produce 25,000 Escort sedans a year; they are only averaging sales of 7,500 cars per year. Most consumers preferred the smaller subcompacts priced at $6,000 rather than the hefty $15,000 for the Escort.[77] The most plausible reasons for the low market demand are culture and overoptimistic projections of demand. Members of the Indian middle class—Ford's the target market—do not trade up to newer and more modern models because labor is cheap and things can be repaired. Second, the buying capacity of Indians and a false image of the middle class as voracious for something foreign, no matter the costs, are probably exaggerated.

For a number of reasons, India still presents a difficult business environment. Tariffs are well above those of developing-world norms, although they have been slashed to a maximum of 65 percent from 400 percent. Inadequate protection of intellectual property rights remains a serious concern. The antibusiness attitudes of India's federal and state bureaucracies continue to hinder potential investors and plague their routine operations. Policy makers have dragged their feet on selling money-losing state-owned enterprises, making labor laws flexible, and deregulating banking.

In addition, widespread corruption and a deeply ingrained system of bribery make every transaction complicated and expensive. One noted authority on India declared that corrupt practices are not the quaint custom of *baksheesh* but pervasive, systematic, structured, and degraded corruption running from the bottom to the top of the political order.[78] Bureaucracy also, from top to bottom, including the once pure Indian Administrative Service, has become thoroughly corrupted.

Nevertheless, a survey of U.S. manufacturers shows that 95 percent of respondents with Indian operations plan on expanding and none say they are leaving. They are hooked on the country's cheap, qualified labor and massive market.[79]

---

[76] Sudeep Chakravarti, "WTO Negotiations: Playing Hardball the US and the EU Are Aggressively Pressing for More Patent Protection and Market Access," *India Today,* November 11, 1997, p. 52.

[77] Roy Ranjan, "Foreigners Find Indian Market Not as Advertised," *The Associated Press,* October 15, 1997.

[78] See, for example, "50 Years of Independence: Progress, Problems and Prospects; Warning," *India Abroad,* June 13, 1997, p. PG.

[79] "India Still Loved," *The Economist,* February 17, 1997, p. 8.

India has the capacity to be one of the more prosperous nations in Asia if allowed to develop and live up to its potential. Some worry, however, that the opportunity could be lost if reforms don't soon reach a "critical mass"—that point when reforms take on a life of their own and thus become irreversible.

Newest Emerging Markets

The United States' decision to lift the embargo against Vietnam and the United Nations' lifting of the embargo against South Africa have resulted in the rapid expansion of these economies. Because of their growth and potential, the Department of Commerce has designated both as BEMs (Vietnam as a member of ASEAN).

Vietnam's economy and infrastructure were in a shambles after 20 years of social-ism and years of war, but this country of nearly 70 million is poised for significant growth. If Vietnam follows the same pattern of development as other Southeast Asian countries, it could become another Asian Tiger. Many of the ingredients are there: the population is educated and highly motivated, and the government is committed to eco-nomic growth. There are some factors that are a drag on development, including poor infrastructure, minimum industrial base, and a lack of capital and technology, which must come primarily from outside the country. Most of the capital and technology are being supplied by three of the Asian Tigers—Taiwan, Hong Kong, and South Korea. In addition, since the U.S. economic embargo has been lifted, U.S. companies are begin-ning to make investments. As full diplomatic relations resume and Vietnam receives the same trade advantages offered to China, South Korea, Taiwan, and other developing countries, more investment will come.[80]

As for South Africa, now that apartheid is officially over and the United Nations has lifted the economic embargo that isolated that nation from much of the industrial-ized world for more than six years, economic growth has increased significantly. Unlike Vietnam, South Africa has an industrial base that will help propel it into rapid economic growth, with the possibility of doubling its GNP in as few as 10 years. The South African market also has developed infrastructure—airports, railways, highways, telecommunications—that make it important as a base for serving nearby African mar-kets too small to be considered individually but viable when coupled with South Africa.

There has been a rush of U.S. companies eager to enter the largest economy on the African continent and to re-establish their pre-embargo market positions. Unfortunately, many of their former competitors remained in South Africa and have had the advantage of eight years to strengthen their market positions. For example, when Eastman Kodak left the country it had 60 percent of the film market. When it returned eight years later, it had only 4 percent—all of it gray-market purchases for professional photographers. Four years later, its market share is only about 12 percent,[81] as Fuji Photo Film Co., Agfa, and Konica had stepped into the gap. Coca-Cola fared somewhat better because it moved operations to Swaziland and distributed through South African Breweries. Pepsi-Cola left entirely and its market share plummeted. Pepsi's come-back strategy is heavy promotion and touting itself as the "drink of liberation."[82]

Vietnam and South Africa have the potential of becoming the newest emerging markets, but their future development will depend on government action and external investment by other governments and multinational firms. In varying degrees, foreign investors are leading the way by making sizable investments.

---

[80] For an interesting article on doing business in Vietnam, see Esmond D. Smith, Jr., and Cuong Pham, "Doing Business in Vietnam: A Cultural Guide," *Business Horizons,* May–June 1996, p. 47.

[81] Donald G. McNeil Jr., "Kodak Focuses on South Africa after 8-Year Absence, Film Company Trying to Increase Exposure," *The New York Times,* November 10, 1997, p. N24.

[82] Although firms that chose to leave South Africa lost market position in that country, a study found that there was a positive rate of return to investment on withdrawal from South Africa. See Judith F. Posnikoff, "Disinvestment from South Africa: They Did Well by Doing Good," *Contemporary Economic Policy,* January 1997, p. 76.

Strategic Implications for Marketing

Surfacing in the emerging markets described above is a vast population whose expanding incomes are propelling them beyond a subsistence level to being viable consumers. As a country develops, incomes change, population concentrations shift, expectations for a better life adjust to higher standards, new infrastructures evolve, and social capital investments are made (see Exhibit 9–9). Foreign and domestic companies seek these new markets or to expand their positions in existing markets. Market behavior changes and eventually groups of consumers with common tastes and needs (i.e., market segments) arise (see Exhibit 9–10).

When incomes rise, new demand is generated at all income levels for everything from soap to automobiles. Officially, per capita income in China is under $400 a year. But nearly every independent study by academics and multilateral agencies puts incomes, adjusted for black market activity and purchasing power parity, at three or four times that level. Further, large households can translate into higher disposable incomes. Young working people in Asia and Latin American usually live at home until they marry. With no rent to pay, they have more discretionary income and can contribute to household purchasing power. Low per capita incomes are potential markets for a large variety of goods; consumers show remarkable resourcefulness in finding ways to buy what really matters to them. In the United States, the first satellite dishes sprang up in the poorest parts of Appalachia. Similarly, the poorest slums of Calcutta are home to 70,000 VCRs, and in Mexico, homes with color televisions outnumber those with running water.

As incomes rise to middle-class range, demand for more costly goods increases for everything from disposable diapers to automobiles. Incomes for the middle class in emerging markets are less than that in the United States, but their spending patterns are different so they have more to spend than comparable income levels in the U.S. would indicate. For example, members of the middle class in emerging markets do not own two automobiles and suburban homes, and health care and housing in some cases are subsidized freeing income to spend on washing machines, TVs, radios, better clothing, and special treats. Exhibit 9–11 illustrates the percent of household income spent on various classes of goods and services. More household money goes for food in emerg-

Exhibit 9–9   Living Standards in Selected Countries (1995)

	Households (000)	Persons per Household	Percent of Households		
			Piped Water	*Flush Toilets*	*Electric Lighting*
Brazil	38,434	4.05	73%	76%	69%
Chile	3,216	4.35	70	59	88
China	357,064	3.40	90	NA	NA
Colombia	8,482	4.14	76	64	87
Ecuador	2,626	4.36	52	33	62
Hong Kong	1,797	3.44	98	80	93
India	185,048	5.00	10	5	16
Indonesia	43,065	4.50	12	15	30
Japan	40,548	3.09	93	65	98
Peru	5,057	4.65	49	43	48
Philippines	12,750	5.37	NA	NA	NA
Singapore	815	3.67	48	42	37
South Korea	13,300	3.37	96	35	90
United States	100,308	2.62	99	99	99

Sources: For additional data, see *Demographic Yearbook 1997* (New York: United Nations, 1997); and *International Marketing Data and Statistics, 1997* (London: Euromonitor Publications, 1997).

EXHIBIT 9–10   Which of the Following Have You Purchased in the Past Three Months?* (percent of 14 to 34 year-olds)

Product	Percent in United States	Percent in Australia	Percent in Brazil	Percent in Germany	Percent in Japan	Percent in United Kingdom
Soft drinks	96%	90%	93%	83%	91%	94%
Fast-food	94	94	91	70	86	85
Athletic footwear	59	40	54	33	30	49
Blue jeans	56	39	62	45	42	44
Beer**	46	50	60	46	57	7
Cigarettes**	24	33	30	38	39	40

* Percent of 14 to 34 year-olds who purchased product within the last three months.

** Among adults 18+. Source: Yankelovich Clancy Shulman.

Source: Nancy Giges, "Global Spending Patterns Emerge," *Advertising Age,* November 11, 1991, p. 64.

CROSSING BORDERS 9–7

Low per Capita Income Means Low Demand? Don't Be So Sure

In China, where per capita income is less than $600, Rado is selling thousands of its $1,000 watches. A Kentucky Fried Chicken (KFC) dinner costs the equivalent of a day's wages, yet one of KFC's highest-volume stores is in Beijing. How can this be? There is a large wealthy group who buys the watches, but there are many others who budget and save their extra income to afford their vision of the "good life."

Mr. Xu is a good example of China's emerging consumer market. Like millions of Chinese middle-class consumers, Mr. Xu strives to afford imports from the West. He and his wife and their 22-year-old daughter live in a modest three-bedroom apartment in north Beijing with no hot water and little heat in winter. His monthly salary as a college English professor is just over $81, and his wife, retired, contributes her $35 monthly pension to family income. The family gets free medical care and pays a minimal $3 each month for rent. Like many Chinese, Mr. Xu earns extra money by doing part-time English translation work. The additional money is saved to go toward occasional family entertainment such as a trip to McDonald's, to help his only daughter who is studying accounting in the United States, and to buy Western luxuries. They buy Hollywood-brand gum, a treat for his daughter, for 70 cents—seven times the cost of a Chinese chewing gum; the family's toothpaste, Colgate, is also luxury priced at $1.41 compared to a local brand at 35 cents. Mr. Xu boasts, "We haven't used a Chinese toothbrush for five years."

Sources: Adapted from Bill Saporito, "Where the Global Action Is," *Fortune,* Autumn–Winter 1993, p. 63; and Sheila Tefft, "Xu's Have Western Taste," *Advertising Age,* April 18, 1994, p. I-10.

EXHIBIT 9–11   Consumption Patterns in Selected Countries (Percent of Household Expenditures)

	U.S.	Germany	Sinagapore	Mexico	Poland	Iran	Kenya	Thailand	India
Food	10%	12%	19%	35%	29%	37%	38%	30%	52%
Clothing	6	7	8	10	9	9	7	16	11
Gross rent	18	18	11	8	6	23	12	7	10
Medical care	14	13	7	5	6	6	3	5	3
Education	8	6	12	5	7	5	10	5	4
Transport/communications	14	13	13	12	8	6	8	13	7
Appliances/other durables	30	31	30	25	35	14	22	24	13

Source: For additional data see Ricardo Sookdeo, "The New Global Consumer," *Fortune,* Autumn–Winter 1993, pp. 68–72.

ing markets than in developed markets, but the next category of high expenditure for emerging and developed countries alike is appliances and other durables.

A London securities firm says a person earning $250 annually in a developing country can afford Gillette razors, and at $1,000, he can become a Sony television owner. A Nissan or Volkswagen could be possible with a $10,000 income. Whirlpool estimates that in Eastern Europe a family with an annual income of $1,000 can afford a refrigerator and with $2,000 they can buy an automatic washer as well.

Recognizing the growth in Asia, Whirlpool has invested $265 million to buy controlling interest in four competitors in China and two in India. The attraction is expanding incomes and low appliance-use ownership rates. Fewer than 10 percent of Chinese households have air conditioners, microwave ovens, or washers. At the same time, incomes are reaching levels where demand for such appliances will grow.[83]

One analyst suggests that as a country passes the $5,000 per capita GNP level, people become more brand conscious and forgo many local brands to seek out foreign brands they recognize. At $10,000, they join those with similar incomes who are exposed to the same global information sources. They join the "$10,000 Club" of consumers with homogeneous demands who share a common knowledge of products and brands. They become global consumers. If a company fails to appreciate the strategic implications of the $10,000 Club, it will miss the opportunity to participate in the world's fastest-growing global consumer segment. There are now over 700 million people in the world whose income is $10,000 or better. In Asia alone, Singapore's average income is over $12,000, Hong Kong is at $14,000, and Taiwan is just over $10,000. Companies that look for commonalties among this 700 million will find a growing market for global brands.[84]

Markets are changing rapidly and in many countries there are identifiable market segments with similar consumption patterns across countries. Emerging markets will be the growth areas of the 21st century.

Summary

The ever-expanding involvement of more and more people with varying needs and wants will test old trading patterns and alliances. The foreign marketer of today and tomorrow must be able to react to market changes rapidly and to anticipate new trends within constantly evolving market segments that may not have existed as recently as last year. Many of today's market facts will likely be tomorrow's historical myths.

Along with dramatic shifts in global politics, the increasing

[83] Robert L. Rose, "For Whirlpool, Asia Is the New Frontier," *The Wall Street Journal,* April 25, 1997, p. B1.
[84] Kenichi Ohmae, "The $10,000 Club," *Across the Board,* October 1996, p. 13.

scope and level of technical and economic growth have enabled many nations to advance their standards of living by as much as two centuries in a matter of decades. As nations develop their productive capacity, all segments of their economies will feel the pressure to improve. The impact of these political, social, and economic trends will continue to be felt throughout the world, resulting in significant changes in marketing practices. Marketers must focus on devising marketing plans designed to respond fully to each level of economic development. China and Russia continue to undergo rapid political and economic changes that have brought about the opening of most socialist-bloc countries to foreign direct investments and international trade. And though Big Emerging Markets present special problems, they are promising markets for a broad range of products now and in the future. Emerging markets create new marketing opportunities for MNCs as new market segments evolve.

Questions

1. Define the following terms:
   underdeveloped   BEM
   economic development   infrastructure
   NICs   economic dualism

2. Is it possible for an economy to experience economic growth as measured by total GNP without a commensurate rise in the standard of living? Discuss fully.

3. Why do technical assistance programs by more affluent nations typically ignore the distribution problem or relegate it to a minor role in development planning? Explain.

4. Discuss each of the stages of evolution in the marketing process. Illustrate each stage with a particular country.

5. As a country progresses from one economic stage to another, what in general are the marketing effects?

6. Locate a country in the agricultural and raw material stage of economic development and discuss what changes will occur in marketing when it passes to a manufacturing stage.

7. What are the consequences of each stage of marketing development on the potential for industrial goods within a country? For consumer goods?

8. Discuss the significance of economic development to international marketing. Why is the knowledge of economic development of importance in assessing the world-marketing environment? Discuss.

9. Select one country in each of the five stages of economic development. For each country, outline the basic existing marketing institutions and show how their stages of development differ. Explain why.

10. Why should a foreign marketer study economic development? Discuss.

11. The infrastructure is important to the economic growth of an economy. Comment.

12. What are the objectives of economically developing countries? How do these objectives relate to marketing? Comment.

13. Using the list of NIC growth factors, evaluate India and China as to their prospects for rapid growth. Which factors will be problems for India? For China?

14. What is marketing's role in economic development? Discuss marketing's contributions to economic development.

15. Discuss the economic and trade importance of the big emerging markets.

16. What are the traits of those countries considered Big Emerging Markets? Discuss.

17. Discuss how the economic growth of BEMs is analogous to the situation after World War II.

18. Discuss the problems a marketer might encounter when considering the Marxist–socialist countries as a market.

19. One of the ramifications of emerging markets is the creation of a middle class. Discuss.

20. The needs and wants of a market and the ability to satisfy them are the result of the three-way interaction of the economy, culture, and the marketing efforts of businesses. Comment.

21. Discuss changing market behavior and the idea that "markets are not, they become."

22. Discuss the strategic implications for marketing in India.

MULTINATIONAL MARKET REGIONS AND MARKET GROUPS

Chapter Learning Objectives

What you should learn from Chapter 10

- The need for economic union and how that need is affected by current events.

- The impact of the Triad powers on the future of international trade.

- Patterns of multinational cooperation.

- The evolution of the European Community (EC) to the European Union (EU).

- The strategic implications for marketing in Europe.

- The evolving patterns of trade as Eastern Europe and the former republics of the USSR embrace a free-market system.

- The trade linkage of NAFTA and South America and its effect on other Latin American major trade areas.

- The development of trade within the Asian Pacific Rim.

- The increasing importance of emerging markets.

GLOBAL PERSPECTIVE

Free Trade Means Losing Jobs, or Does It?

"Another 280 Jobs Go to Mexico," "Euro-skeptics Think the European Union Is Hostile to Free Markets," "Even in Gephardt's Missouri, Low Rate of Joblessness Is Mitigating the Fears." These and comparable headlines reflect the fears that many have about free trade and multinational associations like the North American Free-Trade Area (NAFTA), the European Community (EC), and other trade alliances among nations. Concerns range from jobs being exported to other countries to companies being closed out of once-open and lucrative markets. In short, many fear that free trade will not live up to its promises of open markets, market growth, lower prices, more trade, more jobs. Big multinational companies won't be hurt; the small company and the worker will suffer the brunt of free trade.

Since the economic revolution is still a work in progress, it is much too early to make a definitive evaluation of its success or failure. However, consider these "textbook examples" of how it is supposed to work—and in these cases has:

St. Joseph, Missouri, lost a major employer when the company relocated to Mexico in 1994, taking 280 jobs with it. This was a hefty labor loss for a town of 73,000. Today the city's jobless rate is 3.8 percent, among the lowest in the state. More than 2,000 jobs have been added to local payrolls since that eventful day when Lee Jeans announced it was closing its plant. Where did all those extra jobs come from? Many came from exports. For example, Altec Industries, a manufacturer of mobile hydraulic equipment used to install overhead power lines, has hired nearly 200 more workers because of growing demand in Mexico and Canada. St Joseph Packaging, which sells boxes, cartons, and other packing materials only in the United States, has seen an increase in its business from customers who are involved in exporting to Mexico and Canada. St. Joseph Packaging's largest customer is a medical supply firm that has dramatically expanded its sales since the passage of NAFTA. To fill all the new orders, St. Joseph Packaging has added 30 new employees to its staff of 120. And the story goes on: 50 jobs here and 100 there and before long you have 2,000 additional jobs. In the St. Louis area alone, more than 1,200 companies are now exporting, up from 600 five years ago according to the U.S. Department of Commerce. Nearly three-quarters of them are small or midsize companies, including many low-tech manufacturers that seemed doomed a decade ago.

Yes, international business decisions can and do affect domestic jobs but domestic business decisions also affect the job market. It is inherent in the course of commerce. When the meatpacking industry moved to the epicenter of the cattle market in the rural areas in Nebraska and Colorado from St. Joseph, jobs were also lost. Fortunately for those displaced by NAFTA, the government will provide federal aid to help offset job losses.

Exports by small companies have created thousands of new jobs in the last decade and many are a result of sales to new markets created by free trade and of products and markets where you would least expect it. A Vermont company sells cheddar cheese in the village of Cheddar in southwest England. In France, imports of mozzarella cheese have tripled to 315,172 pounds from 92,568 pounds in six months. Poppers, maker of frozen appetizers such as mozzarella sticks and onion rings, exported 3.2 million pounds of appetizers to Europe in 1996, up from 800,000 pounds a year earlier.

Ten years ago, a Cape Cod, Massachusetts, entrepreneur and his wife began a small business making kettle-fried chips. Today, they are growing at 100 percent per year, selling in markets in Europe, South America and Canada. Their Cape Cod Potato Chips are displayed among nearly 100 other stands hawking American food at the Salon International de l'Alimentation, one of the largest international food trade shows.

These are just a few examples of what is happening all over the United States. Some companies are moving offshore to Mexico and jobs are lost. In other cases, exports to Mexico and Canada are increasing and thus creating new jobs. It is much too early to gauge the success or failure of NAFTA but as you explore the issues in this chapter, consider the consequences of the United States not being an active member of viable multinational trade regions.

Sources: Helene Cooper and Scott Kilman, "Exotic Tastes: Trade Wars Aside, U.S. and Europe Buy More of Each Other's Food," *The Wall Street Journal,* November 11, 1997, p. A1; Robert S. Greenberger, "A Worldview: As U.S. Exports Rise, More Workers Benefit, and Favor Free Trade," *The Wall Street Journal,* September 10, 1997; and Jon Jeter, "Some Initial Losses Followed Free Trade Pact's Passage but Exports Are Now on the Rise," *The Washington Post,* November 29, 1997, p. A6.

A global economic revolution began in 1958 when the EEC was ratified and Europe took the step that would ultimately lead to the Economic and Monetary Union (EMU). Until then, skeptics predicted that the experiment would never work and the alliance would fall apart quickly. It was not until the single market was established that the United States, Japan, and other countries gave serious notice to creating other alliances. This event, coupled with the trend away from planned economies to the free-market system in Latin America, Asia, and eventually the former USSR, created a fertile ground that sparked the drive to establish trade alliances and free markets the world over. Nation after nation embraced the free-market system and began reforms of their economic and political systems with the desire to be part of a multinational market region in the evolving global marketplace. Traditions that are centuries old are being altered, issues that cannot be resolved by decree are being negotiated to an acceptable solution, governments and financial systems are restructuring, and companies are being reshaped to meet new competition and trade patterns.

The evolution and growth of the *multinational market region*—those groups of countries that seek mutual economic benefit from reducing intraregional trade and tariff barriers—are the most important global trends today. Organizational form varies widely among market regions, but the universal orientation of such multinational cooperation is economic benefit for the participants. Political and social benefits sometimes accrue, but the dominant motive for affiliation is economic. The world is awash in economic cooperative agreements as countries look for economic alliances to expand access to free markets.

Regional economic cooperative agreements have been around since the end of World War II. The most successful one is the European Community (EC), the world's largest multinational market region and foremost example of economic cooperation. Multinational market groups form large markets that provide potentially significant market opportunities for international business. As it became apparent in the late 1980s that the EC was to achieve its long-term goal of a single European market, a renewed interest in economic cooperation followed with the creation of several new alliances. The European Economic Area (EEA), a 17-country alliance between the European Union (EU) and members of EFTA (European Free Trade Area), became the world's largest single unified market. The North American Free Trade Agreement (NAFTA) and Mercosur in the Americas, and the Association of Southeast Asian Nations (ASEAN) and Asia-Pacific Economic Cooperation (APEC) of Asia-Pacific Rim are all relatively new or re-energized associations that are gaining strength and importance as multinational market regions. Along with the growing trend of economic cooperation, there is concern about the effect of such cooperation on global competition. Governments and businesses worry that the EEA, NAFTA, and other cooperative trade groups will become regional trading blocs without trade restrictions internally but with borders protected from outsiders. It is too early to determine to what extent trading groups will close their borders to outsiders, but whatever the future, global companies face a richer and more intense competitive environment.

Three global regions—Europe, the Americas, and the Asian Pacific Rim—are involved in forging a new economic order for trade and development that will dominate world markets for years to come. In Kenichi Ohmae's book, *Triad Power,*[1] he points out that the global companies that will be Triad powers must have significant market positions in each of the *Triad regions.* At the economic center of each Triad region will be an economic industrial power: in the European Triad, it is the European Community; in the American Triad, it is the United States, in the Asian Triad, it is Japan.

The Triad regions are the centers of economic activity that provide global companies with a concentration of sophisticated consumer- and capital goods markets. Within each Triad region there are strong single-country markets and/or multicountry markets (such as the European Community) bound together by economic cooperative agreements. Much of the economic growth and development that will occur in these regions

---

[1] Kenichi Ohmae, *Triad Power* (New York: The Free Press, 1985), p. 220.

Although exporting to Japan is often seen as difficult, this Mitsukoshi Department Store has U.S. meat for sale. The man's apron reads, "U.S. Meat Export Federation." (John Nordell/The Image Works)

and make them such important markets will result from single countries being forged into thriving free-trade areas. The focus of this chapter will be on the various patterns of multinational cooperation and the strategic marketing implications of economic cooperation for marketing.

La Raison d'Etre

Successful economic union requires favorable economic, political, cultural, and geographic factors as a basis for success. Major flaws in any one factor can destroy a union unless the other factors provide sufficient strength to overcome the weaknesses. In general, the advantages of economic union must be clear-cut and significant, and the benefits must greatly outweigh the disadvantages before nations forgo any part of their sovereignty. Many of the associations formed in Africa and Latin America have had little impact because there were not sufficient perceived benefits to offset the partial loss of sovereignty.

In the past, a strong threat to the economic or political security of a nation was the impetus for cooperation. The cooperative agreements among European countries that preceded the EC certainly had their roots in the need for economic redevelopment after World War II and the political concern for the perceived threat of communism. Many felt that if Europe was to survive there had to be economic unity; the agreements made then formed the groundwork for the European Community. The more recent creation of multinational market groups has been driven by the fear that not to be part of a vital regional market group is to be left on the sidelines of the global economic boom of the 21st century.

Economic Factors

Every type of economic union shares the development and enlargement of market opportunities as a basic orientation; usually markets are enlarged through preferential tariff treatment for participating members and/or common tariff barriers against outsiders. Enlarged, protected markets stimulate internal economic development by providing assured outlets and preferential treatment for goods produced within the customs union, and consumers benefit from lower internal tariff barriers among the participating countries. In many cases, external as well as internal barriers are reduced because of the greater economic security afforded domestic producers by the enlarged market.

Nations with complementary economic bases are least likely to encounter frictions in the development and operation of a common market unit. However, for an economic union to survive, it must have in place agreements and mechanisms to settle economic disputes. In addition, the total benefit of economic integration must outweigh individual differences that are sure to arise as member countries adjust to new trade relationships. The European Community includes countries with diverse economies, distinctive monetary systems, developed agricultural bases, and different natural resources. It is significant that most of the problems encountered by the EC have arisen over agriculture and monetary policy. In the early days of the European Community, agricultural disputes were common. The British attempted to keep French poultry out of the British market, France banned Italian wine, and the Irish banned eggs and poultry from other member countries. In all cases, the reason given was health and safety, but the probable motive was the continuation of the age-old policy of market protection. Such skirmishes are not unusual but they do test the strength of the economic union. In the case of the EC, the European Commission was the agency used to settle disputes and charge the countries that violated EC regulations.

The demise of the Latin American Free Trade Association (LAFTA) was the result of economically stronger members not allowing for the needs of the weaker ones. Many of the less-well-known attempts at common markets (see Exhibit 10–7) have languished because of economic incompatibility that could not be resolved and the uncertainty of future economic advantage.

Political Factors

Political amenability among countries is another basic requisite for development of a supranational market arrangement. Participating countries must have comparable aspirations and general compatibility before surrendering any part of their national sovereignty. State sovereignty is one of the most cherished possessions of any nation and is relinquished only for a promise of significant improvement of the national position through cooperation.

Economic considerations provide the basic catalyst for the formation of a customs union group, but political elements are equally important. The uniting of the original European Community countries was partially a response to the outside threat of Russia's great political and economic power; the countries of Western Europe were willing to settle their family squabbles to present a unified front to the Russian bear. The communist threat no longer exists but the importance of political unity to fully achieve all the benefits of economic integration has driven EC countries to form the European Union.

Geographic Proximity

Although it is not absolutely imperative that cooperating members of a customs union have geographic proximity, such closeness facilitates the functioning of a common market. Transportation networks basic to any marketing system are likely to be interrelated and well developed when countries are close together. One of the first major strengths of the European Community was its transportation network; the opening of the tunnel between England and France further bound this common market. Countries that are widely separated geographically have major barriers to overcome in attempting economic fusion.

Cultural Factors

Cultural similarity eases the shock of economic cooperation with other countries. The more similar the culture, the more likely a market is to succeed because members understand the outlook and viewpoints of their colleagues. Although there is great cultural diversity in the European Community, key members share a long-established Christian heritage and are commonly aware of being European. Language, as a part of culture, has not created as much a barrier for European Community countries as was expected. Initially there were seven major languages, but such linguistic diversity did not impede trade because European businessmen historically have been multilingual. Nearly every educated European can do business in at least two or three languages; thus, in every relationship, there is likely to be a linguistic common ground.

Patterns of Multinational Cooperation

Multinational market groups take several forms, varying significantly in the degree of cooperation, dependence, and interrelationship among participating nations. There are five fundamental groupings for regional economic integration ranging from regional cooperation for development, which requires the least amount of integration, to the ultimate integration of political union.

Regional Cooperation Groups.   The most basic economic integration and cooperation is the *regional cooperation for development (RCD)*. In the regional cooperation for development arrangement, governments agree to participate jointly to develop basic industries beneficial to each economy. Each country makes an advance commitment to participate in the financing of a new joint venture and to purchase a specified share of the output of the venture. An example is the project between Colombia and Venezuela to build a hydroelectric generating plant on the Orinoco River. They shared jointly in construction costs and they share the electricity produced.

Free-Trade Area.   A *free-trade area (FTA)* requires more cooperation and integration than the RCD. It is an agreement among two or more countries to reduce or eliminate customs duties and nontariff trade barriers among partner countries while members maintain individual tariff schedules for external countries. Essentially, an FTA provides its members with a mass market without barriers that impede the flow of goods and services. The United States has free-trade agreements with Canada and Mexico (NAFTA) and separately with Israel. The seven-nation European Free Trade Association (EFTA), among the better-known free-trade areas, still exists although five of its members also belong to the European Economic Area (EEA).

Customs Union.   A *customs union* represents the next stage in economic cooperation. It enjoys the free-trade area's reduced or eliminated internal tariffs and adds a common external tariff on products imported from countries outside the union. The customs union is a logical stage of cooperation in the transition from an FTA to a common market. The European Community was a customs union before becoming a common market. Customs unions exist between France and Monaco, Italy and San Marino, and Switzerland and Liechtenstein.

Common Market.   A *common market* agreement eliminates all tariffs and other restrictions on internal trade, adopts a set of common external tariffs, and removes all restriction on the free flow of capital and labor among member nations. Thus a common market is a common marketplace for goods as well as for services (including labor) and for capital. It is a unified economy and lacks only political unity to become a political

CROSSING BORDERS 10-1

When Is Sausage Sausage and Chocolate Chocolate? In the European Community, Perhaps Never

A widespread suspicion among many Europeans is that many of the local-country regulations are simply disguised trade restrictions. The problem becomes one of deciding when restrictions are really a protection of health and tradition or just more roadblocks. Consider the cases for bratwurst and chocolate.

At Eduard Kluehspie's snack bar in Nuremberg the talk has turned to sausage, but not the plump and juicy bratwurst, brockwurst, or currywurst that are served together with a slice of bread and a dollop of sweet Bavarian mustard. Today, the regulars are contemplating something that is totally indigestible—something less than pure German wurst.

For generations, Germans have insisted on keeping their sausage more or less pure by limiting the amount of nonmeat additives such as vegetable fat and protein. But EC bureaucrats and other European sausage-makers see the regulations as a clever German plot to keep out imports, and they are demanding change. "I'd rather eat my dog," says one grumpy local at the thought of eating anything but pure sausage.

The EC acted, and so what has happened? Bratwurst or grilled sausage has been on sale for centuries but fake sausages carrying the same name are now competing for the palates of the thousands of visitors who flock to Nuremberg from far and wide to sample the traditional fare.

But then not even locals find it easy to spot the impostors that do not conform with stringent legislation which stipulates that a Nuremberg sausage must be a maximum of eight centimeters long, weigh 25 grams at the most, be flavored with marjoram, and contain no more than 30 percent fat.

A similar debate has roiled around chocolate. In 1973, Britain, Ireland, and Denmark joined the EU, and the debate began over what constitutes "true" chocolate. The three offending countries add a small amount of noncocoa vegetable fat to their chocolate, whereas in Belgium and France chocolate isn't chocolate unless it is only made with cocoa butter.

Companies like Cadbury's make milk chocolate with about 25 percent milk content, while Continental producers use about 14 percent. "Historically, this is the way the British make their chocolate."

After months of fruitless negotiations spurred by the drive to unify European Standards, the European Parliament voted overwhelmingly that chocolate is different from what companies in Britain, Denmark, and the other five countries have produced for decades. The Parliament also voted to force Britain and Ireland to rename their milk chocolate, arguing that it has too much milk by European standards. It voted 316–112 to delete a provision that would allow Britain to use the expression "milk chocolate," and recommended that the product should be renamed something like "chocolate with milk and noncocoa vegetable fats."

Sources: Adapted from Peter Gumbel, "Pure German Sausage Brings Out Wurst in European Community," *The Wall Street Journal*, September 9, 1985, p. 24; Sandra Trauner, "Save Our Sausages," *Deutsche Presse-Agentur*, November 28, 1997; Edmond L. Andrews, "Great Chocolate War Reveals Dark Side of Europe," *The New York Times*, October 24, 1997, p.3; and Charles Bremmer, "All Because the Belgians Do Not Like Milk Tray," *The Times of London*, October 24, 1997, p. 5.

union. The Treaty of Rome, which established the European Economic Community (EEC), called for common external tariffs and the gradual elimination of intramarket tariffs, quotas, and other trade barriers. The treaty also called for elimination of restrictions on the movement of services, labor, and capital; prohibition of cartels; coordinated monetary and fiscal policies; common agricultural policies; use of common investment funds for regional industrial development; and similar rules for wage and welfare payments. The EEC existed until the Maastricht Treaty created the European Union, an extension of the EEC into a political union. Latin America boasts three common markets: the Central American Common Market (CACM), the Andean Common Market, and the Southern Cone Common Market (Mercosur). The three have roughly similar goals and seek eventual full economic integration.

Political Union.   *Political union* is the most fully integrated form of regional cooperation. It involves complete political and economic integration, either voluntary or enforced. The most notable enforced political union was the Council for Mutual Economic Assistance (COMECON), a centrally controlled group of countries organized by the USSR. With the dissolution of the USSR and the independence of Eastern Europe, COMECON was disbanded.

The Commonwealth of Nations is a voluntary organization providing for the loosest possible relationship that can be classified as economic integration. The British Commonwealth is comprised of Britain and countries formerly part of the British Empire. Its members recognize the British Monarch as their symbolic head, although Britain has no political authority over the Commonwealth. Its member states also had received preferential tariffs when trading with Great Britain but, when Britain joined the European Community, all preferential tariffs were abandoned. The Commonwealth can best be described as the weakest of political unions and is mostly based on economic history and a sense of tradition. Heads of state meet every three years to discuss trade and political issues they jointly face, and compliance with any decisions or directives issued is voluntary.

Two new political unions have come into existence in this decade: the Commonwealth of Independent States (CIS), made up of the republics of the former USSR, and the European Union (EU). The European Union was created when the 12 nations of the European Community ratified the Maastricht Treaty. The members committed themselves to economic and political integration. The treaty allows for the free movement of goods, persons, services, and capital throughout the member states; a common currency; common foreign and security policies, including defense; a common justice system; and cooperation between police and other authorities on crime, terrorism, and immigration issues. Although not all the provisions of the treaty have been universally accepted, each year the EU members become more closely tied economically and politically. Once the Economic and Monetary Union (EMU) is put in place in 1999 and participating members share a common currency, the EU will be complete and political union inevitable.

Global Markets and Multinational Market Groups

The globalization of markets, the restructuring of Eastern Europe into independent market-driven economies, the dissolution of the Soviet Union into independent states, the worldwide trend toward economic cooperation, and enhanced global competition make it important that market potential be viewed in the context of regions of the world rather than country by country. Formal economic cooperation agreements such as the EC are the most notable examples of multinational market groups but many new coalitions are forming, old ones are being re-energized, and the possibility of many new cooperative arrangements is on the horizon.

This section will present basic information and data on markets and market groups in Europe, the Americas, Africa, Asia, and the Middle East. Existing economic cooperation agreements within each of these regions will be reviewed. The reader must appreciate that the status of cooperative agreements and alliances among nations has been extremely fluid in some parts of the world. Many are fragile and may cease to exist or may restructure into a totally different form. It will probably take the better part of a decade for many of the new trading alliances that are now forming to stabilize into semipermanent groups.

Europe

The European Union is the focus of the European region of the first Triad. Within Europe, every type of multinational market grouping exists. The European Community (EC), European Union (EU), European Economic Area (EEA), and the European Free Trade Association (EFTA) are the most established cooperative groups (see Exhibit 10–1 and Map 10–1).

Of escalating economic importance are the fledgling capitalist economies of Eastern Europe and the three Baltic States that gained independence from the USSR just prior to its breakup. Key issues center around their economic development and eventual economic alliance with the EC. Also within the European region is the Commonwealth of Independent States. New and untested, this coalition of 12 former USSR republics may or may not survive in its present form to take its place among the other multinational market groups.

European Community

Of all the multinational market groups, none is more secure in its cooperation or more important economically than the *European Community* (Exhibit 10–2). From its beginning, it has made progress toward achieving the goal of complete economic integration and, ultimately, political union. However, many people, including Europeans, had little hope for the success of the European Economic Community, or the European Common Market[2] as it is often called, because of the problems created by integration and the level of national sovereignty that would have to be conceded to the community. After all, there were 1,000 years of economic separatism to overcome and the European Common Market is very uncommon; there are language differences, individual national interests, political differences, and centuries-old restrictions designed to protect local national markets.

Historically, standards were used to effectively limit market access. Germany protected its beer market from the rest of Europe with a purity law requiring beer sold in Germany to be brewed only from water, hops, malt, and yeast. Italy protected its pasta market by requiring that pasta be made only from durum wheat. Incidentally, the European Court of Justice has struck down both the beer and pasta regulations as trade violations. Such restrictive standards kept competing products, whether from other European countries or elsewhere, out of their respective markets. Skeptics, doubtful that such cultural, legal, and social differences could ever be overcome, held little hope for a unified Europe. Their skepticism has proved wrong. Today, many marvel at how far the European Economic Community has come. While complete integration has not been fully achieved, a review of the structure of the EC, its authority over member states, the Single European Act, the European Economic Area, the Maastricht Treaty, and the Amsterdam Treaty will show why the final outcome of full economic and political integration seems certain.

---

[2] The official name was EEC; however EC (European Community) and European Common Market are names that are often used to refer to the EEC, which is now (1998) known as the European Union.

EXHIBIT 10–1   European Trade Areas—1997*

European Economic Community (EEC)		*European Free-Trade Area (EFTA)*	
Belgium	Italy	Iceland	Norway
Denmark	Luxembourg	Liechtenstein	Switzerland
France	The Netherlands		
Greece	Spain		
Germany	Portugal		
Ireland	United Kingdom		
European Union (EU)		*European Economic Area (EEA)*	
EEC Countries and		EU Countries and	
Austria		Norway	Iceland
Finland	Sweden		
In Membership Negotiations		*Second Tier—Awaiting Evaluation*	
Cyprus	Hungary	Bulgaria	Romania
Czech Republic	Poland	Latvia	Slovakia
Estonia	Slovenia	Lithuania	

* Visit **http://europa.eu.int/** (select Abc and then Agenda 2000 for details on requirements of accession).

The Single European Act.   Exhibit 10–3 illustrates the evolution of the EU from its beginnings after WWII to today. Europe Without Borders, Fortress Europe, and EC 92 refer to the *Single European Act*—the agreement designed to finally remove all barriers to trade and make the European Community a single internal market. The ultimate goal of the Treaty of Rome, the agreement that founded the EC, was economic and political union, a United States of Europe. The Single European Act moved the EC one step closer to the goal of economic integration.

The European Commission, the EC's executive body, began the process toward total unification with a White Paper outlining almost 300 pieces of legislation designed to remove physical, technical, and fiscal barriers between member states. The White Paper was incorporated into the Single European Act, providing for the elimination of internal border controls with corresponding strengthening of external border controls, the unification of technical regulations on product standards, procedures to bring national value-added and excise tax systems among member countries closer together, and free migration of the population. The target date for implementation of this series of economic changes was 1992, hence EC 92. It is important to emphasize that the process begun in 1992 was just the beginning of an evolutionary process that will continue until full integration is achieved.

In addition to dismantling the existing barriers, the Single European Act proposed a wide range of new commercial policies including single European standards, one of the more difficult and time-consuming goals to achieve. Technical standards for electrical products are a good example of how overwhelming the task of achieving universal standards is for the EC. There are 29 types of electrical outlets, 10 types of plugs, and 12 types of cords used by EC member countries. The estimated cost for all EC countries to change wiring systems and electrical standards to a single European standard is 80 billion European Currency Units (ECUs), or about 95 billion U.S. dollars. Because of the time it will take to achieve uniform Euro-standards for health, safety, technical, and other areas, the Single European Act provides for a policy of harmonization and mutual recognition.

Under harmonization, the most essential requirements for protection of health, safety, the environment, and product standards are established. Once these EC-wide essential requirements have been met by all members (i.e., *harmonization*), each member

Map 10-1   The European Economic Area: EU, EFTA, and Associates

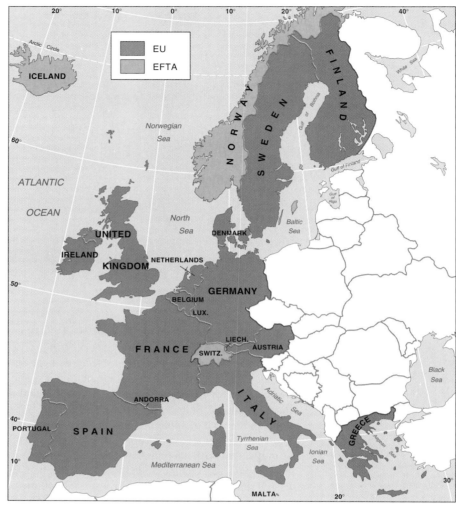

state will be expected to recognize each other's national standards for nonessential characteristics (i.e., *mutual recognition*). In other words, all member countries must adopt the same essential requirements but also accept any different national standards as adequate.

Mutual recognition extends beyond technical or health standards and includes mutual recognition for marketing practices as well. The European Court of Justice's (ECJ) interpretation of Article 30, which establishes the principle of mutual recognition, is that a product put on sale legally in one member state should be available for sale in the same way in all others. The ECJ's landmark decision involved Germany's ban on the sale of Cassis de Dijon, a French liqueur. Germany claimed that selling the low-alcohol drink would encourage alcohol consumption, considered by authorities to be unhealthy. The Court of Justice rejected the argument, ruling that the restriction represented a nontariff barrier outlawed by Article 30. In other words, once Cassis de Dijon was legally sold in France, Germany was obligated, under mutual recognition, to allow it in Germany.

When all the directives are fully implemented, such artificial barriers to trade will be done away with. However, there are still problems to be resolved. Food definition

Exhibit 10–2 European Market Regions

Association	Member	Population (millions)	GDP (U.S. $ billions)	GDP per Capita (U.S. $)	Imports (U.S. $ millions)
European Community (EC)	Belgium	10.1	$ 269.2	$26,653	$ 163,348
	Denmark	5.2	173.3	33,135	43,497
	France	58.0	1,537.9	26,501	274,321
	Germany	81.6	21,126.2	26,044	443,780
	Greece	10.6	114.3	10,785	26,958
	Ireland	3.6	60.4	16,868	32,202
	Italy	57.9	1,070.3	18,482	204,290
	Luxembourg	0.4	12.4	30,244	124,952*
	Netherlands	15.5	395.3	25,584	138,521
	Portugal	10.8	103.7	9,602	32,604
	Spain	39.2	559.2	14,268	114,832
	United Kingdom	58.6	1,106.4	18,880	262,504
European Union (EU)	EC Countries	351.5	7,528.5	21,416	1,861,809
	Austria	8.1	233.3	28,809	67,257
	Finland	5.1	125.0	24,457	28,930
	Sweden	8.8	229.2	25,955	63,422
Central European Free Trade Area (CEFTA)	Czech Republic	10.3	45.7	4,421	23,255
	Hungary	10.2	43.6	4,266	15,483
	Poland	38.6	114.1	2,957	30,370
	Slovakia	5.3	9.3	1,763	9,070

* Includes Luxembourg and Belgium.

Sources: "Indicators of Market Size for 115 Countries," *Crossborder Monitor,* August 27, 1997; and *International Marketing Data and Statistics, 1997* (London: Euromonitor, 1997).

problems in particular have impeded progress in guaranteeing free circulation of food products within the Community. For example, several EC member states maintain different definitions of yogurt, so an EC standard has yet to be established. The French insist that anything called *yogurt* must contain live cultures; thus, they prohibited the sale of a Dutch product under the name *yogurt* because it did not contain live cultures as does the French product. Until a standard for yogurt is established, mutual recognition will not work as intended. There are similar problems elsewhere, especially in the area of health, but the policy of harmonization and mutual recognition will, when fully implemented, eliminate standards as a barrier to trade.

Some of the first and most welcome reforms were the single customs document that replaced the 70 forms originally required for transborder shipments to member countries, the elimination of cabotage rules (which kept a trucker from returning with a loaded truck after delivery), and EC-wide transport licensing. These changes alone were estimated to have reduced distribution costs 50 percent for companies doing cross-border business in the EC.

Approval and adoption of the Single European Act's original 282 directives have been slow. By the end of the first year of the newly formed single market, the Council of Ministers had approved 268 of the 282 directives that make up the Internal Market Program, but only 115 of these laws are in force throughout the member states. Nevertheless, these directives have harmonized or made subject to mutual recognition 100,000 national standards, labeling laws, testing procedures, and consumer-protection measures covering everything from toys to food to stockbroking to teaching. As many as 60,000 customs and tax formalities at frontiers have been scrapped.

A survey showed that there has been considerable benefit from the program over a five-year period. Up to 900,000 jobs have been created, and the gross domestic product of the EU is between 1.1 percent and 1.5 percent higher than it would have been without the effects of the Single European Act. Additionally, price differentials between member

Exhibit 10-3   European Coal and Steel Community to European Union

1951	Treaty of Paris	European Coal and Steel Community (ECSC) (Founding members are Belgium, France, Germany, Italy, Luxembourg, and the Netherlands)
1957	Treaty of Rome	Blueprint for European Economic Community (EEC)
1958	European Economic Community	Ratified by ECSC founding members. Common Market is established
1960	European Free-Trade Area	Established by Austria, Denmark, Norway, Portugal, Sweden, Switzerland, and United Kingdom
1973	Expansion	Denmark, Ireland, and United Kingdom join EEC
1979	European Monetary System	The European Currency Unit (ECU) is created. All members except the UK agree to maintain their exchange rates within specific margins
1981	Expansion	Greece joins EEC
1985	1992 Single Market Program	Introduced to European Parliament "White Paper" for action
1986	Expansion	Spain and Portugal join EEC
1987	Single European Act	Ratified with full implementation by 1992
1992	Treaty on European Union	Also known as Maastricht Treaty. Blueprint for Economic and Monetary Union (EMU)
1993	Europe 1992	Single European Act in force (January 1, 1993)
1993	European Union	Treaty on European Union (Maastricht Treaty) in force with monetary union by 1999
1994	European Economic Area	The EEA was formed with EU members and Norway and Iceland
1995	Expansion	Austria, Finland, and Sweden join EU
1997	Amsterdam Treaty	Established procedures for expansion to Central and Eastern Europe
1999?	Monetary Union	Euro replaces all national banknotes and coins of EMU members

Source: "Chronology of the EU," **http://www.europa.eu.int/** (select Abc). Reprinted with permission from the European Communities.

states have narrowed somewhat.[3] Prior to 1992, the average price differential for consumer goods was 22.5 percent and 33.7 percent for services. These have now fallen to 19.6 percent and 28.6 percent, respectively.

In spite of these successes, the program is still incomplete; several member states are not fully implementing all the measures to which they have agreed.[4] Taxation is an area where reform continues to be necessary. For example, a midsize Mercedes in Haderslev, Denmark, costs $90,000, nearly triple the amount you would pay in Flensburg, Germany, just 30 miles south. Scotch in Sweden has an $18 tax, nine times the amount levied in Italy.[5] The EU Finance Ministers have addressed these issues but not much progress has been made since tax-raising ability is a sacred power of the nation–state. The full implementation of the legislation is expected to take several years. Even though all proposals have not been met, the program for unification has built up a pace that cannot be reversed.

EC Institutions.   The European Community's institutions form a federal pattern with executive, parliamentary, and judicial branches: the European Commission, the Council of Ministers, the European Parliament, and the Court of Justice. Their decision-making processes have legal status and extensive powers in fields covered by common policies. The European Community uses three legal instruments: (1) regulations binding the

---

[3] "Europe's Single Market: Thatcherites in Brussels," *The Economist,* March 15, 1997, p. 32.
[4] "Eye on the EU," *Europe,* April 1997, p. 4.
[5] "Bring On Tax Reform in Europe," *Business Week (International Edition),* July 7, 1997, p. 33.

CROSSING BORDERS 10-2

The Computer Age Has Dawned—If You Have the "Ultimate Connection"

Inspired, I left last month on a trip to the Middle East and Europe, Apple PowerBook 5300 in hand. For two weeks I lugged around this 7.3-pound beast. I also carried four power adapters and a stash of telephone adapters: three-pronged for Jordan; T-shaped for France; one jack for old Israeli buildings; another for new Israeli buildings. I didn't use my PowerBook once the entire trip.

In Paris my modem didn't recognize the strange dial tone. In Jerusalem the hotel phone line was not analog, but digital, which could have fried my modem. In Amman there were no jacks, only a phone cable going straight into a wall.

On my return I tracked down TeleAdapt, Inc., a U.K. firm that does nothing but help folks with laptops communicate from the road. The head of TeleAdapt's U.S. office cheerfully explained that aside from all my adapters, I should also have carried: (1) a thermometer-like instrument to test phone lines for dangerous digital currents; (2) a small box that allows an analog connection on a digital system; (3) a retractable 8.5-foot telephone extension cable; (4) alligator clips, a miniature tool set, and a flashlight to handle phones that are hardwired into the wall (for this I'd have to crawl under the desk, unscrew the telephone faceplate, and attach the clips to the exposed wires); 5) and finally, in case all else fails, an "acoustic coupler" to transmit data through suction cups attached to a telephone receiver. Total cost: about $470.

But I've since learned that even equipped with every product the company sells (TeleAdapt's "Ultimate Connection" pack sells for $950), I wouldn't be all the way out of the woods. Poor phone lines, unexpected interferences, and plain bad luck often conspire to undermine even the best-prepared traveler.

Source: Adapted from Nina Munk, "The Not-So-Virtual Office," *Forbes,* July 23, 1996, p. 37.

member states directly and having the same strength as national laws; (2) directives also binding the member states but allowing them to choose the means of execution; and (3) decisions addressed to a government, an enterprise, or an individual, binding the parties named. Over the years, the Community has gained an increasing amount of authority over its member states.

The European Commission initiates policy and supervises its observance by member states, and it proposes and supervises execution of laws and policies. Commission members act only in the interest of the EC, and their responsibilities are to ensure that the EC rules and the principles of the common market are respected.

The Council of Ministers is the decision-making body of the EC; it is the Council's responsibility to debate and decide which proposals of the Single European Act to accept as binding on EC members. The council can enact into law all proposals by majority vote except for changes in tax rates on products and services, which require unanimous vote. The Council, for example, drafted the Maastricht Treaty that was presented to member states for ratification.

The European Parliament originally had only a consultative role that passed on most community legislation. It can now amend and adopt legislation although it does not have the power to initiate legislation. It also has extensive budgetary powers that allow it to be involved in major EC expenditures.

The European Court of Justice (ECJ) is the Community's Supreme Court. It is responsible for challenging any measures incompatible with the Treaty of Rome and for passing judgment, at the request of a national court, on interpretation or validity of points of EC law. The court's decisions are final and cannot be appealed in national courts. For example, Estee Lauder Cosmetics appealed to the ECJ to overrule a German court's decision to prohibit the company from selling its product called "Clinque." The German court had ruled that the name could mislead German consumers by implying medical treatment. The ECJ pointed out that "Clinque" is sold in other member states without confusing the consumer and ruled in favor of Estee Lauder. This was a landmark case because many member countries had similar laws that were in essence nontariff trade barriers designed to protect their individual markets. If the German court ruling against Estee Lauder had been let to stand, it would have made it difficult for companies to market their products across borders in an identical manner. This is but one example of the ECJ's power in the EC and its role in eliminating nontariff trade barriers.[6]

European Free-Trade Area (EFTA) and European Economic Area (EEA).   Britain, not wanting to join the EEC, conceived the *European Free-Trade Area (EFTA)* for those European nations not willing to join the EEC but wanting to participate in a free-trade area. Britain and other EFTA countries later became members of the European Community in 1973. When Austria, Finland, and Sweden joined the EC in 1985 (Exhibit 10–3) only Iceland, Liechtenstein, Norway, and Switzerland remained in EFTA. EFTA will most probably dissolve as its members join either the EEA or the EU.

Because of the success of the EC and concern that they might be left out of the massive European market, five members of the European Free-Trade Area elected to join the 12 members of the EC in 1994 to form the *European Economic Area (EEA),*[7] a single market with free movement of goods, services, and capital. The EFTA countries joining the EEA adopted most of the EC's competition rules and agreed to implement EC rules on company law; however, they will maintain their domestic farm policies. The EEA is governed by a special Council of Ministers composed of representatives from EEA member nations.

With nearly 400 million consumers and a gross national product of $7 trillion, the EEA is the world's largest consumer market, eclipsing the United States even after the formation of the North American Free Trade Agreement (see Exhibit 10–4). The EEA is a middle ground for those countries that want to be part of the EC's single internal market but do not want to go directly into the EU as full members or do not meet the requirements for full membership. Of the five founding EFTA members of EEA, three joined the EU in 1995. Iceland and Norway chose not to become EU members with the other EFTA countries but did remain members of the EEA. Of the other EFTA members, Switzerland voted against joining the EEA but has formally requested membership in the EU, and Liechtenstein has not joined the EEA or requested admission to the EU.[8] EEA has cooperation agreements and free-trade agreements with several countries, including most of Eastern Europe.

European Union and Maastricht Treaty

The final step in the European Community's march to union was ratification of the Maastricht Treaty. The treaty provided for the Economic and Monetary Union (EMU) and European Union (EU). The Treaty touched on all the missing links needed for a truly European political union, including foreign policy. Because procedures on how foreign policy and social legislation decisions are to be made are so complex, another round of negotiations that was concluded in the Amsterdam Treaty was necessary. Ini-

---

[6] For additional explanation of the institutions of the EU, visit **http://www.europa.eu.int/** (select Institutions).

[7] Sweden, Finland, and Austria later joined the 12 members of the EC to form the EU.

[8] For details on the EFTA and EEA visit **http://www.efta.int/**.

CROSSING BORDERS 10–3

There Are Myths and Then There Are Euromyths

The Austrians feared the EU would force them to eat chocolate made with blood. The French worried about EU plans to ban certain maggots as bait because they suffer "le stresse" on a fishing hook. Italians complained about a fanciful plan to paint all taxis white. Others feared the EU would require nudity on beaches. And the Germans wrung their hands over a nonexistent edict changing the size of trashcans. Brussels sprouted an edict on sexual harassment that struck down Valentine's Day cards. Now the EU wants to do away with Britain's beloved double-decker buses and pull-chain toilets, and classify carrots as fruit. In addition, Brussels outlawed asymmetrical Christmas trees and pronounced that donkeys must wear diapers. By the time EU packaging rules criminalized the curved cucumber, it was clear that the Eurocrats had clearly lost their senses.

"There Is No Absurdity of Which the European Community Is Not Capable," "The Whole Thing Has Turned into a Mad, Bureaucratic Alice in Wonderland Crossed with Kafka," blared the headlines. Yet what is really Kafkaesque is that each of these stories has only a remote relationship to reality. The EU calls them "Euromyths."

The EU didn't actually ban skiing when snow is less than 20 centimeters deep—but the European Parliament did raise the possibility of such a prohibition. Brussels didn't require donkeys to wear diapers on Euro-beaches, but it won't award its Blue Flag to beaches that admit the animals.

Curved cucumbers aren't banned, just classified differently for packaging reasons. The guidelines lay down a "maximum height of arc, 10 mm per 10 cm length of cucumber." Because "if you have straight cucumbers, it's possible to know how many you are getting in a box," is the official EU justification. Symmetrical Christmas trees? A trade association, not the EU, proposed something like this. Carrots are classified as fruit, since this allows the Portuguese to continue their practice of making carrot jam.

Some myths are completely fanciful, like the one about the EU banning square gin bottles; this started as an April Fool's joke in the *Times*. Also in this category is the Valentine's Day warning that the sending of unwanted cards could qualify as sexual harassment under EU law; it was meant to be "tongue in cheek."

The EU blames the British press for 80 percent of Euromyths. Coupled with politicians' perennial hostility toward the EU, the myths seem to be the latest way to express centuries of hostility, particularly toward Germany and France, the drivers of European unity.

So the EU has hired grown men and women to spend their days reassuring an alarmed public that the EU has no plans to do away with paperboys, small bananas, knotty oak trees, saucy postcards, and any pizza that isn't 11 inches in diameter.

Sources: Adapted from Dana Milbank, "Will Unified Europe Put Mules in Diapers and Ban Mini-Pizza?" *The Wall Street Journal*, June 22, 1995, p.1; and Peter Popham and Scott Hughes, "Could This Banana Be Straighter?" *The Independent-London*, February 2, 1996, p.4.

tially, there was considerable doubt about the viability of a European Union. Surrendering more sovereignty beyond that already relinquished with the provisions of the Single European Act seemed too extreme for many. There was concern that monetary union would move monetary policy away from the individual countries to a central power. And even more sovereignty would be lost as the Court of Justice gained more power over business transactions. However, within months of the ratification of the treaty, the EU was expanded to include Austria, Finland, and Sweden—all members of the EEA. Norway voted not to join the EU but remains as a member of the European Economic

EXHIBIT 10–4   **A Comparison of the EU and NAFTA**

Association	Population (millions)	GNP ($millions)	Imports† ($millions)	Exports† ($millions)
EU*	373.5	8,180	1,899,466	1,927,914
NAFTA	387.4	8,061	1,014,211	852,536

* Includes 15 countries.

† Includes intramember trade.

Source: "Indicators of Market Size for 115 Countries," *Crossborder Monitor,* August 27, 1997; and *International Marketing Data and Statistics, 1997* (London: Euromonitor, 1997).

Area. Much of the concern persists even as the Economic and Monetary Union is put into place.

Economic and Monetary Union (EMU).   The EMU, a provision of the Maastricht Treaty, established the parameters of the creation of a common currency for the EU, the Euro, and established a timetable for its implementation.[9] By 2002, a central bank will be established; conversion rates will be fixed; circulation of Euro banknotes and coins will begin; and the legal tender status of participating members' banknotes and coins will be cancelled.[10] To participate, members must meet strict limits on several financial and economic criteria including a member's national deficit, debt, and inflation. At this writing, Finland, Ireland, Germany, France, Belgium, Luxembourg, and the Netherlands seem sure to be part of the EMU zone. Britain, Sweden, and Denmark have elected to wait until sometime later to participate, while the other EU members will be admitted when they meet the criteria.[11]

Predictions about the impact of the Euro range from its high costs and economic and political risk to its positive long-term impact. It is considered to be one of the most important economic events in postwar European history that will have a positive long-term impact, albeit a negative effect on economic growth in the short run.[12] The cost for changing over to Euros will be high for members as well as companies. As an example of the cost a company will incur to convert to Euros, Philips, the Dutch-based MNC, has 35 groups involving about 250 people under a steering committee of 35 senior managers working to convert all intercompany transactions to Euros and issue its annual report in Euros by 1999.[13] All EU-based companies will have to convert as Philips is doing and companies operating in the EU will have to convert prices, billing, and so forth as the Euro will be the currency of the "realm."

Treaty of Amsterdam

The *Treaty of Amsterdam,* concluded in 1997, addressed some of the issues left undone in the Maastricht Treaty. It identifies the priority measures needed to bring the single market fully into effect and to lay a solid foundation for both the single currency and the enlargement into central and Eastern Europe.[14] The treaty's four objectives are: (1) to place employment and citizens' rights at the heart of the Union; (2) to sweep away the

---

[9] "Introducing the Euro," *Business Europe,* June 18, 1997, p. 3.

[10] This schedule could change as several prior dates have. However, this is the plan at this writing. See **http://europa.eu.int/euro/**. See also Helene Cooper, "Bureaucrats Drug Their Feet on Euro," *The Wall Street Journal,* February 3, 1998, p. A18.

[11] Samuel Brittan, "Some EMU Surprises," *Financial Times,* February 5, 1998, p. 18.

[12] Wolfgang Munchau, "Economic Impact: Predictions of Widespread Risk and Reward," *Financial Times Limited,* May 26, 1997, p. 6.

[13] "Euro Conversion to Cost a Fortune," *The Associated Press,* October 22, 1997.

[14] "One More Heave," *Business Europe,* May 7, 1997, p. 1.

Scenes from a unified Europe: (1) in school, (2) on the road, (3) across borders, (4) in the European Parliament. (All photos courtesy European Commission Delegation, Washington, D.C.)

last remaining obstacles to freedom of movement and to strengthen security; (3) to give Europe a stronger voice in world affairs; and (4) to make the union's institutional structure more efficient with a view to enlarging the Union.[15]

The original 40-year-old operating rules were proving to be inadequate in dealing with the problems that confront the EU today. Expansion beyond its present 15 members (Exhibit 10–1 lists countries applying for membership), managing the conversion to the Euro and EMU, and speaking with one voice on foreign policy that directly affects the European continent are all issues that require greater agreement among members and thus more responsibility and authority to the institutions of the EU. The Amsterdam Treaty increases the authority of the institutions of the EU and is designed to accommodate the changes brought about by the monetary union and the new members to be admitted in the next decade.

Strategic Implications for Marketing in Europe

The complexion of the entire world marketplace has been changed significantly by the coalition of nations into multinational market groups. To international business firms, multinational groups spell opportunity in bold letters through access to greatly enlarged markets with reduced or abolished country-by-country tariff barriers and restrictions. Production, financing, labor, and marketing decisions are affected by the remapping of the world into market groups.

---

[15] Details can be found in "The Four Major Objectives of the New Treaty for Europe," at **http:// europa.eu.int/** (select Abc). The complete draft of the Treaty can be found at **http://ue.eu.int/ Amsterdam/en/treaty/main.htm/**.

World competition will intensify as businesses become stronger and more experienced in dealing with large market groups. European and non-European multinationals are preparing to deal with the changes in competition in a fully integrated Europe. In an integrated Europe, U.S. multinationals may have an initial advantage over expanded European firms because U.S. businesses are more experienced in marketing to large, diverse markets and are accustomed to looking at Europe as one market. The advantage, however, is only temporary as mergers, acquisitions, and joint ventures consolidate operations of European firms in anticipation of the benefits of a single European market. Individual national markets will still confront international managers with the same problems of language, customs, and instability, even though they are packaged under the umbrella of a common market. However, as barriers come down and multicountry markets are treated as one common market, a global market will be one notch closer to reality.

Regulation of business activities has been intensified throughout multinational market groups; each group now has management and administrative bodies specifically concerned with business. In the process of structuring markets, rules and regulations common to the group are often more sophisticated than those of the individual countries. Many non-EC countries see such activities as creating a "Fortress Europe" and, in effect, making marketing entry into a single European market more difficult than entering the member countries individually. Despite the problems and complexities of dealing with the new markets, the overriding message to the astute international marketer continues to be opportunity and profit potential.

Opportunities.   Economic integration creates large mass markets for the marketer. Many national markets, too small to bother with individually, take on new dimensions and significance when combined with markets from cooperating countries. Large markets are particularly important to businesses accustomed to mass production and mass distribution because of the economies of scale and marketing efficiencies that can be achieved. In highly competitive markets, the benefits derived from enhanced efficiencies are often passed along as lower prices that lead to increased purchasing power.

Most multinational groups have coordinated programs to foster economic growth as part of their cooperative effort. Such programs work to the advantage of marketers by increasing purchasing power, improving regional infrastructure, and fostering economic development. Despite the problems that are sure to occur because of integration, the economic benefits from free trade can be enormous. One study showed that the EC countries lost at least $250 billion a year as a result of market barriers that impeded productivity and competitiveness. Quotas, border restrictions, and excessive documentation alone are estimated to have cost nearly 7 percent of the value of goods traded annually—in essence, a tax comparable to the average tariff existing on all trade among industrialized countries.

Major savings also will result from the billions of dollars now spent in developing different versions of products to meet a hodgepodge of national standards. Philips and other European companies invested a total of $20 billion to develop a common switching system for Europe's 10 different telephone networks. This compares with the $3 billion spent in the United States for a common system and $1.5 billion in Japan for a single system.

Market Barriers.   The initial aim of a multinational market is to protect businesses that operate within its borders. An expressed goal is to give an advantage to the companies within the market in their dealings with other countries of the market group. Analysis of the intraregional and international trade patterns of the market groups indicates that such goals have been achieved. Intra-EU imports now account for 67.9 percent of total manufacturing imports compared to 61.2 percent before the 1992 program began. Intra-EU service imports also have increased somewhat, from 49.6 percent of the total to 50 percent. This increase of trade among the member states has not been at the expense of third countries.

CROSSING BORDERS 10–4

What a Single Market Means to One Industry: Come In, If You Can!

European standards recently imposed on electronic goods have effectively wiped out the export business of a Connecticut company. The cost of servicing the standards, known as "CE mark" regulations, has caused a manufacturer of high-tech audio conferencing equipment to discontinue European exports, which used to represent nearly 10 percent of the company's growing business. Each type of audio- or video-conferencing unit manufactured must be separately tested to meet the new European standards—at a cost of $4,000 to $5,000 per test.

U.S. manufacturers of electronic or electrical operated products being exported into the 15-nation European Union (EU), as well as Switzerland and Norway, are required to prove product conformance to safety requirements developed in Brussels by the Committee of European Electrotechnical Standards (CENELEC). The products must bear a CE mark to prove they have been adequately tested to meet EU mandates over electromagnetic emissions and susceptibility to emissions. Compliance cannot be established by reliance on U.S. marks such as UL (Underwriters Labs).

The European Union's CE mark regulations can be burdensome. First, U.S. manufacturers must determine which of more than 30 CE directives so far enacted may apply to their products. Second, depending on the type of certification necessary, the manufacturers must establish whether they can certify the goods themselves, or whether they must submit the products to an EU-authorized laboratory for testing. Third, before the tested product can be sold in the EU, documentation demonstrating the efficacy of the testing must be submitted to the appropriate trade agency or sales agent within the EU and each product unit must bear the official CE mark. Based on the complexity of a given product, it can cost from $6,000 to more than $20,000 to receive certification, certainly a burden on smaller companies. A large company can hire a consulting firm to handle the process but, for the smaller business that cannot afford a consultant, it can be a profit-consuming investment.

In one respect, the directives should make it easier for U.S. manufacturers to do business with Europe. Before the standards were adapted, manufacturers were faced with conflicting standards for each of the 15 countries; now one standard can be utilized for the entire European Union. The CE marking represents the first time manufacturers have been forced to meet requirements, since the old standard systems were seldom enforced by any of the various countries.

U.S. manufacturers often are confounded by the EU directives because of differences in philosophy between the two nations. The focus of American safety standards is on fire protection, while the European standards are based on preventing electrical shock.

Sources: Adapted from Timothy Aeppel, "Europe's 'Unity' Undoes a U.S. Exporter," *The Wall Street Journal,* April 1, 1996, p. B1; and Don Dzikowsi, "European Standards Too Costly for Small Businesses to Meet," *Fairfield County Business Journal,* November 4, 1996, p.1.

Extra-EU manufacturing imports have increased their share of EU markets from 12 to 14 percent since the beginning of the single market. Although these changes seem modest, one must appreciate that the program is not fully implemented. With the strengthening of the various institutions of the EU by the Amsterdam Treaty, substantial progress in implementing the directives should occur over the next few years.

Companies willing to invest in production facilities in multinational markets may benefit from protectionist measures as they become a part of the market. Exporters, however, are in a considerably weaker position. This prospect confronts many U.S. exporters who are faced with the possible need to invest in Europe to protect their export markets in the European Community. Trade barriers are always a possibility but the major problem for the small company may be adjusting to the EU standards. A company selling in one or two EU member countries and meeting standards there may find itself in a situation of having to change standards or be closed out when an EU-wide standard is adopted.

A manufacturer of hoses used to hook up deep-fat fryers and other gas appliances to gas outlets faced such a problem when one of its largest customers informed the company that McDonald's was told it could no longer use his hoses in its British restaurants. The same thing happened in EuroDisney. Unfortunately, when the common standards were written, only large MNCs and European firms participated, so they had the benefit of setting a standard to their benefit. The small company has only one choice: change or leave. In this particular case, it appears that competitors are working to keep the company out of the market. There are, however, enough questions about threaded fittings and compatibility that the company is working with individual countries to gain entrance to their markets—just like it was before a single market existed.[16]

The prospect of Europe as one unified internal market has many countries concerned about the EC becoming Fortress Europe—free trade within but highly protectionist to all others. In fact, there is considerable concern that reactions to a single European market by other major trading countries will lead to the creation of regional trading blocs in Europe, East Asia, and North America. As regional trading blocs evolve, the fear is that external tariffs among these blocs will further close their borders to non-trading-bloc members. NAFTA is seen as a trading bloc that could develop protectionist barriers so that businesses outside the group will face ever-intensifying competition for markets within the bloc. Concern for such possibilities may be a major reason why the EU has established a trade link with the Mercosur alliance and is expected to sign a free-trade accord in 1999. European businesses also are taking a large stake throughout Latin America. In Brazil, for example, seven out of the 10 largest supermarkets are European-owned, while just two are U.S.-owned. European firms also are landing major contracts to rebuild South America's infrastructure. Spain's Telefonica de España has spent $5 billion buying telephone companies in Brazil, Chile, Peru, and Argentina.[17] At the same time, U.S. firms are investing heavily in the EU.

The European Commission strongly denies the possibilities of a Fortress Europe and insists that access by outsiders to their common market will not become more difficult than it is now; nevertheless, concerns remain in many countries, especially Japan. In recent trade talks with European Commission members, the Japanese envoy worried that the removal of barriers to internal EC trade could be accompanied by moves to keep out imports from non-EC members. The United States also expressed these same reservations. Will the rules under the Single European Act deny foreign financial institutions, automakers, and others equal market access to Europe? One study indicated that more than 40 percent of Japanese manufacturers felt that aspects of EU integration favor European firms. However, there were others who felt that they stood to benefit from the single market. Reaction from the Japanese is a wait-and-see attitude. It is too early to know whether or not such barriers will materialize. Only when the EU has adjusted to the Euro and new directives and it focuses more on external trade will it be apparent if issues of protectionism arise.

Reciprocity.   Reciprocity is an important part of the trade policy of a unified Europe. If a country does not open its markets to an EC firm, it cannot expect to have access to

---

[16] Timothy Aeppel, "Europe's Unity Undoes a U.S. Exporter," *The Wall Street Journal,* April 1, 1996, p. B1.

[17] Ian Katz, "Is Europe Elbowing the U.S. Out of South America?" *Business Week,* August 4, 1997, p. 18.

the EC market. Europeans see reciprocity as a fair and equitable way of allowing foreign companies to participate in the European market without erecting trade barriers, while at the same time giving Europeans equal access to foreign markets.

There are strong feelings that the Japanese market is not equally accessible to foreign firms and reciprocity addresses such inequities. The community will not grant trade concessions to Japan if Japan fails to reciprocate for European exporters. The desire by some Europeans to force reciprocity on the Japanese was best explained by one who observed, "This time the game will not pit Japan against an individual European country, to be picked off, as was often the case in the past"; now there will be 15 countries with which to deal. Reciprocity is to be directed to all outsiders. A French government-sponsored advertisement on TV captured the European attitude. As the advertisement opens, "a skinny French boxer is squaring off to battle a giant American football player and a menacing Japanese sumo wrestler. Suddenly several buddies—the rest of the EC, of course—rush to his side, and the aggressors turn away."

Marketing Mix Implications

Companies are adjusting their marketing mix strategies to reflect anticipated market differences in a single European market. In the past, companies often charged different prices in different European markets. Nontariff barriers between member states supported price differentials and kept lower-priced products from entering those markets where higher prices were charged. Colgate-Palmolive Company has adapted its Colgate toothpaste into a single formula for sale across Europe at one price. Before changing its pricing practices, Colgate sold its toothpaste at different prices in different markets. Beddedas Shower Gel, for example, is priced in the middle of the market in Germany and as a high-priced product in the United Kingdom. As long as products from lower-priced markets could not move to higher-priced markets, such differential price schemes worked. Now, however, under the EC rules, companies cannot prevent the free movement of goods, and parallel imports from lower-priced markets to higher-priced markets are more apt to occur. Price standardization among country markets will be one of the necessary changes to avoid the problem of parallel imports. With the adoption of the Euro, price differentials will be much easier to spot.[18] And, from the consumer's viewpoint, it will be easier to search for brand-name products at the best bargains. Further, the Euro will make marketing on the Internet a much simpler task for the European than it presently is.[19]

In addition to initiating uniform pricing policies, companies are reducing the number of brands they produce to focus advertising and promotion efforts. For example, Nestlé's current three brands of yogurt in the EC will be reduced to a single brand. A major benefit from an integrated Europe is competition at the retail level. Europe lacks an integrated and competitive distribution system that would support small and midsize outlets. The elimination of borders could result in increased competition among retailers and the creation of Europe-wide distribution channels. Retail giants like France's Carrefour and Germany's Aldi groups are planning huge hypermarkets with big advertising budgets. This could spell the slow death of shopkeepers and midsize retailers who today dominant most European countries.

Ensuring EC Market Entry

Whether or not the European Community will close its doors to outsiders, firms that want to be competitive in the EC will have to establish a presence there. There are four

[18] Thomas Kamm, "A Common Currency in Europe Will Bring Big Changes to Many," *The Wall Street Journal,* March 24, 1997, p. A1.

[19] Allyson L. Stewart-Allen, "How the 'Euro' Will Affect Marketing," *Marketing News,* September 1, 1997, p. 6.

levels of involvement that a firm may have vis-a-vis the EC: (1) firms based in Europe with well-established manufacturing and distribution operations in several European countries; (2) firms with operations in a single EC country; (3) firms that export manufactured goods to the EC from an offshore location; and (4) firms that have not actively exported to EC countries. The strategies for effective competitiveness in the EC are different for each type of firm.

Firms in the first level, those that are fully established in several EC countries with local manufacturing, are the best positioned. However, the competitive structure will change under a single Europe. Marketers will have to exploit the opportunities of greater efficiencies of production and distribution that result from lowering the barriers. They will also have to deal with increased competition from European firms as well as other MNCs that will be aggressively establishing market positions.

A third area of change will require companies to learn how their customers are changing and, thus, how best to market to them. European retailers and wholesalers as well as industrial customers are merging, expanding, and taking steps to ensure their success in this larger market. Nestlé has bought Rowntree, a United Kingdom candy maker, and Britone, the Italian food conglomerate, to strengthen its ties to EC market firms. European banking is also going through a stage of mergers. In one 18-month period, 400 banks and finance firms merged, took stock in one another, or devised joint marketing ventures to sell stocks, mutual funds, insurance, or other financial instruments. These mergers are viewed as necessary to compete with Japanese, U.S., and Swiss financial institutions.

Firms in the second level, those with operations in one European country, are vulnerable as barriers come down and competitors enter the companies' market. For a firm in this situation the biggest problem is not being large enough to withstand the competition from outside the country. The answer is either to become larger or withdraw. There are several choices for this firm: expand through acquisition or merger, enter a strategic alliance with a second company, or expand the company beyond being a local single-country firm to being a pan-European competitor.

The EC and the difficulty of maintaining a significant market share from offshore will face the firm in the third level, an exporter to European markets from a non-European source. This exporter also must deal with the prospects of protectionistic measures. It is this type that will be most susceptible to the principle of reciprocity. Other than continuing business as usual with hopes that things will not change, this firm's alternatives are: establish a European marketing branch (although this may give them a better marketing presence in Europe, it will not exclude the firm from protectionism), acquire a European company, or enter a strategic alliance.

The fourth level, companies with no business in the EC, are the most vulnerable. Even if they stay in their home market they face competition from firms whose experience in global markets will outdistance their ability to remain competitive. Unfortunately, even with a comfortable position in a home market, there is no guarantee against competition from foreign firms. These firms have only one alternative and that is to become involved in global marketing.

The Commonwealth of Independent States (CIS)

In addition to the EU, Europe has two other trade groups that have emerged since the dissolution of the USSR: the Commonwealth of Independent States (CIS) and the Central European Free-Trade Area (CEFTA). The series of events after the aborted coup of Mikhail Gorbachev led to the complete dissolution of the USSR.[20] The first to declare

---

[20] The 12 republics of the former USSR, collectively referred to as the Newly Independent States (NIS), are: Russia, Ukraine, Belarus (formerly Byelorussia), Armenia, Moldova (formerly Moldavia), Azerbaijan, Uzbekistan, Turkmenistan, Tajikistan, Kazakhstan, Kyrgystan (formerly Kirghiziya), and Georgia. These same countries are also members of the CIS.

independence were the Baltic states, which quickly gained recognition by several Western nations. The remaining 12 republics of the former USSR, collectively known as the Newly Independent States (NIS), regrouped into the *Commonwealth of Independent States (CIS)* (see Map 10–2).

The CIS is a loose economic and political alliance with open borders but no central government. The main provisions of the commonwealth agreement are to: (1) repeal all Soviet laws and assume the powers of the old regimes; (2) launch radical economic reforms, including freeing most prices; (3) keep the ruble, but allow new currencies; (4) establish a European Community-style free-trade association; (5) create joint control of nuclear weapons; and (6) fulfill all Soviet foreign treaties and debt obligations.

The 12 members of the CIS share a common history of central planning, and their close cooperation could make the change to a market economy less painful, but differences over economic policy, currency reform, and control of the military may break them apart. How the CIS will be organized and its ultimate importance is anyone's guess.

The three Slavic republics of Russia, Ukraine, and Belarus have interests and history in common, as do the five Central Asian Republics. But the ties between these two core groups of the CIS are tenuous and stem mainly from their former Soviet membership. The three Slavic republics are discussing the establishment of an organization modeled on the European Union to succeed the Commonwealth of Independent States. Kazakhstan and other former Soviet republics may join, which would create a trade bloc that includes most of the former Soviet Union. Moscow would dominate since Russia far outweighs the others in military might and economic resources.[21] Leaders in these countries see reintegration with the Russian economy as the best shot at salvaging falling standards of living; however, Russian behavior may be the cause of disarray in the CIS. As one foreign minister commented, "Moscow is behaving itself as if nothing has changed since the USSR's collapse." It is acting like it has no obligation to the CIS and treats the CIS as its "backyard" rather than as an organization of which it is only one member.

The CIS is by no means coming apart, although it has not solidified to the point that it might not change its membership and purpose.[22] Should the CIS or some variation not survive, many believe the NIS countries may realign in a different pattern. Moldovia may find a natural ally in Romania. Central Asian republics could be drawn toward successful Islamic models such as Turkey. Further east, Kazakhstan could gravitate toward China, from which it has solicited economic advice. Or, if the economic union between Ukraine, Russia, and Belarus does not materialize, Russia, Ukraine, and Kazakhstan, the largest and richest republics, might go it alone as separate countries.

Of all the former republics, Azerbaijan, Georgia, and Armenia have done best economically since leaving the former USSR. After the USSR collapsed, their economies had all imploded to less than half their peak size during Soviet days. Now, however, they are showing sustained signs of commercial renewal. Their economies are all growing at modest rates and inflation has been kept under control.[23]

Central European Free-Trade Area (CEFTA)

The newest free-trade area in Europe is the six-member Central European Free-Trade Area (CEFTA), organized in 1993 by Poland, Hungary, Slovakia, and the Czech Republic and joined by Slovenia and Romania in 1997.[24] Import duties initially were removed

---

[21] Therese Raphael, "Russia's Un-neighborly Relations," *The Wall Street Journal Europe,* September 11, 1997, p. 8.

[22] Oleg Stepanenko, "Commonwealth Requires Overhaul," *Russian Press Digest,* December 2, 1997, p. 4.

[23] Hugh Pope, "Caucasus Awakes from Post-Soviet Nightmare," *The Wall Street Journal,* July 24, 1997, p. A14.

[24] "Romania Signs Central European Free Trade Accord," *Xinhua English Newswire,* April 12, 1997.

MAP 10-2   The Newly Independent States (NIS)

from 60 percent of items, and there was a commitment to abolish all duties and quotas within five years. Unlike the CIS, CEFTA has been successful in its plan to remove barriers to trade. Since 1996, approximately 80 percent of industrial exports among CEFTA members have been duty-free, and in 1997 all tariffs were abolished, except for the Polish auto industry which has an exemption until 2002. Progress in liberalizing agricultural goods had been slower although the goal is to eliminate tariffs completely by 2001.[25]

Economically, CEFTA has been a success story: Tariffs reductions are on schedule and there has been growth in the gross domestic product (GDP), falling unemployment, and a slowdown of inflationary trends for all members of the association.[26] Since all six member–states have requested admission to the EU, CEFTA really serves as a vehicle to get their economies to a level that will allow accession to the EU. Exhibit 10–1 indicates the order that each country will be considered for admission to the EU.

The Americas

The Americas, the second Triad region, have as their center the United States. Within the Americas, the United States, Canada, Central America, and South America have been natural if sometimes contentious trading partners. As in Europe, the Americas are engaged in all sorts of economic cooperative agreements, with NAFTA being the most significant.

---

[25] "CEFTA Leaders/Summit—3: Seek Further Tariff Reductions," *Dow Jones International News,* September 13, 1997.

[26] "GDP Grows, Unemployment Falls in CEFTA Countries," *Czech News Agency,* August 6, 1997, p. 4.

North American Free-Trade Area (NAFTA)

Preceding the creation of the *North American Free-Trade Area (NAFTA)*, the United States and Canada had the world's largest bilateral trade agreement; each was the other's largest trading partner. Despite this unique commercial relationship, tariff and other trade barriers hindered even greater commercial activity. To further support trade activity, the two countries established the *United States–Canada Free-Trade Area (CFTA)*, designed to eliminate all trade barriers between the two countries. The CFTA created a single, continental, commercial market for all goods and most services. The agreement between the United States and Canada was not a customs union such as the European Community; no economic or political union of any kind was involved. It provided only for the elimination of tariffs and other trade barriers.

The agreement removed barriers to trade and investment for most industrial, agricultural, and service sectors. Products were grouped into three categories for removal of tariffs, some for immediate elimination and others gradually eliminated over five and ten years. After being in effect for more than three years, evidence showed that the provisions of the agreement were being met or exceeded. CFTA was, however, to be short lived.

Shortly after both countries had ratified the CFTA, Mexico announced that it would seek free trade with the United States. Mexico's overtures were answered positively by the United States, and talks on a U.S.–Mexico free-trade area began. Canada, initially ambivalent about joining, agreed to participate and the talks were expanded to a North American Free-Trade Area—involving Canada, the United States, and Mexico. CFTA became the model after which NAFTA was designed.

Mexico and the United States have been strong trading partners for decades but Mexico had never officially expressed an interest in a free trade agreement until the President of Mexico, Carlos Salinas de Gortari, announced that Mexico would seek such an agreement with the United States. Since earlier overtures to Mexico from the U.S. had been rebuffed, Salinas' announcement was a surprise to Americans and Mexicans alike. However, those watching the changes in Mexico under Salinas were less surprised; a transformation in Mexico began shortly after Salinas came to office. Suffering from massive foreign debt and inflation, the first signal of change came when Mexico joined the General Agreement on Tariffs and Trade (GATT), a move its leaders had opposed earlier. Salinas then gutted Mexico's bureaucracy and sold more than 1,000 state-owned companies, from steel mills to the telephone company; cut tariffs that averaged 100 percent to an average of 10 percent; and privatized the banks. Mexico was on the move, readying itself to become a partner in the North American Free-Trade Area.

Despite the disparity between Mexico's economy and the economies of the other two countries, there are sound reasons for such an alliance. Canada is a sophisticated industrial economy, resource-rich, but with a small population and domestic market. Mexico, on the other hand, desperately needs investment, technology, exports, and other economic reinforcement to spur its economy. Even though Mexico has an abundance of oil and a rapidly growing population, the number of new workers is increasing faster than its economy can create new jobs. The United States needs resources (especially oil) and, of course, markets. The three need each other to compete more effectively in world markets, and they need mutual assurances that their already dominant trading positions in each other's markets are safe from protection pressures. When the NAFTA agreement was ratified and became effective in 1994, a single market of 360 million peoples with a $6 trillion GNP emerged.

NAFTA requires the three countries to remove all tariffs and barriers to trade over 15 years, but each country will have its own tariff arrangements with nonmember countries. All changes already occurring under CFTA will stand and be built on under the NAFTA agreement. Some of the key provisions of the agreement follow.

Market Access.   Within 10 years of implementation, all tariffs will be eliminated on North American industrial products traded between Canada, Mexico, and the United

States. All trade between Canada and the U.S. not already duty free will be duty free by 1998 as provided for in CFTA. Mexico will immediately eliminate tariffs on nearly 50 percent of all industrial goods imported from the U.S., and remaining tariffs will be phased out entirely within 15 years.

Nontariff Barriers.   In addition to elimination of tariffs, Mexico will eliminate nontariff barriers and other trade-distorting restrictions. U.S. exporters will benefit immediately from the removal of most import licenses that have acted as quotas essentially limiting the importation of products into the Mexican market. NAFTA also eliminates a host of other Mexican barriers such as local content, local production, and export performance requirements that have limited U.S. exports.

Rules of Origin.   NAFTA reduces tariffs only for goods made in North America. Tough rules of origin will determine whether goods qualify for preferential tariff treatment under NAFTA. Rules of origin are designed to prevent "free riders" from benefiting through minor processing or transshipment of non-NAFTA goods. For example, Japan could not assemble autos in Mexico and avoid U.S. or Canadian tariffs and quotas unless the auto had a specific percentage of Mexican (i.e., North American) content. For goods to be traded duty free, they must contain substantial (62.5 percent) North American content. Since NAFTA rules of origin have been strengthened, clarified, and simplified over those contained in the U.S.-Canada Free Trade Agreement, they supersede the CFTA rules. Exhibit 10–5 gives a brief picture of how rules of origin work.

Customs Administration.   Under NAFTA, Canada, Mexico, and the U.S. have agreed to implement uniform customs procedures and regulations. Uniform procedures ensure that exporters who market their products in more than one NAFTA country will not have to adapt to multiple customs procedures. Most procedures governing rules of origin documentation record keeping and origin verification will be the same for all three NAFTA countries. In addition, the three will issue advanced rulings, on request, on whether or not a product qualifies for tariff preference under the NAFTA rules of origin.

Investment.   NAFTA will eliminate investment conditions that restrict the trade of goods and service to Mexico. Among conditions eliminated are the requirements that foreign investors export a given level or percentage of goods or services, use domestic

---

EXHIBIT 10–5   How NAFTA Rules of Origin Work

Each product has a rule of origin that applies to it. The rules are organized according to the Harmonized System (HS) classification of the product. There are two types of rules; both require substantial North American processing, but they measure it differently.

Rule Type	Description	Example
Tariff-Shift Rule	Non-NAFTA imports undergo sufficient manufacture or processing to become products that can qualify under a different tariff classification.	Wood pulp (HS Chapter 47) imported from outside North America is processed into paper (HS Chapter 48) within North America. The wood pulp has been transformed within NAFTA to a product eligible for distribution within NAFTA. In other words, the tariff classification shifted from HS Chapter 47 to HS Chapter 48.
Value-Content Rule	A set percentage of the value of the good must be North American (usually coupled with a tariff classification shift requirement). Some goods are subject to the value-content rule only when they fail to pass the tariff classification shift test because of non-NAFTA imputs.	If perfume (HS #3303), for example, fails the applicable tariff classification shift rule, it must contain 50–60 percent (depending on the valuation method) North American content in order to get preferential tariff treatment.

goods or services, transfer technology to competitors, or limit imports to a certain percentage of exports.

Services.   NAFTA establishes the first comprehensive set of principles governing services trade. U.S. and Canadian financial institutions are permitted to open wholly-owned subsidiaries in Mexico, and all restrictions on the services they offer will be lifted by the year 2000. U.S. and Canadian trucking companies are able to carry international cargo into Mexican border states and, by 1999, they will be able to truck throughout Mexico.

Intellectual Property.   NAFTA will provide the highest standards of protection of intellectual property available in any bilateral or international agreement. The agreement covers patents, trademarks, copyrights, and trade secrets, semiconductor integrated circuits, and copyrights for North American movies, computer software, and records.

Government Procurement.   NAFTA guarantees businesses fair and open competition for procurement in North America through transparent and predictable procurement procedures. In Mexico, Pemex (the national oil company), CFE (the national electric company), and other government-owned enterprises will be open to U.S. and Canadian suppliers.

Standards.   NAFTA prohibits the use of standards and technical regulations used as obstacles to trade. However, NAFTA provisions do not require the United States or Canada to lower existing health, environmental, or safety regulations, nor does NAFTA require the importation of products that fail to meet each country's health and safety standards.

NAFTA: A Progress Report

NAFTA is a comprehensive trade agreement that addresses, and in most cases improves, all aspects of doing business within North America. The elimination of trade and investment barriers among Canada, Mexico, and the United States creates one of the largest and richest markets in the world. However, NAFTA has its detractors and it is safe to say that there has been constant turmoil since its inception—namely, Mexico had a serious financial crisis that led to the devaluation of the peso, and the expansion of NAFTA became a political hot potato in the United States. While none of its members has advocated dropping NAFTA, it did appear that the United States administration directed its attention elsewhere and did not follow through to the second stage—expansion beyond Mexico. There was also a political setback in 1997 when President Clinton sought fast-track authorization that postponed any expansion of NAFTA until 1998, if then.

Depending on the source, NAFTA has been a "wash," a costly creator of deep U.S. trade deficits and job losses, or a modest success. In fact, a survey taken three years after its beginning revealed that 67 percent of the Mexicans surveyed believe that Mexico had had little or no success with NAFTA. In another study, 57 percent of U.S. citizens said they are against any new trade pacts with Latin American countries.[27] It is difficult to evaluate the success or failure of NAFTA because all the provisions will not be in place until 2008. Further, those companies and industries that are adversely affected by lowering tariffs and opening the U.S. market to Mexican and Canadian goods have not had time to adjust to the new trading environment. The problems that NAFTA members have experienced should not be viewed as failure; as history has shown in Europe, it takes time to form a common market. In short, NAFTA is still a work in progress and it

---

[27] Chris McGinn, "NAFTA Numbers: Three Years of NAFTA Facts," *Multinational Monitor,* January/February 1997, **http://www.essential.org/monitor/**.

EXHIBIT 10–6   NAFTA Facts

- Since 1992, U.S. exports of goods and services have risen over 35 percent.
- The U.S. Department of Commerce estimates that every $1 billion increment in U.S. exports creates 22,800 new jobs in the U.S. This means that export growth from 1993 to 1996 was responsible for creating over 5 million U.S. jobs, or 57.7 percent of the 8.8 million net new payroll jobs created by the U.S. economy during the three-year period.
- Despite the temporary peso-related decline in goods exports to Mexico in 1995, U.S. goods exports to Canada were up by 26 percent, while U.S. exports to Mexico were up by 11 percent.
- Trade as a percent of GDP has risen from 13 percent in 1970 to 30 percent in 1996.
- Exports to our NAFTA partners were up by over 34 percent in 1996 over the same period of 1993.
- U.S. exports to Canada were up by 33 percent and by nearly 37 percent to Mexico in 1996.
- Jobs supported by U.S. goods exports to NAFTA countries are up an estimated 311,000 to 2.3 million in 1996 since NAFTA started.
- Mexico's goods imports rose from 71 percent in 1994 to 74 percent in 1995, while Western Europe's, Japan's, and Korea's goods exports to Mexico fell by 25.5 percent, 24.5 percent, and 64 percent, respectively.
- It took only 18 months for U.S. exports to Mexico to fully recover from the December 1994 peso crisis, not the seven years needed after the 1982 peso crisis.
- A poll found that 42 percent of respondents believe NAFTA has had a negative impact on the United States, compared with only 28 percent who believe the 1994 accord was positive.*
- Total North American trade increased during NAFTA's first three years, from $293 billion in 1993 to $429 billion in 1996, a 43 percent gain. In 1996, US. exports to Canada and Mexico, at $190 billion, exceeded U.S. exports to any other area of the world, including the entire Pacific Rim or all of Europe.

* Jim Lobe, "U.S. Americas: Washington's Uncertain Trumpet on Trade," *Inter Press Service,* May 13, 1997.

Sources: "NAFTA and the U.S. Economy," #4012 and "NAFTA and U.S. Jobs" #4014 **http://www.itaiep.doc.gov/ nafta/nafta2.htm** (select NAFTA Facts, a list of documents on NAFTA). The documents listed above and all documents in NAFTA Facts can be ordered from (800) 872-8723 by using a document number. They will be delivered by fax.

will take at least 10 to 15 years for an objective evaluation. Nevertheless, there have been some measurable results (Exhibit 10–6).

One of the major complaints against NAFTA by organized labor was the fear that new investments would be made south of the border instead of in U.S. factories. In fact, however, American direct investment in Mexico has averaged less than $3 billion a year since 1994. That is less than 0.5 percent of American firms' total spending on plant and equipment.[28] It is true that there has been an investment boom in Mexico but not all of it has come from the United States. U.S. and foreign investors with apparel and footwear factories in Asia have been encouraged to relocate their production operations to Mexico. For example, Victoria's Secret lingerie chain opened a new manufacturing plant near Mexico City. The company used to use contractors in the Far East for its lingerie line but now, because of NAFTA, it goes to Mexico. Even with wages in Mexico three times the monthly wages in Sri Lanka, the company will still come out ahead because it's cheaper and faster to move goods from Mexico City to the U.S. than from Colombo—the time it takes to make a sample can be cut from weeks to days. Further, there are no tariffs on Mexican goods, while Sri Lanka goods carry a 19 percent duty.

Mexico's apparel exports to the U.S. have tripled to $3.3 billion since NAFTA began. Last year Mexico surpassed Hong Kong and China to become the U.S.' top source of imported apparel. This is a great boon for U.S. fabric and yarn makers. In years past they have supplied only minuscule amounts of fabric to the vertically integrated Asian apparel markets, but now they supply 70 percent of the raw material going to Mexican sewing shops.[29]

Total foreign direct investment in Mexico reached $7.6 billion in 1996, as companies from all over the world poured money into auto and electronics plants, telecommu-

---

[28] "When Neighbors Embrace," *The Economist,* July 5, 1997, p.18.

[29] Christopher Palmeri and Jose Aguayo, "Good-bye Guangdong, Hello Jalisco," *Forbes,* February 10, 1997, p. 76.

nications, petrochemicals, and a host of other areas. A large chunk of investment is earmarked for factories that will use Mexico as an export platform for the rest of North America, and increasingly the rest of Latin America.[30]

The investment boom in Mexico has been a major source of new demand for U.S. manufacturers of capital goods. The largest post-NAFTA gains in U.S. exports to Mexico have been in such high-technology manufacturing sectors as industrial machinery, transportation and electronic equipment, plastics, rubber, fabricated metal products, and chemicals.[31]

Another complaint of organized labor is the number of jobs that are "exported" to Mexico. Of the 300,000 to 600,000 alleged to have been lost because of NAFTA, the Labor Department has certified only 128,303 U.S. workers who have lost jobs because of increased competition from Mexico and Canada. That compares with 2.2 million jobs created each year since NAFTA took effect. Job losses have not been as drastic as once feared, in part because companies like Lucent Technologies have established *maquiladora* plants[32] in anticipation of the benefits from NAFTA. The plants have been buying more components from U.S. suppliers, while cutting back on Asian sources. Miles Press, a $2 million maker of directory cards, has seen orders from Lucent grow 20 percent in just a few months. Berg Electronics, a $700 million component maker, expects to triple sales to Lucent's Guadalajara plant next year. This ripple effect has generated U.S. service-sector jobs as well. Fisher Price Inc. shifted toy production for the U.S. market from Hong Kong to a plant in Monterey. Celadon Trucking Services Inc., which moves goods produced for Fisher Price from Mexico to the U.S., has added 800 new U.S. drivers to the payroll.[33]

For Valley Drive Systems, manufacturer of automobile front-wheel-drive assemblies, NAFTA has been a success. Because Canadian tariffs on its products were lowered, Valley Drive products are now competitive with Taiwan. The company made its first-ever exports in 1996 and now exports 17 percent of its products.[34]

Expansion of NAFTA—Now or Ever?   The answer to this question rests with the issue of fast-track legislation and a strong desire on the part of the Clinton Administration to focus on Latin America. After successfully gaining the legislation to create NAFTA, the Administration's policies toward Latin America and NAFTA were allowed to drift aimlessly until 1997 when President Clinton went to Congress for fast-track authorization.[35]

Unfortunately, NAFTA was severely politicized during the 1996 presidential elections. There was a consciousness-raising among the electorate as opponents painted a picture of economic doom. One political candidate claimed that NAFTA would produce a "giant sucking sound" of jobs running from the United States to Mexico. Proponents created an equally incorrect picture of economic bliss. Neither side presented a factual picture; first, it was too early to estimate accurately the effect of NAFTA and second, during the short run, it was expected that jobs would be lost and companies displaced. In fact, legislation provided assistance for those whose jobs were displaced by NAFTA.

Further, it was never clearly presented that the flow of jobs to Mexico had started long before NAFTA, when U.S. and Mexican treaties made it advantageous for U.S.

---

[30] Brendan M. Case, "Mexico in Transition," *Latin Trade,* October 1997, p. 36.

[31] "The Success of NAFTA," *The World & I,* October 1997, p. 294.

[32] See Chapter 12 for a complete discussion of the *maquiladora* program.

[33] "NAFTA: Where's That 'Giant Sucking Sound'?" *Business Week,* July 7, 1997, p. 45.

[34] Ellyn Ferguson, "Reviews Mixed on Whether Trade Hurt or Helped U.S. Jobs," *Gannett News Service,* September 6, 1997.

[35] Fast-track authority allows the President to negotiate trade agreements with the assurance that Congress will vote to either accept or reject the agreement without amendments or changes. Without fast track, countries are reluctant to negotiate seriously since the President cannot assure that agreements will survive Congressional approval intact.

Billboard on a highway south of Santiago, Chile. As restrictions on foreign entrance into the long-distance business in Chile were removed, prices dropped as the Baby Bells and others fought it out. Off-peak calls from Chile to the United States fell from $1.50 a minute to 20 cents to 25 cents a minute. (© Larry Luxner 1998)

firms to establish assembly plants in Mexico as part of the *maquiladora* program. Finally, it was never articulated that the importance of NAFTA extended beyond immediate markets and trade opportunities well into the next century when trading regions now forming in Europe and Asia will define global trade. Misinformation prevailed and the general public turned sour on NAFTA. With public opinion turning against the expansion of NAFTA and the Clinton Administration's inability to rally support, it was obvious that a request for fast-track authorization was in jeopardy. When the President finally announced plans to ask Congress for fast track in 1997, it quickly became apparent that the votes were not there, so the request was withdrawn until 1998, if then.

Without fast-track authority, Chile's accession was put on hold. In fact, the administration appears to have given up the idea of adding Chile to NAFTA. A U.S. Trade Representative was quoted as saying, that he was "not so sure about the expansion of NAFTA." The plan now seems to be that the U.S. will go for a bilateral agreement with Chile instead of expanding NAFTA.[36] However, even this scenario appears unlikely without major concessions to Chile.

For one thing, the Chileans have entered into new trade relationships with Mercosur and Canada that complicate if not outright kill the possibilities of NAFTA accession. When Chile joined Mercosur, the agreement stipulated that any favorable tariff concessions Chile may grant to third parties, such as the NAFTA partners, must also be extended to the Mercosur countries. Accordingly, Chile must now answer to Mercosur for anything it may concede to NAFTA. The Chilean-Canadian Free Trade Agreement, signed in 1996, creates further stumbling blocks for Chilean accession to NAFTA. Chile preserved its capital retention program, which requires that capital entering the country cannot be sent abroad for a year. Chile also was able to keep its price band mechanism

---

[36] Jim Lobe, "U.S.-Americas: Washington's Uncertain Trumpet on Trade," *Inter Press Service,* May 13, 1997.

for key agricultural products, which the U.S. has denounced as a protectionist measure. The rule of origin requirement in the Canada-Chile agreement includes a liberal 35 percent regional content[37] requirement, compared to a minimal regional content requirement of 60 percent in NAFTA. Unlike NAFTA, the Canada-Chile FTA makes no provisions for liberalizing cross-border investments in the financial services sector and has no section on intellectual property rights. In sharp contrast to NAFTA, the Canada-Chile agreement also obligates both countries to phase out within six years the use of antidumping duties against imports from either country, a practice that the United States upholds. This is something the Canadians also wanted eliminated within NAFTA but were unsuccessful in securing in the face of opposition by the United States.

Since Chile was able to obtain concessions in its negotiations with Canada, it is unlikely that Chile will agree to drop them in exchange for NAFTA accession. Chile's best interest may be to wait until the rapidly evolving Mercosur-led South American Free-Trade Area (SAFTA) becomes a reality. As a partner, Chile could have more negotiating power with the U.S. to get Canadian- and Mexican-type concessions extended to Chile.

Not bringing Chile into NAFTA may prove to be a major mistake by the U.S. in the short run if not longer. Consider these examples of how Chile being an associate member of Mercosur and not a member of NAFTA affects U.S. business and jobs. Caterpillar Inc., the heavy equipment company, made the decision to move some of its production from the U.S. to Brazil when it became apparent that Chile would not be a NAFTA member. The reason was basic economics: Chile, coupled with the other countries of Mercosur, constitutes a major market for heavy equipment. In Chile alone, Caterpillar sells nearly $100 million worth of bulldozers, excavators, and off-road trucks each year to Chile's mining industry. Further, Chilean and other Mercosur customers do not pay duty on heavy equipment produced in Brazil, but if shipped from the U.S. there is an 11 percent duty. General Electric, Coca-Cola, and Eastman Kodak are just a few of the companies being forced to choose between exporting jobs or losing markets. Chrysler, however, already has manufacturing in Canada,[38] so minivans going to Chile now will be shipped from Canada because of the preferential tariffs between Chile and Canada.

Initially NAFTA was envisioned as the blueprint for a free-trade area extending from Alaska to Argentina. The first country to enter the NAFTA fold was to be Chile, then on south. Now it appears that NAFTA will remain a solid tri-country free-trade area that may or may not become a part of a larger Americas trade area. The important point here is that the U.S. may have lost its leadership role in the creation of a broader and more inclusive Americas trade area. At the time of the Miami Summit for the Free Trade Area of the Americas (FTAA), the United States' leadership was unquestioned. Today, Brazil-led Mercosur is providing the leadership for the creation of the FTAA.

Southern Cone Free Trade Area (Mercosur)[39]

Mercosur is the newest common-market agreement in Latin America. The Treaty of Asuncion, which provided the legal basis for Mercosur, was signed in 1991 and formally inaugurated in 1995. The treaty calls for a common market that would eventually allow for the free movement of goods, capital, labor, and services among the member countries with a uniform external tariff.[40] Because there was concern among Mercosur members about sacrificing sovereign control over taxes and other policy matters, the

---

[37] Regional content refers to the percentage of the product that must be locally produced rather than imported for assembly.

[38] Paul Magnusson, "Beyond NAFTA: Why Washington Mustn't Stop Now," *Business Week,* April 21, 1997, p. 42.

[39] The Mercosur homepage can be reached at **http://mercosur.com/**. However, the site is mostly in Spanish. There is one section (Mercosur Links), and there will be a list of sites, some of which will indicate an English version. Another site for general information in English is **http://algarbull.com.uy/secretariamercosur/**.

[40] An exception that allowed Bolivia and Chile to retain their external tariffs on all imports from non-members of Mercosur was made when they became associate members.

agreement envisioned no central institutions similar to those of the European Common Market institutions.

Since its inception, Mercosur has become the most influential and successful free-trade area in South America. With the addition of Bolivia and Chile in 1996, Mercosur is a market of 212 million people with a combined GDP of nearly $1 trillion. Since 1991, Mercosur has demonstrated greater success than many observers had expected. The success can be attributed to the willingness of the region's governments to confront some very tough issues caused by dissimilar economic policies related to the automobile and textile trade, and antiquated border customs procedures that initially created a bottleneck to smooth border crossings. Additionally, the lack of surface and transportation infrastructure to facilitate trade and communications is a lingering problem that is being addressed at the highest levels.

Nevertheless, intra-Mercosur trade since 1991 has grown 300 percent to $4.5 billion compared to the growth of non-Mercosur trades of $68 billion or about 250 percent. By 1995 Mercosur trade reached $12.5 billion, compared to total non-Mercosur trade of $130 billion. The largest expansion of trade occurred between Argentina and Brazil, as two-way trade increased from $3.7 billion in 1991 to $11.4 billion in 1995.[41] Much of the non-Mercosur trade has come from increases in two-way trade with the EU, which totaled $43 billion in 1995, versus $29 billion with the U.S.

Mercosur has pursued agreements aggressively with other countries or trading groups. Mercosur and Canada are conferring on a free-trade agreement, the second major free-trade deal between Canada and South America. Plans also are underway to enter a tariff-cutting accord with the neighboring Andean pact.[42] In addition, the EU will sign a free-trade agreement with Mercosur in 1999, the first region-to-region free-trade accord. A framework agreement was signed in 1995 and negotiations are to take place with a definitive accord in place at the end of 1999. The two blocs propose a free-trade area, the largest one in the world, before 2005.[43] The advantages of the accord to Mercosur will mainly come from lifting trade barriers on agricultural and agroindustrial products, which account for the lion's share of Mercosur exports to Europe. However, that will also be a major stumbling block if the EU is unwilling to open its highly protected agricultural sector to Brazilian and Argentine imports. Nevertheless, one official of the EU indicated that the EU was already in the process of reforming its Common Agricultural Policy and while negotiations will not be easy, Mercosur and the EU should be able to reach an accord.[44] As we shall see in the next section, Mercosur has assumed the leadership in setting the agenda for the creation of a free-trade area of the Americas or more likely a South America Free Trade Area (SAFTA).

FTAA[45] or SAFTA?

Initially the North American Free Trade Agreement was conceived as the base on which U.S.-led trade expansion in the Western Hemisphere would result in the creation of a *Free Trade Area of the Americas (FTAA)* by 2005. When fast-track authority lapsed in May 1993 and the devaluation of the Mexican peso created a financial crisis in 1994, the Clinton Administration's political will to expand NAFTA to Chile and other countries in the region seemed to be completely derailed.[46]

---

[41] Randy Mye and Lorena Palagonia, "MERCOSUR's Potential Market Is Now Over 200 Million People With a Combined Economy of Nearly $1 Trillion," *Business America,* April 1996, p. 17.

[42] Stephen Fidler and Geoff Dyer, "Mercosur, Andean Pact in Tariff Deal," *Financial Times-London Edition,* October 24, 1997, p. 6.

[43] "Mercosur, EU to Sign Free Trade Accord in 1999," *Xinhua News Agency,* September 14, 1997.

[44] Michael Christie, "EU Seeks Trade Deal with Mercosur in 1999," *Reuters Business Report,* September 12, 1997.

[45] Visit the homepage for FTAA for additional and updated information at **http://www.alca-ftaa.org/**.

[46] John P. Sweeney, "Americas Free Trade Pact," Hearing of the Subcommittee on International Economic Policy and Trade of the House Committee on International Relations, June 11, 1997, *Congressional Testimony by Federal Document Clearing House,* June 11, 1997.

Even though the U.S. lost interest, FTAA continued but with the guidance and influence of a Brazil-led Mercosur. At the first summit on the FTAA in Miami, the U.S. was the undisputed leader but at subsequent meetings and at the second FTAA summit in 1997 at Belo Horizonte, the United States' declining influence was apparent. In a presummit meeting of the various working groups established at the initial meeting in Miami, support for the U.S. blueprint to build a FTAA was only lukewarm. The U.S. plan was seen as a threat to Brazil's[47] burgeoning regional status and, as a consequence, Brazil was pushing its own plan, which differed in timing and process from the United States'. The question of how to proceed toward a free-trade area for the Western Hemisphere was seen as a clash between the two largest economies in the Americas, Brazil and the U.S. The first confrontation came at the meeting in Belo Horizonte, which provided the groundwork for the agenda of the next summit in Santiago, Chile, in 1998.

Two issues on which the United States and Brazil differed at the Belo Horizonte meeting were the timing of tariff reductions and a single binding agreement versus a series of separate undertakings. Brazil, speaking on behalf of its Mercosur partners, favored a gradual buildup to talks on tariffs. Brazil wanted a three-stage approach. Step one, to begin in 1998, would involve negotiations over what it called business facilitation and deregulation. Step two would involve embarking on negotiations on trade-related rules, such as disputes settlement and rules of origin. Step three would involve only then beginning talks on tariffs, perhaps by 2003. The U.S., backed by Canada, wanted to start negotiations on all the issues immediately after the Santiago summit with all tariff reductions in place by 2005. Washington's position of a rapid timetable for tariff reductions and an immediate discussion on other matters is not likely to prevail unless it can convince Latin American governments that it can follow up on its pledges. That depends heavily on fast-track authority for the U.S. President that is not guaranteed.[48]

Another cause for agitation between the U.S. and the rest of Latin America is the United States' insistence that FTAA be used as the basis for a wide-ranging agreement on hemispheric issues such as security, drug trafficking, the environment, and labor issues. Brazil takes a much narrower approach, believing the accords should be limited to trade and trade only. Brazil's response was that the United States "will have to stop using trade as an instrument of political pressure" if it expects to secure the fast-growing Latin American market through the FTAA.

Linking foreign trade with foreign policy is a tactic for which Latin America has continuously faulted the U.S. A recent example cited by Brazil was the politically motivated trade sanction against Argentina when 300 Argentine products were pulled out of a system of preferences that has been operating since 1974, a measure that increased the price of exports from Argentina to the U.S. by more than $260 million annually. Washington said the measure was punishment for unsatisfactory protection of intellectual rights in Argentina.[49] Colombia also has been sanctioned for dumping its flower exports and therefore pays the maximum 76 percent tariff; Ecuador has seen restrictions imposed on its bananas and Brazil is facing problems on textile imports, orange juice, and other agricultural produce.[50] Some say such problems between the U.S. and South American countries over U.S. protectionist measures could lead them to file complaints with the World Trade Organization against the United States.

Not to be an active participant in the FTAA and not to be able to influence the final architecture of the FTAA could be a blow to the U.S. economy and trade. As a market

---

[47] Brazil has a home page that is in English. At this site you can also access information on Mercosur (Mercosul in Spanish). Visit **http://www.netbiz.com.br/**.

[48] Geoff Dyer and Stephen Fidler, "Hare and Tortoise Set for Americas' Free Trade Race," *Financial Times-London Edition,* May 14, 1997, p. 5.

[49] Mario Osava, "Americas: No More Using Trade as Political Tool, Officials Say," *Inter Press Service,* April 17, 1997.

[50] Gustavo Gonzalez, "Americas: U.S. Protectionism Undermines FTAA," *Inter Press Service,* July 15, 1997.

Merchants on Beijing's Chaowal Street, a hot, dusty market alley, offer bargains in fur coats to Russian traders who flock to them. More than 100 stalls line the street and offer garments of mink, rabbit, goat, fox, and even dog. (© 1997, *The Washington Post.* Photo by Kevin Sullivan. Reprinted with permission.)

for U.S. goods, the Western Hemisphere is nearly twice as large as the European Union and nearly 50 percent larger than Asia. Moreover, between 1960 and 1996 U.S. goods exports globally increased 57 percent but U.S. exports to Latin America (excluding Mexico) increased by 110 percent. If these trends were to continue, Latin America alone could exceed Japan and Western Europe combined as an export market for U.S. goods by 2010.

With or without U.S. influence, FTAA continues to evolve but it may evolve into a *South American Free Trade Area (SAFTA)* with Mercosur at the center providing the necessary drive. Mercosur's negotiations with Canada are going smoothly since Canadian business supports the FTAA and the Canadian government is a strong champion of liberalized trade.[51] Negotiations under way with Europe and the rest of South America also seem positive. Other countries also are getting involved with their own negotiations. A meeting with the Pacific Economic Cooperation Council (PECC) was organized by Chile to discuss establishing a partnership between Pacific Asia (East Asia, Australia, and New Zealand) and Latin America. Chile was praised as performing a most laudable role as the gateway for Pacific Asia into Latin America.

In Asia, ASEAN is expanding into other parts of Asia with the creation of the ASEAN Pacific Economic Cooperation (APEC). Within the Americas, Chile has established separate free-trade links with Mexico and has associate membership in Mercosur. One of the objectives in the creation of NAFTA was to expand throughout the Americas and build a unified free-trade area to preclude a piecemeal and complex system of conflicting bilateral and multilateral agreements among nations in the Americas—a situation that could lead to disastrous trade wars. Unfortunately, the direction Latin America is now heading seems to be toward the very situation that NAFTA was intended to avoid.

While the U.S. has remained on the sidelines, the EU is expanding into Central Europe and the Americas and APEC continues its expansion to include other areas of Asia and possibly even China. Inaction on the part of the United States and the lack of fast-track authority for the President to negotiate trade agreements will continue to undermine the ability of U.S. trade negotiators to shape the agenda of the Free Trade Association of the Americas (FTAA). The United States' position will be greatly weakened and further complicated if it has to negotiate to join the FTAA when its own backyard is bound up with free trade treaties with the EU and APEC, and Mercosur has a series of multilateral trade agreements with countries throughout Latin America. Instead of a Free Trade Area

---

[51] "Free Trade for the Americas a Goal Worth Attaining," *The Financial Post,* June 13, 1997, p. 12.

of the Americas as once envisioned, the Western Hemisphere may have a South American Free Trade Area (SAFTA) with strong ties to Europe and Asia and NAFTA.

The critical period for the United States is not the next five or ten years but beyond, when the trading world will be dominated by trading blocs, a process that is well under way. The EU's expansion plans include Eastern and Central Europe and beyond to Latin America. Its negotiations with Mercosur and Mexico[52] for free trade arrangements are well under way. In fact, during a visit to Argentina, the French president was quoted as having said, "Latin America's future does not lie on a North-South axis, but in Europe." And further, "Latin America's essential interests in trade, investment and aid do not lie in the United States but in Europe."[53]

Latin American Economic Cooperation[54]

Prior to 1990, most Latin-American market groups (Exhibit 10–7) had varying degrees of success. The first and most ambitious, the *Latin American Free Trade Association (LAFTA)* gave way to *LAIA (Latin American Integration Association)*. Plagued with tremendous foreign debt, protectionist economic systems, triple-digit inflation, state ownership of basic industries, and over-regulation of industry, most countries were in a perpetual state of economic chaos. Under such conditions there was not much trade or integration among member countries. But, as discussed earlier, sparked by the success of Mercosur,[55] there is a wave of genuine optimism in Latin America about the economic miracle under way propagated by political and economic reforms occurring from the tip of Argentina to the Rio Grande River. Coupled with these market-oriented reforms is a genuine desire to improve trade among neighboring countries by reviving older agreements or forming new ones. In fact, many of the trade groups are seeking ties to Mercosur and/or the European Union.[56]

Keeping track of all the proposed free-trade areas in Latin America is a major endeavor, as almost every country has either signed some type of trade agreement or is involved in negotiations. In addition to new trade agreements, many of the trade accords that have been in existence for decades, such as the Latin American Integration Association, have moved from a moribund to an active state.

Latin American Integration Association (LAIA).   The long-term goal of the LAIA is the establishment, in a gradual and progressive manner, of a Latin American Common Market. One of the more important aspects of LAIA is the differential treatment of member countries according to their level of economic development. Over the years, negotiations among member countries have lowered duties on selected products and eased trade tensions over quotas, local-content requirements, import licenses, and other trade barriers. An important feature of LAIA is the provision that permits members to establish bilateral trade agreements among member countries. It is under this proviso that trade agreements have been developed among LAIA members.

The Andean Common Market (ANCOM).   ANCOM, or the Andean Pact as it is generally called, has served its member nations with a framework to establish rules for foreign investment, common tariffs for nonmember countries, and the reduction or elim-

---

[52] "Mexico, EU Plan Free-Trade Talks," *The Wall Street Journal,* December 9, 1997, p. A14.

[53] Marcela Valente, "Trade-Mercosur: Bloc Resists 'Dissolving' into FTAA," *Inter Press Service,* October 13, 1997.

[54] For information on all Latin American trade agreements visit the Organization of American States home page at **http://www.oas.org/** (select Trade) or go direct to **http://www.sice.oas.org/**.

[55] For a comprehensive review of economic integration in Latin America and the role of Mercosur see Donald G. Richards, "Dependent Development and Regional Integration: A Critical Examination of the Southern Cone Common Market," *Latin American Perspectives,* November 1997, p. 133.

[56] "EU/Andean Pact: President of Ecuador Signs EIB and EU Finance Agreements," *European Report,* October 25, 1997, p. 32.

EXHIBIT 10-7   Latin American Market Groups

Association	Member	Population (millions)	GDP (U.S. $ billions)	GDP per Capita (U.S. $)	Imports (U.S. $ millions)
Andean Common Market (ANCOM)	Bolivia	7.4	$ 7.0	$ 942	$ 1,424
	Colombia	35.1	79.3	2,260	13,859
	Ecuador	11.5	17.9	1,565	4,193
	Peru	23.5	58.9	2,502	9,045
	Venezuela	21.6	75.0	3,467	12,276
	Panama (Assoc)	2.6	7.7	2,928	10,561
Central American Common (CACM)	Guatemala	10.6	14.8	1,392	3,884
	El Salvador	5.7	9.6	1,683	3,042
	Costa Rica	3.4	9.2	2,715	3,656
	Nicaragua	4.5	1.9	421	1,044
	Honduras	6.0	3.6	607	2,541
Caribbean Community and Common Market (CARICOM)	Antigua and Barbuda	0.08	0.418	6,500	326
	Barbados	0.3	1.8	6,923	623
	Belize	0.3	0.373	1,635	194
	Dominica	0.09	0.171	2,000	104
	Grenada	0.08	0.238	2,800	105
	Guyana	0.8	0.5	644	538
	Jamaica	2.5	4.7	1,858	2,694
	Montserrat	0.01	—	—	25
	St. Kitts-Nevis Anguilla	0.04	88	1,544	54
	St. Lucia	0.15	197	1,492	155
	St. Vincent Trinidad-Tobago	1.30	5.5	4,274	1,713
Latin American Integration Association (LAIA)	Argentina	34.6	280.1	8,098	18,352
	Bolivia	7.4	7.0	942	1,424
	Brazil	155.8	717.2	4,603	49,498
	Chile	14.2	67.3	4,739	15,348
	Colombia	35.1	79.3	2,260	13,859
	Ecuador	11.1	17.9	1,565	4,193
	Mexico	94.8	249.9	2,637	75,866
	Paraguay	4.8	8.9	1,838	5,826
	Peru	23.5	58.9	2,502	9,045
	Uruguay	3.2	17.8	5,595	2,867
	Venezuela	21.6	75.0	3,467	12,276

Sources: "Indicators of Market Size for 115 Countries," *Crossborder Monitor,* August 27, 1997; *International Marketing Data and Statistics, 1997* (London: Euromonitor, 1997); and *Statistical Abstract of Latin America* (Los Angeles: UCLA Latin American Center Publications, Vol. 32, 1996).

ination of internal tariffs. The Andean Pact is going through a restructuring as many of its members are either withdrawing or signing bilateral agreements with other groups including Mercosur.[57] There are negotiations under way for the Andean Pact and Mercosur to reach a free-trade agreement. The combined free-trade area of Mercosur and ANCOM would create a market of 310 million with a joint GDP in excess of $1.2 trillion.[58]

Caribbean Community and Common Market (CARICOM).[59] The success of the Caribbean Free Trade Association led to the creation of the Caribbean Community and Common Market. CARICOM member-countries continue in their efforts to achieve true re-

[57] Sally Bowen, "Andean Pact Begins to Crumble," *Financial Times,* April 23, 1997, p. 5.
[58] Raymond Colitt, "Andean Pact, Mercosur Eye Free Trade Area," *Financial Times,* November 10, 1997, p. 5.
[59] CARICOM has a Web page at **http://www.caricom.org/**.

gional integration. The group has worked to establish a single-market economy. The introduction of a common external tariff structure was a major step toward that goal.[60] Of continuing importance is establishing stronger ties with other groups in Latin America; presently CARICOM accounts for only 2 percent of exports in the Latin American and Caribbean region.[61]

Asian Pacific Rim

Countries in the Asian Pacific Rim constitute the third Triad region. Japan is at the center of this Triad region, which also includes many of the world's newly industrialized countries (NICs) whose early economic growth was dependent on exports to U.S. markets. Now, after decades of dependence on the United States and Europe for technology and markets, countries in the Asian Pacific Rim are preparing for the next economic leap, driven by trade, investment, and technology aided by others in the region. Though few in number, trade agreements among some of the Asian NICs are seen as movement toward a region-wide, intra-Asian trade area, with Japan at the center of this activity.

While the United States is Japan's single largest trading partner, markets in China and Southeast Asia are increasingly more important for trade and direct investment by Japanese corporate strategy. Once a source of inexpensive labor for products shipped to Japan or to third markets, these countries are now seen as viable markets. Further, Japanese investment across a number of manufacturing industries is geared toward serving local customers and building sophisticated local production and supplier networks. In 1996, trade with Asia accounted for 46.9 percent of Japan's total exports and imports compared with 30.1 percent in 1990. Foreign direct investment accounted for only 12.4 percent in 1990 and had increased to over 25 percent by 1995. In both 1994 and 1995, more production-related money went into Asia than North America. Japanese manufacturing investment in Asia totaled $8.1 billion in 1995, compared with $7.5 billion in North America[62] Exhibit 10–8 illustrates that a substantial portion of Japanese direct investment was made in China and ASEAN countries.

The pattern of investment by Japan has some observers concerned that Japan is creating a keiretsu-type network in Southeast Asia. One analysis of three ASEAN nations determined, for example, that 60 percent of the Japanese manufacturing affiliates operating in Indonesia have ties to one or more keiretsu groups; the comparable figures for Malaysia and Thailand were 45 percent and 48 percent, respectively. Another study argues that Japanese businesses and the Japanese government are collaborating to export Japan's economic system to Asian nations. The proliferation of these exclusionary business relationships is raising concern, as it could become increasingly difficult for nonkeiretsu suppliers to successfully market in these countries. In any case, Japan is an important participant in the economic growth and development of the trading groups in the Asian Pacific Rim.

Presently, there is one multinational trade group, Association of Southeast Asian Nations (ASEAN),[63] that is evolving into the ASEAN Free Trade Area (AFTA), and one forum, Asia-Pacific Economic Cooperation (APEC), that meets annually to discuss regional economic development and cooperation, which is moving rapidly toward becoming a free-trade area.

---

[60] Wesley Gibbings, "Caribbean-Economy: Region Joins Forces on Trade," *Inter Press Service,* September 18, 1997.

[61] Other Web sites to visit for Latin America and Caribbean region (English) are **http://www.eclac.org/** and **http://www.cepal.org/**.

[62] Christopher B. Johnstone and Atsushi Yamakoshi, "Strength without Dominance; Japanese Investment in Southeast Asia," *JEI Report,* May 16, 1997, p. 16.

[63] The Web page for ASEAN is **http://www.aseansec.org/**.

Exhibit 10–8   Japan's Trade and Investment in ASEAN Countries, 1996 (Millions U.S. Dollars)

	Foreign Direct Investment		Total Trade (Exports & Imports)	
		% Total		% Total
ASEAN	$ 5,467	10.6%	$125,530	16.5%
China	4,472	8.7	62,335	8.2
World	51,398	100	760,337	100

Association of Southeast Asian Nations (ASEAN)[64]

The primary multinational trade group in Asia is *ASEAN*. The goals of the group are economic integration and cooperation through complementary industry programs, preferential trading including reduced tariff and nontariff barriers, guaranteed member access to markets throughout the region, and harmonized investment incentives. Like all multinational market groups, ASEAN has experienced problems and false starts in attempting to unify the combined economies of its member-nations. Most of the early economic growth came from trade outside the ASEAN group. Similarities in the kinds of products they had to export, in their natural resources, and other national assets hampered earlier attempts at intra-ASEAN trade. The steps taken when ASEAN was first created to expand and diversify their industrial base in order to foster intraregional trade have resulted in the fastest-growing economies in the region and an increase in trade among its members. Intra-ASEAN trade has grown to more than $70 billion in 1996 from $27 billion in 1990[65] and average per capita income for the member countries has more than doubled to $1,700, from $700.

Four major events account for the vigorous economic growth of the ASEAN countries and their transformation from cheap-labor havens to industrialized nations: (1) the ASEAN governments' commitment to deregulation, liberalization, and privatization of their economies; (2) the decision to shift their economies from commodity-based to manufacturing-based; (3) the decision to specialize in manufacturing components in which they have a comparative advantage (this created more diversity in their industrial output and increased opportunities for trade); and (4) Japan's emergence as a major provider of technology and capital necessary to upgrade manufacturing capability and develop new industries.

In 1997 Myanmar (formerly Burma) and Laos joined ASEAN, giving the group a combined population of 480 million and a combined gross domestic product of $590 billion.[66] Although there has never been an attempt to duplicate the supranational government of the European Union, each year the group becomes more interrelated. ASEAN Vision 2020 is the most outward-looking commitment to regional goals ever accepted by the group. Among the targets that will lead to further integration is the commitment to implementing fully and as rapidly as possible the *ASEAN Free Trade Area (AFTA).*[67]

Under the AFTA agreement implemented in 1993, tariffs must be reduced on 95 percent of goods originating in member countries to 5 percent or below by 2003.[68]

---

[64] ASEAN countries are Brunei, Indonesia, Malaysia, the Philippines, Singapore, Thailand, Vietnam, Myanmar (Burma), and Laos. Burma and Laos were admitted in 1997.

[65] James Kynge and Ted Bardacke, "ASEAN Agrees to Burma's Membership," *Financial Times,* June 2, 1997, p. 4.

[66] Fauziah Ismail, "Economic Problems Prove to Be a Boon to Regional Solidarity," *The New Straits Times Press,* December 18, 1997, p. 20.

[67] "ASEAN Leaders Define Vision 2020 Targets," *Asia Pulse,* December 17, 1997.

[68] "Malaysia Official Says ASEAN Members Committed to Trade Pact," *Dow Jones News Service,* October 14, 1997.

The two new members, Myanmar and Laos, will be given 10 years to comply with the AFTA[69] tariff schedule. Some leaders proposed a speedier implementation to the year 2000 to demonstrate the group's commitment to free and open trade. Instead, the final decision was to reaffirm the 2003 date with emphasis on accelerating the process.

Just as was the case in the EU, businesses are drafting plans for operation within a free-trade area. The ability to sell in an entire region without differing tariff and non-tariff barriers is one of the important changes that will affect many parts of the marketing mix. Distribution can be centralized at the most cost-effective point rather than having distribution points dictated by tariff restrictions. Some standardization of branding will be necessary since large customers will buy at the regional level rather than bit-by-bit at the country level. Pricing can be more consistent, which will help the reduction of smuggling and parallel importing that occur when there are major price differentials among countries due to different tariff schedules. In essence, marketing can become more regionally and centrally managed rather than by individual country.[70]

Asia-Pacific Economic Cooperation[71]

The other important grouping that encompasses the Asian Pacific Rim is the Asia-Pacific Economic Cooperation (APEC). Formed in 1989, APEC provides a formal structure for the major governments of the region, including the United States and Canada, to discuss their mutual interests in open trade and economic collaboration. APEC is a unique forum that has evolved into the primary regional vehicle for promoting trade liberalization and economic cooperation. The 18 member-nations had a combined gross national product in 1996 of over $22 trillion, accounting for approximately 52 percent of total world output and 40 percent of global trade.[72]

APEC includes the most powerful regional economies in the world (Exhibit 10–9), and as a region constitutes the United States' most important economic partner. APEC has as its common goal a commitment to open trade, to increase economic collaboration, to sustain regional growth and development, to strengthen the multilateral trading system, and to reduce barriers to investment and trade without detriment to other economies.

Representatives from APEC member-nations meet annually to discuss issues confronting the group, to propose solutions to problems arising from the growing interdependence among their economies and to continue their quest for ways to lower barriers to trade. The most recent meeting in Vancouver, British Columbia, resulted in a significant departure from an earlier agreement to achieve free and open trade and investment in the region by 2010 for developed countries and 2020 for developing members. This "voluntary" process of trade liberalization had yielded only modest progress, so in its place the group adopted a new approach: liberalization negotiated sector by sector. Nine sectors, covering $1.5 trillion in global trade, were designated for accelerated negotiations, including energy, chemicals, environmental goods and services, medical equipment, and fish and forest products.

The success of this plan depends on how many nations participate. Mexico and Chile, preferring a comprehensive round of trade negotiations, have declined to play. The United States and Japan differ on how to implement the proposals. The United States is pushing for specific and binding targets to cut tariff liberalization, whereas Japan is agreeable to trade liberalization and tariff reductions on the nine economic sec-

---

[69] More information about AFTA can be reached through the ASEAN Web site. For links to additional information on Southeast Asia visit **http://www.library.wisc.edu/guides/SEAsia/seainint.htm/**.

[70] "Before and After AFTA," *Business Asia,* May 19, 1997, p. 1.

[71] APEC Web site is found at **http://apecsun.apecsec.org.sg/**.

[72] "APEC an Overview," *Asia-Pacific Economic Cooperation,* can be found at **http://apec97.gc.ca/apec/index.html/**.

EXHIBIT 10-9   **Comparison of Export Trade among Members of APEC and the EC**

	Population 1996 (millions)	*Exports, 1990* (U.S. $ millions)	*Exports, 1995* (U.S. $ millions)	*GNP, 1996* (U.S. $ billions)
APEC	2,235.1	732,869	770,097	22,952
Americas*	401.6	306,486	311,085	7,989
Asia	1,811.8	399,455	419,901	6,440
Oceania	21.7	26,928	39,111	342
EC	373.5	515,915	628,606	8,180

* Includes United States, Canada, Mexico, and Chile.

Sources: IMF: International Financial Statistics, Direction of Trade; OECD: National Account, EC Committee; "Indicators of Market Size for 115 Countries," *Crossborder Monitor,* August 27, 1997; and *International Marketing Data and Statistics, 1997* (London: Euromonitor, 1997).

tors, but only if it can liberalize those sectors at its own pace.[73] Although still far from being a free-trade area, each meeting seems to advance another step in that direction, notwithstanding the objections of some members.[74]

In addition to the agenda items, a group that met in Manila prior to the Vancouver meeting proposed an approach to address the financial crisis that was threatening the region's capital markets in 1997. The "Manila Agreement" provided for a richer and more flexible International Monetary Fund (IMF) with programs and resources to counter the instabilities that emerge from the globalized financial markets of the 21st century. The IMF would provide large pools of short-term financing to help countries weather financial problems. Additionally, the Manila framework adds a regional dimension that allows the IMF to coordinate loans from friendly APEC members to assist financially faltering economies. It also creates a regional forum for finance ministries and central banks to examine each other's economies in an attempt to spot potential problems in their early stages, enabling them to apply pressure before a crisis occurs that could adversely affect the entire region. The hope is that crises such as those that occurred in Indonesia, Thailand, and South Korea in 1997 could be avoided or minimized.[75]

At a meeting in Kuala Lumpur, APEC members voted to allow Russia, Vietnam, and Peru to join APEC in 1998. At the same time, the leaders adopted a 10-year "consolidation period," freezing new entries even though eight other countries have applied for membership.[76] APEC is growing in importance and each year's summit creates a stronger union.

Africa[77]

Africa's multinational market development activities can be characterized by a great deal of activity but little progress. Including bilateral agreements, an estimated 200 economic arrangements exist between African countries (Exhibit 10–10). Despite the large number and assortment of paper organizations, there has been little actual economic in-

---

[73] Kenneth McCallum, "U.S., Japan Are Far Apart on APEC Trade-Liberalization Plan," *Dow Jones Online News,* November 11, 1997.

[74] Isao Kubota, "Why APEC Should Not Become a Free Trade Area," *Look Japan,* January 1996, p. 32.

[75] Tim Healy and Alejandro Reyes, "APEC: Asia's Economic Crisis Overshadows the Top-Level Get-Together," *Asiaweek,* December 5, 1997.

[76] "Russia, Vietnam, Peru to Join APEC in 1998," *Asian Economic News,* December 1, 1997.

[77] For a variety of sources of information on Africa visit these two sites: **http://africanews.com/** and **http://usafricanvoice.com/**.

EXHIBIT 10–10 African Market Groups

Association	Member	Population (millions)	GDP (U.S. $ billions)	GDP per Capita (U.S. $)	Imports (U.S. $ millions)
Afro-Malagasy Economic Union	Benin	5.5	$ 2.0	$ 370	$ 493
	Burkina Faso	10.4	2.4	230	549
	Cameroon	13.3	8.6	650	1,241
	Central African Republic	3.3	1.1	340	174
	Chad	6.4	1.2	180	220
	People's Repub. of the Congo	2.6	1.8	680	670
	Cote d' Ivoire	14.0	9.2	660	2,808
	Gabon	1.1	3.8	3,490	882
	Mali	9.8	2.5	250	529
	Mauritania	2.3	1.1	460	700
	Niger	9.0	2.0	220	309
	Senegal	8.5	5.1	600	704
	Togo	4.1	1.3	310	386
East African Customs Union	Ethiopia	56.4	5.6	100	1,033
	Kenya	26.7	7.5	280	2,949
	Sudan	25.0	9.2	398	1,000
	Tanzania	29.6	3.6	120	1,619
	Uganda	19.2	4.6	240	1,058
	Zambia	9.0	3.6	400	1,258
Maghreb Economic Community	Algeria	28.0	44.8	1,600	9,200
	Libya	5.4	30.4	5,630	7,500
	Tunisia	9.0	16.4	1,820	6,500
	Morocco	26.6	29.5	1,110	8,563
Economic Community of West African States (ECOWAS)	Benin	5.5	2.0	370	493
	Burkina Faso	10.4	2.4	230	549
	Cote d' Ivoire	14.0	9.2	660	2,808
	Gambia	1.1	0.35	320	140
	Ghana	17.1	6.7	390	1,580
	Guinea	6.6	3.6	550	690
	Guinea-Bissau	1.1	0.27	250	50
	Liberia	2.58	1.1	467	308
	Mali	9.8	2.5	250	529
	Mauritania	2.3	1.1	460	700
	Niger	9.0	2.0	220	309
	Nigeria	111.3	28.9	260	7,900
West Africa Economic Community (CEAO)	Senegal	8.5	5.1	600	704
	Togo	4.1	1.3	310	386
	Burkina Faso	10.4	2.4	230	549
	Cote d' Ivoire	14.0	9.2	660	2,808
	Mali	9.8	2.5	250	529
	Mauritania	2.3	1.1	460	700
	Niger	9.0	2.0	220	309
Customs and Economic Union of Central Africa (CEUCA)	Cameroon	13.3	8.6	650	1,241
	C. Afric. Repub.	3.3	1.1	340	174
	P. Rep. of Congo	2.6	1.8	680	670
	Gabon	1.1	3.8	3,490	882

Exhibit 10–10   African Market Groups (concluded)

Association	Member	Population (millions)	GDP (U.S. $ billions)	GDP per Capita (U.S. $)	Imports (U.S. $ millions)
Southern African Development	Angola	11.6	$ 11.7	$1,008	$ 1,803
Community (SADC)	Botswana	1.5	4.5	3,000	1,800
	Lesotho	2.0	2.6	1,340	964
	Namibia	1.7	5.8	3,600	1,100
	Malawi	9.8	1.5	150	654
	Mauritius	1.1	3.9	3,508	1,949
	Mozambique	17.4	1.5	86	1,213
	South Africa	41.2	133.6	3,240	28,543
	Swaziland	8.6	0.7	900	637
	Tanzania	30.3	2.8	92	1,659
	Zambia	9.4	3.7	395	836
	Zimbabwe	11.5	6.6	571	2,300

Sources: "Indicators of Market Size for 115 Countries," *Crossborder Monitor,* August 27, 1997; *International Marketing Data and Statistics, 1997* (London: Euromonitor, 1997); and **http://www.stat-usa.gov/**.

tegration. This is generally due to the political instability that has characterized Africa in recent decades and the unstable economic base on which Africa has had to build. The United Nations Economic Commission for Africa (ECA) has held numerous conferences but has been hampered by governmental inexperience, undeveloped resources, labor problems, and chronic product shortages.

The *Economic Community of West Africa States (ECOWAS)* and the *Southern African Development Community (SADC)* are the two most active regional cooperative groups. A 15-nation group, ECOWAS has an aggregate gross domestic product of more than $57.9 billion and is striving to achieve full economic integration. The 20th ECOWAS summit in 1997 approved a plan to accelerate subregional economic integration and development with emphasis on their full commitment to regional monetary integration and the eventual adoption of a single West African currency.[78] Unfortunately, ECOWAS continues to be plagued with financial problems, conflict within the group, and inactivity on the part of some members.[79]

Southern African Development Community (SADC)[80] is the most advanced and viable of Africa's regional organizations. Its 12 members encompass a landmass of 6.6 million square kilometers containing abundant natural resources and a population of over 135 million. South Africa, the region's dominant economy, has a GDP of $125 billion and accounts for 76.8 percent of SADC market share.

Created in 1992, it has its roots in the Southern African Development Coordination Conference (SADCC), which was founded in 1980 as a means to coordinate regional economic and infrastructure development. Following sweeping political changes in South Africa, SADC welcomed that nation as a full member and partner in development in 1994. The primary focus of SADC is to liberalize intraregional trade and to increase economic and political integration among member states. It has as a goal the creation of a free economic-trade zone by 2004, in which goods could cross borders without tariffs and taxes. While there is a fair amount of skepticism about reaching that goal, most agree that of all the regional groups in Africa, SADC is the strongest and the one most apt to make significant advancements.[81]

---

[78] "ECOWAS Approves Plan for Faster Integration," *Xinhua English Newswire,* August 30, 1997.

[79] "Togo: ECOWAS Leaders Agree to Set Up Peacekeeping, Conflict Management," *BBC Worldwide Monitoring,* December 18, 1997.

[80] The Web site for SADC is **http://www.sadc-usa.net/**.

[81] Judith Matloff, "Southern Africa's Other Story: Economies Roar," *Christian Science Monitor,* August 7, 1997, p. 6.

EXHIBIT 10-11   Far East and Middle East Market Groups

Association	Member	Population (millions)	GDP (U.S. $ billions)	GDP per Capita (U.S. $)	Imports (U.S. $ millions)
ASEAN Free Trade Area	Brunei	0.3	$ 5.7	$18,900	
(AFTA)	Indonesia	193.8	198.1	1,022	$ 39,456
	Malaysia	20.1	81.3	4,045	77,662
	Philippines	68.4	74.1	1,083	28,419
	Singapore	3.0	85.1	28,463	124,394
	Thailand	60.2	167.1	2,775	73,959
Arab Common Market	Iraq	21.9	16.8	767	608
	Kuwait	1.7	26.6	15,767	6,629
	Jordan	5.3	6.6	1,236	3,690
	Syria	14.3	57.1	3,990	6,015
	Egypt	59.2	60.5	1,021	17,395
Economic Cooperation	Pakistan	130.3	43.8	453	11,460
Organization (ECO)	Iran	61.1	61.4	1,005	12,311
	Turkey	61.6	167.0	2,709	35,720
	Azerbaijan	7.5	15.5	2,067	240
	Turkmenistan	4.1	13.1	3,280	304
	Uzbekistan	22.6	53.2	2,350	947

Sources: "Indicators of Market Size for 115 Countries," *Crossborder Monitor,* August 27, 1997; *International Marketing Data and Statistics, 1997* (London: Euromonitor, 1997); and **http://www.stat-usa.gov/**.

Middle East

The Middle East has been less aggressive in the formation of successfully functioning multinational market groups (Exhibit 10–11). The *Arab Common Market* has set goals for free internal trade but has not succeeded. The aim is to integrate the economies of the 22 Arab countries, but before that will be feasible a long history of border disputes and persisting ideological differences will have to be overcome.[82] The free trade agreement between Morocco and Egypt may be the first step in forging an Arab common market that would include Egypt. In any case the idea is still alive.[83]

Pakistan, Iran, and Turkey, formerly the Regional Cooperation for Development (RCD), have renamed their regional group the *Economic Cooperation Organization (ECO)*. Since reorganizing, Afghanistan and six of the Newly Independent States were accepted into the ECO. When the RCD was first organized, impressive strides in developing basic industrial production were being made, until the revolution in Iran ended any economic activity. ECO has as its primary goal the development of its infrastructure in order to pave the way for regional cooperation.[84] The other activity in the region, led by Iran, is the creation of an *Organization of the Islamic Conference (OIC),* a common market composed of Islamic countries. A preferential tariff system among the 55 member states of the OIC and the expansion of commercial services in insurance, transport, and transit shipping are among the issues to be debated at the next conference of Islamic countries. The vast natural resources, substantial capital, and a cheap labor force are seen as the strengths of the OIC.[85]

---

[82] Hamoud Salhiof, "UAE-Development: Arab Common Market Well within Reach," *Inter Press Service,* November 14, 1997.

[83] Alison C. Hills, "From Cairo to Casablanca," *Business Today,* November 24, 1997.

[84] "ECO to Promote Cooperation Despite Difficulties," *Xinhua English Newswire,* November 25, 1997.

[85] "Iranian Trade Minister Calls for Islamic Common Market to Be Set Up," *BBC Worldwide Monitoring,* December 3, 1997.

Regional Trading Groups and Emerging Markets

There are two opposing views on the direction of global trade in the future. One view suggests the world is dividing into major regional trading groups like the European Union (EU), the North American Free Trade Area (NAFTA), and the ASEAN Free Trade Area (AFTA) that are now and will continue to be the major markets of the future. The other view is that global economic power may be shifting away from the traditional industrialized markets to the developing world and its emerging markets.

Those who support the first view see the world divided into three regional Triads centered on a major industrialized power: the United States in the Americas, the EC in Europe, and Japan in Asia. Further, these trading blocs will lead the industrialized world to a more protectionist period excluding countries not aligned with a trade group. Speculation is that until the member countries of the EC adjust to a new internal competitive environment there will be a strong tendency to "keep the EC for Europeans." It is also conceivable that the United States and an expanded NAFTA will become more protective of markets in the Americas, and that Japan and ASEAN will dominate Asian markets. Further, it is natural for the dominant countries in each of the regions to focus more of their economic trade within their respective areas. This suggests that these three Triads will dominate trade patterns. Should such a scenario develop, those countries not tied economically to one of these trading blocs will be denied access to markets, capital, and technology, and, thus, to economic growth.

Those who hold the second view see the focus of international trade shifting away from the mature economies of the United States, Europe, and Japan and toward the emerging markets. The most important reason given in support of this view is that developed countries have mature, stable markets dominated by global companies. Thus, their economies will grow more slowly than emerging markets and offer less opportunity for new trade. Conversely, enormous demand will be created as emerging economies continue the rate of economic development experienced over the last decade. These emerging economies will need highways, communications networks, utilities, factories, and the other capital goods necessary for industrialization. And as their economies continue to prosper, consumer goods will be needed to satisfy the demands of a newly affluent consumer market. Rather than international trade being driven by the major industrialized countries, emerging economies may be the engine for global market growth. Many experts predict that over the next 50 years the majority of global economic growth will be in the developing world, principally in those countries identified as emerging markets. While most of the immediate growth will be accounted for by 10 countries now on the threshold of expansion, many of the 120 other developing countries in Europe, Latin America, and Asia are awakening to the desire for economic development and industrialization and may soon be among the future emerging markets.

A shift in global demand may already be occurring. For example, during the last decade the U.S. share of exports going to industrialized countries remained flat, while the share of exports going to emerging markets increased for that same period. A similar pattern has occurred in Japan: In 1988, Japan exported more than 5 percent more to the United States than to Asia, but nearly a decade later, Japan exported nearly 40 percent more to Asia than it did to the U.S.

In reality, both views may be too extreme. What is more likely to occur is that global economic growth will be spurred by both the creation of regional trade groups and the desire for economic growth in the developing world. The future may be as much about sharing in the enormous projected growth of the emerging markets as it is about sharing markets of the industrialized world. It is very likely that the competitive battleground of the future will encompass both the industrialized world and emerging markets. Competitive rivals will be Japan, Europe, and the United States as well as several of the NICs. All the players are in place. Only time will tell which direction global trade will take.

Summary

The experiences of the multinational market groups developed since World War II point up both the successes and the hazards such groups encounter. The various attempts at economic cooperation represent varying degrees of success and failure, but almost without regard to their degree of success, the economic market groups have created great excitement among marketers.

Economic benefits possible through cooperation relate to more efficient marketing and production: Marketing efficiency is effected through the development of mass markets, encouragement of competition, the improvement of personal income, and various psychological market factors. Production efficiency derives from specialization, mass production for mass markets, and the free movement of the factors of production. Economic integration also tends to foster political harmony among the countries involved; such harmony leads to stability, which is beneficial to the marketer.

The marketing implications of multinational market groups may be studied from the standpoint of firms located inside the market or of firms located outside which wish to sell to the market. For each viewpoint the problems and opportunities are somewhat different; regardless of the location of the marketer, however, multinational market groups provide great opportunity for the creative marketer who wishes to expand volume. Market groupings make it economically feasible to enter new markets and to employ new marketing strategies that could not be applied to the smaller markets represented by individual countries. At the same time, market groupings intensify competition by protectionism within a market group but may foster greater protectionism between regional markets. Since there is little question that future global markets will revolve around regional superpowers, tomorrow's marketers must concern themselves with positioning in these trade groupings in order to keep the door open to opportunity. The new Mercosur, for example, suggests the growing importance of economic cooperation and integration. Such developments will continue to confront the international marketer by providing continually growing market opportunities and challenges.

Questions

1. Define:

multinational market region	CEFTA
United States–Canada Free Trade Agreement	regional cooperation group
EMU	free-trade area
Single European Act	customs union
NAFTA	common market
AFTA	political union
Amsterdam Treaty	Maastricht Treaty
Mercosur	Treaty of Amsterdam
APEC	

2. Elaborate on the problems and benefits for international marketers from multinational market groups.

3. Explain the political role of multinational market groups.

4. Identify the factors on which one may judge the potential success or failure of a multinational market group.

5. Explain the marketing implications of the factors contributing to the successful development of a multinational market group.

6. Imagine that the United States was composed of many separate countries with individual trade barriers. What marketing effect might be visualized?

7. Discuss the possible types of arrangements for regional economic integration.

8. Differentiate between a free-trade area and a common market. Explain the marketing implication of the differences.

9. It seems obvious that the founders of the European Community intended it to be a truly common market, so much so that economic integration must be supplemented by political integration to accomplish these objectives. Discuss.

10. The European Commission, the Council of Ministers, and the Court of Justice of the EC have gained power in the last decade. Comment.

11. Select any three countries that might have some logical basis for establishing a multinational market organization and illustrate their compatibility as a regional trade group. Identify the various problems that would be encountered in forming multinational market groups of such countries.

12. U.S. exports to the European Community are expected to decline in future years. What marketing actions may a company take to counteract such changes?

13. "Because they are dynamic and because they have great growth possibilities, the multinational markets are likely to be especially rough and tumble for the external business." Discuss.

14. Differentiate between a customs union and a political union.

15. Why have African nations had such difficulty in forming effective economic unions?

16. Discuss the implications of the European Union's decision to admit Eastern European nations to the group.

17. Discuss the consequences to the United States of not being a part of the SAFTA.

18. Discuss the strategic marketing implications of NAFTA.

19. How is the concept of reciprocity linked to protectionism?

20. Visit the Web pages for NAFTA (**http://www.itaiep.doc. gov/nafta/nafta2.htm/**) and Mercosur (**http:// mercosur.com/** or **http://algarbull.com.uy/ secretariamercosur/**) and locate each group's rules of origin. Which group has the most liberal rules of origin? Why the difference?

21. Using the factors that serve as the basis for success of an economic union (political, economic, social, and geographic), evaluate the potential success of the EC, NAFTA, AFTA, and Mercosur.

22. For each regional trade group—EC, NAFTA, AFTA, and Mercosur—cite which of the factors for success are the strongest and which are the weakest. Discuss each factor.

23. Changes that occurred in APEC after the 1997 Vancouver meeting were discussed in the chapter. Visit the APEC Web site (**http://apecsun.apecsec.org.sg/**) and discuss these changes.

CHAPTER
11

GLOBAL MARKETING MANAGEMENT: PLANNING AND ORGANIZATION

Chapter Learning Objectives

What you should learn from Chapter 11

- How global marketing management differs from international marketing management.

- The increasing importance of strategic international alliances.

- The need for planning to achieve company goals.

- The important factors for each alternative market-entry strategy.

The Nestlé Way—Evolution Not Revolution

Nestlé epitomizes the company that "thinks globally and acts locally." Nestlé has been international almost from its start in 1866, as a maker of infant formula. By 1920, the company was producing in Brazil, Australia, and the United States, and exporting to Hong Kong. Today, it sells more than 8,500 products produced in 489 factories in 193 countries. Nestlé is the world's biggest marketer of infant formula, powdered milk, instant coffee, chocolate, soups, and mineral water. It ranks number two in ice cream, and in cereals it ties Ralston Purina and trails only Kellogg Co. Its products are sold in the most upscale supermarkets in Beverly Hills, California, and in huts in Nigeria, where women sell Nestlé bouillon cubes alongside homegrown tomatoes and onions. Although the company has no sales agents in North Korea, its products somehow find their way into stores there, too.

The "Nestlé way" is to dominate its markets. Its overall strategy can be summarized in four points: (1) think and plan long term, (2) decentralize, (3) stick to what you know, and (4) adapt to local tastes. To see how Nestlé operates, take a look at its approach to Poland, one of the largest markets of the former Soviet bloc. Company executives decided at the outset that it would take too long to build plants and create brand awareness. Instead, the company pursued acquisitions and followed a strategy of "evolution not revolution." It purchased Goplana, Poland's number two chocolate maker (it bid for the number one company but lost out), and carefully adjusted the end product with small changes every two months over a two-year period until it measured up to Nestlé's standards and was a recognizable Nestlé brand. These efforts, along with all-out marketing, put the company within striking distance of the market leader, Wedel. Nestlé also purchased a milk operation and, as it did in Mexico, India, and elsewhere, sent technicians into the field to help Polish farmers improve the quality and quantity of the milk it buys through better feeds and improved sanitation.

Nestlé's efforts in the Middle East are much longerterm. The area currently represents only about 2 percent of the company's worldwide sales, and the markets, individually, are relatively small. Further, regional conflicts preclude most trade among the countries. Nevertheless, Nestlé anticipates that hostility will someday subside, and when that happens the company will be ready to sell throughout the entire region. Nestlé has set up a network of factories in five countries that can someday supply the entire region with different products. The company makes ice cream in Dubai, and soups and cereals in Saudi Arabia. The Egyptian factory makes yogurt and bouillon, while Turkey produces chocolate. And a factory in Syria makes ketchup, a malted-chocolate energy food, instant noodles, and other products. If the obstacles between the countries come down, Nestlé will have a network of plants to provide a complete line to market in all the countries. In the meantime, factories produce and sell mostly in the countries in which they are located.

For many companies such a long-term strategy would not be profitable, but it works for Nestlé because the company relies on local ingredients and markets products that consumers can afford. The tomatoes and wheat used in the Syrian factory, for example, are major local agricultural products. Even if Syrian restrictions on trade remain, there are 14 million people to buy ketchup, noodles, and other products the company produces there. In all five countries as well, on all brands sold by Nestlé, the Nestlé name and the bird-in-a-nest trademark appear on every product.

Nestlé bills itself as "the only company that is truly dedicated to providing a complete range of food products to meet the needs and tastes of people from around the world, each hour of their day, throughout their entire lives."

Sources: Greg Steinmetz and Tar Parker-Pope, "At a Time When Companies Are Scrambling to Go Global, Nestlé Has Long Been There," *The Wall Street Journal Europe,* September 30, 1996, p. R3; and "Nestlé the World Food Company," **http://www.nestle.com/html/home.html/**. Visit the Nestlé Website for a short history of the company, the location of its manufacturing plants, and the markets it serves: **http://www.nestle.com**.

Confronted with increasing global competition for expanding markets, multinational companies are changing their marketing strategies and altering their organizational structures. Their goals are to enhance their competitiveness and to assure proper positioning in order to capitalize on opportunities in the global marketplace.

A recent study of North American and European corporations indicated that nearly 75 percent of the companies are revamping their business processes, that most have formalized strategic-planning programs, and that the need to stay cost competitive was considered to be the most important external issue affecting their marketing strategies. Change is not limited to the giant multinationals but includes midsize and small firms as well.

In fact, the flexibility of a smaller company may enable it to reflect the demands of global markets and redefine its programs more quickly than larger multinationals.[1] Acquiring a global perspective is easy, but the execution requires planning, organization, and a willingness to try new approaches—from engaging in collaborative relationships to redefining the scope of company operations.

This chapter discusses global marketing management, competition in the global marketplace, strategic planning, and alternative market-entry strategies. It also identifies the elements that contribute to effective international or global organization.

Global Marketing Management

Determining a firm's overall global strategy and shaping the organization to achieve goals and objectives are the two central tasks of global marketing management that define the level of international integration of the company. Companies must deal with a multitude of strategic issues including the extent of the internationalization of operations.

Recall from Chapter 1 that a company's international marketing management orientation can be characterized as one of three operating concepts: (1) under the *domestic market extension concept,* foreign markets are extensions of the domestic market and the domestic marketing mix is offered, as is, to foreign markets; (2) with the *multidomestic market concept,* each country is viewed as being culturally unique and an adapted marketing mix for each country market is developed; and (3) with the *global market concept,* the world is the market and, wherever cost- and culturally effective, a standardized marketing mix is developed for entire sets of country markets (whether the home market and only one other or the home market and 100 other countries). The selection of any one of the approaches to internationalization produces different effects on subsequent product, promotion, distribution, and pricing decisions and strategies.

Global versus International Marketing Management

The primary distinction between global marketing management and multinational or international[2] marketing management is orientation (see Exhibit 11–1). *Global marketing management* is guided by the global marketing concept, which views the world as one market and is based on identifying and targeting cross-cultural similarities. On the other hand, *international marketing management,* also known as multinational marketing management, is based on the premise of cross-cultural differences and is guided by the belief that each foreign market requires its own culturally adapted marketing strategy.

---

[1] Mohammad Zafarullah, Mujahid Ali, and Stephen Young, "The Internationalization of the Small Firm in Developing Countries—Exploratory Research from Pakistan," *Journal of Global Marketing,* Vol. 11(3), 1998, p. 21.

[2] Multinational marketing and international marketing are used interchangeably.

**EXHIBIT 11–1   A Comparison of Assumptions about Global
and International Companies**

	Global Companies	*International Companies*
Product Life Cycle	Global product life cycles. All consumers want the most advanced products.	Products are in different stages of the product life cycle in each nation.
Design	International performance criteria considered during design stage.	Adjustments to products initially designed for domestic markets.
Adaptation	Products are adapted to global wants and needs. Restrained concern for product suitability.	Product adaptation is necessary in markets characterized by national differences.
Market Segmentation	Segments reflect group similarities. Group similar segments together.	Segments reflect differences. Customized products for each segment.
	Fewer standardized markets.	Many customized markets.
	Expansion of segments into worldwide proportions	Acceptance of regional/national differences.
Competition	Ability to compete in national markets is affected by a firm's global position.	Domestic/national competitive relationships.
Production	Globally standardized production. Adaptations are handled through modular designs.	Standardization limited by requirements to adapt products to national tastes.
The Consumer	Global convergence of consumer wants and needs.	Preferences reflect national differences.
Product	Emphasis on value-enhancing distinction.	Products differentiated on the basis of design, features, functions, style, and image.
Price	Consumers prefer a globally standardized good if it carries a lower price.	Consumers willing to pay more for a customized product.
Promotion	Global product image, sensitive to national differences and global needs.	National product image, sensitive to national needs.
Place	Global standardization of distribution.	National distribution channels.

Source: Adapted with the authors' permission from Gerald M. Hampton and Erwin Buske, "The Global Marketing Perspective," *Advances in International Marketing,* vol. 2, S. Tamer Cavusgil, ed. (Greenwich, Conn.: JAI Press, 1987), pp. 265–66.

As discussed in an earlier chapter, there is still debate about the extent of global markets today. A reasonable question concerns whether a global marketing strategy is possible only when a completely standardized marketing mix can be achieved. (Keep in mind that the term "global marketing strategy," as used in this text, and the term "globalization of markets" are two separate, although interrelated, ideas. The former has to do with orientation, efficiency of operations, and competitiveness; the latter concerns the homogeneity of demand across cultures.[3] A global marketing strategy can be cost-effective and competitively advantageous without absolute homogeneity in global market demand when standardization across markets is sought. As a result, a company may pursue different orientations in its different businesses.

---

[3] For yet another article on the standardization debate but one that is very well done, see Jeryl Whitelock and Carole Pimblett, "The Standardisation Debate in International Marketing," *Journal of Global Marketing,* Vol. 10(3), 1997, p. 45.

Global strategies do not mean huge companies operating in a single world market. Nor is a global strategy a standard product–market mix that assumes the world to be a single, homogeneous, border–free marketplace. Global strategies are also not about global presence or about large companies. Instead, a company pursuing a global strategy can compete in any market it chooses to compete in and can bring its entire worldwide resources to bear on any competitive situation it finds itself in, regardless of where that might be.[4] A company with a global orientation constantly scours the world for market openings and processes information on a global basis.

There are at least three points that help define a global approach to international marketing: (1) the world is viewed as the market (that is, sets of country markets); (2) homogeneous market segments are sought across country market sets; and (3) standardization of the marketing mix is sought wherever possible but adapted whenever culturally necessary.

It is important to stress that to follow a global strategy does not dictate absolute standardization of all activities. Companies approach decision making with a global orientation to achieve standardization where possible, but the market is the final determinate of what strategy to follow. For example, multinational corporation Procter & Gamble pursues a global orientation for disposable diapers, but for its detergents, it pursues a regional strategy in North America and Europe and a multidomestic one in Asia-Pacific. Even with detergents, however, there is some standardization; for example, the Tide brand is marketed worldwide.

Benefits of Global Orientation

Why globalize? Several benefits are derived from globalization and standardization[5] of the marketing mix, with **economies of scale in production and marketing** being the most frequently cited. As a case in point, Black & Decker Manufacturing Company—makers of electrical hand tools, appliances, and other consumer products—realized significant production cost savings when it adopted a global strategy. It was able to reduce not only the number of motor sizes for the European market from 260 to 8 but also 15 different models to 8. Similarly, Ford estimates that by globalizing its product development, purchasing, and supply activities, it can save up to $3 billion a year.

The savings in the standardization of advertising can be substantial as well. PepsiCo has saved an estimated $10 million per year by using the same film for TV ads in individual national markets.[6] Colgate-Palmolive Company introduced its Colgate tarter-control toothpaste in over 40 countries, each of which could choose one of two ads. The company estimates that for every country where the standardized commercial runs, it saves $1 to $2 million in production costs.

Transfer of experience and know-how across countries through improved coordination and integration of marketing activities is also cited as a benefit of globalization. Unilever, N.V., successfully introduced two global brands originally developed by two subsidiaries. Its South African subsidiary developed Impulse body spray and a European branch developed a detergent that cleaned effectively in European hard water. Aluminum Co. of America's (Alcoa) joint venture partner in Japan produced aluminum sheets so perfect that U.S. workers, when shown samples, accused the company of hand-selecting the samples. Line workers were sent to the Japanese plant to learn the techniques that were then transferred to the United States operations. Because of the benefits of such transfers of knowledge, Alcoa has changed its practice of sending man-

---

4 Vijay Jolly, "Global Strategies in the 1990s," *The Financial Post,* February 15, 1997, p. S6.

5 For an interesting report on the degree of standardization, see Cheng Lu Wang, "The Degree of Standardization: A Contingency Framework for Global Marketing Strategy Development," *Journal of Global Marketing,* Vol. 10(1), 1996, p. 89.

6 Susan Segal-Horn, "The Limits of Global Strategy," *Strategy & Leadership,* November 21, 1996, p. 12.

Exhibit 11-2   International Planning Process

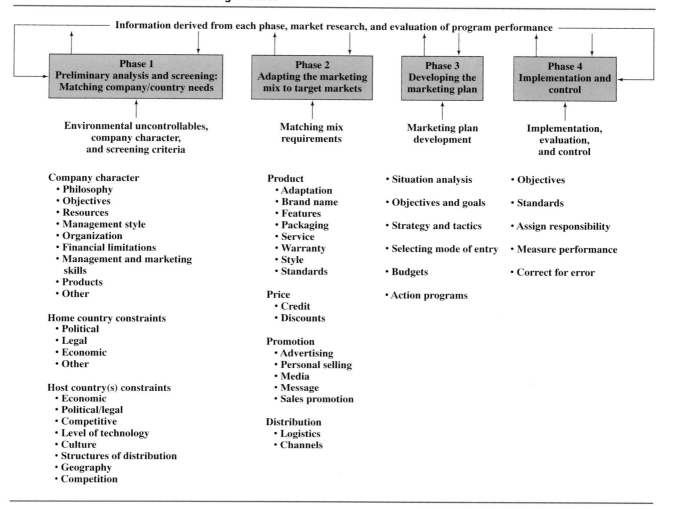

Information derived from each phase, market research, and evaluation of program performance

Phase 1 Preliminary analysis and screening: Matching company/country needs	Phase 2 Adapting the marketing mix to target markets	Phase 3 Developing the marketing plan	Phase 4 Implementation and control
Environmental uncontrollables, company character, and screening criteria	Matching mix requirements	Marketing plan development	Implementation, evaluation, and control

Company character
 • Philosophy
 • Objectives
 • Resources
 • Management style
 • Organization
 • Financial limitations
 • Management and marketing
  skills
 • Products
 • Other

Home country constraints
 • Political
 • Legal
 • Economic
 • Other

Host country(s) constraints
 • Economic
 • Political/legal
 • Competitive
 • Level of technology
 • Culture
 • Structures of distribution
 • Geography
 • Competition

Product
 • Adaptation
 • Brand name
 • Features
 • Packaging
 • Service
 • Warranty
 • Style
 • Standards

Price
 • Credit
 • Discounts

Promotion
 • Advertising
 • Personal selling
 • Media
 • Message
 • Sales promotion

Distribution
 • Logistics
 • Channels

• Situation analysis

• Objectives and goals

• Strategy and tactics

• Selecting mode of entry

• Budgets

• Action programs

• Objectives

• Standards

• Assign responsibility

• Measure performance

• Correct for error

step in the international planning process is deciding in which existing country market to make a market investment. A company's strengths and weaknesses, products, philosophies, and objectives must be matched with a country's constraining factors and market potential. In the first part of the planning process, countries are analyzed and screened to eliminate those that do not offer sufficient potential for further consideration.[14] Emerging markets pose a special problem since many have inadequate marketing infrastructures, distribution channels are underdeveloped, and income level and distribution vary among countries.[15]

The next step is to establish screening criteria against which prospective countries can be evaluated. These criteria are ascertained by an analysis of company objectives, resources, and other corporate capabilities and limitations. It is important to determine the reasons for entering a foreign market and the returns expected from such an invest-

  [14] Lloyd C. Russow and Sam C. Okoroafo, "On the Way towards Developing a Global Screening Model," *International Marketing Review,* Vol. 13(1), 1996, p. 46.

  [15] For an interesting indexing approach for screening emerging markets see, S. Tamer Cavusgil, "Measuring the Potential of Emerging Markets: An Indexing Approach," *Business Horizons,* January–February 1997, p. 87.

ment. A company's commitment to international business and its objectives for going international are important in establishing evaluation criteria. A company guided by the global market concept looks for commonalties among markets and opportunities for standardization, whereas a company guided by the domestic market extension concept seeks markets that accept the domestic marketing mix as implemented in the home market. Minimum market potential, minimum profit, return on investment, acceptable competitive levels, standards of political stability, acceptable legal requirements, and other measures appropriate for the company's products are examples of the evaluation criteria to be established.

Once evaluation criteria are set, a complete analysis of the environment within which a company plans to operate is made. The environment consists of the uncontrollable elements discussed earlier and includes both home-country and host-country restraints, marketing objectives, and any other company limitations or strengths that exist at the beginning of each planning period. Although an understanding of uncontrollable environments is important in domestic market planning, the task is more complex in foreign marketing because each country under consideration presents the foreign marketer with a different set of unfamiliar environmental constraints. It is this stage in the planning process that more than anything else distinguishes international from domestic marketing planning.

The results of Phase 1 provide the marketer with the basic information necessary to: (1) evaluate the potential of a proposed country market; (2) identify problems that would eliminate the country from further consideration; (3) identify environmental elements which need further analysis; (4) determine which part of the marketing mix can be standardized for global companies or which part of and how the marketing mix must be adapted to meet local market needs; and (5) develop and implement a marketing action plan.[16]

Information generated in Phase 1 helps a company avoid the mistakes that plagued Radio Shack Corporation, a leading merchandiser of consumer electronic equipment in the United States, when it first went international. Radio Shack's early attempts at international marketing in Western Europe resulted in a series of costly mistakes that could have been avoided had it properly analyzed the uncontrollable elements of the countries targeted for its first attempt at multinational marketing. The company staged its first Christmas promotion for December 25 in Holland, unaware that the Dutch celebrate St. Nicholas Day and gift giving on December 6. Furthermore, legal problems in various countries interfered with some of their plans; they were unaware that most European countries have laws prohibiting the sale of citizen-band radios, one of the company's most lucrative U.S. products and one they expected to sell in Europe. German courts promptly stopped a free flashlight promotion in German stores because giveaways violate German sales laws. In Belgium, the company overlooked a law requiring a government tax stamp on all window signs, and poorly selected store sites resulted in many of the new stores closing shortly after opening.

With the analysis in Phase 1 completed, the decision maker faces the more specific task of selecting country target markets, identifying problems and opportunities in these markets, and beginning the process of creating marketing programs.[17]

Phase 2—Adapting the Marketing Mix to Target Markets.   A more detailed examination of the components of the marketing mix is the purpose of Phase 2. When target markets are selected, the market mix must be evaluated in light of the data generated in Phase 1. In which ways can the product, promotion, price, and distribution be standardized and in which ways must they be adapted to meet target market requirements? In-

---

[16] See Poul H. Andersen and Jesper Strandskov, "International Market Selection: A Cognitive Mapping Perspective," *Journal of Global Marketing*, Vol. 11(3), 1998, p. 65

[17] For an excellent study on a model for product introduction see James J. Hoffman, "A Two Stage Model for the Introduction of Products into International Markets," *Journal of Global Marketing*, Vol. 11(1), 1997, p. 65.

Responding to Asian preferences, Campbell's "Arnott's" biscuits were packaged in a carton rather than in traditional plastic wrapping. (Courtesy of Campbell Soup Company)

correct decisions at this point lead to costly mistakes through lost efficiency from lack of standardization; products inappropriate for the intended market; and/or costly mistakes in improper pricing, advertising, and promotional blunders. The primary goal of Phase 2 is to decide on a marketing mix adjusted to the cultural constraints imposed by the uncontrollable elements of the environment that effectively achieve corporate objectives and goals.

The process used by the Nestlé Company is an example of the type of analysis done in Phase 2. Each product manager has a country fact book that includes much of the information suggested in Phase 1. The country fact book analyzes in detail a variety of culturally related questions. In Germany, the product manager for coffee must furnish answers to a number of questions. How does a German rank coffee in the hierarchy of consumer products? Is Germany a high or a low per capita consumption market? (These facts alone can be of enormous consequence. In Sweden the annual per capita consumption of coffee is 18 pounds, while in Japan it's half a gram!) How is coffee used—in bean form, ground, or powdered? If it is ground, how is it brewed? Which coffee is preferred—Brazilian Santos blended with Colombian coffee, or robusta from the Ivory Coast? Is it roasted? Do the people prefer dark roasted or blond coffee? (The color of Nestlé's soluble coffee must resemble as closely as possible the color of the coffee consumed in the country.)

As a result of the answers to these and other questions, Nestlé produces 200 types of instant coffee, from the dark robust espresso preferred in Latin countries to the lighter blends popular in the United States. Almost $50 million a year is spent in four research laboratories around the world experimenting with new shadings in color, aroma, and flavor. Do the Germans drink coffee after lunch or with their breakfast? Do they take it black or with cream or milk? Do they drink coffee in the evening? Do they sweeten it? (In France, the answer is clear: in the morning, coffee with milk; at noon, black coffee—i.e., two totally different coffees.) At what age do people begin drinking coffee? Is it a traditional beverage as in France, is it a form of rebellion among the young as in

England where coffee drinking has been taken up in defiance of tea-drinking parents, or is it a gift as in Japan? There is a coffee boom in tea-drinking Japan, where Nescafé is considered a luxury gift item; instead of chocolates and flowers, Nescafé is toted in fancy containers to dinners and birthday parties. With such depth of information, the product manager can evaluate the marketing mix in terms of the information in the country fact book.

Phase 2 also permits the marketer to determine possibilities for standardization. By grouping all countries together and looking at similarities, market characteristics that can be standardized become evident.

Frequently, the results of the analysis in Phase 2 indicate that the marketing mix would require such drastic adaptation that a decision not to enter a particular market is made. For example, a product may have to be reduced in physical size to fit the needs of the market, but the additional manufacturing cost of a smaller size may be too high to justify market entry. Also the price required to be profitable might be too high for a majority of the market to afford. If there is no way to reduce the price, sales potential at the higher price may be too low to justify entry.

On the other hand, additional research in this phase may provide information that can suggest ways to standardize marketing programs among two or more country markets. This was the case for Nestlé when research revealed that young coffee drinkers in England and Japan had identical motivations. As a result, Nestlé now uses principally the same message in both markets.

The answers to three major questions are generated in Phase 2: (1) Which elements of the marketing mix can be standardized and where is standardization not culturally possible? (2) Which cultural/environmental adaptations are necessary for successful acceptance of the marketing mix? and (3) Will adaptation costs allow profitable market entry? Based on the results in Phase 2, a second screening of countries may take place, with some countries dropped from further consideration. The next phase in the planning process is development of a marketing plan.

Phase 3—Developing the Marketing Plan.   At this stage of the planning process, a marketing plan is developed for the target market—whether a single country or a global market set. The marketing plan begins with a situation analysis and culminates in the selection of an entry mode and a specific action program for the market. The specific plan establishes what is to be done, by whom, how it is to be done, and when. Included are budgets and sales and profit expectations. Just as in Phase 2, a decision not to enter a specific market may be made if it is determined that company marketing objectives and goals cannot be met.

Phase 4—Implementation and Control.   A "go" decision in Phase 3 triggers implementation of specific plans and anticipation of successful marketing. However, the planning process does not end at this point. All marketing plans require coordination and control during the period of implementation. Many businesses do not control marketing plans as thoroughly as they could even though continuous monitoring and control could increase their success. An evaluation and control system requires performance objective action, that is, to bring the plan back on track should standards of performance fall short. A global orientation facilitates the difficult but extremely important management tasks of coordinating and controlling the complexities of international marketing.

While the model is presented as a series of sequential phases, the planning process is a dynamic, continuous set of interacting variables with information continuously building among phases. The phases outline a crucial path to be followed for effective, systematic planning.

Although the model depicts a global company operating in multiple country markets, it is equally applicable for a company interested in a single country. Phases 1 and 2 are completed for each country being considered, and Phases 3 and 4 are developed individually for the target market whether it consists of a single country or a series of sep-

their surprise, PicturePhone's sales staff received orders from Israel, Portugal, and Germany.[24]

Other companies have had similar experiences and are actively designing Internet catalogues targeting specific countries with multilingual Web sites. In fact, Dell Computer Corporation's strategy of selling its computers over the Internet has been expanded to foreign sites as well. In 1997, Dell began selling computers via the Internet to Malaysia, Australia, Hong Kong, New Zealand, Singapore, Taiwan, and other Asian countries through a "virtual store" on the Internet. The same selling mode has been launched in Europe.[25] Another high-tech direct marketer with a multilingual Web presence is Sun Microsystems and its aftermarketing company, SunExpress,[26] which lists local language information on more than 3,500 aftermarket products. The company enables visitors in North America, Europe, and Japan to get information online on products and services and place orders directly and securely in their native languages.[27]

As discussed in Chapter 2, the impact of the Internet on international marketing is yet to be determined. However, IIM should not be overlooked as an alternative market-entry strategy by the small or large company. Coupled with the international scope of credit card companies like MasterCard and Visa and international delivery services like UPS and Federal Express, deliveries to foreign countries can be relatively effortless.

Contractual Agreements

*Contractual agreement*s are long-term, nonequity associations between a company and another in a foreign market. Contractual agreements generally involve the transfer of technology, processes, trademarks, or human skills. In short, they serve as a means of transfer of knowledge rather than equity. Contractual agreements include licensing, franchising, joint ventures, and consortia.

Licensing.   A means of establishing a foothold in foreign markets without large capital outlays is *licensing*. Patent rights, trademark rights, and the rights to use technological processes are granted in foreign licensing. It is a favorite strategy for small and medium-sized companies although by no means limited to such companies. Not many confine their foreign operations to licensing alone; it is generally viewed as a supplement to exporting or manufacturing, rather than the only means of entry into foreign markets. The advantages of licensing are most apparent when: capital is scarce, import restrictions forbid other means of entry, a country is sensitive to foreign ownership, or it is necessary to protect patents and trademarks against cancellation for nonuse.

Although licensing may be the least profitable way of entering a market, the risks and headaches are less than for direct investments; it is a legitimate means of capitalizing on intellectual property in a foreign market. Licensing takes several forms. Licenses may be granted for production processes, for the use of a trade name, or for the distribution of imported products. Licenses may be closely controlled or be autonomous, and they permit expansion without great capital or personnel commitment if licensees have the requisite capabilities. Not all experiences with licensing are successful because of the burden of finding, supervising, and inspiring licensees.

Franchising.   *Franchising* is a rapidly growing form of licensing in which the franchisor provides a standard package of products, systems, and management services, and

---

[24] Thomas W. Malone, "Is Empowerment Just Fad? Control, Decision Making, and IT," *Sloan Management Review*, January 1997, p. 23.

[25] Marina Emmanuel, "Dell Strikes Gold Selling Computers via Internet," *The New Straits Times,* April 3, 1997, p. 26.

[26] Visit the Web site at **http://sun.com/sunexpress**.

[27] Rob Yoegel, "Global Selling on the Internet," *Target Marketing,* March 1997, p. 106.

the franchisee provides market knowledge, capital, and personal involvement in management. The combination of skills permits flexibility in dealing with local market conditions and yet provides the parent firm with a reasonable degree of control. The franchisor can follow through on marketing of the products to the point of final sale. It is an important form of vertical market integration. Potentially, the franchise system provides an effective blending of skill centralization and operational decentralization, and has become an increasingly important form of international marketing. In some cases, franchising is having a profound effect on traditional businesses. In England, for example, it is estimated that annual franchised sales of fast-foods are nearly $2 billion, which accounts for 30 percent of all foods eaten outside the home.

Prior to 1970, international franchising was not a major activity. A survey by the International Franchising Association revealed that only 14 percent of its member firms had franchises outside of the United States, and the majority of those were in Canada. By the 1990s, more than 30,000 franchises of U.S. firms were located in countries throughout the world. Franchises include soft drinks, motels, retailing, fast-foods, car rentals, automotive services, recreational services, and a variety of business services from print shops to sign shops. Canada is the dominant market for U.S. franchisors, with Japan and the United Kingdom second and third in importance. The Asian Pacific Rim has seen rapid growth as companies look to Asia for future expansion.

Franchising is the fastest-growing market-entry strategy. It is often among the first types of foreign retail business to open in the emerging market economies of Eastern Europe, the former republics of Russia, and China—McDonald's is in Moscow (their first store seats 700 inside and has 27 cash registers), and Kentucky Fried Chicken is in China (the Beijing KFC store has the highest sales volume of any KFC store in the world). The same factors that spurred the growth of franchising in the U.S. domestic economy have led to its growth in foreign markets. Franchising is an attractive form of corporate organization for companies wishing to expand quickly with low capital investment. The franchising system combines the knowledge of the franchisor with the local knowledge and entrepreneurial spirit of the franchisee. Foreign laws and regulations are friendlier toward franchising because it tends to foster local ownership, operations, and employment.

There are two types of franchise agreements used by franchising firms—master franchise and licensing—either of which can have a country's government as one partner. The master franchise is the most inclusive agreement and the method used in more than half of the international franchises. The *master franchise* gives the franchisee the rights to a specific area (many are for an entire country) with the authority to sell or establish subfranchises. McDonald's franchise in Moscow is a master agreement owned by a Canadian firm and its partner, the Moscow City Council Department of Food Services.

Licensing a local franchisee the right to use a product, good, service, trademark, patent, or other asset for a fee is a second type of franchise arrangement. Coca-Cola licenses local bottlers in an area or region to manufacture and market Coca-Cola using syrup sold by Coca-Cola. Rental-car companies often enter a foreign market by licensing a local franchisee to operate a rental system under the trademark of the parent company.

Lil'Orbits, a Minneapolis-based company that sells donut-making equipment and ingredients to entrepreneurs, is an example of how a small company can use licensing and franchising to enter a foreign market.[28] Lil'Orbits sells a donut maker that turns out $1^1/2$-inch donuts while the customer waits. The typical buyer in the United States buys equipment and mix directly from the company without royalties or franchise fees. The buyer has a small shop or kiosk and sells donuts by the dozen for take away or individually along with a beverage.

---

[28] Curtice K. Cultice, "'Donuts to Dollars' Batter Up: Its Time for the Rest of the World to Make Donuts," *Business America* May 1997, p. 39.

Whirlpool refrigerators, like these in Bangkok, come in bright colors because often they are put in living rooms. (Kraipit Phanyut/SIPA)

Successful in the United States, Lil'Orbits ran an advertisement in *Commercial News USA,* a magazine showcasing products and services in foreign countries, that attracted 400 inquiries. Pleased with the response, the company set up an international franchise operation based on royalties and franchise fees. Now a network of international franchised distributors markets the machines and ingredients to potential vendors. The distributors pay Lil'Orbits a franchise fee and buy machines and ingredients directly from Lil'Orbits or from one of the 28 licensed blenders worldwide from which Lil'Orbits receives a royalty. This entry strategy has enabled the company to enter foreign markets with minimum capital investment outside the home country. The company has 20,000 franchised dealers in 78 countries. About 60 percent of the company's business is international.

Although franchising enables a company to expand quickly with minimum capital, there are costs associated with servicing franchisees. For example, to accommodate different tastes around the world, Lil'Orbits had to develop a more "pastry," less-sweet type of mix than that used in the United States. Other cultural differences have to be met as well. For example, customers in France and Belgium could not pronounce the trade name, Lil'Orbits, so Orbie is used instead. Toppings also have to be adjusted to accommodate different tastes. Cinnamon sugar is the most widely accepted, but in China, cinnamon is considered a medicine, so only sugar is used. In the Mediterranean region, the Greeks like honey and chocolate sauce is popular in Spain. Powdered sugar is more popular than granulated sugar in France, where the donuts are eaten in cornucopia cups instead of on plates.[29]

Joint Ventures.   *Joint ventures (JVs)* as a means of foreign market entry have accelerated sharply since the 1970s. Besides serving as a means of lessening political and economic risks by the amount of the partner's contribution to the venture, JVs provide a less-risky way to enter markets that pose legal and cultural barriers than would be the case in an acquisition of an existing company.[30]

---

[29] Visit the Lil'Orbits Web site at **http://www.lilorbits.com/**.

[30] Robert Miller, Jack Glen, Fred Jaspersen, and Yannis Karmokolias, "International Joint Ventures in Developing Countries," *Finance & Development,* March 1997, p. 26.

CROSSING BORDERS 11-2

Two Companies—Two Strategies

Polaroid and Eastman Kodak have followed different paths to success in Russia. While Polaroid owes its lead in the camera market to early entry, Kodak controls the film market thanks to a pioneering franchising scheme.

Polaroid was one of the first big foreign companies to believe in the Russian market. It opened a Moscow-based joint venture in 1989. The company had everything consumers wanted as the Iron Curtain lifted: The Polaroid cameras were new, "gadgety," and distinctly foreign. They were tied to home and family life, but also offered a cheap way to signal affluence in public. Over 95 percent of sales come from the most inexpensive camera in the line, retailing at about $45. Instant pictures helped to demystify photography, a pursuit which in Soviet times was considered "technical" and largely reserved for devoted hobbyists. Polaroid has outsold all other compact cameras combined in Russia.

Although consumer sales are beginning to level out, Polaroid Russia has barely touched the sector of the business which brings in half of its revenue in other countries—badge, license, and ID photography. Given the Russians' extraordinary fondness for badges and the like, this sector ought to be a new gold mine.

Kodak sells not so much a product as a level of quality, which was widely known and recognized despite the closed-door policy during the Soviet regime. Kodak decided that the best way into Russia was through franchising Kodak Express minilaboratories. It sought its first franchisees through an advertisement in *Kommersant*. No experience was necessary, but $50,000 in cash was.

Kodak quickly found that there was money for small business opportunities, particularly those tied to the prestige of a global leader like Kodak. It originally targeted 25 Kodak Express labs in Moscow. However, as modern processing labs were opened, customers saw they could have better pictures than Polaroid's with not much more trouble. Furthermore, using Kodak film was also cheaper if they chose to print only the best-looking negatives. By late 1996 there were 350 Kodak Express labs all over the country.

The beauty of Kodak's idea to franchise is that it offloads much of the risk and headache of Russian expansion to the franchisees. Kodak simply sells them equipment, film, and chemicals for cash. More ambitious lab operators have evolved into regional distributors. The enterprise award goes to one former photographer who has opened 21 labs in offbeat cities in the Northern Urals. Kodak leads its film/chemical competitors, Fuji and Agfa, as the category-defining brand.

Both photo firms achieved broad consumer awareness with little advertising. Polaroid did it by being early with a product that symbolized the new world and freedom. Kodak traded on its global image and the presence of the labs as living, breathing publicity.

Source: Adapted from "Russia: Photo Finish," *Business Eastern Europe*, March 3, 1997, p. 5. Visit Kodak's and Polaroid's respective Web sites at **http://www.kodak.com** and **http://www.polaroid.com/**.

A joint venture is differentiated from other types of strategic alliances or collaborative relationships in that a joint venture is a partnership of two or more participating companies that have joined forces to create a separate legal entity. Joint ventures are differentiated from minority holdings by a MNC in a local firm.

Four factors are associated with joint ventures: (1) JVs are established, separate, legal entities; (2) they acknowledge intent by the partners to share in the management of the JV; (3) they are partnerships between legally incorporated entities such as companies, chartered organizations, or governments, and not between individuals; and (4) equity positions are held by each of the partners.

Nearly all companies active in world trade participate in at least one joint venture somewhere; many companies have dozens of joint ventures. A recent Conference Board study indicated that 40 percent of Fortune 500 companies were engaged in one or more international joint ventures.

In the Asian Pacific Rim, where U.S. companies face unfamiliar legal and cultural barriers, joint ventures are preferred to buying existing businesses. Local partners can often lead the way through legal mazes and provide the outsider with help in under-standing cultural nuances. A joint venture can be attractive to an international marketer: (1) when it enables a company to utilize the specialized skills of a local partner; (2) when it allows the marketer to gain access to a partner's local distribution system; (3) when a company seeks to enter a market where wholly-owned activities are prohibited; (4) when it provides access to markets protected by tariffs or quotas; and (5) when the firm lacks the capital or personnel capabilities to expand its international activities.

In China, a country considered to be among the riskiest in Asia, there have been 49,400 joint ventures established in the 15 years since the government began allowing JVs. Among the many reasons JVs are so popular is that they offer a way of getting around high Chinese tariffs, allowing a company to gain a competitive price advantage over imports. Manufacturing locally with a Chinese partner rather than importing by-passes China's high tariffs (the tariff on automobiles is 200 percent, 150 percent on cos-metics, and the average on miscellaneous products is 75 percent). Manufacturing locally with a Chinese partner rather than importing achieves additional savings as a result of low-cost Chinese labor. Many Western brands are manufactured and marketed in China at prices that would not be possible if the products were imported.

Recently, however, many of the legal reasons for creating a JV rather than imple-menting direct investment have changed. The changing environment has produced a growing trend toward a new and possibly much more effective way of doing business in China: wholly foreign-owned enterprises (WFOEs). WFOEs take less time to establish than JVs, although they are barred from some sectors where only a JV is permitted.[31]

Consortia. *Consortia* are similar to the joint venture and could be classified as such except for two unique characteristics: (1) they typically involve a large number of par-ticipants; and (2) they frequently operate in a country or market in which none of the participants is currently active. Consortia are developed for pooling financial and man-agerial resources and to lessen risks. Often, huge construction projects are built under a consortium arrangement in which major contractors with different specialties form a separate company specifically to negotiate for and produce one job. One firm usually acts as the lead firm, or the newly formed corporation may exist quite independently of its originators.

Direct Foreign Investment

A fourth means of foreign market development and entry is *direct foreign investment,* that is, investment within a foreign country. Companies may manufacture locally to cap-italize on low-cost labor, to avoid high import taxes, to reduce the high costs of trans-portation to market, to gain access to raw materials, and/or as a means of gaining market entry.

The growth of free-trade areas that are tariff free among members but have a com-mon tariff for nonmembers creates an opportunity that can be capitalized on by direct investment. Companies have avoided significant commitment to Central America, since no single country offers a sufficiently large market. However, trade liberalization among the countries makes it possible to consider a multicountry strategy. With tariffs lowered

---

[31] Wilfried Vanhonacker, "Entering China: An Unconventional Approach," *Harvard Business Review,* March–April 1997, p. 130.

among countries and external tariffs remaining high, companies such as Unilever and Nestlé are making direct investments in manufacturing plants to serve the region.[32]

A hallmark of global companies today is the establishment of manufacturing operations throughout the world. This is a trend that will increase as barriers to free trade are eliminated and companies can locate manufacturing wherever it is most cost effective.[33]

Strategic International Alliances

A *strategic international alliance (SIA)*[34] is a business relationship established by two or more companies to cooperate out of mutual need and to share risk in achieving a common objective. While not strictly a market-entry strategy method, many contractual agreements discussed above can be classified as SIAs. Strategic alliances have grown in importance over the last few decades as a competitive strategy in global marketing management. SIAs are sought as a way to shore up weaknesses and increase competitive strengths. Opportunities for rapid expansion into new markets, access to new technology, more efficient production and marketing costs, and additional sources of capital are motives for engaging in strategic international alliances.

A strategic international alliance implies: (1) that there is a common objective; (2) that one partner's weakness is offset by the other's strength; (3) that reaching the objective alone would be too costly, take too much time, or be too risky; and (4) that together their respective strengths make possible what otherwise would be unattainable. In short, a SIA is a synergistic relationship established to achieve a common goal where both parties benefit.[35]

Company alliances are not new to business enterprises. Joint ventures, licensing, franchising, equity ownership, and other forms of business relationships are well-known cooperative business agreements. Many joint ventures were established for legal and political reasons; before NAFTA, for example, Mexican law required 51 percent local ownership for investments in Mexico. To minimize risk in politically unstable countries, companies sought local partners to help ward off expropriation and other forms of political harassment. While political and legal reasons for SIAs still exist, the growing importance for SIAs today can be attributed more to competition and global expansion.[36]

As discussed in Chapter 2, the competitive environment of international business is changing rapidly. To be competitive in global markets a company must meet or exceed new standards for quality and new levels of technology. There is an increasing change of pace for product development and profitability. Cost-efficient, technologically advanced products are being offered by competitors and demanded in established markets as well as in markets rising from formerly Marxist–socialist economies. Opportunities abound the world over, but to benefit firms must be current in new technology, have the ability to keep abreast of technological change, have distribution systems to capitalize on global demand, have cost-effective manufacturing, and have capital to build new systems as necessary.

The scope of what a company needs to do and what it can do is at a point where even the largest firms engage in alliances to maintain their competitiveness. In an annual report, the president of General Electric shared with stockholders his enthusiasm for

---

[32] "Unilever Central America: Critical Mass," *Business Latin America,* March 17, 1997, p. 6.

[33] For a complete description of the different purposes for FDI in manufacturing plants, see "Charting the Strategic Roles of Foreign Factories," *Harvard Business Review,* March–April 1997, p. 76.

[34] For a complete discussion of the logic of SIAs, see Kenichi Ohmae, *The Borderless World* (New York: Harper Business, 1990), chap. 8, "The Global Logic of Strategic Alliances," pp. 114–36; and Kenichi Ohmae, "Putting Global Logic First," *Harvard Business Review,* January–February 1995, pp. 119–25.

[35] An interesting report on alliances in the telecommunications industry is: Ken Zita, "Grand Alliances," *Infrastructure Finance,* April 1997, p. 27.

[36] See, for example: Desiree Blankenburg Holm, Kent Eriksson, and Jan Johnason, "Business Networks and Cooperation in International Business Relationships," *Journal of International Business Studies,* Special Issue 1996, p. 1033.

Putting their rivalries aside, Nestlé and General Mills have formed a joint venture to market breakfast cereals. The Swiss company brings its global marketing network, and the American company brings the brands. (Susan May Tell/SABA)

alliances when he wrote, "We view [alliances] as a means to expand product lines, make the company more competitive in existing products in existing markets, and to reduce the investment and time it takes to bring good ideas to our customers." Examples of SIAs involving large corporations abound: IBM uses a series of alliances with Japanese suppliers to fill out its product line—Seiko Epson produces several key components for IBM's Proprinter, and an alliance with Canon provides the color printer used in many of IBM's desktop publishing and printing systems. General Motors and Isuzu, and Ford and Nissan are involved in codesigning and coproducing small cars (GM's Geo and Sprint and Ford's Escort line) for the U.S. markets.

Companies enter strategic alliances to acquire the skills necessary to achieve their objectives more effectively, at a lower cost, or with less risk than if they acted alone. For example, a company strong in research and development skills and weak in the ability or capital to successfully market a product may seek an alliance to offset its weakness— one partner to provide marketing skills and capital and the other to provide technology and a product. The majority of alliances today are designed to exploit markets and/or technology.

A SIA with multiple objectives involves C-Itoh (Japan), Tyson Foods (USA), and Provemex (Mexico). It is an alliance that processes Japanese-style *yakatori* (bits of chicken on a bamboo stick marinated and grilled) for export to Japan and other Asian countries. Each company had a goal and made a contribution to the alliance. C-Itoh's goal was to find a lower-cost supply of *yakatori;* because it is so labor intensive, it was becoming increasingly costly and noncompetitive to produce in Japan. C-Itoh's contribution was access to its distribution system and markets throughout Japan and Asia. Tyson's goal was new markets for its dark chicken meat, a by-product of demand for mostly white meat in the U.S. market. Tyson exported some of its excess dark meat to Asia and knew that C-Itoh wanted to expand its supplier base. But Tyson faced the same high labor costs as C-Itoh. Provemex, the link that made it all work, had as its goal expansion beyond raising and slaughtering chickens into higher value-added products for international markets. Provemex's contribution was to provide highly cost-competitive labor.

Through the alliance, they all benefited. Provemex acquired the know-how to debone the dark meat used in *yakatori,* and was able to vertically integrate its operations and secure a foothold in a lucrative export market. Tyson earned more from the sale of surplus chicken legs than was previously possible, and also gained an increased share of the Asian market. C-Itoh had a steady supply of competitively priced *yakatori* for its vast distribution and marketing network. This is a collaborative relationship; three companies with individual strengths created a successful alliance in which each contributes and each benefits.

Many companies also are entering SIAs to be in a strategic position to be competitive and to benefit from the expected growth in the single European market.[37] As a case in point, when General Mills wanted a share of the rapidly growing breakfast-cereal market in Europe, joined with Nestlé to create Cereal Partners Worldwide. The European cereal market was projected to be worth hundreds of millions of dollars as health-conscious Europeans changed their breakfast diet from eggs and bacon to dry cereal. General Mills' main U.S. competitor, Kellogg, has been in Europe since 1920 and controls about half of the market.

It would be extremely costly for General Mills to enter the market from scratch. Although the cereal business uses cheap commodities as its raw materials, it is both capital- and marketing intensive; sales volume must be high before profits begin to develop. Only recently has Kellogg earned significant profit in Europe.

For General Mills to reach its goal alone would have required a manufacturing base and a massive sales force. Further, Kellogg's stranglehold on supermarkets would have been difficult for an unknown to breach easily. The solution was a joint venture with Nestlé. Nestlé had everything General Mills lacked—a well-known brand name, a network of plants, a powerful distribution system—except the one thing General Mills could provide: strong cereal brands.

The deal was mutually beneficial. General Mills provided the knowledge in cereal technology, including some of its proprietary manufacturing equipment, its stable of proven brands, and its knack for pitching these products to consumers. Nestlé provided its name on the box, access to retailers, and production capacity that could be converted to making General Mills' cereals. In time, Cereal Partners Worldwide intends to extend its marketing effort beyond Europe. In Asia, Africa, and Latin America, Cereal Partners Worldwide will have an important advantage over the competition since Nestlé is a dominant food producer.

Of course not all SIAs are successful; some fail, and others are dissolved after reaching their goals. Failures can be attributed to a variety of reasons, but all revolve around lack of perceived benefits to one or more of the partners. Benefits may never have been realized in some cases, and different goals and management styles may have caused dissatisfaction in other alliances. Such was the case with an alliance between Rubbermaid and the Dutch chemical company, DSM—the two differed on management and strategic issues. Rubbermaid wanted to invest in new products and expansion to combat sluggish demand as the result of a European recession, while DSM balked at any new investments. In other cases, an alliance can outlive its usefulness for one of the partners and thus be dissolved. Ford and Volkswagen's Autolatina alliance was entered into to manufacture low-cost automobiles for the Latin American market. The two companies would manufacture cars together for Brazil and Argentina, sharing all the profits and producing no competing models. Unfortunately, Ford elected to make compact size cars and VW, small subcompact cars. Market growth came in subcompacts. It was obvious that Ford was not benefiting from the alliance and in 1997 ended it.[38]

The selection of an entry mode is a critical decision because the nature of the firm's operations in the country market is affected by and depends on the choice made. It affects the future decisions because each mode entails an accompanying level of resource

[37] Allyson L. Stewart-Allen, "Strategic Alliance Is a Good Route to European Market," *Marketing News,* August 12, 1996, p. 15.

[38] Keith Bradsher, "Messy Latin Divorce Splits Ford and VW," *International Herald Tribune,* May 17–18, 1997, p. B1.

commitment and it is difficult to change from one entry mode to another without considerable loss of time and money.[39]

Organizing for Global Competition

An international marketing plan should optimize the resources committed to company objectives. The organizational plan includes the type of organizational arrangements to be used, and the scope and location of responsibility. Because organizations need to reflect a wide range of company-specific characteristics—such as size, the level of policy decisions, length of chain of command, staff support, source of natural and personnel resources, degree of control, centralization, and type or level of marketing involvement—it is difficult to devise a standard organization structure. Many ambitious multinational plans meet with less than full success because of confused lines of authority, poor communications, and lack of cooperation between headquarters and subsidiary organizations.

An organization structure that effectively integrates domestic and international marketing activities has yet to be devised. Companies face the need to maximize the international potential of their products and services without diluting their domestic marketing efforts. Companies are usually structured around one of three alternatives: (1) global product divisions responsible for product sales throughout the world; (2) geographical divisions responsible for all products and functions within a given geographical area; or, (3) a matrix organization consisting of either of these arrangements with centralized sales and marketing run by a centralized functional staff, or a combination of area operations and global product management.

Companies that adopt the global product division structure are generally experiencing rapid growth and have broad, diverse product lines. Geographic structures work best when a close relationship with national and local governments is important.

The matrix form—the most extensive of the three organizational structures—is popular with companies as they reorganize for global competition. A matrix structure permits management to respond to the conflicts that arise between functional activity, product, and geography. It is designed to encourage sharing of experience, resources, expertise, technology, and information among global business units. At its core is better decision making, in which multiple points of view affecting functional activity, product, and geography are examined and shared.

For some companies, however, the matrix structure does not work well. These companies tend to modify the matrix in favor of organizing by product groups or strategic business units, the assumption being that integrating each product's business system on a worldwide basis is the best way to optimize strategy and achieve coherence among different local units.

A company may be organized by product lines but have geographical subdivisions under the product categories. Both may be supplemented by functional staff support. Exhibit 11–3 shows such a combination. Modifications of this basic arrangement are used by a majority of large companies doing business internationally.

As multinational companies face increasing competitive pressure to develop global strategies, adapting the corporate organization to match global objectives is crucial. The rules for doing business in a global market are changing and the organizational structure must change to reflect new opportunities and levels of competitiveness.[40]

The extent of change in organizational structures among multinational companies that are globalizing is reflected in a study of 43 large U.S. companies. The companies indicated they planned a total of 137 organizational changes for their international oper-

---

[39] An excellent study on the entry decision can be found in V. Kumar and Velavan Subramaniam, "A Contingency Framework for the Mode of Entry Decision," *Journal of World Business,* Vol. 31(1), 1997, p. 53.

[40] See, for example, Henry P. Conn and George S. Yip, "Global Transfer of Critical Capabilities," *Business Horizons,* January–February 1997, p. 22.

CROSSING BORDERS 11–3

Many Roads Lead to Globalization

The rules for doing business in global markets are changing and companies are reorganizing to respond to new levels of competitiveness. Consider what some multinational corporations are doing to globalize operations:

• Bristol-Meyers Squibb is revamping its consumer business by installing a new chief responsible for its worldwide consumer medicines business and creating a new business unit with worldwide responsibility for its haircare products.

• Ford is merging its manufacturing, sales, and product development operations in North America and Europe—and eventually in Latin America and Asia. The company is also setting up five program centers with worldwide responsibility to develop new cars and trucks.

• IBM is reorganizing its marketing and sales operations into 14 worldwide industry groups. By moving away from a geography-based organization, IBM hopes to make itself more responsive to customers.

• Rank Xerox is regrouping its operations into nine autonomous worldwide business units in order to enhance customer satisfaction. The traditional top-down style of hierarchical organization will be jettisoned because it takes too long to get products to customers, involves costly duplication, stifles initiative, and discourages individual accountability.

Sources: "Borderless Management," *Business Week,* May 23, 1994, p. 25; "Rank Xerox's New Regional Groups," *Business Europe,* March 28–April 3, 1994, p. 6; and Jerry Flint, "One World, One Ford," *Forbes,* June 20, 1994, p. 40. Visit Bristol-Meyers Squibb's, IBM's, and Xerox's Web sites at **http://www.bms.com/, http://www.ibm.com/,** and **http://www.xerox.com/.**

ations over a five-year period. Included were such changes as: centralizing international decision making, creating global divisions, forming centers of excellence, and establishing international business units. Bausch & Lomb, Inc., one of the companies in the study, has revamped its international organizational structure; it has collapsed its international division into a worldwide system of three regions and set up business management committees to oversee global marketing and manufacturing strategies for four major product lines.[41] Bausch & Lomb's goal was to better coordinate central activities without losing touch at the local level. "Global coordination is essential," according to the company's CEO, "but in a way that maintains the integrity of the foreign subsidiaries."

To the extent that there is a trend, three factors seem to be sought, regardless of the organizational structure: a single locus for direction and control, greater emphasis to functional strategies instead of business-by-business ones, and the creation of a simple line organization that is based on a more decentralized "network" of local companies.[42]

---

[41] "Building Tomorrow's Global Company," *Crossborder Monitor,* October 15, 1997, p. 12.
[42] Vijay Jolly, "Global Strategies in the 1990s," *The Financial Post,* February 15, 1997, p. S6.

EXHIBIT 11–3   **Schematic Marketing Organization Plan Combining Product, Geographic, and Functional Approaches**

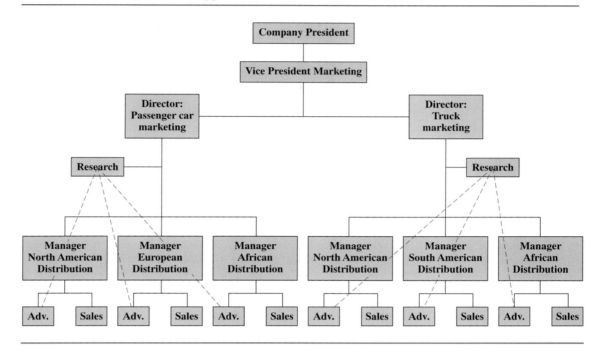

Locus of Decision

Considerations of where decisions will be made, by whom, and by which method constitute a major element of organizational strategy. Management policy must be explicit about which decisions are to be made at corporate headquarters, which at international headquarters, which at regional levels, and which at national or even local levels. Most companies also limit the amount of money to be spent at each level. Decision levels for determination of policy, strategy, and tactical decisions must be established. Tactical decisions normally should be made at the lowest possible level without country-by-country duplication. If a tactical decision applies to several countries, it probably should be made at the regional level, but if it applies to only one country, it should be made at the national level.

Centralized versus Decentralized Organizations

An infinite number of organizational patterns for the headquarters activities of multinational firms exist, but most fit into one of three categories: centralized, regionalized, or decentralized organizations. The fact that all of the systems are used indicates that each has certain advantages and disadvantages. Chief advantages of centralization are the availability of experts at one location, the ability to exercise a high degree of control on both the planning and implementation phases, and the centralization of all records and information.

Some companies affect extreme decentralization by selecting competent managers and giving them full responsibility for national or regional operations. These executives are in direct day-to-day contact with the market but lack a broad company view, which can mean partial loss of control for the parent company.

Multinationals are constantly seeking the "right" organization that will provide it with flexibility, an ability to respond to local needs, and worldwide control over far-flung business units. Not any single one of the traditional organization plans that have evolved is adequate for today's global enterprise seeking to combine the economies of scale of a global company with the flexibility and marketing knowledge of a local company. Companies are experimenting with several different organization schemes, but greater centralization of decisions is common to all.

In many cases, whether or not a company's formal organizational structure is centralized or decentralized, the informal organization reflects some aspect of all organizational systems. This is especially true relative to the locus of decision making. Studies show that even though product decisions may be highly centralized, subsidiaries may have a substantial amount of local influence in pricing, advertising, and distribution decisions.[43] If a product is culturally sensitive, the decisions are more apt to be decentralized.

Summary

Expanding markets around the world have increased competition for all levels of international marketing. To keep abreast of the competition and maintain a viable position for increasingly competitive markets, a global perspective is necessary. Global competition also requires quality products designed to meet ever-changing customer needs and rapidly advancing technology. Cost containment, customer satisfaction, and a greater number of players mean that every opportunity to refine international business practices must be examined in light of company goals. Collaborative relationships, strategic international alliances, strategic planning, and alternative market-entry strategies are important avenues to global marketing that must be implemented in the planning and organization of global marketing management.

Questions

1. Define:

global marketing	franchising
management	joint venture
corporate planning	domestic market extension
direct exporting	concept
strategic planning	multidomestic market concept
indirect exporting	global market concept
tactical planning	SIA
licensing	

2. Define strategic planning. How does strategic planning for international marketing differ from domestic marketing?

3. Discuss the benefits to an MNC of accepting the global market concept. Explain the three points that define a global approach to international marketing.

4. Discuss the effect of shorter product life cycles on a company's planning process.

5. What is the importance of collaborative relationships to competition?

6. In Phases 1 and 2 of the international planning process, countries may be dropped from further consideration as potential markets. Discuss some of the conditions in each phase that may exist in a country that would lead a marketer to exclude a country.

7. Assume that you are the director of international marketing for a company producing refrigerators. Select one country in Latin America and one in Europe and develop screening criteria to use in evaluating the two countries. Make any additional assumptions that are necessary about your company.

8. "The dichotomy typically drawn between export marketing and overseas marketing is partly fictional; from a marketing standpoint, they are but alternative methods of capitalizing on foreign market opportunities." Discuss.

9. How will entry into a developed foreign market differ from entry into a relatively untapped market?

10. Why do companies change their organizations when they go from being an international to a global company?

11. Formulate a general rule for deciding where international business decisions should be made.

12. Explain the popularity of joint ventures.

13. Compare the organizational implications of joint ventures versus licensing.

14. Visit the Web sites of Maytag Corporation (**http://www. maytag.com/**) and the Whirlpool Corporation (**http:// www.whirlpool.com/**), both appliance manufacturers in the United States. Search their Web sites and compare their international involvement. How would you classify each— as exporter, international, or global?

---

[43] Ingo Theuerkauf, David Ernst, and Amir Mahini, "Think Local, Organize . . .?" *International Marketing Review,* 13, no. 3 (1996), p. 7.

15. Using the sources in question above i.e., **http://www. maytag.com/** and **http://www.whirlpool.com/**, list the different alternatives entry modes each uses.

16. Visit the Nestlé Corporation Web site (**http://www.nestle. com/**) and the Unilever N.V. (**http://www.unilever.com/**) Web site. Compare their strategies toward international markets. In what ways do they differ (besides product categories) in their international marketing?

CREATING PRODUCTS FOR CONSUMERS IN GLOBAL MARKETS

Chapter Learning Objectives

What you should learn from Chapter 12

- The importance of offering a product suitable to the intended market.
- The current dichotomy of standardized versus differentiated products in international marketing.
- The relationship between product acceptance and the market into which it is introduced.
- The importance of quality and how quality is defined.
- Country of origin effect on product image.
- Physical, mandatory, and cultural requirements for product evaluation.
- Physical, mandatory, and cultural requirements for product adaptation.
- The need to view all attributes of a product in order to overcome or modify resistance to its acceptance.
- The increasing importance of quality in global marketing.

Snapple Just Can't Get It Right
American Products Don't Suit the Japanese Consumer

As the fractured cliché goes, "It's Déjà Vu all over again." Initially Snapple Beverage Corp. was wildly successful in the U.S. with exotic flavored, New Age-style drinks supported by a shoestring marketing budget that focused on consumer involvement with the brand. Snapple flavors such as kiwi-strawberry appealed to Americans who were turning to more natural beverages. The company was successful enough for Quaker Oats Company to buy it for $1.7 billion. But after two and a half years it was sold back to its original owners for $300 million. What happened during the few short years that Quaker owned the company? Snapple rapidly lost market share in the United States when Quaker Oats restructured its distribution and folded Snapple in with Gatorade. The company also made the decision to go global with the product in Europe and Asia, but it withdrew the brand after less than two years; consumers were turned off.

Snapple looked like a natural in Japan, where consumers were showing a growing thirst for natural soft drinks and teas. The ready-to-drink (RTD) tea market represents the fastest growing drink market in Japan. RTD teas have vaulted to a 22 percent share of Japan's total soft drinks market. Studies of consumer trends indicated an underlying demand for low-calorie, authentic-tasting drinks. In response to these changing consumer tastes, tea drink manufacturers began producing healthy-type drinks coupled with high-quality taste and convenience.

Most tea drinks are packaged in cans—a package best suited to the vending machine channel (around 60 percent of canned drinks are sold through Japan's vending machines). These machines are highly developed and can serve drinks either hot or cold or both, thus covering the full spectrum of tea types on the market—whether ice tea or hot tea drinks. A small but growing volume of tea drinks is sold in paper packs. To date, glass bottle volume has been small. However, the two top-selling brands in the new fruit tea drinks category—Snapple and Nestea—were launched in large (473 ml) glass bottles.

Not only did the market look right for a Snapple-type drink, but Quaker also landed a powerful ally when 7-Eleven Japan Co., Japan's top food-and-beverage retailer and franchiser of 6,400 stores nationwide, agreed to carry the drinks. Initially sales were great, but they soon began falling off. Mr. Takeda, the Snapple representative, surveyed retailers and customers and came back with a diagnosis: Snapple's unusually shaped bottle and its American image which had initially attracted millions of curious buyers were not enough to turn them into repeat purchasers. Comments included: "Snapple had a sticky, sugary sweetness to it that I didn't like" and "Snapple's iced tea was murky-looking with all that sediment floating in it."

Mr. Takeda urged Quaker to quickly modify its flavors, to reduce sweetness, and to filter out the sediment. He also urged Quaker to spend more to market Snapple's name. Quaker had spent only about 200 million yen ($1.86 million), mostly for a late-night television commercial. That was "very insufficient," Mr. Takeda says, in a country where companies routinely spend several billion yen advertising a new drink. Quaker's meager Japanese ad spend on the brand, believed to be under $2 million, was grossly inadequate in a market where food, beverages, and tobacco are the biggest spending ad category—totaling $7.2 billion in 1995, according to Dentsu. "The way they handled Snapple's launch fit right into the stereotypical image of the shortsighted American firm totally preoccupied with immediate results,"

Last spring, when sales fell under 10 bottles a week from a peak of 50, 7-Eleven halted Snapple orders. "We can't tolerate slow-selling products even for a couple of days." Japanese convenience-shop owners are merciless. They stop ordering a product at the first sign of tapering customer interest. Store owners can choose from some 1,000 new soft drinks that are launched each year by foreign and domestic companies, so they can afford to ditch products quickly. Which is what happened to Snapple at stores all over Japan.

Convenience stores are a powerful force in Japan—they outsell large supermarket chains in food and beverages—so failure with that segment of the market can be fatal, with no chance of resurrection. "Our shoppers gave a resounding thumbs down on Snapple." "You'll never see Snapple again in our stores . . . and probably not elsewhere, either."

As you read the chapter, see what lessons can be learned from the Snapple example: distribution, advertising, cultural differences, failing to adapt the product, wrong packaging, knowing your market, alternative modes of entry. A Japanese partner could have helped. Or was it just poor marketing by a company, not very experienced in international marketing? You might want to visit the Quaker Oats Web site (**http://www.quakeroats. com**). How much international experience does Quaker Oats have? Perhaps it was just a fad in the United States as well, and the product would have dropped off even if the original owners had not sold to Quaker Oats. Check and see just how successful Snapple is after being back in

the hands of the original owners. Visit the Snapple Web site at **http://www.snapple.com**.

Sources: Adapted from: Helen Deal, "Quirky Snapple Fails to Make a Splash in Asia," *Advertising Age,* June 10, 1996, p. I30; "Snapple in Japan," *Dow Jones News Service-Wall Street Journal Stories,* April 15, 1996; "Snapple: A US Success Story That Has Failed to Translate," *Marketing,* September 12, 1996, p. 21; Norihiko Shirouzu, "Snapple in Japan: How a Splash Dried Up," *The Wall Street Journal,* April 15, 1996, p. B1; "Ready-to-Drink Teas in Japan," *Gorman's New Product News,* June 12, 1996, p. 10; Laura Tyson, "Tre; Chic in Taiwan," *Financial Times London,* December 16, 1996, p. 14; and Kim Walker, "They Watch, but Do They Buy?" *The American Chamber of Commerce in Japan Journal,* June 1, 1997.

The opportunities and challenges for international marketers of consumer goods today have never been greater or more diverse. New consumers are springing forth in emerging markets from Eastern Europe, the Commonwealth of Independent States, China and other Asian countries, India, Latin America—in short, globally. While some of these emerging markets have little purchasing power today, they promise to be huge markets in the future. In the more mature markets of the industrialized world, opportunity and challenge also abound as consumers' tastes become more sophisticated and complex and as increases in purchasing power provide them with the means of satisfying new demands. A key theme now and in the future in international marketing management is the globalization of markets, with its impact on a firm's strategies and marketing mix.

Never has the question "Which products should we sell?" been more critical than it is today. For the company with a domestic market extension orientation, the answer generally is, "Whatever we are selling at home." The company with a multidomestic market orientation develops different products to fit the uniqueness of each country market; the global company ignores frontiers and seeks commonalties in needs among sets of country markets and responds with a global product.

All three strategies are appropriate somewhere but because of the enormous diversity in global markets, the appropriate strategy for a specific market is determined by the company's resources, the product, and the target market. Consequently, each country market must be examined thoroughly or a firm risks marketing poorly conceived products in incorrectly defined markets with an inappropriate marketing effort.

The trend for larger firms is toward becoming global in orientation and strategy. However, product adaptation is as important a task in a smaller firm's marketing effort as it is for global companies. As competition for world markets intensifies and as market preferences become more global, selling what is produced for the domestic market in the same manner as it is sold at home proves to be increasingly less effective. Some products cannot be sold at all in foreign markets without modification; others may be sold as is but their acceptance is greatly enhanced when tailored specifically to market needs. In a competitive struggle, quality products that meet the needs and wants of a market at an affordable price should be the goal of any marketing firm. For some product category groups and some country markets, this means differentiated products for each market. Other product groups and country market segments do well competitively with a global or standardized product but for both, a quality product is essential.

This chapter explores some of the relevant issues facing an international marketer when planning and developing consumer products for global markets. The questions about product planning and development range from the obvious—which product to sell—to the more complex—when, how, and if products should be adapted for different markets.

Global Markets and Product Development

There is a recurring debate about product planning and development that focuses on the question of standardized or global products marketed worldwide versus differentiated products adapted, or even redesigned, for each culturally unique market. One extreme position is held by those with strong production and unit-cost orientation who advocate global standardization, while at the other extreme are those, perhaps more culturally sensitive, who propose a different product for each market.

Underlying the arguments offered by the proponents of standardized products is the premise that global communications and other worldwide socializing forces have fostered a homogenization of tastes, needs, and values in a significant sector of the population across all cultures. This has resulted in a large global market with similar needs and wants that demands the same reasonably priced products of good quality and reliability.

In support of this argument, a study found that products targeted for urban markets in less-developed countries needed few changes from products sold to urban markets in developed countries. "Modern products usually fit into life-styles of urban consumers wherever they are"; young urban professionals in London have more in common with their contemporaries in Singapore than with middle-class families outside London.[1] Other studies identify a commonality of preferences among population segments across countries. Families in New York need the same dishwashers as families in Paris, and families in Rome make similar demands on a washing machine as do families in Toledo.

Although recognizing some cultural variations, advocates of standardization believe that price, quality, and reliability will offset any differential advantage of a culturally adapted product. Product standardization leads to production economies and other savings that permit profits at prices that make a product attractive to the global market. Economies of production, better planning, more effective control, and better use of creative managerial personnel are the advantages of standardization. Such standardization can result in significant cost savings but it makes sense only when there is adequate demand for the standardized product.

Those who hold the opposing view stress that substantial cultural variation among countries dictates a need for differentiated products to accommodate the uniqueness of cultural norms and product use patterns. For example, Electrolux, the appliance manufacturer, finds the refrigerator market among European countries far from homogeneous. Northern Europeans want large refrigerators because they shop only once a week in supermarkets; Southern Europeans prefer small ones because they pick through open-air markets almost daily. Northerners like their freezers on the bottom, Southerners on top. And Britons, who devour huge quantities of frozen foods, insist on units with 60 percent freezer space. Further, 100 appliance makers compete for that market. To be competitive, Electrolux produces 120 basic designs with 1,500 variations. Compare such differences to the relatively homogeneous United States market where most refrigerators are standardized, have freezers on top, and come in only a few sizes, and where 80 percent are sold by four firms. Can Electrolux standardize its refrigerator line for the European market? Management thinks not, so long as the market remains as it is.

The issue between these two extremes cannot be resolved with a simple either/or decision because the prudent position probably lies somewhere in the middle. Most astute marketers concede that there are definable segments across country markets with some commonalty of product preferences, and that substantial efficiencies can be attained by standardizing, but they also recognize there may be cultural differences that remain important. The key issue is not whether to adapt or standardize, but how much adaptation is necessary and to what point a product can be standardized.

---

[1] John Willman, "No Secret Formula behind Ruling Brands," *The Financial Post,* October 21, 1997, p. 66.

CROSSING BORDERS 12–1

The Muppets Go Global

"One of the interesting things about puppetry and our work is that it crosses cultural lines. . . . We are known around the world."

It's no idle statement. The "Muppet Show" is truly a world product, seen on TV screens in over 100 countries and dubbed in 15 languages. The three Muppet movies have played in nearly 60 countries. The TV series "Fraggle Rock" reached 96 countries in 13 different languages. Jim Hensen's "Big Bird" adapted perfectly to cultural environments around the world. In Arabic-speaking countries, Big Bird became the big camel; in Latin America, a big parrot; in the Philippines, a tortoise; in West Germany, a big brown bear.

In China, Da Niao, literally "big bird" in Mandarin, will debut in 1998. It won't come wholesale from the U.S. with local languages dubbed but will be created especially for China by Chinese production companies. The formula or model will be adapted to a Chinese curriculum created by Chinese. Instead of teaching the ABCs, "Zhima," Sesame Street in Chinese, will teach children their Chinese characters. The plot line will focus on China's rural and urban population, a combination of modern China with convenience stores and the old China of noodle shops. Two new Muppets were created exclusively for "Zhima," a blue pig named Hu Hu Xhu, or Snoring Pig, and a red monster girl named Xiao Meizi, or Little Plum.

There is even a Sesame Street sponsored jointly between Israel and Palestine. Much like real life, each has its own set: a boardwalk with an ice-cream parlor and a view of the Mediterranean for the Israeli street; and for the Palestinian street, a water well, a shop selling Arab sweets, and a backdrop of West Bank-style hills and olive trees. Both languages are spoken. Ernie will ask a question in Hebrew and Bert will answer in Arabic. Producers use a core of 3,000 words that are similar in both Semitic languages. Although the characters visit each other's streets, there is no one place they share. An attempt was made to create a third set, a park where residents of both streets would meet and play. The Israelis were willing to consider the idea but the Palestinians wanted to know who owned the park—they wanted a sign marking the border between Palestine and Israel. The Israelis said no, so there is no place on the show for Palestinians and Israelis to share.

Sources: Adapted from Lily Tung, "How to Get to (China's) Sesame Street," *The Wall Street Journal Interactive Edition,* August 20, 1997; Amy Dockser Marcus, "Ernie Uses Hebrew, Bert Speaks Arabic; Moses, He's a Grouch," *The Wall Street Journal,* June 5, 1997, p. A1.

Most products are adapted to some degree, even those traditionally held up as examples of standardization. Although the substantial portion of its product is standardized worldwide, McDonald's includes vegetarian and lamb burgers in its India stores to accommodate dietary and religious restrictions, and wine and beer in European stores. Campbell's sells many of its soup flavors as standardized products worldwide, but also accommodates taste preferences in China with pork, fig, and date soup, and with Crema de Chile Poblano soup in Mexico. Pepsi Cola reformulated its diet cola to be sweeter and more syrupy, and changed its name from Diet Pepsi to Pepsi Max to appeal to international markets where the idea of "diet" is often shunned and a sweeter taste is preferred.

Even if different products are necessary to satisfy local needs, as in the case of Electrolux, it does not exclude a standardized approach. A fully standardized product may not be appropriate, but some efficiency through standardizing certain aspects of the product may be achieved. Whirlpool faced this problem when it acquired the appliance division of N. V. Philips, the European manufacturer whose approach to the European market was to make a different product for each country market. Whirlpool found that Philips' German plant produced feature-rich washing machines that sold at higher prices, while washers from the Italian plants ran at lower RPMs (revolutions per minute) and were less costly. Each plant operated independently of the other and produced customized products for its respective markets. The washing machines made in the Italian and German facilities differed so much that "they did not have one screw in common"; yet the reality was that the insides of the machines were very similar. Electrolux took immediate steps to standardize and simplify both the German and Italian machines by reducing the number of parts and using as many common parts as possible. New products were developed in a way to ensure that a wide variety of models could be built on a standardized platform. The same approach was taken for dryers and other product categories.[2] Although complete standardization could not be achieved, standardizing the platform (the core product) and customizing other features to meet local preferences attained efficiencies.

As companies gain more experience with the idea of global markets, the approach is likely to be to standardize where possible and adapt where necessary. To benefit from standardization as much as possible and still provide for local cultural differences, companies are using an approach to product development that allows for such flexibility.

The idea is to develop a core platform containing the essential technology, and then base variations on this platform. Sony of Japan has used this approach for its Walkman. The basic Walkman platform gives Sony the flexibility to adjust production rapidly to shifts in market preference. It is interesting to speculate on the possibilities of using this approach for standardizing the refrigerators discussed above.

Going even further to ensure that products meet the needs of local market regions and maintain maximum benefits of globalization, companies are establishing research and development centers within regions, to identify important product trends that can be incorporated into their product lines. Unilever has several centers across the Asian regions where researchers develop local variations of ice cream, shampoo, tea, detergents, and cosmetics. The dividends are not necessarily limited to Asian markets, either; many products are offered globally. One example is Vim floor cleaner. Developed to deal with the number of creeping, crawling pests that invade a tropical Asian home, Unilever's researchers added insect repellent. The reformulated brand did so well in Asia that Unilever is launching it wherever bugs prevail.[3] Nestlé has similar R&D centers where key categories for innovation are identified; when a new innovation is developed, the new product is adapted to local tastes by in-country teams. A case in point is a unit that identified healthy foods as a key category and developed a yogurt containing active bacteria, which helps sustain the body's natural defenses. After the product concept is developed, the product is then offered to all units for adaptation to local tastes.[4]

To differentiate for the sake of differentiation is not a solution, nor is adaptation for the sake of adaptation. Realistic business practice requires that a company strive for uniformity in its marketing mix whenever and wherever possible, while recognizing that cultural differences may demand some accommodation if the product is to be competitive. Later in the chapter, various ways of screening products to determine the extent of necessary adaptation will be discussed.

Global Brands

Hand in hand with global products are global brands. A *global brand* is defined as the worldwide use of a name, term, sign, symbol, design, or combination thereof intended

---

[2] "Did Whirlpool Spin Too Far Too Fast?" *Business Week,* June 24, 1996, p. 134.

[3] Fara Warner, "Unilever Turns to Local Flavor to Lure Asia's Missing Market," *The Wall Street Journal Interactive Edition,* October 10, 1997. See also **http://www.wsj.com**.

[4] "New Products," *Business Europe,* February 12, 1997, p. 9.

Global brands in a French hypermarket. (Guy Le Querrec/Magnum)

to identify goods or services of one seller and to differentiate them from those of competitors. Much like the experience with global products, there is no single answer to the question of whether or not to establish global brands. There is, however, little question of the importance of a brand name.

A successful brand is the most valuable resource a company has. The brand name encompasses the years of advertising, good will, quality evaluation, product experience, and the other beneficial attributes the market associates with the product. Brand image is at the very core of business identity and strategy. Customers everywhere respond to images, myths, and metaphors that help them define their personal and national identities within a global context of world culture and product benefits.[5] Global brands play an important role in that process. The value of Kodak, Sony, Coca-Cola, McDonald's, Toyota, and Marlboro is indisputable.[6] One estimate of the value of Coca-Cola, the world's most valuable brand, places it at over $35 billion. In fact, one authority speculates that brands are so valuable that companies will soon include a "statement of value" addendum to their balance sheets to include intangibles such as the value of their brands.[7]

Naturally, companies with such strong brands strive to use those brands globally. Even for products that must be adapted to local market conditions, a global brand can be

---

[5] Jeanne Binstock van Rij, "Trends, Symbols, and Brand Power in Global Market: The Business Anthropology Approach, " *Strategy & Leadership,* November 21, 1996, p. 18.

[6] For an interesting study on measuring the equity of a brand name, see David A. Aaker, "Measuring Brand Equity across Products and Markets," *California Management Review,* March 1996, p. 102.

[7] "Buying Power, Global Brands of the Future Will Speak to Millions Worldwide in a Voice They Understand as Their Own," *Business Age,* January 1996, p. 34.

successfully used. Heinz produces a multitude of products to meet local tastes that are sold under the Heinz brand all over the world. Many are also adapted to local tastes. In the U.K., for example, Heinz Baked Beans Pizza (available with cheese or sausage) was a runaway hit, selling over 2.5 million pizzas in the first six months after its introduction. In the British market, Heinz's brand of baked beans is one of the more popular products. The British consumer eats an average of 16 cans annually, for a sales total of $1.5 billion a year. The company realizes that consumers in other countries are unlikely to rush to stores for bean pizzas, but the idea could lead to the creation of products more suited to other cultures and markets.[8]

A global brand gives a company a uniform worldwide image that enhances efficiency and cost savings when introducing other products associated with the brand name, but not all companies believe a single global approach is the best. In addition to companies like Kodak, Coca-Cola, Caterpillar, and Levi's that use the same brands worldwide, other multinationals such as Nestlé, Mars, Procter & Gamble,[9] and Gillette have some brands that are promoted worldwide and others that are country specific. Among companies that have faced the question of whether or not to make all their brands global, not all have followed the same path.

Companies that already have successful country-specific brand names must balance the benefits of a global brand against the risk of losing the benefits of an established brand. The cost of reestablishing the same level of brand preference and market share for the global brand that the local brand has must be offset against the long-term cost savings and benefits of having only one brand name worldwide. In those markets where the global brand is unknown, many companies are buying local brands of products that consumers want and revamping, repackaging, and finally relaunching them with a new image.[10] Unilever purchased a local brand of washing powder, Biopan, that had a 9 percent share of the market in Hungary and after relaunching, market share rose to about 25 percent.[11]

When Mars, a U.S. company that includes candy and pet food among its product lines, adopted a global strategy, it brought all its products under a global brand, even those with strong local brand names. In Britain, the largest candy market in Europe, M&Ms, were sold as Treets and Snickers candy was sold under the name Marathon to avoid association with "knickers," the British word for women's underpants. To bring the two candy products under the global umbrella, Mars returned to their original names, M&Ms and Snickers.[12] The pet food division adapted Whiskas and Sheba for cat foods and Pedigree for dog food as the global brand name replacing KalKan. To support this global division that accounts for over $4 billion annually, Mars also developed a Web site for the pet food brands. The Web site (**http://www.petcat.com**) functions as a "global infrastructure" that can be customized locally by any Pedigree Petfoods branch worldwide. For instance, Pedigree offices can localize languages and information on subjects such as veterinarians and cat-owner gatherings.[13]

National Brands

A different strategy is followed by the Nestlé Company, which has a stable of global and country-specific national brands in its product line. The Nestlé name itself is promoted

---

[8] "Baked Beans Pizza Wins Raves in—Where Else?—the U.K.," *Ad Age International,* February 1997, p. 14.

[9] Robert L. Wehling, "Even at P&G, Only 3 Brands Make Truly Global Grade So Far," *Ad Age International,* January 1998, p. 8.

[10] "Asia Offers Brand Opportunities for Western Food Manufacturers," *Brand Strategy,* August 22, 1997, p. 28.

[11] Normandy Madden and Sheryl Lee, "Brands of Past Embraced in Former Eastern Bloc," *Ad Age International,* May 1997, p. 120.

[12] "Developing Uniform Brands," *Business Europe,* March 26, 1997, p. 9.

[13] Juliana Koranteng, "Behind the Strategy: Syzygy's Success Falls into Orchestrated Order: CEO Hunt Sells Web Sites for Marketing While Preaching Online Gospel," *Ad Age International,* July 1997, p. 128.

CROSSING BORDERS 12–2

Cream of Snake Soup? It Might Sell!

Prepared food may be the toughest product to sell overseas. It isn't as universal or as easily marketed as, say, soap, cigarettes, or soda. Regional tastes are involved and food flavors do not always travel well.

Campbell's found that Italians, unsurprisingly, shudder at canned pasta, so Franco-American SpaghettiOs don't fly there. The average Pole consumes five bowls of soup a week—three times the American average—but 98 percent of Polish soups are home-made and Mom is one tough competitor. To get around that problem, Campbell's advertises to working Polish mothers looking for convenience, which just might work. But Campbell's realizes it can't just shove a can in the consumer's face and replace Mom. To encourage customers to ease into canned soups, it typically launches a basic meat or chicken broth which consumers can doctor with meats, vegetables, and spices. Then it brings out more sophisticated soups created to appeal to distinctly regional tastes.

To help develop these new soups, the company conducts taste-tests with consumers around the world. On any weekday morning, a dozen consumers take the elevator to the 19th floor of Cornwall House, home to Campbell Soup Co.'s Hong Kong taste kitchen, opened to help get the right flavors to reach 2 billion Asian consumers. Chosen carefully to get the right demographic mix, such groups are assembled to taste the offerings that Campbell's hopes will ignite consumer interest in China and other parts of Asia. There, they split off into carrels and take their seats before bowls of soup and eager food scientists.

Campbell's has a couple of hits to its credit: scallop and ham soups came out of the Hong Kong lab and watercress and duck-gizzard soup out of a U.S. test kitchen. Local ingredients are always considered, but Campbell's draws the line on some Asian favorites. Dog soup is out, as is shark's fin, since most species of shark are endangered. But the staff keeps an open mind. Snake, for example. One researcher admits, "I have tasted it." Who knows? Campbell's cream of snake could emerge as the chicken noodle of the future. M-M-M Good!!

Sources: Adam Heller, "A Recipe for Success?" *The China Business Review,* July–August 1993, pp. 30–32; Susan Warner, "Campbell Soup Tries New Recipes to Cater to Asian Market," *Journal of Commerce and Commercial,* July 13, 1993, p. 9A; " 'Hmm. Could Use a Little More Snake,' " *Business Week,* March 15, 1994, p. 53, and C. Samuel Craig and Susan P. Douglas, "Developing Strategies for Global Markets: An Evolutionary Perspective," *Columbia Journal of World Business,* March 1996, p. 72.

globally but its global brand expansion strategy is two-pronged. In some markets it acquires well-established national brands when it can and builds on their strengths—there are 7,000 local brands in its family of brands.[14] In other markets where there are no strong brands it can acquire, it uses global brand names.[15] The company is described as preferring brands to be local, people regional, and technology global. It does, however, own some of the world's largest global brands; Nescafé is but one.

Unilever is another company that follows a similar strategy of a mix of national and global brands. In Poland, Unilever introduced its Omo brand detergent (sold in many other countries), but it also purchased a local brand, Pollena 2000. Despite a strong introduction of two competing brands, Omo by Unilever and Ariel by Procter & Gamble,

---

[14] Bill Britt, "For Multinationals, Value Lies in Eyes of Local Consumers," *Ad Age International,* May 1997, p. I18.

[15] John Willman, "No Secret Formula behind Ruling Brands, *The Financial Post,* October 21, 1997, p. 66.

a refurbished Pollena 2000 had the largest market share a year later. Unilever's explanation was that East European consumers are leery of new brands; they want brands that are affordable and in keeping with their own tastes and values. Pollena 2000 is successful not just because it is cheaper but because it chimes with local values.

Multinationals must also consider a rise in nationalistic pride that occurs in some countries and impacts on brands. In India, for example, Unilever considers it critical that its brands, such as Surf detergent and Lux and Lifebuoy soaps, are viewed as Indian brands.[16] Just as is the case with products, the answer to the question of when to go global with a brand is, "It depends—the market dictates." Use global brands where possible and national brands where necessary.

Country of Origin Effect and Global Brands

As discussed earlier, brands are used as external cues to taste, design, performance, quality, value, prestige, and so forth. In other words, the consumer associates the value of the product with the brand. The brand can convey either a positive or a negative message about the product to the consumer and is affected by past advertising and promotion, product reputation, and product evaluation and experience.[17] In short, many factors affect brand image. One factor that is of great concern to multinational companies that manufacture worldwide is the country-of-origin effect on the market's perception of the product.

Country-of-origin effect (COE) can be defined as any influence that the country of manufacture has on a consumer's positive or negative perception of a product. Today a company competing in global markets will manufacture products worldwide and, when the customer becomes aware of the country of origin, there is the possibility that the place of manufacture will affect product/brand image.

The country, the type of product, and the image of the company and its brands all influence whether or not the country of origin will engender a positive or negative reaction. There are a variety of generalizations that can be made about country-of-origin effects on products and brands. Consumers tend to have stereotypes about products and countries[18] that have been formed by experience, hearsay, and myth. Following are some of the more frequently cited generalizations.

Consumers have broad but somewhat vague stereotypes about specific countries and specific product categories that they judge "best": English tea, French perfume, Chinese silk, Italian leather, Japanese electronics, Jamaican rum, and so on. Stereotyping of this nature is typically product specific and may not extend to other categories of products from these countries.

The importance of these types of stereotypes was emphasized recently as a result of a change in U.S. law that requires any cloth "substantially altered" (woven for instance) in another country must identify that country on its label. Designer labels like Ferragamo, Gucci, and Versace are affected in that they now must include on the label "Made in China" since the silk comes from China. The lure to pay $195 and up for shoes "Made in Italy" by Ferragamo loses some of its appeal when accompanied with "Made in China." As one buyer commented, "I don't care if the scarves are made in China as long as it doesn't say so on the label." The irony is that 95 percent of all silk comes from China, which has the reputation for the finest silk but also a reputation of producing cheap scarves. The "best" scarves are made in France or Italy by one of the *haut couture* designers.[19]

---

[16] Sorab Mistry, "To Succeed In India, Marketers Must Look beyond the Numbers," *Ad Age International,* October 1997, p. 16.

[17] See, for example, Chung Koo Kim and Jay Young Chung, "Brand Popularity, Country Image and Market Share: An Empirical Study," *Journal of International Business Studies,* Second Quarter 1997, p. 361.

[18] Ian Jones, "Made in the USA: Sexy and Salable," *World Trade,* March 1997, p. 78

[19] Helene Cooper, "That Gucci Scarf 'Made in Italy' Is Sort of Chinese," *The Wall Street Journal,* May 13, 1997, p. A1.

CROSSING BORDERS 12–3

Logos Sell in Japan, or How to Be a Harvard Man

One key to success for marketing in Japan is to emblazon products with a name. Logos—slapped on everything from umbrellas to socks to toilet seat covers—can never be too obvious. A London-based Japanese casual-wear designer says one of the best-selling items in her business is a winter jacket with the entire back covered with her logo in thick capital letters. The names don't even have to make sense. Other popular Japanese logos include Poshboy, Papas, and Pink House. Levi Strauss and Company's Japanese subsidiary saw its sales soar after launching an advertising campaign that claims James Dean, Marilyn Monroe, and John Wayne wore Levi's jeans.

To capitalize on this Japanese obsession for logos, Harvard University licenses its logo for use outside the United States. One step up are Harvard brand shoes, eyeglass frames, umbrellas, neckties, and briefcases, all embossed with the prestige of "Harvard University."

These items are only available in selected stores in East Asia, mostly Japan, and they aren't the typically logo-laden T-shirts, sweat shirts, and other memorabilia sold at the Harvard Coop. In fact, Harvard students and alumni aren't even aware they exist. Nor are they aware that their school's name sewn into the lining of a blazer or etched into eyeglass frames conveys the "American traditional" look.

A Tokyo footwear company has a line of wingtips, loafers, and deck shoes with a Harvard label. The company is also developing a line of infant clothes called Harvard Baby. Further, the company is negotiating a brand of Harvard-label men's wear in China. "The Chinese follow Japanese trends very closely," says the owner.

Harvard earns about $1 million a year worldwide in licensing fees. Officials say money isn't the goal; rather, they are trying to protect Harvard's image. To protect their trademarks for various categories of products they have to register them from country to country and use the trademarks or lose the protection, which lapses after several years if unused. Harvard has already lost its rights in many countries. There is a "Harvard" cigarette brand sold all over India, for example.

If you are a Harvard alumnus, don't despair, your image is secure—Princeton is a B brand, vastly less well known among the Japanese and not nearly as popular as Harvard.

Sources: Yumiko Ono, "Designers Cater to Japan's Love of Logos," *The Wall Street Journal,* May 29, 1990 p. B1;.and Melinda Beck, "So You Didn't Go to Harvard; You Can Still Wear the Shoes," Reprinted by permission of *The Wall Street Journal,* © 1990 Dow Jones & Companies, Inc. All Rights Reserved Worldwide.

Ethnocentrism can also have country-of-origin effects; feelings of national pride—the "buy American" effect, for example—can influence attitudes toward foreign products.[20] Honda, which manufactures one of its models almost entirely in the United States, recognizes this phenomenon and points out how many component parts are made in America in some of its advertisements. On the other hand, others have a stereotype of Japan as producing the "best" automobiles. A recent study found that U.S. automobile producers may suffer comparatively tarnished in-country images regardless of whether they actually produce superior products.

Countries are also stereotyped on the basis of whether they are industrialized, in the process of industrializing, or developing. These stereotypes are less country-product

---

[20] Craig A. Conrad and Subhra Chakrabarty, "An Empirical Study of Consumers' Ethnocentrism towards Product Classes," *Advances in Marketing,* Southwestern Marketing Association Proceedings 1994, pp. 14–20.

specific; they are more a perception of the quality of goods in general produced within the country. Industrialized countries have the highest quality image, and there is generally a bias against products from developing countries.[21]

In Russia, for example, the world is divided into two kinds of products: "ours" and "imported." Russians prefer fresh, homegrown food products but imported clothing and manufactured items. Companies hoping to win loyalty by producing in Russia have been unhappily surprised. Consumers remain cool toward locally produced Polaroid cameras and Philips irons. On the other hand, computers produced across the border in Finland are considered high quality.[22] For Russians, country-of-origin is more important than brand name as an indicator of quality. South Korean electronics have difficulty convincing Russians that they are as good as Japanese. Goods produced in Malaysia, Hong Kong, or Thailand are more suspect still. Eastern Europe is considered adequate for clothing, but poor for food or durables. Turkey and China are at the bottom of the heap.[23]

One might generalize that the more technical the product, the less positive is the perception of one manufactured in a less-developed or newly industrializing country. There is also the tendency to favor foreign-made products over domestic-made in less-developed countries. Foreign products do not fare equally well since consumers in developing countries have stereotypes about the quality of foreign-made products even from industrialized countries. A survey of consumers in the Czech Republic found that 72 percent of Japanese products were considered to be of the highest quality, German goods followed with 51 percent, Swiss goods with 48 percent, Czech goods with 32 percent, and, last, the United States with 29 percent.

One final generalization about COE involves fads that often surround products from particular countries or regions in the world. These fads are most often product specific and generally involve goods that are themselves faddish in nature. European consumers are apparently enamored with a host of American-made products ranging from Jeep Cherokees, Budweiser beer, and Jim Beam bourbon, to Bose sound systems. In the 1970s and 1980s there was a backlash against anything American, but in the 1990s American is in. In China, anything Western seems to be the fad. If it is Western it is in demand, even at prices three and four times higher than domestic products. In most cases such fads wane after a few years as some new fad takes over.

There are exceptions to the generalizations presented here but it is important to recognize that country of origin can affect a product or brand's image. Further, not every consumer is sensitive to a product's country of origin. A finding in a recent study suggested that more knowledgeable consumers are more sensitive to a product's COE than those less knowledgeable.[24] The multinational company needs to take this factor into consideration in product development and marketing strategy since a negative country stereotype can be detrimental to a product's success unless overcome with effective marketing.

Once the market gains experience with a product, negative stereotypes can be overcome. Nothing would seem less plausible than selling chopsticks made in Chile to Japan, but it happened. It took years for a Chilean company to overcome doubts about the quality of its product, but persistence, invitations to Japanese to visit the Chilean poplar forests that provided the wood for the chopsticks, and a quality product finally overcame doubt; now the company cannot meet the demand for chopsticks.

Country stereotyping can be overcome with good marketing. The image of Korean electronics improved substantially in the United States once the market gained positive experience with Korean brands. All of which stresses the importance of building strong

---

[21] Gopalkrishnan R. Iyer and Jukti K. Kalita, "The Impact of Country-of-Origin and Country-of-Manufacture Cues on Consumer Perceptions of Quality and Value," *Journal of Global Marketing,* Vol. 11(1), 1997, p. 7.

[22] "Laptops from Lapland," *The Economist,* September 6, 1997, p. 67.

[23] Graig Mellow, "Free-Spending Foibles," *Business Eastern Europe,* March 24, 1997, p. 1.

[24] Anja Schaefer, "Consumer Knowledge and Country of Origin Effects," *European Journal of Marketing,* Vol. 31(1), 1997, p. 56.

CROSSING BORDERS 12–4

"Things Go Better with Coke" or Sprite— It Depends on Whether It's Red or White

France—the country of origin? So what? Who cares how the French drink wine. Certainly the Chinese don't. Wine is catching on in China, but it's hardly the stuff that wine lovers dream about.

Western wine is starting to replace cognac at China's bars, weddings, and business banquets. But the drinkers aren't wasting time sniffing and sipping: They're mixing it with soda pop and downing it by the pitcher. Red wine with Sprite and white wine with Coke or fruit soda are easier—and cheaper—to gulp.

Connoisseurs sniff at such wines, retailing for around $6 a bottle. These wines are made from "the fourth or fifth pressing of the grapes," says Timothy Yeo, who among other things runs a wine bar in Singapore.

At a dim Bistro in downtown Shanghai, a waitress offers customers a bottle of Le Elmar 33, "Produit de France," though there's no address on the bottle to identify the vintner. The thin Bordeaux stings going down, inducing a purple-tongued cough from one young drinker. The proprietress offers to mix it with something smoother—7 Up, perhaps. "That's the way I drink it," she says.

One newcomer, a French wine called Chantfleur, advertises itself as an official drink of Shanghai athletes at China's Eighth National Games.

A wine exporter tested the market by importing 20 cases of *Chateau Lafite Rothschild Grand Cru Classe.* At a wholesale price of $150 a bottle, the wine sold out in 10 days—all to one karaoke bar that was mixing it with Sprite. "It sent a shudder through many circles that would have appreciated the product." But another shipment is on the way. "We'll let the wine go where the money is," he says.

Sources: Adapted from Craig S. Smith, "Many Chinese Prefer Their Wine Sparkling with a Bouquet of Coke," *The Wall Street Journal;* and "China's New Tipplekkkk; China's Wine Craze," *The Economist,* April 5, 1997.

global brands like Sony, General Electric, and Levi's. Brands effectively advertised and products properly positioned can help ameliorate a less-than-positive country stereotype.

Private Brands

Private brands owned by retailers are growing as challenges to manufacturers' brands, whether global or country-specific. In the food-retailing sector in Britain and many European countries, private labels owned by national retailers increasingly confront manufacturers' brands. From blackberry jam and vacuum-cleaner bags to smoked salmon and sun-dried tomatoes, private-label products dominate grocery stores in Britain and in many of the hypermarkets of Europe.[25] Private brands have captured nearly 30 percent of the British and Swiss markets and more than 20 percent of the French and German markets. In some European markets, private-label market share has doubled in just the past five years.

Sainsbury,[26] one of Britain's largest grocery retailers with 420 stores, reserves the best shelf space for its own brands. A typical Sainsbury store has about 16,000 products,

---

[25] Gerard O'Dwyer, "Swedes Import Private Label Concept," *Ad Age International*, May 1997, p. I23.
[26] Visit Sainsbury's Web site at **http://www.j-sainsbury.co.uk**.

of which 8,000 are Sainsbury labels. Their labels account for two-thirds of store sales. The company avidly develops new products, launching 1,400 to 1,500 new private-label items each year, and weeds out hundreds of others no longer popular. It launched its own Novon-brand laundry detergent and, in the first year, its sales climbed past Procter & Gamble's and Unilever's top brands to make it the top-selling detergent in Sainsbury stores and the second-best seller nationally with a 30 percent market share. The 15 percent margin on private labels claimed by chains such as Sainsbury helps to explain why their operating profit margins are as high as 8 percent, or eight times the profit margins of their U.S. counterparts.

Private-label brand penetration has traditionally been high in Britain and, more recently, in Europe as well. The success of private labels can be attributed to the few national chains, which tend to dominate. In the U.K. for example, the top four chains account for almost 60 percent of the total grocery market of $95 billion.[27] Private labels, with their high margins, will become even more important as the trend in consolidation of retailers continues and as discounters such as Costco, Wal-Mart of the U.S., and Correfore of France expand throughout Europe, putting greater pressure on prices. U.K.'s Tesco, one of Europe's bigger retailers, and other European retailers are expanding across borders where they may gradually introduce private label programs.

As it stands now, private labels are formidable competitors. They provide the retailer with high margins; they receive preferential shelf space and strong in-store promotion; and, perhaps most important for consumer appeal, they are quality products at low prices. Contrast that with manufacturers' brands, which traditionally are premium priced and offer the retailer lower margins than they get from private labels.

To maintain market share, global brands will have to be priced competitively and provide real consumer value. Global marketers must examine the adequacy of their brand strategies in light of such competition. This may make cost and efficiency benefits of global brands even more appealing.

Quality Products

Global competition is placing new emphasis on some basic tenets of business. It is reducing time frames and focusing on the importance of quality, competitive prices, and innovative products. The power in the marketplace is shifting from a seller's market to customers, who have more choices because there are more companies competing for their attention. More competition, more choices, put more power in the hands of the customer, and that, of course, drives the need for quality. Gone are the days when the customer's knowledge was limited to one or at best just a few different products. Today the customer knows what is best, cheapest, and best quality. It is the customer who defines quality in terms of his or her needs and resources.

American products have always been among the world's best, but competition is challenging us to make even better products. In most global markets the cost and quality of a product are among the most important criteria by which purchases are made. For consumer and industrial products alike, the reason often given for preferring one product brand to another is better quality at a competitive price. Quality, as a competitive tool, is not new to the business world but many believe that it is the deciding factor in world markets. However, we must be clear about what we mean by quality.

Quality Defined

Quality can be defined on two dimensions: market-perceived quality and performance quality. Both are important concepts but consumer perception of a quality product often

---

[27] "When Client Turns Competitor," *Business Europe,* January 29, 1997, p. 9.

has more to do with market-perceived quality than performance quality. The relationship of quality conformance to customer satisfaction is analogous to an airline's delivery of quality. If viewed internally from the firm's perspective (performance quality), an airline has achieved quality conformance with a safe flight and landing. But because the consumer expects performance quality to be a given, quality to the consumer is more than compliance (a safe flight and landing). Rather, cost, timely service, frequency of flights, comfortable seating, and performance of airline personnel from check-in to baggage claim are all part of the customer's experience that is perceived as being of good or poor quality.

Considering the number of air miles flown daily, the airline industry is approaching zero defects in quality conformance, yet who will say that customer satisfaction is anywhere near perfection? These market-perceived quality attributes are embedded in the total product, that is, the physical or core product and all the additional features the consumer expects.

In a competitive marketplace where the market has choices, most consumers expect performance quality to be a given. Naturally if the product does not perform up to standards, it will be rejected. When there are alternative products, all of which meet performance quality standards, the product chosen is the one that meets market-perceived quality attributes. Interestingly, China's leading refrigerator maker recognized the importance of these market-perceived quality attributes when it adopted a technology that enabled it to let consumers choose from 20 different colors and textures for door handles and moldings. For example, a consumer can design an off-white refrigerator with green marble handles and moldings. Why is this important? Because it lets consumers "update the living rooms" where most of the refrigerators are parked. The company's motive was simple: It is positioning its product for competition from the multinational brands by giving the consumer another expression of quality.[28]

Maintaining Quality

Maintaining performance quality is critical, but frequently a product that leaves the factory at performance quality is damaged as it passes through the distribution chain. This is a special problem for many global brands where production is distant from the market and/or control of the product is lost because of the distribution system within the market. When Mars Company's Snickers and other Western confectioneries were introduced to Russia, they were a big hit.[29] Foreign brands like Mars, Toblerone, Waldbaur, and Cadbury were the top brands—indeed, only one Russian brand placed in the top 10. But by late 1996, Russian brands held eight of the top spots and only one U.S. brand, Mars' Dove bars, was in the top 10.

What happened? A combination of factors caused the decline. Russia's Red October Chocolate Factory got its act together, modernized its packaging, product mix, and equipment, and set out to capture the market. Performance quality was also an issue. When the Russian market opened to outside trade, foreign companies anxious to get into the market dumped excess out-of-date and poor-quality products. In other cases, chocolates were smuggled in and sold on street corners, and were often mishandled in the process. By the time they made it to consumers, the chocolates were likely to be misshapen or discolored—poor quality compared to Russian's Red October chocolate.

Market-perceived quality was also an issue. Russian chocolate has a different taste because of its formulation—more cocoa and chocolate liqueur are used than in Western brands, which makes it grittier. Thus, Red October brand appeals more to Russian taste

[28] Fara Warner, "Kelon Electrical to Tout Fridges with a More Homey Appeal," *The Wall Street Journal Interactive Edition,* March 14, 1997. See also **http://www.wsj.com**.

[29] Christian Caryl, "We Will Bury You . . . With a Snickers Bar," *U.S. News & World Report,* January 26, 1998, p. 50.

CROSSING BORDERS 12–5

Unless They're Idaho Potatoes, They Don't Fry Right

Maintaining a quality standard worldwide is, or should be, the hallmark of every company. There is no industry where this is practiced more diligently than the franchise food industry. McDonald's imported frozen french fries, at a high cost, for its Russian and Chinese facilities until it could test several potato varieties in different parts of each country. Once the variety of potato that would produce a french fry which measured up to its quality standards was found, the company trained local farmers, imported the seeds, and shepherded the potato through processing, freezing, and delivery to stores— all for the sake of maintaining quality. Frito-Lay took two years to get its chips to market in China because it had to first get the Chinese farmers to grow the perfect chip-frying potato.

The consequences of not maintaining quality can mean mediocre results. Shakey's Pizza had long lines in its stores in Moscow until it shifted from imported to local ingredients, then sales dropped. Locally made toppings just don't make the same pizza— even for locals. In many countries, a consistent, dependable supply of ingredients is often just not available and companies have to ensure their supply by costly importing, or developing a local supply.

KFC (Kentucky Fried Chicken) trains local farmers in many locations around the world to breed poultry that meet KFC's hygiene and quality standards. Haagen-Dazs' policy of buying the best quality ingredients and getting its milk from cow to factory in less than 72 hours precludes it from making ice cream in Asia. The region's dairy products are just not up to their standards. Instead, the ice cream is shipped from California. If monitors determine that the temperature of a refrigerated container fluctuated too much during shipment, the cargo is considered spoiled. It also brought its own refrigerated trucks into China to ensure a continuous cold-chain from airport to storage and into display cases. This drives up the price to $2.40 for a scoop or $6.50 a pint, about double the price in the United States. Nevertheless, the company sells $400 million annually in Asia in 50,000 retail outlets handling its products and its 150 company-owned stores.

Quality is a serious business when maintaining a global brand.

Sources: Adapted from "Haagen-Dazs More Than a Scoop," *Business Asia,* September 23, 1996, p. 12; "The King of Snacks," *Forbes,* October 20, 1997, p. 213; and "Corporate Strategies: KFC Goes After Pakistan's Yuppies," *Crossborder Monitor,* September 10, 1997, p. 1.

even though it is generally priced above Western brands.[30] As evidenced by this example, quality is not just desirable, it is essential for success in today's competitive global market, and the decision to standardize or adapt a product is crucial in delivering quality.

Products and Culture

To appreciate the complexity of standardized versus adapted products, one needs to understand how cultural influences are interwoven with the perceived value and importance a market places on a product. A product is more than a physical item; it is a bundle of satisfactions (or *utilities*) the buyer receives. This includes its form, taste, color,

---

[30] Maria Atanasov, "In Moscow, 'Red October' Means Chocolate," *Fortune,* June 9, 1997 p. 53.

odor, and texture; how it functions in use; the package; the label; the warranty; manu-facturer's and retailer's servicing; the confidence or prestige enjoyed by the brand; the manufacturer's reputation; the country of origin; and any other symbolic utility received from the possession or use of the goods. In short, the market relates to more than a product's physical form and primary function.

The values and customs within a culture impute much of the importance of these other benefits. In other words, a product is the sum of the physical and psychological satisfactions it provides the user.

Its physical attributes generally are required to create the primary function of the product. The primary function of an automobile, for example, is to move passengers from point A to point B. This ability requires a motor, transmission, and other physical features to achieve its primary purpose. The physical features or primary function of an automobile are generally in demand in all cultures where there is a desire to move from one point to another other than by foot or animal power. Few changes to the physical attributes of a product are required when moving from one culture to another. However, an automobile has a bundle of psychological features as important in providing consumer satisfaction as its physical features. Within a specific culture, other automobile features (color, size, design, brand name, price) have little to do with its primary function, the movement from point A to B, but do add value to the satisfaction received.

The meaning and value imputed to the psychological attributes of a product can vary among cultures and are perceived as negative or positive. To maximize the bundle of satisfactions received and to create positive product attributes rather than negative ones, adaptation of the nonphysical features of a product may be necessary.

Coca-Cola, frequently touted as a global product, found it had to change Diet Coke to Coke Light when it was introduced in Japan. Japanese women do not like to admit to dieting, and further, the idea of diet implies sickness or medicine. So instead of emphasizing weight loss, "figure maintenance" is stressed.

Adaptation may require changes of any one or all of the psychological aspects of a product. A close study of the meaning of a product shows to what extent the culture determines an individual's perception of what a product is and what satisfaction that product provides.

The adoption of some products by consumers can be affected as much by how the product concept conflicts with norms, values, and behavior patterns as by its physical or mechanical attributes. A novelty always comes up against a closely integrated cultural pattern, and it is primarily this that determines whether, when, how, and in what form it gets adopted. Insurance has been difficult to introduce into Moslem countries because the pious could claim that it partook of both usury and gambling, both explicitly vetoed in the Koran. The Japanese have always found all body jewelry repugnant. The Scots have a decided resistance to pork and all its associated products, apparently from days long ago when such taboos were decided by fundamentalist interpretations of the Bible. Filter cigarettes have failed in at least one Asian country because the local life expectancy of 29 years hardly places many people in the age-bracket most prone to fears of lung cancer—even supposing that they shared the Western attitudes about death.[31]

When analyzing a product for a second market, the extent of adaptation required depends on cultural differences in product use and perception between the market the product was originally developed for and the new market. The greater these cultural differences between the two markets, the greater the extent of adaptation that may be necessary.

An example of this involves an undisputed American leader in cake mixes, which tacitly admitted failure in the English market by closing down operations after five unsuccessful years. Taking its most successful mixes in the U.S. market, the company

[31] D. E. Allen, "Anthropological Insights into Customer Behavior," *European Journal of Marketing,* Vol. 5(3), p. 54.

CROSSING BORDERS 12-6

Iced Tea for the British—
"It Was Bloody Awful"

After sampling one of the new canned iced teas, the response by one Brit was, "It tasted like stewed tea that had been left in the pot. It was bloody awful." Such are the challenges faced by iced-tea makers in Britain, a culture where tea, served hot, is the national drink and cold tea borders on the sacrilegious. Iced tea is, after all, an American beverage, where more than 332.7 million gallons, not including home-brewed, is consumed annually.

Unilever and PepsiCo with Liptonice and Snapple Beverage Corp. with Snapple believe they can eventually convince the British that iced tea isn't just hot tea that has gone cold, but a plausible alternative to soft drinks. Each company is approaching this mammoth task differently.

To distinguish iced tea from cold dregs left in the pot, Liptonice is carbonated. "We've tried to bring people around to the idea of looking at tea in a different way." Public reaction is mixed. One response: "Let's say it was unusual. I've never quite tasted anything like it actually. I'll stick with Coke." This is, in fact, the second time Unilever has tried iced tea in the British market. The previous attempt "flopped." The product itself wasn't the problem, "it was just ahead of its time." Now, Unilever points to the growth of carbonated flavored water as an indication that consumers are increasingly receptive to new types of beverages.

Snapple's approach is to ease British consumers into drinking iced tea by enticing them to sample other Snapple products first. Lemonade and other fruit-flavored drinks, including raspberry, peach, and orange, were sold in Britain for about a year before iced tea was introduced. The company's goal was to persuade a nation of tea-lovers to sample a line anchored by a beverage that is not served hot or with milk. When you ask people if they want to try cold tea, their immediate reaction is no. Snapple's approach is to saturate the market to gain awareness by making Snapple available in 15,000 retail outlets from minuscule confectionery, news, and tobacco stores to huge supermarkets. Coupled with extensive distribution, Snapple will offer 250,000 samples in tiny Snapple-labeled cups in all kinds of outlets, including hundreds of service stations. In its first major sales promotion, "Tea for Two," Snapple tackles the tea issue head-on. In point-of-sale displays at 750 Esso service stations, Snapple shows colorful photos of the product and brand name, offering customers who buy two Snapple fruit-flavored drinks a free one-pint tea drink. All of this is supported with advertising.

The third member of the big iced-tea companies, Nestlé and Coca-Cola with Nestea, introduced their product in several European countries but not Britain. Since there is no history of consumption of iced tea in England, changing consumer perception is going to take a long time. Nestlé prefers to wait and see, although there is speculation that it will enter the British market soon.

Different companies with the same goal—change British attitudes about drinking iced tea—and different strategies. Which will win? Maybe all, maybe none.

Sources: Adapted from Tara Parker-Pope, "Will the British Warm Up to Iced Tea? Some Big Marketers Are Counting on It," *The Wall Street Journal*, August 22, 1994, p. B1; and Elena Bowes and Laurel Wentz, "Snapple Beverage War Spills onto Continent, *Advertising Age*, April 18, 1994, p. I-1.

introduced them into the British market. Considerable amounts of time, money, and effort were expended to introduce its variety of cake mixes to this new market. Hindsight provides several probable causes for the company's failure. Traditionalism was certainly among the most important. The British eat most of their cake with tea instead of dinner and have always preferred dry sponge cake, which is easy to handle; the fancy, iced cakes favored in the United States were the type introduced. Fancy iced cakes are accepted in Britain, but they are considered extra special and purchased from a bakery or made with much effort and care at home. The company introduced what it thought to be an easy cake mix. This easy cake mix was considered a slight to domestic duties. Homemakers felt guilty about not even cracking an egg, and there was suspicion that dried eggs and milk were not as good as fresh ones. Therefore, when the occasion called for a fancy cake, an easy cake mix was simply not good enough.

Ironically, this same company had faced almost identical problems, which they eventually overcame, when introducing new easy cake mixes in the U.S. market. There was initial concern about the quality of mixes and the resulting effect on the homemaker's reputation as a baker. Even today there remains the feeling that "scratch" cakes are of special quality and significance and should be made for extra-important occasions. This, in spite of the fact that the uniform quality of results from almost all mixes, and the wide variety of flavors certainly equal, if not exceed, the ability of most to bake from scratch.

Such a cultural phenomenon apparently exists in other cultures as well. When instant cake mixes were introduced in Japan, the consumers' response was less than enthusiastic. Not only do Japanese reserve cakes for special occasions, they prefer the cakes to be beautifully wrapped and purchased in pastry shops. The acceptance of instant cakes was further complicated by another cultural difference: most Japanese homes do not have ovens. An interesting sidebar to this example is the company's attempt to correct for that problem by developing a cake mix that could be cooked in a rice cooker, which all Japanese homes have. The problem with that idea was that in a Japanese kitchen rice and the manner in which it is cooked has strong cultural overtones and to use the rice cooker to cook something other than rice is a real taboo.

Examples are typically given about cultures other than American, but the need for cultural adaptation is often necessary when a foreign company markets a product in the United States. A major Japanese cosmetics company, Shiseido, attempted to break into the U.S. cosmetic market with the same products sold in Japan. After introducing them in more than 800 U.S. stores, the company realized that American taste in cosmetics is very different from Japanese. The problem was that Shiseido's makeup required a time-consuming series of steps, a point that does not bother Japanese women. Success was attained after designing a new line of cosmetics as easy to use as American products.

The problems of adapting a product to sell abroad are similar to those associated with the introduction of a new product at home. Products are not measured solely by their physical specifications. The nature of the new product is in what it does to and for the customer—to habits, tastes, and patterns of life. The problems illustrated in the cake mix example have little to do with the physical product or the user's ability to make effective use of it, but more with the fact that acceptance and use of the cake mixes would have required upsetting behavior patterns considered correct or ideal.

What significance, outside the intended use, might a product have in a different culture? When product acceptance requires changes in patterns of life, habits, tastes, the understanding of new ideas, acceptance of the difficult to believe, or the acquisition of completely new tastes or habits, special emphasis must be used to overcome natural resistance to change.

Innovative Products and Adaptation

An important first step in adapting a product to a foreign market is to determine the degree of newness perceived by the intended market. How people react to newness and how new a product is to a market must be understood. In evaluating the newness of a product, the international marketer must be aware that many products successful in the United States, having reached the maturity or even decline stage in their life cycles, may be perceived as new in another country or culture and, thus, must be treated as innovations. From a sociological viewpoint, any idea perceived as new by a group of people is an innovation.

Whether or not a group accepts an innovation and the time it takes to do so depends on its characteristics. Products new to a social system are innovations, and knowledge about the *diffusion* (i.e., the process by which innovation spreads) of innovation is helpful in developing a successful product strategy. Marketing strategies can guide and control to a considerable extent the rate and extent of new product diffusion because successful new product diffusion is dependent on the ability to communicate relevant product information and new product attributes.

A critical factor in the newness of a product is its effect on established patterns of consumption and behavior. In the preceding cake mix example, the fancy, iced cake mix was a product that required acceptance of the "difficult to believe," that is, that dried eggs and milk are as good in cake as the fresh products; and the "acquisition of new ideas," that is, that easy-to-bake fancy cakes are not a slight to one's domestic integrity. In this case, the product directly affected two important aspects of consumer behavior, and the product innovation met with sufficient resistance to convince the company to leave the market. Had the company studied the target market before introducing the product, perhaps it could have avoided the failure.

Another U.S. cake mix company entered the British market but carefully eliminated most of the newness of the product. Instead of introducing the most popular American cake mixes, the company asked 500 British housewives to bake their favorite cake. Since the majority baked a simple, very popular dry sponge cake, the company brought to the market a similar easy mix. The sponge cake mix represented familiar tastes and habits that could be translated into a convenience item, and did not infringe on the emotional aspects of preparing a fancy product for special occasions. Consequently, after a short period of time, the second company's product gained 30 to 35 percent of the British cake-mix market. Once the idea of a mix for sponge cake was acceptable, the introduction of other flavors became easier.

The goal of a foreign marketer is to gain product acceptance by the largest number of consumers in the market in the shortest span of time. However, as discussed in Chapter 4 and as many of the examples cited have illustrated, new products are not always readily accepted by a culture; indeed, they often meet resistance. Although they may ultimately be accepted, the time it takes for a culture to learn new ways, to learn to accept a new product, is of critical importance to the marketer since planning reflects a time frame for investment and profitability. If a marketer invests with the expectation that a venture will break even in three years and it takes seven to gain profitable volume, the effort may have to be prematurely abandoned. The question comes to mind whether or not the probable rate of acceptance can be predicted before committing resources and, more critically, if the probable rate of acceptance is too slow, whether it can be accelerated. In both cases, the answer is a qualified yes. Answers to these questions come from examining the work done in diffusion research—research on the process by which "innovations spread to the members of a social system."

Diffusion of Innovations

Everett Rogers notes that "crucial elements in the diffusion of new ideas are (1) an innovation, (2) which is communicated through certain channels, (3) over time, (4) among the members of a social system." Rogers continues with the statement that it is the element of time that differentiates diffusion from other types of communications research. The goals of the diffusion researcher and the marketer are to shorten the time lag between introduction of an idea or product and its widespread adoption.[32]

Rogers gives ample evidence of the fact that product innovations have a varying rate of acceptance. Some diffuse from introduction to widespread use in a few years;

---

[32] Everett M. Rogers, *Diffusion of Innovations*, 4th ed. (New York: Free Press, 1995), pp. 204–51. This is a book that should be read by anyone responsible for product development and brand management, domestic or international.

Getting them young: promoting oral hygiene among children in Kenya is one of the many school programs sponsored by Colgate-Palmolive throughout the world. (Courtesy Colgate-Palmolive Company/Photography by Richard Alcorn)

others take decades. Microwave ovens, introduced in the United States initially in the 1950s, took nearly 20 years to become widespread; the contraceptive pill was introduced during that same period and gained acceptance in a few years. In the field of education, modern math took only five years to diffuse through U.S. schools, while the idea of kindergartens took nearly 50 years to gain total acceptance. There is also a growing body of evidence that the understanding of diffusion theory may provide ways in which the process of diffusion can be accelerated. Knowledge of this process may provide the foreign marketer with the ability to assess the time it takes for a product to diffuse—before it is necessary to make a financial commitment.[33] It also focuses the marketer's attention on features of a product that provoke resistance, thereby providing an opportunity to minimize resistance and hasten product acceptance.

At least three extraneous variables affect the rate of diffusion of an object: the degree of perceived newness, the perceived attributes of the innovation, and the method used to communicate the idea. Each variable has a bearing on consumer reaction to a new product and the time needed for acceptance. An understanding of these variables can produce better product strategies for the international marketer.

Degree of Newness

As perceived by the market, varying degrees of newness categorize all new products. Within each category, myriad reactions affect the rate of diffusion. In giving a name to these categories, one might think of (1) congruent innovations, (2) continuous innovations, (3) dynamically continuous innovations, and (4) discontinuous innovations. A *congruent innovation* is actually not an innovation at all because it causes absolutely no disruption of established consumption patterns. The product concept is accepted by the culture and the innovativeness is typically one of introducing variety and quality or functional features, style, or perhaps an exact duplicate of an already existing product— exact in the sense that the market perceives no newness, such as cane sugar versus beet sugar.

---

[33] An interesting study on the effect of learning on diffusion is found in Jaishankar Ganesh and V. Kumar, "Capturing the Cross-National Learning Effect: An Analysis of an Industrial Technology Diffusion," *Journal of the Academy of Marketing Science,* Vol. 24(4), 1966, p. 328.

CROSSING BORDERS 12-7

So This Is What Is Called an Innovation— But Does It Flush?

An American diplomat was at a dinner party in a Japanese home when he excused himself to go to the bathroom. He completed his errand, stood up, and realized he didn't have a clue about how to flush the toilet.

The diplomat spoke Japanese, but he was still baffled by the colorful array of buttons on the complicated keypad on the toilet. This super-high-tech toilet had a control panel that looked like the cockpit of a plane. So he just started pushing.

He hit the noisemaker button that makes a flushing sound to mask any noise you might be making in the john. He hit the button that starts the blow dryer for your bottom. Then he hit the bidet button and watched helplessly as a little plastic arm, sort of a squirt gun shaped like a toothbrush, appeared from the back of the bowl and began shooting a stream of warm water across the room and onto the mirror.

And that's how one of America's promising young Foreign Service officers ended up frantically wiping down a Japanese bathroom with a wad of toilet paper. Other buttons he could have tried automatically open and close the lid; the button for men lifts the lid and seat; the button for women lifts the lid only. Some toilets even have a handheld remote control, sort of a clicker for the loo.

What confounded this diplomat was one of Japan's recent additions to the bathroom: the Toto "Washlit," a toilet of the future at $2,000 to $4,000 depending on the number of functional features. The company sells about $400 million annually of these technological wonders and plans to enter the U.S. market with a less complicated, less expensive model—it will feature only the seat warmer, bottom washer, and deodorizing fan for $400.

Sources: Mary Jordan and Kevin Sullivan, "But Do They Flush?" *The Washington Post,* May 15, 1997, p. 1; and "High Technology Is Now in the Toilet," *Los Angeles Times,* June 18, 1997, p. B4.

A *continuous innovation* has the least disruptive influence on established consumption patterns. Alteration of a product is almost always involved rather than the creation of a new product. Generally the alterations result in better use patterns—perceived improvement in the satisfaction derived from its use. Examples include fluoride toothpaste, disposable razors, and flavors in coffee.

A *dynamically continuous innovation* has more disruptive effects than a continuous innovation, although it generally does not involve new consumption patterns. It may mean the creation of a new product or considerable alteration of an existing one designed to fulfill new needs arising from changes in life-styles or new expectations brought about by change. It is generally disruptive and therefore resisted because old patterns of behavior must change if consumers are to accept and perceive the value of the dynamically continuous innovation. Examples include electric toothbrushes, electric haircurlers, central air-conditioning, cellular telephones, freeze-dried foods.

Finally, a *discontinuous innovation* involves the establishment of new consumption patterns and the creation of previously unknown products. It introduces an idea or behavior pattern where there was none before. Examples include television, the computer, the Internet, ATMs (automatic teller machines), and microwave ovens.[34]

---

[34] Thomas S. Robertson, "The New Product Diffusion Process," in *American Marketing Association Proceedings,* ed. Bernard A. Marvin (Chicago: American Marketing Association, June 1969), p. 81.

Most innovation in the U.S. economy is of a continuous nature. However, a product that could be described as a continuous innovation in the U.S. market could be a dynamically continuous innovation, if not a discontinuous innovation, in many other markets of the world. For example, when the cake mix was first introduced into the American economy, it was a dynamically continuous innovation. However, with time it overcame resistance, consumption and behavior patterns changed, and it was accepted in the U.S. market.

Indeed, there are many continuous innovations involving the cake mix itself, such as the introduction of new flavors, changes in package size, elimination of dried eggs in favor of fresh eggs, and so on. That same cake mix, now a part of U.S. eating habits, is a congruent innovation when a new brand is offered on the U.S. market. If it is offered in a new, unique flavor, it is a continuous innovation; if it is introduced at the same time into a market unfamiliar with cake mixes, it is a dynamically continuous innovation. That same product also could be classified as a discontinuous innovation in a market that had no previous knowledge of cakes. In all cases, we are dealing basically with a cake mix, but in acceptance and marketing success we are dealing with people, their feelings, and their perceptions of the product.

Continuing with the previous example, the second U.S. cake mix company offered the British market a familiar sponge cake mix. This slight adjustment from a fancy cake mix to a sponge cake changed the product from a dynamically continuous innovation to a continuous innovation. One advantage of analyzing a product's degree of innovativeness is to determine what may alter the degree of newness to gain quicker acceptance. Even a tractor must be modified to meet local needs and uses if it is to be accepted in place of an ox-drawn plow.

The time the diffusion process takes, that is, the time it takes for an innovation to be adopted by a majority in the marketplace, is of prime importance to a marketer. Generally speaking, the more disruptive the innovation, the longer the diffusion process takes.

The extent of a product's diffusion and its rate of diffusion are partly functions of the particular product's attributes. Each innovation has characteristics by which it can be described, and each person's perception of these characteristics can be utilized in explaining the differences in perceived newness of an innovation. These attributes can also be utilized in predicting the rate of adoption. The adjustment of these attributes or product adaptation can lead to changes in consumer perception and thus to altered rates of diffusion. Emphasis given to product adaptation for local cultural norms and the overall brand image created are critical marketing decision areas.

Analysis of Characteristics of Innovations

The more innovative a product is perceived to be, the more difficult it is to gain market acceptance. However, the perception of innovation can often be changed if the marketer understands the perceptual framework of the consumer.

Analyzing the five characteristics of an innovation can assist in determining the rate of acceptance or resistance of the market to a product. A product's (1) *relative advantage* (the perceived marginal value of the new product relative to the old); (2) *compatibility* (its compatibility with acceptable behavior, norms, values, and so forth); (3) *complexity* (the degree of complexity associated with product use); (4) *trialability* (the degree of economic and/or social risk associated with product use); and (5) *observability* (the ease with which the product benefits can be communicated) affect the degree of its acceptance or resistance. In general, it can be postulated that the rate of diffusion is positively related to relative advantage, compatibility, trialability, and observability, but negatively related to complexity.

By analyzing a product within these five dimensions, a marketer can often uncover perceptions held by the market, which, if left unchanged, would slow product acceptance. Conversely, if these perceptions are identified and changed, the marketer may be able to accelerate product acceptance.

CROSSING BORDERS 12–8

Here Comes Kellogg—Causing Cultural Change

Marketers become cultural change agents by accident or by design. In Latvia, cultural change is being planned.

As a column of creamy white milk cascades into a bowl of Corn Flakes in the television ad, a camera moves in for a tight shot and the message "eight vitamins" flashes across the screen.

Kellogg Company of Battle Creek, Michigan, is trying to change the way hundreds of millions of Latvians and other former Soviet citizens start their day. Historically, the favorite breakfast in Latvia and in much of the former Soviet Union has been a hearty plate of sausage, cold cuts, potatoes, eggs, and a few slices of thick, chewy bread slathered with wonderfully high-cholesterol butter.

Kellogg is out to change all that and is pressing ahead with one of the more ambitious education programs in the annals of eating. "We have to teach people a whole new way to eat breakfast," said a specialist in Soviet affairs for Kellogg. To win converts, Kellogg is relying mainly on slick television advertisements showing a family joyfully digging into their Corn Flakes, and on demonstrations in grocery stores that the company refers to as "taste testing."

A young sales representative for Kellogg had stacked a table in the immaculate Dalderi grocery store with red and white boxes of Corn Flakes and little white paper bowls. The display was set in front of chest-high deli cases displaying giant blocks of cheese, a dozen varieties of sausage, and glistening slabs of fatty bacon. A cluster of women and children surrounded the Kellogg display. The sales representative held up a bowl and urged a woman to try some. "It's delicious," she said, "it's quite substantial. Normally I would have boiled macaroni with milk and sugar." Another exclaims that her children just adore corn flakes but "we can't afford them—maybe sometimes we buy them for a gift." A man tasted and remarked, "This is not food for man."

Kellogg's marketing plans are best summarized in a Kellogg Company representative's comment: "It took 40 years to develop the Latin American market; Latvia is going to be part of long-term growth." Any wonder that Kellogg is the world's most successful cereal company, with 51 percent of the market? Latvia is its 18th international facility. Today, you would have a hard time finding a store in Latvia that doesn't have Kellogg's Corn Flakes.

In India, however, it is another story. Kellogg Company is getting a cold shoulder from Indians who prefer hot food for breakfast because they feel it infuses them with energy. When Kellogg's Corn Flakes were introduced, Indian consumers indulged their curiosity. After a couple of years, sales fell when Indians returned to their traditional breakfast of flat bread with eggs or cooked vegetables. There is demand for Western food, as Kentucky Fried Chicken and Pizza Hut can attest, but when the new food is a replacement for the main meal, home is where the heart is. As long as a food is for casual eating, you have a good chance of succeeding. But, based on Kellogg's Latin American timetable, it has 38 years left to change Indian eating habits.

Sources: Adapted from Joseph B. Treaster, "Kellogg Seeks to Reset Latvia's Breakfast Table," *The New York Times,* May 19, 1994, p. C1; and Miriam Jordan, "Marketing Gurus Say: In India, Think Cheap, Lose the Cold Cereal," *The Wall Street Journal,* October 11, 1996, p. A7.

The evaluator must remember it is the perception of product characteristics by the potential adopter, not the marketer, that is crucial to the evaluation. A market analyst's self-reference criterion (SRC) may cause a perceptual bias when interpreting the characteristics of a product. Thus, instead of evaluating product characteristics from the foreign user's frame of reference, it is analyzed from the marketer's frame of reference, leading to a misinterpretation of the cultural importance.

Once the analysis has been made, some of the perceived newness or cause for resistance can be minimized through adroit marketing. The more congruent product perceptions are with current cultural values, the less resistance there will be and the more rapid product diffusion or acceptance will be.

A product can often be modified physically to improve its relative advantage over competing products, enhance its compatibility with cultural values, and even minimize its complexity. Its relative advantage and compatibility also can be enhanced and some degree of complexity lessened through advertising efforts. Small sizes, samples, packaging, and product demonstrations are all sales promotion efforts that can be used to alter the characteristics of an innovative product and accelerate its rate of adoption.

The marketer must recognize not only the degree of innovativeness a product possesses in relation to each culture, but marketing efforts must also reflect an understanding of the importance of innovativeness to product acceptance and adoption. One of the values of analyzing characteristics of innovations is that it focuses the efforts of the marketer on those issues that influence the acceptance of a product concept. It is possible to accentuate the positive attributes of an innovation, thus changing the market's perception to a more positive and, therefore, acceptable attitude.

The potential of communicating product innovations can be illustrated with some hypothetical questions about the cake mix example used earlier. Would the company have had the same results if it had analyzed the cake mix as an innovation and then set out to make the idea a more acceptable one? What would have been the result, for example, if the introduction had been the traditional sponge cake, which required minimal communication to gain acceptance? Or, in offering the market a fancy cake mix, what if the company had set out to convince the market of the advantages of that type of cake over the traditional, thus enhancing its relative advantage? The company could also have set out to promote advantages of the "new" cake mix over the old traditional cake so that it would have seemed more compatible with present behavior. There are many "what ifs" to be asked: what if the company had communicated the product's ease of trialability and observability to allay fears as to quality, taste, flavor, and ease of preparation? for example.

In retrospect, the answers to these questions are of little value to the cake mix company, but they illustrate the value of viewing a product in terms of innovation and characteristic analysis and then communicating a positive product picture to the new market.

A similar situation to the cake mix example is one involving Green Giant and frozen vegetables. In this case, however, Green Giant recognized the problem in time to avoid it. Although vegetables are a significant part of the Asian diet, Green Giant discovered that Japanese mothers take pride in the time they take to prepare a family meal and therefore saw frozen vegetables as an unwelcome shortcut. Applying an analysis of the characteristics of innovations highlights two negative attributes: (1) The short-cut in preparing frozen vegetables rather than from scratch is not compatible with the Japanese mothers' self-image and role, that is, carefully preparing meals for the family; (2) there was no perceived relative advantage over the "traditional" way. Much like the cake mix example, with a little convenience comes a little guilt.

Unlike the cake mix company, however, Green Giant recognized the problem and used an advertising theme to convince moms that using frozen vegetable gives them the opportunity to prepare the families' favorite foods more often. To that end they developed a frozen mixture of julienned carrots and burdock root, a traditional favorite root vegetable that requires several hours of tedious preparation.[35]

Green Giant's advertising overcame two problems: negative compatibility was reduced and relative advantage was stressed. It showed the Japanese mother how her role was enhanced by saving meal preparation time that would enable her to spend

---

[35] Tara Parker-Pope, "Custom Made: The Most Successful Companies Have to Realize a Simple Truth: All Consumers Aren't Alike," *The Wall Street Journal,* September 26, 1996, p. R22.

more time with the family. It also created a perceived relative advantage of using frozen over the traditional preparation of vegetables. It amplified both characteristics positively by using a "favorite" version of vegetables that would assuage her guilt by letting her feel good about serving the family's favorite vegetable more often yet have more time for the family. While fresh vegetables still dominate the market, Green Giant reports that frozen varieties have risen to account for half the company's total sales in Japan.

Frequently, the cause of failure for a U.S. marketer abroad is not inadequate marketing practices but failure to employ the right marketing practices against the correct problems.[36]

Physical or Mandatory Requirements and Adaptation

A product may have to change in a number of ways to meet physical or mandatory requirements of a new market, ranging from simple package changes to total redesign of the physical core product. A recent study reaffirmed the often-reported finding that mandatory adaptations were more frequently the reason for product adaptation than adapting for cultural reasons.[37]

Some changes are obvious with relatively little analysis; a cursory examination of a country will uncover the need to rewire electrical goods for a different voltage system, simplify a product when the local level of technology is not high, or print multilingual labels where required by law. Electrolux, for example, offers a cold-wash-only washing machine in Asian countries where electric power is expensive or scarce. Other necessary changes may surface only after careful study of an intended market.

Legal, economic, political, technological, and climatic requirements of the local marketplace often dictate product adaptation. During a period in India when the government was very anti-foreign investment, Pepsi-Cola changed its product name to Lehar-Pepsi (in Hindi lehar means wave) to gain as much local support as possible. The name returned to Pepsi-Cola when the political climate turned favorable.[38] Laws that vary among countries usually set specific package sizes and safety and quality standards. To make a purchase more affordable in low-income countries, the number of units per package may have to be reduced from the typical quantities offered in high-income countries. Razor blades, cigarettes, chewing gum, and other multiple-pack items are often sold singly or two to a pack instead of the more customary 10 or 20. Cheetos, a product of PepsiCo Inc.'s Frito-Lay, is packaged in 15-gram size packages in China so it can be priced at one yuan, about 12 cents. At this price, even children with little spending money can afford them. If the concept of preventive maintenance is unfamiliar to an intended market, product simplification and maintenance-free features may be mandatory for successful product performance.

Changes may also have to be made to accommodate climatic differences. General Motors of Canada, for example, experienced major problems with several thousand Chevrolet automobiles shipped to a Mideast country; it was quickly discovered they were unfit for the hot, dusty climate. Supplementary air filters and different clutches had to be added to adjust for the problem. Even crackers have to be packaged in tins for humid areas. The less economically developed a market is, the greater degree of change a product may need for acceptance. One study found only 1 in 10 products could be mar-

---

[36] See Rogers, *Diffusion of Innovations*, pp. 204–50, for a discussion of the characteristics of an innovation.

[37] Surjit S. Chhabra, "Marketing Adaptations by American Multinational Corporations in South America," *Journal of Global Marketing*, Vol. 9(4), 1996, p. 57.

[38] "The Battle for Identity In the Face of International Branding," *Brand Strategy*, September 19, 1997, p. 22.

Sales of P&G products in China exceeded $1 billion annually, thanks largely to shampoo. A young woman buys a bottle of Pantene, designed for straight Asian hair, at a general store in a small village near the city of Guangzhou. (Greg Girard/CONTACT Press Images)

keted in developing countries without modification of some sort. Because most products sold abroad by international companies originate in home markets and most require some form of modification, companies need a systematic process to identify products that need adaptation.

Product Alternatives

When a company plans to enter a market in another country, careful consideration must be given to whether or not the present product lines will prove adequate in the new culture. Will they sell in quantities large enough and at prices high enough to be profitable? If not, what other alternatives are available? The marketer has at least four viable alternatives when entering a new market: (1) sell the same product presently sold in the home market (domestic market extension strategy); (2) adapt existing products to the tastes and specific needs in each new country market (multidomestic market strategy); (3) develop a standardized product for all markets (global market strategy); or (4) acquire local brands and reintroduce.

An important issue in choosing which alternative to use is whether or not a company is starting from scratch (i.e., no existing products to market abroad), whether it has products already established in various country markets, or whether there are local products that can be more efficiently developed for the local market than other alternatives. For a company starting fresh, the prudent alternative is to develop a global product. If the company has several products that have evolved over time in various foreign markets, then the task is one of repositioning the existing products into global products. In some cases, a company encounters a market where local brands are established and the introduction of a company brand would take too long and be more costly than acquiring the local brand. As discussed earlier in this chapter, Nestlé and Unilever have used this approach effectively in Eastern Europe and Russia.

The success of these alternatives depends on the product and the fundamental need

CROSSING BORDERS 12–11

Where Design and Packaging Are King

One of the prime differences between Japanese and American approaches to packaging is what the Japanese might call "design." The Japanese consider design to be the subliminal and essential aspect of a product. Japanese consumers are much more attuned to the visual and graphic presentation of products than are Americans.

Everything is seen from a design perspective. In a Japanese restaurant, the entire operation is geared around distinct design—the menu, the interior, the food on the plate, even the way waiters and waitresses dress and act. Customers are willing to pay a lot for good design.

An important custom of the Japanese is gift-giving when visiting another's home or business. As a result, Japanese consumers will spend money on well-packaged goods. A Japanese boutique will sell a single honeydew melon wrapped in black velvet. Exquisite tins of cookies, elaborately wrapped, fancy packages of seaweed, or summer noodles are found in many stores. Packaging that requires handcraft and uses natural materials such as leaves or paper-thin slices of wood can be found even for seemingly mundane, staple products such as noodles. In Japan the package is an integral part of the gift. But most U.S. packages don't meet Japanese standards of quality and style.

One U.S. fruit exporter has been successful with the grapefruit it sells in Japan. Each one is wrapped in white tissue paper and labeled with a gold sticker—each individual piece of fruit is like a small gift.

After weak sales in Japan, an American company selling rice crackers changed its packaging and became a success. Initially, the company packaged its rice crackers in California-style packages. The wrappers had bright colors and the word "California" printed on them. The Japanese liked the taste but the packaging flopped. The package was changed to a Japanese-style design, complete with almond blossoms in pastel colors. After the package change, the product "just flew off the shelf."

Sources: Adapted from "Letter from Tokyo: Season for Giving in Japan," *Chicago Tribune,* July 16, 1996, p. 4; Alexander Besher, "Packaging, Design Aren't Frivolous in Japan," *Chronicle Features,* August 24, 1990, p. 26; and Thomas Hine, *The Total Package* (Boston: Little, Brown and Company, Back Bay Books, 1997), p. 31.

Ford tried to sell its Pinto automobile in Brazil, it quickly found out that the car model's name translated to "tiny male genitals."[44] White, the color for purity in Western countries, is the color for mourning in others. In China, P&G packaged diapers in a pink wrapper. The consumer shunned the pink package—pink symbolized a girl, and in a country with a one-child per family rule where the male is preferred, you do not want anyone to think you have a girl, even if you do.[45]

There are countless reasons why a company might have to adapt a product's package. In some countries, law stipulates specific bottle, can, package sizes, and measurement units. If a country uses the metric system, it will probably require that weights and measurements conform to the metric system. Such descriptive words as "giant" or "jumbo" on a package or label may be illegal. High humidity and/or the need for long shelf life because of extended distribution systems may dictate extra-heavy packaging for some products. As is frequently mentioned, the Japanese attitudes about quality include the packaging of a product. A poorly packaged product conveys an impression

---

[44] Jeff Harrington, "P&G Mastering Art of 'Glocalization' Taking Crest into China Typifies How Procter Will Give Global Sales a Local Feel," *The Cincinnati Enquirer,* April 13, 1997, p. I1.

[45] Alecia Swasy, *Soap Opera* (New York: Touchstone Book, Simon & Schuster, 1993), p. 281.

of poor quality to the Japanese. It is also important to determine if the packaging has other uses in the market. Again in Japan, Lever Brothers sells Lux soap in stylish boxes because in Japan more than half of all soap cakes are purchased during the two gift-giving seasons. Size of the package is also a factor that may make a difference to success in Japan. Soft drinks are sold in smaller-size cans than in the United States to accommodate the smaller Japanese hand. In Japan, most food is sold fresh or in clear packaging, while cans are considered dirty. So when Campbell's Soup introduced soups to the Japanese market, it decided to go with a cleaner, more expensive pop-top opener.[46]

Labeling law varies from country to country and does not seem to follow any predictable pattern. In Saudi Arabia, for example, product names must be specific. "Hot Chili" will not do; it must be "Spiced Hot Chili." Prices are required to be printed on the labels in Venezuela, but in Chile it is illegal to put prices on labels or in any way suggest retail prices. Coca-Cola ran into a legal problem in Brazil with its Diet Coke. Brazilian law interprets *diet* to have medicinal qualities. Under the law, producers must give daily-recommended consumption on the labels of all medicines. Coke had to get special approval to get around this restriction. In China until recently Western products could be labeled in a foreign language with only a small temporary Chinese label affixed somewhere on the package. With the new Chinese labeling law, however, food products must have their name, contents, and other specifics listed clearly in Chinese printed directly on the package—no temporary labels.[47]

Labeling laws create a special problem for companies selling products in various markets with different labeling laws and small initial demand in each. In China, for example, there is a demand for American- and European-style snack foods even though the demand is not well developed at this time. The expense of labeling specially to meet Chinese law makes market entry cost prohibitive. Forward-thinking manufacturers with wide distribution in Asia are adopting packaging standards comparable to those required in the European Union, by providing standard information in several different languages on the same package. A template is designed with a space on the label reserved for locally required content, which can be inserted depending on the destination of a given production batch.[48]

Marketers must examine each of the elements of the packaging component to be certain that this part of the product conveys the appropriate meaning and value to a new market. Otherwise they may be caught short, as was the U.S. soft-drink company that incorporated six-pointed stars as decoration on its package labels. Only when investigating weak sales did they find they had inadvertently offended some of their Arab customers who interpreted the stars as symbolizing pro-Israeli sentiments.

Support Services Component

The *support services* component includes repair and maintenance, instructions, installation, warranties, deliveries, and the availability of spare parts. Many otherwise-successful marketing programs have ultimately failed because little attention was given to this product component. Repair and maintenance are especially difficult problems in developing countries. In the United States, a consumer has the option of company service as well as a score of competitive service retailers ready to repair and maintain anything from automobiles to lawn mowers. Equally available are repair parts from company-owned or licensed outlets or the local hardware store. Consumers in a developing coun-

---

[46] Susan Warner, "Campbell's Develops Taste for World M-M-M-arkets," *The Denver Post*, June 15, 1997, p. H6.

[47] "Brand Management in China," *U.S. Department of Agriculture Reports*, January 7, 1997, 7 pages.

[48] "New Food-Labeling Law Comes into Effect: Add the Ingredients," *Business China*, September 30, 1996, p. 3.

try and many developed countries may not have even one of the possibilities for repair and maintenance available in the United States.

In some countries, the concept of routine maintenance or preventive maintenance is not a part of the culture. As a result, products may have to be adjusted to require less-frequent maintenance, and special attention must be given to features that may be taken for granted in the United States.

Literacy rates and educational levels of a country may require a firm to change a product's instructions. A simple term in one country may be incomprehensible in another. In rural Africa, for example, consumers had trouble understanding that Vaseline Intensive Care lotion is absorbed into the skin. *Absorbed* was changed to *soaks into,* and the confusion was eliminated. The Brazilians have successfully overcome low literacy and technical skills of users of the sophisticated military tanks it sells to Third World countries. They include videocassette players and videotapes with detailed repair instructions as part of the standard instruction package. They also minimize spare parts problems by using standardized, off-the-shelf parts available throughout the world.

While it may seem obvious to translate all instructions into the language of the market, many firms overlook such a basic point. "Do Not Step Here," "Danger," or "Use No Oil" have little meaning to an Arab unfamiliar with the English language.

The Product Component Model can be a useful guide in examining adaptation requirements of products destined for foreign markets. A product should be carefully evaluated on each of the three components for mandatory and discretionary changes that may be needed.

Green Marketing and Product Development

An issue of growing importance the world over and especially in Europe and the United States is green marketing. Europe has been at the forefront of the "green movement," with strong public opinion and specific legislation favoring environmentally friendly marketing. *Green marketing* is a term used to identify concern with the environmental consequences of a variety of marketing activities. The European Commission has passed legislation to control all kinds of packaging waste throughout the EC. Two critical issues that affect product development are the control of the packaging component of solid waste and consumer demand for environmentally friendly products.

The EC Commission issued guidelines for eco-labeling that became operational in 1992. Under the EC directive, a product is evaluated on all significant environmental effects throughout its life cycle, from manufacturing to disposal—a cradle-to-grave approach.[49] A detergent formulated to be biodegradable and not to pollute would be judged friendlier than a detergent whose formulation would be harmful when discharged. Aerosol propellants that do not deplete the ozone layer are another example of environmentally friendly products. No country's laws yet require products to carry an eco-label to be sold, however.[50] The designation that a product is "environmentally friendly" is voluntary and its environmental success depends on the consumer selecting the eco-friendly product.

Since the introduction of the eco-label idea, Hoover washing machines are the only products that have gained approval for the eco-label. Interestingly enough, the benefits of winning the symbol have result in trebling Hoover's market share in Germany and doubling its share of the premium sector of the U.K. washing-machine market. The

---

[49] "Packaging Problems," *Business Europe,* June 5, 1996, p. 1.

[50] Ira Teinowitz, "U.S. Government Fights EU on Ecolabel Awards," *Ad Age International,* May 9, 1997, p. I30.

approval process seems to be deterring many European manufacturers, many of whom are using their own, unofficial symbols. The National Consumer Council, a consumer watchdog group, reports that many consumers are so confused and cynical about the myriad symbols that they are giving up altogether on trying to compare the green credentials of similar products.[51]

Laws that mandate systems to control solid waste, while voluntary in one sense, do carry penalties. The EC law requires that packaging material through all levels of distribution, from the manufacturer to the consumer, must be recycled or reused.[52] By 2001 between 50 percent and 65 percent of the weight of packaging must be recovered. From the same date, between 25 percent and 45 percent of the weight of the totality of packaging materials contained in packaging waste will be recycled.

Each level of the distribution chain is responsible for returning, back up stream, all packaging, packing, and other waste materials. The biggest problem is with the packaging the customer takes home; by law the retailer must take back all packaging from the customer if no central recycling locations are available.[53] For the manufacturer's product to participate in direct collection and not have to be returned to the retailer for recycling, the manufacturer must guarantee financial support for curbside or central collection of all materials. The growing public and political pressure to control solid waste is a strong incentive for compliance.[54]

Although the packaging and solid waste rules are burdensome, there have been successful cases of not only meeting local standards but of being able to transfer this approach to other markets. Procter & Gamble's international operations integrated global environmental concerns as a response to increasing demands in Germany. It introduced Lenor, a fabric softener in a super-concentrated form, and sold it in a plastic refill pouch that reduced packaging by 85 percent. This move actually increased brand sales by 12 percent and helped set a positive tone with government regulators and activists. The success of Lenor was transferred to the United States, where P&G faced similar environmental pressures. A superconcentrated Downy, the U.S. brand of fabric softener, was repackaged in refill pouches that reduced package size by 75 percent, thereby costing consumers less, and actually increasing Downy market share.[55] The global marketer should not view green marketing as a European problem; concern for the environment is worldwide and similar legislation is sure to surface elsewhere. This is another example of the need to adapt products for global marketing.

Marketing Consumer Services Globally

During the 1990s one-quarter of the value of all international trade has been derived from the sale of services. The United States' service exports account for almost 40 percent of total exports. In 1996, the most recent year for which data are available, U.S. exports of services reached an all-time high of $237 billion (up from $164 billion in 1991), resulting in a $80 billion trade surplus in that category.[56] That growing surplus has helped counterbalance the $191 billion deficit in merchandise trade. Moreover,

---

[51] Diane Summers, "Green Muddle—Environmental Claims on Packaging Are Becoming Meaningless without Standard Rules," *Financial Times,* March 21, 1996, p. 13.

[52] Richard Ball, "Play It Again: UK's Recycling Law," *Electronics Weekly,* April 23, 1997, p. 22.

[53] "European Packaging Laws Europe: The 14 Member Nations of the European Union Require Manufacturers to Bear the Responsibility for Packaging Waste," *Waste Age,* June 1996, p. 61.

[54] "Packaging: The EU Means Business," *Food Manufacture,* November 1997, p. 56.

[55] James Maxwell, Sandra Rothenberg, Forrest Briscoe, and Alfred Marcus, "Green Schemes: Corporate Environmental Strategies and Their Implementation," *California Management Review,* March 22, 1997, p. 118.

[56] "1996 U.S. Foreign Trade Highlights," U.S. Department of Commerce, June 1997.

numbers on service trade are underestimated by as much as 30 percent because data in the current account do not reflect all categories of services (see Chapter 7 for an explanation). Thus, U.S. services trade may be as high as $300 billion.

The dynamism and competitiveness of American services industries ensures that innovations will continue to emanate from U.S. firms into the next century. Indeed, what the United States has to offer the rest of the world is new ideas, expressed most often in high-technology products *and* services.

In contrast to industrial and consumer goods, services are distinguished by unique characteristics and thus require special consideration. Products are classified as *tangible* or *intangible.* Automobiles, computers, and furniture are examples of tangible products that have a physical presence; they are a thing or object that can be stored and possessed, and whose intrinsic value is embedded within its physical presence. Insurance, dry cleaning, hotel accommodations, and airline passenger or freight service are intangible products whose intrinsic value is the result of a process, a performance, or an occurrence that only exists while it is being created.

The intangibility of services results in characteristics unique to a service: it is *inseparable* in that its creation cannot be separated from its consumption; it is *heterogeneous* in that it is individually produced and is thus virtually unique; it is *perishable* in that once created it cannot be stored but must be consumed simultaneously with its creation. Contrast these characteristics with a tangible product that can be produced in one location and consumed elsewhere, that can be standardized, whose quality assurance can be determined and maintained over time, and which can be produced and stored in anticipation of fluctuations in demand.

As is true for many tangible products, a service can be marketed both as an industrial (business) or consumer service, depending on the motive of, and use by, the purchaser. For example, travel agents and airlines sell industrial or business services to a businessperson and a consumer service to a tourist. Financial services, hotels, insurance, legal services, and others may each be classified as either a business or consumer service.

As one would suspect, the unique characteristics of services result in differences in the marketing of services and the marketing of industrial and consumer products. However, since many of the issues and topics in this and the next chapter on industrial products are applicable to business and consumer services alike, a detailed coverage of services will follow the discussion of industrial products in the next chapter.

Summary

The growing globalization of markets that gives rise to standardization must be balanced with the continuing need to assess all markets for those differences that might require adaptation for successful acceptance. The premise that global communications and other worldwide socializing forces have fostered a homogenization of tastes, needs, and values in a significant sector of the population across all cultures is difficult to deny. However, as one authority notes, "In spite of the forces of homogenization, consumers also see the world of global symbols, company images, and product choice through the lens of their own local culture and its stage of development and market sophistication."[57]

Each product must be viewed in light of how it is perceived by each culture with which it comes in contact. What is acceptable and comfortable within one group may be radically new and resisted within others, depending on the experiences and perceptions of each group. Understanding that an established product in one culture may be considered an innovation in another is critical in planning and developing consumer products for foreign markets. Analyzing a product as an innovation and using the Product Component Model may provide the marketer with important leads for adaptation.

---

[57] Jeanne Binstock van Rij, "Trends, Symbols, and Brand Power in Global Market: The Business Anthropology Approach," *Strategy & Leadership,* November 21, 1996, p. 18.

Questions

1. Define the following terms and show their significance to international marketing:

product diffusion	dynamically continuous
Product Component Model	innovation
trialability	global brand
relative advantage	innovation
quality	green marketing

2. Debate the issue of global versus adapted products for the international marketer.

3. Define the country-of-origin effect and give examples.

4. The text discusses stereotypes, ethnocentrism, degree of economic development, and fads as the basis for generalizations about country-of-origin effect on product perception. Explain each and give an example.

5. Discuss product alternatives and the three marketing strategies: domestic market extension, multidomestic markets, and global market strategies.

6. Discuss the different promotional/product strategies available to an international marketer.

7. Assume you are deciding to "go international," and outline the steps you would take to help you decide on a product line.

8. Products can be adapted physically and culturally for foreign markets. Discuss.

9. What are the three major components of a product? Discuss their importance to product adaptation.

10. How can a knowledge of the diffusion of innovations help a product manager plan international investments?

11. Old products (that is, old in the U.S. market) may be innovations in a foreign market. Discuss fully.

12. "If the product sells in Dallas, it will sell in Tokyo or Berlin." Comment.

13. How can a country with a per capita GNP of $100 be a potential market for consumer goods? What kinds of goods would probably be in demand? Discuss.

14. Discuss the four types of innovations. Give examples of a product that would be considered by the U.S. market as one type of innovation but a different type in another market. Support your choice.

15. Discuss the characteristics of an innovation that can account for differential diffusion rates.

16. Give an example of how a foreign marketer can use knowledge of the characteristics of innovations in product adaptation decisions.

17. Discuss "environmentally friendly" products and product development.

18. Visit the home page of Unilever (**http://www.unilever.com**) and select Unilever Research. From the list of research titles, select No. 4, Europeans and Their Vegetables, and No. 5, Factors Affecting Children's Food Choice. Using this information, discuss how you could adapt frozen vegetables in order to increase sales in the European market.

CHAPTER 13

MARKETING INDUSTRIAL PRODUCTS AND SERVICES

Chapter Outline

Chapter Learning Objectives

What you should learn from Chapter 13

- The importance of derived demand in industrial markets.
- The relationship between a country's environment and its industrial market needs.
- How demand is affected by technology.
- Characteristics of an industrial product.
- The importance of ISO 9000 certification.
- The importance of relationship marketing and industrial products.
- The importance of trade shows in promoting industrial goods.
- The growth of business services and nuances of their marketing.

GLOBAL PERSPECTIVE

How Far Is Up for Intel?

Fortune's cover story, "Intel, Andy Grove's Amazing Profit Machine—and His Plan for Five More Years of Explosive Growth" is capped only by *Time*'s Man of the Year story, "Intel's Andy Grove, His Microchips Have Changed the World —and Its Economy." 1997 was the eighth consecutive year of record revenue ($25.1 billion) and earnings ($6.5 billion) for the company Grove helped found. Yet at the beginning of 1998 the real question was, Will the world change Intel? Judging from Intel's own forecasts for a flat first quarter in 1998, Chairman of the Board Grove and his associates were concerned that the financial meltdown in Asian markets would affect Intel's plans for "five more years of explosive growth." Some 30 percent of the firm's record 1997 revenues had come from Asian markets. Indeed, one pundit had earlier predicted, "I see no clear technology threats. The biggest long-term threat to Intel is that the market growth slows." Others warned there's something wrong out there: computer-industry overcapacity.

Actually Intel had an even longer list of threats all posted as a disclaimer to its published forecast:

"Other factors that could cause actual results to differ materially are the following: business and economic conditions, and growth in the computing industry in various geographic regions; changes in customer order patterns, including changes in customer and channel inventory levels and seasonal PC buying patterns; changes in the mixes of microprocessor types and speeds, motherboards, pur-

chased components and other products; competitive factors, such as rival chip architectures and manufacturing technologies, competing software-compatible microprocessors and acceptance of new products in specific market segments; pricing pressures; changes in end users' preferences; risk of inventory obsolescence and variations in inventory valuation; timing of software industry product introductions; continued success in technological advances, including development, implementation and initial production of new strategic products and processes in a cost-effective manner; execution of manufacturing ramp; excess storage of manufacturing capacity; the ability to successfully integrate any acquired businesses, enter new market segments and manage growth of such businesses; unanticipated costs or other adverse effects associated with processors and other products containing errata; risks associated with foreign operations; litigation involving intellectual property and consumer issues; and other risk factors listed from time to time in the company's SEC reports."

Time's Man of the Year had a lot to worry about—most of all that industrial market booms are always followed by busts. Will the rise truly last five more years?

Sources: Adapted from David Kirkpatrick, "Intel, Andy Grove's Amazing Profit Machine—and His Plan for Five More Years of Explosive Growth," *Fortune*, February 17, 1997, pp. 60–75; "Man of the Year," *Time*, January 5, 1998, pp. 46–99; and Peter Burrows, Gary McWilliams, Paul C. Judge, and Roger O. Crockett, "There's Something Wrong Out There," *Business Week*, December 29, 1997, pp. 38–40. See also **http://www.intel.com**.

The issues of standardization versus adaptation discussed in Chapter 12 have less relevancy to marketing industrial goods than consumer goods since there are more similarities in marketing industrial products across country markets than there are differences. The inherent nature of industrial goods and the sameness in motives and behavior among industrial goods customers create a market where product and marketing mix standardization are commonplace. Photocopy machines are sold in Belarus for the same reasons as in the United States: to make photocopies. Some minor modification may be necessary to accommodate different electrical power supplies or paper size but, basically, photocopy machines are standardized across markets, as are the vast majority of industrial goods. For industrial products that are basically custom made (specialized steel, customized machine tools, and so on), adaptation takes place for domestic as well as foreign markets.

Two basic factors account for greater market similarities among industrial goods customers than among consumer goods customers. First is the inherent nature of the product: industrial services are used in the process of creating other goods and services; consumer goods are in their final form and are consumed by individuals. And second, the motive or intent of the user differs: industrial consumers are seeking profit, whereas the ultimate consumer is seeking satisfaction. These factors are manifest in specific buying patterns and demand characteristics, and in a special emphasis on relationship marketing as a competitive tool. Whether a company is marketing at home or abroad, the differences between industrial and consumer markets merit special consideration.

Along with industrial goods, services are a highly competitive growth market seeking quality and value. Manufactured products generally come to mind when we think of international trade. Yet the most rapidly growing sector of U.S. international trade today consists of business and consumer services—accounting, advertising, banking, consulting, construction, hotels, insurance, law, transportation, travel, television programs, and movies sold by U.S. firms in global markets. The intangibility of services creates a set of unique problems to which the service provider must respond. A further complication is a lack of uniform laws that regulate market entry. Protectionism, while prevalent for industrial goods, can be much more pronounced for the service provider.

This chapter discusses the special problems in marketing industrial goods and services internationally, the increased competition and demand for quality in those goods and services, and the implications for the global marketer.

The Volatility of Industrial Demand

There are numerous reasons why consumer products firms market internationally—exposure to more demanding customers, keeping up with the competition, extending product life cycles, growing sales and profits, to name a few. For firms producing products and services for industrial markets there is an additional crucial reason for venturing abroad: dampening the natural volatility of industrial markets. Indeed, perhaps the single most important difference between consumer and industrial marketing is the huge, cyclical swings in demand inherent in the latter. It is true that demand for consumer durables such as cars, furniture, or home computers can be quite volatile. In industrial markets, however, two other factors come into play that exacerbate both the ups and downs in demand: (1) professional buyers tend to act in concert; and (2) derived demand accelerates changes in markets.

Purchasing agents at large personal computer manufacturers such as IBM, Apple, Acer, Samsung, and Toshiba are responsible for obtaining component parts for their firms as cheaply as possible and in a timely manner. They monitor demand for PCs and prices of components like microprocessors or disk drives, and changes in either customer markets or supplier prices directly affect their ordering. Declines in PC demand or supplier prices can cause these professionals to "slam on the brakes" in their buying; in the latter case they wait for further price cuts. And because the purchasing agents at all the PC companies, here and abroad, are monitoring the same data, they all brake (or accelerate) simultaneously.[1] Consumers do monitor markets as well, but not nearly to the same degree. Purchases of clothing and cars tends to be steadier.

For managers selling capital equipment and big-ticket industrial services, understanding the concept of derived demand is absolutely fundamental to their success. *Derived demand* can be defined as demand dependent on another source. Thus, the demand for Boeing 747s is derived from the worldwide consumer demand for air travel services, and the demand for Fluor Daniel's global construction and engineering services to design and build oil refineries in China is derived from Chinese consumers' demands for gasoline. Minor changes in consumer demand mean major changes in the related industrial demand. In the example in Exhibit 13–1, a 10 percent increase in consumer demand for shower stalls in year 2 translates into a 100 percent increase in demand for the

---

[1] For the most complete discussion, see Robert W. Haas, *Business Marketing,* 6th ed.(Cincinnati, OH: Southwestern, 1995), pp. 111–118.

EXHIBIT 13-1   Derived Demand Example

Time Period	Consumer Demand for Premolded Fiberglass Shower Stalls			Number of Machines in Use to Produce the Shower Stalls			Demand for the Machines		
Year	Previous Year	Current Year	Net Change	Previous Year	Current Year	Net Change	Replacement	New	Total
1	100,000	100,000	—	500	500	—	50	—	50
2	100,000	110,000	+10,000	500	550	+50	50	50	100
3	110,000	115,000	+5,000	550	575	+25	50	25	75
4	115,000	118,000	+3,000	575	590	+15	50	15	65
5	118,000	100,000	−18,000	590	500	−90	—	−40	−40
6	100,000	100,000	—	500	500	—	10	—	10

Source: Adapted from R. L. Vaile, E. T. Grether, and R. Cox, *Marketing in the American Economy* (New York: Ronald Press, 1952), p. 16. Appears in Robert W. Haas, *Business Marketing*, 6th edition (Cincinnati, OH: Southwestern, 1995), p. 115.

machines to make shower stalls. The 15 percent decline in consumer demand in year 5 results in a complete shutdown of demand for shower-stall making machines. For Boeing circa 1998, Asian financial problems directly caused reductions in air travel (both vacation and commercial) to and within the region, which in turn caused cancellations of orders for aircraft. Indeed, the commercial aircraft industry has always been and will continue to be one of the most volatile of all.

Industrial firms can take several measures to manage this inherent volatility, such as maintaining broad product lines, raising prices faster and reducing advertising expenditures during booms, or ignoring market share as a strategic goal and focusing on stability. For most American firms, where corporate cultures emphasize beating competitors, such stabilizing measures are usually given only lip service. Alternatively, in German and Japanese firms employees and stability are more highly valued and they are generally better at managing volatility in markets.[2]

Some U.S. companies, such as Boeing, Intel, and Microsoft, have been quite good at "spreading their portfolio" of markets served. Late 1990s declines in Asian markets were somewhat offset by strong American markets just as late 1980s Japanese demand increases had offset declines in the U.S. Indeed, one of the strange disadvantages of having the previously command economies go private is their integration into the global market. That is, prior to the breakup of the U.S.S.R., Soviets bought industrial products according to a national five-year plan which often had little to do with markets outside of the Communist Bloc. Their off-cycle ordering tended to dampen demand volatility for companies able to sell there. Now privately held Russian manufacturers watch and react to world markets just as their counterparts do all over the globe. The increasing globalization of markets will tend to increase the volatility in industrial markets as purchasing agents around the world act with even greater simultaneity. Managing this inherent volatility will necessarily affect all aspects of the marketing mix including product/service development.

The Industrial Product Market

Because an industrial product is purchased for business use and thus sought not as an entity in itself but as part of a total process, the buyer places high value on service, dependability, quality, performance, and cost. In international marketing, these features are

---

[2] Cathy Anterasian, John L. Graham, and R. Bruce Money, "Are American Managers Superstitious about Market Share?" *Sloan Management Review,* Summer 1996, pp. 67–77.

complicated by cultural and environmental differences, including variations in industrial development found among countries.

Stages of Economic Development

Perhaps the most significant environmental factor affecting the industrial goods market is the degree of industrialization. Although generalizing about countries is imprudent, the degree of economic development in a country can be used as a rough gauge of the market for industrial goods. Because industrial goods are products for industry, there is a logical relationship between the degree of economic development and the character of demand for industrial goods found within a country. One authority suggests that nations can be classified into five stages of development. This classification is essentially a production-oriented approach to economic development in contrast to the marketing-oriented approach used in Chapter 12. A production orientation is helpful because at each stage some broad generalizations can be made about the level of development and the industrial market within the country.

The first stage of development is really a *pre-industrial or commercial stage,* with little or no manufacturing and an economy almost wholly based on the exploitation of raw materials and agricultural products. The demand for industrial products is confined to a limited range of goods used in the simple production of the country's resources, that is, the industrial machinery, equipment, and goods required in the production of these resources. During this stage, a transportation system develops that creates a market for highly specialized and expensive construction equipment that must be imported. One American bank chairman has estimated that China needs to spend $55 trillion to build an infrastructure to support a developed economy.[3] That is three times the world's gross domestic product!

The second stage reflects the development of *primary manufacturing concerned with the partial processing of raw materials and resources,* which in stage one were shipped in raw form. At this level, demand is for the machinery and other industrial goods necessary for processing raw materials prior to exporting. For example, in South Africa there is demand for health services, construction equipment, telecommunications equipment, mining equipment and process facilities, power generating equipment, and technical expertise and training for most of the basic industries.

The third stage of development is characterized by the *growth of manufacturing facilities for nondurable and semidurable consumer goods.* Generally, the industries are small, local manufacturers of consumer goods having relative mass appeal. In such cases, the demand for industrial products extends to entire factories and the supplies necessary to support manufacturing. Most of the Eastern European countries such as Russia, Romania, and Ukraine fit this category. Liberia is another country at this stage of development. The Liberian Development Corporation has been focusing attention on developing small- and medium-sized industries, such as shoe factories and battery and nail manufacturing. This degree of industrialization requires machinery and equipment to build and equip the factories and the supplies to keep them operating. Liberia's chief imports from the United States are construction and mining equipment, motor vehicles and parts, metal structures and parts, and manufactured rubber goods.

A country at stage four is a *well-industrialized economy.* This stage reflects the production of capital goods as well as consumer goods, including products such as automobiles, refrigerators, and machinery. Even though the country produces some industrial goods, it still needs to import more specialized and heavy capital equipment not yet produced there but necessary for domestic industry. Parts of Eastern Europe typify countries at this stage—places like the Czech Republic, Hungary, Poland, and Estonia.[4] The

---

[3] John Naisbitt, *Megatrends Asia* (New York: Simon and Schuster, 1996).
[4] Kevin Godier and Alan Spense, "Market Divides in Two," *Financial Times,* October 9, 1997, p. 17.

needs of their industrial base reflect major revitalization, creating an enormous market as they turn from socialist-managed to market-driven economies.

Another category of countries in this fourth stage are the newly industrialized countries (NICs), many of which were in stages one or two just a few decades ago. South Korea, for example, has risen from a war-torn economy to a major competitor in world markets, offering an ever-increasing number of industrial and consumer products. Even though South Korea is a major exporter of high-tech goods such as petrochemicals, electronics, machines, automobiles, and steel, it is dependent on more industrialized countries for industrial tools, commercial aircraft, information systems, and other technologically advanced products not presently produced in South Korea but necessary to sustain its expanding manufacturing base. Sales from American industrial suppliers such as Boeing, Cisco Systems, and Intel suffered substantially when South Korean growth nose-dived in 1997.[5]

The fifth stage of economic development signifies *complete industrialization* and generally indicates world leadership in the production of a large variety of goods. Many of the industrial goods that had been purchased from others are now produced domestically. Countries that have achieved this level typically compete worldwide for consumer and industrial goods markets.

Japan, the United States, and Germany have all reached the fifth stage of industrial development, and although they are industrialized economies, there is still the need to import goods. Countries in this category are markets for the latest technology as well as for less-sophisticated products that can be produced more economically in other countries. Demand is found for telecommunication equipment, computer chips, electronic testing equipment, and scientific controlling and measuring equipment, as well as for forklifts and lathes. However, products on the cutting edge of technology and goods produced in the most cost-effective manner are the important differential advantages for companies competing for market demand in countries in the fifth stage. Indeed, information technology exports are helping America maintain world economic leadership well into the 21st century.

Success in a fiercely competitive global market for industrial goods depends on building an edge in science and technology. The industrialization of many countries in stages one to four creates enormous demand for goods produced by firms in the most advanced stages of technical development. The Asian worker who can wire 120 integrated circuits for semiconductor chips in one hour is being phased out by automated machines that wire 640 circuits in an hour. As technology develops, countries that have been relying on cheap labor for a competitive advantage have to shift to more sophisticated machines, thus creating markets for products from more technologically advanced countries.

Technology and Market Demand

Another important approach to grouping countries is on the basis of their ability to benefit from and use technology, particularly now that countries are using technology as economic leverage to leap several stages of economic development in a very short time.

Not only is technology the key to economic growth, for many products it is the competitive edge in today's global markets. As precision robots and digital control systems take over the factory floor, manufacturing is becoming more science-oriented and access to inexpensive labor and raw materials is becoming less important. The ability to develop the latest information technology and to benefit from its application is a critical factor in the international competitiveness of managers, countries, and companies.

---

[5] Nelson D. Schwartz and Erick Schonfeld, "Have Nasdaq's Tech Giants Flamed Out?" *Fortune,* February 2, 1998, pp. 164–168; and Maura Griffin Solovar, "Boeing's Big Problem," *Fortune,* January 12, 1998, pp. 96–103.

Three interrelated trends will spur demand for technologically advanced products: (1) expanding economic and industrial growth in Asia, particularly China and India; (2) the disassembly of the Soviet empire; and (3) the privatization of government-owned industries worldwide.

Beginning with Japan, many Asian countries have been in a state of rapid economic growth over the last 25 years. While this growth has recently slowed, the long-term outlook for these countries remains excellent. Japan has become the most advanced industrialized country in the region, while South Korea, Hong Kong, Singapore, and Taiwan (the Four Tigers) have successfully moved from being cheap labor sources to becoming industrialized nations. The Southeast Asian countries of Malaysia, Thailand, Indonesia, and the Philippines are exporters of manufactured products to Japan and the United States now, and once they overcome current financial problems they will continue to gear up for greater industrialization. Countries at each of the first three levels of industrial development demand technologically advanced products for further industrialization that will enable them to compete in global markets.

As a market economy develops in the Newly Independent States (former republics of the USSR) and other Eastern European countries, new privately-owned businesses will create a demand for the latest technology to revitalize and expand manufacturing facilities. The BEMs (big emerging markets) discussed in Chapter 9 are estimated to account for more than $1^{1}/_{2}$ trillion of trade by 2010.[6] These countries will demand the latest technology to expand their industrial bases and build modern infrastructures.

Concurrent with the fall of communism which fueled the rush to privatization in Eastern Europe, Latin Americans began to dismantle their state-run industries in hopes of reviving their economies. Mexico, Argentina, and Venezuela are leading the rest of Latin America in privatizing state-owned businesses. The move to privatization will create enormous demand for industrial goods as new owners invest heavily in the latest technology. Telmex, a $4 billion joint venture between Southwestern Bell, France Telecom, and Telefonos de Mexico, will invest hundreds of millions of dollars to bring the Mexican telephone system up to the most advanced standards. Telmex is only one of scores of new privatized companies from Poland to Patagonia that are creating a mass market for the most advanced technology.

The return to economic growth in Asia, the creation of market economies in Eastern Europe and the republics of the former Soviet Union, and the privatization of state-owned enterprises in Latin America and elsewhere will create an expanding demand particularly for industrial goods and business services well into the next century. The competition to meet this global demand will be stiff; the companies with the competitive edge will be those whose products are technologically advanced, of the highest quality, and accompanied by world-class service.

Attributes of Product Quality

As discussed in Chapter 12, the concept of quality encompasses many factors, and the perception of quality rests solely with the customer. The level of technology reflected in the product, compliance with standards that reflect customer needs, support services and follow-through, and the price relative to competitive products are all part of a customer's evaluation and perception of quality. As noted, these requirements are different for ultimate consumers and for industrial customers because of differing end uses. The factors themselves also differ among industrial goods customers because their needs are varied.

Industrial marketers frequently misinterpret the concept of quality. Good quality as interpreted by a highly industrialized market is not the same as when interpreted by standards of a less-industrialized nation. For example, an African government had been buying hand-operated dusters for farmers to distribute pesticides in cotton fields. The

---

6 "The Big Emerging Markets," *Business America,* March 1994, pp. 4–6.

duster supplied was a finely machined device requiring regular oiling and good care. But the fact that this duster turned more easily than any other on the market was relatively unimportant to the farmers. Furthermore, the requirement for careful oiling and care simply meant that in a relatively short time of inadequate care the machines froze up and broke. The result? The local government went back to an older type of French duster that was heavy, turned with difficulty, and gave a poorer distribution of dust, but which lasted longer because it required less care and lubrication. In this situation, the French machine possessed more relevant quality features and, therefore, in marketing terms, possessed the higher quality.

Likewise, when commercial jet aircraft were first developed, European and American designs differed substantially. For example, American manufacturers built the engines slung below the wings while the British competitor built the engines into the wings. The American design made for easier access and saved on repair and servicing costs, and the British design reduced drag and saved on fuel costs. Both designs were "high quality" for their respective markets. At the time labor was relatively expensive in the U.S. and fuel was relatively expensive in the U.K.

Quality Is Defined by the Buyer

There is a price–quality relationship that exists in an industrial buyer's decision. One important dimension of quality is how well a product meets the specific needs of the buyer. When a product falls short of performance expectations, its poor quality is readily apparent. However, it is less apparent but nonetheless true that a product which *exceeds* performance expectations is also of poor quality. A product whose design exceeds the wants of the buyer's intended use generally means a higher price that reflects the extra capacity. Quality for many goods is assessed in terms of fulfilling specific expectations—no more and no less. Thus, a product that produces 20,000 units per hour when the buyer needs one that produces only 5,000 units per hour is not a quality product in that the extra capacity of 15,000 units is unnecessary to meet the buyer's use expectations. Indeed, this is one of the key issues facing personal computer makers. Many business buyers are asking the question, Do we really need the latest $3,000 PC for everyone? And more and more often the answer is, "No," the $900 machines will do just fine.[7]

This price–quality relationship is an important factor in marketing in developing economies, especially those in the first three stages of economic development described earlier. Standard quality requirements of industrial products sold in the U.S. market that command commensurately higher prices may be completely out of line for the needs of the underdeveloped growth markets of the world. Labor-saving features are of little importance when time has limited value and labor is plentiful. Also of lesser value is the ability of machinery to hold close tolerances where people are not quality-control conscious, where large production runs do not exist, and where the wages of skillful workers justify selective fits in assembly and repair work. Features that a buyer does not want or cannot effectively use do not enhance a product's quality rating.

This does not mean quality is unimportant or that the latest technology is not sought in developing markets. Rather, it means that those markets require products designed to meet their specific needs, not products designed for different uses and expectations, especially if the additional features result in higher prices. This attitude was reflected in a study of purchasing behavior of Chinese import managers who ranked product quality first, followed in importance by price. Timely delivery was third and product style/features ranked eleventh out of 17 variables studied.[8] Hence, a product whose design reflects the needs and expectations of the buyer—no more, no less—is a quality product.

---

[7] Schwartz and Schonfeld, *Fortune,* February 2, 1998.

[8] Kyung-il Ghymn, Paul Johnson, and Weijong Zhang, "Chinese Import Managers' Purchasing Behavior," *Journal of Asian Business,* 9(3), Summer 1993, pp. 35–45.

The design of a product must be viewed from all aspects of use. Extreme variations in climate create problems in designing equipment that is universally operable. Products that function effectively in Western Europe may require major design changes to operate as well in the hot, dry Sahara region or the humid, tropical rain forests of Latin America. Trucks designed to travel the superhighways of the United States almost surely will experience operational difficulties in the mountainous regions of Latin America on roads that barely resemble Jeep trails. Manufacturers must consider many variations in making products that will be functional in far-flung markets.

In light of today's competition, a company must consider the nature of its market and the adequacy of the design of its products. Effective competition in global markets means that over-engineered and overpriced products must give way to products that meet the specifications of the customer at competitive prices. Success is in offering products that fit a customer's needs, technologically advanced for some and less sophisticated for others, but all of high quality. To be competitive in today's global markets, the concept of total quality management (TQM) must be a part of all MNCs' management strategy, and TQM starts with talking to customers.

Service and Replacement Parts

Effective competition abroad not only requires proper product design but effective service, prompt deliveries, and the ability to furnish spare and replacement parts without delay. In the highly competitive European Union, for example, it is imperative to give the same kind of service a domestic company or EU company can give. One U.S. export management firm warned that U.S. business may be too apathetic about Europe, treating it as a subsidiary market not worthy of "spending time to develop." It cites the case of an American firm with a $3 million potential sale in Europe which did not even give engineering support to its representatives when the same sale in the U.S. would have brought out "all the troops."

For many technical products, the willingness of the seller to provide installation and training may be the deciding factor for the buyers in accepting one company's product over another's. South Korean and other Asian businesspeople are frank in admitting they prefer to buy from American firms but the Japanese get the business because of outstanding after-sales service. Frequently heard tales of conflicts between U.S. and foreign firms over assistance expected from the seller are indicative of the problems of after-sales service and support. A South Korean businessman's experiences with an American engineer and some Japanese engineers typify the situation. The Korean electronic firm purchased semiconductor-chip-making equipment for a plant expansion. The American engineer was slow in completing the installation; he stopped work at five o'clock and would not work on weekends. The Japanese, installing other equipment, understood the urgency of getting the factory up and running; without being asked they worked day and night until the job was finished.

Unfortunately this is not an isolated case. In another example, Hyundai Motor Company bought two multimillion-dollar presses to stamp body parts for cars. The presses arrived late, even more time was required to set up the machines, and Hyundai had to pay the Americans extra to get the machines to work correctly. The impact of such problems translates into lost business for U.S. firms. Samsung Electronics Company, Korea's largest chip maker, used U.S. equipment for 75 percent of its first memory-chip plant; when it outfitted its most recent chip plant, it bought 75 percent of the equipment from Japan.

Customer training is rapidly becoming a major after-sales service when selling technical products in countries that demand the latest technology but do not always have trained personnel. China demands the most advanced technical equipment but frequently has untrained people responsible for products they do not understand. Heavy emphasis on training programs and self-teaching materials to help overcome the common lack of skills to operate technical equipment is a necessary part of the after-sales service package in much of the developing world.

A recent study of international users of heavy construction equipment revealed that, next to the manufacturer's reputation, quick delivery of replacement parts was of major importance in purchasing construction equipment. Furthermore, 70 percent of those questioned indicated they bought parts not made by the original manufacturer of the equipment because of the difficulty of getting original parts. Smaller importers complain of U.S. exporting firms not responding to orders or responding only after extensive delay. It appears that the importance of timely availability of spare parts to sustain a market is forgotten by some American exporters. When companies are responsive, the rewards are significant. U.S. chemical production equipment manufacturers dominate sales in Mexico because, according to the International Trade Administration, they deliver quickly. The ready availability of parts and services provided by U.S. marketers can give them a competitive edge.

Some international marketers also may be forgoing the opportunity of participating in a lucrative aftermarket. Certain kinds of machine tools use up to five times their original value in replacement parts during an average life span and thus represent an even greater market. One international machine tool company has capitalized on the need for direct service and available parts by changing its distribution system from "normal" to one of stressing rapid service and readily available parts. Instead of selling through independent distributors, as do most machine tool manufacturers in foreign markets, this company established a series of company stores and service centers similar to those found in the United States. The company can render service through its system of local stores, while most competitors dispatch service people from their home-based factories. The service people are kept on tap for rapid service calls in each of its network of local stores, and each store keeps a large stock of standard parts available for immediate delivery. The net result of meeting industrial needs quickly is keeping the company among the top suppliers in foreign sales of machine tools.

International small-package door-to-door express air services and international toll-free telephone service have helped speed up the delivery of parts and have made after-sales technical service almost instantly available. Amdahl, the giant mainframe computer maker, uses air shipments almost exclusively for cutting inventory costs and ensuring premium customer service, which is crucial to competing against larger rivals. With increasing frequency, electronics, auto parts, and machine parts sent by air have become a formidable weapon in cutting costs and boosting competitiveness. Technical advice is only a toll-free call away, and parts are air-expressed immediately to the customer. Not only does this approach improve service standards, but it also is often more cost effective than maintaining an office in a country, even though foreign language speakers must be hired to answer calls.

Finally, after-sales services are not only crucial in building strong customer loyalty and the all-important reputation that leads to sales at other companies. After-sales services (such as maintenance contracts, parts, repair, and overhaul) are also almost always more profitable than the actual sale of the machinery or product.

Universal Standards

A lack of universal standards is another problem in international sales of industrial products. The United States has two major areas of concern in this regard for the industrial goods exporter: one is a lack of common standards for manufacturing highly specialized equipment such as machine tools and computers, and the other is the use of the inch–pound or English system of measurement. Conflicting standards are encountered in test methods for materials and equipment, quality control systems, and machine specifications. In the telecommunications industry, the vast differences in standards among countries create enormous problems for expansion of that industry.

Efforts are being made through international organizations to create international standards. For example, the International Electrotechnical Commission (IEC) is concerned with standard specifications for electrical equipment for machine tools. The U.S. Department of Commerce participates in programs to promote U.S. standards and is active in the development of the Global Harmonization Task Force, an international effort to harmonize standards for several industry sectors. The U.S. Trade Representative participates in negotiations to harmonize standards as well. During 1997 a key agreement was signed with the European Union to mutually recognize one another's standards in six sectors. The agreements will eliminate the need for double testing (one each on both sides of the Atlantic), inspection or certification in telecommunications, medical devices, electromagnetic compatibility, electrical safety, recreation craft, and pharmaceuticals. The agreements cover approximately $50 billion in two-way trade and are expected to equate to a 2–3 percent drop in tariffs.[9]

In addition to industry and international organizations setting standards, countries often have standards for products entering their markets. Saudi Arabia has been working on setting standards for everything from light bulbs to lemon juice, and it has asked its trading partners for help. The standards, the first in Arabic, will most likely be adopted by the entire Arab world. Most countries sent representatives to participate in the standard setting. For example, New Zealand sent a representative to help write the standards for the shelf life of lamb. Unfortunately, the United States failed to send a representative until late in the discussions, and thus many of the hundreds of standards written favor Japanese and European products. Also, Saudi Arabia adopted the new European standard for utility equipment. The cost in lost sales to just two Saudi cities by just one U.S. company, Westinghouse, could be from $15–$20 million for U.S.-standard distribution transformers.

In the United States, conversion to the metric system and acceptance of international standards have been slow. Congress and industry have dragged their feet for fear conversion would be too costly. But the cost will come from not adopting the metric system; the General Electric Company had a shipment of electrical goods turned back from a Saudi port because its connecting cords were six feet long instead of the required standard of two meters.

As American industry sales are accounted for more and more by foreign customers on the metric system, the cost of delaying standardization mounts. Measurement-sensitive products account for one half to two thirds of U.S. exports, and if the European Union bars nonmetric imports, as expected, many U.S. products will lose access to that market just as the EU is on the threshold of economic expansion. About half of U.S. exports are covered by the EU's new standards program.

To spur U.S. industry into action, the Department of Commerce has indicated that accepting the metric system will not be mandatory unless you want to sell something to the U.S. government; all U.S. government purchases will be conducted exclusively in metrics. All federal buildings are now being designed with metric specifications, and highway construction funded by Washington uses metric units. Since the U.S. government is the nation's largest customer, this directive may be successful in converting U.S. business to the metric system. The Defense Department now requires metrics for all new weapons systems, as well.

Despite the edicts from Washington, the National Aeronautics and Space Administration (NASA), which presides over some of the most advanced technology in the world, resists metrification. The $14 billion space station now being built will contain some metric parts, but most of the major components are made in the U.S. and will be based on inches and pounds. NASA's excuse is it was too far into the design and production to switch. Moreover, the space station is supposed to be an international effort

9 "USTR: U.S.-E.U. MRA Accord to Save U.S. Industry $1B a Year," *Dow Jones News Service,* June 13, 1997.

CROSSING BORDERS 13-1

Your Hoses Are a Threat to Public Security!

Universal standards have made life miserable for Evan Segal. He is president of Dormont Manufacturing Co., which makes hoses that hook up deep-fat fryers and the like to gas outlets and which once sold these hoses throughout Europe. But one day in 1989, one of his top customers, Frymaster Corp. of Shreveport, LA, called to alert him that McDonalds was being told it could no longer use his hoses in its British restaurants. Similar problems popped up elsewhere, including EuroDisney outside Paris; shortly before the theme park opened, French inspectors demanded that Dormont's hoses be replaced with French-approved equipment.

The disparate national standards stemmed from the fact that the hoses are crucial to safe operation of gas appliances and thus fall under the product-safety provisions allowing each country to set up its own standards. . . . In Dormont's case, the specifications were written by committees often dominated by domestic producers. They spell out minutiae of each country's acceptable gas hose design—such as the color of plastic coating or how the end pieces should be attached to the rest of the hose.

Mr. Segal thought he had made a major breakthrough when the British Standards Institute, one of the European agencies that test equipment and hand out approvals, issued Dormont a certificate authorizing the company to paste a seal of approval on its products signifying that the hoses conformed with European Union rules for gas appliances, enabling the company to sell them throughout the region.

But the victory was short-lived. A miffed German competitor fired off a formal complaint to the European Commission, the EU's Brussels-based executive body. Commission officials familiar with the case say the rival argued that the British office erred because hoses are not really part of a gas appliance. The approval was withdrawn.

Source: Adapted from Timothy Aeppel, "Europe's Unity Undoes a U.S. Exporter," *The Wall Street Journal,* April 1, 1996, p. B1. Reprinted by permission from *The Wall Street Journal,* © 1996 Dow Jones & Company, Inc. All Rights Reserved Worldwide.

with Russia as one of the partners, and this creates large problems for systems integration.[10] Yes, it is hard to believe that the only two countries not officially on the metric system are Myanmar and the United States. It is becoming increasingly evident that the United States must change or be left behind.

ISO 9000 Certification: An International Standard of Quality

With quality becoming the cornerstone of global competition, companies are requiring assurance of standard conformance from suppliers just as their customers are requiring the same from them.

ISO 9000s, a series of five international industrial standards (ISO 9000–9004) originally designed by the International Organization for Standardization in Geneva to meet the need for product quality assurances in purchasing agreements, are becoming a quality assurance certification program that has competitive and legal ramifications when doing business in the European Union and elsewhere.

ISO 9000 refers to the registration and certification of a manufacturer's quality system. It is a certification of the existence of a quality control system a company has in place to ensure it can meet published quality standards. ISO 9000 standards do not

---

[10] Malcolm W. Browne, "Kinder, Gentler Push for Metric Inches Along," *The New York Times,* June 4, 1996, p.1.

The ISO 9000 quality assurance program was initiated in the European Union, but now has evolved into an international standard. Here American managers of a Japanese company work on ISO 9000 specifications for printers and copiers to be sold in NAFTA countries. (© 1997 Nation's Business/T. Michael Keza)

apply to specific products. They relate to generic system standards that enable a company, through a mix of internal and external audits, to provide assurance that it has a quality control system. It is a certification of the production process only, and does not guarantee a manufacturer produces a "quality" product. The series describes three quality system models, defines quality concepts, and gives guidelines for using international standards in quality systems.[11]

To receive ISO 9000 certification a company requests a certifying body (a third party authorized to provide an ISO 9000 audit) to conduct a registration assessment—that is, an audit of the key business processes of a company. The assessor will ask questions about everything from blueprints to sales calls to filing. Does the supplier meet promised delivery dates? and Is there evidence of customer satisfaction? are two of the questions asked and the issues explored. The object is to develop a comprehensive plan to ensure minute details are not overlooked. The assessor helps management create a quality manual which will be made available to customers wishing to verify the organization's reliability. When accreditation is granted, the company receives certification. A complete assessment for recertification is done every four years, with intermediate evaluations during the four-year period.

Although ISO 9000 is generally voluntary, except for certain regulated products, the *EU Product Liability Directive* puts pressure on all companies to become certified. The directive holds that a manufacturer, including an exporter, will be liable, regardless of fault or negligence, if a person is harmed by a product that fails because of a faulty component. Thus, customers in the EU need to be assured that the components of their products are free of defects or deficiencies. A manufacturer with a well-documented quality system will be better able to prove that products are defect-free and thus minimize liability claims.

[11] Robert W. Peach, ed., *The ISO 9000 Handbook,* 3rd ed.(Fairfax, VA: CEEM Information Services, 1996).

A strong level of interest in ISO 9000 is being driven more by "marketplace" requirements than by government regulations, and ISO 9000 is becoming an important competitive marketing tool in Europe. As the market demands quality and more and more companies adopt some form of TQM (total quality management), manufacturers are increasingly requiring ISO 9000 registration of their suppliers. Companies manufacturing parts and components in China are quickly discovering that ISO 9000 certification is a virtual necessity,[12] and the Japanese construction industry now requires ISO 9000 as part of the government procurement process.[13] More and more buyers, particularly those in Europe, are refusing to buy from manufacturers that do not have internationally recognized third-party proof of their quality capabilities. ISO 9000 may also be used to serve as a means of differentiating different "classes" of suppliers (particularly in high-tech areas) where high product reliability is crucial. In other words, if two suppliers are competing for the same contract, the one with ISO 9000 registration may have a competitive edge.

While more and more countries (now more than 100) and companies continue to adopt ISO 9000 standards, many have complaints about the system and its spread. For example, 39 electronics companies battled against special Japanese software criteria for ISO 9000. Electronics companies also protested against the establishment of a new ISO Health and Safety Standard.[14] Still others are calling for more comprehensive international standards along the lines of America's Malcolm Baldridge Award, which considers seven criteria—leadership, strategic planning, customer and market focus, information and analysis, human resource development, management, and business results.[15] Perhaps the most pertinent kind of quality standard is now being developed by the University of Michigan Business School and the American Society for Quality Control. Using survey methods, their American Customer Satisfaction Index (ACSI) measures customers' satisfaction and perceptions of quality of a representative sample of America's goods and services. The approach was actually developed in Sweden and is now being considered in other European countries. The appeal of the ACSI approach is its focus on results, that is, quality as perceived by product and service users.[16] So far the ACSI approach has been applied only in consumer product/service contexts; however, the fundamental notion that customers are the best judges of quality is certainly applicable to international industrial marketing settings as well.

Relationship Marketing and Industrial Products

The characteristics that define the uniqueness of industrial products discussed above lead naturally to relationship marketing.[17] The long-term relationship with customers which is at the core of relationship marketing fits the characteristics inherent in industrial products and is a viable strategy for industrial goods marketing. The first and foremost characteristic of industrial goods markets is the motive of the buyer: to make a

---

[12] "Quality: ISO 9000 Certification Standardization," *Business China,* May 30, 1994, p. 4.

[13] Amy Zuckerman, "The Economic Arsenal of the Global Economy," *Management Review,* January 1, 1997, p. 57.

[14] Amy Zuckerman, January 1, 1997.

[15] "Neighborhood Times, Q & A Top of the Class," *St. Petersburg Times,* October 15, 1997, p. 11.

[16] Claes Fornell, Michael D. Johnson, Eugene W. Anderson, Jaesung Cha, and Barbara Everitt Bryant, "The American Consumer Index: Nature, Purpose, and Findings," *Journal of Marketing,* 60(4), October 1996; Daniel Pedersen, "Dissing Customers: Why Service Is Missing from America's Service Economy," *Newsweek,* June 23, 1997, p. 56; and "Consumers Less Satisfied, Survey Finds," *Dallas Morning News,* November 18, 1997, p. 2D.

[17] For a comprehensive review of the literature, see Robert M. Morgan and Shelby D. Hunt, "The Commitment–Trust Theory of Relationship Marketing," *Journal of Marketing,* July 1994, pp. 20–38.

CROSSING BORDERS 13–2

In the European Community, Standards Are a Must for Telecommunications

The hodge-podge of European telephone industry standards is and was one of the most daunting problems facing Continental unification. Even in the early 1990s connections were not being made well: In Spain the busy signal was three pips a second; in Denmark, two. French telephone numbers were 8 and soon to be 10 digits long; Italian numbers were almost any length. German phones ran on 60 volts of electricity; elsewhere, it is 48. The list of differences went on and on; only 30 percent of the technical specifications involved in phone systems were common from one country to the next. In telephones, as in much else in Europe, each country went its own way.

Technical conflicts abounded. Each national telephone authority set different technical requirements for equipment to enter its market. One representative from an electronics company estimated that an average of 50 to 100 labor-years of costly software engineering were needed to rework computerized exchange equipment for each additional European country his company entered.

The Europeans learned their lesson well and have now been adopting the most widely standardized Global System for Mobile Communications (GSM) even faster than American buyers. For some 30 million users from Oslo to Rome there is no problem; cellular is skipping over the spaghetti plate of wires down on the ground. Indeed, "roaming" in Rome is no problem. Compared with Europe, the U.S. system is still in the Dark Ages. In an effort to catch up, American wireless companies are importing rate plans, phone features, marketing strategies, and executives from Europe.

Sources: Adapted from "European Officials Push Idea of Standardizing Telecommunications—But Some Makers Resist," *The Wall Street Journal,* April 10, 1985, p. 28. Reprinted by permission of *THE WALL STREET JOURNAL,* © 1985 Dow Jones & Company, Inc. All Rights Reserved Worldwide; Nittaya Wongtada, John M. Zerio, and Joseph T. Huber, "The Myth of Unified EC Product Standards," *The International Executive,* May 1991, p. 24, and Jon G. Auerbach, "Wireless Warfare: Lessons from Europe Drive Frantic Scramble in Telephone Industry," *The Wall Street Journal,* July 16, 1997, p. A1.

---

profit. Industrial products fit into a business or manufacturing process, and their contributions will be judged on how well they contribute to that process. In order for an industrial marketer to fulfill the needs of its customer, the marketer must understand those needs as they exist today and how they will change as the buyer strives to compete in global markets that call for long-term relationships.

Relationship marketing ranges all the way from gathering information on customer needs to designing products and services, channeling products to the customer in a timely and convenient manner, and following up to make sure the customer is satisfied. For example, SKF, the bearing manufacturer, seeks strong customer relations with postsales follow-through. The end of the transaction is not delivery; it continues as SKF makes sure the bearings are properly mounted and maintained. This helps customers reduce downtime, thus creating value in the relationship with SKF. SKF marketing efforts encompass an array of activities to support long-term relationships which go beyond "merely satisfying the next link in the distribution chain to meeting the more complex needs of the end user, whether those needs are technical, operational, or financial."[18] In short, "the business [SKF does] consists of providing service" to its customers.

---

[18] Rahul Jacob, "Why Some Customers Are More Equal Than Others," *Fortune,* September 19, 1994, p. 215.

The industrial customer's needs in global markets are continuously changing, and suppliers' offerings must also continue to change. The need for the latest technology means that it is not a matter of selling the right product the first time but one of continuously changing the product to keep it right over time. The objective of relationship marketing is to make the relationship an important attribute of the transaction, thus differentiating oneself from competitors. It shifts the focus away from price to service and long-term benefits. The reward is loyal customers that translate into substantial profits.

Focusing on long-term relationship building will be especially important in most international markets where culture dictates stronger ties between people and companies. Particularly in countries with collectivistic[19] and high-context[20] cultures such as those in Latin America or Asia, trust[21] will be a crucial aspect of commercial relationships. Constant and close communication with customers will be the single most important source of information about the development of new industrial products and services. Indeed, in a recent survey of Japanese professional buyers a key choice criterion for suppliers was a trait they called "caring" (those who defer to the requests without argument and recognize that in return buyers will care for the long-term interests of sellers).[22] Longer-term and more communication-rich relationships are keys to success in international industrial markets.

IBM of Brazil stresses stronger ties with its customers by offering planning seminars that address corporate strategies, competition, quality, and how to identify marketing opportunities. One of these seminars showed a food import/export firm how it could increase efficiency by decentralizing its computer facilities to better serve its customers. The company's computers were centralized at headquarters; while branches took orders manually and mailed them to the home office for processing and invoicing. It took several days before the customer's order was entered and added several days to delivery time. The seminar helped the company realize it could streamline its order processing by installing branch office terminals that were connected to computers at the food company's headquarters. A customer could then place an order and receive an invoice on the spot, shortening the delivery time by several days or weeks. Helping a client or supplier identify a problem and its solution also helped IBM sell equipment to the company. Not all participants who attend the 30 different seminars offered annually become IBM customers, but it creates a continuing relationship among potential customers. "So much so," as one executive commented, "when a customer does need increased computer power, he will likely turn to us."[23]

Promoting Industrial Products

The promotional problems encountered by foreign industrial marketers are little different from the problems faced by domestic marketers. Until recently there has been a paucity of specialized advertising media in many countries. In the last decade, however, specialized industrial media have been developed to provide the industrial marketer with

---

[19] Geert H. Hofstede, *Cultures and Organizations: Software of the Mind* (New York: McGraw-Hill, 1991); and Harry C. Triandis, *Individualism and Collectivism* (Boulder, CO: Westview Press, 1995).

[20] Edward T. Hall and Mildred Reed Hall, *Hidden Differences, Doing Business with the Japanese* (New York: Anchor Press, 1985).

[21] For the most comprehensive discussion of the notion of trust see Francis Fukuyama, *Trust* (New York: Free Press, 1995).

[22] Frank Alpert, Michael Kamins, Tomoaki Sakano, Naoto Onzo, and John L. Graham, "Retail Buyer Decision Making in Japan: What U.S. Sellers Need to Know," *International Business Review,* 6(2), 1997, pp. 91–112.

[23] "Brazil: Relationship Building," *Business Latin America,* February 7, 1994, p. 6.

a means of communicating with potential customers, especially in Western Europe and to some extent in Eastern Europe, the Commonwealth of Independent States (CIS), and Asia.

In addition to advertising in print media and reaching industrial customers through catalogs (now including Web sites[24]) and direct mail, the trade show or trade fair has become the primary vehicle for doing business in many foreign countries. As part of its international promotion activities, the U.S. Department of Commerce sponsors trade fairs in many cities around the world. Additionally, there are annual trade shows sponsored by local governments in most countries. African countries, for example, host more than 70 industry-specific trade shows.

Trade shows serve as the most important vehicles for selling products, reaching prospective customers, contacting and evaluating potential agents and distributors, and marketing in most countries. Although important in the United States, they serve a much more important role in other countries. They have been at the center of commerce in Europe for centuries and are where most prospects are found. European trade shows attract high-level decision makers who are not attending just to see the latest products but are there to buy.[25] Preshow promotional expenditures are often used in Europe to set formal appointments. The importance of trade shows to Europeans is reflected in percentage of their media budget spent on participating in trade events and how they spend those dollars.[26] On average, Europeans spend 22 percent of their total annual media budget on trade events, while American firms typically spend less than 5 percent. Europeans tend not to spend money on circuslike promotions, gimmicks, and such; rather, they focus on providing an environment for in-depth dealings. More than 2,000 major trade shows are held worldwide every year. The Hannover Industry Fair (Germany), the largest trade fair in the world, has nearly 6,000 exhibitors who show a wide range of industrial products to 600,000 visitors.

Trade shows provide the facilities for a manufacturer to exhibit and demonstrate products to potential users and to view competitors' products.[27] They are an opportunity to create sales and establish relationships with agents, distributors, and suppliers that can lead to more-permanent distribution channels in foreign markets. In fact, a trade show may be the only way to reach some prospects. Trade show experts estimate that 80 to 85 percent of the people seen on a trade show floor never have a salesperson call on them. Most recently, several Internet Web sites now specialize in virtual trade shows. They often include multimedia and elaborate product display booths that can be virtually toured. Some of these virtual trade shows last only a few days during an associated actual trade show.[28]

The number and variety of trade shows is such that almost any target market in any given country can be found through this medium. In Eastern Europe, fairs and exhibitions offer companies the opportunity to meet new customers, including private traders, young entrepreneurs, and representatives of nonstate organizations. The exhibitions in countries such as Russia and Poland offer a cost-effective way of reaching a large number of customers who might otherwise be difficult to target through individual sales

---

[24] For illustrative examples of the burgeoning information available to industrial customers on Web sites see **www.caterpillar.com**, **www.fluor.com**, **www.hewlett-packard.com**, **www.microsoft.com**, and **www.qualcomm.com**.

[25] Joachim Schafer, "Making the Most of Trade Fairs," *Trade & Culture,* October–November 1996, pp. 60–62.

[26] Marnik G. Dekimpe, Pierre Francois, Srinath Gopalakrishna, Gary L. Lillien, and Christophe Van den Bulte, "Generalizing about Trade Show Effectiveness: A Cross-National Comparison," *Journal of Marketing,* 61, October 1997, pp. 55–64.

[27] Kare Hansen, "The Dual Motives of Participants in Trade Shows," *International Marketing Review,* 13(2), 1996, pp. 39–53.

[28] Russell Shaw, "Computers Made Plain Web Plays Host to Virtual Trade Shows," *Investor's Business Daily,* October 7, 1997, p. A1.

So you want to buy a jet fighter? How about kicking the tires of this Gripen fighter (the product of a Swedish/ British joint venture) at the Paris Airshow, the world's biggest aerospace trade show. (REUTERS/Gareth Watkins/ARCHIVE PHOTOS)

calls. Specialized fairs in individual sectors such as computers, the automotive industry, fashion, and home furnishings regularly take place.[29]

Besides country-sponsored trade shows, U.S. government-sponsored trade shows have proved to be effective marketing events. A U.S.-sponsored show called Made in USA attracted 20,000 South Africans to visit 335 U.S. companies.[30] Thirty-nine American firms participated in a seven-day electronics production equipment exhibition in Osaka, Japan, and came home with $1.6 million in confirmed orders along with estimates for the following year of $10 million. Five of the companies were seeking Asian agent/distributors through the show, and each was able to sign a representative before the show closed. Trade shows and trade fairs are scheduled periodically and any interested business can reserve space to exhibit.[31]

Marketing Services Globally

As mentioned in Chapter 12, exports of services are growing faster than merchandise exports. Additionally, because of the dynamism of the sector, the United States maintains a comfortable trade surplus in services. The growing importance of American ser-

---

[29] Andrew Hope, "Poland, Fairest of the Fairs," *Business Eastern Europe,* February 26, 1996, pp. 6–7; "Trade Fairs: Is Exhibiting Worth It?" *Business Eastern Europe,* May 23, 1994, pp. 6–7; and Valeri Akopov, "Making a Name for Your Product in the New Russia," *Trade & Culture,* March–April 1995, pp. 47–48.

[30] "Africa: Marketing through Trade Shows," *Trade & Culture,* Spring 1994, pp. 55–56.

[31] Information about trade shows is available from the following sources: the U.S. Trade Information Center's *The Export Promotion Calendar,* which lists dates and locations of trade shows worldwide; *Europe Trade Fairs,* which lists European shows including U.S. Department of Commerce-sponsored shows; *Trade Shows Worldwide* (published by Gale Research), a comprehensive listing of more than 6,000 trade shows worldwide; and *International Trade Fairs and Conferences* (published by Co-Mar Management Services), which lists 5,000 shows worldwide.

vices exports clearly reflects the dramatic growth in the services segment of the U.S. economy itself—80 percent of all Americans were employed in the services sector in the late 1990s. Perhaps most amazing, 2.4 million of the 2.6 million jobs created in the U.S. economy in 1997 were in services. Further, most of these jobs were created in such well-paid fields as information, health, education, and social services.[32] Services dominate the economies of other developed nations as well. In OECD countries, services companies employ more than half the labor force and produce more than half the GDP.[33]

Services Opportunities in Global Markets

International tourism is by far the largest services export of the United States, ranking behind only capital goods and industrial supplies when all exports are counted. In 1996 foreigners spent some $64 billion while visiting destinations in the United States.[34] Compare that with Boeing's worldwide sales of jet aircraft at $37 billion for 1996.[35] Worldwide tourists spent some $400 billion in 1996 and an agency of the United Nations projects that number will grow to $2 trillion by 2020. That same agency predicts that China will be followed by the United States, France, Spain, Hong Kong, Italy, Britain, Mexico, Russia, and the Czech Republic as the most popular destinations in the next century. Most tourists will be, as they are today, Germans, Japanese, and Americans; and Chinese will be the fourth largest group.[36] Currently, Japanese tourists contribute the most to U.S. tourism income at some $20 billion.[37]

The dramatic growth in tourism has prompted American firms and institutions to respond by developing new travel services. For example, the Four Seasons Hotel in Philadelphia offers a two-day package including local concerts and museum visits. In addition to its attractions for kids, Orlando, Florida, now sells its Opera Company with performances by Domingo, Sills, and Pavarotti. This year the cities of Phoenix, Las Vegas, and San Diego have formed a consortium and put together a $500,000 marketing budget specifically appealing to foreign visitors to stop at all three destinations in one trip.[38]

Other top services exports include transportation, financial services, education, business services, telecommunications, entertainment, information, and healthcare, in that order. Consider the following examples of each:

- American airlines are falling all over themselves to capture greater shares of the fast expanding Latin American travel market through investments in local carriers.[39]

- Insurance sales are also burgeoning in Latin America with joint ventures between local and global firms making the most progress.[40]

- Banking in China is about to undergo a revolution with National Cash Register ATMs popping up everywhere.[41]

---

[32] Bob Vastine, "Good News for U.S. Trade," *Christian Science Monitor,* March 17, 1997, p. 18.

[33] Mary C. Gilly and John L. Graham, "Chapter 15—International Services Marketing," in Valarie A. Zeithaml and Mary Jo Bitner, *Services Marketing* (New York: McGraw-Hill, 1996).

[34] "1996 U.S. Foreign Trade Highlights," U.S. Department of Commerce, June 1997.

[35] **http://www.boeing.com**, January 1998.

[36] Stephen Kinser, "Expect to Travel in 2020? You'll Have Company," *The New York Times,* December 28, 1997, p. 3.

[37] **http://www.jetro.go.jp**, January 1998.

[38] Edwin McDowell, "Tourists Respond to the Lure of Culture Word Spreads That Art Sells," *The New York Times,* April 24, 1997, p. 1.

[39] Wendy Zellner and Andrea Mandel-Campbell, "The Battle of Argentina, Brazil, Chile, Venezuela. . . . U.S. Carriers in a Dogfight over Lucrative Latin Alliances," *Business Week,* May 19, 1997, p. 56.

[40] Sally Bowen, Raymond Colitt, Tim Coone, and Mac Margolis, "Insuring," *Latin Trade,* October 1996, pp. 76–83.

[41] Joanna Slater, "Let a Million ATMs Bloom," *China Trade Report,* November 1997, p. 5.

Japan's financial markets are opening to foreigners, slowly but surely. The latest sign is these posters advertising foreign-managed mutual funds for sale at a Tokyo brokerage for the first time ever. (© Tom Wagner/SABA)

- Merrill Lynch is going after the investment-trust business expected to take off after Japan allows brokers and banks to enter that business for the first time in 1998.[42]

- Foreign students spend some $7 billion a year in tuition to attend American universities and colleges.[43]

- American engineering consulting firms will provide services to design and manage construction of more than $1 trillion worth of infrastructure development worldwide during the next decade.[44]

- Currently phone rates in markets such as Germany, Italy, and Spain are so high that American companies cannot maintain toll-free information hotlines or solicit phone-order catalogue sales.[45]

- "Xena," "Hercules," and comparably "dumbed-down" (i.e., heavy on action, violence, and sex) video-game heroes are conquering electronic screens worldwide.[46]

- Cable TV is exploding in Latin America. The latest Gallup poll in China indicates that 43 percent of Beijing residents are aware of the Internet.[47]

- Finally, not only are foreigners coming to the United States for health care services in fast growing numbers, but also North American firms are building hospitals abroad as well. Most recently two infants, one from Sweden and one from Japan, received heart transplants at Loma Linda hospital in California—laws in both their countries prohibit such life-saving operations.[48] Beijing Toronto International Hospital will soon open its doors for some 250 Chinese

---

[42] "Japan's 'Big Bang,' Enter Merrill," *The Economist,* January 3, 1998, p. 72.

[43] Bob Vastine, "Good News for U.S. Trade," *Christian Science Monitor,* March 17, 1997, p. 18.

[44] Garrett Wasny, "Engineering Services North of the Border," *World Trade,* January 1998, pp. 42–43.

[45] Daniel B. Moskowitz, "Opening the Services Door," *International Business,* March 1996, pp. 70–71.

[46] Brian Lowry, "Conquer the World," *Los Angeles Times,* August 13, 1997, pp. F1, F11; and "Dip into the Future, Far as Cyborg Eye Can See: and Wince," *The Economist,* January 3, 1998, pp. 81–83.

[47] "The Gallup 1997 Nationwide Survey of Consumer Attitudes and Lifestyles in the People's Republic of China," The Gallup Organization, 1997.

[48] Fox Television News, January 12, 1998.

patients, and the services include a 24-hour satellite link for consultations to Toronto.[49]

Entering Global Markets

Trade creates demands for international services. That is, most U.S. service companies enter international markets to service their U.S. clients, business travelers, and tourists abroad. Accounting and advertising firms were among the earlier companies to establish branches or acquire local affiliations abroad to serve their U.S. multinational clients. Hotels and auto-rental agencies followed the business traveler and tourist abroad. Their primary purpose for marketing their services internationally was to service home-country clients. Once established, many of these *client followers,* as one researcher refers to them, expanded their client base to include local companies. As global markets grew, creating greater demand for business services, service companies became *market seekers* in that they actively sought customers for their services worldwide. Indeed, notice in Exhibit 13–2 how American law firms have expanded overseas in recent years.

Because of the varied characteristics of business services, not all of the traditional methods of market entry discussed in Chapter 12 are applicable to all types of services. Although most services have the inseparability of *creation* and *consumption* just discussed, there are those where these occurrences can be separated. Such services are those whose intrinsic value can be "embodied in some tangible form (such as a blueprint or architectural design) and thus can be produced in one country and exported to another." Data processing and data analysis services are other examples. The analysis or processing is completed on a computer located in the United States and the output (the service) is transmitted via satellite to a distant customer. Some banking services could be exported from one country to another on a limited basis through the use of ATMs. Architecture and engineering consulting services are exportable when the consultant travels to the client's site and later returns home to write and submit a report. In addition to exporting as an entry mode, these services also use franchising, direct investment (wholly owned subsidiaries), joint ventures, and licensing.

Most other services—automobile rentals, airline services, entertainment, hotels, and tourism, to name a few—are inseparable and require production and consumption to occur almost simultaneously, and thus, exporting is not a viable entry method for them. The vast majority of services (some 85 percent) enter foreign markets by licensing, franchising, and/or direct investment.[50]

Market Environment for Business Services

Service firms face most of the same environmental constraints and problems confronting merchandise traders. Protectionism, control of transborder data flows, competition, the protection of intellectual property, and cultural barriers are the most important problems confronting the MNC in today's international services market.

Protectionism. The most serious threat to the continued expansion of international services trade is protectionism. The growth of international services has been so rapid during the last decade it has drawn the attention of local companies and governments. As a result, direct and indirect trade barriers have been imposed to restrict foreign companies from domestic markets. Every reason, from the protection of infant industries to

---

[49] Joanna Slater, "Good Medicine," *China Trade Report,* November 1997, pp. 1–3.

[50] For an insightful study of entry-mode choice by service firms, see M. Krishna Erramilli and C. P. Rao, "Service Firms' International Entry-Mode Choice: A Modified Transaction–Cost Analysis," *Journal of Marketing,* July 1993, pp. 19–38.

Exhibit 13-2   Expansion of U.S. Law Firms Abroad (1989–1994)

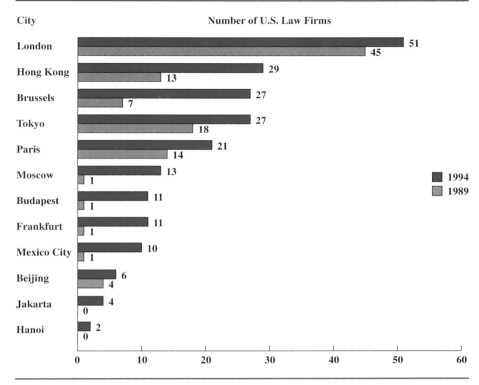

Source: Excerpted from Valarie A. Zeithaml and Mary Jo Bitner, *Services Marketing,* New York: McGraw-Hill, 1996, p. 433.

national security, has been used to justify some of the restrictive practices. A list of more than 2,000 instances of barriers to the free flow of services among nations was recently compiled by the U.S. government. In response to the threat of increasing restriction, the United States has successfully negotiated to open services markets in both NAFTA and GATT.

Until the GATT and NAFTA agreements there were few international rules of fair play governing trade in services. Service companies faced a complex group of national regulations that impeded the movement of people and technology from country to country. The United States and other industrialized nations want their banks, insurance companies, construction firms, and other service providers to be allowed to move people, capital, and technology around the globe unimpeded. Restrictions designed to protect local markets range from not being allowed to do business in a country to requirements that all foreign professionals pass certification exams in the local language before being permitted to practice. In Argentina, for example, an accountant must have the equivalent of a high school education in Argentinean geography and history before being permitted to audit the books of a multinational company's branch in Buenos Aires.

The European Union is making modest progress toward establishing a single market for services.[51] However, it is not now clear exactly how foreign service providers will be treated as unification proceeds. Reciprocity and harmonization, key concepts in the Single European Act, possibly will be used to curtail the entrance of some service industries into Europe. Legal services and the U.S. film industry seem to be two that are

[51] "A Single Market for Services," *Business Europe,* January–February 1994, pp. 1–2.

CROSSING BORDERS 13-3

Garbage Collection an International Service?

The service industry in the United States has a bright future with a variety of services to sell. Ten thousand house-hungry Londoners signed up for more than $500 million of mortgages. When a Wall Street subsidiary of Salomon Brothers has European executives eager to get a package from Amsterdam to Atlanta, increasingly, they are turning to Federal Express, a Memphis company whose international revenues have been doubling every year since it began operating overseas. That is only part of the story; there are many services we don't hear about. For example, Hospital Corporation of America, the biggest operator of private hospitals in the United States, has acquired 28 hospitals abroad and signed contracts to operate 9 others.

In Japan, ServiceMaster of the United States is showing those masters of industry quality control a few things about improving productivity and cutting costs when it comes to scrubbing floors and washing laundry. ServiceMaster has in the past few years launched more than 500 home-cleaning franchises in Japan and won contracts to do the housekeeping for 40 hospitals.

Having persuaded hundreds of local governments in the United States to contract out street cleaning and trash collection, WMX Technologies is collecting trash, cleaning streets, and constructing sanitary landfills in 20 countries, including Argentina, New Zealand, and Saudi Arabia. It also has a 15-year contract to run a hazardous-waste treatment plant that will process all of Hong Kong's industrial and chemical waste.

Sources: Adapted from Richard I. Kirkland, Jr. "The Bright Future of Service Exports," *Fortune*, June 8, 1987, pp. 32 and 38; Ralph T. King, Jr., "Quiet Boom: U.S. Service Exports Are Growing Rapidly, but Almost Unnoticed," *The Wall Street Journal*, April 21, 1993, p. A6; and Susan Moffat and Rajiv M. Rao, "Asia Stinks That's Not a Value Judgment. It's Just That the Region Has Overlooked the Environmental Fallout from Its Explosive Growth. Until Now," *Fortune*, December 9, 1996, pp. 120+.

very difficult to negotiate. A directive regarding Transfrontier Television Broadcasting created a quota for European programs requiring EU member states to ensure that at least 50 percent of entertainment air time is devoted to "European Works." The EU argues that this set-aside for domestic programming is necessary to preserve Europe's cultural identity.[52] The consequences for the U.S. film industry are significant, since over 40 percent of U.S. film industry profits come from foreign revenues.

Transborder Data Flow.   Restrictions on transborder data flows are potentially the most damaging to both the communications industry and other MNCs that rely on data transfers across borders to conduct business. Some countries impose tariffs on the transmission of data and many others are passing laws forcing companies to open their computer files to inspection by government agencies or tightly control transmission domestically. Data transmission was tightly controlled in India via a government monopoly whose high pricing policies limited Internet usage to about 50,000 in 1997. However, now the Indian Cabinet has voted to open the Net to private competitors hoping that usage will expand to 1–2 million users by the turn of the millennium.[53]

Most countries have a variety of laws to deal with the processing and electronic transmission of data across borders. There is intense concern about how to deal with this relatively new technology. In some cases, concern stems from not understanding how

---

[52] "EU Parliament Limits Foreign TV Shows," *Los Angeles Times*, February 2, 1996, p. D2.
[53] Amy Louise Kazmin, "Internet Policy," *Financial Times*, December 3, 1997, p. 4.

best to tax transborder data flows; in other cases, there is concern over the protection of individual rights when personal data are involved. The European Commission is concerned that data on individuals (such as income, spending preferences, debt repayment histories, medical conditions, and employment data) are being collected, manipulated, and transferred between companies with little regard to the privacy of the individuals on whom the data are collected. A proposed directive by the Commission would require the consent of the individual before data are collected or processed. A wide range of U.S. service companies would be affected by such a directive; insurance underwriters, banks, credit reporting firms, direct marketing companies, and tour operators are a few examples. The directive would have wide-ranging effect on data processing and data analysis firms since it will prevent a firm from transferring information electronically to the United States for computer processing if it concerns individual European consumers. Hidden in all the laws and directives are the unstated motives of most countries: a desire to inhibit the activities of multinationals and to protect local industry. As the global data transmission business continues to explode into the next century, regulators will focus increased attention in that direction.[54]

Competition.   As mentioned earlier, competition in all phases of the service industry is increasing as host-country markets are invaded by many foreign firms.[55] The practice of following a client into foreign markets and then expanding into international markets is not restricted to U.S. firms. German, British, Japanese, and service firms from other countries follow their clients into foreign markets and then expand to include local business as well. Telecommunications, advertising, construction, and hotels are U.S. services that face major competition, not only from European and Japanese companies but also from representatives of Brazil, India, and other parts of the world.

Protection of Intellectual Property.   An important form of competition that is difficult to combat is pirated trademarks, processes, and patents. Computer design and software, trademarks, brand names, and other intellectual properties are easy to duplicate and difficult to protect. The protection of intellectual property rights is a major problem in the services industries. Countries seldom have adequate—or any—legislation, and any laws they do have are extremely difficult to enforce. The Trade Related Intellectual Property Rights (TRIPS) part of the GATT agreement obligates all members to provide strong protection for copyright and related rights, patents, trademarks, trade secrets, industrial designs, geographic indications, and layout designs for integrated circuits. The TRIPS agreement is helpful in protection services but the key issue is that enforcement is very difficult without full cooperation of host countries. The situation in China has been particularly bad since that country has not been active in enforcing piracy of intellectual property. The annual cost of pirated software, CDs, books, and movies in China alone totals more than $827 million.[56] Worldwide, industry estimates are that U.S. companies lost $60 billion annually on piracy of all types of intellectual property. Since it is so easy to duplicate software, electronically recorded music, and movies, pirated copies often are available within a few days of their release. In Thailand, for example, illegal copies of movies are available within 10 days of their release in the United States. In Russia, pirated movies are sometimes available before their (legal) U.S. debut!

Cultural Barriers and Adaptation.   Because trade in services more frequently involves people-to-people contact, culture plays a much bigger role in services than in

---

[54] John J. Keller, "Ex-MFS Managers Plan Global Network Based on Internet, Rivaling Phone Firms," *The Wall Street Journal,* January 20, 1998, p. A3.

[55] Scott Donaton and Dagmar Mussey, "Online's Next Battleground: Europe," *Advertising Age,* March 6, 1995, p. 18.

[56] "Will China Scuttle Its Pirates," *Business Week,* August 15, 1994, pp. 40–42.

CROSSING BORDERS 13–4

Homecare Isn't Home Decorating!

Can U.S.-based home healthcare companies expand their services beyond U.S. borders? There are a number of reasons why this might not be a viable idea. First, Home health-care was invented in the United States in response to an aging population and double-digit healthcare inflation in the 1980s giving rise to cost-containment pressures from the government and managed-care payers. The level of home healthcare sophistication in the U.S. has significantly lowered hospital lengths of stay and provided an alternative to hospital admissions resulting in significant cost savings. In Western Europe, however, homecare is viewed as a lower level of care and not accepted as clinically viable for pediatric, oncology, or medically complex patients with co-morbidities. Hence, there is a general reluctance to discharge to home.

Second, exporters of home healthcare are thwarted by the lack of trained clinicians to deliver the care and sales representatives to communicate the viability of homecare. In the United Kingdom, homecare is often confused with "home decorating." Third, there are technological barriers to homecare stemming from electrical incompatibility. In many instances, home medical equipment and diagnostic instruments were designed to meet U.S. specifications, thus making them inoperable in the rest of the world. And finally, medieval traditions stemming from feudal guilds and aristocracies prevent modern companies from utilizing existing distribution systems. For example, in the U.K. the royal postal service cannot be used for the distribution of medications.

Even with these challenges, Western Europe, Asia, and Canada are primary expansion markets for U.S.-based homecare for the next several decades. Moreover, the national healthcare services in these areas of the world are looking for alternatives to institutional care to avoid bankrupting the national coffers for an expanding elderly population.

Source: Sarah Ladd Eames, Executive Vice-President, Transworld Healthcare, 1998.

merchandise trade. Examples are many: Eastern Europeans are perplexed by Western expectations that unhappy workers put on a "happy face" when dealing with customers. But McDonald's requires Polish employees to smile whenever they interact with customers. Such a requirement strikes many employees as artificial and insincere. The company has learned to encourage managers in Poland to probe employee problems and to assign troubled workers to the kitchen rather than to the food counter.[57] As another example, notice if the Japanese student sitting next to you in class ever verbally disagrees with your instructor. Classroom interactions vary substantially around the world. Students in Japan listen to lectures, take notes, and ask questions only after class, if then. In Japan the idea of grading class participation is nonsense. Alternatively, because Spaniards are used to large undergraduate classes (hundreds rather than dozens), they tend to talk to their friends even when the instructor is talking. Likewise, healthcare delivery systems and doctor/patient interactions also reflect cultural differences. Americans ask questions and get second opinions. Innovative healthcare services are developed on the basis of extensive marketing research. However, in Japan the social hierarchy is reflected heavily in the patients' deference to their doctors. While Japanese

---

[57] Dean E. Murphy, "New East European Retailers Told to Put on a Happy Face," *Los Angeles Times,* November 1994, pp. A1, A18.

patient compliance is excellent and longevity is the best in the world, the healthcare system there is quite unresponsive to the expressed concerns of consumers.

Japanese also tend to take a few long vacations—seven to 10 days is the norm. Thus, vacation packages designed for them are packed with activities. Phoenix, Las Vegas, and San Diego or Rome, Geneva, Paris, and London in 10 days makes sense to them. The Four Seasons Hotel chain provides special pillows, kimonos, slippers, and teas for Japanese guests. Virgin Atlantic Airways and other long-haul carriers now have interactive screens available for each passenger, allowing viewing of Japanese (or American, French, etc.) movies and TV.

Managing a global services workforce is certainly no simple task. Just ask the folks at UPS:[58]

> Some of the surprises UPS ran into: indignation in France, when drivers were told they couldn't have wine with lunch; protests in Britain, when drivers' dogs were banned from delivery trucks; dismay in Spain, when it was found that the brown UPS trucks resembled the local hearses; and shock in Germany, when brown shirts were required for the first time since 1945.

And, while tips of 10–15 percent are an important part of services workers' incentives in the United States, this is not the case in Germany, where tips are rounded to the nearest deutsche mark, or in China, where they are considered an insult. Thus, closer management of service personnel is required in those countries to maintain high levels of customer satisfaction.[59]

Clearly opportunities for the marketing of services will continue to grow well into the next century. International marketers will have to be quite creative in responding to the legal and cultural challenges of delivering high-quality services in foreign markets and to foreign customers.

Summary

Industrial goods marketing requires close attention to the exact needs of customers. Basic differences across various markets are less than for consumer goods but the motives behind purchases differ enough to require a special approach. Global competition has risen to the point that industrial goods marketers must pay close attention to the level of economic and technological development for each market to determine the buyer's assessment of quality. Companies that adapt their products to these needs are the ones that should be the most effective in the marketplace. Industrial markets are lucrative and continue to grow as more countries strive for at least a semblance of industrial self-sufficiency.

One of the fastest-growing areas of international trade is services. This segment of marketing involves all countries at every level of development; even the least-developed countries are seeking computer technology and sophisticated data banks to aid them in advancing their economies. Their rapid growth and profit profile make them targets for protectionism and piracy.

Questions

1. Define the following terms and show their significance to international marketing:
   derived demand
   price–quality relationship
   client followers
   market seekers
   ISO 9000
   relationship marketing

2. What are the differences between consumer and industrial goods and what are the implications for international marketing? Discuss.

3. Discuss how the various stages of economic development affect the demand for industrial goods.

4. "Industrialization is typically a national issue, and industrial goods are the fodder for industrial growth." Comment.

5. "The adequacy of a product must be considered in relation to the general environment within which it will be operated rather than solely on the basis of technical efficiency." Discuss the implications of this statement.

---

[58] Dana Milbank, "Can Europe Deliver?" *The Wall Street Journal,* September 30, 1994, pp. R15, R23.
[59] See Gilly and Graham, "Chapter 15—International Services Marketing" for more detail.

6. Why hasn't the United States been more helpful in setting universal standards for industrial equipment? Do you feel that the argument is economically sound? Discuss.

7. What role do service, replacement parts, and standards play in competition in foreign marketing? Illustrate.

8. Discuss the part industrial trade fairs play in international marketing of industrial goods.

9. Describe the reasons an MNC might seek an ISO 9000 certification.

10. What ISO 9000 legal requirements are imposed on products sold in the EU? Discuss.

11 Discuss the competitive consequences of being ISO 9000 certified.

12. Discuss how the characteristics that define the uniqueness of industrial products lead naturally to relationship marketing. Give some examples.

13. Discuss some of the more pertinent problems in pricing industrial goods.

14. What is the price–quality relationship? How does this affect a U.S. firm's comparative position in world markets?

15. Select several countries, each at a different stage of economic development, and illustrate how the stage affects demand for industrial goods.

16. England has almost completed the process of shifting from the inch–pound system to the metric system. What effect do you think this will have on the traditional U.S. reluctance to such a change? Discuss the economic implications of such a move.

17. Discuss the importance of international business services to total U.S. export trade. How do most U.S. service companies become international?

18. Discuss the international market environment for business services.

not dominate supply, supply can be increased or decreased within a given range, and profit maximization occurs at or near production capacity. Generally a buyer's market exists and the producer strives to penetrate the market and push goods out to the consumer, resulting in a highly developed channel structure that includes a variety of intermediaries.

Business attitudes in an import-oriented market system are often the direct opposite of what you would expect. As one observer notes:[1]

> Consumers, retailers, and other intermediaries are always seeking goods. This results from the tendency of importers to throttle the flow of goods, and from this sporadic and uneven flow of imports, inventory hoarding as a means of checking the market can be achieved at relatively low cost, and is obviously justified because of its lucrative and speculative yields.

This import-oriented philosophy permeates all aspects of market activities and behavior. For example, a Brazilian bank had ordered piggy banks for a local promotion; because it went better than expected, the banker placed a reorder of three times the original. The local manufacturer immediately increased the price and, despite arguments pointing out reduced production costs and other supply–cost factors, could not be dissuaded from this action. True to an import-oriented attitude, the notion of economies of scale and the use of price as a demand stimulus escaped the manufacturer who was going on the theory that with demand up, the price also had to go up.

A one-deal mentality of pricing at retail and wholesale levels exists because in an import-oriented market, goods come in at a landed price and pricing is then simply an assessment of demand and diminishing supply. If the importer has control of supply, then the price is whatever the market will bear. Thus, variations in manufacturing costs are of little concern; each shipment is a deal, and when that is gone, the merchant waits for another good deal, basing the price of each deal on landed costs and the assessment of demand and supply at that moment.

This attitude affects the development of intermediaries and their functions. Distribution systems are local rather than national in scope and the relationship between the importer and any middleman in the marketplace is considerably different from that found in a mass-marketing system. The idea of a channel as a chain of intermediaries performing specific activities and each selling to a smaller unit beneath it until the chain reaches the ultimate consumer is not common in an import-oriented system.

In an import-oriented system, an importer may not sell to a specific link in the channel but to a range of other intermediaries that simultaneously assume wholesaling and retailing functions and perform the marketing tasks of sorting, assorting, advertising and promotion, financing, storage, shipping, packaging, and breaking bulk. Since the importer-wholesaler had traditionally performed most marketing functions, independent agencies that provide advertising, marketing research, warehousing and storage, transportation, financing, and other facilitating functions that are found in a developed, mature marketing infrastructure are nonexistent or underdeveloped. Thus, few independent agencies necessary to support a fully integrated distribution system develop.

Obviously, few countries fit the import-oriented model today. Instead, as countries develop economically, their market systems evolve as well. As already discussed, economic development is uneven, and various parts of an economy are at different stages of development. Nevertheless, channel structures in countries that have historically evolved from an import-oriented base will have vestiges of their beginnings reflected in a less-than-fully-integrated system. At the other extreme is the Japanese distribution system with multiple layers of specialized middlemen.

---

[1] A. A. Sherbini, "Import-Oriented Marketing Mechanisms," *MSU Business Topics,* Spring 1968, p. 71. Reprinted by permission of the publisher, the Bureau of Business and Economic Research, Division of Research, Graduate School of Business Administration, Michigan State University.

Japanese Distribution Structure

Distribution in Japan has long been considered the most effective nontariff barrier to the Japanese market.[2] The *Japanese distribution structure* is different enough from its United States or European counterparts that it should be carefully studied by anyone contemplating entry. The Japanese system has four distinguishing features: (1) a structure dominated by many small middlemen dealing with many small retailers; (2) channel control by manufacturers; (3) a business philosophy shaped by a unique culture; and (4) laws that protect the foundation of the system—the small retailer.[3]

High Density of Middlemen.   There is a density of middlemen, retailers, and wholesalers in the Japanese market unparalleled in any Western industrialized country. The traditional Japanese structure serves consumers who make small, frequent purchases at small, conveniently located stores. An equal density of wholesalers supports the high density of small stores with small inventories. It is not unusual for consumer goods to go through three or four intermediaries before reaching the consumer—producer to primary, secondary, regional, and local wholesaler, and finally to retailer to consumer. Exhibit 14–1 illustrates the contrast between shorter U.S. channels and the long Japanese channels.

Other countries have large numbers of small retail stores but the major difference between small stores (nine or fewer employees) in Japan and the United States is the percentage of total retail sales accounted for by small retailers. In Japan, small stores (95.1 percent of all retail food stores) account for 57.7 percent of retail food sales, whereas in the United States, small stores (69.8 percent of all retail food stores) generate 19.2 percent of food sales. A disproportionate percentage of nonfood sales are made in small stores in Japan as well. In the United States, small stores (81.6 percent of all stores) sell 32.9 percent of nonfood items; in Japan, small stores (94.1 percent of all stores) sell 50.4 percent. These small stores serve an important role for Japanese consumers. High population density, the tradition of frequent trips to the store, an emphasis on service, freshness, and quality,[4] and wholesalers who provide financial assistance, frequent deliveries of small lots, and other benefits combine to support the high number of small stores.

Channel Control.   Manufacturers depend on wholesalers for a multitude of services to other members of the distribution network. Financing, physical distribution, warehousing, inventory, promotion, and payment collection are provided to other channel members by wholesalers. The system works because wholesalers and all other middlemen downstream are tied to manufacturers by a set of practices and incentives designed to ensure strong marketing support for their products and to exclude rival competitors from the channel. Wholesalers typically act as agent middlemen and extend the manufacturer's control through the channel to the retail level.

Control is maintained by: (1) inventory financing—sales made on consignment with credits extending for several months; (2) cumulative rebates—rebates given annually for any number of reasons, including quantity purchases, early payments, achieving sales targets, performing services, maintaining specific inventory levels, participating in sales promotions, loyalty to suppliers, maintaining manufacturer's price policies, cooperation, and contribution to overall success; (3) merchandise returns—all unsold mer-

---

[2] For a detailed study on this subject, see Frank Alpert, Michael Kamins, Tomoaki Sakano, Naoto Onzo, and John Graham, "Retail Buyer Decision-Making in Japan: What U.S. Sellers Need to Know," *International Business Review,* Vol. 6(2), 1997, p. 91.

[3] A comprehensive review of the changing character of the Japanese distribution system is presented in John Fahy and Fuyuki Taguchi, "Reassessing the Japanese Distribution System," *Sloan Management Review,* Winter 1995, pp. 49–61.

[4] "A Matter of Convenience: Japanese Retailing/Japan's Convenience Stores," *The Economist,* January 25, 1997.

Exhibit 14-1   Comparison of Distribution Channels between the United States and Japan

Automobile parts: Japan

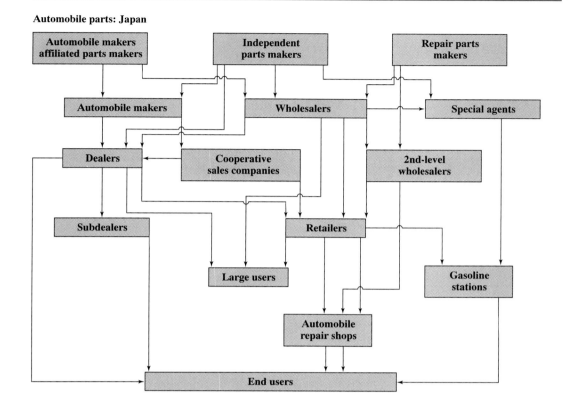

Automobile parts: United States

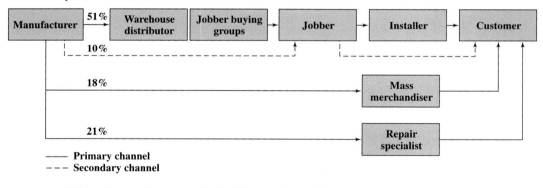

Source: McKinsey industry studies.

chandise may be returned to the manufacturer; and (4) promotional support—intermediaries receive a host of displays, advertising layouts, management education programs, in-store demonstrations, and other dealer aids which strengthen the relationship among middlemen and the manufacturer.

Business Philosophy.   Coupled with the close economic ties and dependency created by trade customs and the long structure of Japanese distribution channels is a unique business philosophy that emphasizes loyalty, harmony, and friendship. The value system supports long-term dealer/supplier relationships that are difficult to change as long as each party perceives economic advantage. The traditional partner, the insider, generally has the advantage.

A general lack of price competition, the provision of costly services, and other inefficiencies render the cost of Japanese consumer goods among the highest in the world; for example, a bottle of 96 aspirin tablets sells for $20. Yet the system is slow to change. The Japanese consumer contributes to the continuation of the traditional nature of the distribution system through frequent buying trips, small purchases, favoring personal service over price, and the proclivity for loyalty to brands perceived to be of high quality. Additionally, Japanese law gives the small retailer enormous advantage over the development of larger stores and competition. All these factors support the continued viability of small stores and the system, although changing attitudes among many Japanese consumers are beginning to weaken the hold traditional retailing has on the market

Large-Scale Retail Store Law.   Competition from large retail stores has been almost totally controlled by *Daitenho*—the *Large-Scale Retail Store Law.* Designed to protect small retailers from large intruders into their markets, the law requires that any store larger than 5,382 square feet (500 square meters) must have approval from the prefecture government to be "built, expanded, stay open later in the evening, or change the days of the month they must remain closed." All proposals for new "large" stores are first judged by MITI (Ministry of International Trade and Industry). Then, if local retailers unanimously agree to the plan, it is swiftly approved. However, without approval at the prefecture level (all small retailers in the area must agree), the plan is returned for clarification and modification that may take several years (10 years is not unheard of) for approval. Designed to protect small retailers against competition from large stores, the law has been imposed against both domestic and foreign companies. It took 10 years for one of Japan's largest supermarket chains to get clearance for a new site. Toys "R" Us fought rules and regulations for over three years before it gained approval for a store.

Besides the Large-Scale Retail Store Law, there are myriad licensing rules. One investigation of the regulations governing the opening of retail stores uncovered 39 different laws, each with a separate license that had to be met to open a full-service store.

Businesspeople in Japan and the United States see the Japanese distribution system as a major nontariff barrier and, by many Japanese, as a major roadblock to improvement of the Japanese standard of living. However, pressure from the United States and the *Structural Impediments Initiative (SII)* negotiations to pry open new markets for American companies is producing strong cracks in the system. As of this writing, it is reported the Japanese government will repeal the Large-Scale Retail Store Law as early as the end of fiscal 1998.[5]

Changes in the Japanese Distribution System.   Agreements between the United States and Japan under the SII have had a profound impact on the Japanese distribution system by leading to deregulation of retailing and by strengthening rules on monopoly business practices. The retailing law has been relaxed to permit new outlets as large as 1,000 square meters without prior permission. Limits on store hours and business days per year have also been lifted. Officially relaxing laws and regulations on retailing is but one of the important changes signaling the beginning of profound changes in how the Japanese shop.

SII and deregulation will undoubtedly have a part in changing Japanese distribution practices, but those merchants willing to challenge traditional ways and give the consumer quality products at competitive, fair prices will bring about the demise of the way department stores and small shops wedded to the traditional distribution system operate. Specialty discounters are sprouting up everywhere and entrepreneurs are slashing prices by buying direct and avoiding the distribution system altogether. For example, Kojima, a consumer electronics discounter, practices what it calls "global purchasing" and buys

---

[5] "Japan Retailing Seen Deregulated in 98-Nihon Keizai Shimbun," *Dow Jones International News,* December 1, 1997.

Traditional Japanese hima dolls are among the 15,000 children's items displayed in one of the 64 Toys "R" Us outlets in Japan. Toys "R" Us was one of the first U.S. retailers to successfully challenge Japan's Large-Scale Retail Store Law. (Chiaki Tsukumo/AP Wide World Photos)

merchandise anywhere in the world as long as it can be done as cheaply as possible. Kojima's tie-up with General Electric enables it to offer a 410-liter GE refrigerator for $640, down from the typical price of $1,925, and the 550-liter model from $3,462 to $1,585.[6]

Japanese consumers, described as brand loyal and more interested in services and quality than price, seem to be willing accomplices to the changes taking place, if the price is right. Japanese consumers have traditionally paid the highest prices in the world for the goods they buy. Before Toys "R" Us changed price levels, toys in Japan cost four times as much as toys in any other country. Japanese-made products imported to the United States can be purchased in the U.S. for less than they cost in Japan. Such inequities did not seem to matter to Japanese consumers when they had no other alternatives. But, more often now, the Japanese consumer has a choice of prices for everything from appliances to beer. Before price competition, a can of Coors beer would cost 240 yen; now it costs 240 yen in a neighborhood liquor store, 178 yen in a supermarket, and 139 yen in a discount store.

The "new" retailers are relatively small and account for no more than 3 percent of retail sales, compared with 14 percent for all specialty discounters in the U.S. But the impact extends beyond their share of market because they are forcing the system to change. Traditional retailers are modifying marketing and sales strategies in response to the new competition as well as to take advantage of changing Japanese lifestyles. There are also indications that some wholesalers are modernizing and consolidating operations

---

[6] Katayama Osamu, "Cheapest in the World," *Look Japan*, May 1997, p. 18.

as retailers demand to buy direct from the manufacturer or from the largest wholesalers. The process is slow because the characteristics of the distribution system are deeply rooted in the cultural history of Japan.

Japanese retailing may be going through a change similar to that which occurred in the United States after World War II. At that time the U.S. retailing structure was made up of many small retailers served by a multilayered wholesaling system, and full-service department stores and specialty stores offering all the needs of the shopper from soup to nuts, including a long list of services. Resale price maintenance laws (also referred to as fair trade laws) allowed national manufacturers to dictate high retail prices necessary to support an inefficient distribution system and amenities, i.e., services, which, when offered the opportunity, the consumer was willing to give up for lower prices. High margins were an attraction to the discounter who offered few, if any, services and priced items well below manufacturers' suggested prices. Department stores and other traditional retailers fought back with attempts to enforce fair trade laws. When that failed, they also began to discount items but found they could not continue to operate in the old way with discounted prices. At that point, retailing in the United States began to change. Some traditional stores went out of business, others downsized and dropped entire lines, others reinvented themselves into different operations, and many of the small mom-and-pop stores went out of business. Thus began a retailing revolution that ultimately spawned new types of retailers like Wal-Mart, Kmart, Target, Price/Costco, Levitz Furniture, Home Depot, Toys "R" Us, and a whole host of other retail store types that did not exist a few decades earlier. Similarly, traditional Japanese retailing is slowly giving ground to specialty stores, supermarkets, and discounters.

If retailing follows a similar pattern in Japan, as it appears to be doing, Japanese retailing will not be recognizable in a decade or two or, perhaps, in even less time. The downturn in the Japanese economy over the last few years has reduced the price of real estate by more than 50 percent and thus opened an opportunity for retail store expansion; not traditional retailing, but for retail malls. American Malls International Corporation plans to spend $165 million building a "retail theme park" outside of Tokyo. And another mall developer from California plans to develop a string of malls on abandoned factory and railway land near large cities. These malls will be entertainment centers as well as locations for a number of discount retailers.[7] What seemed to be an impenetrable retailing system just a few years ago now appears to be on the verge of opening up and creating opportunities for U.S. marketers.

Trends: From Traditional to Modern Channel Structures

Today, few countries are so sufficiently isolated that they are unaffected by global economic and political changes. These currents of change are altering all levels of economic fabric, including the distribution structure. Traditional channel structures are giving way to new forms, new alliances, and new processes—some more slowly than others, but all changing. Pressures for change in a country come from within and without. Multinational marketers are seeking ways to profitably tap market segments that are served by costly, traditional distribution systems. Direct marketing, door-to-door selling, hypermarkets, discount houses, shopping malls, catalog selling, e-commerce via the Internet, and other distribution methods are being introduced in an attempt to provide efficient distribution channels.

Some important trends in distribution will eventually lead to greater commonality than disparity among middlemen in different countries. Wal-Mart, for example, is expanding all over the world—from Mexico to Brazil and from Argentina to Asia.[8]

---

[7] Robert Sterner, "Is Japan Headed for a Revolution in Retailing?" *The Asian Wall Street Journal,* February 24, 1997, p. 1.

[8] Claire Poole, "Ringing Up Sales," *Latin Trade,* January 1997, p. 54.

Amway and Avon are expanding into Eastern Europe, Mary Kay Cosmetics[9] in China, and L. L. Bean and Lands' End have made successful entry into the Japanese market. In Spain, the Southland Corporation's 7-Eleven Stores are replacing many of the traditional mom-and-pop stores. Hypermarkets developed in France, and their many spin-offs are expanding all over Europe, Latin America,[10] and Asia. These huge stores, supplied with computerized inventories, may spell a slow death for small shops and midsize retailers in urban areas.[11] The effect of all these intrusions into the traditional distribution systems is change that will make discounting, self-service, supermarkets, and mass merchandising concepts common all over the world and elevate the competitive climate to a level not known before.

With the single European market a fact and the new monetary unit, the Euro, to become reality in 1999, national and international retailing networks are developing throughout Europe. An example is Sainsbury, the U.K. supermarket giant, which has entered an alliance with Esselunga of Italy (supermarkets), Docks de France (hypermarkets, supermarkets, and discount stores), and Belgium's Delhaize (supermarkets). The alliance provides the opportunity for the four companies to pool their experience and buying power and prepare to expand into other European markets and face growing competition. When the Euro goes into use, easier comparison-shopping will send consumers across borders looking for bargains on big-ticket items and competition will get tougher. As one analyst suggests, "Retailers who don't have low costs and who can't compete on price are going to get slammed."[12]

Expansion outside of the home country as well as new types of retailing is occurring throughout Europe. El Corte Inglés, Spain's largest department store chain, is not only moving into Portugal and other European countries but it has introduced Spain's first virtual supermarket on the Internet (**http://www.elcorteingles.es**) and has signed a deal to sponsor two pioneer 24-hour home shopping channels in Spain.[13] While European retailers see a unified Europe as an opportunity for pan-European expansion, foreign retailers are attracted by the high margins and prices characterized as "among the most expensive anywhere in the world." Costco, the U.S.-based warehouse retailer, saw the high gross margins British supermarkets command, 7–8 percent compared with 2.5–3 percent in the United States, as an opportunity. Costco prices will be 10 to 20 percent cheaper than rival local retailers.

In addition to hypermarkets and other warehouse retailers, companies that specialize in single product lines and market warehouse style like Toys "R" Us and Ikea, the Swedish furniture chain, are scrambling for a European presence. Among department store and other multiproduct retailers, such operations are known as "category killers" in that their prices, variety, and assortment kill the product category for other merchants.[14]

The impact of these and other trends is to change traditional distribution and marketing systems, leading to greater efficiency in distribution. Competition will translate those efficiencies into lower consumer prices and force distribution to become even more innovative.[15]

Exhibit 14–2 gives you an idea of the relative importance of different types of middlemen in the United States, Britain, and Japan.

---

[9] See, for example, "Mary Kay's Direct Marketing," *Business China,* April 14; 1997, p. 4; and "Mary Kay Moves Quickley in China," *Crossborder Monitor,* June 4, 1997, p. 8.

[10] "Retailing in South America," *The Economist,* July 12, 1997.

[11] Al Goodman, "Small Family-Run Stores in Spain Are Fighting to Limit the Hypermarkets," *The New York Times,* January 6, 1996, p. 18.

[12] David Woodruff, Julia Flynn, Mia Trinephi, and William Echikson, "The Euro Effect: The Race to Rule Retailing Heats Up as the New Currency Looms," *Business Week,* January 19, 1998, p. 16.

[13] Derek Cox, "Él Corte Ingles Explores World beyond Homeland," *Ad Age International,* May 1997, p. 14.

[14] "Towards Pan-European Retailing," *Business Europe,* April 9, 1997, p. 9.

[15] Chris Davies, "American No-How," *Marketing Tools,* May 1997, **http://marketingtools.com**.

EXHIBIT 14-2   Cutting Out the Middleman

Number of companies involved in each level of the food industry, % of total, 1993

Source: McKinsey.

Distribution Patterns

International marketers need a general awareness of the patterns of distribution that confront them in world marketplaces. Nearly every international trading firm is forced by the structure of the market to use at least some middlemen in the distribution arrangement. It is all too easy to conclude that, because the structural arrangements of foreign and domestic distribution seem alike, foreign channels are the same as or similar to domestic channels of the same name. This is misleading. Only when the varied intricacies of actual distribution patterns are understood can the complexity of the distribution task be appreciated. The following description should convey a sense of the variety of distribution patterns.

General Patterns

Generalizing about internal distribution channel patterns of various countries is almost as difficult as generalizing about behavior patterns of people. Despite similarities, marketing channels are not the same throughout the world. Marketing methods taken for granted in the United States are rare in many countries.

Middlemen Services.   Service attitudes of tradespeople vary sharply at both the retail and wholesale levels from country to country. In Egypt, for example, the primary purpose of the simple trading system is to handle the physical distribution of available goods. On the other hand, when margins are low and there is a continuing battle for customer preference, both wholesalers and retailers try to offer extra services to make their goods attractive to consumers. When middlemen are disinterested in promoting or selling individual items of merchandise, the manufacturer must provide adequate inducement to the middlemen or undertake much of the promotion and selling effort. Such is the case in China, where wholesalers see their function as storing the goods and waiting for their customers to come to them.

Line Breadth.   Every nation has a distinct pattern relative to the breadth of line carried by wholesalers and retailers. The distribution system of some countries seems to be characterized by middlemen who carry or can get everything; in others, every middleman seems to be a specialist dealing only in extremely narrow lines. Government regulations in some countries limit the breadth of line that can be carried by middlemen and licensing requirements to handle certain merchandise are not uncommon.

Costs and Margins.   Cost levels and middleman margins vary widely from country to country, depending on the level of competition, services offered, efficiencies or inefficiencies of scale, and geographic and turnover factors related to market size, purchasing power, tradition, and other basic determinants. In India, competition in large cities is so intense that costs are low and margins thin; but in rural areas, the lack of capital has permitted the few traders with capital to gain monopolies with consequent high prices and wide margins.

Channel Length.   Some correlation may be found between the stage of economic development and the length of marketing channels. In every country channels are likely to be shorter for industrial goods and for high-priced consumer goods than for low-priced products. In general, there is an inverse relationship between channel length and the size of the purchase. Combination wholesaler-retailers or semiwholesalers exist in many countries, adding one or two links to the length of the distribution chain. In China, for example, the traditional distribution system for over-the-counter drugs consists of large local wholesalers divided into three levels. First-level wholesalers supply drugs to major cities such as Beijing and Shanghai. The second-level services medium-sized cities, while the third level distributes to counties and cities with 100,000 people or less. It can be profitable for a company to sell directly to the two top-level wholesalers and have them sell to the third level which is so small that it would be unprofitable to seek out.

Nonexistent Channels.   One of the things companies discover about international channel-of-distribution patterns is that in many countries adequate market coverage through a simple channel of distribution is nearly impossible. In many instances, appropriate channels do not exist; in others, parts of a channel system are available but other parts are not. In Peru, for example, the informal distribution network accounts for almost a quarter of all retail cash sales. The ubiquitous street markets and ambulatory sellers offer far wider market penetration than formal distribution companies. Further, their prices are generally lower than traditional retailers, partly because of lower overhead costs compared with the higher costs generated by the overextended formal distribution chain of the traditional retailer.[16] Thus, several distinct distribution channels are necessary to reach different segments of a market; channels suitable for distribution in urban areas seldom provide adequate rural coverage.

Eastern Europe presents a special problem. When Communism collapsed, so did the government-run distribution system. Local entrepreneurs are emerging to fill the gap but they lack facilities, training, and product knowledge and they are generally undercapitalized. In Poland, with a population of 38 million, there is an overabundance of middlemen. Food, for example, is sold through 500,000 small shops and kiosks (76 people per shop), supplied by about 30,000 wholesalers (17 stores per wholesaler). Companies that have any hope of getting goods to customers profitably must be prepared to invest heavily in distribution. It is this kind of situation that entices supermarket groups like Tesco, of the U.K., to invest in Eastern Europe, where they can control the sources of their merchandise and provide one source of food for customers.[17]

---

[16] "Peru: Dispensing with the Formalities," *Business Latin America,* September 30, 1996, p. 6.

[17] Alison Maitland, "Food for Thought in Eastern Europe," *Financial Times,* April 18, 1997, p. 10.

Blocked Channels. International marketers may be blocked from using the channel of their choice. Blockage can result from competitors' already-established lines in the various channels and trade associations or cartels having closed certain channels. The classic example of blocked channels is Japan, as discussed above, but it is by no means the only example.

Associations of middlemen sometimes restrict the number of distribution alternatives available to a producer. Druggists in many countries have inhibited distribution of a wide range of goods through any retail outlets except drugstores. The drugstores, in turn, have been supplied by a relatively small number of wholesalers who have long-established relationships with their suppliers. Thus, through a combination of competition and association, a producer may be kept out of the market completely. In the U.K., simple magnifying reading glasses that can be purchased in a dozen different types of stores in the United States can only be purchase by prescription through registered optical stores, which are controlled by a few large companies.

Stocking. The high cost of credit, danger of loss through inflation, lack of capital, and other concerns cause foreign middlemen in many countries to limit inventories. This often results in out-of-stock conditions and sales lost to competitors. Physical distribution lags intensify their problem so that in many cases the manufacturer must provide local warehousing or extend long credit to encourage middlemen to carry large inventories. Often large inventories are out of the question for small stores with limited floor space. Considerable ingenuity, assistance, and, perhaps pressure are required to induce middlemen in most countries to carry adequate or even minimal inventories.

Power and Competition. Distribution power tends to concentrate in countries where a few large wholesalers distribute to a mass of small middlemen. Large wholesalers generally finance middlemen downstream. The strong allegiance they command from their customers enables them to effectively block existing channels and force an outsider to rely on less effective and more costly distribution.

Retail Patterns

Retailing shows even greater diversity in its structure than does wholesaling. In Italy and Morocco, retailing is composed largely of specialty houses which carry narrow lines, while in Finland, most retailers carry a more general line of merchandise. Retail size is represented at one end by Japan's giant Mitsukoshi Ltd., which reportedly enjoys the patronage of more than 100,000 customers every day. The other extreme is represented in the market of Ibadan, Nigeria, where some 3,000 one- or two-person stalls serve not many more customers.

Size Patterns. The extremes in size in retailing are similar to those that predominate in wholesaling. Exhibit 14–3 dramatically illustrates some of the variations in size and number of retailers per person that exist in some countries. The retail structure and the problems it engenders cause real difficulties for the international marketing firm selling consumer goods. Large dominant retailers can be sold direct, but there is no adequate way to directly reach small retailers who, in the aggregate, handle a great volume of sales. In Italy, official figures show there are 865,000 retail stores, or one store for every 66 Italians. Of the 340,000 food stores, fewer than 1,500 can be classified as large. Thus, middlemen are a critical factor in adequate distribution in Italy.

Underdeveloped countries present similar problems. Among the large supermarket chains in South Africa there is considerable concentration. One thousand of the country's 31,000 stores control 60 percent of all grocery sales, leaving the remaining 40 percent of sales to be spread among 30,000 stores. It may be difficult to reach the 40 percent of the market served by those 30,000 stores. Predominantly in Black communities, retailing is on a small scale—cigarettes are often sold singly, and the entire fruit inventory may consist of four apples in a bowl.

CROSSING BORDERS 14–1

Mitsukoshi Department Store, Established 1611—But Will It Be There in 2011?

Japanese department stores have a long history in Japanese retailing; indeed, Mitsukoshi department store, the epitome of Japanese retailing, began as a dry goods store in 1611. To visit a Japanese department store is to get a glimpse of Japanese life. In the basements and subbasements, food abounds with everything from crunchy Japanese pickles to delicate French pastry and soft-colored, seasonally changing forms of Japanese candies. Besides the traditional floors for women's and men's apparel and furniture, most stores have a floor devoted to kimonos and related accessories and another floor dedicated to children's needs and wants. On the roof there may be miniature open-air amusement parks for children.

But wait, there's more. Department stores are not merely content to dazzle with variety, delight with imaginative displays, and accept large amounts of yen for clothes and vegetables. They also seek to serve up a bit of culture. Somewhere between the floors of clothing and the roof, it is likely that you will find a banquet hall, an art gallery, an exhibition hall, and one or two floors of restaurants serving everything from *doria* (creamy rice with cheese) to tempura. Department stores aim to be "total life-style enterprises," says one manager. "We try to be all-inclusive, with art, culture, shopping and fashion. We stress the philosophy of *i-shoku-ju,* the three big factors in life: what you wear, what you eat, and how you live."

Japanese retailing is dominated by two kinds of stores, giant department stores like Mitsukoshi and small neightborhood shops, both kept alive by a complex distribution system that translates into high prices for the Japanese consumer. In exchange for high prices, the Japanese consumer gets variety, services, and, what may be unique to Japanese department stores, cultural enlightenment.

But there are winds of change. Department stores sales have fallen for 45 straight months from 1992 to late 1995. There was a slight increase prior to a sales tax increase but a downward trend started by mid-1997. The Japanese like the amenities of department stores but they are beginning to take notice of the wave of "new" discount stores that are challenging the traditional retail system by offering quality products at sharply reduced prices. Aoyama Trading Company, which opened a discount men's suit store in the heart of Ginza, where Tokyo's most prestigious department stores are located, may be the future. The owner says he can sell suits for two-thirds the department store price by purchasing directly from manufacturers. Another omen may be Toys "R" Us, which has opened 50 discount toy stores and plans to hit 100 by 2000 and is now the largest toy retailer in Japan. Department store response has been to discount toy prices, for the first time, by as much as 30 percent. As one discounter after another "cherry picks" item after item to discount, can department stores continue to be "total life-style enterprises"? Will there be a Mitsukoshi, as we know it today, in 2011?

Sources: "A World in Themselves," *Look Japan,* January 1994, pp. 40–42; "From Men's Suits to Sake, Discounting Booms in Japan," *Advertising Age International,* March 21, 1994, pp. I–4; and Virginia Kouyoumdjian, "Retailing in Japan: The U.S.-Revolution," *The American Chamber of Commerce in Japan Journal, (ACCJ Journal),* http://www.accj.or.jp, September 1997.

Retailing around the world has been in a state of active ferment for several years. The rate of change appears to be directly related to the stage and speed of economic development, and even the least-developed countries are experiencing dramatic changes. Supermarkets of one variety or another are blossoming in developed and underdeveloped countries alike. Discount houses that sell everything from powdered milk and canned chili to Korean TVs and VCRs are thriving and expanding worldwide. Wal-Mart,

Exhibit 14-3   Retail Patterns

Country	Retail Outlets (000)	Population per Outlet	Employees per Outlet
Argentina	199.5	164	4
Australia	160.2	111	5
Canada	157.2	183	9
India	3540.0	253	NA
Japan	1591.2	79	4
Malaysia	170.6	109	8
Mexico	899.3	96	2
Philippines	120.1	547	28
South Africa	60.4	675	7
South Korea	730.0	60	2
U.S.A.	1516.3	170	13

Sources: *International Marketing Data and Statistics,* 21st ed. (London: Euromonitor Publications, 1997); and "Indicators of Market Size for 115 Countries," *Crossborder Monitor,* August 27, 1997.

already in Mexico, is expanding into Brazil,[18] Argentina, Thailand, Hong Kong, and China.

Direct Marketing.   Selling directly to the consumer through the mail, by telephone, or door-to-door is becoming the distribution–marketing approach of choice in markets with insufficient and/or underdeveloped distribution systems. Amway,[19] operating in 42 foreign countries, has successfully expanded into Latin America and Asia with its method of direct marketing. Companies that enlist individuals to sell their products are proving to be especially popular in Eastern Europe and other countries, where many people are looking for ways to become entrepreneurs. In the Czech Republic, for example, Amway Corporation signed up 25,000 Czechs as distributors and sold 40,000 starter kits at $83 each in its first two weeks of business

Direct sales through catalogs have proved to be a successful way to enter foreign markets.[20] In Japan, it has been an important way to break the trade barrier imposed by the Japanese distribution system. For example, a U.S. mail-order company, Shop America, has teamed up with 7-Eleven in Japan[21] to distribute catalogs in its 4,000 stores. Shop America sells items such as compact disks, Canon cameras, and Rolex watches for 30–50 percent less than Tokyo stores. For example, a Canon Autoboy camera sells for $260 in Tokyo and $180 in the Shop America catalog, and a Lady Remington shaver sells for $86 in Tokyo versus $46 in the catalog.

Many catalog companies are finding that they need to open telephone service centers in a country to accommodate customers that have questions or problems. Companies such as Eddie Bauer, Sharper Image, Lands' End, L.L. Bean, and Hanna Andersson actively market in Japan. The volume of sales generated is large enough to justify special attention. Hanna Andersson, for example, received complaints that it was too difficult to get questions answered and to place orders by telephone, So it opened a service center with 24 telephone operators to assist customers that generate over $5 million in

---

[18] Jonathan Friedland and Louise Lee, "Wal-Mart Changes Tactics to Meet International Tastes," *The Wall Street Journal Interactive Edition,* October 8, 1997.

[19] Yumiko Ono, "Amway Grows Abroad, Sending 'Ambassadors' to Spread the Word," *The Wall Street Journal,* May 14, 1997, p. A1.

[20] For a detailed study on adapting catalogs for international marketing, see Fernando Robles and Syed H. Akhter, "International Catalog Mix Adaptation: An Empirical Study," *Journal of Global Marketing,* Vol. 11(2), 1997, p. 65.

[21] Washida Kiyokazu, "Open All Hours" *Look Japan,* June 1997, p. 11.

The grand opening of a Wal-Mart Supercenter in China. Wal-Mart has 603 international stores including the recently acquired 21 outlets of Wertkauf GmbH of Germany. (Greg Girard/CONTACT Press Images)

sales annually.[22] Changing life-styles, acceptance of credit cards, and improved postal and telephone services in many countries support direct marketing.

Resistances to Change.   Efforts to improve the efficiency of the distribution system, new types of middlemen, and other attempts to change traditional ways are typically viewed as threatening and thus resisted. Laws abound that protect the entrenched in their positions. In Italy, a new retail outlet must obtain a license from a municipal board composed of local tradespeople. In a two-year period, some 200 applications were made and only 10 new licenses granted. Opposition to retail innovation prevails everywhere, yet in the face of all the restrictions and hindrances, self-service, discount merchandising, liberal store hours, and large-scale merchandising continue to grow because they offer the consumer convenience and a broad range of quality product brands at advantageous prices.[23] Ultimately the consumer does prevail.

World Wide Web

The use of the Internet is rapidly becoming an important distribution method for multinational companies and a source of products for businesses and consumers. Computer hardware and software companies, and book and music retailers are the most experienced "e-marketers" in using this method of distribution and marketing. Technically, e-commerce is a form of direct selling; however, because of its newness and the unique issues associated with this form of distribution, it is important to differentiate from other types of direct marketing. E-commerce is used to market business-to-business services,

---

[22] Alan K. Ota, "Japanese Turn to Foreign Mail Order Companies," *The Oregonian,* October 1, 1995, p. E1.

[23] Greg Steinmetz, "German Consumers Are Seeing Prices Cut in Deregulation Push," *The Wall Street Journal,* August 15, 1997, p. A1.

consumer services, and consumer and industrial products via the World Wide Web on the Internet. It involves the direct marketing from a manufacturer, retailer, or some other intermediary to a final user.

Some examples of e-marketers that have an international presence include Dell Computer Corporation, which generates revenues of more than $3 million per day; in the U.K., 10 percent of its sales are online.[24] Cisco Systems Inc. generated $1 billion in sales in 1997. Cisco's Web site appears in 14 languages and has country-specific content for 49 nations.[25] Gateway 2000 has global sites in Japan, France, the Netherlands, Germany and Sweden, Australia, the U.K., and the United States (**http://gateway2000. com**). Sun Microsystems and its aftermarketing company, SunExpress, have local language information on more than 3,500 aftermarket products. SunPlaza enables visitors in North America, Europe, and Japan to get information on-line on products and services, and place orders directly and securely in their native languages.

Many services are ideally suited for the Internet. Inventory management, quality control, accounting, secretarial, translation, and legal services are traditionally supplied in-house. However, as outsourcing has become more popular among companies, the Internet providers of these services have grown both in the United States and internationally.[26]

A recent study found that worldwide, shoppers spent about $500 million on-line in 1996 and it is expected to increase to $6.5 billion by 2000. Selling on-line allows retailers to establish a presence beyond their traditional markets. As one Internet customer from the Netherlands commented, "The first time I bought something in the U.S. it was a test." He purchased a pair of brake levers for his mountain bike from Torrance, California-based Price Point. He paid $130 instead of the $190 that the same items cost in a local bike store.

For Fernando Hernandez, buying sheet music used to mean a 400-kilometer trip to Madrid from his home in Pamplona. Now he crosses the Atlantic to shop—and the journey takes less time than a jaunt to the corner store. Via the Internet he can buy directly from specialized stores and high-volume discounters in New York, London, and almost anywhere else. On-line shoppers buy books, music, fishing gear, computers, bicycles, and a host of other products.

Although the Web might not be right for every company, it has become far more than another space to plant billboards promoting a company's products, or even sites from which to make sales. E-commerce is rapidly becoming a business site with companies coming to rely on the Net for numerous complex activities and connections ranging from linking global offices and factories to facilitating data exchange with vendors and customers.

E-commerce is much more developed in the United States than the rest of the world.[27] This is partly because of the vast number of people who own personal computers and because of the much lower cost of access to the Internet than found elsewhere. However, personal computer ownership[28] and Internet access is forecasted to increase substantially in Europe and Japan, as well as other parts of Asia and South America within the next few years.[29]

Internet usage in other parts of the world is modest by U.S. levels, where an estimated 26 million households access the Web.[30] The most recent data available (1997)

---

[24] David Fox. "Death of an Ill-Informed Hardware Salesman," *The Independent—London,* December 9, 1997, p. N9.

[25] "Going Global," November 15, 1997, **http://www.euromktg.com/eng/ed/art/rep-eur4.html**.

[26] Carlos A. Primo Braga, "The Impact of Internationalization of Services on Developing Countries," *Finance & Development,* March 1996, p. 34.

[27] "The Virtual Mall Gets Real," *Business Week,* January 26, 1998, p. 90.

[28] "Japanese Internet Business Worth $245 Million in 1996," *Newsbytes News Network,* June 2, 1997; and "Online Commerce in Asia Will Boom, Analyst Says," *Newsbytes News Network,* January 27, 1997, **http://www.newsbytes.com**.

[29] "Germany: Online Retailing Market Overview," *International Market Insight Reports,* U.S. & Foreign Commercial Service, June 23, 1997.

[30] "The Virtual Mall Gets Real," *Business Week,* January 26, 1998, p. 90.

for other countries show that there are 7 million Japanese[31] and between 3 and 4 million Germans who have access to the Internet. In Finland there are 3 million (60 percent of the population), 2.5 million French speakers (in Canada, France, Switzerland, and Belgium), 2.2 million Swedes (one Swede out of four), 1.5 million Spanish speakers (U.S. Hispanic, Spain, and Latin America), and 1 million Brazilians (Portuguese language.) on-line. These figures are changing rapidly; the most current figures are available from **http://www.euromktg.com/eurostats.html**.

Web Malls.   An indication of the impact U.S. e-retailers have had on retail sales in the U.K. is the E-Christmas mall created to counter Christmas gift sales that have been going to the U.S. In an attempt to provide more opportunity for European e-customers to stay at home, a group of 150 of Europe's best-known retailers organized E-Christmas (**http://www.e-christmas.com**) on-line in time for the Christmas selling season.[32] E-Christmas shoppers can choose from one of six languages and 11 currencies. They are presented with prices that include duty when applicable and delivery charges for the 25 countries served by UPS worldwide. Germany also has an e-mall that operates year-around (**http://www.shopping24.de**); it is, however, only in German. Both of these shopping malls have U.S. stores included in their lineup.[33]

Special Issues.   By its very nature e-commerce has some unique issues that must be addressed if international sales are to be maximized. The following issues need to be addressed if a domestic e-vendor expects to be a viable player in the international cyber marketplace. Many of these issues arise because the host country intermediary who would ordinarily be involved in international marketing is eliminated. An important advantage of selling direct is that total costs can be lowered so the final price overseas is considerably less than it would have been through a distributor. However, doing business in other countries has always required someone who can translate prospective customer inquiries and orders into English, and reply in their language. Often a local distributor in each country, who stocks and provides the local interface between vendor and client, provides these services. Intermediaries can be eliminated but someone, either the seller or the buyer, must assume the functions they perform. Consequently, an e-vendor must be concerned with the following issues:[34]

- **Translation.** Ideally, a Web site should be translated into the languages of the target markets. This may not be financially feasible but at least the most important pages of the site should be translated. A reasonable solution is to use automatic translator software such as that offered by Globalink (**http://www. globalink.com**). The resulting text is not perfect, but you can understand what is being asked, and you can respond easily.

- **Local contact.** Many companies are creating "virtual offices" abroad, whereby a company has a phone number in important cities that doubles as a voicemail/fax contact point.[35] Companies fully committed to foreign markets buy server space and create "mirror sites" in key markets. The feeling is that foreign customers are more likely to visit sites in their own country and in the local language.[36]

---

[31] "Online Commerce in Asia Will Boom, Analyst Says," *Newsbytes News Network,* January 27, 1997, **http://www.newsbytes.com**.

[32] "European Retailers Cast Their Holiday Nets," *Chain Store Age Executive with Shopping Center Age,* December 1997, p. 154.

[33] It might be revealing to check some Web malls in other countries. Try a German mall that will ship to the U.S. (**http://www.my-world.de**) and a shopping mall sponsored by the Singapore government that has shopping sites as well as information about Singapore (**http://www.ech.ncb.gov.sg**).

[34] Bill Dunlap, "Thinking International?" October 29, 1997, **http://www.euromktg.com/eng/ed/art/ repeur5.html**.

[35] For an interesting report on how Europe's many Internet Service Providers are being linked, see "I-Pass to Bring Internet Roaming to Europe," *Newsbytes News Network,* June 3, 1997, **http://newsbytes.com**.

[36] "Report From Europe: Internet Marketing" March 21, 1997, **http://www.euromktg.com/eng/ed/ repeur1.html**.

- **Payment.** For all amounts over $10, the consumer should be able to use a credit card number—either by e-mail (from a secure page on your Web site), by fax, or over the phone. A company not set up to accept credit cards can use companies like First Virtual (**http://www.fv.com**), which provides this service at a reasonable charge. Others, like Thomas Cook (**http://thomascook.com**), are going on-line to offer payment and other financial services.[37]
- **Delivery.** For companies operating in the United States, surface postal delivery of small parcels is the most cost effective but takes the longest time. For more rapid but more expensive deliveries, Federal Express, United Parcel Service, and other private delivery services provide delivery worldwide. For example, Tom Clancy's bestseller, *Executive Orders,* shipped express to Paris from Seattle-based Amazon.com, would cost a reader $55.52. The same book delivered in four to 10 weeks via surface mail costs $25.52—substantial savings over the cost of the book in a Paris bookstore where it sells for $35.[38]

Once sufficient volume in a country or region is attained, container shipments to Free Trade Zones or bonded warehouses can be used as shipping points to customers within the region.[39] These same locations can also be used for such after-sale services as spare parts, defective product returns, supplies, and similar types of services.

Promotion.   Although the WWW is a means of promotion, if you are engaging in e-commerce, you need also to advertise your presence and the products or services offered. The old adage, "build a better mouse trap and the world will beat a path to your door" does not work for e-commerce, just as it does not work with other products unless you tell your target market about the availability of the "better mouse trap." How do you attract visitors from other countries to your Web site? The same way you would at home—except in the local language. Index registration, press releases, local newsgroups and forums, mutual links, and banner advertising are the traditional way.

It is the authors' opinion, however, that one of the weakest links in e-commerce is the promotion of Web sites. It is still a hit and miss proposition for a prospective customer to be exposed to one of the traditional ways that Internet sites are promoted. There is so much clutter on the Web, continually increasing as the Web grows, that an e-vendor needs to attract attention. One method is to advertise via other media to the target market. Some companies do this indirectly by listing their Web address somewhere in an advertisement—generally as a tag line. A more effective way would be to advertise directly to the target market using other media.

A Web site should be seen as a retail store, the only difference between it and a physical store is that the customer arrives over the Internet instead of on foot. Hence, the customer needs to know where your store can be found, what you offer, and why it would benefit the customer to shop there. Further, an e-seller needs to attract those not now shopping on the Web to assure future growth.

The World Wide Web is less than 10 years old and is still evolving. Much of what is standard practice today will be obsolete as new means of data transmission are achieved and costs of accessing the Web decrease all over the world. The WWW is rapidly growing and changing as it grows.

Alternative Middleman Choices

A marketer's options range from assuming the entire distribution activity (by establishing its own subsidiaries and marketing directly to the end user) to depending on inter-

---

[37] "Visa: Smart Commerce Japan Launches World-Leading In-Store and In-Cyberspace Visa Chip Card Pilot," *M2 Press Wire,* October 6, 1997.

[38] David Rocks, "Bargain Surfing: World Wide Web Lets You Mall Hop from the Study," *The Wall Street Journal Europe,* November 25, 1996, p. 30.

[39] Read more about using Free Trade Zones to lower costs in Chapter 15.

EXHIBIT 14-4   International Channel-of-Distribution Alternatives

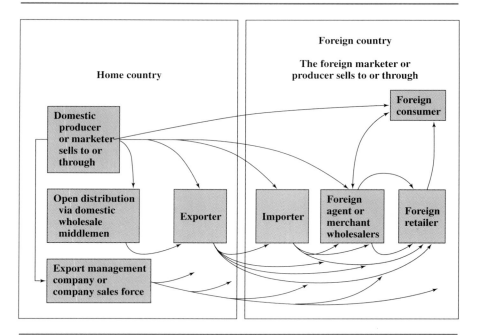

mediaries for distribution of the product. Channel selection must be given considerable thought since once initiated it is difficult to change, and if it proves inappropriate, future growth of market share may be affected.[40]

The channel process includes all activities beginning with the manufacturer and ending with the final consumer. This means the seller must exert influence over two sets of channels, one in the home country and one in the foreign-market country. Exhibit 14–4 shows some of the possible channel-of-distribution alternatives. The arrows show those to whom the producer and each of the middlemen may sell. In the home country, the seller must have an organization (generally the international marketing division of a company) to deal with channel members needed to move goods between countries. In the foreign market, the seller must supervise the channels that supply the product to the end user. Ideally, the company wants to control or be involved in the process directly through the various channel members to the final user. To do less may result in unsatisfactory distribution and the failure of marketing objectives. In practice, however, such involvement throughout the channel process is not always practical or cost effective. Consequently, selection of channel members and effective controls are high priorities in establishing the distribution process.

Once the marketer has clarified company objectives and policies, the next step is the selection of specific intermediaries needed to develop a channel. External middlemen are differentiated on whether or not they take title to the goods—agent middlemen represent the principal rather than themselves, and merchant middlemen take title to the goods and buy and sell on their own account. The distinction between agent and merchant middlemen is important because a manufacturer's control of the distribution process is affected by who has title to the goods in the channel.

Agent middlemen work on commission and arrange for sales in the foreign country but do not take title to the merchandise. By using agents, the manufacturer assumes

---

40 Preet S. Aulakh and Masaaki Kotabe, "Antecedents and Performance Implications of Channel Integration in Foreign Markets," *Journal of International Business Studies,* First Quarter 1997, p. 145.

CROSSING BORDERS 14-2

Distribution in Mexico—By Delivery Van and Donkey

Millions of Latin Americans—many of them active consumers in at least some product segments—live in areas difficult to reach. In Mexico, companies have come up with a number of innovations to service isolated mountain and jungle villages.

Sabritas, Mexico's largest snack-food company, has one of Mexico's most extensive internal distribution networks. The company divides the country into 220 regions serviced by 7,000 vehicles. Routes in the most isolated areas are covered weekly (versus daily in urban areas), usually by vans equipped for rough conditions. Drivers often sleep in their vans or find shelter at stores along the way. Many rural stores serve as distribution centers for the even less-accessible areas. Roadside stores also serve other marketing purposes—they are collection points for product coupons turned in by distant consumers.

In some areas even Sabritas's vans can't get through. Distributors reach out-of-the-way villages in the lake region of Veracruz State by canoe, while in mountainous regions drivers may arrange for transport of goods by donkey from drop-off points where the roads end. Diconsa, another food company, sends boats out on the main rivers to supply small stores or sell to isolated villages and ranches.

Despite the difficulty of servicing the backcountry, Sabritas says sales volumes warrant the added effort in a nation where over 25 percent of the market lives in the countryside.

Source: Abstracted from "How Firms in Mexico Reach Isolated Rural Markets," *Business Latin America*, September 9, 1991, pp. 289–95.

---

trading risk but maintains the right to establish policy guidelines and prices and to require its agents to provide sales records and customer information.

Merchant middlemen actually take title to manufacturers' goods and assume the trading risks, so they tend to be less controllable than agent middlemen. Merchant middlemen provide a variety of import and export wholesaling functions involved in purchasing for their own account and selling in other countries. Because merchant middlemen primarily are concerned with sales and profit margins on their merchandise, they are frequently criticized for not representing the best interests of a manufacturer. Unless they have a franchise or a strong and profitable brand, merchant middlemen seek goods from any source and are likely to have low brand loyalty. Ease of contact, minimized credit risk, and elimination of all merchandise handling outside the United States are some of the advantages of using merchant middlemen.

Middlemen are not clear-cut, precise, easily defined entities. It is exceptional to find a firm that represents one of the pure types identified here. Thus, intimate knowledge of middlemen functions is especially important in international activity because misleading titles can fool a marketer unable to look beyond mere names. What are the functions of a British middleman called a stockist, or one called an exporter or importer? One exporter may, in fact, be an agent middleman, whereas another is a merchant. Many, if not most, international middlemen wear several hats and can be clearly identified only in the context of their relationship with a specific firm. One company may engage in both importing and exporting; act as an agent and a merchant middleman; operate from offices in the United States, Germany, and Great Britain; provide financial services; and act as a freight forwarder. It would be difficult to put this company into an appropriate pigeonhole. Many firms work in a single capacity, but the conglomerate type of middleman described here is a major force in some international business.

Only by analyzing middlemen functions in skeletal simplicity can the nature of the channels be determined. Three alternatives are presented: first, middlemen physically located in the manufacturer's home country; next, middlemen located in foreign countries; and finally, government-affiliated middlemen.

Home-Country Middlemen

Home-country middlemen, or domestic middlemen, located in the producing firm's country, provide marketing services from a domestic base. By selecting domestic middlemen as intermediaries in the distribution processes, companies relegate foreign-market distribution to others. Domestic middlemen offer many advantages for companies with small international sales volume, those inexperienced with foreign markets, those not wanting to become immediately involved with the complexities of international marketing, and those wanting to sell abroad with minimum financial and management commitment. A major trade-off for using home-country middlemen is limited control over the entire process. Domestic middlemen are most likely to be used when the marketer is uncertain and/or desires to minimize financial and management investment. A brief discussion of the more frequently used domestic middlemen follows.

Global Retailers.   As global retailers like Costco, Sears Roebuck, Toys "R" Us, and Wal-Mart expand their global coverage, they are becoming major domestic middlemen for international markets. Wal-Mart, with 603 stores in nine foreign markets, is an attractive entry point to international markets for U.S. suppliers if they can meet Wal-Mart's stringent shipping requirements. For those that can meet the test, Wal-Mart offers an effective way to enter international markets with a minimum of experience. Pacific Connections, for example, a California manufacturer of handbags with $70 million in sales in 1997, ventured into overseas markets in Argentina, Brazil, Canada, and Mexico through its ties to Wal-Mart. Wal-Mart executives say that many U.S. vendors lack global expertise and seem ill prepared to supply the retailer in places like China and Brazil.[41]

Export Management Companies.   The *export management company (EMC)* is an important middleman for firms with relatively small international volume or for those unwilling to involve their own personnel in the international function. EMCs range in size from one person upward to 100 and handle about 10 percent of the manufactured goods exported. An example of an EMC is a Washington, D.C.-based company that has exclusive agreements with 10 U.S. manufacturers of orthopedic equipment and markets these products on a worldwide basis.

Whether handling five clients or 100, the EMC's stock-in-trade is personalized service. Typically, the EMC becomes an integral part of the marketing operations of the client companies. Working under the names of the manufacturers, the EMC functions as a low-cost, independent marketing department with direct responsibility to the parent firm. The working relationship is so close that customers are often unaware they are not dealing directly with the export department of the company (see Exhibit 14–5).

The EMC provides many services for the manufacturer; in all instances, however, the main functions are contact with foreign customers (sometimes through an EMC's own foreign branches) and negotiations for sales. An EMC's specialization in a given field often makes it possible to offer a level of service that could not be attained by the manufacturer without years of groundwork.

---

[41] Wendy Zellner, Louisa Shepard, Ian Katz, and David Lindorff, "Wal-Mart Spoken Here," *Business Week,* June 23, 1997, p. 138.

EXHIBIT 14-5   How Does an EMC Operate?

Most export management companies offer a wide range of services and assistance, including:

Researching foreign markets for a client's products.

Traveling overseas to determine the best method of distributing the product.

Appointing distributors or commission representatives as needed in individual foreign countries, frequently within an already existing overseas network created for similar goods.

Exhibiting the client's products at international trade shows, such as U.S. Department of Commerce-sponsored commercial exhibitions at trade fairs and U.S. Export Development Offices around the world.

Handling the routine details in getting the product to the foreign customer—export declarations, shipping and customs documentation, insurance, banking, and instructions for special export packing and marking.

Granting the customary finance terms to the trade abroad and assuring payment to the manufacturer of the product.

Preparing advertising and sales literature in cooperation with the manufacturer and adapting it to overseas requirements for use in personal contacts with foreign buyers.

Corresponding in the necessary foreign languages.

Making sure that goods being shipped are suitable for local conditions and meet overseas legal and trade norms, including labeling, packaging, purity, and electrical characteristics.

Advising on overseas patent and trademark protection requirement.

Source: "The Export Management Company," U.S. Dept. of Commerce, Washington, D.C.

The export management company may take full or partial responsibility for promotion of the goods, credit arrangements, physical handling, market research, and information on financial, patent, and licensing matters. Traditionally, the EMC works on commission, although an increasing number are buying products on their own account.

Two of the chief advantages of EMCs are (1) minimum investment on the part of the company to get into international markets, and (2) no company personnel or major expenditure of managerial effort. The result, in effect, is an extension of the market for the firm with negligible financial or personnel commitments.[42]

The major disadvantage is that EMCs can seldom afford to make the kind of market investment needed to establish deep distribution for products because they must have immediate sales payout to survive. Such a situation does not offer the market advantages gained by a company that can afford to use company personnel. Carefully selected EMCs can do an excellent job, but the manufacturer must remember the EMC is dependent on sales volume for compensation and probably will not push the manufacturer's line if it is spread too thinly, generates too small a volume from a given principal, or cannot operate profitably in the short run. Then the EMC becomes an order taker and not the desired substitute for an international marketing department.

Trading Companies.   *Trading companies* have a long and honorable history as important intermediaries in the development of trade between nations. Trading companies accumulate, transport, and distribute goods from many countries. In concept, the trading company has changed little in hundreds of years.

The British firm, Gray MacKenzie and Company, is typical of companies operating in the Middle East. It has some 70 salespeople and handles consumer products ranging from toiletries to outboard motors and Scotch whiskey. The key advantage to this type of trading company is that it covers the entire Middle East.

Large, established trading companies generally are located in developed countries; they sell manufactured goods to developing countries and buy raw materials and unprocessed goods. Japanese trading companies *(sogo shosha)*, dating back to the early

---

[42] Stephanie Gruner, "International: Calling the Shots with Export Traders," *Inc. On Line,* **http://www.inc.com/incmagazine**, February 1996, p. 94.

1700s, operate both as importers and exporters. Some 300 are engaged in foreign and domestic trade through 2,000 branch offices outside Japan and handle over $1 trillion in trading volume annually. Japanese trading companies account for 61 percent of all Japanese imports and 39 percent of all exports or about a fifth of Japan's entire GDP.[43]

For companies seeking entrance into the complicated Japanese distribution system, the Japanese trading company offers one of the easiest routes to success. The omnipresent trading companies virtually control distribution through all levels of channels in Japan. Since trading companies may control many of the distributors and maintain broad distribution channels, they provide the best means for intensive coverage of the market.

An increasingly important part of trading company business consists of sales to markets in countries other than Japan; third-nation or offshore deals make up a growing part of trading company business. Mitsui and Company helps export American grain to Europe; Nissho-Iwai Corporation arranges for athletic shoes to be manufactured in South Korea and Taiwan for Nike Inc. of Oregon. The nine largest Japanese trading companies have sales to other nations in excess of 20 percent of their combined sales.

U.S. Export Trading Companies.   The *Export Trading Company (ETC) Act* allows producers of similar products to form export trading companies. A major goal of the ETC Act was to increase U.S. exports by encouraging more efficient export trade services to producers and suppliers in order to improve the availability of trade finance and to remove antitrust disincentives to export activities. By providing U.S. businesses with an opportunity to obtain antitrust preclearance for specified export activities, the ETC Act creates a more favorable environment for the formation of joint export ventures. Through such joint ventures, U.S. firms can take advantage of economies of scale, spread risk, and pool their expertise. In addition, through joint selling arrangements, domestic competitors can avoid inter-firm rivalry in foreign markets. Prior to the passage of the ETC Act, competing companies could not engage in joint exporting efforts without possible violation of antitrust provisions. The other important provision of the ETC Act is to permit bank holding companies to own ETCs. Prior to the ETC Act, banks could not own commercial enterprises.

Immediately after passage of the ETC Act, several major companies (General Electric, Sears Roebuck, Kmart, and others) announced the development of export trading companies. In most cases, these export firms did not require the protection of the ETC Act since they initially operated independently of other enterprises. They provided international sales for U.S. companies to a limited extent, but primarily they operated as trading companies for their own products. To date, many of the trading companies established after passage of the ETC Act have closed their doors or are languishing.[44]

Complementary Marketers.   Companies with marketing facilities or contacts in different countries with excess marketing capacity or a desire for a broader product line sometimes take on additional lines for international distribution; although the generic name for such activities is *complementary marketing*, it is commonly called *piggybacking*. General Electric Company has been distributing merchandise from other suppliers for many years. It accepts products that are noncompetitive but complementary and that add to the basic distribution strength of the company itself.

Most piggyback arrangements are undertaken when a firm wants to fill out its product line or keep its seasonal distribution channels functioning throughout the year. Companies may work either on an agency or merchant basis, but the greatest volume of

---

[43] Robert L. Cutts, "The *Sogo Shosha:* So Much More Than Just Another Global Import-Export Giant," *The American Chamber of Commerce in Japan Journal,* **http://www.accj.or.jp**, May 1997.

[44] For an excellent review of all types of public and private trading companies, see Henry Wichmann, "Private and Public Trading Companies within the Pacific Rim Nations," *Journal of Small Business Management,* January 1997, p. 62.

piggyback business is handled on an ownership (merchant) purchase–resale arrangement.

The selection process for new products for piggyback distribution determines whether (1) the product relates to the product line and contributes to it; (2) the product fits the sales and distribution channel presently employed; (3) there is an adequate margin to make the undertaking worthwhile; and (4) the product will find market acceptance and profitable volume. If these requirements are met, piggybacking can be a logical way of increasing volume and profit for both the carrier and the piggybacker.

Manufacturer's Export Agent.   The *manufacturer's export agent (MEA)* is an individual agent middleman or an agent middleman firm providing a selling service for manufacturers. Unlike the EMC, the MEA does not serve as the producer's export department but has a short-term relationship, covers only one or two markets, and operates on a straight commission basis. Another principal difference is that MEAs do business in their own names rather than in the name of the client. Within a limited scope of operation, the MEAs provide services similar to those of the EMC.

Home Country Brokers.   The term *broker* is a catchall for a variety of middlemen performing low-cost agent services. The term is typically applied to import–export brokers who provide the intermediary function of bringing buyers and sellers together and who do not have a continuing relationship with their clients. Most brokers specialize in one or more commodities for which they maintain contact with major producers and purchasers throughout the world.

Buying Offices.   A variety of agent middlemen may be classified simply as buyers or buyers for export. Their common denominator is a primary function of seeking and purchasing merchandise on request from principals; as such, they do not provide a selling service. In fact, their chief emphasis is on flexibility and the ability to find merchandise from any source. They do not often become involved in continuing relationships with domestic suppliers and do not provide a continuing source of representation.

Selling Groups.   Several types of arrangements have been developed in which various manufacturers or producers cooperate in a joint attempt to sell their merchandise abroad. This may take the form of complementary exporting or of selling to a business combine such as a Webb-Pomerene export association. Both are considered agency arrangements when the exporting is done on a fee or commission basis.

Webb-Pomerene Export Associations (WPEA).   *Webb-Pomerene Export Associations (WPEA)* are another major form of group exporting. The Webb-Pomerene Act of 1918 made it possible for American business firms to join forces in export activities without being subject to the Sherman Antitrust Act. WPEAs cannot participate in cartels or other international agreements that would reduce competition in the United States, but can offer four major benefits: (1) reduction of export costs, (2) demand expansion through promotion, (3) trade barrier reductions, and (4) improvement of trade terms through bilateral bargaining. Additionally, WPEAs set prices, standardize products, and arrange for disposal of surplus products. Although they account for less than 5 percent of U.S. exports, WPEAs include some of America's blue-chip companies in agricultural products, chemicals and raw materials, forest products, pulp and paper, textiles, rubber products, motion pictures, and television.

Foreign Sales Corporation (FSC).   A *Foreign Sales Corporation (FSC)* is a sales corporation set up in a foreign country or U.S. possession that can obtain a corporate tax exemption on a portion of the earnings generated by the sale or lease of export property. Manufacturers and export groups can form FSCs. A FSC can function as a principal,

CROSSING BORDERS 14–3

Tai Fei—Big Flyers—and Chinese Norazi Agents

Smuggling is big business between Hong Kong and China, and big business requires the latest in technology. *Tai fei,* or "big flyers," the Cantonese translation, are custom-made speedboats large enough to hold a full-size Mercedes Benz, or up to 300 VCRs or 150 TV sets. Some 40 feet long and powered by four to six outboard engines of 300 horsepower each, the *tai fei* can carry up to two tons and travel fully loaded at a speed of over 80 miles an hour. *Tai fei* are truly out of a James Bond movie; they can outrun any boat on the sea, are outfitted with steel prows used as battering rams to slice through police boats that get in their way, have bulletproof windscreens, and the driver is shielded with armor plate that will stop an AK-47 round.

A day in the life of a Chinese Norazi may go something like this: A corrupt official in Guangdong, a southern Chinese province, specifies the make, model, and color of a car he wants. The car is promptly stolen in Hong Kong, often at rush hour since the thieves figure Hong Kong police won't set up roadblocks then. The luxury car (a Mercedes or BMW) is whisked away by *tai fei* on the day it is stolen and 90 minutes later is being unloaded in China. Laden with hard currency, the *tai fei* travels to an isolated pickup point on Hong Kong Island for a load of TVs, VCRs, air conditioners, and other consumer goods for the return trip.

Source: Adapted from Peter Fuhrman and Andrew Tanzer, "The *Tai Fei* Know the Way," *Forbes,* December 21, 1992, pp. 172–75.

buying and selling for its own account, or as a commissioned agent. It can be related to a manufacturing parent or can be an independent merchant or broker.

Norazi Agent. *Norazi agents* are unique middlemen specializing in shady or difficult transactions. They deal in contraband materials, such as hazardous waste products or war materials, and in providing strategic goods to countries closed to normal trading channels. The Norazi is also likely to be engaged in black-market currency operations, untaxed liquor, narcotics, industrial espionage, and other illicit traffic. The Norazi exists because tariffs, import taxes, import/export regulations, and excise taxes make illegal movements of goods more profitable than legal movements. Because of high tariffs, the amount of contraband entering Brazil from Paraguay is estimated to be between $4 and $12 billion annually. Cigarette smuggling accounts for over one-fourth of all cigarettes sold abroad according to one estimate.[45] In the last few years, money laundering has become a major activity of Norazi agents; some estimate that $500 billion is laundered worldwide annually.[46]

The volume of business transacted by Norazi is unknown but estimates are in excess of $100 billion, exclusive of illegal drugs. The Norazi has its supporters. In Bolivia, a group called the Union of Minority Businessmen speaks openly in favor of the smuggling trade, and one government official commented, "Smuggling is a social and economic necessity since it allows people to buy goods at lower prices."

---

[45] Raymond Bonner and Christopher Drew, "Cigarette Smuggling Burgeons Worldwide," *The New York Times,* August 25, 1997, p. B12.

[46] Peter J. Quirk, "Money Laundering: Muddying the Macroeconomy," *Finance & Development,* March 1997, p. 7.

Export Merchants.   *Export merchants* are essentially domestic merchants operating in foreign markets. As such, they operate much like the domestic wholesaler. Specifically, they purchase goods from a large number of manufacturers, ship them to foreign countries, and take full responsibility for their marketing. Sometimes they utilize their own organizations, but, more commonly, they sell through middlemen. They may carry competing lines, have full control over prices, and maintain little loyalty to suppliers, although they continue to handle products as long as they are profitable.

Export Jobbers.   *Export jobbers* deal mostly in commodities; they do not take physical possession of goods but assume responsibility for arranging transportation. Because they work on a job-lot basis, they do not provide a particularly attractive distribution alternative for most producers.

Exhibit 14–6 summarizes information pertaining to the major kinds of domestic middlemen operating in foreign markets. No attempt is made to generalize about rates of commission, markup, or pay because so many factors influence compensation. Services offered or demanded, market structure, volume, and product type are some of the key determinants. The data represent the predominant patterns of operations; however, individual middlemen of a given type may vary in their operations.

Foreign-Country Middlemen

The variety of agent and merchant middlemen in most countries is similar to those in the United States. An international marketer seeking greater control over the distribution process may elect to deal directly with middlemen in the foreign market. They gain the advantage of shorter channels and deal with middlemen in constant contact with the market. As with all middlemen, particularly those working at a distance, effectiveness is directly dependent on the selection of middlemen and on the degree of control the manufacturer can and/or will exert

Using foreign-country middlemen moves the manufacturer closer to the market and involves the company more closely with problems of language, physical distribution, communications, and financing. Foreign middlemen may be agents or merchants; they may be associated with the parent company to varying degrees; or they may be temporarily hired for special purposes. Some of the more important foreign-country middlemen are manufacturer's representatives and foreign distributors.

Manufacturer's Representatives.   *Manufacturer's representatives* are agent middlemen who take responsibility for a producer's goods in a city, regional market area, entire country, or several adjacent countries. When responsible for an entire country, the middleman is often called a *sole agent.* As in the United States, the well-chosen, well-motivated, well-controlled manufacturer's representative can provide excellent market coverage for the manufacturer in certain circumstances. The manufacturer's representative is widely used in distribution of industrial goods overseas and is an excellent representative for any type of manufactured consumer goods.

Foreign manufacturer's representatives have a variety of titles, including sales agent, resident sales agent, exclusive agent, commission agent, and indent agent. They take no credit, exchange, or market risk but deal strictly as field sales representatives. They do not arrange for shipping or for handling and usually do not take physical possession. Manufacturers who wish the type of control and intensive market coverage their own sales force would afford, but who cannot field one, may find the manufacturer's representative a satisfactory choice.

Distributors.   A *foreign distributor* is a merchant middleman. This intermediary often has exclusive sales rights in a specific country and works in close cooperation with the manufacturer. The distributor has a relatively high degree of dependence on the supplier companies, and arrangements are likely to be on a long-run, continuous basis. Working

Exhibit 14–6 Characteristics of Domestic Middlemen Serving Overseas Markets

Type of Duties	Agent					Merchant				
	EMC	MEA	Broker	Buying Offices	Selling Groups	Norazi	Export Merchant	Export Jobber	Importers and Trading Companies	Complementary Marketers
Take title	No*	No	No	No	No	Yes	Yes	Yes	Yes	Yes
Take possession	Yes	Yes	No	Yes	Yes	Yes	Yes	No	Yes	Yes
Continuing relationship	Yes	Yes	No	Yes	Yes	No	No	Yes	Yes	Yes
Share of foreign output	All	All	Any	Small	All	Small	Any	Small	Any	Most
Degree of control by principal	Fair	Fair	Nil	Nil	Good	Nil	None	None	Nil	Fair
Price authority	Advisory	Advisory	Yes (at market level)	Yes (to buy)	Advisory	Yes	Yes	Yes	No	Some
Represent buyer or seller	Seller	Seller	Either	Buyer	Seller	Both	Self	Self	Self	Self
Number of principals	Few—many	Few—many	Many	Small	Few	Several per transaction	Many sources	Many sources	Mnay sources	One per product
Arrange shipping	Yes	Yes	Not usually	Yes	Yes	Yes	Yes	Yes	Yes	Yes
Type of goods	Manufactured goods and commodities	Staples and commodities	Staples and commodities	Staples and commodities	Complementary to their own lines	Contraband	Manufactured goods	Bulky and raw materials	Manufactured goods	Complementary to line
Breadth of line	Specialty—wide	All types of staples	All types of staples	Retail goods	Narrow	n.a.	Broad	Broad	Broad	Narrow
Handle competitive lines	No	No	Yes	Yes—utilizes many sources	No	Yes	Yes	Yes	Yes	No
Extent of promotion and selling effort	Good	Good	One shot	n.a.	Good	Nil	Nil	Nil	Good	Good
Extend credit to principal	Occasionally	Occasionally	Seldom	Seldom	Seldom	No	Occasionally	Seldom	Seldom	Seldom
Market information	Fair	Fair	Price and market conditions	For principal not for manufacturer	Good	No	Nil	Nil	Fair	Good

Note: n.a. = not available.

* The EMC may take title and thus becomes a merchant middleman.

433

through distributors permits the manufacturer a reasonable degree of control over prices, promotional effort, inventories, servicing, and other distribution functions. If a line is profitable for distributors, they can be depended on to handle it in a manner closely approximating the desires of the manufacturer.

Foreign-Country Brokers.   Like the export broker discussed in an earlier section, *foreign-country brokers* are agents who deal largely in commodities and food products. The foreign brokers are typically part of small brokerage firms operating in one country or in a few contiguous countries. Their strength is in having good continuing relationships with customers and providing speedy market coverage at a low cost.

Managing Agents and Compradors.   A *managing agent* conducts business within a foreign nation under an exclusive contract arrangement with the parent company. The managing agent in some cases invests in the operation and in most instances operates under a contract with the parent company. Compensation is usually on the basis of cost plus a specified percentage of the profits of the managed company. In some countries, managing agents may be called *compradors* and there are some differences in duties performed (see Exhibit 14–7).

Dealers.   Generally speaking, anyone who has a continuing relationship with a supplier in buying and selling goods is considered a *dealer*. More specifically, dealers are middlemen selling industrial goods or durable consumer goods direct to customers; they are the last step in the channel of distribution. Dealers have continuing, close working relationships with their suppliers and exclusive selling rights for their producer's products within a given geographic area. Finally, they derive a large portion of their sales volume from the products of a single supplier firm. Usually a dealer is an independent merchant middleman, but sometimes the supplier company has an equity in its dealers.

Some of the best examples of dealer operations are found in the farm equipment, earth-moving, and automotive industries. These categories include Massey Ferguson, with a vast, worldwide network of dealers; Caterpillar Tractor Company, with dealers in every major city of the world; and the various automobile companies.

Import Jobbers, Wholesalers, and Retailers.   *Import jobbers* purchase goods directly from the manufacturer and sell to wholesalers and retailers and to industrial customers. Large and small wholesalers and retailers engage in direct importing for their own outlets and for redistribution to smaller middlemen. The combination retailer-wholesaler is more important in foreign countries than in the United States. It is not uncommon to find large retailers wholesaling goods to local shops and dealers. Exhibit 14–7 summarizes the characteristics of foreign-country middlemen.

Government-Affiliated Middlemen

Marketers must deal with governments in every country of the world. Products, services, and commodities for the government's own use are always procured through government purchasing offices at federal, regional, and local levels. As governments undertake more and more social services, the level of government purchasing activity escalates. In The Netherlands, the state's purchasing office deals with more than 10,000 suppliers in 20 countries. About one-third of the products purchased by that agency are produced outside The Netherlands; 90 percent of foreign purchases are handled through Dutch representatives. The other 10 percent are purchased directly from producing companies.

Various patterns of representation are employed in dealing with *government-affiliated middlemen*—the company may deal directly with the government agency or may use an agent middleman. Only rarely are merchant middlemen employed to handle goods for sale to or through government agencies. In some countries, a foreign company

EXHIBIT 14–7 Characteristics of Middlemen in Foreign Countries

Type of Duties	Agent					Merchant		
	Broker	Manufacturer's Representative	Managing Agent	Comprador	Distributor	Dealer	Import Jobber	Wholesaler and Retailer
Take title	No	No	No	No	Yes	Yes	Yes	Yes
Take possession	No	Seldom	Seldom	Yes	Yes	Yes	Yes	Yes
Continuing relationship	No	Often	With buyer, not seller	Yes	Yes	Yes	No	Usually not
Share of foreign output	Small	All or part for one area	n.a.	All one area	All, for certain countries	Assignment area	Small	Very small
Degree of control by principal	Low	Fair	None	Fair	High	High	Low	Nil
Price authority	Nil	Nil	Nil	Partial	Partial	Partial	Full	Full
Represent buyer or seller	Either	Seller	Buyer	Seller	Seller	Seller	Self	Self
Number of principals	Many	Few	Many	Few	Small	Few major	Many	Many
Arrange shipping	No	No	No	No	No	No	No	No
Type of goods	Commodity and food	Manufactured goods	All types manufactured goods	Manufactured goods	Manufactured goods	Manufactured goods	Manufactured goods	Manufactured consumer goods
Breadth of line	Broad	Allied lines	Broad	Varies	Narrow to broad	Narrow	Narrow to broad	Narrow to broad
Handle competitive lines	Yes	No	Yes	No	No	No	Yes	Yes
Extent of promotion and selling effort	Nil	Fair	Nil	Fair	Fair	Good	Nil	Nil usually
Extend credit to principal	No	No	No	Sometimes	Sometimes	No	No	No
Market information	Nil	Good	Nil	Good	Fair	Good	Nil	Nil

Note: n.a. = not available.

435

or agent may deal only with the foreign trading organization; in turn, it attempts to represent the interests of the company to customers in that country. Such arrangements offer little control over the selling effort and are generally unsatisfactory.

Factors Affecting Choice of Channels

The international marketer needs a clear understanding of market characteristics and must have established operating policies before beginning the selection of channel middlemen. The following points should be addressed prior to the selection process.

1. Identify specific target markets within and across countries.
2. Specify marketing goals in terms of volume, market share, and profit margin requirements.
3. Specify financial and personnel commitments to the development of international distribution.
4. Identify control, length of channels, terms of sale, and channel ownership.

Once these points are established, selecting among alternative middlemen choices to forge the best channel can begin. Marketers must get their goods into the hands of consumers and must choose between handling all distribution or turning part or all of it over to various middlemen. Distribution channels vary depending on target market size, competition, and available distribution intermediaries.[47]

Key elements in distribution decisions include: (1) functions performed by middlemen (and the effectiveness with which each is performed), (2) cost of their services, (3) their availability, and (4) extent of control which the manufacturer can exert over middlemen activities.

Although the overall marketing strategy of the firm must embody the company's profit goals in the short and long run, channel strategy itself is considered to have six specific strategic goals. These goals can be characterized as the six Cs of channel strategy: cost, capital, control, coverage, character, and continuity.

In forging the overall channel-of-distribution strategy, each of the six Cs must be considered in building an economical, effective distribution organization within the long-range channel policies of the company.[48]

Cost

There are two kinds of channel cost: (1) the capital or investment cost of developing the channel and (2) the continuing cost of maintaining it. The latter can be in the form of direct expenditure for the maintenance of the company's selling force or in the form of margins, markup, or commissions of various middlemen handling the goods. Marketing costs (a substantial part of which is channel cost) must be considered as the entire difference between the factory price of the goods and the price the customer ultimately pays for the merchandise. The costs of middlemen include transporting and storing the goods, breaking bulk, providing credit, and local advertising, sales representation, and negotiations.

Despite the old truism that you can eliminate middlemen but you cannot eliminate their functions or cost, creative marketing does permit channel cost savings in many

---

[47] For a excellent study of maintaining control when using foreign-country middlemen, see Daniel C. Bello and David I. Gilliland, "The Effect of Output Controls, Process Controls, and Flexibility on Export Channel Performance," *Journal of Marketing,* January 1997, p. 22.

[48] An interesting study on standardizing the process of channel design and management can be found in Bert Rosenbloom, Trina Larsen, and Rajiv Mehta, "Global Marketing Channels and the Standardization Controversy," *Journal of Global Marketing,* Vol. 11(1), 1997, p. 49.

circumstances. Some marketers have found, in fact, that they can reduce cost by using shorter channels. Mexico's largest producer of radio and television sets has built annual sales of $36 million on its ability to sell goods at a low price because it eliminated middlemen, established its own wholesalers, and kept margins low. Conversely, many firms accustomed to using their own sales forces in large-volume domestic markets have found they must lengthen channels of distribution to keep costs in line with foreign markets.

Capital Requirement

The financial ramifications of a distribution policy are often overlooked. Critical elements are capital requirement and cash-flow patterns associated with using a particular type of middleman. Maximum investment is usually required when a company establishes its own internal channels, that is, its own sales force. Use of distributors or dealers may lessen the capital investment, but manufacturers often have to provide initial inventories on consignment, loans, floor plans, or other arrangements. Coca-Cola initially invested in China with majority partners that met most of the capital requirements. However, Coke soon realized that it could not depend on its local majority partners to distribute its product aggressively in the highly competitive, market-share-driven business of carbonated beverages. To assume more control of distribution it had to assume management control and that meant greater capital investment from Coca-Cola.[49] One of the highest costs of doing business in China is the capital required to maintain effective distribution.

Control

The more involved a company is with the distribution, the more control it exerts. A company's own sales force affords the most control but often at a cost that is not practical. Each type of channel arrangement provides a different level of control and, as channels grow longer, the ability to control price, volume, promotion, and type of outlets diminishes.[50] If a company cannot sell directly to the end user or final retailer, an important selection criterion of middlemen should be the amount of control the marketer can maintain.

Coverage

Another major goal is full-market coverage to (1) gain the optimum volume of sales obtainable in each market, (2) secure a reasonable market share, and (3) attain satisfactory market penetration. Coverage may be assessed on geographic and/or market segments. Adequate market coverage may require changes in distribution systems from country to country or time to time. Coverage is difficult to develop both in highly developed areas and in sparse markets—the former because of heavy competition and the latter because of inadequate channels.

Many companies do not attempt full-market coverage but seek significant penetration in major population centers. In some countries, two or three cities constitute the majority of the national buying power. For instance, 60 percent of the Japanese population lives in the Tokyo–Nagoya–Osaka market area, which essentially functions as one massive city.

At the other extreme are many developing countries with a paucity of specialized middlemen except in major urban areas. Those that do exist are often small, with traditionally high margins. In China, for example, the often-quoted 1 billion-person market

[49] "The Right Formula," *Business China*, February 19, 1996, p. 1.

[50] Aviv Shoham, Gregory M. Rose, and Fredric Kropp, "Conflict in International Channels of Distribution," *Journal of Global Marketing*, Vol. 11(2), 1997, p. 5.

CROSSING BORDERS 14-4

Are You Sure That's What "Not Satisfied" Means?

If customers are dissatisfied, they can get a full refund at any time, no questions asked—even if the returned bottles are empty. That is Amway's refund policy—a courtesy to customers and testament that it stands behind its products, and it is the same all over the world. But such capitalistic concepts are somewhat unfamiliar in China.

The best game in town for months among the rising ranks of Shanghai's entrepreneurs was an $84 investment for a box of soaps and cosmetics that they could sell as Amway distributors. Word of this no-lose proposition quickly spread, with some people repackaging the soap, selling it, and then turning in the containers for a refund. Others dispensed with selling altogether and scoured garbage bins instead—showing up at Amway's Shanghai offices with bags full of bottles to be redeemed.

One salesman got nearly $10,000 for eight sacks full of all kinds of empty Amway containers. And at least one barbershop started using Amway shampoos for free and returning each empty bottle for a full refund. In a few weeks refunds were totaling more than $100,000 a day. "Perhaps we were too lenient," said Amway's Shanghai chief.

Amway changed the policy, only to have hundreds of angry Amway distributors descend on the company's offices to complain, "We were cheated out of our money." Amway had to call a press conference to explain that it wasn't changing its refund policy, simply raising the standard for what is deemed dissatisfaction. If someone returns half a bottle, fine, but for empties Amway announced it would check records to see if the person had a pattern of return.

But the company didn't anticipate the unusual sense of entitlement it engendered in China. The satisfaction guaranteed policy doesn't spell out specifically what dissatisfaction means, something people in the Western world understand. "We thought that it would be understood here, too." The change in policy has left some dissatisfied. One distributor protested, "Don't open a company if you can't afford losses."

Source: Abstracted from Craig S. Smith, "In China, Some Distributors Have Really Cleaned Up with Amway," *The Wall Street Journal,* August 4, 1997, p. B1.

---

is, in reality, fewer than 25 to 30 percent of the population of the most affluent cities. Even as personal income increases in China, distribution inadequacies limit marketers in reaching all those who have adequate incomes. In both extremes, the difficulty of developing an efficient channel from existing middlemen plus the high cost of distribution may nullify efficiencies achieved in other parts of the marketing mix.

In China the problem is not too few middlemen but too many. The legacy of communism's highly regional production and distribution system demands that both producers and retail outlets interact with an excess of wholesalers. The contrast between a Watson's pharmacy in Hong Kong, where the distribution structure reflects the British system, and one in Shanghai clearly illustrates the problems facing a manufacturer. In Hong Kong the pharmacy gets its entire product line from just one wholesaler but in Shanghai the Watson's store must deal with more than 200. Shanghai outlets of the Hong Kong-based supermarket chain Park'N'Shop look to more than 1,200 domestic suppliers to fill their stores. Manufacturers are known to sell products directly to up to 40 wholesalers in a single city.[51]

---

[51] "Distribution Remains the Key Problem for Market Makers," *Business China,* May 13, 1996, p. 4.

Vietnamese consumers know and like American goods—but how does IBM control distribution? (REUTERS/ Claro Cortes IV/ARCHIVE PHOTOS)

To achieve coverage, a company may have to use many different channels—its own sales force in one country, manufacturers' agents in another, and merchant wholesalers in still another.

Character

The channel-of-distribution system selected must fit the character of the company and the markets in which it is doing business. Some obvious product requirements, often the first considered, relate to perishability or bulk of the product, complexity of sale, sales service required, and value of the product.

Channel commanders must be aware that channel patterns change; they cannot assume that once a channel has been developed to fit the character of both company and market, no more need be done. Great Britain, for example, has epitomized distribution through specialty-type middlemen, distributors, wholesalers, and retailers; in fact, all middlemen have traditionally worked within narrow product specialty areas. In recent years, however, there has been a trend toward broader lines, conglomerate merchandising, and mass marketing. The firm that neglects the growth of self-service, scrambled merchandising, or discounting may find it has lost large segments of its market because its channels no longer reflect the character of the market.

Continuity

Channels of distribution often pose longevity problems. Most agent middlemen firms tend to be small institutions. When one individual retires or moves out of a line of business, the company may find it has lost its distribution in that area. Wholesalers and especially retailers are not noted for their continuity in business either. Most middlemen have little loyalty to their vendors. They handle brands in good times when the line is making money, but quickly reject such products within a season or a year if they fail to produce during that period. Distributors and dealers are probably the most loyal middlemen, but even with them, manufacturers must attempt to build brand loyalty downstream in a channel lest middlemen shift allegiance to other companies or other inducements.

Locating, Selecting, and Motivating Channel Members

The actual process of building channels for international distribution is seldom easy, and many companies have been stopped in their efforts to develop international markets by their inability to construct a satisfactory system of channels.

Despite the chaotic condition of international distribution channels, international marketers can follow a logical procedure in developing channels. After general policy guides are established, marketers need to develop criteria for the selection of specific middlemen. Construction of the middleman network includes seeking out potential middlemen, selecting those who fit the company's requirements, and establishing working relationships with them.

In international marketing, the channel-building process is hardly routine. The closer the company wants to get to the consumer in its channel contact, the larger the sales force required. If a company is content with finding an exclusive importer or selling agent for a given country, channel building may not be too difficult; but if it goes down to the level of subwholesaler or retailer, it is taking on a tremendous task and must have an internal staff capable of supporting such an effort.[52]

Locating Middlemen

The search for prospective middlemen should begin with study of the market and determination of criteria for evaluating middlemen servicing that market. The company's broad policy guidelines should be followed, but expect expediency to override policy at times. The checklist of criteria differs according to the type of middlemen being used and the nature of their relationship with the company. Basically, such lists are built around four subject areas: (1) productivity or volume, (2) financial strength, (3) managerial stability and capability, and (4) the nature and reputation of the business. Emphasis is usually placed on either the actual or potential productivity of the middleman.

Setting policies and making checklists are easy; the real task is implementing them. The major problems are locating information to aid in the selection and choice of specific middlemen, and discovering middlemen available to handle one's merchandise. Firms seeking overseas representation should compile a list of middlemen from such sources as: (1) the U.S. Department of Commerce; (2) commercially published directories; (3) foreign consulates; (4) chamber-of-commerce groups located abroad; (5) other manufacturers producing similar but noncompetitive goods; (6) middlemen associations; (7) business publications; (8) management consultants; (9) carriers—particularly airlines; and (10) Internet-based services such as Unibex, a global business center (see Exhibit 14–8).

Selecting Middlemen

Finding prospective middlemen is less a problem than determining which of them can perform satisfactorily. Low volume or low potential volume hampers most prospects, many are underfinanced, and some simply cannot be trusted. In many cases, when a manufacturer is not well known abroad, the reputation of the middleman becomes the reputation of the manufacturer, so a poor choice at this point can be devastating.

Screening.   The screening and selection process itself should follow this sequence: (1) a letter including product information and distributor requirements in the native language to each prospective middleman; (2) a follow-up to the best respondents for more specific information concerning lines handled, territory covered, size of firm, number of

---

[52] Perry B. Newman, "The Nuts and Bolts of Product Distribution," *Trade & Culture*, May/July 1997, p. 52.

EXHIBIT 14–8   Unibex and Trade Compass—Examples of Internet Resources

The Internet provides a plethora of information and services available to the international marketer, some free and some fee-based. Here is a brief overview of two.

Unibex (http://www.unibex.com). Unibex Corporation is a Web-based import–export support service, which offers one-stop, on-line shopping for the full range of trade services, from market research to settlement. Subscribers can create offers, negotiate deals, and close business—all on-line. The Global Business Center has three internal sites: The Global Exhibit Center has over 16 million records for companies; The Global Exchange Center has specific business opportunities presented as offers from Unibex Exchange subscribers; and The Global Resource Center provides access to information from over 600 professional sources including company profiles, credit reports, market research, and other data.

Companies like Dun & Bradstreet (country market reports, identifying prospects, commercial risk management), Deloitte & Touche (verification services as to trading partner's credit line, product quality, and business references), and The Chase Manhattan Corporation (credit card and fund transfer services) are among the companies to be found on Unibex.

Trade Compass (http://www.tradecompass.com). Trade Compass is organized into four categories: World Infodesk provides a variety of information sources, U.S. laws and regulations, over 10,000 market reports, and country guides; International Business Center provides insurance, finance, and travel; Strategic Analysis provides market intelligence and trade consulting; and Trade Leads provides sources for projects and prospects, export offer services, and links to potential agents, distributors, joint venture partners, and licensing opportunities. Visit these sites for more detailed information. Both are fee-based but each does provide a free visit.

salespeople, and other background information; (3) check of credit and references from other clients and customers of the prospective middleman; and (4) if possible, a personal check of the most promising firms. It has become easier to obtain financial information on prospective middlemen via such Internet companies as Unibex (Exhibit 14–8), which provides access to Deloitte & Touche International and Dun & Bradstreet client information resources.

Experienced exporters suggest the only way to select a middleman is to go personally to the country and talk to ultimate users of your product to find whom they consider to be the best distributors. Visit each one before selecting the one to represent you; look for one with a key man who will take the new line of equipment to his heart and make it his personal objective to make the sale of that line a success. Further, exporters stress that if you cannot sign one of the two or three customer-recommended distributors, it might be better not to have a distributor in that country because having a worthless one costs you time and money every year and may cut you out when you finally find a good one.

The Agreement.   Once a potential middleman has been found and evaluated, there remains the task of detailing the arrangements with that middleman. So far the company has been in a buying position; now it must shift into a selling and negotiating position to convince the middleman to handle the goods and accept a distribution agreement that is workable for the company. Agreements must spell out specific responsibilities of the manufacturer and the middleman, including an annual sales minimum. The sales minimum serves as a basis for evaluation of the distributor, and failure to meet sales minimums may give the exporter the right of termination.

Some experienced exporters recommend that initial contracts be signed for one year only. If the first year's performance is satisfactory, they should be reviewed for renewal for a longer period. This permits easier termination, and more important, after a year of working together in the market, a more workable arrangement generally can be reached. At this point, success depends on a good product and company reputation, a skilled negotiator or salesperson, and an intimate knowledge of the market, the middleman, and the environment within which they work.

Motivating Middlemen

Once middlemen are selected, a promotional program must be started to maintain high-level interest in the manufacturer's products. A larger proportion of the advertising budget must be devoted to channel communications than in the United States because there are so many small middlemen to be contacted. Consumer advertising is of no value unless the goods are actually available. Furthermore, few companies operating in international business have the strong brand image in foreign environments that they have in their own country. In most countries, retailers and wholesalers are only minimally brand conscious, and yet, to a large degree, they control the success or failure of products in their countries.

The level of distribution and the importance of the individual middleman to the company determine the activities undertaken to keep the middleman alert. On all levels there is a clear correlation between the middleman's motivation and sales volume. The hundreds of motivational techniques that can be employed to maintain middleman interest and support for the product may be grouped into five categories: financial rewards, psychological rewards, communications, company support, and corporate rapport.

Obviously, financial rewards must be adequate for any middleman to carry and promote a company's products. Margins or commissions must be set to meet the needs of the middleman and may vary according to the volume of sales and the level of services offered. Without a combination of adequate margin and adequate volume, a middleman cannot afford to give much attention to a product.

Being human, middlemen and their salespeople respond to psychological rewards and recognition for the jobs that they are doing. A trip to the United States or to the parent company's home or regional office is a great honor. Publicity in company media and local newspapers also builds esteem and involvement among foreign middlemen.

In all instances, the company should maintain a continuing flow of communication in the form of letters, newsletters, and periodicals to all its middlemen. The more personal these are, the better. One study of exporters indicated that the more intense the contact between the manufacturer and the distributor, the better the performance from the distributor. More and better contact naturally leads to less conflict and a smoother working relationship. One factor that was partly responsible for the success of Smith, Kline, and French in building its own channels for Contac was a monthly periodical specifically published for the 1,200 wholesale salespeople dealing in that product.

A company can support its middlemen by offering advantageous credit terms, adequate product information, technical assistance, and product service. Such support helps build the distributors' confidence in the product and in their own ability to produce results.

Finally, considerable attention must be paid to the establishment of close rapport between the company and its middlemen. In addition to methods noted earlier, a company should be certain the conflicts that arise are handled skillfully and diplomatically. Bear in mind that all over the world business is a personal and vital thing to the people involved.[53]

Terminating Middlemen

When middlemen do not perform up to standards or when market situations change, requiring a company to restructure its distribution, it may be necessary to terminate relationships with certain middlemen or certain types of middlemen. In the United States, it is usually a simple action regardless of the type of middlemen; they are simply dismissed. However, in other parts of the world, the middleman typically has some legal protection that makes it difficult to terminate relationships. In Colombia, for example, if

---

[53] The importance of commitment in middlemen relations is discussed in Keysuk Kim and Gary L. Frazier, *International Marketing Review,* Vol. 13(1), 1996, p. 19.

you terminate an agent, you are required to pay 10 percent of the agent's average annual compensation, multiplied by the number of years the agent served, as a final settlement. In some countries, an agent cannot be dismissed without arbitration to determine whether the relationship should be ended. Some companies make all middlemen contracts for one year to avoid such problems. However, there have been cases where termination under these contracts has been successfully contested. Competent legal advice is vital when entering distribution contracts with middlemen. But as many experienced international marketers know, the best rule is to avoid the need to terminate distributors by screening all prospective middlemen carefully. A poorly chosen distributor may not only fail to live up to expectations but may also adversely affect future business and prospects in the country.

Controlling Middlemen

The extreme length of channels typically used in international distribution makes control of middlemen particularly difficult. Some companies solve this problem by establishing their own distribution systems; others issue franchises or exclusive distributorships in an effort to maintain control through the first stages of the channels. Until the various world markets are more highly developed, most international marketers cannot expect to exert a high degree of control over their international distribution operations. Although control is difficult, a company that succeeds in controlling distribution channels is likely to be a successful international marketer. Indeed, the desire for control is a major reason companies initiate their own distribution systems in domestic as well as in international business.

All control systems, of course, originate in corporate plans and goals. Marketing objectives must be spelled out both internally and to middlemen as explicitly as possible. Standards of performance should include sales volume objective, market share in each market, inventory turnover ratio, number of accounts per area, growth objective, price stability objective, and quality of publicity. Obviously the more specific the standards of performance, the easier they are to administer. Ease of administration, however, should not be confused with control.

Control over the system and control over middlemen are necessary in international business. The first relates to control over the distribution channel system per se. This implies overall controls for the entire system to be certain operations are within the cost and market coverage objectives. The specifics of distribution must also be controlled since pricing margins, transshipping, and other specific elements affect the overall system. Some manufacturers have lost control through "secondary wholesaling"—when rebuffed discounters have secured a product through unauthorized outlets. A company's goods intended for one country are sometimes diverted through distributors to another country where they compete with existing retail or wholesale organizations. A manufacturer may find some of the toughest competition from its own products that have been diverted through other countries or manufactured by subsidiaries and exported or bootlegged into markets the parent would prefer to reserve. Such action can directly conflict with exclusive arrangements made with distributors in other countries and may undermine the entire distribution system by harming relationships between manufacturers and their channels.

The second type of control is at the middleman level. When possible, the parent company should know (and to a certain degree control) the activities of middlemen in respect to their volume of sales, market coverage, services offered, prices, advertising, payment of bills, and even profit. All levels of the distribution system cannot be controlled to the same degree or by the same methods, but quotas, reports, and personal visits by company representatives can be effective in managing middleman activities at any level of the channel.

When control fails and the best interests of the company are not being met, the middleman must be terminated. As mentioned earlier, middleman separations can be painful and expensive in other countries. American business is free to hire and fire middlemen with relative abandon unless specific contractual relationships to the contrary exist. In most other countries of the world, however, there is an implied obligation to middlemen who have incurred expenses or helped build distribution.

Summary

From the foregoing discussion, it is evident that the international marketer has a broad range of alternatives for developing an economical, efficient, high-volume international distribution system. To the uninitiated, however, the variety may be overwhelming.

Careful analysis of the functions performed suggests more similarity than difference between international and domestic distribution systems; in both cases there are three primary alternatives of using agent middlemen, merchant middlemen, or government-affiliated middlemen. In many instances, all three types of middlemen are employed on the international scene, and channel structure may vary from nation to nation or from conti-

nent to continent. The neophyte company in international marketing can gain strength from the knowledge that information and advice are available relative to the structuring of international distribution systems and that many well-developed and capable middleman firms exist for the international distribution of goods. Within the past decade, international middlemen have become more numerous, more reliable, more sophisticated, and more readily available to marketers in all countries. Such growth and development offer an ever-wider range of possibilities for entering foreign markets, but the international businessperson should remember that it is just as easy for competitors.

Questions

1. Define:

distribution process	dealer
distribution structure	import jobber
distribution channel	Export Trading Company Act
facilitating agency	(ETC)
agent middlemen	export management company
merchant middlemen	(EMC)
home-country	Webb-Pomerene Export
middlemen	Association (WPEA)
trading company	foreign sales corporation
complementary	(FSC)
marketing	Structural Impediments
manufacturer's export	Initiative (SII)
agent (MEA)	Large-Scale Retail Store
Norazi agent	Law
manufacturer's agents	government-affiliated
foreign distributor	middlemen
foreign-country broker	e-commerce
managing agent	

2. Discuss the distinguishing features of the Japanese distribution system.

3. Discuss the ways Japanese manufacturers control the distribution process from manufacturer to retailer.

4. Describe the Large-Scale Retail Store Law found in Japan and show how the Structural Impediments Initiative (SII) is bringing about change in Japanese retailing.

5. "Japanese retailing may be going through a change similar to that which occurred in the United States after World War II." Discuss and give examples.

6. Discuss how the globalization of markets, especially Europe 1992, affects retail distribution.

7. To what extent, and in what ways, do the functions of domestic middlemen differ from those of their foreign counterparts?

8. Why is the EMC sometimes called an independent export department?

9. Discuss how physical distribution relates to channel policy and how they affect one another.

10. Explain how and why distribution channels are affected as they are when the stage of development of an economy improves.

11. In what circumstances is the use of an EMC logical?

12. Predict whether the Norazi agent is likely to grow or decline in importance.

13. In which circumstances are trading companies likely to be used?

14. How is distribution-channel structure affected by increasing emphasis on the government as a customer and by the existence of state trading agencies?

15. Review the key variables that affect the marketer's choice of distribution channels.

16. Account, as best you can, for the differences in channel patterns which might be encountered in a highly developed country and an underdeveloped country.

17. One of the first things companies discover about international channels-of-distribution patterns is that in most countries it is nearly impossible to gain adequate market coverage through a simple channel-of-distribution plan. Discuss.

18. Discuss the various methods of overcoming blocked channels.

19. What strategy might be employed to distribute goods effectively in the dichotomous small–large middleman pattern which characterizes merchant middlemen in most countries?

20. Discuss the economic implications of assessing termination penalties or restricting the termination of middlemen. Do you foresee such restrictions in the United States?

21. Discuss why Japanese distribution channels can be the epitome of blocked channels.

22. What are the two most important provisions of the Export Trading Company Act?

23. Why are WPEAs considered more risky from an antitrust perspective than are ETCs?

24. Eddie Bauer, a U.S. retailer, has a Web site in the U.S. at **http://www.eddiebauer.com** and is also included in the German Web Mall, **http://www.shopping24.de**. Visit both stores, the one in the U.S. and the one in Germany. Find the same article for sale in each store and compare the price. The German store will list the product in German marks but you can convert to U.S. dollars by visiting the Universal Currency Converter at **http://www.xe.net/ currency**. Does the article you selected cost more in Germany or the United States? What would be the delivered price to your hometown from both stores? Would it be to the advantage of the German to buy the article in the United States? For you to buy in Germany?

25. What are the benefits for a small retail company that wants to get international sales to engage in e-commerce? What are some of the problems that might be encountered? Suggest ways the problems can be overcome.

26. Assume you owned a small manufacturing company that produced widgets. How could you go about finding buyers for your widgets using the Internet? How could commercial Internet companies help you in expanding your business overseas using the Internet?

CHAPTER 15

EXPORTING AND LOGISTICS: SPECIAL ISSUES FOR THE SMALL BUSINESS

Chapter Learning Objectives

What you should learn from Chapter 15

- How the U.S. government helps exporters.
- The steps necessary to move goods across country borders.
- How various import restrictions are used politically.
- Means of reducing import taxes to remain competitive.
- The basic instruments for foreign commercial payments.
- The mechanics of export documents and their importance.
- The logistics and problems of the physical movement of goods.

An Export Sale: From Trade Show to Installation

February 3—The Trade Show and The Order

This is an account of the sale of paper-converting machinery, called a case maker, between Austin Inc., a New Hampshire-based manufacturer, and China Books, a Chinese book publisher. The story begins in Germany at DRUPA, the largest trade show in the world for the printing and paper market, which attracts more than 500,000 visitors each year. Mr. Kang, a representative for China Books, approaches Austin's booth and thinks, "Well, it took a week to find the Americans' booth, but watching their machines run has made it easier to see which equipment serves us best." Kang also muses that it was nice to meet the people who actually design and build the machine and to see how good the relationship is with their Far Eastern sales agent. Kang likes the equipment and signs an order for $500,000, which stipulates a 15 percent deposit ($75,000) and the pledge of a letter of credit for the rest.

March 3—The Financing

Once Mr. Kang returns home he applies for financing and an import license. The import license requirements make the whole deal a chicken-and-egg situation. Kang can't complete the financing until he gets the import license, and once he gets the license, he has only a specified time in which to complete the transaction.

July 3—Import License and the Letter of Credit

Four months later, Mr. Kang finally gets the import license. Because it is only good for six months, he has to be careful that the letter of credit's latest ship and expiry dates are within the effective time of the import permit. He applies for financing and the letter of credit.

In the U.S., Mr. Roberts, Austin Inc.'s controller, is concerned about the sale to China Books. "It's been more than four months since the sales department sent a copy of the signed order, and yet the company still hasn't received the 15 percent deposit," Roberts thinks. "Until they send the money, the customer isn't really committed. Nevertheless, the general manager has decided to release a stock machine to the manufacturing department to begin the necessary adaptations that the Chinese buyer wants. If the company doesn't begin work now, the equipment will not be ready as promised on the order. If this customer doesn't come through, the company will be stuck with a product finished to China Books' specifications—and no cash."

Over the past four months there has been a flurry of fax messages between Austin and China Books. Before the instructions for the letter of credit can be completed, details on the proposed shipment dates (before December 31), terms of sale (CIF-cost, insurance, and freight), and lists of ExIm Bank facilities from the trade resource center in Portsmouth, New Hampshire (China Books wants to finance part of the cost of the purchase with an ExIm Bank-guaranteed loan) have to be confirmed by both parties.

Roberts chooses CIF as the terms of sale so his company can select its regular freight forwarder to handle all the details. This is the company's first sale to China, so CIF gives Roberts some peace of mind—he won't have to rely on unknown people to collect on the letter of credit. It also means Austin Inc. controls selection of the shipping carrier and presumably will get the best shipping rate, too.

In addition, China Books was able to use one of the banks on the ExIm Bank list so the financing should go smoothly, and Roberts is satisfied that China Books will qualify for a loan.

August 1—Closing the Deal

The bank just called Mr. Kang with loan approval. "Now I've got to get wire instructions for the letter of credit and send the 15 percent deposit. They said delivery this December. I'll put down December 31 as the latest shipment date, with an expiry of January 31."

Roberts receives the request for wire instructions from Kang. "It will probably take about three weeks for everything to clear the bank," he thinks. "But the wire instructions must go out now since nothing can be shipped until the original letter of credit is received." Shipping had advised Roberts that if the machinery were shipped through Montreal, the company could avoid some stiff harbor maintenance fees that shipping out of New York would entail. Thus, when Roberts sends the wire instructions to Kang, he asks the Chinese buyer to permit shipment through Montreal.

September 4—Production and Shipment

Mr. Kang thinks to himself, "This faxing across the world is awkward but more efficient than telephoning, because while I'm writing in mid-morning, they're going to bed.

Now we just need to wait for the machine to get here." Kang begins planning for the integration of the new case maker into China Books' production line, and realizes they need to add a counterstacker option to the machine. The extra $20,000 should be worth the plant efficiency that will be gained. Mr. Kang starts to call the bank to have the counterstacker added to the letter of credit but hesitates and thinks, "I'm sick of bank rhetoric, so we'll just wire them the additional funds before shipment. The amendment to the letter of credit will cost too much time and money."

Because a lot rides on this order, Mr. Kang decides he will schedule a trip to New Hampshire for the final acceptance test. He wants to be sure the machine will handle the paper stock the company uses. No one wants the machine to be delivered and then find out it won't work the way they expect. Too many complications arise if the equipment is paid for and delivered and it needs major adjustments.

Back in New Hampshire, Roberts is checking details to make sure the case maker will be shipped on time. "Things are getting hectic—so much to do, so little time. If they expect to ship this year, the customer must accept the machine by December 16. That gives us a week to break it down and skid it (bolt the machine to a wooden pallet) and a week to get it on a boat. We have very little room for error because of the holidays. Besides, the customer wants special packing in desiccant because of climactic conditions. So we'll need to send the shipment to a packing specialist before it goes to port."

November 1—Letter of Credit

Roberts sends the original letter of credit to his freight forwarder by second-day air and includes the bank invoice forms and marine insurance certificate.

December 2—Final Inspection and Shipping Schedules

In China, Kang thinks, "Roberts faxed me possible vessel dates. They're going for Friday, December 20, out of Montreal, and I'm booked to be in New Hampshire December 11–15. The vessel arrives in Shanghai January 25. That would be just right. I hope they'll be ready for the test run because our material will be a challenge for them to run."

Meanwhile, Roberts is thinking, "I'm glad our general manager decided to release the case maker as a stock machine during the DRUPA show. He OK'd it because the China Books deal looked firm. We'd never be able to ship it this year otherwise. Kang seems like a decent person—

very bright. They got their material here two weeks ago for us to try, and since then manufacturing has been working hard trying to meet their specs. I hope we have a good week."

December 13—The Test Run

"The machine looks impressive," Kang observes after he watches the test run take place. "But I'm not convinced we can run a consistent 120 per minute. I insisted we come in tomorrow for one more demo. They're close, so if they don't quite do it, I won't pay the installation bill until we're comfortable with production at our plant. Besides, Roberts told me the boat would probably leave late, so they have a little extra time to get the container to the pier."

A second test run takes place the next day. Kang asks for a few minor adjustments but is otherwise satisfied that China Books will get consistently good production from Austin's case maker.

In his office, Roberts wonders why all foreign shipments seem to occur at year-end. "Cheryl at Fast Forwarder (Austin's freight forwarder) said we should be ready first thing on Monday, December 16, if we want to get the container on board for a December 31 sailing. Since nothing happens during the last week of the year, it needs to be there this Friday morning to be processed by the line. The steamship companies will probably start the holidays at noon on the 24th. Red alert! Call Cheryl immediately and tell her the 40-footer (container) must have a wooden floor—with no room for surprises!"

January 2—It's on the Way

Kang is ecstatic. "Roberts just faxed me the ocean bill of lading. The case maker was on board the vessel *Tiger Shark* December 31, with an estimated arrival in Shanghai on January 30. They just made it!"

Analysis

While this scenario may seem staggering, it is not intended to overwhelm you or make you wary of exporting. The point is that there are specific export mechanics that occur when goods are shipped from one country to another and while they may be tedious, you cannot escape them. The good news is, assistance is available for the exporter from government and private sources. As you read this chapter, identify each of the issues in this scenario and decide where you would find information and assistance.

Source: Abstracted from Robert R. Costa, "Tales of Foreign Sales," *Financial Executive*, Jan–Feb 1997, pp. 43–46.

EXHIBIT 15-1   The Exporting Process

Leaving the Exporting Country	*Physical Distribution*	*Entering the Importing Country*
Licenses	*International*	*Tariffs, taxes*
General	*shipping and*	*Nontariff barriers*
Validated	*logistics*	Standards
Documentation	*Packing*	Inspection
Export declaration	*Insurance*	Documentation
Commercial		Quotas
invoice		Fees
Bill of lading		Licenses
Consular invoice		Special certificates
Special certificates		Exchange permits
Other documents		Other barriers

Exporting is an integral part of all international business, whether the company is large or small, or markets in one country or is a global marketer. Goods manufactured in one country, destined for another, must be moved across borders to enter the distribution system of the target market.

Most countries control the movement of goods crossing their borders, whether leaving (exports) or entering (imports). Export and import documents, tariffs, quotas, and other barriers to the free flow of goods between independent sovereignties are requirements that must be met by either the exporter or importer, or both.[1]

In addition to selecting a target market, designing an appropriate product, establishing a price, planning a promotional program, and selecting a distribution channel, the international marketer must meet the legal requirements of moving goods from one country to another. The exporting process (see Exhibit 15–1) includes the licenses and documentation necessary to leave the country, an international carrier to transport the goods, and fulfillment of the import requirements necessary to get the shipment legally into another country.

Firms often have staff experienced in dealing with export mechanics but when confronted with unfamiliar situations or a task that is too burdensome, there are viable agencies, government and private, available to provide expert assistance. More and more, companies are finding it cost effective to outsource many of the exporting activities. These mechanics of exporting are sometimes considered the essence of foreign marketing; however, while their importance cannot be minimized, they should not be seen as the primary task of international marketing.

There are many reasons why countries impose some form of regulation and restriction on the exporting and importing of goods. *Export regulations* may be designed to conserve scarce goods for home consumption or to control the flow of strategic goods to actual or potential enemies. *Import regulations* may be imposed to protect health, conserve foreign exchange, serve as economic reprisals, protect home industry, or provide revenue in the form of tariffs. To comply with various regulations, the exporter may have to acquire export licenses or permits from the home country and ascertain that the potential customer has the necessary permits for importing the goods. The rules and regulations that cover the exportation and importation of goods and their payment, and the physical movement of those goods between countries, are the special concerns of this chapter.

---

[1] For a detailed explanation of export controls and their effect on commerce, see James B. Burnham, "The Heavy Hand of Export Controls," *Society,* January 11, 1997, p. 39.

Export Restrictions

Although the United States requires no formal or special license to engage in exporting as a business, permission or a license to export may be required for certain commodities and certain destinations. Export licensing controls apply to (1) exports of commodities and technical data from the United States; (2) reexports of U.S.-origin commodities and technical data from a foreign destination to another foreign destination; (3) U.S.-origin parts and components used in foreign countries to manufacture foreign products for exports; and, in some cases, (4) foreign products made from U.S.-origin technical data. Most items requiring special permission or a license for exportation are under the control of the *Bureau of Export Administration (BXA)* of the Department of Commerce.

The volume of exports and the number of companies exporting from the United States has grown spectacularly over the last decade. In the opinion of many observers, this growth has occurred in spite of the cumbersome rules and regulations imposed by the Department of Commerce. In an effort to further fuel the current export boom and to alleviate many of the problems and confusions of exporting, the Department of Commerce has published a revised set of export regulations, the first such revision in 42 years. These regulations, known as the *Export Administration Regulations (EAR)*, became mandatory at the beginning of 1997.[2] They are intended to speed up the export license granting process by removing a large number of items from specific export license control and by concentrating licensing on a very specific list of items, most of which affect either national security, nuclear nonproliferation, and/or chemical and biological weapons. Along with these changes comes a substantial increase in responsibility on the part of the exporter, since the exporter must now ensure that Export Administration Regulations are not violated.

Briefly, the revisions to the export control provisions of the EAR are:

1. A new country and commodity classification system has been devised, making it the exporter's responsibility to select the proper classification number for an item to be exported. The classification number, known as the *Export Control Classification Number (ECCN)*, will lead to a description in the *Commerce Control List (CCL)*, which will indicate the exportability status of the item.

2. The exporter must decide if there are end-use restrictions on the items due to the possibility of their use in the development of nuclear, chemical, and biological weapons. EAR-controlled products that can have a dual use are identified. *Dual-use products* are defined as products that can be used both in military and other strategic uses (e.g., nuclear) and commercial applications. Allergen Inc. had to pay $824,000 to settle a violation over exporting without a special license a medicine legally used as a muscle relaxant. The medicine's ingredients included botulinum, a lethal toxin that can be extracted and used in biological warfare. As a medicine, it could be shipped legally without a special license, but shipment to Iraq, where it could serve a dual-use in the manufacture of biological weapons, required a special license.[3]

3. The exporter now has responsibility to determine the ultimate end-customer and ultimate end-uses, regardless of who may be the initial buyer, or face the legal consequences of doing business with unauthorized trading partners. Under EAR, manufacturers and distributors are responsible for carefully screening end-users and end-uses of their exported products to determine if the final destination of the product

---

[2] "How to Cope with the New Export Regulations." *Laser Focus World,* December 1996, p. 81. For a detailed discussion of these and other issues in this section visit the Bureau of Export Administration (BXA) Web site at **http://www.bxa.doc.gov**.

[3] Barbara Marsh, "Allergen Settles Toxic-Export Allegations Penalty: U.S. Agency Said Irvine Firm Shipped to Iran an Agent That Could be Modified for Use in Biological Warfare," *Los Angeles Times,* January 27, 1998, p. D1.

is to an unapproved user or for an unapproved use. For example, China has shown a willingness to trade with countries of concern to the U.S. for weapons proliferation (e.g., India, Pakistan, and Iraq).[4] U.S. law requires firms to avoid shipments to China if the firm has knowledge that customers will use its products for illegal purposes[5] or resell the products to unauthorized end-users such as India or Iraq.

4. A special category for the control of encryption-related products has been established.[6] Encryption involves the scrambling of documents, computer programs, voice communications, and other data. There is concern that if encryption processes were exported without the U.S. government having the proper codes to unscramble encrypted data, its ability to monitor illegal activities such as money laundering or other nefarious activities would be impaired.[7]

The export control provisions of the Export Administration Regulations are intended to serve the national security, foreign policy, and nonproliferation interests of the United States and, in some cases, to carry out its international obligations. The EAR also includes some export controls to protect the United States from the adverse impact of the unrestricted export of commodities in short supply, such as Western cedar. Items that do not require a license for a specific destination can be shipped with the notation NLR (no license required) on the Shipper's Export Declaration.

Determining License Requirements

As mentioned earlier, the new Export Administration Regulations place on the exporter the responsibility of determining if a license for export is required. This can be a very involved task. For purposes of illustration, suppose you are an exporter of shotguns and you are beginning the process of fulfilling orders from Argentina (20-inch barrel shotguns), Australia (23-inch and 26-inch barrels), and Sudan (26-inch barrels).[8] The first step is to determine the proper Export Control Classification Number (ECCN) for the commodity to be exported. Each ECCN consists of five characters that identify its category, product group, type of control, and country group level (see Exhibit 15–2 for examples of CCL notations).

There are three general ways to determine a product's ECCN. First, if you are the exporter of the product but not its manufacturer, you can contact the manufacturer or developer to see if they already have an ECCN. The second method is to compare the general characteristics of your product to the Commerce Control List and find the most appropriate product category. Once the category is identified, you will then need to go through the entire category and identify the appropriate ECCN by determining the product's particular functions. This can be a time-consuming process.

The third way to determine your ECCN is to ask for a Classification Request from the Bureau of Export Administration (BXA). If requested for a given end-use, end-user, and/or destination, the BXA will also advise you on whether a license is required or likely to be granted for a particular transaction. This type of request is known as an Advisory Opinion. Note that an advisory opinion does not bind the BXA to issuing a license in the future, since government policies may change before a license is actually granted.

Once the proper ECCN has been obtained, the next step is to locate the number in the Commerce Control List. Upon consulting the CCL for your product's ECCN, 0A984, the following description is found:

---

[4] Jonathan S. Landay, "Is China Diverting High Technology to U.S. Foes?" *Christian Science Monitor,* July 11.1997. p. 1.

[5] Larry Christensen, "International Trade Regs: New Burdens for Shippers," *Transportation & Distribution.* November 1997, p. 80.

[6] For a complete discussion of encryption export controls, see "Commercial Encryption Export Controls," **http://www.bxa.doc.gov/encstart.htm**.

[7] "Encryption Proponents Ready Major Capitol Hill Offensive," *New Technology Week,* January 5.1998.

[8] This is an abbreviated example intended to illustrate the general idea of the steps necessary to determine licensing requirements.

.0A984—Shotguns, barrel length 18 inches (45.72 cm) inches or over; buckshot shotgun shells; except equipment used exclusively to treat or tranquilize animals, and except arms designed solely for signal, flare, or saluting use; and parts, n.e.s.

License Requirements	
Reason for Control:	CC, UN
Control(s)	Country Chart
CC applies to shotguns with a barrel length over 18 in. (45.72 cm) but less than 24 in. (60.96 cm) or buckshot shotgun shells controlled by this entry, regardless of end-user.	CC Column 1
CC applies to shotguns with a barrel length over 24 in. (60.96 cm), regardless of end-user.	CC Column 2
CC applies to shotguns with a barrel length over 24 in. (60.96 cm) if for sale or resale to police or law enforcement.	CC Column 3
UN applies to entire entry:	Rwanda

License Exceptions
LVS: N/A
GBS: N/A
CIV: N/A

List of Items Controlled
Unit: $ value
Related Controls: This entry does not control shotguns with a barrel length of less than 18 inches (45.72 cm). See 22 CFR part 121, Category I. These items are subject to the export licensing authority of the Department of State, Office of Defense Trade Controls.
Related Definitions: N/A
Items: The list of items controlled is contained in the ECCN heading.

This description shows that the reason for control is Crime Control (CC) and that there are different restrictions depending on the length of the shotgun barrel.

The third step in determining the licensing requirements for your export product is to consult the *Commerce Country Chart (CCC),* which helps you determine, based on the reason(s) for control associated with your item, if you need a license to export or re-export your item to a particular destination. The CCC contains licensing requirements based on destination and reason for control. In combination with the Commodity Control List, it allows you to determine whether a license is required for items on the CCL to any country in the world. In checking the CCC (Exhibit 15–3), you find Argentina, Australia, and Sudan all listed. Looking at the Crime Control (CC) columns and referencing back to the product description in the Commodity Control List, you see that the Argentine order for shotguns with 20-inch barrels falls into CC Column 1, where the x indicates that the order cannot be shipped without a special license. The Australian orders for 23-inch and 26-inch shotguns (CC Columns 1 and 2) do not require special licenses.

Finally, an examination of the Sudanese order for 26-inch shotguns reveals in CC Column 2 that the product can be exported without a special license; however, CC Column 3 indicates that if the guns are for sale or resale to police or law enforcement, a special license is required. Because you are not sure if the shotguns are to be resold, more information will be needed before the order can be processed. If you determine that the guns will not be resold to police or law enforcement, they can be shipped without special license; otherwise a license will have to be obtained before the shipment can take place.

EXHIBIT 15-2   Notations Used in the Commerce Control List (CCL) for Reasons for Control, Product Categories, and Product Groups

Reason for Control

AT	Anti-Terrorism	NP	Nuclear Nonproliferation
CB	Chemical & Biological Weapons	RS	Regional Stability
CC	Crime Control	SS	Short Supply
EI	Encryption Items	XP	Computers
MT	Missile Technology	SI	Significant Items
NS	National Security		

Product Categories

0-Nuclear Materials, Facilities and Equipment and Miscellaneous
1-Materials, Chemicals, "Microorganisms," and Toxins
2-Materials Processing
3-Electronics
4-Computers
5-Telecommunications and Information Security
6-Lasers and Sensors
7-Navigation and Avionics
8-Marine
9-Propulsion Systems, Space Vehicles, and Related Equipment

Groups

Within each category, items are arranged by group. Each category contains the same five groups. The letters A through E identify each group, as follows:

A-Equipment, Assemblies, and Components
B-Test, Inspection, and Production Equipment
C-Materials
D-Software
E-Technology

Source: Bureau of Export Controls, **http://www.bxa.gov**.

But the challenge is not yet over. An exporter also must establish that the end-user is not listed in the *Table of Denial Orders,*[9] which lists orders that currently deny export privileges; in other words, no shipments may be made to any person or company on the denial orders list.[10] In addition to checking the denial list, the exporter needs to make a general check to be sure there are no indications that the end-user's intentions will lead to an unauthorized use of the product. Unfortunately, you cannot always rely on the buyer's word. Sun Microsystems Inc. sold one of its supercomputers to a Hong Kong firm that claimed the computer was destined for a scientific institute near Beijing, an authorized sale. A trace of the final destination revealed that the computer was at a military research facility in China, an unauthorized end-use and end-user. Since Sun Microsystems monitored the sale and reported the diversion, there were no legal consequences. Negotiations between China and the U.S. government resulted in the return of the computer to Sun Microsystems.[11] To be alert to possible problems like the one Sun faced, the Export Administration Regulations suggest looking for red flags that your customer might be planning an unlawful diversion (Exhibit 15–4).

As is true of all the export mechanics that an exporter encounters, the details of exporting must be followed to the letter. Good record keeping verifying the steps undertaken in establishing the proper ECCN and the evaluation of the intentions of end-users

---

[9] An updated list of new denial orders can be found at **http://www.bxa.doc.gov/Text/1_denial.txt**.

[10] David J. Wallace, "Penalties Can Be Severe for Companies That Don't Keep Tabs on the 'Denied Persons List,'" *Denver Business Journal,* May 16, 1997, p. 25A.

[11] Jana Byron, "Focus on Enforcement," *The Export Practitioner,* October 15, 1997, p. 17.

EXHIBIT 15–3   Commerce Country Chart: Reasons for Control (Selected Countries)

Countries	Chemical & Biological Weapons			Nuclear Nonproliferation		National Security		Missile Tech	Regional Stability		Crime Control			Anti-Terrorism	
	CB Col 1	CB Col 2	CB Col 3	NP Col 1	NP Col 2	NS Col 1	NS Col 2	MT Col 1	RS Col 1	RS Col 2	CC Col 1	CC Col 2	CC Col 3	AT Col 1	AT Col 2
Albania	x*	x		x		x	x	x	x	x	x	x			
Argentina	x					x	x	x	x	x	x				
Australia	x					x		x	x						
Canada															
China	x	x	x	x		x	x	x	x	x	x		x		
France	x					x		x	x						
India	x	x	x	x	x	x	x	x	x	x	x		x		
Mexico	x	x		x		x	x	x	x	x	x		x		
Sudan	x	x		x		x	x	x	x	x	x		x	x	
Syria	x	x	x	x		x	x	x	x	x	x		x	x	x

* x = special license required.

Source: Abstracted from Commerce Country Chart, **http://chaos.fedworld.gov/bxa/search.cgi** (select EAR part name, 738spir), February 2, 1998.

Exhibit 15-4   Red Flags

The exporter has an important role to play in preventing exports and reexports that might be contrary to the national security and foreign policy interest of the United States and to ensure that the shipment is not in violation of Bureau of Export Administration regulations. To assist in determining the motives of a buyer, the BXA proposes these indicators as possible signs that a customer is planning an unlawful diversion:

1. The customer or purchasing agent is reluctant to offer information about the end-use of a product.

2. The product's capabilities do not fit the buyer's line of business; for example, a small bakery places an order for several sophisticated lasers.

3. The product ordered is incompatible with the technical level of the country to which the product is being shipped. For example, semiconductor-manufacturing equipment would be of little use in a country without an electronics industry.

4. The customer has little or no business background.

5. The customer is willing to pay cash for a very expensive item when the terms of the sale call for financing.

6. The customer is unfamiliar with the product's performance characteristics but still wants the product.

7. The customer declines routine installation, training, or maintenance services.

8. Delivery dates are vague, or deliveries are planned for out-of-the-way destinations.

9. A freight-forwarding firm is listed as the product's final destination.

10. The shipping route is abnormal for the product and destination.

11. Packaging is inconsistent with the stated method of shipment or destination.

12. When questioned, the buyer is evasive or unclear about whether the purchased product is for domestic use, export, or reexport.

Source: **http://www.bxa.doc.gov**.

and end-uses is important should a disagreement arise between the exporter and the Bureau of Export Administration. Penalties can entail denial of export privileges and/or fines. For example, a five-year denial of export privileges was imposed on William F. McNeil, of Pittsfield, MA, based on his conviction of illegally exporting 150 riot shields to Romania without the required export license. At the time of the shipment, the riot shields were controlled for export worldwide for foreign policy reasons.[12]

While the procedure described above may seem overwhelming on the first reading, in reality the system is well laid out and an exporter familiar with its regular customers and its product line will find the process simpler and more expeditious than before the Export Administration Regulations revisions.

ELAIN, STELA, and ERIC

Three other innovations have been designed to cut through the paperwork and time necessary to acquire export licenses. They have enabled the Department of Commerce to reduce in-house processing time from an average of 46 days to 14 days or less. First, once exporters have authorization, they are able to submit license applications electronically to the *Export License Application and Information Network (ELAIN)*, via the Internet, for all commodities except supercomputers for all free-world destinations. When approved, licensing decisions are electronically conveyed back to the exporters via the same electronic network.

The second innovation is the *System for Tracking Export License Applications (STELA)*. This is an automated voice response system that can be accessed using a

---

[12] From the "Denied Persons List," **http://www.bxa.doc.gov/Text/1_denial.txt**, January 15, 1998.

CROSSING BORDERS 15–1

Free Trade or Hypocrisy?

There is much written about trade problems between the United States, Japan, and other countries. The impression is that high tariffs, quotas, and export trade subsidies are restrictions used by other countries—that the United States is a free, open market, and the rest of the world's markets are riddled with trade restrictions.

But the United States does engage in trade restrictions. One estimate indicates that trade barriers affect over 25 percent of manufactured goods sold in the United States. The cost to U.S. consumers is $50 billion more annually than if there were not restrictions. Consider these samples of U.S. trade hypocrisy:

Quotas: Sugar quotas imposed by the United States result in a pound of sugar costing 35 cents in the United States versus 10 cents in Canada. U.S. beef quotas cost consumers $873 million a year in higher prices. There are quotas with all major apparel-producing nations and on steel with the European Community.

Tariffs: Tariffs average 26 percent of the value of imported clothing, 40 percent on orange juice, 40 percent on peanuts, 115 percent on low-priced watch parts imported from Taiwan, and 40 percent on leather imports from Japan.

Shipping: Foreign ships are barred from carrying passengers or freight between any two U.S. ports. Food donations to foreign countries cost an extra $100 million because they must be shipped on U.S. carriers.

Subsidies: The U.S. provided export subsidies of 111 percent to U.S. farmers for poultry exports, 78 percent for wheat and flour, and more than 100 percent for rice.

Customs: The Korean Customs Service has complained about barriers to trade with the United States. For example, Korean neckties were delayed for two months because a dog logo on the neckties was similar to the U.S. Disney logo. Korean fabric was denied because the export declaration stated the width of the fabric was between 44 and 46 inches when the actual width was 48 inches.

Many of these restrictions will begin to disappear as the provisions of the Uruguay Round GATT apply, but even then the U.S. will have tariffs, quotas, and other barriers to trade.

Sources: Abstracted from "Import Tariffs Imposed by a Protectionist U.S.," *Fortune,* December 12, 1991, p. 14; James Bovard, "A U.S. History of Trade Hypocrisy," *The Wall Street Journal,* March 8, 1994, p. 36; and Nicholas D. Kristof and Sheryl WuDunn, "Export, Asia's Key to Survival, Could Crash into U.S. Barriers," *The New York Times,* January 15, 1998, p. 1.

---

touch-tone phone. It provides applicants with the status of their license and classification applications and is available 24 hours a day, seven days a week. STELA can give exporters authority to ship their goods for those licenses approved without conditions. The third time- and paperwork reducer is the Electronic Request for Item Classification (ERIC). A supplementary service to ELAIN, ERIC allows an exporter to submit commodity classification requests electronically to the Bureau of Export Administration.

Import Restrictions

When an exporter plans a sale to a foreign buyer, it is necessary to examine the export restrictions of the home country as well as the import restrictions and regulations of the importing country.[13] Although the responsibility of import restrictions may rest with the

---

[13] See, for example, "Customary Practices," *Business Latin America,* January 13, 1997, p. 2.

CROSSING BORDERS 15-2

You Don't Look Like a Mexican Peanut to Me!

The government is serious about its import restrictions, especially on agricultural products. It doesn't look kindly, for example, on peanuts from China being shipped as Mexican peanuts. But how do you tell where peanuts, orange juice, and other agricultural products come from? With an "inductively coupled plasma mass spectrometer," that's how.

U.S. customs uses such a machine to determine whether a peanut headed for Safeway matches a peanut grown in Mexico or Georgia. It's a little like DNA testing for plants. While the machine can't tell exactly whether the peanuts come from a specific country, it can tell if the peanuts in a sample match a sample of peanuts known to come from a specific country. This process began about 10 years ago with the analyzing of frozen orange juice. Since frozen orange juice from different countries has different tariff schedules, transshipment through a lower-tariff country can make a big difference in tariffs paid.

In a little over a year, with the help of the machine, U.S. Customs was able to build a case of "dumping" against Chinese garlic, an illegal transshipment case against Argentine peanuts, and a case against a California coffee distributor who was adulterating Hawaiian Kona coffee with cheaper Central American beans and selling the result as pure Kona.

Source: Guy Gugliotta, "High-Tech Trade Enforcement Tracks Peanuts Across Borders," *Washington Post,* December 4, 1997, p. A21.

importer, the exporter does not want to ship goods until it is certain that all import regulations have been met. Goods arriving without proper documentation can be denied entry.

Besides import tariffs there are many other trade restrictions imposed by the foreign country.[14] A few examples of the 30 basic barriers to exporting considered important by *Business International* include: (1) import licenses, quotas, and other quantitative restrictions; (2) currency restrictions and allocation of exchange at unfavorable rates on payments for imports; (3) devaluation; (4) prohibitive prior import deposits, prohibition of collection-basis sales, and insistence on cash letters of credit; (5) arbitrarily short periods in which to apply for import licenses; and (6) delays resulting from pressure on overworked officials or from competitors' influence on susceptible officials.

The various market barriers that exist among members of the European Community create a major impediment to trade.[15] One study of 20,000 EC exporting firms indicated that the most troublesome barriers were administrative roadblocks, border-crossing delays, and capital controls. One such barrier was imposed by the French government against Japanese VCRs. All Japanese VCRs were directed to land only at one port where only one inspector was employed; hence, just 10 to 12 VCRs could enter France each day.

As the EC becomes a single market, the elimination of many of the barriers that exist among member countries will be erased, although not as rapidly as some expect.[16] The single European market will no doubt make trade easier among its member

---

[14] For a look at some of the import barriers in Korea, see Louis Hau, "Drug Makers Try to Surmount South Korean Import Barriers," *The News & Observer,* January 25, 1998.

[15] Michael Sanchez Rydelski, "German Catch-All Controls and the EU," *The Export Practitioner,* July 15, 1997, p. 10.

[16] "Virtual Warehousing: A New Pan-European Approach May Alleviate Customs Headaches," *Business Europe,* April 23, 1997, p. 5.

countries, but there is rising concern that a fully integrated EC will become a market with even stronger protectionist barriers toward nonmember countries.

The most frequently encountered trade restrictions, besides tariffs, are such nontariff barriers (NTBs) as exchange permits, quotas, import licenses, boycotts, standards, and voluntary agreements.

Tariffs.   Recall that tariffs are the taxes or customs duties levied against goods imported from another country. All countries have tariffs for the purpose of raising revenue and protecting home industries from competition of foreign-produced goods. Tariff rates are based on value or quantity or a combination of both. In the United States, for example, the types of customs duties used are classified as: (1) *ad valorem duties*, which are based on a percentage of the determined value of the imported goods; (2) *specific duties*, a stipulated amount per unit weight or some other measure of quantity; and (3) a *compound duty*, which combines both specific and ad valorem taxes on a particular item, that is, a tax per pound plus a percentage of value. Because tariffs frequently change, published tariff schedules for every country are available to the exporter on a current basis.[17]

Exchange Permits.   Especially troublesome to exporters are exchange restrictions placed on the flow of currency by some foreign countries. To conserve scarce foreign exchange and alleviate balance-of-payment difficulties, many countries impose restrictions on the amount of their currency they will exchange for the currency of another country—in effect, they ration the amount of currency available to pay for imports. Exchange controls may be applied in general to all commodities, or a country may employ a system of multiple exchange rates based on the type of import. Essential products might have a very favorable exchange rate, while nonessentials or luxuries would have a less favorable rate of exchange. South Africa, for example, has a two-tier system for foreign exchange, Commercial Rand and Financial Rand. At times, countries may not issue any exchange permits for certain classes of commodities.

In countries that use exchange controls, the usual procedure is for the importer to apply to the control agency of the importing country for an import permit; if the control agency approves the request, an import license is issued. On presentation to the proper government agency, the import license can be used to have local currency exchanged for the currency of the seller.

Receiving an import license, or even an exchange permit, however, is not a guarantee that a seller can exchange local currency for the currency of the seller. If local currency is in short supply—a chronic problem in some countries—other means of acquiring home-country currency are necessary. For example, in a transaction between the government of Colombia and a U.S. truck manufacturer, there was a scarcity of U.S. currency to exchange for the 1,000 vehicles Colombia wanted to purchase. The problem was solved through a series of exchanges. Colombia had a surplus of coffee that the truck manufacturer accepted and traded in Europe for sugar; the sugar was traded for pig iron, and finally the pig iron for U.S. dollars.

This somewhat complicated but effective countertrade transaction has become more common. As will be discussed in Chapter 18, countertrade deals are often a result of the inability to convert local currency into home-country currency and/or the refusal of a government to issue foreign exchange.

Quotas.   Countries may also impose limitations on the quantity of certain goods imported during a specific period. These quotas may be applied to imports from specific

[17] The entire Harmonized Tariff Schedule of the United States (HTS) can be downloaded or there is an interactive tariff database at USITC: Tariff Affairs and Related Matters at **http://usitc.gov/taffairs.htm**. Quotas and other relevant information can be found at the Web site of the U.S. Customs Service at **http://www.customs.ustreas.gov**.

countries or from all foreign sources in general. The United States, for example, has specific quotas for importing sugar, wheat, cotton, tobacco, textiles, and peanuts; in the case of some of these items, there also are limitations on the amount imported from specific countries.

The most important reasons to set quotas are to protect domestic industry and to conserve foreign exchange. Some importing countries also set quotas to ensure an equitable distribution of a major market among friendly countries.

Import Licenses.   As a means of regulating the flow of exchange and the quantity of a particular imported commodity, countries often require import licenses. The fundamental difference between quotas and import licenses as a means of controlling imports is the greater flexibility of import licenses over quotas. Quotas permit importing until the quota is filled; licensing limits quantities on a case-by-case basis.

Boycott.   A boycott is an absolute restriction against trade with a country, or trade of specific goods. Boycotts sanctioned by the U.S. government must be honored by American firms; however, a U.S. company participating in an unauthorized boycott could be fined for violating the U.S. antiboycott law. For example, U.S. companies are prohibited from participating in the Arab League boycott on trade with Israel. The Arab League boycott has three levels: a primary boycott bans direct trade between Arab states and Israel; a secondary boycott bars Arab governments from doing business with companies that do business with Israel; and a tertiary boycott bans Arab governments from doing business with companies that do business with companies doing business with Israel.

U.S. law forbids U.S. firms to comply with such unauthorized boycotts. If an American firm refuses to trade with Israel in order to do business with an Arab nation, or in any other way participates in the Arab League boycott, it faces stiff fines. For example, a $298,000 civil penalty was imposed on Grove Europe Limited for 120 alleged violations of the antiboycott provisions of the Export Administration Act and Regulations. The Department of Commerce alleged that in connection with sales to Libya, Grove Europe on 15 occasions agreed to comply with the Arab boycott of Israel and knowingly agreed to refuse to do business with Israel or with individuals or companies known or believed to be blacklisted.

Although the six Gulf Cooperation Council nations lifted the boycott in 1994, it remains in effect for the other Arab states. Boycotts are the most restrictive because they ban all trade, whereas other types of restrictions permit some trade.

Standards.   Like many nontariff barriers, standards have legitimacy. Health standards, safety standards, and product quality standards are necessary to protect the consuming public, and imported goods are required to comply with local laws. Unfortunately, standards can also be used to slow down or restrict the procedures for importing to the point that the additional time and cost required to comply become, in effect, trade restrictions.

Safety standards are a good example. Most countries have safety standards for electrical appliances and require that imported electrical products meet local standards. However, safety standards can be escalated to the level of an absolute trade barrier by manipulating the procedures used to determine if products meet the standards. The simplest process for the importing nation is to accept the safety standard verification used by the exporting country, such as Underwriters Laboratories in the United States. If the product is certified for sale in the United States, and if U.S. standards are the same as the importing country's, then U.S. standards and certification are accepted and no further testing is necessary. Most countries not interested in using standards as a trade barrier follow such a practice.

The extreme situation occurs when the importing nation does not accept the same certification procedure required by the exporting nation and demands all testing be done in the importing country. Even more restrictive is the requirement that each item be tested instead of accepting batch testing. When such is the case, the effect is the same as a boycott. Until recently, Japan required all electrical consumer products to be tested in Japan or tested in the United States by Japanese officials. Japan now accepts the Underwriters Laboratories' safety tests, except for medical supplies and agricultural products, which still must be tested in Japan.

Voluntary Agreements.   Foreign restrictions of all kinds abound and the United States can be counted among those governments using restrictions. For over a decade, U.S. government officials have been arranging "voluntary" agreements with the Japanese steel and automobile industries to limit sales to the United States. Japan entered these voluntary agreements under the implied threat that if it does not voluntarily restrict the export of automobiles or steel to an agreed limit, the United States might impose even harsher restrictions including additional import duties. Similar negotiations with the governments of major textile producers have limited textile imports as well. It is estimated that the cost of tariffs, quotas, and voluntary agreements on all fibers is as much as $40 billion at the retail level. This works out to be a hidden tax of almost $500 a year for every American family.

Other Restrictions.   Restrictions may be imposed on imports of harmful products, drugs, medicines, and immoral products and literature. Products must also comply with government standards set for health, sanitation, packaging, and labeling. For example, in the Netherlands all imported hen and duck eggs must be marked in indelible ink with the country of origin; in Spain, imported condensed milk must be labeled to show fat content if it is less than 8 percent fat; and in the European Community, strict import controls have been placed on beef and beef products imported from the U.K. because of mad-cow disease.[18]

Failure to comply with regulations can result in severe fines and penalties. Because requirements vary for each country and change frequently, regulations for all countries must be consulted individually and on a current basis. *Overseas Business Reports,* issued periodically by the Department of Commerce, provides the foreign marketer with the most recent foreign trade regulations of each country as well as U.S. regulations regarding each country.

While sanitation certificates, content labeling, and other such regulations serve a legitimate purpose, countries can effectively limit imports by using such restrictions as additional trade barriers. Most of the economically developed world encourages foreign trade and works through the World Trade Organization (WTO) to reduce tariffs and nontariff barriers to a reasonable rate. Yet in times of economic recession, countries revert to a protectionist philosophy and seek ways to restrict the importing of goods. Nontariff barriers have become one of the most potent ways for a country to restrict trade. The elimination of nontariff barriers has been a major concern of GATT negotiations in both the Tokyo and Uruguay Rounds and continues with the WTO.

Terms of Sale

Terms of sale, or trade terms, differ somewhat in international marketing from those used in the United States. In U.S. domestic trade, it is customary to ship FOB (free on board, meaning that the price is established at the door of the factory), freight collect, prepaid, and/or COD (cash, or collect, on delivery). International trade terms often sound similar to those used in domestic business but generally have different meanings. International terms indicate how buyer and seller divide risks and obligations and, there-

---

[18] "E.U./U.K. Beef-2: Link to Risk Material Ban Seen," *Dow Jones Commodities Service,* January 13, 1998.

CROSSING BORDERS 15-3

Underwear, Outerwear, and Pointed Ears— What Do They Have in Common?

What do underwear, outerwear, and pointed ears have in common? Quotas, that's what!

Call the first one The Madonna Effect. Madonna, the voluptuous pop star, affected the interpretation of outerwear/underwear when the ever-vigilant U.S. Customs Service stopped a shipment of 880 bustiers at the U.S. border. The problem was quota and tariff violations. The shipper classified them as underwear, which comes into the United States without quota and tariff. A quota controls outerwear imports, however, and the Customs official classified the fashion item inspired by Madonna as "outerwear" and demanded the appropriate quota certificates.

"It was definitely outerwear. I've seen it; and I've seen the girls wearing it, and they're wearing it as outerwear." It took the importer three weeks to obtain sufficient outerwear quota allowances to cover the shipment; by that time, several retailers had canceled their orders.

Call the second The Vulcan Effect. EU officials have applied the Vulcan death grip to Star Trek hero Spock. Likenesses of the pointed-eared Spock and other "nonhuman creatures" have fallen victim to an EU quota on dolls made in China. The EU Council of Ministers slapped a quota equivalent to $81.7 million on nonhuman dolls from China—but it left human dolls alone.

British customs officials are in the unusual position of debating each doll's humanity. They have blacklisted teddy bears but cleared Batman and Robin. And although they have turned away Spock because of his Vulcan origins, they have admitted Star Trek's Captain Kirk. The Official Fan Club for Star Trek said the customs officials "ought to cut Spock some slack" because his mother, Amanda, was human. But Britain's customs office said, "We see no reason to change our interpretation. You don't find a human with ears that size."

Sources: Abstracted from Rosalind Resnick, "Busting Out of Tariff Quotas," *North American International Business* (now published as *International Business*), February 1991, p. 10; and Dana Milbank, "British Customs Officials Consider Mr. Spock Dolls to Be Illegal Aliens," *The Wall Street Journal*, August 2, 1994, p. B1.

---

fore, the costs of specific kinds of international trade transactions.[19] When quoting prices, it is important to make them meaningful. The most commonly used international trade terms include:

CIF—(cost, insurance, freight) to a named overseas port of import. A CIF quote is more meaningful to the overseas buyer because it includes the costs of goods, insurance, and all transportation and miscellaneous charges to the named place of debarkation.

C&F—(cost and freight) to named overseas port. The price includes the cost of the goods and transportation costs to the named place of debarkation. The cost of insurance is borne by the buyer.

FAS—(free alongside) at a named U.S. port of export. The price includes cost of goods and charges for delivery of the goods alongside the shipping vessel. The buyer is responsible for the cost of loading onto the vessel, transportation, and insurance.

---

[19] F. John Mathis, "Export Payment Terms Adjust the Risk to Exporters and the Cost to Importers," *Business America*, October 1997, p. 26.

Exhibit 15-5   Who's Responsible for Costs under Various Terms?

Cost Items/Terms	FOB (Free on Board) Inland Carrier at Factory	FOB (Free on Board) Inland Carrier at Point of Shipment	FAS (Free Along Side) Vessel or Plane at Port of Shipment	CIF (Cost, Insurance, Freight) at Port of Destination
Export packing*	Buyer	Seller	Seller	Seller
Inland freight	Buyer	Seller	Seller	Seller
Port charges	Buyer	Buyer	Seller	Seller
Forwarder's fee	Buyer	Buyer	Buyer	Seller
Consular Fee	Buyer	Buyer	Buyer	Buyer†
Loading on vessel or plane	Buyer	Buyer	Buyer	Seller
Ocean freight	Buyer	Buyer	Buyer	Seller
Cargo insurance	Buyer	Buyer	Buyer	Seller
Customs duties	Buyer	Buyer	Buyer	Buyer
Ownership of goods passes	When goods onboard an inland carrier (truck, rail, etc.) or in hands of inland carrier	When goods unloaded by inland carrier	When goods alongside carrier, in hands of air or ocean carrier	When goods on board air or ocean carrier *at port of shipment*

* Who absorbs export packing? This charge should be clearly agreed on. Charges are sometimes controversial.

† The seller has responsibility to arrange for consular invoices (and other documents requested by buyer's government). According to official definitions, buyer pays fees, but sometimes as a matter of practice, seller includes fees in quotations.

FOB—(free on board) at a named inland point of origin, at a named port of exportation, or at a named vessel and port of export. The price includes the cost of the goods and delivery to the place named.

EX—(named port of origin). The price quoted covers costs only at the point of origin (example, EX Factory). All other charges are the buyer's concern.

A complete list of terms and their definitions can be found in *Incoterms,* a booklet published by the International Chamber of Commerce.[20] It is important for the exporter to understand exactly the meanings of terms used in quotations. A simple misunderstanding regarding delivery terms may prevent the exporter from meeting contractual obligations or make that person responsible for shipping costs he or she did not intend to incur. Exhibit 15–5 indicates who is responsible for a variety of costs under various terms.

Getting Paid: Foreign Commercial Payments

The sale of goods in other countries is further complicated by additional risks encountered when dealing with foreign customers.[21] There are risks from inadequate credit reports on customers; problems of currency exchange controls, distance, and different legal systems; and the cost and difficulty of collecting delinquent accounts which require a different emphasis on payment systems. In U.S. domestic trade, the typical payment procedure for established customers is an *open account*—that is, the goods are delivered and the customer is billed on an end-of-the-month basis. However, the most frequently used term of payment in foreign commercial transactions for both export and import sales is a letter of credit, followed closely in importance by commercial dollar drafts or

---

[20] A list of Incoterms can be found at the Web site of I-Trade **http://www.i-trade.com** (select "Index of Free Services"). This is a good site to bookmark for a collection of information on exporting from different sources.

[21] See for example, "Collections," *International Business,* from *Inc. Online,* **http://www.inc.com/ international/recommended_readings/04971071**.

bills of exchange drawn by the seller on the buyer. Internationally, open accounts are reserved for well-established customers, and cash in advance is required of only the poorest credit risks or when the character of the merchandise is such that not fulfilling the terms of the contract may result in heavy loss. Because of the time required for shipment of goods from one country to another, advance payment of cash is an unusually costly burden for a potential customer and places the seller at a definite competitive disadvantage.

Terms of sales are typically arranged between the buyer and seller at the time of the sale. The type of merchandise, amount of money involved, business custom, credit rating of the buyer, country of the buyer, and whether the buyer is a new or old customer must be considered in establishing the terms of sale. The five basic payment arrangements—(1) letters of credit, (2) bills of exchange, (3) cash in advance, (4) open accounts, and (5) forfaiting—are discussed in this section.

Letters of Credit

Export *letters of credit* opened in favor of the seller by the buyer handle most American exports. Letters of credit shift the buyer's credit risk to the bank issuing the letter of credit. When a letter of credit is employed, the seller ordinarily can draw a draft against the bank issuing the credit and receive dollars by presenting proper shipping documents. Except for cash in advance, letters of credit afford the greatest degree of protection for the seller.

The procedure for a letter of credit begins with completion of the contract. See Exhibit 15–6 for the steps in a letter of credit transaction. Then the buyer goes to a local bank and arranges for the issuance of a letter of credit; the buyer's bank then notifies its correspondent bank in the seller's country that the letter has been issued. After meeting the requirements set forth in the letter of credit, the seller can draw a draft against the credit (in effect, the bank issuing the letter) for payment for the goods. The precise conditions of the letter of credit are detailed in it and usually also require presentation of certain documents along with the draft before the correspondent bank will honor it. The documents usually required are: (1) commercial invoice, (2) consular invoice (when requested), (3) clean bill of lading, and (4) insurance policy or certificate.

Letters of credit can be revocable or irrevocable. An *irrevocable letter of credit* means that once the seller has accepted the credit, the buyer cannot alter it in any way, without permission of the seller. Added protection is gained if the buyer is required to confirm the letter of credit through a U.S. bank. This irrevocable, confirmed letter of credit means that a U.S. bank accepts responsibility to pay regardless of the financial situation of the buyer or foreign bank. From the seller's viewpoint, this eliminates the foreign political risk and replaces the commercial risk of the buyer's bank with that of the confirming bank. The confirming bank assures payment against a confirmed letter of credit. As soon as the documents are presented to the bank, the seller receives payment.[22]

The international department of a major U.S. bank cautions that a letter of credit is not a guarantee of payment to the seller. Rather, payment is tendered only if the seller complies exactly with the terms of the letter of credit. Since all letters of credit must be exact in their terms and considerations, it is important for the exporter to check the terms of the letter carefully to be certain that all necessary documents have been acquired and properly completed. Some of the discrepancies found in documents that cause delay in honoring drafts or letters of credit include:

- Insurance defects such as inadequate coverage, no endorsement or countersignature, and a dating later than the bill of lading.

---

[22] For additional examples of the process followed in a letter of credit, see Steve Anderson, "Russia, Despite Woes, Offers Credits," *Idaho Business Review,* March 31, 1997, p. 1A.

- Bill-of-lading defects include the bill lacking an "on board" endorsement or signature of carrier, missing an endorsement, or failing to specify prepaid freight.
- Letter-of-credit defects arise if it has expired or is exceeded by the invoice figure, or when including unauthorized charges or disproportionate charges.
- Invoice defects relate to missing signatures, or failure to designate terms of shipment (C&F, CIF, FAS) as stipulated in the letter of credit.
- Other problems occur with documents that are missing, stalemated, or inaccurate.

Bills of Exchange

Another important international commercial payment form is *bills of exchange* drawn by sellers on foreign buyers. In letters of credit, the credit of one or more banks is involved, but in the use of bills of exchange (also known as dollar drafts), the seller assumes all risk until the actual dollars are received. The typical procedure is for the seller to draw a draft on the buyer and present it with the necessary documents to the seller's bank for collection. The documents required are principally the same as for letters of credit. On receipt of the draft, the U.S. bank forwards it with the necessary documents to a correspondent bank in the buyer's country; then the buyer is presented with the draft for acceptance and immediate or later payment. With acceptance of the draft, the buyer receives the properly endorsed bill of lading that is used to acquire the goods from the carrier.

Bills of exchange or dollar drafts can have one of three time periods—sight, arrival, or date. A *sight draft* requires acceptance and payment on presentation of the draft and often before arrival of the goods. An *arrival draft* requires payment be made on arrival of the goods. Unlike the other two, a *date draft* has an exact date for payment and in no way is affected by the movement of the goods. There may be time designations placed on sight and arrival drafts stipulating a fixed number of days after acceptance when the obligation must be paid. Usually this period is 30 to 120 days, thus providing a means of extending credit to the foreign buyer.

Dollar drafts have advantages for the seller because an accepted draft frequently can be discounted at a bank for immediate payment. Banks, however, usually discount drafts only with recourse; that is, if the buyer does not honor the draft, the bank returns it to the seller for payment. An accepted draft is firmer evidence in the case of default and subsequent litigation than an open account would be.[23]

Cash in Advance

The volume of international business handled on a cash-in-advance basis is not large. Cash places unpopular burdens on the customer and typically is used when credit is doubtful, when exchange restrictions within the country of destination are such that the return of funds from abroad may be delayed for an unreasonable period, or when the American exporter for any reason is unwilling to sell on credit terms.

Although full payment in advance is employed infrequently, partial payment (from 25 to 50 percent) in advance is not unusual when the character of the merchandise is such that an incomplete contract can result in heavy loss. For example, complicated machinery or equipment manufactured to specification or special design would necessitate advance payment, which would be, in fact, a nonrefundable deposit.

Open Accounts

Sales on open accounts are not generally made in foreign trade except to customers of long standing with excellent credit reputations or to a subsidiary or branch of the

---

[23] Parts of this section are taken from "International Trade Finance Services—Collections, Letters of Credit, Acceptances," Worldwide Banking Department, The First National Bank of Chicago.

EXHIBIT 15-6   A Letter-of-Credit Transaction

Here is what typically happens when payment is made by an irrevocable letter of credit confirmed by a U.S. bank.

1. After you and your customer agree on the terms of sale, the customer arranges for his or her bank to open a letter of credit. (Delays may be encountered if, for example, the buyer has "insufficient funds." In many developing countries, foreign currencies, such as the U.S. dollar, may be scarce.)

2. The buyer's bank prepares an irrevocable letter of credit, including all instructions.

3. The buyer's bank sends the irrevocable letter of credit to a U.S. bank requesting confirmation. (Foreign banks with more than one U.S. correspondent bank generally select the nearest one to the exporter.)

4. The U.S. bank prepares a letter of confirmation to forward to you, along with the irrevocable letter of credit.

5. You review carefully all conditions in the letter of credit, in particular, shipping dates. If you cannot comply, alert your customer at once. (Your freight forwarder can help advise you.)

6. You arrange with your freight forwarder to deliver your goods to the appropriate port or airport. If the forwarder is to present the documents to the bank (a wise move for new-to-export firms), the forwarder will need copies of the letter of credit.

7. After the goods are loaded, the forwarder completes the necessary documents (or transmits the information to you).

8. You (or your forwarder) present documents indicating full compliance to the U.S. bank.

9. The bank reviews the documents. If they are in order, it issues you a check. The documents are airmailed to the buyer's bank for review and transmitted to the buyer.

10. The buyer (or agent) gets the documents that may be needed to claim the goods.

Source: "A Basic Guide to Exporting," U.S. Department of Commerce, International Trade Administration, Washington, D.C.

exporter. Open accounts obviously leave sellers in a position where most of the problems of international commercial finance work to their disadvantage. It is generally recommended that sales on open account not be made when it is the practice of the trade to use some other method, when special merchandise is ordered, when shipping is hazardous, when the country of the importer imposes difficult exchange restrictions, or when political unrest requires additional caution.

Forfaiting

Inconvertible currencies and cash-short customers can kill an international sale if the seller cannot offer long-term financing. Unless the company has large cash reserves to finance its customers, a deal may be lost. *Forfaiting* is a financing technique for such a situation.[24]

In a forfait transaction, the seller makes a one-time arrangement with a bank or other financial institution to take over responsibility for collecting the account receivable. The basic idea of a forfaiting transaction is fairly simple. The exporter offers a long financing term to its buyer, but intends to sell its account receivable, at a discount, for immediate cash. The forfaiter buys the debt, typically a promissory note or bill of exchange, on a nonrecourse basis. Once the exporter sells the paper, the forfaiter assumes the risk of collecting the importer's payments. The forfaiting institution also assumes any political risk present in the importer's country.

While forfaiting is similar to factoring, it is not the same. In factoring a company has an ongoing relationship with a bank that routinely buys its short-term accounts

---

[24] Ricardo Beroiza, "Forfaiting in the Emerging Markets: A Financial Alternative for American Exporters," *Business America,* October 1997, p. 47.

receivable at a discount—in other words, the bank is acting as a collections department for its client.[25] In forfaiting, however, the seller makes a one-time arrangement with a bank to buy a specific account receivable.

Export Documents

Each export shipment involves many documents to satisfy government regulations controlling exporting as well as to meet requirements for international commercial payment transactions. The most frequently required documents are export declarations, consular invoices or certificates of origin, bills of lading, commercial invoices, and insurance certificates. In addition, documents such as import licenses, export licenses, packing lists, and inspection certificates for agricultural products are often necessary.

The paperwork involved in successfully completing a transaction is considered by many to be the greatest of all nontariff trade barriers. There are 125 different documents in regular or special use in more than 1,000 different forms. A single shipment may require over 50 documents and involve as many as 28 different parties and government agencies, or require as few as five. Generally, preparation of documents can be handled routinely, but their importance should not be minimized; incomplete or improperly prepared documents lead to delays in shipment.[26] In some countries, there are penalties, fines, and even confiscation of goods as a result of errors in some of these documents. Export documents are the result of requirements imposed by the exporting government, of requirements set by commercial procedures established in foreign trade, and in some cases, of the supporting import documents required by the importing government. Descriptions of the principal export documents follow.

Export Declaration.   To maintain a statistical measure of the quantity of goods shipped abroad and to provide a means of determining whether regulations are being met, most countries require shipments abroad to be accompanied by an *export declaration*. Usually such a declaration, presented at the port of exit, includes the names and addresses of the principals involved, the destination of the goods, a full description of the goods, and their declared value. When manufacturers are exporting from the United States, U.S. Customs and the Department of Commerce require an export declaration for all shipments. If specific licenses are required to ship a particular commodity, the export license must be presented with the export declaration for proper certification. It thus serves as the principal means of control for regulatory agencies of the U.S. government.

Consular Invoice or Certificate of Origin.   Some countries require *consular invoices*. These forms must be obtained from the country's consulate and returned with two to eight copies in the language of the country, along with copies of other required documents (e.g., import license, commercial invoice, and/or bill of lading), before certification is granted. The consular invoice probably produces the most red tape and is the most exacting to complete. Preparation of the document should be handled with extreme care because fines are levied for any errors uncovered. In most countries, the fine is shared with whoever finds the errors, so few go undetected.

Bill of Lading.   The *bill of lading* is the most important document required for establishing legal ownership and facilitating financial transactions. It serves the following purposes: (1) as a contract for shipment between the carrier and shipper, (2) as a receipt

[25] Kenley A. Tarter, "International Factoring: An Effective Financial Strategy," *Business America,* October 1997, p. 40.

[26] Ravi R. Singh Mehta, "Do-Them-Yourself Details: Beware of Discrepancies in Documentary Credits-Based Exports," *International Business,* July/August 1997, p. 8.

from the carrier for shipment, and (3) as a certificate of ownership or title to the goods. Bills of lading are issued in the form of straight bills, which are nonnegotiable and are delivered directly to a consignee, or order bills, which are negotiable instruments. Bills of lading frequently are referred to as being either clean or foul. A clean bill of lading means the items presented to the carrier for shipment were properly packaged and clear of apparent damage when received; a foul bill of lading means the shipment was received in damaged condition and the damage is noted on the bill of lading.

Commercial Invoice. Every international transaction requires a *commercial invoice,* that is, a bill or statement for the goods sold. This document often serves several purposes; some countries require a copy for customs clearance, and it is one of the financial documents required in international commercial payments.

Insurance Policy or Certificate. The risks of shipment due to political or economic unrest in some countries, and the possibility of damage from sea and weather, make it absolutely necessary to have adequate insurance covering loss due to damage, war, or riots. Typically the method of payment or terms of sale require insurance on the goods, so few export shipments are uninsured. The insurance policy or certificate of insurance is considered a key document in export trade.

Licenses. Export or import licenses are additional documents frequently required in export trade. In those cases where import licenses are required by the country of entry, a copy of the license or license number is usually required to obtain a consular invoice. Whenever a commodity requires an export license, it must be obtained before an export declaration can be properly certified.

Other Documents. Sanitary and health inspection certificates attesting to the absence of disease and pests may be required for certain agricultural products before a country allows goods to enter its borders. Packing lists with correct weights are also required in some cases.

Packing and Marking

In addition to completing all documentation, special packing and marking requirements must be considered for shipments destined to be transported over water, subject to excessive handling, or destined for parts of the world with extreme climates or unprotected outdoor storage. Packing that is adequate for domestic shipments often falls short for goods subject to the conditions mentioned. Protection against rough handling, moisture, temperature extremes, and pilferage may require heavy crating, which increases total packing costs as well as freight rates because of increased weight and size. Since some countries determine import duties on gross weight, packing can add a significant amount to import fees. To avoid the extremes of too much or too little packing, the marketer should consult export brokers, export freight forwarders, or other specialists.

All countries regulate the marking of goods and containers on imports, and noncompliance can result in severe penalties. Recently announced Peruvian regulations require all imported foreign products to bear a brand name, country of origin, and an expiration date clearly inscribed on the product. In case of imported wearing apparel, shoes, electric appliances, automotive parts, liquors, and soft drinks, the name and tax identity card number of the importer must also be added. Peruvian customs refuse clearance to foreign products not fulfilling these requirements, and the importer has to reship the goods within 60 days of the customs appraisal date or they are seized and auctioned as abandoned goods. Further, goods already in Peru must also meet the provisions of the decree or be subject to public auction.

The exporter must be careful that all marking on the container conforms exactly to the data on the export documents because discrepancies are often interpreted by customs officials as an attempt to defraud. A basic source of information for American exporters is the Department of Commerce pamphlet series entitled *Preparing Shipment to (Country),* which details the necessary export documents and pertinent U.S. and foreign government regulations for labeling, marking, packing, and customs procedures.

Customs-Privileged Facilities

To facilitate export trade, countries designate areas within their borders as *customs-privileged facilities,* that is, areas where goods can be imported for storage and/or processing with tariffs and quota limits postponed until the products leave the designated areas. Foreign-trade zones (also known as free-trade zones), free ports, and in-bond arrangements are all types of customs-privileged facilities that countries use to promote foreign trade.

Foreign-Trade Zones

The number of countries with *foreign-trade zones (FTZs)* has increased as trade liberalization has spread through Africa, Latin America, Eastern Europe, and other parts of Europe and Asia.[27] Most FTZs function in a similar manner regardless of the host country.[28]

In the United States, FTZs extend their services to thousands of firms engaged in a spectrum of international trade-related activities ranging from distribution to assembly and manufacturing. More than 150 foreign-trade zones are located throughout the United States, including New York, New Orleans, San Francisco, Seattle, Toledo, Honolulu, Mayaques (Puerto Rico), Kansas City, Little Rock, and Sault St. Marie.[29] Goods subject to U.S. custom duties and quota restrictions can be landed in these zones for storage or such processing as repackaging, cleaning, and grading before being brought into the United States or reexported to another country. Merchandise can be held in a FTZ even if it is subject to U.S. quota restrictions. When a particular quota opens up, the merchandise may then be immediately shipped into the U.S. Merchandise subject to quotas may also be substantially transformed within a zone into articles that are not covered by quotas, and then shipped into the United States free of quota restrictions.

In situations where goods are imported into the United States to be combined with American-made goods and reexported, the importer or exporter can avoid payment of U.S. import duties on the foreign portion and eliminate the complications of applying for a "drawback," that is, a request for a refund from the government of 99 percent of the duties paid on imports later reexported. Other benefits for companies utilizing foreign-trade zones include: (1) lower insurance costs due to the greater security required in FTZs; (2) more working capital, since duties are deferred until goods leave the zone; (3) the opportunity to stockpile products when quotas are filled or while waiting for ideal market conditions; (4) significant savings on goods or materials rejected, damaged, or scrapped for which no duties are assessed; and (5) exemption from paying duties on

[27] Japan's version of the FTZ is called Foreign Access Zone (FAZ). Basically it operates much like a FTZ. A complete description of the Japanese FAZ can be found on the JETRO Web site at **http://www.jetro.go.jp/faz-e/top.html**.

[28] For a comprehensive study of the role of FTZs in global marketing, see Patriya S. Tansuhaj and James W. Gentry, "Firm Differences in Perceptions of the Facilitating Role of Foreign Trade Zones in Global Marketing and Logistics," *Journal of International Business Studies,* Spring 1987, pp. 19–33.

[29] John J. DaPonte, Jr., "The Foreign-Trade Zones Act: Keeping Up with the Changing Times," *Business America,* December 1997, p. 22.

CROSSING BORDERS 15-4

Free-Trade Zones Boom in Russia, Eastern Europe, and Cuba

Leningrad hosted a conference aimed at turning the entire city into a free-trade zone (FTZ) where manufacturers can assemble their products without paying tariffs on the imported parts until they enter a country and are for sale. The Russian republics are attempting to create several of these special zones designed to boost industrial production, especially for export, and to create employment. Their efforts are inspired by China's Special Economic Zones (SEZs), which encompass entire regions, rather than the smaller FTZ that may be simply a warehouse or factory.

Bulgaria, Hungary, Poland, Romania, and Yugoslavia are also in the process of setting up FTZs. Some countries designate a factory or a warehouse where goods can be stored or assembled; others designate an entire area as an FTZ. Hungary, for example, has no plans to design special industrial enclaves as FTZs but will designate factories as FTZs.

Cuba has established several free-trade zones in order to attract foreign investment. This move follows the trend in Latin America to use FTZs to lure manufacturing, distribution, and service businesses. In addition to postponing customs duties, the Cuban FTZs offer exemptions and/or reductions on taxes and utilities charges.

Special zones for export processing have existed in the developed world for decades—the United States has some 200. Volkswagen and Nissan operate large automobile assembly plants in an FTZ in Barcelona; Ireland has had an FTZ near Shannon Airport since 1959.

Sources: Abstracted from "Free-Trade Zones in Europe: A Boom in the East, a Burden in the West," *EuroSphere,* KPMG Peat Marwick, August–September 1991, pp. 2–3; and "U.S.-Cuban Trade Battle Takes New Twist," *Crossborder Monitor,* June 12, 1996, p. 1.

labor and overhead costs incurred in an FTZ which are excluded in determining the value of the goods.[30]

Offshore Assembly (Maquiladoras)

Maquiladoras, in-bond companies, or twin plants are names given to a special type of customs-privileged facility that originated in Mexico in the early 1970s. It has since expanded to other countries that have abundant, low-cost labor. Even though in-bond operations vary from country to country, the original arrangement between Mexico and the United States remains the most typical. In 1971, the Mexican and U.S. governments established an in-bond program that created a favorable opportunity for U.S. companies to use low-cost Mexican labor.

The Mexican government allows U.S. processing, packaging, assembling, and/or repair plants located in the in-bond area to import parts and processed materials without import taxes, provided the finished products are reexported to the United States or to another foreign country. In turn, the U.S. government permits the reimportation of the packaged, processed, assembled, or repaired goods with a reasonably low import tariff applied only to the value added while in Mexico. Originally goods processed in *maquiladoras* could not be sold in Mexico without first being shipped back to the

---

[30] See Chapter 18 for a discussion on using FTZs to help reduce price escalation.

CROSSING BORDERS 15–5

When Is a Car a Truck or a Truck a Car?

Chrysler officials were miffed about Japan's fastest-growing class of imports in the United States: four-wheel drive sport-utility vehicles (SUVs) that include the Toyota 4Runner, Isuzu Trooper, and Suzuki Samurai. Some 230,000 such Japanese vehicles were imported into the United States, capturing nearly one-third of the $10 billion SUV market. These vehicles are aimed squarely at the Jeep, America's best-known maker of four-wheel drives.

All Japanese four-wheel drives are imported into the United States without backseats. By doing so, they are able to qualify as trucks instead of cars, thereby avoiding Japan's voluntary limit of 2.3 million passenger-car imports into the United States. As trucks they simply pay a duty and roll onto America's docks.

Trucks? True, the Japanese vehicles don't have backseats when they are imported but they do have carpeting, ashtrays, air-conditioning, vents, and stereo speakers in the back. Most even have rear seat mounts so that backseats—imported separately—can be quickly and easily installed by U.S. dealers.

This is not unlike the 1960s subterfuge the Japanese engaged in when they dodged U.S. truck tariffs by importing pickup trucks as "truck parts." They imported the trucks without the box on the back and once the trucks were in the United States the boxes—again imported separately—were simply bolted on.

As one official stated, "Close the door and they come through the window. Close the window and they come through the door."

Source: Adapted from Edwin A. Finn, Jr., "Look, Ma, No Back Seats," *Forbes,* February 22, 1988, p. 91.

United States and reimported at regular Mexican tariffs. However, Mexican law was changed to allow *maquiladoras,* with special permission, the right to sell a maximum of 50 percent of their products in Mexico if they use some Mexican-made components.

As a result of the NAFTA agreement there will be some changes over a seven-year period in the rules governing *maquiladoras.*[31] By 2001 preferential tariff treatment and all export performance requirements (for example, trade and foreign exchange balancing) will be eliminated for NAFTA countries. Also by 2001, 100 percent of all *maquiladora*-manufactured goods can be sold in Mexico versus the 50 percent permitted prior to NAFTA.[32]

More than 2,600 companies participate in the *maquiladora* program, with finished products valued at more than $30 billion annually. Although still dominated by U.S. companies, the *maquiladoras* are no longer only American. Heavy investments are pouring in from Asia and Europe, spurring expansion at close to 7 percent annually.[33] Products made in *maquiladoras* include electronics, health-care items, automotive parts, furniture, clothing, and toys.[34] In most in-bond arrangements, special trade privileges are also part of the process. The *maquiladora* arrangement is becoming more cost efficient for many companies operating in Asia as Asian wage rates increase. Higher costs

---

[31] Diane Lindquist, "End of Maquiladora Program Is in Sight," *The San Diego Union-Tribune,* August 14, 1997, p. C1.

[32] "Make Room for Mexicans," *Business Latin America,* November 4, 1996, p. 2.

[33] "The Border," *Business Week,* May 12, 1997, p. 64.

[34] Tim Coone and John Otis, "Weaving Away in Maquilaville," *Latin Trade,* January 1997, p. 26.

in Mexico are offset by wage increases in Asia and the higher shipping costs from Asia to the United States than from Mexico.[35]

Logistics

When a company is primarily an exporter from a single country to a single market, the typical approach to the physical movement of goods is the selection of a dependable mode of transportation that ensures safe arrival of the goods within a reasonable time for a reasonable carrier cost. As a company becomes global, such a solution to the movement of products could prove costly and highly inefficient for seller and buyer. At some point in the growth and expansion of an international firm, costs other than transportation are such that an optimal cost solution to the physical movement of goods cannot be achieved without thinking of the physical distribution process as an integrated system.[36] When a foreign marketer begins producing and selling in more than one country and becomes a global marketer, it is time to consider the concept of *logistics management,* that is, a total systems approach to management of the distribution process that includes all activities involved in physically moving raw material, in-process inventory, and finished goods inventory from the point of origin to the point of use or consumption.[37]

Interdependence of Physical Distribution Activities

A *physical distribution system* involves more than the physical movement of goods. It includes location of plants and warehousing (storage), transportation mode, inventory quantities, and packing. The concept of physical distribution takes into account that the costs of each activity are interdependent and a decision involving one affects the cost and efficiency of one or all others. In fact, because of their interdependence, there are an infinite number of "total costs" for the sum of each of the different activity costs. (Total cost of the system is defined as the sum of the costs of all these activities.)

The idea of interdependence can be illustrated by the classic example of air freight. Exhibit 15–7 is an illustration of an actual company's costs of shipping 44,000 peripheral boards worth $7.7 million from a Singapore plant to the U.S. West Coast using two modes of transportation—ocean freight and the seemingly more expensive air freight. When considering only rates for transportation and carrying costs for inventory in transit, air transportation costs are approximately $57,000 higher than ocean freight. But notice that when total costs are calculated, air freight is actually less costly than ocean freight. This is because there are other costs involved in the total physical distribution system. To offset the slower ocean freight and the possibility of unforeseen delays and still ensure prompt customer delivery schedules, the company has to continuously maintain 30 days of inventory in Singapore and another 30 days inventory at the company's distribution centers. Costs of financing 60 days of inventory and additional warehousing costs at both points—that is, real physical distribution costs—would result in the cost of ocean freight exceeding air by more than $75,000. There may even be additional costs associated with ocean freight—for example, higher damage rate, higher insurance, and higher packing rates for ocean freight. Substantial savings can result from systematic examination of logistics costs and the calculation of total physical distribution costs.

[35] Jeff Manning and Steve Duin, "Asia May Lose Grip on Athletic Footwear," *The Oregonian,* January 25, 1998, p. A1.

[36] Steven R. Clinton and Roger J. Calantone, "Logistics Strategy: Does It Travel Well?" *International Marketing Review,* Vol. 13(5), 1996, p. 98.

[37] Tom Andel, "Ready to Go Global?" *Transportation Distribution,* June 1997, p. 34.

Exhibit 15-7   **Real Physical Distribution Costs between Air and Ocean Freight—Singapore to the United States**

In this example, 44,000 peripheral boards worth $7.7 million are shipped from a Singapore plant to the U.S. West Coast. Cost of capital to finance inventories is 10 percent annually: $2,109 per day to finance $7.7 million.

	Ocean	*Air*
Transport costs	$31,790 (in transit 21 days)	$127,160 (in transit 3 days)
In-transit inventory financing costs	$44,289	$ 6,328
Total transportation costs	$76,079	$133,487
Warehousing inventory costs, Singapore and U.S.	(60 days @ $2,109 per day) $126,540	
Warehouse rent	$ 6,500	
Real physical distribution costs	$209,119	$133,487

Source: Adapted from "Air and Adaptec's Competitive Strategy," *International Business,* September 1993, p. 44.

Amdahl, the computer manufacturer, was able to trim more than $50 million from its logistics costs, shrinking spending to 5 percent of sales from 8.5 percent, while improving customer service. The beauty of such savings is that they "go right to the bottom line."

Another example involves a large multinational firm with facilities and customers the world over. This firm shipped parts from its U.S. Midwest plant to the nearest East Coast port, then by water route around the Cape of Good Hope (Africa), and finally to its plants in Asia taking 14 weeks. Substantial inventory was maintained in Asia as a safeguard against uncertain water-borne deliveries. The transportation carrier costs were the least expensive available; however, delivery delays and unreliable service caused the firm to make emergency air shipments to keep production lines going. As a result, air shipment costs rose to 70 percent of the total transport bill. An analysis of the problem in the physical distribution system showed that costs could be lowered by using higher-cost motor carriers to truck the parts to West Coast ports, then ship them by sea. Transit time was reduced, delivery reliability improved, inventory quantities in Asia lowered, and emergency air shipments eliminated. The new distribution system produced annual savings of $60,000.

Although a cost difference will not always be the case, the examples serve to illustrate the interdependence of the various activities in the physical distribution mix and the total cost. A change of transportation mode can affect a change in packaging and handling, inventory costs, warehousing time and cost, and delivery charges.

The concept of physical distribution is the achievement of optimum (lowest) system cost consistent with the customer service objectives of the firm. If the activities in the physical distribution system are viewed separately, without consideration of their interdependence, the final cost of distribution may be higher than the lowest possible cost (optimum cost) and the quality of service may be adversely affected. Additional variables and costs that are interdependent and must be included in the total physical distribution decision heighten the distribution problems confronting the international marketer. As the international firm broadens the scope of its operations, the additional variables and costs become more crucial in their effect on the efficiency of the distribution system.

One of the major benefits of the European Community's unification is the elimination of transportation barriers among member countries. Instead of approaching Europe on a country-by-country basis, a centralized logistics network can be developed. The

Getting the product to market can mean multitransportation modes such as canal boats in China, pedal power in Vietnam, and speed trains in Japan. (Philip R. Cateora; Jerry Alexander/Tony Stone Images; Alain Choisnet/The Image Bank)

trend in Europe is toward pan-European distribution centers.[38] Studies indicate that companies operating in Europe may be able to cut 20 warehousing locations to three and maintain the same level of customer service. A German white goods manufacturer was able to reduce its European warehouses from 39 to 10, as well as improve its distribution and enhance customer service. By cutting the number of warehouses, it reduced total distribution and warehousing costs, brought down staff numbers, held fewer items of stock, provided greater access to regional markets, made better use of transport networks, and improved service to customers, all with a 21 percent reduction of total logistics costs.

Benefits of Physical Distribution Systems

There are more benefits to a system of physical distribution than cost advantages. An effective physical distribution system can result in optimal inventory levels and, in multiplant operations, optimal production capacity, both of which can maximize the use of working capital. In making plant-location decisions, a company with a physical distribution system can readily assess operating costs of alternative locations to serve various markets.

---

[38] "Competing on Logistics," *Business Europe,* February 28, 1996, p. 8.

A physical distribution system may also result in better (more dependable) delivery service to the market; when production occurs at different locations, companies are able to determine quickly the most economical source for a particular customer. As companies expand into multinational markets and source these markets from multinational production facilities, they are increasingly confronted with cost variables that make it imperative to employ a total systems approach to the management of the distribution process to achieve efficient operation. Finally, a physical distribution system can render the natural obstructions created by geography less economically critical for the multinational marketer. Getting the product to market can mean multitransportation modes such as canal boats in China, pedal power in Vietnam, and speed trains in Japan.

Export Shipping and Warehousing

Whenever and however title to goods is transferred, those goods must be transported. Shipping goods to another country presents some important differences from shipping to a domestic site. The goods can be out of the shipper's control for longer periods of time than in domestic distribution; more shipping and collections documents are required; packing must be suitable; and shipping insurance coverage is necessarily more extensive. The task is to match each order of goods to the shipping modes best suited for swift, safe, and economical delivery. Ocean shipping, air freight, air express, and parcel post are all possibilities. Ocean shipping is usually the least expensive and most frequently used method for heavy bulk shipment. For certain categories of goods, air freight can be the most economical and certainly the speediest.

Shipping costs are an important factor in a product's price in export marketing, and the transportation mode must be selected in terms of the total impact on cost—one esti-

A raft of trucks waits to pass customs between Shenzhen, China, and Hong Kong. Before the unification, China and Hong Kong were each other's main trading partners. (Michael Yamashita/ Woodfin Camp & Associates)

EXHIBIT 15-8   Examples of Distribution Costs from Paris to Denver via New York (U.S. dollars per metric ton)

Conventional Cargo Handling	Commodity A per Metric Ton	Commodity B per Metric Ton
Domestic carrier	$ 0.95	$ 0.95
Inland warehouse, 1 month including handling and delivery	12.14	12.14
Transport to port	12.78	12.78
Ship's agent	1.89	5.18
Port forwarder	0.97	2.66
Port warehouse (average 4 days) including handling	2.92	2.92
Stevedore	3.93	5.70
Sea carrier	21.67	80.70
Stevedore + port warehouse	6.32	6.32
Ship's agent	0.94	2.59
Port forwarder	0.79	0.79
Inland transport	46.64	46.64
Unloading	11.50	11.50
Totals	$123.44	$190.87

Containerized Cargo Handling	Commodity A per Metric Ton	Commodity B per Metric Ton
Domestic carrier	$ 0.95	$ 0.95
Inland warehouse, 1 month including handling and delivery	12.14	12.14
Transport to port	5.97	5.97
Ship's agent	1.69	4.65
Port forwarder	0.87	2.39
Stevedore	1.60	1.60
Sea carrier	23.07	78.35
Stevedore + port warehouse	6.32	6.32
Ship's agent	0.85	2.32
Forwarder	0.79	0.79
Inland transport	33.45	35.49
Unloading	11.50	11.50
Totals	$ 99.20	$162.47

Note: Commodity A = Industrial cooking oil in 10-gallon containers (low-tariff cargo).

Commodity B = Industrial chemicals, harmless (high-tariff cargo).

mate is that logistics account for between 19 and 23 percent of the total cost of a finished product sold internationally. One of the important innovations in ocean shipping in reducing or controlling the high cost of transportation is the use of *containerization*. Containerized shipments, in place of the traditional bulk handling of full loads or break-bulk operations, have resulted in intermodal transport between inland points, reduced costs, reduction in losses from pilferage and damage, and simplified handling of international shipments.

With increased use of containerization, rail container service has developed in many countries to provide the international shipper with door-to-door movement of goods under seal, originating and terminating inland. This eliminates several loadings, unloadings, and change of carriers and reduces costs substantially, as illustrated in Exhibit 15–8. Containerized cargo handling also reduces damage and pilferage in transit. Unfortunately, such savings are not always possible for all types of cargo.

For many commodities of high unit value and low weight and volume, international air freight has become important. Air freight has shown the fastest growth rate for freight transportation even though it accounts for only a fraction of total international shipments. While air freight can cost two to five times surface charges for general cargo, some cost reduction is realized through reduced packing requirements, paperwork, insurance, and the cost of money tied up in inventory. Although usually not enough to offset the higher rates charged for air freight, it can, as illustrated in Exhibit 15–7, be a justifiable alternative if the commodity has high unit value or high inventory costs, or if there is concern with delivery time. Many products moving to foreign markets meet these criteria.

In the last decade there has been continuous improvement in the services available to the international shipper both in the home market and abroad. *Intermodal services,* a transportation system that unites various modes of transportation into one seamless movement of goods from factory to the customer's port of entry, have become more efficient as deregulation has allowed the coupling of various modes of transportation. In addition, intermodal marketing companies (IMC) have evolved to broker transportation services so an exporter can make one transaction with an IMC that takes care of the movement of goods from factory to customer, rivaling the simplicity of single-mode freight transportation. The IMC stitches together each of the transportation modes involved in the intermodal freight movements, which may involve as many as four separate transportation modes. All of this can be done within guaranteed time frames, with 98 percent on-time performance schedules more the norm than the exception.[39]

Intermodal services in other parts of the world are not as advanced as in the United States. Europe comes the closest to providing similar services; however, deregulation and barriers that existed before unification have yet to be completely eliminated. Unlike truck transportation, Europe's 26 railways have not capitalized on the removal of borders in Europe's single market. Progress is being made as railroads are beginning to restructure and a pan-European intermodal marketing company similar to those in the United States has been formed.[40] Before long it will be possible to extend the services in the United States to European customers so one transaction can be made to ensure freight delivery from a factory in the United States to a final customer in Europe. Such services are not available in Asia or Latin America, although improvement in transportation services is being made in both areas.[41] Rail transportation between the United States and Mexico should improve as Kansas City Southern railway has purchased a Mexican rail line, creating a direct route owned by one carrier from Chicago to Mexico City.[42] U.S. railroad companies' investments in Brazil, New Zealand, and Britain call for major investments in the improvement of these rail systems.[43] Moving goods rapidly and on a timely schedule is more important today than ever before and the improvement of rail systems and the development of intermodal systems will go along way towards making that possible.

Another innovation in transportation and logistics is the service provided by companies such as United Parcel Service (UPS), Federal Express (FedEx), and others. Besides providing air-express service for packages, these companies are offering complete logistics management services for their clients—truly door-to-door delivery around the world. This service not only includes delivery but other services as well. For example, FedEx provides total logistics support. It will take a manufacturer's product, warehouse it, keep inventory, providing all the labor and technology, and move it throughout the world. FedEx can warehouse a computer system made in Malaysia, move it to Japan to be coupled with components from Taiwan, then deliver a completed product to the final destination in yet another country.[44] One client's experience illustrates how such a ser-

---

[39] John Conley, "Coming of Age," *International Business,* March 1996, p. 36.

[40] Russ Banham, "Getting on Track: Europe's Railways Are Suddenly Moving Fast to Provide Competitive Intermodal Services," *International Business,* March 1997, p. 14.

[41] John Davies, "Gateway to the East," *International Business,* February 1997, p. 11.

[42] Jose Aguayo, "The Little Railroad That Hopes It Can," *Forbes,* April 21, 1997, p. 58.

[43] Anna Wilde Mathews and Jonathan Friedland, "U.S. Railroads' Expansion Plans Gather Steam Overseas," *The Wall Street Journal,* May 20, 1977, p. B4.

[44] David C. Hulme, "The Right Stuff in the Right Place: Japan's Logistics Revolution," *The American Chamber of Commerce in Japan Journal,* May 1997.

CROSSING BORDERS 15–6

If the Shoe Fits Wear It . . . or Abandon It

Pilferage and theft are ongoing problems in shipping. These problems are constantly being addressed with different security strategies. Using containers for shipping is one of the more successful strategies, but containers also can be stolen. Such was the case in Los Angeles, when thieves cut through security fencing at a major container terminal, drove a truck tractor into the area, and broke open a few containers until they found one with sports shoes that sell for $140 a pair in retail stores. They hooked up the container and drove out with their bounty.

But the police had the last laugh. A week later, they found the container abandoned with its cargo intact. The U.S.-based shoe importer routinely ships all its left shoes in one container and all its right shoes in another. The thieves had stolen the container with left shoes.

Source: Adapted from John Davies, "Sneaking Up on Security," *International Business,* February 1997, p. 18.

vice can improve a company's distribution costs and service. A computer parts repair center of one company moved into a FedEx Express Distribution Center in Japan and was able to cut average total turnaround time from 45 days to five days and at less cost. FedEx took over storage, control, and shipment of the parts using its own networks and aircraft. UPS offers similar services, including local parts stocking and defective return services in Europe, the Pacific Rim, and the Americas.[45]

Distribution and its costs are an important part of every international transaction. Cheap labor may make Chinese clothing competitive in the United States, but if delays in shipment tie up working capital and cause winter coats to arrive in April, the advantage may be lost. Similarly, production machinery disabled for lack of a part can affect cost throughout the system, all of which may be avoided with a viable logistics system.[46]

The globalization of marketing and manufacturing component parts made in several countries, assembled in some others, and serviced the world over puts tremendous pressure on a company's ability to physically move goods. A narrow solution to physical movement of goods is the selection of transportation; a broader application is the concept of logistics management or physical distribution.

The Foreign-Freight Forwarder

The *foreign-freight forwarder,* licensed by the Federal Maritime Commission, arranges for the shipment of goods as the agent for an exporter. The forwarder is an indispensable agent for an exporting firm that cannot afford an in-house specialist to handle paperwork and other export trade mechanics.[47]

---

[45] Tom Andel, "Ready to Go Global?" *Transportation Distribution,* June 1997, p. 34.

[46] "Globalization: Freight Industry's Role," *The Economist,* November 15, 1997.

[47] One of the many freight forwarders is Serra International, Inc. Serra has an extensive Web site that lists all the services it provides, in addition to one of the most comprehensive sets of links to almost every government agency and private source of information found anywhere. Visit the Serra Web site at **http://www.serraintl.com.**

Even in large companies with active export departments capable of handling documentation, a forwarder is useful as a shipment coordinator at the port of export or at the destination port. Besides arranging for complete shipping documentation, the full-service foreign-freight forwarder provides information and advice on routing and scheduling, rates and related charges, consular and licensing requirements, labeling requirements, and export restrictions. Further, the agent offers shipping insurance, warehouse storage, packing and containerization, and ocean cargo or air freight space.

An astute freight forwarder will also double-check all assumptions made on the export declaration such as commodity classifications, checking the list of denied parties and end-uses.[48] Both large and small shippers find freight forwarders' wide range of services useful and well worth the fees normally charged.[49] In fact, for many shipments, forwarders can save on freight charges because they can consolidate shipments into larger, more economical quantities. Experienced exporters regard the foreign-freight forwarder as an important addition to in-house specialists.

Summary

An awareness of the mechanics of export trade is indispensable to the foreign marketer who engages in exporting goods from one country to another. Although most marketing techniques are open to interpretation and creative application, the mechanics of exporting are very exact; there is little room for interpretation or improvisation with the requirements of export licenses, quotas, tariffs, export documents, packing, marking, and the various uses of commercial payments. The very nature of the regulations and restrictions surrounding importing and exporting can lead to frequent and rapid change. In handling the mechanics of export trade successfully, the manufacturer must keep abreast of all foreign and domestic changes in requirements and regulations pertaining to the product involved. For firms unable to maintain their own export staffs, foreign-freight forwarders can handle many details for a nominal fee.

With paperwork completed, the physical movement of goods must be considered. Transportation mode affects total product cost because of the varying requirements of packing, inventory levels, time requirements, perishability, unit cost, damage and pilfering losses, and customer service. Transportation for each product must be assessed in view of the interdependent nature of all these factors. To assure optimum distribution at minimal cost, a physical distribution system determines everything from plant location to final customer delivery in terms of the most efficient use of capital investment, resources, production, inventory, packing, and transportation.

Questions

1. Define and show the significance to international marketing of the following terms:

Commerce Control List (CCL)	bill of lading
Commerce Country Chart (CCC)	commercial invoice
export regulations	customs-privileged facilities
import regulations	foreign-trade zone
Export Administrative Regulations (EAR)	maquiladora
terms of sale	Export Control Classification Number (ECCN)
open account	logistics management
letter of credit	physical distribution system
bill of exchange	ELAIN
forfaiting	STELA
export declaration	ERIC
consular invoice	

2. Explain the reasoning behind the various regulations and restrictions imposed on the exportation and importation of goods.

3. What determines the type of license needed for exportation? Discuss.

4. Discuss the most frequently encountered trade restrictions.

5. What is the purpose of an import license? Discuss.

6. Explain foreign-trade zones and illustrate how an exporter may use them. How do foreign-trade zones differ from bonded warehouses?

7. How do in-bond areas differ from foreign-trade zones? How would an international marketer use an in-bond area?

8. Explain each of the following export documents:
   a. Bill of lading
   b. Consular invoice

---

[48] "What to Expect from a Great Freight Forwarder," *Managing Exports, Newsletter,* The Institute of Management and Administration, **http://www.ioma.com**, June 1997.

[49] For a discussion on how large companies use freight forwarders, see Chris Gillis and Philip Damas, "What Should You Outsource?" *American Shipper,* January 1997, p. 25.

c. Commercial invoice

d. Insurance certificate

9. What are the differences between a straight bill of lading and an order bill of lading? What are the differences between a clean bill of lading and a foul bill of lading?

10. Why would an exporter use the services of a foreign-freight forwarder? Discuss.

11. Besides cost advantages, what are the other benefits of an effective physical distribution system?

12. Discuss customs-privileged facilities. How are they used?

13. Why would a company engage the services of an intermodal transportation service instead of performing activities in-house?

14. You are the manager of a small company that manufactures and sells various types of personal restraints (for example, handcuffs and leg irons) that you sell to law enforcement agencies, private security companies, and novelty stores. You receive a large order from an importer in Madrid. You have never done business with this importer although you have previously sold your product in Spain. Do you need a special export license? Outline the steps you would take to ensure that your transaction is legal. (Note: The solution to this problem cannot be completely answered from information in the text. Information will have to be obtained from sources on the Internet.)

15. You are the sales manager of a small company with sales in the United States. About 30 percent of your business is mail order and the remainder from your two retail stores. You recently created an e-store on the Web and a few days later received an order from a potential customer from a city near Paris, France. The shipping charges listed on the Web are all for locations in the United States. You don't want to lose this $350 order. You know you can use the postal service but the customer indicated she wanted the item in about a week. Air Express seems logical but how much will it cost? Consult both the FedEx homepage (**http://www.fedex.com**) and the UPS homepage (**http://www.ups.com**) and get some estimates on shipping costs. Here are some details you will need: value $350; total weight of the package, 2.5 pounds; package dimensions, 4 inches high by 6 inches wide; U.S. Zip Code, 97035; and French Zip Code, 91400. (Note: It's not fair to call UPS or FedEx—use the Internet.)

16. Based on the information collected in Question 15, how practical would it be to encourage foreign sales? Your average order ranges from about $250 to $800. All prices are quoted plus shipping and handling. You handle a fairly exclusive line of Southwestern Indian jewelry that sells for about 15 to 20 percent higher in Europe than in the United States. The products are lightweight and high in value.

THE GLOBAL ADVERTISING AND PROMOTION EFFORT

Chapter Outline

Chapter Learning Objectives

What you should learn from Chapter 16

- Local market characteristics which affect the advertising and promotion of products.
- When global advertising is most effective; when modified advertising is necessary.
- The effects of a single European market on advertising.
- The effect of limited media, excessive media, paper and equipment shortages, and government regulations on advertising and promotion budgets.
- The strengths and weaknesses of sales promotions in global marketing.
- The communication process and advertising misfires.

GLOBAL PERSPECTIVE

Global Advertising Campaigns—A Potpourri of Approaches

The commercial unfolds with a flashback to an elderly Chinese man talking to his granddaughter about values and traditions. Fade to a generation later. The young girl, now grown up, wants the best for her son—in the form of Procter & Gamble's Crest toothpaste. The scene closes with a corporate logo at the end, cognizant that Asians place more weight on the company behind the brand than Americans typically do. Only a master marketer like P&G could introduce a brand into a new country and wrap it in an aura of tradition.

The TV campaign bringing Crest to millions of Chinese is prototypical of how the consumer-goods king plans to turn many of its top North American product brands into global ones. Here's the game plan: Take a well-established brand, like Crest; focus on its core attribute, which is cavity-fighting; and massage the commercial to fit the culture—in this case, Chinese respect for the elderly and tradition.

P&G's so-called "global model" is to use the most successful commercials, wherever originated, and quickly reapply them in other markets—with a twist. Pantene's global model, for instance, came out of Taiwan. P&G took a minor brand, Pantene, retooled it with a vitamin-enriched formula, and stressed its "hair so healthy it shines" campaign in global advertisements. Today, Pantene is the world's top-selling shampoo. The Head & Shoulders commercials now making the rounds originated in Mexico. Campy commercials in Great Britain for Daz dishwashing liquid were replicated in Japan for Joy dishwashing and in the United States for Gain detergent.

The strategy does not always work, however. A case in point is Tide's launch in China. Procter & Gamble tried the successful U.S. campaign idea that included letters to the company from real consumers about their toughest stains. But Chinese housewives were not in the habit of writing to companies, nor did they worry about spaghetti stains on linen blouses. After this apparent failure, P&G made home visits and realized that doing the washing is an ordeal; the Chinese use washboards, which can take the entire day.

P&G went back to the drawing board to create totally different commercials for the Chinese market The new Tide ad begins with black-and-white footage of a woman slaving over her washboard, scrubbing a shirt that won't come clean. A friend arrives with a box of Tide. The woman washing asks if it is expensive. The ad turns to color and kicks into something described as sort of "washing aerobics" that includes a jingle with the phrase, "It cleans really well, and it doesn't cost a lot." P&G ended up with an ad that didn't look like any of its other washing-detergent ads and it hit emotional buttons that could only come from consumer insight.

Sources: Fara Warner, "Researchers Roam Mainland in Search of What Makes Chinese Tick," *The Asian Wall Street Journal,* March 24, 1997, p. 1; Jeff Harrington, "P&G Mastering Art of 'Glocalization' Taking Crest into China Typifies How Procter Will Give Global Sales a Local Feel," *The Cincinnati Enquirer,* April 13, 1997, p. I01; and "China: Consumers Seen Spending Less Freely," *Emerging Markets Report,* March 23, 1997.

Advertising, sales promotion, personal selling, and public relations, the mutually reinforcing elements of the promotional mix, have as their common objective the successful sale of a product. Once a product is developed to meet target market needs and is properly distributed, intended customers must be informed of the product's value and availability. Advertising and promotion are basic ingredients in the marketing mix of an international company.

Of all the elements of the marketing mix, decisions involving advertising are those most often affected by cultural differences among country markets. Consumers respond in terms of their culture, its style, feelings, value systems, attitudes, beliefs, and perceptions. Because advertising's function is to interpret or translate the need/want-satisfying qualities of products and services in terms of consumer needs, wants, desires, and aspirations, the emotional appeals, symbols, persuasive approaches, and other characteristics of an advertisement must coincide with cultural norms if it is to be effective.

Reconciling an international advertising and promotion effort with the cultural uniqueness of markets is the challenge confronting the international or global marketer.

The basic framework and concepts of international promotion are essentially the same wherever employed. Six steps are involved: (1) study the target market(s); (2) determine the extent of worldwide standardization; (3) determine the promotional mix (the blend of advertising, personal selling, sales promotions, and public relations) by national or global markets; (4) develop the most effective message(s); (5) select effective media; and (6) establish the necessary controls to assist in monitoring and achieving worldwide marketing objectives.

In this chapter, a review of some of the global trends that can impact international advertising is followed by a discussion of global versus modified advertising. A survey of problems and challenges confronting international advertisers—including basic creative strategy, media planning and selection, sales promotions, and the communications process—concludes the chapter.

Global Advertising

Intense competition for world markets and the increasing sophistication of foreign consumers have led to a need for more sophisticated advertising strategies. Increased costs, problems of coordinating advertising programs in multiple countries, and a desire for a common worldwide company or product image have caused Multinational Companies (MNCs) to seek greater control and efficiency without sacrificing local responsiveness. In the quest for more effective and responsive promotion programs, the policies covering centralized or decentralized authority, use of single or multiple foreign or domestic agencies, appropriation and allocation procedures, copy, media, and research are being examined.

One of the most widely debated policy areas pertains to the degree of specialized advertising necessary from country to country.[1] One view sees advertising customized for each country or region because every country is seen as posing a special problem. Executives with this viewpoint argue that the only way to achieve adequate and relevant advertising is to develop separate campaigns for each country. At the other extreme are those who suggest that advertising should be standardized for all markets of the world and overlook regional differences altogether.

Debate on the merits of standardization compared to modification of international advertising has been going on for decades. Theodore Levitt's seminal article, "The Globalization of Markets,"[2] caused many companies to examine their international strategies and to adopt a global marketing strategy. Levitt postulated the existence and growth of the global consumer with similar needs and wants, and advocated that international marketers should operate as if the world were one large market, ignoring superficial regional and national differences.

Without discussing the merits of Levitt's arguments, there is evidence that companies may have overcompensated for cultural differences and have modified advertising and marketing programs for each national market without exploring the possibilities of a worldwide, standardized marketing mix. After decades of following country-specific marketing programs, companies had as many different product variations, brand names, and advertising programs as countries in which they did business.

A case in point is the Gillette Company, which sells 800 products in more than 200 countries. Gillette has a consistent worldwide image as a masculine, sports-oriented company, but its products have no such consistent image. Its razors, blades, toiletries, and cosmetics are known by many names. Trac II blades in the United States are more

---

[1] Michael G. Harvey, "Point of View: A Model to Determine Standardization of the Advertising Process in International Markets," *Journal of Advertising Research,* July–August 1993, pp. 57–63.

[2] Theodore Levitt, "The Globalization of Markets," *Harvard Business Review,* May–June 1983, pp. 92–102.

widely known worldwide as G-II, and Atra blades are called Contour in Europe and Asia. Silkience hair conditioner is known as Soyance in France, Sientel in Italy, and Silkience in Germany. Whether or not a global brand name could have been chosen for Gillette's many existing products is speculative. However, Gillette's current corporate philosophy of globalization provides for an umbrella statement, "Gillette, the Best a Man Can Get," in all advertisements for men's toiletries products in the hope of providing some common image.

A similar situation exists for Unilever N. V., which sells a cleaning liquid called Vif in Switzerland, Viss in Germany, Jif in Britain and Greece, and Cif in France. This situation is a result of Unilever marketing separately to each of these countries. At this point, it would be difficult for Gillette or Unilever to standardize their brand names since each brand is established in its market. Yet, with such a diversity of brand names, it is easy to imagine the problem of coordination and control and the potential competitive disadvantage against a company with global brand recognition.

Reebok, a company new to international marketing, has a situation similar to Gillette and Unilever. Reebok is faced with the problem of having confusing messages in its markets—it is known as a running shoe in the U.K., a fashion statement in the U.S., and generally seen as women's fitness and aerobics sneakers. In contrast, Reebok's major competitors, Nike and Adidas, are associated with top athletes. Reebok's approach has placed it in the number two spot in the U.S. market but trailing Nike and Adidas worldwide. To remedy the problem, Reebok plans to launch a $100 million ad campaign and focus on a unified global approach. Included in the global restructuring is a new centralized product development center to develop designs that can cross borders from the Americas to Europe and Asia. The company's plan is to have consumers see the same Reebok designs worldwide almost simultaneously.[3]

The comparison of Reebok, Gillette, and Unilever highlights the situation in which companies can find themselves. In the case of Gillette and Unilever, multiple brand names and different messages are the result of decades of a multidomestic marketing strategy that is being melded into a global strategy. Reebok, on the other hand, appears to have evolved into an international marketer without any apparent thought given to a unified international advertising or marketing strategy. The lesson to be learned by companies contemplating international expansion is to approach it with a global perspective. It is much easier to grow with a global perspective than to correct the situation later.

Recall from previous chapters that there is a fundamental difference between a multidomestic marketing strategy and a global marketing strategy. The former is based on the premise that all markets are culturally different and a company must adapt marketing programs to accommodate the differences; the latter assumes similarities as well as differences and standardizes where there are similarities but adapts where culturally required. A global strategy further assumes that it may be possible to standardize some parts of the marketing mix and not others. Also, the same standardized products may be marketed globally but, because of differences in cultures, require a different advertising appeal in different markets. For instance, Ford's model advertising varies by nation because of language and societal nuances. Ford advertises the affordability of its Escort in the U.S., where the car is seen as entry level. But in India, Ford launched the Escort as a premium car. "It's not unusual to see an Escort with a chauffeur there," said a Ford executive.[4]

A global perspective directs products and advertising toward worldwide markets rather than multiple national markets. The seasoned international marketer or advertiser realizes the decision for standardization or modification depends more on motives for buying than on geography. Advertising must relate to motives. If people in different

[3] Juliana Koranteng, "Reebok Finds Its Second Wind as It Pursues Global Presence," *Advertising Age International,* January 1998, p. 18.

[4] Jean Halliday, " GM, Ford Think Globally for Branding Strategies," *Advertising Age,* January 6, 1997, p. 35.

markets buy similar products for significantly different reasons, advertising must focus on such differences. For example, an advertising program developed by Chanel, the perfume manufacturer, bombed in the United States although it was very popular in Europe. Admitting failure in their attempt to globalize the advertising, one fragrance analyst commented, "There is a French-American problem." The French concept of prestige is not the same as America's. On the other hand, when markets react to similar stimuli, it is not necessary to vary advertising messages for the sake of variation. A Mexican-produced commercial for Vicks VapoRub was used throughout Latin America and then in 40 other countries, including France. The message was totally relevant to the habits and customs of all these countries.

Because there are few situations where either a multidomestic or global marketing strategy alone is clearly the best, most companies compromise with pattern advertising.

Pattern Advertising: Plan Globally, Act Locally

As discussed in the chapter on product development (Chapter 12), a product is more than a physical item; it is a bundle of satisfactions the buyer receives. This package of satisfactions or utilities includes the primary function of the product along with many other benefits imputed by the values and customs of the culture. Different cultures often seek the same value or benefits from the primary function of a product; for example, the ability of an automobile to get from point A to point B, a camera to take a picture, or a wristwatch to tell time. But while agreeing on the benefit of the primary function of a product, other features and psychological attributes of the item can have significant differences.

Consider the different market-perceived needs for a camera. In the United States, excellent pictures with easy, foolproof operation are expected by most of the market; in Germany and Japan, a camera must take excellent pictures but the camera must also be state-of-the-art in design. In Africa, where penetration of cameras is less than 20 percent of the households, the concept of picture-taking must be sold. In all three markets, excellent pictures are expected (i.e., the primary function of a camera is demanded) but the additional utility or satisfaction derived from a camera differs among cultures. There are many products that produce such different expectations beyond the common benefit sought by all. Thus, many companies follow a strategy of *pattern advertising,* a global advertising strategy with a standardized basic message allowing some degree of modification to meet local situations.[5] As the popular saying goes, "Think Globally, Act Locally." In this way, some economies of standardization can be realized while specific cultural differences are accommodated.

Levi Strauss and Company has changed from all localized ads to pattern advertising where the broad outlines of the campaign are given but the details are not. Quality and Levi's American roots are featured worldwide. In each country market, different approaches will express these two points.(See Crossing Borders 16–1 for some examples.)

Similarly, Dannon's brand of yogurt promotes itself as the brand that understands the relationship between health and food but communicates the message differently depending on the market. In the U.S., where Dannon yogurt is seen as a healthy, vibrant food, the brand celebrates its indulgent side. In France, however, Dannon was seen as too pleasure-oriented. Therefore, Dannon created the Institute of Health, a real research center dedicated to food and education. The end result is the same message but communicated differently—a careful balance of health and pleasure.[6]

The Blue Diamond Growers Association's advertising of almonds is an excellent example of the fact that some products are best advertised only on a local basis. Blue

---

5 "Advertising in Asia: Global to Local," *Business Asia,* February 10, 1997, p. 2.

6 Jean-Marie Dru, "Passport to Success: In a Global-Village World, All Advertising Is Local," *Adweek,* April 21, 1997, p. 34.

CROSSING BORDERS 16–2

Electricity Costs Are High, but *That* High?

Just one misunderstood word can lead to amazing misunderstandings. For example, a U.S. firm had negotiated a sale of technology to the People's Republic of China. When the Chinese saw the contract, they complained about the high cost of electricity to run the machinery. The Americans were perplexed; there was nothing about electricity in the sales contract. The Chinese told the Americans to refer to Article 10 of the contract. Sure enough, it said, "The current value of the machinery is $1 million." A high electric bill to say the least! While this example occurred in a contract, it does illustrate how someone who does not read or speak the language can misunderstand simple English words. Imagine the response had this been used in an advertisement, as it well could have been.

Source: Reprinted by permission of the publisher, from *Management Review,* February 1990, © 1990 American Management Association, New York. **http://www.amanet.org**. All Rights Reserved.

standardized advertising program or a standardized product, a company may have a world brand. Nescafé, the world brand for Nestlé Company's instant coffee, is used throughout the world even though advertising messages and formulation (dark roast and light roast) vary to suit cultural differences. In Japan and the United Kingdom, advertising reflects each country's preference for tea; in France, Germany, and Brazil, cultural preferences for ground coffee call for a different advertising message and formulation. Even in this situation, however, there is some standardization; all advertisements have one common emotional link: "Whatever good coffee means to you and however you like to serve it, Nescafé has a coffee for you." The debate between advocates of strict standardized advertising and those who support locally modified promotions will doubtless continue.

Some companies that had taken extreme positions are reassessing those positions. The Colgate-Palmolive Company announced it was decentralizing its advertising; marketing in the 1990s would be tailored specifically to local markets and countries.[8] An industry analyst reported that "There will be little, if any, global advertising." This appeared to be a reversal for Colgate, one of the first companies to embrace worldwide standardized advertising. However, another change in policy came a few years later when the company launched a new shampoo in Thailand. Nouriche, the brand name, will be sold in Australia, Europe, and Latin America as well as Thailand. The same TV, print, and sampling blitz planned for Thailand will run in the other markets.

The seeming reversal in Colgate-Palmolive's earlier policy to decentralize advertising represents what is happening in many companies that initially took extreme positions on standardizing their marketing efforts. Companies have discovered that the idea of complete global standardization is more myth than reality.

As discussed in Chapter 9, markets are constantly changing and are in the process of becoming more alike, but the world is still far from being a homogeneous market with common needs and wants for all products. Myriad obstacles to strict standardization remain. A strong case against standardization in one study suggests that advertising strategies can be transferred but the creative execution must be changed to suit the local context.[9] Nevertheless, the lack of commonality among markets should not deter a marketer from being guided by a global strategy, that is, a marketing philosophy that directs

---

[8] Jay Schulberg, "Successful Global Ads Need Simplicity, Clarity," *Advertising Age,* June 30, 1997, p. 17.

[9] Susan H. C. Tai, "Advertising in Asia: Localize or Regionalize?" *International Journal of Advertising,* Vol. 16, 1997, p. 48.

products and advertising toward a worldwide rather than a local or regional market, seeking standardization where possible, and modifying where necessary.

Pan-European Advertising

The attraction of a single European market will entice many companies to standardize as much of their promotional effort as possible. As media coverage across Europe expands, it will become more common for markets to be exposed to multiple messages and brands of the same product. To avoid the confusion that results when a market is exposed to multiple brand names and advertising messages, as well as for reasons of efficiency, companies will strive for harmony in brand names, advertising, and promotions across Europe.

Mars, the candy company, traditionally used several brand names for the same product but has found it necessary to select a single name to achieve uniformity in its standardized advertising campaigns. As a result, a candy bar sold in some parts of Europe under the brand name Raider was changed to Twix, the name used in the U.S. and the United Kingdom. Similarly, Campbell Biscuits, the cookie subsidiary of Campbell Soup Company, standardized packaging graphics for more than 50 products and put its five cookie brands under a single umbrella brand, Delacre. These changes to standardize brand names and packaging were necessary before Campbell would be able to standardize advertising campaigns throughout Europe. To facilitate pan-European advertising campaigns, a trend toward developing Euro-brands is also occurring. In a recent study, 81 percent of the respondents said they were aiming toward brand standardization while only 18 percent indicated they were localizing brands.

IBM has gradually created a pan-European promotional strategy by moving away from campaigns individually tailored for each European country. Broadcast and print advertisements for its personal computers feature an identical image with text that is translated into local languages. To ensure uniformity in its promotional materials, IBM developed a manual to provide step-by-step instructions on how to achieve a common theme in the design of all the company's product and service brochures.

An important reason for uniform promotional packaging across country markets is cost savings. In IBM's case, one set of European ads versus one set for each country for one of its personal computers saved an estimated $2 million. The company also estimates that a completely unified European advertising strategy will result in stretching its $150 million European budget by an extra 15 to 20 percent

Along with changes in behavior patterns, legal restrictions are slowly being eliminated, and viable market segments across country markets are emerging. While Europe will never be a single homogenous market for every product, that does not mean that companies should shun the idea of developing European-wide promotional programs. A pan-European promotional strategy would mean identifying a market segment across all European countries and designing a promotional concept appealing to market segment similarities. IBM, Campbell Biscuits, and Mars candy, examples discussed earlier, represent pan-European promotional strategies.[10]

With a common language (Brazil being the one exception), Latin America lends itself to regionwide promotion programs as well. Eveready Battery has developed a 16-country campaign with one message instead of the patchwork of messages that previously existed. Whether or not regionwide promotional programs will work depends on a variety of factors. Companies will have to decide whether their promotional strategy should reflect standardization, adaptation, or a combination of the two (pattern advertising). Global market segmentation offers some direction in developing global strategies.

Global Market Segmentation and Promotional Strategy

Rather than approach a promotional strategy decision as having to be either standardized or adapted, a company should first identify market segments. A market segment

---

[10] Juliana Koranteng, "EU Membership Spurs New Ads," *Advertising Age,* January 23, 1995, p. 10.

consists of consumers with more similarities in their needs, wants, and buying behavior than differences, and thus more responsive to a uniform promotional theme. Market segments can be defined within country boundaries or across countries. *Global market segmentation* involves identifying homogeneous market segments across groups of countries. Customers in a global market segment may come from different cultural backgrounds with different value systems and live in different parts of the world, but their commonalities in life-styles and their needs are fulfilled by similar product benefits. Further, while segments in some countries may be too small to be considered, when aggregated across a group of countries, they make a very lucrative total market.

Procter & Gamble has identified mass market segments across the world and designed brand and advertising concepts that apply to all. The company's shampoo positioning strategy, "Pro-V vitamin formula strengthens the hair and makes it shine," was developed for the Taiwan market, and then successfully launched in several Latin American countries with only minor adaptation for hair type and language. L'Oreal's "It's expensive and I'm worth it" brand position also works well worldwide. Unilever's fabric softener's teddy bear brand concept has worked well across borders, even though the "Snuggle" brand name changes in some countries; it's Kuschelweich in Germany, Coccolino in Italy, and Mimosin in France.

Other companies have identified niche segments too small for country-specific development but, when taken in aggregate, they have become profitable markets. The luxury brand luggage, Vuitton, is an example of a product designed for a niche segment. It is marketed as an exclusive, high-priced, glamorous product worldwide to relatively small segments in most countries.

Another approach is to identify niche segments where the same product category is promoted but from a different angle. Gillette sees a tremendous market in Europe, where surveys indicate only 30 percent of the European women wet shave, compared with about 75 percent in the U.S. What's more, there are still large numbers of European women who do not remove hair from their legs and underarms. Gillete's challenge is to introduce these women to hair removal. For those who use some other method (waxing, for example), the challenge is to switch them to wet shaving with Gillette products. For those who shave, the theme "the Two Minute Makeover" implies that shaving should be a part of a regular beauty regime—that is, shave more frequently than you wax and in much less time. For those who do not remove hair at all, the approach is to stress "legs that look and feel good." To communicate this message, Gillette ads feature life-style vignettes such as children caressing their young mother's legs on the beach rather than using a barrage of technical details. "It's a very sensual portrayal that shows the end result—legs that feel and look good," explains an executive.[11] In the U.S., where 75 percent of women wet shave, the goal is to convince them to switch to Gillette products.

There are those who continue to argue the merits of standardization versus adaptation but most agree that identifiable market segments for specific products exist across country markets and that companies should approach promotional planning from a global perspective, standardize where feasible, and adapt where necessary.[12]

Creative Challenges

The growing intensity of international competition, coupled with the complexity of multinational marketing, demands that the international advertiser function at the highest creative level. Advertisers from around the world have developed their skills and

[11] Ernest Beck, "Gillette, Wilkinson Make Inroads, but Obstacles Remain," *The Wall Street Journal Europe,* May 6, 1997, p. 4.

[12] See, for example, Linda C. Ueltschy and John K. Ryans, Jr., "Employing Standardized Promotion Strategies in Mexico: The Impact of Language and Cultural Differences," *The International Executive,* July/August 1997, p. 479.

abilities to the point that advertisements from different countries reveal basic similarities and a growing level of sophistication. To complicate matters further, boundaries are placed on creativity by legal, language, cultural, media, production, and cost limitations.

Legal Considerations

Laws that control comparative advertising vary from country to country in Europe. In Germany, it is illegal to use any comparative terminology; you can be sued by a competitor if you do. Belgium and Luxembourg explicitly ban comparative advertising, whereas it is clearly authorized in the U.K., Ireland, Spain, and Portugal. The directive covering comparative advertising will allow implicit comparisons that do not name competitors, but will ban explicit comparisons between named products. The European Commission has issued several directives to harmonize the laws governing advertising. However, member states are given substantial latitude to cover issues under their jurisdiction.[13] Many fear that if the laws are not harmonized, member states may close their borders to advertising that does not respect their national rules.[14]

Comparative advertising is heavily regulated in other parts of the world, as well. In Asia, an advertisement showing chimps choosing Pepsi over Coke was banned from most satellite television; the term "the leading cola" was accepted only in the Philippines. An Indian court ordered Lever to cease claiming that its New Pepsodent toothpaste was "102% better" than the leading brand. Colgate, the leading brand, was never mentioned in the advertisement although a model was shown mouthing the word "Colgate" and the image was accompanied by a "ting" sound recognized in all Colgate ads as the ring of confidence.[15] Banning explicit comparisons will rule out an effective advertising approach heavily used by U.S. companies at home and in other countries where it is permitted.

Advertising on television is strictly controlled in many countries. In Kuwait, the government-controlled TV network allows only 32 minutes of advertising per day, in the evening. Commercials are controlled to exclude superlative descriptions, indecent words, fearful or shocking shots, indecent clothing or dancing, contests, hatred or revenge shots, and attacks on competition. It is also illegal to advertise cigarettes, lighters, pharmaceuticals, alcohol, airlines, and chocolates or other candy.

There does seem to be some softening of country laws against accessibility to broadcast media. Australia has ended a ban on cable television spots[16] and Malaysia is considering changing the rules to allow foreign commercials to air on newly legalized satellite signals. With rare exception all commercials on Malaysian television must be made in Malaysia.[17]

Companies that rely on television infomercials and television shopping are restricted by the limitations placed on the length and number of television commercials permitted when their programs are classified as advertisements. The levels of restrictions in the European Community vary widely from no advertising on the BBC in the U.K. to member states that limit advertising to a maximum of 15 percent daily. The Television without Frontiers directive permits stricter or more detailed rules to the broadcasters under jurisdiction of each member state. In Germany, for example, com-

---

13 For a complete review of the disparities between regulations in EU member states, see "Part III. Evaluation of Specific Areas for Community Action," May 1996, found at **http://europa.eu.int** and search for advertising and regulation.

14 The European Commission's attempt to harmonize advertising laws is constantly contested in the courts. To see some cases and decisions by the Court of Justice, see "Proceedings of the Court of Justice and the Court of First Instance of the European Communities, July 1997" at **http://europa.eu.int/cj/en/act/9721en.htm**.

15 Mir Maqbool Alam Khan, "Indian Court Tells Lever to Clean Up Ad Claims," *Ad Age International,* January 1998, p. 32.

16 Rochelle Burbury, "Australia Ends Ban on Cable TV Spots," *Ad Age International,* March 1997, p. I22.

17 Tze Yee-Lin, "Malaysia May Allow Foreign Commercials," *Ad Age International,* March 1997, p. I22.

CROSSING BORDERS 16-3

You Try, but Sometimes It Just Doesn't Work

White space in a print advertisement is considered effective in creating contrast, in setting off an illustration and giving it focus. But sometimes, other issues seem more important. Iranian authorities frowned on a Chiquita banana ad because they considered it a waste of space to show only three bananas on a full-page ad. But that wasn't the only obstacle Chiquita faced as one of the first Western brands to advertise heavily in Iran. Soon after Chiquita banana advertising took off, so did sales. Distributors told the ad agency to cut back on the advertising—the bananas sold so well that Iranian authorities became concerned about the popularity of a Western brand. How does the old saying go? "You can't win for losing."

Source: Adapted from "Multinationals Tread Softly While Advertising in Iran," *Advertising Age,* November 8, 1993, p. 121.

mercials must be spaced at least 20 minutes apart and total ad time may not exceed 12 minutes per hour.[18]

Internet services are especially vulnerable as EU member states decide which area of regulation should apply to these services. Barriers to pan-European services will arise if some member states opt to apply television-broadcasting rules to the Internet while other countries apply print-media advertising rules.[19] The good news is that the EU is addressing the issues of regulation of activities on the Internet.[20] Although most of the attention will be focused on domain names and Internet addresses, the Commission does recognize that on-line activities will be severely hampered if subject to fragmented regulation.[21]

Some countries have special taxes that apply to advertising, which might restrict creative freedom in media selection. The tax structure in Austria best illustrates how advertising taxation can distort media choice by changing the cost ratios of various media: In federal states, with the exception of Bergenland and Tyrol, there is a 10 percent tax on ad insertions; for posters, there is a 10–30 percent tax according to state and municipality. Radio advertising carries a 10 percent tax, except in Tyrol where it is 20 percent. In Salzburg, Steiermark, Karnten, and Voralbert, there is no tax. There is a uniform tax of 10 percent throughout the country on television ads. Cinema advertising has a 10 percent tax in Vienna, 20 percent in Bergenland, and 30 percent in Steiermark. There is no cinema tax in the other federal states.

Language Limitations

Language is one of the major barriers to effective communication through advertising. The problem involves different languages of different countries, different languages or dialects within one country, and the subtler problems of linguistic nuance and vernacular.

---

[18] Miriam Hils, "TVINTL German Spot Checks," *Variety,* May 19, 1997, p. 30.

[19] "A Single Market for Advertising," *Business Europe,* May 22, 1996, p. 3.

[20] Jennifer L. Schenker and Rebecca Quick, "EU Is Set to Unveil Plan on Internet Governance," *The Wall Street Journal Europe,* February 2, 1998, p. 3.

[21] Angus MacKinnon, "EU Calls for Global Charter on Internet Regulation," *Agence France-Presse,* February 4, 1998.

Incautious handling of language has created problems in nearly every country. Some examples suffice. Chrysler Corporation was nearly laughed out of Spain when it translated its U.S. theme advertising, "Dart Is Power." To the Spanish, the phrase implied that buyers sought but lacked sexual vigor. The Bacardi Company concocted a fruity bitters with a made-up name, Pavane, suggestive of French chic. Bacardi wanted to sell the drink in Germany, but Pavane is perilously close to *pavian,* which means "baboon." A company marketing tomato paste in the Middle East found that in Arabic the phrase "tomato paste" translates as "tomato glue." In Spanish-speaking countries you have to be careful of words that have different meanings in the different countries. The word "ball" translates in Spanish as *bola. Bola* means ball in one country, revolution in another, a lie or fabrication in another, and, in yet another, it is an obscenity.

Tropicana brand orange juice was advertised as *jugo de China* in Puerto Rico, but when transported to Miami's Cuban community, it failed. To the Puerto Rican, *China* translated into orange, but to the Cuban it was China the country—and the Cubans were not in the market for Chinese juice. One Middle East advertisement features an automobile's new suspension system that, in translation, said the car was "suspended from the ceiling." Since there are at least 30 dialects among Arab countries, there is ample room for error. What may appear as the most obvious translation can come out wrong. "A whole new range of products" in a German advertisement came out as "a whole new stove of products."

Language translation encounters innumerable barriers that impede effective, idiomatic translation and thereby hamper communication. This is especially apparent in advertising materials. Abstraction, terse writing, and word economy, the most effective tools of the advertiser, pose problems for translators. Communication is impeded by the great diversity of cultural heritage and education which exists within countries and which causes varying interpretations of even single sentences and simple concepts. Some companies have tried to solve the translation problem by hiring foreign translators who live in the United States. This often is not satisfactory because both the language and the translator change, so the expatriate in the United States is out of touch after a few years. Everyday words have different meanings in different cultures. Even pronunciation causes problems: Wrigley had trouble selling its Spearmint gum in Germany until it changed the spelling to Speermint.

In addition to translation challenges, low literacy in many countries seriously impedes communications and calls for greater creativity and use of verbal media. Multiple languages within a country or advertising area pose another problem for the advertiser. Even a tiny country such as Switzerland has four separate languages. The melting-pot character of the Israeli population accounts for some 50 languages. A Jerusalem commentator says that even though Hebrew "has become a negotiable instrument of daily speech, this has yet to be converted into advertising idiom."

Cultural Diversity

The problems associated with communicating to people in diverse cultures present one of the great creative challenges in advertising. Communication is more difficult because cultural factors largely determine the way various phenomena are perceived. If the perceptual framework is different, perception of the message itself differs.

Knowledge of cultural diversity must encompass the total advertising project. General Mills had two problems with one product. When it introduced instant cake mixes in the United States and England, it had the problem of overcoming the homemaker's guilt feelings. When General Mills introduced instant cake mixes in Japan, the problem changed; cakes were not commonly eaten in Japan. There was no guilt feeling but the homemaker was concerned about failing. She wanted the cake mix as complete as possible. In testing TV commercials promoting the notion that making cake is as easy as making rice, General Mills learned it was offending the Japanese homemaker who believes the preparation of rice requires great skill.

CROSSING BORDERS 16–4

RTV—CNN, MTV, and the Society Page All Rolled into One

We are all familiar with MTV and CNN, but have you heard of RTV (Rural Television)? RTV is a little different as far as television networks go but not necessarily less effective. It gets the job done and goes where no other television goes—the rural areas of South Africa. RTV is South Africa's only direct communication with the country's large rural population.

The idea for RTV had its roots in the filming of the epic movie *Shaka Zulu.* The founders of RTV had the idea of placing TV sets in rural stores in KwaZulu, the Zulu homeland, when the African extras asked for an opportunity to see themselves in the movie. The showings drew such huge crowds that the idea of bringing entertainment to the rural areas was born.

RTV consists of four parts: 550 rural stores that rent TVs and VCRs; videos of local events; ladies' clubs that organize groups of locals for showings, contests, and product samplings; and an entertainment group that performs local, cultural-specific shows.

In a typical day of RTV "programming" these three events were happening somewhere in "RTV land": "Anchor Yeast! Anchor Yeast!" boomed a crowd of several thousand in one of South Africa's quasi-independent black homelands. The crowd bounced to the beat of rock music, encouraged by an enthusiastic leader chanting and dancing from a banner-festooned stage mounted on a truckbed. Dancing to rock music blasting from the giant speakers, one mother bouncing her baby cries out, "I love the music. This fun. Things like this don't happen often in our little place." One performer moves crowds to a frenzy extolling the virtues of products promoted by RTV and another wows them with expert Zulu dancing.

On the shaded porch of a country store a few miles down the road, 50 women from the local ladies' club, resplendent in tribal dress, cheered as their friends sang jingles and correctly answered questions about Oxo soups to win free samples, T-shirts, bags, and baseball caps.

Meanwhile, 300 miles south, in the Zulu homeland, townspeople jostled and vied for position in front of a TV set perched on the porch of a country store. Anticipation mounted as the storekeeper inserted into the VCR a tape made of a wedding in the little town a month earlier. Women ululated and men applauded as they recognized themselves. Every three minutes, there was a commercial in their own language.

RTV crews film local events, weddings, initiations, coming-of-age ceremonies, gospel music, and sporting events. The raw footage is edited and commercials are inserted. On the next trip through there is a "premiere" of the local tape and a day of fun and games, songs, contests, and giveaways organized by the ladies' clubs. The tape remains with the storeowner to be shown until the next "premiere." RTV representatives visit every month to six weeks with new tapes featuring at least six hours of entertainment and a maximum of 18 minutes of commercials per hour.

RTV clients include Lipton (Oxo soup), Anchor Yeast (yeast), Colgate-Palmolive Co. (Stay Soft fabric softener), Nestlé (Nespray baby milk formula and Gold Cross condensed milk), and Unilever (Van den Bergy Foods' Rama margarine).

RTV claims to reach 3.2 million people a month, or 80 percent of the rural population.

Source: Reprinted with permission from the April 17, 1993, issue of *Advertising Age.* Copyright Crain Communications, Inc., 1993.

Existing perceptions based on tradition and heritages are often hard to overcome. For example, marketing researchers in Hong Kong found that cheese is associated with *Yeung-Yen* (foreigners) and rejected by some Chinese. The concept of cooling and heating the body is important in Chinese thinking; malted milk is considered heating while fresh milk is cooling; brandy is sustaining, whiskey harmful.

Procter & Gamble's initial advertisement for Pampers brand diapers failed because of cultural differences between the United States and Japan. A U.S. commercial that showed an animated stork delivering Pampers diapers to homes was dubbed into Japanese and the U.S. package was replaced by the Japanese package and put on the air. To P&G's dismay the advertisement failed to build the market. Some belated consumer research revealed the consumers were confused about why this bird was delivering disposable diapers. According to Japanese folklore, giant peaches that float on the river bring babies to deserving parents, not storks.[22]

In addition to concerns with differences among nations, advertisers find subcultures within a country require attention as well. In Hong Kong there are 10 different patterns of breakfast eating. The youth of a country almost always constitute a different consuming culture from the older people, and urban dwellers differ significantly from rural dwellers. Besides these differences, there is the problem of changing traditions. In all countries, people of all ages, urban or rural, cling to their heritage to a certain degree but are willing to change some areas of behavior. A few years ago, it was unthinkable to try to market coffee in Japan, but it has become the fashionable drink for younger people and urban dwellers who like to think of themselves as European and sophisticated. Coffee drinking in Japan was introduced with instant coffee and there is virtually no market for anything else.

Media Limitations

Media are discussed at length later, so here we maintain only that limitations on creative strategy imposed by media may diminish the role of advertising in the promotional program and may force marketers to emphasize other elements of the promotional mix.

A marketer's creativity is certainly challenged when a television commercial is limited to 10 showings a year with no two exposures closer than 10 days, as is the case in Italy. Creative advertisers in some countries have even developed their own media for overcoming media limitations. In some African countries, advertisers run boats up and down the rivers playing popular music and broadcasting commercials into the bush as they travel.

Production and Cost Limitations

Creativity is especially important when a budget is small or where there are severe production limitations, poor-quality printing, and a lack of high-grade paper. For example, the poor quality of high-circulation glossy magazines and other quality publications has caused Colgate-Palmolive to depart from its customary heavy use of print media in the West for other media in Eastern Europe. Newsprint is of such low quality in China that a color ad used by Kodak in the West is not an option. Kodak's solution has been to print a single-sheet color insert as a newspaper supplement.[23] The necessity for low-cost reproduction in small markets poses another problem in many countries. For example, hand-painted billboards must be used instead of printed sheets because the limited number of billboards does not warrant the production of printed sheets. In Egypt, static-filled television and poor-quality billboards have led companies such as Coca-Cola and Nestlé

---

[22] Robert L. Wehling, "Even at P&G, Only 3 Brands Make Truly Global Grade So Far," *Ad Age International,* January 1998, p. 8.

[23] Audrey Snee, "Kodak Divides Up China in Order to Conquer It," *Ad Age International,* January 1998, p. 20.

to place their advertisements on the sails of feluccas, boats that sail along the Nile. Feluccas, with their triangle sails, have been used to transport goods since the time of the pharaohs and serve as an effective alternative to attract attention to company names and logos.[24]

The various constraints on advertising creativity can be seen as insurmountable impediments to standardized worldwide promotional campaigns, or they can be seen as the ultimate creative challenge for an advertiser, that is, to develop a promotional campaign that communicates across country markets, is informative, and is persuasive. There are many internationally known advertising agencies that feel they can successfully surmount the obstacles encountered when creating a standardized, global advertising campaign.

In reflecting on what a marketer is trying to achieve through advertising, it is clear that an arbitrary position strictly in favor of either modification or standardization is wrong; rather, the position must be to communicate a relevant message to the target market. If a promotion communicates effectively in multiple-country markets, then standardize; otherwise, modify. It is the message a market receives that generates sales, not whether an advertisement is standardized or modified.

Media Planning and Analysis

Tactical Considerations

Although nearly every sizable nation essentially has the same kinds of media, there are a number of specific considerations, problems, and differences encountered from one nation to another. In international advertising, an advertiser must consider the availability, cost, and coverage of the media. Local variations and lack of market data require added attention.

Imagine the ingenuity required of advertisers confronted with these situations:

- In Brazil, TV commercials are sandwiched together in a string of 10 to 50 commercials within one station break.
- National coverage in many countries means using as many as 40 to 50 different media.
- Specialized media reach small segments of the market only. In the Netherlands, there are Catholic, Protestant, socialist, neutral, and other specialized broadcasting systems.
- In Germany, TV scheduling for an entire year must be arranged by August 30 of the preceding year, with no guarantee that commercials intended for summer viewing will not be run in the middle of winter.
- In Vietnam, advertising in newspapers and magazines is limited to 10 percent of space, and to 5 percent of time, or three minutes an hour, on radio and TV.

Availability. One of the contrasts of international advertising is that some countries have too few advertising media and others have too many. In some countries, certain advertising media are forbidden by government edict to accept some advertising materials. Such restrictions are most prevalent in radio and television broadcasting. In many countries there are too few magazines and newspapers to run all the advertising offered to them. Conversely, some nations segment the market with so many newspapers that the advertiser cannot gain effective coverage at a reasonable cost. Gilberto Sozzani, head of an Italian advertising agency, comments about his country: "One fundamental rule. You cannot buy what you want."

---

[24] Amy Dockser Marcus, "Advertising Breezes Along the Nile River with Signs for Sails," *The Wall Street Journal,* July 18, 1997, p. A1.

EXHIBIT 16-1   Top 10 Global Advertising Markets Percentage Spending by Advertising Media (1997)

	Advertising by Media						
Country	Television	Newspaper	Radio	Magazine	Outdoor	Cinema	Other
United States	38.4	36.4	10.5	12.9	1.7	-0-	-0-
Japan	44.8	28.1	4.9	9.0	13.2	-0-	-0-
Germany	22.3	45.3	3.7	24.6	3.2	0.9	-0-
U.K.	31.9	37.3	3.5	22.5	4.1	0.7	-0-
France	34.0	23.5	7.3	22.9	11.8	0.6	-0-
Brazil	52.0	29.0	4.5	10.5	4.0	-0-	-0-
So. Korea	32.0	37.0	4.0	3.9	-0-	-0-	22.6
China	25.1	25.4	2.6	2.0	-0-	-0-	44.9
Italy	54.5	21.7	3.8	16.6	3.1	0.4	-0-
Mexico	73.8	10.8	8.8	2.9	3.1	0.6	-0-

Source: Abstracted from "Top Global Ad Markets," *Ad Age International,* May 1997, p. I7.

In China the only national TV station, CCTV, has one channel that must be aired by the country's 27 provincial/municipal stations. In 1997 CCTV auctioned off the most popular break between the early evening news and weather; a secured yearlong, daily five-second billboard ad in this break went for $38.5 million. For this price, advertisers are assured of good coverage—over 70 percent of households have TV sets and the government's goal is 90 percent by 2000. One of the other options for advertisers is with the 2,828 TV stations that provide only local coverage.[25] For a comparison on how much of the advertising dollar is spent on different media in the top 10 global markets see Exhibit 16–1.

Cost.   Media prices are susceptible to negotiation in most countries. Agency space discounts are often split with the client to bring down the cost of media. The advertiser may find the cost of reaching a prospect through advertising depends on the agent's bargaining ability. The per-contract cost varies widely from country to country. One study showed the cost of reaching one thousand readers in 11 different European countries ranged from $1.58 in Belgium to $5.91 in Italy; in women's service magazines, the page cost per thousand circulation ranged from $2.51 in Denmark to $10.87 in Germany. Shortages of advertising time on commercial television in some markets have caused substantial price increases. In Britain, prices escalate on a bidding system. They do not have fixed rate cards; instead there is a preempt system in which advertisers willing to pay a higher rate can bump already scheduled spots.

Coverage.   Closely akin to the cost dilemma is the problem of coverage. Two points are particularly important: one relates to the difficulty of reaching certain sectors of the population with advertising and the other to the lack of information on coverage. In many world marketplaces, a wide variety of media must be used to reach the majority of the markets. In some countries, large numbers of separate media have divided markets into uneconomical advertising segments. With some exceptions, a majority of the population of less-developed countries cannot be reached readily through the medium of advertising. In India, Video Vans are used to reach India's rural population with 30-minute infomercials extolling the virtues of a product. Consumer goods companies deploy vans year-round except in the monsoon season. Colgate hires 85 vans at a time and sends them to villages that research has shown to be promising.[26]

---

[25] "China's Media Boom Rewards Those Willing to Endure Growing Pains," *Advertising Age International,* October 1997, p. I6.

[26] Miriam Jordan, "Rural India, Video Vans Sell Toothpaste and Shampoo," *The Wall Street Journal,* January 10, 1996, p. B1.

Because of the lack of adequate coverage by any single media in Eastern European countries, it is necessary for companies to resort to a multimedia approach. In the Czech Republic, for example, TV advertising rates are high, and unavailable prime-time spots have forced companies to use billboard advertising. Outdoor advertising has become popular, and in Prague alone, billboards have increased from 50 in 1990 to over 3,500 in 1994. In Slovenia the availability of adequate media is such a problem that companies resort to some unique approaches to get their messages out. For example, in the summer lasers are used to project images onto clouds above major cities. Vehicle advertising includes cement-mixers, where Kodak ads have appeared. On the positive side, crime is so low that products can be displayed in free-standing glass cabinets on sidewalks; Bosch Siemens (Germany) and Kodak have both used this method.[27]

Lack of Market Data. Verification of circulation or coverage figures is a difficult task. Even though many countries have organizations similar to the Audit Bureau of Circulation, accurate circulation and audience data are not assured. For example, the president of the Mexican National Advertisers Association charged that newspaper circulation figures are grossly exaggerated. He suggested that as a rule agencies divide these figures in two and take the result with a grain of salt. The situation in China is no better; surveys of habits and market penetration are available only for the cities of Beijing, Shanghai, and Guangzhou. Radio and television audiences are always difficult to measure, but at least in most countries, geographic coverage is known. Research data are becoming more reliable as advertisers and agencies demand better quality data.[28]

Even where advertising coverage can be measured with some accuracy, there are questions about the composition of the market reached. Lack of available market data seems to characterize most international markets; advertisers need information on income, age, and geographic distribution, but such basic data seems chronically elusive except in the largest markets. Even the attractiveness of global television (satellite broadcasts) is diminished somewhat because of the lack of media research available.[29]

Specific Media Information

An attempt to evaluate specific characteristics of each medium is beyond the scope of this discussion. Furthermore, such information would quickly become outdated because of the rapid changes in the international advertising media field. It may be interesting, however, to examine some of the particularly unique international characteristics of various advertising media. In most instances, the major implications of each variation may be discerned from the data presented.

Newspapers. The newspaper industry is suffering in some countries from lack of competition and choking because of it in others. Most U.S. cities have just one or two major daily newspapers, but in many countries, there are so many newspapers an advertiser has trouble achieving even partial market coverage. Uruguay, population three million, has 21 daily newspapers with a combined circulation of 553,000. Turkey has 380 newspapers and an advertiser must consider the political position of each newspaper so the product's reputation is not harmed through affiliations with unpopular positions. Japan has only five national daily newspapers, but the complications of producing a Japanese-language newspaper are such that they each contain just 16 to 20 pages. Connections are necessary to buy advertising space; *Asahi,* Japan's largest newspaper, has been known to turn down over a million dollars a month in advertising revenue.

---

27 "Slovenia: Simple Life," *Business Eastern Europe,* January 22, 1996, p. 4.

28 Jane Blennerhassett and Laurel Wentz, "New Study Aims to End Asia's Research Drought," *Ad Age International,* March 1997, p. 116.

29 Joe Mandese, "Cable, Satellite Aim High; Advertisers Stay Grounded," *Ad Age International Special Issue: Cable and Satellite TV,* March 1997, p. 14.

CROSSING BORDERS 16-5

Good Housekeeping in Name Only

When *Good Housekeeping* magazine appeared on Japanese newsstands, many Japanese thought it was a journal for diligent housemaids. To adapt this successful U.S. magazine has been no small task. Almost everything from the name to the content has been changed.

First of all, translation of the title was out of the question. *Kaji,* the closest translation of "housekeeping," literally means "domestic duties" and connotes servants' tasks. So the publishers stuck with the U.S. title to preserve the American cachet but printed the word "good" on the cover triple the size of the word "housekeeping."

The articles typically found in the U.S. version didn't fly either. Harrowing tales of an ordinary woman's triumph over the tragedy of a tornado that leveled her home would put Japanese women off. They are more accustomed to cheery stories. Best-Loved Bible Quotes won't fly either in a largely Buddhist nation. Instead, "aspirational" articles about an idealized America are featured, like the 16-page feature on sparkling New York kitchens that are about the size of an entire Japanese apartment. Although a distant dream of most Japanese, the layout of every pantry, cabinet, and shelf in tiny diagrams was shown. Close-up photos of nooks and crannies such as pullout drawers and custom-made spice racks are useful in even the tiniest kitchens.

The recipes for party snacks, a direct lift from the U.S., were well received. Goat-cheese crostini and roast-beef-and-potato bites were quite tasty and easy to prepare.

But even with all the changes, some women in Japan say they don't see much unique about *Good Housekeeping.* "It has everything that other women's magazines have . . . it should have more practical articles like the sample product-complaint letter, in English, to companies abroad," commented one woman.

Source: Abstracted from Yumiko Ono, "Will *Good Housekeeping* Translate into Japanese?" *The Wall Street Journal,* December 30, 1997, p. B1.

In many countries there is a long time lag before an advertisement can be run in a newspaper. In India and Indonesia, paper shortages delay publication of ads for up to six months. Furthermore, because of equipment limitations, most newspapers cannot be made larger to accommodate the increase in advertising demand.

Separation between editorial and advertising content in newspapers provides another basis for contrast on the international scene. In some countries, it is possible to buy editorial space for advertising and promotional purposes; the news columns are for sale to anyone who has the price. Since there is no indication that the space is paid for, it is impossible to tell exactly how much advertising appears in a given newspaper.

Magazines.   The use of foreign national consumer magazines by international advertisers has been notably low for many reasons. Few magazines have a large circulation or provide dependable circulation figures. Technical magazines are used rather extensively to promote export goods but, as with newspapers, paper shortages cause placement problems. Media planners are often faced with the largest magazines accepting up to twice as many advertisements as they have space to run them in—then they decide what advertisements will go in just before going to press by means of a raffle.

Such local practices may be key items favoring the growth of so-called international media which attempt to serve many nations. Increasingly, U.S. publications are publishing overseas editions. *Reader's Digest International* has added a new Russian-language edition to its more than 20 other language editions. Other American print media available in international editions range from *Playboy* to *Scientific American,*

Exhibit 16-2 Selected International Print Media: Asia Pacific (AP), Europe (E), and Latin America (LA)

Print Media	Region	Web*	Circulation	Advertising Rates†
Channel World (v, cc)	AP	Yes	16,000	N/A
The Chinese (m, p)	AP	No	50,000	4C: $10,000/b&w: $8,000
Cosmopolitan (w, cc)	AP	No	874,816	4C:$39,890
International Herald Tribune (d, p)	AP	Yes	47,500	4C: $24,198/b&w: $18,614
Newsweek Pacific (w,p)	AP	Yes	350,000	4C: $46,000/b&w: $28,025
Reader's Digest (m, p)	AP	No	1.9mil.	4C: $64,383/b7w: $51,735
Yazhou Zhoukan (w, p)	AP	Yes	90,156	4C:$12,762/b&w: $$10,207
Channel World (v, cc)	E	Yes	118,000	N/A
Cosmopolitan (w, cc)	E	Yes	450,000	4C:$141,807
The European (w, p)	E	No	155,000	4C: $19,650/b&w: $16,300
Newsweek (w, p)	E	No	340,000	4C:$43,265/b&w: $25,450
Reader's Digest (m,p)	E	No	7.5 mil	4C: $169,341/b&w: $125,495
Cosmopolitan en Español (m, p)	LA	No	448,602	4C: $29,855/b&w: $22,391
Eres (b,p)	LA	No	566,504	4C: $21,680/b&w: $16,260
Harper's Bazaar en Español (m, p)	LA	No	106,298	4C: $12,15-/b&w $9,113
Mecanica Popular (m, cc)	LA	No	187,218	4C: $12,750/b&w $9,563
Newsweek en Español (w, p)	LA	No	54,100	4C: $10,295/b&w: $6,175
Reader's Digest LA (m, p)	LA	No	1.6 mil.	4C: $58,312/b&w: $43,721
T.V. y Novelas (bw, p)	LA	No	935,751	4C: $27,520/b&w $20,640

Notes: b = bimonthly; bw = biweekly; d = daily; f = fortnightly; m = monthly; v = varies by market; w = weekly; p = paid circulation; cc = controlled circulation.
* Ad supported Web site; † full page, 1x.
Source: "Global Media," *Ad Age International,* February 9, 1998, pp. 15–22.

and even include the *National Enquirer,* recently introduced to the U.K. Advertisers have three new magazines to reach females in China: Hachette Filipachi Presse, the French publisher, is expanding Chinese-language editions of *Elle,* a fashion magazine; *Woman's Day* is aimed at China's "busy modern" woman; and *L'Evenement Sportif* is a sports magazine. These media offer alternatives for multinationals as well as for local advertisers. See Exhibit 16–2 for some examples of circulation and advertising rates for print media.

Radio and Television. Possibly because of their inherent entertainment value, radio and television have become major communications media in most nations. Most populous areas have television broadcasting facilities. In some markets, such as Japan, television has become almost a national obsession and thus finds tremendous audiences for its advertisers. In China, virtually all homes in major cities have a television and most adults view television and listen to radio daily. See Exhibit 16–3 for number of households covered and rates for TV advertising. Radio has been relegated to a subordinate position in the media race in countries where television facilities are well developed. In many countries, however, radio is a particularly important and vital advertising medium when it is the only one reaching large segments of the population.

Television and radio advertising availability varies between countries. Three patterns are discernible: competitive commercial broadcasting, commercial monopolies, and noncommercial broadcasting. Countries with free competitive commercial radio and television normally encourage competition and have minimal broadcast regulations. Elsewhere, local or national monopolies are granted by the government and individual stations or networks may then accept radio or TV commercials according to rules established by the government. In some countries, commercial monopolies may accept all the advertising they wish; in others, only spot advertising is permissible and programs may not be sponsored. Live commercials are not permitted in some countries; in still others, commercial stations must compete for audiences against the government's noncommercial broadcasting network.

EXHIBIT 16-3   Selected International TV Media
Asia Pacific (AP), Europe (E), and Latin America (LA)

Network	Region	Web*	No. Households	Average Rate, :30 Spot
BBC World	AP	Yes	19.1 million	$450
CNN International	AP	Yes	14.5 million	$3,000
Discovery Asia	AP	Yes	21.5 million	N/A
ESPN Star Sports	AP	No	60 million	N/A
MTV Asia	AP	Yes	1.2 million	Varies
TNT/Cartoon Network	AP	Yes	11.2 million	$800
CNN International	E	Yes	68.7 million	$4,000
Euronews	E	No	91 million	$1,625
MTV Networks Europe	E	Yes	60 million	Varies
Orbit Satellite TV & Radio	E	No	3.1 million	$250
CBS Telenoticias	LA	Yes	6.8 million	$1,000
CNN en Espanol	LA	Yes	6.1 million	$1,300
Discovery Channel LA	LA	Yes	8.4 million	$900
Gems International	LA	Yes	11.3 million	$600
MTV Latin America	LA	No	8.2 million	Varies
Nickelodeon Latin America	LA	Yes	4 million	$300-$600
TeleUNO	LA	No	6.6 million	$600 prime time

* Web site support, yes or no.
Source: "Global Media," *Ad Age International,* February 9, 1998, pp. 15–22.

No commercial radio or television is permitted in some countries, but several of the traditional noncommercial countries have changed their policies in recent years because television production is so expensive. Until recently, France limited commercials to a daily total of 18 minutes, but now has extended the time limit to 12 minutes per hour per TV channel. South Korea has two television companies, both government-owned, which broadcast only a few hours a day. They do not broadcast from midnight to 6 A.M. and they usually cannot broadcast between 10 A.M. And 5:30 P.M. on weekdays. Commercials are limited to 8 percent of air time and are shown in clusters at the beginning and end of programs. One advertiser remarked, "We are forced to buy what we don't want to buy just to get on."

Although commercial programming is limited, people in most countries have an opportunity to hear or view commercial radio and television. Entrepreneurs in the radio–television field have discovered that audiences in commercially restricted countries are hungry for commercial television and radio, and that marketers are eager to bring their messages into these countries. A major study in 22 countries revealed that the majority favored advertising. Individuals in former Communist countries were among the more enthusiastic supporters. Egypt was the only country in the survey where the majority of responses were anti-advertising. Only 9 percent of Egyptians surveyed agreed that many TV commercials are enjoyable compared to 80 percent or more in Italy, Uruguay, and Bulgaria.

Because of business and public demand for more programming, countries that had in the past banned private broadcast media have changed their laws in recent years to allow privately owned broadcasting stations. Italy, which had no private/local radio or TV until 1976, currently has some 300 privately owned stations. There also has been some softening of restrictions to allow limited amounts of airtime for commercials in countries where advertising has not been permitted on government-owned stations.

Lack of reliable audience data is another major problem in international marketing via radio and television. Measurement of radio and television audiences is always a precarious business, even with highly developed techniques. In most countries, audience measurement is either unaudited or the existing auditing associations are ineffective. Despite the paucity of audience data, many advertisers use radio and television exten-

EXHIBIT 16–4   **Household Penetration of Cable, Satellite, and Internet Top 10 Media Markets (1997)**

Country	Cable	Satellite	Internet
United States	66.9	4.1	21.3
Japan	22.9	22.9	9.9
Germany	59.9	20.7	11.6
UK	7.0	15.0	5.0
France	7.0	8.0	1.7
Brazil	4.3	5.2	0.003
So. Korea	14.0	N/A	1.8
China	25.8	25.8	N/A
Italy	N/A	3.4	1.9
Mexico	7.5	1.5	0.06

Source: Abstracted from "Top Global Advertising Markets," *Ad Age International,* May 1997, p. 17.

sively. Advertisers justify their inclusion in the media schedule on the inherent logic favoring the use of these media, or defend their use on the basis of sales results.

Satellite and Cable TV. Of increasing importance in TV advertising is the growth and development of satellite TV broadcasting. Sky Channel, a United Kingdom-based commercial satellite television station, beams its programs and advertising into most of Europe via cable TV subscribers. The technology that permits households to receive broadcasts directly from the satellite via a dish the "size of a dinner plate" costing about $350 is adding greater coverage and the ability to reach all of Europe with a single message. The expansion of TV coverage will challenge the creativity of advertisers and put greater emphasis on global standardized messages. For a comparison of household penetration by satellite, cable, and Internet in the top 10 media markets see Exhibit 16–4.

Advertisers and governments are both concerned about the impact of satellite TV. Governments are concerned because they fear further loss of control over their airwaves and the spread of "American cultural imperialism." European television programming includes such U.S. shows as "Roseanne"; "Wheel of Fortune" is the most popular foreign show in the United Kingdom and in France, where both the U.S. and French versions are shown. U.S. imports are so popular in France and Germany that officials fear lowbrow U.S. game shows, sitcoms, and soap operas will crush domestic producers. A major victory for the French in the Uruguay Round of GATT was the exclusion of movies and TV from the free-trade umbrella.

Most European governments are reducing restrictions, adding TV satellites of their own, and privatizing many government-owned channels in an attempt to attract more commercial revenue and to provide independent broadcasters with greater competition. With cable, satellites,[30] privatization of government-owned stations, and the European Commission's directives to harmonize the laws governing broadcast media, broadcasting—as a medium for advertising—will become easier to use and provide greater coverage of the European market.

Parts of Asia and Latin America receive TV broadcasts from satellite television networks. Univision and Televisa are two Latin-American satellite television networks broadcasting via a series of affiliate stations in each country to most of the Spanish-speaking world, including the United States. "Sabado Gigante," a popular Spanish-

---

[30] For an excellent report on the trends of satellites in global communications, see Krysten Jenci, "Satellites: Critical to the New Global Telecommunications Network," *Business America,* July 1997, p. 13.

language program broadcast by Univision, is seen by tens of millions of viewers in 16 countries. Star TV,[31] a new pan-Asian satellite television network, has a potential audience of 2.7 billion people living in 38 countries from Egypt through India to Japan, and from the Soviet Far East to Indonesia. Star TV[32] was the first to broadcast across Asia but was quickly joined by ESPN and CNN. The first Asian 24-hour all-sports channel was followed by MTV Asia and a Mandarin Chinese-language channel that delivers dramas, comedies, movies, and financial news aimed at the millions of overseas Chinese living throughout Asia. Programs are delivered through cable networks but can be received through private satellite dishes.

One of the drawbacks of satellites is their strength, that is, their ability to span a wide geographical region covering many different country markets. That means a single message is broadcast throughout a wide area. This may not be desirable for some products and, further, with cultural differences like language, preferences, and so on, a single message may not be as effective. PVI (Princeton Video Imaging) is an innovation that will make regional advertising in diverse cultures easier than it presently is when using cable or satellite television. PVI allows ESPN, which offers this service, to fill visual "real estate"—blank walls, streets, stadium sidings—with computer-generated visuals that look like they belong in the scene. For instance, if you are watching the "street luge" during ESPN's X-games, you will see the tobogganers appear to pass a billboard advertising Adidas shoes that really is not there. That billboard can say one thing in Holland and quite another in Cameroon. And if you are watching in Portland, Oregon, where Adidas might not advertise, you will see the scene as it really appears—without the billboard. These commercials can play in different languages, in different countries, and even under different brand names.[33]

Most satellite technology involves some government regulation. Singapore, Taiwan, and Malaysia prohibit selling satellite dishes, and the Japanese government prevents domestic cable companies from rebroadcasting from foreign satellites. Such restrictions seldom work for long, however. In Taiwan, there are an estimated 1.5 million dishes in use and numerous illicit cable operators. Through one technology or another, Asian households will be open to the same kind of viewing choice Americans have grown accustomed to and the advertising it brings along.

Direct Mail.   Direct mail is a viable medium in many countries. It is especially important when other media are not available. As is often the case in international marketing, even such a fundamental medium is subject to some odd and novel quirks.[34] For example, in Chile, direct mail is virtually eliminated as an effective medium because the sender pays only part of the mailing fee; the letter carrier must collect additional postage for every item delivered. Obviously, advertisers cannot afford to alienate customers by forcing them to pay for unsolicited advertisements. Despite some limitations with direct mail, many companies have found it a meaningful way to reach their markets. The Reader's Digest Association has used direct-mail advertising in Mexico to successfully market its magazines.

In Southeast Asian markets, where print media are scarce, direct mail is considered one of the most effective ways to reach those responsible for making industrial goods purchases, even though accurate mailing lists are a problem in Asia as well as in other parts of the world. In fact, some companies build their own databases for direct mail.[35]

---

[31] Visit Star TV's Web site for all the services and rate cards at **http://www.startv.com**.

[32] Tze Yee-Lin, "Star TV Finds Its Brilliance in Localization," *Ad Age International,* March 1997, p. 118.

[33] Mark London Williams, "Freeze Frame; ESPN Int'l at 15 Ad Deals Strike a Cultural Match," *Variety,* January 18, 1998, p. A8.

[34] Allyson L. Stewart-Allen, "Keys to Success in Europe's Massive Mail-Order Market," *Marketing News,* January 6, 1997, p. 17.

[35] Suzanne Bidlake, "Nestlé Builds Database in Asia with Direct Mail," *Ad Age International,* January 1998, p. 34.

CROSSING BORDERS 16-6

The Japanese—They Just Don't Get It

You remember the commercials—animated clay raisin figures stepping about smartly to the Motown sound; raisins wearing shades and dancing to choreographed moves, much like the Temptations; raisins singing "I Heard It through the Grapevine," much like Marvin Gaye.

The raisins were such a hit after their introduction that they won several Clio Awards, one of television advertising's highest accolades, and danced right into the National Museum of American History. And the California Raisin Advisory Board reasoned that if it's great in the United States, it's got to work in Japan.

The U.S. Department of Agriculture gave the California Raisin Advisory Board a $3 million grant to promote raisins in Japan. But the campaign failed—it didn't reach the 900-ton export goal. Why? Was it another case of those closed Japanese markets? Or was it poor marketing? Consider these points and judge for yourself:

The commercials were not translated into Japanese; they aired in English. The "dancing raisin" figures (misshapen and shriveled like raisins) frightened children. Some respondents were unable even to discern what product was being advertised and guessed them to be potatoes or chocolates. How can such a mistake be made today? Perhaps poor marketing?

The English-only raisin promotion cost $3,000 per ton of raisins sold to the largely mystified Japanese. U.S. producers earned $1,583 per ton. Now that's a great promotion.

Source: *The Oregonian.* © 1994, Oregonian Publishing Co. All Rights Reserved. Reprinted with permission.

Industrial advertisers are heavy mail users and rely on catalogs and sales sheets to generate large volumes of international business. Even in Japan, where media availability is not a problem, direct mail is successfully used by marketers such as Nestlé Japan and Dell Computer. To promote its Buitoni fresh chilled pasta, Nestlé is using a 12-page, color direct-mail booklet of recipes, including Japanese-style versions of Italian favorites.

Not all attempts have been successful, however. A catalog producer, R. R. Donnelley, suspended *American Showcase,* a collection of a dozen American catalogs sent to Japanese consumers, after receiving only modest responses and orders. Failure to receive sufficient response may reflect more on the *American Showcase* package than on the success of direct mail in the Japanese market. Even though the covering letter and brochure describing the catalogs were in Japanese, the catalogs were all in English. This error was further amplified by the fact that the mailing list did not target English-speaking Japanese.

In Russia, the volume of direct mail has gone from just over 150,000 letters per month to over 500,000 per month in one year. While small by U.S. standards, the response rate to direct mailings is as high as 10–20 percent, compared with only 3–4 percent or less in the United States. One suggestion as to why it works so well is that Russians are flattered by the attention—needless to say that will probably change as the medium grows.[36]

Other Media.   Restrictions on traditional media or their availability cause advertisers to call on lesser media to solve particular local-country problems. The cinema is an im-

---

[36] "Mail Bonding," *Business Europe,* October 28, 1996, p. 1.

Innovation is required to get the advertising message to different markets. Video vans that travel from village to village help Hindustan Lever sell soap in Maharashtra. (Raghu Rai/Magnum)

portant medium in many countries, as are billboards and other forms of outside advertising. Billboards are especially useful in countries with high illiteracy rates.

In Haiti, sound trucks equipped with powerful loudspeakers provide an effective and widespread advertising medium. Private contractors own the equipment and sell advertising space much as a radio station would. This medium overcomes the problems of illiteracy, lack of radio and television set ownership, and limited print media circulation. In Ukraine, where the postal service is unreliable, businesses have found that the most effective form of direct business-to-business advertising is direct faxing.

In Spain, a new medium includes private cars that are painted with advertisements for products and serve as moving billboards as they travel around. This new system, called *Publicoche* (derived from the words *publicidad,* meaning advertising, and *coche,* meaning car), has 75 cars in Madrid. Car owners are paid $230 a month and must submit their profession and "normal" weekly driving patterns. Advertisers pay a basic cost of $29,000 per car per month, and can select the type and color of car they are interested in and which owners are most suited to the campaign based on their driving patterns.[37]

The Internet—A Media Mix Alternative

Though still evolving,[38] the Internet is emerging as a viable medium for advertising and should be included as one of the media in a company's possible media mix.[39] Its use in business-to-business communications and promotion via catalogs and product descriptions is rapidly gaining in popularity.[40] Since a large number of businesses have access to the Internet, the Internet can reach a large portion of the business-to-business market.

Although limited in its penetration of households, the Internet is being used by a growing number of companies as an advertising medium for consumer goods.[41] Many

---

[37] Derek Cox, "Drivers Paid to Carry Ads," *Ad Age International,* April 1997, p. 118.

[38] "The Web Is Crawling in Asia," *Newsbytes News Network,* **http://www.newsbytes.com**, January 22, 1998.

[39] W. Wossen Kassaye, "Global Advertising and the World Wide Web," *Business Horizons,* June/July 1997, p. 33.

[40] Laurie Freeman, "Net Drives B-to-B to New Highs Worldwide," *Business Marketing,* January 1998, p. 1.

[41] Juliana Koranteng, "CEO Hunt Sells Web Sites for Marketing While Preaching Online Gospel," *Advertising Age International,* July 1997, p. 128.

consumer goods companies have e-stores and others use the Internet as an advertising medium to stimulate sales in retail outlets. Waterford Crystal of Ireland has set up its Web site specifically to drive store traffic. The aim is to promote its products and to attract people into stores that sell Waterford Crystal. Sites list and display almost the entire catalogue of the Waterford collection, while stores like Bloomingdales that stock Waterford support the promotional effort by also advertising on the Internet.[42]

Another company that is using the Internet as an advertising medium is Levi Strauss & Company. Levi's is using its Web site as an integral part of a global advertising campaign. At **http://www.levi.com**, customers can surf through North American or European sites, sampling products and brand campaigns. When a new European jeans ad campaign was launched, an accompanying interactive game and mystery story appeared on the European site. In all there are five different games based on one of five Levi's "brand truths," as established in Levi's mainstream advertising campaign.[43] The company has also launched a specific site for Japan, using *kanji,* the Japanese language characters.[44]

For consumer products the major limitation of the Internet is coverage (see Exhibit 16–4). In the United States only a small portion of households have access to a computer, but there are even fewer in other countries. Nevertheless, the small number of Internet households accessible outside the United States generally constitutes a younger, better-educated market segment with higher than average incomes. For many companies, that group is an important market niche. Furthermore, this limitation is only temporary as new technology allows access to the Internet via television and as lower prices for personal computers expand the household base. NetChannel,[45] a new subscription Internet service provider which offers its service via domestic TV sets, will be available initially in the U.K. and the U.S., followed by a rollout across Europe and ultimately into Asia.[46] As an advertising medium it may be the ideal tool for pan-regional areas that cover various languages and cultures. A company's Web site can have as many cultural, linguistic options as it needs. If someone in Thailand lands on the Procter & Gamble site, they can read an ad in Thai for the company's products available in Thailand.[47]

As the Internet grows and countries begin to assert control over what is now virtually a medium without restrictions, limitations will be set. Besides control of undesirable information,[48] issues such as taxes, unfair competition, import duties, and privacy are being addressed all over the world. In Australia, local retailers are calling for changes in laws because of loss of trade to the Internet; under current law Internet purchases do not carry regular import duties.[49] The Internet industry is lobbying for a global understanding on regulation to avoid a crazy quilt of confusing and contradictory rules. As the director of the Asia-Pacific Internet Association commented, "Internationally . . . 1997 has been the year that the Internet has finally been recognized as requiring globally coordinated policy and regulatory understanding and development."[50]

Another limitation that needs to be addressed soon is the competition for Web surfers. The sheer proliferation of the number of Web sites makes it increasingly difficult for a customer to stumble across a particular page. Banners or interceptive sites

---

[42] "Spreading Web: The Wealth Generated by the Internet Is Likely to Be Concentrated in the Hands of a Few," *The Irish Times,* January 26, 1998, p. 19.

[43] John Owen, "The Ultimate Global Medicine but Is It Worth the Effort?" *Campaign,* September 26, 1997.

[44] Jane Weaver, "Them Jeans Are Made for Surfing," *MSNBC Interactive,* December 20, 1997.

[45] Suzanne Bidlake, "Europe Tunes In to Net," *Ad Age International,* September 1997, p. I47.

[46] Visit NetChannel's Web site for information about the company and whether it is available in your area: **http://www.netchannel.net**.

[47] "And Now the Net," *Business Asia,* February 10, 1997, p. 3.

[48] "Internet: Sixth Modified Version Emerges—Need for Legislation Still Faces Questions," *Bangkok Post,* January 21, 1998.

[49] "Australia Internet:Meet Telecom Companies," *Dow Jones News Service,* July 2, 1997.

[50] "Internet Regulation," *Asia Computer Weekly,* January 12, 1998.

advertising the site can help but that venue is also becoming crowded. As discussed earlier, serious Internet advertisers or e-marketers will have to be more effective in communicating the existence of their Internet sites via other advertising media. Some companies are coupling their traditional television spots with a Web site; IBM, Swatch Watches, AT&T, and Samsung electronics are among those going for a one-two punch of on-air and online. TV spots are used to raise brand awareness of product regionally, and to promote the company's Web site. Additionally, the company buys ad banners on the Web that will lead enthusiastic consumers to the company's Web that also promotes the product. Some TV networks offer a package deal, a TV spot and ad banners on the network's Web site. For example, the EBN (European Business News) channel offers cross-media program that includes TV spots and the advertiser's ad banner on the EB Interactive page for $15,000 a quarter.[51]

Sales Promotion

Sales are marketing activities that stimulate consumer purchases and improve retailer or middlemen effectiveness and cooperation. Cents-off, in-store demonstrations, samples, coupons, gifts, product tie-ins, contests, sweepstakes, sponsorship of special events such as concerts and fairs, and point-of-purchase displays are types of sales promotion devices designed to supplement advertising and personal selling in the promotional mix.

Sales promotions are short-term efforts directed to the consumer and/or retailer to achieve such specific objectives as (1) consumer-product trial and/or immediate purchase; (2) consumer introduction to the store; (3) gaining retail point-of-purchase displays; (4) encouraging stores to stock the product; and (5) supporting and augmenting advertising and personal sales efforts. An example of sales promotion is the African cigarette manufacturer who, in addition to regular advertising, sponsors musical groups and river explorations and participates in local fairs in attempts to make the public aware of the product. Procter & Gamble's introduction of Ariel detergent in Egypt included the "Ariel Road Show." The puppet show was taken to local markets in villages, where more than half of the Egyptian population still lives. The show drew huge crowds, entertained people, told about Ariel's better performance without the use of additives, and sold the brand through a distribution van at a nominal discount. Besides creating brand awareness for Ariel, the road show helped overcome the reluctance of the rural retailers to handle the premium-priced Ariel.

In markets where the consumer is hard to reach because of media limitations, the percentage of the promotional budget allocated to sales promotions may have to be increased. In some less-developed countries, sales promotions constitute the major portion of the promotional effort in rural and less-accessible parts of the market. In parts of Latin America, a portion of the advertising-sales budget for both Pepsi-Cola and Coca-Cola is spent on carnival trucks, which make frequent trips to outlying villages to promote their products. When a carnival truck makes a stop in a village, it may show a movie or provide some other kind of entertainment; the price of admission is an unopened bottle of the product purchased from the local retailer. The unopened bottle is to be exchanged for a cold bottle plus a coupon for another bottle. This promotional effort tends to stimulate sales and encourages local retailers, who are given prior notice of the carnival truck's arrival, to stock the product. Nearly 100 percent coverage of retailers in the village is achieved with this type of promotion. In other situations, village stores may be given free samples, have the outsides of their stores painted, or receive clock signs in attempts to promote sales.

---

[51] Juliana Koranteng, "Global Advertisers Value On-Air, Online Combination," *Ad Age International (Special Issue: Cable and Satellite TV)*, March 1997, p. 110.

Nestlé's roadside stops in France are painted in the familiar blue and white company colors and are adorned with the baby food's symbol, teddy bear Pipo. (Courtesy Nestlé France)

An especially effective promotional tool when the product concept is new or has a very small market share is product sampling. Nestlé Baby Foods faced such a problem in France in its attempt to gain share from Gerber, the leader. The company combined sampling with a novel sales promotion program to gain brand recognition and to build goodwill. Since most Frenchmen take off for a long vacation in the summertime, piling the whole family into the car and staying at well-maintained campgrounds, Nestlé provides rest-stop structures along the highway where parents can feed and change their babies. Sparkling clean *Le Relais Bebes* are located along main travel routes. Sixty-four hostesses at these rest stops welcome 120,000 baby visits and dispense 600,000 samples of baby food each year. There are free disposable diapers, a changing table, and high chairs for the babies to sit in while dining.

As is true in advertising, the success of a promotion may depend on local adaptation. Major constraints are imposed by local laws, which may not permit premiums or free gifts to be given. Some countries' laws control the amount of discount given at retail, others require permits for all sales promotions, and in at least one country, no competitor is permitted to spend more on a sales promotion than any other company selling the product. Effective sales promotions can enhance the advertising and personal selling efforts and, in some instances, may be effective substitutes when environmental constraints prevent full utilization of advertising.

Global Advertising and the Communications Process

Promotional activities (advertising, personal selling, sales promotion, and public relations) are basically a communications process. All the attendant problems of developing an effective promotional strategy in domestic marketing plus all the cultural problems just discussed must be overcome for a successful international promotional program. A major consideration for foreign marketers is to determine that all constraints (cultural diversity, media limitations, legal problems, and so forth) are controlled so the right message is communicated to and received by prospective consumers. International communications may fail for a variety of reasons: a message may not get through because of media inadequacy; the message may be received by the intended audience but not be

CROSSING BORDERS 16-7

Promotions: When They're Good, They're Very Good; When They're Bad, They Cost Like the Dickens

Contests, lotteries, and all those schemes designed to get the consumer to buy a product for a chance to win a prize can be effective promotions—when they work right. The operative words here are "work right." Two recent promotional events, Hoover appliances in London and Pepsi Cola in the Philippines, didn't exactly "work right."

Hoover, the appliance and vacuum cleaner manufacturer, launched a promotion campaign in Britain and Ireland to build sales and brand awareness. Hoover offered two round-trip flights to Europe or America free with the purchase of $150 worth of Hoover appliances. (The cheapest airline tickets to New York were $750.) The company expected people to be attracted by the free tickets, but didn't expect many to follow through because of restrictions on travel times and hotel accommodations. No way. It didn't take a rocket scientist to figure out the key: buy the least-expensive appliance and go to the States. Over 200,000 did. Hoover has paid an estimated $72 million to make good on its offer. Now, four years later, a class-action suit has been filed on the behalf of those who have not received free airline tickets.

Coca-Cola and Pepsi were fighting for market share in the Philippines and Pepsi needed a boost. "Number Fever," a cash prize promotion, looked like the winning ticket. It had worked in 10 Latin American countries, and it combined the Filipinos' penchant for gambling and the lure of instant wealth. Buyers of Pepsi products would look under the bottle caps for a three-digit number from 001 to 999, to win cash prizes ranging from 1,000 pesos ($40) to 1 million pesos ($40,000), and a 7-digit security code. Pepsi would announce the winning three digits daily. Although all caps were imprinted with cash prizes, purchasers would not know if they had won until the three-digit number was announced. The more caps they collected, the greater their chance of winning. Over a three-month period, Pepsi seeded 60 winning numbers for cash prizes amounting to a total of 25 million pesos ($1 million).

Number Fever was an immediate success. Sales and market share of Pepsi products rose, and within a month increased sales covered the $4 million in prize money and advertising costs budgeted for the promotion.

At the end of six weeks, Pepsi market share had risen to 24.9 percent. The success prompted the company to extend Number Fever for five more weeks. A computer picked 25 new winning numbers. The consultants were convinced that a nonwinning number in the original promotion period would not come up as a winning number in the extension. They were wrong. They announced 349 as the winning number for May 26.

A jobless man, married with one child, couldn't sleep the night 349 was announced as a winner. He had bottle caps good for 3 million pesos. He dreamed about the house he would buy and the business he might start. But there were as many as 800,000 other people who could be holding 349 from the first contest. Paying the winners would have cost the company $1.6 billion. Pepsi's first move was to replace 349 with a new winning number. The claimants organized, lobbied, boycotted, sued, and even bombed delivery trucks. Pepsi offered to pay all holders of 349 caps 500 pesos as a compromise. Five hundred thousand came forward to claim the 500 pesos, costing the company $10 million. The 349 debacle sapped employee morale, ruined Pepsi's image, scared off potential retail distributors, cost the firm all its market share gains, and an order was issued to arrest the nine executives for swindling. Pepsi appealed to the Philippine Supreme Court and, after more than two years of legal action, the Court has stopped a lower court from ordering the arrest until the Justice Department can review the case.

Sources: Adapted from "Hoover Hopes to Sweep Up Mess from Flights Promotion," *Associated Press,* March 5, 1993; Dirk Beveridge, "Hoover Can't Sweep Ticket Mess under Rug," *Associated Press,* December 12, 1996; "Pepsi in the Philippines: Putting the Fizz Back," *Crossborder Monitor,* April 6, 1994, p. 8; and "Philippine Court Halts Arrest of Pepsi Officials," *Dow Jones News Service,* March 6, 1996.

EXHIBIT 16–5   The International Communications Process

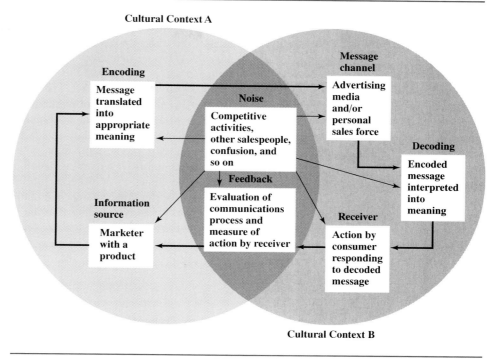

understood because of different cultural interpretations; or the message may reach the intended audience and be understood but have no effect because the marketer did not correctly assess the needs and wants of the target market.

The effectiveness of promotional strategy can be jeopardized by so many factors that a marketer must be certain no controllable influences are overlooked. Those international executives who understand the communications process are better equipped to manage the diversity they face in developing an international promotional program.

In the *international communications process,* each of the seven identifiable segments can ultimately affect the accuracy of the process. As illustrated in Exhibit 16–5, the process consists of (1) an information source—an international marketing executive with a product message to communicate; (2) encoding—the message from the source converted into effective symbolism for transmission to a receiver; (3) a message channel—the sales force and/or advertising media that conveys the encoded message to the intended receiver; (4) decoding—the interpretation by the receiver of the symbolism transmitted from the information source; (5) receiver—consumer action by those who receive the message and are the target for the thought transmitted; (6) feedback—information about the effectiveness of the message which flows from the receiver (the intended target) back to the information source for evaluation of the effectiveness of the process; and, to complete the process, (7) noise—uncontrollable and unpredictable influences such as competitive activities and confusion detracting from the process and affecting any or all of the other six steps.

Unfortunately, the process is not as simple as just sending a message via a medium to a receiver and being certain that the intended message sent is the same one perceived by the receiver. In Exhibit 16–5, the communications-process steps are encased in Cultural Context A and Cultural Context B to illustrate the influences complicating the process when the message is encoded in one culture and decoded in another. If not properly considered, the different cultural contexts can increase the probability of misunderstandings. As one researcher notes, "Effective communication demands that there exist a psychological overlap between the sender and the receiver"; otherwise a message falling outside the receiver's perceptual field may transmit an unintended meaning. It is in this area that even the most experienced companies make blunders.[52]

Most promotional misfires or mistakes in international marketing are attributable to one or several of these steps not properly reflecting cultural influences and/or a general lack of knowledge about the target market. A review of some of the points discussed in this chapter serves to illustrate this. The information source is a marketer with a product to sell to a specific target market. The product message to be conveyed should reflect the needs and wants of the target market; however, as many previous examples have illustrated, the marketer's perception of market needs and actual market needs do not always coincide. This is especially true when the marketer relies more on the self-reference criterion (SRC) than on effective research. It can never be assumed that "if it sells well in one country, it will sell in another." For instance, bicycles designed and sold in the United States to consumers fulfilling recreational-exercise needs are not sold as effectively for the same reasons in a market where the primary use of the bicycle is transportation.[53] Cavity-reducing fluoride toothpaste sells well in the United States, where healthy teeth are perceived as important, but it has limited appeal in markets such as Great Britain and the French areas of Canada, where the reason for buying toothpaste is breath control. From the onset of the communications process, if basic needs are incorrectly defined, communications fail because an incorrect or meaningless message is received even though the remaining steps in the process are executed properly.

The encoding step causes problems even with a proper message. At this step such factors as color, values, beliefs, and tastes can cause the international marketer to symbolize the message incorrectly. For example, the marketer wants the product to convey coolness so the color green is used; however, people in the tropics might decode green as dangerous or associate it with disease. Another example of the encoding process misfiring was a perfume presented against a backdrop of rain which, for Europeans, symbolized a clean, cool, refreshing image, but to Africans was a symbol of fertility. The ad prompted many viewers to ask if the perfume was effective against infertility.

DeBeers, the South African diamond company, found that its stylish ads depicting shadow figures conveying engagement, wedding, and anniversary gifts of diamonds failed among Chinese consumers, some of whom associate shadows with ghosts and death. A totally different ad was developed for the Chinese market. In some Muslim countries the ads had to be altered so that the shadows show silhouettes of women wearing veils, rather than the barefaced women whose shadows are shown in Western markets.[54]

Problems of literacy, media availability, and types of media create problems in the communications process at the encoding step. Message channels must be carefully selected if an encoded message is to reach the consumer. Errors such as using television as a medium when only a small percentage of an intended market is exposed to TV, or using print media for a channel of communications when the majority of the intended users cannot read or do not read the language in the medium, are examples of ineffective media channel selection in the communications process.

Decoding problems are generally created by improper encoding, which caused such errors as Pepsi's "Come Alive" slogan being decoded as "Come out of the grave." Chevrolet's brand name for the Nova model (which means star) was decoded into

---

[52] Sudhir H. Kale, "Culture-Specific Marketing Communications: An Analytical Approach," *International Marketing Review,* Vol. 8(2), 1991, p. 18.

[53] For an interesting study of the problem of matching advertising to culture, see Yong Zhang and Betsy D. Gelb, "Matching Advertising Appeals to Culture: The Influence of Products' Use Conditions," *Journal of Advertising,* September 1996, p. 29.

[54] Tara Parker-Pope, "The Most Successful Companies Have to Realize a Simple Truth: All Consumers Aren't Alike," *The Wall Street Journal,* September 26, 1996, p. R22.

Spanish as *No Va!*, meaning "it doesn't go." In another misstep, a translation that was supposed to be decoded as "hydraulic ram" was instead decoded as "wet sheep."[55] In a Nigerian ad, a platinum blonde sitting next to the driver of a Renault was intended to enhance the image of the automobile but she was perceived as not respectable and so created a feeling of shame. An ad used for Eveready Energizer batteries with the Energizer bunny was seen by Hungarian consumers as touting a bunny toy, not a battery.[56]

Decoding errors may also occur accidentally. Such was the case with Colgate-Palmolive's selection of the brand name Cue for toothpaste. The brand name was not intended to have any symbolism; nevertheless, it was decoded by the French into a pornographic word. In some cases, the intended symbolism has no meaning to the decoder. In an ad transferred from the United States, the irony of a tough-guy actor Tom Selleck standing atop a mountain with a steaming mug of Lipton tea was lost on Eastern Europeans.

Errors at the receiver end of the process generally result from a combination of factors: an improper message resulting from incorrect knowledge of use patterns, poor encoding producing a meaningless message, poor media selection that does not get the message to the receiver, or inaccurate decoding by the receiver so that the message is garbled or incorrect.

Finally, the feedback step of the communications process is important as a check on the effectiveness of the other steps. Companies that do not measure their communications efforts are apt to allow errors of source, encoding, media selection, decoding, or receiver to continue longer than necessary. In fact, a proper feedback system allows a company to correct errors before substantial damage occurs.

In addition to the problems inherent in the steps outlined, the effectiveness of the international communications process can be impaired by *noise.* Noise comprises all other external influences such as competitive advertising, other sales personnel, and confusion at the receiving end that can detract from the ultimate effectiveness of the communications. Noise is a disruptive force interfering with the process at any step and is frequently beyond the control of the sender or the receiver. As Exhibit 16–5 illustrates with the overlapping cultural contexts, noise can emanate from activity in either culture or be caused by the influences of the overlapping of the cultural contexts. The significance is that one or all steps in the process, cultural factors, or the marketer's SRC, can affect the ultimate success of the communication. For example, the message, encoding, media, and the intended receiver can be designed perfectly but the inability of the receiver to decode may render the final message inoperative. In designing an international promotional strategy, the international marketer can effectively use this model as a guide to help ensure all potential constraints and problems are considered so that the final communication received and the action taken correspond with the intent of the source.

The Advertising Agency

Just as manufacturing firms have become international, U.S., Japanese, and European advertising agencies are expanding internationally to provide sophisticated agency assistance worldwide. Local agencies also have expanded as the demand for advertising services by MNCs has developed. Thus, the international marketer has a variety of alternatives available. In most commercially significant countries, an advertiser has the op-

55 Gary P. Ferraro, *The Cultural Dimension of International Business,* 3rd. ed. (Englewood Cliffs, N.J.: Prentice Hall, 1997), p. 48.

56 Tara Parker-Pope, "Ad Agencies Are Stumbling in East Europe," *The Wall Street Journal,* May 10, 1996, p. B1.

portunity to employ (1) a local domestic agency, (2) its company-owned agency, or (3) one of the multinational advertising agencies with local branches. There are strengths and weaknesses with each.

A local domestic agency may provide a company with the best cultural interpretation in situations where local modification is sought, but the level of sophistication can be weak. However, the local agency may have the best feel for the market, especially if the multinational agency has little experience in the market. Eastern Europe has been a problem for the multinational agency that is not completely attuned to the market. In Hungary, a U.S. baby-care company advertisement of bath soap showing a woman holding her baby hardly seemed risqué. But where Westerners saw a young mother, scandalized Hungarians saw an unwed mother. The model was wearing a ring on her left hand; Hungarians wear wedding bands on the right hand. It was obvious to viewers that this woman wearing a ring on her left hand was telling everybody in Hungary she wasn't married. This is a mistake a local agency would not have made.[57]

The best compromise is the multinational agency with local branches because it has the sophistication of a major agency with local representation. Further, the multinational agency with local branches is better able to provide a coordinated worldwide advertising campaign. This has become especially important for firms doing business in Europe. With the interest in global or standardized advertising, many agencies have expanded to provide worldwide representation. Many companies with a global orientation employ one, or perhaps two, agencies to represent them worldwide.

Compensation arrangements for advertising agencies throughout the world are based on the U.S. system of 15 percent commissions. However, agency commission patterns throughout the world are not as consistent as they are in the United States; in some countries, agency commissions vary from medium to medium. Companies are moving from the commission system to a reward by results system, which details remuneration terms at the outset. If sales rise, the agency should be rewarded accordingly. This method of sharing in the gains or losses of profits generated by the advertising is gaining in popularity and it may become the standard.[58] Services provided by advertising agencies also vary greatly but few foreign agencies offer the full services found in U.S. agencies.

Even a sophisticated business function such as advertising may find it is involved in unique practices. In some parts of the world, advertisers often pay for the promotion with the product advertised rather than with cash. Kickbacks on agency commissions are prevalent in some parts of the world and account in part for the low profitability of international advertising agencies. In Mexico, India, and Greece, the advertiser returns half the media commissions to the agencies. In many of the developing countries, long-term credit is used to attract clients.

The global firm with branches and/or joint ventures with local firms dominate advertising globally. Over the last two decades most of the major ad agencies in the United States, the U.K., and Japan have expanded globally and can easily represent a global company almost anywhere in the world. As Exhibit 16–6 shows, the top agency in the world in 1995 and 1996 was a Japanese firm, Dentsu, Inc., followed by the U.S. firm McCann-Erickson Worldwide.[59] If you visit the Web site of some of these agencies you will see how extensive their range is. These companies represent the consolidation of advertising agencies that has been going on over the last decade or so.[60]

---

[57] Ibid.

[58] Julian Lee, "Advertisers Get a Guide to the Money Jungle," *The Times of London,* January 6, 1998, p. 27.

[59] Visit Dentsu at **http://www.dentsu.co.jp** and McCann-Erickson Worldwide at **http://www.interpublic.com/agencies/mccannworldgrop.html** to see how extensive their services and global reach is. Also visit Interpublic, the parent company for McCann-Erickson and a score of other advertising and service companies, at **http://www.interpublic.com**.

[60] Jim Puntasen, "Ad Agencies Look Overseas for Support," *Nation,* January 13, 1998.

CROSSING BORDERS 16-8

Some Advertising Misses and Near-Misses

When translating an advertisement into another language, several missteps are possible: Some words may be euphemisms in another language, a literal translation does not convey the intended meaning, phonetic problems may result in brand names sounding like a different word, or symbols become inappropriate or project an unintended message. Here are a few examples that have shown up on advertisements.

Euphemisms

Parker Pen Company translated a counter display card for its brand of ink which had been very successful in the United States. The card said, "Avoid Embarrassment—Use Quink." The Spanish translation, *"Evite embarazos—Use Quink,"* unfortunately means, idiomatically, "Avoid Pregnancy—Use Quink."

Incorrect translation of phrases

Stepping stone translated into *stumbling block..*
Car wash translated into *car enema.*
High rated translated into *over rated.*
On leather translated into *naked.*

Phonetic problems with brand names

Bardok sounds like the word for brothel in Russian.
Misair sounds like the word for misery in French.

Symbols

An owl was used in an advertisement for India, where the owl is bad luck.
An elephant used in an ad for India was an African elephant, not Indian.
A turbaned model in an Indian ad wore a turban style of Pakistan.

Unintended message

Pictured were soiled clothes on the left, soap in the middle, clean clothes on the right. This is fine, unless you read from right to left. Then the ad seems to say: take clean clothes, use our soap, and they will be soiled.

Source: Compilation by the authors.

International Control of Advertising

Consumer criticisms of advertising are not a phenomenon of the U.S. market. Consumer concern with the standards and believability of advertising may have spread around the world more swiftly than have many marketing techniques. A study of a representative sample of European consumers indicated that only half of them believed advertisements gave consumers any useful information, 6 out of 10 believed that advertising meant higher prices (if a product is heavily advertised, it often sells for more than brands that are seldom or never advertised); nearly 8 out of 10 believed advertising often made them buy things they did not really need, and that ads often were deceptive about product quality. In Hong Kong, Colombia, and Brazil advertising fared much better than in

EXHIBIT 16-6   Top Ten Global Advertising Agencies

Rank '96	Rank '95	Agency	Worldwide Gross Income '96	Worldwide Gross Income '95	'96-'95 % Chg	Worldwide Capitalized Volume '96	Worldwide Capitalized Volume '95	'96-'95 '% Chg
1	1	Dentsu Inc.	$1,929.9	$1,999.1	-3.5	$14,047.9	$14,597.2	-3.8
2	2	McCann-Erickson Worldwide	1,299.0	1,148.0	13.1	9,232.5	7,869.1	17.3
3	3	J. Walter Thompson Co.	1,073.0	1,006.2	6.6	7,288.0	6,765.3	7.7
4	5	BBDO Worldwide	925.2	857.2	7.9	7,456.1	6,759.6	10.3
5	4	Hakuhodo	897.7	958.6	-6.3	6,677.0	6,909.3	-3.4
6	6	Leo Burnett Co.	866.3	805.9	7.5	5,821.1	5,386.7	8.1
7	9	DDB Needham Worldwide	848.3	744.8	13.9	6,629.2	5,909.4	12.2
8	7	Grey Advertising	841.8	777.3	8.3	5,621.9	5,191.1	8.3
9	8	Euro RSCG	823.8	770.3	6.9	6,064.5	5,666.4	7.0
10	10	Ogilvy & Mather Worldwide	793.0	714.1	11.1	6,937.6	6,391.9	8.5

Source: "World's Top 25 Agency Brands," *Advertising Age,* April 21, 1997, **http://www.adage.com**.

Europe. The non-Europeans praised advertising as a way to obtain valuable information about products; most Brazilians consider ads entertaining and enjoyable.

European Community officials are establishing directives to provide controls on advertising as cable and satellite broadcasting expands. Deception in advertising is a thorny issue since most member countries have different interpretations of what constitutes a misleading advertisement. Demands for regulation of advertising aimed at young consumers is a trend appearing in both industrialized and developing countries.

Decency and the blatant use of sex in advertisements also are receiving public attention. One of the problems in controlling decency and sex in ads is the cultural variations around the world. An ad perfectly acceptable to a Westerner may be very offensive to someone from the Mideast, or, for that matter, another Westerner. Standards for appropriate behavior as depicted in advertisements vary from culture to culture. Regardless of these variations, there is growing concern about decency, sex, and ads that demean women and men. International advertising associations are striving to forestall laws by imposing self-regulation, but it may be too late; some countries are passing laws that will define acceptable standards.

The difficulty that business has with self-regulation and restrictive laws is that sex can be powerful in some types of advertisements. European advertisements for Haagen-Dazs, a premium U.S. ice-cream marketer, and LapPower, a Swedish laptop computer company, received criticism for their ads as being too sexy. Haagen-Dazs' ad shows a couple, in various stages of undress, in an embrace feeding ice cream to one another. Some British editorial writers and radio commentators were outraged. One commented that "the ad was the most blatant and inappropriate use of sex as a sales aid." The ad for LapPower personal computers that the Stockholm Business Council on Ethics condemned featured the co-owner of the company with an "inviting smile and provocative demeanor displayed." (She was bending over a LapPower computer in a low-cut dress.)

The bottom line for both these companies was increased sales. In Britain, ice cream sales soared after the "Dedicated to Pleasure" ads appeared, and in Sweden, the co-owner stated, "Sales are increasing daily." Whether laws are passed or the industry polices itself, there is an international concern about advertising and its effect on people's behavior.

Advertising regulations are not limited to Europe; there is an enhanced awareness of the expansion of mass communications and the perceived need to effect greater control in developing countries as well. Malaysia consistently regulates TV advertising to

CROSSING BORDERS 16–9

Harmonization of EC Rules for Children's Advertisements

Creating one advertising campaign for the European Market is almost impossible with the plethora of rules that govern children's advertising. One estimate is that in all of Europe there are at least 50 different laws restricting advertising to children. Here are some samples:

- In the Netherlands, confectionery ads must not be aimed at children, and can't be aired before 8 P.M. or feature children under age 14. Further, a toothbrush must appear on the screen, either at the bottom during the entire spot or filling the whole screen for the last $1^1/2$ seconds.
- There is a ban on toy advertising in Greece on television between 7 A.M. and 10 P.M.
- War toys cannot be advertised in Spain or Germany.
- French law prohibits children from being presenters of a product or to appear without adults. A Kellogg Company spot that runs in the U.K. featuring a child assigning a different day to each box could not be used in France.
- Sweden prohibits TV spots aimed at children under 12 and no commercials of any kind can air before, during, or after children's programs. It's interesting to note that Sweden passed the law at least a year before commercial television was permitted.

Although some advertising laws have been harmonized, there still exists some major differences in advertising laws among the EC countries. The European Commission continues to review these bans, case by case, and it is striving for some agreement on a set of standard directives. As yet this goal has not been achieved.

Sources: Adapted from Laurel Wentz, "Playing by the Same Rules," *Advertising Age,* December 2, 1991, p. S2; and "Part III. Evaluation of Specific Areas for Community Action," **http://europa.eu.int** (search "advertising and regulation"), May 1996.

control the effect of the "excesses of Western ways." The government has become so concerned that it will not allow "Western cultural images" to appear in TV commercials. No bare shoulders or exposed armpits are allowed, nor are touching or kissing, sexy clothing, or blue jeans. These are just a few of the prohibitions spelled out in a 41-page advertising code that the Malaysian government has been adding to for more than 10 years.

The advertising industry is sufficiently concerned with the negative attitudes and skepticism of consumers and governments and with the poor practices of some advertisers that the International Advertising Association and other national and international industry groups have developed a variety of self-regulating codes.[61] Sponsors of these codes feel that unless the advertisers themselves come up with an effective framework

---

[61] For an interesting study of the skepticism toward advertising, see Lawrence Feick and Heribert Gierl, "Skepticism about Advertising: A Comparison of East and West German Consumers," *International Journal of Research in Marketing,* Vol. 13, 1996, p. 227.

for control, governments will intervene. This threat of government intervention has spurred interest groups in Europe to develop codes to ensure that the majority of ads conform to standards set for "honesty, truth, and decency." In those countries where the credibility of advertising is questioned and in those where the consumerism movement exists, the creativity of the advertiser is challenged.[62] The most egregious control, however, may be in Myanmar (formerly Burma), where each medium has its own censorship board that passes judgement on any advertising even before it is submitted for approval by the Ministry of Information. There is even a censorship board for calendars. Content restrictions are centered on any references to the government or military, other political matters, religious themes, or images deemed degrading to traditional culture.[63]

In many countries, there is a feeling that advertising, and especially TV advertising, is too powerful and persuades consumers to buy what they do not need, an issue that has been debated in the United States for many years. South Korea, for example, has threatened to ban advertising of bottled water because the commercials may arouse public mistrust of tap water.

Summary

Global advertisers face unique legal, language, media, and production limitations in every market. These must be considered when designing a promotional mix. As the world and its markets become more sophisticated, there is greater emphasis on global marketing strategy. The current debate among marketers is the effectiveness of standardized versus modified advertising for culturally varied markets. And, as competition increases and markets expand, greater emphasis is being placed on global brands and/or image recognition.

The most logical conclusion seems to be that, when buying motives and company objectives are the same for various countries, the advertising orientation can be the same. When they vary from nation to nation, the advertising effort will have to reflect these variations. In any case, variety in media availability, coverage, and effectiveness will have to be taken into consideration in the advertiser's plans. If common appeals are used, they may have to be presented by a radio broadcast in one country, by cinema in another, and by television in still a third.

A skilled advertising practitioner must be sensitive to the environment and alert to new facts about the market. It is also essential for success in international advertising endeavors to pay close attention to the international communications process and the steps involved.

Questions

1. Define:
   noise
   international communications process
   global market segmentation
   market segment
   pattern advertising

2. "Perhaps advertising is the side of international marketing with the greatest similarities from country to country throughout the world. Paradoxically, despite its many similarities, it may also be credited with the greatest number of unique problems in international marketing." Discuss.

3. Discuss the difference between advertising strategy when a company follows a multidomestic strategy rather than a global market strategy.

4. Someone once commented that advertising is America's greatest export. Discuss.

5. With satellite TV able to reach many countries, discuss how a company can use satellite TV and deal effectively with different languages, different cultures, and different legal systems.

6. Outline some of the major problems confronting an international advertiser.

7. Defend either side of the proposition that advertising can be standardized for all countries.

8. Review the basic areas of advertising regulation. Are such regulations purely foreign phenomena?

9. How can advertisers overcome the problems of low literacy in their markets?

10. What special media problems confront the international advertiser?

11. Discuss the reason for pattern advertising.

62 Kang Siew Li, "Advertising Faces a Major Setback," *The New Straits Times Press,* February 4, 1998, p. 17.
63 "Mandalay via Madison Avenue," *Business Asia,* February 26, 1996, p. 6.

12. After reading the section in this chapter on direct mail, develop guidelines to be used by a company when developing a direct mail program.

13. Will the ability to broadcast advertisements over TV satellites increase or decrease the need for standardization of advertisements? What are the problems associated with satellite broadcasting? Comment.

14. "In many world marketplaces, a wide variety of media must be used to reach the majority of the market." Explain.

15. Cinema advertising is unimportant in the United States but a major medium in such countries as Austria. Why?

16. "Foreign newspapers cannot be considered homogeneous advertising entities." Elaborate.

17. Borrow a foreign magazine from the library. Compare the foreign advertising to that in an American magazine.

18. What is sales promotion and how is it used in international marketing?

19. Show how the communications process can help an international marketer avoid problems in international advertising.

20. Take each of the steps of the communications process and give an example of how cultural differences can affect the final message perceived.

21. Discuss the problems created because the communications process is initiated in one cultural context and ends in another.

22. What is the importance of feedback in the communications process? Of noise?

23. Visit the Adobe Web site (**http://www.adobe.com/ newsfeatures/internationalsites/main.html**). Adobe claims to be one of the best Web sites. Evaluate this Web site and outline the features that make this a good Web site for international marketing.

CHAPTER 17

PERSONAL SELLING AND SALES MANAGEMENT

Chapter Learning Objectives

What you should learn from Chapter 17

- The role of interpersonal selling in international marketing.

- The considerations in designing an international sales force.

- The steps to recruiting three types of international sales people.

- Selection criteria for international sales and marketing positions.

- How culture influences managerial values.

- The special training needs of international personnel.

- Motivation techniques for international sales representatives.

- How to design compensation systems for an international sales force.

- How to prepare Americans for foreign assignments.

- The changing profile of the global sales and marketing manager.

GLOBAL PERSPECTIVE

Sales Force Management and Global Customers

Did IBM *really* need a new sales compensation plan? For proof, just ask Kevin Tucker. Tucker, an IBM global account manager dedicated to Ford Motor Company, closed a $7 million sale with the automotive giant's European operations. Ford wanted Tucker and his team of IBM reps to install networking systems in its engineering facilities. The systems would run the applications that design the company's automobiles.

Ford's installation required help from an IBM sales executive in Germany, the project's headquarters. So Tucker, whose office sits in Ford's Dearborn, Michigan, headquarters, sent an e-mail requesting the executive's assistance. And that's when things turned ugly.

Although the rep in Germany didn't turn his back on the project, his initial reaction was less than enthusiastic. Ford wanted the systems installed throughout Europe, yet the compensation plan for IBM's Germany-based reps rewarded only the systems that were installed in that country. With 80 percent of the work scheduled outside of Germany, the executive was left wondering: Where's the payoff? Tucker and other IBM sales incentive managers wasted three weeks discussing ways to maximize the rep's incentive. Energy that could have been focused on the customer was wasted on a pay plan.

"Ford was world-centric, we were country-centric," Tucker says. "The team in Germany was asking, 'Kevin, how can you make us whole?'"

They weren't the only salespeople asking that question at IBM. Tucker's predicament represents just one of many problems that were rooted in IBM's "$72-billion" sales incentive plan—a plan that had been obviously put on the back burner as the company giant tinkered with its vision.

Bob Wylie, manager of incentive strategies for IBM Canada, says, "There was the attitude that if it's outside my territory and outside my measurements, I don't get paid for it, and I don't get involved. What's in my pay plan defines what I do." Not the best setup for a company that operates in 140 countries.

Source: Excerpted from Michele Marchetti, "Gamble: IBM Replaced Its Outdated Compensation Plan with a Worldwide Framework. It Is Paying Off?" *Sales & Marketing Management,* July 1996, pp. 65–69.

The salesperson is a company's most direct tie to the customer and, in the eyes of most customers, the salesperson is the company. As presenter of company offerings and gatherer of customer information, the sales representative is the final link in the culmination of a company's marketing and sales effort.

Special care needs to be taken to properly select, train, motivate, and compensate an international sales force which is drawn from three sources: qualified personnel from the home country *(expatriates),* qualified local-country personnel, and/or third-country nationals, neither American nor local. With each choice, cultural attributes must be dealt with to ensure effective market representation. Poorly selected sales intermediaries cost the marketer sales and are difficult and costly to terminate.

Increased global competition coupled with the dynamic and complex nature of international business increases the need for closer ties with both customers and suppliers. *Relationship marketing,* built on effective communications between the seller and buyer, focuses on building long-term alliances rather than treating each sale as a one-time event. This approach is becoming increasingly important for successful global marketers.

The tasks of designing, building, training, motivating, and compensating an international marketing group generate unique problems at every stage of management and development. This chapter discusses the alternatives and problems of managing sales and marketing personnel in foreign countries. Indeed, these problems are among the most difficult facing international marketers. In one survey of CEOs and other top executives the respondents most often identified "establishing sales and distribution networks" as a major difficulty in international sales and operations.[1] Others concur that "coordinating global sales teams . . . is a major effort for transnational corporations."[2]

Designing the Sales Force

The first step in managing a sales force is its design. Based on analyses of current and potential customers, the selling environment, competition, and the firm's resources and capabilities, decisions must be made regarding the numbers, characteristics, and assignments of sales personnel. All these design decisions are made more challenging by the wide variety of pertinent conditions and circumstances in international markets. Moreover, the globalization of markets and customers, as illustrated by the IBM–Ford story above, makes the job of international sales manager quite interesting.

As described in previous chapters, distribution strategies will often vary from country to country. Some markets may require a direct sales force where others may not. How customers are approached can differ as well. For example, as noted in Crossing Borders 17–1, automobiles have been sold door-to-door in Japan for years, and only recently are life insurance policies being sold by phone in Europe.[3] The size of accounts certainly makes a difference as well—did you notice in the Global Perspective that an IBM sales representative works *inside* Ford? Selling high-technology products may allow for the greater use of American expatriates, while selling consulting services will tend to require more participation by native sales representatives. Selling in low-context (individualistic/egalitarian) cultures such as Germany may also allow for greater use of expatriates. However, high-context (collectivistic/hierarchical) countries like Japan will require the most complete local knowledge possessed only by natives. Writing about Japan, two international marketing experts agree: "Personal selling as a rule has to be localized for even the most global of corporations and industries."[4]

Once decisions have been made about how many expatriates, local nationals, and/or third-country nationals a particular market requires, then more intricate aspects of design can be undertaken such as territory allocation and customer call plans. Many of the most advanced operations research tools developed in the United States can be applied in foreign markets, of course, with appropriate adaptation of inputs. For example, one company has provided such tools to help international firms create balanced territories and find optimal locations for sales offices in Canada, Mexico, and Australia.[5] However, the use of such high-tech resource allocation tools requires the most intricate knowledge of not only geographical details, but also appropriate call routines. Many things can differ across cultures—length of sales cycles, the kinds of customer relationships,[6] and the

---

[1] Dennis J. Aigner and Kenneth L. Kraemer, *The 1998 Orange County Executive Survey,* The University of Califrnia Graduate School of Management, 1998.

[2] Allan J. Magrath, "From the Practitioner's Desk: A Comment on 'Personal Selling and Sales Management in the New Millennium,' " *Journal of Personal Selling & Sales Management,* 17(1), Winter, 1997, pp. 45–47.

[3] Andrew Jack, "International Company News: CNP Considers Direct Life Insurance Sales," *Financial Times,* March 18, 1996, p. 19.

[4] Johny K. Johansson and Ikujiro Nonaka, *Relentless: The Japanese Way of Marketing* (New York: Harper Business, 1996), p. 97.

[5] See the Web site for TerrAlign Services Group, **www.terralign.com**, for more detailed information.

[6] Frank Alpert, Michael Kamins, Tomoaki Sakano, Naoto Onzo, and John L. Graham, "Retail Buyer Decision Making in Japan: What U.S. Sellers Need to Know," *International Business Review,* 6(2), 1997, pp. 91–112.

CROSSING BORDERS 17–1

Soap and Cars—Door-to-Door in Japan

Coca-Cola is Japan's most profitable American company. Who's number two? It's not IBM, McDonalds, or Microsoft. Surprisingly, it's Amway. About $2 billion worth of the company's soap and other products are sold by direct sales in Japan every year. Amway got started in Japan in 1971, and it has avoided the country's inefficient and expensive retail distribution system by offering alternative ways to shop—via mail-order catalogs and home visits by Amway "distributors" who, as in the U.S., are often neighbors.

Eiko Shiraishi didn't want or need a new car. In fact, she had never set foot inside a dealership nor taken a test drive. So why did she buy one anyway? The car salesman came to her door!

Now she's got a new silver Toyota in her driveway. Indeed, about half the cars sold in Japan are peddled by door-to-door salesmen. This creates a tough problem for GM, Ford, and Chrysler as they try to figure out how to sell cars in Japan.

Sources: Melinda Jensen Ligos, "Direct Sales: The Secret to Success in Japan," *Sales & Marketing Management,* December 1996, p. 54; and Valerie Reitman, "Toyota Calling," *The Wall Street Journal,* September 28, 1994, pp. A1, A6.

kinds of interactions with customers.[7] Indeed, one study has identified substantial differences in the importance of referrals in the sales of industrial services in Japan vis-à-vis the United States.[8] The implications are that in Japan sales calls must be made not only on customers, but also on the key people, such as bankers, in the all-important referral networks.

Recruiting Marketing and Sales Personnel

The number of marketing management personnel from the home country assigned to foreign countries varies according to the size of the operation and the availability of qualified locals. Increasingly, the number of U.S. home-country nationals (expatriates) assigned to foreign posts is smaller as the pool of trained, experienced locals grows.

The largest personnel requirement abroad for most companies is the sales force, recruited from three sources: expatriates, local nationals, and third-country nationals. A company's staffing pattern may include all three types in any single foreign operation, depending on qualifications, availability, and a company's needs. Sales and marketing executives can be recruited via the traditional media of advertising (including newspapers, magazines, job fairs, and the Internet), employment agencies/executive search firms,[9] and the all-important personal referrals. The last source will be even more crucial in many foreign countries, particularly the high-context ones.

Expatriates

The number of companies relying on expatriate personnel is declining as the volume of world trade increases and as more companies use locals to fill marketing positions.

---

[7] Andy Cohen, "Small World, Big Challenge," *Sales & Marketing Management,* June 1996, pp. 69–73.

[8] R. Bruce Money, Mary C. Gilly, and John L. Graham, "National Culture and Referral Behavior in the Purchase of Industrial Services in the United States and Japan," *Journal of Marketing,* 62(4), October 1998.

[9] The largest international executive search firm is Korn/Ferry International. See its Web site at **www.kornferry.com**.

However, when products are highly technical, or when selling requires an extensive background of information and applications, an expatriate sales force remains the best choice. The expatriate salesperson may have the advantages of greater technical training, better knowledge of the company and its product line, and proven dependability. Because they are not locals, expatriates sometimes add to the prestige of the product line in the eyes of foreign customers. And perhaps most important, expatriates usually are able to effectively communicate with and influence headquarters personnel.

The chief disadvantages of an expatriate sales force are high cost, cultural and legal barriers, and a limited number of high-caliber personnel willing to live abroad for extended periods. Companies in the United States are finding it difficult to persuade outstanding employees to take overseas posts. Employees are reluctant to go abroad for many reasons: some find it difficult to uproot families for a two- or three-year assignment;[10] increasing numbers of dual-career couples often require finding suitable jobs for spouses;[11] and many executives believe such assignments impede their subsequent promotions at home.[12] The belief that "out of sight is out of mind" plus the loss of visibility at corporate headquarters are major reasons for the reluctance to accept a foreign assignment. Companies with well-planned career development programs have the least difficulty. Indeed, the best international companies make it crystal clear that a ticket to top management is an overseas stint.[13]

Expatriates commit to foreign assignments for varying lengths of time, a few weeks or months to a lifetime. Some expatriates have one-time assignments (which may last for years) after which they are returned to the parent company; others are essentially professional expatriates, working abroad in country after country. Still another expatriate assignment is a career-long assignment to a given country or region; this is likely to lead to assimilation of the expatriate into the foreign culture to such an extent that the person may more closely resemble a local than an expatriate. Because expatriate marketing personnel are likely to cost substantially more than locals, a company must be certain of their effectiveness.[14]

More and more American companies are taking advantage of American employees who are fluent in languages other than English. For example, many U.S. citizens speak Spanish as their first language—the large numbers of Puerto Ricans working for American multinationals in places like Mexico City is well documented.[15] Recent immigrants and their sons and daughters who learn their parents' languages and about their native cultures will continue to be invaluable assets for firms wishing to enter such markets. Certainly ethnic Chinese- and Vietnamese-Americans are serving and will continue to serve as cultural bridges for commerce with those two nations. Indeed, throughout history commerce has always followed immigration.

Local Nationals

The historical preference for expatriate managers and salespeople from the home country is giving way to a preference for *local nationals*. At the sales level, the picture is

---

[10] Betty Jane Punnett, "Towards Effective Management of Expatriate Spouses," *Journal of World Business,* 32(3), 1997, pp. 243–257.

[11] Michael Harvey, "Dual-Career Expatriates: Expectations, Adjustment, and Satisfaction with International Relocation," *Journal of International Business Studies,* Third Quarter, 1997, pp. 627–658. Alternatively, one author suggests that "global couples" can now be found that "relish adventure, support each other, home-school their children if necessary and get involved in meaningful activities wherever they are stationed." See Sue Shellenbarger, "Families Are Facing New Strains as Work Expands across Globe," *The Wall Street Journal,* October 12, 1997, p. B1.

[12] Linda Grant, "That Overseas Job Could Derail Your Career," *Fortune,* April 14, 1997, p. 166.

[13] Henry P. Conn and George S. Yip, "Global Transfer of Critical Capabilities," *Business Horizons,* January 11, 1997, pp. 22–30; and Joann S. Lublin, "An Overseas Stint Can Be a Ticket to the Top," *The Wall Street Journal,* January 29, 1996, pp. B1, B5.

[14] Some companies are taking steps to reduce the extra costs of expatriate pay. See Michele Marchetti, "Paring Expatriate Pay," *Sales & Marketing Management,* January 1996, pp. 28–29.

[15] "P&G's Workforce Reflects Its Diverse Market Cultures," *Hispanic Times,* June 30, 1996, p. 14; and Larry Luxner, "Straddling Two Cultures," *U.S./Latin Trade,* December 1994, pp. 18–20.

clearly biased in favor of the locals because they transcend both cultural and legal barriers. More knowledgeable about a country's business structure than an expatriate would be, local salespeople are better able to lead a company through the maze of unfamiliar distribution systems and referral networks. Furthermore, in some places there are now pools of qualified foreign personnel available, which cost less to maintain than a staff of expatriates. In Europe, many locals have earned MBA degrees in the United States; thus, a firm gets the cultural knowledge of the local meshed with an understanding of U.S. business management. Although expatriates' salaries may be no more than those of their national counterparts, the total cost of keeping comparable groups of expatriates in a country can be considerably higher because of special cost-of-living benefits, moving expenses, taxes, and other costs associated with keeping an expatriate abroad.

The main disadvantage of hiring local nationals is the tendency of headquarters personnel to ignore their advice. Even though most foreign nationals are careful to keep relationships at the home office warm, their influence is often reduced by their limited English communication skills and lack of understanding of how home office politics influence decision making. Another key disadvantage can be their lack of availability; one CEO of a consulting firm that specializes in recruiting managers in China reports that 10 openings exist for every one qualified applicant.[16] Moreover, while in the U.S. it is common practice to hire away experienced salespeople from competitors, suppliers, and/or vendors, the same approach in other countries will not work. In places like Japan, employees are much more loyal to their companies and therefore are difficult to lure away even for big money.[17] College recruits can also be hard to hire in Japan because the smartest students are heavily recruited by the largest Japanese firms. Smaller firms and foreign firms are seen in Japan as much more risky employment opportunities.

One other consideration makes recruiting of local nationals as sales representatives more difficult in many foreign countries: We all know about Americans' aversion to being a "salesman." Personal selling is often derided as a career and represented in a negative light in American media—Authur Miller's *Death of a Salesman* is of course the best example. Despite the bad press, however, personal selling is the most common job in the U.S. Indeed, the United States has been described as *A Nation of Salesmen.*[18] But, as negatively as the selling profession is viewed in the U.S., in many other countries it's viewed in even worse ways. Particularly in the more hierarchical cultures like Mexico and Japan, sales representatives tend to be on the bottom rung of the social ladder. Thus, it can be very difficult indeed to recruit the brightest people to fill sales positions in foreign operations.

Third-Country Nationals

The internationalization of business has created a pool of *third-country nationals (TCNs),* expatriates from their own countries working for a foreign company in a third country. TCNs are a group whose nationality has little to do with where they work or for whom. An example would be a German working in Argentina for a U.S. company. Historically, there have been a few expatriates or TCNs who have spent the majority of their careers abroad, but now a truly "global executive" has begun to emerge. The recently appointed chairman of a division of a major Netherlands company is a Norwegian who gained that post after stints in the United States, where he was the U.S. subsidiary's chairman, and in Brazil, where he held the position of general manager. At one

---

[16] Ames Gross, "Strategies for Successfully Recruiting Your China Staff," presented at the US/China Joint Commission on Commerce and Trade, Management and Training Symposium, U.S. Department of Commerce, April 25–26, 1996.

[17] Recent bankruptcies in Japan have provided opportunities for American firms to hire very experienced Japanese marketing personnel. See David P. Hamilton, "U.S. Firms in Japan Step In to Hire Workers Fired amid Business Turmoil," *The Wall Street Journal,* December 15, 1997, p. B54.

[18] See Earl Shorris' excellent book *A Nation of Salesmen* (New York: Norton, 1994); also see Charles Butler, "Why the Bad Rap?" *Sales & Marketing Management,* June 1, 1996, pp. 58–62.

CROSSING BORDERS 17-2

Hopping about the Pacific

I would like to explain my model, called the "Japan Management Evolution Model" which I have been using the last several years.

I was born, raised, and educated through college in Japan, and worked as an adult in Japan. I was with IBM Japan selling computer hardware and software to Japanese as well as to foreign companies in Tokyo.

I then resigned from IBM Japan to pursue a graduate degree in the U.S. Upon getting a master's degree, I was recruited by IBM U.S. domestic to market IBM hardware and software to Sears Roebuck in Chicago. Then I was recruited by Storage Technology in Colorado to be responsible for marketing programs for Americas/Asia, which included Canada, Latin America, Japan, Australia, and the Far East. I received two promotions in the next three years, before being sent to Japan as president of Storage Technology Japan to run the subsidiary. I had what you call "headquarters experience" and "country experience."

Source: Quoted from Yoshi Noguchi, "Back and Forth: Who Should Be the Boss? The Answer May Change in a Predictable Pattern," *The Wall Street Journal*, September 26, 1996, p. R18.

time, Burroughs Corporation's Italian subsidiary was run by a Frenchman, the Swiss subsidiary by a Dane, the German subsidiary by an Englishman, the French subsidiary by a Swiss, the Venezuelan subsidiary by an Argentinean, and the Danish subsidiary by a Dutchman.

American companies often seek TCNs from other English-speaking countries to avoid the double taxation cost of their American managers. That is, Americans working in Spain, for example, must pay both Spanish and U.S. income taxes, and most American firms' compensation packages for expatriates adjust accordingly. So, given the same pay and benefits, it is cheaper for an American firm to post a British executive in Spain than an American.

However, overall, the development of TCN executives reflects not only a growing internationalization of business, it also acknowledges that personal skills and motivations are not the exclusive property of one nation. TCNs often are sought because they speak several languages and know an industry or foreign country well. More and more companies feel that talent should flow to opportunity regardless of one's home country.

Host Country Restrictions

The host governments' attitudes toward foreign workers complicate flexibility in selecting expatriate U.S. nationals or local nationals. Concern about foreign corporate domination, local unemployment, and other issues causes some countries to restrict the number of non-nationals allowed to work within the country. Most countries have specific rules limiting work permits for foreigners to positions that cannot be filled by a national. Further, the law often limits such permits to periods just long enough to train a local for a specific position. Such restrictions mean that MNCs have fewer opportunities for sending home-country personnel to management positions abroad.

In earlier years, personnel gained foreign-country experience by being sent to lower management positions to gain the necessary training before eventually assuming top-level foreign assignments. Most countries, including the United States, control the num-

The American press likes to show Japanese looking for work—these middle managers have been laid off. Some American companies have been able to "capture" experienced Japanese managers in this circumstance, but such opportunities remain very unusual, and thus a newsworthy event in Japan. (© 1994 P.J. Griffiths/Magnum)

ber of foreign managers allowed to work or train within their borders. In one year, the United States Immigration Service rejected 37 out of 40 applications of European chefs the Marriott Corporation wanted to bring to the United States for management training in their U.S. hotels.

Selecting Sales and Marketing Personnel

To select personnel for international marketing positions effectively, management must define precisely what is expected of its people. A formal job description can aid management in expressing those desires for long-range needs as well as for current needs. In addition to descriptions for each marketing position, the criteria should include special requirements indigenous to various countries.

People operating in the home country need only the attributes of effective salespersons, whereas a transnational manager can require skills and attitudes that would challenge a diplomat. Personnel requirements for various positions vary considerably, but despite the range of differences, some basic requisites leading to effective performance should be considered because effective executives and salespeople, regardless of what foreign country they are operating in, share certain characteristics. Special personal characteristics, skills, and orientations are demanded for international operations.

Maturity is a prime requisite for expatriate and third-country personnel. Managers and sales personnel working abroad typically must work more independently than their domestic counterparts. The company must have confidence in their ability to make decisions and commitments without constant recourse to the home office, or they cannot be individually effective.

International personnel require a kind of *emotional stability* not demanded in domestic positions. Regardless of location, these people are living in cultures dissimilar to their own; to some extent they are always under scrutiny, and always aware that they are official representatives of the company abroad. They need a sensitivity to behavioral variations in different countries but cannot be so hypersensitive that their behavior is adversely affected.

Managers or salespeople operating in foreign countries need considerable breadth of knowledge of many subjects both on and off the job. The ability to speak one or more other languages is always preferable.

In addition to the intangible skills necessary in handling interpersonal relationships, international marketers must also be effective salespeople. Every marketing person in a foreign position is directly involved in the selling effort and must possess a sales sense that cuts through personal, cultural, and language differences and deals effectively with the selling situation.

The marketer who expects to be effective in the international marketplace needs to have a *positive outlook* on an international assignment. People who do not like what they are doing and where they are doing it stand little chance of success. Failures usually are the result of overselling the assignment, showing the bright side of the picture, and not warning about the bleak side.

An international salesperson must have a high level of *flexibility* whether working in a foreign country or at home. Expatriates working in a foreign country must be particularly sensitive to the habits of the market; those working at home for a foreign company must adapt to the requirements and ways of the parent company.

Successful adaptation in international affairs is based on a combination of attitude and effort. A careful study of the customs of the market country should be initiated before the marketer arrives, and should continue as long as there are facets of the culture that are not clear. One useful approach is to listen to the advice of national and foreign businesspeople operating in that country. *Cultural empathy* is clearly a part of basic orientation because it is unlikely that anyone can be effective if antagonistic or confused about the environment.

Finally, international sales and marketing personnel must be *energetic* and *enjoy travel.* Many international sales representatives spend about two-thirds of their nights in hotel rooms around the world. Going through the long lines of customs and immigration after a 15-hour flight requires a certain kind of stamina not commonly encountered. Some even argue that long flights can damage your health.[19] Even the seductive lights of Paris nights fade after the fifth business trip there.

Most of these traits can be assessed during interviews and perhaps during role-playing exercises. Paper and pencil ability tests, biographical information, and reference checks will be of secondary importance. Indeed, as previously mentioned, in many countries referrals will be the best way to recruit managers and sales representatives, making reference checks during evaluation and selection processes irrelevant.

There is also some evidence that some traits that make for successful sales representatives in the United States may not be important in other countries. In one study sales representatives in the electronics industries in Japan and the United States were compared. For the American representatives, valence for pay and education were both found to be positively related to performance and job satisfaction. In Japan they were not. That is, the Americans who cared more about money and were more educated tended to perform better in and be more satisfied with their sales jobs. Alternatively, the Japanese sales representatives tended to be more satisfied with their jobs when their values were consistent with those of their company.[20] The few systematic studies in this genre suggest that selection criteria must be localized, and American management practices must be adapted in foreign markets.

Finally, selection mistakes are costly. When an expatriate assignment does not work out, hundreds of thousands of dollars are wasted in expenses and lost time. Getting the right person to handle the job becomes especially important in the selection of locals to

---

[19] Rajeev Syal and Mark Hodson, "Airline Inquiry on 'Health-Risk' Seats," *London Sunday Times,* June 29, 1997, p. 1.

[20] R. Bruce Money and John L. Graham, "Sales Performance, Pay, and Job Satisfaction: Tests of a Model Using Data Collected in the U.S. and Japan," *Journal of International Business Studies,* 1998.

CROSSING BORDERS 17–3

The View from the Other Side

The globalization of U.S. markets means that more foreign managers are coming to the United States to live. The problem of cultural adaptation and adjustment is no less a problem for them than for Americans going to their countries to live. Here are a few observations from the other side—from foreigners in the United States.

"There are no small eggs in America," says a Dutchman. "There are only jumbo, extra large, large, and medium." This is no country for humility.

"If you are not aggressive, you're not noticed." "For a foreigner to succeed in the United States . . . he needs to be more aggressive than in his own culture because Americans expect that."

Young Japanese have difficulty addressing American superiors in a manner that shows self-confidence and an air of competence. The essential elements are posture and eye contact, but the Japanese simply cannot stand up straight, puff up their chests, look the Americans in the eyes, and talk at the same time.

Schedules and deadlines are taken very seriously. How quickly one does a job is often as important as how well one does the job. Japanese, who are experts at being members of teams, need help in learning to compete, take initiative, and develop leadership skills.

A Latin American has to refrain from the sort of socializing he would do in Latin countries, where rapport comes before deal making. "Here that is not necessary," he says. "You can even do business with someone you do not like." He still feels uncomfortable launching right into business, but Americans become frustrated when they think they are wasting time.

Americans say, "Come on over sometime," but the foreigner learns—perhaps after an awkward visit—that this is not really an invitation.

"Living alone in the United States is very sad, so much loneliness. Of course, living alone in Japan is also lonely, but in this country we can't speak English so fluently, so it is difficult to find a friend. I miss my boyfriend. I miss my parents. I miss my close friends."

Source: Adapted from Lennie Copeland, "Managing in the Melting Pot," *Across the Board*, June 1986, pp. 52–59; and Eva S. Kras, *Management in Two Cultures*, revised edition (Yarmouth, ME: Interncultural Press, 1995).

work for foreign companies within their home country. Most developing countries and many European countries have stringent laws protecting workers' rights. These laws are specific as to penalties for the dismissal of employees. Perhaps Venezuela has the most stringent dismissal legislation: With more than three months of service in the same firm, a worker gets severance pay amounting to one month's pay at severance notice plus 15 days' pay for every month of service exceeding eight months plus an additional 15 days' pay for each year employed. Further, after an employee is dismissed, the law requires that person be replaced within 30 days at the same salary. Colombia and Brazil have similar laws that make employee dismissal a high-cost proposition.

Impact of Cultural Values on Managing

After the sales force has been established, next come the tasks of training, motivating, and controlling. Several vital questions arise when performing these tasks in other cultures. How much does a different culture affect management practices, processes, and concepts used in the United States? Practices that work well in the United States may not be equally effective when customs, values, and life-styles differ. Transferring management practices to other cultures without concern for their exportability is no less vulnerable to major error than assuming a product successful in the United States will be successful in other countries. Management concepts are influenced by cultural diversity and must be evaluated in terms of local norms. Whether or not any single management practice needs adapting depends on the local culture.

Because of the unlimited cultural diversity in the values, attitudes, and beliefs affecting management practices, only those fundamental premises on which U.S. management practices are based are presented here for comparison. International managers must analyze normally used management practices to assess their transferability to another culture. The purpose of this section is to heighten the reader's awareness of the need for adaptation of management practices rather than to present a complete discussion of U.S. culture and management behavior.

There are many divergent views on the most important ideas on which normative U.S. cultural concepts are based. Those that occur most frequently in discussions of cross-cultural evaluations are represented by the following: (1) "master of destiny" viewpoint, (2) independent enterprise—the instrument of social action, (3) personnel selection and reward based on merit, (4) decisions based on objective analysis, (5) wide sharing in decision making, and (6) never-ending quest for improvement.

The *master of destiny* philosophy underlies much of U.S. management thought and is a belief held by many in our culture. Simply stated, people can substantially influence the future; we are in control of our own destinies. This viewpoint also reflects the attitude that although luck may influence an individual's future, on balance, persistence, hard work, a commitment to fulfill expectations, and effective use of time give people control of their destinies. In contrast, many cultures have a fatalistic approach to life. They believe individual destiny is determined by a higher order and what happens cannot be controlled.

In the United States, approaches to planning, control, supervision, commitment, motivation, scheduling, and deadlines are all influenced by the concept that individuals can control their futures. Recall from Chapter 4 that the U.S. scored highest on Hofstede's individualism scale.[21] In cultures with more collectivistic and fatalistic beliefs, these good business practices may be followed but concern for the final outcome is different. After all, if one believes the future is determined by an uncontrollable higher order, then what difference does individual effort really make?

The acceptance of the idea that *independent enterprise* is an instrument for social action is the fundamental concept of U.S. corporations. A corporation is recognized as an entity that has rules and continuity of existence, and is a separate and vital social institution. This recognition of the corporation as an entity can result in strong feelings of obligation to serve the company. In fact, the enterprise can take priority over personal preferences and social obligations because it is viewed as an entity that must be protected and developed. This concept ties into the master of destiny concept in that, for a company to work and for individuals to control their destinies, they must feel a strong obligation to fulfill the requirements necessary to the success of the enterprise. Indeed, the company may take precedence over family, friends, or other activities which might detract from what is best for the company.

American management theory rests on the assumption that each member of an organization will give primary efforts to performing assigned tasks in the interests of that organization. Thus, in the United States an enterprise takes precedence and receives loyalty and the willingness to conform to its managerial systems. This is in sharp contrast to the attitudes held by Mexicans, who feel strongly that personal relationships are more important in daily life than the corporation.[22]

---

[21] Geert Hofstede, *Culture and Organizations* (London: McGraw-Hill, 1991).

[22] Eva S. Kras' *Management in Two Cultures: Bridging the Gap between U.S. and Mexican Managers* (Yarmouth, ME: Intercultural Press, 1995) provides a clear description of the differences between Mexican and American management.

Consistent with the view that individuals control their own destinies is the belief that personnel selection and reward must be made on *merit.* The selection, promotion, motivation, or dismissal of personnel by U.S. managers emphasizes the need to select the best qualified persons for jobs, retaining them as long as their performance meets standards of expectations, and continuing the opportunity for upward mobility as long as those standards are met. Indeed, the belief that anyone can become the corporate president prevails among management personnel within the United States. Such presumptions lead to the belief that striving and making accomplishments will be rewarded, and conversely, the failure to do so will be penalized. The penalty for poor performance could be, and often is, dismissal. The reward and penalty scheme is a major basis for motivating U.S. personnel.

In other cultures where friendship or family ties may be more important than the vitality of the organization, the criteria for selection, organization, and motivation are substantially different from those in U.S. companies. In some cultures, organizations expand to accommodate the maximum number of friends and relatives.[23] Further, if one knows that promotions are made on the basis of personal ties and friendships rather than on merit, a fundamental motivating lever is lost.

The very strong belief in the United States that business decisions are based on *objective analysis* and that managers strive to be more scientific has a profound effect on the U.S. manager's attitudes toward objectivity in decision making and accuracy of data. While judgment and intuition are important criteria for making decisions, most U.S. managers believe decisions must be supported and based on accurate and relevant information. This scientific approach is not necessarily the premise on which foreign executives base decisions. In fact, the infallibility of the judgment of a key executive in many foreign cultures may be more important in the decision process than any other single factor. If one accepts scientific management as a fundamental basis for decision making, then attitudes toward accuracy and promptness in reporting data, availability and openness of data to all levels within the corporation, and the willingness to express even unpopular judgments become important characteristics of the business process. Thus, in U.S. business, great emphasis is placed on the collection and free flow of information to all levels within the organization and on frankness of expression in the evaluation of business opinions or decisions. In other cultures, such high value on factual and rational support for decisions is not as important; the accuracy of data and even the proper reporting of data are not prime prerequisites. Further, existing data frequently are for the eyes of a select few. The frankness of expression and openness in dealing with data characteristic of U.S. businesses do not fit easily into some cultures.

Compatible with the views that one controls one's own destiny and that advancement is based on merit is the prevailing idea of *wide sharing in decision making.* Although decision making is not truly a democratic process in U.S. businesses, there is a strong belief that individuals in an organization require and, indeed, need the responsibility of making decisions for continued development. Thus, decision making is frequently decentralized, and the ability as well as the responsibility for making decisions are pushed down to lower ranks of management. In this way, employees have an opportunity to grow with responsibility and to prove their abilities. One of the frustrating aspects of an American working for a Japanese corporation is the American's belief that decisions are made "in Tokyo—or in late-night drinking sessions in New York sushi bars that seem to exclude anyone who doesn't speak Japanese." In many cultures, decisions are highly centralized, in part, because of the belief that only a few in the company have the right or the ability to make decisions. In the Middle East, for example, only top executives make decisions.

Finally, all of these concepts culminate in a *never-ending quest for improvement.* The United States has always been a relatively activist society; in many walks of life,

---

[23] S. Gordon Redding, *The Spirit of Chinese Capitalism* (Berlin: Walter de Gruyter, 1993).

the prevailing question is: "Can it be done better?" Thus, management concepts reflect the belief that change is not only normal but also necessary, that no aspects are sacred or above improvement. In fact, the merit on which one achieves advancement is frequently tied to one's ability to make improvements. Results are what count; if practices must change to achieve results, then change is in order. In other cultures, the strength and power of those in command frequently rest not on change but on the premise that the status quo demands stable structure. To suggest improvement implies that those in power have failed; for someone in a lower position to suggest change would be viewed as a threat to another's private domain rather than the suggestion of an alert and dynamic individual.

The views expressed here pervade much of what is considered U.S. management technique. They are part of our self-reference criterion (SRC) and affect our management attitudes, and they must be considered by the international marketer when developing and managing an international sales force.

Training for International Marketing

The nature of a training program depends largely on whether expatriate or local personnel are being trained for overseas positions. Training for the expatriates focuses on the customs and the special foreign sales problems that will be encountered, whereas local personnel require greater emphasis on the company, its products, technical information, and selling methods. In training either type of personnel, the sales training activity is burdened with problems stemming from long-established behavior and attitudes. Local personnel, for instance, cling to habits continually reinforced by local culture. Nowhere is the problem greater than in China or Russia, where the legacy of the communist tradition lingers. The attitude that whether you work hard or not, you get the same rewards, has to be changed if training is going to hold. Expatriates, as well, are captives of their own habits and patterns. Before any training can be effective, open-minded attitudes must be established.

Continual training may be more important in foreign markets than in domestic ones because of the lack of routine contact with the parent company and its marketing personnel. In addition, training of foreign employees must be tailored to the recipients' ways of learning and communicating.[24] For example, the *Dilbert* cartoon characters theme that worked so well in ethics training courses with a company's American employees did not translate well in many of its foreign offices.

Finally, one aspect of training is frequently overlooked: Home-office personnel dealing with international marketing operations need training designed to make them responsive to the needs of the foreign operations. In most companies, the requisite sensitivities are expected to be developed by osmosis in the process of dealing with foreign affairs. However, the best companies provide home-office personnel with cross-cultural training and send them abroad periodically to increase their awareness of the problems of the foreign operations.

The Internet now makes some kinds of sales training much more efficient.[25] Users can study text on screen and participate in interactive assessment tests. Sun Microsystems estimates that its use of the Internet can shorten training cycles by as much as 75 percent. And in some parts of the world where telecommunications facilities are more limited, CD-ROM approaches have proven quite successful. Lockheed-Martin uses an interactive CD-ROM based system to train its employees worldwide on the nuances of the Foreign Corrupt Practices Act and associated corporate policies and ethics.

[24] Andy Cohen, "Small World, Big Challenge," *Sales & Marketing Management,* June 1996, pp. 69–73.

[25] Robert M. Kahn, "21st Century Training (Sales Training on the Internet)," *Sales & Marketing Management,* June 1, 1997, p. 80.

Exhibit 17–1   **The Salespeople Were Asked to: "Distribute 100 points among the Rewards in Terms of their Importance to You"**

Rewards	Relative Importance (mean)	
	Japanese	*Americans*
Job security	18.5	17.6
Promotion	13.7	14.9
Merit increase in pay	24.7	26.2
Feeling of worthwhile accomplishment	18.5	18.2
Social recognition (sales club awards)	8.1	5.2
Personal growth and development	16.6	17.8

Source: R. Bruce Money and John L. Graham, "Salesperson Performance, Pay, and Job Satisfaction: Tests of a Model Using Data Collected in the U.S. and Japan," *Journal of International Business Studies,* 1998.

Motivating Sales Personnel

Motivation is especially complicated because the firm is dealing with different cultures, different sources, different philosophies—and always dealing with individuals. Marketing is a business function requiring high motivation regardless of the location of the practitioner. Marketing managers and sales managers typically work hard, travel extensively, and have day-to-day challenges. Selling is hard, competitive work wherever undertaken, and a constant flow of inspiration is needed to keep personnel functioning at an optimal level. National differences must always be considered in motivating the marketing force. In one study[26] sales representatives in comparable Japanese and American sales organizations were asked to allocate 100 points across an array of potential rewards from work. As shown in Exhibit 17–1, the results were surprisingly similar. The only real difference between the two groups was in Social Recognition, which predictably, the Japanese rated as more important. However, the authors of the study concluded that although individual values for rewards may be similar, the social and competitive contexts still require different motivational systems.

Because the cultural differences reviewed in earlier chapters affect the motivational patterns of a sales force, a manager must be extremely sensitive to the personal behavior patterns of employees. Individual incentives that work effectively in the United States can fail completely in other cultures. For example, with Japan's emphasis on paternalism and collectivism and its system of lifetime employment and seniority, motivation through individual incentive does not work because Japanese employees seem to derive the greatest satisfaction from being comfortable members of a group. Thus, an offer of an individual financial reward for outstanding individual effort could be turned down because an employee would prefer not to appear different from peers and possibly attract their resentment. As such, Japanese bonus systems are based on group effort, and individual commission systems are quite rare. Japanese sales representatives are more motivated by the social pressure of their peers than the prospect of making more money based on individual effort.

Communications are also important in maintaining high levels of motivation; foreign managers need to know the home office is interested in their operations, and, in turn, they want to know what is happening in the parent country. Everyone performs better when well informed.

Because promotion and the opportunity to improve status are important motivators, a company needs to make clear the opportunities for growth within the firm. In truly global firms foreign nationals can aspire to the highest positions in the firm. Likewise,

---

[26] R. Bruce Money and John L. Graham, 1998.

CROSSING BORDERS 17-4

Avon Calling—In the Amazon Basin?

In a gold-mining town near an Amazon tributary, Maria de Fatima Nascimento ambles among mud shacks hawking Honesty and Care Deeply, two beauty products by Avon. She is part of a several-thousand-member Avon army that travels via foot, kayak, river-boat, and small plane through the Amazon basin. Latin America accounts for 35 percent of Avon's total sales and its success can be attributed to the company's willingness to adapt to local conditions. Cash payments aren't required; many Brazilian customers barter for products with fruit, eggs, flour, or wood. Two-dozen eggs buys a Bart Simpson roll-on deodorant, and miners pay from 1 to 4 grams of gold powder or nuggets for fragrances like Sweet Crystal Splash. "Ladies of the evening," who regard the cosmetics as a cost of doing business, are some of Nascimento's better customers. But then, so are miners. One commented, "It's worth $1^1/2$ grams of gold to smell nice."

Avon's latest coup is to launch sales of Mattel's Barbie in China. Avon also hopes to offer Barbie in other markets where distribution systems are undeveloped, including Indonesia, Russia, and Brazil.

Sources: Adapted from "Avon Calling near the Amazon," *U.S. News & World Report,* October 25, 1994, pp. 16–17; and Tara Parker-Pope and Lisa Bannon, "Avon's New Calling: Selling Barbie in China," *The Wall Street Journal,* May 1, 1997, p. B1.

one of the greatest fears of expatriate managers, which can be easily allayed, is that they will be forgotten by the home office. Blending company sales objectives and the personal objectives of the salespeople and other employees is a task worthy of the most skilled manager. The U.S. manager must be constantly aware that many of the techniques used to motivate U.S. personnel and their responses to these techniques are based on the six basic cultural premises discussed earlier. Therefore, each method used to motivate a foreigner should be examined for cultural compatibility.

Designing Compensation Systems

For Expatriates

Developing an equitable and functional compensation plan that combines balance, consistent motivation, and flexibility is extremely challenging in international operations. This is especially true when a company operates in a number of countries, when it has individuals who work in a number of countries, or when the sales force is composed of expatriate and local personnel. Fringe benefits play a major role in many countries.[27] Those working in high-tax countries prefer liberal expense accounts and fringe benefits which are nontaxable instead of direct income subject to high taxes. Fringe-benefit costs are high in Europe, ranging from 35 to 60 percent of salary.

Pay can be a significant factor in making it difficult for a person to be repatriated. Often those returning home realize they have been making considerably more money with a lower cost of living in the overseas market; returning to the home country means a cut in pay and a cut in standard of living.

---

[27] "Living Costs: 60 Percent Personal Goods Tax Hits Expats," *Business Eastern Europe,* May 2, 1994, p. 7.

A strong corporate culture will be crucial in motivating salespeople in collectivistic cultures. Here new employees at China Bicycle Company shout out the company anthem during "morale training." Their salary is about $300 per month. (© Michael Yamashita/Woodfin Camp & Associates)

Conglomerate operations that include domestic and foreign personnel cause the greatest problems in compensation planning. Expatriates tend to compare their compensation with what they would have received at the home office at the same time, and local personnel and expatriate personnel are likely to compare notes on salary. Although any differences in the compensation level may easily and logically be explained, the group receiving the lower amount almost always feels aggrieved and mistreated.

Short-term assignments for expatriates further complicate the compensation issue, particularly when the short-term assignments extend into a longer time. In general, short-term assignments involve payments of overseas premiums (sometimes called *separation allowances* if the family does not go along), all excess expenses, and allowances for tax differentials. Longer assignments can include home-leave benefits or travel allowances for the spouse. Many companies estimate that these expenses equal approximately the base compensation of the employees.

Besides rewarding an individual's contribution to the firm, a compensation program can be used effectively to recruit, develop, motivate, or retain personnel. Most recommendations for developing a compensation program suggest that a program focus on whichever one of these purposes fits the needs in the particular situation. If all four purposes are targeted, it can result in unwieldy programs that have become completely unmanageable for many. International compensation programs also provide additional payments for hardship locations and special inducements to reluctant personnel to accept overseas employment and to remain in the position. Fringe-benefits costs for an annual base salary of $169,000 for a three-year period can range from $210,000 in Argentina to $489,000 in Japan.[28]

An important trend questions the need for expatriates to fill foreign positions. Many companies now feel that the increase in the number and quality of managers in other countries means many positions being filled by expatriates could be filled by locals and/or third-country nationals who would require lower compensation packages. Several major U.S. multinationals, including PepsiCo, Black & Decker Manufacturing

---

[28] "The Cost of Employing U.S. Expatriates," *International Business,* February 4, 1994, p. 88.

Exhibit 17-2   Global Similarity to U.S. Compensation Plans

Countries/Regions		Eligibility	Performance Measures	Weighting	Plan Mechanics	Mix/ Leverage	Payout Frequency
Europe	United Kingdom						
	Scandinavia						
	France						
	Germany						
	Spain/Italy						
Southeast Asia	Hong Kong						
	Korea						
	Taiwan						
	Malaysia						
	Indonesia						
	(Singapore)						
	Australia						
Japan							
Canada							
South America							

Column header: **Degree of Plan Similarity with the United States**

Legend: ▢ Similar   ▢ Varies   ▮ Dissimilar

Data represent multiple client projects conducted by The Alexander Group Inc. for primarily high-technology industry sales organizations.

Source: David G. Schick and David J. Cichelli, "Developing Incentive Compensation Strategies in a Global Sales Environment," *ACA Journal,* Autumn 1996.

Company, and Hewlett-Packard Company, have established policies to minimize the number of expatriate personnel they post abroad. With more emphasis being placed on the development of third-country nationals and locals for managerial positions, companies find they can reduce compensation packages.[29]

For a Global Sales Force

Compensation plans of American companies vary substantially around the globe, reflecting the economic and cultural differences in the diverse markets served. As reflected in Exhibit 17–2, some experts feel compensation plans are most different from the standard U.S. approach in Japan and Southern Europe.

One company has gone possibly the farthest to homogenize its worldwide compensation scheme. Beginning in 1996 IBM rolled out what is perhaps the most global approach to compensating a worldwide sales force.[30] The main features of that plan, which applies to 140,000 sales executives in 140 countries, are presented in Exhibit 17–3. The plan was developed in response to "global" complaints from sales representatives that the old plan was confusing, that it did not provide for work done outside one's

[29] For a still excellent discussion of the problems of constructing a compensation plan for expatriates, nationals, and third-country nationals, see Michael Harvey, "Empirical Evidence of Recurring International Compensation Problems," *Journal of International Business Studies,* Fourth Quarter, 1993, pp. 785–799.

[30] For more details, see Michele Marchetti, *Sales & Marketing Management,* July 1996.

EXHIBIT 17–3   A Compensation Blueprint
How IBM Pays 140,000 Sales Executives Worldwide

Total
Compensation

Benefits		Plan Components	Payout Frequency	Pay Measurements	Number of Measurements Used to Calculate
Variable Pay	→	Corporate Objectives	Annually	Bonus payment (based on) • Profit • Customer satisfaction	2
Incentive Compensation	→	Teamwork	Monthly	20% of incentive compensation • Work team performance • Industry performance	2
		Personal Contribution	Quarterly	60% of incentive compensation • Growth • Solutions • Channels/partners • Profit contribution	1–2
		Challenges/ Contests	As earned	20% of incentive compensation • National • Local	1–4
Recognition					
Base Salary					

Source: Adapted from Michele Marchetti, "Gamble, IBM Replaces Its Outdated Compensation Plan with a World Wide Framework, Will It Pay Off?" *Sales and Marketing Management,* July 1996, pp. 65–69.

territory (such as in the scenario presented at the beginning of this chapter), and therefore did not promote cross-border team work. IBM sales incentive managers from North America, Latin America, Asia Pacific, and Europe worked together with consultants on the design for some nine months. At first glance it may appear that IBM is making the cardinal error of trying to force a plan developed centrally onto sales offices literally spread around the world and across diverse cultures; however, the compensation plan still allows substantial latitude for local managers. Compensation managers in each country determine the frequency of incentive payouts and the split between base and incentive pay, while still following a global scheme of performance measures. Thus, the system allows for a high incentive component in countries like the U.S. and high base-salary components in countries like Japan.

Perhaps the most valuable information provided regards the lessons IBM learned in the process of revamping its sales compensation scheme. The following is a list of the associated "do's and don'ts" of global compensation:[31]

1. Do involve reps from key countries.
2. Do allow local managers to decide the mix between base and incentive pay.
3. Do use consistent performance measures (results paid for) and emphasis on each measure.
4. Do allow local countries flexibility in implementations.
5. Do use consistent communication and training themes worldwide.
6. Don't design the plan centrally and dictate to local offices.
7. Don't create a similar framework for jobs with different responsibilities.

---

[31] Ibid.

8. Don't require consistency on every performance measure within the incentive plan.

9. Don't assume cultural differences can be managed through the incentive plan.

10. Don't proceed without the support of senior sales executives worldwide.

In a similar global move, Levi's recently announced a unique worldwide incentive plan: At the end of six years every one of the company's 37,500 employees in 60 countries, regardless of position, will receive an extra year's pay as a bonus if the firm achieves a cumulative cash flow of $7.6 billion during the period. That will cost the firm some $750 million![32]

Evaluating and Controlling Sales Representatives

Evaluation and control of sales representatives in the U.S. is a relatively simple task. In many sales jobs, emphasis is placed on individual performance, which can easily be measured by sales revenues generated (often compared to past performance, forecasts, and/or quotas). In short, a good sales representative produces big numbers. However, in many countries the evaluation problem is more complex, particularly in the more collectivistic cultures, where teamwork is favored over individual effort. Performance measures require closer observation and may include the opinions of customers, peers, and supervisors. Of course, on the other hand, managers of sales forces operating in more collective cultures may see measures of individual performance as relatively unimportant.

One study comparing American and Japanese sales representatives' performance illustrates such differences.[33] Supervisors' ratings of the representatives on identical performance scales were used in both countries. The distribution of performance of the Japanese was statistically normal—a few high performers, a few low, but most in the middle. The American distribution was different—a few high, most in the middle, but almost no low performers. In the U.S. poor performers either quit (because they are not making any money) or they are fired. In Japan the poor performers stay with the company and are seldom fired. Thus, sales managers in Japan have a problem their American counterparts do not: how to motivate poor performers. Indeed, sales management textbooks in the United States usually include material on how to deal with "plateaued" salespeople, but say little about poor performers because the latter are not a problem.[34]

The primary control tool used by American sales managers is the incentive system. With the Internet and fax machines, more and more American sales representatives operate out of offices in their homes and see supervisors infrequently.[35] Organizations have become quite flat and spans of control increasingly broad in recent years. However, in many other countries spans of control can be quite narrow by American standards—even in Australia[36] and particularly in Japan. In the latter country, supervisors spend much more time with fewer subordinates. Corporate culture and frequent interactions

---

[32] Joan O'C. Hamilton, "Levi's Pot of Gold," *Business Week,* June 24, 1996, p. 44.

[33] R. Bruce Money and John L. Graham, *Journal of International Business Studies,* 1998.

[34] For a complete discussion of sales management issues, see Gilbert A. Churchill, Jr., Neil M. Ford, and Orville C. Walker, Jr., *Sales Force Management,* 5th ed. (Chicago: Irwin/McGraw-Hill, 1997).

[35] Geoffrey Brewer, Ginger Conlon, John F. Yarbrough, Andy Cohen, Michele Marchetti, Tom Dellecave, Chad Kaydo, and Allison Lucas, "The Top (25 Best Sales Forces in the U.S.)," *Sales & Marketing Management,* November 1, 1996, pp. 38–46.

[36] David W. Cravens, Ken Grant, Thomas N. Ingram, Raymond W. LaForge, and Clifford E. Young, "Comparison of Field Sales Management Activities in Australian and American Sales Organizations," *Journal of Global Marketing,* 5(4), 1992, pp. 23–45.

CROSSING BORDERS 17–5

How Important Are Those Meetings?

In Japan, they're real important. A former American sales manager tells this story:

"I worked as general manager of the Japanese subsidiary of an American medical equipment company. Our office was in downtown Tokyo, which made for a two-hour commute for most of our salesmen. Rather than have them come into the office before beginning sales calls everyday, I instructed them to go to their appointments directly from home and to come to the office only for a weekly sales meeting. Although this was a common way for a U.S. sales force to operate, it was a disaster in Japan. Sales fell, as did morale. I quickly changed the policy and had everyone come to the office everyday. Sales immediately climbed as the salesmen reinforced their group identity."

Now contrast that with how sales representatives are managed at Hewlett-Packard in the United States, as described by one of its sales executives:

"We're really looking at this issue of work/family balance. If someone wants to work at home, they can, and we'll outfit their home offices at our expense, provided they have a good reason to want to work at home. If you want to drive productivity, getting people's work lives and home lives in balance is key."

Sources: Clyde V. Prestowitz, *Trading Places—How We Are Giving Away Our Future to Japan and How to Reclaim It* (New York: Basic Books, 1989); and Geoffrey Brewer, et al., "The Top (25 Best Sales Forces in the U.S.)," *Sales & Marketing Management,* November 1, 1996, p. 38.

with peers and supervisors are the means of motivation and control of sales representatives in more collectivistic and hierarchical cultures like Japan.

Preparing U.S. Personnel for Foreign Assignments

Estimates of the annual cost of sending and supporting a manager and the family in a foreign assignment range from 150–400 percent of base salary. The cost in money (some estimates are in the $250,000 to $500,00 range)[37] and morale increases substantially if the expatriate requests a return home before completing the normal tour of duty (a normal stay is two to four years). In addition, if repatriation into domestic operations is not successful and the employee leaves the company, an indeterminately high cost in low morale and loss of experienced personnel results. To reduce these problems, international personnel management has increased planning for expatriate personnel to move abroad, remain abroad, and then return to the home country. The planning process must begin prior to the selection of those who go abroad and extend to their specific assignments after returning home. Selection, training, compensation, and career development policies (including repatriation) should reflect the unique problems of managing the expatriate.

Besides the job-related criteria for a specific position, the typical candidate for an international assignment is married, has two school-aged children, is expected to stay

---

[37] Jennifer Oldham, "The State of Expatriates," *Los Angeles Times,* January 13, 1996, p. B1.

overseas three years, and has the potential for promotion into higher management levels. These characteristics of the typical expatriate are the basis of most of the difficulties associated with getting the best qualified to go overseas, keeping them there, and assimilating them on their return.

Overcoming Reluctance to Accept a Foreign Assignment

Concerns for career and family are the most frequently mentioned reasons for a manager to refuse a foreign assignment. The most important career-related reservation is the fear that a two- or three-year absence will adversely affect opportunities for advancement. This "out of sight, out of mind" fear is closely linked to the problems of repatriation. Without evidence of advance planning to protect career development, better-qualified and ambitious personnel may decline the offer to go abroad. However, if candidates for expatriate assignments are picked thoughtfully, returned to the home office at the right moment, and rewarded for good performance with subsequent promotions at home, companies find recruiting of executives for international assignments eased.

Even though the career development question may be adequately answered with proper planning, concern for family may interfere with many accepting an assignment abroad. Initially, most potential candidates are worried about uprooting a family and settling into a strange environment. Questions about the education of the children, isolation from family and friends, proper health care, and, in some countries, the potential for violence reflect the misgivings a family faces when relocating in a foreign country. Special compensation packages have been the typical way to deal with this problem. A hardship allowance, allowances to cover special educational requirements that frequently include private schools, housing allowances, and extended all-expense-paid vacations are part of compensation packages designed to overcome family-related problems with an overseas assignment. Ironically, the solution to one problem creates a later problem when that family returns to the United States and must give up those extra compensation benefits used to induce them to accept the position.

Reducing the Rate of Early Returns

Once the employee and family accept the assignment abroad, the next problem is keeping them there for the assigned time. The attrition rate of those selected for overseas positions can be very high. One firm with a hospital management contract experienced an annualized failure rate of 120 percent—not high when compared with the construction contractor who started out in Saudi Arabia with 155 Americans and was down to 65 after only two months.

The most important reasons a growing number of companies are including an evaluation of an employee's family among selection criteria are the high cost of sending an expatriate abroad, and increasing evidence that unsuccessful family adjustment is the single most important reason for expatriate dissatisfaction and the resultant request for return home. In fact, a study of personnel directors of over 300 international firms found that the inability of the manager's spouse to adjust to a different physical or cultural environment was the primary reason for an expatriate's failure to function effectively in a foreign assignment. One researcher estimated that 75 percent of families sent to a foreign post experience adjustment problems with children or have marital discord. One executive suggests that there is so much pressure on the family that if there are any cracks in the marriage and you want to save it, think long and hard about taking a foreign assignment.[38]

Dissatisfaction is caused by the stress and trauma of adjusting to new and often strange cultures. The employee has less trouble adjusting than family members; a com-

---

[38] Minda Zetlin, "Making Tracks," *Journal of European Business,* May–June 1994, pp. 40–47.

pany's expatriate moves in a familiar environment even abroad and is often isolated from the cultural differences that create problems for the rest of the family. And about half of American expatriate employees receive cross-cultural training before the trip—much more often than their families.[39] Family members have far greater daily exposure to the new culture but are often not given assistance in adjusting. New consumption patterns must be learned, from grocery shopping to seeking healthcare services.[40] Family members frequently cannot be employed and, in many cultures, female members of the family face severe social restrictions. In Saudi Arabia, for example, the female's role is strictly dictated. In one situation, a woman's hemline offended a religious official who, in protest, sprayed black paint on her legs. In short, the greater problems of culture shock befall the family. Certainly any recruiting and selection procedure should include an evaluation of the family's ability to adjust.

Families that have the potential and the personality traits that would enable them to adjust to a different environment may still become dissatisfied with living abroad if they are not properly prepared for the new assignment. More and more companies realize the need for cross-cultural training to prepare families for their new homes. One- to two-day briefings to two- to three-week intensive programs that include all members of the family are provided to assist assimilation into new cultures. Language training, films, discussions, and lectures on cultural differences, potential problems, and stress areas in adjusting to a new way of life are provided to minimize the frustration of the initial cultural shock. This cultural training helps a family anticipate problems and eases adjustment. Once the family is abroad, some companies even provide a local ombudsman (someone experienced in the country) to whom members can take their problems and get immediate assistance. Although the cost of preparing a family for an overseas assignment may appear high, it must be weighed against estimates that the measurable cost of prematurely returned families could cover cross-cultural training for 300 to 500 families. Companies that do not prepare employees and their families for culture shock have the highest incidence of premature return to the United States.[41]

Successful Expatriate Repatriation

A Conference Board study reported that many firms have sophisticated plans for executives going overseas but few have comprehensive programs to deal with the return home. One consultant noted that too often repatriated workers are a valuable resource neglected or wasted by inexperienced U.S. management.

Low morale and a growing amount of attrition among returning expatriates have many reasons. Some complaints and problems are family related, others are career related. The family-related problems generally deal with financial and life-style readjustments. Some expatriates find that, in spite of higher compensation programs, their net worths have not increased, and the inflation of intervening years makes it impossible to buy a home comparable to the one they sold on leaving. The hardship compensation programs used to induce the executive to go abroad also create readjustment problems on the return home. Such compensation benefits frequently permitted the family to live at a much higher level abroad than at home (for example, yard boys, chauffeurs, domestic help, and so forth). Because most compensation benefits are withdrawn when employees return to the home country, their standard of living decreases and they must readjust. Another objection to returning to the United States is the location of the new assignment; the

---

[39] Erika Rasmusson, "Beyond Miss Manners, the Importance of International Business Ettiquette," *Sales & Marketing Management,* April 1997, p. 84.

[40] Mary C. Gilly, Lisa Penaloza, and Kenneth Kambara, "The Role of Consumption in Expatriate Adjustment and Satisfaction," working paper, Graduate School of Management, University of California, Irvine, 1998.

[41] J. Stewart Black, Hal Gregersen, and Mark Mendenhall, *Global Assignments* (San Francisco: Josey-Bass, 1992).

new location often is not viewed as desirable as the location before the foreign tour. Unfortunately, little can be done to ameliorate these kinds of problems short of transferring the managers to other foreign locations. Current thinking suggests that the problem of dissatisfaction with compensation and benefits upon return can be reduced by reducing benefits when overseas. Rather than provide the family abroad with hardship payments, some companies are considering reducing payments on the premise that the assignment abroad is an integral requirement for growth, development, and advancement within the firm.

Family dissatisfaction, which causes stress within the family on returning home, is not as severe a problem as career-related complaints. A returning expatriate's dissatisfaction with the perceived future is usually the reason many resign their positions after returning to the United States. The problem is not unique to U.S. citizens; Japanese companies have similar difficulties with their personnel. The most frequently heard complaint involves the lack of a detailed plan for the expatriate's career when returning home. New home-country assignments are frequently mundane and do not reflect the experience gained or the challenges met during foreign assignment. Some feel their time out of the mainstream of corporate affairs has made them technically obsolete and thus ineffective in competing immediately on return. Finally, there is some loss of status requiring ego adjustment when an executive returns home.

As discussed earlier, overseas assignments are filled most successfully by independent, mature self-starters. The expatriate executive enjoyed a certain degree of autonomy, independence, and power with all the perquisites of office not generally afforded in comparable positions domestically. Many find it difficult to adjust to being just another middle manager at home. In short, returning expatriates have a series of personal- and career-related questions to anticipate with anxiety back at corporate headquarters. Companies with the least amount of returnee attrition differ from those with the highest attrition in one significant way: personal career planning for the expatriate.[42]

Expatriate career planning begins with the decision to send the person abroad. The initial transfer abroad should be made in the context of a long-term company career plan. Under these circumstances, the individual knows not only the importance of the foreign assignment but also when to expect to return and at what level. Near the end of the foreign assignment, the process for repatriation is begun. The critical aspect of the return home is to keep the executive completely informed—proposed return time, new assignment and an indication of whether it is interim or permanent, new responsibilities, and future prospects. In short, returnees should know where they are going and what they will be doing next month and several years ahead.

A report on what MNCs are doing to improve the reentry process suggests five steps:

1 Commit to reassigning expatriates to meaningful positions.
2. Create a mentor program. Mentors are typically senior executives who monitor company activities, keep the expatriate informed on company activities, and act as liaison between the expatriate and various headquarters departments.
3. Offer a written job guarantee stating what the company is obligated to do for the expatriate on return.
4. Keep the expatriate in touch with headquarters through periodic briefings and headquarters visits.
5. Prepare the expatriate and family for repatriation once a return date is set.

Some believe the importance of preparing the employee and family for culture shock on returning is on a par with preparation for going abroad.

Even though such a program requires considerable preparation prior to and after the assignment, it gives a strong signal of the importance of long-term foreign assignments. If

---

[42] Howard Tu and Sherry E. Sullivan, "Preparing Yourself for an International Assignment," *Business Horizons*, January–February 1994, pp. 67–70.

foreign corporate experience is seen as a necessary prerequisite for personnel development and promotion, reluctance to accept foreign assignments and other problems associated with sending personnel abroad will be lessened. Although this discussion has focused primarily on U.S. personnel, it is equally applicable and important for the assignment of foreign personnel to the United States and the posting of third-country nationals.

Developing Cultural Awareness

Throughout the text, the need to adapt to the local culture has been stressed over and over. Developing cultural sensitivity is necessary for all international marketers. Personnel can be selected with great care, but if they do not possess or are not given the opportunity to develop some understanding of the culture to which they are being assigned, there is every chance they will develop culture shock, inadvertently alienate those with whom they come in contact in the new culture, and/or make all the cultural mistakes discussed in this text.

Many businesses focus on the functional skills needed in international marketing, overlooking the importance of cultural knowledge. Just as the idea "if a product sells well in Dallas it will sell well in Hong Kong" is risky, so is the idea that "a manager who excels in Dallas will excel in Hong Kong." Most expatriate failures are not caused by lack of management skills but rather by lack of an understanding of cultural differences and their effect on management skills. As the world becomes more interdependent and as companies become more dependent on foreign earnings, there is a growing need for companies to develop cultural awareness among those posted abroad.

Just as we remark that someone has achieved good social skills (i.e., an ability to remain poised and be in control under all social situations), so good cultural skills can be developed. These skills serve a similar function in varying cultural situations; they provide the individual with the ability to relate to a different culture even when the individual is unfamiliar with the details of that particular culture. Cultural skills can be learned just as social skills can be learned. People with cultural skills can:

- Communicate respect and convey verbally and nonverbally a positive regard and sincere interest in people and their culture.
- Tolerate ambiguity and cope with cultural differences and the frustration that frequently develops when things are different and circumstances change.
- Display empathy by understanding other people's needs and differences from their point of view.
- Be nonjudgmental by not judging the behavior of others by their own value standards.
- Recognize and control the SRC, that is, recognize their own culture and values as an influence on their perceptions, evaluations, and judgment in a situation.
- Laugh things off—a good sense of humor helps when frustration levels rise and things do not work as planned.

The Changing Profile of the Global Manager

Until recently the road to the top was well marked. Surveys of chief executives consistently report that more than three-quarters had either finance, manufacturing, or marketing backgrounds. As the 45-year postwar period of growing markets and domestic-only competition fades, however, so too does the narrow one-company, one-industry chief executive. Into the new millennium increasing international competition, the globaliza-

Japanese salesmen saving on expenses. Capsule hotel for traveling businessmen, Osaka, Japan.
(Paul Chesley/Tony Stone Images)

tion of companies, technology, demographic shifts, and the speed of overall change will govern the choice of company leaders.[43] It will be difficult for a single-discipline individual to reach the top in the future.

The executive recently picked to head Procter & Gamble's U.S. operations is a good example of the effect globalization is having on businesses and the importance of experience, whether in Japan, Europe, or elsewhere. The head of all P&G's U.S. business was born in the Netherlands, received an MBA from Rotterdam's Eramus University, then rose through P&G's marketing ranks in Holland, the United States, and Austria. After proving his mettle in Japan, he moved to P&G's Cincinnati, Ohio, headquarters to direct its push into East Asia, and then to his new position. Speculation is that if he succeeds in the United States, as he did in Japan, he will be a major contender for the top position at P&G.

Fewer companies today limit their search for senior-level executive talent to their home countries. Coca-Cola's former CEO, who began his ascent to the top in his native Cuba, and the former IBM vice-chairman, a Swiss national who rose through the ranks in Europe, are two prominent examples of individuals who rose to the top of firms outside their home countries.

Businesses are placing a greater premium on international experience.[44] In the past, a foreign assignment might have been considered a ticket to nowhere, but such experience now has come to represent the fast track to senior management in a growing number of MNCs. The truly global executive, an individual who takes on several consecutive international assignments and eventually assumes a senior management position at headquarters, is beginning to emerge. For example, of the eight members of the executive committee at Whirlpool, five have had international postings within three years of joining the committee. In each case, it was a planned move that had everything to do with their executive development.

The executives of 2010, as one report speculates, will be completely different from the CEOs of today's corporations. They will come from almost anywhere, with an

---

[43] Thomas S. Stewart, "Planning a Career in a World without Managers," *Fortune,* March 20, 1995, pp. 72–80.

[44] Lori Ioannou, "Stateless Executives," *Business Europe,* February 14–20, 1995, p. 7.

CROSSING BORDERS 17–6

Koreans Learn Foreign Ways—Goof Off at the Mall

The Samsung Group is one of Korea's largest companies and it wants to be more culturally sensitive to foreign ways. To that end, the company has launched an internationalization campaign. Cards are taped up in bathrooms each day to teach a phrase of English or Japanese. Overseas-bound managers attend a month-long boot camp where they are awakened at 5:30 A.M. for a jog, meditation, and then lessons on table manners, dancing, and avoiding sexual harassment. About 400 of its brightest junior employees are sent overseas for a year. Their mission? Goof off!

Samsung knows international exposure is important, but feels its executives also have to develop international taste. To do this they have to do more than visit; they have to goof off at the mall and watch people, too. The payoff? One executive of Samsung remarked, after reading a report of "goofing off" by an employee who spent a year's sabbatical in Russia, "In 20 years, if this man is representing Samsung in Moscow, he will have friends and he will be able to communicate, and then we will get the payoff."

Japanese companies have a similar program of exposure to foreign markets which comes early in the employees' careers. The day he was hired by Mitsubishi in 1962, a new employee was asked if he wanted to go overseas. Mitsubishi did not need his services abroad immediately but the bosses were sorting out who, over the next 40 years, would spend some time overseas. Japanese executives have long accepted the fact that a stint overseas is often necessary for career advancement. Because foreign tours are so critical for promotions, Japanese companies do not have to offer huge compensation packages to lure executives abroad. The new employee who was asked to go abroad back in 1962 is now on his third U.S. tour and has spent a total of 10 years in the United States. And the beat goes on. Just look at the East Village in Manhattan as one example. Now some 2,000 young Japanese expatriates are living there and soaking up American culture the easy way—shopping and partying in their new neighborhood.

Sources: Abstracted from "Sensitivity Kick: Korea's Biggest Firm Teaches Junior Execs Strange Foreign Ways," *The Wall Street Journal,* December 30, 1992, p. A1; "Why Japan's Execs Travel Better," *Business Week,* November 1993, p. 68; and Weld Royal, "Japanese Expatriates Live Hip Life in New York," *Cleveland Plain Dealer,* September 4, 1997, p. 5E.

education that will include an undergraduate degree in French literature as well as a joint MBA/engineering degree. Starting in research, these executives for the 21st century will quickly move to marketing and then on to finance. Along the way there will be international assignments taking them to Brazil, where turning around a failing joint venture will be the first real test of ability that leads to the top. These executives will speak Portuguese and French, and will be on a first-name basis with commerce ministers in half a dozen countries.

While this description of tomorrow's business leaders is speculative, there is mounting evidence that the route to the top for tomorrow's executives will be dramatically different from today's. A Whirlpool Corporation executive was quoted as saying that the CEO of the 21st century "must have a multi-environment, multi-country, multi-functional, and maybe even multi-company, multi-industry experience."

The fast pace of change in today's international markets demands continuous training throughout a person's career. Many companies, faced with global competition and the realization that to continue to grow and prosper means greater involvement in international marketing, are getting serious about developing global business skills. For those destined for immediate overseas posting, many companies offer in-house training or rely on the many intensive training programs offered by private companies.[45]

Some companies, such as Colgate-Palmolive, believe that it is important to have international assignments early in a person's career, and international training is an integral part of their entry-level development programs. Colgate recruits its future managers from the world's best colleges and business schools. Acceptance is highly competitive and successful applicants have a BA or MBA with proven leadership skills, fluency in at least one language besides English, and some experience living abroad. A typical recruit might be a U.S. citizen who has spent a year studying in another country, or a national of another country who was educated in the United States.

Trainees begin their careers in a two-year, entry-level, total-immersion program that consists of stints in various Colgate departments. A typical rotation includes time in the finance, manufacturing, and marketing departments and an in-depth exposure to the company's marketing system. During that phase, trainees are rotated through the firm's ad agency, marketing research, and product management departments and then work seven months as a field salesperson. At least once during the two years, trainees accompany their mentors on business trips to a foreign subsidiary. The company's goal is to develop in their trainees the skills they need to become effective marketing managers, domestically or globally.

On completion of the program, trainees can expect a foreign posting, either immediately after graduation or soon after an assignment in the United States. The first positions are not in London or Paris, as many might hope, but in developing countries such as Brazil, the Philippines, or maybe Zambia. Because international sales are so important to Colgate (60 percent of its total revenues are generated abroad), a manager may not return to the United States after the first foreign assignment but rather move from one overseas post to another, developing into a career internationalist, which could open to a CEO position. Commenting on the importance of international experience to Colgate's top management, the director of management and organization said, "The career track to the top—and I'm talking about the CEO and key executives—requires global experience. . . . Not everyone in the company has to be a global manager, but certainly anyone who is developing strategy does."

Companies whose foreign receipts make up a substantial portion of their earnings, and who see themselves as global companies rather than as domestic companies doing business in foreign markets, are the most active in making the foreign experience an integrated part of a successful corporate career. Indeed, for many companies a key threshold seems to be that when oversees revenues surpass domestic revenues, then the best people in the company want to work on international accounts. Such a global orientation then begins to permeate the entire organization—from personnel policies to marketing and business strategies. Such is the case with Gillette, which in the early 1990s made a significant recruitment and management-development decision when it decided to develop managers internally.[46] Gillette's international human resources department implemented its international-trainee program, designed to supply a steady stream of managerial talent from within its own ranks. Trainees are recruited from all over the world, and when their training is complete they will return to their home countries to become part of Gillette's global management team.

Not all companies share the global outlook of Colgate or Gillette. Many problems associated with getting personnel to accept a foreign assignment, keeping them there, and having a successful repatriation stem from concerns managers have about what their companies consider important. If personnel in some companies really are "out of sight, out of mind" when sent abroad, if they are not provided with the training needed to be

[45] Visit **www.natwestoffshore.com** for a quick review of the kinds of services provided by expat preparation companies.

[46] Jennifer J. Laabs, "How Gillette Grooms Global Talent," *Personnel Journal,* August 1993, pp. 65–75.

CROSSING BORDERS 17–7

A Look into the Future: Tomorrow's International Leaders? An Education for the 21st Century

A school supported by the European Community teaches Britons, French, Germans, Dutch, and others to be future Europeans. The European School in a suburb of Brussels has students from 12 nations who come to be educated for life and work, not as products of motherland or fatherland but as Europeans. The EC runs nine European Schools in Western Europe, enrolling 15,000 students from kindergarten to 12th grade. Graduates emerge superbly educated, usually trilingual, and very, very European.

The Schools are a linguistic and cultural melange. There are native speakers of 36 different languages represented in one school alone. Each year students take fewer and fewer classes in their native tongue. Early on, usually in first grade, they begin a second language, known as the "working language," which must be English, French, or German. A third language is introduced in the seventh year and a fourth may be started in the ninth.

By the time students reach their 11th year, they are taking history, geography, economics, advanced math, music, art, and gym in the working language. When the students are in groups talking, they are constantly switching languages to "whatever works."

Besides language, students learn history, politics, literature, and music from the perspective of all the European countries—in short, European cultures. The curriculum is designed to teach the French, German, Briton, and other nationalities to be future Europeans.

This same approach is being taken at the MBA level as well. The well-respected European School of Management has campuses in several different cities—Berlin, Paris, Oxford, and Madrid. Students spend part of their time in each of the campuses.

Sources: Abstracted from Glynn Mapes, "Polyglot Students Are Weaned Early off Mother Tongue," *The Wall Street Journal*, March 6, 1990, p. A1. Reprinted by permission of *THE WALL STREET JOURNAL*, © 1990 Dow Jones & Company, Inc. All Rights Reserved Worldwide; and Della Bradshaw, "Full-time MBAs," *Financial Times*, January 19, 1998, p. 3.

successful in another culture, and/or if the reentry is not positive, then the international experience will be perceived as having little value and managers will be reluctant to accept a foreign assignment. While not all companies value foreign experience, more and more companies are facing the problem of not having sufficient numbers of managers with international experience to staff their expanding global reach.

Foreign Language Skills

Reviews are mixed on the importance of a second language for a career in international business. There are those whose attitude about another language is summed up in the statement that "the language of international business is English." Others feel that even if you speak one or two languages, you may not be needed in a country whose language you speak. So, is language important, or not?

Proponents of language skills argue that learning a language improves cultural understanding and business relationships. Others point out that, to be taken seriously in the business community, the expatriate must be at least conversational in the host language. Particularly when it comes to selling in foreign countries, languages are important—says a Dutch sales training expert, "People expect to buy from sales reps they can relate to, and who understand their language and culture. They're often cold towards Americans trying to sell them products."[47]

Some recruiters want candidates who speak at least one foreign language, even if the language will not be needed in a particular job. Having learned a second language is a strong signal to the recruiter that the candidate is willing to get involved in someone else's culture.

Though most companies offer short, intensive language-training courses for managers being sent abroad, many are making stronger efforts to recruit people who are bi- or multilingual. According to the director of personnel at Coca-Cola, when his department searches its data base for people to fill overseas posts, the first choice is often someone who speaks more than one language.

The authors feel strongly that language skills are of great importance; if you want to be a major player in international business in the future, learn to speak other languages or you might not make it—your competition will be those European students described in Crossing Borders 17–7. There is a joke that foreigners tell about language skills. It goes something like this: What do you call a person who speaks three or more languages? Multilingual. What do you call a person who speaks two languages? Bilingual. What do you call a person who speaks only one language? An American! Maybe the rest of the world knows something we don't.

Summary

An effective international personnel force constitutes one of the international marketer's greatest concerns. The company's sales force represents the major alternative method of organizing a company for foreign distribution and, as such, is on the front line of a marketing organization.

The role of marketers in both domestic and foreign markets is rapidly changing, along with the composition of international managerial and sales forces. Such forces have many unique requirements that are being filled by expatriates, locals, third-country nationals, or a combination of the three. In recent years, the pattern of development has been to place more emphasis on local personnel operating in their own lands. This, in turn, has highlighted the importance of adapting U.S. managerial techniques to local needs.

The development of an effective marketing organization calls for careful recruiting, selecting, training, motivating, and compensating of expatriate personnel and their families to ensure maximization of a company's return on its personnel expenditures. The most practical method of maintaining an efficient international sales and marketing force is careful, concerned planning at all stages of career development.

Questions

1. Define:

   relationship marketing   TCN
   expatriate   "master of destiny" philosophy
   local nationals   separation allowance

2. Why may it be difficult to adhere to set job criteria in selecting foreign personnel? What compensating actions might be necessary?

3. Why does a global sales force cause special compensation problems? Suggest some alternative solutions.

4. Under which circumstances should expatriate salespeople be utilized?

5. Discuss the problems that might be encountered in having an expatriate sales manager supervising foreign salespeople.

6. "To some extent, the exigencies of the personnel situation will dictate the approach to the overseas sales organization." Discuss.

7. How do legal factors affect international sales management?

---

[47] Andy Cohen, *Sales & Marketing Management,* June 1996.

8. How does the sales force relate to company organization? To channels of distribution?

9. "It is costly to maintain an international sales force." Comment.

10. Adaptability and maturity are traits needed by all salespeople. Why should they be singled out as especially important for international salespeople?

11. Can a person develop good cultural skills? Discuss.

12. Describe the six attributes of a person with good cultural skills.

13. Interview a local company that has a foreign sales operation. Draw an organization chart for the sales function and explain why that particular structure was used by that company.

14. Evaluate the three major sources of multinational personnel.

15. Which factors complicate the task of motivating the foreign sales force?

16. Discuss how the "master of destiny" philosophy would affect attitudes of an American and a Mexican toward job promotion. Give an example.

17. Discuss the basic ideas on which U.S. management practices are based.

18. Why do companies include an evaluation of an employee's family among selection criteria for an expatriate assignment?

19. Discuss how a family can affect the entire process of selecting personnel for foreign assignment.

20. "Concerns for career and family are the most frequently mentioned reasons for a manager to refuse a foreign assignment." Why?

21. Discuss and give examples of why returning U.S. expatriates are dissatisfied. How can these problems be overcome?

22. If "the language of international business is English," why is it important to develop a skill in a foreign language? Discuss.

23. The global manager of 2010 will have to meet many new challenges. Draw up a sample resume for someone who could be considered for a top-level executive position in a global firm.

CHAPTER

18

PRICING FOR INTERNATIONAL MARKETS

Chapter Outline

Chapter Learning Objectives

What you should learn from Chapter 18

- Components of pricing as competitive tools in international marketing.

- The pricing pitfalls directly related to international marketing.

- How to control pricing in parallel imports or gray markets.

- Price escalation and how to minimize its effect.

- Countertrading and its place in international marketing policies.

- The mechanics of price quotations.

The Price War

The battle between P&G and Kimberly-Clark is creating a global duopoly, bringing Pampers and Huggies, respectively, to places they never had been before, forcing down diaper prices worldwide and sending smaller rivals scurrying for survival. The two rivals are targeting new markets in China, India, Israel, and Russia, spurring rapid growth in what is already a $10 billion annual business. Worldwide, P&G holds the commanding heights; its 40 percent market share far exceeds Kimberly's 27 percent. But as they compete for market share from country to country, market position shifts. A battle in Brazil between the two giants gives an interesting glimpse of what it may be like as companies vie for the global markets of tomorrow:

Disposable diapers are still considered a luxury by the vast majority of Brazil's 160 million people, whose average annual income is under $4,000. Before P&G and Kimberly arrived, rich and poor alike generally made do with cloth or nothing at all. The disposables that were available were not only expensive but also bulky and leaky. Cheaper ones were even more primitive; mom-and-pop stores made them with do-it-yourself kits. Since P&G and Kimberly landed, however, the market for disposable diapers has increased 12-fold. In just one year (1994–1995), the number used on Brazilian babies doubled to 1.4 billion, and the total was projected to hit 3 billion in 1996.

In 1993 when less than 5 percent of the Brazilian mass market used disposable diapers, P&G launched Pampers Uni, a no-frills, unisex diaper. The strategy was to hook parents on the inexpensive Uni and then push them toward costlier versions. Johnson & Johnson, the only competitor with multinational muscle and one that P&G had already run out of the U.S. market, chose not to respond with a lower price. Thus, P&G quickly grabbed market share. The introduction of the relatively cheap, high-quality Uni fundamentally changed the economics of the diaper market for most middle-class Brazilians. Before Uni, it cost more to pay for disposable diapers than to pay for a maid to wash cloth ones.

Around the time that P&G introduced Uni, Kimberly-Clark was examining the 10 major growth markets around the world and its position in each of them. Brazil was empty, and that was a problem since P&G was entrenching itself in Brazil just as Brazil's new economic-stabilization plan was taking hold. The plan was to put such nonessentials as disposable diapers within the reach of millions of Brazilians for the first time.

Inflation had subsided in Brazil and overnight the purchasing power of the poor increased by 20 percent. Low-priced products flew off the shelves. To handle the surge in demand, P&G began trucking in diapers from Argentina as it struggled to open new production lines. A few local companies also jumped into the breach.

But the good days didn't last. Kimberly-Clark teamed up with Unilever. Unilever's arch rival in soap was P&G and Kimberly-Clark's arch rival in diapers was P&G. Unilever and Kimberly-Clark had a deal, a global alliance to look for win–win situations where it was in both their best interests to partner and help each other from a competitive standpoint.

Kimberly began importing Huggies from Argentina and a Unilever unit acted as distributor in Brazil, which gave Kimberly immediate distribution across the country. With Unilever's help, Kimberly quickly made deep inroads. Its Argentine commercial, dubbed into Portuguese, trumpeted Huggies as the "revelation of the year." The distributors "push girls" invaded markets to demonstrate the diaper's absorption. Sales rose, but not enough to justify building production facilities. Kimberly had to do something to level the playing field, so it formed an alliance with Kenko do Brazil. Kenko do Brasil, which was P&G's largest home-grown rival, built a factory in 1990 and licensed Brazil's most popular cartoon character, Monica, as the Kenko diaper brand. Monica and her pals, who are a bit like the Peanuts characters in U.S. comic books, are featured in "Monica's Gang" and sell four million copies monthly. Monica diapers were a big hit. Through aggressive pricing and innovative packaging, Kenko managed to hang on against Pampers Uni by redesigning and launching a cheaper and better version of Monica. But when Kimberly entered the market, Kenko couldn't compete. So Kimberly bought controlling interest in Kenko. This gave Kimberly the ability to leapfrog P&G, and with the help of Kenko, Kimberly became number one in the Brazilian market.

It was a tough blow to P&G. The company had devoted an entire page of its 1995 annual report to how Pampers Uni had tripled its market share in Brazil, helping P&G "retain the number one position in a market that has grown fivefold." Now it suddenly found itself on the defensive. First it cut prices, a step P&G loathes. "Price cutting is like violence: No one wins," says the head of its Brazilian operation. Then it broadened its product range, rolling out an up-market diaper called Super-Seca, priced 25 percent higher than Pampers Uni. Later, in a flanking move, it also unveiled Confort-Seca, a bikini-style diaper originally developed for Thailand and priced 10–15 percent lower than the already-inexpensive Uni.

Kimberly fired back, matching the price cut and then introducing a cheaper version of Monica called Tippy Basic. Four weeks later P&G cut prices another 10 percent on Super-Seca and Confort-Seca. But for all the price cuts, the two are still relatively expensive, and a wave of really cheap diapers arrived. Carrefour SA, a French retailer that is now Brazil's biggest supermarket chain, sells crudely made Bye-Bye Pipi diapers from Mexico. P&G doesn't sell its diapers at Carrefour because of the retailer's insistence on special terms from suppliers. But, despite their inferior quality, retailers say the cheap imports are pulling down diaper prices across the board.

While both U.S. giants are taking hits on price, they also are pouring millions into advertising and direct marketing. P&G, whose Pampers dominate U.S. hospitals, tried to replicate that strategy in Brazil; it hired a Florida direct-marketing firm that specializes in hospitals, to canvass São Paulo maternity wards.

Kimberly countered, and in April São Paulo malls were crowded with thousands of kids waiting to get an Easter photo taken with actors in Monica suits, an honor that required the purchase of three packs of diapers. The pitches filter down to include an aisle in a supermarket on the outskirts of São Paulo where a Kimberly representative tries to explain to a grandmother cradling a package of Puppet, the cheapest brand in the store, that with diapers, like most products, you get what you pay for. First, he touts the merits of Kimberly's top-of-the-line Huggies and then, getting nowhere, tries to sell her on the cheaper Monica. Both are superior diapers that last for hours and don't leak, he says. The grandmother isn't swayed. "My grandson needs frequent changes," she says, heading for the checkout counter, with Puppet in hand.

As the companies have taken turns slashing prices to capture new customers, disposables now cost about 33 cents, down from $1 just six years ago, when they were barely available. A further drop can't be ruled out, since Americans pay about 23 cents a diaper. The market is still growing. "The real war starts when the market flattens out."

Sources: Raju Narisetti and Jonathan Friedland, "Disposable Income: Diaper Wars of P&G and Kimberly-Clark Now Heat Up in Brazil," *The Wall Street Journal*, June 4, 1997, p. A1. For more information, see Johnson & Johnson's Web site at **http://www.jnj.com**; Kimberly-Clark's at **http://www.kimberly-clark.com**; and Procter & Gamble's at **http://www.pg.com**.

Even when the international marketer produces the right product, promotes it correctly, and initiates the proper channel of distribution, the effort fails if the product is not properly priced. Setting the right price for a product can be the key to success or failure. While the quality of U.S. products is widely recognized in global markets, foreign buyers, like domestic buyers, balance quality and price in their purchase decisions. A product's price must reflect the quality/value the consumer perceives in the product. Of all the tasks facing the international marketer, determining what price to charge is one of the most difficult. It is further complicated when the company sells its product to customers in different country markets.

A unified Europe, economic reforms in Eastern Europe and the Newly Independent States, and the economic growth in Pacific Rim and Latin American countries are creating new marketing opportunities. As these markets grow, the competition has intensified among multinational companies and home-based companies, all of whom seek a solid market position so they can prosper as markets reach full potential. As global companies vie for these markets, price becomes increasingly important as a competitive tool. Whether exporting or managing overseas operations, the international marketing manager is responsible for setting and controlling the actual price of goods as they are traded in different markets. The marketer is confronted with new sets of variables to consider with each new market: different tariffs, costs, attitudes, competition, currency fluctuations, methods of price quotation, and the marketing strategy of the firm.

This chapter focuses on pricing considerations of particular concern in the international marketplace. Basic pricing policy questions that arise from the special cost, market, and competitive factors in foreign markets are reviewed. A discussion of price escalation and its control and factors associated with price setting and leasing is followed by discussion of the use of countertrade as a pricing tool and a review of the mechanics of international price quotation.

Price competition and sales are an integral part of the pricing strategies of Wal-Mart supercenters as they expand globally. (Dannemiller/SABA)

Pricing Policy

Active marketing in several countries compounds the number of pricing problems and variables relating to price policy.[1] Unless a firm has a clearly thought-out, explicitly defined price policy, expediency rather than design establishes prices. The country in which business is being conducted, the type of product, variations in competitive conditions, and other strategic factors affect pricing activity. Price and terms of sale cannot be based on domestic criteria alone.[2]

Pricing Objectives

In general, price decisions are viewed two ways: pricing as an active instrument of accomplishing marketing objectives, or pricing as a static element in a business decision. If prices are viewed as an active instrument, the company uses price to achieve a specific objective, whether a targeted return on profit, a targeted market share, or some other specific goal. The company that follows the second approach, pricing as a *static element,* probably exports only excess inventory, places a low priority on foreign business, and views its export sales as passive contributions to sales volume. Profit is by far the most important pricing objective. When U.S. and Canadian international businesses were asked to rate, on a scale of one to five, several factors important in price setting, total profits received an average rating of 4.7, followed by return on investment (4.41), market share (4.13), and total sales volume (4.06). Liquidity ranked the lowest (2.19).

The more control a company has over the final selling price of a product, the better it is able to achieve its marketing goals. However, it is not always possible to control

[1] Matthew B. Myers, "The Pricing Processes of Exporters: A Comparative Study of the Challenges Facing U.S. and Mexican Firms," *Journal of Global Marketing,* Vol. 10(4), 1997, p. 95.

[2] S. Tamer Cavusgil, "Unraveling the Mystiques of Export Pricing," Chapter 71 in Sidney J. Levy et. al., eds., *Marketing Manager's Handbook* (New York: The Dartnell Corporation, 1994), pp. 1357–1374.

end prices. The broader the product line and the larger the number of countries involved, the more complex the process of controlling prices to the end user.

Parallel Imports

Besides having to meet price competition country by country and product by product, companies have to guard against competition from within the company and by their own customers. If a large company does not have effective price and distribution controls, it can find its products in competition with its own subsidiaries or branches.[3] Because of different prices that can exist in different country markets, a product sold in one country may be exported to another and undercut the prices charged in that country. For example, to meet economic conditions and local competition, an American pharmaceutical company sells its drugs in a developing country at a low price then discovers these discounted drugs are exported to a third country where they are in direct competition with the same product sold for higher prices by the same firm.[4] These *parallel imports* (sometimes called a *gray market*) upset price levels and result from lack of control and ineffective management of prices.[5]

Parallel imports develop when importers buy products from distributors in one country and sell them in another to distributors who are not part of the manufacturer's regular distribution system. This practice is lucrative when wide margins exist between prices for the same products in different countries. A variety of conditions can create the profitable opportunity for a parallel market.

Variations in the value of currencies between countries frequently lead to conditions that make parallel imports profitable. Because of the weaker strength of the Italian lira relative to the German mark, for example, German and Austrian citizens can buy Volkswagens and Audi cars cheaper in Italy than in Germany. Similarly, because of Asian currencies adversely affected by the 1997–98 Asian stock market crisis, Asian-assembled Mercedes-Benzes were being sold in Hong Kong (whose currency remained relatively strong) at discounts of up to 30 percent over local dealers.[6]

Restrictions brought about by import quotas and high tariffs also can lead to parallel imports and make illegal imports attractive. India has a three-tier duty structure on computer parts ranging from 50–80 percent on imports. As a result, estimates are that as much as 35 percent of India's domestic computer hardware sales are accounted for by the gray market.

Large price differentials between country markets are another condition conducive to the creation of parallel markets. Japanese merchants have long maintained very high prices for consumer products sold within the Japanese market.[7] As a result, prices for Japanese products sold in other countries are often lower than they are in Japan. The Japanese can buy Canon cameras from New York catalog retailers and have them shipped to Japan for a price below that of the camera purchased in Japan. When the New York price for Panasonic cordless telephones was $59.95, they cost $152 in Tokyo, and when the Sony Walkman was $89, it was $165.23 in Tokyo.

Foreign companies doing business in Japan generally follow the same pattern of high prices for the products they sell in Japan, thus creating an opportunity for parallel

---

[3] For a complete and thorough discussion of parallel markets, see Robert E. Weigand, "Parallel Import Channels—Options for Preserving Territorial Integrity," *The Columbia Journal of World Business,* Spring 1991, pp. 53–60.

[4] "Parallel Drug Imports: Tougher Rules Urged," *Singapore Straits Times,* March 17, 1997.

[5] For a discussion on how companies deal with the problem of parallel imports, see Soo J. Tan, Guan H. Lim, and Khai S. Lee, "Strategic Responses to Parallel Importing," *Journal of Global Marketing,* Vol. 10(4), 1997, p. 45.

[6] Nisha Gopalanun, "Asia Dumps Cut-Price Luxury Cars in HK," *South China Morning Post,* January 4, 1998, p. 1.

[7] See, for example, Carol Howard and Paul Herbig, "Japanese Pricing Policies," *Journal of Consumer Marketing,* Vol. 13(4), 1996, p. 5.

markets in their products. Eastman Kodak prices its film higher in Japan than in other parts of Asia. Enterprising merchants buy Kodak film in South Korea for a discount and resell it in Japan at 25 percent less than the authorized Japanese Kodak dealers. For the same reason, Coca-Cola imported from the United States sells for 27 percent less through discounters than Coke's own made-in-Japan product.

The possibility of a parallel market occurs whenever price differences are greater than the cost of transportation between two markets. In Europe, because of different taxes and competitive price structures, prices for the same product vary between countries.[8] When this occurs, it is not unusual for companies to find themselves competing in one country with their own products imported from another European country at lower prices. Pharmaceutical companies face this problem in the European Community, where pharmaceuticals are priced lower in Italy, Greece, and Spain. Presumably such price differentials will cease to exist once all restrictions to trade are eliminated in the European Union.

Exclusive distribution, a practice often used by companies to maintain high retail margins to encourage retailers to provide extra service to customers, to stock large assortments, and/or to maintain the exclusive-quality image of a product, can create a favorable condition for parallel importing. Perfume and designer brands such as Gucci and Cartier are especially prone to gray markets. To maintain the image of quality and exclusivity, prices for such products traditionally include high profit margins at each level of distribution, differential prices among markets, and limited quantities, as well as distribution restricted to upscale retailers. In the United States, wholesale prices for exclusive brands of fragrances are often 25 percent more than wholesale prices in other countries. These are ideal conditions for a lucrative gray market for unauthorized dealers in other countries who buy more than they need at wholesale prices lower than U.S. wholesalers pay. They then sell the excess at a profit to unauthorized U.S. retailers, but at a price lower than the retailer would have to pay to an authorized U.S. distributor.

The high-priced designer sportswear industry is especially vulnerable to such practices. Nike, Adidas, and Calvin Klein were incensed to find their products being sold in one of Britain's leading supermarket chains, Tesco. Nike's Air Max Metallic trainers, which are priced at £120 ($196) in sports shops, could be purchased at Tesco for £50 ($80). Tesco had bought £8 million in Nike sportswear from overstocked wholesalers in the United States.[9]

To prevent parallel markets from developing when such marketing and pricing strategies are used, companies must maintain strong control systems. These control systems are difficult to maintain and there remains the suspicion that some companies are less concerned with controlling gray markets than they claim. For example, in one year a French company exported $40 million of perfume to Panamanian distributors. At that rate, Panama's per capita consumption of that one brand of perfume alone was 35 times that of the United States.

Companies that are serious about restricting the gray market must establish and monitor controls that effectively police distribution channels. In some countries they may get help from the courts. A Taiwan court ruled that two companies that were importing Coca-Cola from the United States to Taiwan were violating the trademark rights of both the Coca-Cola Company and its sole Taiwan licensee. The violators were prohibited from importing, displaying, or selling products bearing the Coca-Cola trademark. In other countries, the courts have not always come down on the side of the trademark owner. The reasoning is that once the trademarked item is sold, the owner's rights to control the trademarked item are lost. In Japan, for example, parallel imports are not illegal.

[8] Greg Steinmetz, "Mark Down: German Consumers Are Seeing Prices Cut in Deregulation Push," *The Wall Street Journal,* August 15, 1997, p. A1.

[9] Emily Moore, "A Grey Area: Big Supermarkets Have Designs on Designer Labels, Much to the Fury of the Manufacturers," *The Guardian,* February 10, 1998, p. 9.

CROSSING BORDERS 18−1

How Do Levi's 501s Get to International Markets?

Levi Strauss sells in international markets; how else would 501s get to market? Well, another way is via the gray market or "diverters." Diverters are enterprising people who legally buy 501s at retail prices, usually during sales, and then resell them to foreign buyers. It is estimated that millions of dollars of Levi's are sold abroad at discount prices—all sales authorized by Levi Strauss. In Germany, Levi's 501s are sold to authorized wholesalers for about $40 and authorized retailers sell them at about $80, compared with U.S. retail prices of $30 to $40 a pair. The difference of $40 or so makes it economically possible for a diverter to buy 501s in the U.S. and sell them to unauthorized dealers who then sell them for $60 to $70, undercutting authorized German retailers. Similar practices happen around the world. How do diverters work?

One way is to legally buy 501s at retail prices. A report on diverters in Portland, Oregon, is an example of what is repeated in city after city all over the United States. "They come into a store in groups and buy every pair of Levi's 501 jeans they can," says one store manager. He says he has seen two or three vans full of people come to the store when there is a sale and buy the six-pair-a-day limit, and return day after day until the sale is over. In another chain store having a month-long storewide sale, Levi's were eliminated as a sale item after only two weeks. A group of "customers" was visiting each store daily to buy the limit, and the store wanted to preserve a reasonable selection for its regular customers. All these Levi's are channeled to a diverter who exports them to unauthorized buyers throughout the world. What makes this practice feasible is the lower markups and prices of U.S. retailers compared with the higher costs and the resulting higher markups and prices retailers charge in many other countries (Levi's has a higher wholesale price for foreign sales than for domestic sales).

Retail prices in the U.S. are often more competitive than in other countries where, historically, price competition is not as widely practiced and markups along the distribution chain are often higher. Thus, prices for imported goods frequently are substantially higher in foreign markets than in domestic markets. One recent study of retail prices in Britain reported that some of the differences in prices between the U.S. and Britain were "staggering." For example, besides blue jeans, which sell for $90 in Britain versus $30 in the U.S., disposable contact lenses are $225 versus $87 and a tennis racket is $225 versus $78. Some, but not all, of the price differences can be attributed to price escalation—that is, tariffs, shipping, and other costs associated with exporting—but that portion of the difference attributable to higher margins creates an opportunity for profitable diverting.

Sources: Jim Hill, "Flight of the 501s," *The Oregonian*, June 27, 1993, p. G1; and "Consumers in Britain Pay More," *The Wall Street Journal*, February 2, 1994, p. A13.

Hong Kong recently passed a law that bans parallel imports of all copyrighted material, such as movie videos and compact disks, from sources other than a local, licensed distributor or from the holder of the copyright. Violators could be subject to a maximum of four years in prison and a HK $40,000 fine.[10]

Where differences in prices between markets occur, the Internet makes it easy for individuals to participate in the gray market. Music CDs are especially vulnerable be-

---

[10] Kristi Heim, "Distributors, Retailers Battle over Ban on Parallel Imports," *The Asian Wall Street Journal*, June 16, 1997, p. 1.

cause of the price differentials. Six foreign-owned record companies that maintain high prices through limited distribution dominate the Australian market and create a situation ripe for the gray market. CDs retail there for an average of $24 but can be purchased for about 25–30 percent less from the many e-stores on the Internet. It is estimated that CDs purchased directly from the U.S. over the Internet have led to a 5 percent fall in Australian retail sales.[11] In the U.K., gray market CDs come from Italy, were they are about 50 percent cheaper and account for between 15 and 20 percent of sales in some releases. Sony believes over 100,000 copies of Celine Dion's best-selling album sold in the U.K. were from parallel imports.[12]

Parallel imports can do long-term damage in the market for trademarked products. Customers who unknowingly buy unauthorized imports have no assurance of the quality of the item they buy, of warranty support, and of authorized service or replacement parts. In the case of automobiles, those produced for cooler climates may have different thermostats, radiators, and electrical systems, which could have problems and not function well in the summer heat of Hong Kong, for instance. When the product fails, the consumer blames the owner of the trademark and the quality image of the product is sullied. Further, the owner may not be able to get parts or changes made since authorized dealers have no obligation to service these vehicles.[13]

The European Commission will not restrict parallel imports and, further, will enforce its laws if companies try to force distributors to refuse sales across borders. As a case in point, Volkswagen Group was fined $111.3 million for systematically forcing its Italian dealers to refuse to sell VW or Audi cars to customers living outside Italy. Dealers who went against such orders were threatened with cuts in bonuses or cancellation of their contracts.[14] Until companies harmonize prices across Europe, the possibility of parallel imports remains. Since the European Commission is cracking down on any attempt to prevent wholesalers or retailers from selling across borders, harmonization is the only answer. BMW has harmonized its prices and thus was not confronted with the same problem that faced Volkswagen. Further, the pharmaceutical industry has reached an agreement with the health ministers of EU states to end all artificial government price fixing and thus to harmonize drug pricing across Europe. That should end most of the opportunity for parallel importing.[15] In Denmark, a recently passed law requires that pharmacists inform patients filling a prescription that an identical parallel-imported drug is available if the price difference exceeds a set notification threshold—originally five kroner (0.72 cents U.S.).[16]

Companies doing business in the European Community will either have to harmonize prices among member states or contend with parallel imports from member country markets where there are differences in selling prices that make it profitable. As companies continue to focus on developing global brands that make comparisons easier, it will become increasingly difficult for companies to price-differentiate. So brand harmonization and price harmonization must be addressed simultaneously.[17]

Approaches to International Pricing

Whether the orientation is toward control over end prices or over net prices, company policy relates to the net price received. Both cost and market considerations are impor-

---

[11] Brook Turner, "Woolies Backs Alston's CD Fight," *Australian Financial Review,* February 5, 1998, p. 4.

[12] Alice Rawsthorn, "Flood of Imports Threatens CD Market," *Financial Times,* January 7, 1998, p. 4.

[13] Kristi Heim, "Gray-Market Cars Cutting into Official Dealers' Sales," *The Asian Wall Street Journal,* January 19, 1998, p. 2.

[14] "VW Fined DM 201 Million," *Borsen-Zeitung,* January 29, 1998, p. 7.

[15] "Pharmaceuticals: Europe Moves towards Pricing Consensus," *Chemical Business News,* January 20, 1998.

[16] "Parallel Trade: Price Lists Proliferate," *Dow Jones News Service,* January 2, 1997.

[17] "Developing Uniform Brands," *Business Europe,* March 26, 1997, p. 9.

tant; a company cannot sell goods below cost of production and remain in business for very long, and neither can it sell goods at a price unacceptable in the marketplace. Firms unfamiliar with overseas marketing and firms producing industrial goods orient their pricing solely on a cost basis. Firms that employ pricing as part of the strategic mix, however, are aware of such alternatives as market segmentation from country to country or market to market, competitive pricing in the marketplace, and other market-oriented pricing factors.

Full-Cost versus Variable-Cost Pricing.   Firms that orient their price thinking around cost must determine whether to use variable cost or full cost in pricing their goods. In *variable-cost pricing,* the firm is concerned only with the marginal or incremental cost of producing goods to be sold in overseas markets. Such firms regard foreign sales as bonus sales and assume that any return over their variable cost makes a contribution to net profit. These firms may be able to price most competitively in foreign markets, but because they are selling products abroad at lower net prices than they are selling them in the domestic market, they may be subject to charges of dumping. In that case, they open themselves to antidumping tariffs or penalties that take away from their competitive advantage. Nevertheless, variable- or marginal-cost pricing is a practical approach to pricing when a company has high fixed costs and unused production capacity. Any contribution to fixed cost after variable costs are covered is profit to the company.

On the other hand, companies following the *full-cost pricing* philosophy insist that no unit of a similar product is different from any other unit in terms of cost and that each unit bears its full share of the total fixed and variable cost. This approach is suitable when a company has high variable costs relative to its fixed costs. In such cases, prices are often set on a cost plus basis, that is, total costs plus a profit margin. Both variable-cost and full-cost policies are followed by international marketers.

Skimming versus Penetration Pricing.   Firms must also decide when to follow a skimming or a penetration pricing policy. Traditionally, the decision of which policy to follow depends on the level of competition, the innovativeness of the product, and market characteristics.

A company uses *skimming* when the objective is to reach a segment of the market that is relatively price-insensitive and thus willing to pay a premium price for the value received. If limited supply exists, a company may follow a skimming approach in order to maximize revenue and to match demand to supply. When a company is the only seller of a new or innovative product, a skimming price may be used to maximize profits until competition forces a lower price. Skimming often is used in those markets where there are only two income levels, the wealthy and the poor. Costs prohibit setting a price that will be attractive to the lower-income market, so the marketer charges a premium price and directs the product to the high-income, relatively price-inelastic segment. Apparently this was the policy of Johnson & Johnson's pricing of diapers in Brazil before the arrival of P&G. Today, such opportunities are fading away as the disparity in income levels is giving away to growing middle-income market segments. The existence of larger markets attracts competition and, as is often the case, the emergence of multiple product lines, thus price competition.

A *penetration pricing* policy is used to stimulate market growth and capture market share by deliberately offering products at low prices. Penetration pricing most often is used to acquire and hold share of market as a competitive maneuver. However, in country markets experiencing rapid and sustained economic growth, and where large shares of the population move into middle-income classes, penetration pricing may be used to stimulate market growth even with minimum competition. Penetration pricing may be a more profitable strategy than skimming if it maximizes revenues and builds market share as a base for the competition that is sure to come.

Regardless of the formal pricing policies and strategies a company uses, it must never be forgotten that the market sets the effective price for a product. Said another way, the price has to be set at a point at which the consumer will perceive value received and the price must be within reach of the target market. As a consequence, many products are sold in very small units in some markets in order to bring the unit price within reach of the target market. Warner-Lambert's launch of its five-unit-pack of Bubbaloo bubble gum in Brazil failed—even though bubble gum represents over 72 percent of the overall gum sector—because it was priced above the target market. A re-launch of a single-unit "pillow" pack brought the price within range and enabled it to quickly gain a respectable market share.[18]

As growth trends in many country markets that were set in place in the early 1990s begin to pay dividends with more equitable distribution of wealth and the emergence of distinct market segments, the pricing policies of companies will change to reflect a more competitive market environment. Such issues as multiple price levels and price/quality perceptions will increase in importance as markets develop multiple income levels that become distinct market segments. As an example, the market for electronic consumer goods in China changed in just a few years. Instead of a market for imported high-priced and high quality electronic goods aimed at the new rich and cheaper, poorer quality Chinese-made goods for the rest of the market, a multitiered market reflecting the growth of personal income has emerged. Sony of Japan, the leading foreign seller of the high-priced consumer electronic goods, was upstaged when Aiwa recognized the emergence of a new middle tier for good quality and modestly priced electronic goods. As part of a global strategy focused on slim margins and high turnover, Aiwa began selling hi-fi systems at prices closer to Chinese brands than to Sony's. Aiwa's product quality was not far behind that of Sony, better than top Chinese brands, and the product looked similar to Sony's high-end systems. Aiwa's recognition of a new market segment and its ability to tap into it resulted in a huge increase in overall demand for Aiwa products.[19]

Similarly, for years Mattel has been successful in selling its Barbie dolls to the upper-end market in much of the world. However, sales of new product extensions such as the Holiday Barbie that were highly successful in the United States did not generate enough foreign sales to justify its marketing abroad. Simply adapting U.S. products for foreign markets has resulted in overpriced merchandise in some market segments. The company estimates that the potential for Barbie in lower-priced market segments is $2 billion. To capture that market, along with brand extensions of a collector Barbie, Mattel will introduce lower-priced dolls, a line called "Global Friends," which features a different doll for each major global city.[20]

Pricing decisions that were appropriate when companies directed their marketing efforts toward single market segments will give way to more sophisticated practices. As incomes rise in many foreign markets, the pricing environment companies encounter will be similar to that which they face in the United States. The one exception is a phenomenon unique to international marketing: price escalation.[21]

Price Escalation

People traveling abroad often are surprised to find goods that are relatively inexpensive in their home country priced outrageously higher in other countries. Because of the natural tendency to assume that such prices are a result of profiteering, manufacturers often resolve to begin exporting to crack these new, profitable foreign markets only to find

---

[18] "Brazil: A Sweet Market for Warner-Lambert," *Crossborder Monitor,* February 28, 1996, p. 9.

[19] "Selling Tactics: The Price Is What?" *Business China,* January 8, 1996, p. 12.

[20] Lisa Bannon, "Mattel Plans to Double Sales Abroad," *The Wall Street Journal,* February 11, 1998, p. A3.

[21] For the results of an interesting study on export pricing, see Matthew B. Myers, "The Pricing of Export Products: Why Aren't Managers Satisfied with the Results?" *Journal of World Business,* Fall 1997, p. 277.

that, in most cases, the higher prices reflect the higher costs of exporting. A case in point is the pacemaker for heart patients that sells for $2,100 in the United States. Tariffs and the Japanese distribution system add substantially to the final price in Japan. Beginning with the import tariff, each time the pacemaker changes hands an additional cost is incurred. First, the product passes through the hands of an importer, then to the company with primary responsibility for sales and service, then to a secondary or even a tertiary local distributor, and finally to the hospital. Markups at each level result in the $2,100 pacemaker selling for over $4,000 in Japan. This inflation results in price escalation, one of the major pricing obstacles facing the MNC marketer.

Costs of Exporting

Excess profits exist in some international markets, but generally the cause of the disproportionate difference in price between the exporting country and the importing country, here termed *price escalation,* is the added costs incurred as a result of exporting products from one country to another. Specifically, the term relates to situations where ultimate prices are raised by shipping costs, insurance, packing, tariffs, longer channels of distribution, larger middlemen margins, special taxes, administrative costs, and exchange-rate fluctuations.[22] The majority of these costs arise as a direct result of moving goods across borders from one country to another and combine to escalate the final price to a level considerably higher than in the domestic market.

Taxes, Tariffs, and Administrative Costs.   "Nothing is surer than death and taxes" has a particularly familiar ring to the ears of the international trader because taxes include tariffs, and tariffs are one of the most pervasive features of international trading. Taxes and tariffs affect the ultimate consumer price for a product and, in most instances, the consumer bears the burden of both. Sometimes, however, consumers benefit when manufacturers selling goods in foreign countries reduce their net return in order to gain access to a foreign market. Absorbed or passed on, taxes and tariffs must be considered by the international businessperson.

A tariff, or duty, is a special form of taxation. Like other forms of taxes, a tariff may be levied for the purpose of protecting a market or for increasing government revenue. A tariff is a fee charged when goods are brought into a country from another country. Recall from Chapter 15 that the level of tariff is typically expressed as the rate of duty and may be levied as specific, ad valorem, or compound. A specific duty is a flat charge per physical unit imported, such as 15 cents per bushel of rye. Ad valorem duties are levied as a percentage of the value of the goods imported, such as 20 percent of the value of imported watches. Compound duties include both a specific and an ad valorem charge, such as $1 per camera plus 10 percent of its value.

Tariffs and other forms of import taxes serve to discriminate against all foreign goods. Fees for import certificates or for other administrative processing can assume such levels that they are, in fact, import taxes. Many countries have purchase or excise taxes, which apply to various categories of goods, value-added or turnover taxes, which apply as the product goes through a channel of distribution, and retail sales taxes. Such taxes increase the end price of goods but, in general, do not discriminate against foreign goods. Tariffs are the primary discriminatory tax, which must be taken into account in reckoning with foreign competition.

In addition to taxes and tariffs, there are a variety of administrative costs directly associated with exporting and importing a product. Acquiring export and import licenses and other documents and the physical arrangements for getting the product from port of entry to the buyer's location mean additional costs. While such costs are relatively small, they add to the overall cost of exporting.

---

[22] Michael Daly and Hiroaki Kuwahara, "Examining Restraints on Trade," *The OECD Observer,* December/January 1997, p. 27.

A prospective buyer checks out a GE Hotpoint refrigerator in a Mexico City chain store. Such customers
will help keep U.S. exports growing as long as prices can be kept within the reach of the local market.
(Sergio Dorantes)

CROSSING BORDERS 18–2

Thunderbird: The American Classic

Tariff structures in a country can lead to some peculiar opportunities for products. In some situations, they can even dictate taste. In Kuala Lumpur, Malaysia, Ms. Muthu, on her way to a party, stops by a premier supermarket for a favorite California wine to help ring in the New Year. She heads straight for the Thunderbird and Night Train Express, cheap fortified apple wines often associated with skid-row drinking in the U.S. "We like the taste of it" as well as the low price, she says.

Thunderbird, which promotes itself as "The American Classic," and Night Train Express don't have much of an image problem in Kuala Lumpur. They are prominently displayed in upscale department stores and at some of the toniest supermarkets in this affluent capital. "They sell like hot cakes," says the liquor department head. Night Train Express (label instructions: serve very cold) was such a hot seller that the store ran out of stock in the crucial days before the long New Year's holiday weekend.

The popularity of these two wines shows how a tariff system can help dictate taste. Malaysia's bureaucrats decided years ago that so-called "beverage wines"—those made from fruit other than grapes—should be taxed at a significantly lower rate than grape wines. As a result, cheap table wine, until recently, sold at more than twice the price of Thunderbird, which retails for less than $5. Night Train Express is a little more expensive. Obviously the wine market in Kuala Lumpur has little understanding of the nuances of wine and that makes price differences critical.

Source: Adapted from Dan Biers, "What's a Malaysian's Favorite Whine? The Store's All Out of Thunderbird," *The Wall Street Journal*, January 8, 1996, p. A9.

While these prices reflect some of the differences among countries, the much higher prices, traditional in Japan, are beginning to come down as protections by regulations, informal cartels, and legal sanctions against discounting are being abolished. As a consequence, J. Crew wool sweaters that sold for $130 a year earlier are now $72, Coca-Cola in a 350-ml can has gone from $1.10 to $0.83, and the Jeep Cherokee Limited has dropped from $33,000 to $31,000. The changes in Japan reflect the shifts that are occurring in markets elsewhere. As discussed in this chapter, pricing approaches for global companies are becoming more standardized because markets are becoming more alike.

Inflation.   The effect of inflation on cost must be taken into account. In countries with rapid inflation or exchange variation, the selling price must be related to the cost of goods sold and the cost of replacing the items. Goods often are sold below their cost of replacement plus overhead, and sometimes are sold below replacement cost. In these instances, the company would be better off not to sell the products at all. When payment is likely to be delayed for several months or is worked out on a long-term contract, inflationary factors must be figured into the price. Inflation and lack of control over price were instrumental in the unsuccessful new product launch in Brazil by the H. J. Heinz Company; after only two years, they withdrew from the market. Misunderstandings with the local partner resulted in a new fruit-based drink being sold to retailers on consignment; that is, they did not pay until the product was sold. Faced with a rate of inflation of over 300 percent, just a week's delay in payment eroded profit margins substantially. Soaring inflation in many developing countries (Latin America in particular) makes widespread price controls a constant threat.

Because inflation and price controls imposed by a country are beyond the control of companies, they use a variety of techniques to inflate the selling price to compensate for inflation pressure and price controls. They may charge for extra services, inflate costs in transfer pricing, break up products into components and price each component separately, or require the purchase of two or more products simultaneously and refuse to deliver one product unless the purchaser agrees to take another, more expensive item as well.

Exchange-Rate Fluctuations.   At one time, world trade contracts could be easily written and payment was specified in a relatively stable currency. The American dollar was the standard and all transactions could be related to the dollar. Now that all major currencies are floating freely relative to one another, no one is quite sure of the future value of any currency. Increasingly, companies are insisting that transactions be written in terms of the vendor company's national currency, and forward hedging is becoming more common. If exchange rates are not carefully considered in long-term contracts, companies find themselves unwittingly giving 15–20 percent discounts. The added cost incurred by exchange rate fluctuations on a day-to-day basis must be taken into account, especially where there is a significant time lapse between signing the order and delivery of the goods. Exchange-rate differentials mount up. Whereas Hewlett-Packard gained nearly half a million dollars additional profit through exchange-rate fluctuations in one year, Nestlé lost a million dollars in six months; other companies have lost and gained even larger amounts.

Varying Currency Values.   In addition to risks from exchange-rate variations, other risks result from the changing values of a country's currency relative to other currencies. Consider the situation in Germany for a purchaser of U.S. manufactured goods from the mid-1980s to the mid-1990s. During this period, the value of the U.S. dollar relative to the German mark went from a very strong position ($1 U.S. to 2.69 DM) in the late 1980s to a weaker position in 1994 ($1 U.S. to 1.49 DM). A strong dollar produces price resistance because it takes a larger quantity of local currency to buy a U.S. dollar. Conversely, when the U.S. dollar is weak, demand for U.S. goods increases because

jewelry. For example, a U.S. customs inspector could not decide whether to classify a $2.7 million Fabergé egg as art or jewelry. The difference was zero tariff versus $700,000. An experienced freight forwarder/customs broker saved the day by persuading the customs agent that the Fabergé egg was a piece of art. Since the classification of products varies among countries, a thorough investigation of tariff schedules and classification criteria can result in a lower tariff.

Besides having a product reclassified into a lower tariff category, it may be possible to modify a product to qualify for a lower tariff rate within a tariff classification. In the footwear industry, the difference between "foxing" and "foxlike" on athletic shoes makes a substantial difference in the tariff levied. To protect the domestic footwear industry from an onslaught of cheap sneakers from the Far East, the tariff schedule states that any canvas or vinyl shoe with a foxing band (a tape band attached at the sole and overlapping the shoe's upper by more than $1/4$ inch) be assessed at a higher duty rate. As a result, manufacturers design shoes so that the sole does not overlap the upper by more than $1/4$ inch. If the overlap exceeds $1/4$ inch, the shoe is classified as having a foxing band; less than $1/4$ inch, a foxlike band. A shoe with a foxing band is taxed 48 percent and one with a foxlike band ($1/4$ inch or less overlap) is taxed a mere 6 percent.

There are often differential rates between fully assembled, ready-to-use products and those requiring some assembly, further processing, the addition of locally manufactured component parts, or other processing that adds value to the product and can be performed within the foreign country. For example, a ready-to-operate piece of machinery with a 20 percent tariff may be subject to only a 12 percent tariff when imported unassembled. An even lower tariff may apply when the product is assembled in the country and some local content is added.

Repackaging also may help to lower tariffs. Tequila entering the United States in containers of one gallon or less carries a duty of $2.27 per proof gallon; larger containers are assessed at only $1.25. If the cost of rebottling is less than $1.02 per proof gallon, and it probably would be, considerable saving could result. As will be discussed shortly, one of the more important activities in foreign-trade zones is the assembly of imported goods, using local and, frequently, lower-cost labor.

Lower Distribution Costs.   Shorter channels can help keep prices under control. Designing a channel that has fewer middlemen may lower distribution costs by reducing or eliminating middleman markup. Besides eliminating markups, fewer middlemen may mean lower overall taxes. Some countries levy a value-added tax on goods as they pass through channels. Each time goods change hands, they are taxed. The tax may be cumulative or noncumulative. A cumulative value-added tax is based on total selling price and is assessed every time the goods change hands. Obviously, in countries where value-added tax is cumulative, tax alone provides a special incentive for developing short distribution channels. Where that is achieved, tax is paid only on the difference between the middleman's cost and the selling price.

Using Foreign-Trade Zones to Lessen Price Escalation

Some countries have established foreign- or free-trade zones (FTZs) or free ports to facilitate international trade. There are more than 300 of these facilities in operation throughout the world where imported goods can be stored or processed. As free-trade policies in Africa, Latin America, Eastern Europe,[24] and other developing regions expand there has been an equally rapid expansion in the creation and use of foreign-trade zones.[25] Recall from Chapter 15 that in a free port or FTZ, payment of import duties is postponed until the product leaves the FTZ area and enters the country. An FTZ is, in

---

[24] "Hungary: Less Outlandish-Customs Free Zones," *Business Eastern Europe,* October 21, 1996, p. 5.

[25] " Emirates: Although Nation Currently Boasts 9 Free Trade Zones, Demand for Them Is Still Growing," *International Freighting Weekly,* January 12, 1998, p. 12.

CROSSING BORDERS 18–4

I Tell You I'm a Car, Not a Truck!!

In 1989 the U.S. Customs Service classified multipurpose vehicles as trucks, i.e., vehicles designed to transport cargo or other goods. Trucks pay a 25 percent tariff while passenger vehicles pay only a 2.5 percent tariff. The import classification was challenged by the manufacturer of the 2-door Nissan Pathfinder, classified as a truck rather than as a passenger vehicle, and Nissan won.

The Justice Department argued that the Pathfinder was built with the same structural design as the Nissan pickup truck despite all the options added later in production, and should be considered a truck for tariff purposes. The Court said that doesn't matter; it's how the vehicle is used that counts. The judge declared that the Pathfinder "virtually shouts to the consumer, 'I am a car, not a truck!'"

The case has implications in settling the long-standing controversy over whether imported minivans and sport-utility vehicles should be considered cars or trucks. The ruling means a $225 savings for every $1,000 the consumer spends on a Pathfinder.

Source: "Nissan Wins U.S. Customs Suit," Associated Press release, September 9, 1994.

essence, a tax-free enclave and not considered part of the country as far as import regulations are concerned. When an item leaves an FTZ and is imported officially into the host country of the FTZ, all duties and regulations are imposed.

Price escalation resulting from the layers of taxes, duties, surcharges, freight charges, and so forth, can to some extent be controlled by utilizing FTZs. The benefits of foreign-trade zones permit many of these added charges to be avoided, reduced, or deferred so that the final price is more competitive. One of the more important benefits of the FTZ in controlling prices is the exemption from duties on labor and overhead costs incurred in the FTZ in assessing the value of goods.

By shipping unassembled goods to an FTZ in an importing country, a marketer can lower costs in a variety of ways:

1. Tariffs may be lower because duties are typically assessed at a lower rate for unassembled versus assembled goods.
2. If labor costs are lower in the importing country, substantial savings may be realized in the final product cost.
3. Ocean transportation rates are affected by weight and volume, thus, unassembled goods may qualify for lower freight rates.
4. If local content, such as packaging or component parts, can be used in the final assembly, there may be a further reduction of tariffs.

All in all, a foreign- or free-trade zone is an important method for controlling price escalation. Incidentally, all the advantages offered by an FTZ for an exporter are also advantages for an importer. U.S. importers use over 100 FTZs in the United States to help lower their costs of imported goods.

Dumping

A logical outgrowth of a market policy in international business is goods priced competitively at widely differing prices in various markets. Marginal (variable) cost pricing, as discussed above, is one way prices can be reduced to stay within a competitive price

CROSSING BORDERS 18-5

How Are Foreign-Trade Zones Used?

There are more than 100 foreign-trade zones (FTZs) in the United States, and FTZs exist in many other countries as well. Companies use them to postpone the payment of tariffs on products while they are in the FTZ. Here are some examples of how FTZs in the United States are used.

- A Japanese firm assembles motorcycles, jet skis, and three-wheel all-terrain vehicles for import as well as for export to Canada, Latin America, and Europe.
- A U.S. manufacturer of window shades and miniblinds imports and stores fabric from Holland in a FTZ, thereby postponing a 17 percent tariff until the fabric leaves the FTZ.
- A manufacturer of hair dryers stores its product in a FTZ, which it uses as its main distribution center for products manufactured in Asia.
- A European-based medical supply company manufactures kidney dialysis machines and sterile tubing using raw materials from Germany and U.S. labor. It then exports 30 percent of its products to Scandinavian countries.
- A Canadian company assembles electronic teaching machines using cabinets from Italy; electronics from Taiwan, Korea, and Japan; and labor from the United States, for export to Colombia and Peru.

In all these examples, tariffs are postponed until the products leave the FTZ and enter the U.S. Further, in most situations the tariff is at the lower rate for component parts and raw materials versus the higher rate that would have been charged if imported directly as finished goods. If the finished products are not imported into the U.S. from the FTZ but shipped to another country, no U.S. tariffs apply.

Sources: Lewis E. Leibowitz, "An Overview of Foreign Trade Zones," *Europe,* Winter–Spring 1987, p. 12; and "Cheap Imports," *International Business,* March 1993, pp. 98–100.

range. The market and economic logic of such pricing policies can hardly be disputed, but the practices often are classified as dumping and are subject to severe penalties and fines. *Dumping* is defined differently by various economists. One approach classifies international shipments as dumped if the products are sold below their cost of production. The other approach characterizes dumping as selling goods in a foreign market below the price of the same goods in the home market. Even rate-cutting on cargo shipping has been called dumping.

Dumping and Countervailing Duty: The law authorizes the imposition of a dumping duty when goods are sold at a price lower than the normal export price or less than the cost in the country of origin increased by a reasonable amount for the cost of sales and profits, and when this is likely to be prejudicial to the economic activity of the country. A *countervailing duty* [italics added for emphasis] may be imposed on foreign goods benefiting from subsidies in production, export, or transport.

Before countervailing duties can be invoked, it must be shown not only that prices are lower in the importing country than in the exporting country but also that producers in the importing country are being directly harmed by the dumping.

In the 1960s and 1970s, dumping was hardly an issue because world markets were strong. As the 1980s began, however, dumping became a major issue for a large number of industries. Excess production capacity relative to home-country demand caused many companies to price their goods on a marginal-cost basis figuring that any contribution above variable cost was beneficial to company profits. In a classic case of dumping, prices are maintained in the home-country market and reduced in foreign markets. For example, the European Community charged that differences in prices between Japan and EC countries ranged from 4.8 to 86 percent. To correct for this dumping activity, a special import duty of 33.4 percent was imposed on Japanese computer printers.

Today, tighter government enforcement of dumping legislation is causing international marketers to seek new routes around such legislation. Some of the strategies include subsidies by governments to exporting companies, kickbacks to purchasers, and model-year changes to permit discounting. Assembly in the importing country is another way companies attempt to lower prices and avoid dumping charges. However, these "screwdriver plants," as they are often called, are subject to dumping charges if the price differentials reflect more than the cost savings that result from assembly in the importing country. For example, the EC imposed a $27 to $58 dumping duty per unit on a Japanese firm that assembled and sold electronic typewriters in the EC. The firm was charged with valuing imported parts for assembly below cost. The increased concern and enforcement in the European Community reflects the changing attitudes among all countries toward dumping.[26] The EC has had antidumping legislation from its inception, but the first antidumping duties ever imposed were on Taiwanese bicycle chains in 1976. Since then, the Department of Trade of the EC has imposed duties on a variety of products.

The U.S. market is currently more sensitive to dumping than in the recent past.[27] In fact, the Uruguay Round of the GATT included a section on antidumping that grew out of U.S. insistence for stricter controls on dumping of foreign goods in the U.S. at prices below those charged at home.[28] Changes in U.S. law have enhanced the authority of the Commerce Department to prevent circumvention of antidumping duties and countervailing duties that have been imposed on a country for dumping. Previously, when an order was issued to apply antidumping and countervailing duties on products, companies charged with the violation would get around the order by slightly altering the product or by doing minor assembly in the United States or a third country. This created the illusion of a different product not subject to the antidumping order. The new authority of the Department of Commerce closes many such loopholes.

Another loophole used in price competition is government subsidies. Subsidies have long been unacceptable devices used by governments to aid exporters. Increasingly protectionist attitudes have caused the United States to add countervailing duties when government subsidies are involved. For example, the United States imposed countervailing duties of 19.6 percent for cotton yarn and 15.8 percent for scissors, imported from Brazil. Exported scissors had received exemption from Brazilian industrial product tax, value-added tax, and income tax. Cotton yarn had benefited from preferential government financing, and regional investment incentives provided for building plants in remote areas of northeastern Brazil. The pressure of higher duties eventually forced Brazil to eliminate the subsidies, and the U.S. government correspondingly reduced the countervailing duties.

Kickbacks are another device used to get around antidumping legislation. In the case of Japanese television tubes imported into the United States, the export price matched the Japanese price (thus avoiding any possible notion of dumping), but the producer provided under-the-table payments to the importer. Zenith officials charged that

---

[26] "Anti-dumping: Assault on 'Fortress Europe,'" *Business Europe*, January 15, 1996, p. 4.

[27] "Trade Commission Backs Cray on Dumping Dispute," *The Wall Street Journal (Interactive Edition)*, September 26, 1997.

[28] For a discussion of the World Trade Organization and GATT position on dumping and countervailing duties, read David M. Gould and William C. Gruben, "Will Fair Trade Diminish Free Trade?" *Business Economics*, April 1997, p. 7.

during one period nearly every television set brought into the United States benefited from such kickbacks, much to the detriment of Zenith and other domestic companies.

Model-year discounts that make price variations possible from country to country have also come to the attention of antidumping authorities. The model-year device works this way: An exported item is designated as the previous year's model and discounted in the foreign country but still sold at the current model-year prices in the home country. These dumping devices are cheerfully winked at in times of soft world competition, but receive careful attention when competition is intense and antidumping commissions take a hard line against subterfuge.

Leasing in International Markets

An important selling technique to alleviate high prices and capital shortages for capital equipment is the leasing system. The concept of equipment leasing has become increasingly important as a means of selling capital equipment in overseas markets. In fact, it is estimated that $50 billion worth (original cost) of U.S.- and foreign-made equipment is on lease in Western Europe.

The system of leasing used by industrial exporters is similar to the typical lease contracts used in the United States. Terms of the leases usually run one to five years, with payments made monthly or annually; included in the rental fee are servicing, repairs, and spare parts. Just as contracts for domestic and overseas leasing arrangements are similar, so are the basic motivations and the shortcomings. For example:

1. Leasing opens the door to a large segment of nominally financed foreign firms that can be sold on a lease option but might be unable to buy for cash.
2. Leasing can ease the problems of selling new, experimental equipment, since less risk is involved for the users.
3. Leasing helps guarantee better maintenance and service on overseas equipment.
4. Equipment leased and in use helps to sell other companies in that country.
5. Lease revenue tends to be more stable over a period of time than direct sales would be.

The disadvantages or shortcomings take on an international flavor. Besides the inherent disadvantages of leasing, some problems are compounded by international relationships. In a country beset with inflation, lease contracts that include maintenance and supply parts (as most do) can lead to heavy losses toward the end of the contract period. Further, countries where leasing is most attractive are those where spiraling inflation is most likely to occur. The added problems of currency devaluation, expropriation, or other political risks are operative longer than if the sale of the same equipment is made outright. In the light of these perils, there is greater risk in leasing than in outright sale; however, there is a definite trend toward increased use of this method of selling internationally.

Countertrade as a Pricing Tool

Countertrade is a pricing tool that every international marketer must be ready to employ, and the willingness to accept a countertrade will often give the company a competitive advantage. The challenges of countertrade must be viewed from the same perspective as all other variations in international trade. Marketers must be aware of which markets will likely require countertrades just as they must be aware of social customs and legal requirements. Assessing this factor along with all other market factors will en-hance a marketer's competitive position.[29]

Ben and Jerry's Homemade Ice Cream Inc., the well-known U.S. ice-cream vendor, manufactures and sells ice cream in Russia. With the rubles they earn, they are buying Russian walnuts, honey, and matryoshky (Russian nesting dolls) to sell in the United States. This is the only means of getting their profit out of Russia because there is a shortage of hard currencies in Russia that makes it difficult to convert rubles to dollars. The Philippines barters coconut oil and fertilizers in exchange for rice from its neigh-boring Asian rice suppliers.[30] In neither transaction does cash change hands; these are barter deals, a type of countertrade. Although cash may be the preferred method of pay-ment, countertrades are an important part of trade with Eastern Europe, the Newly Inde-pendent States,[31] China, and, to a varying degree, some Latin American and African na-tions. Today, an international company must include in its market-pricing toolkit some understanding of countertrading.

Types of Countertrade

Countertrade includes four distinct transactions: barter, compensation deals, counterpur-chase, and buy-back.

Barter is the direct exchange of goods between two parties in a transaction.[32] One of the largest barter deals to date involved Occidental Petroleum Corporation's agree-ment to ship super-phosphoric acid to the former Soviet Union for ammonia urea and potash under a two-year, $20-billion deal. No money changed hands nor were any third parties involved. Obviously, in a barter transaction, the seller must be able to dispose of the goods at a net price equal to the expected selling price in a regular, for-cash transac-tion. Further, during the negotiation stage of a barter deal, the seller must know the mar-ket and the price for the items offered in trade. In the Occidental Petroleum example, the price and a market for the ammonia urea and potash were established because Occi-dental could use the products in its operations. But bartered goods can range from hams to iron pellets, mineral water, furniture, or olive oil—all somewhat more difficult to price and market when potential customers must be sought.

Because of the almost limitless range of goods and quality grades possible and a lack of expertise or necessary information, sellers rely on barter houses to provide infor-mation and find potential buyers for goods received. Barter houses are particularly help-ful to the small exporter. As an example, suppose a Russian company orders 10 meat-cutting machines from a Western firm, which is paid for with a shipment of reindeer antlers, a valuable commodity in Asia. The machinery maker, with the help of a barter house, might then sell the antlers to a South Korean company that uses them to make fertility potions and other traditional Asian medicines.[33]

Compensation deals involve payment in goods and in cash. A seller delivers lathes to a buyer in Venezuela and receives 70 percent of the payment in convertible currency and 30 percent in tanned hides and wool. In an actual deal, General Motors Corporation sold $12 million worth of locomotives and diesel engines to Yugoslavia and took cash and $4 million in Yugoslavian cutting tools as payment. McDonnell Douglas agreed to a

---

[29] Most countertrade is found in countries with shortages of foreign exchange, which is often given as the reason why countertrades are mandated by these countries. An interesting study, however, casts some doubt on this thesis and suggests instead that countertrades may be a reasonable way for countries to minimize transaction costs. For an insightful report on this research, see Jean-François Hennart and Erin Anderson, "Countertrade and the Minimization of Transaction Costs: An Empirical Examination," *The Journal of Law, Economics, & Organization* 9, no. 2 (1993), p. 29.

[30] "RP Mulls Countertrade Scheme on Rice Imports," *Manila Times,* January 27, 1998.

[31] "Use of Barter on the Increase in Ukraine," *BBC Worldwide Monitoring,* January 12, 1998.

[32] Christopher Bobinski, "Poland in Barter Agreement," *Financial Times,* January 20, 1998, p. 8.

[33] Janet Aschkenasy, "Give and Take," *International Business,* September 1996, p. 10.

compensation deal with Thailand for eight top-of-the-range F/A-18 strike aircraft. Thailand agreed to pay $578 million of the total cost in cash, and McDonnell Douglas agreed to accept $93 million in a mixed bag of goods including Thai rubber, ceramics, furniture, frozen chicken, and canned fruit.[34] In a move to reduce its current account deficit, the Thai government requires that 20–50 percent of the value of large contracts be paid for in raw and processed agricultural goods.

An advantage of a compensation deal over barter is the immediate cash settlement of a portion of the bill; the remainder of the cash is generated after successful sale of the goods received. If the company has a use for the goods received, the process is relatively simple and uncomplicated. On the other hand, if the seller has to rely on a third party to find a buyer, the cost involved must be anticipated in the original compensation negotiation if the net proceeds to the seller are to be equal to the market price.

Counterpurchase, or *offset trade,* is probably the most frequently used type of countertrade. For this trade, the seller agrees to sell a product at a set price to a buyer and receives payment in cash. However, two contracts are negotiated. The first contract is contingent on a second contract that is an agreement by the original seller to buy goods from the buyer for the total monetary amount involved in the first contract or for a set percentage of that amount. This arrangement provides the seller with more flexibility than the compensation deal since there is generally a time period—6 to 12 months or longer—for completion of the second contract. During the time that markets are sought for the goods in the second contract, the seller has received full payment for the original sale. Further, the goods to be purchased in the second contract are generally of greater variety than those offered in a compensation deal. Even greater flexibility is offered when the second contract is nonspecific; that is, the books on sales and purchases need to be cleared only at certain intervals. The seller is obligated to generate enough purchases to keep the books balanced or clear between purchases and sales.

Offset trades are becoming more prevalent among economically weak countries. Several variations of a counterpurchase or offset have developed to make it more economical for the selling company. For example, the Lockheed Corporation goes so far as to build up offset trade credits before a counterpurchase deal is made. Knowing that some type of countertrade would have to be accepted to make aircraft sales to Korea, for example, Lockheed actively sought the opportunity to assist in the sale of Hyundai personal computers even though there was no guarantee that Korea would actually buy Lockheed's aircraft. Lockheed has been involved in countertrades for over 20 years. During that time countertrade agreements have totaled over $1.3 billion and have included everything from tomato paste to rugs, textiles, and automotive parts.

McDonnell Douglas actively engages in all types of countertrades, as well. A $100 million sale of DC-9s to Yugoslavia required McDonnell Douglas to sell or buy $25 million in Yugoslavian goods. Some of its commitment to Yugoslavia was settled by buying Yugoslavian equipment for its own use, but it also sold items such as hams, iron castings, rubber bumper guards, and transmission towers to others. McDonnell Douglas held showings for department store buyers to sell glassware and leather goods to fulfill its counterpurchase agreement. Twice a year, company officials meet to claim credits for sales and clear the books in fulfillment of the company's counterpurchase agreements.

Product buy-back agreement is the last of the four countertrade transactions. This type of agreement is made when the sale involves goods or services that produce other goods and services, that is, production plant, production equipment, or technology. The buy-back agreement usually involves one of two situations: (1) the seller agrees to accept as partial payment a certain portion of the output, or (2) the seller receives full price initially but agrees to buy back a certain portion of the output. One U.S. farm equipment manufacturer sold a tractor plant to Poland and was paid part in hard

---

[34] Ted Bardacke and Bernard Gray, "World Trade: Thais in Swap Deal for Fighter Aircraft," *Financial Times,* May 31, 1996, p. 6.

currency and the balance in Polish-built tractors. In another situation, General Motors built an auto manufacturing plant in Brazil and was paid under normal terms but agreed to the purchase of resulting output when the new facilities came on stream. Levi Strauss took Hungarian blue jeans, which it sells abroad, in exchange for setting up a jeans factory near Budapest.

A major drawback to product buy-back agreements comes when the seller finds that the products bought back are in competition with its own similarly produced goods. On the other hand, some have found that a product buy-back agreement provides them with a supplemental source in areas of the world where there is demand but where they have no available supply.

U.S. Firms Reluctant to Countertrade

Countertrade transactions are on the increase in world trade; some estimates of countertrade in international trade go as high as 30 percent, although more conservative estimates place the amount closer to 20 percent. Regardless, a significant amount of all international trade now involves some type of countertrade transaction, and this percentage is predicted to increase substantially in the near future. Much of that increase will come in trading with Third World countries; in fact, some countries require countertrades of some sort with all foreign trade.[35] Countertrade arrangements are involved in an estimated 50 percent or more of all international trade with Eastern European and Third World countries.

Western European and Japanese firms have the longest history of countertrade. Western Europe has traded with Eastern Europe and Japan through its *soga shosha* (trading companies) worldwide. U.S. firms have been slow to accept countertrade until recently. The attitude has been one of preferring to lose a sale rather than become involved in an unfamiliar situation. However, as demands for countertrades have increased in those parts of the world that offer the greatest potential, U.S. businesses have concluded that they have little choice but to cope with countertrade to be competitive in world markets. As Exhibit 18–3 illustrates, countertrade will continue to be important in the future.

While some U.S. firms shun barter or countertrade arrangements, others are profitably involved. Pepsi-Cola Company was one of the pioneers in using countertrade arrangements in Russia and Eastern European countries. Pepsi-Cola's expansion in that region has been made possible by its willingness to accept vodka (sold under the brand name Stolichnaya) from Russia and bottled wines (sold under the brand name of Permiat) from Romania to finance Pepsi-Cola bottling plants in those countries. From all indications, this has been a very profitable arrangement for Russia, Romania, and Pepsi-Cola. Pepsi-Cola continues to use countertrade to expand its bottling plants. In a recent agreement between Pepsi and Ukraine, Pepsi agreed to market $1 billion worth of Ukrainian-made commercial ships over an eight-year period. Some of the proceeds from the ship sales will be reinvested in the shipbuilding venture, and some will be used to buy soft-drink equipment and build five Pepsi bottling plants in Ukraine. Pepsi dominates the cola market in Russia and all the former republics of the USSR in part because of its exclusive countertrade agreement with Russia, which locked Coca-Cola out of the Russian cola market for more than 12 years. Since entering Russia in 1985, Coca-Cola has had to play catch-up.

Problems of Countertrading

The crucial problem confronting a seller in a countertrade negotiation is determining the value of and potential demand for the goods offered. Frequently there is inadequate time

35 "South Korea to Promote Barter Trade with Indonesia, Thailand," *Asia Pulse*, January 22, 1998.

EXHIBIT 18-3   **Why Purchasers Impose Countertrade Obligations**

To Preserve Hard Currency. Countries with nonconvertible currencies look to countertrade as a way of guaranteeing that hard currency expenditures (for foreign imports) are offset by hard currency (generated by the foreign party's obligation to purchase domestic goods).

To Improve Balance of Trade. Nations whose exports to the West have not kept pace with imports increasingly rely on countertrade as a means to balance bilateral trade ledgers.

To Gain Access to New Markets. As a nonmarket or developing country increases its production of exportable goods, it often lacks a sophisticated marketing channel to sell the goods to the West for hard currency. By imposing countertrade demands, foreign trade organizations utilize the marketing organizations and expertise of Western companies to market their goods for them.

To Upgrade Manufacturing Capabilities. By entering compensation arrangements under which foreign (usually Western) firms provide plant and equipment and buy back resultant products, the trade organizations of less-developed countries can enlist Western technical cooperation in upgrading industrial facilities.

To Maintain Prices of Export Goods. Countertrade can be used as a means to dispose of goods at prices that the market would not bear under cash-for-goods terms. Although the Western seller absorbs the added cost by inflating the price of the original sale, the nominal price of the counterpurchased goods is maintained, and the seller need not concede what the value of the goods would be in the world supply-and-demand market. Conversely, if the world price for a commodity is artificially high, such as the price for crude oil, a country can barter its oil for Western goods (e.g., weapons) so that the real "price" the Western partner pays is below the world price.

Source: Leo G. B. Welt, "Countertrade? Better Than No Trade," *Export Today,* Spring 1985, p. 54.

to conduct a market analysis; in fact, it is not unusual to have sales negotiations almost completed before countertrade is introduced as a requirement in the transaction.

Although such problems are difficult to deal with, they can be minimized with proper preparation. In most cases where losses have occurred in countertrades, the seller has been unprepared to negotiate in anything other than cash. Some preliminary research should be done in anticipation of being confronted with a countertrade proposal. Countries with a history of countertrading are identified easily and the products most likely to be offered in a countertrade can often be ascertained. For a company trading with developing countries, these facts and some background on handling countertrades should be a part of every pricing toolkit. Once goods are acquired, they can be passed along to institutions that assist companies in selling bartered goods.

Barter houses specialize in trading goods acquired through barter arrangements and are the primary outside source of aid for companies beset by the uncertainty of a countertrade. While barter houses, most of which are found in Europe, can find a market for bartered goods, it requires time, which puts a financial strain on a company because capital is tied up longer than in normal transactions. Seeking loans to tide it over until sales are completed usually solves this problem.

In the United States, companies are being developed to assist with bartered goods and their financing. Citibank has created a countertrade department to allow the bank to act as a consultant as well as to provide financing for countertrades. Universal Trading Exchange, a New York company, acts as a clearinghouse for bartered goods. Members can trade products of unequal value with other members or they have the option of settling accounts in cash. It is estimated that there are now about 500 barter exchange houses in the United States.

Barter houses serve a vital role in countertrade, but some companies with high volumes of barter have organized their own in-house trading groups to provide the assistance needed to effectively deal in countertrades. One such inside group, perhaps a forerunner of many to come, is Motors Trading Company, a wholly owned subsidiary of General Motors Corporation. It is designed to develop markets for GM products in countries where cash deals or capital investments are not practical. General Motors has countertrade deals with 20 countries, accounting for more than 50 percent of all the business it does with former Eastern-bloc nations. General Electric Co., McDonnell Douglas, and several other major U.S. corporations also have their own special departments to help dispose of countertraded goods. In many situations, these companies have been able to deal with countertrades when the competition has been less flexible.

There are many examples of companies losing sales to competitors willing to enter into countertrade agreements. A U.S. oil-field equipment manufacturer claims it submitted the lowest dollar bid in an Egyptian offer but lost the sale to a bidder that offered a counterpurchase arrangement. Incidentally, the successful company was Japanese, with a sizable established trading company to dispose of the Egyptian goods received in the counterpurchase arrangement. In the request for bid on a significant purchase of military equipment, the government of South Africa indicated that "the government will be partial to bidding firms that can offer a combination of favorable financing, countertrade options and job-creation opportunities."[36] Companies not prepared or willing to accept countertrade as part of the payment run the risk of losing sales to competitors who can match the financing and job creation yet also accept some countertrade options.

Proactive Countertrade Strategy

Currently most companies have a reactive strategy; that is, they use countertrade when they believe it is the only way to make a sale. Even when these companies include countertrade as a permanent feature of their operations, they use it to react to a sales demand rather than using countertrade as an aggressive marketing tool for expansion. Some authorities suggest, however, that companies should have a defined countertrade strategy as part of their marketing strategy rather than be caught unprepared when confronted with a countertrade proposition.[37]

A proactive countertrade strategy is the most effective strategy for global companies that market to exchange-poor countries. Economic development plans in Eastern European countries, the Commonwealth of Independent States (CIS), and much of Latin America will put unusual stress on their ability to generate sufficient capital to finance their growth. Further, as they encounter financial crises such as in Latin America in 1996 and Asia in 1998, countertrade is especially important as a means of exchange.[38] To be competitive, companies must be willing to include some countertraded goods in their market planning. Companies with a proactive strategy make a commitment to use countertrade aggressively as a marketing and pricing tool. They see countertrades as an opportunity to expand markets rather than as an inconvenient reaction to market demands.

Successful countertrade transactions require that the marketer accurately establish the market value of the goods being offered and dispose of the bartered goods once they are received. Most countertrades judged unsuccessful result from not properly resolving one or both of these factors.[39]

In short, unsuccessful countertrades are generally the result of inadequate planning and preparation. One experienced countertrader suggests answering the following questions before entering into a countertrade agreement: (1) Is there a ready market for the goods bartered? (2) Is the quality of the goods offered consistent and acceptable? (3) Is an expert needed to handle the negotiations? (4) Is the contract price sufficient to cover the cost of barter and net the desired revenue?

---

[36] "South Africa Government Narrows Arms Search to 6 Countries," *Dow Jones International News,* January 7, 1998.

[37] For an excellent study on countertrade practices, see Aspy P. Palia and Peter W. Liesch, "Survey of Countertrade Practices in Australia," *Industrial Marketing Management,* Vol. 26, 1997, p. 301.

[38] See, for example, Sopon Onkgara, "Political View: New Year Greets Baht with a Sledgehammer," *Nation,* January 6, 1998; and "Trade Finance: Indonesia's IPTN Looks to Countertrade," *Project & Trade Finance,* January 1998, p. 57.

[39] Aviv Shoham and Dorothy A. Paun, "A Study of International Modes of Entry and Orientation Strategies Used in Countertrade Transactions," *Journal of Global Marketing,* Vol. 11(3), 1998, p. 5.

Capital-poor countries striving to industrialize will account for much of the future demand for goods. Companies not prepared to seek this business with a proactive countertrade strategy will miss important market opportunities.[40]

Intracompany Pricing Strategy

As companies increase the number of worldwide subsidiaries, joint ventures, company-owned distributing systems, and other marketing arrangements, the price charged to different affiliates becomes a preeminent question. Prices of goods transferred from a company's operations or sales units in one country to its units elsewhere, known as intracompany pricing or transfer pricing, may be adjusted to enhance the ultimate profit of the company as a whole. The benefits are:

1. Lowering duty costs by shipping goods into high-tariff countries at minimal transfer prices so duty base and duty are low.

2. Reducing income taxes in high-tax countries by overpricing goods transferred to units in such countries; profits are eliminated and shifted to low-tax countries. Such profit shifting may also be used for "dressing up" financial statements by increasing reported profits in countries where borrowing and other financing are undertaken.

3. Facilitating dividend repatriation when dividend repatriation is curtailed by government policy. Invisible income may be taken out in the form of high prices for products or components shipped to units in that country.

Government authorities have not overlooked the tax and financial manipulation possibilities of transfer pricing. Transfer pricing can be used to hide subsidiary profits and to escape foreign market taxes. Intracompany pricing is managed in such a way that profit is taken in the country with the lowest tax rate. For example, a foreign manufacturer makes a VCR for $50 and sells it to its U.S. subsidiary for $150. The U.S. subsidiary sells it to a retailer for $200, but it spends $50 on advertising and shipping so it shows no profit and pays no U.S. taxes. Meanwhile, the parent company makes a $100 gross margin on each unit and pays at a lower tax rate in the home country. If the tax rate was lower in the country where the subsidiary resides, the profit would be taken in the foreign country and no profit taken in the home country.

When customs and tax regimes are high, there is a strong incentive to trim fiscal liabilities by adjusting the transaction value of goods and service between subsidiaries. Pricing low cuts exposure to import duties; declaring a higher value raises deductible costs and thereby lightens the corporate tax burden. The key is to strike the right balance that maximizes savings over all.[41]

The overall objectives of the intracompany pricing system include (1) maximizing profits for the corporation as a whole; (2) facilitating parent-company control; and (3) offering management at all levels, both in the product divisions and in the international divisions, an adequate basis for maintaining, developing, and receiving credit for their own profitability. Transfer prices that are too low are unsatisfactory to the product divisions because their overall results look poor; prices that are too high make the international operations look bad and limit the effectiveness of foreign managers.

An intracompany pricing system should employ sound accounting techniques and be defensible to the tax authorities of the countries involved. All of these factors argue against a single uniform price or even a uniform pricing system for all international operations.

---

[40] For an excellent discussion of the countertrading process of successful firms, see Dorothy A. Paun, "An International Profile of Countertrading Firms," *Industrial Marketing Management,* Vol. 26, 1996, p. 41.

[41] "Not at Any Price," *Business Eastern Europe,* August 25, 1997.

Four arrangements for pricing goods for intracompany transfer are:

1. Sales at the local manufacturing cost plus a standard markup.
2. Sales at the cost of the most efficient producer in the company plus a standard markup.
3. Sales at negotiated prices.
4. Arm's-length sales using the same prices as quoted to independent customers.

Of the four, the arm's-length transfer is most acceptable to tax authorities and most likely to be acceptable to foreign divisions, but the appropriate basis for intracompany transfers depends on the nature of the subsidiaries and market conditions.

While the practices described above are not necessarily improper, they are being scrutinized more closely by both home and host countries concerned about the loss of potential tax revenues from foreign firms doing business in their countries as well as domestic firms underreporting foreign earnings.[42] The United States government is paying particular attention to transfer pricing in tax audits. This has led to what some have described as a "tax war" between the U.S. and Japan over transfer pricing by its MNCs—each country bringing charges against the foreign MNC for underpayment of taxes because of transfer pricing practices. For example, the U.S. claimed that Nissan U.S. had inflated the prices it paid to its parent for finished cars it was importing to lower U.S. taxes. As a result, the U.S. levied a hefty multi-million-dollar tax penalty against Nissan. Japan retaliated by hitting Coca-Cola with a $145-million tax deficiency.

Governments are seeking tax revenues from their domestic MNCs as well. Prior to PepsiCo's decision to spin-off the restaurant division into a separate company, the IRS charged PepsiCo with an $800-million bill after an audit of its foreign operations of Taco Bell, Pizza Hut, and Kentucky Fried Chicken indicated an underreporting of profits of their foreign operations. Penalties can be as high as 40 percent of the amount underreported. The only certain way to avoid such penalties is to enter an *advanced pricing agreement (APA)* with the IRS. An APA is an agreement between the IRS and a taxpayer on transfer pricing methods that will be applied to some or all of a taxpayer's transactions with affiliates. Such agreements generally apply for up to five years and offer better protection against penalties than other methods. Otherwise, once the IRS charges underreporting, the burden of proof that a transfer price was "fair" rests with the company.

Price Quotations

In quoting the price of goods for international sale, a contract may include specific elements affecting the price, such as credit, sales terms, and transportation. Parties to the transaction must be certain that the quotation settled on appropriately locates responsibility for the goods during transportation and spells out who pays transportation charges and from what point. Price quotations must also specify the currency to be used, credit terms, and the type of documentation required. Finally, the price quotation and contract should define quantity and quality. A quantity definition might be necessary because different countries use different units of measurement. In specifying a ton, for example, the contract should identify it as a metric or an English ton, and as a long or short ton. Quality specifications can also be misunderstood if not completely spelled out. Furthermore, there should be complete agreement on quality standards to be used in evaluating the product. For example, "customary merchantable quality" may be clearly understood among U.S. customers but have a completely different interpretation in another country.

---

[42] Suk H. Kim, Eugene Swinnerton, and Gregory Ulferts, "1994 Final Transfer Pricing Regulations of the United States," *Multinational Business Review,* April 1997, p. 17.

At an exchange rate of $1.50/British pound, the six-pack of Coke is a bargain at $1.15 but, not so with gasoline, which is about $4.00 a gallon. The high price of gas is a point of friction between the Scots and the English since the Scots figure that the close-by North Sea oil should make prices at the pump much cheaper. (John Graham)

The international trader must review all terms of the contract; failure to do so may have the effect of modifying prices even though such a change was not intended.

Administered Pricing

Administered pricing relates to attempts to establish prices for an entire market. Such prices may be arranged through the cooperation of competitors, through national, state, or local governments, or by international agreement. The legality of administered pricing arrangements of various kinds differs from country to country and from time to time. A country may condone price fixing for foreign markets but condemn it for the domestic market, for instance.

In general, the end goal of all administered pricing activities is to reduce the impact of price competition or eliminate it. Price fixing by business is not viewed as an acceptable practice (at least in the domestic market), but when governments enter the field of price administration, they presume to do it for the general welfare to lessen the effects of "destructive" competition.

The point when competition becomes destructive depends largely on the country in question. To the Japanese, excessive competition is any competition in the home market that disturbs the existing balance of trade or gives rise to market disruptions. Few countries apply more rigorous standards in judging competition as excessive than Japan, but no country favors or permits totally free competition. Economists, the traditional champions of pure competition, acknowledge that perfect competition is unlikely and agree that some form of workable competition must be developed.

The pervasiveness of price-fixing attempts in business is reflected by the diversity of the language of administered prices; pricing arrangements are known as agreements, arrangements, combines, conspiracies, cartels, communities of profit, profit pools, licensing, trade associations, price leadership, customary pricing, or informal interfirm agreements. The arrangements themselves vary from the completely informal, with no spoken or acknowledged agreement, to highly formalized and structured arrangements. Any type of price-fixing arrangement can be adapted to international business, but of all the forms mentioned, cartels are the most directly associated with international marketing.

Cartels

A *cartel* exists when various companies producing similar products or services work together to control markets for the types of goods and services they produce. The cartel association may use formal agreements to set prices, establish levels of production and sales for the participating companies, allocate market territories, and even redistribute profits. In some instances, the cartel organization itself takes over the entire selling function, sells the goods of all the producers, and distributes the profits.

The economic role of cartels is highly debatable, but their proponents argue that they eliminate cut-throat competition and "rationalize" business, permitting greater technical progress and lower prices to consumers. However, in the view of most experts, it is doubtful that the consumer benefits very often from cartels.

The Organization of Petroleum Exporting Countries (OPEC) is probably the best-known international cartel. Its power in controlling the price of oil resulted from the percentage of oil production it controlled. In the early 1970s, when OPEC members provided the industrial world with 67 percent of its oil, OPEC was able to quadruple the price of oil. The sudden rise in price from $10 or $12 a barrel to $50 or more a barrel was a primary factor in throwing the world into a major recession. Non-OPEC oil-exporting countries benefited from the price increase while net importers of foreign oil suffered economic downturns. Among Third World countries, those producing oil prospered while oil importers suffered economically from the high prices.

One important aspect of cartels is their inability to maintain control for indefinite periods. Greed by a cartel member and other problems generally weaken the control of the cartel. OPEC's control began to erode as member nations began violating production quotas, users were taking effective steps for conservation, and new sources of oil production by non-OPEC members were developed.[43]

A lesser-known cartel but one that has a direct impact on international trade is the shipping cartel that exists among the world's shipping companies. Every two weeks about 20 shipping-line managers gather for their usual meeting to set rates on tens of billions of dollars of cargo. They do not refer to themselves as a cartel but rather operate under such innocuous names as "The Trans-Atlantic Conference Agreement." Regardless of the name, they set the rates on about 70 percent of the cargo shipped between the United States and Northern Europe. Shipping between the United States and Latin American ports and between the United States and Asian ports also is affected by shipping cartels. Not all shipping lines are members of cartels, but a large number are and thus they have a definite impact upon shipping. Although legal, shipping cartels are coming under scrutiny by the U.S. Congress, and new regulations may soon be passed.[44]

---

[43] Kathryn Graddy, " Cartels and Collusion," *Financial Times,* January 1996, p. IX.
[44] Anna Wilde Mathews, "Making Waves: As U.S. Trade Grows, Shipping Cartels Get a Bit More Scrutiny," *The Wall Street Journal,* October 7, 1997, p. A1.

The legality of cartels at present is not clearly defined. Domestic cartelization is illegal in the United States, and the European Community also has provisions for controlling cartels.[45] The United States, however, does permit firms to take cartel-like actions in foreign markets although it does not sanction foreign market cartels if the results have an adverse impact on the United States economy. Archer Daniels Midland Company, the U.S. agribusiness giant, was fined $205 million for its role in fixing prices for two food additives, lysine and citric acid. German, Japanese, Swiss, and Korean firms were also involved in the cartel.

The group agreed on prices to charge and then allocated the share of the world market each company would get down to the tenth of a decimal point. At the end of the year, any company that sold more than its allotted share was required to purchase in the following year the excess from a co-conspirator that had not reached its volume allocation target.[46] Increasingly, it has become apparent that many governments, concluding they cannot ignore or destroy cartels completely, have chosen to establish ground rules and regulatory agencies to oversee the cartel-like activities of businesses within their jurisdiction.[47]

Government-Influenced Pricing

Companies doing business in foreign countries encounter a number of different types of government price setting. To control prices, governments may establish margins, set prices and floors or ceilings, restrict price changes, compete in the market, grant subsidies, and act as a purchasing monopsony or selling monopoly. The government may also influence prices by permitting, or even encouraging, businesses to collude in setting manipulative prices.

The Japanese government traditionally has encouraged a variety of government-influenced price-setting schemes. However, in a spirit of deregulation that is gradually moving through Japan, Japan's Ministry of Health and Welfare will soon abolish regulations of business hours and price setting for such businesses as barbershops, beauty parlors, and laundries. Under the current practice, 17 sanitation-related businesses can establish such price-setting schemes, which are exempt from the Japanese Anti-Trust Law.[48]

Governments of producing and consuming countries seem to play an ever-increasing role in the establishment of international prices for certain basic commodities. There is, for example, an international coffee agreement, an international cocoa agreement, and an international sugar agreement. And the world price of wheat has long been at least partially determined by negotiations between national governments.

Despite the pressures of business, government, and international price agreements, most marketers still have wide latitude in their pricing decisions for most products and markets.

Summary

Pricing is one of the most complicated decision areas encountered by international marketers. Rather than deal with one set of market conditions, one group of competitors, one set of cost factors, and one set of government regulations, international marketers must take all these factors into account, not only for each country in which they are operating, but often for each market within a country. The continuing growth of Third World markets coupled with their lack of investment capital has increased the importance of countertrades for most marketers, making it an important tool to include in pricing policy.

---

[45] "Cart Europe's Cartel Away," *Business Week,* February 2, 1998, p. 60.

[46] Michael J. Sniffen, "More Than 20 Grand Juries Probe International Price-Fixing Cartels," *The Associated Press,* October 16, 1997.

[47] Thane Peterson and David Woodruff, "Death of the Cartels," *Business Week,* February 2, 1998, p. 14.

[48] "Japan Health Min to End Barbers, Laundries Regulatory Cartels, " *Dow Jones News Service,* February 11, 1998.

Market prices at the consumer level are much more difficult to control in international than in domestic marketing, but the international marketer must still approach the pricing task on a basis of established objectives and policy, leaving enough flexibility for tactical price movements. Pricing in the international marketplace requires a combination of intimate knowledge of market costs and regulations, an awareness of possible countertrade deals, infinite patience for detail, and a shrewd sense of market strategy.

Questions

1. Define:

dumping	variable-cost pricing
parallel imports	full-cost pricing
exclusive distribution	skimming
buy-back agreement	price escalation
administered pricing	barter
countervailing duty	counterpurchase
compensation deal	transfer pricing
subsidy	advanced pricing agreement
cartel	(APA)
countertrade	

2. Discuss the causes of and solutions for parallel imports and their effect on price.

3. Why is it so difficult to control consumer prices when selling overseas?

4. Explain the concept of "price escalation" and tell why it can mislead an international marketer.

5. What are the causes of price escalation? Do they differ for exports and goods produced and sold in a foreign country?

6. Why is it seldom feasible for a company to absorb the high cost of international transportation and reduce the net price received?

7. Price escalation is a major pricing problem for the international marketer. How can this problem be counteracted? Discuss.

8. Changing currency values have an impact on export strategies. Discuss.

9. "Regardless of the strategic factors involved and the company's orientation to market pricing, every price must be set with cost considerations in mind." Discuss.

10. "Price fixing by business is not generally viewed as an acceptable practice (at least in the domestic market); but when governments enter the field of price administration, they presume to do it for the general welfare to lessen the effects of 'destructive' competition." Discuss.

11. Do value-added taxes discriminate against imported goods?

12. Explain specific tariffs, ad valorem tariffs, and compound tariffs.

13. Suggest an approach a marketer may follow in adjusting prices to accommodate exchange-rate fluctuations.

14. Explain the effects of indirect competition and how they may be overcome.

15. Why has dumping become such an issue in recent years?

16. Cartels seem to rise, phoenixlike, after they have been destroyed. Why are they so appealing to business?

17. Develop a cartel policy for the United States.

18. Discuss the various ways in which governments set prices. Why do they engage in such activities?

19. Discuss the alternative objectives possible in setting prices for intracompany sales.

20. Why do governments so carefully scrutinize intracompany-pricing arrangements?

21. Why are costs so difficult to assess in marketing internationally?

22. Discuss why countertrading is on the increase.

23. Discuss the major problems facing a company that is countertrading.

24. If a country you are trading with has a shortage of hard currency, how should you prepare to negotiate price?

25. Of the four types of countertrades discussed in the text, which is the most beneficial to the seller? Explain.

26. Why should a "knowledge of countertrades be part of an international marketer's pricing toolkit"? Discuss.

27. Discuss the various reasons purchasers impose countertrade obligations on buyers.

28. Discuss how FTZs can be used to help reduce price escalation.

29. Why is a proactive countertrade policy good business in some countries?

30. Differentiate between proactive and reactive countertrade policies.

31. One free trade zone is ZFM of Montevideo. Visit **http://www.zfm.com** and discuss how it might be used to help solve the price escalation problem of a product being exported from the United States to one of the Mercosur countries.

32. Select, "What is an FTZ" from the Web page of USCAN (**http://www.uscan.com/main/wtftz.htm**). How does the description of this FTZ differ from the discussion in the text? Discuss how an exporter from the United States could use this FTZ to lower distribution costs.

A Japanese *Aisatsu*

It is not so much that speaking only English is a disadvantage in international business. Instead, it's more that being bilingual is a huge advantage. Observations from sitting in on an *Aisatsu* (a meeting or formal greeting for high-level executives typical in Japan) involving the president of a large Japanese industrial distributor and the marketing vice-president of an American machinery manufacturer are instructive. The two companies were trying to reach an agreement on a long-term partnership in Japan:

Business cards were exchanged and formal introductions made. Even though the president spoke and understood English, one of his three subordinates acted as an interpreter for the Japanese president. The president asked everyone to be seated. The interpreter sat on a stool between the two senior executives. The general attitude between the parties was friendly but polite. Tea and a Japanese orange drink were served.

The Japanese president controlled the interaction completely, asking questions of all Americans through the interpreter. Attention of all the participants was given to each speaker in turn. After this initial round of questions for all the Americans, the Japanese president focused on developing a conversation with the American vice-president. During this interaction an interesting pattern in nonverbal behaviors developed. The Japanese president would ask a question in Japanese. The interpreter then translated the question for the American vice-president. While the interpreter spoke, the American's attention (gaze direction) was given to the interpreter. However, the Japanese president's gaze direction was at the American. Thus, the Japanese president could carefully and unobtrusively observe the American's facial expressions and nonverbal responses. Alternatively, when the American spoke the Japanese president had twice the response time. Because he understood English, he could formulate his responses during the translation process.

What is this extra response time worth in a strategic conversation? What is it worth to be able to carefully observe the nonverbal responses of your top-level counterpart in a high-stakes business negotiation?

Source: Adapted from John L. Graham, "Vis-à-Vis: International Business Negotiations," in Pervez N. Ghauri and Jean-Claude Usunier, *International Business Negotiations* (Oxford: Pergamon, 1996).

Face-to-face negotiations are an omnipresent activity in international commerce.[1] Once global marketing strategies have been formulated, once marketing research has been conducted to support those strategies, and once products, pricing, promotion, and place decisions have been made, then the focus of managers turns to implementation of the plans. In international business such plans are almost always implemented through

---

[1] Several excellent books have been published recently on the topic of international business negotiations. Among them are Camille Schuster and Michael Copeland, *Global Business, Planning for Sales and Negotiations* (Fort Worth, TX: Dryden, 1996); Robert T. Moran and William G. Stripp, *Dynamics of Successful International Business Negotiations* (Houston: Gulf, 1991); and Pervez Ghauri and Jean-Claude Usunier (eds.), *International Business Negotiations* (Oxford: Pergamon, 1996). Additionally Roy J. Lewicki, Joseph A. Litterer, John W. Minton, and David M. Saunder's *Negotiation,* 2nd edition (Burr Ridge, IL: Irwin, 1994) is an important book on the broader topic of business negotiations. The material from this chapter draws extensively on John L. Graham and Yoshiro Sano's *Smart Bargaining, Doing Business with the Japanese,* 2nd edition (New York: Harper Collins, 1989); and John L. Graham s article in the Ghauri and Usunier book, "Vis-à-Vis International Business Negotiations," Chapter 3, pp. 69–91.

face-to-face negotiations with business partners and customers from foreign countries. The sales of goods and services, the management of distribution channels, the contracting for marketing research and advertising services, licensing and franchise agreements, and strategic alliances all require managers from different cultures to sit and talk with one another to exchange ideas and express needs and preferences. Executives must also negotiate with representatives of foreign governments who might approve a variety of their marketing actions[2] or in fact be the actual ultimate customer for goods[3] and services. In many countries governmental officials may also be joint venture partners, and in some cases vendors. For example, negotiations for the television broadcast rights for the 1998 Winter Olympics in Nagano, Japan, included CBS, the International Olympic Committee, and Japanese governmental officials.[4]

One authority on international joint ventures suggests that a crucial aspect of all international commercial relationships is the negotiation of the original agreement. The seeds of success or failure often are sown at the negotiation table, *vis-a-vis* (face-to-face), where not only are financial and legal details agreed to, but perhaps more important, the ambiance of cooperation is established. Indeed, the legal details and the structure of international business ventures are almost always modified over time, and usually through negotiations. But the atmosphere of cooperation initially established face-to-face at the negotiation table persists—or the venture fails.

Business negotiations between business partners from the same country can be difficult. And the added complication of cross-cultural communication can turn an already daunting task into an impossible one. On the other hand, if cultural differences are taken into account, oftentimes wonderful business agreements can be made that lead to long-term, profitable relationships across borders.[5] The purpose of this final chapter is to help prepare managers for the challenges and opportunities of international business negotiations. To do this, we will discuss the dangers of stereotypes, the impact of culture on negotiation behavior, and the implications of culture for managers and negotiators.

The Dangers of Stereotypes

The images of John Wayne, the cowboy, and the *samurai,* the fierce warrior, often are used as cultural stereotypes in discussions of international business negotiations. There is almost always a grain of truth to such representations—an American cowboy kind of competitiveness versus a *samurai* kind of organizational (company) loyalty. One Dutch expert on international business negotiations argues, "The best negotiators are the Japanese because they will spend days trying to get to know their opponents. The worst are Americans because they think everything works in foreign countries as it does in the USA."[6] There are, of course, some Americans who are excellent international negotia-

---

[2] John D. Daniel and Lee H. Radebaugh, *International Business, Environments and Operations,* 8th ed. (Reading, MA: Addison-Wesley, 1998). Their Chapter 12, "International Business Negotiations and Diplomacy," is quite useful.

[3] Stephen E. Weiss, "The IBM-Mexico Microcomputer Investment Negotiations," reprinted in Ghauri and Usunier (eds.), *International Business Negotiations,* 1996; the original version is "The Long Path to the IBM-Mexico Agreement: An Analysis of the Microcomputer Investment Negotiations," *Journal of International Business Studies,* 21(4), 1990.

[4] Robert Neff, William Echikson, Mark Hyman, and David Greising, "The Risks and Rewards of Going for the Gold," *Business Week,* February 9, 1998, pp. 64–65.

[5] Geert Hofstede, "Forward," in Herbert J. Davis and William D. Schulte, Jr. (eds.), *National Culture and International Management in East Asia* (London: International Thomson Business Press, 1997).

[6] Samfrits Le Poole comments on the American cowboy stereotype in "John Wayne Goes to Brussels," in Roy J. Lewicki, Joseph A. Litterer, David M. Saunders, and John W. Minton (eds.), *Negotiation: Readings, Exercises, and Cases* 2nd ed. (Burr Ridge, IL: Irwin, 1993). The quote is translated from the Spanish newspaper *Expansion,* November 29, 1991, p. 41.

The open-air pedicabs make pre-meeting strategizing a challenge for these General Motors executives in Hanoi negotiating a car deal with the Communist government. (© Catherine Karnow/Woodfin Camp & Associates)

tors and some Japanese who are ineffective. The point is that negotiations are not conducted between national stereotypes; negotiations are conducted between people and cultural factors often make huge differences.

Recall our discussion on the cultural diversity within countries from Chapter 4,[7] and consider its relevance to negotiation. For example, we might expect substantial differences in negotiation styles between English-speaking and French-speaking Canadians. The genteel style of talk prevalent in the American Deep South is quite different from the faster speech patterns and pushiness more common in places like New York City. Experts tell us that negotiation styles differ across genders in America, as well.[8] Still others tell us that the urbane negotiation behaviors of Japanese bankers are very different from the relative aggressiveness of those in the retail industry in that country. Finally, age and experience can also make important differences. The older Chinese executive with no experience dealing with foreigners is apt to behave quite differently from her young assistant with undergraduate and MBA degrees from American universities.[9]

The focus of this chapter is culture's influence on international negotiation behavior. However, it should be clearly understood that individual personalities and backgrounds also heavily influence behavior at the negotiation table—and it is the manager's responsibility to consider these factors. Remember: Companies[10] and countries do not negotiate, people do. Consider the culture of your customers and business partners, but treat them as individuals.

The Pervasive Impact of Culture on Negotiation Behavior

The primary purpose of this section is to demonstrate the extent of cultural differences in negotiation styles, and how these differences can cause problems in international business

---

[7] Yasmine Bahrani provides an eloquent description of the pitfalls of cultural identification in "Why Does My Race Matter?" *Los Angeles Times,* February 1, 1998, p. M5.

[8] Deborah Tannen, *Talking from 9 to 5, Women and Men in the Workplace: Language, Sex and Power* (New York: Avon Books, 1994).

[9] Rone Tempest, "China's New Communists Juggle Business and Politics," *Los Angeles Times,* September 20, 1997, p. A3.

[10] See Allyson L. Stewart-Allen, "Europe Lacks Business Culture Necessary for Marketing Success," *Marketing News,* February 16, 1998, p. 5.

negotiations. The material in this section is based on a systematic study[11] of the topic over the last two decades in which the negotiation styles of more than 1,000 businesspeople in 16 countries (18 cultures) were considered. The countries studied were: Japan, Korea, Taiwan, China (northern and southern), Hong Kong, the Philippines, Russia, the Czech Republic, Germany, France, the United Kingdom, Spain, Brazil, Mexico, Canada (English-speaking and French-speaking), and the United States. The countries were chosen because they comprise America's most important present and future trading partners.

Looking broadly across the several cultures two important lessons stand out. The first is that regional generalizations usually are not correct. For example, Japanese and Korean negotiation styles are quite similar in some ways, but in other ways they could not be more different. The second lesson learned from this study is that Japan is an exceptional place: On almost every dimension of negotiation style considered, the Japanese are on or near the end of the scale. Sometimes, Americans are on the other end. But actually, most of the time Americans are somewhere in the middle. The reader will see this evinced in the data presented below. The Japanese approach, however, is most distinct, even *sui generis*.

Cultural differences cause four kinds of problems in international business negotiations—at the levels of:

1. Language
2. Nonverbal behaviors
3. Values
4. Thinking and decision-making processes

The order is important; the problems lower on the list are more serious because they are more subtle. For example, two negotiators would notice immediately if one is speaking Japanese and the other German. The solution to the problem may be as simple as hiring an interpreter or talking in a common third language, or it may be as difficult as learning a language. Regardless of the solution, the problem is obvious. Cultural differences in nonverbal behaviors, on the other hand, are almost always hidden below our awareness. That is to say, in a face-to-face negotiation participants nonverbally—and more subtly—give off and take in a great deal of information. Some experts argue that this information is more important than verbal information. Almost all this signaling goes on below our levels of consciousness. When the nonverbal signals from foreign partners are different, negotiators are most apt to misinterpret them without even being conscious of the mistake. For example, when a French client consistently interrupts, Americans tend to feel uncomfortable without noticing exactly why. In this manner, interpersonal friction often colors business relationships, goes on undetected, and, consequently, uncorrected. Differences in values and thinking and decision-making processes are hidden even deeper and therefore are even harder to cure. We discuss these differences below, starting with language and nonverbal behaviors.

Differences in Language and Nonverbal Behaviors

Americans are clearly quite near the bottom of the languages skills list, although Australians assert that Australians are even worse. It should be added, however, that American

---

[11] The following institutions and people have provided crucial support for the research upon which this material is based: U.S. Department of Education; Toyota Motor Sales USA, Inc.; Solar Turbines, Inc. (a division of Caterpillar Tractors Co.); the Faculty Research and Innovation Fund and the International Business Educational Research (IBEAR) Program at the University of Southern California; Ford Motor Company; The Marketing Science Institute; Madrid Business School; and Professors Nancy J. Adler (McGill University), Nigel Campbell (Manchester Business School), A. Gabriel Esteban (University of Houston—Victoria), Leonid I. Evenko (Russian Academy of the National Economy), Richard H. Holton (University of California, Berkeley), Alain Jolibert (Universite de Sciences de Grenoble), Dong Ki Kim (Korea University), C. Y. Lin (National Sun-Yat Sen University), Hans-Gunther Meissner (Dortmund University), Alena Ockova (Czechoslovak Management Center), Sara Tang (Mass Transit Railway Corporation, Hong Kong), and Theodore Schwarz (Monterrey Institute of Technology).

undergrads recently have begun to see the light and are flocking to language classes. Unfortunately, foreign language teaching resources in the U.S. are inadequate to satisfy the increasing demand. In contrast, the Czechs are now throwing away a hard-earned competitive advantage: Young Czechs will not take Russian anymore. It is easy to understand why, but the result will be a generation of Czechs who cannot leverage their geographic advantage because they will not be able to speak to their neighbors to the east.

The language advantages of the Japanese executive in the description of the *Aisatsu* that opened the chapter were quite clear. However, the most common complaint heard from American managers regards foreign clients and partners breaking into side conversations in their native languages. At best, it is seen as impolite and, quite often, American negotiators are likely to attribute something sinister to the content of the foreign talk—"They're plotting or telling secrets or . . ."

This is a frequent American mistake. The usual purpose of such side conversations is to straighten out a translation problem. For instance, one Korean may lean over to another and ask, "What'd he say?" Or, the side conversation can regard a disagreement among the foreign team members. Both circumstances should be seen as positive signs by Americans, because getting translations straight enhances the efficiency of the interactions, and concessions often follow internal disagreements. But because most Americans speak only one language, neither circumstance is appreciated. By the way, people from other countries are advised to give Americans a brief explanation of the content of their first few side conversations to assuage the sinister attributions.

Data from simulated negotiations are also informative.[12] In our study, the verbal behaviors of negotiators in 14 of the cultures (six negotiators in each of the 14 groups) were videotaped. The numbers in the body of Exhibit 19–1 represent the percentages of statements that were classified into each category listed. That is, 7 percent of the statements made by Japanese negotiators were classified as promises, 4 percent were threats, 7 percent were recommendations, and so on. The verbal bargaining behaviors used by the negotiators during the simulations proved to be surprisingly similar across cultures. Negotiations in all 14 cultures studied were comprised primarily of information-exchange tactics—questions and self-disclosures. Note that the Japanese appear on the low end of the continuum of self-disclosures. Their 34 percent (along with the Spaniards and the English-speaking Canadians) was the lowest across all 14 groups, suggesting that they are the most reticent about giving information. Overall, however, the verbal tactics used were surprisingly similar across the diverse cultures.

Exhibit 19–2 provides the analyses of some linguistic aspects and nonverbal behaviors for the 14 videotaped groups. While these efforts merely scratch the surface of these kinds of behavioral analyses, they still provide indications of substantial cultural differences. Note that, once again, the Japanese are at or next to the end of the continuum on almost every dimension of the behaviors listed. Their facial gazing and touching are the least among the 14 groups. Only the Northern Chinese used the words "no" less frequently and only the Russians used more silent periods than did the Japanese.

A broader examination of the data in Exhibits 19–1 and 19–2 reveals a more meaningful conclusion: The variation across cultures is greater when comparing linguistic aspects of language and nonverbal behaviors than when the verbal content of negotiations is considered. For example, notice the great differences between Japanese and Brazilians in Exhibit 19–1 vis-a-vis Exhibit 19–2.

Following are further descriptions of the distinctive aspects of each of the 14 cultural groups videotaped. Certainly, conclusions about the individual cultures cannot be drawn from an analysis of only six business people in each culture, but the suggested cultural differences are worthwhile to consider briefly:

---

[12] The analysis approach used is detailed in Michael Kamins, Wesley Johnston, and John L. Graham, "A Multi-Method Examination of Buyer-Seller Interactions among Japanese and American Businesspeople," *Journal of International Marketing* 6 (1), 1998, pp. 8–32.

EXHIBIT 19–1 Verbal Negotiation Tactics (The "What" of Communications)

Bargaining Behaviors and Definitions	Cultures (in each group, n = 6)													
	JPN	KOR	TWN	CHN*	RUSS	GRM	UK	FRN	SPN	BRZ	MEX	FCAN	ECAN	USA
Promise. A statement in which the source indicated its intention to provide the target with a reinforcing consequence, which source anticipates target will evaluate as pleasant, positive, or rewarding.	7†	4	9	6	5	7	11	5	11	3	7	8	6	8
Threat. Same as promise, except that the reinforcing consequences are thought to be noxious, unpleasant, or punishing.	4	2	2	1	3	3	3	5	2	2	1	3	0	4
Recommendation. A statement in which the source predicts that a pleasant environmental consequence will occur to the target. Its occurrence is not under source's control.	7	1	5	2	4	5	6	3	4	5	8	5	4	4
Warning. Same as recommendation, except that the consequences are thought to be unpleasant.	2	0	3	1	0	1	1	3	1	1	2	5	0	1
Reward. A statement by the source that is thought to create pleasant consequences for the target.	1	3	2	1	3	4	5	3	3	2	1	1	3	2
Punishment. Same as reward, except that the consequences are thought to be unpleasant.	1	5	1	0	1	2	0	3	2	3	0	2	1	3
Positive normative appeal. A statement in which the source indicates that the target's past, present, or future behavior was or will be in conformity with social norms.	1	1	0	1	0	0	0	0	0	0	0	1	0	1
Negative normative appeal. Same as positive normative appeal except that the target's behavior is in violation of social norms.	3	2	1	0	0	1	1	0	1	1	1	2	1	1
Commitment. A statement by the source to the effect that its future bids will not go below or above a certain level.	15	13	9	10	11	9	13	10	9	8	9	8	14	13
Self-disclosure. A statement in which the source reveals information about itself.	34	36	42	36	40	47	39	42	34	39	38	42	34	36
Question. A statement in which the source asks the target to reveal information about itself.	20	21	14	34	27	11	15	18	17	22	27	19	26	20
Command. A statement in which the source suggests that the target perform a certain behavior.	8	13	11	7	7	12	9	9	17	14	7	5	10	6

* Northern China (Tianjin and environs).

† Read "7 percent of the statements made by Japanese negotiators were promises."

Source: Reprinted from John L. Graham, *International Business Negotiations*, Copyright 1996, pp. 69–91, with permission from Elsevier Science.

EXHIBIT 19–2   Linguistic Aspects of Language and Nonverbal Behaviors ("How" Things Are Said)

Bargaining Behaviors (per 30 minutes)	Cultures (in each group, n = 6)													
	JPN	KOR	TWN	CHN*	RUSS	GRM	UK	FRN	SPN	BRZ	MEX	FCAN	ECAN	USA
Structural aspects														
"No's." The number of times the word "no" was used by each negotiator.	1.9	7.4	5.9	1.5	2.3	6.7	5.4	11.3	23.2	41.9	4.5	7.0	10.1	4.5
"You's." The number of times the word "you" was used by each negotiator.	31.5	34.2	36.6	26.8	23.6	39.7	54.8	70.2	73.3	90.4	56.3	72.4	64.4	54.1
Nonverbal behaviors														
Silent periods. The number of conversational gaps of 10 seconds or longer.	2.5	0	0	2.3	3.7	0	2.5	1.0	0	0	1.1	0.2	2.9	1.7
Conversational overlaps. Number of interruptions.	6.2	22.0	12.3	17.1	13.3	20.8	5.3	20.7	28.0	14.3	10.6	24.0	17.0	5.1
Facial gazing. Number of minutes negotiators spent looking at opponent's face.	3.9	9.9	19.7	11.1	8.7	10.2	9.0	16.0	13.7	15.6	14.7	18.8	10.4	10.0
Touching. Incidents of bargainers touching one another (not including handshaking).	0	0	0	0	0	0	0	0.1	0	4.7	0	0	0	0

* Northern China (Tianjin and environs).

Source: Reprinted from John L. Graham, *International Business Negotiations*, Copyright 1996, pp. 69–91, with permission from Elsevier Science.

Japan. Consistent with most descriptions of Japanese negotiation behavior, the results of this analysis suggest their style of interaction is among the least aggressive (or most polite). Threats, commands, and warnings appear to be deemphasized in favor of the more positive promises, recommendations, and commitments. Particularly indicative of their polite conversational style was their infrequent use of "no" and "you" and facial gazing, as well as more frequent silent periods.

Korea. Perhaps one of the more interesting aspects of the analysis is the contrast of the Asian styles of negotiations. Non-Asians often generalize about the Orient; the findings demonstrate, however, that this is a mistake. Korean negotiators used considerably more punishments and commands than did the Japanese. Koreans used the word "no" and interrupted more than three times as frequently as the Japanese. Moreover, no silent periods occurred between Korean negotiators.

China[13] (Northern). The behaviors of the negotiators from Northern China (i.e., in and around Tianjin) are most remarkable in the emphasis on asking questions at 34 percent. Indeed, 70 percent of the statements made by the Chinese negotiators were classified as information-exchange tactics. Other aspects of their behavior were quite similar to the Japanese, particularly the use of "no" and "you" and silent periods.

Taiwan. The behavior of the businesspeople in Taiwan was quite different from that in China and Japan but similar to that in Korea. The Chinese on Taiwan were exceptional in the time of facial gazing—on the average almost 20 out of 30 minutes. They asked fewer questions and provided more information (self-disclosures) than did any of the other Asian groups.

Russia. The Russians' style was quite different from that of any other European group, and, indeed, was quite similar in many respects to the style of the Japanese. They used "no" and "you" infrequently and used the most silent periods of any group. Only the Japanese did less facial gazing, and only the Chinese asked a greater percentage of questions.

Germany. The behaviors of the western Germans are difficult to characterize because they fell toward the center of almost all the continua. However, the Germans were exceptional in the high percentage of self-disclosures at 47 percent and the low percentage of questions at 11 percent.

United Kingdom. The behaviors of the British negotiators are remarkably similar to those of the Americans in all respects.

Spain. *Diga* is perhaps a good metaphor for the Spanish approach to negotiations evinced in our data. When you make a phone call in Madrid, the usual greeting on the other end is not *hola* (hello) but is, instead, *diga* (speak). It is not surprising, then, that the Spaniards in the videotaped negotiations likewise used the highest percentage of commands (17 percent) of any of the groups and gave comparatively little information (self-disclosures, 34 percent). Moreover, they interrupted one another more frequently than any other group, and they used the terms "no" and "you" very frequently.

France. The style of the French negotiators is perhaps the most aggressive of all the groups. In particular, they used the highest percentage of threats and warnings (together,

---

[13] For an excellent article on the Chinese style of negotiation, see David Strutton and Lou Pelton, "Scaling the Great Wall: The Yin and Yang of Resolving Business Conflicts within China," *Business Horizons,* September–October 1997, pp. 22–34.

8 percent). They also used interruptions, facial gazing, and "no" and "you" very frequently compared to the other groups, and one of the French negotiators touched his partner on the arm during the simulation.

Brazil. The Brazilian businesspeople, like the French and Spanish, were quite aggressive. They used the second highest percentage of commands of all the groups. On average, the Brazilians said the word "no" 42 times, "you" 90 times, and touched one another on the arm about 5 times during 30 minutes of negotiation. Facial gazing was also high.

Mexico.[14] The patterns of Mexican behavior in our negotiations are good reminders of the dangers of regional or language-group generalizations. Both verbal and nonverbal behaviors are quite different than those of their Latin American (Brazilian) or continental (Spanish) cousins. Indeed, Mexicans answer the telephone with the much less demanding *bueno* (short for good day). In many respects, the Mexican behavior is very similar to that of the negotiators from the United States.

French-Speaking Canada. The French-speaking Canadians behaved quite similarly to their continental cousins. Like the negotiators from France, they too used high percentages of threats and warnings, and even more interruptions and eye contact. Such an aggressive interaction style would not mix well with some of the more low-key styles of some of the Asian groups or with English speakers, including English-speaking Canadians.

English-Speaking Canada. The Canadians who speak English as their first language used the lowest percentage of aggressive persuasive tactics (threats, warnings, and punishments totaled only 1 percent) of all 14 groups. Perhaps, as communications researchers suggest, such stylistic differences are the seeds of interethnic discord as witnessed in Canada over the years. With respect to international negotiations, the English-speaking Canadians used noticeably more interruptions and "no's" than negotiators from either of Canada's major trading partners, the United States and Japan.

United States. Like the Germans and the British, the Americans fell in the middle of most continua. They did interrupt one another less frequently than all the others, but that was their sole distinction.

These differences across the cultures are quite complex, and this material *by itself* should not be used to predict the behaviors of foreign counterparts. Instead, great care should be taken with respect to the aforementioned dangers of stereotypes. The key here is to be aware of these kinds of differences so the Japanese silence, the Brazilian "no, no, no . . . ," or the French threat are not misinterpreted.

Differences in Values[15]

Four values—objectivity, competitiveness, equality, and punctuality—which are held strongly and deeply by most Americans seem to frequently cause misunderstandings and bad feelings in international business negotiations.

Objectivity. "Americans make decisions based upon the bottom line and on cold, hard facts." "Americans don't play favorites." "Economics and performance count, not people." "Business is business." Such statements well reflect American notions of the importance of objectivity.

---

[14] For a good quick summary of the Mexican negotiation style, see "Getting Cozy, Negotiating Successfully in Mexico," *International Business*, February 1997, p. 15.

[15] Larry A. Samovar, Richard E. Porter, and Lisa A. Stefani, *Communication between Cultures*, 3rd ed. (Belmont, CA: Wadsworth, 1998).

The single most important book on the topic of negotiation, *Getting to YES,*[16] is highly recommended for both American and foreign readers. The latter will learn not only about negotiations but, perhaps more important, about how Americans think about negotiations. The authors are quite emphatic about "separating the people from the problem," and they state, "Every negotiator has two kinds of interests: in the substance and in the relationship." This advice is probably quite worthwhile in the United States or perhaps in Germany, but in most places in the world such advice is nonsense. In most places in the world, personalities and substance are not separate issues and cannot be made so.

For example, consider how important nepotism is in Chinese or Hispanic cultures. Experts[17] tell us that businesses don't grow beyond the bounds and bonds of tight family control in the burgeoning "Chinese Commonwealth." Things work the same way in Spain, Mexico, and the Philippines by nature. And, just as naturally, negotiators from such countries not only will take things personally but will be personally affected by negotiation outcomes. What happens to them at the negotiation table will affect the business relationship regardless of the economics involved.

Competitiveness and Equality.   Simulated negotiations can be viewed as a kind of experimental economics wherein the values of each participating cultural group are roughly reflected in the economic outcomes. The simple simulation used in the study represents the essence of commercial negotiations—it has both competitive and cooperative aspects. At least 40 businesspeople from each culture played the same buyer–seller game, negotiating over the prices of three products. Depending on the agreement reached, the "negotiation pie" could be made larger through cooperation (as high as $10,400 in joint profits) before it is divided between the buyer and seller. The results are summarized in Exhibit 19–3.

The Japanese were the champions at making the pie big. Their joint profits in the simulation were the highest (at $9,590) among the 18 cultural groups. The American pie was more average-sized (at $9,030), but at least it was divided relatively equitably (51.8 percent of the profits went to the buyers). Alternatively, the Japanese (and others) split their pies in strange ways, with buyers making higher percentages of the profits (53.8 percent). The implications of these simulated business negotiations are completely consistent with the comments of other authors and the adage that in Japan the buyer is "kinger." By nature, Americans have little understanding of the Japanese practice of giving complete deference to the needs and wishes of buyers. That is not the way things work in America. American sellers tend to treat American buyers more as equals, and the egalitarian values of American society support this behavior. Moreover, most Americans will, by nature, treat Japanese buyers more frequently as equals. Likewise, American buyers will generally not "take care of" American sellers or Japanese sellers. The American emphasis on competition and individualism represented in these findings is quite consistent with the work of Geert Hofstede[18] detailed in Chapter 5, which indicated that Americans scored the highest among 40 other cultural groups on the individualism (versus collectivism) scale.

Finally, not only do Japanese buyers achieve higher results than Americans buyers, but compared to American sellers ($4,350), Japanese sellers also get more of the commercial pie ($4,430), as well. Interestingly, when shown these results, Americans in executive seminars still often prefer the American seller's role. In other words, even

---

[16] Roger Fisher, William Ury, and Bruce Patton, *Getting to YES: Negotiating Agreement without Giving In* (New York: Penguin, 1991); in its original edition, Roger Fisher and William Ury, *Getting to YES* (New York: Penguin, 1981).

[17] John Kao, "The Worldwide Web of Chinese Business," *Harvard Business Review,* March–April 1993, pp. 24–36.

[18] Geert Hofstede, *Cultures and Organizations: Software of the Mind* (Maidenhead, Berkshire: McGraw-Hill, 1991).

EXHIBIT 19-3   Cultural Differences in Competitiveness and Equality

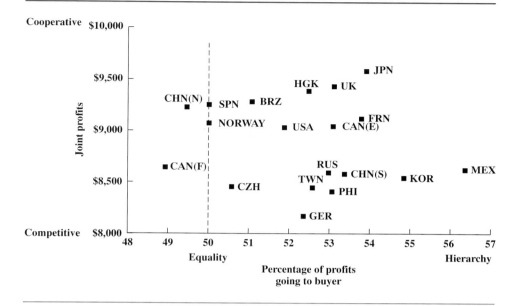

Based upon at least 40 business people in each cultural group.
Source: Reprinted from John L. Graham, *International Business Negotiations,* copyright 1996, pp. 69–91, with permission from Elsevier Science.

though the American sellers make lower profits than the Japanese, many American managers apparently prefer lower profits if those profits are yielded from a more equal split of the joint profits.

Time. "Just make them wait." Everyone else in the world knows no negotiation tactic is more useful with Americans, because no one places more value on time, no one has less patience when things slow down, and no one looks at their wristwatches more than Americans do. The material from Chapter 5 on P-time versus M-time is quite pertinent here. Edward T. Hall in his seminal writing[19] is best at explaining how the passage of time is viewed differently across cultures and how these differences most often hurt Americans.

Even Americans try to manipulate time to their advantage however. As a case in point, Solar Turbines Incorporated (a division of Caterpillar) once sold $34 million worth of industrial gas turbines and compressors for a Russian natural gas pipeline project. Both parties agreed that final negotiations would be held in a neutral location, the south of France. In previous negotiations, the Russians had been tough but reasonable. But in Nice, the Russians were not nice. They became tougher and, in fact, completely unreasonable, according to the Solar executives involved.

It took a couple of discouraging days before the Americans diagnosed the problem, but once they did, a crucial call was made back to headquarters in San Diego. Why had the Russians turned so cold? They were enjoying the warm weather in Nice and weren't interested in making a quick deal and heading back to Moscow! The call to California was the key event in this negotiation. Solar's headquarters people in San Diego were sophisticated enough to allow their negotiators to take their time. From that point on, the routine of the negotiations changed to brief, 45-minute meetings in the mornings, with afternoons at the golf course, beach, or hotel, making calls and doing paperwork.

---

[19] Edward T. Hall, "The Silent Language in Overseas Business," *Harvard Business Review,* May–June 1960, pp. 87–96.

CROSSING BORDERS 19–1

Changing Your Internal Clock

Vincente Lopez spent five years making the Tijuana-to-San Diego commute. Each time he crossed the border, it felt like a button was pushed inside him. When entering the United States, he felt his whole being switch to rapid clock-time mode: he would walk faster, drive faster, talk faster, and meet deadlines. When returning home, his body would relax and slow the moment he saw the Mexican customs agent. "There is a large group of people like me who move back and forth between the times," Lopez observes. Many, he believes, insist on keeping their homes on the Mexican side precisely because of its slower pace of life.

Source: Reprinted from *American Demographics* magazine with permission. © 1998, Cowles Business Media, Ithaca, New York.

Finally, during the fourth week, the Russians began to make concessions and to ask for longer meetings. Why? They could not go back to Moscow after four weeks on the Mediterranean without a signed contract. This strategic reversal of the time pressure yielded a wonderful contract for Solar.

Differences in Thinking and Decision-Making Processes

When faced with a complex negotiation task, most Westerners (notice the generalization here) divide the large task up into a series of smaller tasks. Issues such as prices, delivery, warranty, and service contracts may be settled one issue at a time, with the final agreement being the sum of the sequence of smaller agreements. In Asia, however, a different approach is more often taken wherein all the issues are discussed at once, in no apparent order, and concessions are made on all issues at the end of the discussion. The Western sequential approach and the Eastern holistic approach do not mix well.

For example, American managers report great difficulties in measuring progress in Japan. After all, in America, you are half done when half the issues are settled. But in Japan, nothing seems to get settled. Then, surprise, you are done. Often, Americans make unnecessary concessions right before agreements are announced by the Japanese. For example, one American department store buyer traveling to Japan to buy six different consumer products for his chain lamented that negotiations for his first purchase took an entire week. In the United States, such a purchase would be consummated in an afternoon. So, by his calculations, he expected to have to spend six weeks in Japan to complete his purchases. He considered raising his purchase prices to try to move things along faster. But before he was able to make such a concession, the Japanese quickly agreed on the other five products in just three days. This particular businessman was, by his own admission, lucky in his first encounter with Japanese bargainers.

This American businessman's near blunder reflects more than just a difference in decision-making style. To Americans, a business negotiation is a problem-solving activity, the best deal for both parties being the solution. To a Japanese businessperson, on the other hand, a business negotiation is a time to develop a business relationship with the goal of long-term mutual benefit. The economic issues are the context, not the content, of the talks. Thus, settling any one issue really is not that important. Such details will take care of themselves once a viable, harmonious business relationship is established. And, as happened in the case of our retail goods buyer, once the relationship was established—signaled by the first agreement—the other "details" were settled quickly.

American bargainers should anticipate such a holistic approach and be prepared to discuss all issues simultaneously and in an apparently haphazard order. Progress in the talks should not be measured by how many issues have been settled. Rather, Americans must try to gauge the quality of the business relationship. Important signals of progress can be:

- Higher-level foreigners being included in the discussions.
- Their questions beginning to focus on specific areas of the deal.
- A softening of their attitudes and position on some of the issues—"Let us take some time to study this issue."
- At the negotiation table, increased talk among themselves in their own language, which may often mean they're trying to decide something.
- Increased bargaining and use of the lower level, informal, and other channels of communication.

Implications for Managers and Negotiators

Considering all the potential problems in cross-cultural negotiations, it is a wonder that any international business gets done at all. Obviously, the economic imperatives of global trade make much of it happen despite the potential pitfalls. But an appreciation of cultural differences can lead to even better international commercial transactions—it is not just business deals but highly profitable business relationships that are the real goal of international business negotiations.

Four steps lead to more efficient and effective international business negotiations. They are: (1) selection of the appropriate negotiation team; (2) management of preliminaries, including training, preparations, and manipulation of negotiation settings; (3) management of the process of negotiations, that is, what happens at the negotiation table; and (4) appropriate follow-up procedures and practices. Each is discussed below.

Negotiation Teams

One reason for global business successes is the large numbers of skillful international negotiators. These are the managers who have lived in foreign countries and speak foreign languages.[20] In many cases, they are immigrants to the United States or those who have been immersed in foreign cultures in other capacities (Peace Corps volunteers and Mormon missionaries are common examples). Thankfully, more business schools are beginning to reemphasize language training and visits abroad. Indeed, it is interesting to note that the original Harvard Business School catalogue of 1908–09 listed German, French, and Spanish correspondence within its curriculum.

The selection criteria for international marketing and sales personnel previously detailed in Chapter 17 are applicable in selecting negotiators as well. Traits such as maturity, emotional stability, breadth of knowledge, optimism, flexibility, empathy, and stamina[21] are all important, not only for marketing executives involved in international negotiations, but also for the technical experts who often accompany and support them. In studies conducted at Ford Motor Company and AT&T, three additional traits were found to be important predictors of negotiator success with international clients and partners: willingness to use team assistance, listening skill, and influence at headquarters.

---

[20] Gunnar Beeth, "Multicultural Managers Wanted," *Management Review,* May 1, 1997, pp. 17–20.

[21] The wear and tear of international negotiators' travel can also be reflected in anxieties expressed about time away from families. See Paul Blustein, "Top U.S. Negotiators to Leave China Talks," *Washington Post,* April 15, 1997, pp. E1 and E3.

Willingness to use team assistance is particularly important for American negotiators. Because of a cultural heritage of independence and individualism Americans often make the mistake of going it alone against greater numbers of foreigners. One American sitting across the negotiation table from three or four Chinese negotiators is unfortunately an all too common sight. The number of brains in the room does make a difference. Moreover, business negotiations are social processes, and the social reality is that a larger number of nodding heads can exercise greater influence than even the best arguments. It is also much easier to gather detailed information when teams are negotiating rather than individuals. For example, the Japanese are quite good at bringing along junior executives for the dual purposes of training via observation and careful note taking. Compensation schemes that overly emphasize individual performance can also get in the way of team negotiating—a negotiation *team* requires a split commission, which many Americans naturally eschew. Finally, negotiators may have to request the accompaniment of senior executives to better match up with client's and partner's negotiation teams. Particularly in high-context, hierarchical cultures rank speaks quite loudly in both persuasion and the demonstration of interests in the business relationship.

The single most important activity of negotiations is listening.[22] The negotiator's primary job is collecting information with the goal of enhancing creativity. This may mean assigning one team member the sole responsibility of taking careful notes and not worrying about speaking during the meetings. This may also mean that knowing the language of clients and partners will be crucial for the most complete understanding of their needs and preferences. The importance of listening skills in international business negotiations cannot be overstated.

Bringing along a senior executive is important because influence at headquarters is crucial to success. Indeed, many experienced international negotiators argue that half the negotiation is with headquarters. The representatives' lament goes something like this, "The better I understand my customer, the tougher time I have with headquarters." Of course, this misery associated with boundary spanning roles is precisely why international negotiators and sales executives make so much money.

Finally, it is also important to reiterate a point made in Chapter 5: Gender should not be used as a selection criterion for international negotiation teams. This is so despite the great differences in the roles of women across cultures. Even in countries where women do not participate in management, American women negotiators are treated as foreigners first. For obvious reasons it may not be appropriate for women managers to participate in some forms of business entertainment—common baths in locker rooms at Japanese golf course club houses, for example. However, it is still important for women executives to establish personal rapport at restaurants and other informal settings. Indeed, one expert on cross-gender communication suggests that women may actually have some advantages in international negotiations:[23]

> In general, women are more comfortable talking one-on-one. The situation of speaking up in a meeting is a lot closer to boys' experience of using language to establish their position in a large group than it is to girls' experience using language to maintain intimacy. That's something that can be exploited. Don't wait for the meeting; try to make your point in advance, one-to-one. This is what the Japanese do, and in many ways American women's style is a lot closer to the Japanese style than to American men's.

Negotiation Preliminaries

Many companies in the United States provide employees with negotiations training. For example, through his training programs, Chester Karrass[24] has taught more people to

---

[22] Hal Lancaster, "You Have to Negotiate Everything in Life, So Get Good at It," *Wall Street Journal,* January 27, 1998, p. B1.

[23] Deborah Tannen, *You Just Don't Understand: Men and Women in Conversation* (New York: William Morrow, 1990).

[24] See Karrass's firm's Web site for information regarding his programs: **www.karrass.com.**

CROSSING BORDERS 19-2

Ford Trains Executives for Negotiations with Japanese

Proactive and direct is the approach Ford uses to develop competence in employees who interact with the Japanese. This occurs through a variety of practices, including programs that help Ford personnel better understand the Japanese culture and negotiating practices, and by encouraging the study of the spoken language. By designing training that highlights both the pitfalls and the opportunities in negotiations, Ford increases the chance to "expand the negotiation pie."

Back in 1988, the key personnel on Ford's minivan team attended one of the first sessions of the Managing Negotiations: Japan (MNJ) program at the Ford Executive Development Center. Its negotiations with the Nissan team improved immediately. But perhaps the best measure of the usefulness of the MNJ program is the success of the Nissan joint-venture product itself. Reflected in the Villager/Quest are countless hours of effective face-to-face meetings with Ford's Japanese partners.

Not everyone negotiating outside the U.S. has the advantages of in-house training. However, many sources of information are available—books (particularly, on Japan), periodicals, and colleagues with first-hand experience. To succeed, negotiators have to be truly interested in and challenged by the international negotiating environment. Structuring negotiations to achieve win–win results *and* building a long-term relationship takes thoughtful attention and commitment.

Source: Reprinted from John L. Graham, *International Business Negotiations,* copyright 1996, pp. 69–91, with permission from Elsevier Science.

negotiate than any other purveyor of the service—see his ads in almost all in-flight magazines of domestic air carriers. However, very few companies provide training for negotiations with managers from other countries.[25] Ford Motor Company is an exception.

Ford does more business with Japanese companies than any other firm. Ford owns 33 percent of Mazda, it built a successful minivan with Nissan, and it buys and sells component parts and completed cars from and to Japanese companies. But perhaps the best measure of Ford's Japanese business is the 8,000 or so U.S. to Japan round-trip airline tickets the company buys annually! Ford has made a large investment in training its managers with Japanese responsibilities. More than 1,500 of its executives have attended a three-day program on Japanese history and culture and the company's Japanese business strategies. More than 1,000 Ford managers who work face-to-face with Japanese have attended a three-day program, "Managing Negotiations: Japan" (MNJ). The MNJ program includes negotiation simulations with videotape feedback, lectures with cultural differences demonstrated via videotapes of Japanese/American interactions, and rehearsals of upcoming negotiations. The company also conducts similar programs on Korea and the Peoples Republic of China.

In addition to MNJ, the broader Japan training efforts at Ford must be credited for their successes in Japan. Certainly, MNJ alumni can be seen exercising influence across and up the ranks regarding Japanese relationships. But the organizational awareness of

---

[25] Erika Rasmusson, "Beyond Miss Manners," *Sales & Marketing Management,* April 1997, p. 84; Andy Cohen, "Small World, Big Challenge," *Sales & Marketing Management,* June 1996, pp. 69–73.

the cultural dimensions of the Japanese business system was quickly raised as well by their broader, three-day program on Japanese business strategies. Remember the story about the Russians in Nice? Two critical events took place. First, the Solar Turbines (Inc.) negotiators diagnosed the problem. Second, and equally important, their California superiors appreciated the problem and approved the investments in time and money to outwait the Russians. So it is that the Ford programs have targeted not only the negotiators working directly with the Japanese but also their managers who spend most of their time in the company's Detroit headquarters. Negotiators need information specific to the cultures in which they work. Just as critical, their managers back in the United States need a basic awareness and appreciation for the importance of culture in international business so that they will be more apt to listen to the "odd-sounding" recommendations coming from their people in Moscow, Rio, or Tokyo.

Any experienced business negotiator will tell you that there is never enough time to get ready. Given the time constraints of international negotiations, preparations must be accomplished efficiently—the homework must be done before the bargaining begins. We recommend the following checklist to ensure proper preparation and planning for international negotiations:

1. Assessment of the situation and the people.
2. Facts to confirm during the negotiation.
3. Agenda.
4. Best alternative to a negotiated agreement (BATNA).
5. Concession strategies.
6. Team assignments.

Preparation and planning skill is at the top of almost everyone's list of negotiator traits, yet it seems many Americans are still planning strategies during over-ocean flights when they should be trying to rest. Quick wits are important in business negotiations, and arduous travel schedules and jet lag dull even the sharpest minds. Obviously information about the other side's goals and preferences should be sought ahead of time. Also important are clear directions from headquarters and detailed information about market conditions.

No matter how thorough the preliminary research, negotiators should always make a list of key facts to reconfirm at the negotiation table. Information gathered about foreign customers and markets almost always includes errors, and things can change during those long airline flights. Next, anticipate that managers from other cultures may put less emphasis on a detailed agenda, but it still makes sense to have one to propose and help organize the meetings.

The most important idea in *Getting to YES*[26] is the notion of the *best alternative to a negotiated agreement (BATNA)*. This is how power in negotiations is best measured. Even the smallest companies can possess great power in negotiations if they have many good alternatives and their large-company counterparts do not. It is also important to plan out and write down concession strategies. Concessions can often snowball, and writing them down ahead of time helps negotiators keep them under control.

Finally, specific team assignments should be made clear—who handles technical details, who takes notes, who plays the tough guy, who does most of the talking for the group, etc. Obviously this last consideration presumes a negotiation team is involved.

There are at least seven aspects of the negotiation setting that should be manipulated ahead of time if possible:

1. Location.
2. Physical arrangements.

---

[26] Fisher and Ury, *Getting to YES,* 1981.

3. Number of parties.
4. Number of participants.
5. Audiences (news media, competitors, fellow vendors, etc.).
6. Communications channels.
7. Time limits.

Location speaks loudly about power relations. Traveling to a negotiating counterpart's home turf is a big disadvantage, and not just so because of the costs of travel in money and fatigue. A neutral location may be preferred—indeed, many trans-Pacific business negotiations are conducted in Hawaii. The weather and golf are nice and the jet lag is about equal. Location is also an important consideration because it may determine legal jurisdictions if disputes arise. If you must travel to your negotiating counterpart's city, then a useful tactic is to invite clients or partners to work in a meeting room at your hotel. You can certainly get more done if they are away from the distractions of their offices.

Physical arrangements can affect cooperativeness in subtle ways. In high-context cultures the physical arrangements of rooms can be quite a source of embarrassment and irritation if handled improperly. To the detriment of their foreign business relationships, Americans tend to be casual about such arrangements. Furthermore, views about who should attend negotiations vary across cultures. Americans tend to want to get everyone together to "hammer out an agreement" even if opinions and positions are divergent. Japanese prefer to talk to everyone separately, then once everyone agrees more inclusive meetings are scheduled. Russians tend toward a cumulative approach, meeting with one party, reaching an agreement, then both the first two call on a third party, and so on. In addition, the importance of not being outnumbered in international business negotiations has already been mentioned.

Audiences can have crucial influences on negotiation processes. Purchasing executives at PetroBras, the Brazilian national oil company, were well known for putting competitive bidders in rooms adjacent to one another to increase competitive pressures

In countries where personal relationships are crucial in business negotiations, teleconferencing will often be less appropriate than it is in the United States. (Jon Riley/Tony Stone Images)

on both vendors. Likewise, news leaks to the press played a crucial role in pushing along the negotiations between General Motors and Toyota regarding a joint-venture production agreement.

As electronic media become more available and efficient, more business can be conducted without face-to-face communication. However, Americans should recognize that their counterparts in many other countries do not necessarily share their attraction to the Internet and teleconferencing. Indeed, a conversation over a long dinner may be the most efficient way to communicate with clients and partners in places like Mexico and Malaysia.

Finally, it is important to manipulate time limits. Recall the example about the Russians and Americans in Nice. The patience of the home office may be indispensable, and major differences in time orientation should be planned for when business negotiations are conducted in most other countries.

At the Negotiation Table

The most difficult aspect of international business negotiations is the actual conduct of the face-to-face meeting. Assuming that the best representatives have been chosen, and assuming those representatives are well-prepared and that situational factors have been manipulated in one's favor, things can still go sour at the negotiation table. Obviously, if these other preliminaries have not been managed properly, things will go wrong during the meetings. Even with great care and attention to preliminary details, managing the dynamics of the negotiation process is almost always the greatest challenge facing Americans seeking to do business in other countries.

Going into a business negotiation, most people have expectations about the "proper" or normal process of such a meeting. Based on these expectations, progress is measured and appropriate bargaining strategies are selected. That is, things may be done differently in the latter stages of a negotiation than they were in the earlier. Higher risk strategies may be employed to conclude talks—as in the final two minutes of a close soccer match. But all such decisions about strategy are made relative to perceptions of progress through an expected course of events.

Differences in the expectations held by parties from different cultures are one of the major difficulties in any international business negotiation. Before these differences are discussed, however, it is important to point out similarities. Everywhere around the world we have found that business negotiations proceed through four stages:

1. Nontask sounding.
2. Task-related exchange of information.
3. Persuasion.
4. Concessions and agreement.

The first stage, nontask sounding, includes all those activities that might be described as establishing a rapport or getting to know one another, but it does not include information related to the "business" of the meeting. The information exchanged in the second stage of business negotiations regards the parties' needs and preferences. The third stage, persuasion, involves the parties' attempts to modify one another's needs and preferences through the use of various persuasive tactics. The final stage of business negotiations involves the consummation of an agreement, which is often the summation of a series of concessions or smaller agreements.

Despite the consistency of this process across diverse cultures, the content and duration of the four stages differ substantially. For example, Exhibit 19–4 details such procedural differences in Japan and the United States, as well as differences in language, nonverbal behavior, and values.

Nontask Sounding.   Americans always discuss topics other than business at the negotiation table (for example, the weather, family, sports, politics, and business conditions in general), but not for long. Usually the discussion is moved to the specific business at

EXHIBIT 19–4   **Summary of Japanese and American Business Negotiation Styles**

Category	Japanese	Americans
Language	Most Japanese executives understand English, although interpreters are often used.	Americans have less time to formulate answers and observe Japanese nonverbal responses because of a lack of knowledge of Japanese.
Nonverbal behaviors	The Japanese interpersonal communication style includes less eye contact, fewer negative facial expressions, and more periods of silence.	American businesspeople tend to "fill" silent periods with arguments or concessions.
Values	Indirectness and face saving are important. Vertical buyer/seller relationships, with sellers depending on goodwill of buyers (*amae*), is typical.	Speaking one's mind is important. Buyer/seller relationships are horizontal.

Four Stages of Business Negotiations

1. Nontask sounding	Considerable time and expense devoted to such efforts is the practice in Japan.	Very short periods are typical.
2. Task-related exchange of information	This is the most important step— high first offers with long explanations and in-depth clarifications.	Information is given briefly and directly. "Fair" first offers are more typical.
3. Persuasion	Persuasion is accomplished primarily behind the scenes. Vertical status relations dictate bargaining outcomes.	The most important step: Minds are changed at the negotiation table and aggressive persuasive tactics are often used.
4. Concessions and agreement	Concessions are made only toward the end of negotiations—a holistic approach to decision making. Progress is difficult to measure for Americans.	Concessions and commitments are made throughout—a sequential approach to decision making.

John L. Graham and Yoshihiro Sano, *Smart Bargaining, Doing Business with the Japanese, 2nd ed.* (New York: Harper Collins, 1989), p. 32.

hand after five to ten minutes. Such preliminary talk, known as nontask sounding, is much more than just friendly or polite; it helps to learn how the other side feels that particular day. One can determine during nontask sounding if a client's attention is focused on business or distracted by other matters, personal or professional.

Learning about a client's background and interests also provides important cues about appropriate communication styles. To the extent that people's backgrounds are similar, communication can be more efficient. Engineers can use technical jargon when talking to other engineers. Sports enthusiasts can use sports analogies. Those with children can compare the cash drain of "putting a kid through college," and so on.

During these initial stages of conversation, judgments, too, are made about the "kind" of person(s) with whom one is dealing: Can this person be trusted? Will he be reliable? How much power does she have in her organization? All such judgments are made before business discussions ever begin.

There is a definite purpose to these preliminary nontask discussions. Although most people are often unaware of it, such time almost always is used to size up one's clients. Depending on the results of this process, proposals and arguments are formed using different jargon and analogies. Or it may be decided not to discuss business at all if clients are distracted by other personal matters or if the other person seems untrustworthy. All

CROSSING BORDERS 19–3

Fishing for Business in Brazil

How important is nontask sounding? Consider this description about an American banker's meeting in Brazil, as told by an observer.

Introductions were made. The talk began with the usual "How do you like Rio?" questions—Have you been to Ipanema, Copacabana, Corcovado, etc? There was also talk about the flight down from New York. After about five minutes of this chatting, the senior American quite conspicuously glanced at his watch, and then asked his client what he knew about the bank's new services.

"A little," responded the Brazilian. The senior American whipped a brochure out of his briefcase, opened it on the desk in front of the client, and began his sales pitch.

After about three minutes of "fewer forms, electronic transfers, and reducing accounts receivable," the Brazilian jumped back in, "Yes, that should make us more competitive . . . and competition is important here in Brazil. In fact, have you been following the World Cup *fútbol* (soccer) matches recently? Great games." And so the reel began to whir, paying out that monofilament line, right there in that hot high-rise office.

After a few minutes' dissertation on the local *fútbol* teams, Pélé, and why *fútbol* isn't popular in the United States, the American started to try to crank the Brazilian back in. The first signal was the long look at his watch, then the interruption, "Perhaps we can get back to the new services we have to offer."

The Brazilian did get reeled back into the subject of the sale for a couple of minutes, but then the reel started to sing again. This time he went from efficient banking transactions to the nuances of the Brazilian financial system to the Brazilian economy. Pretty soon we were all talking about the world economy and making predictions about the U.S. presidential elections.

Another look at his Rolex, and the American started this little "sport fishing" ritual all over again. From my perspective (I wasn't investing time and money toward the success of this activity), this all seemed pretty funny. Every time the American VP looked at his watch during the next 45 minutes, I had to bite my cheeks to keep from laughing out loud. He never did get to page two of his brochure. The Brazilian just wasn't interested in talking business with someone he didn't know pretty well.

Source: Reprinted from John L. Graham, *International Business Negotiations,* copyright 1996, pp. 69–91, with permission from Elsevier Science.

this sounds like a lot to accomplish in five to ten minutes, but that's how long it usually takes in the United States. This is not the case in other high-context countries like China[27] or Brazil; the goals of the nontask sounding are identical, but the time spent is much, much longer.[28]

In the United States, firms resort to the legal system and their lawyers when they've made a bad deal because of a mistake in sizing up a customer or vendor. In most other countries the legal system cannot be depended upon for such purposes. Instead, executives in places like Korea and Egypt spend substantial time and effort in nontask sounding so that problems do not develop later. Americans need to reconsider, from the foreigner's perspective, the importance of this first stage of negotiations if they hope to succeed in Seoul or Cairo.

---

[27] Michele Marchetti, "Selling in China? Go Slowly," *Sales & Marketing Management,* January 1997, pp. 35–36.

[28] "And Never the Twain Shall Meet . . ." *The Economist,* March 29, 1997, pp. 67–68.

Task-Related Information Exchange.   Only when nontask sounding is complete and a trusting personal relationship established, should business be introduced. American executives are advised to let the foreign counterpart decide when such substantive negotiations should begin, to let them bring up business.

A *task-related information exchange* implies a two-way communication process. However, observations suggest that when Americans meet executives from some cultures across the negotiation table, the information flow is unidirectional. Japanese, Chinese, and Russian negotiators all appear to ask "thousands" of questions and to give little feedback. The barrage of questions severely tests American negotiators' patience, and the latter causes them great anxiety. Both can add up to much longer stays in these countries, which means higher travel expenses.

Certainly it is an excellent negotiation tactic to drain information from one's negotiation counterparts. But the oft-reported behaviors of Chinese, Japanese, and Russians may not necessarily represent a sophisticated negotiation ploy. Indeed, reference to Exhibit 19–2 provides some hints that differences in conversational styles—silent periods occurred more frequently in negotiations in all three cultures—may be part of the explanation. Indeed, in careful studies of conversational patterns of Americans negotiating with Japanese, the Americans seem to fill the silent periods and do most of the talking.[29] These results suggest that American negotiators must take special care to keep their mouths shut and let foreign counterparts give them information.

Exchanging information across language barriers can be quite difficult as well. Most of us understand about 80–90 percent of what our same-culture spouses or roommates say—that means 10–20 percent is misunderstood or misheard. That latter percentage goes up dramatically when someone is speaking a second language, no matter the highest fluency levels and length of acquaintance. And when the second language capability is limited, entire conversations may be totally misunderstood. Using multiple communication channels during presentations—writing, exhibits, speaking, repetition—works to minimize the inevitable errors.

In many cultures negative feedback is very difficult to obtain. In high-context cultures like Mexico and Japan, speakers are reluctant to voice objections lest they damage the all-important personal relationships. Some languages themselves are by nature indirect and indefinite. English is relatively clear, but translations from languages like Japanese can leave much to be understood. In more collectivistic cultures like China, negotiators may be reluctant to speak for the decision-making group they represent, or they may not even know how the group feels about a particular proposal. All such problems suggest the importance of having natives of customer countries on your negotiation team and/or spending extra time in business and informal entertainment settings trying to understand better the information provided by foreign clients and partners. Alternatively, low-context German executives often complain that American presentations include too much "fluff"—they are interested in information only, not the hyperbole and hedges so common in American speech. Negative feedback from Germans can seem brutally frank to higher-context Americans.

A final point of potential conflict in information exchange has to do with first offers. Price padding varies across cultures, and Americans' first offers tend to come in relatively close to what they really want. "A million dollars is the goal, let's start at $1.2 million," seems about right to most Americans. Implicit in such a first offer is the hope that things will get done quickly. Americans do not expect to move far from first offers. Negotiators in many other countries do not share the goal of finishing quickly, however. In places like China, Brazil, or Spain the expectation is for a relatively longer period of haggling, and first offers are more aggressive to reflect these expectations. "If the goal is one million, we better start at two," makes sense there. Americans react to such aggressive first offers in one of two ways: They either laugh or get mad.

---

[29] Michael Kamins, Wesley Johnston, and John L. Graham, *Journal of International Marketing*, 1998.

CROSSING BORDERS 19–4

Who Adapts to Whom?

It depends on the capabilities on both sides of the table and power relationships.

For their discussions over construction of the tunnel under the English Channel, British and French representatives agreed to partition talks and alternate the site between Paris and London. At each site, the negotiators were to use established, local ways, including the language. The two approaches were thus clearly punctuated by time and space. Although each side was able to use its customary approach some of the time, it used the script of the other culture the rest of the time.

At the outset of a meeting to discuss the telecommunications policies of France's Ministry of Industry and Tourism, the minister's chief of staff and his American visitor each voiced concern about speaking in the other's native language. They expressed confidence in their listening capabilities and lacked immediate access to an interpreter, so they agreed to proceed by each speaking in his own language. Their discussion went on for an hour that way, the American speaking in English to the Frenchman, and the Frenchman speaking French to the American.

Source: Reprinted from "Negotiating with Romans—Part 2," by Stephen E. Weiss, *Sloan Management Review,* 35(3), Spring 1994, pp. 85–99, by permission of publisher. Copyright 1994 by Sloan Management Review Association. All Rights Reserved.

And when foreign counterparts' second offers reflect deep discounts, Americans' ire increases.

A good example of this problem regards an American CEO shopping for a European plant site. When he selected a $20 million plot in Ireland, the Spanish real estate developer he had visited earlier called wondering why the American had not asked for a lower price for the Madrid site before choosing Dublin. He told the Spaniard that his first offer "wasn't even in the ball park." He wasn't laughing when the Spaniard then offered to beat the Irish price. In fact, the American executive was quite mad. A potentially good deal was forgone because of different expectations about first offers. Yes, numbers were exchanged, but information was not. Aggressive first offers made by foreigners should be met with questions, not anger.

Persuasion. In Japan, a clear separation does not exist between task-related information exchange and persuasion. The two stages tend to blend together as each side defines and refines its needs and preferences. Much time is spent in the task-related exchange of information, leaving little to "argue" about during the persuasion stage. Alternatively, Americans tend to lay their cards on the table and hurry through the information exchange to persuasion. After all, the persuasion is the heart of the matter. Why hold a meeting unless someone's mind is to be changed? A key aspect of sales training in the U.S. is "handling objections." So the goal in information exchange among Americans is to quickly get those objections out in the open so they can be handled.

This handling can mean providing clients with more information. It can also mean getting mean. As suggested by Exhibit 19–2, Americans make threats and issue warnings in negotiations. They do not use such tactics often, but negotiators in other cultures use such tactics even less frequently and in different circumstances.[30] For example, notice how infrequently the Mexican and English-speaking Canadians used threats and

---

[30] Roger Volkema, "Perceptual Differences in Appropriateness and Likelihood of Use of Negotiation Behaviors: A Cross-Cultural Analysis," *The International Executive,* 39(3), May–June 1997, pp. 335–350.

warnings in the simulated negotiations. In China the use of such aggressive negotiation tactics can result in the loss of face and the destruction of important personal relationships.[31] Such tough tactics may be used in Japan, but by buyers only and usually only in informal circumstances—not at the formal negotiation table. Americans also get mad during negotiations and express emotions that may be completely inappropriate in foreign countries. Such emotional outbursts may be seen as infantile or even barbaric behavior in places like Hong Kong and Bangkok.

The most powerful persuasive tactic is actually asking more questions. Foreign counterparts can be politely asked to explain why they must have delivery in two months or why they must have a 10 percent discount. Chester Karrass, in his still useful book *The Negotiation Game,*[32] suggests that it is "smart to be a little dumb" in business negotiations. Repeat questions, for example, "I didn't completely understand what you meant—can you please explain that again?" If clients or potential business partners have good answers, then perhaps it is best to compromise on the issue. Often, however, under close and repeated scrutiny their answers are not very good. When their weak position is exposed, they are obliged to concede. Questions can elicit key information, being the most powerful yet passive persuasive devices. Indeed, the use of questions is a favored Japanese tactic, one they use with great effect on Americans.

Finally, third parties and informal channels of communication are the indispensable media of persuasion in many countries. Meetings in restaurants and/or with references and mutual friends who originally provided introductions may be used to handle difficult problems with partners in other countries. The value of such informal settings and trusted intermediaries is greatest when problems are emotion laden. They provide a means for simultaneously delivering difficult messages and saving face. Although American managers may eschew such "behind the scenes" approaches, they are standard practice in many countries.

Concessions and Agreement.   Comments made previously about the importance of writing down concession-making strategies and differences in decision-making styles—sequential versus holistic—are pertinent here. Americans often make concessions early, expecting foreign counterparts to reciprocate. However, in many cultures no concessions are made until the end of the negotiations. Americans often get frustrated and express anger when foreign clients and partners are simply following a different approach to concession making, one that can also work quite well when both sides understand what is going on.

After Negotiations

Contracts between American firms are often longer than 100 pages and include carefully worded clauses regarding every aspect of the agreement. American lawyers go to great lengths to protect their companies against all circumstances, contingencies, and actions of the other party. The best contracts are ones written so tightly that the other party would not think of going to court to challenge any provision. The American adversarial system requires such contracts.

In most other countries, particularly the high-context ones, legal systems are not depended upon to settle disputes. Indeed, the term "disputes" does not reflect how a business relationship should work. Each side should be concerned about mutual benefits of the relationship, and therefore should consider the interests of the other. Consequently, in places like Japan written contracts are very short—two to three pages—are purposely loosely written, and primarily contain comments on principles of the relationship. From the Japanese point of view, the American emphasis on tight contracts is tantamount to planning the divorce before the wedding.

---

[31] Robert R. Gesteland, "Business Negotiation in Greater China," *Trade & Culture,* May–July, 1997, pp. 37–38.

[32] Chester Karrass, *The Negotiation Game* (New York: Crowell, 1970).

Women can get the job done. Indeed, U.S. Trade Representative Charlene Barshefsky has been quite effective in her negotiations with foreign counterparts. Her successes in reducing foreign trade barriers has earned her the nickname, "The Velvet Crowbar." (REUTERS/Will Burgess/ ARCHIVE PHOTOS)

In other countries such as China contracts are more a description of what business partners view their respective responsibilities to be. For complicated business relationships they may be quite long and detailed. However, their purpose is different from the American understanding. When circumstances change, then responsibilities must also be adjusted, despite the provisions of the signed contract. The notion of *enforcing* a contract in China makes little sense.

Informality being a way of life in the United States, even the largest contracts between companies are often sent through the mail for signature. In America, ceremony is considered a waste of time and money. But when a major agreement is reached with foreign companies, their executives may expect a formal signing ceremony involving CEOs of the respective companies. American companies are wise to accommodate such expectations.

Finally, follow-up communications are an important part of business negotiations with partners and clients from most foreign countries. Particularly in high-context cultures, where personal relationships are crucial, high-level executives must stay in touch with their counterparts. Letters, pictures, and mutual visits remain important long after contracts are signed. Indeed, "warm" relationships at the top often prove to be the best medicine for any problems that may arise in the future.

Conclusions

Despite the litany of potential pitfalls facing international negotiators, things are getting better. The "innocents abroad" and cowboy stereotypes of American managers are becoming less accurate. Likewise, we hope it is obvious that the stereotypes of the reticent

Japanese or the pushy Brazilian evinced in the chapter may no longer hold so true. Experience levels are going up worldwide, and individual personalities are important. So you can find talkative Japanese, quiet Brazilians, and effective American negotiators. But culture still does, and always will, count. Hopefully, it is fast becoming the natural behavior of American managers to take it into account.

English author Rudyard Kipling said some one hundred years ago: "Oh, East is East, and West is West, and never the twain shall meet." Since then most have imbued his words with an undeserved pessimism. Some even wrongly say he was wrong.[33] The problem is that not many have bothered to read his entire poem, *The Ballad of East and West:*

> Oh, East is East, and West is West, and never the twain shall meet,
> Till Earth and Sky stand presently at God's great Judgment Seat;
> But there is neither East nor West, border, nor breed, nor birth,
> When two strong men stand face to face, though they come from the ends of the earth!

The poem can stand some editing for these more modern times. Now should be included the other directions, North is North and South is South. And the last line properly should read, "When two strong *people* stand face to face." But Kipling's positive sentiment remains. Differences between countries and cultures, no matter how difficult, can be worked out when people talk to each other in face-to-face settings. Kipling rightly places the responsibility for international cooperation not on companies or governments, but instead directly on the shoulders of individual managers, present and future, like you. Work hard!

Summary

Because styles of business negotiations vary substantially around the world, it is important to take cultural difference into account when meeting clients, customers, and business partners across the international negotiation table. In addition to cultural factors, negotiators' personalities and backgrounds also influence their behavior. Great care should be taken to get to know the *individuals* that represent client and customer companies. Cultural stereotypes can be quite misleading.

Four kinds of problems frequently arise during international business negotiations—problems at the level of—(1) language, (2) nonverbal behaviors, (3) values, and (4) thinking and decision-making processes. Foreign language skills are an essential tool of the international negotiator. Nonverbal behaviors vary dramatically across cultures, and because their influence is often below our level of awareness, problems at this level can be quite serious. While most Americans value objectivity, competitiveness, equality, and punctuality, many foreign executives may not. As for thinking and decision making, Western business executives tend to address complex negotiations by breaking deals down to smaller issues and settling them sequentially; in many Eastern cultures a more holistic approach is taken in discussions.

Much care must be taken in selecting negotiation teams to represent companies in meetings with foreigners. Listening skills, influence at headquarters, and a willingness to use team assistance are important negotiator traits. Americans should be careful to try to match foreign negotiation teams in both numbers and seniority. The importance of cross-cultural training and investments in careful preparations cannot be overstated. Situational factors such as the location for meetings and the time allowed must also be carefully considered and managed.

All around the world business negotiations involve four steps (1) nontask sounding, (2) task-related information exchange, (3) persuasion, (4) concessions and agreement. The time spent on each step can vary considerably from country to country. Americans spend little time on nontask sounding or getting to know foreign counterparts. Particularly in high-context cultures, it is important to let the customer bring up business when they feel comfortable with the personal relationship. Task-related information goes quickly in the U.S. as well. In other countries such as Japan the most time is spent on the second stage, and careful understandings of partners are focused upon. Persuasion is the most important part of negotiations from the American perspective. Aggressive persuasive tactics (threats and warnings) are used frequently. Such persuasive tactics, while they may work well in some cultures, will cause serious problems in others. Finally, because American tend to be deal oriented, more care will have to be taken in follow-up communications with foreign clients and partners who put more emphasis on long-term business relationships.

---

[33] Michael Elliot, "Killing off Kipling," *Newsweek*, December 29, 1997, pp. 52–55.

Questions

1. Define:
   BATNA
   nontask sounding
   task-related information exchange

2. Why can cultural stereotypes be dangerous? Give some examples.

3. List three ways that culture influences negotiation behavior.

4. Describe the kinds of problems that usually come up during international business negotiations.

5. Why are foreign language skills important for international negotiators?

6. Describe three cultural differences in nonverbal behaviors and explain how they might cause problems in international business negotiations.

7. Why is time an important consideration in international business negotiations?

8. What can be different about how a Japanese manager might address a complex negotiation compared to an American negotiator?

9. What are the most important considerations in selecting a negotiation team? Give examples.

10. What kinds of training are most useful for international business negotiators?

11. Name three aspects of negotiation situations which might be manipulated before talks begin. Suggest how this might be done.

12. Explain why Americans spend so little time on nontask sounding and Brazilians so much.

13. Why is it difficult to get negative feedback from counterparts in many foreign countries? Give examples.

14. Why won't getting mad work in Mexico or Japan?

15. Why are questions the most useful persuasive tactic?

THE COUNTRY NOTEBOOK—A GUIDE FOR DEVELOPING A MARKETING PLAN

The first stage in the planning process is a preliminary country analysis. The marketer needs basic information to (1) evaluate a country-market's potential; (2) identify problems that would eliminate a country from further consideration; (3) identify aspects of the country's environment that need further study; (4) evaluate the components of the marketing mix for possible adaptation: and (5) develop a strategic marketing plan. One further use of the information collected in the preliminary analysis is as a basis for a country notebook.

Many companies, large and small, have a *country notebook* for each country in which they do business. The country notebook contains information a marketer should be aware of when making decisions involving a specific country-market. As new information is collected, the country notebook is continually updated by the country or product manager. Whenever a marketing decision is made involving a country, the country notebook is the first data base consulted. New product introductions, changes in advertising programs, and other marketing program decisions begin with the country notebook. It also serves as a quick introduction for new personnel assuming responsibility for a country-market.

This section presents four separate guidelines for collection and analysis of market data and preparation of a country notebook: (1) guideline for cultural analysis; (2) guideline for economic analysis; (3) guideline for market audit and competitive analysis; and (4) guideline for preliminary marketing plan. These guidelines suggest the kinds of information a marketer can gather to enhance planning.

The points in each of the guidelines are general. They are designed to provide direction to areas to explore for relevant data. In each guideline, specific points must be adapted to reflect a company's products. The decision as to the appropriateness of specific data and the depth of coverage depends on company objectives, product characteristics, and the country-market. Some points in the guidelines are unimportant for some countries and/or some products and should be ignored. Preceding chapters of this book provide specific content suggestions for the topics in each guideline.

I. Cultural Analysis

The data suggested in the cultural analysis include information that helps the marketer make market planning decisions. However, its application extends beyond product/market analysis to an important source of information for someone interested in understanding business customs and other important cultural features of the country.

The information in this analysis must be more than a collection of facts. Whoever is responsible for the preparation of this material should attempt to interpret the meaning of cultural information. That is, how does the information help in understanding the effect on the market? For example, the fact that almost all the populations of Italy and Mexico are Catholic is an interesting statistic but not nearly as useful as understanding the effect of Catholicism on values, beliefs, and other aspects of market behavior. Furthermore, even though both countries are predominantly Catholic, the influence of their individual and unique interpretation and practice of Catholicism can result in important differences in market behavior.

Guidelines

    I. Introduction.
        Include short profiles of the company, the product to be exported, and the country with which you wish to trade.
   II. Brief discussion of the country's relevant history.
  III. Geographical setting.
       A. Location.
       B. Climate.
       C. Topography.

IV. Social institutions.
    A. Family.
        1. The nuclear family.
        2. The extended family.
        3. Dynamics of the family.
            a. Parental roles.
            b. Marriage and courtship.
        4. Female/male roles (are they changing or static?).
    B. Education.
        1. The role of education in society.
            a. Primary education (quality, levels of development, etc.).
            b. Secondary education (quality, levels of development, etc.).
            c. Higher education (quality, levels of development, etc.).
        2. Literacy rates.
    C. Political system.
        1. Political structure.
        2. Political parties.
        3. Stability of government.
        4. Special taxes.
        5. Role of local government.
    D. Legal system.
        1. Organization of the judiciary system.
        2. Code, common, socialist, or Islamic-law country?
        3. Participation in patents, trademarks, and other conventions.
    E. Social organizations.
        1. Group behavior.
        2. Social classes.
        3. Clubs, other organizations.
        4. Race, ethnicity, and subcultures.
    F. Business customs and practices.
V. Religion and aesthetics.
    A. Religion and other belief systems.
        1. Orthodox doctrines and structures.
        2. Relationship with the people.
        3. Which religions are prominent?
        4. Membership of each religion.
        5. Are there any powerful or influential cults?
    B. Aesthetics.
        1. Visual arts (fine arts, plastics, graphics, public art, colors, etc.).
        2. Music.
        3. Drama, ballet, and other performing arts.
        4. Folklore and relevant symbols.
VI. Living conditions.
    A. Diet and nutrition.
        1. Meat and vegetable consumption rates.
        2. Typical meals.
        3. Malnutrition rates.
        4. Foods available.
    B. Housing.
        1. Types of housing available.
        2. Do most people own or rent?
        3. Do most people live in one-family dwellings or with other families?
    C. Clothing.
        1. National dress.
        2. Types of clothing worn at work.

    D. Recreation, sports, and other leisure activities.
        1. Types available and in demand.
        2. Percentage of income spent on such activities.
    E. Social security.
    F. Health care.
  VII. Language.
    A. Official language(s).
    B. Spoken versus written language(s).
    C. Dialects.
  VIII. Executive summary.

After completing all of the other sections, prepare a *two-page* (maximum length) summary of the major points and place it at the front of the report. The purpose of an executive summary is to give the reader a brief glance at the critical points of your report. Those aspects of the culture a reader should know to do business in the country but would not be expected to know or would find different based on his or her SRC should be included in this summary.

  IX. Sources of information.
  X. Appendixes.

II. Economic Analysis

The reader may find the data collected for the economic analysis guideline are more straightforward than for the cultural analysis guideline. There are two broad categories of information in this guideline: general economic data that serve as a basis for an evaluation of the economic soundness of a country; and, information on channels of distribution and media availability. As mentioned earlier, the guideline focuses only on broad categories of data and must be adapted to particular company/product needs.

Guidelines

  I. Introduction.
  II. Population.
    A. Total.
        1. Growth rates.
        2. Number of live births.
        3. Birthrates.
    B. Distribution of population.
        1. Age.
        2. Sex.
        3. Geographic areas (urban, suburban, and rural density and concentration).
        4. Migration rates and patterns.
        5. Ethnic groups.
  III. Economic statistics and activity.
    A. Gross national product (GNP or GDP).
        1. Total.
        2. Rate of growth (real GNP or GDP).
    B. Personal income per capita.
    C. Average family income.
    D. Distribution of wealth.
        1. Income classes.
        2. Proportion of the population in each class.
        3. Is the distribution distorted?

    E. Minerals and resources.

    F. Surface transportation.

        1. Modes.

        2. Availability.

        3. Usage rates.

        4. Ports.

    G. Communication systems.

        1. Types.

        2. Availability.

        3. Usage rates.

    H. Working conditions.

        1. Employer–employee relations.

        2. Employee participation.

        3. Salaries and benefits.

    I. Principal industries.

        1. What proportion of the GNP does each industry contribute?

        2. Ratio of private to publicly owned industries.

    J. Foreign investment.

        1. Opportunities?

        2. Which industries?

    K. International trade statistics.

        1. Major exports.

            a. Dollar value.

            b. Trends.

        2. Major imports.

            a. Dollar value.

            b. Trends.

        3. Balance-of-payments situation.

            a. Surplus or deficit?

            b. Recent trends.

        4. Exchange rates.

            a. Single or multiple exchange rates?

            b. Current rate of exchange.

            c. Trends.

    L. Trade restrictions.

        1. Embargoes.

        2. Quotas.

        3. Import taxes.

        4. Tariffs.

        5. Licensing.

        6. Customs duties.

    M. Extent of economic activity not included in cash income activities.

        1. Countertrades.

            a. Products generally offered for countertrading.

            b. Types of countertrades requested (i.e., barter, counterpurchase, etc.).

        2. Foreign aid received.

    N. Labor force.

        1. Size.

        2. Unemployment rates.

    O. Inflation rates.

IV. Developments in science and technology.

    A. Current technology available (computers, machinery, tools, etc.).

    B. Percentage of GNP invested in research and development.

    C. Technological skills of the labor force and general population.

V. Channels of distribution (macro analysis).

This section reports data on all channel middlemen available within the market. Later, you will select a specific channel as part of your distribution strategy.

A. Middlemen.
1. Retailers.
a. Number of retailers.
b. Typical size of retail outlets.
c. Customary markup for various classes of goods.
d. Methods of operation (cash/credit).
e. Scale of operation (large/small).
f. Role of chain stores, department stores, and specialty shops.
2. Wholesale middlemen.
a. Number and size.
b. Customary markup for various classes of goods.
c. Method of operation (cash/credit).
3. Import/export agents.
4. Warehousing.
5. Penetration of urban and rural markets.

VI. Media.

This section reports data on all media available within the country/market. Later, you will select specific media as part of the promotional mix/strategy.

A. Availability of media.
B. Costs.
1. Television.
2. Radio.
3. Print.
4. Other media (cinema, outdoor, etc.).
C. Agency assistance.
D. Coverage of various media.
E. Percentage of population reached by each of the media.

VII. Executive summary.

After completing the research for this report, prepare a two-page (maximum) summary of the major economic points and place it at the front.

VIII. Sources of information.

IX. Appendixes.

III. Market Audit and Competitive Market Analysis

Of the guidelines presented, this is the most product- or brand-specific. Information in the other guidelines is general in nature, focusing on product categories, whereas data in this guideline are brand-specific and are used to determine competitive market conditions and market potential.

Two different components of the planning process are reflected in this guideline. Information in Parts I and II, Cultural Analysis and Economic Analysis, serve as the basis for an evaluation of the product/brand in a specific country market. Information in this guideline provides an estimate of market potential and an evaluation of the strengths and weaknesses of competitive marketing efforts. The data generated in this step are used to determine the extent of adaptation of the company's marketing mix necessary for successful market entry and to develop the final step, the action plan.

The detailed information needed to complete this guideline is not necessarily available without conducting a thorough marketing research investigation. Thus, another purpose of this part of the country notebook is to identify the correct questions to ask in a formal market study.

Guidelines

  I. Introduction.

  II. The product.

    A. Evaluate the product as an innovation as it is perceived by the intended market.

      1. Relative advantage.

      2. Compatibility.

      3. Complexity.

      4. Trialability.

      5. Observability.

    B. Major problems and resistances to product acceptance based on the preceding evaluation.

  III. The market.

    A. Describe the market(s) in which the product is to be sold.

      1. Geographical region(s).

      2. Forms of transportation and communication available in that (those) region(s).

      3. Consumer buying habits.

        a. Product-use patterns.

        b. Product feature preferences.

        c. Shopping habits.

      4. Distribution of the product.

        a. Typical retail outlets.

        b. Product sales by other middlemen.

      5. Advertising and promotion.

        a. Advertising media usually used to reach your target market(s).

        b. Sales promotions customarily used (sampling, coupons, etc.).

      6. Pricing strategy.

        a. Customary markups.

        b. Types of discounts available.

    B. Compare and contrast your product and the competition's product(s).

      1. Competitor's product(s).

        a. Brand name.

        b. Features.

        c. Package.

      2. Competitor's prices.

      3. Competitor's promotion and advertising methods.

      4. Competitor's distribution channels.

    C. Market size.

      1. Estimated industry sales for the planning year.

      2. Estimated sales for your company for the planning year.

    D. Government participation in the marketplace.

      1. Agencies that can help you.

      2. Regulations you must follow.

  IV. Executive summary.

    Based on your analysis of the market, briefly summarize (two-page maximum) the major problems and opportunities requiring attention in your marketing mix, and place the summary at the front of the report.

  V. Sources of information.

  VI. Appendixes.

IV. Preliminary Marketing Plan

Information gathered in Guidelines I through III serves as the basis for developing a marketing plan for your product/brand in a target market. How the problems and opportunities that surfaced in the preceding steps are overcome and/or exploited to produce maximum sales/profits are presented here. The action plan reflects, in your judgment, the most effective means of marketing your product in a country market. Budgets, expected profits and/or losses, and additional resources necessary to implement the proposed plan are also presented.

Guidelines

I. The marketing plan.
   A. Marketing objectives.
      1. Target market(s) (specific description of the market).
      2. Expected sales 20—.
      3. Profit expectations 20—.
      4. Market penetration and coverage.
   B. Product adaptation, or modification—Using the product component model as your guide, indicate how your product can be adapted for the market.
      1. Core component.
      2. Packaging component.
      3. Support services component.
   C. Promotion mix.
      1. Advertising.
         a. Objectives.
         b. Media mix.
         c. Message.
         d. Costs.
      2. Sales promotions.
         a. Objectives.
         b. Coupons.
         c. Premiums.
         d. Costs.
      3. Personal selling.
      4. Other promotional methods.
   D. Distribution: From origin to destination.
      1. Port selection.
         a. Origin port.
         b. Destination port.
      2. Mode selection: Advantages/disadvantages of each mode.
         a. Railroads.
         b. Air carriers.
         c. Ocean carriers.
         d. Motor carriers.
      3. Packing.
         a. Marking and labeling regulations.
         b. Containerization.
         c. Costs.
      4. Documentation required.
         a. Bill of lading.
         b. Dock receipt.
         c. Air bill.
         d. Commercial invoice.

e. Pro forma invoice.
f. Shipper's export declaration.
g. Statement of origin.
h. Special documentation.
5. Insurance claims.
6. Freight forwarder.
   If your company does not have a transportation or traffic management department, then consider using a freight forwarder. There are distinct advantages and disadvantages to hiring one.
E. Channels of distribution (micro analysis).
   This section presents details about the specific types of distribution in your marketing plan.
1. Retailers.
   a. Type and number of retail stores.
   b. Retail markups for products in each type of retail store.
   c. Methods of operation for each type (cash/credit).
   d. Scale of operation for each type (small/large).
2. Wholesale middlemen.
   a. Type and number of wholesale middlemen.
   b. Markup for class of products by each type.
   c. Methods of operation for each type (cash/credit).
   d. Scale of operation (small/large).
3. Import/export agents.
4. Warehousing.
   a. Type.
   b. Location.
F. Price determination.
1. Cost of the shipment of goods.
2. Transportation costs.
3. Handling expenses.
   a. Pier charges.
   b. Wharfage fees.
   c. Loading and unloading charges.
4. Insurance costs.
5. Customs duties.
6. Import taxes and value-added tax.
7. Wholesale and retail markups and discounts.
8. Company's gross margins.
9. Retail price.
G. Terms of sale.
1. Ex works, fob, fas, c&f, cif.
2. Advantages/disadvantages of each.
H. Methods of payment.
1. Cash in advance.
2. Open accounts.
3. Consignment sales.
4. Sight, time, or date drafts.
5. Letters of credit.
II. Pro forma financial statements and budgets.
A. Marketing budget.
1. Selling expense.
2. Advertising/promotion expense.
3. Distribution expense.
4. Product cost.
5. Other costs.
B. Pro forma annual profit and loss statement (first year and fifth year).

III. Resource requirements.
   A. Finances.
   B. Personnel.
   C. Production capacity.
IV. Executive summary.
   After completing the research for this report, prepare a two-page (maximum) summary of the major points of your successful marketing plan, and place it at the front of the report.
V. Sources of information.
VI. Appendixes.

The intricacies of international operations and the complexity of the environment within which the international marketer must operate create an extraordinary demand for information. When operating in foreign markets, the need for thorough information as a substitute for uninformed opinion is equally as important as it is in domestic marketing. Sources of information needed to develop the country notebook and answer other marketing questions are discussed in Chapter 8 and appendix.

Summary

Market-oriented firms build strategic market plans around company objectives, markets, and the competitive environment. Planning for marketing can be complicated even for one country, but when a company is doing business internationally, the problems are multiplied. Company objectives may vary from market to market and from time to time; the structure of international markets also changes periodically and from country to country; and the competitive, governmental, and economic parameters affecting market planning are in a constant state of flux. These variations require international marketing executives to be specially flexible and creative in their approach to strategic marketing planning.

AN OVERVIEW

Outline of Cases

Case 1–1
Selling U.S. Ice Cream in Korea

Effect of Controllable and Uncontrollable Factors

The call from Hong Kong was intriguing: Go to South Korea and be the franchisee of an American premium ice cream to capitalize on the Koreans' new disposable income and their growing appetite for Western fast-food products.

Within six months of my application, the government granted me permission to bring the ice cream, Hobson's, to Seoul with only two nontariff trade conditions: Make my ice cream in Korea after a year of operation and at the same time take on a Korean partner who had at least a 25 percent stake in the company.

I agreed, and chose Itaewon for my site, figuring that between the Korean bar girls and the U.S. Army up the road it would give me a good cross-section of East and West.

The Early Years—Getting Started. Almost a half-year after start-up, I still thought it was a timely idea but it certainly hadn't been easy pickings. The Korean bar girls, for instance, thought my ice cream was too expensive, and Koreans in general are highly suspicious of new products. Government red tape has always been horrendous and foreigners are not welcome.

But because internationalization and economic progress are hard to separate, Seoul had been coming to accept foreigners and their products as a necessary ingredient for their own growth.

The irony, however, is that Korean intransigence was not the only problem a Yankee entrepreneur faced here: Washington trade-bashing can take its toll as well. In the mid-1990s the U.S. government had been pressuring this country to raise the value of the won, to make Korean exports more expensive and U.S. imports less. On top of this was Congress's omnibus trade bill, which forces Korea to open its markets or face punitive sanctions on its own exports to the United States. Although these efforts were designed to help American traders like me, I have seen all too often how the best-laid political plans can actually make it more difficult for us to maintain a foothold in these countries.

In fairness, it also must be said that some American companies often bring this on themselves. Evidence indicates that American companies are badly outclassed by their failure to take Asian markets seriously and a tendency to follow the laws of least resistance by concentrating on selling within the borders of the United States.

American companies have tried to cheat by getting Congress to force not only Korea, but also Japan, Hong Kong, Singapore, and other countries to raise the value of their currency. Those forces drove the won to a value of 590 to 600 won for one dollar by the end of 1994, when just two years earlier $1 would buy 890 won. I thus found myself importing more dollars just to stay even with my original projections when it was 800 won to the dollar. In other words, it cost me 16 percent more dollars just to get started operating, and that was the margin I was hoping I could apply toward profits. Any price increase to recoup losses risked pricing my ice cream out of the Korean market.

Another result of exchange-rate jiggling was inflation. This was a by-product of the won's strengthening against the dollar, reflected in the many outside investment dollars trying to find a home in Korea's currency and stock market.

Consequently, everything came with a price tag that equaled or exceeded what one could buy in the United States. On top of this were import taxes, tariffs, and nontariff barriers on imported capital goods and, in my case, finished ice cream. Duties, for example, ranged from 20–38 percent additional money.

U.S. trade bullying also fans the flames of anti-Americanism here, and American business pays for that. Even though Washington had some legitimate gripes about closed Korean markets, Koreans felt that they were being pushed around and that the United States didn't recognize the great strides they had made. For me this resentment translated into vandalism of my storefront property, such as knocked-down signs, broken patio tables and chairs, pane-glass windows smeared with soda and dirt, and even human feces left on my doorstep. It also manifested itself by Koreans staying away from buying my ice cream.

The Korean bureaucracy seemed to share the suspicion of foreigners trying to do business here. When I made arrangements for the arrival of my first ice cream shipment into Pusan a month before the scheduled opening of my store, the authorities informed me that they couldn't care less about my ice cream and that I was illegally in the country. The upshot was my lawyers spent three weeks trying to persuade some second-echelon bureaucrat that I was here under valid reasons, to no avail. Desperate, and a day away from packing my bags and buying a one-way ticket to California, I called the one friend I had in the government. By a one-in-a-thousand chance, he knew the second-echelon bureaucrat and was able to clear away his "mental block" about me.

But this was a fluke. I have no doubt that the mental block was the Korean dairy farmers complaining about foreign imports of ice cream, which in turn was part of the bigger picture of pressure that Korean agriculture was receiving from U.S. trade negotiators to open its market.

Finally, coinciding with the Olympic Games in Seoul the Korean economy really began to take off. By the mid-1990s South Koreans were buying more products from all over the world. The efforts of our trade negotiators and trade policies apparently were finally having some effect. A few American companies like mine were at last enjoying moderate successes in South Korea, but some were still not.

The question was whether all American companies could take advantage of the "much broader access" into the Korean market. Some Korean business leaders criticized the level of effort of some American managers. Woo Choong Kim, founder of the Daewoo business empire, said: "In the old days, Americans worked hard to challenge new frontiers. But as their economy got mature, they became more interested in nice houses, jogging, and having a good time than in doing business. How can you compete without dedication? It is not the management system that is not working in American companies, it is the people not working hard."

Adapted from Jay R. Tunney, "U.S. Ice Cream Fares Poorly in Korea," *The Asian Wall Street Journal Weekly,* February 13, 1989, p. 13; Henry Shyn, "Doing Business the Korean Way," *Trade & Culture,* March–April 1995, pp. 28–29; and "Harmful Bacteria Found in More U.S. Ice Cream Imported by South Korea," *Associated Press,* November 3, 1997.

Indeed, one U.S. Commerce Secretary lamented at the time that although Americans are great at coming up with new inventions, they "are not good at getting them into products to be sold."

Establishing a Beachhead.   For example, in the early 1990s Korean executives were almost throwing machine-tool and welding-machine orders at American companies—with the U.S. concerns dropping the ball almost every time. The reasons given by Koreans were various: inflexibility about the terms of a contract, poor service, or just plain not trying hard enough (e.g., not working on Saturdays). The one American company that did measure up was Varian Associates. Its management team had projected that the bulk of world manufacturing would be done in Asia in the next few decades and that U.S. companies were missing out on Asia's rush to outfit the factories building more and more of the world's cars, computers, and fast-food plants.

Varian installed 18 Korean nationals and several expatriates in a Seoul office to market its equipment and match Japanese service. Unlike many other American companies, Varian had accommodated the Korean culture and way of doing business by establishing a beachhead presence in one of the world's fastest-growing markets.

Surviving the New Disasters.   For almost 10 years now the business partnership in South Korea has been rewarding. Yes, there have been ups and downs, but I myself have learned that it is important to be here and to learn their ways. In doing so, we have helped each other. The Korean company I chose to do business with, for example, is learning from me an ice cream-making technology and formula that enhances its competitiveness in that industry at home and abroad. I, in turn, am learning from my partner how to be competitive in Korea.

Despite what we have gained from our South Korean adventure two new problems challenge us now. First is the meltdown of the Korean won during the winter of 1997–98. In that time period the won's value halved from 860 to the dollar to 1710 to the dollar. This has proven to be a disaster for our imports of ice cream, and for our fellow American competitors as well. We are somewhat more competitive because part of our production is local, thank goodness. But the general consumers' reaction against imports in a time of financial crisis has made the whole ice cream category less appealing.

Then throw on top of that the contamination scare and our sales really tanked. This last problem got started in October 1997 when E. coli bacteria were discovered on the surface of some imported American beef here in South Korea. When Hong Kong authorities found bacteria contaminating American ice cream shipments there, Korean authorities began to check here as well. Sure enough, they found a different form of dangerous bacteria in one American brand. Now all brands are receiving more scrutiny from government health officials and concerned consumers alike.

Exhibit 1   The International Marketing Task

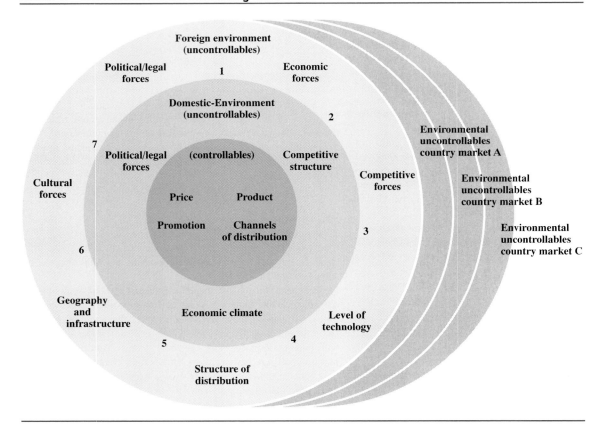

Questions

As a guide use Exhibit 1, and the description (as Exhibit 1–3) in Chapter 1, and do the following:

1. Identify each of the domestic and foreign uncontrollable elements that this U.S. ice cream franchisee encountered in Korea.

2. Describe how problems encountered with each uncontrollable element may have been avoided or compensated for had the element been recognized in the planning stage.

3. Identify other problems the franchisee may encounter in the future.

CASE 1–2
UNILEVER AND NESTLÉ—AN ANALYSIS

While Unilever and Nestlé have engaged in international marketing their entire corporate existence, they are very different companies in their approaches to international marketing and corporate philosophies. Both companies maintain very extensive Web sites. Your challenge in this case is to visit both Web sites, carefully read the information presented, and write a report comparing the two companies on the points that follow.

1. Philosophies on international marketing.
2. Corporate objectives.
3. Global coverage, that is, number of countries in which they do business.
4. Production facilities.

Unilever's Web site is **http://www.unilever.com** and Nestlé's is **http://www.nestle.com**.

5. Number of product categories and number of brands within each category.
6. Number of standardized versus global brands for each.
7. Product categories and brands where the two companies compete.
8. Brands that are standardized, that is, what is standardized in each brand and what is localized in each brand.
9. Product research centers.
10. Organization.
11. Environmental concerns.
12. Research and development.

After completing your analysis, write a brief statement about the area(s) where Unilever is stronger than Nestlé and vice versa, and where Unilever is weaker than Nestlé and vice versa.

CASE 1–3
NESTLÉ—THE INFANT FORMULA INCIDENT

Nestlé Alimentana of Vevey, Switzerland, one of the world's largest food-processing companies with worldwide sales of over $8 billion, has been the subject of an international boycott. For over 20 years, beginning with a Pan American Health Organization allegation, Nestlé has been directly or indirectly charged with involvement in the death of Third World infants. The charges re-

volve around the sale of infant feeding formula which allegedly is the cause for mass deaths of babies in the Third World.

In 1974 a British journalist published a report that suggested that powdered-formula manufacturers contributed to the death of Third World infants by hard-selling their products to people incapable of using them properly. The 28-page report accused the

This case is an update of "Nestlé in LDCs," a case written by J. Alex Murray, University of Windsor, Ontario, Canada, and Gregory M. Gazda and Mary J. Molenaar, University of San Diego. The case originally appeared in the 5th edition of this text.

The case draws from the following: "International Code of Marketing of Breastmilk Substitutes," World Health Organization, Geneva, 1981; *INFACT Newsletter,* Minneapolis, Minn., February 1979; John A. Sparks, "The Nestlé Controversy—Anatomy of a Boycott," Grove City, Pa., Public Policy Education Funds, Inc.; "Who Drafts a Marketing Code," *World Business Weekly,* January 19, 1981, p. 8; "A Boycott over Infant Formula," *Business Week,* April 23, 1979, p. 137; "The Battle over Bottle-Feeding," *World Press Review,* January 1980, p. 54; "Nestlé

and the Role of Infant Formula in Developing Countries: The Resolution of a Conflict" (Nestlé Company, 1985); "The Dilemma of Third World Nutrition" (Nestlé S.A., 1985), 20 pp.; Thomas V. Greer, "The Future of the International Code of Marketing of Breastmilk Substitutes: The Socio-Legal Context," *International Marketing Review,* Spring 1984, pp. 33–41; James C. Baker, "The International Infant Formula Controversy: A Dilemma in Corporate Social Responsibility," *Journal of Business Ethics,* no. 4 (1985), pp. 181–90; and Shawn Tully, "Nestlé Shows How to Gobble Markets," *Fortune,* January 16, 1989, p. 75. For a comprehensive and well-balanced review of the infant formula issue, see Thomas V. Greer, "International Infant Formula Marketing: The Debate Continues," *Advances in International Marketing* 4 (1990), pp. 207–25. For a discussion of the HIV/breast feeding complication see "Back to the Bottle?" *The Economist,* February 7, 1998, p. 50.

industry of encouraging mothers to give up breast feeding and use powdered milk formulas. The report was later published by the Third World Working Group, a lobby in support of less-developed countries. The pamphlet was entitled, "Nestlé Kills Babies," and accused Nestlé of unethical and immoral behavior.

Although there are several companies that market infant baby formula internationally, Nestlé received most of the attention. This incident raises several issues important to all multinational companies. Before addressing these issues, let's look more closely at the charges by the Infant Formula Action Coalition (INFACT) and others and the defense by Nestlé.

The Charges.   Most of the charges against infant formulas focus on the issue of whether advertising and marketing of such products have discouraged breast feeding among Third World mothers and have led to misuse of the products, thus contributing to infant malnutrition and death. Following are some of the charges made:

- A Peruvian nurse reported that formula had found its way to Amazon tribes deep in the jungles of northern Peru. There, where the only water comes from a highly contaminated river—that also serves as the local laundry and toilet—formula-fed babies came down with recurring attacks of diarrhea and vomiting.

- Throughout the Third World, many parents dilute the formula to stretch their supply. Some even believe the bottle itself has nutrient qualities and merely fill it with water. The result is extreme malnutrition.

- One doctor reported that in a rural area, one newborn male weighed 7 pounds. At four months of age, he weighed 5 pounds. His sister, aged 18 months, weighed 12 pounds, what one would expect a 4-month-old baby to weigh. She later weighed only 8 pounds. The children had never been breast-fed, and since birth their diets were basically bottle feeding. For a four-month baby, one tin of formula should have lasted just under three days. The mother said that one tin lasted two weeks to feed both children.

- In rural Mexico, the Philippines, Central America, and the whole of Africa, there has been a dramatic decrease in the incidence of breast feeding. Critics blame the decline largely on the intensive advertising and promotion of infant formula. Clever radio jingles extol the wonders of the "white man's powder that will make baby grow and glow." "Milk nurses" visit nursing mothers in hospitals and their homes and provide samples of formula. These activities encourage mothers to give up breast feeding and resort to bottle feeding because it is "the fashionable thing to do or because people are putting it to them that this is the thing to do."

The Defense.   The following points are made in defense of the marketing of baby formula in Third World countries:

- First, Nestlé argues that the company has never advocated bottle feeding instead of breast feeding. All its products carry a statement that breast feeding is best. The company states that it "believes that breast milk is the best food for infants and encourages breast feeding around the world as it has done for decades." The company offers as support of this statement one of Nestlé's oldest educational booklets on "Infant Feeding and Hygiene," which dates from 1913 and encourages breast feeding.

- However, the company does believe that infant formula has a vital role in proper infant nutrition as (1) a supplement, when the infant needs nutritionally adequate and appropriate foods in addition to breast milk and, (2) a substitute for breast milk when a mother cannot or chooses not to breast feed. One doctor reports, "Economically deprived and thus dietarily deprived mothers who give their children only breast milk are raising infants whose growth rates begin to slow noticeably at about the age of three months. These mothers then turn to supplemental feedings that are often harmful to children. These include herbal teas and concoctions of rice water or corn water and sweetened, condensed milk. These feedings can also be prepared with contaminated water and are served in unsanitary conditions."

- Mothers in developing nations often have dietary deficiencies. In the Philippines, a mother in a poor family who is nursing a child produces about a pint of milk daily. Mothers in the United States usually produce about a quart of milk each day. For both the Philippino and U.S. mothers, the milk produced is equally nutritious. The problem is that there is less of it for the Philippino baby. If the Philippino mother doesn't augment the child's diet, malnutrition develops.

- Many poor women in the Third World bottle feed because their work schedules in fields or factories will not permit breast feeding. The infant feeding controversy has largely to do with the gradual introduction of weaning foods during the period between three months and two years. The average well-nourished Western woman, weighing 20 to 30 pounds more than most women in less-developed countries, cannot feed only breast milk beyond five or six months. The claim that Third World women can breast feed exclusively for one or two years and have healthy, well-developed children is outrageous. Thus, all children beyond the ages of five to six months require supplemental feeding.

- Weaning foods can be classified as either native cereal gruels of millet or rice, or commercial manufactured milk formula. Traditional native weaning foods are usually made by mixing maize, rice, or millet flours with water and then cooking the mixture. Other weaning foods found in use are crushed crackers, sugar and water, and mashed bananas.

    There are two basic dangers to the use of native weaning foods. First, the nutritional quality of the native gruels is low. Second, microbiological contamination of the traditional weaning foods is a certainty in many Third World settings. The millet or the flour is likely to be contaminated, the water used in cooking will most certainly be contaminated, the cooking containers will be contaminated, and therefore, the native gruel, even after it is cooked, is frequently contaminated with colon bacilli, staph, and other dangerous bacteria. Moreover, large batches of gruel are often made and allowed to sit, inviting further contamination.

- Scientists recently compared the microbiological contamination of a local native gruel with ordinary reconstituted milk formula prepared under primitive conditions. They found both were contaminated to similar dangerous levels.

- The real nutritional problem in the Third World is not whether to give infants breast milk or formula; it is how to supplement mothers' milk with nutritionally adequate foods when they are needed. Finding adequate locally produced, nutritionally sound supplements to mothers' milk and teaching people how to prepare and use them safely is the issue. Only effective nutrition education along with improved sanitation and good food that people can afford will win the fight against dietary deficiencies in the Third World.

The Resolution.   In 1974, Nestlé, aware of changing social patterns in the developing world and the increased access to radio and television there, reviewed its marketing practices on a region-by-region basis. As a result, mass media advertising of infant formula began to be phased out immediately in certain markets and, by 1978, was banned worldwide by the company. Nestlé then undertook to carry out more comprehensive health education programs to ensure that an understanding of the proper use of their products reached mothers, particularly in rural areas.

"Nestlé fully supports the WHO (World Health Organization) Code. Nestlé will continue to promote breast feeding and ensure that its marketing practices do not discourage breast feeding anywhere. Our company intends to maintain a constructive dialogue with governments and health professionals in all the countries it serves with the sole purpose of servicing mothers and the health of babies."—this quote is from *Nestlé Discusses the Recommended WHO Infant Formula Code.*

In 1977, the Interfaith Center on Corporate Responsibility in New York compiled a case against formula-feeding in developing nations, and the Third World Institute launched a boycott against many Nestlé products. Its aim was to halt promotion of infant formulas in the Third World. The Infant Formula Action Coalition (IN-FACT, successor to the Third World Institute), along with several other world organizations, successfully lobbied the World Health Organization (WHO) to draft a code to regulate the advertising and marketing of infant formula in the Third World. In 1981, by a vote of 114–1 (three countries abstained and the United States was the only dissenting vote), 118 member nations of WHO endorsed a voluntary code. The eight-page code urged a worldwide ban on promotion and advertising of baby formula and called for a halt to distribution of free product samples and/or gifts to physicians who promoted the use of the formula as a substitute for breast milk.

In May 1981 Nestlé announced it would support the code and waited for individual countries to pass national codes that would then be put into effect. Unfortunately, very few such codes were forthcoming. By the end of 1983, only 25 of the 157 member nations of the WHO had established national codes.

Accordingly, Nestlé management determined it would have to apply the code in the absence of national legislation, and in February 1982 issued instructions to marketing personnel, delineating the company's best understanding of the code and what would have to be done to follow it.

In addition, in May 1982 Nestlé formed the Nestlé Infant Formula Audit Commission (NIFAC), chaired by former Senator Edmund J. Muskie, and asked the commission to review the company's instructions to field personnel to determine if they could be improved to better implement the code. At the same time, Nestlé continued its meetings with WHO and UNICEF (United Nations Children's Fund) to try to obtain the most accurate interpretation of the code.

NIFAC recommended several clarifications for the instructions that it believed would better interpret ambiguous areas of the code; in October 1982, Nestlé accepted those recommendations and issued revised instructions to field personnel.

Other issues within the code, such as the question of a warning statement, were still open to debate. Nestlé consulted extensively with WHO before issuing its label warning statement in October 1983, but there was still not universal agreement with it. Acting on WHO recommendations, Nestlé consulted with firms experienced and expert in developing and field-testing educational materials, so that it could ensure that those materials met the code.

When the International Nestlé Boycott Committee (INBC) listed its four points of difference with Nestlé, it again became a matter of interpretation of the requirements of the code. Here, meetings held by UNICEF proved invaluable, in that UNICEF agreed to define areas of differing interpretation—in some cases providing definitions contrary to both Nestlé's and INBC's interpretations.

It was the meetings with UNICEF in early 1984 that finally led to a joint statement by Nestlé and INBC on January 25. At that time, INBC announced its suspension of boycott activities, and Nestlé pledged its continued support of the WHO code.

Nestlé Supports WHO Code.   The company has a strong record of progress and support in implementing the WHO Code, including:

- Immediate support for the WHO Code, May 1981; and testimony to this effect before the U.S. Congress, June 1981.
- Issuance of instructions to all employees, agents, and distributors in February 1982 to implement the code in all Third World countries where Nestlé markets infant formula.
- Establishment of an audit commission, in accordance with Article 11.3 of the WHO Code, to ensure the company's compliance with the code. The commission, headed by Edmund S. Muskie, was composed of eminent clergy and scientists.
- Willingness to meet with concerned church leaders, international bodies, and organization leaders seriously concerned with Nestlé's application of the code.
- Issuance of revised instructions to Nestlé personnel, October 1982, as recommended by the Muskie committee to clarify and give further effect to the code.
- Consultation with WHO, UNICEF, and NIFAC on how to interpret the code and how best to implement specific provisions, including clarification by WHO/UNICEF of the definition of children who need to be fed breast milk substitutes, to aid in determining the need for supplies in hospitals.

Nestlé Policies.   In the early 1970s Nestlé began to review its infant formula marketing practices on a region-by-region basis. By 1978 the company had stopped all consumer advertising and direct sampling to mothers. Instructions to the field issued in February 1982 and clarified in the revised instructions of October 1982 to adopt articles of the WHO Code as Nestlé policy include:

- No advertising to the general public.
- No sampling to mothers.
- No mothercraft workers.

- No use of commission/bonus for sales.
- No use of infant pictures on labels.
- No point-of-sale advertising.
- No financial or material inducements to promote products.
- No samples to physicians except in three specific situations: a new product, a new product formulation, or a new graduate physician; limited to one or two cans of product.
- Limitation of supplies to those requested in writing and fulfilling genuine needs for breast milk substitutes.
- A statement of the superiority of breast feeding on all labels/materials.
- Labels and educational materials clearly stating the hazards involved in incorrect usage of infant formula, developed in consultation with WHO/UNICEF.

Even though Nestlé stopped consumer advertising, it was able to maintain its share of the Third World infant formula market. By 1988 a call to resume the seven-year boycott was called for by a group of consumer activist members of the Action for Corporate Accountability. The group claimed that Nestlé was distributing free formula through maternity wards as a promotional tactic that undermines the practice of breast feeding. The group claims that Nestlé and others including American Home Products, have continued to dump formula in hospitals and maternity wards and that, as a result, "babies are dying as the companies are violating the WHO resolution."[1] As late as 1997 the Interagency Group on Breastfeeding Monitoring (IGBM) claims Nestlé continues to systematically violate the WHO code. Nestlé's response to these accusations is included on their Web site (see **www.nestlé.com** for details).

The boycott focus is Taster's Choice Instant Coffee, Coffeemate Nondairy Coffee Creamer, Anacin aspirin, and Advil.

Representatives of Nestlé and American Home Products rejected the accusations and said they were complying with World Health Organization and individual national codes on the subject.

The New Twist.   A new environmental factor has made the entire case more complex: Circa 1998 it was believed that some 3.8 million children around the world have contracted HIV at their mothers' breasts. In affluent countries mothers can be told to bottle feed their children. However, 90 percent of the child infections occur in developing countries. There the problems of bottle feeding remain. Further, in even the most infected areas, 70 percent of the mothers do not carry the virus, and breast feeding is by far the best option. And the vast majority of pregnant women in the developing countries have no idea whether they are infected or not. One concern is that large numbers of healthy women will switch to the bottle just to be safe. Alternatively, if bottle feeding becomes a badge of HIV infection, mothers may continue breast feeding just to avoid being stigmatized. In Thailand, pregnant women are offered testing, and if found HIV positive, are given free milk powder. But in some African countries where women get pregnant at three times the Thai rate and HIV infection rates are 25 percent compared to the 2 percent in Thailand, that solution is much less feasible.

The Issues.   Many issues are raised by this incident and the ongoing swirl of cultural change. How can a company deal with a worldwide boycott of its products? Why did the United States decide not to support the WHO Code? Who is correct, WHO or Nestlé? A more important issue concerns the responsibility of an MNC marketing in developing nations. Setting aside the issues for a moment, consider the notion that, whether intentional or not, Nestlé's marketing activities have had an impact on the behavior of many people. In other words, Nestlé is a cultural change agent. And, when it or any other company successfully introduces new ideas into a culture, the culture changes and those changes can be functional or dysfunctional to established patterns of behavior. The key issue is, What responsibility does the MNC have to the culture when, as a result of its marketing activities, it causes change in that culture? Finally, how might Nestlé now participate in the battle against the spread of HIV and AIDS in developing countries?

Questions

1. What are the responsibilities of companies in this or similar situations?

2. What could Nestlé have done to have avoided the accusations of "killing Third World babies" and still market its product?

3. After Nestlé's experience, how do you suggest it, or any other company, can protect itself in the future?

4. Assume you are the one who had to make the final decision on whether or not to promote and market Nestlé's baby formula in Third World countries. Read the section titled "Ethical and Socially Responsible Decisions" in Chapter 5 (pp. 138–39) as a guide to examine the social responsibility and ethical issues with the marketing approach and the promotion used. Were the decisions socially responsible? Were they ethical?

5. What advice would you give to Nestlé now in light of the new problem of HIV infection being spread via mothers' milk?

---

[1] "Boycotts: Activists' Group Resumes Fight against Nestle, Adds American Home Products," *Associated Press,* October 5, 1988.

THE CULTURAL ENVIRONMENT OF GLOBAL MARKETING

Outline of Cases

CASE 2-1
THE NOT-SO-WONDERFUL WORLD OF EURODISNEY—THINGS ARE BETTER NOW AT PARIS DISNEYLAND

Bon Jour, Mickey!

In April 1992, EuroDisney SCA opened its doors to European visitors. Located by the river Marne some 20 miles east of Paris, it was designed to be the biggest and most lavish theme park that Walt Disney Company (Disney) has built to date—bigger than Disneyland in Anaheim, California, Disneyworld in Orlando, Florida, and Tokyo Disneyland in Japan. In 1989, "EuroDisney" was expected to be a surefire moneymaker for its parent Disney, led by Chairman Michael Eisner and President Frank Wells. Since then, sadly, Wells was killed in an air accident in spring of 1994, and EuroDisney lost nearly $1 billion during the 1992–93 fiscal year.

Much to Disney management's surprise, Europeans failed to "go goofy" over Mickey, unlike their Japanese counterparts. Between 1990 and early 1992, some 14 million people had visited Tokyo Disneyland, with three quarters being repeat visitors. A family of four staying overnight at a nearby hotel would easily spend $600 on a visit to the park. In contrast, at EuroDisney, families were reluctant to spend the $280 a day needed to enjoy the attractions of the park, including *les hamburgers* and *les milkshakes*. Staying overnight was out of the question for many because hotel rooms were so high priced. For example, prices ranged from $110 to $380 a night at the Newport Bay Club, the largest of EuroDisney's six new hotels and one of the biggest in Europe. In comparison, a room in a top hotel in Paris costs between $340 and $380 a night.

In 1994, financial losses were becoming so massive at Euro-Disney that Michael Eisner had to step in personally in order to structure a rescue package. EuroDisney was put back on firm ground. A two-year window of financial peace was introduced, but not until after some acrimonious dealings with French banks had been settled and an unexpected investment by a Saudi prince had been accepted. Disney management rapidly introduced a range of strategic and tactical changes in the hope of "doing it right" this time. Analysts are presently trying to diagnose what went wrong and what the future might hold for EuroDisney.

A Real Estate Dream Come True.   Expansion into Europe was supposed to be Disney's major source of growth in the 1990s, bolstering slowing prospects back home in the United States. "Europe is our big project for the rest of this century," boasted Robert J. Fitzpatrick, chairman of Euro Disneyland in spring 1990. The Paris location was chosen over 200 other potential sites stretching from Portugal through Spain, France, Italy, and into Greece. Spain thought it had the strongest bid based on its year-long, temperate, and sunny Mediterranean climate, but insufficient acreage of land was available for development around Barcelona.

In the end, the French government's generous incentives, together with impressive data on regional demographics, swayed

This case was prepared by Professor Lyn S. Amine and graduate student Carolyn A. Tochtrop, Saint Louis University, St. Louis Mo., as a basis for class discussion rather than to illustrate either effective or ineffective handling of a situation.

Eisner to choose the Paris location. It was calculated that some 310 million people in Europe live within two hours' air travel of EuroDisney, and 17 million could reach the park within two hours by car—better demographics than at any other Disney site. Pessimistic talk about the dismal winter weather of northern France was countered with references to the success of Tokyo Disneyland, where resolute visitors brave cold winds and snow to enjoy their piece of Americana. Furthermore, it was argued, Paris is Europe's most-popular city destination among tourists of all nationalities.

According to the master agreement signed by the French government in March 1987, 51 percent of EuroDisney would be offered to European investors, with about half of the new shares being sold to the French. At that time, the project was valued at about FFr 12 billion ($1.8 billion). Disney's initial equity stake in EuroDisney was acquired for FFr 850 million (about $127.5 million). After the public offering, the value of Disney's stake zoomed to $1 billion on the magic of the Disney name.

Inducements by the French government were varied and generous:

- Loans of up to FFr 4.8 billion at a lower-than-market fixed rate of interest.
- Tax advantages for writing off construction costs.
- Construction by the French government, free of charge, of rail and road links from Paris out to the park. The TGV *(très grande vitesse)* fast train was scheduled to serve the park by 1994, along with road traffic coming from Britain through the Channel Tunnel, or "Chunnel."
- Land (4,800 acres) sold to Disney at 1971 agricultural prices. Resort and property development going beyond the park itself was projected to bring in about a third of the scheme's total revenues between 1992 and 1995. As one analyst commented, "EuroDisney could probably make money without Mickey, as a property development alone." These words would come back to haunt Disney in 1994 as real estate development plans were halted and hotel rooms remained empty, some even being closed during the first winter.

Spills and Thrills.   Disney had projected that the new theme park would attract 11 million visitors and generate over $100 million in operating earnings during the first year of operation. Euro-Disney was expected to make a small pretax profit of FFr 227 million ($34 million) in 1994, rising to nearly FFr 3 billion ($450 million) in 2001. By summer 1994, EuroDisney had lost more than $900 million since opening. Attendance reached only 9.2 million in 1992, and visitors spent 12 percent less on purchases than the estimated $33 per head. European tour operators were unable to rally sufficient interest among vacationers to meet earlier commitments to fill the park's hotels, and demanded that Euro-Disney renegotiate their deals. In August 1992, Karen Gee, marketing manager of Airtours PLC, a British travel agency, worried about troubles yet to come: "On a foggy February day, how appealing will this park be?" Her winter bookings at that time were dismal.

If tourists were not flocking to taste the thrills of the new EuroDisney, where were they going for their summer vacations in 1992? Ironically enough, an unforeseen combination of transatlantic airfare wars and currency movements resulted in a trip to Disneyworld in Orlando being cheaper than a trip to Paris, with guaranteed good weather and beautiful Floridian beaches within easy reach.

EuroDisney management took steps to rectify immediate problems in 1992 by cutting rates at two hotels up to 25 percent, introducing some cheaper meals at restaurants, and launching a Paris ad blitz that proclaimed "California is only 20 miles from Paris."

An American Icon.   One of the most worrying aspects of EuroDisney's first year was that French visitors stayed away; they had been expected to make up 50 percent of the attendance figures. Two years later, Dennis Speigel, president of the International Theme Park Services consulting firm, based in Cincinnati, Ohio, framed the problem in these words: "The French see EuroDisney as American imperialism—plastics at its worst." The well-known, sentimental Japanese attachment to Disney characters contrasted starkly with the unexpected and widespread French scorn for American fairy-tale characters. French culture has its own lovable cartoon characters such as Astérix, the helmeted, pint-sized Gallic warrior who has a theme park located near EuroDisney. Parc Astérix went through a major renovation and expansion in anticipation of competition from EuroDisney.

Hostility among the French people to the whole "Disney idea" had surfaced early in the planning of the new project. Paris theater director Ariane Mnouchkine became famous for her description of EuroDisney as "a cultural Chernobyl." A 1988 book, *Mickey: the Sting,* by French journalist Gilles Smadja, denounced the $350 million that the government had committed at that time to building park-related infrastructure. In fall 1989, during a visit to Paris, Michael Eisner was pelted with eggs by French Communists. Finally, many farmers took to the streets to protest against the preferential sales price of local land. The joke going around at the time was, "For EuroDisney to adapt properly to France, all seven of Snow White's dwarfs should be named Grumpy *(Grincheux)*."

Early advertising by EuroDisney seemed to aggravate local French sentiment by emphasizing glitz and size, rather than the variety of rides and attractions. Committed to maintaining Disney's reputation for quality in everything, Chairman Eisner insisted that more and more detail be built into EuroDisney.

For example, the centerpiece castle in the Magic Kingdom had to be bigger and fancier than in the other parks. He ordered the removal of two steel staircases in Discoveryland, at a cost of $200–300,000, because they blocked a view of the Star Tours ride. Expensive trams were built along a lake to take guests from the hotels to the park, but visitors preferred walking. An 18-hole golf course, built to adjoin 600 new vacation homes, was constructed and then enlarged to add another 9 holes. Built before the homes, the course cost $15–20 million and remains under-used. Total park construction costs were estimated at FFr 14 billion ($2.37 billion) in 1989 but rose by $340 million to FFr 16 billion as a result of all these add-ons. Hotel construction costs alone rose from an estimated FFr 3.4 billion to FFr 5.7 billion.

EuroDisney and Disney managers unhappily succeeded in alienating many of their counterparts in the government, the banks, the ad agencies, and other concerned organizations. A barnstorming, kick-the-door-down attitude seemed to reign among the U.S. decision makers. Beatrice Descoffre, a French construction industry official, complained that "They were always sure it would work because they were Disney." A top French banker involved in setting up the master agreement felt that Disney executives had tried to steamroller their ideas. "They had a formidable image and convinced everyone that if we let them do it their way, we would all have a marvelous adventure."

Disney executives consistently declined to comment on their handling of management decisions during the early days, but point out that many of the same people complaining about Disney's aggressiveness were only too happy to sign on with Disney before conditions deteriorated. One former Disney executive voiced the opinion, "We were arrogant—it was like 'We're building the Taj Mahal and people will come—on our terms.'"

Storm Clouds Ahead

Disney and its advisors failed to see signs at the end of the 1980s of the approaching European recession. As one former executive said, "We were just trying to keep our heads above water. Between the glamour and the pressure of opening and the intensity of the project itself, we didn't realize a major recession was coming." Other dramatic events included the Gulf War in 1991, which put a heavy brake on vacation travel for the rest of that year. The fall of Communism in 1989 after the destruction of the Berlin Wall provoked far-reaching effects on the world economy. National defense industries were drastically reduced among western nations. Foreign aid was requested from the West by newly emerging democracies in Eastern Europe. Other external factors that Disney executives have cited in the past as contributing to their financial difficulties at EuroDisney were high interest rates and the devaluation of several currencies against the franc.

Difficulties were also encountered by EuroDisney with regard to competition. Landmark events took place in Spain in 1992. The World's Fair in Seville and the 1992 Olympics in Barcelona were huge attractions for European tourists. In the future, new theme parks are planned for Spain by Anheuser-Busch, with its $300 million Busch Gardens near Barcelona, as well as Six Flags Corporation's Magic Mountain park to be located in Marbella.

Disney management's conviction that it knew best was demonstrated by its much-trumpeted ban on alcohol in the park. This proved insensitive to the local culture because the French are the world's biggest consumers of wine. To them a meal without *un verre de rouge* is unthinkable. Disney relented. It also had to relax its rules on personal grooming of the projected 12,000 cast members, the park employees. Women were allowed to wear redder nail polish than in the U.S., but the taboo on men's facial hair was maintained. "We want the clean-shaven, neat and tidy look," commented David Kannally, director of Disney University's Paris branch. The "university" trains prospective employees in Disney values and culture by means of a one-and-a-half-day seminar. EuroDisney's management did, however, compromise on the question of pets. Special kennels were built to house visitors' animals. The thought of leaving a pet at home during vacation is considered irrational by many French people.

Plans for further development of EuroDisney after 1992 were ambitious. The initial number of hotel rooms was planned to be 5,200, more than in the entire city of Cannes on the Cote d'Azur. This number was supposed to triple in a few years as Disney opened a second theme park to keep visitors at the EuroDisney resort for a longer stay. There would also be a huge amount of office space, 700,000 square meters, just slightly smaller than France's largest office complex, La Defense in Paris. Also planned were shopping malls, apartments, golf courses, and vacation homes. EuroDisney would design and build everything itself, with a view to selling at a profit. As a Disney executive commented with hindsight, "Disney at various points could have had partners to share the risk, or buy the hotels outright. But it didn't want to give up the upside."

Disney management wanted to avoid two costly mistakes it had learned from the past: letting others build the money-making hotels surrounding a park (as happened at Disneyland in Anaheim); and letting another company own a Disney park (as in Tokyo where Disney just collects royalties). This time, along with 49 percent ownership of EuroDisney, Disney would receive both a park management fee and royalties on merchandise sales.

The outstanding success record of Chairman Eisner and President Wells in reviving Disney during the 1980s led people to believe that the duo could do nothing wrong. "From the time they came on, they had never made a single misstep, never a mistake, never a failure," said a former Disney executive. "There was a tendency to believe that everything they touched would be perfect." This belief was fostered by the incredible growth record achieved by Eisner and Wells. In the seven years before EuroDisney opened, they took Disney from being a company with $1 billion in revenues to one with $8.5 billion, mainly through internal growth.

Dozens of banks, led by France's Banque Nationale de Paris, Banque Indosuez, and Caisse des Depots & Consignations, eagerly signed on to provide construction loans. One banker who saw the figures for the deal expressed concern. "The company was overleveraged. The structure was dangerous." Other critics charged that the proposed financing was risky because it relied on capital gains from future real estate transactions.

The Disney response to this criticism was that those views reflected the cautious, Old World thinking of Europeans who didn't understand U.S.-style free-market financing. Supporters of Disney point out that for more than two years after the initial public offering of shares, the stock price continued to do well, and that initial loans were at a low rate. It was the later cost overruns and the necessity for a bailout at the end of the first year that undermined the initial forecasts.

Optimistic assumptions that the 1980s boom in real estate in Europe would continue through the 1990s and that interest rates and currencies would remain stable led Disney to rely heavily on debt financing. The real estate developments outside EuroDisney were supposed to draw income to help pay down the $3.4 billion in debt. That in turn was intended to help Disney finance a second park close by—an MGM Studios film tour site—which would draw visitors to help fill existing hotel rooms. None of this happened. As a senior French banker commented later in 1994, EuroDisney is a "good theme park married to a bankrupt real estate company—and the two can't be divorced."

Telling and Selling Fairy Tales.   Mistaken assumptions by the Disney management team affected construction design, marketing and pricing policies, and park management, as well as initial financing. For example, parking space for buses proved much too small. Restroom facilities for drivers could accommodate 50 people; on peak days there were 200 drivers. With regard to demand for meal service, Disney executives had been erroneously informed that Europeans don't eat breakfast. Restaurant breakfast service was downsized accordingly, and guess what? "Everybody showed up for breakfast. We were trying to serve 2,500 breakfasts in a 350-seat restaurant (at some of the hotels). The lines were horrendous. And they didn't just want croissants and coffee. They wanted bacon and eggs," lamented one Disney executive. Disney reacted quickly, delivering prepackaged breakfasts to rooms and other satellite locations.

In contrast to Disney's American parks where visitors typically stay at least three days, EuroDisney is at most a two-day visit. Energetic visitors need even less time. Jeff Summers, an analyst at debt broker Klesch & Co. in London, claims to have "done" every EuroDisney ride in just five hours. "There aren't enough attractions to get people to spend the night," he commented in summer of 1994. Typically many guests arrive early in the morning, rush to the park, come back to their hotel late at night, then check out the next morning before heading back to the park. The amount of check-in and check-out traffic was vastly underestimated when the park opened; extra computer terminals were installed rapidly in the hotels.

In promoting the new park to visitors, Disney did not stress the entertainment value of a visit to the new theme park. The emphasis on the size of the park "ruined the magic," said a Paris-based ad agency executive. But in early 1993, ads were changed to feature Zorro, a French favorite; Mary Poppins; and Aladdin, star of the huge money-making movie success. A print ad campaign at that time featured Aladdin, Cinderella's castle, and a little girl being invited to enjoy a "magic vacation." A promotional package was offered—two days, one night, and one breakfast at an unnamed EuroDisney hotel—for $95 per adult and free for kids. The tagline said, "The kingdom where all dreams come true."

Early in 1994 the decision was taken to add six new attractions. In March the Temple of Peril ride opened; Storybook Land followed in May; and the Nautilus attraction was planned for June. Donald Duck's birthday was celebrated on June 9. A secret new thrill ride was promised in 1995. "We are positioning EuroDisney as the No. 1 European destination of short duration, one to three days," said a park spokesperson. Previously no effort had been made to hold visitors for a specific length of stay. Moreover, added the spokesperson, "One of our primary messages is, after all, that EuroDisney is affordable to everyone." Although new package deals and special low season rates substantially offset costs to visitors, the overall entrance fee has not been changed and is higher than in the U.S.

With regard to park management, seasonal disparities in attendance have caused losses in projected revenues. Even on a day-to-day basis, EuroDisney management has had difficulty forecasting numbers of visitors. Early expectations were that Monday would be a light day for visitors, and Friday a heavy one. Staff allocations were made accordingly. The opposite was true. EuroDisney management still struggles to find the right level of staffing at a park where high-season attendance can be 10 times the number in the low season. The American tradition of "hiring and firing" employees at will is difficult, if not impossible, in France where workers' rights are stringently protected by law.

Disney executives had optimistically expected that the arrival of their new theme park would cause French parents to take their children out of school in midsession for a short break. It did not happen, unless a public holiday occurred over a weekend. Similarly, Disney expected that the American-style short but more frequent family trips would displace the European tradition of a one-month family vacation, usually taken in August. However, French office and factory schedules remain the same, with their emphasis on an August shutdown.

Tomorrowland.   Faced with falling share prices and crisis talk among shareholders, Disney was forced to step forward in late 1993 to rescue the new park. Disney announced that it would fund EuroDisney until a financial restructuring could be worked out with lenders. However, it was made clear by the parent company, Disney, that it "was not writing a blank check."

In November 1993, it was announced that an allocation of $350 million to deal with EuroDisney's problems had resulted in the first quarterly loss for Disney in nine years. Reporting on fourth-quarter results for 1993, Disney announced its share of EuroDisney losses as $517 million for fiscal 1993. The overall performance of Disney was not, however, affected. It reported a profit of nearly $300 million for the fiscal year ending September 30, 1993, thanks to strong performance by its U.S. theme parks and movies produced by its entertainment division. This compared to a profit of $817 million for the year before.

The rescue plan developed in fall 1993 was rejected by the French banks. Disney fought back by imposing a deadline for agreement of March 31, 1994, and even hinted at possible closure of EuroDisney. By mid-March, Disney's commitment to support EuroDisney had risen to $750 million. A new preliminary deal struck with EuroDisney's lead banks required the banks to contribute some $500 million. The aim was to cut the park's high-cost debt in half and make EuroDisney profitable by 1996, a date considered unrealistic by many analysts.

The plan called for a rights offering of FFr 6 billion (about $1.02 billion at current rates) to existing shareholders at below-market prices. Disney would spend about $508 million to buy 49 percent of the offering. Disney also agreed to buy certain EuroDisney park assets for $240 million and lease them back to EuroDisney on favorable terms. Banks agreed to forgive 18 months of interest payments on outstanding debt and would defer all principal payments for three years. Banks would also underwrite the remaining 51 percent of the rights offering. For its part, Disney agreed to eliminate for five years its lucrative management fees and royalties on the sale of tickets and merchandise. Royalties would gradually be reintroduced at a lower level.

Analysts commented that approval by EuroDisney's 63 creditor banks and its shareholders was not a foregone conclusion. Also, the future was clouded by the need to resume payment of debt interest and royalties after the two-year respite.

Prince Charming Arrives.   In June 1994, EuroDisney received a new lifeline when a member of the Saudi royal family agreed to invest up to $500 million for a 24 percent stake in the park. Prince Al-Walid bin Talal bin Abdul-Aziz Al-Saud is a well-known figure in the world of high finance. Years ago he expressed the desire to be worth $5 billion by 1998. Western-educated, His Royal Highness Prince Al-Walid holds stock in Citicorp worth $1.6 billion and is its biggest shareholder. The Prince has an established reputation in world markets as a "bottom-fisher," buying into potentially viable operations during crises when share prices are low. He also holds 11 percent of Saks Fifth Avenue, and owns a chain of hotels and supermarkets, his own United Saudi Commercial Bank in Riyadh, a Saudi construction company, and part

of the new Arab Radio and Television Network in the Middle East. The prince plans to build a $100 million convention center at EuroDisney. One of the few pieces of good news about EuroDisney is that its convention business exceeded expectations from the beginning.

The Prince's investment could reduce Disney's stake in EuroDisney to as little as 36 percent. The Prince has agreed not to increase the size of his holding for 10 years. He also agreed that if his EuroDisney stake ever exceeds 50 percent of Disney's, he must liquidate that portion.

The Prince loves Disney culture. He has visited both EuroDisney and Disneyworld. He believes in the EuroDisney management team. Positive factors supporting his investment include the continuing European economic recovery, increased parity between European currencies, the opening of the "Chunnel," and what is seen as a certain humbling in the attitude of Disney executives. Jeff Summers, analyst for Klesch & Co. in London, commented on the deal, saying that Disney now has a fresh chance "to show that Europe really needs an amusement park that will have cost $5 billion."

Management and Name Changes

Frenchman Philippe Bourguignon took over at EuroDisney as CEO in 1993 and has navigated the theme park back to profitability. He was instrumental in the negotiations with the firm's bankers, cutting a deal that he credits largely for bringing the park back into the black.

Perhaps more important to the long-run success of the venture were his changes in marketing. The pan-European approach to marketing was dumped and national markets were targeted separately. This new "localization" took into account the differing tourists' habits around the continent. Separate marketing offices were opened in London, Frankfurt, Milan, Brussels, Amsterdam, and Madrid, and each was charged with tailoring advertising and packages to its own market. Prices were cut by 20 percent for park admission and 30 percent for some hotel room rates. Special promotions were also run for the winter months.

The central theme of the new marketing and operations approach is that people visit the park for an "authentic" Disney day-out. They may not be completely sure what that means, except that it entails something American. This is reflected in the transformation of the park's name. The "Euro" in EuroDisney was first shrunk in the logo, and the word "land" added. Then in October 1994 the "Euro" was eliminated completely, and the park is now called Disneyland Paris.

In 1996 Disneyland Paris became France's most visited tourist attraction ahead of both the Louvre Art Museum and the Eiffel Tower. 11.7 million visitors (a 9 percent increase from the previous year) allowed the park to report another profitable year. However, the architect of this remarkable recovery has now left the firm. Despite a promotion to Executive Vice President of Disney's European operations, Mr. Bourguignon has resigned to become chairman of Club Mediterranee SA. Some say he's interested in another turn-around project—Club Med has had big problems recently including huge losses in customers and profits. Others conjecture Mr. Bourguignon's departure had more to do with big challenges facing Disneyland Paris in the immediate future. That is, financial concessions given by bankers and shareholders as part of the restructuring are gradually beginning to expire, and some analysts see storm clouds again on the horizon.

References

"An American in Paris," *Business Week,* March 12, 1990, pp. 60–61, 64.

"A Charming Prince to the Rescue?" *Newsweek,* June 13, 1994, p. 43.

"EuroDisney Rescue Package Wins Approval," *The Wall Street Journal,* March 15, 1994, pp. A3, A13.

"EuroDisney Tries to End Evil Spell," *Advertising Age,* February 7, 1994, p. 39.

"EuroDisney's Prince Charming?" *Business Week,* June 13, 1994, p. 42.

"Disney Posts Loss: Troubles in Europe Blamed," *Los Angeles Times,* November 11, 1993, pp. A1, A34.

Thomas Kamm and Douglas Lavin, "Architect of EuroDisney's Turnaround Resigns to Be Chairman of Club Med," *The Wall Street Journal,* February 24, 1997, p. B6.

"How Disney Snared a Princely Sum," *Business Week,* June 20, 1994, pp. 61–62.

"Mickey Goes to the Bank," *The Economist,* September 16, 1989, p. 38.

"The Mouse Isn't Roaring," *Business Week,* August 24, 1992, p. 38.

"Mouse Trap: Fans Like EuroDisney but Its Parent's Goofs Weigh the Park Down," *The Wall Street Journal,* March 10, 1994, p. A12.

"Saudi to Buy as Much as 24% of EuroDisney," *The Wall Street Journal,* June 2, 1994, p. A4.

"The Kingdom inside the Republic (New Management Strategy at EuroDisney)," *The Economist,* April 13, 1996, p. 66.

www.disney.com

Questions

1. What factors contributed to EuroDisney's poor performance during its first year of operation?

2. To what degree do you consider that these factors were (a) foreseeable and (b) controllable by either EuroDisney or the parent company, Disney?

3. What role does ethnocentrism play in the story of EuroDisney's launch?

4. How do you assess the cross-cultural marketing skills of Disney?

5. *a.* Do you think success in Tokyo predisposed Disney management to be too optimistic in their expectations of success in France? Discuss.

   b. Do you think the new theme park would have encountered the same problems if a location in Spain had been selected? Discuss.

6. Now that Disney has succeeded in turning around Disneyland Paris, where should it go next? The company is now expanding its Tokyo and U.S. facilities; however, the company is also considering other locations around the world. Assume you are a consultant hired to give Disney advice on the issue of where to go next. Pick three locations and select the one you think will be the best new location for Disneyland X. Discuss.

7. Given your choice of local "X" for the newest Disneyland, what are the operational implications of the history of EuroDisney described above for the new park?

CASE 2–2
WHO GOES TO SAUDI ARABIA—BILL OR JANE?

Two senior vice presidents, Robert Donner, VP of International Sales, and Jeanette Falcon, VP of Personnel, disagree on whom to send to Saudi Arabia to negotiate the sale of two major computer installations worth approximately $35 million. Colorado Computing Company (CCC) has an excellent product and enjoys a good reputation in the area. With effective negotiations they are certain they can make a profitable sale. There are two candidates for the job, Jane Adams and Bill Smith. As soon as Jane heard about the possible sale in Saudi Arabia, she asked senior management to send her.

Jane has an MBA in international business and six years' experience with CCC, and she has negotiated two major sales to firms in Norway and Sweden. Bill Smith has been in the marketing/sales department with CCC for five years. He has an excellent reputation and he has a broad understanding of the product line, as does Jane. His only international experience was two years ago when he accompanied a senior executive to Japan to help negotiate a major sale. Bill's assistance was considered crucial in making the sale. Bill would be happy to go to Saudi Arabia but, if he isn't sent, he won't be upset.

At this point, the two vice presidents are not certain who should represent CCC. The vice presidents agree that Jane has the most experience and that, in almost any other part of the world, they could send her as the chief negotiator. Even though Jane has always been a team player, both VPs agree that Jane could consider that management has a lack of confidence in her if she is not picked. The positions of the two VPs are:

Robert Donner: I feel this position must be given to Bill Smith. Although Jane is more qualified in international business, I feel her gender could possibly affect the negotiations.

This is the largest international sale we have ever negotiated and, according to our sources, we are the front-runners. We are confident that we will be awarded the contract with a competent and professional presentation. Bill, who may not have the experience that Jane has, will do a professional and competent presentation and he should bring home a signed contract. I feel that Jane's presence in negotiations will leave questionable impressions on our Arab counterparts. We know her work is excellent, but, because she is a woman, we are not sure she will be seen as a "heavy hitter" by the Saudis. I suggest we send Bill to Saudi Arabia and consider Jane for upcoming negotiations in countries more receptive to businesswomen.

Jeanette Falcon: I believe the position should be awarded to the most capable person, who is Jane Adams. It is true that women in Saudi Arabia are treated unequally, but this pertains to local women and not to foreigners working in Saudi Arabia. When working abroad, a woman is treated first as a business associate and then as a woman. I believe the Saudi government officials are professional enough not to discriminate against Jane.

Studies have shown that women often have advantages over men in some situations: (1) Women tend to be more motivated than men. (2) Women are better able to draw a consensus among groups. (3) Many will consider a woman representing a company in a foreign assignment as outstanding since a company wouldn't risk sending a woman if she wasn't the best.

Jeanette and Bill cannot agree so they have asked you, president of CCC, to make the choice.

Questions

1. How valid are the two positions taken by Robert and Jeanette?

2. List the pros and cons for Bill going; for Jane going.

3. What is your decision? Why?

CASE 2–3
STARNES-BRENNER MACHINE TOOL COMPANY—TO BRIBE OR NOT TO BRIBE

The Starnes-Brenner Machine Tool Company of Iowa City, Iowa, has a small one-man sales office headed by Frank Rothe in Latino, a major Latin-American country. Frank has been in Latino for about 10 years and is retiring this year; his replacement is Bill Hunsaker, one of Starnes-Brenner's top salesmen. Both will be in Latino for about eight months, during which time Frank will show Bill the ropes, introduce him to their principal customers, and, in general, prepare him to take over.

Frank has been very successful as a foreign representative in spite of his unique style and, at times, complete refusal to follow company policy when it doesn't suit him. The company hasn't really done much about his method of operation, although from time to time he has angered some top company people. As President McCaughey, who retired a couple of years ago, once remarked to a vice president who was complaining about Frank, "If he's making money—and he is (more than any of the other foreign offices)—then leave the guy alone." When McCaughey retired, the new chief immediately instituted organizational changes that gave more emphasis to the overseas operations, moving the company toward a truly worldwide operation into which a loner like Frank would probably not fit. In fact, one of the key reasons for selecting Bill as Frank's replacement, besides Bill's record as a top salesman, is Bill's capacity as an organization man. He understands the need for coordination among operations and will cooperate with the home office so the Latino office can be expanded and brought into the mainstream.

The company knows there is much to be learned from Frank, and Bill's job is to learn everything possible. The company certainly doesn't want to continue some of Frank's practices, but much of his knowledge is vital for continued, smooth operation. Today, Starnes-Brenner's foreign sales account for about 25 percent of the company's total profits, compared with about 5 percent only 10 years ago.

The company is actually changing character, from being principally an exporter, without any real concern for continuous foreign market representation, to worldwide operations, where the foreign divisions are part of the total effort rather than a stepchild operation. In fact, Latino is one of the last operational divisions to be assimilated into the new organization. Rather than

try to change Frank, the company has been waiting for him to retire before making any significant adjustments in their Latino operations.

Bill Hunsaker is 36 years old, with a wife and three children; he is a very good salesman and administrator, although he has had no foreign experience. He has the reputation of being fair, honest, and a straight shooter. Some back at the home office see his assignment as part of a grooming job for a top position, perhaps eventually the presidency. The Hunsakers are now settled in their new home after having been in Latino for about two weeks. Today is Bill's first day on the job.

When Bill arrived at the office, Frank was on his way to a local factory to inspect some Starnes-Brenner machines that had to have some adjustments made before being acceptable to the Latino government agency buying them. Bill joined Frank for the plant visit. Later, after the visit, we join the two at lunch.

Bill, tasting some chili, remarks, "Boy! This certainly isn't like the chili we have in America." "No, it isn't, and there's another difference, too. The Latinos are Americans and nothing angers a Latino more than to have a 'Gringo' refer to the United States as America as if to say that Latino isn't part of America also. The Latinos rightly consider their country as part of America (take a look at the map) and people from the United States are North Americans at best. So, for future reference, refer to home either as the United States, States, or North America, but, for gosh sakes, not just America. Not to change the subject, Bill, but could you see that any change had been made in those S-27s from the standard model?"

"No, they looked like the standard. Was there something out of whack when they arrived?"

"No, I couldn't see any problem—I suspect this is the best piece of sophisticated bribe-taking I've come across yet. Most of the time the Latinos are more 'honest' about their *mordidas* than this." "What's a *mordida?*" Bill asks. "You know, *kumshaw, dash, bustarella, mordida;* they are all the same: a little grease to expedite the action. *Mordida* is the local word for a slight offering or, if you prefer, bribe," says Frank.

Bill quizzically responds, "Do we pay bribes to get sales?"

"Oh, it depends on the situation but it's certainly something you have to be prepared to deal with." Boy, what a greenhorn,

Frank thinks to himself, as he continues, "Here's the story. When the S-27s arrived last January, we began uncrating them and right away the *jefe* engineer (a government official)—*jefe,* that's the head man in charge—began extra-careful examination and declared there was a vital defect in the machines; he claimed the machinery would be dangerous and thus unacceptable if it wasn't corrected. I looked it over but couldn't see anything wrong, so I agreed to have our staff engineer check all the machines and correct any flaws that might exist. Well, the *jefe* said there wasn't enough time to wait for an engineer to come from the States, that the machines could be adjusted locally, and we could pay him and he would make all the necessary arrangements. So, what do you do? No adjustment his way and there would be an order cancelled; and, maybe there was something out of line, those things have been known to happen. But for the life of me, I can't see that anything had been done since the machines were supposedly fixed. So, let's face it, we just paid a bribe, and a pretty darn big bribe at that—about $1,200 per machine. What makes it so aggravating is that that's the second one I've had to pay on this shipment."

"The second?" asks Bill.

"Yeah, at the border, when we were transferring the machines to Latino trucks, it was hot and they were moving slow as molasses. It took them over an hour to transfer one machine to a Latino truck and we had 10 others to go. It seemed that every time I spoke to the dock boss about speeding things up, they just got slower. Finally, out of desperation, I slipped him a fistful of pesos and, sure enough, in the next three hours they had the whole thing loaded. Just one of the local customs of doing business. Generally, though, it comes at the lower level where wages don't cover living expenses too well."

There is a pause and Bill asks, "What does that do to our profits?"

"Runs them down, of course, but I look at it as just one of the many costs of doing business—I do my best not to pay, but when I have to, I do."

Hesitantly, Bill replies, "I don't like it, Frank, we've got good products, they're priced right, we give good service, and keep plenty of spare parts in the country, so why should we have to pay bribes? It's just no way to do business. You've already had to pay two bribes on one shipment; if you keep it up, the word's going to get around and you'll be paying at every level. Then all the profit goes out the window—you know, once you start, where do you stop? Besides that, where do we stand legally? The Foreign Bribery Act makes paying bribes like you've just paid illegal. I'd say the best policy is to never start; you might lose a few sales but let it be known that there are no bribes; we sell the best, service the best at fair prices, and that's all."

"You mean the Foreign Corrupt Practices Act, don't you?" Frank asks, and continues, in a I'm-not-really-so-out-of-touch tone of voice, "Haven't some of the provisions of the Foreign Corrupt Practices Act been softened, somewhat?"

"Yes, you're right, the provisions on paying a *mordida* or grease have been softened, but paying the government official is still illegal, softening or not," replies Bill.

Oh boy! Frank thinks to himself as he replies, "Look, what I did was just peanuts as far as the Foreign Corrupt Practices Act goes. The people we pay off are small, and, granted we give good service, but we've only been doing it for the last year or so. Before that I never knew when I was going to have equipment to sell. In fact, we only had products when there were surpluses stateside. I

had to pay the right people to get sales, and besides, you're not back in the States any longer. Things are just done different here. You follow that policy and I guarantee that you'll have fewer sales because our competitors from Germany, Italy, and Japan will pay. Look, Bill, everybody does it here; it's a way of life and the costs are generally reflected in the markup and overhead. There is even a code of behavior involved. We're not actually encouraging it to spread, just perpetuating an accepted way of doing business."

Patiently and slightly condescendingly, Bill replies, "I know, Frank, but wrong is wrong and we want to operate differently now. We hope to set up an operation here on a continuous basis; we plan to operate in Latino just like we do in the United States. Really expand our operation and make a long-range market commitment, grow with the country! And one of the first things we must avoid is unethical . . ."

Frank interrupts, "But really, is it unethical? Everybody does it, the Latinos even pay *mordidas* to other Latinos; it's a fact of life—is it really unethical? I think that the circumstances that exist in a country justify and dictate the behavior. Remember man, 'When in Rome, do as the Romans do.'"

Almost shouting, Bill blurts out, "I can't buy that. We know that our management practices and relationships are our strongest point. Really, all we have to differentiate us from the rest of our competition, Latino and others, is that we are better managed and, as far as I'm concerned, graft and other unethical behavior have got to be cut out to create a healthy industry. In the long run, it should strengthen our position. We can't build our futures on illegal and unethical practices."

Frank angrily replies, "Look, it's done in the States all the time. What about the big dinners, drinks, and all the other hanky-panky that goes on? Not to mention PACs' (Political Action Committee) payments to congressmen, and all those high speaking fees certain congressmen get from special interests. How many congressmen have gone to jail or lost reelection on those kinds of things? What is that, if it isn't *mordida* the North American way? The only difference is that instead of cash only, in the United States we pay in merchandise and cash."

"That's really not the same and you know it. Besides, we certainly get a lot of business transacted during those dinners even if we are paying the bill."

"Bull, the only difference is that here bribes go on in the open; they don't hide it or dress it in foolish ritual that fools no one. It goes on in the United States and everyone denies the existence of it. That's all the difference—in the United States we're just more hypocritical about it all."

"Look," Frank continues almost shouting, "we are getting off on the wrong foot and we've got eight months to work together. Just keep your eyes and mind open and let's talk about it again in a couple of months when you've seen how the whole country operates; perhaps then you won't be so quick to judge it absolutely wrong."

Frank, lowering his voice, says thoughtfully, "I know it's hard to take; probably the most disturbing problem in underdeveloped countries is the matter of graft. And, frankly, we don't do much advance preparation so we can deal firmly with it. It bothered me at first; but then I figured it makes its economic contribution, too, since the payoff is as much a part of the economic process as a payroll. What's our real economic role, anyway, besides making a profit, of course? Are we developers of wealth, helping to push the country to greater economic growth, or are we missionaries? Or should we be both? I really don't know, but I don't think we can be both simultaneously, and my feeling is that, as the company prospers, as higher salaries are paid, and better standards of living are reached, we'll see better ethics. Until then, we've got to operate or leave, and if you are going to win the opposition over, you'd better join them and change them from within, not fight them."

Before Bill could reply, a Latino friend of Frank's joined them and they changed the topic of conversation.

Questions

1. Is what Frank did ethical? Whose ethics? Latino's or the United States'?

2. Are Frank's two different payments legal under the Foreign Corrupt Practices Act as amended by the Omnibus Trade and Competitiveness Act of 1988?

3. Identify the types of payments made in the case; that is, are they lubrication, extortion, or subornation?

4. Frank seemed to imply that there is a similarity between what he was doing and what happens in the United States. Is there any difference? Explain.

5. Are there any legal differences between the money paid to the dock-workers and the money paid the *jefe* (government official)? Any ethical differences?

6. Frank's attitude seems to imply that a foreigner must comply with all local customs, but some would say that one of the contributions made by U.S. firms is to change local ways of doing business. Who is right?

7. Should Frank's behavior have been any different had this not been a government contract?

8. If Frank shouldn't have paid the bribe, what should he have done, and what might have been the consequences?

9. What are the company interests in this problem?

10. Explain how this may be a good example of the SRC (self-reference criterion) at work.

11. Do you think Bill will make the grade in Latino? Why? What will it take?

12. How can an overseas manager be prepared to face this problem?

CASE 2-4
WHEN INTERNATIONAL BUYERS AND SELLERS DISAGREE

No matter what line of business you're in, you can't escape sex. That may have been one conclusion drawn by an American exporter of meat products after a dispute with a West German customer over a shipment of pork livers. Here's how the disagreement came about:

The American exporter was contracted to ship "30,000 lbs. of freshly frozen U.S. pork livers, customary merchandisable quality, first rate brands." The shipment had been prepared to meet the exacting standards of the American market, so the exporter expected the transaction to be completed without any problem.

But when the livers arrived in West Germany, the purchaser raised an objection: "We ordered pork livers of customary merchantable quality—what you sent us consisted of 40 percent sow livers."

"Who cares about the sex of the pig the liver came from?" the exported asked.

"We do," the German replied. "Here in Germany we don't pass off spongy sow livers as the firmer livers of male pigs. This shipment wasn't merchantable at the price we expected to charge. The only way we were able to dispose of the meat without a total

loss was to reduce the price. You owe us a price allowance of $1,000."

The American refused to reduce the price. The determined resistance may have been partly in reaction to the implied insult to the taste of the American consumer. "If pork livers, whatever the sex of the animal, are palatable to Americans, they ought to be good enough for anyone," the American thought.

It looked as if the buyer and seller could never agree on eating habits.

Questions

1. In this dispute which country's law would apply, that of the United States or of West Germany?

2. If the case were tried in U.S. courts, who do you think would win? In German courts? Why?

3. Draw up a brief agreement which would have eliminated the following problems before they could occur.

   a. Whose law applies?

   b. Whether the case should be tried in U.S. or German courts.

   c. The difference in opinion as to "customary merchandisable quality."

4. Discuss how SRC may be at work in this case.

CASE 2–5
MARKETING SWEET CORN TO THE FRENCH

Jean LaRoche of Strasbourg had worked in the United States for over 10 years. While living on Long Island, he acquired a taste for sweet corn on the cob, which he grew in his own garden.

When he first came to the United States Jean knew there were two American delights he was going to resist: Coca-Cola with meals instead of wine, and iced cold water. He was quick to add a third item to his list when offered corn on the cob at a summer outing.

At first, he wasn't too surprised that Americans ate "pig food"; after all, they invented the hamburger and ate french fries with catsup, or is it ketchup? He knew about corn; it was grown as animal feed, not fit for human consumption. In fact, he had once tried the field corn grown for animal food and was put off by its toughness and taste. Nevertheless, after repeated entreaties by his Long Island neighbors, and not wanting to continue to refuse their hospitality, he reluctantly tried some real American corn on the cob and has eaten it ever since.

Jean returned to Strasbourg a few years ago, took a supply of his sweet corn seed with him, and immediately planted a garden. He has introduced some of his French friends to the wonders of summer sweet corn. Once they agree to taste it, they come back for more. His original 10 rows of corn have grown to nearly a half-acre much of which he sells to friends and neighbors.

Being an entrepreneur at heart, Jean has been considering the idea of commercially growing sweet corn and selling it in Europe. After all, he can't keep his friends supplied, so why not import the hybrid seed and commission farmers to grow the corn which he will market?

He has made preliminary inquiries and can import the hybrid seed, which grows well in France. He sees three different markets: fresh corn during the season; frozen corn kernels throughout the year; and corn cobs pressed into briquettes that burn like charcoal. The idea of corn-cob briquettes came from stories his father used to tell him about how they used corn cobs for heat during the war.

He can get an exclusive contract with a U.S. seed company for the Super Sweet hybrid in which genetic manipulation dramatically retards the conversion of the corn's sugar into starch. Super Sweet varieties contain genes that completely block the sugar-to-starch process on the plant and so retard it that a properly refrigerated picked ear of corn stays perfectly fresh-tasting for four to five days. This accounts for its super sweetness. The hybrid is about 30 percent more expensive to grow than other types of sweet corn and yields only half as many ears per hectare, about 20,000, as the other hybrids he has tried.

The hardest part of selling sweet corn to Europeans is simply getting them to taste it. Jean constantly has to fight the misconception that sweet corn is the same as the field corn grown to feed livestock. He has had friends who have tried field corn thinking it was the same as sweet corn. Their response has been that "It's only good for pig food."

He is excited about the prospects of this new business and its potential. In the United States, the average per capita consumption of sweet corn on the cob is 10 ears per person. He does not know how much is sold as frozen kernels but suspects it is considerably higher.

He needs some help in making a preliminary market analysis for his sweet corn business. Using the guidelines in "The Country Notebook—A Guide for Developing a Marketing Plan," prepare a preliminary market analysis for marketing sweet corn in France. You may also want to look at a research report done by Unilever on the consumption of vegetables, which can be found at **http://www.unilever.com**. Select the science & innovation button, then understanding innovation, and then examples. The article is under "Frozen Vegetables, It's Your Choice." Note: A more direct route to the information is **http://www.unilever.com/public/unilever/science/innovait/scin0001.htm** and select "research," which appears in the body of the text. However, this address may change and if it has, you can reach the information via the first Web address.

CASE 2–6
COPING WITH CORRUPTION IN TRADING WITH CHINA

Corruption is on the rise in China, where the country's press frequently has detailed cases of, and campaigns to crack down on, corruption. The articles primarily have focused on domestic economic crimes among PRC citizens, and local officials who have been fired and other penalties assessed. Indeed, China has been rated by Transparency International[1] as # 41 of the 52 countries

[1] **www.transparencey.de**, 1998.

Originally adapted from "Coping with Corruption in Trading with China," *Business Asia*, June 24, 1991, p. 217, and updated via Skip Kaltenheuser, "The Real Cost of Doing Business," *World Trade*, June 1997, pp. 80–83.

the German organization rates on its "Corruption Perception Index." Denmark is rated the least corrupt at #1 and Nigeria as the most corrupt at #52.

Corruption's long arm now is reaching out to touch China's foreign business community. Traders, trade consultants, and analysts have said that foreign firms are vulnerable to a variety of corrupt practices. While some of these firms said they had no experience with corruption in the PRC, the majority said they increasingly were asked to make payments to improve business; engage in black-market trade of import and export licenses; bribe officials to push goods through customs or the Commodity Inspection Bureau; or engage in collusion to beat the system. The Hong

Kong Independent Commission Against Corruption reports that outright bribes as well as gifts or payment to establish *guanxi,* or "connections," average in the PRC 3 to 5 percent of operating costs, or $3 billion to $5 billion of the $100 billion of foreign investments that have been made there.[2] The most common corrupt practices confronting foreign companies in China are examined below.

Paying to Improve Business.   Foreign traders make several types of payments to facilitate sales in China. The most common method? Trips abroad. Chinese officials, who rarely have a chance to visit overseas, often prefer foreign travel to cash or gifts. (This was especially true when few PRC officials had been abroad.) As a result, traders report that dangling foreign trips in front of their PRC clients has become a regular part of negotiating large trade deals that involve products with a technological component. "Foreign travel is always the first inducement we offer," said an executive involved in machinery trade. In most cases, traders built these costs into the product's sale price. Some trips are "reasonable and bona fide expenditures directly related to the promotion, demonstration, or explanation of products and services, or the execution of a contract with a foreign government agency." But other trips, when officials on foreign junkets are offered large per diems and aren't invited specifically to gain technical knowledge, may be another matter.

Foreign travel isn't always an inducement—it also can be extorted: In one case, a PRC bank branch refused to issue a letter of credit for a machinery import deal. The Chinese customer suggested that the foreign trader invite the bank official on an overseas inspection tour. Once the invitation was extended, the bank issued the L/C.

Angling for Cash.   MNCs also are asked sometimes to sponsor overseas education for children of trading officials. One person told a Chinese source that an MNC paid for his/her U.S. $1,500-a-month apartment, as well as a car, university education, and expenses.

Firms find direct requests for cash payments—undeniably illegal—the most difficult. One well-placed source said that a major trader, eager for buyers in the face of an international market glut, has fallen into regularly paying large kickbacks into the Honduran, U.S., and Swiss accounts of officials at a PRC foreign trade corporation (FTC).

Refusing to make payments may not only hurt sales, it also can be terrifying. A U.S. firm was one of several bidders for a large sale; a Chinese official demanded the MNC pay a 3 percent kickback. When the company representative refused, the official threatened: "You had better not say anything about this. You still have to do business in China, and stay in hotels here." Not surprisingly, the U.S. company lost the deal.

Traders of certain commodities may be tempted to purchase on the black market those import and export licenses that are difficult to obtain legally. A fairly disorganized underground market, for instance, exists for licenses to export China-made garments to the United States.

Some branches of the Commodity Inspection Bureau (CIB) also have posed problems for some traders. Abuses have emerged in the CIB since it started inspecting imports in 1987. A Japanese company, for instance, informed CIB officials of its intention to bring heavy industrial items into China—items that had met Japanese and U.S. standards. The officials responded that they planned to dismantle the products on arrival for inspection purposes. The problem was resolved only after the firm invited the officials to visit Japan.

Some traders get around such problems by purchasing inspection certificates on the black market. According to press accounts, these forms, complete with signatures and seals, can be bought for roughly U.S. $200.

Some claim that, for the appropriate compensation, customs officials in a southern province are most willing to reduce the dutiable value of imports as much as 50 percent. Because the savings can far exceed transport costs, some imports that would logically enter China through a northern port are redirected through the southern province.

Questions

1. List all the different types of bribes, payments, or favors, etc., represented in this case and say why each is either legal or illegal.

2. For those that you say are illegal, classify each as either lubrication, extortion, or subornation, and tell why.

3. Which of the payments, favors, or bribes are illegal under the Foreign Corrupt Practices Act (FCPA)?

4. Assuming that the FCPA did not exist, what is the ethical response to each of the payments, favors, or bribes you have identified. Read the section titled "Ethical and Socially Responsible Decisions" in Chapter 5 (pp. 138–39) as a guide to assist you in your decision.

5. Now that the OECD has approved a FCPA-like treaty to ban commercial bribery by firms in member countries[3] do you think bribery will become less prevalent in markets like China?

6. List alternatives to paying bribes in international markets and discuss the pluses and minuses of each.

[2] "The Destructive Costs of Greasing Palms," *Business Week,* December 6, 1993, p. 136.

[3] Edmund L. Andrews, "29 Industrial Nations Agree to Ban Bribery of Foreign Officials," *International Herald Tribune,* November 22–23, 1997, p. 11.

ASSESSING GLOBAL MARKET OPPORTUNITIES

Outline of Cases

CASE 3–1
ASIAN YUPPIES—HAVING IT ALL

Young, urban professionals (Yuppies) in Asian markets appear to have found the right combination for "having it all." Due to high housing costs, most young people continue to live with their parents after starting work and even after getting married. Income from their high-paying professional jobs is therefore available to spend on a wide range of expensive, upscale consumer items such as cars, clothes, consumer electronics, and club memberships. Prestigious European brand-name apparel is the most sought after, such as Ungaro, Hugo Boss, Ermenegildo Zegna, and Gianni Versace.

In the Sunrise Department Store of Taipei (Taiwan), Timberland deck shoes sell for $172; Ralph Lauren shorts for $90; Allen Edmonds shoes for $306; and Giorgio Armani sports jacket for $1,280.[1] Dickson Concepts of Hong Kong concentrates on luxury brand-name products such as Bulgari and Hermes watches, Guy Laroche and Charles Jourdan clothing and accessories, and a variety of Ralph Lauren/Polo products. Sales have grown 50 percent each year for the last five years. Tang's of Singapore takes upscale shopping one step further by targeting a subgroup of Yuppies which it calls NOPEs—not outwardly prosperous or educated consumers—whose goal is to create an understated, discreet image of wealth and success.[2]

Not all Asian Yuppies are able to spend extravagantly even though they want to project an upscale image. Seagrams launched a whiskey in Seoul (South Korea) called "Secret." It sold for $9 a bottle and achieved a 5 percent share of the total whiskey market, against the big-name brands of Chivas Regal and Johnnie Walker Black Label, which usually sell for about $100 a bottle. Also in South Korea, Hyundai introduced the flamboyant, brightly-col-

ored Scoupe sports car for $10,000, aimed at those Yuppies who cannot yet afford a BMW.

Surprisingly, Asian big-spenders may not be considered wealthy by Western standards. As an illustration, average annual income in 1995 for a 32-year old banker ranged from $12,000 in Bangkok (Thailand), to $18,000 in Taipei, $31,000 in Seoul, $32,000 in Singapore, and $35,000 in Hong Kong. Nevertheless, Yuppies' incomes have been rising in these markets by 15–20 percent annually in recent years.[3] Other factors that promote big spending are relatively low taxes, fringe benefits such as company cars and housing allowances, and big end-of-year bonuses. This relatively high level of disposable income becomes even more significant when one remembers that there are about a million people in their 20s and 30s in professional, managerial, or technical jobs in the four markets of Singapore, Hong Kong, Taipei, and Seoul. In addition, single, young, college-educated women in Japan are rapidly gaining a worldwide reputation as conspicuous consumers.[4]

Questions

1. What do you think is the most appropriate way to segment the market for upscale products in Asian markets (i.e., using geographic, demographic, psychographic, or product-related bases)?

2. Which segmentation strategy is likely to be most effective (i.e., concentration on individual market niches or a multi-segment strategy)?

[1] "Today's 'Born to Shop' Asians," *Market Asia Pacific*, October 1997.
[2] Ng Kang-Chung, "Asian Yuppies' Love for West Only Skin Deep," *South China Morning Post*, May 14, 1997, p. 3.

This case was prepared by Lyn S. Amine, Associate Professor of Marketing and International Business, Saint Louis University.

[3] Noel Fung, "Affluent Asians Provide Good News for Publishers," *South China Morning Post*, October 15, 1997, p. 8.
[4] Juliana Koranteng, "The New Asia: Building Brand Loyalty among Hip Asian Teens," *Advertising Age*, June 10, 1996, p. I28.

CASE 3–2
GE LIGHTING ATTACKS THE TRIAD MARKETS

GE Lighting (GEL) is the largest electric lightbulb manufacturer in the United States and has occupied this position since the invention of the electric lamp in 1879 by Thomas Edison, founder of the General Electric Company. GEL is positioning itself to become the world's largest lighting manufacturer. In order to accomplish this goal, GEL must position itself as a viable player in each

part of The Triad. "The Triad" is the name used by Kenichi Ohmae[1] for the three largest markets in the world, North America, the European Community (EC), and Japan. Strength in all three markets is essential to becoming the world lighting leader. Recently, GEL has made moves in the EC and Japan toward attaining the leadership goal.

This case was prepared by Lyn S. Amine, Associate Professor of Marketing and International Business, Saint Louis University.

[1] Kenichi Ohmae, *Triad Power: The Coming Shape of Global Competition* (New York: The Free Press, 1985).

In the United States, GEL has approximately 45 percent market share. Its closest competitors are Philips (of North America) and Sylvania Lighting, who each have about 20 percent market share. Philips purchased its North American Lighting division from Westinghouse Electric.[2] It was, at that time, the number three lighting manufacturer in the United States, behind Sylvania, which is a division of GTE, a global conglomerate. The balance of the U.S. market is made up of numerous other world players such as Siemens/Osram, Toshiba, Panasonic, Ushio, and Mitsubishi. GEL attributes part of its large market share to continued technological advances, astute marketing, and product leadership. A major strength lies in the relationship that GEL has established with the best distribution channels in the industry.

Maintaining its market dominance in the United States has, however, not been easy for GEL. With the continuing reduction of barriers to world trade during the late 1980s and rapidly increasing transfers of technology, GEL is experiencing threats to domestic market share from overseas competitors who continually attack GEL's market share with new technologies, niche marketing, and competitive pricing. European companies have led the way in technological breakthroughs, with Philips N.V. (of The Netherlands) and Osram leading the main thrust of innovation in the U.S. market.

Consolidation of the European market after full integration is expected to present even more problems for GEL's domestic stronghold. Reduction of trade barriers within the EC will enhance European companies' competitiveness through economies of scale, strategic alliances, and the benefits achieved through the restructuring of company operations. As a result, European companies' export strengths are also expected to be enhanced. Aware of these coming changes, GEL has made a move to protect U.S. market share and create new opportunities in the EC.

GEL had not previously been a strong player in the European lighting market, due in part to the effects of strong nationalist procurement policies and trade barriers. The EC market leader is Philips N.V., followed by Siemens, GTE, Thorn/EMI, and Tungsram. GEL held only about 2 percent of the EC bulb market while all other manufacturers held a combined share of about 98 percent. Past export performance had not produced significant market share for GEL, so it was clear that alternative strategies would be necessary to achieve the desired leadership position in the EC.

GEL's solution was bold and creative. GEL agreed to purchase 50 percent plus one share of the state-owned company, Tungsram Lighting of Hungary, for $150 million. Tungsram anticipated sales to reach $370 million with earnings in the order of $30 million. GEL also had the option to buy an additional 25 percent of Tungsram within the following two years. The option was so GEL now owns 75 percent of Tungsram. The Hungarian Credit Bank provided financing.

This large purchase presented several challenges to GEL. First, a plan was needed to allow Tungsram to absorb GE Europe (GEE) into its corporate structure. This move had three results. It gave GEE a source of supply in Eastern Europe, replacing previous imports from the United States; it brought GEL's EC market share up to 9 percent; and it gave Tungsram improved market access through GEE's distribution channels.

Second, it was necessary to upgrade Tungsram's operations. Tungsram was excellent by East European standards but there was much room for improvement by Western standards. Estimates predict that GEL will need to invest between $50 million and $200 million during 1991–95 to transform Tungsram into a strong European competitor.

Third, new management was needed to accomplish the necessary innovations. GE Corporate called on George F. Varga to head the new operation. Varga had emigrated from Hungary some 30 years earlier and had been with GE for 28 years. He proceeded to replace half of Tungsram's[3] management with U.S. executives but was careful with his choices. "We did not want any young tigers, we need people to form a cultural marriage." Varga's staff changes aimed to facilitate the inflow of new ideas and change while still preserving a workable continuity throughout the Tungsram organization.

Although the Tungsram acquisition provided a precious base for operations serving the EC, it could not give GE the "insider" status it needed to become a major player in the newly integrated EC market, challenging Philips N.V. and Siemens "in their own backyard." GEL had therefore carried forward a second plan contemporaneously with the Tungsram deal.

When GTE's attempts to purchase Thorn/EMI Lighting (TEL) broke down in the summer, GEL had stepped in. GEL agreed to pay $136 million to Thorn/EMI for their lightbulb division. GEL would initially buy 51 percent of TEL, with the balance being purchased within the next three years. TEL's European market share for sales of bulbs was 8 percent, worth some $360 million. Included in the TEL purchase were two plants in the United Kingdom, an automotive-lamp manufacturer and supplier in Germany, and 51 percent of a lighting business in Italy. No major management changes were announced.

The Thorn/EMI Lighting purchase gave GEL the local presence needed to compete in the EC after 1992. By owning one of the U.K.'s oldest lighting manufacturers, GEL has become an instant "insider" in the EC. Thus, within two years, GEL transformed itself from being an insignificant factor in the EC to the number three players. Combined market share from the Tungsram and TEL purchases amounted to 17 percent. By means of these two purchases, GEL gained local sources of production, access to established channels of distribution, greater market penetration, and substantially increased market share in two of the Triad markets.

In the remaining Triad market (Japan), GEL could not follow the same strategy of acquisition. Strong market protection and government intervention have made penetration of the Japanese market very difficult, if not impossible, for most foreign companies. But GEL has not given up. Instead of tackling the Japanese challenge head-on, GEL has followed a "back door" strategy.

Toshiba and GEL agreed to combine their resources to build a fluorescent lamp plant in Circleville, Ohio. The plant was funded on a 50/50 basis and features the latest high-speed fluorescent lamp technology combined with computerized automation. Output of the plant is intended for sale in both the domestic U.S. market and Japan, again with a 50–50 split. The domestic product will be sold under the GE Lighting brand name, while the foreign product will be exported to Japan under the Toshiba name.

[2] Thomas A. Stewart, "Welcome to the Revolution," *Fortune*, December 13, 1993, p. 66.

[3] Jonathan B. Levine, "GE Carves Out a Road East," *Business Week*, July 30, 1990, pp. 32–33.

This strategic alliance offers multiple benefits. GEL and Toshiba have been able to increase their individual capacity with only half the investment normally required. Toshiba was able to test the U.S. waters, decrease its risk of U.S. market entry through cost-sharing with GEL, and bolster its own market presence in Japan. Follow-on strategies may emerge. It is possible that Toshiba and GEL may collaborate to make product in Japan for export throughout Asia. Such an alliance would give GEL the localization required to become an insider in the Asian market.

GE Lighting is one of 13 core businesses in the General Electric Company. As CEO Jack Welch stated, "We built and shaped a company of 13 large, healthy businesses—each number one or number two in its global markets." GEL's pursuit of dominance in the Triad markets appears to be becoming a reality.

Questions

1. What other options might GEL have considered in the EC in order to accomplish its market penetration and growth objectives?

2. Can GEL repeat its European strategies in Japan?

3. What limits to growth might GEL encounter in its Triad markets?

4. Is GEL likely to have to face up to similar growth strategies being used by foreign competitors in the domestic U.S. market?

CASE 3–3
KONARK TELEVISION INDIA

In December, Mr. Ashok Bhalla began to prepare for a meeting scheduled for next week with his boss, Mr. Atul Singh. The meeting would focus on distribution strategy for Konark Television Ltd., a medium-sized manufacturer of television sets in India. At issue was the nature of immediate actions to be taken as well as long-range strategy. Mr. Bhalla was managing director of Konark, responsible for a variety of activities, including marketing. Mr. Singh was president.

TV Industry in India. The television industry was started in India in late 1959 with the Indian government using a UNESCO grant to build a small transmitter in New Delhi. The station soon began to broadcast short programs promoting education, health, and family planning.

Numerous changes took place over the next 30 years. Programming increased with the addition of news and entertainment offerings; commercials aired for the first time in 1976. Hours of broadcasting have grown to almost 12 hours per day. The number of transmission centers reached 300, sufficient to cover over 75 percent of India's population. Television was clearly the most popular medium of information, entertainment, and education in India. The network itself consisted of one channel except in large metropolitan areas, where a second channel was also available. Both television channels were owned and operated by the Indian government.

Despite this growth, many in the TV industry would still describe the Indian government's attitude toward television as conservative. In fact, some would say that it was only the pressure of TV broadcasts from neighboring Sri Lanka and Pakistan that forced India's rapid expansion. The prevailing policy was to view the indus-

try as a luxury industry capable of bearing heavy taxes. Thus, the government charged Indian manufacturers high import duties on foreign-manufactured components that they purchased, plus heavy excise duties on sets that they assembled; in addition, state governments charged consumers sales taxes that ranged from 1 to 17 percent. The result was that duties and taxes accounted for almost one half of the retail price of a color TV set and about one third of the retail price of a black and white set. Retail prices of TV sets in India were estimated at almost double the prevalent world prices.

Such high prices limited demand. The number of sets in use in 1995 was estimated at about 25 million. This number provided coverage to about 15 percent of India's population, assuming five viewers per set. To increase coverage to 75 percent of the population would require over 100 million additional TV sets, again assuming five viewers per set. This figure represented a huge latent demand—almost 17 years of production at 1993 levels. Many in the industry expected production and sales of TV sets would grow quite rapidly, if only prices were reduced.

Indian Consumers. The television market in India is concentrated among the affluent middle and upper social classes, variously estimated at some 12 to 25 percent of India's population (850 million). Members of this upscale segment exhibited a distinctly urban lifestyle. They owned videocassette recorders, portable radio-cassette players, motor scooters, and compact cars. They earned MBA degrees, lived in dual-income households, sent their children to private schools, and practiced family planning. In short, members of the segment exhibited tastes and behaviors much like their middle-class, professional counterparts in the United States and Europe.

While there was no formal marketing research available, Mr. Bhalla thought he knew the consumer fairly well. The typical purchase probably represented a joint decision by the husband and wife. After all, they would be spending over one month's salary for Konark's most popular color model. That model was now priced at retail at Rs. 11,300, slightly less than retail prices of many national brands. However, a majority in the target segment

This case was written by Fulbright Lecturer and Associate Professor James E. Nelson, University of Colorado at Boulder, and Dr. Piyush K. Sinha, Associate Professor, Xavier Institute of Management, Bhubaneswar, India. The authors thank Professor Roger A. Kerin, Southern Methodist University, for his helpful comments in writing this case. The case is intended for educational purposes rather than to illustrate either effective or ineffective decision making. Some data in the case are disguised. ©James E. Nelson

probably did not perceive a price advantage for Konark. Indeed, the segment seemed somewhat insensitive to differentials in the range of Rs. 10,000 to Rs. 14,000, considering their TV sets to be valued possessions that added to the furnishing of their drawing rooms. Rather than price, most consumers seemed more influenced by promotion and by dealer activities.

TV Manufacturers in India.   Approximately 140 different companies manufactured TV sets in India. However, many produced fewer than 1,000 sets per year and could not be considered major competitors. Further, Mr. Bhalla expected that many would not survive—the trend definitely was toward a competition between 20 or 30 large firms. Most manufacturers sold in India only, although a few had begun to export sets to nearby countries.

All TV sets produced by the different manufacturers could be classified into two basic sizes, 51 centimeters and 36 centimeters. The larger size was a console model while the smaller was designed as a portable. Black and white sets differ little in styling but greatly in terms of product features. Black and white sets came with and without handles, built-in voltage regulators, and built-in antennas, electronic tuners, audio and videotape sockets, and on-screen displays. Warranties differed in terms of coverage and time periods. Retail prices for black and white sets across India ranged from about Rs. 2,000 to Rs. 3,500, with the average thought by Mr. Bhalla to be around Rs. 2,600.

Differences between competing color sets were more pronounced. Styling was more distinctive, with manufacturers supplying a variety of cabinet designs, cabinet finishes, and control arrangements. Differences in features also were substantial. Some color sets featured automatic contrast and brightness controls, on-screen displays of channel tuning and time, sockets for video recorders and external computers, remote control devices, high-fidelity speakers, cable TV capabilities, and flat-screen picture tubes. Retail prices were estimated to range from about Rs. 7,000 (for a small-screen portable) to Rs. 19,000 (large-screen console), with an average around Rs. 12,000.

Advertising practices varied considerably. Many smaller manufacturers used only newspaper advertisements that tended to be small in size. Larger manufacturers, including Konark, advertised also in newspapers, but used quarter-page or larger advertisements. Larger manufacturers also spent substantial amounts on magazine, outdoor, and television advertising. Videocom, for example, was thought to have spent about Rs. 25 million, or about 4 percent of its sales revenue, on advertising in 1993; Onida's percentage might be as much as twice this amount. Most advertisements for TV sets tended to stress product features and product quality, although a few were based primarily on whimsy and fantasy. Most ads would not mention price.

Konark TV Ltd.   Konark TV Ltd. began operations in 1973 with the objective of manufacturing and marketing small black and white TV sets to the Orissa state market. The state is located on the east coast of India, directly below the state of West Bengal (containing Calcutta). Early years of operation found production leveling at about 5,000 sets per year. However, the company adopted a more aggressive strategy and grew rapidly. Sales revenues reached Rs. 640 million in 1993, based on sales of 290,000 units. Revenues and unit volume were expected to increase by 25 percent and 15 percent, respectively. Company headquarters remained in Bhubaneswar, Orissa's capital.

Manufacturing facilities were located also in Bhubaneswar except for some assembly performed by three independent distributors. Distributor assembly was done to save state sales taxes and to lower the prices paid by consumers. That is, many Indian states charged two levels of sales taxes depending upon whether or not the set was produced within the state. The state of Maharashtra (containing Bombay), for example, charged a sales tax of 4 percent for TV sets produced within the state and 16.5 percent for sets produced outside the state. Sales taxes for West Bengal (Calcutta) were 6 percent and 16.5 percent, while rates for Uttar Pradesh (New Delhi) were 0 percent and 12.5 percent. State governments were indifferent as to whether assembly was performed by an independent distributor or by Konark, as long as the activity took place inside state borders. Manufacturing capacity at Konark was around 400,000 units per year but could be easily expanded by 80 percent with a second shift.

The Konark product line was designed by engineers at Grundig, Gmbh., a German manufacturer known for quality electronic products. This technical collaboration resulted in a line considered by many in the industry to be of higher quality than those of many competitors. Circuitry was well designed and engineers at Konark paid close attention to quality control. In addition, each Konark set was operated for 24 hours as a test of reliability before being shipped. The entire line reflected Konark's strategy of attempting to provide the market with a quality product at prices below the competition. In Orissa, the lowest priced black and white model marketed by Konark sold to consumers for about Rs. 2,200, while its most expensive color set sold for about Rs. 15,000. Promotion literature describing two of Konark's black and white models appears in Exhibit 1.

Konark had a well-established network of more than 500 dealers located in 12 Indian states. In eight states, Konark sold its products directly to dealers through branch offices operated by a Konark area manager. Each branch office also contained two or three salesmen who were assigned specific territories. Together, branch offices were expected to account for about 30 percent of Konark's sales revenues and cost Konark about Rs. 10 million in fixed and variable expenses for 1994. In three states, Konark used instead the service of independent distributors to sell to dealers. The three distributors carried only Konark TV sets and earned a margin of 3 percent (based on cost) for all their activities, including assembly. All dealers and distributors were authorized to service Konark sets. The branch offices monitored all service activities.

In Orissa, Konark used a large branch office to sell to approximately 250 dealers. In addition, Konark used company-owned showrooms as a second channel of distribution. Konark would lease space for showrooms at one or two locations in larger cities and display the complete line. The total cost of operating a showroom was estimated at about Rs. 100,000 per year. Prospective customers often preferred to visit a showroom because they could easily compare different models and talk directly to a Konark employee. However, they seldom purchased—buyers preferred instead to buy from dealers because dealers were known to bargain and to sell at a discount from the list price. In contrast, Konark showrooms were under strict orders to sell all units at list price. About half of Konark's 1990 sales revenues would come from Orissa; about 95 percent of Orissa's unit sales would come from dealers.

The appointment of dealers, either by Konark or its distributors, was made under certain conditions (Exhibit 2). Essential

EXHIBIT 1   Konark Promotion Literature

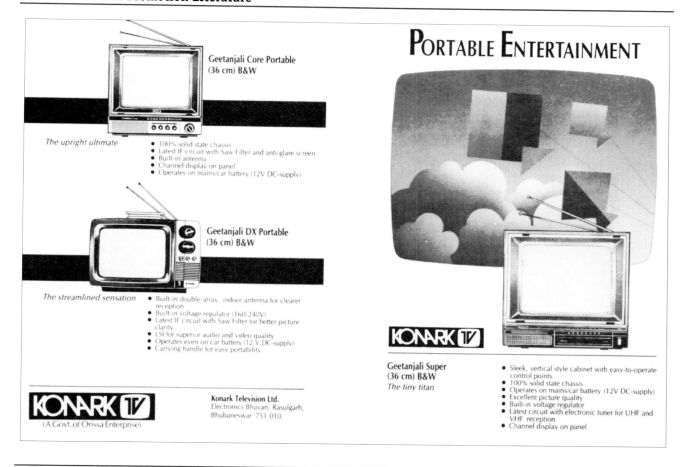

among them was the dealer's possession of a suitable show-room for the display and sale of TV sets. Dealers were also expected to sell Konark TV sets to the best of their ability, at fixed prices, and in specified market areas. Dealers were not permitted to sell sets made by other manufacturers. Dealers earned margins ranging from Rs. 100 (small black and white model) to Rs. 900 (large color model) for every set they sold. Mr. Bhalla estimated that the average dealer margin would be about Rs. 320 per set.

The Crisis.   Unit demand for TV sets in 1994 was expected to grow at only 10 percent, compared to almost 40 percent for 1992 and 1991. Industry experts attributed the slowing growth rate to a substantial hike in consumer prices. The blame was laid almost entirely on increases in import duties, excise duties, and sales taxes, plus devaluation of the rupee—despite election year promises by government officials to offer TV sets at affordable prices! In addition, Konark was about to be affected by the Orissa government's decision to revoke the company's sales tax exemption beginning January 1, 1995. "Right now we are the clear choice, as Konark is the cheapest brand with a superior quality. But with the withdrawal of the exemption, we will be in the same price range as the 'big boys' and it will be a real run for the money

to sell our brand," remarked Mr. Bhalla. Konark's market share in Orissa might fall from its present level of 70 percent of units sold to as low as 50 percent.

Some immediate actions were needed to counter the sales tax decision, improve dealer relations, and stimulate greater sales activity. An example was Konark's quarterly "Incentive Scheme," which had begun in April 1993. The program was a rebate arrangement based on points earned for a dealer's purchases of Konark TV sets. Reaction was lukewarm when the program was first announced. However, a revision in August 1993 greatly increased participation. Other actions yet to be formulated could be announced at a dealers conference that Mr. Bhalla had scheduled for the next month.

All such actions would have to be consistent with Konark's long-term distribution strategy. The problem was that this strategy had not yet been formulated. Mr. Bhalla saw this void as his most pressing responsibility, as well as a topic of great interest to Mr. Singh. Mr. Bhalla hoped to have major aspects of a distribution strategy ready for discussion for next week's meeting. Elements of the strategy would include recommendations on channel structure— branch offices or independent distributors, company showrooms or independent dealers—in existing markets as well as in markets identified for expansion.

EXHIBIT 2   Terms and Conditions for Dealers of Konark TV Products

1. The Dealer shall canvass for, secure orders, and affect sales of Konark Television Sets to the best of his ability and experience and he will guarantee sale of minimum of sets during a calendar month.
2. The Company shall arrange for proper advertisement in the said area and shall give publicity of their product through newspapers, magazines, cinema slides, or by any other media and shall indicate, wherever feasible, the Dealer's name as their Selling Agents. The cost of such advertisements may be shared by the Company and the Dealer as may be mutually agreed to.
3. The appointment shall be confirmed after 3 months and initially be in force for a period of one year and can be renewed every year by mutual consent.
4. The Company reserves the right to evaluate the performance of a Dealer.
5. This appointment may be terminated with a notice of one month on either side.
6. The Company shall deliver the Konark Television Sets to the Dealer at the price agreed upon on cash payment at the factory at Bhubaneswar. On such delivery, the title to the goods would pass on to the Dealer and it will be the responsibility of the Dealer for the transportation of the sets to their place at their cost and expenses.
7. The Company may, however, at their discretion allow a credit of 30 (thirty) days subject to furnishing a Bank Guarantee or letter of credit or security deposits towards the price of Konark Television Sets to be lifted by the Dealer at any time.
8. The Company shall not be responsible for any damage or defect occurring to the sets after delivery of the same to the Dealer or during transit.
9. The Dealer shall undertake to sell the sets to customers at prices fixed by the Company for different models. Dealer margins will be added to wholesale prices while fixing the customer's price of the television sets.
10. The Dealer will not act and deal with similar products of any other company so long as his appointment with Konark Television continues.
11. The Dealer shall not encroach into areas allotted to any other Dealer.
12. Any dispute or difference arising from or related to the appointment of Dealership shall be settled mutually and, failing amicable settlement, shall be settled by an Arbitrator to be appointed by the Chairman of the Company whose decision shall be final and binding upon the parties. The place of arbitration shall be within the State of Orissa and the Court in Bhubaneswar (Orissa) only shall have jurisdiction to entertain any application, suit, or claim arising out of the appointment. All disputes shall be deemed to have arisen within the jurisdiction of the Court of Bhubaneswar.
13. Essential requirements to be fulfilled before getting Dealership:
    a. The Dealer must have a good showroom for display and sale of Television Sets.
    b. The Dealer should have sufficient experience in dealing with Electronics Products (Consumer Goods).

CASE 3–4
SWIFTER, HIGHER, STRONGER, DEARER[1]

Television and Sport Are Perfect Partners. Each Has Made the Other Richer. But Is the Alliance Really So Good for Sport?

Back in 1948, the BBC, Britain's public broadcasting corporation, took a fateful decision. It paid a princely £15,000 (£27,000 in today's money) for the right to telecast the Olympic Games to a domestic audience. It was the first time a television network had paid the International Olympic Committee (IOC, the body that runs the Games) for the privilege.

But not the last. The rights to the Olympics, which opened in Atlanta on July 19, 1996, raised $900m from broadcasters round the world. And the American television rights to the Olympiads up to and including 2008 have been bought by America's NBC network for an amazing $3.6 billion (see Exhibit 1).

The Olympics are only one of the sporting properties that have become hugely valuable to broadcasters. Sport takes up a growing share of screen time (as those who are bored by it know all too well). When you consider the popularity of the world's great tournaments, that is hardly surprising. *Sportsfests* generates audiences beyond the wildest dreams of television companies for anything else. According to Nielsen Media Research, the number of Americans watching the 1996 Super Bowl, the main annual football

---

[1] From *The Economist*, July 20, 1996, pp. 17–19.

EXHIBIT 1   Chariots for Hire: Olympic Broadcast Rights Fees,* $bn

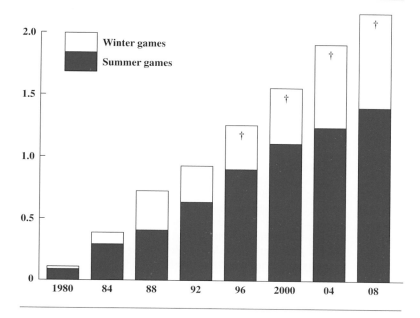

* Rights for 2000–08 Games negotiated to March 1996.
† Two years earlier.
Source: IOC.

EXHIBIT 2   Sport First

Top 10 TV Programmes in America, Sep 95–Jul 96, %*	
Super Bowl	46.0
Super Bowl Kickoff	35.5
Super Bowl Post	35.0
NFC Championship	33.3
AFC Championship	27.1
NFC Playoff-Sunday	25.4
AFC Championship-Sunday	25.4
NFC Playoff-Saturday	22.2
E.R.	22.0
Seinfeld	21.2

*% of American households tuning into the average minute of the programme
Source: Nielsen Media Research

championship, averaged 94m. The top eight television programmes in America are all sporting events (see Exhibit 2). A staggering 3¹/₂ billion people are likely to watch some part of the 1996 Olympiad—two-thirds of mankind.

The reason television companies love sport is not merely that billions want to tele-gawk at ever-more-wonderful sporting feats. Sport also has a special quality that makes it unlike almost any other sort of television programme: immediacy. Miss seeing a particular episode of, say, "E.R." and you can always catch the repeat, and enjoy it just as much. Miss seeing your team beat hell out of its biggest rival, and the replay will leave you cold. "A live sporting event loses almost all its value as the final whistle goes," saves Steve Barnett, author of a British book on sport. The desire to watch sport when it is

happening, not hours afterwards, is universal: a study of South Korea by Spectrum, a British consultancy, finds that live games get 30 percent of the audience while recordings get less than 5 percent.

This combination of popularity and immediacy has created a symbiotic relationship between sport and television in which each is changing the other. As Stephen Wenn, of Canada's Wilfrid Laurier University, puts it, television and the money it brings have had an enormous impact on the Olympic Games, including on the timing of events and their location. For instance, an Asian Olympics poses a problem for American networks: viewers learn the results on the morning news.

The money that television has brought into professional basketball has put some of the top players among the world's highest-paid entertainers: a few are getting multiyear contracts worth over $100m. Rugby has begun to be reorganised to make it more television-friendly; other sports will follow. And, though soccer and American football draw the largest audiences, television has also promoted the popularity of sports which stir more local passions: rugby league in Australia, cricket in India, table tennis in China, snooker in Britain.

What is less often realised is that sport is also changing television. To assuage the hunger for sports, new channels are being launched at a tremendous pace. In America, ESPN, a cable network owned by Capital Cities/ABC, is starting a 24-hour sports news network in the autumn; in Britain, BskyB, a satellite broadcaster partly owned by Rupert Murdoch, has two sports channels and is about to launch a third. Because people seem more willing to pay to watch sport on television than to pay for any other kind of programming, sport has become an essential part of the business strategy of television empire-builders such as Mr. Murdoch. Nobody in the world understands the use of sports as a bait for viewers better than he.

In particular, sport suggests an answer to one of the big problems that will face television companies in the future: how can viewers, comfortable with their old analogue sets, be persuaded to part with the hefty price of a new digital set and a subscription to an untried service? The answer is to create an exclusive chance to watch a desirable event, or to use the hundreds of channels that digital television provides to offer more variety of sports coverage than analogue television can offer. This ploy is not new. "Radio broadcasts of boxing were once used to promote the sale of radios, and baseball to persuade people to buy television sets," points out Richard Burton, a sports marketing specialist at the Lundquist College of Business at Oregon University. In the next few years, the main new outlet for sports programmes will be digital television.

Going for Gold

To understand how these multiple effects have come about, go back to those vast sums that television companies are willing to pay. In America, according to Neal Weinstock of Weinstock Media Analysis, total spending on sports rights by television companies is about $2 billion a year. Easily the most valuable rights are for American football. One of the biggest sporting coups in the United States was the purchase by Fox, owned by Mr. Murdoch's News Corp, of the rights to four years of National Football League games for $1.6 billion, snatching them from CBS. Rights for baseball, basketball, and ice hockey are also substantial (see Exhibit 3).

Americans are rare in following four main sports rather than one. America is also uncommon in having no publicly owned networks. As a result, bidding wars in other countries, though just as fierce as in America, are different in two ways: they are often fought between public broadcasters and new upstarts, many of them pay channels; and they are usually about soccer.

Nothing better illustrates the change taking place in the market for soccer rights than the vast deal struck in early July by Kirch, a German group owned by a secretive Bavarian media mogul. The group spent $2.2 billion for the world's biggest soccer-broadcasting rights: to show the finals of the World Cup in 2002 and 2006 outside America. That is over six times more than the amount paid for the rights to the World Cups of 1990, 1994, and 1998.

Such vast bids gobble up a huge slice of a television company's budget. In America, reckons London Economics, a British consultancy, sport accounts for around 15 percent of all television-programme spending. For some television companies, the share is much larger. BSkyB spends £100m ($155m) a year on sports, about a third of its programming budget.

This seems to pose a threat to public broadcasting, for, in any bidding war outside America, public broadcasting companies are generally the losers. A consortium of mainly public broadcasters bought the rights to the 1990–98 World Cups for a total of $344m. This time around, the consortium raised its bid to around $1.8 billion, and still lost. Public broadcasters often do not have the money to compete: in Britain, the BBC spends about 4 percent of its programme budget on sport in a non-Olympic year, about £15m a year less than BSkyB.

The problem is that the value of sport to viewers ("consumer surplus," as economists would put it) is much larger than the value of most other sorts of programming. Public broadcasters have no way to benefit from the extra value that a big sporting event offers viewers. But with subscription television and with pay-TV, where viewers are charged for each event, the television company will directly collect the value viewers put on being able to watch.

Because of this, many people (especially in Europe) worry that popular sports will increasingly be available only on subscription television, which could, they fear, erode the popular support upon which public broadcasters depend. In practice, these worries seem excessive. Although far more sport will be shown on subscription television, especially outside America's vast advertising market, the most popular events are likely to remain freely available for many years to come, for two reasons.

First, those who own the rights to sporting events are rarely just profit-maximisers: they also have an interest in keeping the appeal of their sport as broad as possible. They may therefore refuse to sell to the highest bidder. Earlier this year, the IOC turned down a $2 billion bid from Mr. Murdoch's News Corp for the European broadcasting rights to the Olympic Games between 2000 and 2008 in favour of a lower bid from a group of public broadcasters. Sometimes, as with the sale of World Cup rights to Kirch, the sellers may stipulate that the games be aired on "free" television.

EXHIBIT 3   Big Deals Europe and America

Event	Date	Buyer	$bn
Olympic Games	1996–2008*	NBC	4.00
World Cup soccer	2002–06	Kirch	2.36
NCAA basketball	1995–2002	CBS	1.73
National Football League (NFL)	1995–98†	Fox	1.58
Olympic Games	1996–2008	EBU	1.44
English Premier League soccer	1997–2001†	BSkyB	0.96
NFL	1995–98†	ABC	0.92
NFL	1995–98†	NBC	0.87
National Basketball Association	1995–98†	NBC	0.75
Dutch Premier League soccer	1996–2004	Sport 7	0.65

* 1998 Winter Games bought by CBS.
† Season ending.
Sources: *Broadcasting & Cable;* Kagan World Media.

Second, the economics of televising sport mean that the biggest revenues are not necessarily earned by tying up exclusive rights. Steven Bornstein, the boss of ESPN, argues that exclusive deals to big events are "not in our long-term commercial interest." Because showing sport on "free" television maximises the audience, some advertisers will be willing to pay a huge premium for the big occasion. So will sponsors who want their names to be seen emblazoned on players' shirts or on billboards around the pitch.

It is not only a matter of audience size. Sport is also the most efficient way to reach one of the world's most desirable audiences from an advertiser's point of view: young men with cash to spend. Although the biggest audiences of young men are watching general television, sporting events draw the highest concentrations. So advertisers of products such as beer, cars, and sports shoes can pay mainly for the people they most want to attract.

There are other ways in which sport can be indirectly useful to the networks. A slot in a summer game is a wonderful opportunity to promote a coming autumn show. A popular game wipes out the audience share of the competition. And owning the rights to an event allows a network plenty of scope to entertain corporate grandees who may then become advertisers.

For the moment, though, advertising revenue is the main recompense that television companies get for their huge investments in sport. Overall, according to *Broadcasting & Cable,* a trade magazine, sport generated $3.5 billion, or 10 percent, of total television advertising revenues in America last year. The biggest purchasers of sports rights by far in America are the national networks. NBC alone holds more big sports rights than any other body has held in the history of television. It can, obviously, recoup some of the bill by selling advertising: for a 30-second slot during the Super Bowl, NBC asked for $1.2m.

Such deals, however, usually benefit the networks indirectly rather than directly. The Super Bowl is a rarity: it has usually made a profit for the network that airs it. "Apart from the Super Bowl, the World Series [for baseball] and probably the current Olympics, the big sports don't usually make money for the networks," says Arthur Gruen of Wilkowsky Gruen, a media consultancy. "But they are a boon for their affiliate stations, which can sell their advertising slots for two or three times as much as other slots." Although Fox lost money on its NFL purchase, it won the loyalty of affiliate stations (especially important for a new network) and made a splash.

Almost everywhere else, the biggest growth in revenues from showing sports will increasingly come from subscriptions or pay-per-view arrangements. The versatility and huge capacity of digital broadcasting make it possible to give subscribers all sorts of new and lucrative services.

In America, DirectTV and Primestar, two digital satellite broadcasters, have been tempting subscribers with packages of sporting events from distant parts of the country. "They have been creating season tickets for all the main events, costing $100–150 per season per sport," says John Mansell, a senior analyst with Paul Kagan, a Californian consultancy. In Germany DF1, a satellite company jointly owned by Kirch and BSkyB and due for launch at the end of July, has the rights to show Formula One motor racing. It plans to allow viewers to choose to follow particular teams, so that Ferrari fanatics can follow their drivers, and to select different camera angles.

In Italy, Telepiu, which launched digital satellite television in February, plans to offer viewers a package in September which will allow them to buy a season ticket to live matches played by one or more teams in the top Italian soccer leagues. The system's "electronic turnstile" is so sophisticated that it can shut off reception for subscribers living in the catchment area for a home game, to assuage clubs' worries that they will lose revenue from supporters at the gate. In fact, top Italian clubs usually have to lock out their fanatical subscribers to avoid overcapacity.

Most skillful of all at using sports rights to generate subscription revenue is BSkyB. It signed an exclusive contract with the English Premier League which has been the foundation of its success. Some of those who know BSkyB well argue that £5 billion of the business's remarkable capital value of £8 billion is attributable to the profitability of its soccer rights.

Winner Take All

Just as the purchase of sporting rights enriches television companies, so their sale has transformed the finances of the sports lucky enough to be popular with viewers. On the whole, the biggest beneficiaries have not been the clubs and bodies that run sports, but the players. In the same way as rising revenues from films are promptly dissipated in vast salaries to stars in Hollywood, in sport the money coming in from television soon flows out in heftier payments to players.

In America, the market for sportsmen is well developed and the cost of players tends to rise with the total revenues of the main sporting organizations (see Exhibit 4). Elsewhere, the market is newer and so a bigger slice of the revenues tend to stick to the television companies. "The big difference between sports and movies is the operating margins," says Chris Akers, chairman of Caspian, a British media group, and an old hand at rights negotiations. "Hollywood majors have per-subscriber deals. No sports federation has yet done such a deal."

Guided by the likes of Mr. Akers, they soon will. Telepiu's latest three-year soccer contract gives the television firm enough revenue to cover its basic costs, guarantees the soccer league a minimum sum and then splits the takings down the middle. In Britain, BSkyB is locked in dispute with the Premier League over the terms of the second half of its rights deal: should the league then be able to opt for half the revenue from each subscriber on top of or instead of a fixed hunk of net profits?

The logical next step would be for some clubs or leagues to set up their own pay-television systems, distributing their games directly by satellite or cable. A few people in British soccer are starting to look with interest at America's local sports networks, such as the successful Madison Square Garden cable network, and to wonder whether Europe might move the same way.

If it does, not all teams will benefit equally. In America, football has an elaborate scheme to spread revenues from national television across teams. But in other sports, including baseball, the wealth and size of a team's local market mean large differences in rights from local television. The New York Yankees make almost $50m a year from local television rights, says Brian Schechter, a Canadian media analyst. At the other end of the scale, the Kansas City Royals make $4m–5m a year.

Not all players benefit equally, either. Television has brought to sport the "winner-take-all" phenomenon. It does not cost substantially more to stage a televised championship game than a run-of-the-week, untelevised match. But the size of the

EXHIBIT 4   To the Winner the Spoils: National Football League, $bn

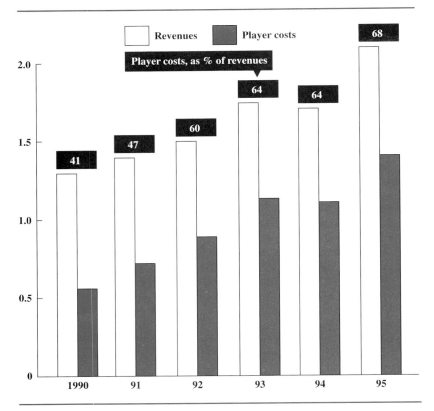

Source: SportsValue.

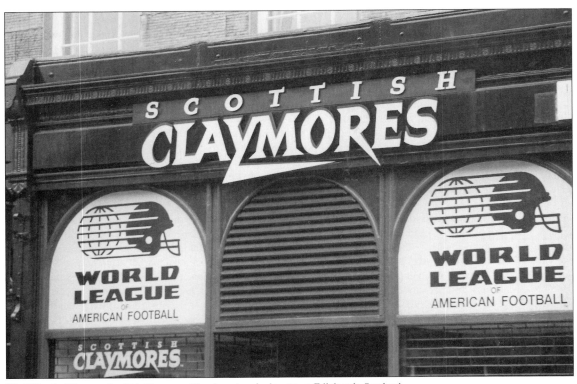

World Football League Scottish Claymores' headquarters in downtown Edinburgh, Scotland.

audience, and therefore the revenue generated, may be hugely different. As a result, players good enough to be in the top games will earn vastly more than those slightly less good, who play to smaller crowds.

The Referee's Whistle

The lure of money is already altering sport and will change it more. Increasingly, games will be reorganised to turn them into better television. British rugby-union officials are squabbling over the spoils from television rights. Rugby league, whose audiences had been dwindling, won a contract worth £87m over five years from BSkyB earlier this year in exchange for switching its games from winter to summer. Purists were aghast.

Other reorganisations for the benefit of television will surely come. Mr. Murdoch wants to build a rugby superleague, allowing the best teams around the world to play each other. A European superleague for soccer is possible. "At the moment, Manchester United plays AC Milan every 25 years: it's a joke," complains one enthusiast.

Sports traditionalists resist changing their ways for the likes of Mr. Murdoch. So far, the big sporting bodies have generally held out against selling exclusive pay-television rights to their crown jewels, and have sometimes deliberately favoured public broad-casters. Regulators have helped them, intervening in some countries to limit exclusive deals with pay-television groups. Britain has just passed a law to stop subscription channels tying up exclusive rights to some big events, such as the Wimbledon tennis championship. In Australia in March, a court threw out News Corp's attempt to build a rugby superleague as the lynchpin of its pay-television strategy.

But the real monopolists are not the media companies, but the teams. Television companies can play off seven or eight Holly-wood studios against each other. But most countries have only one national soccer league, and a public that loves soccer above all other sports. In the long run, the players and clubs hold most of the cards. The television companies are more likely to be their ser-vants than their masters.

Questions

1. The following are the prices paid for the American television broadcasting rights of the summer Olympics since 1980:[2] Moscow—NBC agreed to pay $85 million; 1984 in Los Angeles—ABC paid $225 million; 1988 in Seoul—NBC paid $300 million; 1992 in Barcelona—NBC paid $401 million; 1996 through 2008—NBC will pay $3.6 billion. You have been charged with the responsibility of determining the IOC and local Olympic Committee's asking prices for the 2004 television broadcast rights to five different markets: Japan, China, Australia, the European Union, and Brazil. Determine a price for each and justify your decisions.

2. Your instructor may assign you to represent either the IOC or any one of the television networks in each of the five countries that have been asked to bid for the broadcast rights for the 2004 Games. Prepare to negotiate prices and other organizational details.

3. The World Football League (WFL), a joint venture between the National Football League (NFL) and Fox Television (owned by Rupert Murdoch's News Corp.), has offered you the Edinburg, Scotland, Claymores franchise. Your Scottish Claymores, should you choose to invest, will be playing against the other five WFL teams from London, Barcelona, Amsterdam, Frankfurt, and Dusseldorf. What would you be willing to pay for the Claymores? The interested investor will note that a previous incarnation of the WFL with three teams in Europe and seven in the United States folded in its second season in 1992 having lost $50 million.[3]

---

[2] See Roy J. Lewicki, Joseph A. Litterer, David M. Saunders, and John W. Minton, *Negotiation: Readings, Exercises, and Cases,* 2nd ed. (Burr Ridge, IL: Irwin, 1993), and John L. Graham and Yoshihiro Sano, *Smart Bargaining: Doing Business with the Japanese,* 2nd ed., (New York: Harper-Collins, 1989), for details regarding the negotiations.

[3] Roger Thurow and A. Craig Copetas, "NFL Goes Long in Its Attempt to Sell World League in Europe," *The Wall Street Journal,* March 28, 1997, p. B7.

DEVELOPING GLOBAL MARKETING STRATEGIES

Outline of Cases

CASE 4-1
GLOBAL STRATEGIES—WHAT ARE THEY?

Global strategies do not mean huge companies operating in a single world market. They are much more complex. Global competitive strategies are a bit like supernatural creatures: they can be imagined by each individual to suit his or her own reality while evoking a common concern. The best illustrations are the slogans companies use to describe themselves. These range from "Think Local, Act Global" all the way to its opposite "Think Global Act Local, with everything in between."[1]

Defining Global Strategies

Some 15 years have gone by since the term "global strategy" entered our vocabulary, enough time to bring some clarity to its definition. We now know what it is and what it is not.

Consider first what it is not. Global strategies are not standard product–market strategies that assume the world to be a single, homogeneous, border-free marketplace. The Uruguay Round of trade and investment liberalization notwithstanding, the world is still a collection of different independent economies, each with its own market characteristics. Each, moreover, has its own societal aspirations that occasionally find expression in protectionist policies of one form or another.

Global strategies are also not about global presence or about large companies. A company can very well operate in all countries of the world; but if what it does in one country has no meaning for what it does in another, it is no different from the domestic companies it competes with in each location.

To qualify as pursuing a global strategy, a company needs to be able to demonstrate two things: that it can contest any market it chooses to compete in, and that it can bring its entire worldwide resources to bear on any competitive situation it finds itself in, regardless of where that might be.

Selective Contestability.   Just as companies possessing a certain set of technologies and business competencies choose particular market segments to concentrate on, a global company can be selective about the countries in which it operates.

Many small, high-technology companies and luxury good manufacturers do just that. They compete where there is adequate demand to justify the investments needed to access the market; they focus their investments to achieve critical mass only in those markets they are interested in.

The important thing is that they can and are prepared to contest any and all markets should circumstances warrant. They constantly scour the world for market openings, they process information on a global basis, and they constitute a "potential" threat even in places they have not yet entered.

Markets where such contestability exists, as a corollary, start to behave almost as if the company had already entered—provided,

of course, the threat of entry is a credible one. This explains why telecom markets the world over are so fiercely competitive from the day they are no longer government or private monopolies. The handful of international players in the equipment business not only are waiting in the wings but have products that conform to international standards and resources they can deploy for market access as soon as opportunity arises.

Global Resources for Each Main Street.   The corner shop that carries products by IBM, Philips, Coca-Cola, or Du Pont knows from experience that there is something special about these products compared with those supplied by a small local company. In comparison, products from companies such as Nestlé, Unilever, or even Procter & Gamble did not seem so special—in the past at least. Their names, formulations, and the way they were produced and marketed were not too different from domestic ones.

Just being present in several countries, in other words, does not constitute a global strategy. Globalism is an earned notion rather than being entitlement created by the fact of operating in several countries.

A basic characteristic of a global company is its ability to bring its entire worldwide capabilities to bear on any transaction anywhere regardless of the products it makes. This underlies the importance of organizational integration in global strategies. Transporting capabilities across borders on an as-needed basis requires all local units to be connected and permeable, not isolated from one another.

This is also what allows global strategies to be "within-border" strategies while, at the same time, being "cross-border" ones. They are manifest on each Main Street, with local companies sensing they are dealing with a worldwide organization even while the latter employs a local competitive formula.

Main Attributes of Global Strategy

This dual notion of market contestability and bringing global resources to bear on competition wherever a company is present is really what global strategies are about. Industries where such strategies are prevalent assume a character of their own in which strategies that are geared to one country alone cannot be adopted. What companies do in one country has an inevitable consequence for what they do in others.

There is, of course, nothing absolute about global strategies. Being near-cousins of multidomestic strategies, the best way to judge them is in terms of "degrees of globalness." At the risk of oversimplification, the more a company scores in each of the following five attributes, the more it can be considered a global competitor based on the definition just given. These include possessing a standard product (or core) that is marketed uniformly across the world; sourcing all assets, not just production, on an optimal basis; and achieving market access in line with the break-even volume of the needed infrastructure.

- *Standard products and marketing mix.* While the advantages of having a standard product and marketing mix are obvious, this attribute involves several trade-offs in practice.

---

[1] Note: The authors do not offer this presentation as the definitive piece on global strategies or global companies but only as a basis for discussion.

Source: Vijay Jolly, "Global Strategies in the 1990s," *The Financial Post,* February 15, 1997, p. S6

Economies of scale in design, production, and promotion need to be compared to the greater market acceptance that local adaptation often provides.

If a general conclusion can be drawn, it would be the need at least to aim for a standard "core" in the product and limiting marketing adaptations to those absolutely necessary. The more integrated countries become economically, the less latitude there is anyway for things such as price discrimination and channel selection. The same applies to situations where buyers themselves are global and expect similar products and terms on a worldwide basis.

- *Sourcing assets, not just products.* Sourcing products and components internationally based on comparative advantage and availability has long been a feature of international business. What is new is the possibility to source assets or capabilities related to any part of the company's value chain. Whether it is capital from Switzerland or national credit agencies, software skills from Silicon Valley or Bangalore, or electronic components from Taiwan, global companies now have a wider latitude in accessing resources from wherever they are available or cost-competitive.

The implication of this is that global strategies are as much about asset deployment for market access purposes as they are about asset accumulation abroad. The latter include local capital, technical skills, managerial talent, and new product ideas, as well as the host competencies that local partners and institutions can provide. Also, whereas previously assets accumulated locally were mainly to support a local business, it is increasingly possible—and desirable—to separate those needed for local market access from those intended to support the company's business elsewhere.

It is here that we associate partnerships and alliances with global strategy. They can supplement what a company already possesses by way of assets or complement what is missing, thereby speeding up the creation of the needed infrastructure as well as reducing costs and risks.

- *Market access in line with break-even.* For a company to be a credible global competitor it does not need to be among the biggest in its industry. But it has to be big enough to generate the volume of sales the required infrastructure demands and to amortize up-front investments in R&D and promotion.

Today, it is the latter investments that count most. In the pharmaceutical industry, for example, it now costs around US$400 million to come up with a successful new drug. This puts a natural floor on the amount of sales to be generated over the life of the drug. The greater the presence of a company in all of the large markets, and the greater its ability to launch the drug simultaneously in them, the higher the likelihood of profiting from the investment made.

The same argument applies to other investments in intangibles such as brands. If we associate global competitiveness with size, it is chiefly on account of these types of investments. Unlike investments in plants and physical infrastructure, which can result in diminishing returns to scale, intangibles almost always translate into "big is better."

- *Contesting assets.* Another distinguishing feature of a global company is its ability to neutralize the assets and competencies of its competitors. If a competitor switches its supply from a high-cost to a low-cost factory it too can do so; if a competitor gains access to a critical technology it can do the same. Similarly, if a competitor is using one market to generate excess cash flow in order to "invest" in another, it is able to neutralize this advantage by going to the relatively more profitable market itself.

Purely domestic companies and even those that are run on a multidomestic basis, lack such arbitrage possibilities. Just as in sourcing, to exploit these requires a global view of the business and the capacity to manage it in an integrated fashion.

- *All functions have a global orientation.* As much of the foregoing suggests, global competition today is a lot more than simple cross-border competition at the product or service level. It is equally about building and managing a multinational infrastructure. Frequently, the latter means internationalizing all of the competencies and functions of a company: its R&D, procurement, production, logistics, and marketing, as well as human resources and finance.

These functions are all geared to providing customers with superior products and services on a worldwide basis. The more they have a global orientation of their own, the greater their contribution to the overall effort. Hence, even if their focus may be primarily national in scope, supporting a local business with no trade, for example, any contribution they can make to other units of the company helps.

These five attributes, taken together, operationalize a global strategy. The degrees of globalness in a strategy are the extent to which each is fulfilled in practice. The fact of not having a standard global product, for example, diminishes the scope of a global strategy but does not entirely destroy it, provided the company scores high on the other attributes. If anything, stressing one attribute to the exclusion of others can even be counterproductive and unfeasible. A good balance between all of them is needed.

Local Adaptation

Another important point to make about these attributes is that they do not assume a single, open global marketplace. Trade and investment liberalization coupled with improvements in transportation and communications are what have made global strategies possible. Trade protection, labor policies, investment incentives, and a host of regulations continue to force a country-by-country adaptation of strategies.

It is also these realities, along with the sociocultural differences between countries, that have caused many companies to stress the "local" dimension in their business. And rightly so. If all companies confront the same set of market conditions, advantage goes to those that adapt their strategies best.

The best way to reconcile these local differences with the attributes required of a global strategy is to see them as constraints to global optimization. Localness, in other words, is another variable to incorporate in decision making. Considering it as the basis for the strategy itself, however, is to deny all of the advantages a global company possesses. This is perhaps the biggest conundrum companies face today.

While adapting strategies to local conditions offers greater opportunities for revenue generation, it has two main impacts: it causes overinvestment in the infrastructure needed to serve markets, and brings about a lack of consistency in whatever strategy is being pursued.

Neither is intrinsically bad. They can even contribute positively to the end result if approached correctly. All that is needed is to factor them in as variables to be considered, without losing sight of the overall objective of competing effectively both within and across borders.

Consider the issue of overinvestment, especially in capital-intensive businesses such as semiconductors. Companies such as Texas Instruments, NEC, and Mitsubishi Electric have consciously located abroad. This not only permits them to benefit from generous investment incentives provided by local governments that want such facilities, but also means they can mobilize local companies as co-investors to share the capital burden and help with market access.

More contentious is the issue of strategic focus. Should local subsidiaries be allowed to modify products and diversify into businesses that make sense for them only? Or should they be consistent with what the parent company focuses on? The answer to this depends on several things: a company's definition of its business scope and growth vectors; the subsidiary's domain within the overall organization; and the locus of its strategy-making process.

Business scope and growth vectors pertain to a company's attitude to diversification generally. If its products and technologies provide adequate growth opportunities on a worldwide basis, it is probably better off restricting each subsidiary to just those. If, on the other hand, growth is primarily driven through exploring and creating new market opportunities, then local initiatives are usually welcome.

Logitech SA, a world leader in pointing devices for the personal computer industry, for example, permitted and even encouraged its Taiwanese company to develop special software products for the Chinese market because that would be an additional product to fuel its growth, reduce its dependence on the mouse and, incidentally, facilitate access to a new market. A company that comes up with a new cancer treatment, on the other hand, is likely to want to invest all its resources in commercializing that worldwide as quickly as possible.

The more a company's infrastructure and skills become dispersed and the more global responsibilities individual subsidiaries take on, the greater the need to see the initiation of strategies as a global process. What the parent knows and sees may not be the same as subsidiary management. Giving subsidiaries too narrow a mission based on a centralized notion of between-country competition not only constrains their potential for accumulating local resources but diminishes their potential for competing within their country.

Organizational Implications

How companies ought to structure and manage their international operations has been debated as long as the debate on strategy itself. Because organizations need to reflect a wide range of company-specific characteristics—such as size, diversity, age, culture, technology—in addition to their global posture, it has proven hard to be normative. There are, however, certain key design considerations related to global posture that have dominated thinking and practice in recent years.

The most important consideration has to do with the greater need for organizational integration that global strategies require.

Hence, when companies first tried to adapt their structures in the 1970s and early 1980s, most of them created elaborate matrix organizations giving equal status to products, geography, and functions. While such organizations worked well for some companies, ABB being the leading example, they did not for others. ABB succeeded because of the nature of its business, its superior information system (called Abacus), its investment in developing a number of globally minded managers, and a small but highly effective top management team. What ABB was able to do was to balance finely the need for local autonomy in decision making with the strategic and organizational integration that managing the business on a global basis demanded.

Others that were not able to achieve this balance opted for tilting their matrix in favor of one or the other dimension. Most often, the dominant dimension became product groups or strategic business units, the assumption being that integrating each product's business system on a worldwide basis was the best way to optimize strategy and achieve coherence among different local units.

Where these "product headquarters" were located mattered less and many companies consciously spread them around as a better way to integrate country organizations, give particular local managers a broader domain to look after, and exploit country-specific assets or competencies. Such dispersal had the attendant benefit of also reducing the role (and size) of corporate headquarters.

This fine-tuning of structures continues today. To the extent one can discern a trend for the 1990s it would be one consisting of three things: reverting to a single locus of direction and control, giving greater emphasis to functional strategies instead of business-by-business ones, and creating simple line organizations based on a more decentralized "network" of local companies.

The move to a single locus is partly on account of the difficulty companies have experienced in managing dispersed product headquarters.

The complex interactions between units they gave rise to, the lack of global reach on the part of some country organizations, and the potential for confusion between corporate roles and business unit functions were apparently not compensated by whatever advantage they offered. But it is equally on account of the recognition of the importance of a coherent set of values, goals, and identity, as well the need to avoid duplication of functions across the world.

Having functions as the primary dimension to coordinate global strategies also reflects the dual nature of the latter, combining asset deployment for market-access reasons and asset accumulation for sourcing purposes. Another virtue of a functional orientation is that it is usually at this level that global alliances and asset accumulation takes place—the R&D function cooperating with other companies' R&D departments, procurement with suppliers, finance with local finance companies, and so on.

While marketing can and should be managed nationally or regionally, R&D, finance, and manufacturing lend themselves better to global coordination. Texas Instruments Inc., for example, used to manage its business, including manufacturing, on a regional basis. Four years ago, it introduced the notion of the "virtual fab," linking all its 17 manufacturing sites around the world into a single organization.

In addition to standardizing equipment and procedures across plants, this allows the company to transfer expertise across units efficiently, allocate production optimally, and interact with development on a global basis. Whereas previously the company had country-by-country sales forces, it now has market-based teams with global responsibility for a product's success. The latter has proved particularly effective in serving the needs of global customers who expect similar conditions worldwide.

Whether to have a single set of global functions or to have them specialized by business unit depends on how diverse the latter are. The lesson companies have learned, however, is to avoid overly complex matrix structures and to allow local units sufficient autonomy at the business level.

The last point refers to the way individual units in a global company need to be treated. Based on the arguments made earlier, what one is seeing is an upgrading of their role, both as a locus for independent entrepreneurial effort and as contributors to the business worldwide.

To perform this expanded role coherently they need greater empowerment coupled with all of the things that a network organization possesses: a commonly shared knowledge base, common values and goals, a common understanding of priorities and precommitments others have made, and a common set of measures to judge performance.

Shared values are known to replace the need for elaborate direction and control. Rather than planning for the synergies and interdependencies that are at the heart of a global strategy, effective networks create them voluntarily and in real time. Global strategies in their present form have proved far too complex and demanding to be implemented in a centralized manner.

Questions

1. Write a critique of each of the major points presented in this case. Based on this critique, write your own definition of a global strategy.

2. What do the authors mean by selective contestability? How practical is this idea for a small international company?

3. The case discusses five attributes that, taken together, operationalize a global strategy. How would you use these attributes to define a global company? A global strategy?

4. Evaluate one of the following companies as to its degree of globalness: Nestlé, Procter & Gamble, Unilever, or a company of your choice. Be sure to discuss both why you believe or why you do not believe the company is a global company, has a global product, and/or has a global strategy. You may find some information that is helpful at the Web sites for Nestlé: **http://www.nestle.com**; Procter & Gamble: **http://www.pg.com**; and Unilever: **http://www. uilever.com**.

CASE 4-2
TAMBRANDS—OVERCOMING CULTURAL RESISTANCE

Tampax, Tambrands' only product, is the best-selling tampon in the world with 44 percent of the global market. North America and Europe account for 90 percent of those sales. The company saw earnings drop 12 percent to $82.8 million on revenues of $662 million in 1996. The stakes are high for Tambrands because tampons are basically all it sells, and in the U.S., which currently generates 45 percent of Tambrands' sales, the company is mired in competition with such rivals as Playtex Products Inc. and Kimberly-Clark. What's more, new users are hard to get because 70 percent of women already use tampons. In the 52 weeks ended Feb. 22, 1996, Tambrands' U.S. sales fell 0.6 percent to $335.8 million, according to A. C. Nielsen.

In the overseas market, Tambrands officials talk glowingly of a huge opportunity. Only 100 million of the 1.7 billion eligible women in the world currently use tampons. In planning for expansion into a global market, Tambrands divided the world into three clusters, based not on geography, but on how resistant women are to using tampons. The goal is to market to each cluster in a similar way.

Most women in *Cluster One,* including the U.S., the United Kingdom, and Australia, already use tampons and may feel they know all they need to know about the product. In *Cluster Two,* which includes countries such as France, Israel, and South Africa, about 50 percent of women use tampons. Some concerns about virginity remain and tampons are often considered unnatural products that block the flow. Tambrands enlists gynecologists' endorsements to stress scientific research on tampons. Potentially the most lucrative—but infinitely more challenging—group is *Cluster Three,* which includes countries like Brazil, China, and Russia. There, along with tackling the virginity issue, Tambrands must also tell women how to use a tampon without making them feel uneasy. While the advertising messages differ widely from country to country, Tambrands is also trying to create a more consistent image for its Tampax tampons. The ads in each country show consecutive shots of women standing outside declaring the tampon message, some clutching a blue box of Tampax. They end with the same tagline, "Tampax. Women Know." While marketing consultants say Tambrands' strategy is a step in the right direction, some caution that tampons are one of the most difficult products to market worldwide.

"The greatest challenge in the global expansion of tampons is to address the religious and cultural mores that suggest that insertion is fundamentally prohibited by culture," says the managing director of a consulting company. "The third market [Cluster 3] looks like the great frontier of tampons, but it could be the seductive noose of the global expansion objective."

Sources: Yumiko Ono, "Tambrands Ads Aim to Overcome Cultural and Religious Obstacles," *The Wall Street Journal,* March 17, 1997, p. B8; Sally Goll Beatty and Raju Narisetti, "P&G's Plan for Tambrands Sparks Questions about Account Switch," *The Wall Street Journal,* April 10, 1997, p. B15; Sharon Walsh, "Procter & Gamble Bids to Acquire Tambrands; Deal Could Expand Global Sales of Tampax," *The Washington Post,* April 10, 1997, p. C01; and Kelley Holland, "A New Home for Tambrands," *Business Week,* April 21, 1997, p. 48.

A Tambrands spokeswoman says the company is aware that even within **Cluster Three,** cultural and religious barriers vary. While the company's sales are increasing in some countries like Russia, Tambrands isn't targeting Muslim countries, she says. While Tambrands gears up for international expansion, it is also increasing ad spending in its mainstay U.S. market. Its new focus in the United States: encouraging women to use tampons overnight. Using the **Cluster One** approach of pitching to an already educated and jaded audience, a new ad tries to tease women with a provocative question, "Should I sleep with it, or not?"

The company's new global campaign for Tambrands is a big shift from most feminine-protection-product ads which often show frisky women dressed in white pants biking or turning cartwheels, while discreetly pushing messages of comfort. The new campaign features local women talking frankly about what has been a taboo subject in many countries. A recent Brazilian ad shows a close-up of a tampon while the narrator chirps, "It's sleek, smooth and really comfortable to use."

For years Tambrands has faced a delicate hurdle selling Tampax tampons in Brazil because many young women fear they'll lose their virginity if they use a tampon. When they go to the beach in tiny bikinis, tampons aren't their choice. Instead, hordes of women use pads and gingerly wrap a sweater around their waist. Now, the No. 1 tampon maker hopes a bold new ad campaign will help change the mind-set of Brazilian women. "Of course, you're not going to lose your virginity," reassures one cheerful Brazilian woman in a new television ad. Tambrands' risky new ads are just part of a high-stakes campaign to expand into overseas markets where it has long faced cultural and religious sensitivities. The new ads feature local women being surprisingly blunt about such a personal product. In China, another challenging market for Tambrands, a new ad shows a Chinese woman inserting a tampon into a test tube filled with blue water. "No worries about leakage," declares another.

"In any country, there are boundaries of acceptable talk. We want to go just to the left of that," says the creative director of the New York advertising agency which is creating Tambrands' $65 million ad campaign worldwide. "We want them to think they have not heard frankness like this before." In the next three months the agency plans to launch new Tampax ads in 26 foreign countries and the U.S. However, being a single product company, it is a risky proposition for Tambrands to engage in a global campaign and to build a global distribution network all at the same time.

Tambrands concluded that the company could not continue to be profitable if its major market was the United States and that to launch a global marketing program was too risky to go it alone. The company approached Procter & Gamble about a buyout, and

the two announced a $1.85 billion deal. The move puts Procter back in the tampon business for the first time since its Rely brand was pulled in 1980 after two dozen women who used tampons died from toxic shock syndrome. Procter plans to sell Tampax as a complement to its existing feminine-hygiene products, particularly in Asia and Latin America.

P&G, known for its innovation in such mundane daily goods as disposable diapers and detergent, has grown in recent years by acquiring products and marketing them internationally. "Becoming part of P&G—a world-class company with global marketing and distribution capabilities—will accelerate the global growth of Tampax and enable the brand to achieve its full potential. This will allow us to take the expertise we've gained in the feminine protection business and apply it to a new market with Tampax." Market analysts applauded the deal. "P&G has the worldwide distribution that Tampax so desperately needs," said a stock market analyst. "Tambrands didn't have the infrastructure to tap into growth in the developing countries and P&G does." Market analysts estimate that in some countries, such as those in Asia and Latin America, only about 5 percent of eligible women use tampons. In addition, P&G has expertise in the sanitary protection market as the world's biggest seller of sanitary pads under the Always brand name.

The company said it would use its strong research and development arm to improve the existing Tampax product and develop others. Procter & Gamble's $1.85 billion purchase of Tambrands Inc. will make the consumer product giant, already the biggest maker of feminine pads, the leader in the tampon market. Visit Tampax's Web site for some examples of their Web advertising in various countries at **http://tampax.com/suite**. Procter & Gamble can be reached at **http://www.pg.com**.

Questions

1. Evaluate the wisdom of Tambrands becoming part of Procter and Gamble.

2. The company indicated that the goal of the global advertising plan was to "market to each cluster in a similar way." Discuss this goal. Should P&G continue with the stated goal? Why? Why not?

3. For each of the three clusters identified by Tambrands, identify the cultural resistance that must be overcome. Suggest possible approaches to overcoming the resistance you identify.

4. In reference to the approaches you identified in question 3, is there an approach that can be used to reach the goal, "market to each cluster in a similar way"?

Case 4–3
Baby Apparel and Dubai Fashions—Letter of Credit as an Export Payment

Baby Apparel

Baby Apparel was incorporated in December 1981. From a 1,500-square-meter factory in Manila employing 35 people with U.S.$181,398 in export sales, the company has grown to two factories employing over 1,400 workers with sales of U.S.$8,230,199 (FOB Manila) in 1996.

Baby Apparel, a leading children's wear exporter, specializes in handsmocked children's wear. Handsmocking is a skill that was taught to Filipinos by Spanish nuns during the Spanish regime in the Philippines. To this day, it is said that the Filipinos do better handsmocking than the Spanish. Buyers the world over look to the Philippines for handsmocked dresses because of the quality of the work. Thailand, Malaysia, and Indonesia produce handsmocked children's dresses, but buyers are said to prefer the quality of Philippine handsmocking. Baby Apparel customers include England's Princess Eugenie and Princess Beatrice, daughters of Princess Fergie and Prince Andrew.

Baby Apparel's exports to the U.S. and U.K. account for 90 percent of its production. Its biggest buyer is Norman Marcus, Ltd., a U.K.-based manufacturer and importer. Baby Apparel also sells to JC Penney Company, one of the world's biggest retailers.

Dubai Fashions

September 1, 1996, Mr. Abdul Alih, managing director of Dubai Fashions, visited Manila to look for a supplier of children's wear with smocking. Dubai Fashions is a garment importer based in the United Arab Emirates; it has shops in Dubai, Sharjah, and Alain. Before going to the Philippines, Dubai Fashions had sourced its children's wear from Spain and the United Kingdom. Having heard that the handsmocked children's wear in Spain and U.K. were imported from the Philippines, Dubai Fashions decided to cut the distribution channel by importing directly from the Philippines. Mr. Alih obtained a list of recommended children's wear exporters from the Philippine Commercial Office in Dubai. On top of this list was Baby Apparel.

The Transaction

Although Dubai Fashions liked Baby Apparel's handsmocked dresses instantly, product revisions had to be made to suit the Arab market. Unlike the children's summer dresses sold to JC Penney which had no sleeves and no lining, children's dresses to be sold to Dubai Fashions had to have sleeves and linings. Further, utmost care had to be taken to ensure that designs did not include stars and crosses. A sales contract amounting to U.S. $22,710 covering 2,700 pieces, to be delivered no later than November 15, 1996, was signed by Mr. Alih and Baby Apparel. On August 7, 1996, the

This case was developed by Professor Luz T. Suplico, De La Salle University, Manila, Philippines. The case is based on a true incident but the persons, figures, and data have been disguised.

Bank of Oman, the issuing bank, sent an irrevocable Letter of Credit (LC) at sight to the Philippine National Bank, the negotiating bank. The following were some of the LC's terms:

1. Shipment.
   1.1 Port of discharge: Manila.
   1.2 Port of destination: Dubai.
   1.3 Partial shipment: Allowed.
   1.4 Transshipment: Allowed.
   1.5 Shipment expiry date: November 28, 1996.
   1.6 Shipping documents should be presented to the issuing bank within 10 days of issuance but within the validity of the credit.

2. Special Instructions.
   2.1 Invoice should show the manufacturer's name.
   2.2 Bill of Lading should show Bank of Oman as notify party.
   2.3 Shipment is to be effected by the United Arab Shipping Co. (UASC) line vessel or conference and/or regular line vessel only and a certificate to this effect from the shipping company or its agent must accompany the negotiated documents.
   2.4 A certificate from the owner/master or agent of the vessel or from the manufacturer/exporter is to be presented stating "To Whom It May Concern" and "We certify that the vessel is allowed by Arab authorities to call at Arab ports and is not scheduled to call at any Israeli port during its trip to Arab countries." This certificate is not applicable if shipment was effected on UASC vessel.
   2.5 An inspection certificate is to be issued and signed by the authorized buying agent.

After the receipt of the LC, Baby Apparel produced the reference samples, which were airshipped to Dubai Fashions. Dubai approved the reference samples without any revision. Thus, Baby Apparel began production as soon as the reference samples were approved. Because of its tight production schedule for its major buyers, Baby Apparel notified Dubai that it was having difficulties in shipping the goods before November 15, 1996.

In the Middle East, all business activities are suspended during Ramadan. Dubai had made an urgent request for shipment no later than November 28, 1996, to assure arrival in UAE before the start of Ramadan January 11, 1997. Shipment after December 12, 1996, would mean arrival during Ramadan, and Dubai Fashions would be unable to move the merchandise out of the warehouse until Ramadan was over. The order was shipped on December 15, 1996, and was short four pieces. The buying agent and Dubai Fashions agreed to waive the short-shipment discrepancy on condition that Baby Apparel send the remaining four pieces by courier.

Ocean shipment from Manila to Dubai takes about 30 days on a regular vessel. Since the goods were shipped based on an Irrevocable Letter of Credit at sight, Baby Apparel only had to send the complete set of documents as specified in the LC to the Bank of Oman to be paid. It had expected payment no later than January 15, 1997.

As nonpayment of LCs from the Middle East was a rampant practice, Baby Apparel became increasingly concerned when the Philippine National Bank reported that it could not pay them despite the submission of complete documents. On January 20, Baby Apparel faxed Dubai Fashions to send proof of shipment to the Philippine National Bank as it was not able to receive payment. Dubai Fashions followed up the payment at the Bank of Oman and the following discrepancies in the documents were reported:

1. The LC had expired.
2. The presentation of shipping documents was late.
3. The invoice did not show the manufacturer's name.
4. The Bill of Lading did not show that Bank of Oman was the notifying party.

Dubai Fashions agreed to waive these discrepancies and the Bank of Oman remitted payment to Baby Apparel through the Philippine National Bank.

Questions

1. Why is it important to follow the terms of the LC? What measures should have been taken by Baby Apparel to prevent the discrepancies found in the LC?

2. If you were the production manager of Baby Apparel, how would you try to prevent a potential short-shipment problem in the next order of Dubai Fashions?

3. What were the special arrangements that Baby Apparel had to make in dealing with Arab importers in terms of the products and shipment?

CASE 4-4
BLAIR WATER PURIFIERS INDIA*

"A pity I couldn't have stayed for Diwali," thought Rahul Chatterjee. "But anyway it was great to be back home in Calcutta." The Diwali holiday and its festivities would begin in early November 1996, some two weeks after Chatterjee had returned to the United States. Chatterjee worked as an international market liaison for Blair Company, Inc. This was his eighth year with Blair Company and easily his favorite. "Your challenge will be in moving us from just dabbling in less developed countries (LDCs) to our thriving in them," his boss had said when Chatterjee was promoted to the job last January. Chatterjee had agreed and was thrilled when asked to visit Bombay and New Delhi in April. His purpose on that trip was to gather background data on the possibility of Blair Company entering the Indian market for home water purification devices. Initial results were encouraging and prompted the second trip.

Chatterjee had used his second trip primarily to study Indian consumers in Calcutta and Bangalore and to gather information on possible competitors. The two cities represented quite different metropolitan areas in terms of location, size, language, and infrastructure—yet both suffered from similar problems in terms of water supplied to their residents. These problems could be found in many LDCs and were favorable to home water purification.

Information gathered on both visits would be used to make a recommendation on market entry and on elements of an entry strategy. Executives at Blair Company would compare Chatterjee's recommendation to those from two other Blair Company liaisons who were focusing their efforts on Argentina, Brazil, and Indonesia.

Indian Market for Home Water Filtration and Purification

Like most aspects of India, the market for home water filtration and purification took a good deal of effort to understand. Yet despite expending this effort, Chatterjee realized that much remained either unknown or in conflict. For example, the market seemed clearly a mature one, with four or five established Indian competitors fighting for market share. Or was it? Another view portrayed the market as a fragmented one, with no large competitor having a national presence and perhaps 100 small, regional manufacturers, each competing in just one or two of India's 25 states. Indeed, the market could be in its early growth stages, as reflected by the large number of product designs, materials, and performances. Perhaps with a next generation product and a world-class marketing effort, Blair Company could consolidate the market and stimulate tremendous growth—much like the situation in the Indian market for automobiles.

Such uncertainty made it difficult to estimate market potential. However, Chatterjee had collected unit sales estimates for a 10-year period for three similar product categories—vacuum cleaners, sewing machines, and color televisions. In addition, a Delhi-based research firm had provided him with estimates of unit sales for Aquaguard, the largest-selling water purifier in several Indian states. Chatterjee had used the data in two forecasting models available at Blair Company along with three subjective scenarios—realistic, optimistic, and pessimistic—to arrive at the estimates and forecasts for water purifiers shown in Exhibit 1. "If anything," Chatterjee had explained to his boss, "my forecasts are conservative because they describe only first-time sales, not any replacement sales over the 10-year forecast horizon." He also pointed out that his forecasts applied only to industry sales in larger urban areas, which was the present industry focus.

One thing that seemed certain was that many Indians felt the need for improved water quality. Folklore, newspapers, consumer activists, and government officials regularly reinforced this need

*This case was written by Professor James E. Nelson, University of Colorado at Boulder. He thanks students in the Class of 1996 (Batch 31), Indian Institute of Management, Calcutta, for their invaluable help in collecting all data needed to write this case. He also thanks Professor Roger Kerin, Southern Methodist University, for his helpful comments in writing this case. The case is intended for educational purposes rather than to illustrate either effective or ineffective decision making. Some data as well as the identity of the company are disguised. ©1997 by James E. Nelson. Used with permission.

EXHIBIT 1   Industry Sales Estimates and Forecasts for Water Purifiers in India, 1990–2005 (000 units)

| | Unit Sales | Unit Sales Forecast Under . . . | | |
Year	Estimates	Realistic Scenario	Optimistic Scenario	Pessimistic Scenario
1990	60			
1991	90			
1992	150			
1993	200			
1994	220			
1995	240			
1996		250	250	250
1997		320	370	300
1998		430	540	400
1999		570	800	550
2000		800	1,200	750
2001		1,000	1,500	850
2002		1,300	1,900	900
2003		1,500	2,100	750
2004		1,600	2,100	580
2005		1,500	1,900	420

by describing the poor quality of Indian water. Quality suffered particularly during the monsoons because of highly polluted water entering treatment plants and because of numerous leaks and unauthorized withdrawals from water systems. Such leaks and withdrawals often polluted clean water after it had left the plants. Politicians running for national, state, and local government offices also reinforced the need for improved water quality through election campaign promises. Governments at these levels set standards for water quality, took measurements at thousands of locations throughout the nation, and advised consumers when water became unsafe.

During periods of poor water quality, many Indian consumers had little choice but to consume the water as they found it. However, better educated, wealthier, and more health conscious consumers took steps to safeguard their family's health and often continued these steps year-round. A good estimate of the number of such households, Chatterjee thought, would be around 40 million. These consumers were similar in many respects to consumers in middle- and upper-middle-class households in the United States and the European Union. They valued comfort and product choice. They saw consumption of material goods as a means to a higher quality of life. They liked foreign brands and would pay a higher price for such brands, as long as purchased products outperformed competing Indian products. Chatterjee had identified as his target market these 40 million households plus those in another four million households who had similar values and lifestyles, but as yet took little effort to improve water quality in their homes.

Traditional Method for Home Water Purification.   The traditional method of water purification in the target market relied not on any commercially supplied product but instead on boiling. Each day or several times a day, a cook, maid, or family member would boil two to five liters of water for 10 minutes, allow it to cool, and then transfer it to containers for storage (often in a refrigerator). Chatterjee estimated that about 50 percent of the target market used this procedure. Boiling was seen by consumers as inexpensive, effective in terms of eliminating dangerous bacteria, and entrenched in a traditional sense. Many consumers who used this method considered it more effective than any product on the market. However, boiling affected the palatability of water, leaving the purified product somewhat "flat" to the taste. Boiling also was cumbersome, time-consuming, and ineffective in removing physical impurities and unpleasant odors. Consequently, about 10 percent of the target market took a second step by filtering their boiled water through "candle filters" before storage. Many consumers who took this action did so despite knowing that water could become recontaminated during handling and storage.

Mechanical Methods for Home Water Filtration and Purification.   About 40 percent of the target market used a mechanical device to improve their water quality. Half of this group used candle filters, primarily because of their low price and ease of use. The typical candle filter comprised two containers, one resting on top of the other. The upper container held one or more porous ceramic cylinders (candles) which strained the water as gravity drew it into the lower container. Containers were made of plastic, porcelain, or stainless steel and typically stored between 15 and 25 liters of filtered water. Purchase costs depended on materials and capacities, ranging from Rs.350 for a small plastic model to Rs.1,100 for a large stainless steel model (35 Indian Rupees were equivalent to U.S. $1.00 in 1996). Candle filters were slow, producing 15 liters (one candle) to 45 liters (three candles) of filtered water each 24 hours. To maintain this productivity, candles regularly needed to be removed, cleaned, and boiled for 20 minutes. Most manufacturers recommended that consumers replace candles (Rs.40 each) either once a year or more frequently, depending on sediment levels.

The other half of this group used "water purifiers," devices that were considerably more sophisticated than candle filters. Water purifiers typically employed three water processing stages. The first removed sediments, the second objectionable odors and colors, and the third harmful bacteria and viruses. Engineers at Blair Company were skeptical that most purifiers claiming the latter benefit actually could deliver on their promise. However, all purifiers did a better job here than candle filters. Candle filters were totally ineffective in eliminating bacteria and viruses (and might even increase this type of contamination), despite advertising claims to the contrary. Water purifiers generally used stainless steel containers and sold at prices ranging from Rs.2,000 to Rs.7,000, depending on manufacturers, features, and capacities. Common flow rates were one to two liters of purified water per minute. Simple service activities could be performed on water purifiers by consumers as needed. However, more complicated service required units to be taken to a nearby dealer or an in-home visit from a skilled technician.

The remaining 10 percent of the target market owned neither a filter nor a purifier and seldom boiled their water. Many consumers in this group were unaware of water problems and thought their water quality acceptable. However, a few consumers in this group refused to pay for products that they believed were mostly ineffective. Overall, Chatterjee believed that only a few consumers in this group could be induced to change their habits and become customers. The most attractive segments consisted of the 90 percent of households in the target market who boiled, boiled and filtered, only filtered, or purified their water.

All segments in the target market showed a good deal of similarity in terms of what they thought important in the purchase of a water purifier. According to Chatterjee's research, the most important factor was product performance in terms of sediment removal, bacteria and virus removal, capacity (either in the form of storage or flow rate), safety, and "footprint" space. Purchase price also was an important concern among consumers who boiled, boiled and filtered, or only filtered their water. The next most important factor was ease of installation and service, with style and appearance rated almost as important. The least important factor was warranty and availability of finance for purchase. Finally, all segments expected a water purifier to be warranted against defective operation for 18 to 24 months and to perform trouble-free for five to ten years.

Foreign Investment in India

India appeared attractive to many foreign investors because of government actions begun in the 1980s during the administration of Prime Minister Rajiv Gandhi. The broad label applied to these actions was "liberalisation." Liberalisation had opened the Indian economy to foreign investors, stemming from recognition that protectionist policies had not worked very well and that western economies and technologies—seen against the collapse of the Soviet Union—did. Liberalisation had meant major changes in approval requirements for new commercial projects, investment policies, taxation procedures, and, most importantly, attitudes of government officials. These changes had stayed in place through the two national governments that followed Gandhi's assassination in 1991.

If Blair Company entered the Indian market, it would do so in one of three ways: (1) joint working arrangement, (2) joint venture

company, or (3) acquisition. In a joint working arrangement, Blair Company would supply key purifier components to an Indian company that would manufacture and market the assembled product. License fees would be remitted to Blair Company on a per unit basis over the term of the agreement (typically five years, with an option to renew for three more). A joint venture agreement would have Blair Company partnering with an existing Indian company expressly for the purpose of manufacturing and marketing water purifiers. Profits from the joint venture operation would be split between the two parties per the agreement, which usually contained a clause describing buy/sell procedures available to the two parties after a minimum time period. An acquisition entry would have Blair Company purchasing an existing Indian company whose operations then would be expanded to include the water purifier. Profits from the acquisition would belong to Blair Company.

Beyond understanding these basic entry possibilities, Chatterjee acknowledged that he was no expert in legal aspects attending the project. However, two days spent with a Calcutta consulting firm had produced the following information. Blair Company must apply for market entry to the Foreign Investment Promotion Board, Secretariat for Industrial Approvals, Ministry of Industries. The proposal would go before the Board for an assessment of the relevant technology and India's need for the technology. If approved by the Board, the proposal then would go to the Reserve Bank of India, Ministry of Finance, for approvals of any royalties and fees, remittances of dividends and interest (if any), repatriations of profits and invested capital, and repayment of foreign loans. While the process sounded cumbersome and time-consuming, the consultant assured Chatterjee that the government usually would complete its deliberations in less than six months and that his consulting firm could "virtually guarantee" final approval.

Trademarks and patents were protected by law in India. Trademarks were protected for seven years and could be renewed on payment of a prescribed fee. Patents lasted for 14 years. On balance, Chatterjee had told his boss that Blair Company would have "no more problem protecting its intellectual property rights in India than in the United States—as long as we stay out of court." Chatterjee went on to explain that litigation in India was expensive and protracted. Litigation problems were compounded by an appeal process that could extend a case for easily a generation. Consequently, many foreign companies preferred arbitration, as India was a party to the Geneva Convention covering Foreign Arbitral Awards.

Foreign companies were taxed on income arising from Indian operations. They also paid taxes on any interest, dividends, and royalties received, and on any capital gains received from a sale of assets. The government offered a wide range of tax concessions to foreign investors, including liberal depreciation allowances and generous deductions. The government offered even more favorable tax treatment if foreign investors would locate in one of India's six Free Trade Zones. Overall, Chatterjee thought that corporate tax rates in India probably were somewhat higher than in the United States. However, so were profits—the average return on assets for all Indian corporations in recent years was almost 18 percent, compared to about 11 percent for United States corporations.

Approval by the Reserve Bank of India was needed for repatriation of ordinary profits. However, approval should be obtained easily if Blair Company could show that repatriated profits were being paid out of export earnings of hard currencies. Chatterjee thought that export earnings would not be difficult to realize, given India's extremely low wage rates and its central location to wealthier South Asian countries. "Profit repatriation was really not much of an issue, anyway," he thought. Three years might pass before profits of any magnitude could be realized; at least five years would pass before substantial profits would be available for repatriation. Approval of repatriation by the Reserve Bank might not be required at this time, given liberalisation trends. Finally, if repatriation remained difficult, Blair Company could undertake crosstrading or other actions to unblock profits.

Overall, investment and trade regulations in India in 1996 meant that business could be conducted much easier than ever before. Hundreds of companies from the European Union, Japan, Korea, and the United States were entering India in all sectors of the country's economy. In the home appliance market, Chatterjee could identify 11 such firms—Carrier, Electrolux, General Electric, Goldstar, Matsushita, Singer, Samsung, Sanyo, Sharp, Toshiba, and Whirlpool. Many of these firms had yet to realize substantial profits but all saw the promise of a huge market developing over the next few years.

Blair Company, Inc.

Blair Company was founded in 1975 by Eugene Blair, after he left his position in research and development at Culligan International Company. Blair Company's first product was a desalinator, used by mobile home parks in Florida to remove salts from brackish well water supplied to residents. The product was a huge success and markets quickly expanded to include nearby municipalities, smaller businesses, hospitals, and bottlers of water for sale to consumers. Geographic markets also expanded, first to other coastal regions near the company's headquarters in Tampa, Florida, and then to desert areas in the southwestern United States. New products were added rapidly as well and, by 1996, the product line included desalinators, particle filters, ozonators, ion exchange resins, and purifiers. Industry experts generally regarded the product line as superior in terms of performance and quality, with prices higher than those of many competitors.

Blair Company sales revenues for 1996 would be almost $400 million, with an expected profit close to $50 million. Annual growth in sales revenues averaged 12 percent for the past five years. Blair Company employed over 4,000 people, with 380 having technical backgrounds and responsibilities.

Export sales of desalinators and related products began at Blair Company in 1980. Units were sold first to resorts in Mexico and Belize and later to water bottlers in Germany. Export sales grew rapidly and Blair Company found it necessary to organize its International Division in 1985. Sales in the International Division also grew rapidly and would reach almost $140 million in 1996. About $70 million would come from countries in Latin and South America, $30 million from Europe (including shipments to Africa), and $40 million from South Asia and Australia. The International Division had sales offices, small assembly areas, and distribution facilities in Frankfurt, Germany; Tokyo, Japan; and Singapore.

The Frankfurt office had been the impetus in 1990 for development and marketing of Blair Company's first product targeted exclusively to consumer households—a home water filter. Sales engineers at the Frankfurt office began receiving consumer and distributor requests for a home water filter soon after the fall of

the Berlin wall in 1989. By late 1991, two models had been designed in the United States and introduced in Germany (particularly to the eastern regions), Poland, Hungary, Romania, the Czech Republic, and Slovakia.

Blair Company executives watched the success of the two water filters with great interest. The market for clean water in LDCs was huge, profitable, and attractive in a socially responsible sense. However, the quality of water in many LDCs was such that a water filter usually would not be satisfactory. Consequently, in late 1994, executives had directed the development of a water purifier that could be added to the product line. Engineers had given the final design in the project the brand name, "Delight." For the time being, Chatterjee and the other market analysts had accepted the name, not knowing if it might infringe on any existing brand in India or in the other countries under study.

Delight Purifier

The Delight purifier used a combination of technologies to remove four types of contaminants found in potable water—sediments, organic and inorganic chemicals, microbials or cysts, and objectionable tastes and odors. The technologies were effective as long as contaminants in the water were present at "reasonable" levels. Engineers at Blair Company had interpreted "reasonable" as levels described in several World Health Organization (WHO) reports on potable water and had combined the technologies to purify water to a level beyond WHO standards. Engineers had repeatedly assured Chatterjee that Delight's design in terms of technologies should not be a concern. Ten units operating in the company's testing laboratory showed no signs of failure or performance deterioration after some 5,000 hours of continuous use. "Still," Chatterjee thought, "we will undertake a good bit of field testing in India before entering. The risks of failure are too large to ignore. And, besides, results of our testing would be useful in convincing consumers and retailers to buy."

Chatterjee and the other market analysts still faced major design issues in configuring technologies into physical products. For example, a "point of entry" design would place the product immediately after water entry to the home, treating all water before it flowed to all water outlets. In contrast, a "point of use" design would place the product on a countertop, wall, or at the end of a faucet and treat only water arriving at that location. Based on cost estimates, designs of competing products, and his understanding of Indian consumers, Chatterjee would direct engineers to proceed only with "point of use" designs for the market.

Other technical details were yet to be worked out. For example, Chatterjee had to provide engineers with suggestions for filter flow rates, storage capacities (if any), unit layout, and overall dimensions, plus a number of special features. One such feature was the possibility of a small battery to operate the filter for several hours in case of a power failure (a common occurrence in India and many other LDCs). Another might be one or two "bells or whistles" to tell cooks, maids, and family members that the unit indeed was working properly. Yet another might be an "additive" feature, permitting users to add fluoride, vitamins, or even flavorings to their water.

Chatterjee knew that the Indian market would eventually require a number of models. However, at the outset of market entry, he probably could get by with just two—one with a larger capacity for houses and bungalows and the other a smaller capacity

EXHIBIT 2

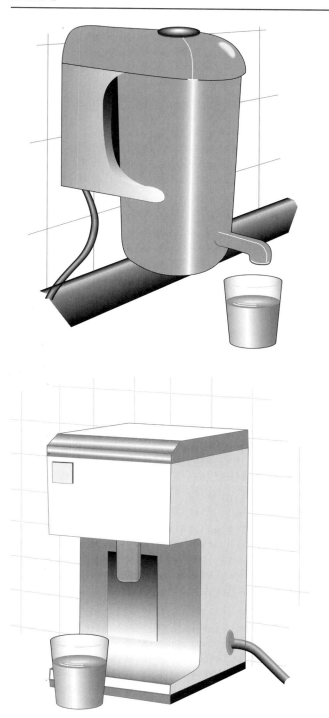

model for flats. He thought that model styling and specific appearances should reflect a western, high technology school of design in order to distinguish the Delight purifier from competitors' products. To that end, he had instructed a graphics artist to develop two ideas that he had used to gauge consumer reactions on his last

visit (see Exhibit 2). Consumers liked both models but preferred the countertop design to the wallmount design.

Competitors

Upwards of 100 companies competed in the Indian market for home water filters and purifiers. While information on most of these companies was difficult to obtain, Chatterjee and the Indian research agencies were able to develop descriptions of three major competitors and brief profiles of several others.

Eureka Forbes.   The most established competitor in the water purifier market was Eureka Forbes, a joint venture company established in 1982 between Electrolux (Sweden) and Forbes Campbell (India). The company marketed a broad line of "modern, lifestyle products" including water purifiers, vacuum cleaners, and mixers/grinders. The brand name used for its water purifiers was "Aquaguard," a name so well established that many consumers mistakenly used it to refer to other water purifiers or to the entire product category. Aquaguard, with its 10-year market history, was clearly the market leader and came close to being India's only national brand. However, Eureka Forbes had recently introduced a second brand of water purifier called "PureSip." The PureSip model was similar to Aquaguard except for its third stage process, which used a polyiodide resin instead of ultraviolet rays to kill bacteria and viruses. This meant that water from a PureSip purifier could be stored safely for later usage. Also in contrast to Aquaguard, the PureSip model needed no electricity for its operation.

However, the biggest difference between the two products was how they were sold. Aquaguard was sold exclusively by a 2,500 person salesforce that called directly on households. In contrast, PureSip was sold by independent dealers of smaller home appliances. Unit prices to consumers for Aquaguard and PureSip in 1996 were approximately Rs.5,500 and Rs.2,000, respectively. Chatterjee believed that unit sales of PureSip were much smaller than unit sales for Aquaguard but growing at a much faster rate.

An Aquaguard unit typically was mounted on a kitchen wall, with plumbing required to bring water to the purifier's inlet. A two-meter long power cord was connected to a 230 volt AC electrical outlet—the Indian standard. If the power supply were to drop to 190 volts or lower, the unit would stop functioning. Other limits of the product included a smallish amount of activated carbon, which could eliminate only weak organic odors. It could not remove strong odors or inorganic solutes like nitrates and iron compounds. The unit's design did not allow for storage of treated water and its flow rate of one liter per minute seemed slow to some consumers.

Aquaguard's promotion strategy emphasized personal selling. Each salesman was assigned to a specific neighborhood and was monitored by a group leader who, in turn, was monitored by a supervisor. Each salesman was expected to canvass his neighborhood, select prospective households (e.g., those with annual incomes exceeding Rs.70,000), demonstrate the product, and make an intensive effort to sell the product. Repeated sales calls helped to educate consumers about their water quality and to reassure them that Aquaguard service was readily available. Television commercials and advertisements in magazines and newspapers supported the personal selling efforts. Chatterjee estimated that Eureka Forbes would spend about Rs.120 million on all sales activities in 1996 or roughly 11 percent of its sales revenues. He estimated that about Rs.100 million of the Rs.120 million would be spent in the form of sales commissions. Chatterjee thought the company's total advertising expenditures for the year would be only about Rs.1 million.

Eureka Forbes was a formidable competitor. The salesforce was huge, highly motivated, and well managed. Moreover, Aquaguard was the first product to enter the water purifier market, and the name had tremendous brand equity. The product itself was probably the weakest strategic component—but it would take much to convince consumers of this. And, while the salesforce offered a huge competitive advantage, it represented an enormous fixed cost and essentially limited sales efforts to large urban areas. More than 80 percent of India's population lived in rural areas, where water quality was even lower.

Ion Exchange.   Ion Exchange was the premier water treatment company in India, specializing in treatments of water, processed liquids, and wastewater in industrial markets. The company began operations in 1964 as a wholly-owned subsidiary of British Permutit. Permutit divested its holdings in 1985 and Ion Exchange became a wholly-owned Indian company. The company presently served customers in a diverse group of industries, including nuclear and thermal power stations, fertilizers, petrochemical refineries, textiles, automobiles, and home water purifiers. Its home water purifiers carried the family brand name, ZERO-B (Zero-Bacteria).

ZERO-B purifiers used a halogenated resin technology as part of a three-stage purification process. The first stage removed suspended impurities via filter pads, the second eliminated bad odors and taste with activated carbon, and the third killed bacteria using trace quantities of polyiodide (iodine). The latter feature was attractive because it helped prevent iodine deficiency diseases and permitted purified water to be stored up to eight hours without fear of recontamination.

The basic purifier product for the home carried the name "Puristore." A Puristore unit typically sat on a kitchen counter near the tap, with no electricity or plumbing hookup needed for its operation. The unit stored 20 liters of purified water. It sold to consumers for Rs.2,000. Each year the user must replace the halogenated resin at a cost of Rs.200.

Chatterjee estimated that ZERO-B captured about 7 percent of the Indian water purifier market. Probably the biggest reason for the small share was a lack of consumer awareness. ZERO-B purifiers had been on the market for less than three years. They were not advertised heavily nor did they enjoy the sales effort intensity of Aquaguard. Distribution, too, was limited. During Chatterjee's visit, he could find only five dealers in Calcutta carrying ZERO-B products and none in Bangalore. Dealers that he contacted were of the opinion that ZERO-B's marketing efforts soon would intensify—two had heard rumors that a door-to-door salesforce was planned and that consumer advertising was about to begin.

Chatterjee had confirmed the latter point with a visit to a Calcutta advertising agency. A modest number of 10-second TV commercials soon would be aired on Zee TV and DD metro channels. The advertisements would focus on educating consumers with the position, "It is not a filter." Instead, ZERO-B is a water purifier and much more effective than a candle filter in preventing health problems. Apart from this advertising effort, the only other form of promotion used was a point-of-sale brochure that dealers could give to prospective customers (see Exhibit 3).

On balance, Chatterjee thought that Ion Exchange could be a major player in the market. The company had over 30 years'

experience in the field of water purification and devoted upwards of Rs.10 million each year to corporate research and development. "In fact," he thought, "all Ion Exchange really needs to do is to recognize the market's potential and to make it a priority within the company." However, this might be difficult to do, given the company's prominent emphasis on industrial markets. Chatterjee estimated that ZERO-B products would account for less than 2 percent of Ion Exchange's 1996 total sales, estimated at Rs. 1,000 million. He thought the total marketing expenditures for ZERO-B would be around Rs.3 million.

Singer.   The newest competitor to enter the Indian water purifier market was Singer India Ltd. Originally, Singer India was a subsidiary of The Singer Company, located in the United States, but a minority share (49 percent) was sold to Indian investors in 1982. The change in ownership had led to construction of manufacturing facilities in India for sewing machines in 1983. The facilities were expanded in 1991 to produce a broad line of home appliances. Sales revenues for 1996 for the entire product line—sewing machines, food processors, irons, mixers, toasters, water heaters, ceiling fans, cooking ranges, and color televisions—would be about Rs.900 million.

During Chatterjee's time in Calcutta, he had visited a Singer Company showroom on Park Street. Initially he had hoped that Singer might be a suitable partner to manufacture and distribute the Delight purifier. However, much to his surprise, he was told that Singer now had its own brand on the market, "Aquarius." The product was not yet available in Calcutta but was being sold in Bombay and Delhi.

A marketing research agency in Delhi was able to gather some information on the Singer purifier. The product contained nine stages (!) and sold to consumers for Rs.4,000. It removed sediments, heavy metals, bad tastes, odors, and colors. It also killed bacteria and viruses, fungi, and nematodes. The purifier required water pressure (8 PSI minimum) to operate but needed no electricity. It came in a single counter top model that could be moved from one room to another. Life of the device at a flow rate of 3.8 liters per minute was listed as 40,000 liters—about four to six years of use in the typical Indian household. The product's life could be extended to 70,000 liters at a somewhat slower flow rate. However, at 70,000 liters, the product must be discarded. The agency reported a heavy advertising blitz accompanying the introduction in Delhi—emphasizing TV and newspaper advertising, plus outdoor and transit advertising as support. All 10 Singer showrooms in Delhi offered vivid demonstrations of the product's operation.

Chatterjee had to admit that photos of the Aquarius purifier shown in the Calcutta showroom looked appealing. And, a trade article he found had described the product as "state of the art" in comparison to the "primitive" products now on the market. Chatterjee and Blair Company engineers tended to agree—the disinfecting resin used in Aquarius had been developed by the United States government's National Aeronautics and Space Administration (NASA) and was proven to be 100 percent effective against bacteria and viruses. "If only I could have brought a unit back with me," he thought. "We could have some test results and see just how good it is." The trade article also mentioned that Singer hoped to sell 40,000 units over the next two years.

Chatterjee knew that Singer was a well-known and respected brand name in India. Further, Singer's distribution channels were superior to those of any competitor in the market, including those

EXHIBIT 3

Purity and Safety. Now on Store. ZERO-B puristore

When it comes to pure and safe drinking water for your family, filtration alone is not enough. A filter removes only the suspended impurities. That's why you need Zero-B Puristore. Zero-B Puristore not only purifies water, but also stores it free from recontamination for several hours.

Zero-B Puristore - Stage Purification Process
• A special three-layer synthetic filter removes suspended impurities from water.
• The *Bac* (Bacteriostatic Activated Carbon) removes bad odour, taste and colour.
• Iodine impregnated *PU* (Purifying Unit) eliminates disease causing bacteria and viruses (Polio, Coxsackie, ECHO).

Inspite of the 3-stage process, the flow of water is considerably faster.

Zero-B Puristore container is made of Stainless Steel AISI 304. Its special valve type tap and other quality components make this product a step ahead of others.

Zero-B is certified in India and abroad by institutions like King Edward VII Hospital, UK, Singapore Institute of Standards and Industrial Research, Enterovirus Research Centre (Indian Council of Medical Research), Bombay and many other reputed international organisations.*

*Certificate copies can be made available on request.

Zero-B is a Registered Trademark of

ION EXCHANGE (INDIA) LTD
THE POWER BEHIND WATER

Consumer Products Division
502 Veer Savarkar Marg, Prabhadevi, Bombay 400 025.
Tel.: (91) 22-4306329/4301736 Tlx.: 011-74458 IONX IN.
Cable: IONTREAT Fax: (91) 22-430 1840

---

of Eureka Forbes. Most prominent of Singer's three distribution channels were the 210 company-owned showrooms located in major urban areas around the country. Each sold and serviced the entire line of Singer products. Each was very well kept and staffed by knowledgeable personnel. Singer products also were sold throughout India by over 3,000 independent dealers, who received inventory from an estimated 70 Singer-appointed distributors. According to the marketing research agency in Delhi, distributors earned margins of 12 percent of the retail price for Aquarius while dealers earned margins of 5 percent. Finally, Singer employed over 400 salesmen who sold sewing machines and food processors door-to-door. Like Eureka Forbes, the direct salesforce sold products primarily in large urban markets.

Other Competitors.   Chatterjee was aware of several other water purifiers on the Indian market. The Delta brand from S & S Industries in Madras seemed a carbon copy of Aquaguard, except for a more eye pleasing, counter top design. According to promotion literature, Delta offered a line of water-related products—purifiers, water softeners, iron removers, desalinators, and ozonators. Another competitor was Alfa Water Purifiers, Bombay. The company offered four purifier models at prices from Rs.4,300 to Rs.6,500, depending on capacity. Symphony's Spectrum brand sold well around Bombay at Rs.4,000 each but removed only suspended sediments, not heavy metals or bacteria. The Sam Group in Coimbatore recently had launched its "Water Doctor" purifier at Rs.5,200. The device used a third stage ozonator to kill bacteria and viruses and came in two attractive countertop models, 6 and 12-liter storage. Batliboi was mentioned by the Delhi research agency as yet another competitor, although Chatterjee knew nothing else about the brand. Taken all together, unit sales of all purifiers at these companies plus ZERO-B and Singer probably would account for around 60,000 units in 1996. The remaining 190,000 units would be Aquaguards and PureSips.

At least 100 Indian companies made and marketed candle filters. The largest of these probably was Bajaj Electrical Division, whose product line also included water heaters, irons, electric lightbulbs, toasters, mixers, and grillers. Bajaj's candle filters were sold by a large number of dealers who carried the entire product line. Candle filters produced by other manufacturers were sold mostly through dealers who specialized in small household appliances and general hardware. Probably no single manufacturer of candle filters had more than 5 percent of any regional market in the country. No manufacturer attempted to satisfy a national market. Still, the candle filters market deserved serious consideration—perhaps Delight's entry strategy would attempt to "trade-up" users of candle filters to a better, safer product.

Finally, Chatterjee knew that sales of almost all purifiers in 1996 in India came from large urban areas. No manufacturer targeted rural or smaller urban areas and at best, Chatterjee had calculated, existing manufacturers were reaching only 10 to 15 percent of the entire Indian population. An explosion in sales would come if the right product could be sold outside metropolitan areas.

Recommendations

Chatterjee decided that an Indian market entry for Blair Company was subject to three "givens" as he called them. First, he thought that a strategic focus on rural or smaller urban areas would not be wise, at least at the start. The lack of adequate distribution and communication infrastructure in rural India meant that any market entry would begin with larger Indian cities, most likely on the west coast.

Second, market entry would require manufacturing units in India. Because the cost of skilled labor in India was around Rs.20 to Rs.25 per hour (compared to $20 to $25 per hour in the United States), importing complete units was out of the question. However, importing a few key components would be necessary at the start of operation.

Third, Blair Company should find an Indian partner. Chatterjee's visits had produced a number of promising partners: Polar Industries, Calcutta; Milton Plastics, Bombay; Videocon Appliances, Aurangabad; BPL Sanyo Utilities and Appliances, Bangalore; Onida Savak, Delhi; Hawkins India, Bombay; and Voltas, Bombay. All companies manufactured and marketed a line of high-quality household appliances, possessed one or more strong brand names, and had established dealer networks (minimum of 10,000 dealers). All were involved to greater or lesser degrees with international partners. All were medium-sized firms—not too large that a partnership with Blair Company would be one-sided, not too small that they would lack managerial talent and other resources. Finally, all were profitable (15 to 27 percent return on assets in 1995) and looking to grow. However, Chatterjee had no idea if any company would find the Delight purifier and Blair Company attractive or if they might be persuaded to sell part or all of their operations as an acquisition.

Field Testing and Product Recommendations. The most immediate decision Chatterjee faced was whether or not he should recommend a field test. The test would cost about $25,000, placing 20 units in Indian homes in three cities and monitoring their performance for three to six months. The decision to test really

was more than it seemed—Chatterjee's boss had explained that a decision to test was really a decision to enter. It made no sense to spend this kind of time and money if India were not an attractive opportunity. The testing period also would give Blair Company representatives time to identify a suitable Indian company as a licensee, joint venture partner, or acquisition.

Fundamental to market entry was product design. Engineers at Blair Company had taken the position that purification technologies planned for Delight could be "packaged in almost any fashion as long as we have electricity." Electricity was needed to operate the product's ozonator as well as to indicate to users that the unit was functioning properly (or improperly, as the case might be). Beyond this requirement, anything was possible.

Chatterjee thought that a modular approach would be best. The basic module would be a countertop unit much like that shown in Exhibit 2. The module would outperform anything now on the market in terms of flow rate, palatability, durability, and reliability, and would store two liters of purified water. Two additional modules would remove iron, calcium, or other metallic contaminants that were peculiar to particular regions. For example, Calcutta and much of the surrounding area suffered from iron contamination, which no filter or purifier now on the Indian market could remove to a satisfactory level. Water supplies in other areas in the country were known to contain objectionable concentrations of calcium, salt, arsenic, lead, or sulfur. Most Indian consumers would need neither of the additional modules, some would need one or the other, but very few would need both.

Market Entry and Marketing Planning Recommendations. Assuming that Chatterjee recommended proceeding with the field test, he would need to make a recommendation concerning mode of market entry. In addition, his recommendation should include an outline of a marketing plan.

Licensee Considerations.   If market entry were in the form of a joint working arrangement with a licensee, Blair Company financial investment would be minimal. Chatterjee thought that Blair Company might risk as little as $30,000 in capital for production facilities and equipment, plus another $5,000 for office facilities and equipment. These investments would be completely offset by the licensee's payment to Blair Company for technology transfer and personnel training. Annual fixed costs to Blair Company should not exceed $40,000 at the outset and would decrease to $15,000 as soon as an Indian national could be hired, trained, and left in charge. Duties of this individual would be to work with Blair Company personnel in the United States and with management at the licensee to see that units were produced per Blair Company's specifications. Apart from this activity, Blair Company would have no control over the licensee's operations. Chatterjee expected that the licensee would pay royalties to Blair Company of about Rs.280 for each unit sold in the domestic market and Rs.450 for each unit that was exported. The average royalty probably would be around Rs.300.

Joint Venture/Acquisition Considerations.   If entry were in the form of either a joint venture or an acquisition, financial investment and annual fixed costs would be much higher and depend greatly on the scope of operations. Chatterjee had roughed out some estimates for a joint venture entry, based on three levels of

Exhibit 4   Investments and Fixed Costs for a Joint Venture Market Entry

	Operational Scope		
	Two Regions	*Four Regions*	*National Market*
1998 market potential (units)	55,000	110,000	430,000
Initial investment (Rs. 000)	4,000	8,000	30,000
Annual fixed overhead expenses (Rs.000)			
Using dealer channels	4,000	7,000	40,000
Using direct salesforce	7,200	14,000	88,000

scope (see Exhibit 4). His estimates reflected what he thought were reasonable assumptions for all needed investments plus annual fixed expenses for sales activities, general administrative overhead, research and development, insurance, and depreciation. His estimates allowed for the Delight purifier to be sold either through dealers or through a direct, door-to-door salesforce. Chatterjee thought that estimates of annual fixed expenses for market entry via acquisition would be identical to those for a joint venture. However, estimates for the investment (purchase) might be considerably higher, the same, or lower. It depended on what was purchased.

Chatterjee's estimates of Delight's unit contribution margins reflected a number of assumptions—expected economies of scale, experience curve effects, costs of Indian labor and raw materials, and competitors' pricing strategies. However, the most important assumption was Delight's pricing strategy. If a skimming strategy was used and the product sold through a dealer channel, the basic module would be priced to dealers at Rs.5,500 and to consumers at Rs.5,900. "This would give us about a Rs.650 unit contribution, once we got production flowing smoothly," he thought. In contrast, if a penetration strategy was used and the product sold through a dealer channel, the basic module would be priced to dealers at Rs.4,100, to consumers at Rs.4,400, and yield a unit contribution of Rs.300. For simplicity's sake, Chatterjee assumed that the two additional modules would be priced to dealers at Rs.800, to consumers at Rs.1,000, and would yield a unit contribution of Rs.100.

To achieve unit contributions of Rs.650 or Rs.300, the basic modules would employ different designs. The basic module for the skimming strategy would be noticeably superior, with higher performance and quality, a longer warranty period, more features,

and a more attractive appearance than the basic module for the penetration strategy. Positioning, too, most likely would be different. Chatterjee recognized several positioning possibilities: performance and taste, value for the money/low price, safety, health, convenience, attractive styling, avoiding diseases and health related bills, and superior American technology. The only position he considered "taken" in the market was that occupied by Aquaguard—protect family health and service at your doorstep. While other competitors had claimed certain positions for their products, none had devoted financial resources of a degree that Delight could not dislodge them. Chatterjee believed that considerable advertising and promotion expenditures would be necessary to communicate Delight's positioning. He would need estimates of these expenditures in his recommendation.

If a direct salesforce was employed instead of dealers, Chatterjee thought that prices charged to consumers would not change from those listed above. However, sales commissions would have to be paid in addition to the fixed costs necessary to maintain and manage the salesforce. Under a skimming price strategy, the sales commission would be Rs.550 per unit and the unit contribution would be Rs.500. Under a penetration price strategy, the sales commission would be Rs.400 per unit and the unit contribution would be Rs.200. These financial estimates, he would explain in his report, would apply to 1998 or 1999, the expected first year of operation.

"If we go ahead with Delight, we'll have to move quickly," thought Chatterjee. "The window of opportunity is open but if Singer's product is as good as they claim, we'll be in for a fight. Still, Aquarius seems vulnerable on the water pressure requirement and on price. We'll need a product category 'killer' to win."

CASE 4–5
SALES NEGOTIATIONS ABROAD FOR MRIS

International sales of General Medical's Magnetic Resonance Imaging (MRI) Systems have really taken off in recent months. Your representatives are about to conclude important sales contracts with customers in both Tokyo and Rio de Janeiro. Both sets of negotiations require your participation, particularly as final details are worked out. The bids you approved for both customers are identical—shown here. Indeed, both customers had contacted you originally at a medical equipment trade show in Las Vegas, and you had all talked business together over drinks at the conference hotel. You expect your two new customers will be talking together again over the Internet about your products and prices as they had in Las Vegas. The Japanese orders are potentially larger because the doctor you met works in a hospital which has nine other units in the Tokyo/Yokohama area. The Brazilian doctor represents a very large hospital in Rio which may require more than one unit. Your travel arrangements are now being made. Your local representatives will fill you in on the details. Best of luck!

NOTE: Your professor will provide you with additional material, which you will need to complete this case.

Price Quotation

DeepVision 2000 MRI (basic unit) Product options	$1,200,000
• 2D and 3D time-of-flight (TOF) angiography for capturing fast flow	150,000
• Flow analysis for quantification of cardiovascular studies	70,000
• X2001 software package	20,000
Service contract (2 years normal maintenance, parts, and labor)	60,000
Total price	$1,500,000

Standard Terms and Conditions

Delivery	6 months
Penalty for late delivery	$10,000/month
Cancellation charges	10% of contract price
Warranty (for defective machinery)	parts, one year
Terms of payment	COD

CASE 4–6
MEDICO-DEVICES, INC.—OXYGEN CONCENTRATOR

You were recommended to the president of a small company, Medico-Devices, Inc., as someone who could help the company get started in international marketing. You were invited to meet with the president and general sales manager to find exactly what was needed and whether or not you could help. The major points covered at the meeting are described here.

The Product

The Aire-I oxygen concentrator is basically a simple device. It consists of a motor-powered compressor that forces the ambient air through sieve beds containing a chemical that extracts the nitrogen, dust, and bacteria from room air; it delivers 95-percent-pure oxygen at a rate of one to five liters per minute (LPM) to patients who must have oxygen because of some type of respiratory illness.

All oxygen concentrators in the United States are essentially the same except for appearance, compressor, sieve-bed material, or assembly. A basic concentrator consists of the following components:

1. A compressor that must move a minimum of 100 liters of air per minute through the system at 9 to 15 pounds of pressure.

2. An air-cooling device to lower the temperature of the compressed air since the performance level of the molecular sieve is reduced at high operating temperatures.

3. A system of solenoid valves to direct air into the sieve beds so that accumulated nitrogen is purged from the system.

4. A measurement system to regulate oxygen flow for the patient coupled with required alarms to indicate malfunction.

The major advantage Aire-I has over the competition is its aluminum sieve beds designed to eliminate the granulation of the sieve material, thus giving it an unlimited life span. PVC is used in competitive units that have an average life of two years. The Medico-Devices sieve beds should last indefinitely if excessive moisture is not allowed to contaminate the material within the beds.

A remote patient control unit allows patients to be 70 feet from the unit yet have all operating controls at their fingertips. A 30-foot nasal cannula (tube) extends the overall distance to 100 feet. Other product features include:

EXHIBIT 1   Aire-I Oxygen Concentrator Specifications

Overall System

Output flow (oxygen-enriched air):	0–5 LPM.	System operating pressures:	—Proto-Flo system operates at between 9–11 psig.
Oxygen concentration (±3%)	1–5 LPM 95%.		
Power consumption:	330 watts (approx.).		—Low system pressure means fewer leaks; less purging noise and increased component life.

Main Unit		*Patient Control Unit*	
Dimensions:	Height: 26″	Weight:	3 lbs. 6 oz.
	Length: 17¼″	Power requirements:	15 Volt DC.
	Width: 18½″	Safety features:	Bacteria filter provides
Weight:	94 lbs.		sterile oxygen.
Power requirements:	115 volts, 60 Hz.		
Safety features:	• Thermal cutout to prevent overheating of drive motor.	Indicators:	• Power on/off.
	• H.E.P.A. filter to provide bacteria-free oxygen.		• Auxiliary power on.
			• Power interrupt.
	• Warning circuit to indicate power failure.		• Audible power interrupt warning.
	• Warning circuit to indicate when air intake is blocked.	Output pressure:	5 psig.
Portability:	Large casters on base and convenient top handle simplify movement of main unit.		

A compressor that pushes far beyond expectations. The Aire-I's compressor utilizes a unique low-pressure/high-flow system. Air volume exceeds 300 litres per minute. The special pump design facilitates easy and fast servicing.

There is something very smart about simple valves. Much of the Aire-I's simplicity is due to its deflector valve, a device which eliminates solenoids and venturi problems. The advanced design integrates the deflector valve with the compressor and motor for peak oxygen production efficiency and rapid nitrogen purging from sieve beds.

Crossover valve. The crossover valve is also specially designed to ensure balanced sieve beds for improved oxygen production and simplified repairs—if ever needed.

Patients have more control over their lives. The portable patient control unit, with controls and patient alerts, includes an audible alarm. It remains within reach of the patient even though he may be as much as 70 feet from the air pumping system. Life is easier for the patient. And oxygen use is safer.

What's good for the patient is good for the dealer. The many design features of the Aire-I which make the unit more convenient, efficient, and reliable for patients also result in simplified service requirements. All components are easily accessible. Service time is minimal.

---

1. Operating costs are 60 percent less than competitive products.
2. The Aire-I produces up to 5 liters of 95-percent-pure oxygen per minute.
3. The unit weighs 20 percent less and is 15 percent smaller than other units.
4. All components are accessible and service personnel may enter the components within minutes.
5. Internal adjustments require minimal training.
6. Any component can be replaced within less than an hour of service time.

The Aire-I weighs 94 pounds and operates on 115 v, 60 Hz (see Exhibit 1 for product specifications). It is designed to operate continuously but needs servicing about every six weeks. Servicing is mostly preventive in nature although the sieve beds may need replacing to ensure maximum output if the concentrator is operated under high-humidity conditions. Operating history indicates oxygen output under the most adverse humidity never drops below three liters of 80-percent-pure oxygen, although for some patients this would be insufficient oxygen output. Each unit has two sieve beds weighing about three pounds each. Replacement is simple, requiring only the removal of two clamps. The sieve beds contain the chemical that filters the nitrogen out of the ambient air.

Company records show the effective life of a machine to be about three years; that is, after three years, the compressor and motor have a high incidence of malfunction. Company policy is to overhaul machines after three years at the owner's expense. An overhaul generally includes a new compressor and motor and new sieve beds if necessary.

The Problem

Medico-Devices, Inc., is a small manufacturing company. Its product line consists of several medical devices, one of which is the oxygen concentrator. The company employs about 150 in manufacturing and has been in business about five years. It has made a modest profit for the last two years. The company has other products but wants to sell only the oxygen concentrator internationally. The U.S. market is estimated at about 120,000 units per year and is valued at approximately $100 million. The company has about 25 percent of the U.S. market and has the capacity to produce another 5,000 to 10,000 units in its present facilities. Since the unit is assembled from component parts, production can be increased quickly if demand exceeds present plant capacity. With the exceptions of the cabinet, one special valve, and the sieve beds, the concentrator's parts are available off the shelf from a variety of sources. The basic technology cannot be protected by patents, so many small assemblers have been attracted to the market by the initial high margins available in the U.S. market.

Sales have grown rapidly over the last five years, but the company believes they have about topped out and forecast sales of 25,000 to 30,000 units per year over the next few years with little growth. Although the total market is projected to grow 10 percent per year, the number of other companies producing the oxygen concentrator has made price competition so severe that the company feels it would be unprofitable to attempt to expand its market share at this time. Medico-Device's Aire-I is more efficient than others due to the patentable construction of its sieve beds. In spite of its more efficient product and relatively lower costs of manufacturing (the company believes its costs are 10 to 15 percent lower than competitors'), it does not feel it has the resources necessary to engage in a price battle for market share. (See Exhibit 2.)

The strategy is to sell the Aire-I as a premium-priced, quality product, and maintain a market presence while others engage in price competition. When the timing is right, the company plans to step up marketing efforts and expand market share slowly. Management realizes this could be a high-risk strategy unless it can enter the European market, where margins are high and there is less price competition. The company wants to capture a share of that emerging market while waiting for the U.S. market to settle down; there is evidence that the market is beginning to settle out, with 10 companies leaving the market in the last six months.

As a result of its unique design, the Aire-I has a lower operating cost for the patient, requires less maintenance (sieve-bed replacement is rarely necessary in the Aire-I versus a two-year replacement for the competition), and has lower overall weight (94 pounds versus 110 pounds for the competition).

Exhibit 2   Aire-I Cost per Unit (5,000–10,000 units)

Parts	$420
Labor*	300
Quality control	30
Packaging	20

* Based on labor assembly cost at current average rates of $14.20 per hour including benefits.

The Market

Most patients in the United States using an oxygen concentrator suffer from emphysema (the inability of the lungs to absorb sufficient oxygen from the ambient air, requiring their air intake to be enriched with pure oxygen). There are other ailments where oxygen therapy is used, but emphysema sufferers are by far the largest users. (Smoking and/or exposure to pollutants are the major causes of emphysema.) If a patient does not use an oxygen concentrator such as the Aire-I, oxygen must be supplied from an oxygen cylinder. Convenience is the major advantage of the oxygen concentrator versus an oxygen cylinder. Cylinders are large and have to be replaced on a schedule, whereas the Aire-I fits into a cabinet and looks like a piece of furniture. (See Exhibit 3.) If properly maintained, there is no problem of running out of oxygen as is the case with the cylinder. Furthermore, the detachable control station can be moved easily around a room, giving the patient more flexibility than offered by a cylinder.

Medical candidates for home use of oxygen are those with heart disease, chronic obstructive pulmonary disease (COPD, which includes emphysema, severe asthma, and bronchitis), or a number of other pulmonary disorders that totally debilitate the patient unless ancillary oxygen is available. Patients with lung disease need supplemental oxygen 24 hours a day in order to extend life and make it more pleasant. Patients who use concentrators comprise 80 percent of the market. The oxygen is delivered to the patient through cannula inserted into the patient's nostrils.

In the United States, the market for patients eligible for home oxygen use is difficult to estimate accurately. However, there are 47 million Americans suffering from some type of lung ailment. In fact, respiratory disorders are the most common reason people visit their physicians. Between 1979 and 1985, the age-adjusted prevalence of COPD increased 17 percent among men and 35 percent among women. During that same period, the age-adjusted death rate for COPD increased 18 percent and 60 percent among men and women, respectively. The total number of persons in the United States suffering from COPD is 16 million. The American Lung Association puts these diseases into three major categories to account for most of that number.

Emphysema	2,000,000
Asthma	6,000,000
Chronic bronchitis	7,100,000

Medical studies indicate that smoking is a major contributor to emphysema. Heavy smokers suffer from some loss of lung function after 15 to 20 years of heavy smoking (heavy smoking is defined as more than one pack of cigarettes per day).

The Aire-I

Medico-Devices, Inc., and most other suppliers of concentrators sell directly to distributors who lease or rent to patients. In the United States, there are approximately 11,000 medical-equipment companies handling oxygen concentrators. Trade shows are an important source of contacts for potential customers.

Patients rent the machine from hospitals, pharmacies, respiratory therapists, medical-equipment supply houses, and other companies specializing in medical equipment. In the United States, oxygen can be supplied only if the patient has a prescription for therapeutic oxygen therapy from a medical doctor.

Exhibit 3   The Aire-I

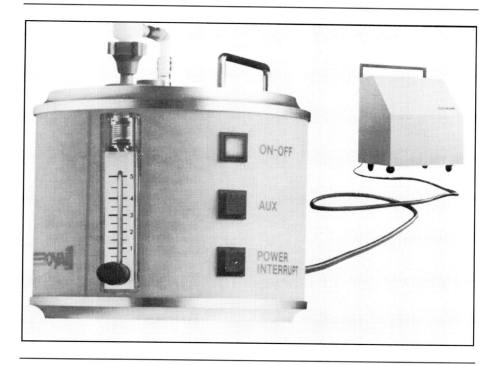

Competition

Domestic prices have been driven down over the last 18 months. Machines comparable to the Aire-I ranged in price from $1,500 to $2,200, f.o.b. manufacturing plant, 18 months ago. Today, prices range from a low of $1,200 to $1,700, with average market price at $1,500, f.o.b. manufacturer. Once marketing and other costs are accounted for, there is little profit at today's market prices.

Company Plans

The company is interested in selling its product in foreign markets. It has no idea where to start selling or how to approach the process. The company does have a medical study that indicates emphysema exists throughout the world in about the same ratio to population distribution as in the United States. The research also revealed that oxygen therapy for emphysema and other COPD is not as widely used elsewhere in the world as in the United States.

THE PROBLEM

Part I.   Since your first meeting with Medico-Devices was general and they were not sure what they needed, you agreed to present management with some guidelines. The idea is to give the company a format that shows the steps necessary to develop a successful export program, raises questions about exporting, and provides some ideas of the kinds of information (and possible sources) it needs to make a decision. Prepare a report for Medico-Devices.

Part II.   You have completed the report in Part I and the company is satisfied with your work; it wants you to continue to assist.

It has been decided to enter the German market first; like most countries, Germany has its share of people with COPD. Further, oxygen therapy is at the early stages of acceptance within the German medical profession. You have agreed to do a complete market analysis and preliminary marketing plan for the German market for the Aire-1. See Exhibits 4 and 5 for some preliminary data on the United States and Germany.

Part III.   Assume two years have elapsed since you completed Parts I and II, and the company has had reasonable success in Germany. However, other U.S. companies have also sought markets in Europe and thus have driven the price down. The company must find ways to remain price competitive in both the U.S. market and in Europe. Prices have stabilized in the United States at an average price of $1,100. Prices in Germany have fallen from an average of $2,200 per unit to $1,500 today. Can you help the company?

Exhibit 4   Deaths from Respiratory Diseases per 100,000—Germany and U.S.A.

	Germany	USA
Acute bronchitis and bronchiolitis	510	548
Acute upper respiratory infection	442	294
Bronchitis (chronic and unspecified), emphysema, and asthma	25,467	22,424
Over 55 years old	24,351	20,400

EXHIBIT 5   **Percent Smokers, Exsmokers, and Nonsmokers, by Male/Female and Age Group**

The United States

	Men (by age)				Women (by age)			
	25–34	*35–44*	*45–54*	*55–64*	*25–34*	*35–44*	*45–54*	*55–64*
Regular	35.5%	51.0%	34.5%	31.1%	34.0%	44.8%	33.0%	30.0%
Other	1.0	2.0	3.1	4.9	0.0	0.0	0.7	0.4
Exsmokers	22.6	19.5	35.7	43.2	15.9	15.1	15.6	18.9
Nonsmokers	40.9	27.5	26.7	20.8	50.1	40.1	50.7	50.7

Germany

	Men (by age)				Women (by age)			
	25–34	*35–44*	*45–54*	*55–64*	*25–34*	*35–44*	*45–54*	*55–64*
Regular	51.4%	40.0%	33.8%	32.0%	30.4%	18.5%	17.8%	13.0%
Other	4.3	3.8	5.1	5.8	3.7	1.7	1.7	1.1
Exsmokers	20.9	25.1	32.5	42.1	9.7	7.2	6.4	9.8
Nonsmokers	23.4	31.2	28.6	20.0	56.2	72.5	74.1	76.0

CASE 4–7
CATERPILLAR IN EUROPE

Caterpillar Incorporated is a worldwide leader in earth-moving equipment and heavy machinery. Founded in 1904 by Daniel Best and Benjamin Holt, Caterpillar (Cat) traces its roots back to the first track-type tractor of its kind. Since then Cat has grown to be the 39th largest company in the United States. Its 1997 sales were more than $18.9 billion,[1] with about half of those sales coming from outside the United States.

Cat's first non-U.S. subsidiary was formed in the U.K. in 1950. As Cat grew in Europe, it developed a "single market" plan for product sourcing, supplier access, and customer support. Today about 12,000 of Cat's 57,000 worldwide employees are located in the EC, making it the company's most important employment base outside the United States. Caterpillar has an extensive network of production, distribution, and sales units throughout the EC. Its marketing headquarters are in Geneva; manufacturing facilities in Belgium, France, Germany, Hungary, Italy, Poland,

Russia, and the U.K.; a design center in Germany; a training center in Spain; and sales offices and service centers throughout the continent (see Exhibit 1). A further 11,000 people work for Caterpillar's 25 independent dealerships in the EC. Cat's dominant position as market leader is amply demonstrated by the following statistics: $1.1 billion worth of EC assets; some $2.4 billion of sales in 1996 to European dealers; and a market share of about 35 percent in the construction equipment sector. Thus Caterpillar has a major stake in the emerging, integrated European market.

Problems and Solutions in the EU

In the past, the most notorious nontariff barriers that divided EU member markets were the mandatory, national technical product standards. These differed sharply from country to country and gave local manufacturers a built-in advantage in their home market. Exhibit 2 illustrates the great complexity of changes involved in the single-market integration program with respect to technical standards. An example will demonstrate the problem. Caterpillar builds wheel loaders in Aurora, Illinois, and in Grosselies, Bel-

[1] **www.caterpillar.com**, 1998.

This case was prepared by Lyn S. Amine, Associate Professor of Marketing and International Business, Saint Louis University.

EXHIBIT 1   Caterpillar in the European Community

gium. If five model 980 wheel loaders go down the line at the Aurora plant, they are built to the same technical standards, even if they are destined for delivery in different regions of the United States. That is not the case at the plant in Grosselies. Five 980s bound for five different EU member states currently have to meet five different sets of technical requirements: different standards for lighting if headed for Italy, special access systems if bound for Germany or the U.K., special engine guards if intended for France, and so on.

In the past, varying standards across the EU meant higher inventories, greater manufacturing complexity, different requirements for quality control, and extra training for employees. A coordinated multimarket marketing strategy was difficult to plan and operate. On the other hand, local manufacturers had the advantage of being close to their home market and knowing all its particularities. Thus, variations in technical standards contributed to a type of market protectionism which discouraged penetration by non-EC companies.

As plans for market integration proceed, technical standards for lift trucks and noise emission devices have already been put in place. The current focus is on resolution of conflicting "roading standards," the safety requirements that must be met before machinery can be driven on the highway.

Due to market-distorting regulations, air freight costs have traditionally been about 50 percent higher in Europe than in the United States. Deregulation will be extremely important to Caterpillar, which is one of the largest commercial users of the Belgian national airlines as a source of incoming supplies for its distribution center near Brussels. Similarly, road transportation in Europe was expensive and time-consuming due to administrative delays at the multiple border crossings. The new Single Administrative Document (SAD) relieved truckers of the need to deal with each country's dispatch and entry documents. Caterpillar estimated that with the improved efficiencies flowing from use of the SAD, savings of some $1.5 to $2 million could be achieved each year on transportation costs, along with significant reductions in transit time and the

Exhibit 2   1992 at a Glance

By 1992, the European Community intends to have implemented 285 regulations to create a single internal market. The following specific changes represent the major part of the 1992 program.

In standards, testing, certification
Harmonization of standards for:
Simple pressure vessels
Toys
Automobiles, trucks and
motorcycles and their emissions
Telecommunications
Construction products
Personal protection equipment
Machine safety
Measuring instruments
Medical devices
Gas appliances
Agricultural and forestry tractors
Cosmetics
Quick-frozen foods
Flavorings
Food emulsifiers
Extraction solvents
Food preservatives
Infant formula
Jams
Modified starches
Fruit juices
Food inspection
Definition of spirited beverages
and aromatised wines
Coffee extracts and chicory
extracts
Food additives
Materials and articles in contact
with food
Tower cranes (noise)
Household appliances (noise)
Tire pressure gauges
Hydraulic diggers (noise)
Detergents
Liquid fertilizers and secondary
fertilizers
Lawn mowers (noise)
Medicinal products and medical
specialties
Radio interferences
Earthmoving equipment
Lifting and loading equipment

New rules for harmonizing packing, labeling, and processing requirements
Ingredients for food and beverages

Irradiation
Extraction solvents
Nutritional labeling
Classification, packaging, labeling
of dangerous preparations
Food labeling

Harmonization of regulations for the health industry (including marketing)
Medical specialties
Pharmaceuticals
Veterinary medicinal products
High-technology medicines
Implantable electromedical devices
Single-use devices (disposable)
In-vitro diagnostics

Changes in government procurement regulations
Coordination of procedures on the
award of public works and supply
contracts
Extension of EC law to
telecommunications, utilities,
transport
Services

Harmonization of regulation of services
Banking
Mutual funds
Broadcasting
Tourism
Road passenger transport
Railways
Information services
Life and nonlife insurance
Securities
Maritime transport
Air transport
Electronic payment cards

Liberalization of capital movements
Long-term capital, stocks
Short-term capital

Consumer protection regulations
Misleading definitions of products
Indications of prices

Harmonization of laws regulating company behavior
Mergers and acquisitions
Trademarks
Copyrights
Cross-border mergers

Accounting operations across
borders
Bankruptcy protection of computer
programs
Transaction taxes
Company law

Harmonization of taxation
Value-added taxes
Excise taxes on alcohol, tobacco,
and other

Harmonization of veterinary and phytosanitary controls
Harmonization of an extensive list of
rules covering items such as:
Antibiotic residues
Bovine animals and meat
Porcine animals and meat
Plant health
Fish and fish products
Live poultry, poultry meat, and
hatching eggs
Pesticide residues in fruit and
vegetables

Elimination and simplification of national transit documents and procedures for intra-EC trade
Introduction of the Single
Administrative Document
(SAD)
Abolition of customs presentation
charges
Elimination of customs formalities
and the introduction of common
border posts

Harmonization of rules pertaining to the free movement of labor and the professions within the EC
Mutual recognition of higher
educational diplomas
Comparability of vocational
training qualifications
Specific training in general medical
practice
Training of engineers
Activities in the field of pharmacy
Activities related to commercial
agents
Income taxation provisions
Elimination of burdensome
requirements related to residence
permits

amount of inventory on the road. Typically, trucks carrying Caterpillar goods cross European borders over 300 times daily.

The European Commission in Brussels estimated that before 1992 trucks ran empty over 33 percent of the time due to restrictions on "cabotage"—the right of a truck from one member state to make a domestic haul within another member state. Deregulation allows Caterpillar to use a Belgian hauler to ship goods from its Belgian plant to Grenoble in France. Then that same truck, on its way back to Belgium, will be able to drop off goods from Grenoble in Paris and Vernon on its way north.

Caterpillar's New Challenges

Caterpillar Overseas S.A. (COSA) covers markets in the EU, the CIS, Africa, and the Middle East. EU dealers working with COSA coordinate marketing strategies and responses to environmental changes and competitive challenges. Cat faces more competition in Europe than in any other area of the world.

Caterpillar's competitors are a significant presence in their respective regions due to joint ventures and partnerships. Japanese competition is encountered throughout the EU. Komatsu Ltd. of Japan is Cat's main competitor in the EU and in world markets. Komatsu plans to increase European sales by some 50 percent by the year 2000 and has invested some $170 million developing its plants in Europe.[2] Locally, Cat faces competition from Fiat in Italy, Spain, France, and Denmark; Volvo in Scandinavia; J.C. Bamford in the U.K.; and Mercedes Benz in Germany. Cat also faces merger competition from Linde-Lansing in the lift-truck business and from Fiat-Hitachi in the excavator business.

As European manufacturers find it easier to sell in more than one member state, customers can be expected to compare prices across different countries. Caterpillar currently has one dealer per member country with the exception of the U.K., which supports four. In the future, dealers will find themselves competing directly with other Cat dealers as well as with competitors' dealers. All dealers will need to become more conversant with international financing opportunities as capital flows across borders come into force with the completion of the single European market. Again, customers will be shopping for the best rates wherever they may be offered.

Dealers in Spain and Portugal have already seen economic activity benefit significantly from huge inflows of EU funds aimed at smoothing out regional inequalities within the EU. Elsewhere, member governments have increased investments in infrastructure, and private investment in new equipment has accelerated This should result in new demand for Caterpillar's goods, such as construction and materials handling equipment, as well as logistical services.

Pan-European versus Local Marketing Strategies

Caterpillar Inc. is well positioned to maintain its strong market position well into the next century. Pan-European marketing strategies will facilitate economies of scale, streamlining of production, and reduction of inventories and operating costs. Cat's focus on individual country dealerships (except in the U.K.) will remain in place. In order to integrate the two strategies, Caterpillar recently underwent a massive company reorganization. Fourteen individual profit centers were created, each responsible for its own resources, marketing, operational costs, and personnel. Among these profit centers are geographic centers (such as COSA) and product centers (such as Cat's new "Challenger" line). Set-up of the profit centers was intended to align the company more closely with customers and dealers. These "equal control" measures facilitate implementation of Pan-European strategies while allowing country dealers to compensate for local nuances in their market. Thus, Caterpillar is attempting to balance two perspectives—the single-market focus of its Pan-European strategy, with an eye on problems such as multicountry logistics and the introduction of new EU-wide technical standards, counterbalanced by a country-level focus, with an eye on adaptation of local sales strategies to changing market factors.

Questions

1. For a long time, Caterpillar has relied on local country dealerships as a source of competitive strength. Now it is combining this with a Pan-European marketing strategy. Do you think that this combined strategy approach is a temporary measure as Caterpillar progresses toward a fully integrated European strategy? Or would you expect Caterpillar to maintain its two-tier approach? Discuss the implications of these and other options in the light of (a) Caterpillar's own constraints and opportunities, and (b) those of the competition.

2. Does European unification make non-European companies less competitive on the continent? Discuss.

---

[2] Peter Marsh, "Komatsu Plans Sales Push in Europe," *Financial Times,* July 14, 1997, p. 19.

CASE 4–8
RALLYSPORT INTERNATIONAL—PROMOTING RACQUETBALL IN JAPAN

Racquetball grew from an obscure sport played in just a few cities in the United States to the fastest-growing participatory sport on the American scene. In 1975 there were fewer than 30 private court clubs in the entire nation featuring racquetball. By 1985 every major city had a number of clubs devoted exclusively to racquetball or to racquetball and squash.

Rallysport International was started in 1975 by Dana Edwards to capitalize on the trend. It was his expressed intention that Rallysport International would become "the McDonald's of the racquetball world." To do so, Rallysport developed several sets of plans, a packaged marketing and promotional program, an entire management and management control system, and subsidiaries devoted to court construction and supervisory management. The company's plans called for a three-stage expansion: the first in prime markets throughout the United States; the second into less-desirable but substantial markets in the United States; the third into developed countries outside the United States.

Three five-year plans were developed; 1985 to 1990—Phase I, 1990 to 1995—Phase II, 1995 to 2000—Phase III (International). During the second five-year plan, however, Edwards observed that competition in the United States was growing so quickly that the company would not have enough time to establish its primacy in domestic market categories and decided to enter the international markets before they became saturated.

Tobby Lewis, the company's development manager, was given responsibility for determining whether first to enter Japan or Germany, the company's two target markets. His research led him to the conclusion that the character of the game was ideally fitted to the Japanese who, he said, "are competitive, fast, sports oriented, and tuned into American athletics." He also pointed out that expensive land costs and relative lack of urban land made the racquetball business ideal for Japan because it took so little space. A few squash courts exist in Japan and are considered very exclusive. This is because they are fully enclosed heavy construction, which is expensive and unusual in Japan.

I. A. Savant and Company was hired to conduct a study of the Japanese market and make general recommendations concerning market entry. The company discovered that there are some 125 million Japanese spread among some 45 million households, 90 percent of whom classified themselves as middle class. Sixty percent of the national population inhabit an area adjacent to three major cities: Tokyo, Nagoya, and Osaka, which essentially constitute one major metropolitan area. Savant's conclusion was that the metro market alone could support at least 27 racquet clubs, averaging 10 courts each. That would represent only one club per 1 million households.

Their report pointed out that the average per capita income in 1998 was more than that in the U.S. and more than $32,000, two-thirds of which came from the male head of household's regular monthly income, 20 percent from a semiannual bonus, 6 percent from wives, 3 percent from other family members, and 3 percent from other sources. Savant pointed out that Japanese like new things, are particularly addicted to U.S. products and activities (although that attraction may have eroded somewhat in recent years), and had shown consistent ability to spend on products that were meaningful to them while saving in other areas.

Approximately 20 percent of the population is in the 20- to 35-year age bracket, which is considered to be a prime market for racquetball in the United States. The consultant saw no reason to question the acceptance of the game in Japan. Volleyball is extremely popular with housewives, who have formed many large leagues.

Tobby Lewis developed an overall plan for invading the Japanese market. He first recommended that at least four clubs be built simultaneously for the following reasons. (1) The market is segmented and should be tested thoroughly. Therefore one club would be built in a purely business location, one in a business–residential combination area, and two in residential areas—one close in, and one further out. One of the locations was to be in the Kanto region, where the head offices of most major Japanese companies are located. (2) Advertising expenditures must be heavy enough to make strong initial impact—one club alone could not support heavy advertising in such a high-cost market. (3) Rallysport's Japanese joint venture partners are prepared to finance four clubs. (4) Building four clubs establishes a market presence, making market entry difficult for other firms. (5) Because of the immense demand potential, each of the four clubs should be immediately profitable.

Savant did foresee some problems. One is that many industrial companies have extensive recreational programs for their employees so that those employees might not be in the market for private recreation. The second problem was that the clubs need to be operated 10 to 11 hours per day to function profitably. Clubs in the United States often operate above that range, but Savant suggested that there were some cultural questions to be considered. Counteracting these issues, the consultant suggested, was a recent survey showing that the target youth market had four primary interests—music, sports, fashion, and travel. The same study pointed out that youth were particularly concerned with health and environmental problems, and that the nation's general shift to a five-day week had placed more emphasis on sports and recreation.

The primary contributions of Rallysport International were to be promotional programs, developmental activities, managerial systems, and construction advice. Among other activities, Edwards and Lewis structured an advertising and promotional campaign plan for review by their Japanese joint-venture partner, a major financial institution with extensive experience in industrial goods but limited involvement in the consumer arena. Because the international expansion is of such importance to the company, the board of directors was asked to review the total development program before showing it to the Japanese partner.

At the board meeting when it was reviewed, Dave Irwin raised several questions; specifically he mentioned his concern about the cultural fit of the game. He also suggested that the promotional program made basic assumptions about the way the Japanese market would react. He personally questioned, although he admitted he did not know the answers, whether the promotional program was appropriate for the Japanese market or whether it reflected U.S. thinking patterns. He therefore recommended that someone thoroughly familiar with the Japanese culture be asked to review the promotion plan to try to identify problem areas and inconsistencies. He was particularly concerned that Rallysport not present a program that would cause the company to lose face when it was presented to the Japanese partner.

Following are the main items included in the advertising and promotional plan devised by Dana Edwards and Tobby Lewis:

Promotion

1. All clubs will tie into the Rallysport name: Rallysport-Tokyo, Rallysport-Osaka, and so forth.
2. Club use will be restricted to members only. (In the United States, some have restricted and some have open-member policies.)
3. Members will be charged a flat monthly fee rather than an hourly rate (both systems are used in the United States).
4. Primary target market will be white-collar workers, 25 to 35 years old, upper-middle income.
5. Secondary target market will be Japanese housewives and female office employees.
6. Low-cost, one-month trial memberships will be widely used.
7. Celebrities will be widely used in promotion. A championship U.S. racquetball player may be utilized, or we may tie in with someone such as Sadeharu Oh and the Yomiuri Giants (leading baseball player and team in Japan, presently endorsing Sogo department stores, Toshiba watches, Nichiban plastic bandages, Kyo-Komachi rice cakes, and Pepsi-Cola. Oh and the Giants would be very expensive, perhaps as much as 30 million yen per year for full tie-in).

Advertising

1. Themes: Three types of advertising are widely used in Japan—follow-the-leader advertising, celebrity tie-ins, and mood advertising. Rally will use the celebrity mode.
2. Multiple themes: Different themes will be used for each market segment, but all will tie to some general themes. The three major market segments to be appealed to will be middle-management executives, clerical workers, and housewives.
3. Overall theme: "Economical Fun and Health with America's Fastest-Growing Sport."
4. Subthemes: Exclusive Clubs; a New Sport; Health and Fitness—stressing cardiovascular benefits; "You Don't Have to Leave the City to Have Fun"; "Easy to Learn, After Just One Hour You Can Have Fun."
5. Campaign will utilize heavy copy and active photography which will explain the game, its benefits, and popularity in the United States. Above all, stress fun.

Media Policy and Timing

1. Timing: A significant segment of the budget will be devoted to a long build-up, teaser-type campaign to establish interest and familiarity and, hopefully, encourage membership presales.
2. Budget allocation: Twenty percent of the total budget will be used for endorsements and for exhibitions by endorsers of the new clubs. Forty percent of the budget will be devoted to television commercials utilizing 60-second spots rather than the more typical 15-second spots. The 60-second spots will give time to show plenty of action and explain the game and benefits of club membership. Twenty-five percent of the budget will be devoted to newspapers, spread between the nationwide dailies, which reach some 90 percent of all households, or local dailies, which reach over 40 percent of the market, and sports newspapers such as those owned by Chunichi Shimbum. Ten percent of the budget will be allocated to develop publicity in television, newspapers, and magazines, and 5 percent to direct mail. Overall media expenditures in Japan are as follows: 35 percent television, 31 percent newspapers, 6 percent magazines, 6 percent direct mail, 5 percent radio, and 17 percent outdoor and all other.

Graphics

Graphics will emphasize racquetball play. They will focus on (1) celebrities who are sponsored by the company, (2) American players in tournament competition, and (3) playing women or husband-and-wife combinations showing the game's broad appeal.

Questions

1. You have been appointed promotional consultant. Analyze the general promotion policy, the budget, advertising themes, and the graphics approach.
2. What other areas or activities should be included in the promotional advertising program?
3. Evaluate other aspects of the proposal.
4. Who else should review this proposal before it is presented to the joint-venture partner?

CASE 4-9
SPERRY/MACLENNAN ARCHITECTS AND PLANNERS MARKETING SERVICES

Mitch Brooks, a junior partner and director of Sperry/MacLennan (S/M), a Dartmouth, Nova Scotia, architectural practice specializing in recreational facilities, is in the process of developing a plan to export his company's services. He intends to present the plan to the other directors at their meeting the first week of October. The regional market for architectural services is showing some signs of slowing and S/M realizes that it must seek new markets. As Sheila Sperry, the office manager and one of the directors, said at their last meeting: "You have to go wider than your own backyard. After all, you can only build so many pools in your own backyard."

About the Company

Drew Sperry, one of the two senior partners in Sperry/MacLennan, founded the company in 1972 as a one-man architectural practice. After graduating from the Nova Scotia Technical College (now the Technical University of Nova Scotia) in 1966, Sperry worked for six years for Robert J. Flinn before deciding that it was time to start his own company. By then he had cultivated a loyal clientele and a reputation as a good design architect and planner. In the first year, the business was supported part-time by a contract with the Province of Prince Edward Island Department of Tourism to undertake parks planning and the design of parks facilities from park furniture to interpretive centers. At the end of its first year, the company was incorporated as H. Drew Sperry and Associates; by then Sperry had added three junior architects, a draftsman, and a secretary. One of those architects was John MacLennan, who would later become a senior partner in Sperry/MacLennan.

Throughout the 1970s, the practice grew rapidly as the local economy expanded, even though the market for architectural services was competitive. The architectural program at the Nova Scotia Technical College (TUNS) was graduating more architects wishing to stay in the Maritimes than could be readily absorbed. But that was not the only reason why competition was stiff; there was a perception among businesspeople and local government personnel that, if you wanted the best, you had to get it from Toronto or New York. The company's greatest challenge throughout this period was persuading the local authorities that they did not have to go to Central Canada for first-class architectural expertise.

With the baby-boom generation entering the housing market, more than enough business came their way to enable Sperry's to develop a thriving architectural practice, and by 1979 the company had grown to 15 employees and had established branch offices in Charlottetown and Fredericton. These branch offices had been established to provide a local market presence and meet licensing requirements during their aggressive growth period. The

one in Charlottetown operated under the name of Allison & Sperry Associates, with Jim Allison as the partner, while in Fredericton, partner Peter Fellows was in charge.

But the growth could not last. The 1980s were not an easy time for the industry and many architectural firms found themselves unable to stay in business through a very slow period. For Sperry/MacLennan, it meant a severe reduction in staff and it also marked the end of the branch offices. Financially stretched and with work winding down on a multipurpose civic sports facility, the Dartmouth Sportsplex, the company was asked to enter a design competition for an aquatics center in Saint John, New Brunswick. It was a situation where they had to win or close their doors. The company laid off all but the three remaining partners, Drew and Sheila Sperry and John MacLennan. However, one draftsman and the secretary refused to leave, working without pay for several months in the belief that the company would win; their faith in the firm is still appreciated today.

Their persistence and faith were rewarded. Sperry won the competition for the aquatics facility for the Canada Games to be held in Saint John. The clients in Saint John wanted to build a new aquatic center, which would house the Canada Games competition and provide a community facility, which was self-supporting, after the Games were over. The facility needed to reflect a forward-thinking image to the world and act as a linchpin in the downtown revitalization plan. Therefore, it was paramount that the facility adhere to all technical competition requirements and that the design include renovation details for its conversion to a community facility sporting a new Sperry design element, the "indoor beach."

The Saint John Canada Games Society decided to use Sperry's for the contract and was very pleased with the building, the more so since the building won two design awards, the Facility of Merit Award for its "outstanding design" from Athletics Business and the Canadian Parks and Recreation Facility of Excellence Award. Sperry's had gained national recognition for its sports facility expertise and its reputation as a good design firm specializing in sports facilities was secured.

From the beginning, the company found recreational facilities work to be fun and exciting. To quote Sheila Sperry, this type of client "wants you to be innovative and new. It's a dream for an architect because it gives him an opportunity to use all the shapes and colors and natural light. It's a very exciting medium to work in." So they decided to focus their promotional efforts to get more of this type of work and consolidate their "pool designer" image by associating with Creative Aquatics on an exclusive basis. Creative Aquatics provided aquatics programming and technical operations expertise (materials, systems, water treatment, safety, and so on) to complement the design and planning skills at Sperry's.

The construction industry rebounded; declining interest rates ushered in a mini building boom which kept everyone busy. Jim Reardon joined the company and quickly acquired the experience and knowledge that would ease the company through its inevitable expansion. John MacLennan, by then a senior shareholder in the firm, wanted to develop a base in the large Ontario market and establish an office in Toronto. Jim Reardon was able to take over John's activities with very little difficulty as he had been working

This case has been prepared by Dr. Mary R. Brooks, of Dalhousie University, as a basis for classroom discussion rather than to illustrate effective or ineffective handling of an administrative situation. The assistance of the Secretary of State and the Canadian Studies Program in developing the case is gratefully acknowledged. Copyright Mary R. Brooks.

very closely with John in the recreational facilities aspect of the business.

Mitch Brooks joined the practice as a partner, albeit a junior one. Brooks was a good production architect, and work under his supervision came in on budget and on time, a factor compatible with the Sperry/MacLennan emphasis on customer service.

In late August, and with the weather cooling, Mitch Brooks reflects on his newest task, planning for the coming winter's activities. The company's reputation in the Canadian sports facility market is secure. The company has completed or has in construction five sports complexes in the Maritimes and five in Ontario, and three more facilities are in design. The awards have followed and, just this morning, Drew was notified of their latest achievement—the company has won the $10,000 Canadian Architect Grand Award for the Grand River Aquatics and Community Center near Kitchener, Ontario. This award is a particularly prestigious one as it is given by fellow architects in recognition of design excellence. Last week, Sheila Sperry received word that the Amherst, Nova Scotia, YM-YWCA won the American National Swimming Pool and Spa Gold Medal for pool design against French and Mexican finalists, giving them international recognition. Mitch Brooks is looking forward to his task ahead. The partners anticipate a slight slowdown and economists are predicting a recession the coming year. With 19 employees to keep busy and a competitor on the West Coast, they decided this morning that it was time to consider exporting their hard-won expertise.

The Architecture Industry

In order to practice architecture in Canada, an architect must graduate from an accredited school and serve a period of apprenticeship with a licensed architect, during which time he or she must experience all facets of the practice. At the end of this period, the would-be architect must pass an examination similar to that required of U.S. architects.

Architects are licensed provincially and these licenses are not readily transferable from province to province. Various levels of reciprocity are in existence. For this reason, joint ventures are not that uncommon in the business. In order to cross provincial boundaries, architecture firms in one province often enter into a joint venture arrangement with a local company. For example, the well-known design firm of Arthur Erickson of Vancouver/Toronto often engages in joint ventures with local production architects, as was the case for their design of the new Sir James Dunn Law Library on the campus of Dalhousie University.

In the United States, Canadian architects are well respected. The primary difficulty in working in the United States has been founded in immigration policies, which limit the movement of staff and provide difficulties in securing contracts. These policies will be eliminated with the U.S.-Canada Free Trade Agreement and the reciprocity accord signed between the American Institute of Architects and the Royal Architecture Institute of Canada, a voluntary group representing the provincial associations.

As architects in Nova Scotia are ethically prohibited from advertising their services, an architect's best advertisement is a good project, well done and well received. The provincial association (Nova Scotia Association of Architects—NSAA) will supply potential clients with basic information about licensed firms, their area of specialization, and so on. NSAA guidelines limit marketing to announcements of new partners, presentations to targeted

potential clients, advertisements of a business card size with "business card" information, and participation in media events.

The provincial association also provides a minimum schedule of fees, although many clients view this as the maximum they should pay. Although architects would like to think that the client chooses to do business with them because they like their past work, the price of the service is often the decision point. Some developers prefer to buy services on a basis other than the published fee schedule, such as a lump sum amount or a per-square-foot price. Although fee cutting is not encouraged by the professional organization, it is a factor in winning business, particularly when interest rates are high and construction slow.

As the "product" of an architecture firm is the service of designing a building, the marketing of the "product" centers on the architect's experience with a particular building type. Therefore, it is imperative that the architect convince the client that he has the necessary experience and capability to undertake the project and complete it satisfactorily. S/M has found with its large projects that the amount of time spent meeting with the client requires some local presence, although the design need not be done locally.

The process of marketing architectural services is one of marketing ideas. Therefore, it is imperative that the architect and the client have the same objectives and ultimately the same vision. Although that vision may be constrained by the client's budget, part of the marketing process is one of communicating with the client to ensure these common objectives exist.

Architects get business in a number of ways. "Walk-in" business is negligible and most of S/M's contracts are a result of one of the following five processes:

1. By referral from a satisfied client.

2. A juried design competition will be announced. (S/M has found that these prestigious jobs, even though they offer "runners-up" partial compensation, are not worth entering except to WIN, as costs are too high and the compensation offered other entrants too low. Second place is the same as last place. The Dartmouth Sportsplex and the Saint John Aquatic Center were both design competition wins.)

3. A client will publish a "Call for Proposals" or a "Call for Expressions of Interest" as the start of a formal selection process. (S/M rates these opportunities; unless they have a 75 percent chance of winning the contract, they view the effort as not worth the risk.)

4. A potential client invites a limited number of architectural firms to submit their qualifications as the start of a formal selection process. (S/M has a prepared qualification package which it can customize for a particular client.)

5. S/M hears of a potential building and contacts the client, presenting its qualifications.

The fourth and fifth processes are most common in buildings done for institutions and large corporations. As the primary buyers of sports facilities tend to be municipalities or educational institutions, this is the way S/M acquires a substantial share of its work. While juried competitions are not that common, the publicity possible from success in landing this work is important to S/M. The company has found that its success in securing a contract is often dependent on the client's criteria and the current state of the local market, with no particular pattern evident for a specific building type.

After the architect signs the contract, there will be a number of meetings with the client as the concept evolves and the drawings and specifications develop. On a large sports facility project, the hours of contact can run into the hundreds. Depending on the type of project, client meetings may be held weekly or every two weeks; during the development of working drawings and specifications for a complex building, meetings may be as often as once a day. Therefore, continuing client contact is as much a part of the service sold as the drawings, specifications, and site supervision and, in fact, may be the key factor in repeat business.

Developers in Nova Scotia are often not loyal buyers, changing architects with every major project or two. Despite this, architects are inclined to think the buyer's loyalty is greater than it really is. Therefore, S/M scrutinizes buyers carefully, interested in those that can pay for a premium product. S/M's philosophy is to provide "quality products with quality service for quality clients," and thus produce facilities which will reflect well on the company.

The Opportunity

The Department of External Affairs and the Royal Architectural Institute of Canada commissioned a study of exporting opportunities for architects on the assumption that free trade in architectural services is possible under the Free Trade Agreement. The report, entitled *Precision, Planning, and Perseverance: Exporting Architectural Services to the United States,* identified eight market niches for Canadian architects in the United States, one of which was educational facilities, in particular postsecondary institutions.

State governments and private organizations control this niche, identified by Brooks as most likely to match S/M's capabilities. Universities are known not to be particularly loyal to local firms and so present a potential market to be developed. The study reported that "post-secondary institutions require design and management competence, whatever the source" (p. 39). Athletic facilities were identified as a possible niche for architects with mixed-use facility experience. Finally, the study concluded, "there is an enormous backlog of capital maintenance and new building requirements facing most higher-education institutions"

In addition to the above factors, the study indicated others that Brooks felt were of importance:

1. The United States has 30 percent fewer architectural firms per capita than Canada.
2. The market shares many Canadian values and work practices.
3. The population shift away from the Northeast to the Sunbelt is beginning to reverse.
4. Americans are demanding better buildings.

Although Brooks knows that Canadian firms have always had a good reputation internationally for the quality of their buildings, he is concerned that American firms are well ahead of Canadian ones in their use of CADD (computer-assisted design and drafting) for everything from conceptual design to facility management. S/M, in spite of best intentions, has been unable to get CADD off the ground but is in the process of applying to the Atlantic Canada Opportunities Agency for financial assistance in switching over to CADD.

Finally, the study cautions that "joint ventures with a U.S. architectural firm may be required but the facility managers network of the APPA [Association of Physical Plant Administrators of Universities and Colleges] should also be actively pursued."

Under free trade, architects will be able to freely engage in trade in services. Architects will be able to travel to the United States and set up an architectural practice without having to become qualified under the American Institute of Architects; as long as they are members of their respective provincial associations and have passed provincial licensing exams and apprenticeship requirements, they will be able to travel and work in the United States and import staff as required.

Where to Start?

In a meeting in Halifax in January, the Department of External Affairs had indicated that trade to the United States in architectural services was one positive benefit of the Free Trade Agreement. As a response, S/M has targeted New England for its expansion, because of its geographical proximity to S/M's home base in the Halifax/Dartmouth area, and also because of its population density and similar climatic conditions. However, with all the hype about free trade and the current focus on the United States, Brooks is quite concerned that the company might be overlooking some other very lucrative markets for his company's expertise. As part of his October presentation to the Board, he wants to identify and evaluate other possible markets for S/M's services. Other parts of the United States, or the affluent countries of Europe where recreational facilities are regularly patronized and design is taken seriously, might provide a better export market, given their string of design successes at home and the international recognition afforded by the Amherst facility design award. Brooks feels that designing two sports facilities a year in a new market would be an acceptable goal.

As part of searching for leads, Brooks notes that the APPA charges $575 for a membership which provides access to their membership list once a year. But this is only one source of leads. And of course there is the U.S. Department of Commerce, Bureau of the Census, as another source of information for him to tap. He wonders what other sources are possible.

S/M looks to have a very good opportunity in the New England market with all of its small universities and colleges. After a decade of cutbacks on spending, corporate donations and alumni support for U.S. universities have never been so strong, and many campuses have sports facilities which are outdated and have been poorly maintained. But Mitch Brooks is not sure that the New England market is the best. After all, a seminar on exporting that he attended last week indicated that the most geographically close market, or even the most psychically close one, may not be the best choice for long-run profit maximization and/or market share.

Questions

1. What types of information will Brooks need to collect before he can even begin to assess the New England market? Develop a series of questions you feel are critical to this assessment.

2. What selection criteria do you believe will be relevant to the assessment of any alternative markets? What preliminary market parameters are relevant to the evaluation of S/M's global options?

3. Assuming that S/M decides on the New England market, what information will be needed to implement an entry strategy?

CASE 4-10
TOUGH DECISIONS AT BOEING

In 1957 Boeing Co. launched the world's first commercial jet airliner, the 707.[1] Followed by the 727 trijet in 1962, the 737 twinjet in 1967, and the 747 in 1970, Boeing has continued to offer a complete product line of commercial jet airliners. Through its recent merger with McDonnell Douglas, Boeing now builds a family of planes that spans seating capacities for 100 to 600 passengers. The current passenger jet product line is represented in Exhibit 1.

The 737 actually has seven models with only the two ends of the product line (smallest and largest) listed below. Both the 767 and 777 include three models, each of which only the largest is represented in Exhibit 1.

Based on a forecasted world GDP growth rate of 3.2 percent per annum and air travel growth at 5.5 percent per annum,

Boeing predicts dramatic growth in demand for commercial jet aircraft between now and 2006. Their estimates are listed in Exhibit 2.

Forty percent of the world's commercial jetliners serve the North American regional market. Since deregulation of the airline industry in the United States in 1986, a travel network dominated by large banks of connecting flights at about 20 hubs has developed. The industry appears to have reached a fairly stable state with new routes pretty much equaling canceled old routes. Thus, during the next decade the North American market will require a mix of smaller- and intermediate-sized planes.

Europe's travel growth exceeds North America's, particularly as Eastern Europe develops and the EU deregulates more commercial airliners of a variety of sizes. Asian requirements are the most varied of the three major regions. Operations range from once-a-week services to Western China using small jets, to half-hourly flights within Japan using high-density 747 shuttles. The rapid growth of the Chinese domestic market will be the dominant

---

[1] Much of the information in this case was taken from Boeing's informative Web site in March 1998: **www.boeing.com**.

EXHIBIT 1   Boeing's 1998 Product Line

Model	Seating Capacity	Range (miles)	1998 Price (millions)
717-200 (formerly MD-95)	106	1800	$30.5–34.5
737-300	126	2600	$38.5–44.5
737-900	189	3100	$50.5–57.5
747-400	420	8300	$158.5–176.5
757-200	194	4500	$62.0–69.0
757-300	290	4000	$69.0–76.0
767-400ER	269	7000	$108.5–120.0
777-300	328	8300	$151.0–173.5
MD-80	172	3200	$41.5–48.5
MD-90	155	2400	$47.5–55.0

EXHIBIT 2   Forecasted Demand for New Airplane Deliveries, 1997–2006

	Number of Airplanes			
	Single-Aisle	Intermediate Twin-Aisle	747 & Larger	Total
N. America	1933	452	76	2461
Europe	1542	373	151	2066
Asia Pacific	923	625	196	1744
Rest of world	774	243	40	1057
Totals	5172	1693	463	7328

EXHIBIT 3   U.S. Shipments of Commercial Aircraft (> 15,000 kg)

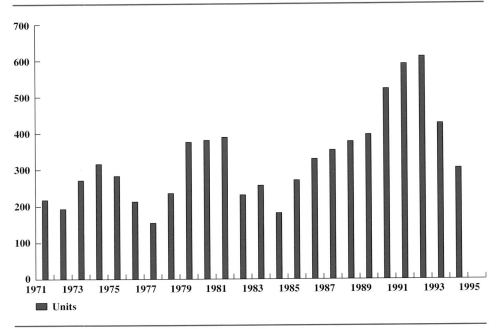

Source: U.S. Commerce Department.

demand factor, pushing demand more in the direction of single-aisle airliners. Boeing has a big advantage in the China market given the U.S./China joint venture to produce MD-90s in Shanghai it inherited via the McDonnell Douglas merger.[2] In 1996 Boeing had turned down the opportunity to work with the Chinese to develop a 100-seat aircraft. The only complication appears to be the MD-90's technical shortcomings in the 140–150 seat range compared to the 737 and Airbus 320.

During 1997 Boeing experienced $1.6 billion in charges due to delays and production bottlenecks severely eating into the firm's profits. Such problems are signs of its struggle to keep up with the boom in orders the industry is now experiencing. Boeing, while trying to absorb McDonnell Douglas, is ramping up production from 19 planes per month in 1996 to over 40 per month in 1998. Current plans call for more than 500 deliveries per year for the next few years.

All these plans are based on pre-Asian financial crisis forecasts.[3] Most recently company officials have estimated that cancelled Asian orders will amount to only 20 planes per year. But the extent of the Asian problems is still quite unclear. Some predict that the "Asian flu" may affect the global boom in commercial aircraft demand dramatically. Indeed, the industry has been one of the most volatile in the past (see Exhibit 3).

Questions

Two immediate and one long-term question are facing executives at Boeing:

1. How to pair down a product line which is apparently too long after the takeover of McDonnell Douglas;

2. How to respond to British Airways' (BA) request for bids for 100 short-haul jets.[4] BA's specifications fit best Boeing's 737 family and Airbus's A320 family—seating capacity between 110–160. They are asking for "innovative" financing and deliveries to begin as soon as 1999; and

3. Given the current global boom in aircraft orders, should Boeing prepare for the traditional unforeseen bust? If so, how? Can the firm do anything to dampen the apparently natural volatility of demand for commercial jetliners?

Act as a consultant to Boeing and make recommendations regarding the three questions.

---

[2] Stanley Holmes, "Boeing Will Likely Phase Out MD-80, MD-90 Jet Production Lines," *Knight Ridder Tribune Business News,* October 1, 1997.
[3] "Boeing Executive Warns of Asian Impact on Aircraft Sales," *Dow Jones News Service,* February 3, 1998.

[4] Charles Goldsmith, "British Airways Seeks Airbus, Boeing Bids for Jets," *The Wall Street Journal,* February 24, 1998, p. A16.

CASE 4–11
CREATING A GLOBAL PERSPECTIVE

Levi Strauss & Co. markets brand-name apparel in more than 60 countries. The company employs a staff of about 1,900 people at its San Francisco headquarters, and approximately 37,500 people worldwide. It operates 53 production facilities and 32 customer service centers in more than 50 countries. The company manufactures and markets product under the Levi's, Dockers, and Slates brands.

The company is now in the process of changing its advertising from a localized campaign for each country in which it sells its products to a worldwide strategy for all advertising. Levi Strauss & Co. announced global sales of $6.9 billion for the fiscal year ending November 30, 1997. Sales for the year were 4 percent below the company's record 1996 sales of $7.1 billion.

Sales for the company's North and South American operations (Levi Strauss, the Americas) totaled $4.6 billion for fiscal year 1997. Levi Strauss Europe posted revenues of $1.8 billion for the year. Sales for the company's Asia/Pacific Division were $468 million.

Comparable divisional sales figures for fiscal 1996 are not available, as this is the first year that Levi Strauss & Co. has reported revenues under its new "Triad" global organization. The company is a privately held corporation. It does not disclose corporate earnings, quarterly revenues, or competitive data on specific business units or brands.

You have been asked to evaluate its present programs and to make recommendations that will assist management in deciding whether it is better (1) to create advertising campaigns locally or regionally but with a good deal of input and influence from headquarters, as they presently do; (2) to allow campaigns to be created independently by local advertising companies; or (3) to centralize all advertising at national headquarters and develop a consistent worldwide advertising campaign.

You are asked to do the following:

1. Prepare a report listing the pros and cons of each of the three approaches.

2. Make a recommendation about the direction the company should take.

3. Support your recommendation and outline major objectives for whichever approach you recommend.

4. Evaluate all new ads using the SERT test.

The following information should be of assistance in completing this assignment:

Sources: "Exporting a Legend," *International Advertising*, November–December 1981, pp. 2–3; "Levi Zipping Up World Image," *Advertising Age*, September 14, 1981, pp. 35–36; David Short, "Speeding Up the Message by Jumping across Borders," *The European*, June 6, 1996, p. 23; "Levi's Launches 'Dream-Logic' Brand Image Campaign," *Reuters Business Report*, July 30, 1997; Eleftheria Parpis, "Searching for the Perfect Fit," *ADWEEK Eastern Edition*, September 15, 1997, p. 23; and the following from Levi Strauss & Co.'s Web site: **http://www.levi.com**, "Responsible Commercial Success," "General Information," "Levi Strauss & Co., Fact Sheet," "Levi Strauss & Co.'s Brand Advertising History," and "Levi Strauss & Co. Announces 1997 Sales Results," February 9, 1998.

Business Vision

Levi Strauss & Co. will strive to achieve responsible commercial success in the eyes of our constituencies, which include stockholders, employees, consumers, customers, suppliers, and communities. Our success will be measured not only by growth in shareholder value, but also by our reputation, the quality of our constituency relationships, and our commitment to social responsibility. As a global company, our businesses in every country will contribute to our overall success. We will leverage our knowledge of local markets to take advantage of the global positioning of our brands, our product and market strengths, our resources, and our cultural diversity. We will balance local market requirements with a global perspective. We will make decisions which will benefit the Company as a whole, rather than any one component. We will strive to be cost effective in everything we do and will manage our resources to meet our constituencies' needs. The strong heritage and values of Levi Strauss & Co. as expressed through our Mission and Aspiration Statements will guide all of our efforts. The quality of our products, services and people is critical to the realization of our business vision.

Products

We will market value-added, branded casual apparel with Levi's branded jeans continuing to be the cornerstone of our business. Our brands will be positioned to ensure consistency of image and values to our customers around the world.

Unlike some competitors, Levi Strauss International does not, in its normal markets, seek targets of opportunity, that is, large one-time shipments to customers it may never serve again. Rather, the goal is to develop sustainable and growing shipment levels to long-term customers.

Business Operations

Levi Strauss & Co. is a global corporation made up of three business units that reflect its "Triad" global organization:

Levi Strauss, the Americas (LSA) employs approximately 28,000 people throughout the United States, Mexico, Canada, Brazil, Argentina, and other countries in Central and South America, and the Caribbean. It manufactures and markets products under the Levi's, Dockers, and SLATES™ brands throughout the region and includes five wholly owned-and-operated businesses: Levi Strauss U.S., Levi Strauss & Co. (Canada) Inc., Levi Strauss Mexico, Levi Strauss do Brasil, and Levi Strauss Argentina.

Levi Strauss Europe (LSE) employs approximately 7,000 people in a region which is divided into three geographic areas: Europe, Africa, and the Mideast. LSE markets and sells its products in the following countries: Austria, Belgium, Croatia, Czech Republic, Denmark, Finland, France, Germany, Greece, Hungry, Ireland, Italy, Luxembourg, the Netherlands, Norway, Poland, Portugal, Russia, South Africa, Spain, Sweden, Switzerland, Tunisia, Turkey, and the United Kingdom.

Asia Pacific Division (APD) employs approximately 2,400 people and manufactures and markets products for Asia and the Pacific. The division consists of 10 wholly owned-and-operated businesses in Japan, South Korea, Hong Kong, Taiwan, Malaysia, the Philippines, Indonesia, India, Australia, and New Zealand; with licensees and distributors in Saipan/Guam, Singapore, and Thailand. The Asia/Pacific Division had its beginning in the 1940s when jeans reached this market through U.S. military exchanges. In 1965, a sales facility was established in Hong Kong.

The Levi's trademark is the most recognized apparel brand and one of the most famous consumer brand names in the world.

Comments

The director of advertising and communications for International shares with you the following thoughts about advertising:

- The success of Levi Strauss International's advertising derived principally from their judging it consistently against three criteria: (1) Is the proposition meaningful to the consumer? (2) Is the message believable? and (3) Is it exclusive to the brand?
- A set of core values underlies advertising wherever it is produced and regardless of strategy: honesty/integrity, consistency/reliability, relevance, social responsibility, credibility, excellence, and style. The question remains whether a centralized advertising campaign can be based on this core of values.
- Levi Strauss' marketing plans include 70 countries and recognize the cultural and political differences affecting advertising appeals. Uniform advertising (i.e., standardized) could ignore local customs and unique product uses, while locally prepared advertising risks uneven creative work, is likely to waste time and money on preparation, and might blur the corporate image. Consistency in product image is a priority.
- Levi's is not satisfied with some of the creative work in parts of Latin America. The company wants consistency in Latin-American strategy rather than appearing to be a different company in different countries. The company is not satisfied with production costs and casting of commercials, and the fact that local agencies are often resistant to outside suggestions to change. It feels there is a knee-jerk reaction in Latin America that results in the attitude that everything must be developed locally.
- The risks of too closely controlling a campaign result in uninteresting ads compared with decentralizing all marketing, which produces uneven creative quality.

Competition

At the same time that Levi's is looking at more centralized control of its advertising, another jeans maker is going in the opposite direction. Blue Bell International's Wrangler jeans company has just ended a six-month review of its international advertising and decided against coordinating its advertising more closely in Europe.

The concept of one idea that will work effectively in all markets is attractive to Wrangler. Yet the disadvantages are just as clear; the individual needs of each market cannot be met, resistance from local managers could be an obstacle, and the management of a centralized advertising campaign would require an organizational structure different from the present one.

To add to the confusion, a leading European jeans manufacturer, the Spanish textile company Y Confecciones Europeas, makers of Louis jeans, recently centralized its marketing through one single advertising agency. Louis, fourth-largest jeans maker after Levi's, Lee Cooper, and Wrangler, is intent on developing a worldwide international image for its Louis brand.

Diesel, another major international competitor, has grown from $12 million in U.S. sales in 1995 to $24 million in 1996 with a different vision of Americana, a mix of '50s kitsch and '90s techno styles. Its "Successful Living" campaign, created by Paradiset DDB, Stockholm, Sweden, has established the brand worldwide with an edgy, trendsetting consumer. The "Heritage" ads, which focused on the Western themes often found in jeans ads, won top film honors at the 1997 International Advertising Festival at Cannes.

"Our advertising has always been provocative, different and humorous. One of the things you don't see very much in fashion advertising is humor. We use irony to the point where we make fun of ourselves."

The company's most recent campaign features the fictitious firm "Brand O" advertising its ice cream, diet, and newspaper products in impoverished North Korea. For example, pictured above a crowd of people waiting in what appears to be a food line is a billboard showing a frolicking couple wearing Diesel Jeans next to a headline that reads, "Brand O ice cream. For a better tomorrow."

Diesel's funky retail stores, which feature DJs spinning the latest hip-hop and techno music, only further reinforce the irreverent personality it has built through its image advertising.

Review of Current Ads

A review of a selection of Levi's advertisements from around the world provided the following notes:

- European television commercials for Levi's were supersexy in appeal, projecting, in the minds of some at headquarters, an objectionable personality for the brand. These commercials were the result of allowing complete autonomy to a sales region.
- Levi's commercials prepared in Latin America projected a far different image than those in Europe. Latin-American ads addressed a family-oriented, Catholic market. However, the quality of the creative work was far below the standards set by the company.
- Ads for the United Kingdom, emphasizing that Levi's is an American brand, star an all-American hero, the cowboy, in fantasy Wild West settings. In Northern Europe, both Scandinavian and the United Kingdom consumers are buying a slice of America when they buy Levi's.
- In Japan, where an attitude similar to that in the U.K. prevails, a problem confronted Levi's. Local jeans companies had already established themselves as very American. To overcome this, Levi's positioned itself against these brands as legendary American jeans with commercials themed "Heroes Wear Levi's," featuring clips of cult figures such as James Dean. These commercials were very effective and carried Levi's from a 35 percent to a 95 percent awareness level in Japan.

- In Brazil, unlike the United Kingdom, consumers are more strongly influenced by fashion trends emanating from the European Continent rather than from America. Thus, the Brazilian-made commercial filmed in Paris featured young people, cool amidst a wild traffic scene—very French. This commercial was intended to project the impression that Levi's is the favored brand among young, trend-setting Europeans.

- Australian commercials showed that creating brand awareness is important in that market. The lines "fit looks tight, doesn't feel tight, can feel comfortable all night" and "a legend doesn't come apart at the seams" highlighted Levi's quality image, and "since 1850 Levi jeans have handled everything from bucking broncos . . ." amplified Levi's unique positioning. This campaign resulted in 99 percent brand awareness among Australians.

Levi's is attempting to refine its image this year (1997) with a bold, new television and print campaign. Scenes from the campaign: A lanky European woman orders a hot dog, a plain hot dog, from a New York City street vendor for a friend's dog because "he likes it plain." A young man whose car is filled with carnival toys says goodbye to his friend, a small-town disc jockey dreaming of spinning in the big city. A taxi driver lives out a fantasy of a high-speed car chase. Lenny Kravitz changes his clothes in a gas station. What do any of these scenarios have to do with jeans? Nothing at all—and everything.

The six spots, whose tagline is "They go on," constitute the first general branding effort undertaken by the 144-year-old company. Backed by an estimated $90 million in media spending, the commercials, directed by Tarsem, teeter between the real and surreal and eschew traditional storytelling structure. Instead, a shared scene connects the ads, and each spot includes circuitous glimpses of the lives of the perennially hip Levi's wearer. The fabric that holds the characters together is the Levi's label and the spirit the red tag represents.

Here was an opportunity to market the brand overall, focusing on the originality and the youthfulness inherent in the overall brand values.

Levi's, says the director of advertising, "is always going to be the real deal. We won't want to be a flashy, hyped brand. We have a quiet strength in a way. We have to balance that authenticity and stay current."

Levi's "Launderette" commercial, featuring Marvin Gaye's classic song "Grapevine," aired in Europe and boosted sales there by 800 percent. This spot—now a classic—was satirized twice the following year in advertising and comedy programming, and the song became popular again. Levi's Europe "Drugstore" TV spot won advertising awards in Berlin, London, Cannes, and Milan. European consumers rated "Drugstore" the second best commercial from Levi's this decade. They rank Levi's "Taxi" TV spot, featuring a sexy cross-dresser, the best of the decade.

"Clayman," an animated tale of a winsome hero clad in Levi's 501 jeans who rescues a beauty trapped in a burning building, is the company's first global commercial. It runs in countries on all five continents. These commercials celebrate the Levi's brand and its core values of originality and youthfulness. According to Derek Bowden, chief executive officer of Saatchi Europe, all ads have to meet what is called the "SURT" test; the commercials have to be Simple, Universally Recognized, and Truthful."

CASE 4–12
NATIONAL OFFICE MACHINES—MOTIVATING JAPANESE SALESPEOPLE: STRAIGHT SALARY OR COMMISSION?

National Office Machines of Dayton, Ohio, manufacturers of cash registers, EDP equipment, adding machines, and other small office equipment, has recently entered into a joint venture with Nippon Cash Machines of Tokyo, Japan. Last year, National Office Machines (NOM) had domestic sales of over $1.4 billion and foreign sales of nearly $700 million. Besides in the United States, it operates in most of Western Europe, the Mideast, and some parts of the Far East. In the past, it has had no significant sales or sales force in Japan, although the company was represented there by a small trading company until a few years ago. In the United States, NOM is one of the leaders in the field and is considered to have one of the most successful and aggressive sales forces found in this highly competitive industry.

Nippon Cash Machines (NCM) is an old-line cash register manufacturing company organized in 1882. At one time, Nippon was the major manufacturer of cash register equipment in Japan but it has been losing ground since 1970 even though it produces perhaps the best cash register in Japan. Last year's sales were 9 billion yen, a 15 percent decrease from sales the prior year. The fact that it produces only cash registers is one of the major problems; the merger with NOM will give them much-needed breadth in product offerings. Another hoped-for strength to be gained from the joint venture is managerial leadership, which is sorely needed.

Fourteen Japanese companies have products that compete with Nippon, plus several foreign giants such as IBM, National Cash Register, and Unisys of the United States, and Sweda Machines of Sweden. Nippon has a small sales force of 21 men, most of whom have been with the company their entire adult careers. These salesmen have been responsible for selling to Japanese trading companies and to a few larger purchasers of equipment.

Part of the joint-venture agreement included doubling the sales force within a year, with NOM responsible for hiring and training the new salesmen who must all be young, college-trained Japanese nationals. The agreement also allowed for U.S. personnel in supervisory positions for an indeterminate period of time and retaining the current Nippon sales force.

One of the many sales management problems facing the Nippon/American Business Machines Corporation (NABMC—the name of the new joint venture) was which sales compensation plan to use; that is, should it follow the Japanese tradition of straight salary and guaranteed employment until death with no individual incentive program, or the U.S. method (very successful for NOM in the United States) of commissions and various incentives based on sales performance, with the ultimate threat of being fired if sales quotas go continuously unfilled?

The immediate response to the problem might well be one of using the tried-and-true U.S. compensation methods, since they have worked so well in the United States and are perhaps the kind of changes needed and expected from U.S. management. NOM management is convinced that salespeople selling its kinds of products in a competitive market must have strong incentives to produce. In fact, NOM had experimented on a limited basis in the United States with straight salary about 10 years ago and it was a bomb. Unfortunately, the problem is considerably more complex than it appears on the surface.

One of the facts to be faced by NOM management is the traditional labor–management relations and employment systems in Japan. The roots of the system go back to Japan's feudal era, when a serf promised a lifetime of service to his lord in exchange for a lifetime of protection. By the start of Japan's industrial revolution in the 1880s, an unskilled worker pledged to remain with a company all his useful life if the employer would teach him the new mechanical arts. The tradition of spending a lifetime with a single employer survives today mainly because most workers like it that way. The very foundations of Japan's management system are based on lifetime employment, promotion through seniority, and single-company unions.[1] There is little chance of being fired, pay raises are regular, and there is a strict order of job-protecting seniority.

Japanese workers at larger companies still are protected from outright dismissal by union contracts and an industrial tradition that some personnel specialists believe has the force of law. Under this tradition, a worker can be dismissed after an initial trial period only for gross cause, such as theft or some other major infraction. As long as the company remains in business, the worker isn't discharged, or even furloughed, simply because there isn't enough work to be done.

Besides the guarantee of employment for life, the typical Japanese worker receives many fringe benefits from the company. Bank loans and mortgages are granted to lifetime employees on the assumption that they will never lose their jobs and therefore the ability to repay. Just how paternalistic the typical Japanese firm can be is illustrated by a statement from the Japanese Ministry of Foreign Affairs which gives the example of A, a male worker, who is employed in a fairly representative company in Tokyo.

> To begin with, A lives in a house provided by his company, and the rent he pays is amazingly low when compared with average city rents. His daily trips between home and factory are paid by the company. A's working hours are from 9 A.M. to 5 P.M. with a break for lunch which he usually takes in the company restaurant at a very cheap price. He often brings home food, clothing, and other miscellaneous articles he has bought at the company store at a discount ranging from 10 percent to 30 percent below city prices. The company store even supplies furniture, refrigerators, and television sets on an installment basis, for which, if necessary, A can obtain a loan from the company almost free of interest.

In case of illness, A is given free medical treatment in the company hospital, and if his indisposition extends over a number of years, the company will continue paying almost his full salary. The company maintains lodges at seaside or mountain resorts where A can spend the holidays or an occasional weekend with the family at moderate prices. . . . It must also be remembered that when A reaches retirement age (usually 55) he will receive a lump-sum retirement allowance or a pension, either of which will assure him a relatively stable living for the rest of his life.

Even though A is only an example of a typical employee, a salesperson can expect the same treatment. Job security is such an expected part of everyday life that no attempt is made to motivate the Japanese salesperson in the same manner as in the United States; as a consequence, selling traditionally has been primarily an order-taking job. Except for the fact that sales work offers some travel, entry to outside executive offices, the opportunity to entertain, and similar side benefits, it provides a young person with little other incentive to surpass basic quotas and drum up new business.[2] The traditional Japanese bonuses are given twice-yearly, can be up to 40 percent of base pay, and are no larger for salespeople than any other functional job in the company.

As a key executive in a Mitsui-affiliated engineering firm put it recently: "The typical salesman in Japan isn't required to have any particular talent." In return for meeting sales quotas, most Japanese salespeople draw a modest monthly salary, sweetened about twice a year by bonuses. Manufacturers of industrial products generally pay no commission or other incentives to boost their businesses.

Besides the problem of motivation, a foreign company faces other different customs when trying to put together and manage a sales force. Class systems and the Japanese distribution system with its penchant for reciprocity put a strain on the creative talents of the best sales managers, as Simmons, the U.S. bedding manufacturer, was quick to learn.

In the field, Simmons found itself stymied by the bewildering realities of Japanese marketing, especially the traditional distribution system which operates on a philosophy of reciprocity that goes beyond mere business to the core of the Japanese character. It's involved with *on,* the notion that regards a favor of any kind as a debt that must be repaid. To *wear* another's *on* in business and then turn against that person is to lose face, abhorrent to most Japanese. Thus, the owner of large Western-style apartments, hotels, or developments buys his beds from the supplier to whom he owes a favor, no matter what the competition offers.

In small department and other retail stores, where most items are handled on consignment, the bond with the supplier is even stronger.[3] Consequently, all sales outlets are connected in a complicated web that runs from the largest supplier, with a huge national sales force, to the smallest local distributor, with a handful of door-to-door salespeople. The system is self-perpetuating and all but impossible to crack from the outside.

However, there is some change in attitude taking place as both workers and companies start discarding traditions for the job mobility common in the United States. Skilled workers are willing to

---

[1] Robert Heller, David Kilburn, et al., "The Managers' Dilemmas," *Management Today,* January 1994, pp. 42–48.

[2] R. Bruce Money and John L. Graham, "Salesperson Performance, Pay, and Job Satisfaction: Tests of a Model Using Data Collection in the U.S. and Japan," *Journal of International Business Studies,* 1998.

[3] Frank Alpert, Michael Kamins, Tomoaki Sakano, Naoto Onzo, and John L. Graham, "Retail Buyer Decision Making in Japan: What U.S. Sellers Need to Know," *International Business Review,* 6(2), 1997, pp. 91–112.

bargain on the strength of their experience in an open labor market in an effort to get higher wages or better job opportunities; in the United States it's called shopping around. And a few companies are showing a willingness to lure workers away from other concerns. A number of companies are also plotting how to rid themselves of deadwood workers accumulated as a result of promotions by strict seniority.

Toyo Rayon company, Japan's largest producer of synthetic fibers, started reevaluating all its senior employees every five years with the implied threat that those who don't measure up to the company's expectations have to accept reassignment and possibly demotion; some may even be asked to resign. A chemical engineering and construction firm asked all its employees over 42 to negotiate a new contract with the company every two years. Pay raises and promotions go to those the company wants to keep. For those who think they are worth more than the company is willing to pay, the company offers retirement with something less than the $30,000 lump-sum payment the average Japanese worker receives at age 55.

More Japanese are seeking jobs with foreign firms as the life-time-employment ethic slowly changes. The head of student placement at Aoyama Gakuin University reports that each year the number of students seeking jobs with foreign companies increases. Bank of America, Japan Motorola, Imperial Chemical Industries, and American Hospital Supply are just a few of the companies that have been successful in attracting Japanese students. Just a few years ago, all Western companies were places to avoid.

Even those companies that are successful work with a multitude of handicaps. American companies often lack the intricate web of personal connections that their Japanese counterparts rely on when recruiting. Further, American companies have the reputation for being quick to hire and even quicker to fire, while Japanese companies still preach the virtues of lifelong job security. Those U.S. companies that are successful are offering big salaries and promises of Western-style autonomy. According to a recent study, 20- to 29-year-old Japanese prefer an employer-changing environment to a single lifetime employer. They complain that the Japanese system is unfair because promotions are based on age and seniority. A young recruit, no matter how able, has to wait for those above him to be promoted before he too can move up. Some feel that if you are really capable, you are better off working with an American company.

Some foreign firms entering Japan have found that their merit-based promotion systems have helped them attract bright young recruits. In fact, a survey done by *Nihon Keizai Shimbun,* Japan's leading business newspaper, found that 80 percent of top managers at 450 major Japanese corporations wanted the seniority promotion system abolished.[4] But, as one Japanese manager commented, "We see more people changing their jobs now, and we read many articles about companies restructuring, but despite this, we won't see major changes coming quickly."

A few U.S. companies operating in Japan are experimenting with incentive plans. Marco and Company, a belting manufacturer and Japanese distributor for Power Packing and Seal Company, was persuaded by Power to set up a travel plan incentive for sales-people who topped their regular sales quotas. Unorthodox as the idea was for Japan, Marco went along. The first year, special one-week trips to Far East holiday spots like Hong Kong, Taiwan, Manila, and Macao were inaugurated. Marco's sales of products jumped 212 percent, and the next year sales were up an additional 60 percent.

IBM also has made a move toward chucking the traditional Japanese sales system (salary plus a bonus but no incentives). For about a year, it has been working with a combination that retains the semiannual bonus while adding commission payments on sales over preset quotas.

"It's difficult to apply a straight commission system in selling computers because of the complexities of the product," an IBM Japan official said. "Our salesmen don't get big commissions because other employees would be jealous." To head off possible ill feeling, therefore, some nonselling IBM employees receive monetary incentives.

Most Japanese companies seem reluctant to follow IBM's example because they have doubts about directing older salesmen to go beyond their usual order-taking role. High-pressure tactics are not well accepted here, and sales channels are often pretty well set by custom and long practice (e.g., a manufacturer normally deals with one trading company, which in turn sells only to customers A, B, C, and D). A salesman or trading company, for that matter, is not often encouraged to go after customer Z and get him away from a rival supplier.

The Japanese market is becoming more competitive and there is real fear on the part of NOM executives that the traditional system just won't work in a competitive market. On the other hand, the proponents of the incentive system agree that the system really has not been tested over long periods or even adequately in the short term since it has been applied only in a growing market. In other words, was it the incentive system that caused the successes achieved by the companies or was it market growth? Especially there is doubt since other companies following the traditional method of compensation and employee relations also have had sales increases during the same period.

The problem is further complicated for Nippon/American because it will have both new and old salespeople. The young Japanese seem eager to accept the incentive method but older ones are hesitant. How do you satisfy both since you must, by agreement, retain all the sales staff?

A recent study done by the Japanese government on attitudes of youth around the world suggests that younger Japanese may be more receptive to U.S. incentive methods than one would anticipate. In a study done by the Japanese Prime Minister's Office there were some surprising results when Japanese responses were compared with responses of similar-aged youths from other countries. Exhibit 1 summarizes some of the information gathered on life goals. One point that may be of importance in shedding light on the decision NOM has to make is a comparison of Japanese attitudes with young people in 11 other countries—the Japanese young people are less satisfied with their home life, school, and working situations, and are more passive in their attitudes toward social and political problems. Further, almost a third of those employed said they were dissatisfied with their present jobs primarily because of low income and short vacations. Asked if they had to choose between a difficult job with responsibility and authority or an easy job without responsibility and authority, 64 percent of the Japanese picked the former, somewhat less than the 70–80 percent average in other countries.

---

[4] David Kilburn, "The Sun Sets on Japan Lifers," *Management Today,* September 1993, pp. 44–47.

EXHIBIT 1   Life Goals

	(Unit: %)				
Japan	35.4	5.8	41.2	6.8	10.8
US	6.2 / 5.1	77.3			9.5 / 1.8
UK	11.2	13.9	63.4		8.6 / 2.9
Germany	9.0	17.8	60.6	5.5	7.5
France	7.1	16.4	62.2	10.9	3.4
Switzerland	3.7 / 9.2	72.3		11.9	3.0
Sweden	2.5 / 1.7	84.8		7.5	3.4
Australia	6.7 / 5.1	76.0		10.5	1.6
India	22.3	33.3	16.2	26.3	1.8
Philippines	21.7	9.6	46.2	22.0	0.5
Brazil	7.7	16.7	63.2	11.9	0.5
Key:	To get rich*	To acquire social position	To live as I choose	To work on behalf of society	No answer

Note: The respondents were asked to choose one answer.
* The literal translation of the question asked the Japanese pollees is close to "to be well-off economically." Had the Japanese respondents been asked the more blunt "to get rich," probably fewer of them would have chosen this alternative.
Source: Prime Minister's Office: "How Youth See Life," *Focus Japan.*

Another critical problem lies with the nonsales employees; traditionally, all employees on the same level are treated equally whether sales, production, or staff. How do you encourage competitive, aggressive salesmanship in a market unfamiliar to such tactics, and how do you compensate salespeople to promote more aggressive selling in the face of tradition-bound practices of paternalistic company behavior?

Questions

1. What should they offer—incentives or straight salary? Support your answer.

2. If incentives are out, how do you motivate salespeople and get them to compete aggressively?

3. Design a U.S.-type program for motivation and compensation of salespeople. Point out where difficulties may be encountered with your plan and how the problems are to be overcome.

4. Design a pay system you think would work, satisfying old salespeople, new salespeople, and other employees.

5. Discuss the idea that perhaps the kind of motivation and aggressiveness found in the United States is not necessary in the Japanese market.

6. Develop some principles in motivation that could be applied by an international marketer in other countries.

CASE 4–13
ALAN AEROSPACE—COMMUNICATIONS SATELLITE SALES TO JAPAN

Japanese managers don't get mad, and they certainly don't pound on negotiation tables. At least that's the conventional wisdom. Yet in February 1995, Takeshi Suzuki, General Manager of the Marketing and Sales Division of Space Systems Corporation (SSC) of Japan, was expressing himself in precisely that manner in response to price and delivery proposals made by Alan AeroSpace Corporation for a multimillion-dollar communications satellite. Ordinarily, such responses on the Japanese side of trans-Pacific negotiations mean just one thing: the deal is dead. However, Alan AeroSpace and SSC have been able to work out their differences, and their Silverbird satellite is scheduled for launch in the spring of 1999. To save the relationship between the companies, managers on both sides of the table took decisive actions at the time and have since followed up with patience, hard work, and true international business acumen. The details of the story provide important insight into the right way to manage negotiations and relationships between Japanese and American firms.

A little background is helpful first. Suzuki-san has been kind enough to provide the following details. In the early 1980s Sakano Corporation, SSC's parent, agreed to act as Alan AeroSpace's agent in Japan. So, the relationship between the two companies goes back almost twenty years. At the beginning of that relationship, Suzuki was assigned to work at Alan AeroSpace in Palo Alto, California, as a trainee. Thus, he knows the executives well and describes his relationships with them as "almost family." Also, in the 1980s Alan AeroSpace and Sakano were awarded a satellite study contract by the National Space Development Agency (or NASDA, the Japanese equivalent of NASA). And soon thereafter Alan was awarded the CS-111 (Ichikawa) project, one of Japan's first communications satellite. Since then, Alan AeroSpace via Sakano has sold seven more satellites to NASDA.

In 1994 Sakano, realizing the importance of pursuing a new high-technology business, decided to commit to the space development program. On March 23, 1995, after securing a license from the Ministry of Post and Telecommunications, SSC was established, with Sakano Corporation owning 60 percent and Sakano Electric Corporation owning 40 percent of the 100 billion-yen venture (about $800 million, at 125¥/$1.00). Shortly thereafter, executives from Alan AeroSpace, SSC, and SSC's parent companies convened to study the anticipated deregulation of the Japanese space program and the feasibility of launching a privately owned communications satellite. SSC asked Alan AeroSpace to submit a technical proposal. Suzuki-san stated four reasons for preselecting Alan AeroSpace as the sole supplier: (1) they had a long and personal relationship; (2) Alan AeroSpace had been reliable and had the requisite experience; (3) the proposal process could be handled more efficiently; and (4) "We expected them to be fair."

Alan AeroSpace's proposal was quite different from that expected by Suzuki—a 45-month delivery schedule (12 months longer than that advertised by a competitor), with a price tag 30–40 percent greater than anticipated. He felt that Alan AeroSpace was taking advantage of its sole source position. However, Suzuki went ahead and signed the Authorization to Proceed (ATP), including a $2–4 million down payment, not wanting to delay further the launch date.

Then came the February 1996 meeting. The Alan AeroSpace team was headed up by a project manager, and included a project engineer and others. The Japanese side included Suzuki and others from SSC, and Carl Onzo, in charge of the Aerospace Department in Sakano's trading company offices in Palo Alto. Suzuki-san began to get upset when he learned that work had not begun on the project despite the ATP. The Alan AeroSpace position was that substantial work could not begin, since the specifications and requirements for the satellite had not yet been clearly defined. Alan AeroSpace refused to budge on the price and delivery schedule and offered no alternatives. At that point Suzuki "blew up" and walked out of the meeting. What happened next was crucial to this particular negotiation, as well as quite instructive about the Japanese approach to such problems: Suzuki called an Alan AeroSpace vice president and director of the space systems operation, and asked him to replace the Alan project management team.

Questions

1. Assume you are the vice president and director of space systems. What immediate actions do you take and what instructions do you give your people? Explain and justify.

Case 4–14
AIDS, Condoms, and Carnival

Brazil

Half a million Brazilians are infected with the AIDS virus, and millions more are at high risk of contracting the incurable ailment, a federal study reported. The Health Ministry study is Brazil's first official attempt to seek an estimate of HIV-infected residents. Many had doubted the government's prior number of 94,997. The report by the National Program for Transmissible Diseases/AIDS said 27 million Brazilians are at high risk to contract AIDS, and another 36 million are considered to be at a medium risk. It said Brazil could have 7.5 million AIDS victims in the next decade.

"If we are going to combat this epidemic, we have to do it now," said Pedro Chequer, a health ministry official. Chequer said the Health Ministry would spend $300 million next year, distributing medicine and 250 million condoms and bringing AIDS awareness campaigns to the urban slums, where the disease is most rampant. Last month, Brazil became one of the few countries to offer a promising AIDS drug free to those who need it. The drug can cost as much as $12,000 a year per patient.

AIDS cases in Brazil have risen so dramatically for married women that the state of São Paulo decided that it must attack a basic cultural practice in Latin America: Their husbands don't practice safe sex. Last month, the government of Brazil's megalopolis started promoting the newly released female condom.

Many of the new AIDS cases in Brazil are married women who have children, according to a report released last month at the Pan-American Conference on AIDS in Lima, Peru. Worldwide, women constitute the fastest-growing group of those diagnosed with HIV. And of the 30.6 million people who are diagnosed with the HIV virus, 90 percent live in poor countries.

One Brazilian mother, Rosana Dolores, knows well why women cannot count on male partners to use condoms. She and her late husband never thought of protecting their future children against AIDS. "We were married. We wanted to have kids," says Mrs. Dolores, both of whose children were born with HIV. "These days, I would advise young people to always use condoms. But married couples . . . who is going to?"

Brazil, with its 155 million people and the largest population in South America, has the second-highest number of reported HIV infections in the Americas, after the United States, according to a report released November 26 by the United Nations agency, UNAIDS.

Public health officials say one reason why AIDS prevention efforts have failed is many Brazilians just don't like condoms. While use in Brazil has quadrupled in the past six years, it is still the least popular method of birth control—a touchy issue in the predominantly Roman Catholic country. Another reason is that condoms cost about 75 cents each, making them more expensive here than anywhere else in the world, health officials say.

Plus, Latin-style machismo leaves women with little bargaining power. Only 14 percent of Brazilian heterosexual men used condoms in 1996, according to AIDSCAP, an AIDS-prevention program funded by the U.S. Agency for International Development. In other studies, many women said they would not ask their partner to use a condom, even if they knew he was sleeping with others.

"Women are afraid of asking their men to have safe sex, afraid of getting beaten, afraid of losing their economic support," says Guido Carlos Levi, a director at the health department at Emilio Ribas Hospital. "This is not Mexico, but we're quite a machistic society here."

The frequency with which Latin men stray from monogamous relationships has compounded the problem. In studies conducted in Cuba by the Pan American Health Organization, 49 percent of men and 14 percent of women in stable relationships admitted they had had an affair in the past year.

In light of statistics showing AIDS as the number one killer of women of childbearing age in São Paulo state, public health officials here launched a campaign in December promoting the female condom.

The hope is that it will help women—especially poor women—protect themselves and their children. But the female condom seemed unlikely to spark a latex revolution when it hit city stores January 1. The price is $2.50 apiece—more than three times the price of most male condoms.

The Family Health Association is asking the government to help subsidize the product and to cut the taxes on condoms that make them out of reach for many poor Brazilians. "We're looking for a pragmatic solution to prevent the transmission of HIV-AIDS," group President Maria Eugenia Lemos Fernandes said. "Studies show there is a high acceptance of this method because it's a product under the control of women."

While 75 percent of the women and 63 percent of the men in a pilot study on the female condom said they approved of the device, many women with AIDS say they would have been no more likely to have used a female condom than a conventional one.

Part of the problem is perception: 80 percent of women and 85 percent of men in Brazil believe they are not at risk of contracting HIV, according to a study conducted by the Civil Society for the Well-Being of the Brazilian Family.

Also at risk are married women, 40 percent of whom undergo sterilization as an affordable way of getting around the Catholic church's condemnation of birth control, health officials noted.

"It's mostly married women who are the victims. You just never think it could be you," says a former hospital administrator who was diagnosed with the virus after her husband had several extramarital affairs. He died two years ago.

"I knew everything there was to know about AIDS—I worked in a hospital—but I never suspected he was going out like that. He always denied it," she says.

While the HIV virus is making inroads in rural areas and among teenagers in Brazil, Fernandes says it doesn't have to reach epidemic proportions as in Uganda or Tanzania. "There is a very big window of opportunity here."

Brazil's Health Ministry is adding a new ingredient to the heady mix that makes up the country's annual Carnival—condoms. The ministry will distribute 10 million condoms next month along with free advice on how to prevent the spread of AIDS at places like Rio de Janeiro's sambadrome, where bare-breasted dancing girls attract millions of spectators every year.

"It's considered as a period of increased sexual activity," a spokeswoman at the ministry's AIDS coordination department said on Monday. "The euphoria provoked by Carnival and the excessive consumption of alcohol make it a moment when people are more likely to forget about prevention," she explained.

Tourists descend on Brazil for Carnival, which is viewed as a time when inhibitions fall away and anything goes.

India

S. Mani's small barber shop in this southern Indian city looks like any other the world over. It's equipped with all the tools of the trade: scissors, combs, razors—and condoms, too.

A blue box full of free prophylactics stands in plain view of his customers as Mr. Mani trims hair and dispenses advice on safe sex, a new dimension to his 20-year career. "I start by talking about the family and children," Mr. Mani explains, snipping a client's moustache. "Slowly, I get to women, AIDS, and condoms."

Many Indian men are too embarrassed to buy condoms at a drugstore or to talk freely about sex with health counselors and family members. There's one place where they let down their hair: the barbershop. So, the state of Tamil Nadu is training barbers to be frontline soldiers in the fight against AIDS.

Programs like the barber scheme are what make Tamil Nadu, a relatively poor Indian state that's home to 60 million people, a possible model for innovative and cost-effective methods to contain AIDS in the developing world.

Six years after it was first detected in India, the AIDS virus is quickly spreading in the world's second most-populous nation. Already, up to 5 million of India's 920 million people are infected with HIV—more than in any other country, according to UN-AIDS, the United Nations' AIDS agency.

But faced with more immediate and widespread health woes, such as tuberculosis and malaria, officials in many Indian states are reluctant to make AIDS prevention a priority. And in some states, the acquired immune deficiency syndrome is regarded as a Western disease of decadence; officials deny that prostitution and drug use even exist in their midst.

"Some Indian states are still in total denial or ignorance about the AIDS problem," says Salim Habayeb, a World Bank physician who oversees an $84 million loan to India for AIDS prevention activities.

Tamil Nadu, the state with the third-highest incidence of HIV infection, has been open about its problem. Before turning to barbers for help, Tamil Nadu was the first state to introduce AIDS education in high school and the first to set up a statewide information hotline. Its comprehensive AIDS-education program targets the overall population, rather than only high-risk groups.

In the past two years, awareness of AIDS in Tamil Nadu has jumped to 95 percent of those polled, from 64 percent, according to Operations Research Group, an independent survey group. "Just two years ago, it was very difficult to talk about AIDS and the condom," says P.R. Bindhu Madhavan, director of the Tamil Nadu State AIDS Control Society, the autonomous state agency managing the prevention effort.

The AIDS fighters take maximum advantage of the local culture to get the message across. Tamils are among the most ardent moviegoers in this film-crazed country. In the city of Madras, people line up for morning screenings even during weekdays. Half of the state's 630 theaters are paid to screen an AIDS-awareness

short before the main feature. The spots are usually melodramatic musicals laced with warnings.

In the countryside, where cinemas are scarce, a movie mobile does the job. The concept mimics that used by multinationals, such as Colgate-Palmolive Co., for rural advertising. Bright red-and-blue trucks ply the back roads, blaring music from well-known movie soundtracks whose lyrics have been rewritten to address AIDS issues. In villages, hundreds gather for the show, on a screen that pops out of the rear of the truck.

In one six-minute musical, a young husband's infidelity leads to his death from AIDS, the financial ruin of his family, and then the death of his wife, also infected. The couple's toddler is left alone in the world. The heart-rending tale is followed by a brief lecture by an AIDS educator—and the offer of a free pack of condoms and an AIDS brochure.

Tamil Nadu's innovations have met with obstacles. It took several months for state officials to persuade Indian government television, Doordarshan, to broadcast an AIDS commercial featuring the Hindu gods of chastity and death. Even then, Mr. Madhavan says, Doordarshan "wouldn't do it as a social ad, so we have to pay a commercial rate."

Later, the network refused to air a three-minute spot in which a woman urges her husband, a truck driver, to use a condom when he's on the road. Safe infidelity was deemed "inappropriate for Indian living rooms," says Mr. Madhavan. A number of commercial satellite channels have been willing to run the ad.

Tamil Nadu has met little resistance recruiting prostitutes for the cause. For almost a year, 37-year-old prostitute Vasanthi has been distributing condoms to colleagues. With state funding, a nongovernmental agency has trained her to spread the word about AIDS and other sexually transmitted diseases. As an incentive, the state pays participants like Ms. Vasanthi, a mother of three, the equivalent of $14 a month, about what she earns from entertaining a client.

Before Ms. Vasanthi joined the plan, she didn't know that the condom could help prevent HIV infection. These days, if any client refuses to wear a condom, "I kick him out, even if it takes using my shoes," she says. "I'm not flexible about this." More men are also carrying their own condoms, she says.

Thank barbers such as Mr. Mani for that. Especially in blue-collar areas of Madras, men "trim their hair and beard before frequenting a commercial sex worker," says Mr. Madhavan. They can pick up their condom on the way out.

Tamil Nadu launched the barber program in Madras last March. So far, it has enlisted 5,000 barbers, who receive AIDS education at meetings each Tuesday—the barbers' day off. The barbers aren't paid to be AIDS counselors, but they appear to take pride in their new responsibility.

Over the generations, India's barbers have been respected as traditional healers and trusted advisers. "If you want to get to the king's ears, you tell his barber," says Mr. Madhavan, the state AIDS director. Reinforcing the image of barbers as healers, the local trade group is called the Tamil Nadu Medical Barber Association.

"I first talked about AIDS with my barber," says Thiyagrajan, an electrician in his 40s. "I don't have multiple partners, so I don't need a condom, but I take them for my friends."

One recent night, a man in his 30s walked into Aruna Hair Arts, greeted Mr. Swami, then headed out the door with a fistful of condoms scooped from the plastic dispenser. "That's OK," Mr. Swami says approvingly. "He's a regular customer."

A local nongovernmental organization helps barbers replenish condom stocks by providing each shop with self-addressed order forms. But the central government hasn't always been able to meet supply, for reasons ranging from bureaucracy to price disputes with manufacturers.

Tamil Nadu has started sourcing condoms from elsewhere. But they're too expensive to give away. So the next stage of the barber scheme, just under way, is to charge two rupees (six cents) for a two-condom "pleasure pack." The barbers will get a 25 percent commission. Thus far, the only perk of participating has been a free wall calendar listing AIDS-prevention tips.

Roughly 30 percent of barbers approached by Tamil Nadu have refused to participate in the AIDS program, fearing that they would alienate customers. But those who take part insist that carrying the AIDS message hasn't hurt business. "We give the message about AIDS, but we still gossip about women," says barber N.V. Durairaj at Rolex Salon.

London International Group

London International Group (LIG) is recognized worldwide as a leader in the development of latex and thin film barrier technologies. The Group has built its success on the development of its core businesses: the Durex family of branded condoms, Regent Medical gloves, and Marigold household and industrial gloves. These are supported by a range of noncore health and beauty products.

With operational facilities in over 40 countries, 12 manufacturing plants, either wholly or jointly owned, and an advanced research and development facility based in Cambridge, England, LIG is well placed to expand into the new emerging markets of the world.

Durex is the world's number one condom brand in terms of quality, safety, and brand awareness. The Durex family of condom brands includes Sheik, Ramses, Hatu, London, Kohinoor, Dua Lima, Androtex, and Avanti. Sold in over 130 countries worldwide and leader in more than 40 markets, Durex is the only global condom brand.

The development of innovative and creative marketing strategies is key to communicating successfully with our target audiences. Consumer marketing initiatives remain focused on supporting the globalization of Durex. A series of innovative yet cost effective projects have been used to communicate the global positioning "Feeling Is Everything" to the target young adult market, securing loyalty.

The Durex Global Survey, together with a unique multi-million-pound global advertising and sponsorship contract with MTV have successfully emphasized the exciting and modern profile of Durex and presented significant opportunities for local public relations and event sponsorship, especially in emerging markets like Taiwan.

LIG continues to focus on education, using sponsorship of events such as the XI Annual AIDS Conference held last summer in Vancouver and other educational initiatives to convey the safer sex message to governments, opinion formers, and educators worldwide.

Japan

London Okamoto Corporation, the joint venture company between London International Group, plc (LIG) and Okamoto Industries Inc. (Okamoto), recently announced the Japanese launch in spring 1998 of DUREX AVANTI, the world's first polyurethane male condom.

This is the first time an international condom brand will be available in Japan, the world's most valuable condom market, which is estimated to be worth £260 million ($433 million). DUREX AVANTI has already been successfully launched in the U.S.A. and Great Britain, and will be launched in Italy and other selected European countries during the next 12 months.

DUREX AVANTI condoms are made from Duron, a unique polyurethane material twice as strong as latex, which enables them to be made much thinner than regular latex condoms thereby increasing sensitivity without compromising safety. In addition, DUREX AVANTI condoms are also able to conduct body heat, creating a more natural feeling, and are the first condoms to be totally odourless, colorless, and suitable for use with oil-based lubricants.

Commenting on the launch, Nick Hodges, chief executive of LIG, said: "Japan is a very important condom market; with oral contraceptives still not publicly available, per capita usage rates for condoms are among the highest in the world. Our joint venture with Okamoto, Japan's leading condom manufacturer, gives us instant access to this strategically important market."

The joint venture with Okamoto, which is the market leader in Japan with a 53 percent share, was established in 1994 with the specific purpose of marketing DUREX AVANTI. Added Mr. Takehiko Okamoto, president of Okamoto, "We are confident that such an innovative and technically advanced product as DUREX AVANTI, coupled with our strong market franchise, will find significant consumer appeal in Japan's sophisticated condom market."

DUREX AVANTI, which is manufactured at LIG's research and development center in Cambridge, England, has taken over 10 years to develop and represents an investment by LIG of approximately £15 million.

Questions

1. Comment on the Brazilian and Indian governments' strategies for the prevention of AIDS via the marketing of condoms.

2. How is the AIDS problem different in the United States compared to Brazil and India?

3. Would the approaches described in Brazil and India work in the U.S.? Why or why not?

4. Suggest additional ways that London International Group could promote the prevention of AIDS through the use of condoms worldwide.

References

"Half a Million Brazilians Are Infected with the AIDS Virus," *Associated Press*, December 21, 1996.

Andrea McDaniels, "Brazil Turns to Women to Stop Dramatic Rise in AIDS Cases. São Paulo Pushes Female Condom to Protect Married Women from Husbands. But Costs of Devices Are High," *Christian Science Monitor*, January 9, 1998, p. 7.

"Brazil to Hand Out 10 Million Condoms during Carnival," *Chicago Tribune*, January 19, 1998, p. 2.

Miriam Jordan, "India Enlists Barbers in the War on AIDS," *The Wall Street Journal*, September 24, 1996, p. A18.

See for example, **www.lig.com**.

Visit **www.durex.com**.

CASE 4-15

MAKING SOCIALLY RESPONSIBLE AND ETHICAL MARKETING DECISIONS: SELLING TOBACCO TO THIRD WORLD COUNTRIES

Strategic decisions move a company toward its stated goals and perceived success. Strategic decisions also reflect the firm's social responsibility and ethical values on which such decisions are made. They reflect what is considered important and what a company wants to achieve.

Mark Pastin, writing on the function of ethics in business decisions, observes:

> There are fundamental principles, or ground rules, by which organizations act. Like the ground rules of individuals, organizational ground rules determine which actions are possible for the organization and what the actions mean. Buried beneath the charts of organizational responsibility, the arcane strategies, the crunched numbers, and the political intrigue of every firm are sound rules by which the game unfolds.[1]

The following situations reflect different decisions made by multinational firms and governments and also reflect the social responsibility and ethical values underpinning the decisions. Study the following situations in the global cigarette marketplace carefully and assess the ground rules that guided the decisions of firms and governments.

Exporting U.S Cigarette Consumption

In the United States, 600 billion cigarettes are sold annually, but sales are shrinking rapidly. Unit sales have been dropping at about 1 to 2 percent a year, and sales have been down by almost 5 percent in the last six years. The U.S. Surgeon General's campaign against smoking and the concern Americans have about general health have led to the decline in tobacco consumption.

Faced with various class-action lawsuits, success states have had in winning lawsuits, and pending federal legislation, tobacco companies have stepped up their international marketing activities to maintain profits.[2]

Even though companies have agreed to sweeping restrictions in the United States on cigarette marketing and secondhand smoke and to bolder cancer-warning labels, they are fighting as hard as ever in the Third World to convince the media, the public, and policy makers that similar changes are not needed. At seminars in luxury resorts worldwide tobacco companies invite journalists, all expenses paid, to participate in programs that play down the health risks of smoking. It is hard to gauge the influence of such seminars, but in the Philippines a government plan to reduce smoking by children was "neutralized" by a public relations campaign of cigarette companies to remove "cancer awareness and prevention" as a "key concern." A slant in favor of the tobacco industry's point of view seemed to prevail.[3]

At a time when most industrialized countries are discouraging smoking,[4] the tobacco industry is avidly courting consumers throughout the developing world, using catchy slogans, obvious image campaigns, and single cigarette sales that fit a hard-pressed customer's budget. The reason is clear: The Third World is an expanding market. As an example, Indonesia's per capita cigarette consumption quadrupled in less than 10 years. Increasingly, cigarette advertising on radio and television is being restricted in some countries; however, other means of promotion, especially to young people, are not controlled.

Recently, a major U.S. tobacco company signed a joint-venture agreement with the Chinese government to produce cigarettes in China. The $21 million factory will employ 350 people and produce 2.5 billion cigarettes annually when fully operational.

China, with more than 300 million smokers, produces and consumes about 1.4 trillion cigarettes per year, more than any other country in the world. The company projects that about 80 percent of the cigarettes produced under the joint venture will be for the domestic market, with the remainder for export.

By using China's low-cost labor, this factory will put cigarettes within easy reach of 1.1 billion consumers. The tobacco company estimates that China has more smokers than the United States has people. Just 1 percent of that 1.4 trillion cigarette market would increase the U.S. tobacco company's overseas sales by 15 percent and would be worth as much as $300 million in added revenue.

American cigarette companies have received a warm welcome in Russia, where at least 50 percent of the people smoke. Consumers are hungry for most things Western and tobacco taxes are low. Unlike the United States and other countries that limit or ban cigarette advertising, there are few effective controls on tobacco products in Russia.

Advertising and Promotions

In Gambia, smokers send in cigarette box tops to qualify for a chance to win a new car. In Argentina, smoking commercials fill

---

[1] Mark Pastin, *The Hard Problems of Management* (San Francisco: Jossey-Bass Publishers, 1986), p. 24.

[2] Jeffrey Taylor and Brian Duffy, "Bipartisan Bill over Tobacco Is in the Works," *The Wall Street Journal*, February 27, 1998, p. A3.

Sources: Philip Shenon, "Tobacco Giants Turn to Asia for the Future," *The New York Times News Service*, May 19, 1994; Marcus W. Brauchli, "Ad Ban in China Makes Tobacco Tricky Business," *The Wall Street Journal*, December 28, 1994, p. B1; "Special Report: America's New Merchants of Death," *Reader's Digest*, April 1993, pp. 50–57; "U.S. Makers Aiming to Get China in the Habit," *The Wall Street Journal*, May 27, 1994, p. B1; Gene R. Laczniak and Jacob Naor, "Global Ethics: Wrestling with the Corporate Conscience," *Business*, July, August, September 1985; Jeffrey Taylor and Brian Duffy, "Bipartisan Bill over Tobacco Is in the Works," *The Wall Street Journal*, February 27, 1998, p. A3; Barry Meier, "Tobacco Industry, Conciliatory in the U.S., Goes on the Attack in the Third World," *The New York Times*, January 18, 1998, p. 14; Toby Helm, "International: EU Plans Stronger Anti-smoking Laws," *The Daily Telegraph London*, January 10, 1998, p. 18; Anna Dolgov, "Russia Is Tobacco's New Frontier Western Companies Find Growing Source of Revenue in Smoker-Friendly Nation," *Milwaukee Journal Sentinel*, March 1, 1998, p. 5; "High-Nicotine Smokes Sold Overseas," *The News & Observer*, February 2, 1998, p. A12; "Bulgartabac to Export Some 40,000 T of Cigarettes to Russia," *Bulgarian Business News*, January 30, 1998; "China's 1997 Tobacco Exports Hit Record $480 Million," *Dow Jones News Service*, January 20, 1998; and David E. Rosenbaum, "U.S. Officials Abroad to Stop Promoting Tobacco Products," *The New York Times*, February 16, 1998, p. 12.

---

[3] Barry Meier, "Tobacco Industry, Conciliatory in the U.S., Goes on the Attack in the Third World," *The New York Times*, January 18, 1998, p. 14.

[4] Toby Helm, "International: EU Plans Stronger Anti-smoking Laws," *The Daily Telegraph London*, January 10, 1998, p. 18.

20 percent of television advertising time. And in crowded African cities, billboards that link smoking to the good life tower above the sweltering shantytowns. Latin American tobacco consumption rose by more than 24 percent over a 10-year period. In the same period, it rose by 4 percent in North America.

Critics claim that sophisticated promotions in unsophisticated societies entice people who cannot afford the necessities of life to spend money on a luxury—and a dangerous one at that.

The sophistication theme runs throughout the smoking ads. In Kinshasa, Zaire, billboards depict a man in a business suit stepping out of a black Mercedes as a chauffeur holds the door. In Nigeria, promotions for Graduate brand cigarettes show a university student in his cap and gown. Those for Gold Leaf cigarettes have a barrister in a white wig and the slogan, "A very important cigarette for very important people." In Kenya, a magazine ad for Embassy cigarettes shows an elegant executive officer with three young men and women equivalent to American yuppies. Some women in Africa, in their struggle for women's rights, defiantly smoke cigarettes as a symbol of freedom.

Billboards all over Russia features pictures of skyscrapers and white sandy beaches and slogans like "Total Freedom" or "Rendezvous with America." They aren't advertising foreign travel but American cigarette brands."[5]

Every cigarette manufacturer is in the image business, and tobacco companies say their promotional slant is both reasonable and common. They point out that in the Third World a lot of people cannot understand what is written in the ads anyway, so the ads zero in on the more understandable visual image.

The scope of promotional activity is enormous. In Kenya, a major tobacco company is the fourth-largest advertiser. Tobacco-sponsored lotteries bolster sales in some countries by offering as prizes expensive goods that are beyond most people's budgets. Gambia has a population of just 640,000, but in 1987 a tobacco company lottery attracted 1.5 million entries (each sent in on a cigarette box top) when it raffled off a Renault car.

Evidence is strong that the strategy of tobacco companies has targeted young people as a means of expanding market demand. Report after report reveals that adolescents receive cigarettes free as a means of promoting the product. For example, in Buenos Aires, a Jeep decorated with the yellow Camel logo pulls up in front of a high school. The driver, a blond woman wearing khaki safari gear, begins handing out free cigarettes to 15- and 16-year-olds on lunch recess.

At a video arcade in Taipei, free American cigarettes are strewn atop each game. "As long as they're here, I may as well try one," says a high-school girl.

In Malaysia, Gila-Gila, a comic book popular with elementary-school students, carries a Lucky Strike ad. Attractive women in cowboy outfits who hand them Marlboros regularly meet teenagers going to rock concerts or discos in Budapest. Those who accept a light on the spot also receive Marlboro sunglasses.

In Russia, a United States cigarette company sponsors disco parties where thousands of young people dance to booming music. Admission is the purchase of one pack of cigarettes. In other cigarette-sponsored parties, attractive women give cigarettes away free.

In many countries, foreign cigarettes have a status image that also encourages smoking. A 26-year-old Chinese man says he switched from a domestic brand to Marlboro because "You feel a higher social position" when you smoke foreign cigarettes. "Smoking is a sign of luxury in Czechoslovakia as well as in Russia and other Eastern countries," says an executive of a Czech tobacco firm that has a joint venture with a U.S. company. "If I can smoke Marlboro, then I'm a well-to-do man."

The global tobacco companies insist that they are not attempting to recruit new smokers. They say they are only trying to encourage smokers to switch to foreign brands. "The same number of cigarettes are consumed whether American cigarettes or not," was the comment of one executive.

Another source of concern is the tar and nicotine content of cigarettes. A 1979 study found three major U.S. brands with filters had 17 milligrams of tar in the U.S., 22.3 in Kenya, 29.7 in Malaysia, and 31.1 in South Africa. Another brand with filters had 19.1 milligrams of tar in the U.S., 28.8 in South Africa, and 30.9 in the Philippines.

Although cigarette companies deny they sell higher tar and nicotine cigarettes in the Third World, one British tobacco company does concede that some of its brands sold in developing countries contain more tar and nicotine than those sold in the United States and Europe. This firm leaves the tar- and nicotine-level decisions to its foreign subsidiaries, which tailor their products to local tastes. The firm says that Third World smokers are used to smoking their own locally made product, which might have several times more tar and nicotine.

A recent legal deposition by an official of the third-largest U.S. cigarette maker testified that American cigarettes contain a genetically altered high-nicotine tobacco that is exported to Asia, the Middle East, and Western Europe. More than twice as much nicotine-rich leaf is added to cigarettes sold overseas as sold in the U.S.[6]

Smokers from the poorest countries often buy cigarettes one at a time and consume fewer than 20 a day. However, even these small quantities represent a serious drain on resources in a country like Zimbabwe, where average monthly earnings are the equivalent of $70 U.S. and a single cigarette costs the equivalent of about 2 U.S. cents.

A study published in Lancet, the British medical journal, reported that Bangladesh smokers spent about 20 percent of their income on tobacco. It asserted that smoking only five cigarettes a day in a poor household in Bangladesh might lead to a monthly dietary deficiency.

It is hard to judge how smoking may be affecting Third World health. In Kenya, for instance, a physician in only one in ten cases certifies the cause of death. Some statistics do suggest an increase in smoking-related diseases in Shanghai. According to the World Health Organization, lung cancer doubled between 1963 and 1975, a period that followed a sharp increase in smoking in the 1950s.

C. Everett Coop, the retired U.S. Surgeon General, was quoted in a recent news conference as saying, "Companies' claims that science cannot say with certainty that tobacco causes cancer were flat-footed lies" and that "sending cigarettes to the Third World was the export of death, disease, and disability." An Oxford Uni-

---

[5] Anna Dolgov, "Russia Is Tobacco's New Frontier Western Companies Find Growing Source of Revenue in Smoker-Friendly Nation," *Milwaukee Journal Sentinel,* March 1, 1998, p. 5.

[6] "High-Nicotine Smokes Sold Overseas," *The News & Observer,* February 2, 1998, p. A12.

versity epidemiologist has estimated that, because of increasing tobacco consumption in Asia, the annual worldwide death toll from tobacco-related illnesses will more than triple over the next two decades. He forecasts about 3 million a year to 10 million a year by 2050, a fifth of them in China.

Government Involvement

Third World governments often stand to profit from tobacco sales. Brazil collects 75 percent of the retail price of cigarettes in taxes, some $100 million a month. The Bulgarian state-owned tobacco company, Bulgartabac, contributes annually almost $30 million in taxes to the government. Bulgartabac is a major exporter of cigarettes to Russia and exported 40,000 tons of cigarettes to Russia in 1997.[7]

Tobacco is Zimbabwe's largest cash crop. One news report from a Zimbabwe newspaper reveals strong support for cigarette companies. "Western anti-tobacco lobbies verge on the fascistic and demonstrate unbelievable hypocrisy," notes one editorial. "It is relatively easy to sit in Washington or London and prattle on about the so-called evils of smoking, but they are far removed from the day-to-day grind of earning a living in the Third World." It goes on to comment that it doesn't dispute the fact that smoking is addictive or that it may cause diseases, but "smoking does not necessarily lead to certain death. Nor is it any more dangerous than other habits." Unfortunately, tobacco smoking has attracted the attention of a particularly "sanctimonious, meddling sector of society. They would do better to keep their opinions to themselves."

Generally, smoking is not a big concern of governments beset by debt, internal conflict, drought, or famine. It is truly tragic, but the worse famine becomes, the more people smoke—just as with war, when people who are worried want to smoke. "In any case," says one representative of an international tobacco company, "People in developing countries don't have a long enough life expectancy to worry about smoking-related problems. You can't turn to a guy who is going to die at age 40 and tell him that he might not live up to 2 years extra at age 70." As for promoting cigarettes in the Third World, "If there is no ban on TV advertising, then you aren't going to be an idiot and impose restrictions on yourself," says the representative, "and likewise, if you get an order and you know that they've got money, no one is going to turn down the business."

Cigarette companies figure China's self-interest will preserve its industry. Tobacco provides huge revenues for Beijing since all tobacco must be sold through the China National Tobacco Company monopoly. Duty on imported cigarettes is nearly 450 percent of their value. Consequently, tobacco is among the central government's biggest source of funding, accounting for more than $6 billion a year in income. China is also a major exporter of tobacco. In 1997 China's exports of tobacco were a record $480 million, an increase of 22.5 percent from a year earlier.[8]

National self-interest is not limited to Third World countries alone. The United States sends mixed reactions as well. On the one hand, the State Department sent a directive to all United States diplomatic posts in 1998 instructing them not to promote American tobacco products abroad. According to the directive, tobacco will be treated as a danger to health. At the same time, the directive also stated that the government would continue to *oppose trade policies abroad that favor local tobacco products over those made in the United States.*[9] Unfortunately, even unambiguous directives have not always been followed. In 1994, the Administration promised to work toward lowering smoking around the world but worked hand in hand with tobacco companies against an effort by the Government of Thailand to require tobacco companies to disclose the ingredients in each brand of cigarettes. In 1994, the Ambassador to Romania attended the opening of a new U.S. cigarette company plant and declared, "I'm sure that the splendid products of the (Company name) company will prosper in Romania."

Assessing the Ethics of Strategic Decisions

Ethical decision making is not a simplistic "right" or "wrong" determination. Ethical ground rules are complex, tough to sort out and to set priorities, tough to articulate, and tough to use.

The complexity of ethical decisions is compounded in the international setting—comprising different cultures, different perspectives of right and wrong, different legal requirements, and different goals. Clearly, when U.S. companies conduct business in an international setting, the ground rules become further complicated by the values, customs, traditions, ethics, and goals of the host countries that have developed their own ground rules for conducting business.

Three prominent American ethicists have developed a framework to view ethical implications of strategic decisions by American firms. They identify three ethical principles that can guide American managers in assessing the ethical implications of their decisions and the degree to which these decisions reflect these ethical principles or ground rules. They suggest asking, "Is the corporate strategy acceptable according to the following ethical ground rules?"

Principles	*Question*
Utilitarian ethics (Bentham, Smith)	Does the corporate strategy optimize the "common good" or benefits of all constituencies?
Rights of the parties (Kant, Locke)	Does the corporate strategy respect the rights of the individuals involved?
Justice or fairness (Aristotle, Rawls)	Does the corporate strategy respect the canons of justice or fairness to all parties?

These questions can help uncover the ethical ground rules embedded in the tobacco consumption situation described above. These questions lead to an ethical analysis of the degree to which this strategy is beneficial or harmful to the parties, and ultimately, whether it is a "right" or "wrong" strategy, or whether the conse-

---

[7] "Bulgartabac to Export Some 40,000 T of Cigarettes to Russia," *Bulgarian Business News,* January 30, 1998.
[8] "China's 1997 Tobacco Exports Hit Record $480 Million," *Dow Jones News Service,* January 20, 1998.

[9] David E. Rosenbaum, "U.S. Officials Abroad to Stop Promoting Tobacco Products," *The New York Times,* February 16, 1998, p. 12.

**EXHIBIT 1   A Decision Tree for Incorporating Ethical
and Social Responsibility Issues
into Multinational Business Decisions**

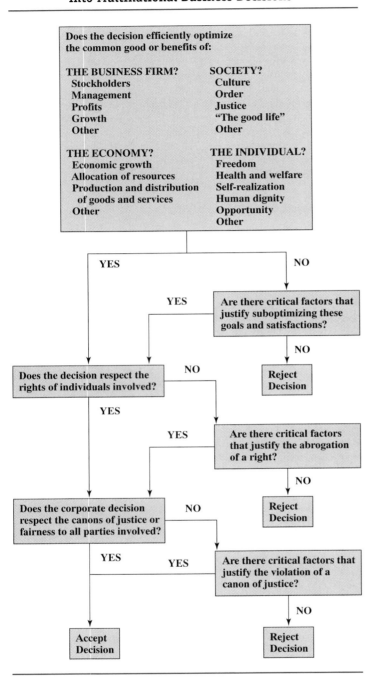

Sources: This decision tree is an adaptation of Figure 1, "A Decision Tree for Incorporating Ethics into Political Behavior Decision," in Gerald F. Cavanagh, Dennis J Moberg, and Manuel Velasquez, "The Ethics of Organizational Politics," *Academy of Management Review*, 1981, p. 368; and Exhibit 1: The Value Hierarchy—A Model for Management Decision, in Wilmar F. Bernthal, "Value Perspectives in Management Decisions," *Journal of the Academy of Management*, December 1962, p. 196.

quences of this strategy are ethical or socially responsible for the parties involved. These ideas are incorporated in the decision tree in Exhibit 1.

Laczniak and Naor discuss the complexity of international ethics or, more precisely, the ethical assumptions that underlie strategic decisions for multinationals. They suggest that multinationals can develop consistency in their policies by using federal law as a baseline for appropriate behavior as well as respect for the host country's general value structure. They conclude with four recommendations for multinationals:

1. Expand codes of ethics to be worldwide in scope.
2. Expressly consider ethical issues when developing worldwide corporate strategies.

3. If the firm encounters major ethical dilemmas, consider withdrawal from the problem market.
4. Develop periodic ethics-impact statements, including impacts on host parties.

Questions

1. Using the model in Exhibit 1 as a guide, assess the ethical and social responsibility implications of the situation described.
2. Can you recommend alternative strategies or solutions to the dilemmas confronting the tobacco companies? To governments? What is the price of ethical behavior?

Indexes

NAME INDEX

SUBJECT INDEX